World Population Policy: An Annotated Bibliography

World Population Policy: An Annotated Bibliography

Edwin D. Driver
University of Massachusetts

with the assistance of
Shirnavaz Driver, Shanta Driver
and Cyrus Driver

Lexington Books
D.C. Heath and Company
Lexington, Massachusetts
Toronto London

Published simultaneously in Canada.

Printed in the United States of America.

International Standard Book Number: 0-669-81711-2.

Library of Congress Catalog Card Number: 73-184302.

To Shavaksha Jhabvala and Meherban Jhabvala

"The Hermitage", Khar, Bombay

for their selfless devotion to all humanity

TABLE OF CONTENTS

TABLE OF CONTENTS

TABLE OF CONTENTS

TABLE OF CONTENTS

TABLE OF CONTENTS

TABLE OF CONTENTS

TABLE OF CONTENTS

PREFACE

The increasing interest of demographers, social scientists, the health professions, and other scholars in population policy is shown by the great growth in recent years of publications on this subject. An indicator of this growth is the expansion in the classificatory system of the Population Index, the major bibliography on demography. Publication of the Index began in 1935 and in the early years it contained little information under its category M, Policies. Over time the increase in writings on policies necessitated the dividing of this category into five subclasses: general population policy, measures affecting fertility, policy on internal redistribution, policy on international migration, and policy on quality. This increase has also affected another major category, Fertility and Natural Increase. Until 1968 it consisted of five subclasses: general fertility, differential fertility, sterility and other pathology, fertility controls, and natural increase. In 1968, fertility controls had to be subdivided into: action programs, clinical studies, use-effectiveness studies, and socioeconomic and other relations.

In the face of what is virtually a "literature explosion", an official of the National Science Foundation says that "reference works ... assume a new importance but bring with them a new danger".[1] They provide researchers and practitioners with quick access to a wide range of studies of interest and benefit to them. But the danger is that the reader may falsely infer that comprehensive coverage means that every publication of value to him is included in the reference work. This danger, which O'Dette calls the "paradox of plenty",[2] may be minimized if readers would observe, rather than ignore, the stated limitations of each reference work.

This reference work has several limitations. It contains information on only two of the types of population policy mentioned in the Population Index: general population policy, and measures

---

[1]Ralph E. O'Dette, "A Note on the Literature Problem," in Community Mental Health and Social Psychiatry: A Reference Guide by Harvard Medical School and Psychiatric Service, Massachusetts General Hospital. Cambridge: Harvard University Press, 1952, xv.

[2]Ibid.

affecting fertility and family size.[3] General population policy consists of two or more of the other types of population policy. Secondly, this work covers the literature for the various countries of the world for the years 1940 to 1969. The coverage is both comprehensive and systematic. The year 1940 was selected as the starting point because the little literature that existed before then is quite well covered in Glass' early book on population policy.[4] Furthermore, since 1940, except for Eldridge's excellent but highly selective review of some literature,[5] the materials on population policy have not been organized. Our coverage of the published materials ends with the year, 1969. The reason for this is that our searching of bibliographic sources which were available through 1970 usually carried items which had been published in 1969, if not a bit earlier. In order to ensure that we had found most of the important items published through 1969, we made a check of the contents of recent volumes of journals such as _Demography_, _Population_, and _Population Studies_. _Population_ was especially useful because it reviews the contents of many other population journals and contains an excellent and up-to-date bibliography on books.

The selection of bibliographic sources and their searching were guided by a definition of population policy which is broader than the more popular one offered by Eldridge. She says that "population policies may be defined as legislative measures, administrative programs, and other governmental action intended to alter or modify existing population trends in the interest of national survival and welfare".[6] Berelson's definition is virtually identical to Eldridge's.[7] Quite different are the views of Borrie and Myrdal who regard population policy as being inseparable from a more comprehensive social policy.[8] Social

---

[3]A volume on the other types of policies is planned.

[4]D.V. Glass, _Population Policies and Movements in Europe_. London: Oxford University Press, 1940.

[5]Hope T. Eldridge, _Population Policies: A Survey of Recent Developments_. Washington: International Union for the Scientific Study of Population, 1954.

[6]Hope T. Eldridge, "Population Policies," _International Encyclopedia of the Social Sciences_ 12(1968):381-388.

[7]Bernard Berelson, "Population Policy:Personal Notes," _Population Studies_ 25(1971):173.

[8]W.D. Borrie, _Population Trends and Policies_. Sydney: Australasian Company, 1948; Alva Myrdal, _Nation and Family: The Swedish Experiment in Democratic Family and Population Policy_. Cambridge: Massachusetts Institute of Technology Press, 1968 (paperback edition).

policy, according to Marshall, may be defined as "the policy of governments with regard to action having a direct impact on the welfare of the citizens, by providing them with services or income. The essential core consists, therefore, of social insurance, public (or national) assistance, the health and welfare services, and housing policy. Education obviously belongs... So also... the treatment of crime".[9] My view of population policy, while closer to that of Myrdal than that of Eldridge, is the broadest of all. Population policy is conceived of as both direct and indirect measures, formulated and implemented by the whole range of social institutions including government, which, whether intended or not, may influence the size, distribution, or composition of human population.[10]

Given this definition, the procedure in searching a bibliographic source was to first list all the concepts from its index which presumably were related to our topic. Next the titles of all the references included under each concept were read and those which clearly did not refer to policy or population were eliminated. The remaining references or existing abstracts of them were read and the ones which still fitted our definition of population policy were selected for inclusion in our bibliography. And, finally, abstracts were prepared where needed, provided that the item could be obtained and translated. Some of the bibliographic sources which were systematically searched include the: _Cumulative Book Index_, _Biological Abstracts_, _Current Publications in Population/Family Planning_, _Dissertation Abstracts_, _Index to the Humanities and Social Sciences_, _Index to Legal Periodical Literature_, _Index to Periodical Literature Relative to Law_, _Index Medicus_, _Legal Abstracts_, _NICHD Research Reports and Abstracts_, _Population Index_, _Psychological Abstracts_, _Reader's Guide to Periodical Literature_, _Sociological Abstracts_, and the _South Asia Social Science Abstracts and Bibliography_. Each of these sources had numerous key concepts which had to be reviewed for entries on population policy. For example, there were 55 concepts in the Public Affairs Information Service bibliography and 68 concepts in the _Index to Legal Periodical Literature_ which we selected to guide our examination of all volumes of these

---

[9] T.H. Marshall, _Social Policy_. London: Hutchinson University Library, 1965, p. 7.

[10] For an extended discussion of this conceptualization of population policy, see: Edwin D. Driver, _Essays on Population Policy_. Lexington (Massachusetts): D.C. Heath and Company, 1972, Ch. 2; R. Titmuss and B. Abel-Smith, _Social Policies and Population Growth in Mauritius_. London: Methuen and Company, 1960.

works published between 1940 and 1970. Some of the concepts from these and other sources are: abortion, adoption, adultery, alimony, annulment, anthropology, bigamy, birth control, birth rate, child labor, churches, community development, comparative law, contraception, criminal law, descent and distribution, desertion, development, divorce, domestic relations, ecclesiastical law, eugenics, family, family allowances, family assistance, health, Hindu law, husband and wife, illegitimacy, inheritance, Islamic law, Jewish law, legislation, marriage, marriage property, married woman, maternal welfare, maternity benefit, maternity protection, native law, parent and child, policy, polygamy, population, pregnancy, prostitution, sex crimes, social change, social insurance, social legislation, social security, social welfare, sterilization, support of dependents, taxation, wages, widows, and workmen's compensation.

In addition to these bibliographic sources, there was a searching of several general books on demography. They include Eldridge's Population Policies, and her Materials of Demography: A Selected and Annotated Bibliography (New York: Columbia University Press, 1959); Legeard's Guide de Recherches Documentaires on Demographie (Paris: Gauthier-Villars, 1966); and Tabah and Viet's Demographie: Tendances Actuelles et Organisation de la Recherches, 1955-1965 (Paris: Mouton, 1966).

The organization of entries in our book, as shown by the Table of Contents, is primarily geographic. It follows the scheme found in the United Nations Demographic Yearbook for classifying nations under major areas and component regions of the world. Most entries refer to just one nation and they are, of course, placed under the section where that nation is the topical heading. When an entry refers to two nations, it is listed under the nation which, according to the abstract, suggests that it is the central concern. But where two nations are equally central, the entry is placed under the nation whose name appears first in the title of the entry. The same rules apply when two regions or areas are the subject of the entry. Now, when the entry refers to more than two nations, regions, or areas, it is put under the next larger geographic subdivision. Thus for example, an entry referring to Guinea, the Ivory Coast, and Liberia would be put under Western Africa (general); and one referring to Western Africa, Eastern Africa, and Northern Africa, or specific countries from these different regions, would be put under Africa (general).

Finally, we should note that our manuscript is less than perfect. It was not possible to abstract every entry. The main reason is that various publications could not be obtained despite our best efforts and the magnificent assistance given by many libraries. Stylistically the manuscript could be better but this improvement would have required financial and manpower resources far beyond our command. But these are minor matters. Our real concern and hope is that we have provided the many researchers and practitioners in the field of population policy with the kind of comprehensive reference work that will meet their needs and advance our knowledge.

ACKNOWLEDGEMENTS

The completion of this volume has required cooperation and financial support from several sources. I am most indebted to my three children for their enthusiastic and skillful searching of bibliographic sources, translating and abstracting of items, and proofreading and editing of the manuscript. Such is my debt that I have listed them as co-authors. Next, I wish to thank my secretary, Mrs. Jane Wood, for her patience, perserverance, and superb handling of an extremely difficult task. Thirdly, I appreciate the assistance given by many undergraduate and graduate students in translating materials into English and performing other tasks. Major assistance was given by two of them, Mrs. Lynn Millard and Mrs. Nancy Biron. I wish also to thank the many reference librarians at the University of Massachusetts Library for their great assistance.

Financial support came from three sources. I wish to thank the Research Council of the University of Massachusetts for its support of this project and continued support over the past dozen years. I wish to acknowledge, too, the very timely grant provided by the Population Council, Inc. I am especially indebted to the Ford Foundation for financial assistance and to Dr. Oscar Harkavy and his colleagues in the Population Office of the Foundation for their continued and sincere interests in my efforts in population policy.

Lastly, a special note of appreciation is owed my wife, Aloo Jhabvala Driver, who for many years has encouraged my every scholarly activity even though it has meant a sacrifice of the usual leisure-time pursuits. Further she remains my best critic and friend.

Edwin D. Driver
Amherst, Massachusetts
1972

World Population Policy: An Annotated Bibliography

I INTER-REGIONAL

General population policies

1 Admunson, Robert H. Population Problems and Policies in Puerto Rico, India, and Japan. Publication No. 18,072. Ann Arbor: University Microfilms, 1956. 424 pp.

Compares the rapid growth of population in Puerto Rico, India, and Japan. Describes and evaluates the methods of population control fostered by recent programs or policies. Considers the practical and ethical aspects of these programs or policies.

2 Back, Kurt W., and Winsborough, Halliman H. "Population Policy: Opinions and Actions of Government," Proc. Amer. Assn. Pub. Opinion Res., 1967

This study is based on a survey of 113 governments. It is concerned with a topic that is not dependent solely on ideological or bloc positions, namely population policy. It attempts to construct a model by which government reports can be analyzed like individual interviews. The content of the reports reflects the opinions of many individuals and usually a compromise between them; its exact meaning may be an accident of bureaucratic procedure. Some formal characteristics of the report may be independent of personal idiosyncrasies. Illustrations of this type of analysis are given.

3 Balfour, Marshall C. "Administrative Problems in Connection with Aid to Underdeveloped Areas," pp. 159-69 in: Milbank Memorial Fund, Approaches to Problems of High Fertility in Agrarian Societies . New York: Milbank Memorial Fund, 1952. 171 pp.

Discusses the concept of planning in such programs as that of Point IV, the needs for and difficulties of securing a balanced and multi-disciplinary approach to problems of underdeveloped areas, and the steps in research and action that should be taken toward meeting the problem of high fertility in agrarian societies.

4 Barnett, H.J. "Population and World Politics," World Politics 12(4):640-50. July 1960.

A review of Philip M. Hauser, ed. Population and World Politics, 1958. Rapid rates of population increase in the major, economically aspiring, non-Communist nations imperil their economic progress, and this in turn threatens world peace. The economic difficulty is not significantly related to the classical conception of limited natural resources and diminishing returns attributable thereto. The difficulty is primarily due to limitation of capital needed to exploit technological advance. A problem to begin with because the poor, non-totalitarian nation finds it hard to save, it is rendered most acute by two other phenomena: the drain on capital supplies for purposes which do not directly improve industrial productivity, such as cultural education and the drain incident to converting agrarian economies into urban ones. Finally, to this is joined the dilemma that presents high fertility rates and consumers to the society relatively faster than workers. This reduces per capita incomes and thereby the volume of savings. Per capita income could increase more than twice as fast in the next two generations from the single influence of a 50% reduction in fertility rates and its effect on population numbers, age distribution, and capital formation. Relevant policies for the U.S. and other rich nations are indicated.

5 Benson, Wilfrid. "A People's Peace in the Colonies," Internat. Labour Rev. 47(2):141-68. February 1943.

This survey of the developments with reference to the general principles of colonial policy, its social objectives, and the economic possibilities, considers possible policies in the fields of health, nutrition, labor and industry.

6 Berelson, Bernard. "Population Policy: Current Issues" Paper presented at the Annual Meeting of the Population Association of America, 10 April 1969, Atlantic City.

A review of what some of the leading demographers put forth as some of the important policy issues in the field and on which the scientific and professional effort might best be placed. There is a need to consider policies in a context broader than the economic or demographic, to examine "hidden policies", and to learn how policies come to be formulated. There is also need to clarify the different demographic means by which non-demographic objectives may be achieved.

7 Bertram, G.C.L. "Eugenics in the Age of Crowding," Eugenics Rev. 50(1):41-50. April 1958.

The author presents a case for the limitation of world population to an optimal population size and contends that an extensive proportion of the world has already exceeded optimal growth. The inevitability of population control is stressed, with reference to the two options available for such control -- continued action of factors making up haphazard limitation, which should be avoided, or acceptable human deliberation. Whichever of these two modes of control may operate in limiting human numbers, the qualitative and quantitative aspects of differential reproduction must remain the primary concern.

8 Bie, Pierre de, "Politique Familiale et Politique Demographique" [Family Policy and Demographic Policy], Popul. Fam./Bevolk. Gezin. 1:6-17, 1963.

A study to define the concepts of family and demographic policy, to see if they converge or diverge, and to examine whether it is possible and/or desirable to dissociate them. A distinction is established between the objectives of the two policies. Family policy is directed at the state and development of the family and includes all of the measures of assistance and protection which permit the family to fulfill its functions. Demographic policy concerns human collectivism and is based on the data gathered by demographic studies (quantitative and qualitative). The policies are also distinguished by the methods they employ. Although some measures are used exclusively by the one or the other, others can serve for both. It is shown historically that a clear distinction cannot always be established between the two, and that they are both interdependent and necessary.

9 Borgstrom, George. Too Many: A Study of Earth's Biological Limitations. New York: The Macmillan Company, 1969. 368 pp.

An overview of the world food situation by the author of The Hungry Planet, dealing with deforestation, pollution, and the over-utilization of all our resources. No fast or easy solution to the agricultural situation is predicted. The use of reprocessed sewage to fertilize algae beds upon which yeasts will grow and supplement man's diet is examined as a partial answer to overpopulation. Population control is presented as the only final answer. Included are 24 chapters and 54 figures, such as growth of world population, utilization of the world's wood resources, hydrological cycle of the earth, water balance of West Germany, a designer's vision of an algae factory, and the global energy balance, 1960-1962.

10 Borrie, W.D. Population Trends and Policies. A Study in Australian and World Demography. Sydney: Australasian Publishing Co., 1948. xx, 263 pp.

Part IV, Population Policy, has a chapter on the main techniques of the population policies of France, Italy, Germany, the USSR, and Sweden. With the exception of Sweden, these policies have been, or are avowedly expansionist in aim. The other chapter discusses a population policy for Australia with respect to aims and forms. A major conclusion is that a fundamental aim of Australia's policy must be an improvement in quality, and a social redirection that enable the rising generation to breed to the limit of their volition and not compel them to breed to the limit of their capacity.

11 Boserup, M. "Prospects for Population Policies," Paper presented at the International Union for the Scientific Study of Population, General Conference, 3-11 September 1969, London.

Six papers on population policy, presented at a IUSSP session in 1969, are analyzed with regard to: general trends in attitudes and policies, potential policies, regional contrasts in policies and broad problems of population control in the future.

12 Bourdon, Jean. "Remarques sur les Doctrines de la Population depuis Deux Siècles" [Comments on the Population Doctrines of Two Centuries], Population 2(3):481-95. July - September 1947.

13 Boverat, Fernand. Directives Generales d'une Politique de Natalite [General Directives of a Pro-Natalist Policy]. Congrès International de la Famille et de la Population, IX. Bruxelles: Editions "Familia," 1946, 23 pp.

14 Brown, Harrison. "Science, Technology, and World Development," Bull. Atomic Scientists 14(10):409-12. December 1958.

Section,"How will we feed people?"discusses population growth. The author suggests the establishment of an International Institute of World Development staffed by physical, biological, and social scientists, and engineers. A part of the effort in such an institute might be devoted to devising techniques of fertility control applicable in specific unindustrialized areas, and studies of ways and means of spreading knowledge of these techniques.

15 Brugarola, Martin, S.J. El Drama de la Poblacion [The Drama of Population]. Barcelona: Ed. Lumen, 1958. 445 pp.

Considers the interrelations of economic development and population growth and relevant issues of policy, especially on fertility controls.

16 Burch, Guy I. "Relation of Population to National and International Policies," World Affairs 3(4):217-26. Winter 1948.

Argues that over-population caused World Wars I and II and will cause III; that the United Nations should encourage an environment in which contraceptive information is easily available, advocate sterilization laws on social as well as hereditary criteria, and let the world know that lax marriage laws are related to poverty.

17 Burch, Guy I., and Pendell, Elmer. Human Breeding and Survival. New York: Penquin Books, 1947.

Presents four general suggestions as a program for United Nations actions on the population problem: encourage an environment in which information concerning means of population control for married people is easily available; emphasize the responsibility of each nation to keep its population in check and encourage migration restrictions against any country which fails to do so; encourage sterilization laws on the basis of social and hereditary laws; and emphasize the need for adoption and enforcement of appropriate marriage and reproduction qualifications.

18 Cadbury, George W. "Population Planning: Some Suggestions for Emphasis in Future Research," in Vol. 2, pp. 314 of United Nations Department of Economic and Social Affairs, Proceedings of the World Population Conference, Belgrade, 30 August - 10 September 1965. 4 vols. New York: United Nations, 1967.

Practical policies discussed are divided between those relevant to a situation where a simple reduction of the birth rate is the immediate goal and those in which more complex considerations are involved. Suggests a dozen areas of needed research.

19 Carolina Population Center, University of North Carolina. Approaches to the Human Fertility Problem. Prepared for the United Nations Advisory Committee on the Application of Science and Technology to Development, October 1968. 143 pp.

Chapter V, Demogenic Policy, defines population policy rather broadly, and discusses the process by which policy develops and the economic, familial, and socio-psychological variables which enter into policy implementation. Chapter VI, Program Organization, considers the organizational, evaluative, and training aspects of fertility control programs.

20 Carolina Population Center, University of North Carolina. Cracking the World Population Problem: A U.S. Goal for the 70's. Prepared for the Presidential Task Force on International Development, December 1969. 32 pp.

Part I, Present Situation, stresses the challenges which population growth at home and elsewhere pose for the U.S. government. Part II, Population Program Policy for the '70s, discusses specific goals, expressions of policy, and budgetary and organizational considerations. In Part III, Elements of a World Program, specific national and international programs are suggested and there is a discussion of the role of the U.S. government and institutions, the United Nations, and private international organizations.

21 Chandrasekhar, S. "Cultural Barriers to Family Planning in Under-Developed Countries," Popul. Rev. 1(2):44-51. 1957.

In order to disseminate birth control information, the population must be literate; this in turn indicates a relatively high aspiration level, which in many areas is not the case. The filtering down of sterilization as a birth control method from the upper classes to the lower classes in Puerto Rico is used as an example of cultural communication. The extended family is seen as a "cultural barrier to birth control." Religious attitudes, not only toward birth control, but also toward the political and economic institutions, will play a part in determining the population size. This is due to the desire of most major religions to be in the numerical majority. A population policy is primarily an economic policy of balancing a nation's resources with the people's needs. Family policy implies a planned family in a more or less planned economy.

22 Chandrasekhar, S. "Population Growth, Socio-Economic Development and Living Standards," Internat. Labour Rev. 69(6):527-46. June 1954.

Discusses the population pressure on the means of subsistence in countries where living standards are low and population is increasing rapidly. The author contends that even with economic development and higher production the living standards in these countries will not improve if the present rate of population growth continues. A forceful plea for a world population policy constitutes the major portion of the article. Stressed is the need for a policy which would include the universal adoption of birth control as well as political freedom for all colonial peoples, planned international migration, and the industrialization and agricultural development of underdeveloped areas.

23 Clark, Colin. "Population and Progress: the Problem of Birth Control," Queens Quart. 62:411-22. Autumn 1955.

Attacks the prevailing "myth" that fertility control is the solution to the enormous population pressures of Asia and Africa.

24 Cook, Robert C. "The World Bank Tackles Population," Popul. Bull. 24(3):57-80. November 1968.

Contains the speech of Robert McNamara as President of the International Bank for Reconstruction and Development to the Board of Governors of the Bank. Also reactions of Governors and Robert C. Cook of Population Reference Bureau to the three point program on population recommended by McNamara.

25 Davis, Kingsley. "Population Policy: Will Current Programs Succeed?" Science 153:730-39. November 1967.

The world's population problem cannot be solved by pretense and wishful thinking. The unthinkable identification of family planning with population control is an ostrich-like approach in that it permits people to hide from themselves the enormity and unconventionality of the task. There is no reason to abandon family-planning programs; contraception is a valuable technological instrument. But such programs must be supplemented with equal or greater investment in research and experimentation to determine the required socioeconomic measures.

26 "Declaration on Population," Stud. Fam. Planning, No. 16. January 1967, p. 1.

On Human Rights Day, December 10, 1966, Secretary General U. Thant of the United Nations issued a Declaration on Population developed on the initiative of Mr. John D. Rockefeller 3rd, Chairman of the Board, Population Council, and signed by the heads of state of twelve countries.

27 "Declaration on Population: The World Leaders Statement," Stud. Fam. Planning, No. 26. January 1968, pp. 1-3.

The Declaration was originally signed by the heads of state of twelve countries. During the year, an additional eighteen heads of state signed the Declaration. Their signing was the occasion for special ceremonies and speeches at the United Nations.

28 Douglas, Mary. "Population Control in Primitive Groups," Brit. J. Sociol. 17(3):263-73. September 1966.

A study of four groups which attempt to control fertility: (1) the Pelly Bay Eskimos, who kill off a percentage of their female babies; (2) the Rendille, camel herders in the Kenya highlands who postpone the age of marriage of females and kill off boys; (3) the Tilopia, inhabitants of a small Pacific island who used to use abortion, contraception, infanticide and suicide migration; and (4) the Nambudiri Brahmins of India, who only allow the eldest son in each family to contract marriage and maintain a large percent of female population in spinsterhood. The groups are used as a basis for considering V.C. Wynne-Edwards' hypothesis (Animal Dispersion in Relation to Social Behaviour, 1962) that in primitive human groups social conventions operate homeostatic controls on population, and certain concepts of Carr-Saunders in The Population Problem (1922). It is concluded that population homeostasis does occur in human groups. The kind of relation to resources that is sought is more often a relation to limited social advantages than to resources crucial to survival. It is stressed that the focus of demographic inquiry should be shifted from subsistence to prestige, and to the relation between the prestige structure and the economic basis of prosperity. A small primitive population which is homogeneously committed to the same pattern of values and to which the ladders of social status offer a series of worthwhile goals which do not require large families for their attainment is likely to apply restrictive demographic policies. In a stratified population it is those sections which are most advantageously placed regarding power and prestige in which policies of population control are spontaneously applied.

29 Duke University. Rule of Law Research Center, Law and Population: a Preliminary Report. Prepared for the Population Council. Arthur Larsen, Director of the Center and Luke T. Lee, Project Supervisor.

Brief history of government policies and actions; laws dealing with birth, family planning education and services, marriage and divorce, and economic factors related to the family, general observations and suggested improvements in laws affecting population. Covers Japan, Korea, Thailand, Tunisia, Egypt, and the Soviet Union.

30 Duke University. School of Law. "A Symposium on Population Control," Law and Contemporary Problems 25(3):377-629. Summer 1960. Reprinted as: Shimm, Melvin G., and Robinson, O. Everett, eds. Population Control: the Imminent World Crisis. New York: Oceana Publications, 1961. 254 pp.

Contents: Shimm, Melvin G., Foreword; Cook, Robert C., World Population Growth; Stamp, L. Dudley, World Resources and Technology; Loon, Henry B. van, Population, Space and Human Culture; Osborn, Frederick, Qualitative Aspects of Population Control: Eugenics and Euthenics; Tietze, Christopher, The Current Status of Fertility Control; St. John-Stevas, Norman, A Roman Catholic View of Population Control; Fagley, Richard M., A Protestant View of Population Control; Mauldin, W. Parker, Population Policies in the Sino-Soviet Bloc; Jaffe, A.J., Population Trends and Controls in Underdeveloped Countries; Bronfenbrenner, Martin, and Buttrick, John A., Population Control in Japan: Economic Theory and its Application; Back, Kurt W., et al., Population Control in Puerto Rico: the Formal and Informal Framework; Agarwala, S.N., Population Control in India: Progress and Prospects; Sulloway, Alvah W., The Legal and Political Aspects of Population Control in the United States; Miller, Arthur S., Some Observations on the Political Economy of Population Growth.

31 Dunn, Stephen P., and Kvasha, A. IA. "Comments on Demography and Population Policy in the Developing Countries," Soviet Sociology 6(3):47-51. Winter 1967.

In the first part, by Stephen P. Dunn, pp. 47-48, are comments on article [Some problems of population in the economically developing countries of Asia and Africa], by A. IA. Kvasha in Soviet Sociology 4(4):3-11, 1966. The second part is Kvasha's reply, pp. 48-51.

32 Eldridge, Hope T. "Population Policies," in: Vol. 12, pp. 381-88 of David L. Sills, ed. International Encyclopedia of the Social Sciences. New York: Macmillan Company and Free Press, 1968. 16 vols.

Brings up to date the earlier statement found in her book.

33 Eldridge, Hope T. Population Policies: a Survey of Recent Developments. Washington: The International Union for the Scientific Study of Population, 1954. vi, 154 pp.

A survey of data, by country, on national population policies, with particular consideration of recent developments in (1) measures affecting the integrity and health of the family, (2) policies concerning emigration and immigration, and (3) policies concerning the control of natality. Geographically classified bibliography.

34 Enke, Stephen. "Birth Control for Economic Development," Science 164(3881):798-802. 16 May 1969.

It is calculated that money spent each year on birth control can be 100 times more effective in raising output per head than money spent each year on traditional productive investments. An economic-demographic computer model is applied to a typical less developed country: the benefit cost ratio is 22 to 1 in the fifth year, 82 to 1 in the 30th year. It is questioned whether enough people will voluntarily practice effective contraception. The role of government in encouraging contraceptive use is discussed.

35 Enke, Stephen. "The Economic Aspects of Slowing Population Growth," Economic J. 76(301):44-56. March 1966.

Aspects considered with reference to less developed countries: effect on per capita incomes of allocating a given unit of economic resources to retarding population growth rather than to accelerating production; estimates of per capita cost of adequate birth-control program; use of resources for education and bonuses in cash or kind to increase participation in family planning.

36 Enke, Stephen. "The Economic Case for Birth Control in Underdeveloped Nations," Challenge 15:30 ff. May - June 1967.

One dollar to slow population can be 100 times more effective in raising income per head than one dollar to expand output.

37 Enke, Stephen. "Economic Programmer to Prevent Births," in Vol. 2, pp. 314-15 of United Nations Department of Economic and Social Affairs, Proceedings of the World Population Conference , Belgrade, 30 August - 10 September 1965. 4 Vols. New York: United Nations, 1967.

The economic worth of preventing a birth in over-populated, less developed countries is calculated to be one to two times the annual per capita income of that country. In a typical country, the cost of such a national program would be about ten U.S. cents annually per head of population, or about one per cent of the cost of the country's overall development program.

38 Etzioni, Amitai. "Sex Control, Science and Society," Science 161(3846):1107-12. September 1968.

The possibility within the next decade or so of sex control, the ability to control whether a newborn infant will be a male or a female, raises the question of whether in certain circumstances societal well-being justified some limitation on the freedom of scientific research. The history, possible administration, and societal consequences of sex control are outlined. The scientific community must take the responsibility of asking what effects its endeavors, such as sex control, would have on the community by setting up a system of self-regulation that builds on the difference between science and technology and identifies and controls those technologies that are likely to cause significantly more damage than payoffs. Such control would not be an opening wedge leading to deeper penetration of society into scientific activity but, on the contrary, might prevent such a social "backlash."

39 Fabre-Luce, Alfred. Les Hommes de l'an 2000: Six Milliards d'Insectes [Mankind in the Year 2000: Six Billion Insects]. Collection Notre Temps, 4. Paris: Arthaud, 1962. 246 pp.

Chapters on: the approach to saturation; two worlds; investors in human beings; whom to abolish? birth control; some guide lines for action.

40 Farmer, Richard N., _et al_., eds. _World Population -- The View Ahead_. Graduate School of Business, Indiana University, 1968. 310 pp.

A collection of 11 papers and discussions of them presented at the Conference on World Population Problems, Indiana University, 3-6 May 1967, by participants representing several disciplines. Sections include economic, technological, and sociological aspects; "quality of life;" death and birth control; and ethical issues of control.

41 Federici, Nora. _Politica Della Popolazione_ [Population Policy]. Rome: Institute of Statistics, University of Rome, 1941. 386 pp.

One of the earliest, general discussions of population policy. Part I defines population policy, optimum population, policies concerned with optima quantity and quality; it also criticizes Anglo-Saxon conceptions of optimum population. Part II considers the legitimacy of the State's intervention in demographic processes through population and general policies. In Part II demographic problems and population policies from pre-historic times to the 19th century are discussed. Part IV discusses the demographic viewpoint and policies prevailing in Italy, Germany, Spain, France, U.S.S.R., other European nations, the United States, and Latin America.

42 "First Inter-American Demographic Congress," _Popul. Index_ 10:13-14, 1944.

At the invitation of the Mexican government, representatives of the countries of the American hemisphere participated in a First Inter-American Demographic Congress, which was held in Mexico City during October 12-21, 1943. Twenty-one republics and the Dominion of Canada sent delegates. The main purpose of the conference was to express and coordinate the points of view of the American countries with reference to postwar migration, and to formulate demographic policies that could be recommended for this period of emergency. Accordingly, immigration was the chief topic of discussion, with particular reference to the possibilities of heavy immigration from Europe at the close of the war. Although it was the general feeling that cooperative action in meeting the problem was desirable, the various delegates repeatedly affirmed the principle that each country should maintain its own sovereign right to determine its immigration policy. Despite the attention given to immigration, a wide range of topics was considered, including racial, economic, and health problems, under the three sections into which the program was divided - (1) Demography, (2) Ethnology and Eugenics, and (3) Demographic Policy. Out of the discussions arose numerous resolutions. These for the most part recommended means for attracting, assisting, selecting, and controlling immigrants; eliminating race prejudice and improving the political and economic conditions of the indigenous races; guaranteeing full employment and industrial development to American nations; improving the health, level of living, and heredity of the population; and planning for the cooperation of the American countries in the standardization of records, definition of terms, exchange of information, and improvement of techniques with reference to demographic statistics. Perhaps the most important resolution was that providing for the establishment in Mexico City of a committee of representatives from certain countries, this committee to form the nucleus of a group devoted to the study of demographic problems, especially the problem of immigration.

43 "Focus on Population," _Mid East, A Middle East-North African Rev._ 8(5), September - October 1968. 39 pp.

This special issue includes articles by A.R. Omran on Iran, H. Shanawany on the U.A.R., W. Spencer on Algeria, W. Spencer on Morocco, and B. Tuncer on Turkey. Each article discusses, with varying degrees of emphasis, the demographic characteristics of the country concerned, the history of the formulation of its population policies and the family planning program currently in progress.

44 Gannage, Elias. "Population et Politique de Croissance au Moyen-Orient" [Population Growth Policy in the Middle East], _Rev. Econ._ 9(1):127-43. January 1958.

Examines available statistical information on demographic structure (mortality rates, fertility rates, rates of natural increase), living conditions (public health, cost of subsistence, education), proposals for improving the economic level (birth control, direct aid in matters of health and hygiene, housing, education), the need for basic investment for a program of industrialization. Data on Egypt, Iraq, Israel, Jordan, and Syria.

45 Gardner, Richard N. "The Politics of Population," _Dept. State Bull._ 48:906-14. June 1963.

A blueprint for international cooperation; growing concern with the population problem; U.N. involvement in population field; principal viewpoints revealed in U.N. debate; U.S. program for international cooperation.

46 Gardner, Richard N. "Population Growth, Economic Development and the United Nations," _Dept. State Bull._ 48(1228):14-20. 7 January 1963.

Two statements by the Deputy Assistant Secretary for International Organization Affairs in Committee II (Economic and Financial) during debate on the item Population growth and economic development, together with text of resolution adopted in plenary session, December 18.

47 Gerasimov, Gennady. "Without Prejudice," _Current Digest of the Soviet Press_ 18(9):11-12. 23 March 1966. Complete text translated from _Literaturnaya Gazeta_ (Moscow), 3 March 1966.

Part of the continuing discussion of population policy in the Soviet Union in Literaturnaya Gazeta. The acknowledgement of the decisive role of socioeconomic reforms for the solution of the population problem should be supplemented by the acknowledgement of the necessity for examining without prejudice auxiliary measures, which are called population policies. Suggests substitution of terms "guidance of the birth rate" and "planned parenthood" [literally, "deliberate motherhood"] for the term "birth control."

48 Germain, Pierre. "Surpopulation du Monde et Deshumanisation" [Overpopulation of the World and Dehumanization], Rev. Administrative 13(76):389-98. August 1960.

Proposal of a world conference for demographic disarmament, to be initiated by the United Nations, to determine for each country its optimum population and to establish an international agreement obliging each country to respect the optimum worked out for it, and to furnish underdeveloped countries with assistance in establishing contraceptive programs.

49 Gini, Corrado. "Le Rôle du Facteur Demographique dans la Politique Internationale" [The Role of the Demographic Factor in International Policy], Affaires Danubiennes 4(3-4):67-94, 1941.

Nations which are confronted with increasing pressure of population on resources are in need and will seek greater living space. The conquest of neighboring or distant territories serves both as emigration outlets and as sources of natural resources. Political and military policies are in this sense linked to population policies.

50 Glass, David V. "Population Growth and Population Policy," pp. 3-24 in: Sheps, Mindel C., and Ridley, Jeanne C., eds. Public Health and Population Change: Current Research Issues. Pittsburgh: University of Pittsburgh Press, 1965. xvii, 557 pp. Also in: J. Chron. Dis. 18:1079-94, 1965.

Discusses aspects of the question, How far can we, as demographers or more generally as social scientists, offer pertinent suggestions about the kinds of action which may help to produce the desired changes in the rate of population growth?

51 Glass, David V. "Population Policies and Their Objectives," J. Heredity 33(3):107-12, 1942.

By historical review the author shows that population policies have been established by ancient as well as modern nations and that democratic as well as authoritarian governments have actively promoted them. Some have been repressive instead of population-boosting programs which have received more prominence. With the exception of Sweden none of the countries have looked at the population problem as a whole. There have been marked similarities in the use of large-scale immigration and such measures as (1) propaganda to encourage marriage and parenthood; (2) repression of the use of individual control of conception and child-bearing; and (3) the granting of cash and other allowances. Legislators have refused consistently to recognize that the population trend is part of the economic and social environment and cannot be changed without changing that environment.

52 Golding, Martin P. "Ethical Issues in Biological Engineering," UCLA Law Rev. 15(267):443-79, 1968.

There will soon be a need for legislative solutions to population size and quality and other problems, solutions that will reflect broad policy decisions on whether to encourage, discourage, permit, or prohibit various social tendencies and practices. In this article, the ethical issues which arise in connection with social programs of biological engineering are discussed.

53 Granda, Antonio Garcia, de la. "Las Politicas de la Poblacion en relacion a la Politica de Salarios" [The Politics of Population in Relation to the Politics of Wages], Rev. Int. Sociol. 13(51):323-51. July - September 1955.

Three solutions have been offered for the problem of overpopulation: (1) reduction of natality, (2) emigration, and (3) increased production. (1) is a false remedy since it results in an unwholesome aging of the population. Neither is emigration a solution, since emigrants are always at the age of high productivity both economically and biologically; their loss decreases economic production and contributes to the aging of the population. The only valid remedy for overpopulation is the increase of disposable national income and an increase of real wages. Contrary to common belief it is possible for money wages to increase without their beneficial results being cancelled out by increase in profits.

Any intelligent population policy must take account of the mobility of labor since uneconomic disposition of labor reduced the total output and thus impedes the increase of real wages. One of the possible approaches to increased wages as well as increased natality is the family allowance, which has become a substantial percent of total income in several European countries.

54 Hauser, Philip M. "Interrelationships of Manpower Policy and Population Policy," pp. 288-92, Vol. 4 of United Nations, Department of Economic and Social Affairs, Proceedings of the World Population Conference, Belgrade, 30 August - 10 September 1965. 4 Vols. New York: United Nations, 1967.

Population and manpower policy must be closely coordinated as elements in national economic planning. Policies designed to reduce rates of population growth seem to be consistent with desirable manpower policies as they affect growth, density and age structure of the labor force. Policies in respect of population distribution are, in a more complex fashion, related to general economic policy as well as to manpower policy, and much remains to be learned about their interrelationships.

55 Hauser, Philip M., ed. Population and World Politics. Glencoe, Ill.: Free Press, 1958. 297 pp.

Part III, Population Policy and Politics, contains essays by: Kingsley Davis, Population policy and power in a free world; Frank Lorimer, Population policies and politics in the communist world; Irene Taeuber, Population and political instabilities in underdeveloped areas; and Quincy Wright, Population and U.S. foreign policy.

56 Hooz, Stefan. [Some Theoretical Aspects of Population Policy], Studia Demograficzne, No. 15 (1968), pp. 23-38.

Against the background of recent trends in population growth in the socialist countries, the determining factors in such growth and the role of policy designed to influence them are systematically described.

57 Huxley, Julian. "The Impending Crisis," Eugenics Rev. 53:135-38. October 1961.

An evolutionary biologist views the population crisis, which is described as one in which quantity is threatening quality and the present is threatening the future. More specifically, the crisis is one in which the immense gap between the privileged and the under-privileged is widening instead of narrowing. As agents or leaders of evolution on this earth our ultimate aim must be to hold in trust, to conserve and to cultivate the resources of the earth and the resources of nature and, at the same time, to increase the richness of life and enhance its quality. The feeling that Science -- Science with a capital S -- will solve the population crisis is seen as a great myth of the present day, since science cannot find a way of successfully industrializing underdeveloped countries if their birth rate is too high. The author contends that the solution lies in discovering better methods of birth control and that the control of population by means of birth control applied on a large scale is a prerequisite for anything that might be called progress and advance in human evolution, even in the immediate future. The need for each country to formulate a population policy is heavily stressed, and one of the major goals of the United Nations must be that of achieving a realistic and international policy on population.

58 Huxley, Julian. "Population Planning and Quality of Life," Eugenics Rev. 51(3):149-54. October 1959. Also in: J. Fam. Welf. 5(3):19-27. March 1959.

To the questions "What are people for? What is the aim of human life?" the author replies, "It cannot be merely increase in quantity...It surely must be increased quality of life, and its progressive enrichment" (p. 150). Some thirteen threats to human fulfillment that arise from excessive population increase are enumerated: undernourishment; deforestation and erosion; inadequate water supply; increased numbers of illiterates; destruction of cultural variety; restricted human liberty, resulting from the degree of organization necessary if efficiency is to be maintained; growth of cities to sizes far beyond the optimum for efficiency and for human living; in technologically advanced countries, heavy pressure on space; export of suffering and discontent from crowded countries to those receiving immigrants; reduced possibilities of satisfying employment; in underdeveloped, densely populated countries, reduced possibility of saving enough capital to achieve a higher standard of living; curtailed possibilities of wonder, enjoyment, and adventure; frustration of human need to feel in some harmonious relation with nature. To attack the population problem, the author suggests that government ministries of health should be enlarged into ministries of health and population with equal importance given to each of the two branches. Economic motivation for population control should be provided by systems of family allowances in which the amount allowed decreases sharply after the second child. Supporting modifications of the tax structure might also be introduced. Individuals should be encouraged to aspire to higher standards of living and to realize the advantages of family limitation both for the family itself and for the nation.

59 International Labour Office. Director's Report. International Labour Conference. Twenty-seventh Session, Paris, 1945. First item on the agenda. Montreal: International Labour Office, 1945. 163 pp.

The section on migration, pp. 101-106, summarizes international and national developments; the section on population policy, pp. 106-108, stresses that current population trends deserve closer investigation and study than they have yet received.

60 International Labour Office. Minimum Standards of Social Policy in Dependent Territories. Supplementary provisions. International Labour Conference, Twenty-seventh session, 1945. Montreal: International Labour Office, 1945. 46 pp.

At its nineteenth sitting, on May 12, 1944, the twenty-sixth session of the International Labour Conference adopted a Recommendation concerning minimum standards of social policy in dependent territories. A questionnaire was distributed which included the subject of supplementary provisions regarding social security. Articles 37-40 of the standing orders of the conference cover the following questions: improvement of health and nutrition; the responsibility of the competent authority for insuring the establishment of satisfactory housing conditions; and the housing obligations of operations employing labour where such operations are situated in an area where satisfactory housing accommodation is not available. The office's text had proposed "that compulsory insurance for the protection of employed persons and their dependants in cases of sickness and maternity, old age, death of the breadwinner, and unemployment shall be introduced as soon as necessary conditions for the operation of such insurance are present" and that "it shall be an object of policy to introduce for the more developed and industrialised communities in dependant territories schemes of compulsory insurance for the protection of employed persons and their dependants.

61 Janssens, Louis. Morale et Problemes Demographiques [Ethics and Population Problems]. Louvain: Societe d'Etudes Morales, Sociales et Juridiques, 1953.

A professor at the Catholic University of Louvain places demographic problems on the plane of morals and of universal conscience.

62 Kamerschen, D.R. "Population Policies in Underdeveloped Countries," Soc. Econ. Stud. 17(1):70-74. March 1968.

Some recent hypotheses regarding population and population policies are examined critically. In particular, empirical evidence is brought to bear on the following proposition: rates of population growth in the developing countries are generally high, generally rising and generally higher than those experienced by the industrial countries at a comparable stage of economic development. The first two of these propositions are shown to be suspect and the third is untestable within the confines of our present data limitations. In an appendix some basic economic data for the less developed noncommunist areas are presented on such important variables as total population, rate of growth of population, total land area, percent of the total area that is fertile, amount of arable land per capita, GNP per capita, electric power per capita, literacy rate, pupils as a percent of population, people per physician and main export products.

63 Kiser, Clyde V. "Implications of Population Trends for Postwar Policy," Milbank Memorial Fund Quart. 23(2):111-30. April 1944.

This is an analytical report of the discussions at the Round Table on "Implications of Population Trends for Postwar Policy," held in connection with the Twenty-first Annual Conference of the Milbank Memorial Fund in New York City, April 1943. A general resume of the demographic outlook was given by the Chairman, Frank W. Notestein. The individual contributions summarized by Kiser are as follows: Lorimer, Frank. Implications of Demographic Trends in Europe and the USSR; Dublin, Louis I., Implications of the Demographic Position of Minority Groups in Europe; Thompson, Warren S., Implications of Population Trends in the Far East; Fairchild, Henry P., Implications Regarding Postwar Problems of Immigration; Whelpton, P.K., Needed Factual Basis for Pronatalist Policies; Woofter, T.J., Jr., Some Considerations Regarding Programs of Child Security.

64 Kozlowski, Zygmunt. [Concerning Overpopulation and the Population Policy Under Capitalism and Under Socialism], _Wies Wspolczesna_ 4(10):12-29. October 1960.

It is not realistic or correct to interpret population pressure as a cause of the economic underdevelopment of countries or to declare the problem of pressure as unsolvable by a national policy of economic development under both capitalism and socialism. This is what Malthusian theorists do. Admittedly, nations coming out of capitalism have deficiencies in the means of production and the quick elimination of overpopulation is not possible if there is a high increment annually to the population. Socialism tries to overcome some antagonistic aims, e.g., increasing the standard of living and the means of production along with an emphasis on high reproduction.

65 Kvasha, A. IA. "Some Problems of the Demography of the Developing Countries of Asia and Africa," _Soviet Sociology_ 4(4):3-11. Spring 1966.

One of the important problems of development of the young states of Asia and Africa is the fact that population is increasing out of proportion to economic development. The author rejects the Neo-Malthusian solution and emphasizes a program of economic development that will result in growth several times as great as the high natural population growth arising from a high birth rate and a declining death rate.

Involvement of women in production and education will probably intensify the process of conscious family planning. It is maintained that the general indices for a country's birth rate are, to a certain degree, dependent upon the age structure of its population. The author concludes that the dynamics of birth rate processes in Asia and Africa are determined by a developmental complex composed of social, economic and cultural features.

66 Lestapis, Stanislas de. "Population, Living Standards and Sense of Responsibility," Internat. Labour Rev. 70(5): 442-45. November 1954.

The author contends that although the importance of a humanistic approach to the problem has been brought out and accepted, neither the advocates of an economic solution of plenty nor those who recommend a demographic solution through birth control, faced with a hypothetical or real incompatibility between population growth and higher living standards, have paid sufficient attention to the growth of a personal and democratic sense of responsibility in the community. Stressed is the need for a clearer distinction between education and propaganda so that members of a community can make conscious decisions based on mature reflection and altruism. To make a people too exclusively aware of the disadvantages of unduly rapid growth without at the same time drawing their attention to the undesirability of the aging of the population that inevitably follows from slower growth is unworthy of the science of demography. Nor should any economist attempt to spread the idea that a policy of plenty will provide a universal panacea automatically bestowing happiness.

67 Lorimer, Frank, et al. "An Inquiry Concerning Some Ethical Principles Relating to Human Reproduction," Soc. Kompas 4(5/6): 91-212, 1957.

The treatment of population questions has been distorted by cultural conflicts, involving the confused interplay of scientific, religious, political, and personal elements. Divergence of policy in this field stems from deep differences in religious principles and ethical values that cannot be ignored. Progress has been made in recognizing the distinction between scientific issues and ethical issues relating to population in exploring the implications of information about actual conditions, and in the spread of mutual respect, tolerance and courtesy. The basic principles of cooperative action recognized by the World Population Conference at Rome in 1954 are endorsed: (1) Recognize the limitations of science; (2) respect scientific investigations of social conditions and the free exchange of ideas on the implications of knowledge for social policy; and (3) respect different religions and ethical values, and attempt to promote mutual understanding. The authors seek to enlarge the areas of cooperative action: believing this possible, especially in the spheres of scientific inquiry and of social action; affirming that an unprejudiced empirical investigation of the role of the family in various cultures supports the principle that for normal persons parenthood is an essential aspect of marriage; giving larger recognition to variation in personal needs and to freedom of individual action than seems to be accorded by Catholic tradition.

68 Lorimer, Frank. "Issues of Population Policy," pp. 143-78 in: Hauser, Philip M., ed. The Population Dilemma. Englewood Cliffs, N.J.: Prentice-Hall, 1963. iv, 188 pp.

Propositions are set forth as a basis for international policies regarding the less developed countries: (1) rapid population increase hinders socio-economic development in low-income countries; (2) socio-economic advances along other lines facilitate the control of fertility. Conversely the formation of rational ideals about parenthood favors the adoption of new techniques in agriculture, the treatment of disease, etc; (3) well-planned and actively promoted family limitation programs sponsored by national governments, in conjunction with other progressive measures, can be expected to achieve significant results; (4) the efficiency of such programs can be appreciably increased by external financial and technical assistance; and (5) discoveries in biological research may strongly affect future population trends. Today there is a general trend toward the purposive regulation of fertility. There is no longer any conflict in this sphere between European and Asian interests. Communist policy in this matter is now ambiguous or indifferent. Reformed Christianity strongly supports a positive position. There have been significant developments in Catholic doctrine on marriage and parenthood during the twentieth century, though no major change can be expected in the near future. Major issues of population policy were brought to the UN General Assembly by a resolution in its 17th Session on "Population growth and economic development," which was approved after prolonged and vigorous debate. It established the positive interest of the world organization in this field. The most important issues of national population policy in the U.S. today concern: (A) the implications of internal migration, (B) the need for a rational immigration policy to replace the obsolete quota system, and (C) the problem of chronic unemployment and the increasing number of 'marginal workers' in U.S. society.

69 Mayer, J. "Toward a Non-Malthusian Population Policy," Columbia Forum 12(2):5-13. Summer 1969.

The contention that the present rate of population growth is carrying the world to the brink of starvation is unwarranted. Potential food supplies, through improved methods of agriculture and the exploitation of new methods of food production, will be adequate for increasing populations for some time to come. Nor is population density a useful concept since it is related to such factors as agricultural and economic development, and complicated by esthetic and social considerations. The increase in disposable income is a greater threat to the ecology of the world than the Malthusian concept of widespread poverty created by unchecked population growth. "For rich people occupy much more space, consume more of each natural resource, disturb the ecology more, and create more land, air, water, chemical, thermal, and radioactive pollution than poor people." The author concludes that: "If we believe, like Plato and Aristotle, in trying for excellence rather than in rejoicing in numbers, we need a population policy now, for the rich as well as the poor. Excellent human beings will not be produced without abundance of cultural as well as material resources and, I believe, without sufficient space. We are likely to run out of certain metals before we run out of food; of paper before we run out of metals. And we are running out of clear streams, pure air, and the familiar sights of Nature while we still have the so-called 'essentials' of life. Shall we continue to base the need for a population policy on a nutritional disaster to occur at some hypothetical date, when it is clear that the problem is here, now, for us as well as for others? Shall we continue to hide the fact that a rational policy may entail in many countries not only a plateauing of the population to permit an increase in disposable income, but a decrease of the population as the disposable income rises?"

70 Meadows, Paul. "Toward a Socialized Population Policy," Psychiatry 11(2):193-202. May 1948.

The article discusses a socialized conception of population and the high value generally placed on the perpetuation of traditional population purposes and methods. The requirements of a sound population policy will vary from country to country, and for the American people, from time to time and from region to region. In general, a "numbers" policy which places emphasis on the increasing rate of births regardless of the circumstances has been rejected in favor of a "family-centered" policy which respects personality and the conditions under which children are born and reared. Again and again it has been stressed here that population policy cannot be separated from social policy in general. The methodology to solve the socio-economic problems center on the man-land ratio. "Population (P) times "Standards" (S) equals "Land" (L) times "Technology" (T); this suggests the range of techniques available for relief of "population pressure." Several suggestions for a population policy are (1) aim at replacement, (2) voluntary parenthood, (3) merge both quantitative and qualitative population measures, (4) fit into optimum population, and (5) balance, particularly in the reproductive behavior of various social classes.

71 Milbank Memorial Fund Approaches to Problems of High Fertility in Agrarian Societies: Papers Presented at the 1951 Annual Conference.New York: Milbank Memorial Fund, 1952.

The papers in this volume were given to the 1951 Annual Conference of the Milbank Memorial Fund, under the chairmanship of Professor Frank W. Notestein. After an introductory talk on the demographic gap by Dr. Rupert B. Vance, of the University of North Carolina, which he subtitled "the dilemma of modernization programs," the conference discussed the problems under three headings, cultural bases of agrarian fertility patterns, means of fertility control and implications for research and policy.

72 Mudd, Stuart, ed. The Population Crisis and the Use of World Resources. World Academy of Arts and Sciences, The Hague: W. Junk, 1963. xx, 563 pp.

The volume as a whole deals with the population resources complex, including a good deal of pure demography, and discourses on abortion, sterilization and other forms of fertility control, together with chapters on land use, mineral resources, etc. The further problems, beyond the population and resources imbalance, are not treated in detail.

73 Muhsam, H.V. "The Utilization of Alternative Population Forecasts in Planning," Bull. Res. Coun. Israel 5C(2-3): 133-46. March - June 1956.

For many purposes it would be desirable for policy planners to have accurate knowledge of what the population of a given area will be at some future date. Unfortunately available techniques for population forecasting do not furnish such precise knowledge. The article outlines a procedure by which uncertain population forecasts might be set forth and used in such a way as to permit their uncertainty to be taken specifically into account. The scheme involves three phases: (1) assignment of probabilities to alternative population forecasts; (2) establishment of a quantitative loss function for each use of the forecasts, stating the cost involved if the forecast chosen turns out to be in error by various amounts; and (3) agreement upon a policy criterion stating what risks the policy planner would prefer to run. Some hypothetical examples of this sort of analysis are presented to illustrate the method.

74 Muntendam, P. "The World Population Problem and Human Rights," Higher Education and Research in the Netherlands 12(2):3-13, 1968.

The focus is on the recognition of human rights in relation to the world population explosion. Data on population growth, food resources, and the economics of birth control are cited. Governments must enter a course of action in population policy. It is noted that Japan has been successful in its struggle against population growth because it has a highly educated population, a high degree of industrialization, and a rapid expansion of communication media, in sharp contrast with India, where many sociocultural problems, e.g., illiteracy, lack of health, education, etc., intervene. Extensive research is necessary, particularly into sociocultural problems. Social and behavioral research is just as necessary as scientific research and the two must be combined. Priority must be given to research whose application can lead in the shortest time to a real restriction of population growth. The Government of the Netherlands, in its aid to a number of countries (Kenya, Pakistan, and Tunisia) has paid attention to birth control in these countries. More such efforts are needed. Social medicine must establish a connection between medicine and the social and human sciences, all of which have operated too long beside and without one another. Population control is necessary to protect the most elemental human rights.

75 Myrdal, Alva, and Vincent, Paul. Are There Too Many People? Published under the auspices of UNESCO, Food and People Series, No. 5. New York: Manhattan Publishing Co., 1950 [9]. 48 pp.

The population problem; rejecting the fallacies; world population as we know it; population policies.

76 Myrdal, Gunnar. Population: A Problem for Democracy. The Godkin Lectures, 1938. Cambridge: Harvard University Press, 1940. 237 pp.

The population problem is held to be a political problem of social goals and planned political action. Preliminary chapters sketch the inter-relationships of the great secular swings in population and economic theory, and stress the basic importance of population replacement in the long-time destinies of democracies. The population situation in Sweden and the ideological crisis produced by the severe decline in reproduction form the background for an analysis of the attitudes of individuals toward the population problem as they are influenced by conservative or radical affiliation, family status, and national identification. The effects of population decline on the economy of a nation are then discussed. With 100 per cent net reproduction as a goal, an attempt is made to outline the broad general principles for a positive population policy in a democratic country.

77 Nevett, Albert. "Population Growth and Living Standards," Internat. Labour Rev. 70(5):445-49. November 1954.

A reply to S. Chandrasekhar's paper "Population Growth, Socio-Economic Development and Living Standards "(Internat.

Labour Rev. 69(6):527-46. June 1954). The author enlarges on the points made by Dr. Chandrasekhar in regard to means to meet population growth other than birth control. Stressed is the fact that while birth control is constantly being hailed as the solution to the world population problem, there are economic, educational, social, political and moral aspects of the population problem which must also be faced.

78 Notestein, Frank W. "The Needs of World Population," Bull. Atomic Scientists 7(4):99-101, 128. April 1951.

Points out the consequences of attempting to increase the life expectancy of people in nonindustrialized countries without regard for the resulting population growth.

79 Notestein, Frank W. "Problems of Policy in Relation to Areas of Heavy Population Pressure," Milbank Memorial Fund Quart. 22(4):424-44. October 1944.

This paper deals with the serious population problems of the densely-settled regions with high growth potentials, including Egypt, India, China, Korea, Formosa, Java, much of the Caribbean, and to a lesser extent the Philippine Islands. The demographic situation, the possibilities for checking growth, solutions to the problem, and finally problems of policy, are considered. The analysis indicates that a continuation of past policies toward the technologically undeveloped regions of dense settlement would almost certainly yield on intensification of population pressures. Escape from the rising population pressure lies in a highly complex and integrated program of modernization, which would amount to giving a practical demonstration for decades of the possibility of achieving an internal solution to the most serious problems of population pressure on the basis of industrial production, increasingly efficient agriculture, and world trade. Some of the changes needed for a decline in fertility are suggested: (1) substitution of a rounded for a colonial economy, (2) education to create new wants for physical and material well-being, (3) propaganda directed to developing an interest in the health and welfare of children in favor of controlled fertility, (4) advancement in public health, (5) native leadership with new values, (6) break down of cast and other barriers to the advancement of the individual, and (7) encouragement of migration.

80 Notestein, Frank W., _et al_. "The Problem of Population Control," pp. 125-42 in: Hauser, Philip M., ed. _The Population Dilemma_. Englewood Cliffs, N.J.: Prentice-Hall, Inc., 1963. iv, 188 pp.

A discussion of the necessity and prospects of world-wide population control by voluntary reduction of births. The present situation is examined against the background of the decline in fertility in 19th century Europe, which can be attributed not to changes in reproductive capacity or to the development of improved contraceptives, but to social changes in the wake of technological modernization and reduced mortality. The practical prospects of population control are good. International cooperation need not offend political sensitivities, since the immediate need is for well-developed services in maternal and child health, health, education and community development. In the short run these will reduce the death rate and aggravate the problem, but better health and lowered mortality lie at the root of the necessary motivational changes. The task is made difficult by high population density, low income, high birth rates, and rapidly decreasing death rates in the developing countries. On the hopeful side is the widespread governmental readiness to take measures to control population growth; Japan, India, Pakistan, Taiwan, Singapore, Korea, Turkey, and Egypt are cited. Substantial growth of population is inevitable, but the force of government leadership, plus the emergence of new methods, points to the curtailment of rates of growth as a realistic goal.

81 Organski, Katherine, and Organski, A.F.K. _Population and World Power_. New York: Alfred A. Knopf, 1961. 263 pp.

Chapter 7, National Population Policies - defines population policy as the deliberate attempt to influence fertility, mortality, or migration so as to change the course of events. Considerations of power and welfare are important factors in determining population policy. In this framework, the population policies of Nazi Germany, France, Sweden, Britain, Russia, Japan, India and Pakistan, and China are considered. Chapter 8, Population and the Problem of War and Peace - discusses the inconsistency and the plausibility of the doctrine of _Lebensraum_, pointing out the contradictions between Axis propaganda and Axis policy. It is not true that political domination of new territory provides the most likely cure for overpopulation. However, the assets of the theory are its great simplicity and the fact that the "use of the population argument as a justification for expansion ... would be believed, not only within the complaining nation itself, but also by its competitors." While it is "possible that China and India will threaten world peace when they become powerful enough to do so, it will be their power and not their population pressure that leads them into trouble." Chapter 9, Conclusion - reiterates the interrelationship between population and power and asserts that "a knowledge of the importance of population in the struggle for power and peace will enable us to understand the problems which lie ahead."

82 Osborn, Frederick. Preface to Eugenics. Revised edition. New York: Harper and Brothers, 1951. xiv, 333 pp.

The material of the 1940 edition has been reorganized, expanded and brought up to date. This book attempts to set forth briefly what science knows about heredity as a factor in individual differences, what is taking place in the growth of population, what Europe has done to control population, and what the author believes may be the place of eugenics in a world which, more than ever in the past, requires character and intelligence for the solution of its problems. Since the specific eugenics program will be determined by the form of population policy adopted in the United States it will be well to attempt a forecast of the population policies likely to develop in the near future under the influence of American public opinion. After a survey of population policies in Germany, France, and Sweden, attention is turned to present governmental activities in the United States which actually constitute the beginnings of a national population policy. A eugenic policy is held to imply three steps: 1. General improvement of the environment, in order to permit some freedom of choice as to size of family and that selection may take place at a relatively high environmental level. 2. Completion of the change now taking place to make parenthood voluntary. 3. The introduction of eugenic measures of a psychological and cultural sort which will tend to encourage births among parents most responsive to the possibilities of their environment, and to diminish births among those least responsive, thus bringing about a process of eugenic selection through variations in size of family.

Since the crux of the eugenic problem is insuring that the majority of the large families of the future should occur among eugenically desirable stocks, the psychological aspects of a eugenic environment are analyzed in detail. The eugenic reorientation of social policies is then discussed with relation to nutrition, housing, medical care, recreation, and research. The final section indicates the significance of the eugenics philosophy for the democratic ideal.

83 Petersen, William. "Marx Versus Malthus," Popul. Rev. 1(2):21-32. July 1957.

Compares the views of Marx and Malthus and finds considerable agreement between them.

84 Petersen, William. The Politics of Population. New York: Doubleday, 1964. x, 350 pp.

A collection of essays on the subject of population with each also relating to social policy in some way. Analysis of social policy includes an attempt, in some of the essays, to delineate the inherent limitations of planning with respect to such demographic processes as international migration or urbanization. Population theories are analyzed so as to emphasize their policy implications, or to show how the value commitments of theorists have on occasion influenced their scientific objectivity. Part I has the general heading of population growth and family planning and includes essays on malthusian theory; Keynes' theories of population and the concept of "optimum"; the evolution of Soviet family policy; the socialist position on birth control; and the demographic transition in the Netherlands. Part II has the general heading of migration and acculturation and includes essays on internal migration and economic development; the concept of urbanization planning; the "scientific" basis of U.S. immigration policy; and acculturation and group prejudice.

85 Pod"jacsih, Petr G. [Pod'iachikh, P.G.]. "A Nepesseg-politika Szerepe a Nepesseg Novekedesenek Szabalyozasaban" [Impact of Demographic Policy on the Growth of Population], Demografia 11(1):84-103, 1968.

The growth of population in the world and in the socialist and capitalist countries since World War II is interpreted in the context of Marxist-Leninist doctrine.

86 Population Reference Bureau. "Needed: A Population Policy for the World," Popul. Bull. 21(2):17-47. May 1965.

Notes and comment on recent developments in policy, especially toward fertility controls, on the part of agencies of the United States and of the United Nations.

87 Rimlinger, Gaston V. "Eastern and Western Patterns of the Development of Social Rights" Paper presented at the Annual Meetings of American Sociological Association, August 1968, Boston.

A comparison is made of the development of the individual's rights to income protection by the state in the USSR and in Western countries. A fundamental factor in this development is the extent to which these social rights are granted as a matter of status -- either to all citizens or to specific status groups -- and the extent to which the rights have to be earned in a contractual manner. Soviet ideology and the Soviet Constitution treat the right to protection as a prerequisite of citizenship. The dominant U.S. concept, on the other hand, has been the "contributory-contractual principle", according to which the individual earns whatever benefits he receives. Both of these approaches have inherent limitations and cannot be consistently followed in practice. The principal difficulty with egalitarian protection granted as a matter of status is its adverse incentive effects. Where protection is based on previous economic performance, the main limitation is inadequacy. Both East and West have therefore combined, although in different ways, the status and contractual principles in the development of their social rights. But different ideological points of departure and different economic and political systems have led to differences in the timing, extent, and conditions of protection.

88 Saraceno, Pasquale. Lo Sviluppo Economico dei Paesi Sovrapopolati [The Economic Development of Overpopulated Countries]. Roma: Editrice Studium, 1952. 163 pp.

An attempt by the Director of Research in the Italian Industrial Reconstruction Institute to establish the main lines for an economic development policy in countries where the imbalance between population and resources is not offset by industrial development.

89 Sauvy, Alfred. Fertility and Survival: Population Problems from Malthus to Mao Tse-Tung. Translated by Christine Brooke-Rose. New York: Criterion Books, 1961. 232 pp.

The first part is an exposition of the nature and extent of present trends of population growth, their causes and consequences. In Part 2, the discussion of the economic solution is chiefly concerned with the developing countries. The thesis is that the cost of population growth must first be met by "demographic investment" before one can even plan for raising the levels of living. The demographic investment can be assessed at four times the annual rate of population increase. With a population growth rate of 2.5 percent per annum, national income is therefore already "amputated" by one-tenth before any savings can be employed for economic investments to improve the level of living. Judging by the last ten years slight improvements have occurred only in the less populated, developing countries. Part 3, the demographic solution, states that a reduction in births is the only acceptable measure because emigration and a return to an increased death rate are unacceptable. Reviews the anti-natalist policies of India, China and Japan, Communist doctrine and attitude, and the phenomenon of aging. The long-term effect of a reduction in births is an increased aging of the population which brings with it a set of social problems. What is needed is a comprehensive social policy based on an intricate system of social action.

90 Sauvy, Alfred. "Marx et les Problèmes Contemporains de la Population" [Marx and the Contemporary Population Problems], Soc. Sci. Information 7(4):27-38. August 1968.

It is stated that Karl Marx strongly disagreed with Malthus and maintained that under a collectivist system there would be no population problem. Marx's theory that the utilization of the world's resources and expanded production through modern techniques would take care of all the needs of men, regardless of number is examined. Three notions in Marx's thinking are dealt with: the apparent abundance of a free-market economy; the concept of need; and progress in science and technology. Regarding the institution of the family, Marx felt that true monogamy was only possible under socialism. The historical and economical developments in the 19th and 20th centuries are reviewed in the light of Marx's population theory. Three major positions on population control exist now in the countries of the world, as became apparent during the General Assembly of the UN in 1962; for birth control, against it, and abstention. The Soviet countries now are in principle no longer hostile to birth control but accord it secondary importance, with economic development taking priority. Cuba, on the other hand, according to declarations by Fidel Castro, strongly opposes the efforts to reduce the birth rate of the Latin American countries, thereby following the ideas of Marx and the early socialists. China experienced a change from absolute orthodox attitudes in favor of contraception around 1956; but around 1958 orthodox ideas on population were revived. Shortly thereafter, the Chinese government discreetly returned to a policy of birth limitation, arguing that too many births reduced the economic productivity of women. It is concluded that the best disciples of Marx are trying to liberate from their oppressors the millions who are deprived of the essential necessities and who do not know yet how to overcome nature.

91 Sauvy, Alfred. "Politique de Population" [Population Policy], Revue des Sciences Politiques 11:203-10. October - December 1964.

The declared policy in all countries is to reduce mortality as much as possible; the differences are with regard to the policy on natality. The conservatives, who have been largely concerned about the question of domination, have been dubious about the material benefit as well as the religious, moral and patriotic position of the Malthusians. By the end of the 19th century, various groups differing in political philosophy as well as in Malthusianism had emerged. It is clear that a judicious population policy cannot be divorced from economic, social, and political considerations.

92 Shirras, G. Findlay. "The British Association Conference and Economic Planning," Econ. J. 51(204):515-23. December 1941.

An International Conference on Science and World Order, held in London, September 26-28 1941, attended by representatives of some twenty countries, considered planning in its various aspects. Lord Hailey, speaking of the need of a new planning policy for the colonies, stressed the need for more demographic information and research. G. Findlay Shirras considered population and planning within countries, coordinated planning for and by the self-governing dominions, and planning industrialization and international trade to increase levels of living and thus ultimately reduce the rate of increase of the rapidly growing regions of Asia.

93 Sinha, J.N. "Differential Fertility and Population Policy," pp. 43-47 in: International Conference on Planned Parenthood, New Delhi, 14-21 February 1959. London: International Planned Parenthood Federation, 1959.

The questions of size and composition are inextricably connected in population policy. Excessive preoccupation with the problems of numbers arises from an unquestioned reliance on formal economic models, built around aggregates of resources, output and labour supply, for drawing policy objectives. More detailed analysis on a disaggregated plane suggests that compositional adjustments are at least as important as quantitative regulation. Birth reduction may be a necessary goal of population policy in underdeveloped economies, but it should not be bought at the cost of a heavy reduction in the quality of population. People will be inclined to reduce fertility because of more economic opportunities and raising new aspirations among them. Population policy must be an integral part of social policy.

94 Smulevich, B. Ya. [A Critique of Bourgeois Theories and Population Policy]. Moscow: Publishing House of Socio-Economic Literature, 1959. 430 pp.

This is an investigation and an argument with the objective of presenting a Marxist critique of bourgeois population theories and policy and providing broad groups of economists, sociologists, and medical personnel with the special data and materials of demography and social hygiene which will assist them in the struggle with pseudo-scientific theories of demography and social hygiene. Section I describes the basic regularities of population development under capitalism and socialism. By the analysis of factual material, it is shown that the problem of population and public health is fully resolved only in a socialist society. Section II is devoted to an analysis of sanitation and demographic processes in capitalist countries, where an apolitical interpretation serves as one of the bases of bourgeois theories of population. Sections III and IV are also devoted to a critique of bourgeois theories of population and public health. They reveal the anti-scientific essence of the naturalistic theories of population and public health: Malthusianism, organic theories, and racism. There is obvious interest in the critical analysis of the population theories of W. Sombart, K. Kautsky, O. Bauer, Keiks [sic], Beveridge, Dublin, and others. The concluding Section V of the book is devoted to an analysis of the bourgeois policy of population and public health. It analyzes the situation of insolubility of population and public-health problems within the framework of capitalism and exposes false assertions of reformists and revisionists concerning the superclass character of the bourgeois state. Counteracting the distortions of population problems in the bourgeois literature, the author also presents an attempt to solve a number of urgent problems of social hygiene.

95 Spengler, Joseph J. "Socioeconomic Theory and Population Policy," Amer. J. Sociol. 61:129-33. September 1955.

In all treatments of policy, it is essential to distinguish between policy objectives and policy instruments, that is, between avowed purposes and social instruments specifically contrived to realize these purposes or to make them realizable.

96 Spengler, Joseph J. "Some Economic Aspects of the Subsidization by the State of the Formation of 'Human Capital'," Kyklos 4:316-43, 1950.

The main purpose is to discover what types of family allowances or subsidies are most economical in terms of their effects upon the rate at which human capital is formed (i.e., the rate at which children are reproduced and reared to adulthood). Concern is with methods designed to operate within a given pattern of taste rather than to change this pattern; also ruled out are methods which seek to alter the tastes of a people through force, repression, or propaganda. All consumer goods and services are divided into two types, X, which are complementary to the formation of human capital, and Y, which comprises all other consumer goods and services; and it is assumed that whatever causes the productive power of a nation to be shunted toward the formation of X, particularly if away from the creation of Y, is conducive to an increase in the rate at which human capital is formed. Uses many assumptions to suggest methods of state subsidy.

97 Spengler, Joseph J. "Welfare Economics and the Problem of Over-Population," Scientia 89:128-38, 166-75. April and July 1954.

In this essay the population question is considered in terms of modern welfare economics. It is suggested also that an approach to the population question in terms of modern welfare economics lies within the framework of the Malthusian tradition when this tradition is broadly conceived. The present essay is composed of seven parts: I, devoted to production theory; II, devoted to the Malthusian conception of the population-adjustment process; III, devoted to distinguishing the impact of population growth upon per capita income from its impact upon per capita welfare; IV, devoted to a restatement of the optimum theory in terms of the welfare theory developed in III; V, devoted to consideration of the variability of optimum magnitudes; VI, devoted to the fact that concomitants of dynamic change tend to obscure increases in population maladjustment; and VII, devoted to an inquiry respecting the existence of a tendency toward over-population in human societies.

98 Spengler, Joseph J., and Duncan, Otis Dudley, eds. Population Theory and Policy: Selected Readings. Glencoe, Ill.: Free Press, 1956. x, 522 pp.

Chapter 9 contains papers on Population Policy. Contents: Toward a Socialized Population Policy by Paul Meadows; Socioeconomic Theory and Population Policy by Joseph J. Spengler; Population Policy for the United States by P.K. Whelpton; Problems of Policy in Relation to Areas of Heavy Population Pressure by Frank W. Notestein; Mobility as a Field of Economic Research by D. Gale Johnson; Family Subsidies in the Netherlands by William Petersen; and The Economic Consequences of the Present Trend of Population: Summary of the Conclusions by the Royal Commission on Population.

99 Stassart, Joseph. "Fondements Economiques d'une Politique Démographique" [Economic Basis for a Demographic Policy], Revue des Sciences Economiques 40(144):205-26. December 1965.

Presents and discusses two arguments favorable to the Malthusian thesis and four arguments favorable to the natalist thesis.

100 "Statements on Population Policy," Stud. in Fam. Planning, No. 16, January 1967, pp. 2-12.

Recently a number of countries have initiated steps to deal with population growth. In most cases this development has been based upon official population policies, embodied in laws or pronouncements of various kinds. Provides statements made by several countries and the United Nations and its related organizations.

101 Stycos, J. Mayone. "The Outlook for World Population," Science 146(3650):1435. 11 December 1964.

Aspects considered: Short-run prospects of fertility decline; Birth control and death control; Unconventional methods (sterilization of both sexes, abortion, intrauterine devices); The desired family size; National birth control programs; The case of India; The role of research.

102 Symonds, Richard, and Carder, Michael. International Organizations and Population Control (1947-1967). Sussex: Institute of Development Studies, University of Sussex, 1968.

The international organizations concerned with population control, especially in the developing nations, have greatly increased in number from 1947 to 1967 and include the United Nations, UNESCO, the International Planned Parenthood Federation, the Office for Economic Cooperation and Development, the Swedish Development Organization, and several others. Their scope, financing, and procedures are detailed.

103 Taylor, Carl E. "Five Stages in a Practical Population Policy," Internat. Development Rev., December 1968, pp. 2-7.

A practical population policy requires consideration of five program components: 1) a direct response to existing demand; 2) good technology and convenient administration; 3) health care for mothers and children; 4) economic control methods; 5) modification of socio-cultural factors.

104 Taylor, Wallis. Control of World Population. Manchester, England: Manchester Statistical Society, 1967. 26 pp.

Review of past and prospective growth rates of world population. Sections on: Mortality; Fertility; Population distribution and migration; The possibilities of fertility control in developing countries; Research into new methods of fertility control; Costs; The motivation for family planning.

105 Thompson, Warren S. Plenty of People. Pennsylvania: J. Cattell Press, 1944. x, 246 pp.

Chapter XIV describes population policies particularly of certain selected countries (China, Germany, other European countries). Chapter XV is an essay on factors to be considered in a population policy for the United States.

106 Thompson, Warren S. Population Problems. New York: McGraw-Hill Book Co., Inc., 1942. xi, 471 pp.

"National Population Policies" are handled as chapters XXV and XXVI, and topically by countries: France, Belgium, Italy, Sweden, USSR, Germany, Japan - and "Some Reflections on a Population Policy for the United States."

107 Thompson, Warren S. "Some Implications of Population Changes for National Policies," Statistical Reporter 5(3):12-17. July 1961.

Discussion of the need to promote social as well as economic change and of the difficulties to be overcome.

108 Ungern-Sternberg, Roderick von. "Kunstliche Gerburteinschrankung oder Starkung der Existenzgrundlage der Weltbevolkerung?" [Artificial Birth Control in Strengthening of the Livelihood Base of the Population of the World?] Jahrbucher fur Nationalokonomie und Statistik 174(3): 246-57. June 1962.

The article considers the cultural-ethnic problems of artificial birth control, especially in non-Western countries where, for cultural or religious reasons, there is high resistance to this, in spite of great efforts to the contrary by the national governments. Increase of agricultural output is suggested as one means of partially solving the growing overpopulation problem. Japan and the Soviet Union are cited as examples where agricultural output was sharply increased once more modern methods and means were put to use and the attitudes of the farming community were won over to them. The conclusion is that world agricultural output must and can match or exceed the world birth rate and that this must be achieved through high-geared, worldwide organization.

109 "UNESCO: Report of the Special Committee of Experts on the Definition of UNESCO's Responsibilities in the Field of Population," Stud. Fam. Planning, No. 28, April 1968.

Decision reached is that UNESCO should continue to center its efforts on education, as a general matter, and, now where education is applicable to population.

WORLD POPUALTION POLICY

110 United Nations. Department of Economic and Social Affairs, Proceedings of the World Population Conference, Belgrade, 30 August - 10 September 1965. New York: United Nations, 1967. 4 vols.

Selected papers and summaries: fertility family planning, mortality, migration, urbanization, economic development, population policy.

111 United Nations. Economic and Social Council, Inquiry Among Governments on Problems Resulting from the Reciprocal Action of Economic Development and Population Changes. Report of the Secretary General. [New York], 18 May 1964. [89] pp. including appendixes.

Appendix C contains outline of present demographic activities of the United Nations.

112 United Nations. Economic and Social Council, Population and Its Relation to Economic and Social Development. Note by the Secretary General. Forty-fifth session, Provisional Agenda Item 5. New York, June 21 and July 26 1968. 4 pp.

Note on the report of the Population Commission and recommended action. Annex 1. Declaration on population by world leaders. Annex 2. Projects financed through the United Nations Trust Fund for Population Activities.

113 United Nations. Programme Appraisal, 1959-1964. Work of the United Nations in the Economic, Social, and Human Rights Fields. Note by the Secretary General. New York, 21 December 1959. 80 pp.

Chapter II, Needs and opportunities for international action, includes as the first item, Population pressure. Chapter III, Main developments envisaged in United Nations programmes, includes section, Population problems.

114 United Nations. Population Committee. Basic Considerations in National Programmes of Analysis of Population Census Data as an Aid to Planning and Policy-Making. Note by the Secretary General, New York: United Nations, 1962. (mimeogr.)

The governments of developing countries have acquired significant knowledge in planning economics and other disciplines, but knowledge concerning population and its role in economic and social development is insufficient. This is one of the main reasons for the incomplete understanding of population problems and policies, which in turn causes difficulties in the planning and execution of policy. Census data need to be analyzed so to provide more information on population in relation to a variety of social and economic variables.

115 Universite de Louvain. Justice dans le Monde [Justice in the World]. Louvain, Belgium, September 1963. 144 pp.

Contents: Anciaux, P. Aspects ethiques de la politique démographique [Ethical Aspects of Demographic Policy]; Janssens, L. Régulation des naissances et collaboration des catholiques avec les non catholiques [Birth Control and Collaboration of Catholics with Non-Catholics]; Venegan, R. Problèmes de developpement économique et social en Amérique Latine [Problems of Economic and Social Development in Latin America]; Zimmerman, A.F. La réglementation des naissances au Japon [Birth Control in Japan].

116 Vobornik, Bohumil. "Zakladni Problemy Demografie a Populacni Politika za Socialismu " [Fundamental Problems of Demography and Population Policy Under Socialism], Demografie 1(3):129-34, 1959.

A theoretical approach to the solution of basic problems of demography regarding the needs of population policy in the socialist state. The task of demography to work out such analyses is stressed, and to create a basis that could serve as a solid support for political functionaries in executing practical measures significant for the development of the population. The significance of labor reproduction, a long term prospective plan of economic development, and the determination of population policy measures that influence future population development are pointed out. An analysis of labor reproduction conditions shows that the complex of such conditions is generally expressed under the concept of the living standard. The determination of the living standard as a complex of labor reproduction conditions enables us to explain consistently the relation of demographic indicators to those of the living standard and to evaluate the development of individual demographic indicators, e.g., birth rate, number of weddings, death rate.

117 Wharton, Clifton R., Jr. "The Green Revolution: Cornucopia or Pandora's Box?" Foreign Affairs 47:464-76. April 1969.

The new foodcrop technology will not spread as widely or as rapidly as supposed, because (1) irrigation systems are needed for the new strains, (2) the market system must be expanded to handle the increased product, (3) adoption of new technology will be slower where the crop is a basic food staple, grown by a farmer for family consumption, (4) farmers must learn new skills, (5) multiple cropping will involve special problems, and (6) institutional reforms are also needed. Early adopters of the new technology will be in regions that are already more advanced, and richer farmers will become richer. Plant disease or infestation could produce massive losses if large areas are planted with single strains. Steps needed to avoid catastrophes are: (1) diversified breeding programs, (2) development of a system of agriculturally related industries to support the new methodology, (3) government pricing policies to provide price incentives to farmers, (4) plans to market the increased production, (5) increased incomes so that the greater production entering the market can be purchased, and (6) diversification of the agriculture of food exporting nations, since most developing nations promoting the new methodology are eager to achieve self-sufficiency in food production. The expanding population will soon overtake the new developments.

118 Zlotnick, Jack. "Population Pressure and Political Indecision," Foreign Affairs 39:683-94. July 1961.

Political aspects of the phenomenal population increase throughout the world with particular reference to the Christian and Communist doctrine and dogma. The rapid increase in the population of many poorer nations is a crucial factor preventing "take off" from the stage of sustained economic advance. In the underdeveloped countries, rates of population growth exceeding three percent annually are becoming increasingly common. The food sector is a particularly critical one for free-world and Communist countries alike. The birth control policies of the Roman Catholic church and of Communist countries are examined with emphasis on the contradictions between sacred scripture and stern necessity.

Policies on fertility and family size

119 "Abortion," Med. World January 1966, pp. 104-ff.

Several aspects of induced abortion are presented in a series of short articles by various authors. Topics discussed are: the present reform movement in Britain in its historical perspective; an argument against the Catholic position on abortion and for abortion law reform; physicians attitudes toward legal reform; social indications for induced abortions; case studies of suicides and attempted suicides of pregnant women; and somatic sequelae to illegal abortions resulting from poor asepsis and primitive technique.

120 "Abortion and the Law," J. Amer. Med. Assn. 199:211-ff., 1967.

The current irregular position on the legal status of abortion in the United States is examined in regard to the Bill before the British Parliament and the statement of position from the Royal Medico-Psychological Association of Great Britain.

121 Afriat, S.N. "People and Population," World Politics 17(3): 431-39. April 1965.

A principle is available: it is merely that to replace oneself is a right, a liberty without infringement; but to exceed replacement is a crime, a failing in regard to mankind as a whole, having the nature of an aggression which, if universally practiced, brings universal loss.

122 Ahmadullah, A.K. "Family Planning in an Islamic Polity," Ummah 1(4):22-25. August 1964.

The author begins by discussing Pakistan's increasing poverty and its concurrent problems with population growth, especially in East Pakistan where the density of population is seven times that of West Pakistan. He contends that there cannot be a concentration only on economic development as a measure for combating the country's poverty because the population problem itself offers a serious obstacle to any rapid economic growth. In addition, East Pakistan appears to have reached already the optimum population beyond which its people cannot be fed without penalty. The author discusses the question of whether the living faith in God, in the ideology of Islamic, is compatible or consistent with family planning and subsequently concludes that it can be and that there is room for extensive use of "Ijtihad" (deductive method) in matters of modern national concern. Family planning which does not involve the killing of lives in any way would be in perfect harmony with the essential spirit of Islam when economic conditions justify its humanitarian use for control of population growth.

123 Anderson, James N.D. Family Law in Asia and Africa. New York: Praeger, 1968.

This volume represents a collaborative work by members of the Department of Law at the School of Oriental and African Studies, together with a number of distinguished visitors. It is based on a series of lectures under the same general title given during the academic year 1965/66. The first group of papers discuss marriage, divorce and matrimonial causes in Africa, China and India. The next section is concerned with family property and the law of succession in West Africa, South Africa, Malaysia and Singapore, and Burma. The last section is general in character and includes: the patriarchal family in contemporary Islamic law; religious law and the modern family in Israel; family law in Southern Africa; and the family law of the Parsis of India.

124 Anderson, Richmond K. "World Trends in Population Control," Canadian J. Public Health, February 1966, pp. 51-54.

The author discusses the rate of population growth in relation to economic resources and development and suggests the need to channel resources toward economic investment instead of into marginal levels of consumption by a burgeoning population. The increasing awareness of this relationship between population and economic development has influenced a number of countries to adopt national population policies and several, aided by recent technological advances, have embarked on programs which may reduce high rates of population increase. The intrauterine contraceptive device is suggested as an effective, safe method of birth control. The government-supported family planning programs of India,

Pakistan, South Korea, Tunisia, and Turkey are examined and the limited programs under government auspices of other countries are discussed. Latin American and African countries have recently expressed a need for national population planning programs, and it seems likely that this interest will increase, especially in the Latin American countries where religion has previously blocked its introduction.

125 Annales de Medicine Legale [A Group of Articles on Policies Affecting Fertility]. Annales de Medicine Legale 47:395-547. September - October 1967.

Partial contents: Michaus, M.P. [The Problem of Birth Control: Medicolegal and Medicosocial Aspects], pp. 395-495; Muller, M. [Some Reflections Apropos of Contraception in France in 1966], pp. 496-97; Dourlen-Rollier, A.M. [Juridical and Social Aspect of Abortion in France], pp. 501-505; Bucic, M., and Knezevic, J. [The Problem of Abortion in Birth Control in Yugoslavia], pp. 513-18; Budvari, R. [The Campaign Against Criminal Abortion and Birth Control in Hungary], pp. 519-20; Popielski, B. [Birth Control in Poland], pp. 521-26; Chroscielewski, E., and Simm, S. [Social and Medicosocial Aspect of the Problem of Birth Control in Poland], pp. 527-32; Palmieri, L. [Clinical and Medicolegal Considerations on the Use of Contraceptives in a Population Sample in Naples], pp. 533-36; Ruolt, G. [The Problem of Birth Control (With Regard to Penal Legislation in Morocco)], pp. 537-39; L'Epee, P., et al. [The Problem of Birth Control in Black Africa (Medicolegal and Medicosocial Aspects)], pp. 540-47.

126 Augenstein, Leroy. Come, Let Us Play God. New York: Harper and Row, 1969. ix, 150 pp.

This book attempts to show how man can use constructively the powers being put into his hands by new developments in science. It is intended for the layman. The present range of knowledge, its accumulation, and the dilemmas that are opening up are outlined, together with the timetables involved. Also offered are specific recommendations on how to handle the crucial problems that are looming up for mankind. Discussions are included on genetic defects, organ transplants, the population explosion and control, mind and behavior manipulation, and abortion legislation. Case illustrations are used in presenting the issues.

127 Austin, F.E. Governments and Birth Control. Hanover, N.H.: Austin Workshops, 1940.

Argues that there is no moral, religious, or economic necessity for an increase in the present population of any nation. Only militarism and nationalism are logical justifications. Various sections of the Old Testament are quoted in support of the moral justification of governments to limit a continual increase in the populations under their jurisdiction.

128 Bagley, Christopher. "Incest Behavior and Incest Taboo," Soc. Problems 16(4):505-19. Spring 1969.

Some recent theories on incest taboo are critically examined. Then 425 published cases of incest behavior are reviewed. Five types of incest emerge: (1) functional; (2) accidental or disorganized; (3) pathological; (4) object fixation; and (5) psychopathic. Twenty-one cases could not be classified. Data contradict J.R. Fox, "Sibling Incest." There does not appear to be any natural revulsion to incest in the child. The taboo on incest is not universal and incest for functional reasons can sometimes override strong taboos. Mental disorder and low intelligence are atypical of this type of incest. It most frequently occurs in rural environments and the persistence of the feudal family system there seems to be a contributing factor. Japan, in particular, seems to have a great tolerance for functional incest behavior, aided by the sleeping arrangements in Japanese households. This type of incest can be accepted by the younger partner with equanimity, as shown by the evidence.

129 Bagramov, L.A. "Neomal'Tuzianstvo na Slujbje Amerikano Anglijskovo Imperializma" [Neo-Malthusianism in the Service of Anglo-American Imperialism], Voprosy Economiki, No. 8 (1952), pp. 80-91.

The great achievements of the Soviet Union in the building of communism represent a nice disproof of the malthusianistic 'ideas and theories.' The victory of socialism in the U.S.S.R. totally destroys the malthusianistic lie about the absolute overpopulation, which is supposed to be inherent in all the socio-economic systems. The broad acceptance of the neo-malthusianism in the United States and in England prove that the bourgeois social sciences are merely a servant in the services of the imperialists. The tasks of these servants is to justify and prove the theorems of their anti-people policy, and the exploitation of the working class.

130 Bailey, S. Sherwin. "The Lambeth Conference and the Family," Eugenics Rev. 50(4):239-45. January 1959.

Discussion of the action taken by the world-wide Anglican assembly in 1958.

131 Baird, Dugald. "A Fifth Freedom?" Eugenics Rev. 58(4): 195-204. December 1966.

In addition to the four basic freedoms, the freedom from the tyranny of excessive fertility is suggested as a fifth one. The world population problem as it refers to some different types of society is discussed: (a) the island of Mauritius, where the population in the last 20 years rose by 40%; (b) India, whose population is increasing by about eight million a year; (c) Pakistan; (d) Africa. A more positive policy of aid by advanced countries to backward countries is necessary. The population problem in industrialized societies is also examined. Japan has reduced its birth rate from 34 to 18 per 1,000 between 1948 and 1959 under laws which legalized abortion and family planning. The U.S.A. is faced with the problem of an ever-slowing death rate and an annual increase in population by two percent, in spite of an average family size of only 3.0. The United Kingdom's rising birth rate will result in a population of 65 million in 2003. Next, the point of view of the individual regarding excessive fertility is considered. Tables show preferences in birth control methods and conception patterns in the United Kingdom. Psychological consequences, perinatal mortality and maternal mortality of excessive childbearing are examined. It is stated that no matter which method of contraception is used, unplanned pregnancies will occur and sometimes their continuance will seriously endanger the mother's health. Such cases should be carefully assessed and pregnancy terminated when evidence strongly points to the advantages of this step. Women should not be forced to endure the tyranny of unwanted pregnancies.

132 Balfour, Marshall C. "Chairman's Report of a Panel Discussion on Comparative Acceptability of Different Methods of Contraception," pp. 373-86 in: Research in Family Planning, Kiser, Clyde V., eds. Princeton: Princeton University Press, 1962. xvi, 664 pp.

Five determinants of acceptability were proposed: physiological safety, aesthetic factors and ease of use, clinical and use effectiveness, cost, and factors regarding organization and distribution. These criteria were discussed regarding different methods of contraception: natural, chemical, mechanical, surgical and systemic. Degrees of acceptance were recognized, ranging from professed interest, through acceptance of teaching and materials, to continued and effective use. The consensus was that acceptability can be defined and measured at various stages, but the relative importance of factors that determine usage are not understood. Little is known of the reasons behind individual attitudes and behavior. Until research provides more data on the relative effectiveness of a variety of educational approaches and methods of distribution, family planning programs must continue to rely on empirical hit-or-miss procedures.

133 Bardis, Panos D. "A Pill Scale: A Technique for the Measurement of Attitudes Toward Oral Contraception," Soc. Science 44(1):35-42. January 1969.

Report on the construction and testing of a 25-item scale employing the Likert scaling technique.

134 Behrman, S.J., et al., eds. Fertility and Family Planning: A World View. Ann Arbor: University of Michigan Press, 1969. 503 pp.

Publication of the proceedings of a conference at the University of Michigan, 15-17 November 1967, containing papers by 23 authors organized under six major headings as follows: (1) fertility trends: A.J. Coale, D.V. Glass, D. Kirk and N.B. Ryder; (2) causes and consequences of fertility trends: R.A. Easterlin, S. Kuznets, H. Brown and A.H. Hawley; (3) biologic aspects of fertility control: J. Sutter, C.R. Garcia, S.J. Segal, and C. Tietze; (4) public programs for family planning: B. Berelson, C. Westoff and N.B. Ryder, R.G. Potter, and L. Baumgartner; (5) fertility planning in the developing world during the next decade: L.P. Chow and S.C. Hsu, N.H. Fisek, and M. Requena B.; (6) needed priorities in population control: John D. Rockefeller 3rd.

135 Bennett, John C. "Protestant Ethics and Population Control," Daedalus, Summer 1959, pp. 454-59.

The concern is over the permissible means of control and the moral basis for their permissibility. The Protestant finds no cumulative body of moral laws related to specific situations by means of a tradition of casuistry. Protestant writers believe marriage should normally involve parenthood and that the sexual function has the functions of procreation and manifestation of love between the partners. But the second function is not to be subordinated to the first. As a solution for the world population problem, Protestants find the use of contraception not only acceptable but mandatory. Nations and even the United Nations may encourage family planning.

136 Berelson, Bernard. "Beyond Family Planning," Science 163(3867):533-43. 7 February 1969.

Presents and discusses a classification of proposals for the reduction of the birth rate that have been made, mainly in English language publications during the period 1959-1968. The scheme distinguishes eight categories of proposal other than family planning programs and rates each category in comparison with family planning programs on a six-point scale for each of six criteria. (1) scientific, medical, technological readiness, (2) political viability, (3) administrative feasibility, (4) economic capability, (5) moral, ethical, philosophical acceptability, and (6) presumed effectiveness.

137 Berelson, Bernard, ed. Family-Planning Programs: An International Survey. New York: Basic Books, 1969. x, 310 pp.

Twenty-six contributors who review developments in several countries around the world. There are also statements on the roles of international organizations.

138 Berelson, Bernard. "National Family Planning Programs: A Guide," Stud. Fam. Planning, No. 5 (Supplement), December 1964, pp. 1-12.

This is an attempt to distill present principles of best practice from the experience gained so far with programs designed to implement family planning in large populations in the developing countries.

139 Berelson, Bernard. "National Family Planning Programs: Where We Stand," Stud. Fam. Planning, No. 39 (Supplement), March 1969.

This paper deals with large, organized, more or less official programs that bring family planning information, services, and supplies to mass populations in the developing world in order to promote effective family planning practices, for the welfare of the individual family and for the national community. Although such programs vary widely in their specifics, as is only to be expected from the variety of local circumstances, there is a characteristic progression of events.

140 Berelson, Bernard. "National Population Programs and the Medical Community," J. Med. Education 43(9):953-60. September 1968.

Reviews the growth of world population and its potential harm to health, nutrition, and the quality of life. The problems are most acute in the developing countries and solutions are urgently needed. Emigration must be ruled out because there are not facilities or funds for large scale movement. Birth control is essential, given the continuing control over death, and medical educators can contribute by giving training, service, and leadership to programs.

141 Berelson, Bernard. "A Review of Major Governmental Programs" [in Family Planning], in Vol. 2, pp. 253-56 of United Nations Department of Economic and Social Affairs, Proceedings of the World Population Conference Belgrade, 30 August - 10 September 1965. 4 Vols. New York: United Nations, 1967.

Reviews the programs of the five countries which are known at the end of 1964 to have governmentally approved and administered national programs to implement family planning. Covers India, Pakistan, the Republic of Korea, Tunisia, and Turkey.

142 Berelson, Bernard, et al., eds. Family Planning and Population Programs: A Review of World Developments. Proceedings of the International Conference on Family Planning Programs, Geneva, August 1965. Chicago: University of Chicago Press, 1966. xvi, 848 pp.

Text of 61 papers and reports presented at the first International Conference on Family Planning Programs, Geneva, August 1965, under the joint sponsorship of the Ford Foundation and the Population Council and with additional support from the Rockefeller Foundation. Parts: National programs: achievements and problems [21 papers]; Organization and administration of programs [7 papers]; Contraceptive methods: programmatic implications [14 papers]; Research and evaluation [17 papers]; Summary [2 reports and closing remarks].

143 Berg, J. van den. "Nieuwe Theologische Literatuur op het Terrein Van Huwelijk en Sexualiteit" [New Theological Literature in the Area of Marriage and Sex], Gereformeerd Theol. Tijd. 64:163-74, 1964.

A survey of recent books on marriage, sex, divorce, and homosexuality. Receiving treatment are: (1) Schillebeechx, het Huwelijk (Marriage); (2) B. Maarsingh, het Huwelikj in het Oude Testament (Marriage in the Old Testament); (3) A. Bieler, L'Homme et la Femme dans la Morale Calviniste (Man and Woman in the Calvinistic Morality); (4) V.A. Demant, Christian Sex Ethics; (5) J. Rinzema, Huwelikj en Echtscheiding in Bijbel en Moderne Samenleving (Marriage and Divorce in Modern Living Together; (6) W. Lohff, Die Ehe Nach Evangelischer Auffassung (Marriage According to the Protestant Conception); (7) Symposiums: De Homosexuele Naaste (The Homosexual Neighbor). RTA

144 Bergues, Helene. "Etudes Concernant La Planification de La Famille" [Studies Concerning Family Planning], Population 20(6):1025-36. November - December 1965.

A discussion grouping the studies on family planning has been added to those foreseen by the World Congress on Population which took place at Belgrade, from August 13 - September 10 1965. The papers primarily concerned the programs of birth control in developing countries. At the end of 1964 five countries had governmental programs (India,

Pakistan, South Korea, Tunisia, Turkey, and perhaps China), and others were practicing official encouragement or were presenting a limited program. Hong Kong, Formosa, Korea and Tunisia appeared especially interested in intrauterine methods. The studies on India and Ceylon showed the complexity of the problem. In other countries, family planning leads to the improvement of conditions for a fraction of the poorest of the population: Latin America, the United States. Certain papers, of a more general character, treated the effectiveness of methods, the economic aspect of the question, and its human aspect. The papers and discussion permitted the Eastern European countries to specify their attention by placing the accent on a more effective economic aid, presenting contraception as a means of individual and family well-being, and a means of protecting the health of the mother against the dangers of abortion unsuppressed by legislation and illegally performed. Japan is of special interest in this regard.

145 Berry, Paul C. Origins of Positive Population Control, 1970-2000, Working Paper, Appendix to The Next Thirty-Four Years: A Context for Speculation. Hudson Institute. February 1966.

Account of biological developments and potential impact for fertility control.

146 Bidwell, C.E.A. "Family Allowances," Comparative Legis. Internat. Law, November 1940, pp. 199-202.

The article reviews the origins and motivations for family allowances in several European countries, Chile and New Zealand. Most countries advocated family allowances specifically to increase their populations, and the programs were tried out on government officials before they were put into general practice. As early as 1870, Japan established a form of family allowances with the objective of arousing interest in and providing funds for larger families, by offering a financial reward for childbirth. Discussion centers on the thoughts of various individuals on family allowances: the political polemic view; the public health problem stand; intervention for over-population; and the difficulties with distribution of laws. The institution of marriage or family loans as a more effective measure in the demographic campaign is examined and the five classifications of family allowances are outlined, i.e., allowances paid by the employer; mutual aid programs for those other than wage earners; and the 1939 family aid process in France.

147 Birmingham, William, ed. What Modern Catholics Think About Birth Control: A New Symposium. New York: New American Library, 1964. 256 pp.

The admonitions of Pius XI's Casti Connubii and the recommendations of Pius XII on birth control are discussed in this symposium. A variety of views are expressed by the participants on the basis of their experiences. Participants include John J. Kane, Michael Novak, and others.

148 Blacker, Charles P. "Family Planning and Eugenic Movements in the Mid-Twentieth Century," Eugenics Rev. 47:225-33. January 1956.

The author reviews and relates to each other the histories of the birth control and eugenics movements and attempts to assess their respective positions today. The major emphasis is on developments in Britain, with references to activities in the U.S., France and Germany. The independent developments of the two movements between the years 1830 and 1930 are briefly outlined, and the changes in standpoint, which occurred in both movements during the period between 1930 and 1955, are described. The paper concludes with a tentative consideration of some of the problems of the future.

149 Blacker, Charles P. "The International Planned Parenthood Federation: Aspects of Its History," Eugenics Rev. 56(3): 135-42. October 1964.

Relates the developments of the movement to the successive world events to which it has reacted; describes how closely the United States and the United Kingdom have worked together; and gives some first-hand experience of people and events.

150 Blacker, Charles P. "Population, Religion and Birth Control," Eugenics Rev. 51(5):217-20, 1960.

A report on the Conference of the Marriage Guidance Commission of the International Union of Family Organizations held in Zurich, June 17 - 20 1959. Despite misgivings that fundamental issues of birth control would be side-tracked at this conference it appears that a wide airing of diverse opinions took place. A whole morning of the three day conference was devoted to a discussion of the religious position on population growth and family planning. Further themes discussed included causes of population growth, the concept of demographic pressure and the position of India.

151 Blacker, Charles P. "Voluntary Sterilization: Transitions Throughout the World," Eugenics Rev. 54(3):143-62. October 1962.

A rapid transition is taking place throughout the world in the practice of sterilization moving from a view concerned with limiting reproduction of the 'unfit' to one now increasing in Asia of voluntary sterilization to limit population growth. An intermediate position maintains the advantages of voluntary sterilization for physical, social, and psychological well-being of individuals and families. Changes in practice are reflected in changes of opinion as to the legality of voluntary and compulsory sterilization. Examination of findings in a number of countries including Sweden, Japan, India and the United States indicates on follow-up enquiries satisfaction in the large percentage of cases. The application of this review to the situation in Great Britain suggests the desirability but unlikelihood of enabling legislation which would permit voluntary sterilization on both medical and non-medical grounds. In the absence of this, Great Britain might follow the example of the United States and set up an organization like the American Human Betterment Association to advise and support the doctors concerned and their patients.

152 Blake, Judith. "Demographic Science and the Redirection of Population Policy," pp. 41-69 in: Sheps, Mindel C., and Ridley, Jeanne C., eds. Public Health and Population Change: Current Research Issues. University of Pittsburgh Press, 1965. xvii, 557 pp.

Reviews what is known of reproductive motivation through research concerning family-size declines and present levels in industrial countries as a basis for exploring available alternatives for reducing population growth by means of direct policy.

153 Blake, Judith. "Parental Control, Delayed Marriage, and Population Policy," in: Vol. 2, pp. 132-36 of United Nations Department of Economic and Social Affairs, Proceedings of the World Population Conference, Belgrade, 30 August - 10 September 1965. 4 Vols. New York: United Nations, 1967.

More extended sociological analysis of the role of family structure in family formation might point the way to making marital postponement an object of effective population policy.

154 Blayo, Chantel. "Facteurs et Structures de la Fécondité dans les Régions ou elle est Relativement Elevée" [Factors and Structures of Fertility in Regions Where it is Relatively High], Population 20(6):977-85. November - December 1965.

Customs and practices affecting fertility are of two orders: those relative to marriage (age at marriage, frequency of celibacy, remarriage of widows, frequency of divorces and remarriage of divorcees, and polygamy), and those which deal with the formation of the family (sexual taboos limiting the frequency of sex relations, provoked abortion, infanticide, contraceptive practices, and sterilization). Other factors, more generally, are cultural heritage, change in social and economic conditions, attention toward the family and number of offspring desired, and the effects of national birth control programs. Another approach to factors considers urban or rural residence, regions of the country being studied, profession of the husband, activity of the wife, race or ethnic group, and religion.

155 Bogue, Donald J. "The Demographic Break-Through from Projection to Control," Popul. Index 30:449-54, 1964.

Lists the governments which have adopted family planning as an official policy. Defines the scientific predictions and controls which demography has in its grasp and points to new research opportunity.

156 Bogue, Donald J. "The End of the Population Explosion," The Public Interest 7:11-20. Spring 1967.

The population crisis of the 20th century will be solved by the time humanity moves into the 21st century and mankind will be able to abolish hunger. While the present population situation is indeed serious, demographers are criticized for having terrorized themselves, each other, and the public at large with the essential hopelessness and inevitability of the 'population explosion'. The predicted major trends have not continued nor are they likely to do so. Population trends before 1960 are considered largely irrelevant in predicting what will happen in the future. Major social developments justifying this view are listed as (1) grass roots approval of limiting family size; (2) aroused political leadership in fertility control; (3) accelerated professional and research activity in developed and developing countries and the relaxing of religious objections; (4) the slackening of progress in death control; (5) a variety of sociological and psychological phenomena, previously unknown or underappreciated, which are promoting the rapid adoption of family planning by the mass of the people; and (6) improved technology in contraception which promotes massive adoption by uneducated people at a rapid pace. The accuracy of these points is illustrated by recent experiences in fertility planning in Korea. It is concluded that the trend of the worldwide movement toward fertility control has already reached a state where declines in death rates are being surpassed by declines in birthrates. Thus the world has already entered a situation where the pace of population growth has begun to slacken. This is estimated to have occurred at about 1965. From 1965 onward, therefore, the rate of world population growth may be expected to decline with each passing year.

157 Bonilla, Marin Gabriel. "Subsidios Familiares" [Family Allowances], pp. 549-676 in: Segundo Congreso Mexicano de Ciencias Sociales, Memoria Vol. IV. 1946.

A resume of the economic, demographic and social reasons for granting subsidies to families is followed by a history of such grants and their major provisions in various countries. There is a bibliography, arranged by country.

158 Boschi, Alfredo. Problemi Morali del Matrimonio, in Due Importanti Discorsi di Pio XII, 20 Ottobre - 26 Novembre, 1952 [Moral Problems of Marriage: Two Important Communications of Pope Pius XII, October 20 - November 26 1952]. Torino: Marietti, 1953. xiii, 481 pp.

The first communication is the discourse delivered by the Pope to the Italian Catholic Union of Midwives. The midwives are told that their professional and moral duties confer on them certain responsibilities for advising mothers on the rhythm method and abortion. His comments created considerable controversy. The second communication, delivered to the Italian Family Front, tries to clear up the misunderstandings.

159 Bottelier, P. "Een Notitie Over Demografische Politiek in Nietwesterse Landen" [A Note about Demographic Policy in Non-Western Countries], Sociologische Gids 12(3):175-78. May - June 1965.

A note on methods to be used to decrease family size in underdeveloped countries. An example from India is analyzed: to make propaganda for smaller families, the government distributed posters showing a big family in miserable circumstances and an affluent family with only two children. The reaction of the people was unexpected: they tended to pity the poor large family or to express their indignation at the symbols of progress exhibited by the small family. It is suggested that the reaction is due to the prevalence of the "enlarged family" in India. This example is used to stress the need of sociological and anthropological studies in underdeveloped countries that would develop methods of overcoming resistance to birth control in countries where the "enlarged family" pattern is dominant.

160 Boudet, Robert. "An International Union of Family Organization," Eugenics Rev. 44(1):34-38. April 1952.

The International Union of Family Organizations was established when representatives of twenty-seven nations met in a conference in Paris in 1947. Its objective was to represent family interests and family needs on a world scale and to do so in close cooperation with other international organizations in allied fields. The progress that the Union has made since its brief existence to help maintain healthy family life is examined.

161 Bourgeois-Pichat, M.J. "Les Facteurs de la Fécondité Non Dirigée" [The Factors in Uncontrolled Fecundity], Population 20(3):383-424, 1965.

Research over the last 20 years has enriched knowledge of the biological and social mechanisms regulating the reproduction of human populations. The works of M.L. Henry and P. Vincent are outstanding. The present paper is concerned only with those populations not practicing any form of contraception as it is understood in European civilization. It is seen, however, that these populations may limit family size, but this is not accomplished through the deliberate will of the couple; it is the consequence of a group of customs and thus an effect of the society rather than the individual. Factors in reproduction are considered and marriage is discussed by type for Africa south of the Sahara, North Africa and the Middle East, Asia, Latin America and Europe. Infertility of couples is dealt with. Statistics are presented in tabular form. A critique of the results provides information regarding the types of infertility, effects of variations of infertility on reproduction, duration of pregnancy, temporary infertility after childbirth, delay of conception, comparison of models and observations, observed delays of conception, foetal deaths, fecundability, rates of fecundity of fertile females in eight types of combinations, frequency of sexual relations, the decline of rates of fecundity of fertile females with age, effect of variations of the proportion of fecundable ovules, effects of variations of the period of temporary infertility, and the duration of the fertile life of the ovule. It is emphasized that further research is necessary.

162 Bousquet, G.H. "L'Islam et la Limitation Volontaire des Naissances. Brèves Réflexions sur un Grand Problème Social" [Islam and the Voluntary Limitation of Births. Brief Consideration of a Great Social Problem], Population 5(1): 121-28. January - March 1950.

The author discusses the views of the moralists of Islam, such as El-Bochari, Abou-Sa'id-Alkhodri, Ech-Cha'rani, and Ghazali (1359). These authorities were naturally unaware of appliance methods of birth control: they were solely concerned with non-appliance methods. Ghazali distinguishes five motives for recourse to contraceptive practice. Ghazali discusses these extenuating motives as follows: "In the third place is the fear of falling into extreme want because of the large number of children, and also the need to guard oneself against exhaustion in the pursuit of money or against taking up sinful occupations." Human acts can be judged according to a hierarchy of virtues; to neglect the highest is not a sin. Much depends on the motive. The intention to practise coitus interruptus "is bad if it is a question of a fear of procreating daughters, or if the woman refuses motherhood out of coquetterie, or else out of an excessive desire for cleanliness or to avoid labour or lactation." On the other hand the practice is in no way forbidden if, being the master of a concubine, "one wishes to guarantee oneself against the fact that her childbearing would destroy in any way one's right of property over her; or likewise, if the husband fears, for his wife, fatal consequences of delivery or, for himself, the fact that she would lose attractiveness, thus impairing the continuation of his sexual enjoyment." Considerations so outrageous to the feminist of today date from the remote past; yet they shape the theory of Islamic law. The writer concludes by drawing a contrast between, on the one hand, France which is Catholic, wherein birth-control propaganda is forbidden by law, and which yet has an insufficiency of births, and, on the other, the over-populated Muslim countries where extreme poverty reigns, but wherein the prevailing theology is not in principle opposed to birth control.

163 Brown, B.F. "Natural Law, the Marriage Bond and Divorce," Jurist 15:24-ff. January 1955.

Brendan Brown discusses the conception of the family under the natural law in regard to the marriage bond and divorce. He believes that natural law dictates monogamy and that polyandry contravenes the most important purpose of marriage, for it curtails generation, casts doubt on paternity, and interferes with the proper upbringing of children. He finds marriage according to natural law as a lawful, exclusive, and lifelong contract between a man and a woman. He also finds it parodoxical for those nations which refuse to accept simultaneous polygamy to legalize successive polygamy in the way of easy divorce with the right of remarriage. By allowing divorce with remarriage, monogamy is destroyed in principle, as well as in practice. Brown then discusses what he considers the responsibility of the legal profession in assisting in the maintenance of the stability of family life. He believes that divorce should be discouraged by making it more difficult to obtain.

164 Brown, L.W. "The Law and the Problem of Abortion," New Zealand Med. J. 59:93-ff., 1960.

A study of abortion laws in Britain and New Zealand where abortion is permitted only to preserve the life of the mother. The author urges that the law be revised to include the threat to the mental and physical health of the mother and eugenic and humanitarian indications.

165 Buckman, Rilma. "Social Engineering: A Study of the Birth Control Movement," Soc. Forces 22(44):420-28, 1944.

Analysis of the Birth Control Movement under the leadership of Margaret Sanger. The movement is discussed in terms of its history, methods, plan, organization, educational effort, and achievements.

166 Callaghan, Hubert C. The Family Allowance Procedure: An Analysis of the Family Allowance Procedure in Selected Countries, The Catholic University of America, Studies in Sociology, Vol. 23. Washington: The Catholic University of America Press, 1947. xiii, 262 pp.

Provides a descriptive and analytical study of the family allowance procedure as it is to be found in the recent history of the major European countries, England and Canada. This is accomplished through a study of laws and proposals embodying family allowances or the family allowance principle. The results of this study are then applied to the United States in order to discuss in the broadest terms the legal, ethical and socio-economic feasibility of a family allowance procedure in the U.S.A.

167 Camano Rosa, Antonio. El Delito de Abortio; Conforme al Derecho Uruguayo con Especial Referencia al Decrecho Italiano y Argentino. [The Crime of Abortion; According to Uruguayan Law, with Special Reference to Italian and Argentinian Law]. Montevideo: Editorial Bibliografica Uruguaya, 1958. 130 pp.

168 Camelbeke, M. van. [Birth Control in the Eyes of the Law], Rev. Praticien 13:2217-ff., 1963.

The legislation on contraception, abortion, and sterilization in France, other Western countries, and Japan is studied.

169 Campbell, Flann. "Birth Control and the Christian Churches," Popul. Stud. 14(2):131-47. November 1960.

For centuries the attitude of the Christian Churches toward birth control was clear-cut and unambiguous - any artificial interference with the normal processes of coition and conception was contrary to the laws of God and must be condemned as gravely sinful. During the last 80 years, however, as a result of the progress in medical science, the steady increase in world population, and the failure of the Churches to enforce discipline (with regard to contraception) among their own flocks, theologians have been forced to modify their traditional doctrines. Christian literature on the subject of marriage, the family, and sexual relationships is now extensive, and reflects a growing awareness of current demographic problems. Protestant and Roman Catholic spokesmen now talk of a population "crisis," and all the major Christian Churches are actively trying to develop new demographic policies which will be doctrinally sound, and at the same time realistic in a period of rapid population growth.

170 Casey, Thomas J. "Catholics and Family Planning," Amer. Cath. Sociol. Rev. 21(2):125-35. Summer 1960

A number of social trends have influenced the having and raising of children. Are Catholics resorting to contraceptive birth control in spite of the Church's norms? Freedman, Whelpton and Campbell have shown that three of ten Catholics do; also they found that one of two were doing so who had been married ten years or more and were still fecund. Catholic-Protestant birth rate differentials as studied by Stouffer (1935), Kelly (1935), Mayer & Marx (1956), indicate sharp declines in Catholic fertility. Kiser reports, however, that Catholics have larger size of completed families (1959). Brooks & Henry report that though Catholic-non-Catholic differentials were declining previously, they seem to be increasing now (1958). The decline in Catholic birth rates may be explained in lower marriage rate of Catholics or in later age at marriage. The effect of rhythm is doubtful at best. Voluntary control, however, seems to be the common explanation. Fortune (1943) magazine found on Catholic attitude toward family planning, that 69% of Catholic women thought knowledge of birth control should be available to all married women. Recent study of college women showed 18% would consider contraception to control births (1958). The 1952 Catholic national study reported only 51% of Catholics in clear agreement on the Church's stand. Non-random studies of Pearl (1939) found that 33% of Catholic women used some form of birth control. Riley & White (1940) reported 43% of Catholics admitted to family planning practices other than safe period, withdrawal or plain douche. Both Kanin (1956) and Sanienfink presented similar results. Correlates in Catholic religious attitudes and practices show the decline of religious values as controls over behavior. Fichter, Thomas, *et al.*, found secularization, marginality and religious training deficiencies to be common. This adds credibility to previous studies showing large percentages of Catholics using forbidden forms of birth control.

171 Cavan, R.S., and Zemans, E.S. "Marital Relationships of Prisoners in Twenty-Eight Countries," *J. Crim. Law Criminol. Police Sci.* 49:133-ff. July - August 1958.

This article surveys the policies and practices concerning relationships of prisoners in 28 countries of Europe, Asia, Africa, and the Americas. The general impression is that many countries hold a more humanitarian attitude toward prisoners than do many groups in the United States. The prisoner's right to and need for marriage is recognized; deprivation of marital contacts is less likely to be made a part of punishment than in the United States. However, in only a few countries are provisions for marital contacts extended equally to all categories of prisoners. Marital contacts may have some connotation of a privilege granted only to cooperative and conforming prisoners. In general the countries examined do not favor private or conjugal visits within the prison, with the exception of Mexico. However, home leaves and family residence, which emphasize the whole complex of married life and family relationships, are being expanded by most of these countries.

172 Cavanagh, John R. The Popes, the Pill, and the People: A Documentary Study. Milwaukee: Bruch Publishing Co., 1965. xi, 128 pp.

After sketching the historical background of oral contraceptives, the pill is discussed in its therapeutic and contraceptive aspects.

173 Cavanaugh, J.A. "Demographic and Family Planning Research Needs for Less-Developed Areas," pp. 501-6 in: International Union for the Scientific Study of Population, Sydney Conference, 21 - 25 August 1967.

Research and study findings are needed to help less-developed countries assess their population problems, develop policies and establish efficient action programs within the limitations of their resources and political surroundings.

174 Chakerian, Charles G., and Dupre, Louis. "Two Theological Views on Population Control," PRB Selection No. 21. Washington: Population Reference Bureau. July 1967. 8 pp.

Contents: Chakerian, Charles G. The Population Crisis, Conception Control, and Christian Response. pp. 2-6. Reprinted from: McCormick Quarterly 20(2):3-14. Jan. 1967; Dupre, Louis. Testimony of ... Hearings on the Foreign Aid Bill Before the Committee on Foreign Affairs, House of Representatives, pp. 7-8. May 9 1967.

175 Chamber of Commerce of the United States, Economic Policy Committee. World Population: Prospects and Problems. A report to the Economic Policy Committee, Washington, February 1966. v, 22 pp.

Sections include: Controlling population growth (Developing improved birth control methods; Establishing family-planning programs; Motivating underdeveloped peoples to limit family size); U.S. policy on population problems.

176 Chambers, Rosaline. "Family Allowances in Great Britain, Canada, Australia, and New Zealand," Eugenics Quart. 1(1):21-27, 1954.

Family allowances in the countries discussed are similar in that they do not require a needs test or specific contributions as in social insurance in order to obtain benefits. New Zealand, Australia and Canada finance their program by special taxation. Great Britain achieves this by the combined use of general revenue and social insurance. In Great Britain the first child is excepted from benefit, Australia gives a reduced allowance for the first child. In all countries except Great Britain the allowances are not considered part of taxable income. Allowances have not kept pace with the rising cost and consequently have fallen farther away from meeting the cost of bearing and rearing a child. Although the allowances may contribute sufficiently to those in the lower economic groups, they play a negligible part in the upper economic groups. None of the national schemes take into account differential needs as far as total income is concerned, but Canada does vary their rates according to number of children. Although there has been recommendations for higher allowances, they have been slow in coming.

177 Chand, A. "Legalizing Abortion for Birth Control," J. Indian Med. Assn. 45:95, 1965.

Following a review of the abortion situation in Japan and Eastern Europe, the author argues against the legalization of abortion in India on the grounds that it is contrary to a basic respect for human life and that the limited medical facilities in India could provide only a small number of medically safe abortions.

178 Chandrasekhar, S. "Should We Legalize Abortion in India?" Popul. Rev. 10(2):2-22. July 1966.

This paper examines the case for legalization of abortion in India against the background of official attitude towards it in Sweden, Denmark, the Soviet Union and the East European countries, the United States and the United Kingdom. The paper recommends abortion not as a major solution to India's population problem, but as a last resort when other contraceptives fail.

179 Chandrasekaran, C. "Problem of Research Design and Methods in Studies of Effectiveness of Policy Measures Aimed at Influencing Fertility," in: Vol. 2, pp. 260-64 of United Nations Department of Economic and Social Affairs, Proceedings of the World Population Conference, Belgrade, 30 August - 10 September 1965. 4 Vols. New York: United Nations, 1967.

Even when a population policy is clear-cut, the program is often flexible. Changes in program makes it difficult to single out a policy measure whose effectiveness is to be studied, and, on the other hand, of describing precisely the over-all program.

180 Chao, Paul Kwang-Yi. "Analysis of Marxist Doctrine on the Family with Testing Its Validity in Soviet Russia and Communist China," Dissertation Abstract 26:7484, 1965-66. Abstract of Ph.D. Thesis . New York: University of New York, 1963.

In the early years after the Russian Revolution the leaders attempted to move the family system in the direction of Marxist doctrine. Since 1936, however, Russian official statements stressed a new form of stable, socialist family, i.e., a restoration of the pre-revolutionary type of family on a new "socialist" basis. On the Chinese mainland, the new Marriage Law promulgated in 1950 was an impetus to changing family relationships. Women were encouraged to participate in the labor force and children were forcibly committed to state nurseries and kindergartens. Despite the encouragement of youth to be more loyal to the state than to their families, the duties of the family members to provide security for the aged and the socialization of the young remain unaltered.

181 Cicourel, Aaron V. "Fertility, Family Planning, and the Social Organization of the Family: Some Methodological Issues," J. Soc. Issues 23(4):57-81. October 1967.

Based upon recent field research on fertility and family planning in Argentina, problems of gathering data and coding information are discussed. The discussion revolves around two issues: (1) what is the link between social processes within the family and structural notions about population growth and economic development, and (2) how are practical family problems and social organizations connected with demographically defined problems of population growth? Various approaches to the structure of and process within families are reviewed. A description of field research problems and how they were handled in the Argentine study is presented. The general framework of a survey design with a small sample (number equals 298 families) was used, and the families were interviewed using open-ended questions along the lines used in J. Blake's study (*Family Structure in Jamaica*, New York: Free Press, 1961). The research context is described, and some interpretations of responses are given. Reasons for only minor reliance on a fixed-choice questionnaire administered towards the end of the study are given. Two general problems brought to light through the research relate to the substantive issue of what kinds of problems within the family the researcher would face, and the problem of identifying language and interactional categories that inform the researcher of how family interaction is motivated, how the language takes cognizance of particular structural features of the society, and the routine grounds for decision-making during family interaction. Brief descriptions are presented of interviews with five of the families studied, and problems of interview schedules, interviewer-respondent relations, and coding operations are mentioned.

182 Cicourel, Aaron V. "Kinship, Marriage, and Divorce in Comparative Family Law," *Law and Society Rev.* 1(2):103-30. June 1967.

The causes of indistinctness in sociological studies of the family, ethnographic studies of kinship and marriage, and legal accounts of family law are located in linguistic confounding and an apparent infinite regress. Sources of research data; measurement and comparative research; kinship, marriage, and divorce as formal categories; and family organization as structural meanings and practical activities are discussed. It is concluded that questions about the impact of divorce upon the 'family,' the 'sacred institution of marriage,' and kinship arrangements pertaining to family members' 'rights and obligations,' become contingent upon a study of the interaction between normative talk by members and their actual practices in seeking further inference and action.

183 Clarke, Helen I. *Social Legislation*. 2nd. ed., New York: Appleton, 1957.

Part 1. Marriage, the family and the state; part 2. Parent, child and the state; part 3. The dependent and the state.

184 Coale, Ansley J. "The Voluntary Control of Human Fertility," Amer. Philosophical Soc. Proc. 111: 164-69. June 1967

Deliberate resort to behavior that controls human fertility appears to be directly related to the level of societal modernization: societies with urbanization, exposure to communication, literacy or education, and patterns of employment other than agriculture and fishing have low and steady birth rates. Less modernized societies have high and wavering birth rates. The author discusses total fertility and the reasons for its variations, gives a brief description of fertility control methods and outlines a short history of the voluntary control of fertility throughout the world. While there seems to be no self-evident single feature of modernization that can be identified as necessary for the adoption of controlled fertility in any society, the author cites several possible reasons for its development. He speculates as to whether there will be controlled fertility in populations where it is not yet general and concludes with a discussion of three specific aspects of the current scene which suggest that birth control programs will be rapidly and effectively implemented: the progress with IUD, governmental recognition of the importance of reduced fertility, and the success of birth control programs already organized in a few underdeveloped countries.

185 Coale, Ansley J., and Tye, C.Y. "The Significance of Fertility in High Fertility Populations," Milbank Memorial Fund Quart. 39(4):631-46. October 1961.

Age at marriage affects the size of completed family and the age pattern of child-bearing. Much speculation on the effect of postponement of marriage on population growth has been in terms of the probable magnitude of the first factor and comparatively little attention has been directed at the second. The authors show that in high fertility populations differences in average age of child-bearing can account for variations in the stable rate of population growth to an extent equivalent to some 20% differential in fertility, even if completed family size is identical in each child-bearing pattern. This suggests that postponement of marriage can be an important component of population control.

186 Collins, Oral. "Divorce in the New Testament," Gordon Rev. 7:158-69, 1964.

The New Testament teaches that marriage should be a permanent union, and that remarriage following divorce is explicitly prohibited. Although marriage may be dissolved, for the purpose of divine judgment, God regards it as permanent and the one who marries a divorcee commits adultery. Regarding the exception clause in Matthew 19:9, the Roman Catholic, traditional Protestant, and interpolation approaches are rejected; the Jewish interpretation is adopted. The latter interprets porneia as a violation of the Mosaic law which prohibited marriage to one's near of kin and is included in Matthew's gospel for the benefit of Jewish readers. Paul's teaching on divorce is to the same effect.

187 Cook, Robert C. Human Fertility: The Modern Dilemma. New York: William Sloan Association Publishers, 1951. vii, 380 pp.

Chapters 15 and 16 include discussion of the eugenics movement, the Swedish experiment in population control, the dysgenic effect produced by the Canadian Family Allowance Law, the fallacy of assuming that scientific increase in food supplies can forever keep ahead of population pressure if present growth rates continue (on a global basis the per-capita ration is smaller now than in 1940), and the Soviet genetics controversy. Timing is the all-important element in the dilemma of human fertility. The crucial question is whether or not the revolt against tradition will develop fast enough. However, recognition of the problem, at both national and international levels, is a primary requirement.

188 Corsa, L. "Abortion -- A World View," in: Guttmacher, A.F., ed. The Case for Legalized Abortion Now. Berkeley, Calif.: Diablo Press, 1967.

An analysis of the legal practice and frequency of abortion throughout the world indicates that the majority of the people of the world are obtaining abortion, legally or illegally, as a method of birth control. The author advocates the legalization of abortion and making contraception methods freely available.

189 Cosgrove, S.A. "Lack of Relation Between Therapeutic and Criminal Abortion," Quart. Rev. Sur. Obstet. Gynec. 16: 223-ff., 1959.

A study of the effects on criminal abortion of broadening the indications for therapeutic abortion. The author reviews the comments of others on the situation in the United States and the Scandinavian countries and concludes that broad indications do not affect the incidence of illegal abortion. The obstetrician's independence in making the decision to abort is stressed.

190 Cutler, S.O. "Sexual Offenses - Legal and Moral Considerations," Catholic Law 9:94. Spring 1963.

After reviewing the classifications and ambiguities of the term "sexual offense", the author outlines recent trends for legal reform in the field of criminal law and its enforcement with special references to and descriptions of Great Britain's Wolfenden proposals published in 1957, and the American Law Institute's Model Penal Code, approved in 1962. General moral norms and Catholic ethics are discussed as they relate to the area of homosexual offenses and the author covers the general relationship of law to morality, the question of criminal responsibility, problems of terminology and conflicting solutions and attitudes. The author concludes with a discussion of two specific problem areas, prostitution and obscenity, from the viewpoint of law and morality, and some general considerations which cannot be ignored if current proposals for legal reform are to have any practical value.

191 Das Gupta, Ajit. "Fact Finding for Birth Control Action Programs," pp. 435-42 in Kiser, C.V., ed. Research in Family Planning. Princeton: Princeton University Press, 1962. xvi, 664 pp.

Birth control programs must be integrated with the overall program of development planning of the country. The fact finding should comprise both the statistical macro and the case study micro type of inquiries. The problems of fact finding through large-scale surveys for initial benchmarks and successive evaluation, and through case or other specialized studies for understanding at depth and decision-making are given special attention. In countries with a low literacy level, surveys have to be done by interviews.

Continuing rounds with a time sample provide a better estimate of the trend, and the maintenance of a permanent field force is thereby made feasible. The choice of the most efficient approaches for mass extension and acceptance of birth control calls for research. In India another possible agent of mass extension is the Community Development Program. The importance of the response error and bias in birth control surveys is stressed.

192 Davies, P.M.C. "Love and Contraception in Christian Marriage," Irish Theological Quart. 33(4):327-51, 1966.

New developments in theology will establish the truly sacramental nature of intercourse in marriage and will confirm that it is here that husband and wife encounter the risen Christ. By its nature intercourse is symbolically fertile; intercourse would lose this symbolism if contraception was practiced and hence its sacramentality would be lost.

193 Davis, Kingsley. "Institutional Patterns Favoring High Fertility in Underdeveloped Areas," Eugenics Quart. 2(1): 33-39. March 1955.

In analyzing high fertility in underdeveloped areas basic uniformities rather than superficial differences are stressed. The relationship of the nuclear family to the rest of society is the social factor affecting the level of fertility. Although the underdeveloped areas possess a high rate of fertility, they are agrarian societies and the nuclear family of procreation tends to be controlled by other kinship groups. This results in the joint household and the composite family functioning as an economic unit. The nuclear family is a less independent unit in agrarian societies than in industrialized societies. The relationship of the nuclear family with other kinship groups results in high reproduction because: (1) cost of rearing children does not rest completely on the parents but is shared by the common household; (2) with an extended family the problem of child care may be shared by many; (3) the age at marriage may be at a young age, consequently, women's potential reproduction period is longer; (4) the greater dependence of the nuclear family on other kinship groups often exerts strong social pressure to marry; (5) in societies of patrilocal residence the wife, as an outsider, may gain prestige by having children as early as possible and in considerable numbers; and (6) the family gains political and economic strength by having many children. Segregation of female and male roles in agrarian societies is another influence on fertility. The institutional restriction of women to the home and reproduction and the lack of communication between husbands and wives, particularly on sexual topics, provide attitudes favorable to high fertility.

194 Davis, Kingsley. "The Theory of Change and Response in Modern Demographic History," Popul. Index 29(4):245-66. October 1963.

The process of demographic change and response is not only continuous but also reflexive. Taking Japan as an example, abortion is seen along with contraception, sterilization, migration, and postponement of marriage, as developing rapidly in a short period of time in response to declines in mortality and sustained natural increase. This multiphasic response cannot be explained regarding spreading poverty or diminishing resources, but regarding behavior prompted by personal rather than national goals. Northwestern Europe's response was similar. Under a prolonged drop in mortality with industrialization, people found that their accustomed demographic behavior was handicapping them in their efforts to take advantage of the opportunities being provided by the emerging economics. They accordingly began changing their behavior. Thus, it was in a sense the rising prosperity itself, viewed from the standpoint of the individual's desire to get ahead and appear respectable, that forced a modification of his reproductive behavior. The motivational linkage between change and response depends on fear of absolute poverty. If each family is concerned with its prospective group, it can be understood why the peoples of the industrializing and hence prospering countries altered their demographic behavior in numerous ways, reducing the population growth brought about by lowered mortality.

195 Deverell, Colville. "The International Planned Parenthood Federation - Its Role in Developing Countries," Demography 5(2):574-77, 1968.

The main purpose of IPPF is to convert people and their governments to an acceptance of the need to persuade humanity to regulate its fertility in a fully responsible manner in the interests of individual families and mankind.

196 Deverell, Colville. "Recent Changes in Official, Legal and Political Attitudes to Contraception." Paper presented at the International Union for the Scientific Study of Population, General Conference, 3-11 September 1969.

Significant anti-contraceptive legislation is now largely confined to countries which have inherited the 1920 French law introduced in an attempt to avert the decline in population following the First World War. But the recent amendment to the French law permits French assistance to some developing countries. Legal restrictions, as opposed to motivational, logistic and religious considerations, are not normally serious obstacles to the practice of family planning in developing countries. The tendency in developing countries is for new legislation to facilitate rather than impede fertility reduction. In most countries, most parents wish to curtail their maximum fertility. The extent to which they will do so depends as much on the strength of their motivation as on the access to knowledge and facilities. Legislation to restrict or liberalize the practice of abortion may have a marked influence on fertility.

197 Devereux, George. A Study of Abortion in Primitive Societies: A Typological, Distributional and Dynamic Analysis of the Prevention of Birth in 400 Pre-Industrial Societies. New York: Julian Press, 1955.

An extensive review of abortion illustrating political, social, economic and sociological aspects. Although statistics are generally unavailable, abortion is thought to vary in societies just as do primitive and non-primitive measures. Few groups openly approve of abortion.

198 Doublet, Jacques. "Apercu sur les Législations Etrangeres en Matière Dèmographique" [Summary of Foreign Legislation on Demographic Subjects], Population 1(2):283-98. April - June 1946.

An appendix presents French translations of the Soviet decree of July 8, 1944, and the Canadian family allowance law of August 15, 1944.

199 Dourlen-Rollier, A.M. Le Planning Familial dans le Monde: Aspect Demographique [Family Planning in the World: the Demographic Aspect], Realisations. Petite Bibliotheque Payot, Vol. 129, 1969. 266 pp.

A world-wide review, country by country, consisting of two parts: (1) the background, causes, and nature of the "population explosion" with emphasis on fertility trends; (2) the current situation, including the status of family planning-policy and program.

200 Draper, Elizabeth. Birth Control in the Modern World: The Role of the Individual in Population Control. Baltimore: Penguin Books, 1966. xxx, 333 pp.

A book of IV Parts and 13 Chapters on the facts, problems and issues of birth control. Part I - Introducing the Problem - presents 1. Why Control? examines the attitudes behind the use of the different terms, 'population control', 'family planning' and 'planned parenthood'; chapter 4, Methods of Control, considers rational and irrational methods to restrict population growth or promote fertility. Part III - Society and the Individual - considers chapter 5, Interactions, containing a discussion of influences and opportunities with society and the individual's reactions; chapter 6, Education, discusses the correlation between the effective use of contraception and education; chapter 7, Attitudes of Different Religions, is concerned with the teachings of Judaism, the Christian religions at different times, Islam, Hinduism and Buddhism on birth control; chapter 8, Attitudes of States and Their Laws, examines the policies of governments in West and East Europe, the U.S., Russia and China and mentions the activities of the UN regarding planned parenthood. Part IV - Practice and Prospects - includes, The Search for new methods and evaluation of effectiveness of contraceptive methods and surveys research in new methods; extent of use of contraception; promotion, manufacture, and distribution; future prospects.

201 Dubois-Dumee, J.P. Va-t-on Contrôler les Naissances? [Are We Going to Control Births?] Paris: Bibliothèque de l'Homme d'Action, 1956. 128 pp.

After a brief history of birth control and a glance at the situation in other countries, the demographic, social, psychological, and moral aspects to the question are examined. An answer to the questions raised by Derogy is given from the Catholic point of view. The text of the projected law and a bibliography are included.

202 Duhamel, Joseph S., S.J. The Catholic Church and Birth Control. New York: Paulist Press, 1962. 24 pp.

The factors and elements which have brought about a renewed interest in the problems connected with birth control are reviewed briefly, since it is within the ambience of changing moral views on such problems that the modern Catholic must lead his life in this country. The official condemnation of artificial birth control, or the use of illegitimate means of limiting family size, is examined in terms of definition and Papal documents, and then this individual doctrine is evaluated within the context of the total teaching of the Church on the dignity of marriage and its sacred nature and purposes. The article concludes with a discussion of the moral norms that determine and justify the practice of periodic continence by the rhythm method.

203 Dumas, André. Le Contrôle des Naissances. Opinion Protestantes [Birth Control. Protestant Opinion]. [Cahors], Les Bergers et les Mages, 1965. 164 pp.

Contents: Absence of the problem in Christian tradition; Recent evolution of protestant declarations; The Contestations of the Catholic doctrine; The mystery of sex according to the Bible; Protestants and family planning; Responsibility and demography; The sanctification of the body; Orthodox theology and birth control.

204 Ebling, E.J. ed. Biology and Ethics. London: Academic Press, 1969. 145 pp.

Proceedings of a symposium held 26-27 September 1968 by the Institute of Biology at the Royal Geographical Society in London. Papers were presented by M.R.A. Chance, C.A. Clarke, B.M. Foss, J.E. Hall Williams, J.H. Humphrey, R.P. Michael, B. Mitchell, A.S. Parkes, D.A. Pond, M. Potts, A.I. Richards, and M.F.A. Woodruff on such topics as the problem of abortion, the ethics of organ transplantation, and the right to reproduce in an overcrowded world. Four of the papers are followed by a discussion among several of the conference participants.

205 Egner, G. Birth Regulation and Catholic Belief: a Study in Problems and Possibilities, Stagbooks, London: Sheed and Ward, 1966. xi, 283 pp.

This book is a contribution to the examination of the Roman Catholic beliefs on birth regulation. The first chapter discusses the philosophical background to the concept of nature often used in arguments about the Roman Catholic position. The next four chapters analyze the rational arguments used in support of the Roman Catholic position; the values claimed to be bound up in it; the accordance of it with nature; the distinction it preserves between artificial and natural sterility; and the protection alleged to be afforded by it by the virtue of chastity. The account of the place held by the virtue of chastity in argument for the Roman Catholic position links the analyses of its rational apologetic with the study of its chief dogmatic defense - the appeal to tradition. The author suggests that the appeal to tradition, while uniquely powerful, might not be as irremovable an obstacle in the way of change as is usually supposed. He concludes by stating that the appeal as it stands is indecisive, so that an authoritative intervention of the Church is needed to resolve its ambiguities.

206 Ehrlich, Paul R. The Population Bomb, New York: Ballantine Books, 1968. xiii, 223 pp.

Attempts to give awareness to the ultimate destruction inevitable from over-population. The existence of too many people and too little food is brought to light. Present attempts at family planning and increased food production are reviewed. The necessary policies for the U.S. to implement to control its own population and to influence population control in the rest of the world are presented. An appendix contains letters that have been sent urging action related to the population problem. Contains several proposals for controlling fertility: national satellite television systems for direct informational effect on population and family planning; prizes for each five years of childless marriage or vasectomy before the third child; tax benefits to favor the unmarried or parents of few children; marriage grants to couples where each partner is at least 25 years old at time of first marriage; and establish in the United States a powerful federal agency to take whatever steps are necessary to bring the population to a reasonable size.

207 Ellis, Havelock. "Birth-Control and Eugenics," Eugenics Rev. 60(2):76-81. June 1968.

Various arguments in favor of birth control are outlined: economic or Malthusian; evolutionary or zoological; humanitarian or social reform; purely medical and eugenic. The eugenic argument is not new, "but today, when so many of the chief branches of the white stock are being sapped in their racial vitality by influences of previously unknown virulence...this aspect of the problem assumes the gravest significance of all." Eugenists view birth control as an invaluable instrument not merely for social betterment but for the elevation of the race. Hence they should foster it by: (1)increasing and promoting the knowledge of the laws of heredity; (2) popularizing a knowledge of the methods of birth control; and (3) by acting in accordance with their knowledge.

208 English, J.F. "Married Women and Their Property Rights: A Comparative View," Catholic University Law Rev. 10:75-86. May 1961.

The author outlines the history of the legal relations between husband and wife in regard to property rights, beginning with Roman law, which emphasized the individuality and separateness of the marriage partners, and Anglo-Saxon concepts and developments in early English law, which centered on the independence and rights of the husband and the incapacity and subordination of the wife. Present trends in continental property law, which stresses the fact that marriage creates a conjugal community and thus a system of community property, are described, as well as the American woman's current status of independence and equality. The constant element throughout history is the progression of the wife's position, from one of subjection to her husband to that of complete equality with him in matters of proprietary and legal capacity.

209 Erskine, Hazel Gaudet "The Polls: The Population Exposion, Birth Control, and Sex Education," Publ. Opin. Quart. 30(3): 490-501. Fall 1966-67.

Data of public opinion polls are assembled from various sources regarding the population explosion, birth control, birth control in other countries, sterilization and abortion, and sex education.

210 "Existing Conditions with Respect to the Traffic in Persons and Prostitution in Selected British Trust and Non-self-Governing Territories," Internat. Rev. Criminal Policy, July 1956, pp. 58-67.

This note is based on reports supplied by governments in reply to a questionnaire, approved by the Economic and Social Council. The reports are for 1951-1952 and 1953-1954 but some of the 28 territories did not report for both periods. Information is provided on the traffic in women, extent of prostitution and brothels, and criminal actions taken against these practices. Described, too, are measures aimed at preventing prostitution and venereal diseases. There is little indication of any need for United Nations' action.

211 Fabre, H., and Sutter, J. [Medical Opinion on Contraception and Abortion], Population 21:51-ff., 1966.

Questionnaires concerning birth control were sent to 2490 physicians in many countries. Only 365 responded and many of their answers were incomplete. In response to a question concerning how the legalization of contraception would affect the rate of induced abortion, the difference of opinion was great.

212 Fagley, Richard. "Verantwortliche Elternschaft und das Problem der Ubervolkerung der Erde" [Responsible Parenthood and the Problem of the Overpopulation of the Earth], Z. Evang. Ethik 113-21. March 1960.

A report on the international development of the population problem given to the central committee of the Ecumenical Council by the secretary of the church's Commission for Internation Affairs in 1959. There follows the report of the special ecumenical study group which met at Oxford in 1959 to discuss responsible parenthood and the population problem. This latter report appeared in the Ecumenical Review, October 1959.

213 Fagley, Richard M. Population Explosion and Christian Responsibility, New York: Oxford University Press, 1960. 260 pp.

The author describes the accelerated growth of world population, especially in the underdeveloped areas of Asia, Africa and Latin America, as the chief enemy of free society in the world today. He points out that there is no real answer to this problem unless it includes a slowing down of the population explosion through family planning. The problem posed by an uncontrolled birth rate, particularly in the overpopulated areas of the world, may have consequences as far-reaching as atomic explosions. According to the author, the solution must be found at the religious level. Stressing the need for a more widely held and vigorously supported Christian doctrine of responsible parenthood, the book discusses growing awareness in the Church of population problems, the persistent neglect at the governmental level, religious obstacles and the need for a clear and conscientious stand on the matter.

214 Family Planning Association of Pakistan. Birthright. 1969. 58 pp.

Report on the Pakistan International Family Planning Conference at Dacca, 28 January - 4 February 1969. Each session is reviewed, and texts of five papers are presented: E. Adil, "Pakistan Family Planning Programme"; P.M. Hauser, "Non-Family Planning Methods of Population Control"; M. Potts, "Induced Abortion - The Experience of Other Nations"; and S.J. Segal, "New Frontiers in Contraceptive Technology." Also B. Berelson, "Beyond Family Planning."

215 Feldman, David M. Birth Control in Jewish Law. New York: University Press, 1968. 322 pp.

A study of Judaism's principles concerning marital relations, contraception, and abortion as revealed by an examination of the Talmud, Codes, and Commentaries: the Jewish mystic and moral literature; and the rabbinic Responsa (many of which are made available for the first time). Specific topics covered by written sources spanning the history of Judaism include: sexual pleasure in marriage, "irregular" or "unnatural" sex acts, rights of marriage partners, preferred methods of contraception, and the question of the "ensoulment" of the fetus as related to the subject of abortion and foeticide. These principles are examined with respect to the simultaneous existence of both the strict and the more normative Jewish traditions, and also in contrast to the traditions of Christianity. Many past decisions made by rabbis were situational in nature, and the principles thus revealed are specific. The assimilation of the several hundreds of these Responsa, which provide most of the book's source material, results in a number of general precepts: the sanctity of marital sex; the duty of procreation as the "first mitzvah" of the Torah, with the inadmissibility of abstinence and the legitimacy of oral contraception as alternatives; and the primacy of avoiding physical risk to the wife or mother.

216 Flournoy, Henri. Nouvelles Données et Réflexions Psychologiques sur les Avortements Médicaux. Pour une Attitude Liberale plus Equitable et plus Humaine et contre les Avortements Clandestins [New Data and Psychological Considerations on Medical Abortions. In Favor of a More Equitable and Humane, Liberal Policy and Against Clandestine Abortions]. Geneva: Ed. Médecine et Hygiene, 1955. 106 pp.

217 Ford, Clellan S. *A Comparative Study of Human Reproduction.* New Haven: Yale University Press, Yale University Publications in Anthropology, No. 32, 1945. 111 pp.

Presents available fragmentary evidence about child-bearing, pregnancy, contraception in a sample of primitive societies in Yale cross-cultural files.

218 Ford, Clellan S. "Fertility Controls in Underdeveloped Areas," pp. 841-49 in: Vol. 1, *Proceedings of the World Population Conference.* New York: United Nations, 1955.

The gravity of rapid population increase warrants far more research than is presently being undertaken. It requires the skills of the human biologist, demographer, psychologist, sociologist, economist, political scientist, and the anthropologist. There is noted the directions which anthropological research might take, given the existing knowledge about fertility controls in underdeveloped areas.

219 Frederiksen, Harald, and Brackett, James W. "Demographic Effects of Abortion," *Public Health Reports* 83(12):999-1010. December 1968.

Presents graphs showing annual total fertility rates in comparison with estimated rates for pregnancies, legal abortions, and other abortions for periods of varying length since World War II for selected countries (Bulgaria, Hungary, East Germany, Japan). Notes on the literature and discussion of the data in the light of prototype situations related to the practice of abortion and contraception as alternatives.

220 Freedman, Ronald. "Family Planning Programs Today: Major Themes of the Geneva Conference," *Stud.Fam. Planning,* Number 8 (Supplement), October 1965, pp. 1-7.

In August 1965, the first International Conference on Family Planning Programs was held in Geneva under the sponsorship of The Ford Foundation and the Population Council, with additional support from The Rockefeller Foundation. Ronald Freedman summarizes the major themes and implications of the Conference Papers.

221 Freedman, Ronald, and Whelpton, P.K. "The Relationship of General Planning to Fertility Planning and Fertility Rates," Vol. 3, pp. 549-74 of Kiser, C.V., and Whelpton, P.K., eds. Social and Psychological Factors Affecting Fertility. 5 vols. New York: Milbank Memorial Fund, 1955.

Examines the empirical relation between general planning attitudes and behaviors and the planning of fertility specifically. Planning is conceived as a form of rational, secular behavior.

222 Fryer, Peter. The Birth Controllers. London: Secker and Warburg, 1965. 384 pp.

This is an illustrated biographical history of an important social revolution of modern times. The careers of two famous pioneers, Margaret Sanger and Marie Stopes, along with others are brought to life. The pre-history of this revolution is discussed beginning with primitive techniques and ending with our age of modern techniques. The growing desire for women's rights and freedom is discussed.

223 Gebhard, Paul H., et al. Pregnancy, Birth and Abortion. New York: Harper and Bros. and P.B. Hoeber, 1958. xiii, 282 pp.

Volume 3 of a series of the Institute for Sex Research founded by Alfred C. Kinsey in 8 Chapters. Chapter (1) describes the Terms and Methods used by the Kinsey groups. (2) The Sample, details the constitution of the total sample (7,074 women), and sources of the sample by: age, education, marital status. (3) The Single Woman, describes pregnancy among them as related to: age, marital status at interview, coital experience, age at marriage, educational level, decade of birth, and degree of religious devoutness; the outcome of the pregnancy (live birth, spontaneous abortion including stillbirth, and induced abortion), by the categories in (2) above. The general finding is that: "Of the pre-marital pregnancies that ended before marriage, 6% were live births, 5% spontaneous abortions, and 89% induced abortion. Of 2,221 ever-married females almost 3% were pregnant when they married." (4) The Married Woman, details the same information as in (3) above but for the married group.

224 Geijerstam, G.K., af, ed. An Annotated Bibliography of Induced Abortion. Ann Arbor: Center for Population Planning, University of Michigan, 1969. 359 pp.

Lists and annotates 1175 current works (mainly since 1960) on biological and medical, statistical, legal and administrative, psychiatric, demographic, religious, cultural, and political aspects of induced abortion. Of the original items, 790 are in English, 133 in German, 54 in French, 40 in Czechoslovakian, 48 in Danish, Swedish, Norwegian, and Finnish, 23 in Spanish, and 87 in other languages. Contains a section on epidemiology of induced abortion by continent, and author and special subject indices.

225 Geijerstam, G.K., af "Family Planning and Induced Abortion," in: Westin, B., and Wiqvist, N., eds. Fertility and Sterility. New York: Excerpta Medica Foundation, 1967.

Abortion as a family limitation device is discussed with regard to Japan and the Eastern European countries which have liberal legal abortion laws, Sweden which has restricted legal authorization, and Chile which has none. Also examined are some problems that may accompany the substitution of contraception for abortion and future methods of induced abortion as by oral birth control drugs taken after conception.

226 Geisendorf, W. "Family Planning," J. Internat. Fed. Gynaecol. Obstet. 2(2/3):141-49, 1964.

Following a review of the techniques of contraception, the psychological and social objectives of family planning are discussed. The work of the International Planned Parenthood Federation is discussed, and a description of an ideal family planning center is presented.

227 Geisert, Harold L. The Control of World Population Growth. Population Research Project of the George Washington University Publication. Washington, 1963. 50 pp.

Reviews trends in fertility and mortality for each country in Africa and the Near East, Southcentral Asia, the Far East, and Latin America. There is also a discussion of the variables which influence fertility and the acceptance of birth control. Generally, the spread of ideas concerning birth control is limited by low literacy and a lack of communication. While the overpopulated nations must decide for themselves whether to limit population growth, the developed nations should stand prepared to aid them in implementing their decisions.

228 Gerard, Hubert. "Quelques Orientations de Recherches à propos des Politiques Antinatalistes" [Some Directions of Research on the Subject of Anti-Natalist Policies], Recherches Economiques de Louvain 33(4):477-82. September 1967.

Author suggests that research in the area of anti-natalist policies include study of norms, values, and objectives underlying motivations of societies. Studies of anti-natalist policies should consider their efficacy, feasibility, relationship to traditional cultures, and compatibility with other social and economic objectives of societies.

229 Gibbons, William J. "Fertility Control in the Light of Some Recent Catholic Statements: I," Eugenics Quart. 3(1): 9-15, 1956.

The Roman Catholic Church recognizes the motivation for fertility regulation which has arisen as a result of the Industrial Revolution and a great decline of mortality. Further motivation to limit offspring has arisen owing to the changing socio-economic structure of urbanized society, whereby a large family size came to be regarded as an obstacle. The Church feels, however, as custodian of morality, that the ends of marriage should, as in the past, be so formulated as to include primarily the procreation and education of children, secondarily, the advantages accruing to the spouses from communal bed and life. Recent writers, both non-Catholic and some professed Catholics, have emphasized the psychological values and personality development aspects to spouses which, however important, remain secondary purposes of marriage. The only form of fertility regulation sanctioned by the Church is that of use of the female sterile period. Thus the Sacred Penitentiary in a reply of June 16 1880 to the question: "Is it licit to use marriage only on those days when conception is less likely," indicated that spouses who acted thus were not to be disturbed in conscience.

230 Gibbons, William J. "Fertility Control in the Light of Some Recent Catholic Statements: II," Eugenics Quart. 3(2):82-87, 1956.

The only form of fertility control recognized by the Church is the use of marriage during the female sterile period for reasons not trivial, frivolous, or purely selfish, but significant; i.e., of a medical, eugenic, economic, or social character. It is acknowledged that the effectiveness of the rhythm method of fertility control depends on the technical efficiency of means of detecting the approach of ovulation and on the self-discipline of the marriage partner. The Church disapproves of abortion, regarding it as murder. Likewise the Church disapproves of sterilization as a means of contraception because this is a wilful destruction of a natural function. Furthermore, the Church does not approve of the use of artificial insemination when the husband is not the donor.

231 Gibbons, William J., and Burch, Thomas K. "Physiologic Control of Fertility: Process and Morality," Amer. Ecclesiastical Rev. 138(4):246-77. April 1958.

The impending development of methods of controlling fertility which secure their effect through the elimination or modification of physiological processes essential to reproduction, by administration of drugs, serums, and the like, and which therefore equally require no further interference with coitus immediately before, during, or immediately after its performance raises moral questions for Roman Catholics. It is probable that some persons will fail to see the distinctions involved and hence may believe such methods to be lawful in the eyes of the Church. It is proposed that the various forms of physiological control can appropriately be considered as either (a) sterilization [perhaps temporary or reversible], or (b) abortion or feticide. The relevant moral principles do not deny that much research on fertility may be valuable and have acceptable applications. However, the rise of physiological control measures -- and thus of sterilization, infanticide, or abortion -- for the express purpose of preventing conception or destroying its product is not acceptable.

232 Gille, Halvor. [The Role of the United Nations in Action Programs in the Population Area], Demografia 10(3-4): 365-67, 1967.

Shows the development of ideas on family planning programs which could involve the United Nations and its allied agencies.

233 Glass, David V. "Fertility and Birth Control in Developed Societies and Some Questions of Policy for Less Developed Societies," Malayan Econ. Rev. 8:29-39. April 1963. Also in: J. Fam. Welf. 9(3):6-18, March 1963.

Comments on a number of misconceptions: 1) Birth control does not adequately account for the fall in Western birth rates, biological factors also being involved; 2) Primary cause of the fall was the availability of reliable contraceptive techniques. Briefly traces the demographic history of the West with special attention to Britain, France, and U.S.A. Purpose: 1) to show birth control has worked and in a relatively short period and 2) Western married couples did not avail themselves of modern techniques of contraception. Birth control campaigns and their sponsors should be linked more closely with other measures designed to promote economic and social development.

234 Graham, Leroy S. "An Examination and Analysis of the Relevance of the Christian Ethic of Sex with Respect to Premarital Sexual Intercourse: An Inquiry Based on the Thought of Reinhold Niebuhr and Emil Brunner in View of the Findings of Alfred Kinsey and Margaret Mead," Dissertation Abstr. 26:2890-91, 1965/66. Abstract of Ph.D. Thesis, Drew University, 1965.

The dissertation is organized into an introduction, four parts (containing a total of nine chapters), two appendices and a bibliography. The introduction points out the lack of any extensive Protestant ethical analysis of premarital coitus by reviewing the literature produced since 1948. It also describes the author's research methods and delimitations. Chapter I reports the widespread deviation in practice from the traditional Christian norm of premarital chastity, notes the evidence of a major trend toward greater deviation in the twentieth century in the U.S., and supports the data by summarizing findings of the larger studies on the subject. The widespread theoretical challenge to the traditional norm is documented by brief quotations from a large number of writers in various fields. Chapter II focuses upon the factual data presented by Alfred Kinsey and associates, with sections on male behavior, female behavior, the meaning of their personal behavior to Kinsey's subjects, and the effects of the deviation. Coitus is analyzed in relation to other types of premarital sex activity, and to age, religious devotion, educational level and other factors. The third chapter treats premarital coitus in cultural context and cross-cultural contrast as reported and interpreted by Margaret Mead. Her writings on five South Sea societies and the United States are analyzed to discover the extent to which premarital coitus is approved or forbidden and the way this regulation is intergrated into the entire society and its culture. In Chapters IV and V the focus shifts to separate analysis of the sex ethics of Protestant theologians Emil Brunner and Reinhold Niebuhr. In each case the writer's thoughts concerning human sexuality and its various meanings and expressions are set in systematic order, with a focus upon the meaning of premarital intercourse in the light of God's will. The next progression in the study involves a testing of the relevance of the ethic of sex presented by each theologian to the factual data provided by Kinsey and Mead.

235 Greenhill, J.P. "World Trends of Therapeutic Abortion and Sterilization," Clin. Obstet. Gynecol. 7(1):37-42, 1964.

Legal abortions have increased enormously in many countries, both in countries without any surplus population and in countries in which there is frightful over-population. In the first category are Sweden, Denmark, Hungary, Czechoslovakia, Bulgaria, Poland and Yugoslavia. In the latter group are Denmark, Sweden, Switzerland, Chile, Russia and Japan. The chief indications for legal abortions should be medical illnesses including dubious psychiatric disturbances; however,most legal abortions are being performed for eugenic, economic, or sociologic reasons. Likewise, sterilization operations are increasing especially on males.

236 Grisez, Germain G. Contraception and the Natural Law, Milwaukee: Bruce Publishing Co., 1964. xiii, 245 pp.

The author examines the meaning of natural law. He predicates certain basic inclinations of man, affirming these from anthropological and psychological data. Man's understanding of these inclinations points practical reasoning toward basic human goods which a man should want freely to achieve. The author rejects situationalism as requiring man to act against substantive goods in order to maximize reflexive goods. Conversely, he rejects conventional Catholic natural law theory because the negative legalism of this system results from a basic exclusion of moral evils rather than a derivative exclusion of irrational preferences. He concludes that contraception is intrinsically immoral as a destruction of the procreative good which man should pursue.

237 Gronseth, Erik. "The Decision to Marry: Editorial Introduction," Acta Sociol. 8(1-2):1-6, 1964.

The connection of the 'decision to marry' theme to research in more specific fields as decision making in small groups and as mate selection, premarital sexual relations, dating, engagement, etc., is pointed out, as well as the present lack of integration of those fields. Five main types of substantive content are found in one or more of the papers discussed: (1) outlook, responsibilities and influence of family researchers regarding people's decision to marry, (2) the decision to marry and not to marry as process and its determinants from the point of view of the potential marrier, (3) the decision about when to marry: age at marriage in Finland, Norway, the U.S. and Yugoslavia; differential frequencies and their social and psychological determinants, (4) the decision about whom to marry: mate selection homogamy, socially and symbolically, and (5) consequences of differentially based decisions to marry upon later course of marriage and personality development. The main question addressed by each of the 13 papers and their mutual relation regarding problems covered is indicated as well as their main concepts scope.

238 Guttmacher, A.F. "Abortion," in: Genne, E.S., and Genne, W.H., eds. Foundations for Christian Family Policy. New York: National Council of the Churches of Christ in the U.S.A., 1961.

A review of the status of abortion, of its relation to population situations and of the experiences of Japan, Eastern Europe, Russia and Scandinavia. The author cites the inadequacies of the present laws and advocates a new law to permit non-Catholic physicians to practice modern medicine. Illegal abortion ought to be considered a grave social and medical disease.

239 Guttmacher, A.F. "The Legal and Moral Status of Therapeutic Abortion," in: Meigs, J.V., and Sturgis, S.H., eds. Progress in Gynecology, Vol. IV. New York: Grune and Stratton, 1963.

An examiniation of the historical legal and religious background of abortion; the effects of liberal laws in Japan, Eastern Europe and Scandinavia; and abortion in the United

States giving data from several studies on abortion. The author urges new abortion statutes or at least the broadening of existing laws -- the latter being the most difficult to achieve.

240 Guttmacher, Alan F., _et al._ _The Complete Book of Birth Control._ New York: Ballantine Books, 1961. 152 pp.

Information is included on methods of birth control as well as a discussion of infertility. The chapter on the churches and family planning deals with Protestant, Jewish and Catholic positions. States that all religious denominations approve of some method of birth control, disagreement being as to method. Thus a permissible method of birth control is available for all, whatever their religious belief.

241 Guttmacher, M.S. "The Legal Status of Therapeutic Abortion," in: Rosen, H., ed. _Abortion in America._ Boston: Beacon Press, 1967.

A review of the history of abortion, Russian and Japanese experience, and abortion legislation in the United States and other countries with respect to various interpretations as the Bourne case. Dr. F. Taussig's five principles to be incorporated into an ideal abortion law are quoted.

242 Guzevaty, Y. "Population Problems in Developing Countries," _International Affairs_ (Moscow), No. 9, September 1966, pp. 52-58.

Considers effects of rapid rates of population growth and mal-distribution of population in relation to resources. Comments on national family-planning policies in the United Arab Republic, India, Pakistan, and other countries.

243 Haider, S.M. "Population Pressure in Under-Developed Countries and the Need for Population Control," _Pakistan Horizon_ 10(3):144-56. September 1957.

The author believes that control of population growth will be essential to the improvement of the standard of living of many countries including his own. To develop a foundation for this position, he brings together a substantial number of quotations from leading writers on demographic subjects of the last thirty years. The persistence of the population problem in recent decades despite human advances on many fronts is made more apparent by the major place Haider is able to give to ideas presented by E.A. Ross in 1927.

244 Hammons, Helen G. "International Family Legislation," Eugenical News 37(4):65-85, 1952.

Owing to economic hardships borne by large families, every western European democracy has been forced to institute legislation designed to promote family size. The legislation has arisen largely owing to the threat of war and the inability of the countries to maintain armies large enough for protection. The benefits of the social laws include the following: cash family allowances, income tax relief, aids in providing family food, housing, clothing, education of children, transport, differential savings advantages, preferential admission to employment, advantages in purchasing land, livestock, etc., and exemptions from military service. The author includes detailed tables showing such economic measures in favor of family size in the following countries: Argentina, Belgium Brazil, Canada, France, Greece, Sweden, United States, the United Kingdom and the U.S.S.R. The United States has less family legislation than the other countries. It is hoped that the United States will use eugenic foresight in designing further family benefit legislation rather than consider size of family only.

245 Hankinson, R.K.B., and Soewondo, Nani, eds. Family Planning and National Development, London: International Planned Parenthood Federation, 1969.

Several papers given at a conference in Bandung, Indonesia June 1969. The family planning movement is discussed in terms of governmental and voluntary efforts and benefits for Asia in general, Indonesia, India, Pakistan, United Arab Republic, Hungary, and several other countries.

246 Hardin, Garrett, ed. Population, Evolution and Birth Control: A Collage of Controversial Readings. W.H. Freeman and Co., 1964. 341 pp.

Utilization of the collage technique in arranging articles to stress the idea that some sort of effective birth control technique is urgently needed.

247 Hardin, Garrett. "The Tragedy of the Commons," Science 162(3859):1243-48. 13 December 1968.

The population problem has no technical solution; it requires new social arrangements. A finite world can only support a finite population; population growth must eventually equal zero. Ways are needed to identify the optimum population. Decisions made by individual families cannot be expected to result in the right overall birth rate. The "invisible hand" of Adam Smith does not function in a commons, because the individual gets 100 per cent gain from the resources he depletes while the loss is distributed among all members of the commons, and has negligible effect on him. Combining the concept of freedom to breed with the belief that everyone has an equal right to the world's resources--the commons--locks the world into a tragic course. Appeals to conscience will not affect people's decisions. The world must abandon the freedom to breed and mutually agree on mutual coercion to govern breeding.

248 Harmsen, Hans, ed. Beitrage zur Bevolkerungsentwicklung Sowjetrusslands, Osteuropaischer Volksdemokratien und Mitteldeutschlands unter besonderer Berucksichtigung des Abortproblemes [Contributions on Population Change in the USSR, the East European Peoples' Republics, and East Germany, with Special Reference to Abortion Problems]. Deutsche Akademie fur Bevolkerungswissenschaft an de Universitat Hamburg, Akademie-Veroffentlichung Reihe A, No. 5. Hamburg, 1961 [iii], 205 pp.

Twenty-four contributions on population growth and policy on fertility controls in the USSR, Bulgaria, Hungary, Poland, Czechoslovakia, Yugoslavia, and the German Democratic Republic.

249 Harmsen, Hans. ed. Zur Entwicklung und Organisation des Gersundheitswesens in Sowjetrussland, in Osteuropaischen Volk-Demokratien und in Mitteldeutschland, Band 8. Zur Sozialhygienischen Problematik der Gesetzgebung Betreffend Schwangerschaftsunterbrechang und Abtreibung in Mitteldeutschland [On the Development and Organization of the Health Services in Soviet Russia, in the East European People's Republics and in East Germany. Vol. 8. On the Social-H-gienic Implications of the Legislation on Pregnancy Interruption and Abortion in East Germany]. Hamburg: Akademie fur Staatsmedizin in Hamburg, 1957.

The development of legislation concerning abortions in the Soviet Union and East Germany in comparison with West Germany. It presents the various laws passed in the 1940's and early 1950's and considers the sociological and legal problems of this legislation.

250 Harmsen, Hans. "Fertility and the Law," pp. 108-10 in: Proceedings of the Seventh Conference of International Planned Parenthood Federation, February 10-16 1963, Singapore.

All cultures are governed by their laws and ordinances, no matter whether it be written laws or traditions passed on by mouth from father to son. By such laws and ordinances the inter-human relations of this particular circle are regulated and influenced.

251 Harmsen, Hans. "Lasst sich der Illegale Abort durch Erweiterung der Indikationsstellung zum Schwangerschaftsabbruch Bekampfen? Ein Beitrag zur Neuesten Entwicklung in der USSR" [Can Illegal Abortion be Curtailed by a Broadening of the Position Toward Indications for Pregnancy Interruption? A Contribution on the Latest Developments in the U.S.S.R.], Gesundheitsfursorge - Gesundheitspolitik 6(1):14-19. April 1956. Separately reprinted.

Texts of West German and East German laws on abortion. Comparison of abortion rates in East Germany, 1946-1956, with those in Moscow, 1909-1931. Texts and comment on the USSR decrees of November 18, 1920; June 1, 1922; November 3 1924; June 27, 1936; August 5, 1954; and November 23, 1955.

252 Hauser, Philip M. "On Design for Experiment and Research in Fertility Control," pp. 463-74 in: Kiser, Clyde V., ed. Research in Family Planning. Princeton: Princeton University Press, 1962.

A proposal for an experiment designed to permit the observation and evaluation of the play of cultural, personal, and social psychological factors in effecting changes in behaviour leading to fertility control. Principles of the experimental design, sampling scheme, the dependent variable, "control" independent and the experimental independent variables are the five items that have been emphasized.

253 Havel, J.E. La Condition de la Femme [The Status of Women]. Paris: Librairie Armand Colin, 1961. 221 pp.

A study of the status of women in the past and modern societies. Of particular interest are chapters on prostitutes, woman and maternity, woman and marriage, and women in non-European civilizations.

254 Heiss, Herbert. Die Abortsituation in Europa und in Aussereuropaischen Landern: Eine Medizinisch-Rechtsvergleichende Studie [The Abortion Situation in Europe and in Non-European Countries: A Comparative Medico-Legal Study]. Zeitschrift fur Geburtschilfe, Beilageheft, 166. Stuttgart: Enke, 1967. 256 pp.

The discussion of the philosophy of abortion and its legalistic condensation in each country is preceded by a 33-page general part. In the special part of the book, comprising 207 pages, the legal status of abortion and its historical development in each country [24 European and 8 non-European states] are shown in detail. The effect of legislation on public mores is examined. Quotations of the law, vital statistics, and significant statements by professional leaders are offered. An annex, containing the history of abortion legislation from the Old Testament through ancient, and modern Europe to Northern, Middle, and South America, and Japan concludes the book.

255 Henry, Louis. "Essai de Calcul de l'Efficacité de la Contraception" [Attempt to Compute the Effectiveness of Contraception], Population 23(2):265-78. March - April, 1968.

Examines the way in which the distribution of married women according to residual fecundability (probability of conception during a calendar month) enters into the relation between the improved Pearl index (i.e., his failure rate limited to 12 months) and the effectiveness of contraception and, should the occasion arise, how to pass from a value of the Pearl index to a value, or an order of magnitude, of effectiveness. Appendix presents the general case of the calculation of the failure rate for a period since exposure to risk of conception in terms of the distribution of residual fecundability.

256 Henry, Louis. "Intervals Between Confinements in the Absence of Birth Control," Eugenics Quart. 5(4):200-11, 1958.

Variations of birth intervals within families were studied for a population living in the village of Crulai (in Normandy), including 46 couples married in the years from 1674 to 1742. Completed families with at least six children were studied. Comparisons were confined to intervals where the preceding child had attained at least one year of age, thus eliminating the variation in birth interval owing to infant mortality. Although previous studies of populations practicing no birth control show the effect of birth order (or of mother's age) to be negligible, among the families of Crulai, intervals between successive confinements tend to increase with the order of birth. Further, some families were found to bear children within shorter intervals than other families. Intervals between confinements depend on three factors: (1) the woman's fecundability; (2) the frequency of uninduced miscarriages and still-births; (3) the time-lapse between a confinement and the next onset of ovulation. The data obtained favor the third factor since a constant shape of the successive birth interval curve occurs. Either birth order or mother's age has an effect on the interval between births, there apparently being an increasing delay in the resumption of ovulation after a confinement. There is a marked variation in individual procreative ability as shown by inter-family differences.

257 Henshaw, Paul S. Adaptive Human Fertility. New York: McGraw-Hill, 1955. xii, 332 pp.

Problems of human fertility and population growth; fertility and population growth; fertility management practices and other population policies.

258 Hill, Reuben. "Research on Human Fertility," Internat. Soc. Sci. J. 20(2):226-62, 1968.

A critical summary is presented of the emergent field of family planning research commissioned by UNESCO for the "Science of Man" series. The methodological stances of the range of disciplines contributing are noted, from the macro-emphasis of demography and economy to the micro-concerns of family sociology and psychology. Viewed world-wide, the output is greatest for descriptive baseline surveys of the levels of contraceptive information, family size preferences, and family planning practices now completed in over forty countries. Less wide-spread and more recent are explanatory studies which examine conditions at the macro-societal level necessary to change the perception of population growth as a problem by the "problem definers" and to precipitate social action in the form of national programs on the one hand, and changes in the value orientations and decision-making properties of the country's child-bearing couples on the other. Least frequently reported but of high significance are experimental evaluative researches designed to assess the impacts of educational and mass communication programs on attitudes and adoption of family planning practices. Changes in research emphases are noted. At the macro-societal level, the focus of research is changing from the study of conditions favoring countries recognizing problems of population growth to the multi-faceted dimension of the comparative success of different organizational strategies for reducing population growth. At the micro-familial level, four new dimensions of research are emerging: (1) operational research on non-adopters utilizing feedback to change the programs of persuasion and service to win the "hard-to-reach" as a new clientele; (2) operational research on "drop-outs" to discover the contexts of discontinuance; (3) study of the timing dimension, the timing of marriage, of learning about birth control, and of crystallizing a desired family size, and its consequences for success in family planning; and (4) the study of the social and psychological consequences of family planning.

259 Hiller, A. "Trends Towards Recognition of Polygamous Marriages in Common Law Countries and Matters Incidental Thereto," *J. Family Law* 3:219, 1962.

260 Himes, Norman E. *Medical History of Contraception*. New York: Gamut Press, 1963. liii, 521 pp.

Hime's *Medical History of Contraception* was first published in England in 1936. It is the classic history of birth control methods: it ranges from population control in preliterate societies, through the techniques used in antiquity -- dealing separately with Western and Eastern cultures, the Middle Ages and early modern times to "the democratization of technique since 1800 in England and the United States" and "democratization and its future effects." The new edition is enriched by a twenty-page Preface by Alan F. Guttmacher, President of the Planned Parenthood Federation of America, who disclaims any attempt to bring the book up to date. Guttmacher does, however, give a review of the chief milestones between 1936 and 1963. He starts with the legal position in the United States, from Dr. Hannah Stone's well-known court case in 1936 following the seizure by the Customs authorities of a packet of diaphragms from Japan, to the stringent anti-contraception laws of Massachusetts and of Connecticut, in which State a case was pending for re-argument at the time this Preface was written. Under "Governmental Attitudes" Guttmacher contrasts the wide ranges of official policies in countries with a rapidly expanding population: the positive attitude of Japan, India, Pakistan, Puerto Rico, Singapore, Egypt, Korea and Taiwan on the one hand with the almost complete absence of fertility control policies in the Republics of South and Central America, most of Africa and the Philippines. He also gives the position in the nations with more or less stable populations and suggests that in the Iron Curtain countries contraception and abortion policies are influenced by considerations of maternal welfare rather than by the fear of overpopulation. There is a brief statement of the present-day attitudes of the great religions of the world, and a history of the development of the leading family planning organizations.

261 Hoffner, Claire. "El Desarrollo de la Legislacion Sobre los Subsidios Familiares en los Ultimos Anos," [The Development of Legislation on Family Allowances in Recent Years], Informaciones Sociales 5(3):177-97. March 1941.

History, with special reference to Belgium, France, Italy; new systems in Chile (1937), Hungary (1938), Spain (1938). Tendencies and trends in scope, benefits, and costs.

262 Hoffner, Claire. "Recent Developments in Compulsory Systems of Family Allowances," Internat. Labour Rev. 41(4):337-60. April 1940.

Legislation on family allowances is summarized for stabilized schemes (New Zealand and New South Wales), evolutionary schemes (France and Italy), and new schemes (Chile, Hungary, Spain). Attention is given to the nature of the allowances; to their scope, beneficiaries, and amount; and to the equalization funds and other methods of financing them.

263 Horne, Herbert H., Jr. "World Population Problems and the Catholic Point of View," Internat. J. Fertility 8(1):415-18. January - March 1963.

Report delivered at the Fourth World Congress of the International Fertility Association, Rio de Janeiro, August 1962, concerning efforts to find new means of fertility control acceptable alike to Catholics and non-Catholics.

264 Houghton, Vera. "International Planned Parenthood Federation (I.P.P.F.)," Eugenics Rev. 53(3):149-53 and 53(4):201-7. October 1961 and January 1962.

Traces the development of the international organization from the International Neo-Malthusian Conference held in

Paris in 1900; through a long series of international conferences, organizations and committees; to the formation of the I.P.P.F. in 1952.

265 Houghton, Vera. "Responsibilities of Voluntary Organizations," Eugenics Rev. 57:16-20, 1965.

The term 'voluntary organization' covers bodies which provide some form of social service, control their own policy and depend, in part at least, on financial support from private subscribers or donors. In the planned parenthood movement, the responsibilities are: (1) to the individual, to help him (or her) to take the vital responsible decision in the interests of the well-being of the family. It is essentially a problem of communication; (2) the best possible medical advice and treatment must be provided; (3) harmless and psychologically acceptable contraceptives suited to the individual need must be provided; and (4) special problems, i.e., treatment of infertility, sex education, promsicuity and illegitimacy, marriage problems, abortion and sterilization, should be publicly aired and investigated.

266 Houghton, Vera. Why Family Planning? September, 1959. 33 pp. (Mimeographed).

Various aspects of family planning have been covered, including the motivation factors - individual, national and international - the growing necessity for birth control, and the attempts made in different countries and their results.

267 Hoyt, Robert G., ed. The Birth Control Debate. The National Catholic Reporter Publishing Company, 1968. 224 pp.

Some selected, reportedly authentic documentation of the controversy within the Catholic Church about the use of artificial contraception in marriage, with commentary by the editor on the background issues, and people involved. Texts include translations of reports from the fifth and final session of the Papal Commission, meeting in the spring of 1966 (two working papers, "Status Quaestionis" and "Documentum Syntheticum," one expressing the conservative, the other the liberal view, and the final report,

"Schema Documenti" with an introductory pastoral statement, "Indications Pastorales"); the encyclical letter of Pope Paul VI, "Humanae Vitae," issued 29 July 1968; and responses to "Humanae Vitae" from the episcopate in Belgium, Canada, and the U.S., individual theologians, pro and con, and members of the Church. Except for explanation and introductory matter, almost all the elements of the book appeared previously in the _National Catholic Reporter_.

268 Huard, L.A. "Law of Adoption: Ancient and Modern," _Vanderbilt Law Rev._ 9:743. June 1956.

After a general outline, beginning with primitive societies, of the origins and development of adoption and references to historical influences on United States adoption law, the author assesses the state of current American law on adoption and discusses the substantive provisions of a District of Columbia statute thought to be typical of the enlightened adoption legislation in most states. The problem of religious belief and adoption, or the conflict between the importance of spiritual welfare to the best interests of the child and the fact that a secular system of law lacks a suitable tribunal in which to try the matter, is then examined in light of the continuing uncertainty as to what legal emphasis should be placed on the religious beliefs of the parties in proceedings for adoption, custody and guardianship. There are, at present, some 43 states which have enacted legislation making religious belief pertinent to the judicial determination of adoption, and recent judicial decisions and interpretation of such legislation are described. The author concludes with an analysis of the Catholic position on adoption and a brief discussion of what he contends are two pressing quasi-legal problem areas: the black market and the gray market in adoptions and the question of adoption by blood relatives.

269 Hulme, William E. "Theological Approach to Birth Control," _Past. Psych._ 32(11):25-30. April 1960.

The purposes of marriage and sex fit together, and the accomplishment of such a union indicates the need for some type of conception control. The theological issue is whether conception control is not man's responsibility under God. The controversy over birth control is not simply a question over method but a question of differing conceptions of marriage and of the role of sex in marriage.

270 Huxley, Julian. "Population and Human Fulfillment," Popul. Rev. 2(2):17-34. July 1958.

The increase of the world's population threatens to outstrip food supplies, and to destroy natural beauty and local culture because of the need to import Western industrialization to maintain the expanded population. A plan for establishing a balance in the world population is needed. Japan, in 1954, passed a strong resolution urging Government encouragement of birth control, with widespread propaganda and the provision of birth-control facilities as part of the Health Services, as well as research and family planning in the medical curriculum. In India, research grants are given for: (1) studying new contraceptives, and the effectiveness of the old ways, (2) the study of demographic problems, (3) the establishment of training centers for family planning workers, and (4) education of public opinion regarding family planning. These attempts are just beginnings and do not meet the problem sufficiently.

271 Hyrenius, Hannes. "Evaluating the Effectiveness of a Family Planning Program: Opening Discussion," pp. 420-22 in: Kiser, C.V., ed. Research in Family Planning. Princeton: Princeton University Press, 1962. xvi, 664 pp.

There is often a confusion between attitudes and motivations. Further, attitudes regarding the general acceptability of contraceptive methods may be different from those relating to a single case. We may find that an individual will have one general attitude, one about his family in the long run, and one about his family right now. In field studies, it is difficult to get an inventory of the situation.

272 International Labour Office. "Family Allowances Schemes in 1947," Internat. Labour Rev. 57(4):315-33. April 1948; 57(5):456-77. May 1948.

A survey of existing schemes of family allowances which takes account of wartime and postwar changes in the older schemes as well as the introduction of new schemes. The study deals with the prevalence of plans, objectives of family allowances, including the demographic aims, families covered, and children covered.

273 International Planned Parenthood Federation. The Fifth International Conference on Planned Parenthood: Report of the Proceedings, Tokyo, 24-29 October 1955. London: I.P.P.F. xxvii, 1956. 315 pp.

The papers which form the main body of the Report are arranged in sections dealing with topics such as world population and resources; family planning in relation to sociology, eugenics, health, etc.; contraception in its clinical and in its research aspects; and so on. The group of papers which occupies the greatest number of pages is entitled "Research into Reproductive Processes and into Biological Methods of Controlling Fertility." Parker, Pincus and Zuckerman are prominent here. The papers brought together as "Family Planning and Eugenics: Policies and Movements," is notable for its accounts of Japanese experience. This section ends with an expectedly acid and valuable paper by Blacker on "Family Planning and Eugenics Movements in the Mid-Twentieth Century."

274 International Planned Parenthood Federation. The Sixth International Conference on Planned Parenthood: Report of the Proceedings, New Delhi, 14-21 February 1959. London: I.P.P.F. viii, 1959. 374 pp.

The theme of the Conference was family planning motivations and methods. Population growth, cultural patterns and motivations, biological aspects of fertility control, education for family life, oral methods, laboratory testing of contraceptive effectiveness and family planning programmes were the main topics covered in the different sessions.

275 International Social Security Association. "The General Principles on Which Scales for Family Allowances are Determined: Progressive or Regressive Scale, Age, Order of Birth," Internat. Social Sec. Assn. Bull. 18:405-41. July - September 1965.

Report 17 adopted by the General Assembly, International Social Security Association, Washington, D.C., 26 September-3 October, 1964.

276 International Social Security Association. Reports. Eleventh General Meeting, Paris, 7-11 September 1953. Geneva, 1954. In 4 parts. 106, 312, 170, 67 pp.

Report I. Recent development in the field of social security. Report II. Family allowances. Report III. The evaluation of invalidity. Also [IV] Reports of the Permanent Committees.

277 International Union of Family Organizations. Compensations en Faveur des Familles dans le Monde [Family Allowances in the World]. Rome: Italian Committee of the I.U.F.O., 1951. 425 pp.

The World Congress of the Family and Population met in Paris in June 1947 and showed its interest in the problems confronting the family and children throughout the world. At the conclusion of this Congress, the International Union of Family Organizations (U.I.O.F.) was established for the purpose of considering all opinions and bringing together all organizations concerned with the family. It held its first general assembly in 1948 at Geneva and took up the problem of juvenile delinquency in relation to the family. Next it organized an International Conference on the Family which met in Rome from the 19th to 24th of September 1949. Twenty-six nations attended it. This volume reports on the proceedings of the conference, which had the general theme, family economics during the insecurity of the modern world. The three chapters cover: 1) housing, food, and clothing; 2) home help, education, holiday and leisure; and 3) fiscal matters affecting the family. Each chapter is introduced by a general statement and this is followed by reports from the representatives of particular countries. The most numerous reports pertain to France and Italy. At the end of the entire report is a summary of the conference findings which the President of the International Union of Family Organizations prepared for his address to the United Nations.

278 Jackson, L.N., ed. Overpopulation and Family Planning: Report of the Proceedings of the Fifth International Conference on Planned Parenthood, Tokyo, 24-29 October 1955. London: International Planned Parenthood Federation, 1955.

Seven chapters are concerned with aspects of family planning related to sociology and health, to eugenics, to methods of contraception, to sterilization and abortion, and artificial insemination. There is also a chapter on population policies and pressures which describes the situation in Bermuda, Britain, Ceylon, Egypt, Hawaii, Hong Kong, China, India, Japan, and the Western Hemisphere.

279 Jackson, L.N. "Passport to Tokyo: The Fifth International Conference on Planned Parenthood, Tokyo, 1955," Eugenics Rev. 48(1):41-44, 1956.

Some of the highlights of the Conference are given. Of special interest is the family planning experiment carried out over a period of five years in three villages in Japan and the fashion of abortion since legalization.

280 Jaffe, A.J. "Population Trends and Controls in Underdeveloped Countries," Law and Contemporary Problems 25:508-35. Summer 1960.

Population growth in virtually all underdeveloped areas is rapid and promises to become more rapid as death rates are further reduced while birth rates remain at their present high levels. At present rates, the populations of the underdeveloped parts of the world could increase by as much as 175 per cent. What is significant about such a rapid growth rate is that it is difficult to force an economy to grow at a rate very much faster than this. There are many factors influencing lower fertility levels: (1) growth of the economy, (2) increased schooling, (3) heightened aspirations from urban life, modern means of communication, etc. Within this framework of a changing socioeconomic matrix, the provision of adequate contraceptive techniques will make it easier to achieve lower fertility. The provision of birth control information and materials by itself will contribute little. The implication of these remarks seem to be that under the best circumstances, it will still take at least one generation before there may be a decided slackening in the rate of population growth.

281 Jain, Anrudh K. "Relative Fecundability of Users and Non-Users of Contraception," Soc. Biol. 16(1):39-43. March 1969.

Estimates of fecundability (monthly probability of conception in the absence of contraception, outside the gestation period and the period following the termination of pregnancy) are derived by fitting a Type I geometric model to the frequency distribution of conceptive delays immediately following marriage.

282 James, T.E. Prostitution and the Law. London: William Heinemann, Ltd., 1951. x, 160 pp.

Attempt has been made in this work to state the law in England and a number of other countries relating to factors which are considered basic in precipitating prostitution. The subject is treated under the following headings: introduction, prostitution and kindred offences in their historical setting, the law relating to prostitution and kindred offences in England, the law relating to some subjects collateral to that of prostitution and kindred offences in England, U.S.A., and France, the problem considered in relation to the U.S.S.R., the treatment of prostitutes by the law in England and elsewhere, and the problem and conclusions in relation thereto. Appendices contain details of the laws affecting regulation and abolition in a number of European and American countries, the texts of relevant English statutes, and a general outline of the methods and laws adopted in the various states of the U.S.A. in relation to prostitution and kindred offences.

283 James, William H. "Parameters of the Menstrual Cycle and the Efficiency of Rhythm Methods of Contraception," Popul. Stud. 19(1):45-64. July 1965.

A study, based on various published data, testing the theoretical efficiency of the systems of Ogino and Knaus. The properties of some menstrual parameters are considered and estimates are made of the error variance of the Basal Body Temperature Test of ovulation. An evaluation of the theoretical efficiency of various rhythm methods is offered, including the author's own system. Ten points of conclusion assert the following: The Farris Test and the Basal Body Temperature Test do not seem to be biased, but they do not accurately predict ovulation day. Contrary to Ogino and Knaus, the post-ovulatory phase varies considerably with total cycle length. The correlation of mean post-ovulatory phase with mean total cycle is greater than the correlation between mean pre-ovulatory phase and total cycle. Tentative explanations are offered for the discrepancy between this and the conclusions of earlier works. The author's method of locating the period of prescribed abstinence appeared (on indirect statistical evidence) to be less demanding and more efficient than that of Ogino and Knaus..

284 Jayewardene, C.H.S. "Pregnancy Rates in the Evaluation of Family Planning Programs," pp. 406-11 in: International Union for the Scientific Study of Population, Contributed Papers, Sydney Conference, Australia, 21 - 25 August 1967.

Devises a model which takes into account (1) the number of children a woman would have at different times of her married life if she fell into each of the groups practicing contraception at different levels of effectiveness and (2) the proportion of women in each age group getting married while in the different age groups.

285 J.G. [Islam and Birth Control], Confluent 50:302-ff., 1965.

The author interprets the laws of the Koran with respect to abortion and states that it is clear that the condemnation of infanticide extends to the crime of abortion. However, one passage in the collection of Bukhari states that the soul does not enter the body of the fetus until the eightieth day of gestation. This law would justify the interruption of pregnancy performed within this time limit. In general the Moslem priests have condemned abortion but more recent literature indicates that it is permissible in some cases if performed in various periods after conception before the instilling of a soul.

286 Joblin, J.M., S.J. "The Papal Encyclical 'Mater et Magistra'," Internat. Labour Rev. 84(3):127-43. September 1961.

The following article starts by explaining the relationship of the new encyclical to Catholic social doctrine, and then outlines its main concepts and the way in which these are applied to certain present-day aspects of the social problem.

287 Jones, Gavin W. The Economic Effect of Declining Fertility in Less Developed Countries. Occasional Paper of the Population Council, New York, 1969, iv, 30 pp.

Presents the case for investment in family planning programs. Topics: Family size and family welfare; Population growth and per capita income; Supply of the factors of production over a 20-year period; The longer run -- after 20 years; Some common arguments in favor of high fertility.

288 Jones, Gavin, and Nortman, Dorothy. "Roman Catholic Fertility and Family Planning: A Comparative Review of the Research Literature," Stud. Fam. Planning, No. 34, October 1968, pp. 1-27.

Reviews the official Catholic Church position on contraception and brings together the empirical data on Catholic fertility, family size ideals, knowledge and attitudes toward fertility matters, and the practice of contraception.

289 Jurgens, Hans W. "Geburtenkontrolle als Instrument Internationaler Bevolkerungspolitik" [Birth Control as an Instrument of International Population Politics], Muenchen Med. Wochenschr 110(48):2833-39, 1968.

The unsatisfactory development of the so-called world population problem shows that hitherto the available scientific facilities of population politics have only been utilized inadequately. The experience of the European population explosion prior to the turn of the century is used just as little as the recognition of modern population science and social biology. The present, exceedingly contradictory concepts of population politics in the industrialized as well as in the underdeveloped countries and the failures which were obtained are due to very heterogeneous factors: social disintegration of birth control in the underdeveloped countries, nationalism in these countries, erroneous concepts of the thinking and behavior of peoples, and feminism in the birth control movement. New experiences from a stepwise population-political approach in East Africa as well as in India offers itself as a starting point for the solution of these problems.

290 Kasdon, David I. International Family Planning, 1966-1968: A Bibliography. Bethesda, Maryland: National Institute of Mental Health, 1969. 62 pp.

217 citations of books and articles with abstracts, listed alphabetically by author. A cross index by subject matter and one by country are appended, as well as a list of the 44 journals scanned for entries.

291 Kelleher, S.J. "Ecclesiastical Annulments and Dissolutions of Marriage," Catholic Law 12:13-ff. Winter 1966.

After defining the terms annulment and dissolution according to Church law, the author considers cases for dissolution and, more specifically, those dissolutions which, under present law, can be granted only in Rome. The bases or reasons for annulment are described in terms of those which are processed in a summary judicial procedure and those tried in formal process or the Church court. The author concludes with a general review of the types of cases considered by the Archdiocese of New York in an ordinary year.

292 Kelly, G.A. Birth Control and Catholics. Garden City: Doubleday, 1963. 264 pp.

Chapters: What marriage is all about; What Christian parenthood does not mean; The problems of married people; The world's answer - contraception; The Christian solution for these problems; The place of sex in marriage; Justification for a small family; The medical basis of fertility control; The providence of God.

293 Kelly, G.A. The Catholic Marriage Manual. New York: Random House, 1958.

Health or life is rarely endangered by pregnancy and where there is danger, Caesarian section usually saves the mother and offspring. The Church teaches that intentional taking of life violates the fifth commandment; abortion is not permitted under any conditions. Studies show that abortions are more numerous among users of contraceptives. Thus the starting point for abortions is the use of contraceptives and the use of contraceptives begins with contraceptive mentality. It is this mentality that denies the fundamental truth that the primary purpose of marriage is the procreation of children.

294 Ketchel, Melvin M. "Fertility Control Agents as a Possible Solution to the World Population Problem," Perspectives in Biology and Medicine 11(4):687-803, 1968.

Improvements in the technology of contraception may not effectively reduce birth rate, as it would still depend upon how many children people wanted rather than how many were required to stabilize population growth. Fertility control agents would provide a practical solution to the problem. The advantages of using fertility control agents would more than offset the considerable objections to them. Fertility control agents should be developed and tested seriously; methods of introducing them into the intake of populations, and a consensus arrived at which will dictate whether such agents will be utilized when they are developed.

295 Ketchel, Melvin M. "Should Birth Control be Mandatory?" Med. World News 18:66-71. October 1968.

The article is concerned with mandatory or government-enforced fertility control and the moral-political questions connected to its possible actualization. The author begins by discussing the unlikelihood of a world wide demographic revolution occurring today, especially with conditions as they are in underdeveloped countries. Since methods of controlling the fertility of entire populations will be discovered within 15 years, the author outlines the characteristics a fertility control drug would need to be useful and discusses whether such drugs are necessary and the morality of their use as a function of government. Various alternatives are viewed in terms of their effectiveness and/or limitations. The author concludes that the world population problem has no single, simplistic solution, but the immorality of present starvation and poverty levels indicates the need for developing and testing large-scale fertility control measures and methods for their dissemination over and above the need for deciding their moralor political implications.

296 Kirk, Dudley. "Factors Affecting Moslem Natality," in Vol. 2, pp. 149-52 of United Nations Department of Economic and Social Affairs, Proceedings of the World Population Conference, Belgrade, 30 August - 10 September 1965. 4 Vols. New York: United Nations, 1967.

Moslem natality is almost universally high and relatively uniform. Three reasons are the marriage institutions, emphasis on sexuality, and subordination of women. Population policies and programs to affect the national birth rate are not yet adequate.

297 Kirk, Dudley. "Methods and Results of Surveys for Evaluation of Family Planning." Paper Presented at the International Union for the Scientific Study of Population, General Conference, 3-11 September 1969, London.

Present methodology, though rapidly gaining in sophistication, is still inadequate to provide a reliable measure of the direct effects of a family planning program and the demographic impact is probably exaggerated by methods of analysis now widely used. The demographic impact of family planning programs rests on estimates of "what might have been" in the absence of the program. This is not subject to precise measurement. Improving methodology can do no more than give successively more plausible approximations. Despite methodological limitations, family planning surveys provide a wealth of information for the evaluation of family planning and of family planning programs. These results may be generalized as follows: All populations surveyed are moving toward more awareness, more approval, and more practice of birth control. This is true of areas of great diversity in culture and degree of technological development (e.g., Nigeria, Japan and the United States). The surveys further demonstrate that programs are reaching women of high potential natality (despite selectivity with reference to higher age and parity); that they are progressively reaching younger women; and that they are indeed making headway among the rural and the illiterate. Despite these encouraging evidences of progress, the surveys show that the direct effects of program efforts in reducing births are commonly exaggerated.

298 Kirk, Dudley. "Population Research in Relation to Population Policy and National Family Planning Programs." Paper Presented at Annual Meeting of the American Sociological Association, Boston, August 1968.

Focuses upon policies designed to check the rate of population growth, usually through family planning programs. It indicates the relevancy of social science research and knowledge to policy and programs; makes some general comments on the reasons for receptivity or lack or receptivity to the findings of research; and speculates on some ways in which policies might be different or programs strengthened if available knowledge were taken as a basis for action.

299 Kirk, Dudley. "Prospects for Reducing Natality in the Underdeveloped World," Annals Amer. Acad. Polit. Soc. Sci. 369: 48-59. January 1967.

The prospects for reductions in birth rates in the less industrialized countries are improving owing to the increasingly favorable climate of opinion relating to birth control, the invention of better contraceptives, and the adoption of national family planning programs. Some 23 countries, including over 50 percent of the population in the developing countries, now have such programs. These are too new to have had a measurable effect on the birth rate in most countries. Nevertheless, the birth rate is already falling in a few of the economically more progressive countries in East Asia such as Taiwan, Korea, and Singapore. These reductions in the birth rates may be expected to deepen and spread, accelerated by national family programs operating within the context of rapid socio-economic change. In two decades the solutions to the world population problem may well be in sight, though not yet fully achieved. But these changes will not occur fast enough to forestall massive population growth and continuing critical problems of population at least through the next decade.

300 Kirk, Dudley, and Nortman, Dorothy. "Population Policies in Developing Countries," Econ. Develop. Cult. Change 15(2, Part I):129-42. January 1967.

The now widely prevalent view that population control is a legitimate and proper function of government finds expression in governmental policy to reduce population growth by means of family planning. Today the roster of nations with family planning programs covers some 62.5% of the 2.3 billion people in the developing world. The list includes India, Pakistan, and Mainland China; South Korea, Ceylon, Singapore, Hong Kong, and Malaysia; Turkey, Egypt, Tunisia, Morocco, and Mauritius; and Honduras. Taiwan has no formal policy, but its island-wide program has already reached a substantial part of the population. Elsewhere -- the Philippines, Thailand, Indonesia, Nepal, Afghanistan, Iran, Kenya, Chile, Colombia, Peru, and Venezuela -- at least the beginning of governmental interest is visible. A growing group of institutions is ready to help developing countries implement their population policies. Aid from the technologically advanced nations is also increasing. The major bottlenecks, however, are less a matter of finances and supplies than of internal organization and administration. A review of specific programs reveals the difficulties of reaching masses of illiterate people in remote villages. On the positive side are the favorable attention of the people toward family planning, the priorities accorded family planning in health service programs, augmented training, research and evaluation programs in hospitals, clinics, university and governmental ministries, increasing availability and local manufacture of supplies, development of more effective means of communication, increasing per capita appropriations and expenditures, and the growing body of knowledge associated with different cultural settings. In view of the newness of these programs, measurable progress to date relates more to attitudes and policy than to action and achievement.

301 Kiser, Clyde V., ed. Research in Family Planning. Princeton: Princeton University Press, 1962. xvi, 664 pp.

A collection of essays dealing with the current state of research regarding family planning and the probability of future progress in this area, in 10 Parts and 40 Chapters, with a Foreword by the editor. Part I, Studies in India; II, Studies in Other Asiatic Countries and the Middle East; III, Studies in the United States; IV, Studies in Latin America and Europe; V, Research in Methods of Fertility Control; VI, Acceptability of Methods; VII, Problems of Measurement; VIII, Problems of Research Design; IX, Problems of Motivation and Communication; X, Summary of the Conference.

302 Klinger, Andras. "Demographic Aspects of Abortion." Paper Presented at the International Union for the Scientific Study of Population, General Conference, 3-11 September 1969, London.

One can state that the legalization of induced abortions influences the number of live births considerably, and thus is an important means of family planning. Induced abortion, however, cannot be viewed as a proper and suitable means of birth control. It can be regarded only as an interim, auxiliary method pending the adoption by the population of proper means of birth prevention. Under present circumstances, inasmuch as contraceptive methods are still primitive in most developed countries, induced abortion is applied as one of the chief means of birth control. Its deleterious effect on health is a sufficient reason for changing the present-day situation. This, however, cannot be achieved by administrative measure prohibiting induced abortions but only by disseminating knowledge of modern contraceptive methods, making supplies readily available, and teaching effective use. The health policy of individual countries now takes cognizance of these needs so that women may prevent conception rather than interrupt unwanted pregnancies.

303 Knox, John B., and Hill, Vicky M. "Family Size, Status and Mobility: Some Argentine and American Data," _Eugen_. _Quart_. 11(2):90-95, 1964.

The data reveal a remarkable similarity in family size and intergenerational reductions in family size. Available facts indicate that family planning is the explanation in the U.S.; however, in Argentina it is unlikely that family planning after marriage is as prevalent as in the U.S. and thus it is probably that age at marriage is a partial explanation. When family size is related to occupational status and mobility, the two samples are found to be different. In Tennessee, family size is negatively related to status and mobility; in Buenos Aires the relationship is in the opposite direction. Most of the relationships are not strong enough to be regarded as significant, but the observation of an opposite direction in each case is noteworthy. If control of the family size is accomplished by different means, opposite direction of these relationships might be expected.

304 Kraatz, H. "Grundsatzliche Gedanken zur Frage der Schwangerschaftsunterbrechung" [Basic Ideas on the Problem of Abortion], Das Deutsche Gesundheitswesen 13(5):138-45. January 30, 1958.

Discussion of policies in the Soviet Union, Scandinavia, and Eastern Europe, including the German Democratic Republic.

305 Krause, H.D. "Bastards Abroad -- Foreign Approaches to Illegitimacy," Amer. J. Comparative Law 15:726, 1966-67.

The fifty jurisdictions of the United States differ widely on the subject of illegitimacy, and it is contended that these differences rest on legislative and judicial accident rather than intelligent design. Since foreign experience may be of value in laying the groundwork for new and more uniform state laws on illegitimacy, the author describes briefly the active and extensive movements toward reform of illegitimacy law under way in several foreign countries and then, with occasional reference to the Norwegian precedent and Swiss law, reviews the most recent of European reform efforts -- a detailed West German proposal which seeks to implement a provision of West Germany's 1949 Constitution. This provision centers on equality, through legislation, for the illegitimate child so that he will be given the same conditions for development and position in society as the legitimate child. Included are sections on the definition of equality, the definition of illegitimacy, the mother's relationship with her illegitimate child (support, inheritance, custody, legitimation, etc.), the father's relationship with his illegitimate child, imposition of parental responsibility on the father, and the relationship between unmarried mother and father. The author concludes with a brief survey of American law on illegitimacy and an analysis of the German reform effort.

306 Kumar, V. "Abortion," Singapore Med. J. 5:49-ff., 1964; Also in: Malaya Law Rev. 6:17-ff., 1964.

The abortion legislation of Singapore, England, Sweden, Denmark, Finland, and Japan are compared. Medical terms are defined in regard to the Singapore Penal Code and English law and the guidelines set by the Royal College of Physicians with respect to therapeutic abortion are also included. Legalized abortion in Sweden, Finland and Denmark is discussed as is the increase in abortions for psychiatric-social indications in Sweden. The Eugenic Protection Law of 1948 of Japan and data on studies on abortion and sterilization are given. The author recommends a more clear definition of the Singapore abortion laws and urges centers for contraceptive instruction.

307 Lacinova, Valerie. "Prehled o Rodinnych Fridavcich v Ruznych Statech Sveta" [Survey of Family Allowances in Various Countries of the World], _Demografie_ 4(3):273-76, 1962.

This article deals with the special family allowances, i.e., with the amount of money which is regularly, repeatedly granted to the head of the household in order to help him keep the persons (children, wife, parents) who do not have their own sufficient income. Those entitled to family allowances in various countries in the world; the circumstances affecting the origin and development of family allowance systems; evaluation of systems; age limits for eligibility and the financing of family allowance systems are reviewed for each country.

308 Lader, Lawrence. _The Margaret Sanger Story and the Fight for Birth Control_. New York: Doubleday, 1955. 352 pp.

Traces the efforts and successes of Margaret Sanger in gaining social and legal acceptance of birth control in the United States and various other countries. The work begins with a description of the series of articles on the physiology of reproduction, published in the newspaper _Call_ in 1912, and ends with the tribute paid Margaret Sanger by the Japanese Government in 1954 in having her become the first non-Japanese woman to ever address the House of Councillors.

309 Lasok, D. "Legal Concept of Marriage and Divorce: A Comparative Study in Polish and Western Family Law," _Internat. Comparative Law Quart_. 9:53- 95. January 1960.

The concept of marriage in contemporary Polish law has been modeled upon the Soviet pattern. Marriage is an institution of immense ideological importance, and "socialist marriage" is considered superior to "bourgeois marriage." In the

Socialist view, "bourgeois marriage" is prima facie a restriction on the wife and is a result of cold calculations based on class and material considerations. As a result of removal of all vestiges of inequality, the wife has become in the "socialist marriage" an absolutely equal partner in all respects. While the West is moving toward a contractual form of marriage, the East is concentrating on the institutional and social aspects of marriage. Marriage must fulfill a social function and divorce is harmful to society and the children.

310 Lebel, R. "Les Allocations Familiales dans le Monde " [Family Allowances in the World], Familles dans le Monde, March 1960, pp. 3-34.

The scope and purpose of family allowances; the various formulas adopted.

311 Lehfeldt, Hans. "Psychological Aspects of Planned Parenthood," J. Sex Res. 1(2):97-103. July 1965.

Investigating the high incidence of accidental pregnancies which are blamed on failure of the contraceptive method used, it is found that the protective action of contraception is often thwarted by emotional factors. This phenomenon is called "willful exposure to unwanted pregnancy." Willful exposure to unwanted pregnancy is no female perogative but is also frequently traced to the male; in many cases it may be considered the joint responsibility of both partners. Another factor in contraceptive failure is iatrogenic:the prescribing physician may lack specialized training in this field, or he may have a negative attitude to the problem of birth control, resulting in incomplete or wrong instruction of his patients. Of 100 case histories analyzed, ten fall under the definition of willful exposure to unwanted pregnancy female, seven under willful exposure to unwanted pregnancy male, and in five cases willful exposure to unwanted pregnancy may be considered the joint responsibility of both partners. In the remaining 78 cases, iatrogenic factors, shyness, anxiety, and other elements were found responsible for contraceptive failure.

312 Lehfeldt, Hans, ed. "Symposium on Aspects of Female Sexuality," Quart. Rev. Sury Obstet. Gynec. 16:217-ff., 1959.

A series of short papers presented at the Symposium on Aspects of Female Sexuality discuss: the definition of the term abortion; the estimated abortion rates for the United States; evidence based on data from Scandinavia that liberalization of abortion laws does not decrease criminal abortions; the liberal legislation and administration of abortion in Sweden, Denmark and Norway; the methods for reporting suspected illegal abortions and dealing with complications that result from them; an argument stating that laws in the United States should be altered to conform with current medical practice; and a description of the committee system at Mt. Sinai Hospital in New York.

313 Leitch, A. "Male Homosexuality as a Medico-Legal and Sociological Problem in the United Kingdom," Internat. J. Soc. Psychiat. 5(2):98-106. Autumn 1959.

A.C. Kinsey's findings on the incidence of homosexuality in the U.S. are discussed. The medico-legal problems of homosexuality in the United Kingdom are assessed in three aspects: (1) are the existing laws wise and effective? (2) should the law interfere in homosexual activities any more than it does in heterosexual activities, or in homosexual activities between females? and (3) should the law relating to homosexual activities be altered, and if so, what alterations are desirable? Reasons given by the advocates of changing the law are enumerated. The problem of homosexuality is seen as a part of the greater problem of achieving sexual outlets which are consistent with the aims and ideals of a responsible organized society based on the family unit. If society is reluctant to abandon its present laws, we should begin to tackle the problem by reducing the severity of the penalties. Treatment facilities should be improved perhaps in terms of some special therapeutic institution or community. The recommendations of the Wolfenden Report are reviewed in this context.

314 Leonard, Joseph T. "Artificial Insemination," Amer. Eccl. Rev. 140:301-7, 1959.

Pope Pius XII had frequently stated that artificial insemination is opposed to the sixth commandment, just as fornication and adultery, even though there is no sensual delectation. This condemnation applies to all situations in which there is real artificial insemination, whether it be an unmarried or a married women utilizing homologous or heterologous insemination. It seems that the malice of these acts is the violation of social justice, since God has intended conception to be the result of a human act in human society.

315 Lesinski, J. "Abortion Indications and Procedures," in: Proceedings of the Fourth Conference of the Region for Europe, Near East and Africa of the IPPF. New York: Excerpta Medica Foundation, 1965.

Twenty-eight European, Eastern and African countries were divided into three categories: those with medical indications; those with liberal tendencies; and those which recognize a variety of indications. Results indicate that twelve countries permit abortion for medical and medico-social reasons and that seven of the twelve include the social indications alone. Twenty-six countries require hospitalization, whereas Japan and Poland permit the procedure to be performed in a private office. Commissions regulate the procedures for abortion applicants in all countries and Bulgaria, Poland and Japan permit the decision to be made by private physicians.

316 Lestapis, Stanislas de. "La Conscience Humaine devant le Problème des Accroissements de Population" [Human Awareness of the Problem of Population Growth], Revue de l'Action Populaire 82:947-55. November 1954.

Population growth becomes a problem which is capable of solution only when there is a general social awareness of its harmful consequences. Creating social awareness is one of the objectives of population education. Persons may be aware of their own family size but may need information on population dynamics at the societal level.

317 Lestapis, Stanislas de. "L'Eglise Catholique et les Problèmes de Population. Textes Pontificaux Récents" [The Catholic Church and the Problems of Population. Recent Pontifical Texts], Population 7(2):289-306. April - June 1952.

318 Lestapis, Stanislas de. Family Planning and Modern Problems: A Catholic Analysis. New York: Herder and Herder, 1961. 326 pp. Published in France under title, La Limitation des Naissances. Abridged English edition, published under title, Birth Regulation: The Catholic Position, London: Burns Oates, 1963. 128 pp.

The author starts with a survey of the viewpoints and arguments that favour the use of contraceptives for family planning throughout the world - from Malthus to modern India. He then makes a critical assessment of the results and implications of contraception where it is officially accepted. He also explains the true meaning of the Catholic position and its relevance to the world-wide anxiety concerning the increase in population.

319 Lestapis, Stanislas de. "A Moral Catolica e o Problema Demografico," [Catholic Morality and the Demographic Problem], Sintese Politica Economica Social 7(26):11-46. April - June 1965.

Comment on policies and results observable in 1963. Statement of positions and proposal of the Roman Catholic Church concerning the demographic challenge.

320 Lestapis, Stanislas de. "Problemes de Population et Conscience Chretienne. Parts I-III " [Population Problems and the Christian Conscience. Parts I-III], Revue de l'Action Populaire, August-October 1951, pp. 543-56; November, 1951, pp. 614-34; December 1951, pp. 696-710.

321 Levy, Claude. "Facteurs et Structures de la Fecondité dans les Régions ou Elle est Relativement Faible " [Factors and Structures of Fertility in Regions Where it is Relatively Low], Population 20(6):986-91. November - December 1965.

The fall in mortality and numerous other factors, some of which still remain obscure, have led to a decrease in fertility. In order to better understand the phenomenon of fertility control, which has been provisionally restricted to the countries of Western civilization, but which is beginning (under diverse pressures) to infiltrate the rest of the world, the discussion is concentrated on 4 themes: (1) the general characteristics which determine fertility in countries where it is low, (2) the regulation of fertility in industrialized countries, (3) the present structure of fertility, and (4) reasons for this low fertility. Besides certain well-known socio-demographic factors which have contributed to the disappearance of differential fertility, there is a lack of quantitative and comparative measures among countries with different dimensions and structures. It is necessary to study these countries more closely. Also, the importance of biological factors has hardly been investigated. There is also the development of the role of the State in family planning. In Hungary, Rumania and the Ukraine, the progress of industrialization has affected the birthrate, while the religious factor has had no influence. It is necessary to pursue the demographic consequences resulting from the use of contraceptives, oral or others. Also, an investigation in Czechoslovakia after the legalization of abortion showed that if it did not lead to sterilization, abortion would increase the number of premature and still births.

322 Lipstein, K. "Adoption in Private International Law: Reflections on the Scope and the Limits of a Convention," Internat. Comparative Law Quart. 12:835-49. July 1963.

The rules governing the law and procedure of international adoptions differ from country to country to such an extent that it seems practically impossible to find common denominators. Yet, in adoption, where private and public interests are interwoven and where the cooperation of public social services is called upon increasingly, it is essential that conflicts of law and of jurisdiction be resolved before the act of adoption. An international division of competences appears to be best suited to achieve this purpose.

323 Lloyd, Raymond. "Proposal for a World Family Plan," Internat. Develop. Rev. 7(4):21-23. December 1965.

The objective of the World Family Plan here proposed would be to assist participating countries to reduce their current population increase by one third by 1970 and by one half in 1975. To achieve this goal, some 170 million couples in the developing countries would have to be provided with effective means of family planning. At a very rough guess the cost of a World Family Plan, assuming that at least half of the 170 million couples concerned are provided with the intrauterine loop, would be somewhere in the region of one billion dollars over the five to ten year period. A World Family Plan would have two main elements, a world declaration of intent stating the targets, and various forms of international assistance to participants.

324 Long, W. Newton. Fertility and Population Control, Session 31, Meetings of Southern Sociological Society. 1969.

Fertility rates vary throughout the world depending on the stage of economic development. In the U.S. and other economically advanced nations the birthrate has shown a general decline since the middle of the 19th century with a brief rise after the Second World War. Elsewhere, however, birthrates have either remained unchanged or have actually advanced. It is doubted that any substantial natural change will occur until widespread malnutrition will reduce fertility. Present and proposed methods of contraception including permissive abortion are discussed. The aims of family planning movements in this country are at variance with the concept of population control. The former considers its role in the supplying of contraception for females with medical contraindications to pregnancy, to females with temporary problems who wish to postpone pregnancy, and to females who wish to limit family size. The latter must devote itself to popularizing the "minifamily." Demographers pointing out the diminishing death rate, particularly in people below age 40, show that in order to stabilize population couples should not have more than two children. Present family planning activists are not capable of this task. The present program of India is reviewed as a pioneer venture in government population control.

325 Lopez-Rey y Arrojo, M. [The Offense of Abortion in Spain and Latin America], Bol. Inst. Derecho Comp. Mexico 17:31-ff., 1964.

The abortion laws of Spain and Latin America are compared, and the author concludes that these laws do not correspond to current social necessity in these countries. A large segment of abortion statutes is listed under the Offenses of the Person section of the penal codes demonstrating the individualistic orientation of the laws. Recommends that abortion should be regarded as an offense against the community. An examination of the indications in the Spanish and Latin American legislation (e.g., medical, family honor) demonstrates the need for a more flexible abortion law. Author advocates a law which would punish abortion patients but would provide flexible penalties to be altered according to the individual case; or a law which would punish only defined illegal abortions. In Appendices, statistics on legal and illegal abortions in various countries are given.

326 Loraine, John A., and Bell, E. Trevor. Fertility and Contraception in the Human Female. Baltimore: Williams and Wilkins Company, 1968. vii, 384 pp.

A comprehensive account of the subjects of fertility and contraception was presented. The first two chapters are concerned with the physiology of the ovary and with the mechanisms controlling ovulation. The third describes recent advances in methods for the quantitative determination of hormones and their metabolites in blood and urine, special attention being given to estrogens, androgens and human pituitary gonadotropins. The fourth and fifth chapters are devoted to the normal menstrual cycle, the former dealing with hormone assays in normally menstruating women and the latter with other factors which are believed to be under hormonal control. Advances in the endocrinology of gynecological disorders are discussed in chapter six, special attention being given to recent findings in patients with amenorrhoea, dysmenorrhoea and oligomenorrhoea. Chapters seven and eight respectively with the gonadotrophic hormones and Clomiphene, compounds capable of stimulating ovarian function and of producing ovulation in a proportion of infertile women. The ninth and tenth chapters are devoted to methods of birth control, the former reviewing the field of oral and the latter of intra-uterine contraception. Certain aspects of the world population crises are described and the need for remedial action is emphasized.

327 Louros, N.C. "Fertility, Sterility, and Overpopulation," Internat. J. Fertility 5(2):171-74, 1960.

The rapid increase of world population is pointed out and it is recommended to the gynecologists to take the initiative for planned parenthood. The author calls attention to the insufficiencies and dangers of some methods for this purpose, and points out the necessity of international understanding.

328 Luchaire, F. "Les Prestations Familiales et la Polygamie dans les Territoires d'Outre-Mer " [Family Subsidies and Polygamy in the Overseas Territories], Droit Social 18(6): 393-98. June 1955.

Most of the French possessions overseas have followed the practice of France in granting family allowances to employed persons.

329 Marotta, Michele. "Aspetti Demografici e di Planificazione " [Demographic and Planning Aspects of the Family], Rass. Ital. Sociol. 2(2):273-88, 1961.

Birth rates during and after World War II are examined. Family planning has occurred by: diffusion of information on family planning, sexual education, new marital orientation and scientific developments regarding sterility. Family planning is compared among the United States, U.S.S.R., India, Africa and Japan.

330 Marquard, Elva. "Dependents in Social Security Systems of Great Britain, New Zealand, Australia, and Canada," Soc. Security Bull. 11(9):3-15. September 1948.

Family allowances and maternity benefits are included in the provisions made for the dependents of workers covered by social security systems.

331 Mars, John. "A Population Stop Policy for Developing Countries," Nigerian J. Econ. Soc. Stud. 5(2):145-85. July 1963.

Advocates a "terminable" population stop policy: for holding numbers constant or at a lower rate of growth until desired objectives are fulfilled.

332 Marshall, J. "Population Policies in the Light of the Recent Papal Encyclical." Paper Presented at the International Union for the Scientific Study of Population, General Conference, 3-11 September 1969, London.

Although the publication of Humane Vitae is unlikely to halt the adoption of population policies by governments as a whole and their implementation by the spread of contraceptive methods, it will create delicate situations in some parts of the world. It may somewhat retard the adoption and implementation of policies, and the scientific study of population. Further the assessment of programs and research into the various problems which will arise will not proceed as openly and as quickly as they might.

333 Matras, Judah. "Social Strategies of Family Formation: Some Comparative Data for Scandinavia, the British Isles, and North America," _Internat. Social Science J._ 17(2):260-75, 1965.

Societal norms governing age at marriage, reproductive patterns, etc. Includes a procedure for estimating the extent to which fertility control is practiced.

334 Mattelart, Armand. _El Reto Espiritual de la Explosion Demografica_. [The Spiritual Challenge of the Demographic Explosion]. Santiago de Chile: Editorial del Pacifico, 1966. 96 pp.

Parts: historical survey of demographic doctrines from Malthus to the Neo-Malthusians, and the reaction to them; survey of present world situation with regard to ethics and policy on natality; proposal of a series of concrete measures.

335 Mauldin, W. Parker. "Fertility Control in Communist Countries: Policy and Practice," pp. 179-215 in: Milbank Memorial Fund, _Population Trends in Eastern Europe, the USSR and Mainland China_. New York, 1960. 336 pp.

A survey of policy and practice in the U.S.S.R., Eastern Europe (Czechoslovakia, Poland, Hungary, Bulgaria), and Mainland China. Appendix lists Soviet legislation on abortion, fertility awards, and differential taxation.

336 Mauldin, W. Parker. "Population Policies in the Sino-Soviet Bloc," _Law and Contemporary Problems_ 25(3):490-507. Summer 1960.

Declines in the birth rate accompanied urbanization and industrialization in the communist world prior to the establishment of communist control. Women are being emancipated in the process. The little information, primarily from the Soviet Union is that the process of change, of education, of emancipation of women, of industrialization, modernization, leads to values among the individuals that bring about a reduction in the birth rate. Most of the communist countries have adopted family-allowance programs and honor awards for mothers of many children - pronatalist policies. Anti-natalist measures have been enacted, including legalization of abortion, spread of supplies of and information on contraceptives, maximizing the female labor force, etc. Above all, there is a stress on improving health of mothers and children, of a woman giving birth only when she wants a child and is able to rear one. Population needs and population policy vary among the various communist countries, pro-natalist and anti-natalist sometimes existing side by side. There is increasing evidence of a rational consideration of the relationship between rates of population growth and economic development in many of the communist countries.

337 Mauranges, P. "Sterilisation et Legislation dans Certains Pays" [Sterilization and Legislation in Certain Countries], Semaine Medicale 31(45): 1448-ff. December 6, 1955.

338 Maury, Marian, ed. Birth Rate and Birth Right. New York: Macfadden Books, 1963. pp. 222.

The editor of this anthology has contributed a preface to the thirty papers which have been chosen for the light they throw on different aspects of the problems which have arisen through the weight of expanding populations pressing on world resources. The first section, "Witnesses for the World," consists of twenty-one articles. All are by authorities in their own fields, as may be seen in a few names picked at random from the list of contributors: William Vogt, Harrison Brown, Aldous Huxley, Robert C. Cook, John F. Kennedy, Arnold Toynbee, S. Chandrasekhar, Lady Rama Rau, Jacquetta Hawkes and Eleanor Mears. Some deal with the overall situation, some discuss the problems which face their own countries, others explain contraceptive techniques. The second section is headed "Witnesses for the United States" and deals for the most part with the personal and domestic, and the nation-wide economic angles in America. Then follows an editorial summing-up which closes with a tribute to the International Planned Parenthood Federation, the Family Planning Association and the Planned Parenthood Federation of America. There is also a list of supplementary reading. The influence of the Roman Catholic hierarchy is dealt with editorially and other religious opinions are put forward, in the second section, in an excerpt from the 1961 Statement of the National Council of Churches, amplified by Dr. James A. Pike, Bishop of California, while Rabbi Roland B. Gittelsohn speaks for liberal Judaism in a sermon preached in Boston, Massachusetts in 1959 and reiterated at the Reform Jewish Conference in 1962.

339 McElroy, William D. "Biomedical Aspects of Population Control," Bioscience 19(1):19-23, 1969.

The current rate of growth of the world population cannot be allowed to continue. The United States and other developed countries must take the leadership in setting up world-wide institutions in which maternal and child health care is intimately coupled with family planning and population control advice.

340 Mead, Margaret. "Spiritual Issues in the Problem of Birth Control," Pastoral Psychol. 4(34):39-44, 1953.

It is argued that to reach full spiritual stature man -- and woman -- must be free to choose between one course of action and another, and that contraception gives women control over their own fertility, a freedom denied them when a wedded wife was held to owe conjugal duties to her husband, whatever the outcome in long series of unwanted pregnancies -- many of them bound to end in miscarriage -- still births, and early infant deaths. On the public health side, it is argued that reductions in birth rates and infant deaths will enable persons in the poverty areas of the world to obtain a measure of economic dignity.

341 Mehlan, K.H. "The Effects of Legalization of Abortions," in: Proceedings of the Third Conference in the Region for Europe, Near East and Africa of the IPPF. New York: Excerpta Medica Foundation, 1962.

A review of statistics particularly from Hungary and Japan illustrate the increase in legal abortions following the legalization of abortion. A survey of medical literature demonstrates a reduction of criminal abortion by the liberalization of abortion laws, since legalization of abortion. Also discussed are: maternal mortality rates in North European and Eastern European countries; complications and sequelae after legal abortion based on data from Hungary, 1958, Bulgaria, 1958, and the German Democratic Republic 1948/1950. The author contends that the effect of legalization of abortion on the dissemination of contraception, is not as some officials feel, an inhibitory one. He cited data from Japan which indicates that the ratio of 3:1 in 1950 for percentage of births prevented by abortion to the percentage prevented by contraception decreased to 1:1 due to the growing influence of contraceptives.

342 Mehlan, K.H. [Legalization of Interruption of Pregnancy: Yes or No], Deutsch Gesundh 15:1206-ff., 1960.

An analysis of the status of induced abortion in Japan, Hungary, Czechoslovakia, Yugoslavia and the German Democratic Republic indicates that the desire to limit the number of children per family to two or three appears to be universal and that this goal is frequently attained through criminal or legal abortion wherever contraceptive methods are inadequately used or known. Special attention is given to the abortion law and to the incidence and effects of legal and illegal abortions in East Germany. Author does not advocate further liberalization of the abortion law, but urges the knowledge and use of contraceptives.

343 Meier, Richard L. "Concerning Equilibrium in Human Population," _Soc. Probl._ 6:163-75. Fall 1958.

Possible means for the regulation of birth through the exercise of authority external to the family.

344 Meier, Richard L. "Is Birth Control Enough? The Technical Problem Solved, the Social Problem Remains," _The Humanist_ 18(2):69-76. March - April 1958.

Considers problems of introducing birth control devices on a world scale: costs, acceptability, the role of governments, measures to influence motivation on family size when control has become effective, eugenic equilibrium.

345 Meier, Richard L. _Modern Science and the Human Fertility Problem._ New York: John Wiley, 1959. xii, 263 pp.

The author examines new scientific possibilities in the control of human fertility. He has explored their potential impact on population growth as well as on the social institutions and the economies of various societies. Studies relating to vulnerable points in the reproductive processes and recent research on oral contraceptives are discussed in the appendix.

346 Mertens, C.S.J. "Régulation des Naissances: Pour Une Pastorale d'Ensemble " [Birth Control: for a General Pastoral], _Nouvelle Révue Théologique_ 85(2):176-88. February 1963.

A consideration of the background and content of pastoral counsel for Roman Catholic laity adapted to the size and complexity of the problem of birth control in the world of today.

347 Meyer, Boniface. "A Roman Catholic Interpretation of Contraception," _Luth. Quart._ 16:303-19, 1964.

A discussion of the historical position of various religious attitudes on the question of birth limitation. The

Roman Catholic position is stated, and the gradual development that has occurred among theologians in arriving at a more positive appreciation of the procreative function in marital life is elaborated. Credit for the liberalization of Roman Catholic moral theology must be given to Bernard Haring in _The Law of Christ_.

348 Mihanovich, Clement S., _et al_. _Marriage and the Family_. Milwaukee: Bruce, 1952. 502 pp.

Chapter XIV, "Contraception and the 'Safe Period'," states the Catholic position.

349 Montanari, Antonio. "In Tema di Natalita Controllata " [Trends in Birth Control], _Statistica_ 16(3):603-46. July - September 1966.

On the basis of recent literature, the main aspects of birth control are traced, with special attention being given to the industrialized societies during the last two centuries. The causes and consequences of this progressive diffusion of birth control are also analyzed. Research is indispensible for the development of population policy.

350 Moorens, Leon. "Family Allowances," _Relations_ 12(141):220-21. August 1952.

The International Congress on Family Allowances was held at Brussels from May 26-30 1952. Thirty nations of Europe, Asia Minor and Latin America were represented, and five international organizations sent observers. A dozen topics were classified under three headings: general principles and technical problems; living standards and family needs; and social problems. A large volume of the speeches and discussions was compiled. Part of the discussion was on the subject of social security in general, women's work, birthrate, housing, family budgets, etc. Efficiency was a prime question. The Belgian system of compensation for each child (a bonus at birth of 1,800 francs for the first child and 900 for each other one and a monthly allowance of 315 francs for the first and second, 430 francs for the third, 525 for the fourth and 695 francs for each child after that) did not cover the actual expenses of birth and maintenance of the child. There were arguments on economic, social and psychological bases. The article cites a couple of these arguments.

351 Moss, J. Joel. "Teenage Marriage: Crossnational Trends and Sociological Factors in the Decision of When to Marry," Acta Sociol. 8(1-2):98-117, 1964. Also in: J. Marr. Fam. Living 27(2):230-42. May 1965.

A summary of papers given at the Eighth International Family Research Seminar in Oslo, Norway, 1963, which describe and explain differential frequencies of those decisions to marry which result in teenage marriage. The summary seeks to (1) compare demographic data on age at marriage for the countries reporting and (2) categorize the proposed explanatory factors of teenage marriage according to the theoretical frameworks from which they apparently proceed. Teenage marriage refers to husband or wife or both being under 20 years old at marriage. Trends in average age at marriage in various countries and trends in teenage marriage are illustrated in graphs and analyzed. Consequences of teenage marriage trends have not been adequately pinned down, but may be: a higher divorce rate, a higher fertility rate, and, in the U.S., greater instability and potential neglect of children born to teenage couples. The papers reflect differing conceptual frameworks regarding emphasis on the social system, the cultural system or the personality system. Work on early marriages in the U.S. reflects a sociological-psychological model focusing on the development of personal motivations as influenced by social change and social disorganization. European studies use more an 'institutional' sociological model. Another model emphasizes the cultural system and the processual pressures appearing in the involvement process with the opposite sex. Specific generalizations pertinent to some of these conceptual frameworks were drawn from the reports and categorized according to three different areas of sociological concern. More definitive explanations of teenage marriage on an international scale are encouraged.

352 Muller, C. [Do Our Laws Offer Sufficient Protection for Nascent Life?] Praxis 54:1138-ff., 1965.

An examination of selected international articles on abortion illustrates the author's argument that liberalization of the indications for legal abortion does not lessen the number of criminal abortions but instead generates an abortion mentality and more numerous interruptions, legal and illegal. Abortion should be lawful only on medical indications and the physician should be the guardian of the nascent human life. The author advocates contraceptive centers and facilities for prenatal care to promote responsible family planning.

353 Muller-Dietz, H. "Abortion in the Soviet Union and in the East European States," Rev. Soviet Med. Sci. I (2), 1964.

Surveys abortion legislation and practice in the Soviet Union and the Eastern European countries. The Soviet Union permitted legal abortion in 1920 but condemned it in 1936 because this did not curtail illegal abortion and added to the social disintegration. In 1954 the penalty was again rescinded for the aborting woman and in 1955 penalties were reduced for the performance of an abortion. The Soviet woman was given the right of abortion on demand. The official reason for this is the emancipation of women to join the work force. The author believes it was an attempt to curtail illegal abortion which was excessively high. The Soviet Union has been imitated by the satellite nations and for the same reasons. Bulgaria instituted abortion on demand in 1956 (censure of the women lifted in 1951). Yugoslavia lifted censure in 1951 and now has liberal legalized abortion. Poland legalized abortion in 1956 and instituted abortion on demand in 1959. Rumania, Czechoslovakia and Hungary closely follow the Soviet pattern. East Germany followed the Soviets until 1950. Illegal abortions were keeping pace with legal until in 1950 there were 90 abortions to every 100 births. After eliminating abortion on social and ethical grounds and taking steps to spread information on contraception the ratio dropped to 30 per 100 live births in 1954. The author maintains that legalization in Eastern Europe has had little or insufficient effect on the rate of criminal abortion.

354 Muramatsu, Minoru, and Harper, Paul A., eds. Population Dynamics: International Action and Training Programs. Baltimore: Johns Hopkins Press, 1966. viii, pp. 248.

The Proceedings are divided into three sections. In the first and longest, Action Programs, four papers deal with the situations in India, Pakistan and Puerto Rico, followed by twelve pages of an apparently verbatim report of the comment and discussion on them. There are then a further four papers dealing with Japan, Korea, Taiwan and the Chinese population of East Asia, which again are commented upon. Part II of the Conference was on Programs in the Western Hemisphere, opening with an account of Voluntary Agencies by Alan F. Guttmacher followed by papers on family planning programmes in the U.S., on "Provoked Abortion in Santiago, Chile" and on population control in Latin America. Here again, one discussion covers all the subjects dealt with in this section. Part III deals with three aspects of the training of professional personnel in population dynamics. After the ensuing discussion there is a final chapter on "Population and Public Health Policy."

355 Murray, D.E. "Ancient Laws on Adultery- A Synopsis," J. Family Law 1:89-104. Spring 1961.

This article studies the ancient laws pertaining to adultery and presents a chronological and geographical exposition of this perplexing ever-present sociological-legal phenomenon. The Middle East, Far East, Greek, Roman and Germanic laws are described and analyzed.

356 Naamani, I.T. "Marriage and Divorce in Jewish Law," J. Family Law 3:177. Fall 1963.

A general outline of Jewish precepts regarding marriage and the family is given, with references to the historical sources from which the study is drawn and present religious-legal injunctions on marriage and divorce. There are subsequent sections describing Jewish law and marriage eligibility, polygamy and monogamy, forbidden alliances and consanguinity, permanent and temporary interdictions on marriage (mostly on grounds of chastity and morality), proscriptive days, traditions and regulations concerning engagement, betrothal and marriage, the marriage contract, duties of husband and wife, the wife's property, and finally divorce. Included is a discussion of marriage and divorce in Israel.

357 Nag, Moni. Factors Affecting Human Fertility in Non-Industrial Societies. New Haven: Yale University Publications in Anthropology No. 66, 1962. 227 pp.

This monograph represents a great deal of statistical work on a mass of information presented in the form of a cross-cultural analysis, using a two point scale, of the fertility data from sixty-one non-industrial societies -- twenty from Africa, sixteen from America, thirteen from Asia and twelve from the Pacific. Eight somewhat primitive and isolated communities are considered in detail including their sexual habits and taboos, their attitude to fertility and family size, and their desire to control or enhance fertility, their approval or disapproval of abortion and so forth. The author then goes on to discuss the various factors that emerge from a study of all the sixty-one societies which may have a possible bearing on fertility levels. These are related 1. to the probability of coitus as affected by natural frequency, voluntary and involuntary abstinence, age at marriage, polygamy and the loss of sexual partner; 2. to the probability of conception dependent on fecundity which in turn is limited by the natural reproductive span, altered or damaged by nutritional levels, certain diseases and psychological factors -- and of course controlled to some extent by various contraceptive measures (nearly always withdrawal); and 3. the influence, if any, of abortion, stillbirth and infant mortality. The author concludes that of all these factors probably veneral disease has the most marked effect on fertility levels.

358 Nazer, I.R. "Abortion in the Near East," In: Proceedings of the Eighth International Conference of the International Planned Parenthood Federation. Hertford, England: International Planned Parenthood Federation, 1967.

The preservation of family honor is recognized as a mitigating circumstance in the prosecution of abortion in Jordan and Lebanon. Medical indications, however, are not permitted. In Egypt, Iran and Sudan interruption of pregnancy is allowed only when the life of the mother is endangered. Syria, Morocco and Algeria do not recognize abortion on any indications. In July 1965, the Tunisian government passed a legislation allowing abortions in government hospitals and authorized clinics if the health of the mother is threatened, if the parents have five living children, or if a mother fitted with an IUD becomes pregnant. In general these laws are not enforced. Islam forbids the interruption of pregnancy; yet, the Grand Mufti of Jordan has stated that abortion is allowed as long as the embryo is unformed in the human shape (during the first 120 days). The author observes that middle and upper class women are most likely to resort to illegal abortion, while lower class women accept an unwanted pregnancy as being inevitable. Statistics on the incidence of admitted illegal abortion in a private clinic considered to be middle class (35%) and in a family planning clinic considered to be lower class (19%) are given to support this statement.

359 Nortman, Dorothy. "Population and Family Planning Programs: A Factbook," Reports on Population/Family Planning. The Population Council, December 1969. 48 pp.

Classification and organization from basic sources of present information on national family planning policies and programs throughout the world. Twelve tables and eight figures contain the data around which discussion centers, organized into three sections: (1) a worldwide overview of information on population, economic development, and governmental positions on family planning for broad geographical regions; (2) demographic, social, and economic characteristics, for individual countries in both the developing and developed world; and (3) national family planning policy and program data, including such information as personnel allocated to services or estimated current users of such services.

360 Nortman, Dorothy. "Population Policies in Developing Countries and Related International Attitudes," Eugenics Quart. 11(1): 11-29. March 1964.

A review of the position in selected countries whose national governments either support or at least permit experimental, pilot family planning programs. These are: India, Pakistan, Korea, Malaysia, Hong Kong, Ceylon, Puerto Rico, Barbados, Taiwan, Tunisia, Turkey, United Arab Republic, Chile, Thailand, and Mainland China. Observations also on other areas of interest and on current attitudes and activities in the United Nations.

361 Novo, Rodolfo de. "Adoption in Comparative Private International Law," pp. 69-158, Vol. 3 of Hague Academy of Internation Law, Recueil des Cours, 1961.

The rules on adoption vary from one country to another and are often incompatible with another. The rules for several countries are reviewed and points of convergence and difference are indicated, along with suggestions for reconciling some differences.

362 O'Callaghan, Denis. Moral Principles of Fertility Control. Dublin: Clonmore and Reynolds, 1960. 40 pp.

The booklet analyses from the ethical standpoint the use of hormonal preparations in the control of fertility.

363 O'Keefe, John A. "Tradition and Conceptive Selection," J. Washington Acad. Sci. 47(8):273-74, 1957.

Contraception as a selective force in man, and cultural traditions affecting it.

364 Ohlin, Goran. "Un Tournant dans l'Evolution Démographique " [A Turning-Point in Demographic Change], Observateur de l'O.C.D.E., September 1966, pp. 7-11.

Discusses possibilities of fertility control in developing countries through the adoption of intrauterine contraceptive devices made available in part through foreign aid.

365 Olender, T.J. "Divorce Oddities Around the World," Women Law 52:110. Summer 1966.

Divorce laws vary widely throughout the world, according to the United Nations Commission on the Status of Women. The article deals with questionnaires concerning such laws sent by the Commission to all U.N. member nations. Seventy-one replied, excluding fifty quasi-autonomous states and the U.S., which has no uniform divorce laws. The author has divided the article into three parts: Divorce proceedings, Annulment of Marriage, and Remarriage after Divorce or Annulment. Generally, divorce statutes appear to be similar among those nations that returned the questionnaire, although there are exceptions which strongly discriminate against women.

366 Osborn, Fairfield. The Limits of the Earth. Boston: Little, Brown and Co., 1953. x, 238 pp.

Chapters V, "Africa"; VI, "South Africa"; VII, "The Amazon"; and VIII, "Beyond Europe and East of Suez"; contain many facts and figures, with details on local and peculiar problems in each region, which indicate the practical impossibility of any considerable increase in agricultural production. Shortage of water is an important factor limiting further development, in many places. The urgent need for government-sponsored birth control policies, as the only adequate means of dealing with the problem, is pointed out.

367 Osborn, Frederick. "The World Crisis in Population Growth," Clin. Obstet. Gynecol. 7(3):753-70, 1964.

The cumulative rate of world population growth is the result of reduced death rates. Figures are given for the world, the U.S.A. and a number of undeveloped countries. Prospects for a rapid reduction in births are discussed by areas. An account is given of programs in a number of underdeveloped countries. Future growth rates and ultimate world population are tentatively forecast. If by 1990 average births per woman were cut to replacement only, world population might be stabilized at 6.74 billion by 2060.

368 Paquin, Jules. "Avortement et Stérilisation " [Abortion and Sterilization], Rélations 12(137):118-21. May 1952.

Reviews the positions of Pope Pius XI and XII on direct and indirect abortion, direct or contraceptive sterilization, and curative sterilization. Also provides a few references to the position taken by old Canon Law.

369 Paquin, Jules. "Limitation et Régulation des Naissances" [Limitation and Regulation of Births], Rélations 12(139): 173-76. July 1952.

Pius XII condemned all contraceptive methods, all procedures which directly and positively opposed procreation; he condemned them as contrary to Divine and Natural Law. According to Paquin, violations of Divine Law are justified on false pretexts. He finds people cloaking the avoidance of marriage responsibilities and pure sensual appetite under the name of morality. Acts of marriage which are based on an avoidance of children are immoral and illicit. Abstention is an answer, but qualified. Abstention is immoral and illicit if 1) one spouse does not consent to it (marriage contract = agreement to procreate); neither spouse can limit sex to "sterile days". 2)the couple wish to get rid of any "fruit of conception" (they can be guilty of the sin of abortion on their heads). 3) if either sins by not being abstinent during the period of abstinence, either by adultery, or masturbation. Regulation of births is right, as opposed to control of births. Regulation must be in line with God's law. For economic or social order, eugenic and medical reasons, one may abstain, (e.g., during the recovery after a pregnancy.) God's blessing equals happiness. No blessing for those who are against any procreation. To abstain, purely to avoid children, is a sin.

370 Paupert, Jean Marie, ed. Contrôles des Naissances et Théologie, le Dossier de Rome. Traduction, Présentation et Notes de Jean-Marie Paupert [Birth Control and Theology, the Brief of Rome. Translation, Introduction and Notes by...]. Paris: Editions du Seuil, 1967. 192 pp.

In April 1967 the French press carried resumes and excerpts from some Council documents concerning certain problems facing the Christian conscience because of changes in the attitudes and conditions of birth control. These documents, which presumably reported council and pontifical secret deliberations, were first publicly aired in an American Catholic journal, The National Catholic Reporter, and a British Catholic journal, The Tablet. In this book, the Church's position with regard to the morality of birth control and medical-social arguments in favor of it are reviewed. The authority and philosophical foundations of the Church's doctrines are discussed. It suggest that a demographic policy must give consideration to the fundamental values of marriage and to the concept of responsible parenthood.

371 Peel, John. "Contraception and the Catholic Conscience," New Society 4(103):7-8. September 1964.

As a historical background to the contemporary Roman Catholic debate on contraception, the changing attitude of the Catholic Church on this subject during the last 100 years is surveyed and the concessions to *coitus reservatus* and the 'safe period' are examined. It is suggested that Catholic doctrine on this subject has been more flexible than many would suppose and a plea is entered for a realistic appraisal, by the Vatican Council, of the difficulties facing Catholics and of the urgency of the world population problem.

372 Peel, John, and Potts, Malcolm. Textbook of Contraceptive Practice. Cambridge: Cambridge University Press, 1969. 297 pp.

A textbook for physicians, easily understood by laymen also, giving a detailed description of all commonly available contraceptive measures including sterilization and abortion. Chapters are devoted to each method, to the medical history of contraception, to legal and administrative aspects of birth control, and to medical aspects. Methods are discussed in terms of history, types available, use and application, side effects (where applicable), and evaluation. Charts, diagrams, tables, and five appendices supplement the text.

373 Perkin, Gordon W. "Family Planning: A Factor in the Reduction of Maternal and Child Morbidity and Mortality," pp. 59-67 in: R.K.B. Hankinson and N. Soewondo, eds. Family Planning and National Development. International Planned Parenthood Federation, 1969.

New national family planning programs should give priority to recruiting older, higher parity women as IUD acceptors.

The health justification is that the risks of maternal and infant mortality increase with age of mother and that those risks are affected by other interrelated factors such as anemia due to closely spaced births, and such socioeconomic variables as urban-rural residence and educational levels. The demographic justification is based on the concept of a "balanced" strategy, which simultaneously reduces both the number of births and deaths; the greater acceptance and longer retention of the IUD by older women compared with the young, thus increasing the period of use; and the greater likelihood of older women being limiters than spacers. Data are presented on births averted by programs focused on older acceptors compared with younger acceptors. Administrative implications, which should be considered, include training courses for physicians and paramedical personnel, establishment of postpartum services, and organization and extension of effective services to rural areas, including supplementary family planning services to complement those available through official health programs.

374 Perkin, Gordon W. "Measuring Clinic Performance," Family Planning Perspectives 1(1):36-38. Spring 1969.

A patient/staff index is suggested as a comparative measure of family planning clinic performance. It is designed for self-evaluation and requires minimal staff time. The results obtained from the use of this index are intended to be of practical use to clinic administrators in pointing to possible need for modifications in staffing patterns, clinic hours, or location. It is not a measure of quality of medical care. The index has been used in four Affiliates of Planned Parenthood.

375 "Pharmaceutical Advertising: A Survey of Existing Legislation," Internat. Digest Health Legis. 19:457-552, 1968.

This comparative survey of health legislation is based on such source material as was available, for each country, at the headquarters of the World Health Organization up to the end of July 1968. It supplements the 1961 survey. After a general review of legislation, the legislation for each of several countries is described. Included is the advertisement of abortifacients and contraceptives.

376 Phelps, Edmund S. "Population Increase," Canadian J. Econ. 1(3):497-518. August 1968.

Deals mainly with a somewhat hypothetical and avant-garde question: in a laissez-faire economy with universal birth-control knowledge, is the number of children that present parents would choose to have, in view of their knowledge of the private costs and benefits, equal to the number they would choose to have under accurate information on the full 'social' costs and benefits? Topics include: Consumption per head and lifetime family utility; Pseudo-externalities and interdependence; Genuine externalities. Discussion of policy aspects. Mathematical appendixes.

377 Pius XII, Pope. Famiglia: dai Discorsi di Pio XII Aglisposi [The Family: Discourses of Pius XII to Married People]. A cura del Fronte della Famiglia. Roma: Famiglia Italiana, 1950 vii, 226 pp.

Condemns therapeutic abortion and mechanical methods of contraception.

378 Pius XII, Pope. Marriage and the Moral Law. Addresses of Pope Pius XII: "Vegliare con Sollecitudine" and "Nell' Ordine Della Natura," 1951. London: Catholic Truth Society, 1960. 36 pp.

Addresses to the Congress of the Italian Association of Catholic Midwives and to the Congress of the Association Known as the 'Family Campaign' and other Family Associations. In arguing against artificial methods of contraception, the following themes are discussed: the value and inviolability of human life; the immorality of birth prevention and direct sterilization; natural sterility or the "infertile period"; the morality of complete abstinence and the dignity of virginity; God's gift of conjugal joy and the Church's concern for the family.

379 Planned Parenthood Federation of America."Family Allowances and Human Fertility." Human Fertility 10(4):112-13. December 1945.

A review of the principal provisions of family allowance programs in Russia, Canada, and Great Britain, and a discussion of the possible effect of such programs on reproduction.

380 Ploscowe, Morris. "Report to the Hague: Suggested Revisions of Penal Laws Relating to Sex Crimes and Crimes Against the Family," Cornell Law Quart. 50:425-45. Spring 1965.

Discusses resolutions considered and adopted by the Association Internationale de Droit Penal at its International Congress of Criminal Law Held at the Hague, August 1964.

381 Pohlman, Edward W. "'Birth Planning' Versus 'Family Planning'," Popul. Rev. 12(1&2):18-22. January - December 1968.

The phrase "birth planning" avoids the negative connotations of control; emphasizes the positive, planning; can include pro-natalist as well as anti-natalist efforts; can be used to refer to the efforts of individual couples as well as national and other organizations; and is broad enough to include birth promotion methods as well as methods for birth limitation. In addition, the term can refer not only to number of births, but to the planning of sex, spacing, timing, and quality of offspring.

382 Pohlman, Edward W. "Mobilizing Social Pressures Toward Small Families," Eugenics Quart. 13(2):122-27. June 1960.

Harnessing population growth may become less a matter of contraception and more a matter of influencing people to want fewer children. A direct appeal to people to volunteer to curtail family size in the interests of national or world population or economic problems would probably be relatively ineffective. Instead, if in any subgroup small families were widely regarded as a patriotic duty, or an obligation, parents might curtail family size because of what other people would think. Studies suggest that many parents regard large families as basically 'good' and small families as cause for apology. This might be reversed. To some extent the desire for larger families is the result of social pressures; some parents might welcome a climate of opinion that permitted smaller families. It might be made fashionable for parents to adopt children after having two or three of their own, especially if their own children were all of the same sex.

383 Pohlman, Edward W. "A Psychologist's Introduction to the Birth Planning Literature," J. Soc. Issues 23(4):13-27. October 1967.

This review of literature of family planning, with 98 references, is divided into (a) major research projects, (b) bibliographies and leads to finding material, (c) publications touching on special topics, and (d) sources of funds and information. Special topics include the history of birth planning, religious aspects, legal aspects, population growth, psychological effects of unwanted conceptions, preferences for sex of children, particular contraceptive methods, abortion, sterilization, and "psychological" discussions.

384 Pohlman, Edward W. "Some Effects of Being Able to Control Sex of Offspring," Eugenics Quart. 14(4):274-81. December 1967.

Parents in many cultures prefer at least one child of each sex, and two children of a particular sex, often male. A review of existing research permits projection of the effects to be expected if humans become able to select sex offspring. Direct psychological effects would seem to be considerable and almost wholly positive. The birth of children of an undesired sex may lead to some degree of rejection and/or sex-role confusion, and is often undesirable from a mental health standpoint. Ability to control sex of offspring would probably reduce population growth rates somewhat, although the magnitude and even the existence of this relationship is conjectural, since the prediction rests on so many different and unquantified variables. Countries with strong preferences for males -- among them developing countries with acute population problems -- might experience important reductions in population growth. A general desire for sons (or daughters) in a particular culture might lead to a drastic imbalance in sex ratio. A generation later, such an imbalance might mean a shortage of marriage partners and a resulting reduction in births. Sharp changes in a nation's sex ratio would affect personal, family, and societal life. Polygamy or polyandry, parenthood without wedlock, and widespread voluntary or enforced celibacy, might become more common. Excess males in a militaristic build-up might be increasingly viewed as cannon-fodder. A government determined to keep the sex ratio approximately equal or at some other desirable level might be able to do so by controlling the supplies and services which made sex choice possible. How religious, political, and other powerful organizations would view boy-girl choice is conjectural.

385 Polgar, Steven. "Population Theory, Anthropology and Family Planning." Mimeographed paper . Carolina Population Center, University of North Carolina, Chapel Hill.

Little use has been made of anthropological knowledge in the formulation of population theory. In this article data from prehistory and cross-cultural studies are used to examine the theoretical assumptions leading to the belief that policies should focus on counteracting an ingrained desire of families for a large number of children. This policy recommendation depends greatly on a homeostatic model of human population dynamics governed by mortality, on the assumption of a rigid deterministic relationship between social organization and family size desires, on a simplistic view of factors influencing natality regulating practices, and on a disregard of the differential costs involved in using different methods and services for birth control. Offers an alternative view on how to proceed with the urgent task of population planning.

386 Population Association of America. "Progress and Problems of Fertility Control Around the World." Demography 5(2), 1968. 462 pp.

A special issue containing 44 papers on fertility control programs around the world, national and international, in Africa, the Near East, Asia, Central and Latin America, and the United States. The role of foundations and government agencies is discussed. A medical and methodological section includes an international bibliography of family planning research 1955-68 and papers on the statistical evaluation of contraceptive methods, commercial distribution of contraceptives in the developing world, births prevented, and awareness sources in the adoption of contraception.

387 "Population Problems and Educational Policy," Nature 147 (3724):305-7. March 25,1941.

The international and national importance of adequate reproduction are outlined and the necessity for other than short-range empirical policies stressed. The reorientation of education is held to be the only approach offering any possibilities of permanent success.

388 Population Reference Bureau. "United Nations: Population Opinion Survey," Popul. Bull. 20(6):141-71. October 1964.

Excerpts from the report of the Secretary-General which summarizes a survey conducted by the Economic and Social Council among the member nations. The report is divided into six sections: introduction; demographic conditions and trends; general views; views on particular problems; sources of information; and action programs. Less than half of the nations contacted by the Council responded and most of these were interested in effective action in birth regulation to check population growth and to improve the standard of living.

389 Population Reference Bureau. "The United Nations on Population -- 1966, the Year of the Breakthrough," Popul. Bull. 23(1):1-23. February 1967.

Contains editorial comment and texts of documents and statements relating to the debate on the population resolution, December 1966.

390 Population Reference Bureau. "The Vatican and the Population Crisis," Popul. Bull. 21(1):1-15. February 1964.

Since the first Vatican Council in 1961, ever-increasing population problems appear to have been a concern of the assembled Church Fathers. Three years later, Pope Pius VI, addressing a group of cardinals, acknowledged that the leadership of the Catholic Church could not continue to bypass the important question of population control. The Pope's speech, a paper on the Vatican Council's discussion on birth control, and three statements by Council Fathers are presented here.

391 Potter, Robert G., Jr. "Additional Measures of Use-Effectiveness in Contraception," Milbank Memorial Fund Quart. 41(4, 1):400-18. October 1963.

Any groups' practice of contraception during a single pregnancy interval may be viewed as a selective process wherein, as exposure time elapses, the more pregnancy-prone are progressively removed by accidental conception, and perhaps also by self-removal, leaving behind a more and more homogeneously low-risk remainder. Consequently, when a series of pregnancy rates are calculated for successive segments of the total exposure period, these subinterval rates typically decline. It is attempted here to extend methods for describing and testing the significance of differences between such declines. As an additional way of describing a decline of pregnancy risk, one may consider the percent of a hypothetical cohort that would remain protected for specified durations of exposure if (1) they were subject to successive monthly risks of pregnancy, empirically observed, and if (2) all continued contraception until pregnant. One advantage of this life-table approach is that it is accompanied by formulas for estimating standard errors.

392 Potter, Robert G., Jr. "Length of the Observation Period as a Factor Affecting the Contraceptive Failure Rate," Milbank Memorial Fund Quart. 38(2):140-52. April 1960.

Gives a distribution curve for fecundability and also two possible distributions of efficiency: one assuming all couples to be equally efficient and the other assuming that some couples are fully efficient while others are totally inefficient. On this model he shows that in both cases the number of pregnancies per couple steadily declines as the length of the observation period increases.

393 Potter, Robert G., Jr. "Some Problems in Predicting a Couple's Contraceptive Future," Eugenics Quart. 6(4): 254-59, 1959.

A discussion of the possibilities of deriving a specific prognosis for contraceptive success for the individual from a group contraceptive failure rate. A simplified model relating risk of subsequent pregnancies to (1) regularity of contraceptive practice, and (2) number of years during which protection is sought is also presented. Specific discussions are included on the likelihood of an entirely successful contraceptive; individual prediction through extrapolation from group experience; protection during long risk periods; and omissions of contraceptives.

394 Potter, Robert G., Jr., _et al_. "Improvement of Contraception During the Course of Marriage," _Popul. Stud_. 16(2): 160-74 · November 1962.

The authors develop a technique for estimating how pregnancy risks vary among married couples from time to time. They then use this in connection with the data obtained from the survey of Family Growth in Metropolitan America and show that contraceptive effectiveness improves considerably as the length of a marriage increases. This is especially so both before and after the second birth, mainly owing to a more regular practice of contraception.

395 Potter, Robert G., and Sagi, Philip C. "Some Procedures for Estimating the Sampling Fluctuations of a Contraceptive Failure Rate," pp. 389-407 in: Kiser, Clyde V., ed. _Research in Family Planning_. Princeton: Princeton University Press, 1962.

An approximate formula for estimating the standard errors of a contraceptive failure rate is derived on the basis that the failure rate is a ratio of two random, dependent variables. On the assumption that the contraceptive failure rate behaves as a simple proportion, a binomial formula has also been considered. The capacity of these two formulas to produce useful confidence interval is tested by means of a series of sampling experiments.

396 Potter, Robert G., Jr., and Sakoda, James M. "Family Planning and Fecundity," _Popul. Stud_. 20(3):311-28. March 1967.

A statistical model of family-building is described which allows for the following items: length of reproductive period, chance of spontaneous abortion, chance of still-birth, length of gestation period, anovulation and fecundability. The model is a stochastic one and is evaluated on a computer. It is used to evaluate success in family-planning, and the incidence of unsought births, according to the level of natural fecundability and according to the effectiveness of contraceptive practice. The authors emphasize that, even with average fecundity, unwanted births can be avoided only by very efficient contraceptive practice.

397 Pradervand, Pierre. "La Course Economique " [The Economic Course], Developpement & Civilisations 36:5-30. December 1968.

A summary article, focusing on Asia, Africa, and Latin America, consisting of four major sections: (1) the current population problem: past and future growth, causes, effects on food production, urbanization, and education; (2) the concept of family planning: political and economic implications, contraceptive methods; (3) attitudes toward family planning: general trends and obstacles to its diffusion; (4) the urgency of the problem.

398 Pressat, Roland. "Observations Exceptionnelles en Demographie " [Notes on Exceptional Occurrences in Demography], Concours Médical 90(11):2365-71. March 16, 1968.

Considers several modern examples of anomalies, in the effect of economic crises on mortality and in the effect of government policy on fertility in developed countries.

399 Pressat, Roland. [Population Policies in the U.S.S.R. and in the Peoples' Republics: Birth Rate-Contraception-Abortion], Concours Médical 85:1775-84. March 16, 1963.

Despite a high natality rate between 1917-1959, Soviet Union has had a low growth rate, due to such factors as famine, war and civil war. The Soviet Union did not have liberal abortion laws for many years. The laws were changed and contraception was also introduced in 1956-57. Yugoslavia, Poland, Bulgaria, and Rumania have an increasing fertility level, while Czechoslovakia, Hungary and East Germany have a rate similar to France and England. All have legalized abortion. Tables and graphs show natality rates, abortion, etc. Also discussed are medical aspects of birth control, contraception, etc.

400 Pyle, Leo, ed. The Pill and Birth Regulation: the Catholic Debate, Including Statements, Articles, and Letters from the Pope, Bishops, Priests, and Married and Unmarried Laity. Baltimore: Helicon Press, 1964. x, 225 pp.

Central to the debate in this book is whether within the sacrament of marriage a couple is mated primarily or only for breeding purposes or whether within their own mutual right that of intercourse as a normal and necessary marital activity is not essential to the happiness of the parents and of the entire family. Millions of Catholic couples torn between their faith and their daily needs, await an answer to this question. At least dialogue now exists, and compassion on the part of much of the hierarchy.

401 Rainwater, Lee. "Family Planning in Cross-National Perspectives: An Overview," J. Soc. Issues 23(4):1-11. October 1967.

Social science research and the development of contraceptive techniques has made population control attainable, even in underdeveloped countries with modest resources. Previous research indicates that among the poor in the United States and the underdeveloped nations the ideal family is realistically, small, thereby making it much more possible for governments to embark on family planning programs. Constraints and inefficiencies in the institutional sector prevent knowledge of and facilities for birth control from filtering down. Although family planning information and services are available to middle class Americans, their ideal family size is relatively large. Crucial to the development of effective programs, is research which will illuminate the reasons for large (four children instead of two) family preference in the middle class and make provisions for functional alternatives to gratifications received.

402 Raulet, Harry M. Family Planning and Population Control in Developing Countries. East Lansing: Institute of International Agriculture, Michigan State University, November 1968. 51 pp.

An essay which covers the family planning movement and the determination of fertility, population growth and economic development in underdeveloped areas, and the achievements of family planning and prospects for the future.

403 Ravenholt, R.T. "An Overview of Population Policies and Programs in Developing Countries. Part Two: Methods of Family Planning," War On Hunger 2(5):4-5. May 1968.

Includes brief sections: IUD's - pro and con; Oral contraceptives.

404 Reiterman, Carl. "Birth Control and Catholics," J. Sci. Study Relig. 4(2):213-33. Spring 1966.

A study which sees the conflict on the subject of birth control as an internal struggle within the Church, initially between the clergy and a minority of the laity, and subsequently involving the hierarchy at higher levels. The position of the Church and its theologians and laity on birth control as expressed in 55 years of the Jesuit weekly America is discussed in two sections: (1) the period before the appearance of the rhythm method, and (2) the period following the appearance of rhythm and continuing to the latest available issue of America at the time the article was written (May 9, 1964).

405 Rettig, John. "Problèmes et Evolution de la Planification de la Famille en Europe et au Proche Orient " [Problems and Development of Family Planning in Europe and the Near East], Demografia 10(3/4):409-15, 1967.

Recalls the objectives of the International Planned Parenthood Federation, founded in Bombay in 1952, which are to reduce the increase in population, make parents conscious of their responsibilities in the interest of their families and the entire community, and to bring about a substitution of contraception for induced abortion. Reviews developments in family planning in various European and Near Eastern countries and changes in attitudes of religious and governmental officials.

406 Ridley, Jeanne C., et al. "On the Apparent Sub-Fecundity of Non-Family Planners," Soc. Biol. 16(1):24-28. March 1969.

The hypothesis was tested that factors other than sterility could contribute to observed differentials in the natality of family planners and non-family planners. A computer simulation model, REPSIM-A, was employed to simulate four experimental cohorts of 1,000 females each. A factorial design was followed with each of two experimental factors, age at marriage and sterility, being assumed to operate independently at two levels. Age at marriage was held constant in two of the simulated cohorts and was allowed to vary in the other two. Likewise, in two cohorts no sterility was assumed before the age of 40 and in the remaining two cohorts sterility was allowed to vary with age. Identical assumptions were made for each cohort regarding level of fetal loss, infant mortality, lengths of the non-susceptible periods associated with pregnancy, natural fecundability and contraceptive practice. Since the aim was to simulate survey-type data on surviving married women, divorce, widowhood, and mortality were assumed not to occur. Simulated data for the four cohorts at ages 25, 30, 35, and 40 were obtained. The results supported the hypothesis that sterility is not the only factor contributing to the low natality of non-planners. Consistently lower natality of non-planners than of planners was observed in the four simulated cohorts. The factors studied were found to have effects at each simulated age, but their relative importance was found to change with age. It was concluded that differentials in natality between planners and non-planners observed in survey data may be produced by a variety of causes. Therefore, explanations based on sterility are likely to be erroneous. Further, the role of chance variation was found to be not unimportant, having the effect of depressing the natality of some women. Thus, chance variation has a role in the selection of family planners and hence in the natality difference between planners and non-planners.

407 Riviere, M. [Medico-Sociological Study of Induced Abortion in France and in the Principal Countries of the World], _Rev. Praticien_ 13:2263-ff., 1963.

Criminal and legal abortions are discussed with particular attention given to countries where more liberal policies are observed as in Eastern Europe, Japan, Switzerland and Scandinavia.

408 Roberts, Thomas D., ed. _Contraception and Holiness: the Catholic Predicament_. New York: Herder and Herder, 1964. 346 pp.

A collection of essays on the relationship of natural law to contraception from the vantage of theology, philosophy, law, sociology and biology. Topics include conscience and contraception; sexuality and contraception; responsible parenthood and the population dilemma; and the question of whether the Catholic Church can change her position on birth control. It is contended in the introductory section that every cultural and spiritual tradition should be examined and all the resources of all the specialized sciences should be called upon before attempting to determine how natural law relates to contraception. Stressed is the necessity that non-Western attitudes, customs, and traditions, as well as those of the rest of the Christian world, be allowed to supply evidence in support of their particular nations of what is "intrinsically unnatural and immoral."

409 Rock, John. The Time Has Come. London: Longmans, 1963. xvi, 216 pp.

Main argument is that by perfecting the therapeutic and regulative properties of the pill, medical science could ensure in all cases the complete stability of the menstrual cycle, thus enabling all married couples to use the theologically-approved rhythm method of family planning with entire confidence and success. But also envisages the remote possibility that the moral theologians themselves may determine eventually that the use of the pill for contraceptive purposes is not contra naturam. Further, the accidental suspension of ovulation as a result of steroid treatment for various gynaecological conditions creates temporary sterility as a side-effect of medical treatment; but the effect is contraceptive. Contends that there is a case for reconsideration of the Thomist natural law theory in its application to contraception, since "frustration of nature is man's vocation" (a quotation from a Roman Catholic moralist), and may well be consonant with Man's nature as a rational being.

410 Rockefeller, John D., 3rd. "Population: Decision by Default," Popul. Bull. 19(4):86-93. July 1963.

Text of speech delivered before the American Association of University Women Convention, Denver, June 24 1963. Presentation of the case for a worldwide, government-sponsored program of education in family planning.

411 Roemer, Ruth. "Abortion Law: The Approaches of Different Nations," Amer. J. Public Health 57(11):1906-22, 1967.

The abortion laws of different countries are classified into five categories, with illustrative examples: laws authorizing abortion on demand (USSR, Bulgaria, Hungary); laws authorizing abortion on social grounds (Japan, Poland,

Czechoslovakia, Yugoslavia); laws authorizing abortion on sociomedical grounds (Iceland, Sweden, Denmark, Norway); laws authorizing abortion on medical grounds (Syria, Honduras, Switzerland, England, and several American states); and laws authorizing abortion only to save the life of the woman (majority of American states, western Australia, Venezuela, Chile, and France). The trend in maternal death rates in France and Holland, countries with restrictive statutes, is compared with that in Denmark and Norway, countries with more liberal legislation. During the period that Danish and Norwegian legislation was only slightly more liberal than that of France and Holland, maternal death rates in all four countries declined by about the same proportion. After liberalization of the Scandinavian laws to permit abortion on sociomedical grounds, the decline in maternal deaths in Denmark and Norway far exceeded that in France and Holland. Since criminal abortions account for a significant percentage of maternal deaths in countries with restrictive abortion laws, it is reasonable to assume that a substantial portion of the greater maternal death rate reduction in the Scandinavian countries can be attributed to a lessened resort to criminal abortion after their laws were liberalized. If the American states take only the limited step of the Model Penal Code, as in the 1967 legislation of Colorado, North Carolina, and California, they will be faced with the same problem that the Scandinavian countries faced -- a persistently high criminal abortion rate necessitating further amendment of the law. More than the Model Penal Code is required to combat the problem of criminal abortion.

412 Ross, John A., et al. A Handbook for Service Statistics in Family Planning Programs. New York: The Population Council, July 1968. 151 pp.; Manual de Estadisticas de Servicios en los Programs de Planificacion Familiar. Asociacion Colombiana de Facultades de Medicina, Division de Estudios de Poblacion, March 1969. 162 pp.

A handbook, in English and Spanish versions, suggesting guidelines for collecting day-to-day statistics and records in a large family planning program, including such data as number and characteristics of clients, frequency of various types of service provided, program personnel records, supply levels, and costs for different phases of the program. Chapters cover the coupon system, the clinic monthly report, the client report, follow-up staff, inventories and supply lines, costs and resources, and summary rates, such as acceptance rates and births averted, with illustrative computations by the life table method of live birth rates for contraceptive acceptors and "demographic effectiveness-all contraception" pregnancy rates. Also included are appendices on use-effectiveness and continuation of contraception by C. Tietze and S. Lewit, on the multiple decrement life table by R.G. Potter, and on a variety of reporting forms, questionnaires, and special purpose analyses.

413 Roux, Jean. Précis Historique et Théorique de Marxisme-Leninisme [Historical and Theoretical Summary of Marxism-Leninism]. Paris: Robert Laffont, 1969. 399 pp.

Describes the fundamentals of historical materialism, as represented in Marxism-Leninism, finding their way into the legislation of socialist countries concerning the family. This legislation has undergone important changes. After the October Revolution the enfranchisement of women, the secularization of marriage, the easing of divorce in the code of 1926, the removal of polygamy as a crime, and the legalization of abortions by physicians are among the changes. The results were demographically and ethically disastrous. In reaction, abortions were limited in 1936 and *de facto* marriages were abolished in 1949. There has been an oscillation between natalism and Malthusianism.

414 Ryder, Norman B. "The Character of Modern Fertility," *Annals Amer. Acad. Polit. Soc. Sci.* 369:26-36. January 1967.

One characteristic shared by all modern industrialized and urbanized nations is low fertility. From different initial levels, beginning at different times, the birth rates have declined slowly in some industrialized and urbanized countries and rapidly in others, but have now settled down on a common low plateau a little above what is required for replacement. The regulation of fertility has been achieved by widely variant strategies, involving different combinations of nuptiality control, contraception, and abortion. In every case the small family size has represented the intent of the individual couple and not the guidance of government or church. The explanation of fertility decline advanced here places stress on a normative change in the relationship between parent and children under conditions of declining mortality and urban economic development.

Although the fertility of modern industrialized and urbanized nations is not expected to change much in the long run, these societies will probably have difficulty in avoiding costly fertility fluctuations and in keeping the reproductive goals of individual couples from eventuating in too little or too much population growth.

415 Saigal, M.D. "Some Observations on the Complications of Graefenburg Ring," Fam. Planning News 3(3):59-61. March 1962.

Complications observed in 13 cases following the use of Graefenburg ring are described. The author observes that as a contraceptive it has nothing to commend itself and must be discarded outright.

416 Saunders, Lyle. "Family Planning, the Worldwide View," pp. 312-43 in Liu, William T., ed. Family and Fertility. Notre Dame: Notre Dame University Press, 1967.

After a brief discussion of the concept of family planning, its definitions and historical approaches, there follows a list of sources from which information and inferences concerning family planning throughout the world can be drawn and a view of national fertility rates and world population figures and their relevance or irrelevance to the extent of organized attempts to promote contraception and social-cultural changes. The history and present activities of organized family planning programs, both private and IPPF-supported, are covered with mention of their many social functions and connection to general interest in population control policies. Government-sponsored family planning programs throughout the world are described, with special reference to national fertility rates and abortion laws. There is a summary of world family planning by geographic region. The author concludes with a discussion of the urgent need to curtail world population growth and the conditions and prospects for successful action and effective fertility control programs. Several tables with pertinent data are included.

417 Savel, L.E. "Adjudication of Therapeutic Abortion and Sterilization," Clin. Obstet. Gynec. 7:14, 1964.

An analysis of the Danish, Swedish, and American methods of justification for therapeutic abortion and sterilization. Also provides a detailed account of the system used at Newark Beth Israel Hospital in New Jersey.

418 Schaffer, Helen B. "Status of Birth Control," Editorial Research Reports, October 15 1958, pp. 775-92.

Contents: Controversy over birth control therapy; American and foreign birth control law; Obstacles to acceptance of birth control.

419 Schieffelin, Olivia, ed. Muslim Attitudes Toward Family Planning. New York: The Population Council, 1967.

Divided into three parts: statements by religious leaders; statements by political leaders and governments; commentary on factors affecting Muslim natality by various scholars.

420 Schwelb, Egon. "Marriage and Human Rights," Amer. J. Comparative Law 12:337-83. Summer 1963.

Marriage law in various countries, related to the United Nations convention on consent to marriage, minimum age for marriage, and registration of marriage.

421 Seklani, Mahmoud. "Efficacité de la Contraception: Methodes et Résultats " [The Efficacy of Contraception: Methods and Results], Population 18(2):329-48. April - June 1963.

An ordered presentation of older and recent ideas and works on the measurement of the efficacy of contraception, from the statistical point of view. It is demonstrated that the measure of this efficacy depends on: (1) the differential fecundity of the group of women studied, (2) contraceptive practices, (3) length of observation, (3) individual efficiency, (4) length of exposure to the risk of pregnancy, etc. Interpretation poses arduous problems, the solution of which must affect the collation of data. No experiment should be undertaken in this area regarding a preliminary examination of the manner in which the results will be utilized. It is probably one of the best examples of how statistics serves the physician in aiding the resolution of problems which, a priority, might seem purely medical.

422 Semmens, James P. "Population Explosion," Obstet. Gynecol. 25(3):430-34, 1965.

The various demographic factors influencing the current population trend in the world are emphasized and the fact that the teenage segment of this population may represent as high as 40% of the total in certain land areas is pointed out. Various governmental programs to control the population are discussed and evaluated with regard to causes of failure or success. Particular note is made of the importance of motivation and understanding and the role of publicity and education in the awakening of the populace as being of paramount importance for the success of any program.

423 Sengupta, B. "Liberalisation of Abortion as a Population Control Measure," Indian J. Public Health 9:69-ff., 1965.

The population situation of India and the efforts to control its increase through contraception and sterilization are examined. Following an analysis of the relationship between legal abortion, the birth rate and population increase in Japan and Eastern Europe, the author concludes that induced abortion is safe and that abortion legalization would result in a decrease in the rate of population increase within a short period.

424 Sills, David L., and Sheldon, Richard C. "Discussion of: Survey Research and Population Control in Latin America, by J. Mayone Stycos; Sample Surveys for Family Planning Research in Taiwan, by Ronald Freedman; and The Sample Survey in a National Population Program, by Leslie Corsa, Jr.," Pub. Opin. Quart. 28(3)389-94. Fall 1964.

The function of the social survey for population control and family planning is discussed. Sills summarized the effects of the Taiwan survey, predicting that "the proliferation of social research in the developing countries will have an impact as profound as the introduction of Western technology. Deals with some of the latent functions of family planning studies anticipated by Stycos; and discusses the fertility control problem in Pakistan. Sheldon discusses the value of sample surveys for the observation of changes in the system, and advocates that pilot experiments precede the instituting of action programs.

425 Simon, Julian L. "A Huge Marketing Research Task -- Birth Control," J. Marketing Research 5:21-27. February 1968.

A progress report on research for selling family planning, especially in underdeveloped countries.

426 Simon, Julian L. "The Role of Bonuses and Persuasive Propaganda in the Reduction of Birth Rates," Econ. Development Cult. Change 16(3):404-11. April 1968.

Considers the issues in current experiments in the employment of bonuses and propaganda persuasion in underdeveloped countries and presents the case for regarding them as supplements to each other rather than as alternatives.

427 Simon, Julian L. "The Value of Avoided Births to Underdeveloped Countries," Popul. Stud. 23(1):61-68. March 1969.

Comments on the reasoning of Stephen Enke and of other estimates, particularly those of Coale and Hoover for India.

428 Smith, C.E. Papal Enforcement of Some Medieval Marriage Laws. Baton Rouge: Louisiana State University Press, 1940.

The Christian legislation imposing the impediments of relationship to marriage derived its precedents from the Roman law and the Scriptures. The seventh degree usually was stipulated as the limit of the prohibition, and this limit doubtless was suggested by the Roman law of intestate succession. There were many instances of papal intervention to secure enforcement or relaxation of the law, with relaxation being more numerous.

429 Smith, T. Lynn. "A Demographic Study of Widows," Sociologia 24(2):95-106. June 1962.

The examination of about 650 titles of articles in professional journals, brochures, monographs and books uncovered very few significant studies of the demographic aspects of widowhood. From the world-wide materials available in the 1955 issue of the Demographic Yearbook of the United Nations, three general types or patterns regarding the importance of widows in the population were identified: (1) the pattern prevailing in such countries as India, Ceylon, and Egypt, in which females marry young, few females remain unmarried throughout life, the mortality rates are high, widows are to be found a very high percent; (2) a Latin American type, which prevails in most of the 20 Latin American countries, in which the failure of a large percentage of the population to marry, either legally or consensually, reduces the widows to very small percentages of the population; and (3) an intermediate type characteristic of such societies as Canada, Australia, New Zealand, the U.S., and many of the countries of Western Europe. In the U.S.,widows are increasing more rapidly than the general population, solely as a result of the aging of the population. They also are concentrated to a considerable degree in certain sections of the nation, and especially in the District of Columbia, Florida, the New England states, New York, and New Jersey. Females who have lost their husbands also tend to congregate in small villages and towns, and in the central cities of the nation's major urbanized areas. In 1950 the median age of white widows was 66.4 years and that of nonwhite widows was 58.8 years.

430 St. John-Stevas, Norman. Birth Control and Public Policy. A Report to the Center for the Study of Democratic Institutions, Santa Barbara, 1960. 83 pp.

A part of a larger study of law and morals sponsored by the Fund for the Republic. Chapters deal with: history of contraception, English law, United States law, extent of contraception in England and the United States, religious opinion toward it with special reference to the Roman Catholic Church. The author concludes that the rhythm method could be employed more widely, being the only possible method of international family planning acceptable to all major religions, and that the United Nations policy of neutrality on contraception is unavoidable. The Roman Catholic community in England and the United States would be wise not to urge a total legislative ban on contraceptives. A statute forbidding contraception such as that in Connecticut violates Catholic principles of jurisprudence.

431 St. John-Stevas, Norman. The Right to Life. New York: Holt, Rinehart and Winston, 1964.

The author discusses the principle of the sanctity of life in regard to abortion; euthanasia, suicide, capital punishment and warfare killings. Chapter Two includes the religious and legal aspects of abortion and refutes arguments for the extension and liberalization of legal abortion in Britain. The author concludes that any gains forthcoming to the community as the effect of liberal abortion laws would be doubtful in view of the weakening of the principle of respect for the sanctity of life.

432 Stein, Herman D. "Planification en Faveur de l'Enfance dans les Pays en Voie de Développement. Rapport d'Une Conférence de la Table Rond " [Policies Favoring Children in Countries Undergoing Development. Report of a Round Table Conference], 1-7 April 1964, Bellagio, Italy. Geneva: UNICEF [1965], 264 pp.

Efforts at development are not yet successful in meeting the needs of the next generation. This conference in 1964 was intended to formulate precise plans concerning youngsters and adolescents which need to be implemented immediately so as to structure their future roles. Demographic factors are naturally relevant to this matter and attention was given to reports on trends, in particular the statements of A. Sauvy on education.

433 Stephan, Frederick F. "Possibilities and Pitfalls in the Measurement of Attitudes and Opinions on Family Planning," pp. 423-34, Chpt. in: Kiser, D.V., ed. Research in Family Planning. Princeton: Princeton University Press, 1962. xvi, 664 pp.

There is a great opportunity for research on attitudes regarding family planning, but serious difficulties have arisen in similar fields of attitude research. Planning is more complicated than we tend to assume. There may not be any single variable or a small number of variables that dominate other important variables affecting motivation in family planning. The social context of the couples studied should not be ignored. Techniques of measurement must be improved well beyond the present state of the art.

434 Stern, Loren G. "Abortion: Reform and the Law," J. Crim. Law Criminol. Police Sci. 59(1):84-95. March 1968.

The presentation and justification of a proposed statute to legalize abortion whose adoption is urged. The British and U.S. legislation on abortion is reviewed in detail, and it is concluded that the major purpose of the statutes is to protect the mother's life. Religious attitudes are examined in detail, and it is suggested that while the Catholic Church still opposes abortion, most Protestants and Jews have no religious objection to its legalization. The proposed statute is given in full in an appendix and contains six articles.

435 Stone, Abraham. "Present-Day International Trends in Family Planning," Annals New York Acad. Sciences 54:769-75. May 2 1952.

The growing interest the world over in planned parenthood stems from many realizations, including a growing social awareness that a better balance between populations and resources, between human fertility and soil fertility, is essential for the welfare of nations and the peace of the world. The fertility of man is increasing at a rate faster than ever before in the history of the world and, at the same time, the fertility of the soil is rapidly declining. In light of the above, the author reviews the present status of planned parenthood in the various major countries of the world. Included are sections on England, the Scandinavian countries, Holland, Germany and Austria, France, Italy and Belgium, the Near East, Israel, the Far East, India, Russia and its Satellites, and the United States. The author concludes that the worldwide need today in the area of family planning is twofold: mass education, and mass production of a simple, practical, reliable, and inexpensive contraceptive method.

436 Stopes, Marie. Birth Control Today. London: Hogarth Press, 1957. 178 pp.

Discusses all aspects of fertility control, its necessity, the biological functioning and various stages at which attempt can be made to control spermatozoa or ovum. The author has specified male methods and female methods.

437 Stycos, J. Mayone. "Birth Control. The Restrictions of the Modern Approach," Lancet, No. 7424, 1965, pp. 1231-32.

There are several limitations of traditional Western medicine in the application of birth control to underdeveloped areas. The average physician knows little about contraception. The clinical medicine usually has more prestige than public health, and a certain mystique about the necessity for a close doctor-patient relation emerges. There is also a feeling among doctors of the unsuitability of public service or educational programs on birth control. The newly developing countries seek large scale programs to control population, and Western medicine is not prepared to assist.

438 Stycos, J. Mayone. "A Critique of the Traditional Planned Parenthood Approach in Underdeveloped Areas." Chpt. in: Kiser, C.V., ed. Research in Family Planning. Princeton: Princeton University Press, 1962. xvi, 664 pp.

An examination of the proceedings of various Planned Parenthood professional meetings discloses three major ideological biases: medical, middle class, and feminist. These biases imply that: (1) the primary argument for planned parenthood concerns its salutary effects on maternal health; (2) the distribution of the means for family planning rests with medically directed clinics; (3) methods encouraged and distributed are those placing control of conception with the female; (4) emphasis is placed on spacing as opposed to limiting pregnancies; and (5) abortion, withdrawal and sterilization generally meet with disapproval and the condom tends to be accepted only grudgingly. More emphasis should be placed on male methods of fertility control; a transitional stage of contraceptive behavior should be explicitly recognized during which male and female sterilization is made available. New approaches to the dissemination of ideas and methods are needed, with a less formalized approach. It is concluded that the uncritical exportation of traditional Planned Parenthood ideas to other countries will almost certainly fail in the short run, and may very well be irrelevant in the long run.

439 Stycos, J. Mayone. "Obstacles to Programs of Population Control - Facts and Fancies," Marr. Fam. Living 25(1):5-13, 1963.

Programs of fertility control can assist or accelerate economic development, but face major obstacles in elite beliefs about population dynamics and lower class culture, and in the dominance of ideas about family planning programs imported from the United States and Great Britain. Nationalistic attitudes relating to population control include pride in numbers, suspicions of genocidal intentions on the part of colonial powers, and the use of population pressure as a rationalization for territorial expansion, foreign aid, or support for social reform programs. Elite theories about lower class fertility include such erroneous beliefs as: (1) lower class couples desire large families, (2) religious values are a serious deterrent to the use of birth control techniques, (3) a high frequency of sex relations can be deduced from high fertility, and (4) illegitimacy is a cause of high fertility. Planned parenthood groups have been dominated by a female orientation. This may be even more misplaced in underdeveloped areas than in the U.S., since male dominance in general and specifically in the sexual sphere is much more marked than in the Western societies. The clinical approach is rarely successful because the methods offered are not those most popular with most people, the clinical atmosphere is an embarrassing one, and the clinics are not known to most of the population. Other factors deterring programs of fertility control include ignorance of sexual psysiology and contraceptive techniques among lower class groups, ambivalence regarding ideal family size, and late development of motivation for birth control. A fertility control program should include information and education of elite groups, be government sponsored, and involve non-medical personnel in policy formation and administration. It should give attention and services to males and females, put more resources into non-clinical channels of education and contraceptive distribution, attempt to reach young couples, and de-emphasize the consequences to health of rapid child bearing. Sterilization for women and men should be provided for those who have had all the children they desire.

440 Sulloway, Alvah W. Birth Control and Catholic Doctrine. Boston: Beacon Press, 1959. xxiii, 257 pp.

The official Church position on birth control as contained in Church publications and pronouncements is examined in three sections and eight chapters. Part I reviews the legislative history of contraception in the United States and the Catholic Church's position. Part II, on doctrines, contains the Church's justifications for opposing birth control and the effect of the Ogino-Knaus discovery of the sterility-fertility cycle of the female on the Church's attitude. Part III, on rationalizations, details the Church's adjustment to the use of the rhythm method.

441 Sutter, Jean. "Le Mouvement dans le Monde en Faveur de la Limitation des Familles, 1945-1954 " [The World Movement on Behalf of Limitation of Families, 1945-1954], Population 10(2):277-94. April - June 1955.

Neo-Malthusianism limits its activities to the following social measures: the diffusion of means favorable to birth control and to planned parenthood, (creation of clinics, efforts to combat physiological sterility, sexual education in schools, marriage counseling, legal abortions, and sterilization). Its main argument is still the disproportion between population growth and economic expansion. The development of the movement in the past ten years is described in a paragraph for each of the following countries: (1) In Europe: Germany, Austria, Belgium Denmark, Finland, France, Holland, Italy, Norway, Sweden, Switzerland; (2) in the Middle-East: Egypt, Israel, Turkey; (3) in Asia: Ceylon, China, Formosa, Hong Kong, India, Indonesia, Japan, Pakistan, Singapore, Malaysia, Thailand; (4) in the Pacific: Australia, New Zealand; (5) in America: U.S., Caribbean Islands; and (6) in Africa: South Africa.

442 "Symposium: Abortion and the Law," Western Law Rev. 17: 369-ff., December 1965.

Contents: Introduction by O.G. Schroeder Jr., Current abortion laws: proposals and movements for reform by B.J. George, Jr.; Medical abortion practices in the United States by K.R. Niswander; Humane abortion laws and the health needs of society by K.J. Ryan; Psychiatric implications of abortion: a case study in social hypocrisy by

H. Rosen; The inviolability of the right to be born by R.F. Drinan; Jewish views on abortion by I. Jakobovits; Abortion legislation in Denmark by V. Skalts and M. Norgaard; Medical aspects of the Danish legislation on abortion by H. Hoffmeyer; Abortion in the German-speaking countries of Europe by L. Breitenecker and R. Breitenecker.

443 Tabah, Leon. "La Contraception dans le Tiers Monde " [Contraception in Developing Countries], Population 22(6):999-1030, 1967.

Ignored for a long time or reserved to a very small but highly educated minority (like the Parsis in India), contraception is spreading today in developing countries. Already in 1962, the vote at the United Nations General Assembly had pointed out the way covered, during a few years, by the governments of these countries who were opposed for a long time to the very principle of restriction of births. Since that period, the movement is growing still faster. In regard to birth-rates, the results are yet perceptible nowhere, on a national scale, except in a limited area of the Far East. Moreover, for a long time it was considered that a poor couple, unlearned and living in a precarious lodging, was not able to apply properly the methods of which European populations make already imperfect use. But the discovery of new technics, particularly the intra-uterine ring, has deeply modified this problem.

444 Tabbarah, Riad B. "Birth Control and Population Policy," Popul. Stud. 18(2):187-96. November 1964.

The aim of this article is: (1) to formalize the concept of general acceptability of contraception through the formulation of an arithmetic index of acceptability based on the desired number of children; (2) to demonstrate with the use of the index that especially in underdeveloped rural communities, it is possible that contraceptive methods, irrespective of their effectiveness and cost, may be completely unacceptable; (3) to suggest that even when the desire for limiting births is positive among a certain proportion of married couples, the investment in birth control education may not be justified by its expected effect on the birth rate; and (4) to illustrate other uses of the index in evaluating population policy measures, namely through its application to the policies of raising the minimum age at marriage and the abolition of polygamy.

445 Taeuber, Irene B. "Policies, Programs, and the Decline of Birth Rates: China and Chinese Populations of East Asia," pp. 99-104 in Muramatsu, M., and Harper, Paul A., eds. Population Dynamics: International Action and Training Programmes. Baltimore: Johns Hopkins Press, 1965.

An overview of worldwide events shows that fertility decline is independent of governmental type, religion, and culture and continent. On the positive side, fertility decline is associated with social change which is disruptive of tradition; induced abortion; and programs built on values pertaining to the health of mothers and opportunities for children rather than on macroeconomic arguments. China and Chinese overseas are expected to lower their fertility because of the achievement orientation, potential for change and modernization, and the pragmatic orientation.

446 Taylor, Howard C., and Berelson, Bernard. "Maternity Care and Family Planning as a World Program," Amer. J. Obstet. Gynec. 100(7):885-93. 1 April 1968.

First results from a post-partum approach to family planning show that supervised maternity service would be a successful vehicle for providing education and service in family planning to uninformed people in developing countries for the following reasons: fertile women would be identified, particularly those groups at "high risk" of pregnancy; the relevant audience (and, of great demographic importance, those women of low parity) could be reached when they have just delivered a child and are highly motivated to learn about family planning; the "image" of family planning would be enhanced by its association with a system of infant and maternal welfare, which would in itself build the medical infrastructure and lower child mortality, both useful for subsequent work in family planning. Implementation centers around four essential but minimal requirements: (1) an attendant present at all deliveries to instruct the women in contraception; (2) a maternity health center for the area, where expert medical attention is available; (3) a system of detecting, recording and reporting pregnancy and birth; (4) within the maternity center, a clinic for ante- and post-partum examinations and for family planning instructions.

447 Thomas, John L. "The Catholic Position on Birth Control," Daedalus, Summer 1959, pp. 444-45.

After a brief discussion of ethics, including the Catholic concept of ethical judgment and the basic principles upon which Catholic ethical positions are formulated, the author summarized the premises that underlie the Church's stand on birth control. The complexity of population problems is outlined, followed by a description of the Catholic view of parenthood. The means of population control which Catholics reject are discussed as well as the ethical reasons for rejection, alternatives and possible acceptions. The author presents some practical solutions, offered by Catholic thinkers, to current population problems and concludes that gradual, piecemeal reforms such as birth control act to hinder, rather than promote, the idea of the need for broader and more lasting social, economic and cultural changes.

448 Tietze, Christopher. "The Condom as a Contraceptive," Fam. Planning News 8(4):83-91. April 1962.

Following a discussion of the production and distribution of condoms in selected countries, the author explains the results of inflation tests conducted in the United States to evaluate the quality of the product. From the data collected in various studies, the author concludes that the condom may prove to be a highly acceptable, effective and practicable method of contraception in many areas of the world.

449 Tietze, Christopher. "The Current Status of Fertility Control," Law and Contemporary Problems 25(3):425-44. Summer 1960.

Methods of fertility control, grouped in four basic biological categories: abstinence, contraception, sterilization, and abortion: and the extent and effectiveness of their use in the U.S. and other countries are discussed. The section on contraception sketches the history of most of the known methods of contraception: coitus interruptus, sponges and tampons, condoms, douches, diaphragms, the rhythm or safe period, spermicides, vaginal tablets, and oral contraceptives. Data from recent population surveys, conducted in the U.S. and the United Kingdom, are presented on the acceptance of the better-known methods, and effectiveness by type of method is discussed regarding pregnancy rates. In discussing sterilizations, it is estimated that in 1955 there were 1.2 million surgically sterilized women in the U.S. and that about 75,000 operations for the purpose of family limitation were annually performed in the decade 1945-54. Data on legal abortions are presented for Denmark, Sweden, and Japan. Estimates of illegal abortions in the U.S. range from 200,000 per year to 1.2 million per year.

450 Tietze, Christopher. "Differential Fecundity and Effectiveness of Contraception," Eugenics Rev. 50(4):231-37. January 1959.

To illustrate the time patterns according to which pregnancies will occur under specified assumptions as to fecundity and the use of contraception, the author considers a hypothetical population of couples some of whom are highly fecund, some moderately fecund, and some sub-fecund. Later in the analysis, a proportion of sterile couples is added. If it is assumed that the hypothetical population employs contraception that produces a 90 per cent reduction in the probability of conception for each couple, the total number of pregnancies experienced by the population over a two-year period is about 47 per cent below the number when no contraception is used. Contraception that is 99 per cent effective for individual couples reduces the number of pregnancies in two years for the entire group by about 92 per cent. A complication in the study of contraceptive effectiveness is the period of post-partum sterility. Since the distribution of the length of this period is not fully known, it is often not clear in the case of contraception used within a few months after the termination of a pregnancy whether temporary sterility or the contraception is to be credited for any reduction in the level of fertility. On the other hand, as the analysis of the hypothetical population showed, once fecundity is reestablished, the probability of conception for a group of couples declines from month to month, which further confuses efforts to obtain measures of contraception effectiveness. To help minimize the distortion in such measures that may thus result from early or late starting of contraceptive practice after the termination of pregnancy, the author proposes certain criteria for the inclusion of couples in studies of contraceptive effectiveness and for the length of time that couples should be observed.

451 Tietze, Christopher. "The Effect of Breast Feeding on the Rate of Conception." Paper presented at the International Population Conference, New York, 11-16 September 1961. New York: International Union for Scientific Study of Population and Population Association of America, 1961. 8 pp. (Mimeographed).

The relation between lactation and conception is reviewed on the basis of demographic studies of birth intervals in a population not practicing contraception. The analysis shows that all months of post-partum amenorrhoea should be excluded from consideration while computing pregnancy rates. Also, breast-feeding prolongs the interval between births and provides better protection than ineffective contraceptive practices for about ten months following confinement.

452 Tietze, Christopher. "Fertility Controls," pp.382-88 of Vol.5 in Sills, David L., ed. _International Encyclopedia of the Social Sciences_. New York: Macmillan Free Press, 1968.

After defining "fertility control" as used in the article, the author discusses the traditional four categories of fertility control methods, the increasingly unclear boundaries between them and takes a brief look at the use of the term birth control and the history of the general practice of birth control. An elaboration of the classifications of non-permanent contraceptive measures follows with references to folk, vaginal, rhythm, oral and intrauterine methods. Surveys, tables and official investigations are cited in a discussion of the extent and effectiveness of contraceptive practice in several countries. After considering sterilization and abortion, the author concludes with a list of possible future methods and a selected bibliography in the field of fertility control.

453 Tietze, Christopher. "History of Contraceptive Methods," J. Sex Research 1(2):69-85. July 1965.

A survey is presented of the development of contraception from coitus interruptus, mentioned in the Bible, to modern mechanical and chemical methods. Prescriptions for the use of the rhythm method from the Hippocratic period to the formulas of K. Ogino and H. Knaus are discussed. Current developments in oral and in intra-uterine contraception are emphasized.

454 Tietze, Christopher. "Oral and Intrauterine Contraceptions: Effectiveness and Safety," Internat. J. Fertility 13(4): 377-84. October - December 1968.

Presents estimates as of mid-1967 of the extent of use, effectiveness, and side effects of oral contraceptives and IUD's in the United States, Great Britain, and the rest of the world.

455 Tietze, Christopher. "Some Facts About Legal Abortion," in: Greep, R.O., ed. Human Fertility and Population Problems. Cambridge: Schenkman Publishing Co., 1963.

Statistical data, policies, and indications for legal abortion in New York City, Japan and Eastern Europe during the last two decades are compared.

456 Tietze, Christopher. "The Use-Effectiveness of Contraceptive Methods," pp. 357-71, Chpt. in: Kiser, C.V., ed. Research in Family Planning. Princeton: Princeton University Press, 1962. xvii, 664 pp.

Evaluation of effectiveness of contraceptive methods requires distinction between theoretical effectiveness and practical effectiveness. Theoretical effectiveness can be measured under laboratory conditions only. Effectiveness in practice, or use-effectiveness, is obtainable from clinical and demographic surveys. The standard measure of use-effectiveness is the pregnancy or failure rate per 100 years of exposure, derived by the following formula developed by R. Pearl in the early 1930's: $R = \frac{\text{Accidental pregnancies} \times 1200}{\text{Months of Exposure}}$ The months of exposure cover all months during which contraception was used and conception was possible. The usual procedure is to exclude from the months of exposure nine months for each pregnancy carried to term, 3 months for each abortion, one additional month for the puerperal period, and all months during which contraception was voluntarily discontinued. Comparison of the results from 20 studies of the contraceptive practice of human populations show that certain groups, presumably adequately motivated and generally with a level of education above the minimum, have achieved relatively low pregnancy rates with a variety of contraceptive methods: condom, diaphragm and jelly, foam tablets, jelly alone, suppositories, and withdrawal. Other groups have been far less successful in their efforts to control fertility with the same methods. There can be no doubt that the most important reason for contraceptive failure is irregular practice. Use-effectiveness of a method thus becomes, to a considerable extent, a function of its acceptance.

457 Tietze, Christopher, and Potter, Robert G. "Statistical Evaluation of the Rhythm Method," _Amer_. _J_. _Obstet_. _Gynec_. 84(5):692-98. September 1962.

The effectiveness of the rhythm method has been examined here with the help of a statistical model. Several assumptions are made as to the variability of menstrual cycles and the relative contributions of the follicular and luteal phases to the variation in a total cycle length. According to the authors, the Knaus formula affords substantially less protection than the Ogino formula.

458 Trehan, P.L. "Population Control by Sterilization in Underdeveloped Countries," _J_. _Fam_. _Welf_. 5(2):55-56. December 1958.

Taking into consideration some of the drawbacks of the currently used mechanical and chemical contraceptives, the author pleads for sterilization as the most simple, economical, harmless and effective method of family limitation, especially for people in underdeveloped countries.

459 Tutunji, Djamil. "Population Control and World Health," Human Fertility 11(3):78-79, 1946.

A plea for birth control generally.

460 United Nations, Children's Fund. Executive Board. Family Planning. Report of the Executive Director on the possible role of UNICEF, New York, March 17 1966. 51 pp. plus 13-page Annex.

Sections: The socio-economic background; Relationship of family size to the health and welfare of children; Elements of population programs having a particular bearing on family and child welfare; International cooperation and types of assistance needed; Conclusions and recommendations. Annex: Notes on existing family planning programs.

461 United Nations, Commission on Information from Non-Self-Governing Territories. Social Measures for Economic Welfare of the Family. Report prepared by the Secretariat. New York: United Nations, 1958. 42 pp. (mimeogr.)

Social security and welfare services are established in some of the Territories. In the Trust Territory of Nauru, for example, child endowment is payable to persons who have children under their care, custody or control. The scale of payment is 10s. a week for each of the first two dependent children, and 15s. a week for each subsequent child.

462 United Nations, Department of Economic Affairs. Measures for the Economic Development of Under-Developed Countries. Report by a Group of Experts Appointed by the Secretary-General of the United Nations. New York: United Nations, 1951. ix, 108 pp.

Part 2, Measures requiring domestic action, includes a brief chapter on population growth in which the nature of the economic, financial, and welfare problems are indicated for types of countries, and study is recommended of ways and means, which are consistent with the values and culture of each of the peoples concerned, of speeding up the reduction of fertility rates.

463 United Nations, Department of Economic and Social Affairs. Nationality of Married Women. Report submitted by the Secretary-General. New York: United Nations, 1963. vi, 121 pp.

Part I provides a classification of legal systems and points to sources of conflict in the laws. International conventions are also discussed. In Part II, the constitutional and other legal references to the nationality of married women are briefly described for each of several countries.

464 United Nations, Department of Social Affairs. Economic Measures in Favour of the Family. A Survey of Laws and Administrative Regulations Providing for Economic Measures in Favour of the Family in Various Countries. New York: United Nations, 1952. xx, 175 pp.

Systematically presents the legislation to benefit the family which was in force as of 30 June 1949 in twenty-four countries. The legislation is grouped into three large chapters. The first one concerns measures intended to enlarge the family's income: family allowances, marriage grants, birth grants, and taxation. The second chapter considers health, housing, education, transportation and other aids to the family. In the third chapter, special measures affecting salary workers, rural proprietors, and the military services are considered.

465 United Nations, Economic Commission for Asia and the Far East. Administrative Aspects of Family Planning Programs: Report of a Working Group. Asian Population Studies Series No. 1. New York: United Nations, 1966. vi, 64 pp.

Report on deliberations of meeting at Bangkok, March 16-24 1966, organized by the United Nations Development Program in cooperation with the Population Council. Includes individual reports on ten member countries and proposals for cooperative arrangements.

466 United Nations, Economic and Social Council. Commission on the Status of Women. Bride-Price, Polygamy and Rights of the Mother with Respect to Her Children. Report by the Secretary-General. New York: United Nations, 1957. Mimeogr.

The greater part of the report relates to women living in less-developed countries. Bride-price and polygamy are regarded unfavorably, and it is suggested that these practices would end if the woman's consent to marriage were legally required. The registration of marriage is regarded as necessary if there is to be legal enforcement of changes in customary marriage customs. A minimum age of marriage of 14 years is recommended for girls.

467 United Nations, Economic and Social Council. Commission on the Status of Women. Consent to Marriage and Age of Marriage. Report by the Secretary-General. New York: United Nations, 1958. (Mimeogr.)

Contains the recommendations of the International Federation of Women Lawyers: 1) a minimum age of marriage for all countries, an age which shall in no case be less than fourteen years for both parties; 2) the consent of both parties to a marriage should be freely expressed and duly recorded in the presence of a competent civil or religious authority; and 3) all marriages should be registered and a permanent record kept of all such marriages.

468 United Nations, Economic and Social Council. Commission on the Status of Women. Dissolution of Marriage, Annulment of Marriage and Judicial Separation. Report of the Secretary-General. New York: United Nations, 1963.

Legal conditions and effects of such proceedings. Based on replies of member nations to a questionnaire.

469 United Nations, Commission on the Status of Women. Economic Rights and Opportunities for Women: Facilities for Assisting Employed Mothers in Child-Care. Memorandum by the Secretary-General. New York: United Nations, 1966. 21 pp. (Mimeogr.)

A report on the most important approaches and facilities in assisting employed mothers in child care, namely home-aid services, visiting nurses, creches, day nurseries for children, and other assistance. Information was provided by the World Health Organization, the International Labour Organization, and the International Children's Centre.

470 United Nations, Commission on the Status of Women. Economic Rights and Opportunities for Women: ILO Activities Related to Repercussions of Technological Change on Employment and Conditions of Women Workers. Report by the International Labour Office. New York: United Nations, 1967. (Mimeogr.)

Automation may create unemployment and occupational readjustments. In order to lessen the severe impact of automation, the ILO recommends the adoption of public policies and services to the changing needs of the employment situation, and, in particular, a review of policies relative to vocational guidance, employment and protection against unemployment, and social security.

471 United Nations, Economics and Social Council. Commission on the Status of Women. Eighteenth Session, Beginning 1 March 1965, Teheran, Iran. (Mimeogr.)

Contains a major report of the Activities of the Inter-American Commission of Women. In addition, there are the regular reports on the political rights of women, status of women in private law, economic rights and opportunities of women, and the access of women to education. There is also a report on The International Year for Human Rights.

472 United Nations, Economic and Social Council. Commission on the Status of Women. Equal Pay for Equal Work: Methods Used in Campaigns for Equal Pay for Equal Work and Information on the Present Status of the Application in Various Countries. New York: United Nations, 1956. 46 pp. (Mimeogr.)

473 United Nations, Economic and Social Council. Commission on the Status of Women. Family Planning and the Status of Women. Interim report of the Secretary-General. Item 7 of the provisional agenda, Twenty-first session, Commission on the Status of Women. New York: United Nations, 1968. 27 pp.

The present report contains the following three chapters: Chapter I (Recent policy of the United Nations, the specialized agencies and UNICEF in the fields of population and family planning), which summarizes recently expressed policies of the organizations within the United Nations system; Chapter II (National family planning programmes), which briefly describes existing national family planning programs; Chapter III (Family planning and the status of women), which indicates certain factors which appear to be relevant in considering family planning in relation to the status of women.

474 United Nations, Economic and Social Council. Commission on the Status of Women. Inheritance Laws as They Affect the Status of Women. New York: United Nations, 1962. (Mimeogr.)

475 United Nations, Economic and Social Council. Commission on the Status of Women. Observations of Governments on the Draft Convention and Draft Recommendation on the Minimum Age of Consent to Marriage and Registration of Marriages. Memorandum by the Secretary-General. New York: United Nations, 1961.

Resolution calling for a minimum age at marriage of fourteen years for a girl and sixteen years for a boy and requiring that marriages be registered was passed by the Commission. There were objections by some states to the formulation of a resolution rather than a recommendation, setting any minimum age whatsoever or setting the minimum so low. Objections were few and came mainly from Finland, Japan and the Soviet Union.

476 United Nations, Economic and Social Council. Commission on the Status of Women. Seventeenth Session, 11 to 29 March 1963, New York. 76 pp. (Mimeogr.)

In this Session stress is given to the economic rights and opportunities for women; and the status of women in laws on marriage and the dissolution of marriage.

477 United Nations, Economic and Social Council. Commission on the Status of Women. Status of Women in Family Law. Report of the Secretary-General. New York: United Nations, 1958. 35 pp.

478 United Nations, Economic and Social Council. Commission on the Status of Women. Tax Legislation Applicable to Women. New York: United Nations, 1959.

479 United Nations, Economic and Social Council. Commission on the Status of Women. Twenty-First Session, 29 January to 19 February 1968, New York City. (Mimeogr.)

A variety of topics is richly documented for many nations of the world. The topics most related to fertility are: status of women in private law (legal capacity, marriage customs); social and economic status (employment, social security and welfare service, maternal and child care); the abolition of slavery; family planning; and education. There is also discussion of the role of the U.N. in population policy and family planning.

480 United Nations, Economic and Social Council. Commission on the Status of Women. United Nations Assistance for the Advancement of Women. Unified Long-Term Programme: the Role of Women in the Economic and Social Development of Their Countries. Report of the Secretary-General. New York: United Nations, 1968.

This document includes the text of the questionnaire on the role of women in the economic and social development of their countries and the replies of governments to that questionnaire. The present role of women in such areas as agriculture, industry, government, education, health, population, employment, social security and social welfare are examined. Also given in the report are replies to the areas of economic and social development where women's role might be increased; the problems that must be mounted; measures designed to increase women's contribution; assistance required and the role of non-governmental organizations.

481 United Nations, Human Rights Commission. Subcommittee on the Prevention of Discrimination and Protection of Minorities. Study of Discrimination Against Persons Born Out of Wedlock. New York: United Nations, 1967. vii, 227 pp.

Discrimination against persons born outside the accepted family structure dates many centuries back in the history of mankind. The present survey of states in the United Nations compares persons born out of wedlock with those born in wedlock in order to ascertain discriminations in the establishment of filiation, maintenance, inheritance, legal status, and social position. It also considers the etiology of illegitimacy and the institution of adoption as a means of improving the position of persons born out of wedlock. The last part provides some general principles and proposals for action.

482 United Nations, Population Branch. Survey of Legislation on Marriage, Divorce and Related Topics Relevant to Population. New York: United Nations, 1956. 292 pp., processed.

Contains summaries of the legislation in force in twenty-four countries on the following topics which may influence the changes in population: marriage and divorce, contraceptive measures, abortion and sterilization. These summaries were based primarily on the material supplied by the governments of the countries concerned, in response to a request from the Secretary-General of the United Nations which was circulated in March 1949. The present volume represents a shortened version of a longer report prepared by the Institut National d'Etudes Démographiques.

483 United Nations, Social Commission. *The Suppression of the Traffic in Persons and of the Exploitation of the Prostitution of Others.* Report prepared by the Secretariat. New York: United Nations, 1959.

The Economic and Social Council, by resolution 43 (IV) of 29 March 1947, instructed the Secretary-General, *inter alia*, to resume the study of the League of Nations' draft convention of 1937, to make any necessary amendments in order to bring it up to date, and to introduce any desirable improvement in view of the changes in the general situation since 1937. This led to the adoption by the United Nations General Assembly on 2 December 1949 of the Convention for the Suppression of the Traffic in Persons and of the Exploitation of the Prostitution of Others. This Convention consolidates earlier instruments and embodies the abolitionist policy upon which should be based any program of action against the traffic in persons and the exploitation of the prostitution of others. The purpose of the present report is not to initiate new policies and practices, but to develop the program of action which is already embodied in the Consolidated Convention.

484 United States. Bureau of Labor Statistics. "Recent Developments in the Family-Allowance Movement," *Monthly Labor Rev.* 50(4):867-68. April 1940.

Brazil (decree of November 10, 1939); United Kingdom (private schemes); Japan (system approved February 16 1940) are briefly described.

485 United States. Office of the War on Hunger. Population Service. *Population Program Assistance: Aid to Developing Nations by the United States, Other Nations, and International and Private Agencies*, Washington, September 1968. vi, 175 pp.

Publication prepared with the assistance of A.I.D.'s regional offices in Latin America, Near East-South Asia, Africa, East Asia and Vietnam includes: 1. The latest basic demographic data available on the less developed countries. 2. Summary statements of the overseas programs of family planning assistance carried out by private and international organizations, and by the United States and other countries. 3. Summaries by country, of national family planning programs under way and of external assistance being made available from private and public sources.

486 United States Catholic Conference. Documentary Service. _Encyclical on the Regulation of Birth, July 29 1968, By Pope Paul VI._ Washington: United States Catholic Conference, Press Department, 1968.

In the first part, rapid population growth and some of the problems which result from it are discussed. To gain further understanding of these matters, Pius XIV has enlarged the study commission which Pius XIII instituted in March, 1963. But, whatever the findings of the commission, the Church is obliged to give its views on population and birth control. In Part II, various doctrinal principles are discussed. These include: conjugal love, responsible parenthood, the insepara-bility of union and procreation, the licitness of the rhythm method, and the grave consequences of methods of artificial birth control. The last part contains some pastoral directives.

487 Vadakin, James C., ed. _Children, Poverty, and Family Allowances_. New York: Basic Books, 1968. xxxii, 222 pp.

Chapters: The case for family allowances; A survey of family allowances in the United States; Family allowances through-out the world; Family allowances in Canada; The crisis in existing programs; Guaranteed annual income proposals; Family allowances: United States plan. Appendix: House Resolution 14496, Ninetieth Congress of the United States, December 14, 1967, A bill to provide family allowances.

488 Valensin, G. _Fecondazione Artificiale e Naturale Della Donna_ [Artificial and National Insemination in Women]. Milan: Ed. Feltrinelli, 1959. 280 pp.

An exposition of the history of artificial insemination and current issues in various countries.

489 Vliet, A.A., van. _Marriage and Canon Law_. London: Burns and Oates, 1964.

This book is primarily intended for the busy priest. Part I, Christian Marriage, has chapters on: General Provisions, Preliminaries of Marriage, Impediments and Dispensations, Matrimonial Consent, Dissolution of Marriage, and Remarriage. Part II, Dissolution of Marriage in Favor of the Faith, is concerned with Marriage to a pagan or unbaptisted person, the Pauline Privilege, and the three Apostolic Constitutions of Canon.

490 Waggaman, Mary J. "Family Allowances; Experiments to Date," America, May 29, 1948, pp. 189-91.

Study of family allowances in forty-six countries.

491 Waggaman, Mary J. "Family Allowances in Various Countries," Monthly Labor Rev. 57(2):265-76. August 1943.

Developments in family allowance schemes other than those for armed forces are reviewed for the period 1939-1942, during which more or less important changes occurred in 24 countries.

492 Waggaman, Mary J. Family Allowances in Various Countries, 1944-45. Bureau of Labor Statistics. Bulletin No. 853. Washington: Government Printing Office, 1946. ii, 21 pp.

Reviews the progress in child-welfare programs during 1944-45. During the war three family-allowance measures for civilians were enacted in the British Empire - the Australian Act of 1941, the Canadian Act of 1944, which became effective July 1, 1945, and the British Act of 1945. Discusses family allowances in New Zealand, South Africa, Southern Rhodesia, Belgium, France, Czechoslovakia, Rumania, Soviet Union, Spain, Swiss Cantons, Denmark, Norway, Sweden, Argentina, Bolivia, Brazil, Chile, Uraguay, Columbia, and the United States. There appears to be a growing tendency to correlate family allowances with credit for dependents under income-tax legislation, which emphasizes the fact that children of parents in the very low economic brackets receive little or no benefit from such exemptions. The controversy between the advocates of family allowances in cash and of allowances in kind seems to be developing into a compromise which would provide for both types of benefits.

493 Waggaman, Mary J. "Mid-War Developments in Civilian Family Allowances," Monthly Labor Rev. 59(5):982-93. November 1944.

Summary data on very recent developments in the family allowance movement in 23 countries. (Argentina, Australia, Brazil, Canada, Chile, Eire, Finland, France, Germany, Great Britain, Italy, Luxemburg, New Zealand, Norway, Paraguay, Portugal, the Soviet Union, Spain, Sweden, Switzerland, the Union of South Africa, the United States, and Uruguay.) The recommendations of the Twenty-Sixth International Labor Conference held in Philadelphia in April are summarized.

494 Williams, G., The Sanctity of Life and the Criminal Law. New York: Alfred A. Knopf, 1966.

The ethical and legal aspects of the criminal statutes, case law and medical practice on induced abortion particularly in the United States and Great Britain are examined. Mentioned also is the interpretation of statutes dealing with therapeutic abortion.

495 Wood, Frederick C. "Sex Within the Created Order," Theol. Today 22(3):394-401, 1956.

If one looks at sex from the perspective of "the new morality," he will see that there are no rules given in the Bible to guide him in its use. Sex is: (1) good, (2) fun, (3) funny, and (4) natural. There are no laws attached to sex. We all ought to stop feeling guilty about our sexual activity, whether that activity be heterosexual, homosexual, or autosexual. About all the Bible has to say is that sex is good and creative (as a means of self-fulfillment and self expression). The Bible also adds that sex is inter-personal, which entails a high degree of responsibility to one's partner in the act. In short, a Christian should prefer chastity but there are no biblical rules or sanctions regarding sex outside of marriage. If one acts out the law of love, he will find the best way for him to express his sexuality.

496 World Conference on the Family and Population. Proceedings. Paris: National Union of Family Organizations, 1949. 142 pp.

The First World Congress on the Family and Population met in Paris in June 1947 and manifested an interest in solutions to problems concerning the family and infants. Papers were presented by various delegates under the following general topics: policies and government's role in programs for housing, clothing, and food, and governmental aids to mothers and provisions for education, leisure, and vacations. The last section considers fiscal measures in various countries. Represented are Canada, Egypt, Turkey, and several European countries.

497 Zalba, M. "The Catholic Church's Viewpoint on Abortion," World Med. J. 13:88-ff., 1966.

The Catholic Church forbids all abortion except: indirect abortion, due to medical treatment of an illness which is not exclusively a result of pregnancy; extrauterine conception, a remedy of anomalous condition by giving technical assistance to the tissue in danger of fatal hemorrhage; doubt whether tumor or fetus, whether a living or a dead fetus; successive animation in which pregnancy may be terminated before it is animated with a human soul. Now it is considered that the soul is present from the moment of conception and therefore this condition cannot justify induced abortion.

498 Zatuchni, G.I. "International Postpartum Family Planning Program: Report on an Action-Research Demonstration Study," Amer. J. Obstet. Gynec. 100:1028-41. April 1968.

The first fifteen months of the Postpartum Program demonstrates that the integration of family planning education and services with a hospital's maternity and postpartum service is an effective approach. This is the situation more in the urban areas of the world, including the developing nations, than in the rural areas. By identifying currently pregnant women, the Program assures a systematic approach to potential acceptors and if services are offered, many women will begin to practice contraception.

499 Ziadeh, F.J. "Equality (Kafa'ah) in the Muslim Law of Marriage," Amer. J. Comparative Law 6:503. Autumn 1957.

The problem of social stratification in Muslim society is a subject too wide in scope to be dealt with in a single paper. This paper, therefore, is an attempt to discover only how far social stratification is reflected in the doctrine of Kafa'ah (equality) in the Muslim law of marriage. After some preliminary observations, the author discusses, in relation to

Muslim marriage, the origin of Kafa'ah, Islamic religion and Kafa'ah, effect of Kafa'ah, constituents of Kafa'ah and instances of Kafa'ah. In general, it would seem that the doctrine of Kafa'ah has ceased to be of major importance in determining or reflecting social stratification in Muslim society, and that a field (marriage) once regulated by legal rules has gradually come to be governed by social rules and considerations.

500 Zimmerman, Anthony. Catholic Viewpoint on Overpopulation. New York: Hanover House, 1961. 214 pp.

National campaigns to lower fertility - whether using periodic continence, or *a fortiori*, contraception, sterilization, or abortion - are ethically unjustifiable and practically unwise. Married couples everywhere should have as many children as they personally can support and they are not allowed, much less obliged to limit the number because of problems of the nation or the community.

501 Zimmerman, Anthony. "Some Reasons Why the Church Opposes Contraception," Amer. Eccl. Rev. 150:251-62, 1964.

The Catholic Church realizes that a situation of overpopulation is a disorder which demands correction. It does not believe that it is wise to promote contraception to achieve this purpose. The Church teaches that the elements which constitute man as a reasonable being and as a member of society give rise to the prohibition against contraception. The prohibition preserves essential human values and wards off evils which are prohibitive. It is necessary for normal human development and for the smooth functioning of society.

502 Zuckerman, Solly. "The Control of Human Fertility," Impact of Science on Society 9(2):61-78, 1958.

This general discussion presents historical, biological, sociological, and economic aspects of fertility control as a world problem. The essential points are quite unequivocally stated: the well-being of the world's people will depend upon wide-spread effective family limitation; all existing methods for controlling reproduction leave much to be desired; the prospects that a really satisfactory method will be developed are improving, but as yet there is no certainty of success in this endeavor, much less of success in the near future; even if an "ideal" contraceptive, perhaps an oral pill, were perfected, the difficulties of securing its world-wide adoption would be enormous.

II NORTH AMERICA

CANADA

General population policies

503 Desmond, Annabelle. "Canada: Land of Plenty," Popul. Bull. 14:37-60. May 1958.

While Canada is the second largest country on earth with a land area of 3,846,000 square miles, her population of about 17 million scarcely exceeds that of New York State. However, Canada's population is now growing at an extremely high rate, with a mid-decennial census taken in 1956 revealing that the annual rate of growth was 2.8% during the period 1951-56. Heavy immigration and a comparatively high birth rate account for the increasing population growth. The author reviews the historical and current situation in regard to population and resources, with sections on Canada's early history; the country's dual cultural pattern; population growth to 1911; the reduction in growth during the period 1911-1941; the factor of migration during this period; and the enormous growth between the years 1941 and 1956. Also discussed are the fact that Canada's fertility level today is considerably higher than that of any other industrial nation; natural increase as the largest component of the country's population growth between 1941 and 1956; fertility differentials between the two cultures; the moderate-sized family trend; the role of the family allowances program; the roles of ethnic origin and religion; and the immigration factor, with references to postwar immigration, immigrants as producers and consumers, and immigration policy. The author concludes with some questions regarding how fast the country's population can grow without straining its capacity for absorption and its abundant resources.

504 Henripin, Jacques. "From Acceptance of Nature to Control: The Demography of French Canadians Since the Seventeenth Century," Canadian J. Econ. Polit. Sci. 23:10-19, 1957.

When a population has a natural, spontaneous, or non-controlled behavior, it lives in a cultural situation which makes it virtually incompatible with a system which allows the gathering of statistics needed to analyze population phenomena. Fortunately data were gathered over a twenty-five year period in the nineteenth century from the parish records of North America by Mgr. Tanguay which can depict the early Canadian situation. Tanguay gathered 1,200,000 certificates and constructed the genealogies of 120,000 families from 1621 to the British Conquest. By these records, Canada's early population policy may be characterized as emphasizing high fertility, late age at marriage, low immigration (because of France's control over her emigration), and low mortality. In the nineteenth century, new land and immigration policies brought an influx of new arrivals and, along with the continued high fertility, raised the size of the total population considerably. But emigration to France kept the population much below the level that it might have reached. In the twentieth century, low nuptiality and some adoption of birth control have resulted in a drastic decrease in total fertility rates. The English-French differential in fertility favors the French by about twenty-five _per cent_.

505 Newton-White, E. _Canadian Restoration_. Toronto: Ryerson Press, 1944. viii, 227 pp.

Planned and integrated postwar development is regarded as essential if Canada is to solve her problems of unemployment, underpopulation, mislocated population, etc. The possible total population of Canada is placed at 35 to 40 million as a very modest estimate.

Policies on fertility and family size

506 Allingham, J.D., _et al_. "Time Series of Growth in Use of Oral Contraception and the Differential Diffusion of Oral Renovulents," _Popul Stud_. 23(1):43-51. March 1969.

This paper is based on data derived from a probability sample of once married women under age 46 in 1967 currently living with their husbands in the Toronto metropolitan area. The sample yielded 1,632 interviews. The study, called the Canadian Family Growth Study, was sponsored by the Canada Council and the University of Western Ontario. Main purpose in this paper is to illustrate three possible sources of 'bias' in a time series, 1963-1967, through a study of differential diffusion of oral contraception among women classified by education, national origin, and religion.

507 Bartholomew, G.W. "Recognition of Polygamous Marriages in Canada," Internat. Comparative Law Quart. 10:305-27. April 1961.

Since the vast majority of legal discussions of the polygamous marriage problem has thus far centered almost exclusively on well-known English cases, the author examines Canadian decisions dealing with polygamous marriages and demonstrates that these decisions are very far from being a mere pale reflection of the English decisions. The Canadian decisions fall into two well-defined and distinct groups: those dealing with the problem of marriages between or with members of the Indian tribes and those dealing with the problem of the recognition of Chinese marriages. Both groups of decisions are considered in detail.

508 Beck, Murray J. "The Canadian Parliament and Divorce," Canadian J. Econ. Polit. Sci. 23:297-312. August 1957.

Public bills on divorce are enacted with the greatest difficulty in Canada even when they are merely procedural in nature. The Canadian Parliament has continued to function as a divorce court. From Confederation up to the end of 1956 it had passed 6,626 private divorce bills, 3,548 of them since 1946. There is considerable pressure to place all divorce matters under the provincial governments. Other possibilities are legislative reforms which would expedite the work of Parliament in divorce cases.

509 Black, E.F.E. "Abortion and Sterilization," Manitoba Bar News 33:33-ff., 1961.

The medical and psychiatric indications for abortion and the definition of sterilization are examined. Sterilization is permissible in Canada only if the health or life of the individual is endangered, and only by approval of a hospital committee established to review abortion and sterilization cases.

510 Breul, Frank R. "The Genesis of Family Allowances in Canada," Social Service Rev. 27(3):269-80, 1953.

Some of the forces which led to the passage in Canada of the Family Allowances Act have been described in this article. From the review of the history of the family allowances movement in Canada it is quite apparent that the legislation was not the result of prolonged consideration. The Government, when proposing family allowances, certainly had in mind their eventual role in a comprehensive social security program and then stabilizing consumption. Because of the trend in the interpretation of the British North America Act by the courts, the Government had to avoid any scheme which might possibly be considered as affecting contracts between employers and employees on "Property and Civil Rights in the Province." The Family Allowances Act of 1944 constitutes the first attempt by Canada to pay benefits to all persons within a certain age bracket without regard to the financial means of the recipient or to payments previously made to a social insurance fund.

511 Canada. Department of Labour. Women's Bureau. Maternity Protection for Women Workers in Canada. Ottawa: Queen's Printer, 1967. 63 pp.

This monograph first indicates the increase of the number of working mothers in the labour force, and then considers the Conventions and Recommendations of the I.L.O., which since 1919 have continued to be instrumental in raising standards of maternity protection throughout the world. Provisions made for maternity leave of federal and provincial civil servants are examined and there is a survey of maternity leave in business and industry. It will be seen that maternity protection in the form of cash and medical benefits is rare in Canada.

512 Canada. Department of National Health and Welfare. Research and Statistics Division. Mothers' Allowances Legislation in Canada. Memorandum No. 1. Social Security Series, revised edition. Ottawa, February 1960. vi, 94 pp. processed.

Initially there is a review of legislation, the administration and financing, eligibility, and rates pertaining to Mothers' Allowances. This is followed by descriptions of programs for each province.

513 Cassidy, Harry M. "The Canadian Social Services," Annals Amer. Acad. Polit. Soc. Sci. 253:190-99. September 1947.

Includes a summary of the provisions of the Family Allowances Act of 1944 and present status of the scheme.

514 Cassidy, Harry M. "Childrens Allowances in Canada," Public Welfare 3:171-77. August 1945.

Discussion of the arguments for and against the Canadian program.

515 Charbonneau, Hubert, and Mongeau, Serge. Naissances Planifiées. Pourquoi? Comment? [Birth Planning. Why? How?] Montreal: Editions du Jour, 1966. 160 pp.

The emphasis is on some essential truths. The end of marriage is to bind the union of two persons in love. By this logic the time has come to rescind the legality of birth control and to encourage fertility. Canada is not overpopulated. Moreover neither contraception nor sterilization allows a couple to organize their reproduction in relation to the changing material status of their family. If one defines an ideal contraceptive as one that is safe, efficient, reversible, and acceptable, then each of the current methods fails in some one or more of these respects. Thus, couples cannot obtain a contraceptive which is suitable to birth planning as it might occur in French Canada.

516 Chicanot, E.L. "Quebec Pioneers in Family Allowances," America 69(19):516-17, 1943.

Recent legislation on family allowances encouraging large families is described with some mention of the social and economic aspects involved. Quebec is the first Canadian Province, and apparently the first section of North America to lay the groundwork for a system of family allowances.

517 Cimbura, G. "Studies of Criminal Abortion Cases in Ontario," J. For. Sci. 12:223-29. April 1967.

Data -- obtained by Toronto's Centre of Forensic Studies in the period between 1961 and 1965 -- on materials and methods used in 120 suspected criminal abortion cases are presented. Of the total number of cases examined, thirteen implicated suspects with some to considerable medical knowledge, who preferred instrumental methods. Lay abortionists used the procedures involving injection of fluids. Nineteen cases involved death, and a great majority of the victims became ill and had to be hospitalized.

518 Cook, R.C. "Family Allowances in Canada," J. Heredity 36(12):362-66, 1945.

Presents some comparisons between the Canadian plan for family allowances to children which has been put into effect recently and other attempts to accomplish the same purposes. Population data pertinent to an understanding of the Canadian plan are presented in chart form.

519 Davidson, George F. Family Allowances -- An Installment on Social Security. Ottawa: Canadian Welfare Council, 1944. 19 pp.

The Canadian family allowance programs were introduced as a means of relieving the economic pressure on low family incomes. At the time of the writing of this article, the broad outlines of the Bill were known - to pay an allowance from tax funds to all children in Canada living in a family unit. Provision is made for the scaling down of the allowance as the size of the family grows larger. Part I views the proposal from its fiscal and economic implications; Part II is interested in the social impact; and Part III deals with the administrative and other implications of family allowances. Part II raises several questions vital to the population problem. It discusses the effect of family allowances on the overall birth rate, on the birth rates of certain sections of population, and its effect on the present rates of reproduction of various racial or religious groups.

520 Deutsch, Antal. Income Redistribution Through Canadian Federal Family Allowances and Old Age Benefits. Ottawa: Queen's University, 1968. x, 133 pp.

This study investigates the magnitude and direction of income redistribution arising out of the Family Allowances Act (R.S.C. 1952, C. 109 as amended by 1957, C. 14), the Old Age Security Act (R.S.C. 1952, C. 200, as amended by 1957, C. 14, 1957-58, C. 3), and the federal government's share of the old age assistance program in 1961. An attempt is made to measure the net benefit or burden of these programs by income group, by family type, and by geographic region. The effects of the two programs are considered separately and jointly, and the author shows that family allowances have a much weaker distributive effect, from rich to poor, than old age benefits.

521 Fisher, T.L. "Legal Implications of Sterilization," _Canad. Med. Assn. J._ 91:1363-65, 1964.

Sexual sterilization is legal when it is an integral part of a procedure for the preservation of the life or health of a patient. Done for other reasons it may not be illegal, but this has not been tested in Canadian courts. It is, broadly speaking, a surgical procedure; it is commonly but not always successful; complications, while rare, do occur; the results tend to be irreversible. The same end, the prevention of pregnancy, may be attained by other methods which are safer, less liable to complications, less permanent and so should be used unless contraindicated. Patients' statements that they do not like contraceptives should not be accepted as a reason for sterilization. Sexual sterilization should be reserved for those occasions when it is necessary for the preservation of the health or life of the individual who is to be sterilized.

522 Fisher, T.L. "Sexual Sterilization," _Canad. Med. Assn. J._ 76(9):785-87, 1957.

The author discusses the legality of sexual sterilization for eugenic or financial reasons, or for any reasons other than medical or surgical indications which make sterilization inevitable. The generally applicable rule is that sexual sterilization is legal only when it is an integral part of some procedure itself necessary for the preservation of the health or life of the individual concerned. The possible legal problems which may follow male sterilization are outlined, and the author feels that reasons other than medical are not valid and requests for sterilization based on such reasons should be met with immediate and firm refusals. The liability of physicians in sterilization cases is noted and the article concludes with a brief discussion of sterilization on eugenic grounds. If there are no laws allowing sterilization to prevent the transmission of inheritable diseases, (some provinces do have specific Acts), the author contends that doctors would be wise to refuse to perform the operation.

523 Goodhart, A.L. "Cruelty, Desertion and Insanity in Matrimonial Law," Law Quart. Rev. 79:98-125. January 1963.

The uncertainty surrounding the Canadian law relating to divorce and maintenance is outlined, using three illustrative cases, each concerned with a different aspect of the law (matrimonial cruelty, desertion and insanity) although all are closely interrelated. Problems of interpretation and/or definition are reviewed and the author concludes with a brief summary of the reasons behind such legal uncertainty and some suggestions for placing the law of divorce on a more satisfactory basis, without the need for any new legislation.

524 Gould, Margaret. Family Allowances in Canada. Toronto: Ryerson Press, 1945. 38 pp.

This pamphlet attempts to deal with the principle objections that have been raised against family allowances for Canada. The objections are examined in the light of Canadian conditions and practical questions are answered. Pertinent issues (population - demographic factors, etc.) raised and discussed: critics imply that family allowances can best be applied where there is "purity" of race. But the "pure race" theory has been thoroughly discredited. Canada might, within one generation, achieve a homogeneous character, if all the people had the opportunity to enjoy a "Canadian standard of living." Critics imply that "inferior" people will multiply through family allowances. But much ability and talent is suppressed because of poverty. The Family Allowance Act will help to release creative energies. It will help to improve the quality and efficiency of the Canadian people. Critics imply that the Act is a "bonus" for child-bearing. But mothers in Canada, or anywhere else in the world, do not undertake to bear children to earn $5 or $8 a month. It is a cynical thought that women bear children for gain. The author outlines who is eligible, the amount of the allowances, family allowances, and income tax exemptions, and possible economic and social effects of the allowances.

525 Goulet, J. "La Protection Juridique de L'Amour " [Juridicial Protection of Love], Cahiers de Droit 7:243-ff., 1965-66.

After commenting on the traditional injustice for illegitimate children, e.g., absence of the right of inheritance and other economic sanctions, the author suggests a change from the concept of the family household to the family group and that the family group be given allowances according to its needs, especially to provide security for illegitimate children.

526 Green, Bernard. "Family Planning and Canadian Law," Applied Therapeutics 6:331-34. April 1964.

The author analyzes the provisions of Canadian criminal law concerning contraceptive devices, abortion and voluntary sterilization as methods of birth control. Difficulties of interpretation and definition are illustrated by hypothetical cases and the author comments on the legal and moral problems involved. The author concludes that the ambiguous and conservative nature of these provisions is due to the result of a lack of courage in the legislature and those charged with the administration of criminal justice and that unless members of the health professions establish their legal rights, reform of the law is unlikely within the next twenty-five years. A summary of pertinent legislation is included.

527 Harrison, C.P. "The Doctor and the Patient Under Legalized Abortion," Canadian Med. Assn. J. 97:249-ff., 1967.

The author recommends more liberalization of present abortion law reforms to provide abortion on demand or, at least at the discretion of the doctor. Both patient and physician, he feels, are being subjected to the discriminatory control of the law which is an insult and an infringement upon their right of freedom.

528 Harrison, C.P. "The Issue of Legalized Abortion," Canadian Med. Assn. J. 88:329-30. February 9, 1963.

A conservative view of the question of legalizing abortion. The author stresses the need for the establishment of some generally acceptable principles upon which the arguments for and against legalizing abortion can be developed. Three typical arguments for legalization are reviewed briefly, none of which, it is felt, is based on a rationally acceptable premise. The premise put forward for consideration by the author is that each person has the right not to have his life unjustly taken from him, that human life is sacred and must not be willfully taken, most particularly by those upon whom it is dependent. The inconsistency of those who fight against capital punishment and, at the same time, beg for the death of the guiltless fetus is emphasized. The thalidomide therapeutic abortion cases are cited as examples of situations in which parents and physicians used their unhappiness as a ground for abortion and ignored the fact that the child was not unhappy at the time of its murder and not yet capable of appreciating its own deformity. It is argued that if we abandon our respect for the life of the fetus, we may as well legalize infanticide.

529 Harrison, C.P. "On the Futility of Legalizing Abortion," _Canadian Med. Assn. J._ 95:360-66, 1966.

It has been shown that no matter how ineffective the present abortion law might be, there will be no modification, however great, that will reduce the number of criminal abortions. The author argues that there is an underlying moral imperative that must be examined and recommends wider dissemination of contraceptive information and encouragement of greater idealism and sexual responsibility.

530 Katz, B. "Exploring the Abortion Problem in Canada," _J. Sex Res._ 4:36, 1968.

According to the Canadian Penal Code of 1953-54, induced abortion is permissible only to preserve the life of the mother. Sentences of life imprisonment can be imposed upon the abortionist and up to two years imprisonment may be levied on the woman. It is estimated that there are 50,000 criminal abortions performed in Canada per year. However, in 1950 there were only 41 charges of abortion with 26 convictions; and in 1960, only 48 charges with 32 convictions.

531 LaMarsh, J. "Family and Youth Allowances in Canada," Public Welf. 23:223-26. October 1965.

The public welfare family allowances program in Canada is described, with references to its establishment and first year of operation, its unique factors as compared to similar programs in other countries (i.e., payment made for all children, including the first), its emphasis on family welfare as opposed to child welfare, its decentralized administration, and the fact that payments begin automatically at time of registration of a child's birth. The development of two related programs is also outlined: family assistance (allowances equal to family allowances paid for children of immigrants and settlers arriving in Canada, when they are not yet eligible for benefits under the family allowance program) and youth allowances (allowances paid to all children 16 and 17 years of age, providing they are still in full-time attendance in school).

532 Lebel, Leon. "Après Deux Ans d'Allocations Familiales " [After Two Years of Family Allowances], Relations, No. 80, August 1947, pp. 228-30.

Statistics on distribution of families by size of allowances. Recommends amendments to the law to give particular attention to the needs of large families.

533 Lederman, J.J. "The Doctor, Abortion, and the Law: A Medicolegal Dilemma," Canadian Med. Assn. J. 87:216-ff., 1962.

The law of Canada and England related to the procurement of abortion and the English case of Rex vs. Bourne are examined and discussed. The author concludes that abortion is a crime in all instances according to the law of Canada, and therefore, therapeutic abortion is also unlawful. The absence of a specific exception in criminal legislation in favor of therapeutic abortion, represents a glaring defect in the law and a serious impediment to sound medical practice.

534 Lederman, J.J., and Parker, G.E. "Therapeutic Abortion and the Canadian Criminal Code," Crim. Law Quart. 6:36-85. June 1963.

This work exposes the uncertainties of the Canadian abortion law from both a medical and legal point of view. The principal grievances expressed are related to the failure of the law to clearly define relevant terms ("unlawful", bona fide, mens rea, "teleological" necessity). Court cases are analyzed to reveal the indiscriminate application of these terms and how this in tern leaves too much to the discretion of the judge. Comparisons are made between the Canadian abortion law and the clearer, more specific abortion laws of England and America.

535 Madison, Bernice. "Canadian Family Allowances and Their Major Social Implications," _J. Marr. Fam._ 26(2):134-41. May 1964.

The Family Allowances program in Canada is described and analyzed. First, the history of the program is presented as it has evolved since its inception in 1944. A discussion follows of the major impact made by the program on the welfare of Canadian children and on selected social factors. Finally, areas that need further research before an evaluative conclusion can be reached are pointed up.

536 Majury, A.S. "Therapeutic Abortion in the Winnipeg General Hospital," _Amer. J. Obstet. Gynec._ 82:10-ff., 1961.

A study of 77 therapeutic abortion cases performed at the Winnipeg General Hospital during 1953 to 1959 is presented. The abortion ratio was 1:373. Psychiatric indications accounted for 35% of the cases; hypertensive disease 13%; neurological disease 10%; and heart disease 10%. There were no deaths, and only four cases of complications. The author recommends more careful assessment of each case in order to reduce the frequency of therapeutic abortion.

537 Maxwell, I.D. "Medical-Legal Inquiries," _Nova Scotia Med. Bull._ 46:116-ff., 1967.

A review of Canada's laws on sterilization and abortion, with recommendations for possible reform. Prior to 1955, Section 303 of the Criminal Code was almost identical to the 1861 British Act's Section 58; presumably this meant that the _Rex v. Bourne_ case was applicable in Canada.

In 1955 the Canadian Criminal Code was revised and the word "unlawfully" taken out of the abortion statute, leaving the status of abortion to save the mother's life and the Bourne case's applicability in question.

538 Mongeau, Serge, and Cloutier, Renée. L'Avortement [Abortion]. Montreal: Editions du Jour, 1968. 175 pp.

A memorandum presented by the Center of Family Planning to the permanent Committee on Health and Welfare, charged with studying modifications in the Canadian Code on abortion. Estimates 100,000 to 250,000 induced abortions for Canada, of which 10,000 to 25,000 occur in Quebec. Examines the situation in other countries and makes several recommendations: avoid both laizze-faire and repressive approaches; more support for family planning and sexual education; development of organizations to aid the woman who in the last analysis is interrupting pregnancy for medical-social-psychological reasons. As it is now, doctors do not directly or indirectly advise contraceptive practice even if another pregnancy threatens the mother's life or health.

539 O'Brien, Cliffton. "Eskimo Native Marriage - Common Law Marriage - Marriage Ordinance - Intestate Succession Ordinance [In Re Noah Estate (1961-62) 36 W W R 577]," Alberta Law Rev. 2:121-25, 1962.

Using the recent case of Re Noah Estate as an example, this paper states that the Eskimo marriage conformed to a marriage recognized as valid at common law and the Marriage Ordinance of the Northwest Territories did not invalidate such a marriage. Reference is given to the history of the common law marriage and the English statutes stemming from Lord Hardwicke's Marriage Act of 1753.

540 Perrault, Antonio. "Condition Juridique de la Femme Mariée " [Judicial Status of a Married Woman], Rélations 12(135):58-61. March 1952.

In 1952 Quebec women are still not given full judicial status as men are. Describes previous laws, and inequalities: in Quebec, to be a notary, one must be masculine. In France, by 1942 the head of a family was still considered the husband legally, but he must exercise this function in collaboration with his wife and for the good of the family. A woman ought to be able to initiate legal procedures without having to appeal to her husband's authorization or judicial authorization. She should be able to conclude transactions independent of her husband's or a judge's consent. She should have the right to do business to enter a profession or have a career.

541 Routledge, J.H., et al. "The Present Status of Therapeutic Abortion," Obstet. Gynec. 17:168-ff., 1961.

A study of 122 therapeutic abortions performed at the Montreal General Hospital during 1935 through 1959. In 29% of the cases, the method used was digital evacuation or curettage, and in 71% the abdominal approach associated with sterilization was performed. A decrease in therapeutic abortion was noted; however, an increase in psychiatric indications for abortions was reported. Morbidity from abortions performed by the vaginal route was 8% compared to 5% morbidity rate of the abdominal route.

542 Smith, D.E. "Therapeutic Abortion -- Should the Law be Changed?" Nova Scotia Med. Bull. 46:118-ff., 1967.

Data show that from 1963 to 1965 the therapeutic abortion ratio to live births in Nova Scotia was 1:2193. However, during the same period, there were 3464 women admitted to hospitals in Nova Scotia for all types of abortions -- an approximate incidence of one abortion per ten live births. The author proposes several abortion law reforms with extensive reference to the Canadian Bar Association Resolution Regarding Therapeutic Abortion. This proposal would permit abortions if the pregnancy endangered the life or health of the mother, if the child were likely to be born deformed or if the pregnancy resulted from rape. All applications for therapeutic abortions would be approved by a "Termination Board" committee.

543 Spivak, M.M. "Therapeutic Abortion," Amer. J. Obstet. Gynec. 97:316-ff., 1967.

A review of 262 therapeutic abortions performed at the Toronto General Hospital during 1954-1965. The overall incidence of abortion was 5.8 per 1,000 deliveries, nearly the same for private and other patients. The author suggests the establishment of an abortion committee and urges more liberalization of existing abortion laws.

UNITED STATES

General population policies

544 Baumgartner, Leona. "Population and Public Health Policy," pp. 231-40 in: M. Muramatsu and Paul A. Harper eds. , Population Dynamics: International Action and Training Programmes. Baltimore: Johns Hopkins Press, 1965.

The population policy which makes sense in a pluralistic society with a democratic government, such as the United States is one which strikes a balance between numbers and resources; appropriately provides for economic, social, and family relationships; permits other nations their freedom of choice; and meets the need for research in all fields related to population.

545 Bell, Winifred. "Relatives' Responsibility: A Problem in Social Policy," Soc. Work 12(1):32-39. January 1967.

Regulations governing the responsibility of family members for each other's support, their history and background, the provisions now in effect and their inequity, and the arguments for and against the continuance of these regulations are presented. While public funds are conserved by burdening the family with primary liability, a few questions must be considered regarding the overall value of this practice: (1) Is it sound social policy for an affluent nation, warring however feebly against poverty, to finance public aid and services in a way that deters people from using them? (2) Is it sound long-range financing to force families at the poverty level to pay special assessments for restorative services, over and above their taxes? (3) Is help reluctantly given and forcefully extracted good for the giver or recipient? (4) Should not families already jeopardized by poverty, mental illness, mental retardation, tuberculosis, and any number of other ills be the last, rather than the first, to pay twice?

546 Bonser, Howard J. "A Postwar Population Policy for the Southeast," Soc. Forces 23(1):38-41. October 1944.

This is a concise statement of the quantitative and qualitative aspects of a population policy, with consideration both of immediate postwar and long-time plans.

547 Brayer, Franklin T., ed. World Population and U.S. Government Policy and Programs. Washington: Georgetown University Press, 1968. 116 pp.

Seven papers with an introduction by the editor, from a symposium sponsored by the Center for Population Research of Georgetown University, 12-14 July 1967: L.V. van Nort, "The Development of a U.S. Population Policy"; M.H. Merrill, "Current Activities"; J.M. Stycos, "American Goals and Family Planning"; A.E. Hellegers, "Medical and Public Health Aspects"; P. Demeny, "An Economic Assessment"; N. St. John-Stevas, "An Ethical Appraisal"; R.L. and G. Meier, "New Directions: A Population Policy for the Future".

548 Burch, Guy I. A Democratic Population Policy, With Special References to Business, Health, and National Defense. Washington: Population Reference Bureau, 1941. 46 pp.

A democratic population policy is the business of every citizen and group in the nation. This policy should include measures which will enable all groups, no matter how poor or handicapped, to limit the size of their families if they want to do so. But the adoption of such measures have thus far been obstructed by the fear of race suicide and the primitive reproductive urge. Another obstruction is the lack of knowledge among the lower income groups, who now carry more than their share of the economic and physical responsibilities of reproduction, about the benefits of family limitation to them.

549 Carter, Luther J. "The Population Crisis. Rising Concern at Home," Science 166(3906):722-26. 7 November 1969.

Attitudes of American politicians toward birth control and the population problem have changed rapidly in the last ten years. Many members of Congress are proposing new legislation in this area, and last July, President Richard M. Nixon showed his concern over mounting population pressures in a message to Congress devoted exclusively to the population issue. An alliance has developed between population groups and conservation groups, and a congress on population and the environment will be held in June 1970. At a hearing held by the House Conservation and Natural Resources Subcommittee in September 1969, witnesses testified that the need to limit population growth is no less urgent in the rich countries than in the poor countries, and that the national and world population growth rates must be reduced to zero by the end of the century by whatever means are practicable. Recommendations included establishing social conditions conducive to two-child families, changing tax and welfare laws, allowing abortions on request, and dropping legal restraints on homosexual unions. The average American still looks forward to having a large family, but the sudden interest within Congress and among conservation groups suggests that "complacency is coming to be replaced with growing alarm."

550 Cleveland, Harlan. "The Requisites of Abundance," Department State Bull. 50(1293):550-55. April 6, 1964.

Includes section, The population problem.

551 Coffin, Frank M. Witness for AID. Boston: Houghton Mifflin, 1964. xi, 273 pp.

The author who has served as Deputy Administrator of the Agency for International Development and also as a Congressman with four years of service on the House Foreign Affairs Committee, explains what AID is, how it works, how it is viewed on Main Street and Capitol Hill, its purposes, achievements, problems, and prospects. Chapter, The forces of despair, has section, The population problem, pp. 154-60.

552 Galloway, George B. Postwar Planning in the United States. New York: Twentieth Century Fund, 1942. 158 pp.

This report gives the results of a preliminary survey of research that was being carried on or planned in the field of American postwar (World War II) problems, in 1941. The survey covered hundreds of agencies. Agencies concered with population policy and trends include the Labor Department; League of Nations (Economic, Financial and Transit Department); National Resources Planning Board; Office of Population Research; State Planning Boards; and Tolan Committee on Interstate Migration.

553 Galloway, George B., *et al*. *Planning for America*. New York: Holt, 1941. 713 pp.

This book is a cooperative inquiry into the progress of economic and social planning in the United States: its principles, practices, and problems; its achievements, present status, and potentialities. There are parts devoted to resources, economic and social area, and defense planning. Part 4, (Social planning), Chapter 18 (pp.347-61), Population policy and social planning in a democracy, by Frank Lorimer, states the problem of democratic population planning, and sketches trends in total population, distribution, differential reproduction, and migration, with special reference to the United States. The general types of population policies desired are then outlined in the fields of distribution, quality, and trend of total population.

554 Gardner, Richard N. *Population Growth: A World Problem*. Department of State Publication 7485. International Organization and Conference Series 36. Washington: Government Printing Office, 1963. 16 pp.

Two statements made in Committee II (Economic and Financial) of the U.N. General Assembly during debate on the item "Population growth and economic development" together with the text of a resolution adopted in plenary session on December 18, 1962.

555 Georgia. General Assembly. Joint Committee on the Operations of the General Assembly. *"Population" Acts Since 1870*. Prepared by the Joint Committee on the Operations of the General Assembly and Office of Legislative Counsel, Atlanta, 1960, 369 pp.

Population is defined in the most general way and there is a cataloguing of the several Acts passed by the Georgia General Assembly pertaining to population.

556 Hesburgh, Theodore M., and Fagley, Richard M. "What Should U.S. Do About World Population Problem?" *Foreign Policy Bull*. 39:132-34. May 15, 1960.

Hesburgh suggests that U.S. limit itself to aiding underdeveloped areas in their economic development. Fagley concurs in this recommendation and also suggests that the U.S. provide assistance in education and community organization and promote the consideration of demography in intergovernmental debates and programs concerned with development.

557 Jackson, Henry M. "Public Policy and Environmental Administration," Bioscience 17(12):883-85, 1967.

It is only in comparatively recent years that the growing power of a rich and technologically oriented society to work change upon its natural environment was recognized as a problem of public policy. Some of these problems and the role of federal and local government as well as private industry in making environmental management decisions which are compatible with man's future well-being are discussed.

558 Johnson, Lyndon B. "The Advancement of Peace: Remarks by President Johnson at Independence, Missouri, January 20, 1966," Department State Bull. 54(1389):186-89. February 7, 1966.

The United States will increase its efforts in the great field of human population. It will give help and support to nations which make their own decision to insure an effective balance between the number of their people and the food they have to eat. And it will push forward the frontiers of research in this important field.

559 Lamson, Robert. "Needed Research for Population Policy," Amer. Behavioral Scientist 9(6):23-25. February 1966.

Comment on President Johnson's statements in the State of the Union messages of January 4, 1965, and January 12, 1966. Sections: Population growth and problems of national security; resources and welfare; The range of goals and means; Needed research.

560 Levy, Marion J., Jr. "The Problem of Our Policy in China," Virginia Quart. Rev. 25(3):348-64. Summer 1949.

United States policy in China is related to the possibilities of industrialization and the demographic factors of mortality and fertility.

561 Livi, Livio. "Alcune Osservazioni Sulla Politica Demo-Grafica degli Stati Uniti " [Some Observations on the Population Policy of the United States], Rivista Internazionale di Scienze Sociali 33(2):113-18. March - April 1962.

Livi does not agree with C.E. McGuire about the indifference the United States should show regarding the increase of a population disequilibrium that at present cannot be reduced. He advocates a sort of solidarity between economically advanced and underdeveloped peoples having an excessive natality. It may diffuse, along with economic progress, a social and moral progress which can lead, respecting human values, natality to more normal rates. It is advocated that the U.S. and every other civilized nation, encourage propaganda aiming at procreation within a stable and indissoluble family, and at the prohibition of marriages between very young people. The problem is to be solved on a spiritual level: We can therefore hold it helpful to the U.S. as to any other country, that a sound social education should lead the underdeveloped peoples to procreation levels more adequate to human dignity.

562 Lorimer, Frank, et al. Foundations of American Population Policy. New York: Harper and Bros., 1940. xiii, 178 pp.

This volume, prepared under the auspices of the National Economic and Social Planning Association, represents a systematic attempt to state possible lines of population policy, to clarify basic issues, and to reveal critical areas requiring further study. The first chapter develops the thesis that contemporary American society is inherently self-destructive in the sense that it does not provide conditions and motivations that are adequate to assure the permanent self-replacement of the population on a voluntary basis. Succeeding chapters offer broad critical analyses of recent research in the United States and state its implications for population policy. Chapter II presents the facts of the decline in fertility, with its social-economic and regional variations. Chapter III covers the supply of labor, employment opportunities, and natural resources. Chapter IV concerns the relation of consumption patterns and income levels to family size. Chapter V considers the long-run problem of the relation of population to investment and economic enterprise, and the alternative adjustments possible. Chapter VI surveys such social aspects of population change as health, education, and recreation, while Chapter VII describes the changing pattern of the family. The final chapter, Toward a national population policy, attempts to outline the positive measures needed to adapt the American economy to changing population trends, and to achieve voluntary reproduction adequate from both the quantitative and qualitative standpoint, at the same time maintaining a democratic society.

563 Mann, Thomas C. "Coordination of Policy on Population Matters," Department State Bull. 54(1403):784-87. May 16, 1966.

Statement on goals and activities, 1962-1965, in the Department of State (including the U.S. Delegation to the United Nations, the Agency for International Development, the Bureau of Inter-American Affairs, the Office of Research and Analysis, and the office of the Under-Secretary of State for Economic Affairs).

564 McGuire, Constantine E. "L'Improvvisazione della Politica Demografica negli Stati Uniti " [The Improvization of Population Policy in the United States], Revista Internazionale di Scienze Sociali 32(3):193-212. May - June 1961.

An article critical of recent efforts to promote planned parenthood and to include contraceptive information in the foreign aid program.

565 McGuire, Constantine E. "Ulteriori Osservazioni sulla Improvvisazione della Politica Demografica negli Stati Uniti," [Further Observations on the Improvization of Population Policy in the United States], Rivista Internazionale di Scienze Sociali 33(2):121-28. March - April 1962.

Rejoinder to the comment cited in Livie Livi [Some Observations on the Population Policy of the United States], Rivista Internazionale di Scienze Sociali 33(2):113-18. March - April 1962.

566 National Academy of Sciences. National Research Council. Committee on Science and Public Policy. The Growth of World Population: Analysis of the Problems and Recommendations for Research and Training. Washington: National Research Council, 1963. 38 pp.

A committee of the Academy reviews world population growth, and gives its support to the universal acceptance of planning and controlling family size. Science and technology must provide knowledge and techniques of reproductive control. Five recommendations for strengthening scientific activities are presented.

567 National Academy of Sciences. National Research Council. Committee on Use and Care of National Resources, Division of Biology and Agriculture. Present Needs for Research on the Use and Care of Natural Resources. Publication No. 288, Washington, 1953. 35 pp.

Chapter XII. Tentative statement on the need for a population policy, by Stanley A. Cain and Robert C. Cook.

568 National Planning Association. For a Better Post-War Agriculture. Planning Pamphlets No. 11. Washington, 1942. 47 pp.

One of the concepts basic to post-war planning is that of the number of farms and size of population desired. Possibilities for a better agriculture include consideration of resettlement, distress migration, improved levels of living, and movement from agriculture in their relation to possibilities and goals of planning with reference to agriculture.

569 Nort, Leighton van. "The Development of a U.S. Population Policy," pp. 1-5 in: Brayer, Franklin T., ed. , World Population and U.S. Government Policy and Programs. Washington: Georgetown University Press, 1968. 116 pp.

A review of the government's position on population policy during the Eisenhower, Kennedy and Johnson administrations shows a shift from a negative to a positive attitude on the government's role.

570 Nunley, William T. "World Population Problems and the U.S.A.," _J. Fam. Welfare_ 8(3):1-6. March 1962.

Explains the current attitudes of the Department of State with respect to international population problems. The Department is attempting to stimulate individuals, organizations, and governments to increase their knowledge of population and it is prepared to consider on their merits certain types of requests for assistance to other governments.

571 Osborn, Frederick. "Directives for Private and Public Population Policy in New England," _J. Heredity_ 31(9): 399-402, 1940.

The average number of children necessary to replace the present population in the next generation can be attained only if at least 30% of all married couples have four or more children. At present in the U.S. approximately 17% of married couples are having more than five children with an average of seven; but, these couples are among the least educated and the economically most deprived of our population. Budget analyses show some of the economic deterrents to larger families. High costs of medical care and adequate education are restraining influences which society should remove from prospective parents; especially from post-graduate students and young professional people.

572 Paddock, William, and Paddock, Paul. _Famine -- 1975? America's Decision: Who Will Survive?_ Boston: Little, Brown and Company, 1967. x, 276 pp.

Parts: Inevitability of famine in the hungry nations; Nor can the resources and talents of the developed world avert famine from the hungry nations; Potential role of the United States during the time of famines. Proposes that the United States allot food aid in accordance with the military thesis of "triage," translated into power politics.

573 Popov, A., and Semenov, I. "Chtoskryvaetsia az Sovremenngmi Mal'tuzianskimi'Teoriiami?" [What Is Hidden Behind the Contemporary Malthusian "Theories"?] Isvestiia, June 8, 1950.

An attack of Neo-Malthusian war-mongering in the United States and Great Britain.

574 Population Reference Bureau. "The Emerging Consensus: The Courts, the Congress, and the Administration Move Toward a U.S. Population Policy," Popul. Bull. 21(3):49-71. August 1965.

Notes on recent pronouncements and excerpts from hearings of witnesses on Senate Bill 1676, June 1965.

575 Population Reference Bureau. "Population and International Cooperation at the White House Conference," Popul. Bull. 21(6):137-55. December 1965.

Text of report by a committee of thirteen citizens presented to a panel at the White House Conference on International Cooperation, November 1965, together with statements by John D. Rockefeller, 3rd, and Richard N. Gardner.

576 Rockefeller Panel. Prospect for America. The Rockefeller Panel Reports. Garden City, New York: Doubleday, 1961. xxvi, 486 pp.

Present and projected population is considered in relation to military aspects of international security, foreign economic policy, and education.

577 Roosevelt, James. "U.S. Presents Views on Population Growth and Economic Development," Department State Bull. 54(1388): 175-78. January 31, 1966.

Statement made in Committee II (Economic and Financial) of the United Nations General Assembly, December 15, 1965, detailing United States policy in providing aid to developing countries in population control, while emphasizing that the rapid population-expansion problem is one that affects the United States itself.

578 Rusk, Dean. "Food for Freedom Act of 1960," Statement by Secretary Rusk. Department State Bull. 54(1396):496-503. March 28, 1966.

Press releases on statements of February 25 and March 27 before the House Committee on Agriculture and the Senate Committee on Agriculture and Forestry, respectively. Includes recommendations on family planning, p. 501.

579 Sadowski, Z. "Neomaltuzjanizm -- Antyludzka Teoria w Sluzbie Amerykanskiego Imperializmu " [Neo-Malthusianism: An Inhuman Theory in the Service of American Imperialism], Sprawy Miedzynarodowe 6(2):99-108. March - April 1953.

Demographers, especially in the United States, are viewed as serving the purposes of militarists and industrialists in their approaches to nations in Asia, Africa, and Latin America. Specific reference is made to Elmer Pendell, Robert C. Cook, M.L. Jordan, Vincent M. Whitney, and William Vogt. Among the non-Americans particular attention is given to the writings of Paul Reboux of France and R. Sandwell of Canada. The main disagreement is over the causes of poverty and poor economic development. While the Malthusians emphasize the role of population growth in creating economic difficulties, Sadowski emphasizes the role of economic policy and ideology in creating poverty. The books on economics by Karl Marx, W.I. Lenin, and J.W. Stalin are used to support his arguments.

580 Spengler, Joseph J. "Population Policy in the United States: The Larger Crisis in American Culture," Vital Speeches January 1, 1941, 4 pp.

Recommends a population policy based on: a redefinition of "success" which includes familial values, race replacement, and the obligation not to pursue individual interests to the detriment of the commonweal; an educational system which incorporates this new definition of success; earlier marriage and procreation especially in the upper classes; public expression which idealizes the family of three to four children; private and public employment policies which are congenial to familial values; state support to enable the well-to-do to meet extra costs of large families; and the right of the family to aid.

581 Thomlinson, Ralph. Demographic Problems: Controversy Over Population Control. Belmont, California: Dickenson Publishing Co., 1967. x, 117 pp.

The text prepared for introductory course in social problems. Chapters present background material on: demographic orientation; differential growth trends; control of births, deaths, and migration; population structure. Concluding chapter, National policies, discusses international and national programs.

582 United States. Agency for International Development. Guidlines for Assistance to Population Programs, Washington, September 15, 1967.

This manual order provides guidance for AID assistance for population programs. It sets forth what are now higher levels of priority in U.S. policies relating to the provision of this assistance, emphasizing aid for the self-help activities of less-developed countries in coping with problems of rapid population growth and the need for cooperation with other assisting agencies and institutions. Information is also given on the type of AID assistance in this field, as well as on assistance channels and procedures.

583 United States Congress, Senate. Committee on Government Operations. A Bill to Provide for Certain Reorganizations in the Department of State and the Department of Health, Education, and Welfare, and for Other Purposes. By [Ernest H.] Gruening et al. (89th Congress, 1st Session, S. 1676). Washington, April 1, 1965. 13 pp.

Text of bill read twice and referred to the Committee on Government Operations, to provide for the creation of an office for population problems and an assistant secretary in both departments and for a White House Conference on Population in January 1967.

584 United States Congress, Senate. Government Operations Committee. Subcommittee on Foreign Aid Expenditures. Hearings Before the Subcommittee on Foreign Aid Expenditures of the Committee on Government Operations, United States Senate, 90th Congress, 2nd Session, on S. 1676, A Bill to Reorganize the Department of State and the Department of Health,

<u>Education</u>, <u>and</u> <u>Welfare</u>. Washington, 1967.

Part 1, November 2, 1968. pp. i-v, 1-268; Part 2, January 31, 1968. pp. i-iv, 269-511; Part 3, February 1, 1968. pp. i-v, 513-852; Part 4, Index, 1967-68 (conclusion of 1967-68 hearings), 1968. pp. i-iii, 1-146. Reorganization served to administratively and financially include population as a concern of both departments.

585 United States. International Development Advisory Board. <u>Partners in Progress: A Report to the President</u>. Washington: Government Printing Office, 1951. v, 120 pp.

The problems of the U.S. responsibilities for the underdeveloped areas are assessed on the assumption that strengthening the economies of the underdeveloped regions and an improvement in their living levels must be considered a vital part of the United States' defense mobilization. There is consideration of food, health, strategic material location, etc., and recognition of population increase as a fact but without consideration of the relations between the programs recommended and the ratio of natural increase consequent thereon.

586 United States President. Committee on Population and Family Planning. <u>Population and Family Planning: The Transition from Concern to Action</u>. Government Printing Office, 1968. 43 pp.

This is a report by a committee of citizens and government officials appointed by President Johnson in July 1968, to review United States policies and programs with regard to domestic and world population. It contains twenty-nine recommendations including expansion of U.S. family planning programs and of U.S. international assistance in population, establishment of an advisory group of specialists from other countries for U.S. programs, provision of federal support for population studies centers, appointment of a Commission on Population and development of a National Institute for Population Research. The report, which was submitted in late 1968, appears in a condensed version in The Population Council, <u>Studies in Family Planning</u>, April 1969.

587 Vance, Rupert B. "Human Resources and Public Policy: An Essay Toward Regional - National Planning," Soc. Forces 22(1):20-25. October 1943.

The future of the physical and human resources of the South is discussed in relation to the development of those agricultural, industrial, and demographic policies which will contribute to higher utilization of resources and higher levels of living for both nation and region.

588 Whelpton, Paschal K. "Population Policy for the United States," pp. 462-69 in: Spengler, Joseph J., and Duncan, Otis Dudley, eds. , Population Theory and Policy: Selected Readings. Glencoe, Ill.: Free Press, 1956. xi, 522 pp.

This paper offers a qualitative-quantitative policy, the goal of which is to gradually improve the quality of our population and forestall too rapid a shift from population growth to population decline. Qualitative need is for measures for giving sound contraceptive advise to those groups which have not yet been able to obtain it, in addition to providing materials and supplies free by the Government. To prevent a too rapid decline, a policy of lessening the cost of children to the parents rather than to pay money to people for having large families is suggested. An increase of population helps to give a high level of living only when a nation is underpopulated judging from the ratio of people to resources, or when it is somewhat over-populated but does not know how to regulate its economic life. The United States falls in the latter category. Since our economic education may proceed slowly, it may do well to adopt a population policy which will retard somewhat the slowing up of growth, thus prolonging the period during which increasing numbers may help our economic system.

Policies on fertility and family size

589 "Abortion Law Reform in New York: A Study of Religious, Moral, Medical and Legal Conflict," Albany Law Rev. 31:290, June 1967.

The effect of the abortion controversy in New York has been the proposed modification of the state's abortion law. After reviewing the new proposals and their relation to current legislation on abortion, the author outlines the relevant legal, religious, moral and medical arguments involved in the quest for abortion law reform in New York. The author concludes that the legislature has a duty to carry out the will of the people of the state on this issue and that the proposed revisions are permissive -- no woman will be forced to compromise her religious beliefs or to undergo abortion without her consent.

590 Albrecht, David G. von. Divorce in the "Liberal" Jurisdictions -- Alabama, Florida, Mexico, Nevada and the Virgin Islands, Proceedings of the Special Committee on Marriage and Divorce Law, Federal Bar Association of New York, New Jersey and Connecticut, April 19, 1955, in New York City [N.Y.]. New York: Federal Legal Publications, 1955. 48 pp.

Each chapter is by a different author and each describes the situation in a given jurisdiction. Each author stresses the particulars of divorce which interest him.

591 American Baptist Convention. "American Baptist Resolution on Abortion," Amer. Baptist Convention, Boston. May 31, 1968.

The American Baptists urge that legislation be enacted to provide that the termination of a pregnancy prior to the end of the 12th week (first trimester) be at the request of the individual(s) concerned and be regarded as an elective medical procedure governed by the laws regulating medical practice and licensure.

592 "AMA [American Medical Association] Policy on Therapeutic Abortion," J. Amer. Med. Assn. 201:544. August 14, 1967.

The AMA's Committee on Human Reproduction, in a report prepared in 1967 and transmitted to the AMA House of Delegates, recommended that the AMA adopt a policy on therapeutic abortion, which, essentially, was a modification of the Model Penal Code of the American Law Institute. The statement on therapeutic abortion finally adopted as the policy of the AMA is listed in full, as well as the basic premises underlying the House's approval of the statement.

593 American Medical Association. "Medicolegal Aspects of Sterilization, Artificial Insemination, and Abortion," J. Amer. Med. Assn. 166(6):645-48. February 8, 1958.

Operations to produce sterility, when necessary for therapeutic reasons, may lawfully be performed. But little can be said with any degree of assurance concerning the medicolegal aspects of artificial insemination because of the absence of appellate court hearings. Abortion, like sterilization, must be therapeutic in order to be lawful.

594 American Medical Association. "The People's Bill," J. Amer. Med. Assn. 197(5):263. August 1, 1966.

Comment on possibilities of population control through government action to require all women aged 16-36 to take the pill kept at approximately 75 per cent of totally effective level.

595 American Medical Association. Committee on Human Reproduction. "Birth Control in Comprehensive Health Care," J. Amer. Med. Assn. 196(12):1084-85. June 20, 1966.

Note, prepared by Secretary of the Committee, on lack of implementation at the local level of earlier recommendations that contraceptive information be provided to the indigent as part of public health services.

596 American Public Health Association. "Abortion," American Public Health Association Governing Council, November, 1968.

Resolution on abortion of the APHA Governing Council. Passed in November 1968 at the 96th annual meeting.

597 American Public Health Association. Program Area Committee on Population and Public Health. "Public Health Programs in Family Planning," [A group of 15 papers.] Amer. J. Public Health 56(1, Part 2):i-ii, 1-93. January 1966.

Brings together under the committee's auspices a 'sampler' on programs (both old and new). All contributors were asked to cover the historical development of their program, its administrative aspects, and an evaluation of results achieved. Contents: Corsa, Leslie, Jr., Introduction, pp. 1-5; Eliot, Johan W., et al., The development of family planning services by state and local health departments in the United States, pp. 6-16; Parks, L.L., and Crane, D.L., Florida's family planning program, pp. 17-21; Tepper, Sheri E., A "package" plan for extension of birth control services, pp. 22-28; Huppman, Anne G., and Whitridge, John Jr., Family planning in Maryland, pp. 29-33; Gross, Stewart B., et al., The Alameda County Health Department family planning program, pp. 34-39; Corkey, Elizabeth C., The birth control program in the Mecklenburg County Health Department, pp. 40-47; Willoughby, Joseph L., et al., The organization of a pilot family planning clinic in Tennessee, pp. 48-51; Grant, Murray, Family planning in the nation's capital, pp. 52-56; Lippes, Jack, and Randall, Clyde, Participation of area hospitals in family planning, pp. 57-60; Ten Have, Ralph, and Collver, Andrew, Family planning clinics for the urban fringe, pp. 61-66; Snyder, John C., The education of experts for the 1970's, pp. 67-73; Taylor, Howard C., Jr., Evaluation of recent developments in contraceptives technology, pp. 74-79; Notestein, Frank W., Population growth--a challenge to public health, pp. 80-84; Bogue, Donald J., and Farley, Reynolds, Population growth, problems, and trends in the United States, pp. 85-93.

598 American Public Welfare Association. "Policy Statement: Family Planning," Public Welfare 23(1):57. January 1965.

This policy statement was prepared by the Committee on Public Welfare Policy and adopted by the Board of Directors on November 23, 1964. If an individual client requests information about family planning, he should be referred for the appropriate service which is compatible with his religious and ethical beliefs.

599 American Social Hygiene Association. State Laws to Protect Family Health. 3rd ed. New York: The American Social Hygiene Association, Inc., 1949. 28 pp.

This is a summary of State legislation requiring pre-marital and pre-natal examinations for venereal diseases. It contains a short historical survey of the development of such legislation, a reprint of an article entitled "Premarital examination for syphilis" (J. Amer. Med. Assn. 1949, 139, 310) as well as tables together with explanations of State pre-natal examination legislative requirements for syphilis, maps, legal references and a list of other publications on social hygiene laws and legislation.

600 Anderson, G.C.A. "Abortion, Artificial Insemination, and Sterilization," pp. 125-34 in: Barnes, A.C., ed. The Social Responsibility of Gynecology and Obstetrics. Baltimore: Johns Hopkins Press, 1965.

Reviewed briefly is the current legal status of abortion in the United States, with special reference to Maryland's abortion law. The Model Penal Code's provisions are described as probably the most desirable standards on which to base the changes that must be made in our abortion statutes.

601 Andrews, F. Emerson. "Family Allowances for America?" pp. 216-26 in: National Conference of Social Work. Proceedings... New Orleans, Louisiana, May 10-16, 1942. New York: Columbia University Press, 1942. 670 pp.

The plan for allotments to the families of service men is held to constitute a revolutionary principle in the United States. Policies are needed to avert the consequences of the tendency of the economic burden of child care to produce "the survival of the unfittest". Foreign systems are noted, and a critical examination of possibilities recommended for this country, with careful birth records to be kept as the first policies are introduced in order that family allowances may be adjusted to our population policy, or abandoned if it develops unhappy consequences.

602 Andrews, F. Emerson. "What Price Children?" Atlantic Monthly 172(5):94-99. November 1943.

A system of children's allowances is advocated, primarily as a fiscal war measure and secondarily as an aid to family life.

603 Arizona. State Department of Health. [Notes on the family planning program.] Arizona's Health 1(2):1-4, 12-17. August - September 1966.

Contents: Spendlove, George A., Time is running out, p. 1; Moore, William J., Explosion--what are the stakes? Population dynamics and the challenge to public health, pp. 2-4, 12-16; Policy statement by the Arizona State Board of Health, November 26, 1965, p. 17.

604 Bahr, Gary L. "Fraudulent Representation of Pregnancy - Marriage and Annulment," South Dakota Law Rev. 13:146-58, 1968.

This paper explores United States case law in the area of the annulment of marriages on the ground of a fraudulent representation of pregnancy. The basic situation concerns a man and a woman who have had premarital sexual intercourse. Subsequently, either with the knowledge that she is not pregnant or with no reason to suspect that she is, the woman falsely represents to the man that she is pregnant. The man relies on this misrepresentation and marries the woman. After the marriage, he gains knowledge that his newly acquired wife is not pregnant and he sues for annulment. The question is: "Will either law or equity grant the annulment?" There are twelve jurisdictions which have not granted an annulment in this situation. The author's research indicates thirty-six jurisdictions have not decided the question. Two states, Kentucky and Wisconsin, have granted the annulment prayed for in this situation. One state, New York, apparently is not sure how it should answer.

605 Baker, James N. "A State Program for Planned Parenthood in Alabama," Human Fertility 6(5):29-33. October 1941.

The planned parenthood program carried out by the State Department of Health in cooperation with private physicians and county health departments is described.

606 Bakker, Cornelis B., and Dightman, Cameron R. "Physicians and Family Planning: A Persistent Ambivalence," Obstetrics Gynecology 25(2):279-84, 1965.

Contraception is a medical concern which the medical profession has accepted with ambivalence. The response of 109 physicians which rates medical school and internship inadequate in the area of training for family planning bears this out. It is underscored by the almost total absence of research in psychiatric problems of birth control, tubal ligation and vasectomy. As a result, the help extended to couples in need of family planning is inefficient. Interviews with 100 young married women revealed that only 37% had received their most useful information from a physician. Forty-five per cent of the women had become pregnant in spite of contraceptives.

607 Balfour, Marshall. "Population and Family Planning Programs in U.S. Schools of Public Health," Stud. in Fam. Planning, No. 29, April 1968, pp. 12-16.

Greater appreciation that public health is an applied social science and the growing concern about the population problem have prompted a number of public health schools to train staff for population-family planning teaching and research. The author stresses that the public health aspects of population and family planning are not a neat block of knowledge and experience, but draw from several disciplines and departments. Reviewed briefly are developments at several U.S. public health schools: California School of Public Health (Berkeley), Johns Hopkins School of Hygiene and Public Health, Harvard School of Public Health, Michigan School of Public Health, and North Carolina School of Public Health. Brief mention is also made of the programs at Pittsburgh, Tulane and Hawaii. Studies or action in the area of fertility control and population with public health schools did not develop before the post-war period, with the exception of the pioneering studies at Johns Hopkins.

608 Ball, George W. "A Birthright With Every Birth," Amer. J. Econ. Sociol. 21(4):58. October 1962.

The author discusses the "population explosion" problem and its effects on economic advancement, on volume of resources, and on national programs required to achieve rapid development in less developed areas in the world. Even given favorable circumstances, the less developed nations will fight a losing battle unless they can obtain, and use with maximum efficiency, a huge volume of capital and technical skills. Areas with plentiful manpower must emphasize development activities of a labor-intensive nature; whereas nations with small population relative to resources must consider labor-saving activities. The author concludes that the problem of rapid growth, although it conditions the prospects for achieving the true objectives of economic development, is a social and cultural dilemma and calls increasingly for the exercise of the most mature wisdom.

609 Bare, Samuel L. "Significance of Puberty in Nonage Marriages " [State v. Graves (Ark.) 307 S W 2d 545], Wash. Lee Law Rev. 16:87-92. Spring 1959.

Statutes in every state have raised the age required at common law to contract a valid marriage. Originally, this was the age of puberty, 12 years for the female and 14 years for the male. By thus raising the required age, legislatures have created a gap between the age at which the parties are deemed to have physical capacity to consummate a marriage and the age required by statute for legal capacity to contract a valid marriage. The author examines and describes several Arkansas court cases involving nonage marriages in which one of the parties had reached the age of puberty but not the age required by statute. The major problem the courts face is that of classifying such marriages as either valid, voidable or void. The author concludes that by raising the age of consent, as it existed at common law, modern statutes have created a new age of consent that is unrelated to physical development and rests solely on public policy as interpreted by the legislature.

610 Barnard, Thomas H., Jr. "Analysis and Criticism of the Model Penal Code Provisions on the Law of Abortion," Western Res. Law Rev. 18:540-64. January 1967.

In this critical analysis, the author first calls attention to the many reasons necessitating an examination of the Model Penal Code's abortion provisions. It is his view that the American Law Institute followed the sociological jurisprudential approach in drafting the Code's abortion section, and he points to the Advisory Committee's comments in support of this proposition. Mr. Barnard also believes that the Swedish and Danish abortion statutes exerted significant influence upon the American Law Institute but that the effects of these laws were not given sufficient consideration, with the result that no attempt was made to eliminate the problems caused by their enactment. Finally, the author raises several probing questions which must be considered by those who would change the law of abortion and concludes that the Code represents a commendable though imperfect attempt to answer them.

611 Barnes, Allan C., ed. _Proceedings of a Conference on the Social Responsibility of Gynecology and Obstetrics._ Baltimore: Johns Hopkins Press, 1965. xiv, 210 pp.

The book is for the minister, the social worker, the physician, and the layman. It stresses the social responsibility of gynecology and obstetrics in the problem of controlling birth rate in a world with impressively decreasing death rate. With reference to the problem of population explosion and eugenics, methods to motivate people to limit their offspring, and the probable considerable improvements in quality as a result, are emphasized.

612 Barnett, Larry D. "Religious Differentials in Fertility Planning and Fertility in the United States," _Fam. Life Coordinator_ 14(3):161-70. October 1965.

A review of the literature on the differences between religions in terms of fertility planning and fertility yields the following conclusions: (1) The extent of favorable attitudes toward birth control, the extent of actual use of contraception, and the degree of effectiveness of contraceptive practice among birth control users is today greatest among Jewish and least among Catholic couples, with Protestant couples occupying an intermediate position. (2) Controlling for socio-economic status appears to wipe out the differences between Protestants and Jews in attitudes toward birth control and in actual use of contraceptive methods, but such a control does not appear to markedly change the relative position of Catholics in attitudes and practice of contraception or eliminate differences between the three religious groups in birth control effectiveness. Controlling for differences in several other variables, the differentials tended to remain.

613 Barret, George. "Catholics and Birth Control," Popul. Rev. 8(1):53-72. January 1964.

An article noting the challenge to the traditional Catholic belief that birth control measures other than the rhythm system should not be used. The conservative Catholic view argues that rapid population growth is inherently temporary and that it stimulates economic growth. Projects such as the "Center for Population Research" at Georgetown University, which is linked with a research program seeking ovulation signals at Beth Israel Hospital in Boston, the Buffalo Catholic rhythm clinic, and the St. Vincent's Hospital rhythm center in New York are church supported means of dealing with the problem. In Puerto Rico the Family Planning Association has had some success in its program (a sample survey of 1,097 rural couples showed a 50% decrease in pregnancies). Liberals in the Church feel that there can be changes in the attitude to birth control just as the attitude to the taking of interest on money has changed.

614 Barrett, Donald N., ed. The Problem of Population: Moral and Theological Considerations. Notre Dame, Ind.: University of Notre Dame Press, 1964. xiv, 161 pp.

A collection of papers presented by a group of Catholic scholars at a 1963 conference on the moral and theological aspects of the overpopulation problem held at the University of Notre Dame. Topics included Christian marriage and family planning; marriage and sexuality -- the Catholic position; family size, rhythm and the "pill"; birth control, abortion, sterilization and public policy; and natural law and contraception. The editor presents an integrated outline of conference principles as a concluding chapter, with references to the empirical situations demanding solutions, development in theology, normative and responsible parenthood, love and the conjugal act, the means of responsible parenthood, basic issues on public birth control policy, and problems of state involvement.

615 Bartholomew, Geoffrey W. "Recognition of Polygamous Marriages in America," Internat. Comparative Law Quart. 13: 1022-75. July 1964.

The American decisions relating to the recognition of polygamous and potentially polygamous marriages are examined and the attitude of the American courts on this matter is compared with that of the English courts. Two major groups of cases concerned with the recognition of polygamy are considered: those dealing with American-Indian marriages and those dealing with foreign marriages. The problem of Mormon marriages is also considered because of the peculiar historical significance of such marriages in the development of the English attitude toward polygamy.

616 Baumgartner, Leona. "Family Planning," J. Amer. Med. Assn. 196(6):487. May 9, 1966.

Note based on a paper read before the White House Conference for Health on November 4, 1965. This was the first governmentally sponsored conference to have a special panel devoted to "family planning," and the author summarizes the panel's findings. The problem was approached largely from the points of view of the individual and his preferences, and of helping those who want help and are not getting it, with discussion confined to the United States. The need for family planning in the disadvantaged groups is stressed, as well as for research and larger public and private resources committed to birth control programs. Five initial steps were suggested by the panel: information on family planning offered to every obstetrical patient desiring it at the time of the postpartum check; family planning a part of the health services offered by each hospital to its outpatients; family planning advice and services included as an integral part of the various insurance plans for medical care; every social worker instructed to deal with the problems of family planning in the same way he deals with other familial problems; and the widest possible discussion of responsible parenthood promoted, since this is fundamental to the well-being of the family and the nation.

617 Beaney, William M. "The Griswold Case and the Expanding Right to Privacy," Wisconsin Law Rev., Fall 1966, pp. 979-95.

A comprehensive review of the court cases leading up to the Griswold v. Connecticut case, and of the principles laid down by the Court in concluding that the anti-contraceptive statute was invalid. A lengthy discussion of the overall potentialities of these principles for limiting government policies and actions in the future includes the meaning and portents of a constitutional right to privacy.

618 Beasley, Joseph D. "View from Louisiana," Fam. Planning Perspectives 1(1):2-15. Spring 1969.

Ten principles of operation which need to be observed to develop an effective community-wide family planning program are given, with illustrations drawn from the Louisiana Family Planning Program. The ten principles are: (1) study the population; (2) develop a strong leadership organization; (3) design a goal-oriented preliminary plan; (4) locate and coordinate all existing facilities and services; (5) allow time for development after funding; (6) contact all eligible patients within specific time limit; (7) expand family planning services as a critical first step in improving total health care; (8) value the individual patient's privacy, dignity, and right to choose; (9) use modern management techniques to develop and maintain administrative efficiency; and (10) obtain, evaluate, and report program results.

619 Beasley, Joseph D., et al. "The Orleans Parish Family Planning Demonstration Program," Milbank Memorial Fund Quart. 57(3), Part 1:225-53. July 1969.

A detailed description of program begun in June 1967 in metropolitan New Orleans with the goal of reaching the entire indigent population by June 1969. During the first year, 12,000 contacts were made, resulting in acceptance of some method of family planning by 9,000 patients. The family planning acceptance rate is estimated to be between 18.4 and 26.4 acceptors per 100 eligible females. Evaluation of program impact will continue through the third year (June 1970). Experience of the first year indicates that the indigent will utilize family planning services if they are made available in an acceptable manner -- i.e., the problem is design and provision of service rather than persuading the indigent to accept such services. The program model represented by the program is intended to incorporate methodology of sufficient generality and flexibility for successful adaptation to other populations.

620 Beasley, Joseph D., and Parrish, Vestal W., Jr. "Family Planning and the Reduction of Fertility and Illegitimacy: A Preliminary Report on a Rural Southern Program," Soc. Biology 16(3):167-78. September 1969.

The number of births to medically indigent in the Lincoln Parish Family Planning Research and Demonstration Program decreased 32 per cent in 1967 compared with a decrease of six per cent between 1966 and 1967 for indigent women in the four contiguous parishes, with populations having similar demographic and socioeconomic characteristics, but without similarly organized family planning services. The number of out-of-wedlock births among women in the Lincoln Parish program decreased 40 per cent in 1967 compared with 1966, while in the four adjoining parishes it rose two per cent. The ratio of illegitimate births to total live births in Lincoln Parish declined from 157 per 1,000 in 1966 to 121 per 1,000 in 1967. In the "control" parishes, it rose from 173 per 1,000 in 1966 to 184 per 1,000 in 1967. The Lincoln Parish Family Planning Program, inaugurated in September 1965, was designed to provide adequate family planning services to medically indigent parish residents through systematic identification and contact. Of the 793 women eligible for the program, 472, or 60 per cent, participated. Of the 402 eligible women with one or more out-of-wedlock pregnancies, 133 are still in the program. The authors state that the data in this report are preliminary and caution that the two years of experience presented is not sufficient to rule out the effect of chance variation on the observed trends.

621 Beilenson, A.C. "The Therapeutic Abortion Act: A Small Measure of Humanity," Los Angeles Bar Assn. Bull. 41:316, 1966.

Legislation is needed that will extend the indications for and availability of therapeutic abortion and make the procedure and approval of such abortions less problematic. It is contended that current laws are completely outdated in terms of contemporary morality and are representative of socio-economic discrimination.

622 Ben-Or, Joseph Baruch. "The Relation Between Legal Development and Social Change: Adoption of Children Laws and Adoption Services in Massachusetts," Dissertation Abstr. 29A: 4509, 1968-1969. Abstract of Ph.D. Thesis, Brandeis University, Waltham, Massachusetts, 1968. 241 pp.

The adoption of children is quite common in contemporary United States. As a social process and a legal institution, adoption dates far back in history. For reasons elaborated in the present study, it never formed part of the English

Common Law. The fact, which is amply documented, is that adoption was a legally recognized practice of over 150 years standing in Massachusetts at the time of the enactment of the statute of 1851. Since this study concerns children, about whom the question of what kind of people they will be, and what their affiliations, is answered by social policy -- legislation and practice in the arena of adoption is both a product of this policy and an arena for the processes that produce change in social policy.

623 Berelson, Bernard. "American Attitudes on Population Policy," Stud. Fam. Planning, No. 9, January 1966, pp. 5-8.

A report of the survey on American attitudes toward population sponsored by the Population Council and administered by the Gallup Organization, Inc. The respondents were selected as a modified probability sample and were divided into two separate interview groups with identical questions. The questions used in the survey and their results are given. The questionnaire included topics centered on the United States' present population, the seriousness of rapid population growth, birth control, and foreign aid family planning programs. The social differentials; sex, education and religion are examined in regard to the answers on the questionnaire. It was shown that the impact of the Pope's visit to the United Nations on October 4, did influence some Catholic opinion, at least directly after the event. However, this may not indicate what lasting effect the occasion may have had upon American opinion with regard to population policy.

624 Berle, Beatrice Bishop. "Sterilization and Birth-Control Practices in a Selected Sample of Puerto Ricans Living in a Manhattan Slum," Fertility and Sterility 8(3):267-81, 1957.

The continued pattern of preferring sterilization to birth control in a group of Puerto Rican migrants has been demonstrated. Second-generation Puerto Rican women, however, show a greater prevalence of induced abortions and the more effective use of contraceptive measures.

625 Beyrer, J. Benjamin. "Are Family Allowances on the Way?" Public Welfare 7:87-90. April 1949.

Discusses family allowance programs and suggests ways of inaugurating such a program in the United States.

626 Binavince, Emilio S. "Adoption and the Law of Descent and Distribution: A Comparative Study and a Proposal for Model Legislation," Cornell Law Quart. 51:152-92. Winter 1966.

The author examines civil-law and common-law rules of descent and distribution in adoptive filiation and concludes that these rules fail to reflect the recognized function of adoption and the prevailing theory of inheritance. He questions the validity of the underlying policy of legislation that formulates an inheritance arrangement in adoptive filiation different from that accepted in natural filiation. Observing that inheritance in adoptive filiation finds its justification along with the other effects of adoption in the function of adoption itself, he offers a model law of the effects of adoption that completely equates adoptive filiation with natural legitimate filiation.

627 Biskind, Elliott L. "Legitimacy of Children Born by Artificial Insemination," J. Family Law 5:39-50. Spring 1965.

The basic problem is the necessity to overcome, by clear and convincing evidence, the presumption of legitimacy. What will overcome this presumption is irrefutable proof of the husband's sterility, or impotence to a degree that he cannot emit semen. Terms defined; if any type of sterility is claimed, it must be proven to have existed at the approximate time when the artificial insemination occurred. Birth of a child through artificial insemination donor appears to be more difficult to prove when impotence is claimed rather than sterility. The trend today is to narrow rather than enlarge the area in which children are labeled illegitimate. Children born of heterologous insemination should not be stigmatized with illegitimacy when the husbands of their mothers had freely consented to the practice which resulted in their births, and had permitted their names to be registered as fathers. It is rare to find adultery committed with the consent of a spouse while heterological insemination occurs almost invariably with the active and written consent of the husband. It may be too early to expect state legislatures to establish the legitimacy of an artificial insemination donor when the husband executes his written consent to the process.

628 Biskind, Elliott L., ed. Boardman' New York Family Law. New York: Clark Boardman Co., Ltd., 1964. 2197 pp.

Chapters on the marriage contract; remarriages; rights and obligations arising from the marriage contract; privileged communications (competency of spouses and infants as witnesses); common law marriages; domicile; adoptions; legitimacy, parternity proceedings, and artificial insemination; ante-and post-nuptial agreements; separation agreements; matrimonial actions (general provisions); annulment actions; divorce actions; separation actions; dissolution of marriage on ground of five year absence (Enoch Arden Divorce); presumption of death after seven year absence; foreign divorces; alimony and counsel fees; custody; and the family court. Included are copies of all pertinent forms to be filed in any of the above cases, a table of statutes and a table of cases.

629 Blake, Judith. "Letter to the Editor re: O. Harkavy, et al., 'Family Planning and Public Policy: Who Is Misleading Whom?' " Science 165(3899):1203-4. 19 September 1969.

Response to the article by Harkavy, et al. which criticized Blake's paper on "Population Policy for Americans: Is the Government Being Misled?" Blake asserts that the article constitutes the first explicit admission by family planning leaders that their interest in contraception, is not to be equated in any way with population 'planning', 'control', or 'policy'. In part her response is also a criticism of technical aspects of the evidence presented by the authors. It is asserted, for example, that the estimate that five million women "want" and "need" birth control includes sterile women, birth control users, objectors, and woman seldom or never having intercourse. If these women are eliminated, it is claimed, there are substantially fewer than two million women in need of federal birth control services.

630 Blake, Judith. "Population Policy for Americans: Is the Government Being Misled?" Science 164(3879):522-29. 2 May 1969.

The prevailing view (as set forth in four governmental or private reports), that in the United States high priority should be given to governmentally-aided birth control programs for the poor, is challenged. Evidence from Gallup

Poll data on opinions toward dissemination of birth control information is cited to show that, since the late 1930's, birth control has not been a tabooed topic of public discussion. Data from Whelpton _et al._, _Fertility and Family Planning in the United States_, are presented to show that the explanation for the larger families of the poor is not primarily that they have less access to birth control and birth control information, and that most fecund lower class couples now use birth control methods when they want to prevent pregnancy. The list of possible consequences of a massive governmental program includes loss of an important inducement to marriage if unmarried girls are provided with easy access to birth control pills; threats to health from long time pill use; and exposure of the program to charges of genocide. Since poverty-oriented birth control programs are said to make sense neither as a welfare measure nor as an inhibitor of population growth, it is urged that attention be focused upon the reproduction behavior of the majority of Americans who want families of three or more children. It is proposed that the behavior of this majority can be most effectively altered by "relieving the coercion" upon women that now prevents them from adopting life styles different from marriage and parenthood, and it is concluded that the programs advocated in these reports merely trivialize the problem of population control. What is needed instead are basic changes in the social organization of reproduction that will make non-marriage, childlessness, and small (two-children) families far more prevalent than they now are. The four reports that are challenged are: (1) _Hearings on S. 1676, U.S. Senate Subcommittee on Foreign Aid Expenditures_. (The 1965 and 1966 Hearings each comprise seven volumes, and the 1967-1968 Hearings, to date, comprise three volumes.) U.S. Government Printing Office. (2) "The Growth of U.S. Population." National Academy of Science - Natural Research Council Publication 1279. 1965. (3) O. Harkavy, F.S. Jaffe, S.M. Wishik. "Implementing DHEW Policy on Family Planning and Population." _Population Crisis_, Part 1; 163-207. U.S. Government Printing Office, 1967. (4) President's Committee on Population and Family Planning. _Population and Family Planning: The Transition from Concern to Action_, U.S. Government Printing Office, 1968.

631 Blake, Robert R., _et al._ _Beliefs and Attitudes About Contraception Among the Poor_. Monograph 5, Carolina Population Center. Chapel Hill: University of North Carolina, 1969. 38 pp.

Develops a methodology and instrument whereby the attitudes and beliefs of contraceptors and non-contraceptors can be compared systematically. Such a comparison is intended to show the costs and benefits that are perceived by a group in practicing contraception and to suggest some generalizations and implications for family planning educational programs. Poor women, white and non-white, in North Carolina were selected for study.

632 Bowden, Aneta E. Summary of Recent State Legislation Requiring Premarital and Prenatal Examinations as of January 1, 1941. Washington: Public Health Service, 1941. 19 pp.

A brief history of the laws is followed by a tabular analysis of the specific provisions by states.

633 Brackett, Morris E. "Role of the State Health Department in Family Planning," Obstet. Gynec. 29:590-96. April 1967.

Georgia's Department of Public Health, believing that family planning is an important part of any total health effort, has offered a statewide family planning program since 1939. After listing the benefits of such a program and describing briefly the history of Georgia's activities and progress, the author outlines the data obtained and studied by an advisory committee set up to recommend priorities for program expansion in the area of family planning. By considering the trends in the various obstetric data and then relating them to the parous patient, need was established, primarily the need for IUD utilization. The author concludes with a discussion of plan development: essential criteria, requisites to putting the plan into operation and problem areas to anticipate.

634 Bradley, William L. "Birth Control Laws in Connecticut and Massachusetts," Soc. Action 26(8):20-23. April 1960.

This article deals with efforts to change the Connecticut and Massachusetts birth control laws in the states' General Assembly and to test its constitutionality. The opposition of the church to change is emphasized. The laws appear to be most restrictive in establishment of clinics, causing women to sometimes go to other states for advise. Two prospects for a change in the law are proposed: (1) courts rule them unconstitutional or (2) a change of attitude on the part of religious leaders occurs.

635 Brainard, Margaret. "Cancelled Marriage-License Applications," Sociol. Soc. Res. 25:321-31, 1941.

Close to 700 of the 25,566 applications for a marriage license in Los Angeles County in 1938 were cancelled, after thirty days, because the applicants either did not return at the end of the three-day waiting period or meanwhile had been found to be ineligible. An investigation of 221 couples reveals that about thirty per cent had later married or planned to do so and that almost one-half had not married or did not intend to do so. Thus the law on a waiting-period is viewed as having some impact in reducing the frequency of marriage on a somewhat long-term basis. But this effect is most noticeable on older and once-married couples.

636 Broel-Plateris, Alexander. "Associations Between Marriage Disruption, Permissiveness of Divorce Laws, and Selected Social Variables," pp.512-26, Chpt.33 in:Burgess,E.W.,and Bogue, D.J., eds. Contributions to Urban Sociology. Chicago: University of Chicago Press, 1964. xv, 683 pp.

Association of the prevalence of marriage disruption with strictness of divorce laws and selected social variables was investigated. Percentages of divorced and separated females were used as indices of marriage disruption. These percentages and measures of most other variables were computed from 1950 census data. Law permissiveness scores were assigned on the basis of a survey of family law teachers. Matrices of correlated coefficients were computed for large cities, other urban, rural non-farm and rural farm population, but discussion was limited to urban areas. Geographic distribution of the divorced and the separated indicates low association between these variables. For large cities $r = -.25$. Permissive laws are associated with high prevalence of disruption ($r=.60$) and of divorce in large cities ($r=.79$), but with low prevalence of separation ($r=-.44$). In other residence areas association is lower. r c's with other variables indicate that disruption is associated with lack of social stability. Areas of early settlement, little migration and high percent of Catholics tend to have strict laws, low prevalence of divorce and of total disruption.

637 Brown, L. Neville. "Shotgun Marriage," Tulane Law Rev. 42:837-60. June 1968.

The term "shotgun marriage" is popularly used today to denote a marriage which takes place for the primary purpose of conferring the status and consequent respectability of birth in lawful wedlock upon a child conceived as a result of premarital intercourse. There is also likely to be the desire to save the mother from disgrace or at least embarrassment. Whilst American cases abound of marriages under duress, the English courts have only infrequently been presented with this problem. Hence the interest of the recent English decision in Buckland v. Buckland (1967). After an examination of that case, the present state of the common law authorities, both English and American, is reviewed and the author questions how well the law is suited to modern attitudes towards the act of marriage and the marital relationship. Where relevant, comparisons are made with the civil law of France and Louisiana. It is concluded that reform of the civil and criminal law in this neglected area of domestic relations will help to reduce the number of situations in which the legal process can be used as a means to compel a marriage. Nevertheless, occasions will still sometimes arise when pressure of this kind may be lawful. Thus in Buckland v. Buckland, if the man had in fact seduced the girl, the marriage could have been upheld as not vitiated by duress. But whether it is socially desirable, as distinct from legally permissible, is increasingly open to question. A different answer may be appropriate in a different society.

638 Brunner, Endre K. "The Outcome of 1556 Conceptions: A Medical and Sociological Study," Human Biology 13(2): 159-76, 1941.

Gynecologic consultation with 979 well-educated New York women of the economic middle class showed that 74.3% were married, the rest single. They experienced a total of 1556 conceptions of which 55.8% reached viability, 13.6% aborted spontaneously and 30.5% were terminated artificially. 60.7% of the intra-marital, 18.1% of the extra-marital conceptions were carried to viability, most of the latter being born in wedlock. The percent of spontaneous abortion was exactly the same in both intra- and extra-marital pregnancies: 13.6%. The occurrence of induced abortion was: intra-marital, 25.7%; extra-marital, 68.9%. Spontaneous abortion was most frequent in youth and the older couples. Induced abortion was most frequent in the multiparous. Church affiliation was of negligible significance. Contraception was much more effective in the unmarried, of which 65.9% were sexually experienced. Marriage occurred at the average age of 24. At the arbitrary age of 30, all married couples regardless of religion had an average of one child and taking

all ages, 1.2 children. Of the induced abortions, 78.9% were performed by physicians with instruments and were followed by significant morbidity.

639 Bruno, Hal. "Birth Control, Welfare Funds, and the Politics of Illinois," Reporter 28:32-35. June 20, 1963.

A chronological account of the efforts of Arnold Maremont, chairman of the Illinois Public Aid Commission, to gain legislative and public acceptance of his proposed solutions to the state's complex welfare problems. Main solution was a state-supported birth-control program for recipients of public aid.

640 Bukes, J.S., and Hewson, W.C. "The Legal Status of Therapeutic Abortion," Univ. Pittsburgh Law Rev. 27:669, 1966.

Reference is made to the 1860 Pennsylvania abortion law which is identical to that of English law. Liberal interpretations of both English and Massachusetts laws are outlined. The author urges that the Pennsylvania law be given explicit legal recognition through judicial opinion.

641 Buxton, C. Lee. "Birth Control Problems in Connecticut. Medical Necessity, Political Cowardice and Legal Procrastination," Conn. Med. 28:581-84. August 1964.

This article attacks Section 53-32 of the Connecticut General Statutes which prohibits the use of any drugs or instruments to prevent contraception. The author charges that the law is medically and economically discriminating in preventing the establishment of contraceptive clinics for lower socio-economic groups. The tragic implications of the law are shown by several case histories and the Supreme Court's stand on the issue of the constitutionality of the statute is outlined, with reference to comments taken from the Appellate Court.

642 Byrn, R.M. "The Abortion Question: A Nonsectarian Approach," Catholic Lawyer 11:316-ff., 1965.

The morality and equity of the abortion bill proposed by the American Law Institute is disputed by the author who charges its proponents with unwarranted emotionalism. Public education is urged to guard against radical liberalization in the legal order and to effect public opposition to legalizing abortions.

643 Byrn, R.M. "Abortion II - A Legal View," Commonweal 85: 679-ff., 1967.

This article argues against all legalized abortions in order to protect the rights of a "voiceless, voteless minority."

644 Byrn, R.P. " A Critical Look at Legalized Abortion," Los Angeles Bar Bull. 41: 320-ff., 1966 .

The highly debated issue of whether human life exists before birth, at the time of conception, or exactly when it begins, is used to criticize the emotionalism of the proponents of the Therapeutic Abortion Act. The author notes the increase of non-therapeutic abortions and concludes that abortions performed for economic, social or eugenic purposes are inhumane and disrespectful of human life.

645 Calderone, Mary Steichen, ed. Abortion in the United States. New York: Hoeber, 1958. vii, 224 pp.

A report of a 1955 conference on illegal and therapeutic abortion sponsored by the Planned Parenthood Federation of America. Included are chapters on the background of the conference; abortion in the Scandinavian countries; legal aspects of abortion in the United States; illegal abortion in the United States (incidence, methods used, causes of death); therapeutic abortion in the United States; other aspects of the abortion problem (psychiatric, sociologic); and abortion and contraception. There are also five appendixes: abortion laws in the United States; birth control laws in the United States; abortion in Japan, Germany, U.S.S.R. and Finland; demographic characteristics of females interviewed by the Staff of the Institute for Sex Research, compared with the urban, white population; and bibliographies.

646 Calderone, Mary Steichen. "Illegal Abortion as a Public Health Problem," Amer. J. Public Health 50:948-ff., 1960.

Abortion must be recognized as a national public health problem, and a problem that merits more intensive investigation and attention than it has been given previously in the United States. A partial solution may lie in better contraceptive and sex education.

647 California. State Population Study Commission. Report to the Governor, 1966. Sacramento, 1966. x, 73 pp.

A number of recommendations focus on accelerating the pace by which family planning information and services actually reach Californians. The Commission devoted a substantial portion of its deliberations to three subjects: the merits of family life education in guiding young persons toward responsibility and mastery of their biological capabilities; the age and marital status of persons to whom contraceptives should be made available; and California's law on therapeutic (induced) abortion.

648 California. State Population Study Commission. Report to the Governor, 1967. Berkeley, California, 1967.

Recommendations regarding family planning services in the state and local communities.

649 Callahan, B. "AMA to Restudy Abortion Proposal," Hosp. Progr. 47:6-ff., 1966.

The abortion proposal of the AMA's Special Committee on Human Reproduction is reviewed, with references to the opposition from some AMA members, who contend that a re-examination of the Committee's recommendations is necessary. Reasons for such a re-examination include conflicting testimony, weakening of authority of state board of medical examiners, and the question of whether psychiatric indications are sufficient cause for abortion.

650 Callahan, Parnell J.T. The Law of Separation and Divorce. Dobbs Ferry (N.Y.): Oceana Publications, 1967.

Covers the laws of all the states of the United States with regard to common-law marriage, age at marriage with and without parental consent, prenuptial medical examination, the application for a license, and consanguinity between the potential spouses.

651 Callahan, Parnell J.T. New York's Divorce Law. New York: Oceana, 1966.

The author explains and describes New York's new divorce law which went into effect on September 1, 1967. After this date New York recognized grounds for divorce other than adultery, but expressed its distaste for out-of-state divorces by providing that a New York resident claiming the benefits of an out-of-state divorce must be absent from the state for a period of thirty months (twelve months before the divorce and eighteen months after the divorce). Included are sections on the old law; trial by jury; procedures under the new law; defense eliminated by the new law; commencement of the divorce action; special guardians; conciliation commissioners and conciliation counselors; procedure to obtain a divorce; temporary alimony, child support and counsel fees; remarriage after divorce; and agreements to obtain a divorce. The author also includes a glossary.

652 Callow, William G. "Teen-age Marriage, Misconduct and the Law," J. Amer. Bar Assn. 53:541-43. June 1967.

Young people who have not reached the age of consent for marriage and who engage in immoral conduct are faced with serious consequences under Wisconsin laws. After a brief description of the absolute age requirement for marriage and the provision on marriage with consent in Wisconsin, the author discusses the legal and social penalties for those involved in a marriage in which sufficient age has not been reached, with references to the penalty on persons who, ineligible to marry in Wisconsin, leave the state for the purpose of attempting to evade Wisconsin law and marry in another state, and the legal-social consequences of immoral conduct or irresponsible behavior, such as the statutory rape charge and the paternity suit.

653 Campbell, Arthur A. "Fertility and Family Planning Among Non-White Married Couples in the United States," Eugenic Quart. 12(3):124-31, 1965.

The rapid cultural change that the nonwhite population is undergoing has left its mark on fertility differences between whites and nonwhites. Nonwhite couples expect more births than do white couples, partly because of the unusually high fertility of a minority of nonwhites living in the rural south, and partly because of the moderately high fertility of the many nonwhite couples who have southern farm origins. Nonwhite couples with no rural southern background expect the same number of births as similar white couples. These data suggest that as the influence of southern rural patterns of mating and childbearing diminishes, the fertility differences between whites and nonwhites will decline. Nonwhite wives do not want as many children as they expect to have. A lower proportion of nonwhites than whites have used contraception, and nonwhites are less successfull in controlling fertility than are white couples. This seems to be true in all socioeconomic groups.

654 Campbell, Arthur A. "The Role of Family Planning in the Reduction of Poverty," J. Marr. Fam. 30(2):236-45. May 1968.

The costs of publicly supported family planning programs serving the population living in poverty in the United States are estimated to average $300 to prevent every unwanted birth that would otherwise have occurred, on the assumption that services for ten women at $30 each a year equal the avoidance of one unwanted birth. Over the years the prevention of an unwanted birth brings two major economic benefits -- avoiding the costs of child care and permitting the wife to work -- that, when discounted to the year in which the unwanted births were prevented, would be at least 26 times greater than the program costs.

655 Carver, M.A. "Therapeutic Abortion and Sterilization: Experience With Committee Control," Bull. Millard Fillmore Hosp. 8:43-ff., 1961.

Examined are the actions and operation , over the period 1957-1960, of the Committee on Abortion and Sterilization at Millard Fillmore Hospital, Buffalo, N.Y. Ninety-nine applications for abortion and/or sterilization were received during the three years and 80% of the cases were approved by the Committee. Twenty-six abortions were performed, with an abortion:delivery ratio of 1:623. Indications for the performed abortions included 58% psychiatric, 12% "fetomaternal" (rubella, Rh incompatability, etc.) and 12% cardiovascular. Reports issued by other hospitals are used for comparison.

656 Cassel, William J. "Family Planning Clinical Services are Increasing," California's Health 23(2):43-44. August 1965.

Notes on expansion in services provided by health departments or county hospitals in California between October, 1963 and July 1.

657 Center for Family Planning Program Development, Planned Parenthood-World Population. Need for Subsidized Family Planning Services: United States, Each State and County, 1968. Office of Economic Opportunity, 1969. 255 pp.

A systematic assessment of the adequacy of existing family planning programs in the United States and a summary by region, state, and county of the need for subsidized family planning services, current service levels, related health, social and demographic indices, and available resources for expansion of family planning programs.

658 "Changing Abortion Laws in the United States," J. Fam. Law 7:496-ff. Fall 1967.

An appeal to amend abortion laws, facts and consequences relating to present laws are reviewed: The majority of women who obtain abortions are married, with children, not "teenagers in trouble". Four states adopted liberalized abortion laws in 1967. Four of the remaining 46 states provide no statutory exceptions to general prohibitions against abortions. All but four states permit therapeutic abortion only where pregnancy endangers mother's life. The majority of laws do not distinguish between abortions performed by physicians and those performed by any person. There is much ambivalence about the validity and usefulness of laws against non-therapeutic or out-of-hospital abortions. Rarely is a conviction obtained and then it is usually a suspended sentence or fine. While ensoulment (life before birth) is a question of theology, not law, recent attempts to solve the abortion problem through legislation have been frustrated by pressures from the Catholic Church. Reviewing these facts, these conclusions are arrived at: The question is not whether to legalize abortion but when; that is, in which instances and under what circumstances will abortion be permitted; abortion should be a crime when performed by an individual who is not a duly licensed physician; abortion laws should be amended to enable physicians to treat the medical problem without fear, or threat of losing their licenses; to ensure that criminal abortion will not be the only means available to women in need of medical attention.

659 Chilman, Catherine S. "Fertility and Poverty in the United States: Some Implications for Family Planning Programs, Evaluation and Research," J. Marr. Fam. 30(2):207-27, 1968.

Population problems and family-planning attitudes in the United States are examined through an overview and analysis of national data and large bodies of related social and psychological research. Studies indicate that low-income families express favorable attitudes towards small family size and contraception. Certain groups tend to be ineffective family planners, especially those of southeastern rural residence or rural origins who possess less than an eighth grade education. Implications for program and policy are suggested, proposing needed research. It is suggested that family-planning programs, policies, and research should include equal considerations of males along with females and that they should be considered in dynamic context with the total family and social and economic factors.

660 Chilman, Catherine S., "Poverty and Family Planning in the United States," Welfare in Review 5(4):3-15. April 1967.

An overview and analysis of selected social and psychological research related to family planning and poverty reveals that: (1) at all socio-economic levels in this and other countries the average family desires between two and four children; (2) the arrival of the fourth child often precipitates a family crisis; (3) economic reasons are most often given for family size limitation; (4) poor people of rural residence or origins with little education are least likely to be effective family planners; and (5) this lack of effectiveness is related to ignorance, the conditions and frustrations of poverty, lack of available free services, and the life styles more typical of the very poor. While the newer contraceptives are more acceptable and usable for low-income groups, difficulties remain in terms of the above factors including the greater tendency for poor males and females to live in separate social psychological worlds and to regard each other with hostile, exploitative attitudes. The implications of related social and psychological research for family planning programs include: (a) the need for a comprehensive program approach that includes a consideration of social, psychological, and economic, as well as medical factors; (b) the use of a program team that includes physicians, nurses, social workers, and family life educators as well as trained and supervised "indigenous personnel;" (c) a family centered service that includes males as well as females; (d) a family planning program that is seen as but one strand in a network of services and programs that are indicated to help people move out of poverty; (e) further research, especially action studies related to the comparative costs and benefits of various program and service models.

661 Chilman, Catherine S., and Liu, William T. "Family Planning and Fertility Control," J. Marr. Fam. 30(2):189-366. May 1968.

Partial contents: Sussman, Marvin B. Editor's comments, pp. 189-90; Landman, Lynn. United States, underdeveloped land in family planning, pp. 191-201; Campbell, Arthur A. Population dynamics and family planning, pp. 202-6; Chilman, Catherine S. Fertility and poverty in the United States: some implications for family-planning programs, evaluation, and research, pp. 207-27; Jaffe, Frederick S., and Polgar, Steven. Family planning and public policy: is the "culture of poverty" the new cop-out?, pp. 228-35; Campbell, Arthur A. The role of family planning in the reduction of poverty, pp. 236-45; Hardin, Garrett. Abortion--or compulsory pregnancy?, pp. 246-51; Thimmesch, Nick. Puerto Rico and birth control, pp. 252-62; Potvin, Raymond H., et.al. Factors affecting Catholic wives' conformity to their church Magisterium's position on birth control, pp. 263-72.

662 Clark, Homer H. Jr. "Laws as an Instrument of Population Control," University Colorado Law Rev. 40:179-98. Winter 1968.

Sufficient evidence has accumulated to suggest the need for social controls to sharply and quickly reduce the birth rate in the U.S.A. The most obvious instrument of social control is the law. Yet, specific legal solutions are largely unavailable. Either they will be opposed by a large segment of the population, or they run counter to the conception of individual freedom, or they are likely to be unconstitutional. Only the most limited version of a statute, one which would make the necessary information and techniques available seem to have any chance of enactment.

663 Clark, Tom C. "Religion, Morality, and Abortion: A Constitutional Appraisal," Loyola University Law Rev. 2 (1969). Reprint.

There is disagreement among doctors, social scientists, and other groups as to the morality of abortions. Accommodation of conflicting doctrine is more difficult to achieve in the judicial than in the legislative process. Legislatures, on the other hand, have such facilities for investigation as hearings and may address themselves to the necessities of broad social needs and the correction of evils, both probable and existing. It is for the legislature to determine the proper balance, i.e., that point between prevention of conception and viability of the fetus which would give the State the compelling subordinate interest so that it may regulate or prohibit abortion without violating the individual's constitutionally protected rights.

664 Coale, Ansley. "Should the United States Start a Campaign for Fewer Births," Population Index 34(4):467-74. October 1968.

Discusses what policy on population might be appropriate in the United States and considers, within the national context, only policies directed toward influencing the growth of population, not its location or quality. The effectiveness of a policy of extended planned parenthood is reviewed, with an examination of ways to affect the number of children people want. Described also are some of the properties a good program should have and some of the pitfalls it must avoid. A major consideration is the effects the program might have other than on the birth rate. Preoccupation with population growth should not serve to justify measures more dangerous or of higher social cost than population growth itself. The author feels that an ideal policy would permit a maximum of individual freedom and diversity.

665 Coburn, Vincent P. "Homosexuality and the Invalidation of Marriage," Jurist 20:441-59. October 1966.

Although a complete survey of the incidence of homosexuality as a cause for ecclesiastical annulment in this country has not been undertaken, priests actively engaged in tribunal work indicate a greater and greater recurrence of cases involving homosexuality and marital problems. After a discussion of the varying definitions and classifications of homosexuality, the general theories as to its cause, and the difficulties connected to determining the extent and type of possible-actual homosexuality in premarital counseling, the author examines homosexuality from a moral viewpoint in terms of matrimonial obligations, ecclesiastical law, and the manner in which homosexuality might figure in cases for annulment. Explored, with special references to Canons 104 and 1092, are the nature of impotence and its relation to homosexuality and marriage, the characteristics of homosexuality which effect the intellect and the will, homosexuality as a mental disease, and the concept of premarital intention or the question of whether errors regarding personal identity equate with an invalid matrimonial contract. A list of pertinent Rota decisions since 1925 is included, as well as a brief corollary concerning the options of twenty-eight Catholic physicians who answered a questionnaire on homosexuality.

666 Cogen, Joel, and Feidelson, Kathryn. "Rental Assistance for Large Families: An Interim Report: New Haven's Low-Income Housing Demonstration," Pratt Planning Pas. 3:9-20. June 1964.

Government assistance with rent payments, to enable large-size, low-income families to find adequate space in privately owned housing; New Haven, Connecticut.

667 Cohen, Nathan E., and Connery, Maurice F. "Government Policy and the Family," J. Marr. Fam. 29(1):6-17. February 1967.

Proceeding from the premise that governmental policy inevitably reflects a position regarding the family as a social institute, an attempt is made to describe some of the current explicit and implicit components of this policy, as well as the factors which have contributed to its development. The changing role of the government is considered and the position is developed that government policy regarding the family should be made more visible and clearly articulated. Finally, some guidelines for the formulation of this policy as well as strategies for its realization are developed.

668 Cohen, Wilbur J. "Family Planning: One Aspect of Freedom to Choose," _Health, Education, and Welfare Indicators_, June 1966, pp. 1-16.

Report on current government policy and activities in the United States. Sections: Federal policy; Family planning research and training in the Department of Health, Education, and Welfare; Provision of family planning services; Family planning as an integral part of health, education, and welfare services.

669 Cohen, Wilbur J., "Freedom of Choice," _Stud. Fam. Planning_, No. 23, October 1967, pp. 2-5.

Reviews the contribution of the United States government to family planning through the Department of Health, Education, and Welfare; the Office of Economic Opportunity; and the Agency for International Development. Suggests additional efforts and research needs.

670 Coil, E.J. "Quality of Population as Necessary for National Defense," _J. Heredity_ 32(3):97-99, 1941.

The health of the industrial workers is as important in modern military activities as the health of the army. Present data indicate that the general health level in the population of the U.S. has not materially changed since 1918. Family allowances are recommended to help overcome the effects of the well-known inverse relationship between size of income and the number of children in the family. Another positive approach through the establishment of child welfare centers in every community is recommended. Each center should have a competent birth-control section.

671 Comfort, Alex. "Institutions Without Sex," Soc. Work 12(2): 107-8, 1967.

There is in U.S. culture a deep association between institutional good order and the exclusion of heterosexual intercourse. Jails are perhaps the archetype of the no-sex institution, because in our society the jail has an odd way of being the model for the institution generally.

672 "Congress May Approve First Birth Control Bill in 1966: Background; President's Positions; Legislation; Federal Programs," Cong. Quart. Weekly Rept. 24:1235-38. June 10 1966.

Developments leading up to increased federal activity in the area of birth control programs are viewed, with special mention of growing public support and a brief background on official attitudes and involvement in the past. There is a review of the Presidents' positions on the issue since Eisenhower and a discussion of policy since 1965, when the Johnson administration supported and endorsed birth control efforts and programs and recognized the need for a check on United States and world population growth. A history of pertinent legislation is given as well as descriptions of the major federal birth control programs carried out by HEW, OEO, Department of Interior and AID. The article concludes with a list of other recent developments concerning birth control, such as the official Catholic position and foreign and private efforts.

673 Connell, Elizabeth B., et al. "Growth and Development of a Family Planning Service at a Large Municipal Hospital," Amer. J. Public Health 57(8):1314-21, 1967.

In January 1964, the Family Planning Clinic at Metropolitan Hospital was officially opened, offering help to anyone wishing contraceptive advice. The hospital is a 1,000 bed municipal teaching institution of New York Medical College, located in the section of New York City known as Spanish Harlem. The area served by the hospital is one of economic deprivation, poor housing and low educational level. The growth and development of the clinic is described including clinic administrative and procedural organization. Abortions at the hospital declined from 1,175 in 1960 to 805 in 1966, deliveries from 4,360 to 3,100. The unrestricted contraceptive service is probably a contributing factor. The broader and currently unmet needs and objectives of the program as part of a total maternal and infant care service are discussed.

674 Connor, James E. "The Invalidity of Marriage in the Roman Catholic Church and the Civil Laws of the United States," Dissertation Abstr. 29A:4509, 1968-69. Abstract of J.C.D. Thesis, Catholic University of America, Washington, D.C., 1968. 458 pp.

As the title indicates, the purpose of this dissertation is to compare the legislation of the Roman Catholic Church with that of the fifty states of the United States and the District of Columbia in those areas of law which involve the validity or invalidity of marriage. With respect to the marriage laws of the Roman Catholic Church, consideration is given to (a) the competent authority in matters respecting marriage, (b) the nature of marriage, (c) the concept of valid and invalid marriages, (d) invalidating matrimonial impediments: in general and in particular, (e) defects of consent which invalidate marriage, (f) lack of juridical form, (g) marriage by proxy. In setting forth the civil laws of the United States, consideration is given to (a) the competent authority, (b) the nature of marriage, (c) valid, void and voidable marriages, (d) defects of consent which invalidate marriage, (e) lack of lawful officiant, (f) various circumstances which invalidate marriage, (g) common law marriage, (h) irregular solemnization, (i) marriage by proxy. Specific information is given regarding the marriage laws of each state and the District of Columbia in several appendices. Of special interest to canonists should be the dissertation's treatment of the concept of marriages which are "voidable" in American law. Not only is the ambiguity of the world alluded to, but it is pointed out that the term is not used univocally in all statutes or interpreted univocally by all courts. Consequently a warning is given against generalizations which would classify all "voidable" marriages as either valid or invalid in the canonical sense. Sources used in the exposition of the Church's marriage legislation include the Codex Iuris Canonici, Crebrae Allatae, recent decrees of the Holy See and numerous canonical commentaries. In setting forth the legislation of the several jurisdictions of the United States, use was made of the compiled statutes of the several jurisdictions, pertinent decisions of the State and Federal Courts, and commentaries on matrimonial law.

675 Cooper, George M., *et al*. "Four Years of Contraception as a Public Health Service in North Carolina," *Amer. J. Public Health* 31(12):1248-52, 1941.

Four years after the beginning of the state-wide contraceptive program under the North Carolina State Board of Health, pregnancy-spacing services have been provided for underprivileged women in 47 centers, serving 61 counties, which constitute 75% of those having health centers. In 1940 those receiving contraceptive instruction numbered 3,233, being approximately one out of every 100 married women of childbearing age, or about four out of every 100 underprivileged women in the area served by the health centers.

676 Corkey, Elizabeth Conrad. "A Family Planning Program for the Low Income Family," *J. Marr. Fam.* 26(4):478-80. November 1964.

A B C clinic has been conducted by the Charlotte Health Department since 1937. Since November 1960, an oral contraceptive has been made available free of charge to married and parous single low income females. Intrauterine devices are also being rapidly accepted. 5700 females of child bearing age in this community are medically indigent and will need this service when they reach their desired family size. Results of a study done in 1963 indicate that females in the clinic during its first two years averaged 4.8 children though the average number desired was stated to be between one and two. Several unanswered questions are posed regarding family stability as it may relate to limitation of family size.

677 Cornish, Mary Jean, *et al*. *Doctors and Family Planning*. New York: National Committee on Maternal Health, Inc., 1963. 100 pp.

In June 1937, the American Medical Association gave its official endorsement to birth control. Although some physicians had supported it, the medical profession had, officially, been less than cooperative in spite of Margaret Sanger's repeatedly expressed conviction that physicians should be responsible for providing contraceptive information and advice. The present study is based on the interviewing of 551 practising physicians in 1957 to discover just what role was in fact played by the doctors twenty years later. The first general theme is that the extent and kind of family planning information depends on what a patient requests and on what each doctor believes appropriate rather than on any definition by the profession of what a doctor should do.

678 Corsa, Leslie. "United States: Public Policy and Programs in Family Planning," Stud. Fam. Planning, No. 27, March 1968, pp. 1-4.

The principal issue in the United States now is the priority of family planning for public sector support (i.e., the level of family planning expenditures relative to public need and to total public expenditures). Because of its great centralized taxing power, through the income tax, and its ability to equalize economic differences among the states, the role of the federal government in financing services is vital. While the United States waits for its organization and financing of medical care for the poor to catch up with that of Western Europe, perhaps this country can learn from some of the developing nations that it is possible to equalize opportunity for family planning for all citizens despite inadequate health services. This is one national deficiency we should wait no longer to correct.

679 Coughlan, Robert. "World Birth Control Challenge," Life 47(21):159-76. November 22 1959.

The magnitude of the problem of world population growth and possible approaches to its solution are at last being put before the general public of the U.S. in detail. After a summary of the evidence that improved mortality conditions now make birth control an 'inescapable necessity', two issues are considered: whether a satisfactory method will be available in time; and whether religious and social customs will permit its acceptance. All in all, the chances seem to favor a positive answer to both questions. This leaves the question of how to focus science, public policy, and individual behavior on the solution of the population problem. It is implied that the preservation of Western beliefs, including those of Christianity, will be rendered more likely if U.S. foreign aid programs include assistance in the area of population control.

680 Coughlin, John J. "Sterilization in Oregon," Northwest Med. 66:966-67, 973. October 1967.

The article is concerned with the legal problems and questions surrounding compulsory and voluntary sterilization in Oregon. Senate Bill 344 is described and analyzed in terms of its constitutionality and provisions. The possible grounds of physician liability are listed, along with the conditions of and a suggested form for consent.

681 "Criminal Law -- Abortion -- the 'Morning-After Pill' and Other Pre-Implantation Birth-Control Methods and the Law," Oregon Law Rev. 46:211-ff. Fall 1967.

The author begins by discussing the experimental "morning-after" birth-control pill, which prevents implantation of the fertilized ovum or zygote on the wall of the uterus, as opposed to the "pill-intercourse" sequence of birth-control pills presently in use, which prevents the occurrence of ovulation. Since the new retro-active pill can be taken as late as six days after intercourse, control of fertility involves the termination of pregnancy after conception but before implantation. The author continues by describing the legality, under current abortion laws, of terminating pregnancy between conception and implantation; the language of current abortion laws is felt to be broad enough to include the sanction or condemnation of pre-implantation methods of birth-control. The author divides the abortion statutes in the U.S. into two main categories: those which expressly make pregnancy an element of the offense and those which do not. Each category is broken down in terms of its typical language and the author presents two or three statutes representative of each type for analysis and interpretation. The author concludes that the legislatures and courts must come to a decision in regard to public use of the "morning-after" pill and its relation to abortion statutes and/or overpopulation problems. The author supports the contention that destruction of a fertilized ovum before implantation is hardly distinguishable from other commonly used contraceptive methods today.

682 "Criminal Law -- Abortion -- the New North Carolina Abortion Statute," North Carolina Law Rev. 46:585-ff. April 1968.

The North Carolina General Assembly substantially amended, in 1967, the state's therapeutic abortion laws by adopting essentially intact, the provisions of the American Law Institute's Model Penal Code relating to abortion and kindred offenses. By this enactment, the range of circumstances under which physicians may legally terminate pregnancies was expanded significantly. The new justifications include threat to life or grave danger to health of the pregnant woman; substantial risk of grave physical or mental defects for the child; or pregnancy as a result of rape or incest. The author considers briefly the essential provisions of the new amendments, and concludes that even with the broadest interpretation of the new law, abortion may not now be had in North Carolina for the sake of mere convenience, or on the basis of a woman's desire not to have a child. Very specific evidence, supported by the opinion of three physicians, is needed to justify an abortion. It would appear that this narrowness of purpose will cause the new law to have only the most minimal effects upon criminal abortion, even though the statute would seem to place the state in the vanguard of abortion reform in the U.S.

683 "Criminal Law: Prosecution of Adultery and Bigamy in Oklahoma," Oklahoma Law Rev. 14:203. May 1961.

Oklahoma has two basic statutes dealing with bigamy, both before and after divorce, and one dealing with adultery. The author describes the legislative development of the divorce-bigamy statute since 1921, with references to the 1925 and 1957 amendments, the criminal aspects of bigamy, and problems of enforcement, particularly in regard to the bigamy statute. Since the only sanction available to the state for enforcement of its bigamy laws is prosecution for adulter, the prerequisite conditions for such prosecution are outlined and the question of what constitutes "open and notorious" adultery is examined. The author concludes with the hope that the Oklahoma legislature will either apply the remedial procedures to the bigamy statute as it has already done to the divorce-bigamy statute, or that it will alleviate the almost impossible burden of proving open and notorious adultery so that the state can effectively prosecute persons cohabiting bigamously and/or adulterously.

684 Curran, W.J. "Privacy, Birth Control and 'An Uncommonly Silly Law'," New England J. Med. 273:322-ff, 1965.

A report of the U.S. Supreme Court decision declaring unconstitutional the Connecticut statute barring the use of contraceptive devices or drugs on the grounds that the statute invaded the "right of privacy" protected by the Constitution. The author speculates that this decision may, in the future, affect other medicolegal issues. For a state to prohibit abortions or sterilization of married women may well be some day considered a similar breach of the privacy of the marriage relationship.

685 Custis, Douglass L. "Sex Laws in Ohio: A Need for Revision," University Cinncinati Law Rev. 35:211-41. Spring 1966.

Perhaps no area of the law is so concerned with the regulation of private conduct as that which attempts to control sexual behavior. In general, it can be said that our society has eschewed the idea that all "immoral" sex conduct should be subject to the criminal law. But, beyond this there seems to be a great deal of ambivalence inherent in the contemporary approach to regulating sexual conduct. The author attempts to demonstrate that the laws governing sex conduct form an important but incoherent part of our legal framework and are enacted with more heat than light, making enforcement haphazard. They should, therefore, be generally revised. Further examination is limited to the laws of Ohio, and such laws are grouped in the categories of rape, statutory rape, exhibitionism, sodomy, incest, adultery and fornication and the so-called habitual offender act. Some problems in penal administration and the area of sex-psychopath laws are also examined, as well as some general characteristics of the sex offender.

686 Dahlberg, C.C. "Abortion," pp.379-93 in Slovenko,R., ed. Sexual Behavior and the Law. Springfield, Ill.: Charles C. Thomas, 1965.

Author discusses the problem of abortion with respect to four classes of potential abortion cases: single women; divorced or widowed women; married women after accidental pregnancy; and women with medical contraindications. The consequences of bearing an unwanted child are shown to be widespread when compared to the minimal effects of legal abortions. Liberal legislation as in the Scandinavian countries should be adopted as the most practical method of avoiding misinterpretation of the law.

687 Davies, Vernon. "Fertility Versus Welfare: the Negro American Dilemma," Phylon 27(3):226-32. Fall 1966.

Survey statistics on fertility trends of whites and nonwhites, 1850-1960, and on variations of nonwhite fertility by region and rural-urban residence in 1960. Proposes population control program for rural Negroes in the South.

688 Davis, Clarice M. "Common-Law Marriage in Texas," Southwestern Law J. 21(3):647-63. Fall 1967.

Texas is one of the few U.S. states which still recognizes common-law marriage as legal if a man and woman live together and hold themselves out to the public as being married. Recently, however, it has been suggested that Texas should follow the rule of most states by statutorily abolishing common-law marriage. In this context, the institution of common-law marriage, its historical origins, its legal requirements, the advantages and disadvantages of abolishing it, and alternative devices which could be substituted for it are investigated. A number of rulings in Texas court cases involving common law marriages are discussed. Under Texas law a common-law widow is legally entitled to workmen's compensation benefits upon the death of her husband, can inherit from her husband under the laws of interstate succession, and is entitled to be administratrix of her husband's estate. She is entitled to temporary support from her husband pending divorce and is entitled to 50% of their common property in case of divorce. A woman who enters a common-law marriage in good faith with no knowledge that an impediment exists acquires the rights of a putative wife if the marriage should turn out to be invalid. Modified legal acceptance of common-law marriages existing in New Hampshire, Oregon, Tennessee, Virginia is examined. It is concluded that continued recognition, with statutory regulation of the abuses, appears to be advisable.

689 Davis, Kingsley, and Blake, Judith. "Birth Control and Public Policy," Commentary 29(2):115-21. February 1960.

The authors analyze the questions of civil liberty and church-state relations in this country as they connect to the tensions and misconceptions surrounding the Catholic birth control issue, brought to the surface in 1959, when Catholic bishops in the United States attacked the idea of

American money going to assist underdeveloped countries in lowering their birth rates. Discussed are several surveys which have shown repeatedly that a surprising number of Catholics favor the use of birth control methods other than the technically problematic and unreliable rhythm method and the increasing pressures facing today's Catholic, who is often forced by his clergy to choose between loyalty to country and its democratic values and loyalty to Church doctrine. Reports and studies are cited in a discussion of the misapprehension in regard to the attitudes of people in underdeveloped countries toward birth control, and the inadequacies of the Catholic bishops' alternatives for birth control, i.e., economic development and migration are viewed. The authors conclude that the main issue, over and above foreign involvement, is that of avoiding division within the United States, which will continue to grow unless the individual consciences of Catholic laymen restrain the clergy from equating doctrine with law and public policy.

690 Day, Lincoln H., and Day, Alice T. Too Many Americans. Boston: Houghton Mifflin, 1964. xii, 298 pp.

This book enumerates the reasons why early attainment of population stability in the United States would be in the best interest of Americans, and discusses how, given the predominant values of American culture, this goal might best be achieved. It includes a general discussion of those religious and secular beliefs and values that seem most influential in shaping American attitudes toward family building and population control. It also discusses the arguments against cessation of population growth in the United States.

691 DeMallie, Bayard T. "Sodomy Between Husband and Wife - Grounds for Divorce?" J. Fam. Law 3:124-37. Spring 1963.

A review of the English law pertaining to sodomy as a special ground for divorce demonstrates how judicial interpretation can unecessarily create bad law. The author feels that the United States should benefit from the British experience. The presence of sodomy as a separate ground for divorce is justified when limited to homosexuality or unnatural acts with third parties. The author urges divorce laws to be revised similar to those suggested in the Wolfenden Report and the Model Penal Code. This would permit divorce for perverted acts to which the complaining spouse was not a party and which resulted in a morally and legally offensive situation; however, it would not permit divorce to the petitioner, who irrespective of his consent, was an accomplice to the acts presently termed objectionable and who seeks a divorce solely on those acts. The author advocates that the courts of Alabama, North Carolina and Virginia adopt a similar approach to the divorce law.

692 Dembitz, Nanette. "Law and Family Planning," Fam. Law Quart. 1:103-13. December 1967.

In light of the contention that basic to the resolution of the social and economic problems involved in family planning is determination of the applicable legal principles, the views of the Committee on Law and Family Planning (Section of Family Law -- American Bar Association) on law and family planning are reported, for the assistance of the Bar, Government agencies, and the general public. Part I deals with current public concern over family planning, and includes discussions of the ignorance of the poor as to the availability of family planning, protection against coercion as stated in the statutes, rules and directives recently adopted to facilitate dissemination of birth control information, the function of juvenile and family courts, and measures for the encouragement of family planning. Part II deals briefly with the wide-spread changes in decisional and statutory law in regard to restrictions on dissemination of birth control information or distribution of birth control devices and the fact that scarcely any legislative limitations remain in effect. Part III deals with current issues respecting effectuation of the right to free choice as to family planning, with references to the need of the poor for information on the possibility of family planning, eligibility criteria for birth control information (adults and minors), and the role of the attorney. Part IV consists of six general recommendations, submitted with the entire report to the ABA House of Delegates for consideration in 1968.

693 Dembitz, Nanette, et al. "Report of American Bar Association on Law and Family Planning," J. Amer. Med. Wom. Assn. 23:173-79. February 1968.

In light of the legal developments as to family planning, and the recognition of the right to individual freedom of choice with respect thereto, as well as the right of the impoverished to equality with the affluent in the exercise of basic freedoms -- it is recommended that: (1) Workers in public welfare departments as well as others in contact with the poor be authorized to initiate discussion of the availability of family planning and birth control in order to overcome the ignorance on this matter found to be associated with poverty. (2) In all discussions and all referrals for birth control assistance, the individual's moral and religious convictions be respected. (3) Protection against any coercion to use birth control, through an explicit or implicit threat of any curtailment of public assistance or any public benefit, be assured. (4) Discussion be initiated with any adult under appropriate circumstances; and in special situations, after consideration of individual circumstances, with minors as well. (5) Those rendering counseling, probation, psychiatric, or medical services in the juvenile and family courts be authorized to initiate discussions of family planning in appropriate cases, because of its pertinence to the problems treated in those courts. (6) Positive steps to encourage family planning and birth control be taken to avert the birth of illegitimate children and when either parent has been found responsible for abusing or neglecting his children, provided however that no economic threat or any type of condemnation be employed because such measures would tend to result in a child's rejection and damage. (7) Attorneys become aware of the availability of family planning, because of the possibility that their clients might find it helpful in situations of domestic difficulty.

694 "Desperate Dilemma of Abortion," Time, 13 October 1967, p. 32.

Essay on abortion law reform. Terminations of unwanted pregnancies will occur whether or not abortion is legalized, and piecemeal reform of existing laws on abortion will not provide the enormous number of abortions desired by women today. The abortion problem might be alleviated by making information on birth control more available, increasing the amount of financial aid for families, and allowing the physician to play a greater role in advising and assisting the woman with an unwanted pregnancy.

695 "Deviate Sexual Behavior Under the New Illinois Criminal Code," Washington University Law Quart. April 1965. pp. 220-35.

The five major problem areas of the old (prior to 1961) Illinois statute on deviate sexual behavior are outlined: lack of definition or notice that conduct in a particular situation was illegal; uneven enforcement; the offender's liability to blackmail; the creation of serious guilt feelings in the offender; and the problem of penalizing uncontrollable deviate behavior. The new Illinois statute attempts to solve the above problems by clearly defining terms and clarifying the language and content of the various criminal law sections.

696 Diamond, P.A. "Negative Taxes and the Poverty Problem - A Review Article," _Nat. Tax J._ 21:288-303. September 1968.

This review raises issues central to the choice of negative taxes as stated in _Negative Taxes and the Poverty Problem_ (1967) a book by Christopher Green. (Green includes, incidently, a discussion of the problem of incentives for family planning.) Several possible programs are considered: (1) lump-sum transfer; (2) proportional negative income taxes; and (3) non-proportional negative income taxes. The author concludes that some form of negative income tax would be an extremely valuable addition to our social legislation. Put in its simplest form, the case for such an addition is inherent in a listing of the major defects of our current welfare system.

697 Dienes, Charles T. "Conceptualizing Interactive Behavior Toward Legal Change: Perspectives on Birth Control and Artificial Insemination," _Dissertation Abstr._ 29A:2730, 1968-69. Abstract of Ph.D. Thesis, Northwestern University, Evanston, Illinois, 1968. 556 pp.

The basic purpose of this study is to formulate a conceptual framework for analyzing and evaluating the manner in which the legislature and the judiciary respond to changing social conditions. These legal actors are perceived as elements in a _system of action_ -- a coordinated, functioning whole made up of a set of interrelated, interacting parts. Legal action, the product of these interactions, in turn, influences the environment to which these actors respond. An attempt is made to delineate the manner in which social problems are communicated to the legal actors, the process through which they react (a decision-making model based on the writings of Richard Snyder and Harold Lasswell is used), and the role of decisional outputs as inputs for subsequent social and legal behavior. Part I involves the construction of the conceptual framework utilizing six propositions indicating the interactions which take place between the two legal actors. Part II seeks to apply the framework to two substantive areas of inquiry: (1) the changing status of laws relating to the dissemination of birth control services; (2) the legal problems posed by artificial insemination by donor (AID). The former focuses on legal policy formation in the national jurisdiction and in New York, Connecticut and Massachusetts, i.e., where the most extensive legislative and judicial interaction has occurred from the enactment of restrictive laws in the latter part of the nineteenth century to their recent demise. There is also a chapter devoted to the newly-emerging problem of publicly-supported birth control.

698 Dienes, Charles T. "Moral Beliefs and Legal Norms: Perspectives on Birth Control," St. Louis University Law J. 11:536-69. Summer 1967.

In attempting to deal with the proper relation of conscience, obligation and law, writers are forced to confront severe problems of freedom and authority facing our society. Numerous questions are posed by the intersection of law and morality in the civil law. The author inquires further into the proper relation among the above factors by applying selected jurisprudential thought, both Catholic and non-Catholic, to a modern social problem. More particularly, the competing jural considerations that might be applied to the continuing controversy over the proper legal status to be accorded contraceptive services are indicated and the jural analysis focuses on two central problems: (1) the extent to which moral beliefs may properly be embodied in legal norms, and (2) the right, obligation and prudential judgments involved in opposing a law which violates conscience. Examined are: law in support of the moral consensus (imposition by the majority of its moral beliefs on a minority), law opposed to the moral consensus (right of a dissenting minority to use law to impose its beliefs on the majority), demands of conscience and resistance to law, and applications to birth control (the controversy over the use of public funds for the dissemination of birth control services and an outline of the manner through which government became involved and the present extent of its involvement). Excellent sections on the birth control controversy: contrasting Catholic positions, financial funding problems, government policy, basic ethical questions, and the problem itself: two primary issues -- the need to assure equality of access to birth-control services and the effect of continuing population expansion on the quality of American life, differential fertility patterns among differing socio-economic classes, racial justice, etc. Two problems, indigency and population, have provided the case for government's entrance into the family planning field.

699 Dingle, J.T., and Tietze, Christopher. "Comparative Study of Three Contraceptive Methods: Vaginal Foam Tablets, Jelly Alone, and Diaphragm with Jelly or Cream," Amer. J. Obstet. Gynec. 85:1012-22. April 1963.

The use-effectiveness of three contraceptive methods was studied in a low socio-economic-status clinic population. Excluding the months of use during postpartum amenorrhea, the pregnancy rate as calculated by Pearl's formula was 22.5 per 100 woman-years of use for (1) the foam tablet, 24.0 for (2) the jelly alone, and 14.5 for (3) the diaphragm contraceptive method. Omissions or incorrect use were responsible for a majority of the pregnancies. The failure rate for each prescribed contraceptive method was higher during the first six months of use than during later months. This study demonstrated reasonable effectiveness and acceptability for (1) and (2) as contraceptive methods. Therefore, the suitability of these simple contraceptive methods, especially (1), for large scale family planning programs is suggested.

700 "Dispensing of Birth Control Information, Devices and Medications in College Health Services," J. Amer. Coll. Health Assn. 16:233-35. February 1968.

458 institutional members of the American College Health Association were sent questionnaires concerning their policies on the dispensing of birth control information, devices and medications; 338 (73.8%) completed the questionnaires, with 15 all-male college returns excluded from the final report. Of the 323 colleges remaining, 143 (44.28%) will dispense contraceptives to married students, 13 (4%) to unmarried students over 21, and 12 (3.6%) to unmarried students under 21. 28 (8.6%) will prescribe contraceptives for pre-marital purposes, 35 (10.8%) for medical reasons, and 246 (76.1%)will not prescribe for any purpose for

unmarried students. Comments were received from a substantial number of health services, and these are summarized. Those services which do not prescribe "the pill" for contraceptive purposes feel that this is not an appropriate responsibility of a college health service. Most indicated, however, that they offer a program of sex education and premarital counseling, but that those who request contraceptive drugs or devices are referred to private physicians and specialists. Those health services which prescribe "the pill" for contraceptive purposes felt that contraceptive drugs were like any other drug and that prescribing them was a matter of individual judgment and responsibility between the patient and her physician. A number of services in this category reported that a public policy on contraception was undesirable.

701 "Divorce - American Style: Another Legal Profession Cancer," New York State Bar J. 39:501-14. December 1967.

Contents: New York's new divorce law, particularly as it affects Mexican divorces and the so-called September 1st, 1967 "deadline" by Jason R. Berke and Morris Plosowe.

702 "Divorce Reform in New York, Harvard J. Legis. 4:149-60. December 1966.

The 1967 statutory amendments, which added several new grounds for divorce in New York and established a conciliation bureau to work with the courts in the individual divorce actions, are outlined and evaluated. Attention is given to major features of the new amendments, and the provision on conciliation is described in terms of its deficiencies, benefits,and the problems of compulsory counseling, with suggestions for future changes.

703 Dixon, Robert G., Jr., *et al*. "Symposium on the Griswold Case and the Right of Privacy," Michigan Law Rev. 64:197-288. December 1965.

The principle of an affirmative right of access to birth control information is discussed in regard to the recent case of *Griswold v. Connecticut*. Support for this principle may be founded jointly on the first amendment and on the new constitutionally recognized "penumbral" right of marital privacy. Additional support might be gained from the ninth amendment 'other right' of private self-help and self-control regarding an intimate sphere of private life.

704 "Domestic Relations --Conflict of Laws-- Marriage of First Cousins" [In re Mortenson's Estate (Ariz.) 316 P 2d 1106], South Carolina Law Quart. 10:505-ff. Spring 1958.

Under Arizona statute, marriages by parties of designated degrees of consanguinity are "incestuous and void"; therfore marriage between persons who are first cousins and who are residents of Arizona are void even though the marriage was solemnized in New Mexico where first cousin marriages are permitted. The prohibition of marriage of persons in direct lineal consanguinity is traced from early Christendom and Roman law through the English law to United States laws. Among the states there is considerable controversy over first cousin marriages and particularly with regard to whether they are void or voidable. A recent development in some states is the enactment of statutes which make such marriages void ab initio but make offspring of void marriages legitimate.

705 "Domestic Relations -- Effect of Remarriage on Prior Decree of Divorce Providing for Alimony Payment " [Bean v. Bean (RI) 134 A 2d 146], Boston University Law Rev. 38:152-ff. Winter 1958.

The author discusses a general misconception on the part of many laymen, that their obligation to continue to make alimony payments, which are in the nature of a common law obligation of support, is terminated immediately on remarriage of the divorced wife. The actual fact remains that, in absence of statute, or express judicial decision, the obligation to pay continues, and the remarriage of the wife does not operate ipso facto to put an end to the husband's liability. The questions and problems facing the courts in considering the effect of remarriage of a wife upon the continuance of alimony are described, with references to legislative enactments in Rhode Island and public policy rationale.

706 "Domestic Relations -- Separation -- Wife's Unjustified Refusal to Have Sexual Relations Held Constructive Abandonment -- Improper Designation of Grounds Not Fatal to Pleadings " [Diemer v. Diemer (NY) 168 N E 2d 654], New York Law Rev. 7:113-ff. February 1961.

In reversing a decision of the Appellate Division, the New York Court of Appeals held that a wife's refusal to have sexual relations with her husband until he participated in a religious ceremony was tantamount to abandonment and justified a decree of separation. The theory of the Heermance case, that an abandonment (statuatory grounds for judicial separation) can take place without physical separation. "The refusal of husband or wife to have ordinary marriage relations with the other strikes at the basic obligations springing from the marriage contract when viewed from the State and society at large. The mere fact that the law provides that physical incapacity for sexual relationship shall be grounds for annulling a marriage is of itself a sufficient indication of the public policy that such relationship shall exist with the result and for the purpose of begetting offspring."

707 "Domestic Relations: A Symposium," Vanderbilt Law Rev. 9:593-ff. June 1956.

Contents: The Law of Infants' Marriages, R. Kingsley; Marriage in the conflict of laws, C.W. Taintor, II; The law of divorce and the problem of marriage stability, M. Rheinstein; Divorce litigation and the welfare of the family, J.S. Bradway; Divorce - a suggested approach with particular reference to dissolution for living separate and apart, W.E. McCurdy; Support rights and duties between husband and wife, M.G. Paulsen; The law of adoption: Ancient and modern, L.A. Huard; Model will, with explanatory comments, of the father of a closely-knit family group, designed to minimize family estate and income taxes, W.J. Bowe; Bankruptcy from a family law perspective, G.S. Joslin; Family responsibility in tort, W.J. Harbison; Personal torts within the family, V. Sanford.

708 Donahue, John F., et al., "The Status of Illegitimates in New England," Boston University Law Rev. 38:299-315. Spring 1958.

The illegitimate's rights, privileges and disabilities in the New England states are outlined in relation to the transition from early common laws in these states concerning illegitimacy to present rules, since many of the common law regulations have either been changed or modified by statutes. Discussed are determination and presumption of illegitimacy, obligation of the parents (custody and control versus duty to support), the statutory bastardy proceeding, the illegitimate's right to receive property, and the conflict of laws problem or the question of what law is to control in certain areas. Pertinent court cases are cited, and the varying attitudes and statutes of the different states are reviewed.

709 Donnelly, R.C., and Ferber, W.L. "The Legal and Medical Aspects of Vasectomy," J. Urology 81(2):259-63. February 1959.

The authors focus primarily upon non-institutional sterilizations done as a therapeutic measure. It is contended that in states not specifically permitting therapeutic sterilitions the courts would look with favor on such an operation if a physician should become involved in a legal proceeding when the sterilization was performed on solid medical grounds. The case of Christensen v. Thornby (Minnesota Supreme Court, 1934) is cited as an example, and the authors use analogies from other fields of the law that point the same way. Some medical indications and aspects of therapeutic sterilizations when they are legal and not contrary to public policy are outlined, as well as the procedure that should be followed when the operation is indicated. The authors feel that physicians have been too timid and cautious in not taking a strong stand for a broad and humane interpretation of such terms as "medical necessity" and "sound therapeutic reasons." In addition, the legal aspects and basic issues of sterilization for contraceptive purposes alone are briefly considered, with references to the problem of recanalization and divorce cases involving sterilizations of convenience. A list of legal and medical conclusions is included.

710 Donovan, John A.K. "The Virginia Voluntary Sterilization Act of 1962," Soc. Order 13(4):38-40. April 1963.

Sterilization is being increasingly advocated as a method of attacking such problems as mental illness, illegitimacy, burgeoning relief rolls, the population explosion, etc. The Voluntary Sterilization Act was adopted by the Virginia General Assembly during its regular 1962 session. This act provides that any person who has the consent of the spouse, has received a reasonable explanation from a physician, and completed a 30-day waiting period, can, by merely expressing the desire, be sterilized. This radical change is seemingly abhorrent to the principles of Anglo-American legal jurisprudence because it allows, without legal and/or medical causes, the voluntary sterilization of the human male and female. Virginia is the first jurisdiction in the English-speaking world to make such legislative provision. Sterilization is compulsory in 23 states, voluntary in two. The justification for the operation is that the person concerned is defective. Operations under compulsory statutes are decided by medical opinion; under the voluntary statutes, usually by the consent of a committee or a guardian. Experience under the Virginia Act of 1924 shows that Virginia, with 6,811 operations, has the highest per cent even though more sterilization (19,998), took place in California. Against this background, the Act of 1962 is alarming. It is objectionable on legal, moral, ethical, practical, medical and constitutional grounds. Each one is sufficient to bar consideration of establishing the Act as a valid precedent.

711 Dorsey, Joseph L. "Changing Attitudes Toward the Massachusetts Birth-Control Law," New England J. Med. 271:823-27. October 15, 1964.

Massachusetts and Connecticut remain the only states with laws that effectively make it a criminal offense to sell, distribute or advertise a contraceptive. The author gives a brief historical outline of the birth control controversy in Massachusetts and describes several test cases involving the state's law on contraception. The 1942 and 1948 referenda to amend the law are discussed, with references to the arguments for reform led by the Parenthood League of Massachusetts, the Catholic anti-reform movement, motives of the proponents of each side, and reasons, primarily political, for the defeat of the two referenda. The current situation and attitudes are described in terms of non-observance of the law by physicians, Catholic attitude changes, and the fact that today there is not a consensus against contraception, although the Massachusetts law remains a source of intellectual disagreement and emotional friction. The author concludes with a discussion of methods by which change might occur and bitterness of or division among Catholics be avoided.

712 Dr. X., The Abortionist. New York: Doubleday, 1962.

The author, a physician-abortionist, describes his thirty years of practice and the 25,000 abortions he performed during this time. He recommends that there is a need for wider indications in regard to therapeutic abortions and stresses the role special hospital committees should play in the decision-making process.

713 Drinan, Robert F. "The Inviolability of the Right to be Born," in: Smith D.T., ed. Abortion and the Law. Cleveland: Western Reserve University Press, 1967.

Allowing abortion on the grounds of preserving the mother's life or fetal defect undermines, according to the author, the unborn child's basic right of life. Terminations of pregnancy on such grounds equate with the promotion of one individual's health or happiness while denying even the chance for health or happiness to another.

714 Drinan, Robert F. "Loving [Loving v. Virginia, 87 Sup Ct 1817] Decision and the Freedom to Marry," Ohio State Law J. 29:358-98. Spring 1968.

The United States Supreme Court has recently entered the area of marriage control by holding that a Virginia anti-miscegenation statute violated constitutionally-protected rights. The author traces the meaning of this decision through the maze of state regulatory systems, reaching some conclusions and proposals and illustrating the need for a total rethinking of the role of the state in marriage regulations.

715 Droegemueller, William E., et al. "The First Year of Experience with the New Abortion Law," Amer. J. Obstet. Gynec. 103(5):694-702. 1 March 1969.

In April 1967 Colorado became the first state to enact a modernized abortion law. Equally available and applicable to all socio-economic groups, the law provides the reasons for which and the conditions under which abortions may legally take place. After its first year in effect, 72 per cent of the legal abortions performed in Colorado were for psychiatric reasons, followed in frequency by fetal indications, rape, and physical health of the mother.

716 Dubin, L. "The Antiquated Abortion Laws," Temple Law Quart. 34:146-ff., 1961.

Referring specifically to lack of legal definition of permissible circumstances for therapeutic abortion in the Pennsylvania Abortion Law, this article suggests that legislature should be informed of the medical, fetal, and psychiatric indications. Recommendation of the proposed statute of the American Law Institute - Modern Penal Code is given as a legislative act which will clarify and liberalize the abortion law.

717 Dudley, Florence C., and Allan, William. "Mating Customs in North Carolina," J. Heredity 33(9):331-32. September 1942.

Two samples of the population in North Carolina were studied to determine people's marriage customs in order to formulate eugenic programs. Both populations examined, the Mecklenburg Congregation and the Three Forks Baptist Congregations are composed of the descendants of immigrants from the British Isles and Germany. They differ only in length of time that they have inhabited the areas. Background history of the foundations of these two communities is given as well as figures on the marriages recorded within the separate groups. However, very little is known regarding the size of mating isolates in other parts of the country, and until such knowledge is available, it is hardly possible to assess the conditions given for North Carolina as being representative.

718 Durbin, Winfield T. "Tax Considerations in Marriage, Separation, and Divorce Settlements," University Illinois Law Rev., Fall 1955, pp. 489-533.

Since marriage is a relationship with important income, estate and gift tax consequences, any alteration of the relationship creates tax consequences also of drastic importance. The author's purpose is to clarify and put in order the difficult and confusing tax considerations involved in marriage, separation and divorce settlements. Some attention is paid to matters of substantive law, because of the interaction between substantive law and tax law and the fact that tax objectives can only be sought in the framework of what is permissible under local law. Major sections include: income tax status before decree of divorce or separate

maintenance; property transfers in separation and divorce; tax and local law problems in setting up separation and divorce settlements; whether periodic payments must be for support; child support payments; dependency exemptions and head-of-household status; periodic payments, payments of a principal sum, and installment payments; trust and annuity payments; and tax problems in the use of life insurance in divorce settlements. The author concludes with suggestions for amendments to the 1954 Internal Revenue Code.

719 Dykstra, John W. "The United States and Population Control Programs," Popul. Rev. 6(1):65-68. January 1962.

This paper represents an effort to summarize some of the factors behind the American government's reluctance to act on the urgent matter of providing assistance for population-control programs abroad.

720 Edwards, Angell. "Legal Status of Artificial Insemination: An Opinion by Legal Counsel of the Society," Rhode Island Med. J. 42:668-70. October 1959.

There is no statutory or case law on artificial insemination in Rhode Island. Elsewhere, too, it is so new that it has not acquired any settled legal status. Only four or five cases in other jurisdictions have gotten to the courts but none of them went to the highest court. Therefore, comment is made on only some of the consequences which might follow when a child is born by virtue of artificial insemination. The consequences, which are discussed, are criminal or civil and will depend on whether the insemination is accomplished with the husband's sperm (AIH) or with the sperm of a third party (AID). The criminal consequences include adultery, fornication, forgery, and accessory. The civil ones are illegitimacy, negligence and malpractice, and divorce.

721 Edwards, Olivia Corbett, and Ring, Abraham Eric. "A Demonstration Project on Fertility Control," Dissertation Abstr. 26:2572-73, 1965. Abstract of Ed. D. Thesis, Columbia University, New York, New York, 1964. 132 pp.

The purpose of this demonstration project was to determine whether the small group discussion method could effect a change in the contraceptive behavior patterns of working class Negro mothers. Additional objectives of the study were to develop effective recruitment and retainment procedures for this target population and to identify specific barriers to purposive family planning. All personal data were classified under thirty-six items. The data obtained in the pre-group home interviews and in the group meetings were examined to determine the Obstacles to Fertility Control. Nine obstacles were identified in the target population and were classified under three Primary Categories: Knowledge and Beliefs, Sexual Attitudes, and Values and Motivation with Respect to Family Planning. Statements made by the respondents were rated and analyzed in these three Primary Categories. Four secondary categories were also selected for analysis: Verbal Participation, Group Attendance, Number of Children (Family Size), and Educational Level. The three Primary and the four Secondary Categories were analyzed with respect to degree of Contraceptive Change. The leader behavior was evaluated by description and analysis of the leaders' roles in each group.

722 Ehrmann, Winston. "Changing Sexual Mores," pp. 53-70 in: Ginzberg, Eli, ed. Values and Ideals of American Youth New York: Columbia University Press, 1961. 323 pp.

A discussion of the sexual attitudes and behavior of adolescents, presenting a discussion of: (1) the cultural and historical setting of sexual mores in the United States, (2) the 'sexual revolution' in the United States, (3) studies regarding premarital sexual relations, and (4) the relationship between premarital sexual activity and the following factors: religion and church attendance; rural-urban residence, race, decade of birth; social position; marital intentions, number of partners, type of romantic relationship; juvenile delinquency; and pregnancy, abortion, and illegitimacy.

723 Elgin, H. "Should Abortion be Legalized?" Justice of the Peace 127:532-ff., 1963.

Argues that abortion should be legalized on the grounds that criminal abortion and the physician's fear of jeopardy endanger the lives of many women. It is contended that a more liberal law would not increase immorality, for 90% of illegal abortions are had by married women who do not want more children.

724 Eliot, Johan W., et al. "Family Planning Activities of Official Health and Welfare Agencies, United States, 1966," Amer. J. Public Health 58(4):700-12. March 1968.

The continuing development of family planning services for persons of low income through local health and welfare departments was studied cooperatively by the American Public Welfare Association and the American Public Health Association. Continuing progress in enactment of laws and policies, consultation, educational programs, and reporting of services was traced. However, a slowing of expansion of services was noted, with the number of local health units known to be offering family planning services advancing only from 815 to 896 between mid-1965 and mid-1966. This slowing was coincident with failure of federal funds to materialize in support of new federal policies favoring development of family planning services.

725 Eliot, Johan W., et al. "Fertility Control in Hospitals With Residencies in Obstetrics and Gynecology: An Exploratory Study," Obstet. Gynec. 28:582-91. October 1966.

An exploratory study of family planning services rendered by hospitals with residencies in obstetrics and gynecology. The role of obstetric and gynecology departments and the teaching and clinical experience received by residents in regard to family planning are discussed. The different policies, methods and patterns of family planning assistance are described and rated according to their popularity. Situations and factors which impede as well as those which promote services are investigated. The types of assistances offered are categorized and the conditions that determine the type that is utilized are explained. The characteristics of the obstetric department chiefs who gave the most comprehensive assistance are described. The study attempts to show, finally, that the extent of inclusion of family planning in residency training is reflected in better, more comprehensive service to patients.

726 Ellis, Albert. "Psychological Aspects of Discouraging Contraception," Realist 1(7):11-13. April 1959.

Anti-contraceptive statutes and mores that are effective result in many disadvantages, especially that of curtailing human freedom. Anti-contraceptive statutes and mores that are ineffective and that do not actually restrain people from using birth control devices tend to result in even more human disadvantages, among which are: (1) the use of widespread hypocrisy, lying, and other forms of dishonesty; (2) the appearance of deep-seated feelings of guilt and shame; (3) development of neurotic symptoms, such as depression, anxiety and sexual impotence or frigidity; (4) a consequent ineffective use of contraceptives themselves, which result in unwanted pregnancies and abortions, leading to (5) further self-hatred, hostility to members of the other sex, and sexual difficulties stemming from the unpleasant effects of ineffective employment of birth control methods, etc.

727 Emerson, Luther, *et al*. "Acceptance of Family Planning Among a Cohort of Recently Delivered Mothers," *Amer. J. Public Health* 58(9):1738-45, 1968.

A cohort of 107 women, who had recently given birth to their second child on the ward service of the Sloane Hospital of Columbia Presbyterian Medical Center, was interviewed in an attempt to determine their family planning status and the reasons for that status. This population possessed a very cohesive and stable family structure despite low mean income. Eighty-seven per cent of the sample were married and living with their husbands and 95% of these husbands were employed. There was an interest in family life and a concern for medical care and 96% of the sample had prenatal and postpartum medical care and 95% made provision for care of the new baby. Sixty-four per cent of the sample was of Latin American origin mainly Puerto Rican. A high percentage (90%) used birth control after the second child. A large increase in the use of birth control followed the birth of the second child (from 52% to 90%). Results from the provision of birth control integrated with maternity care seemed to be highly successful. There was a high proportion of users of effective methods of birth control compared to previous practices of the group. Among the non-users of birth control, a greater proportion were dissatisfied with the adequacy of the educational efforts about birth control than among birth control users. The Latin American members of the group, although nominally Catholic and frequently recent arrivals from Latin America, possessed ideals of family size which differed little from those of the rest of the group. The ideal family size for birth control users was small (2.35 children). For non-users of birth control this was higher (3.2 children). For Latin

Americans religion seemed to have little effect on their acceptance of methods of birth control not approved by the church. The effectiveness and the widespread acceptance of a family planning service integrated with a hospital maternity care program is pointed out.

728 Enke, Stephen. "Changing View in America on Birth Control," Popul. Rev. 8(2):21-28. July 1964.

The 'American Assemblies' of 1963-64 discussed population questions with the aim of formulating policy recommendations for the United States government. Regional Assemblies were held near Washington, New York, Los Angeles, San Francisco and New Orleans. Each involved from 60-200 people. Those attending included educators, legislators, clergymen, writers, and a few businessmen. Each Assembly was subdivided into panels of about twenty persons. Each panel was given five sets of questions. Subject titles were (1) World Population Policy, (2) Population and Economic Development, (3) U.S. Policy and the Less Developed Nations, and (4) Population Policy for the United States. Close agreement prevailed among the recommendations of these five American Assemblies: (A) birth rates must be reduced through out the world, and especially in poor and over-populated countries; (B) foreign aid to such countries is largely being nullified by high birth rates and the extent of future U.S. aid should be influenced in part by the willingness and ability of recipient countries to reduce birth rates; (C) U.S. aid should include technical assistance and specific devices directed to reducing births where such help is requested by a developing nation; (D) domestic policy favored repeal of state laws preventing adults from obtaining information about birth control or purchasing contraceptive devices. An interesting feature of these conferences was the opportunity to observe what the layman does and doesn't know about population control. By and large, participants lacked technical knowledge of population processes, causes of rapid population growth, and of possible ways to bring populations under control. It is concluded that a bonus payment to young adult males willing to undergo vasectomies stands as the most possible and effective means for developing countries to limit births.

729 Ernst, M.L. "There is Desperate Need of Medical Wisdom to Deal With the Problem of 'Abortion'," New Med. Materia 4:21-ff., 1962.

This article encourages intelligent reform of the United States abortion laws through advice by members of the medical profession.

730 Erskine, Hazel G. "The Polls: More on Morality and Sex," Public Opinion Quart. 30:116-28, 1966.

Polls reported in the Fall and Winter 1966 issues of the Quarterly concerned the population explosion, birth control, sex, and morality. In this and the Spring 1967 issues of the Quarterly are summaries of some of the attitudes on morality and sex based on the survey which the Gallup organization conducted in February 1965 for Look magazine. In addition to the Look study, questions asked nationally since 1936 on venereal disease are summarized from Roper's Fortune poll and polls of some Gallup affiliates.

731 Erskine, Hazel G. "The Polls: More on the Population Explosion and Birth Control," Public Opinion Quart. 31(2):303-13. Summer 1967.

Findings and cross-tabulations are presented from a public opinion survey by Look magazine on the population explosion, birth control, sex and morality. LOOK questions regarding the population explosion and birth control are reproduced. The following results emerged: (1) "Have you read or heard about the great increase in population which is predicted for the world during the next few years?" (82%--yes, 16%--no, 2%--don't know). (2) "Are you worried or not worried about this population increase?" (29%--yes, 65%--no, 6%--don't know). (3) "What, if anything, do you think should be done to control the increase in population?" (33% advocated the use of birth control methods, 25% of education and advice on birth control, 22% held that it is up to the individual). (4) "Do you favor or oppose the distribution of birth control information?" (76%--favor, 15%--oppose, 9%--don't know). 80% felt that birth control information should be available to anyone who wants it, 13% that it should not, and 7% didn't know. (5) 55% thought the Roman Catholic Church will change its position on birth control, 20% thought it would not, 25% didn't know. 50% felt the Roman Catholic Church tries to prevent distribution of birth control information in the U.S., 21% felt it did not, 29% didn't know. 27% approved of the Roman Catholic Church's position, 61% did not, 12% didn't know. 62% felt that most Roman Catholics would like to see the Church change its position, 11% felt they would not, 27% didn't know. (6) 78% were in favor of the UN supplying birth control information to people of different nations, 14% were opposed, 8% didn't know. (7) 62% thought birth control pills should be made available free to all females on relief of childbearing age, 28% thought it should not, 10% had no opinion. (8) 64% approved of sterilization operations for females who have more children than they can provide for, 24% disapproved, 12% had no opinion. (9) 67% considered it harder for the average man to lead a good moral life today than 50 years ago, 15% thought it depends, 12% that it was harder 50 years ago, 6% had no opinion.

732 Erskine, Hazel G. "The Polls: The Population Explosion, Birth Control, and Sex Education," Public Opinion Quart. 30:490-501, 1966.

Topics cover attitudes toward the population, birth control (including questions involving the Roman Catholic Church and the United Nations), and sex education.

733 Falco, James F. "Preventive Law and Family Law: Pre-Marital Phases and Purposes," Villanova Law Rev. 12(4): 839-59. Summer 1967.

An examination of the concept of preventive law in its application to family disputes. Preventive law, which has existed for a century but was formally reorganized only in 1961, is defined as "a branch of law that endeavors to minimize the risk of litigation or to secure more certainty as to legal rights and duties." It is contended that preventive law should operate in the field of domestic relations law; also, that there is an obligation not only on the part of preventive lawyers but also of the entire legal profession to analyze the difficulties which the preventive law movement has encountered, to correlate its analysis with domestic relations law problems, to recommend specific preventive law objectives in this field, and to consider the advantages in applying preventive law. In particular, it is recommended that a statute be enacted using the "legal check-up" technique. It would require a "pre-marital legal check-up" by an attorney with the parties to the intended marriage. The primary function of the lawyer would be to apprise the couple of the state's interest in their marriage, its regularity and integrity; he would also examine the legal elements of the marriage and inform the couple of them, emphasizing that they each would assume, through the marriage, a new and different legal status, personality, and capacity.

734 "Family Planning and Public Policy," World View 3:5-14. January 1960.

Contents: The need for discussion, by Stephen F. Bayne, Jr.; Birth control and foreign aid, by James O'Gara; The moral question, by John C. Bennett; On clarifying issues, by William Esty; A Catholic candidate? by Robert Lekachman; The need for consensus, by Will Herberg.

735 Farley, Arthur N., "Conception. Contraceptives and the Law: A Connecticut Problem," University Pittsburg Law Rev. 22: 91-103. October 1960.

The author deals with the problem of the "competing claims" of Connecticut's ban upon dissemination of contraceptive information as a proper exercise of the police power, and of the liberty of the physician to prescribe, and the patient to use, such devices as a proper means to safeguard their health and preserve the state of their marriage, regardless of the moral attitude of the community. The Supreme Court will face this problem in the present term when it hears arguments in Buxton vs. Ullman and Poe vs. Ullman, companion suits on appeal from the Connecticut Supreme Court of Errors by three young married couples and their attending medical practitioner, C. Lee Buxton, M.D., an eminent specialist in obstetrics and gynecology. This appeal to the highest court in the land follows the Connecticut tribunal's action again upholding the constitutionality of a state statute forbidding the use and prescription of conception preventives. The relevant Connecticut statutes are described, as well as the situation and arguments of the couples involved. There follow discussions of the general development and repeal of the contraceptive ban, the Connecticut experience, the modern problem (that of conflicting interests -- namely, those of the individual, the theologian, the physician and the state), theological influences, psychiatric and physiological considerations, and the constitutional issue, with an analysis of the Connecticut decision. It is concluded that this Connecticut statute, which regulates the most intimate and personal relationship of married couples, is an unjustified and arbitrary use of the police power, to the extent that it confuses the public interest in protecting the youth of the state from promiscuous activities with the individual interest of a class of citizens entitled by law to enjoy, without fear, the intimacy of the conjugal act. The Supreme Court of Errors of Connecticut ignores not only the necessity for sexual intercourse as a fundamental cohesive factor in promoting the stability of marriage, but also denies the veracity of medical statistics indicating the efficacy of contraceptive devices to preserve life by preventing impregnation. It is felt that the U.S. Supreme Court will reverse the Connecticut tribunal on this point.

736 Farney, Dennis. "Cash Premium to Break Up the Family," Wall Street J. 170:18. November 30, 1967.

Effects of state laws denying aid to families with dependent children when the parents are unemployed and the father is able-bodied and living at home.

737 "Federal Stand on Population Control May Be Nearing," Cong. Quart. Weekly Rept. 23:1181-84. June 18, 1965.

Congress appears nearing an open discussion on population control that may pave the way for a federal stand on the issue. Most bills introduced propose establishing offices in the Department of State and the Department of Health, Education and Welfare to collect and disseminate at home and abroad information on family planning programs and population growth. The federal government which has been restrained, has recently moved into the field with: The Agency of International Development, The National Institute of Health, The HEW Department and The Office of Economic Opportunity. Progress, developments related to population problems and action taken are discussed. The content of, and the legislative action on bills introduced is reviewed. The future "outlook" is examined: Gruening's bill has some chance of passage mainly because it will not provide federal controls over population matters. Todd's bill is likely to be opposed by those who do not want any federal interferance. There appears to have been a change in attitude since Eisenhower indicated birth control was off-limits for the government. There is reason to believe the federal government will become more involved with the problem of overpopulation.

738 Fisher, R.S. "Criminal Abortion," in: Rosen, H., ed. Abortion in America. Boston: Beacon Press, 1967.

This article points out the incidence of abortion, noting a conservative estimate of 30% due to artificial interference. Criminal abortions were estimated as 34-69% of all abortions by Taussig in 1936. The conditions of therapeutic and criminal abortions including causes of maternal mortality are reviewed. Methods for collection of evidence in cases of illegal abortion are outlined.

739 Fleck, Stephen. "Family Welfare, Mental Health and Birth Control," J. Family Law 3:241-47. Fall 1963.

From the reservoir of undesired and ill-cared for offspring derive an unduly large proportion of mentally ill and other disabled persons. Those parts of the population who rely on clinics and other public agencies for their health and welfare are being discriminated against because they often need birth control advice most urgently to prevent further medical and psycho-social disability, but even in states where no laws pertaining to birth control exist, public policy often parallels the restrictive laws that do exist in Connecticut and Massachusetts, forbidding physicians even to advise about birth control matters. The laws interfere with the physician's freedom of action and speech and specifically interfere with established standards of medical practice, of public health, and mental hygiene. The physician and the psychiatrist in particular, must be free to recommend that method of pregnancy prevention which he judges to be optimal for a particular couple.

740 Foote, C., et al. Cases and Materials on Family Law. Boston: Little, Brown & Co., 1966.

Included in the article are: (1) MacNaghten's summary in the Rex vs. Bourne case (1938), (2) the proposed legislation in the Model Penal Code (1958), (3) the California Penal Code, (4) articles by Williams, Packer, and Gampbell, and (5) the Proposal of the 1962 official draft of the Model Penal Code.

741 Forster, George F., and Shaughnessy, Howard J. "Premarital Examination Laws in the United States," J. Amer. Med. Assn. 118(10):790-97. March 27, 1942.

This summary presents a tabular analysis of scope, laboratory tests required, examining personnel, time limitations, and restrictions, for the thirty states having such laws.

742 Foster, Henry H., Jr. "Current Trends in Divorce Law," Family Law Quart. 1:21-39. June 1967.

The author examines briefly the recent studies on divorce reform and makes some general observations about the family law of Wisconsin in order to evaluate the significance of current trends in divorce reform. Examined also are: California's recommendations (the Governor's Commission on the Family), England's Law Commission report, and the New York Divorce Reform Law. It is concluded that the task of adapting law to changing social needs is never finished. The long history of marriage and divorce laws amply demonstrates that both the public interest and legitimate private concerns must be recognized and a workable compromise effected. If reform is desirable, there is an initial policy question of whether codification of a new marriage and divorce law, or a piecemeal patching of the old law, is the more practicable. Wisconsin by the enactment of its Family Code set a standard by which to measure subsequent divorce reform. Especially the protections and safeguards for children merit emulation by other states. Suggestions for additional reform: 1) a functional non-fault ground for divorce should be added and the interval of living apart should be reduced to a reasonable period. 2) defenses to divorce should be mitigated or eliminated and perhaps it should be possible to decree divorce to both parties. 3) legal separation should not be imposed except where both parties consent to it. 4) the "cooling-off" period after divorce should be eliminated. 5) obsolete and perhaps unconstitutional provisions regarding the recognition of foreign marriages or divorces should be repealed. 6) a detailed survey and study of the actual workings of the restrictive provisions of the present Wisconsin law should be undertaken so that we may know to what extent local procedure is being evaded or avoided by persons who leave Wisconsin, temporarily or for good, in order to utilize the more lax divorce procedures of other states. The absence of workable non-fault grounds inevitably means that the poor who cannot afford migratory divorce and those who are joined by the "bonds of acrimony to spiteful and estranged spouses" are denied remedy.

743 Foster, Henry H., Jr. "Divorce Law Reform: The Choices for the States," State Government, Spring 1969, pp. 112-19.

This discussion of divorce reform relates almost exclusively to the problems of middle and upper class families and not to the marriage failures of the poor who have been priced out of the divorce market. Reform must reckon with the economic consequences and custodial incidents of divorce as well as the grounds for terminating marriage.

744 Foster, Henry H., Jr. and Freed, Doris J. Law and the Family. 2 Vols. Rochester, N.Y.: Lawyers Co-operative Publishing Co., 1966.

The economic aspects of marriage and divorce are perhaps the most neglected area of domestic relations law. In these volumes an attempt is made to record existing New York law and to evaluate it in terms of current social and economic values. Tax aspects with regard to general principles are included.

745 Foster, J.T. "Abortion -- Three States Have New Laws and More are Coming," Mod. Hospital 109(2):90-ff., 1967.

This article foresees new administrative responsibilities and liabilities being created by the new abortion laws of North Carolina, California, and Colorado, although the actual number of abortions in American hospitals should not increase greatly. A review of the conditions of the laws in the three states is given.

746 Freedman, A.L., and Freedman, M. Law of Marriage and Divorce in Pennsylvania. Second ed. 3 Vols. Philadelphia: Bisel, 1957. xvii, 1862 pp.

The authors present a comprehensive and critical statement of the Law of Marriage and Divorce in Pennsylvania. Court decisions and the various statutes are analyzed and subjected to independent criticism with suggestions for reform. The historical background of the law is examined and frequent reference is made to the decisions of the English ecclesiastical courts. The laws of other states are used as a guide in the solution of problems not yet authoritatively determined in Pennsylvania. In their preface to the second edition, the authors supply information on the changes and developments in both the substantive and procedural law which have occurred in the twenty years since the original edition was published. Notwithstanding these changes, however, the great body of marriage and divorce law in Pennsylvania remains substantially the same despite the unending flow of reported decisions.

747 Freedman, Ronald. "American Studies of Family Planning and Fertility: A Review of Major Trends and Issues," pp. 211-30, Chpt. in Kiser, C.V., ed. Research in Family Planning. Princeton: Princeton University Press, 1962. xvi, 664 pp.

U.S. studies on fertility and family planning based on government data are reviewed. The GAF and Princeton Studies and others on a smaller scale indicate a remarkable consensus in the U.S. population on a moderate size family of two to four children. The Princeton and GAF Studies have also demonstrated that contraception is used almost universally by fecund couples in the U.S. to make their desires for a moderate size family a reality. There are several plausible theories for the contraction of status or rural/urban differentials: (1) contraceptive practice has spread through all strata of the population, diminishing the role of differential contraceptive practice as a basis for differential fertility. (2) There is evidence that the higher fertility of the lower status groups in the past may have been largely a function of their recent rural origin. (3) Class differences may be becoming blurred in the U.S. as the working class takes on middle class characteristics. Studies which bring to light economic factors, wife's labor force participation, religious differentials and social psychological factors are discussed. The difficulty in predicting variations among individual couples in fertility may result partly from the fact that most of the variation is in a narrow range within which the significance of the differentials is not great.

748 Freedman, Ronald, et al. Family Planning, Sterility and Population Growth. New York: McGraw-Hill, 1959. xi, 515 pp.

Report of interviews with 2,713 young married women concerning the past and prospective growth of their families. The interviews covered such topics as births and miscarriages, sterility, methods of avoiding pregnancy, and the desired and expected number of children. It is found that most American couples have used contraception at some time but the patterns of fertility planning have many variations. There is a significant minority of couples who have more pregnancies than they want. But most couples want and are having families of two to four children. The methods used to avoid pregnancy and their success are described in detail.

749 Furie, Sidney. "Birth Control and the Lower-Class Unmarried Mother," Soc. Work 11(1):42-49. January 1966.

The paper examines contradictions in prevailing attitudes toward the lower-class unmarried mother and existing programs both in the U.S. and abroad that view illegitimacy as a result of social deprivation. Recourse to abortion is often not available to the lower-class unmarried woman. In addition, there is a wider social acceptance of unwed motherhood in lower-class Negro and Puerto Rican families living under deprived social conditions. Social deprivation not only inhibits opportunity for a stable marriage, it also deprives the woman of the opportunity for family planning because birth control information is not available to her. It is felt that birth control has been given too little attention by social workers who in the past have overemphasized psychological motivation. Furthermore, the traditional case work approach to unmarried mothers seems to be inappropriate for the lower-class and may be inhibiting the development of more meaningful and creative programs for this group. Informal discussion groups if led by public health or social work personnel, might create the climate for free discussion. It may also be possible to set up a program in conjunction with family planning clinics to follow up women who have not returned to the clinic after an initial contact. It is believed that if the support of public health personnel could be enlisted, unwanted pregnancies could be combatted as part of the war on poverty.

750 Gampbell, R.J. "Legal Status of Abortion and Sterilization in the United States," Clin. Obstet. Gynec. 6:22-ff., 1964

After reviewing the statutes regulating induced abortion in the U.S., this article cites Packer's study of the conformity of 26 California hospitals to abortion laws. It was discovered that the hospitals authorized abortions despite knowledge of the non-compliance with the law, that there was confusion over what justified abortions, and that growing concern with the hospitals' responsibility was highlighted by instituting abortion committees. Three possibilities exist in the split between law and social conduct: (1) attempt to make action conform with law, which is not the will of society; (2) remain the same, jeopardizing the position of the physician; or (3) change the law to coincide with current practices. Abortions restricted to hospitals under given procedural requirements with medical circumstances determined by physicians is suggested.

751 Gaud, William S. "New Opportunities in Asia," Department State Bull. 57(1479):579-84. October 30, 1967.

Address by the Administrator, U.S. Agency for International Development, before the 1967 conference on Asia of the Far East-American Council, New York, October 4, 1967. Includes statement of policy on aid for birth rate reduction in developing countries.

752 Gebhard, P.H., et al. Pregnancy, Birth and Abortion. New York: Harper and Brothers, and P.B. Hoeber, 1958. xiii, 282 pp.

Taking data from the portion of the "Kinsey Report" on 5,293 white, non-prison females, in addition to 572 Negro, non-prison females, and 309 Negro and 900 white women interviewed in prison, the third major report from the Institute for Sex Research of Indiana University examines the incidence of abortion and birth out of wedlock. One-quarter to one-fifth of the total sample had an induced abortion, commonly the outcome of a premarital pregnancy. 89% of premarital abortions were induced. The number of induced abortions in marriage was highest at younger ages and in the late reproductive life. Although a smaller percentage of marital pregnancies were intentionally aborted, the greatest number of induced abortions come from them. Single Negro women had a low percentage of induced abortions, but a high number of births out of wedlock. Most of the abortions were performed operatively by "physicians" with few ill effects. Prices ranged from nothing to thousands of dollars. The abortion situation of the Soviet Union, Japan, the Scandanavian countries, Germany, and France is discussed in the appendix.

753 George, B.J., Jr. "Current Abortion Laws: Proposals and Movements for Reform," in: Smith, D.T., ed. Abortion and the Law. Cleveland: Western Reserve University Press, 1967.

The author proposes the modification of existing abortion laws through the removal of legal threat to physicians who perform abortions in hospitals, through the extension of grounds for therapeutic abortions and through elimination of legal regulation, substituted by medical regulation. Also recommended is the placing of requirements for therapeutic abortion in the affirmative context of statutes regulating hospitals rather than in the negative context of licensing regulation statutes.

754 George, B.J., Jr. "Legal Medical and Psychiatric Consideration in the Control of Prostitution," Michigan Law Rev. 60:717-60. April 1962.

An investigation of the legal, medical and psychiatric factors involved in reducing the incidence of prostitution is given. The author contends that if a cure for the causes of prostitution and related offenses is to be found and applied, it will be through administrative activities: the efforts of social workers to prevent the dissolution of family units and to aid children of broken homes and those physically or mentally handicapped; the control measures against disease taken by public health officials; the therapy administered by staff members of mental institutions and out-patient clinics; and the supervision of probation and patrol officers. Application of penal law for other than indirect enforcement of the preventative and remedial activities of administrative organs or the contacting of those who need help to those who can give them aid thus keeping the disease-bearing contacts as small as possible, is either a neutral factor in the solution of the underlying problem or a hinderance to such solution.

755 Georgetown Law Journal Association. "Sterilization and Family Planning: The Physician's Civil Liability," Georgetown Law J. 56(5):976-96. May 1968.

This note focuses upon whether a physician should be liable to his patient when, following the performance of a sterilization operation for family planning purposes, a child is born. Although this note will discuss liability in terms of the traditional legal theories available to a plaintiff, the nature of the injury alleged is sufficiently unique to make considerations of public policy of great importance.

756 Giannella, Donald A. "The Difficult Quest for a Truly Humane Abortion Law," Villanova Law Rev. 13(2):257-302. Winter 1968.

It is stated that participants in the current controversy have not advanced arguments that illuminate the most challenging aspect of a humane abortion law: at what point the law should consider the fetus as a human being entitled to the basic right to survive. The most significant proposal is that recommended by the American Law Institute in its Model Penal Code. It is heavily oriented toward a utilitarian approach and is based on selective liberalization of the abortion law, both of which are questioned here. The criteria to be used in selecting the cases where abortion should be granted are found to be unclear and arbitrary and would lead to an excessively broad interpretation. The only principled justification for abortion must rest on the right of the pregnant woman to determine her own body processes. Although the principles of utility and the jurisprudence of interests are usually the best tools for setting public policy in a pluralistic society, it is maintained that avoidance of the ultimate issue is improper in the area of abortion. The state must adopt an official view on the basic ethical question of valuing the fetus, and the integrity of a free and democratic society demands that the matter be resolved only after a searching and full public exploration of the issue. Outlines are offered for an evaluation of the life of the fetus different from that provided in the Model Penal Code.

757 Ginsberg, M. On Justice in Society, Ithaca, N.Y.: Cornell University Press, 1965.

The author considers briefly whether there is a fetal right to life and whether there should be a legal protection of the fetus. Qualified physicians who perform abortions should not be viewed as having committed a criminal offense.

758 Girardeau, J.L. "The Abortion Law," Georgia Med. Assn. J. 56:340-ff., 1967.

A discussion of revisions of abortion law and attempts to legalize abortion in Georgia during 1967 meeting of state legislature which failed because of religious objections and the lack of resources to provide adequate statewide supervision. The AMA proposal and its terms are cited and author urges physicians to be influential in their communities and the state legislature so that better laws will be enacted.

759 Gobble, Fleetus L., et al. "A Nonmedical Approach to Fertility Reduction," Obstet. Gynec. 34(6):888-91. December 1969.

Preliminary report of storefront walk-in contraceptive service units established in low income communities in the southern United States in an attempt to lower the out-of-wedlock pregnancy rate. The three established units were each staffed by one non-medical woman trained in family planning techniques and had visiting hours in the evenings. Ninety per cent of the client visits were by males.

760 Goda, Paul J. "Historical Evolution of the Concepts of Void and Voidable Marriages," J. Family Law 7:297-308. Summer 1967.

The distinction between void and voidable marriages arose in cases where property was the main issue and as a result of conflicts of jurisdiction between ecclesiastical and temporal courts. If the marriage could be civilly attacked after the death of one of the spouses, then it had been a void marriage; if it could not be attacked, even though canonically invalid, the marriage was voidable but not avoided. Property cases were usually handled by temporal courts, whereas cases involving the validity of the marriage were heard in ecclesiastical courts. However, after the Reformation property and relational aspects of marriage were no longer heard separately. This was necessitated by Henry VIII's predicament: in order to obtain his annulment(s) he had to forbid appeals to Rome; thus he had to put marriage under the same procedure as property claims. Not until 1598 was the term voidable used in an issue between husband and wife and not after the death of one of them. From this point, old property solutions to problems after the death of one of the partners became applicable to the marriage itself during the life of the partners. Early American courts accepted the distinction between canonical and civil disabilities as the rationale for void (civilly disabled) and voidable (canonically disabled) marriages. But the modern basis for the distinction should be the seriousness of the defect. Whatever the rationale, society's interest in the status of marriage as a support for firm family relationships is still partially borne by the distinction between void and voidable marriages, although historically the distinction was never meant to be such a buttress.

761 Gold, E.M. "Observations on Abortion," World Med. J. 13:76-ff., 1966.

This article constitutes a summary of the findings of Gold, Erhardt and Nelson, who studied the incidence of therapeutic abortions in New York City during the period 1943 to 1962. Legal reform and expanded sex and birth control education programs were stressed after analysis of the data.

762 Gold, E.M., et al. "Therapeutic Abortions in New York City: A 20-Year Review," Amer. J. Public Health 55:964-ff., 1965.

This study of the incidence of therapeutic abortions performed in New York City hospitals between 1943-1962 indicates that although there has been a consistent downward trend over this period for all ethnic groups, therapeutic abortions are still most frequently performed for the white population, more frequently performed in proprietary hospitals and mental disorders are most frequent indications for abortions. The authors contend that their study indicates a need for equalizing opportunities for therapeutic abortions among ethnic groups, for alerting the public about the dangers of criminal abortions and the need for abortion law reform in New York.

763 Goldscheider, Calvin, and Uhlenberg, Peter R. "Minority Group Status and Fertility," Amer. J. Sociol. 74(4):361-72. January 1969.

Most studies of minority group fertility assume that, as assimilation proceeds, the fertility of minority and majority populations will converge. Empirical evidence, however, does not fully support this explanation. The fact that Jews and segments of the Negro and Japanese-American populations show lower fertility may be explained on the basis of the interaction between minority group status and social status and economic status. Minority group fertility must be treated within a broader context of other social behavior characterizing these groups. A key element in the relationship between minority group status and fertility is the degree of, and desire for, acculturation. It is suggested that: The insecurities of minority group membership operate to depress fertility below majority levels when (1) acculturation of minority group members has occurred in conjunction with the desire for acculturation; (2) equalization of social and economic characteristics occurs, particularly at middle class and upper class levels, and/or there is a desire for social and economic mobility; and (3) there is no pronatalist ideology associated with the minority group and no norm discouraging the use of efficient contraceptives.

764 Goldstein, Joseph, and Katz, Jay. The Family and the Law: Problems for Decision in the Family Law Process. New York: Free Press. Collier-Macmillan, 1965. xxxviii, 1229 pp.

The book is divided into three large chapters, each of which is made up of many parts. Chapter 1 is an introduction to the family and law and to methods, concepts and techniques for analyzing substantive and procedural problems for decisions in the family law process. Chapter 2 is concerned with decisions on husband-wife relationships. Chapter 3 is concerned with decisions on child-parent and parent-child relationships. Each chapter contains excerpts from cases and articles.

765 Goode, William J. "The Socio-Economic Framework, Family Patterns and Human Rights," Internat. Soc. Sci. J. 18(1): 41-54, 1966.

The central sociological problem is to ascertain what social patterns will maximize the protection of human rights. These rights are conceived as a specific part of the social structure and examined, at the family level, as a set of role obligations. The following areas in which human rights within the family have been recently extended are summarized: mate choice, bride price or dowry, inter-caste and inter-class marriage, control by elders and other kin, inheritance, contraception, abortion, divorce, and egalitarianism within the family. The trends noted are steps toward the securing of human rights.

766 Goodman, Irv S. "Bedroom Should Not be Within the Province of the Law," California Western Law Rev. 4:115-31. Spring 1968.

The author presents arguments supporting a repeal and revision of those statutes proscribing consensual sexual behavior. Considered are: the history of sodomy laws in England and the United States, the development of the right of privacy on Constitutional grounds, the legal philosophy which is the basis for those Constitutional grounds, the enforcement of present laws relating to sodomy, and proposals for future legislation. It is concluded that there is now legal precedent for limiting the scope of laws pertaining to sexual morality. The Supreme Court has declared that the right of privacy is an independent constitutional right. Furthermore, the American Law Institute has drafted a Model Penal Code which expressly recognized the right of privacy in man's sexual activities. Illinois has already taken the first step. California and all other states should preserve human dignity by revising their sex laws in the manner suggested by the American Law Institute.

767 Gordon, D.A. "The Unborn Plaintiff," Michigan Law Rev. 63:579-ff., 1965.

The question of whether there is a "uterine personality" is examined, with reference to differing religious and medical opinions on the issue. Since there has been increasing recognition and discussion of the legal rights of the unborn child, the author reviews the various interpretations of the laws on abortion in regard to such rights.

768 Gould, George. "Laws Against Prostitution and Their Use," J. Soc. Hyg. 27:335-43, 1941.

A survey of the state and federal laws dealing with the traffic.

769 Gould, George, and Dickerson, R.E. Digest of State and Federal Laws Dealing with Prostitution and Other Sex Offenses. New York: American Social Hygiene Assn., 1942.

The digest was written with the motivation of preventing wastage of human resources resulting from prostitution. All the laws passed up to and including September 11, 1941 were examined. Each state is considered under four headings: Sections One to Three concern prostitution and certain sex offenses; Section Four deals with other legislation effective in fighting prostitution, including (1) authorizing state officials to intervene where law enforcement authorities are derelict and (2) suspending or revoking liquor licenses if prostitution is permitted on the premises. Under the heading of Addenda, following the Digests under each state, are included definitions and other incidental data relating to the laws discussed and to the whole subject.

770 Graham, John B. "The 'Population Explosion' and North Carolina's Response," North Carolina Med. J. 29:41-51. February 1968.

Reasons are given to justify discussion of the "population explosion" in a medical journal, and there follows a general overview of population growth and population problems. Examined briefly are: the history of human population growth (with an extrapolation to the year 2000), how a population grows in mathematical terms, a representative example of a "developing" country's population growth, the effects of rapid growth on society, economic development and social welfare, the effect of educational achievement on growth rates, growth rate projections for various continents, the concept of demographic transition, the current population growth rate situation in various countries, and family planning, with references to national programs, fertility control and the basic purposes and principles of such planning. The University of North Carolina's response is outlined, and its Population Program is discussed. The article concludes with a review of developments in the state of North Carolina.

771 Greenberg, Daniel S. "Population: Planning Group Hears Encouraging Reports on Efforts to Start Latin American Programs," Science 144(3618):513-15. May 1, 1964.

A review of the efforts of the United States Foreign Aid program to stimulate government and Church officials in Latin America to adopt family planning programs. As a result of the broadened knowledge of the relationship between population growth and economic development, the Latin American government is becoming aware of their monumental birth rate and is willing to do anything substantial to alleviate the situation; this may conceivably result in a clash with the Catholic Church. The Church is torn between a long-held position on contraception and a growing understanding of the doctrine's foreseeable economic disadvantages. The U.S. Agency for International Development (AID) has stated that while the conditions are changing and can be encouraged to change even more, it must be recognized that even if the Church and Latin American governments were to reverse their opinions, no facilities are available to give impoverished, low-literacy populations motivation for small families. More important than the lack of a technology to effect rapid changes is the awareness that nothing can happen until the ruling groups become activated. It is to these problems that AID is directing its efforts.

772 Greenberg, Daniel S. "Population Planning: 1963 Marked by Reduction of Controversy and Shift in Government Attitude," <u>Science</u> 142:1554-56. December 20,1963.

The author views 1963 as the year when the efforts of population-planning organizations and the enormity of the population problem overwhelmed long-established and tenaciously held ideological positions, and opened the way for beginning substantial efforts toward turning down the world's population curve. It is felt that efforts have now shifted from the polemics of birth control to the technology and social acceptance of birth control. Discussed are current and past developments in the area, with references to Church reaction to the Draper Report, which concluded in 1959 that population control assistance should be incorporated into the U.S. foreign aid programs; moves in Congress for federal support of population planning; changes in public and Church attitudes toward U.S. involvement in foreign birth control programs (including Eisenhower's change of opinion on the subject); and initial efforts and policy of the Kennedy Administration. The problem remains, however, that foreign nations have been slow to realize the change in climate in the U.S. AID officials state that such governments, aware of this country's longstanding sensitivities on the subject, automatically look elsewhere when they seek birth control assistance. The author stresses the need for organized attempts to convince nations in need of assistance that the U.S. is now ready to help.

773 Groob, Irving. "'Get': Divorce Jewish Style," Connecticut Bar J. 40:594-601. December 1966.

The lore and law of the "Get" - the Jewish divorce - are highlighted, with references to the Jewish concept of marriage, grounds for divorce, illegal marriages where no divorce is required, the divorce procedure, jurisdiction, the text of the divorce and some general characteristics of Jewish divorce.

774 Grossman, Harry, and Cole, Robert H. "Distribution of Family Allowance Benefits," Soc. Service Rev. 19:359-72. September 1945.

After a brief description of the Servicemen's Dependents Allowance Act of 1942 in terms of its operation and dependents eligible to receive a family allowance, with reference to the rates of allowance payments for the various categories of dependents, the authors present and analyze six tables which reflect the geographical distribution of allowances payable to dependents as of June 30, 1944 and which show the various categories of dependents and the various percentages of payments as compared with the populations of the various states. The analysis and data on distribution represent the first study of its kind made in connection with the family allowance benefit program operative in World War II. In order to insure a uniform interpretation of the statistics contained in the tables, certain approved definitions of the terms employed are listed. Also described are the four types of family allowance accounts involving dependents with payees residing outside the United States.

775 Grove, Daniel G. "Independent Adoption: The Case for the Gray Market," Villanova Law Rev. (1):116-36. Fall 1967.

The practice of independent adoption -- those adoptions arranged and consummated solely by private persons without any institutional supervision -- is discussed. Such adoptions are broken into two categories: (1) black market, and (2) gray market. The black market is found completely lacking in justification since it is based upon the profit motive with complete disregard for the individual's welfare. The gray market is justified, however, because sociological surveys indicate that favorable results (under existing statutes) occur in such adoptions almost as frequently as in cases of agency supervised adoptions and because agency adoptions cannot now accommodate all of the children and parents existing as potential participants. The statutes of the 50 states are surveyed and criticized primarily because of inadequate investigation before placement. Changes are suggested to bring private adoptions up to parity with agency adoptions -- at least for gray market adoptions; black market adoptions have been abolished.

776 Gruening, Ernest. "The Birth Control Revolution," The Progressive 30(9):25-28. September 1966.

Account of the introduction and progress in the U.S. Senate of the bill on birth control.

777 Gruening, Ernest. What the Federal Government is Now Doing in the Field of Population Control and What is Needed. Speech of Hon. Ernest Gruening of Alaska in the Senate of the United States, Wednesday, May 3, 1967. Washington: Government Printing Office, 1967. 13 pp.

The involvement of the Federal Government in population control has been extremely limited. The Department of Defense has provided contraceptive information and materials to men in military service for sometime. The Department of Health, Education and Welfare and the Office of Economic Opportunity provide some grants to aid family planning clinics. Senator Gruening proposes considerable extension of the Federal Government's contribution to family planning programs.

778 Guthmann, Bernice J. The Planned Parenthood Movement in Illinois. Chicago: Planned Parenthood Association, Chicago Area, 1965. 28 pp.

This book gives a history of the Planned Parenthood movement in Illinois, offering a knowledge of past errors and triumphs.

It makes clear the striking progress that has been made in the social acceptance of family planning since the days of Margaret Sanger's beginnings - a half century before publication. It also emphasizes that, while the scale of operation has grown vastly, the basic problems of organizing people devoted to the common welfare and educating the public are often very similar.

779 Guttmacher, A.F. "Abortion Laws Make Hypocrites of All of Us," New Med. Materia, February 1962, p. 56.

Liberalization of the laws on abortion is needed which would allow physicians to use the ground of preservation of the mother's health as well as preservation of her life in performing abortions.

780 Guttmacher, A.F. "Abortion -- Yesterday, Today, and Tomorrow," in: Guttmacher, A.F., ed. The Case of Legalized Abortion Now. Berkeley, Calif.: Diablo Press, 1967.

After a historical examination of the legal status of abortion, the author contends that current laws ignore the mother's mental health, the quality of the off-spring and impregnation circumstances (rape, incest, etc.). The inequities of the abortion statutes are stressed, such as the ability of those on a higher economic level to obtain safer abortions.

781 Guttmacher, Alan F., ed. The Case for Legalized Abortion Now. Berkeley, Calif.: Diablo Press, 1967. vi, 154 pp.

In editing the book, Dr. Guttmacher sought to include the full range of thinkers who support reform: a woman who has been aborted, a survey researcher, a social critic, an anthropologist, a biologist, a minister, an attorney, a psychiatrist, a public health specialist, two professors of law, and a crusader. Contents: Guttmacher, Alan F., Abortion-yesterday, today, and tomorrow, pp. 1-14; Finkbine, Sherri, The Lesser of two evils, pp. 15-25; Rossi, Alice S., Public views on abortion, pp. 26-53; Mannes, Marya, A woman views abortion, pp. 54-60; Newman, Lucile, Between the ideal and reality: values in American society, pp. 61-68; Hardin, Garrett, Abortion and human dignity, pp. 69-86; Lion, Felix D., Abortion and theology, pp. 87-96; Pilpel, Harriet F.,

The abortion crisis, pp. 97-113; Kummer, Jerome M., A psychiatrist views our abortion enigma, pp. 114-24; Tietze, Christopher, Abortion--a world view, pp. 125-30; Maginnis, Patricia, Elective abortion as a woman's right, pp. 131-44; Tietze, Christopher, Abortion in Europe, pp. 145-46; Packer, Herbert L., and Gampell, Ralph J., Therapeutic abortion: a problem in law and medicine, pp. 147-54.

782 Guttmacher, Alan F. "Conception Control and the Medical Profession," Human Fert. 12(1):1-11, 1947.

Questionnaire to 15,000 physicians brought 3,381 completed replies, showing that three-fourths received no medical school instruction in contraception control. While 96% approved of contraception on medical indications, only 80% approved it for child-spacing. Average minimum safe interval between babies was considered to be 23 months. Diaphragm with jelly or cream was prescribed most frequently, with condom second.

783 Guttmacher, Alan F. "The Shrinking Non-Psychiatric Indications for Therapeutic Abortion," in: Rosen, H., ed. Abortion in America. Boston: Beacon Press, 1967.

The author reviews the history and incidence of therapeutic abortion, and discusses the process of obtaining and the justifications for such an abortion. Appropriate indications are classified into three groups: fetal, systemic and gynecologic. Also discussed are those justifications the author feels would not qualify as sufficient for the performance of a therapeutic abortion.

784 Guttmacher, Alan F. "Therapeutic Abortion in a Large General Hospital," Surg. Clin. North Amer. 37:459-ff., 1957.

Results of a committee plan for validation of abortions to be performed at Mount Sinai Hospital in New York City during 1952-1956. All abortions performed must be unanimously approved by the five members of the committee. During the period studied, 84% of all applicants have been approved by the committee; however, the author states that under this system, most questionable cases are never formally presented to the committee. He also claims that in only 13 of the 85 abortions performed was the New York State abortion law carried out. Psychiatric indications account for 39% of abortions, eugenic for 27%, malignancy for 12% and cardiovascular for 7%. The author urges abortion law reform for it is impossible for most non-Catholic physicians to practice what they believe to be good medicine.

785 Guttmacher, Alan F. "Therapeutic Abortion: The Doctor's Dilemma," J. Mount Sinai Hosp. N.Y. 21:111-ff., 1954.

The author describes the five problem areas which constitute the doctor's dilemma when involved with therapeutic abortion: interpretation of existing laws; decisions concerning socio-economic factors and their relation to purely medical indications; the legitimacy of the incidence for the operation; indications for sterilization in addition to the abortion; and the roles of the hospital and doctor. The importance of the Abortion Committee -- in this case, at Mt. Sinai Hospital -- is emphasized; such committees should evaluate all of the above questions for each individual case. There were 40 applications for therapeutic abortion during the Mt. Sinai Committee's first 17 months of operation, 31 of which were approved: 15 for psychiatric indications, five on the ground of malignancy, and four on the ground of maternal rubella.

786 Hakanson, E.Y. "An Obstetrician's View of Therapeutic Abortion," Minnesota Med. 50:23-ff., 1967.

The approaches of other countries to the abortion problem are mentioned, and the situation in the U.S. is evaluated, with reference to the increase in fetal and psychiatric indications for therapeutic abortion. It is contended that liberalization of present laws is needed, as well as abortion consultation centers and extended sex and family life programs in the public schools.

787 Hall, M.-Francoise. "Field Effectiveness of the Oral and Intra-Uterine Methods of Contraception: The Baltimore Public Program, 1964-1966," Milbank Memorial Fund Quart. 47(1, Part 1):55-71. January 1969.

The clinical records of all women [12,092] ever given oral or intrauterine contraception in Baltimore public clinics were analyzed. The data were collected from April to July 1966. Comparison is made of oral and device users as to socio-demographic characteristics and age-adjusted probabilities of continuing contraception.

788 Hall, Robert E. "Abortion in American Hospitals," Amer. J. Public Health 57(11):1933-36, 1967.

With minor exceptions the laws in all 50 states permit abortion only "if necessary to preserve the life of the mother." Yet, as medicine has progressed, it has become apparent that considerations other than the preservation of maternal life are involved in the practice of abortion. The principal indications for therapeutic abortions today are rubella and psychiatric disease. The overall abortion-delivery ratio in the U.S.A. is 1:500, whereas in Scandinavia it is 1:20 and in Japan 1:1. One of the medical factors responsible for our low rate is the establishment of the therapeutic abortion boards. The board at Sloane Hospital in New York City, for example, resulted in reducing the abortion rate by one third. Individuals and organizations have recently recognized the enormity of this problem and to recommend the abortion law reform necessary as a first step in its solution. All of these groups have given public support to proposals at least as liberal as that recommended by the American Law Institute in its Model Penal Code, which provides that abortion should be permitted when the mother's mental or physical health is endangered, when there is a significant risk of fetal deformity, and in cases of rape and incest.

789 Hall, Robert E. "New York Abortion Law Survey," Amer. J. Obstet. Gynec. 93:1182-83. December 1965.

The article describes and lists the results of a survey taken in 1965 of all New York State physicians registered with the AMA as obstetricians and/or gynecologists. The survey concerned the current state abortion law and asked whether that law should remain unchanged or be modified in accordance with the recommendation of the American Law Institute. Of the 1350 physicians who responded, 85.3% favored a liberalization of the law and the author concludes that a vast majority of this country's non-Catholic citizens would favor abortion law liberalization if informed of the many issues involved and helped in this educational process by those most familiar with the problem, namely, obstetricians. A table presenting a detailed breakdown of survey results is included.

790 Hall, Robert E. "Therapeutic Abortion, Sterilization, and Contraception," Amer. J. Obstet. Gynec. 91(4):518-32. February 1965.

In an effort to assess the current birth control practices in the United States, the experience of the Sloane Hospital for Women in New York was analyzed for the years 1951 through 1960 and a survey of 65 major American hospitals was made. The data obtained is presented in three separate sections -- Therapeutic Abortion, Sterilization and Contraception -- and each section includes comments on the data's medicolegal implications and a consideration of future responsibility and action.

791 Hammond, H. "Therapeutic Abortion: Ten Years' Experience with Hospital Committee Control," Amer. J. Obstet. Gynec. 89:349-ff., 1964.

An analysis of the practice of the Therapeutic Abortion Committee established at Marin General Hospital in 1952. In over a ten-year period, the committee has approved twelve abortions and rejected six. The ratio of abortion to deliveries is 1:1247 but this does not provide an accurate rate of the entire San Francisco Bay area because the policies of abortion committees in San Francisco hospitals are certainly more liberal and many physicians will send their patients to these other hospitals when abortion is contemplated.

792 Hanley, J.B. "The Rights of the Unborn Child," Western J. Surg. Obstet. Gynec. 6:113-ff., 1959.

The author discusses the question of whether the unborn child has certain rights, with references to the moral issues raised by therapeutic abortion, the role of the physician, who observes the growth and development of the fetus, and the basic dignity of human nature received by the fetus from the mother.

793 Hardin, Garrett. "Abortion and Human Dignity," in: Guttmacher, A.E., ed. The Case for Legalized Abortion Now. Berkeley, Calif.: Diablo Press, 1967.

Objections to legalized abortion on demand are evaluated from a liberal viewpoint.

794 Hardin, Garrett. "Blueprints, DNA, and Abortion: A Scientific and Ethical Analysis," Med. Opin. Rev., February 1967, p. 74.

The author argues for abortion on demand of any woman with an unwanted pregnancy, with references to the overemphasized dangers of abortion and the fact that contraceptive failure or lack of proper use of contraceptives will always generate a great number of unwanted pregnancies. It is contended that abortion can in no way be considered murder, since normal development of an infant is possible only if a great deal of love and attention is bestowed upon it and restrictions on or total prohibition of abortion point toward "the spiritual mutilation" of the unwanted child.

795 Hardin, Garrett. "Semantic Aspects of Abortion," ETC 24: 263, 1967.

The author defends the contention that more liberal abortion legislation is needed in this country. The arguments against eugenic, humanitarian and social indications are reviewed, as well as the more general premise that abortion equates with the termination of innocent life.

796 Harkavy, Oscar, _et al_. "Family Planning and Public Policy: Who is Misleading Whom?" _Science_ 165(3891):367-73. 25 July 1969.

This is a reply to arguments presented by Judith Blake challenging four governmental and private reports on the need for government-aided birth control programs for the poor in the United States ("Population Policy for Americans: Is the Government Being Misled?" _Science_ 164, 3879, 2 May 1969). The reply is by the three authors of one of these reports ("Implementing DHEW Policy on Family Planning and Population," _Population Crisis_ Part 1, 163-207, U.S. Government Printing Office, 1967). Evidence is cited from national surveys (largely the Growth of American Family Studies of 1955 and 1960 and the National Fertility Study of 1965) and other sources to show that the five propositions Blake states are either "misleading" or "in error." Her assertion that the reduction of U.S. population growth is "virtually unchallenged as an official national goal" is countered by both personal testimony and official statements; both of these sources indicate that population control has never been an official national goal. Her assertion that it is in pursuit of this goal that the reports recommend publicly-financed family planning is countered by direct quotations from the reports indicating that health and social welfare, not population control, are the underlying purposes of the recommendations. Her assertion that advocates of this policy contend that the poor have been denied family planning services because of "the prudery and hypocrisy of the affluent" is countered by evidence indicating that family planning services have been withheld for political reasons rather than those given by Blake. Her assertions that the poor both desire larger families than do higher income families and are significantly less inclined to favor birth control are countered by evidence from surveys that the poor want either no more or fewer children than do the non-poor. Her assertion that the estimate of 5 million poor women in need of subsidized family planning service is exaggerated is countered by a description of the procedures followed by two independent research groups, who arrived at the figures of 4.6 million and 5.3 million respectively.

797 Harkavy, Oscar, _et al_. _Implementing DHEW Policy on Family Planning and Population: A Consultant's Report_. Washington: U.S. Dept. of Health, Education, and Welfare, 1967.

The consultants undertook a wide ranging examination of progress made to date by DHEW in implementing Secretary Gardner's policy statement of January 24, 1966. Interviews were conducted with DHEW officials in Washington and in the regional offices. Sixteen recommendations for increasing family planning work are made. These pertain to funding, services, training, and research.

798 Harkavy, Oscar, et al. "An Overview of the Ford Foundation's Strategy for Population Work," Demography 5(2):541-52, 1968.

Since 1952 the Ford Foundation has devoted $100 million to programs dealing with world population programs. The Foundation believes that in helping nations reduce their fertility it must also assist with developmental work in education, agriculture, industry and government. The Foundation has been a major force in three general areas of population work: research and training in reproductive biology; the establishment and/or expansion of university population studies centers in the United States; and assistance to population programs in developing countries. It has also contributed to experimental programs designed to improve family planning in the United States. Activities in each of these areas are briefly reviewed, with descriptions of the status of family planning in several countries where the Foundation is directly engaged to demonstrate some aspects of the nature and scope of support. Greatest expenditures in population outside the United States have been in Asia, particularly for aid to the family planning programs of India and Pakistan, and Europe, primarily for research and training in reproductive biology. About two-thirds of expenditures in population have gone to American institutions, although the activities supported by these grants are directed for the most part toward population programs in developing countries. Only in the past three years has it been Foundation policy to assist family planning in the United States.

799 Harrison, C.P. "Legalized Abortion: Utopia or Disaster?" Med. Sci. 18:36-ff, 1967.

If all legislation on abortion were abolished, abortion would be a surgical procedure, to be performed only when medical indications make it a natural medical necessity. Viewing abortion in this way would not compel the physician to perform an abortion for social indications or on the basis of the woman's decision alone. Abortion would not be condoned legally, nor would it be generally condemned. Discussed are the probable detrimental effects on society and public, e.g., increases in the number of criminal abortions and the total morbidity of abortions, lowering of the birth rate, if abortion were to be legalized for sociologic reasons or indications.

800 Hart, H.L.A. Law, Liberty and Morality. Stanford: Stanford University Press, 1963. 88 pp.

Theoretical and philosophic aspects of the use of the criminal law to enforce morality, in particular sexual morality.

801 Harter, Carl L. "A Survey Concerning Induced Abortions in New Orleans," Amer. J. Public Health 57:1937-ff., 1967.

The author reviews the results of two opinion surveys taken in the New Orleans area concerning attitudes toward induced abortion. A representative sample was used for one survey, and the other involved women admitted to the Charity Hospital of New Orleans and discharged with a diagnosis of abortion. Both groups of women rejected, to a large degree, the notion that "too many children" might be used as an indication or justification for abortion, and the belief that abortion should be available to any women who decides she needs one was held by 40% of the representative sample and 60% of the hospital sample. The belief that abortion is indicated by rape, physical ailment, incest and mental illness was held by the majority of women in both groups.

802 Harting, Donald, et al. "Family Planning Policies and Activities of State Health and Welfare Departments," Public Health Reports 84(2):127-34. February 1969.

Findings of a 1967 survey sponsored by the American Public Health Association and the American Public Welfare Association -- part of a continuing enquiry begun in 1963 -- show an increase in the number of States that include costs of contraceptive services in medical care provided by welfare agencies for Aid to Families with Dependent Children from

24 in fiscal 1966 to 33 in fiscal 1967. Clinic locations were increased by 10 per cent and the number of clinic services by 20 per cent in the 19 States in which family planning services were provided in local health departments in 1966 and for which comparable data were available for 1967.

803 Hatcher, Robert A., and Tiller, Mary J. "Acceleration of a Public Health Department Family Planning Program: Referral from Well-Baby Clinics in Muscogee County, Georgia," Amer. J. Public Health 59(4):1217-25. July 1969.

Referrals from all types of public pediatric clinics doubled the patient load at the Muscogee County Health Department family planning clinic within two months. Of 500 women interviewed at pediatric clinics, 244 were pleased with their present means of contraception, and 152 made appointments with a family planning clinic; 97, or 64 per cent of those making appointments were seen at family planning clinics. A system of follow-up reminders, by post card, telephone, and home visits, was used to encourage those making appointments to keep them. The advantages of this type of referral system are that both mother and staff at pediatric clinics are highly motivated to receive and encourage family planning respectively. Referrals can be made inexpensively and with minimal effort through the various public pediatric clinics serving a community.

804 Heffernan, R.J., and Lynch, W.A. "Is Therapeutic Abortion Scientifically Justified?" Linacre Quart. 19:11-ff., 1952.

Therapeutic abortion is held to be immoral, constituting a deliberate destruction of innocent life with no scientific justification. The authors, in coming to this conclusion, review the medical, psychiatric and fetal indications for therapeutic abortion with reference to modern methods of management.

805 Hellegers, A.E. "Abortion, the Law and the Common Good," Med. Opin. Rev., 26 May 1967, p. 76.

Concise arguments are offered against liberalization of U.S. abortion laws, with reference to reasons commonly used in promoting such liberalization. Special attention is given to the argument that more liberal abortion laws would diminish significantly the number of illegal abortions performed each year and especially the number of deaths connected with these abortions. The author contends that criminal abortion will continue even with abortion law liberalization.

806 Hellegers, A.E. "Law and the Common Good," Commonweal 86:418-ff., 1967.

The author contends that proposed liberalization of current abortion statutes will qualify only a minimal number of those women wanting an abortion, and that, while liberalization in other countries has greatly increased the number of legal abortions, the number of illegal abortions has not significantly decreased.

807 Heller, Abraham, and Whittington, H.G. "The Colorado Story: Denver General Hospital Experience with the Change in the Law on Therapeutic Abortion," Amer. J. Psychiat. 125(6): 809-16, 1968.

Cautious implementation of Colorado's newly liberalized abortion law has obviated initial fears that the state might become an "abortion mecca." Denver General Hospital, a typical public hospital which had rarely performed therapeutic abortion, now has a major involvement in this procedure. In this report of early experience with the new law, it is concluded that few clinical guidelines exist. A major clinical subtype among those reported -- unemancipated teenagers -- requires more adequate study and special consideration. The lower socioeconomic groups continue to underutilize therapeutic abortion. A registry is planned to standardize information and provide the basis for further objective studies.

808 Hellman, Louis M. "One Galileo is Enough: Some Aspects of Current Population Problems," Eugenics Res. 57(4):161-66. December 1965.

A discussion of world public opinion and the attitude of the Catholic Church toward birth control. It is pointed out that the bitter controversy in New York City in 1958 over the distribution of birth control information in public institutions may have marked a turning point in U.S. thinking on the subject. The archdiocese issued a statement reiterating traditional Roman Catholic positions, as against the near unanimity of the rest of the community. The influence of two new developments in the field of contraception, the pill and the reintroduction of intrauterine devices, is evaluated. It is estimated that over 45,000 indigent mothers will receive contraceptive information and services from the municipal hospitals of New York City this year, a marked contrast with the situation of a few years ago and even more marked when one considers that the dropout rate with the diaphragm during the early years was 50% with a pregnancy rate greater than 20%. Lack of motivation among the indigent thus appears to be a myth.

809 Henker, F.O. "Abortion and Sterilization from Psychiatric and Medico-Legal Viewpoints," Arkansas Med. Assn. J. 57: 368-ff., 1961.

The Arkansas law on therapeutic abortion requires that in order for the operation to be performed, the mother's life must be endangered. However, this law does not account for the fact that pregnancy can be one of the most stressful events in our culture and may constitute the precipitating stress which activates mental illness. Reviewed are the more liberal laws of other countries and literature concerning lessening stress following pregnancy.

810 Herbert, J.G. "Is Legalized Abortion the Solution to Criminal Abortion?" University Colorado Law Rev. 37:283-ff., 1965.

Some medical, ethical and theological aspects are examined with regard to proposals for abortion law reform. Statistical data from Ekblad's study of Swedish women is used to demonstrate that the risk of psychiatric sequelae must be considered as well as psychiatric indications for abortion. The author contends that abortion disregards human life and does not deter criminal abortions.

811 Herrera, Lee F., and Kiser, Clyde V. "Social and Psychological Factors Affecting Fertility. XIII. Fertility in Relation to Fertility Planning and Health of Wife, Husband and Children," Milbank Memorial Fund Quart. 29(3):331-76, 1951.

The study was conducted by the questionnaire method and the material gathered from suitably selected couples of the Indianapolis Study. More adequate measures of health of wife, husband and children must be developed for more rigorous testing but the present data fail to confirm the hypotheses that the poorer the health of wife, husband or children the higher is the proportion of couples practicing contraception effectively and the smaller are the planned families. In most cases the opposite type of relationship is found. To some extent the relationship observed between health and fertility-planning status can be accounted for by the interrelation of socio-economic status, health and fertility-planning status.

812 Hershey, Nathan, et al. "Facts on Family Planning Policies in the United States." Mimeographed Paper. Graduate School of Public Health, University of Pittsburgh, June 1968. 24 pp.

This report constitutes a state-by-state summary of the characteristic features of family planning policies. General program direction and content within each state are indicated but some details are omitted. In reviewing these policies, the following criteria were used: (1) eligibility of women to receive the services; (2) ability of case workers to initiate discussion of the need for family planning with the patient; and (3) extent to which payment is made by the state for medical services, drugs and devices. Listed also are criteria for judging whether the state programs are liberal or restrictive; there are programs which contain both elements and should be classified as moderate.

813 Herst, R.E. Chapel Sermon. San Francisco: Society of Humane Abortion, Inc., 1964.

The author argues for liberalization of abortion statutes through the two fundamental principles inherent in the Torah codes. First, they realized in the Nishnah that the woman's life has priority over that of the unborn child. Secondly, they affirmed in the Codes that the embryo is not human for it requires neither formal burial nor mourning rites should it die. This, he contends, should be the basis for all Reform Jews to press for: intelligently controlled and performed therapeutic abortion.

814 Hicks, Nathaniel W. "By 'Planned Parenthood' the People May Perish," America, A Catholic Review of the Week 48(26): 709-11. 3 April 1943.

Figures from the Thompson-Whelpton estimates form the major material for the statement of the Catholic position.

815 Hildebrand, Dietrich von. "Marriage and Overpopulation," Thought 36:81-100. Spring 1961.

The author explores the meaning and value which marriage possesses in itself and the link between this love union and procreation. The sinfulness of artificial birth control is discussed and the suggestion that this is the proper means to avert the threat of overpopulation is clearly repudiated. Urges science to provide us with a means of detecting the days of fecundity in such a strict manner that the use of rhythm will become a reliable method of avoiding conception.

816 Hill, G.W., and Tarver, J.D. "Marriage and Divorce Trends in Wisconsin, 1915-1945," Milbank Memorial Fund Quart. 30: 5-17. January 1952.

A descriptive statistical study based upon all divorces and every tenth marriage contracted in the years 1915, 1920, 1935, 1940, and 1945 in the state of Wisconsin.

817 Hines, Don C., and Goldzieher, Joseph W. "Large-Scale Study of an Oral Contraceptive," Fertility and Sterility 19(6): 841-66. November - December 1968.

A cooperative study of an oral contraceptive agent of the sequential type (C-Quens) included 8895 women treated for 148,998 cycles (12,416 woman-years) in 27 centers. Of the total patients, two had completed 63 cycles and 193 had completed 54 or more. Topics include: use effectiveness, influence of interval between courses and of body weight, effects on menstrual cycle, side effects.

818 Hoheisel, P. "Abortion -- A Complex Issue Today Calling for More Discussion," Michigan Med. 66:900-ff., 1967.

Report of the pros and cons for legalizing abortions which were raised at the Maternal Health Conference of the Michigan State Medical Society.

819 Holman, Edwin J. "Medico-Legal Aspects of Sterilization, Artificial Insemination, and Abortion," J. Amer. Med. Assn. 156(14):1309-11. 4 December 1954.

The author discusses the civil or criminal liability incurred by a physician who performs a sterilization on eugenic, therapeutic or nontherapeutic grounds, with references to pertinent court cases and the problem of valid consent. He feels that the laws on sterilization are still not settled, and the question of legal liability of the physician in the absence of therapeutic necessity or according to eugenic sterilization statutes is not clear. In regard to the medico-legal aspects of artificial insemination, there is little that can be said with any degree of assurance, since such aspects have not been explored satisfactorily by any court of appellate jurisdiction in the United States. Discussed briefly are questions relating to legitimacy, inheritance and liability in connection with the selection of donors. A short section on abortion concludes the article.

820 Homes, Robert O. "Putative Marriage Doctrine in Louisiana," Loyola Law Rev. 12:89-127, 1966.

The theory of putative marriage is formulated in Article 117 and 118 of Louisiana's Civil Code: "The marriage which has been declared null, produces nevertheless its civil effects as it relates to the parties and their children, if it has been contracted in good faith." (117) "If only one of the parties acted in good faith, the marriage produces its civil effects only in his or her favor, and in favor of the children born of the marriage." (118) The author first considers, before the question of putative marriage, several points in regard to determining whether a particular relationship is to be given effect as a valid marriage and then divides the putative marriage problem into two areas: (1) existence of a putative marriage (creation-ceremony, good faith and termination -- bad faith vs. annullment); and (2) effects of a putative marriage (in general -- election of effects, effects as to bad-faith party, effects after termination and particular effects of putative marriages -- children, good-faith spouse). Pertinent court cases are described.

821 Hopper, Columbus B. "Conjugal Visiting: A Controversial Practice in Mississippi," Criminal Law Bull. 3:289-99. June 1967.

The author discusses the objections to conjugal visiting in the United States as expressed by many penologists and describes the practice as it operates in the Mississippi State Penitentiary. The article is based on research which began in 1959. Included are sections on the unusual structure of the Penitentiary itself, the liberal visitation program, the development on conjugal visiting privileges (still best described as an informal, unofficial practice), evaluations of conjugal visiting by camp sergeants, inmate opinion on the program, and the recidivism rate. The author feels that the experience in Mississippi calls for consideration and evaluation and that conjugal visiting should be studied not only in comparison with but also in conjunction with other types of marital relationships and visiting programs and in a variety of institutions. He concludes that an important element in the Parchman system of conjugal visiting appears to be the small community-camp arrangement, since it affords more freedom of visitation in general, each camp being somewhat isolated.

822 Horty, J.F. "Ignorance of Abortion Law Can Lead to Court," Mod. Hosp. Law 99:107-ff. September 1962.

Hospitals are warned to obey state laws on abortion and to avoid performing criminal abortions. The author reviews the statutes of various states and their exceptions and makes several recommendations which might assist hospitals in maintaining their legal obligations.

823 Huddleston, H. Martin. "Law of Therapeutic Abortion: A Social Commentary on Proposed Reform," J. Public Law 15: 386-400, 1966.

After a brief historical review of the laws and attitudes concerning abortion, the author examines the present status of therapeutic abortion laws, primarily in the United States and Britain, and outlines more extensively the relevant attitudes and practices of the two professional groups which have been most influential in the field: medical doctors and religious leaders. Their approaches are discussed in the context of apparent social needs and the proposed and existing legal reforms. The author concludes that as abortion laws exist today they are ineffective and that the most efficient solution would be the alteration of current laws to fit current practice combined with careful administration of new laws and workable preventive measures.

824 Hull, Addis E. "Federal Tax Problems in Marriage, Divorce, and Separation," Taxes 41:722-41. December 1963.

The author describes the federal tax consequences -- income, gift and estate -- of transfers of money and property between spouses incident to marriage, divorce and separation.

825 Hutchinson, James M. "The Present Birth Control Controversy," Humanist 20:42-43, 1960.

In the present birth control controversy a number of important factors are being overlooked. Played as basically a "religious" question, particularly as a difference of opinion between Roman Catholics and Protestants, there are, however, 68 million Americans who are non-church members and who have a vital concern here. The Committee on Church and State of the American Humanist Association insists that birth control and family planning are individual matters of moral choice and should not be limited by governmental statute. The individual whose church teaches him that mechanical contraception is against "the natural law" is free to so choose where materials and information are freely a·ailable to those who wish to use them for family planning.

826 Hyatt, Jim. "Legalized Abortions," Wall Street J. 170:1. 18 August 1967.

Colorado's cautious use of liberalized statute may spur similar laws. Doctors turn down requests of many women. Twenty-eight other states now mull over changes but controversy still exists.

827 Ibrahim, Afaf, F.A.B. "Self-Concept and Family Planning," Dissertation Abstr. 29A:1953, 1968-69. Abstract of Ph.D. Thesis, University of California, Los Angeles, California, 1968. 279 pp.

The purpose of the study is to investigate why some families are effective in family planning and others are not. It investigates the problem within a social-psychological frame of reference. The design of the research is based on the interactionist approach to the study of dyadic members in a family constellation. The main theory used is that of role and its importance in the establishment of self-conception. Consequently, the study investigates the effect of high cosmopolitan and low cosmopolitan self-conceptions, interaction patterns in the family, powerlessness, and the role of women in society, as they are related to the degree of subjective effectiveness and objective success in family planning. The total sample is comprised of 126 wives and of 72 of their husbands. The findings from the investigation indicate that, as hypothesized, wives who perceived themselves as high cosmopolitan were more effective in planning their families than those who saw themselves as low cosmopolitan. The diversification of the roles of a wife influenced her to investigate and effectively follow a successful regimen of family planning. Husband-wife interactions considered in terms of intimacy, preference, and trust are shown to have a significant relationship and effectiveness in family planning. The higher the husband-wife interactions, the higher the degree of effectiveness in family planning. As hypothesized, effectiveness in family planning is predicted by the degree of powerlessness the wife manifests. The husband's degree of powerlessness was not correlated with the degree of effectiveness in family planning as was initially predicted. Neither the identification of the wife nor of the husband with community-oriented roles of women in society had any effect on the degree of effectiveness in family planning. It is tentatively concluded that the wife's self-conception has the strongest effect on effectiveness in family planning.

828 "Illegitimacy -- Growing Problem for the Taxpayer," U.S. News 46:86-ff. 15 June 1959.

Some of the proposals being considered by local governments to minimize rising costs of caring for illegitimate children.

829 Illinois State Medical Society. "Symposium on Medical Implications of the Current Abortion Law in Illinois," Illinois Med. J. 131:662-700, 1967.

Eight Illinois physicians discuss the possibilities for abortion law reforms. Some aspects considered are: the pursuit of proper medicine; the validity of medical and social indications; the incidences of illegal abortion; right of fetal life; psychiatric conditions and fetal malformation; the public health problem; the susceptibility of medicine to external factors and the scientific, religious and emotional forces which affect the abortion situation.

830 "Income Tax That Pays the Poor," Bus. Week, 13 November 1965, pp. 105-6.

How a negative income tax plan might work; most people would continue to pay taxes but those with incomes below the poverty line would receive a subsidy.

831 Jacobson, Paul H. "Differentials in Divorce by Duration of Marriage and Size of Family," Amer. Sociol. Rev. 15: 235-44. April 1950.

Provisional data on the involvement of children in cases of divorce and annulment and analysis of the differentials in divorce and annulment according to family size and length of marriage based upon all available data from county and state records and National Office of Vital Statistics for period from 1890 to 1948.

832 Jaffe, Frederick S. "Family Planning and the Medical Assistance Program," Medical Care 6(1):69-77. January - February 1968.

Assesses the potential impact of Medicaid on the delivery of family planning services for the 32 State Medicaid Programs thus far [April 4, 1967] approved by the Department of Health, Education and Welfare. The stated provisions of these programs, and the manner in which they are being administered, are analyzed in an attempt to establish both the potentialities and the limits of Medicaid for the extension of family planning.

833 Jaffe, Frederick S. "Family Planning and Poverty," J. Marr. Fam. 26(4):467-70. November 1964.

There is a significant gap between lower class fertility aspiration and performance. Data are cited to show that low-income white and nonwhite families want as few or fewer children than those of higher socio-economic status, but unwanted pregnancies and large families are a severe problem. This paradox is explained in part by the unequal access of poor families to effective birth control instruction and guidance, since public medical and welfare facilities do not make these services routinely available. Recent evidence also suggests that impoverished parents accept contraception especially the oral pills if it is sympathetically and energetically offered. Attention is drawn to other aspects of the institutional and social mechanisms governing birth control services which are amenable to modification and correction by the serving professions, especially to questionable attitudes and biases on the part of the professions.

834 Jaffe, Frederick S. "Family Planning, Public Policy and Intervention Strategy," J. Soc. Issues 23(4):145-63. October 1967.

Despite important changes in public policy on family planning, it is felt that public agencies in the United States have yet to develop adequate programs. Shifts in policy are reviewed with particular reference to New York, where birth control clinics in New York City serve more patients than all the clinics of many states, and in federal policies, which are reviewed from 1959 through 1964. Most developments are found to relate to administrative policies rather than to legislation. The inadequacy of current programs is illustrated. It is emphasized that birth control programs are voluntary medical programs, and in no way coercive. Extension of services to those who need them to effectuate their family size preferences is inhibited to some degree by continuous religious opposition, but more significantly by stereotyped views of the poor among the serving professions and by the generally inadequate state of available medical care. It is suggested that public voluntary programs must be extended rapidly to prevent compulsory measures, i.e., coercive, punitive responses to problems of illegitimacy and mothers receiving welfare for dependent children.

835 Jaffe, Frederick S. "Financing Family Planning Services," Amer. J. Public Health 56(6):912-17. June 1966.

Suggests the nature and priority of questions to be asked at the outset in any community, concerning type of service, location, auspices, source of funds, and target groups.

836 Jaffe, Frederick S. "A Strategy for Implementing Family Planning Services in the United States," Amer. J. Public Health 58(4):713-25, 1968.

Fertility studies and experiences in U.S. family planning programs are analyzed to provide a strategy to guide resource allocation and establishment of priorities for a national effort to provide services in approximately five years to those who are presently without access to them. Detailed analysis is presented of New York City programs which increased from 15% of target population served in 1961 to 51% in 1966, primarily through making services geographically and economically more accessible. A diffusion model of the response of low-income families to different program inputs is proposed. The resulting strategy assigns first priority to changing behavior by increasing availability of services to accommodate existing desire of many poor parents for effective fertility control. As services are established in central and neighborhood health facilities, educational activities are intensified and efforts are initiated to identify and reach those who experience greatest difficulty in adopting modern family planning. A corollary is that family planning requires special attention until it is fully integrated in present health services and much higher priority in staff, budgets and facilities.

837 Jaffe, Frederick S., and Guttmacher, Allan F. "Family Planning Programs in the United States," Demography 5(2): 910-23, 1968.

In the last several years, acknowledgment of the long-term denial of family planning services to low-income couples has resulted in efforts to create an adequate network of facilities providing modern services. Because health services for the poor are financed principally with public funds, the implementation of this program has become the key issue of domestic public policy on family planning.

838 Jaffe, Frederick S., and Polgar, Steven. "Family Planning and Public Policy: Is the 'Culture of Poverty' the New Cop-Out?" J. Marr. Fam. 30(2):228-35, 1968.

The application of the culture-of-poverty concept to family planning is reviewed. Two approaches to program development are contrasted: accessibility versus cultural-motivational. Experience appears to support the accessibility approach, which seeks to create services where none exist or to remove obstacles which make services inaccessible (distance, crowding, eligibility and fee practices, scheduling, lack of information, and depersonalized delivery). Yet the cultural-motivational view dominates the thinking of many health and welfare professionals and is employed to rationalize slow progress. This anomaly is analyzed as an example of the resistance of institutions to change and in terms of its historical antecedents in upper-class biases about lower-class fertility. The implications for public policy are explored, particularly the potential use of the culture-of-poverty concept to justify selective compulsory fertility control if health and welfare agencies continue to lag in developing voluntary programs.

839 Jain, Sagar, and Sinding, Steven. North Carolina Abortion Law 1967: A Study in Legislative Process. Monograph 2, Carolina Population Center. Chapel Hill: University of North Carolina, 1968.

During 1967, abortion bills were introduced in twenty-eight state legislatures. North Carolina was one of these states. This retrospective study of the legislative process is based on interviews with legislators, reporters, physicians, and witnesses at the hearings. The first chapter describes the North Carolina setting in which the course of the bill was chartered. Chapters two to five trace step by step progress of the bill, examines strategies and tactics used by the proponents and opponents, and gives details of roles played by key individuals and groups. Chapter six provides a summary of the total process and then attempts to abstract out critical factors which influenced the course of events.

840 Jakobovits, I. "Abortion and Embryotomy," in: Jewish Medical Ethics. New York: Philosophical Library, 1959.

The author reviews Jewish attitudes toward abortion and the termination of fetal human life.

841 Jakobovits, I. "Jewish Views on Abortion," in Smith,D.T., ed. Abortion and the Law. Cleveland: Western Reserve University Press, 1967.

The author reviews the Orthodox Jewish position on abortion. Interpretation of the Talmud reveals that preservation of the mother's life allows the performance of an abortion, and that Jewish interpretation of the Bible reveals that abortion does not equate with murder. However, the use of humanitarian and eugenic grounds for abortion is clearly condemned in later rabbinical writings. The Jewish position views the maintenance of order in society and the supreme value of each human life as major arguments for limiting induced abortion.

842 Jarrett, William H. "Family Size and Fertility Patterns of Participants in Family Planning Clinics," Sociol. Anal. 25(2):113-20. Summer 1964.

The family size and fertility of participants in a Catholic family planning clinic is compared with similar national data. Family size is positively related to wife's education and secondarily to husband's occupation. Generally, the relationships from national studies are confirmed in this sample of high fertility couples, though length of marriage is still the primary determinant of fertility. The large family size of these couples suggests that attendance at the clinic is probably their first serious exposure to fertility control, though their family size remains smaller than the 'unplanned' families reported in national studies of fertility.

843 Jessee, R.W. "Family Planning Services in Virginia," _Public Health Reports_ 82(4):292-96. April 1967.

Presents and discusses, against a background of the history of state activity, statistics on family-planning services supplied by the State Department of Health, 1960-1966, and trends in birth, marriage, and illegitimacy rates, 1916 to 1965.

844 Kaltreider, D.F. "Changing Attitudes Toward Abortion, Sterilization, and Contraception," _Texas Med_. 62:40-45, 1966.

Partial reform of existing abortion laws will not lessen the number of criminal abortions in the United States unless socio-economic considerations are included. Since contraception is more widely preferred by the public, the development of a perfect contraception would improve the situation.

845 Kane, John J. _Marriage and the Family: A Catholic Approach_ New York: Dryden Press, 1952. 341 pp.

The section on birth control, pp. 268-77, begins with a discussion of the differences between birth control, which can include failure to marry and abstinence from copulation, and artificial contraception, the use of which the Roman Catholic Church views as a perversion of a natural act. The general decline in the birth rate and the increased percentage of childless marriages are examined, and Pearl's study, which demonstrated that contraceptive effort varies considerably in regard to economic circumstances is reviewed. Artificial contraception is practiced for a variety of reasons, some of which are undoubtedly rationalizations, and the roots of its use go deep into personal and group attitudes, characteristic of a materialistic society. The prevalence of contraception is but another index of society's lack of a consistent value system, and the two basic questions for Catholics today involve the problem of how Catholic families can live according to their value system in a society which not only ignores or ridicules it, but actually places serious barriers in the way of such a practice, and the extent to which Catholic families can play an active part in assisting others to achieve an integrated value system. It would appear that the matter of contraception is much more emotional than logical and that contraception fits into the psychic needs of many Americans because of the false system of values available to them.

846 Kantner, John, and Allingham, John D. "American Attitudes on Population Policy: Recent Trends," Stud. Fam. Planning, No. 30, May 1968, pp. 1-6.

Changes in the way the public regards the population program are examined according to the findings of a 1967 survey taken by the Gallup Organization. The 1967 findings are compared with the results of a previous survey completed in 1965. Viewed first is the over-all opinion profile, and then variations in opinions by age, sex, education and religion of the respondents. The authors also review the events of the period between the two surveys which may have influenced public attitudes. In summarizing the results, the authors conclude that change is perceptible in how the public views the problem of population generally, in opinions regarding policy and programs, and in attitudes toward abortion. Some liberalization is evident while at the same time the population problem has waned somewhat in relation to other issues of public concern. There is widespread support for many programs and policies -- providing birth control information to adults, married and single, giving aid to states and cities and to foreign countries, revising the laws on abortion. On the whole, the evidence suggests a growing acceptance of the need to take steps necessary to meet the problem of population growth, a view against which there is no major center of popular opposition.

847 Kantner, John F., and Kiser, Clyde V. "Social and Psychological Factors Affecting Fertility. xxii. The Interrelation of Fertility, Fertility Planning and Intergenerational Social Mobility," Milbank Memorial Fund Quart. 32(1):69-103, 1954.

This survey investigates the hypothesis of Arsene Dumont which states that there is a relationship between social mobility and reproduction. The data used in the survey were collected as part of the Indianapolis Study which utilized data collected from 1444 couples included in previous studies. Although exceptions are noted, the data support the hypothesis in that families exhibiting intergeneration mobility upward tend to be smaller than nonmobile families of comparable status. Within the same limits, a second hypothesis that planned families of socially mobile couples are smaller than families of socially nonmobile couples of comparable status is confirmed. The third hypothesis that socially mobile couples are more effective in fertility planning than socially nonmobile couples of comparable status could not be confirmed. There is some evidence that social mobility partially overcomes resistances to contraception, giving upwardly mobile couples a position intermediate in fertility planning effectiveness between the level of effectiveness demonstrated by their origin and destination groups. Consistent with this is the greater regularity of contraception among upwardly mobile couples. This is taken as a desire to regulate conception but a desire that is handicapped by relatively ineffective practices.

848 Kantner, John F., and Potter, Robert G., Jr. "Social and Psychological Factors Affecting Fertility. xxiv. The Relationship of Family Size in Two Successive Generations," Milbank Memorial Fund Quart. 32(3):294-311, 1954.

The data obtained from the Indianapolis Study have been analyzed to test the hypothesis "Family and childhood situations and attitudes affect the proportion of couples practicing contraception effectively and the size of the planned families." No correlation was seen between number of biological siblings and the type of family-size control practiced, the socio-economic status or feeling of economic security of husband and wife.

849 Kantner, John F., and Whelpton, P.K. "Social and Psychological Factors Affecting Fertility. xvi. Fertility Rates and Fertility Planning by Character of Migration," Milbank Memorial Fund Quart. 30:153-58, 1952.

This study deals with some of the relationships between physical mobility and patterns of reproductive behavior. Specifically, frequency of movement is studied in relation to (a) number of live births and (b) the extent to which fertility is planned. In addition, the relationship of the size and locations of the migrant's community of origin to his fertility and fertility planning is investigated. Some attempt will also be made to deal with the interaction among these variables.

850 Katz, N. "Judicial and Statutory Trends in the Law of Adoption," Georgetown Law J. 51:64-95. Fall 1962.

A review of the recent developments in American adoption laws, stressing the complexity of the adoption process and its traditional concern for the welfare of the child. The author contends that the adoption of a child is no longer a simple legal act, but rather a legal and social process. Reference to the model adoption legislation drawn up by the Department of Health, Education, and Welfare indicate that the present tendency is toward greater recognition of the need for safeguarding the interests of all of the parties to an adoption proceeding.

851 Kelley, Dean, and Pemberton, John de J., Jr. Birth Control and the Legislation of Morality. [New York], National Conference of Christians and Jews, 1962. 46 pp.

This symposium organized by the National Conference of Christians and Jews is concered with birth control as a part of the more general problem: what forms and forums should conscientious moral convictions manifest for the enrichment rather than the disruption of our civil commonwealth? The four papers published in this volume are employed to generate discussion among the many participants. They are: Reflections on Birth Control and the Legislation of Morality by Rev. Dean M. Kelley; Birth Control and the Law by John de J. Pemberton Jr.; Remarks by Donald B. Straus; and Remarks by Harriet F. Pilpel. Most of the participants are clergymen, educators, or members of Planned Parenthood.

852 Kennedy, David Michael. "Birth Control: Its Heroine and Its History in America -- The Career of Margaret Sanger," Dissertation Abstr. 29A:3953, 1968-1969. Abstract of Ph.D. Thesis, Yale University, New Haven, Connecticut, 1968. 428 pp.

This dissertation is a history of the birth control movement in the United States. It is necessarily, therefore, in part a biography of the movement's leader, Margaret Sanger. The following pages examine the factors which impelled Mrs. Sanger to begin her career; the heritage of nineteenth-century attitudes toward the family, women, and sexuality which influenced the reception given to her proposed reform; the organizational development of the birth control movement; the rhetoric which Mrs. Sanger employed to justify her cause; the responses she evoked; the growing public acceptance of the practice of contraception and the consequent adjustments in the positions of American churches; the relationship of the medical profession to the birth control movement; and the history of state and federal laws with regard to contraception. The dissertation argues that Mrs. Sanger presented an idea which was neither altogether new nor altogether progressive. The birth control movement in large part capitalized on long-developing social practices and attitudes, though the emergence of an organized movement to promote contraception in the early twentieth century was symptomatic of the quickening of those developments. And contrary to accepted belief, birth control has gained increasing acceptance not simply as a liberating device, but in perhaps larger measure as a conservative one.

853 Kennedy, J.L. "Mississippi Marriages and Legislation," Public Admin. Survey, March 1957, pp. 1-6.

In 1955, Mississippi was second only to Nevada in terms of marriage rates for the country, and of the total number of licenses issued in that year, 65.6% went to couples from other states and 47.1% went to teenagers. The author describes Mississippi's present marriage law, which has no required blood test and provisions on proof of age and a waiting period that goes largely unnoticed, and discusses legislative attempts to strengthen this law. The laws on marriage in neighboring states are outlined briefly, and opposition to reform is explained in terms of the economy of certain counties in Mississippi, whose marriage license businesses benefit from out-of-state applications. The author concludes with a discussion of the part lax marriage laws play in encouraging a high divorce rate for the state.

854 Kennedy, R.B. "Abortion: Issue of the Shadows, Dilemma of Antiquity," J. Mississippi Med. Assn. 8:661-ff., 1967.

The medical, legal and religious aspects of abortion law reform are examined.

855 Kennedy, R.B. "Malthus and Welfare: A Public Policy on Contraception?" J. Mississippi Med. Assn. 4:551-52. December 1963.

Editorial comment. In the Malthusian dispute, it seems that Malthus was more nearly correct about the supply of welfare funds than that of food. The crucial question is whether a state can provide contraceptive services under programs in which federal funds are involved. The National Institutes of Health and the Public Health Service have granted funds for birth control research. Except for policies relating to sterilization, most medical organizations have been silent on public sponsorship of contraceptive services for welfare recipients. But the Illinois action formally raises the issue to the extent that medicine in that state must soon speak.

856 Kenney, D.J. "Thalidomide Catalyst to Abortion Reform," Arizona Law Rev. 5:105, 1963.

The difficulty of establishing legal justification for abortion, the abortion laws, and opposition to them are examined. The author contends that the thalidomide incidents may center public attention on the problem and affect changes of the present abortion laws.

857 Kim, Han Young. "Structural Balance and Adoption and Diffusion of an Innovation: A Study of Adoption and Diffusion of the Intrauterine Contraceptive Device," Dissertation Abstr. 28A:3779-80, 1967-68. Abstract of Ph.D. Thesis, University of Washington, Seattle, Washington, 1967. 202 pp.

This study examines the applicability of "balance" theory in the explanation of the adoption and diffusion of an innovation. The research is specifically concerned with the cognitive process of the potential adopter which is assumed to have a bearing on the pattern of adoption and further diffusion of an innovation by the individual. The formulation proposes that the adoption and diffusion of an innovation by an individual depends not only on his perception of the attributes of the innovative item but also upon the perception of his "significant others" opinion toward the item. It asserts that these two factors have an "interaction" effect on adoption and diffusion. An alternative set of propositions specifically pertaining to post-decisional behavior is also set forth on the basis of "dissonance" theory, and the explanatory utility of the implications of conventional "balance" theory and "dissonance" theory with specific reference to post-decisional behavior is comparatively examined. These propositions were tested empirically with regard to the adoption and diffusion of an innovative contraceptive method, i.e., the intrauterine device, among female clients of Public Health Clinics in King County, Washington.

858 Kinsolving, L. "What About Therapeutic Abortion?" Christian Century 81:632-ff., 1964.

A review of the arguments from the Roman Catholic opponents to changes in the California statute on induced abortion. The author cites the disagreement in the Church that life starts at conception and opposes the view that the fetus has human rights equal to those after birth. In a conflict situation the mother's life should be the primary concern. The author contends that a minority opposition should not be allowed to obstruct a needed revision in the abortion law.

859 Kirkendall, Lester A. "Sex and Social Policy," Clin. Pediat. 3(4):236-46. April 1964.

Profound alterations in non-marital sexual standards and practices have resulted from (a) waning power of fear-evoking deterrents; (b) greater capacity of people through better health, earlier pubescence and later climacteric for enjoying the pleasures of sexual activities; (c) cultural interchanges which challenges existing and conventional practices; (d) changing sex roles; and (e) rise of scientific inquiry. A redirection of thinking regarding management of the sexual impulse can be attained by eliminating: (1) an unreasoning and irrational fear of sex; (2) the view that the sexual problem is a youth, rather than an adult problem; and (3) attitudes of marked repressiveness which have made rational procedures impossible. A growing body of evidence indicates that the individual who is using sex exploitively is very likely seeking satisfactions through sex that he could not find through other more acceptable ways. One aid would be a value framework for moral decision-making which emphasizes those attitudes and acts which have implications for the improvement of interpersonal relations.

860 Kirsch, R.M. "How Does Epilepsy Affect the Validity of Marriages," Wyoming Law J. 10:244-48. Spring 1956

The author examines legislation and pertinent court cases dealing with epilepsy and marriage since 1895, when Connecticut enacted a statute which provided for the imprisonment (up to three years) of any man or woman with epilepsy who married or entered into a common law relationship when the woman was under forty-five years of age. In the absence of a statute prohibiting marriage between persons either of whom is epileptic, the courts have generally held that if the afflicted person conceals the fact of epilepsy, a fraud results which betrays the marriage relationship. In states which do have statutes the courts generally agree that such marriage is voidable, not void, although the courts in such states do not agree as to the circumstances under which they will grant a decree of annulment. The author stresses that only the idiopathic (genetic) type of epilepsy is transmissible to offspring and that the law should not be concerned with symptomatic (acquired) epilepsy, although in practice few courts make a distinction between the two.

861 Kiser, Clyde V. "Implications of Population Trends for Postwar Policies," Milbank Memorial Fund Quart. 22(2): 111-30, 1944.

An abstract of a round table discussion by some 25 participants with final emphasis on the necessity of child security programs.

862 Kiser, Clyde V., and Whelpton, P.K. "Social and Psychological Factors Affecting Fertility: ix, Fertility Planning and Fertility Rates by Socio-Economic Status," Milbank Memorial Fund Quart. 27(2):188-244, 1949.

This survey included data from a survey of 41,498 native-white, once married couples with the wife under 45 which indicated that these couples exhibit fertility rates by age and age at marriage quite similar to those for comparable couples in all cities of 250,000 population and over in this country. A sample of 1,977 Protestant couples with at least an elementary school education are on an average 15% less fertile than couples in cities of 250,000 or over. Study of this group shows little relation of fecundity status to socio-economic class. About 73% are classed as relatively fecund and the rest as relatively sterile. These average proportions remain much the same in various socio-economic subdivisions. Further breakdown of the data reveal that of all the subdivisions erected the relatively fecund group varies most widely with economic status. The higher the socio-economic status, the higher the proportion of couples practicing contraception effectively, but at the same time the size of the family may or may not be depressed by this planning.

863 Kling, S.G. Sexual Behavior and the Law. New York: Geis, 1965.

A popular presentation of legal aspects of abortion, adultery, annulment, aphrodisiacs, artificial insemination, birth control and contraceptives, homosexuality, impotency and frigidity, incest and prostitution.

864 Kramer, Leonard J., ed. Man Amid Change in World Affairs. New York: Friendship Press, 1964. 175 pp.

The major part of this book originated in the discussions of five study commissions comprised of over a hundred authorities on various aspects of world affairs and convened by the Department of International Affairs of the National Council of the Churches of Christ in the U.S.A. Chapter, Challenge of the developing nations has section, The problem of population, which advocates government aid in family planning programs.

865 Krause, Harry D. "Bringing the Bastard into the Great Society -- A Proposed Uniform Act on Legitimacy," Texas Law Rev. 44:829-59. April 1966.

The inadequacy of illegitimacy laws in the United States is discussed, with references to the procession of the courts in an uneven fashion from common-law principles which were strongly influenced by ancient moral taboos, the failure of the legislatures to provide a full-scale statutory treatment of illegitimacy, the lack of uniformity among the states which has created an acute conflict of laws problem, and failure of the laws to protect the interests of the illegitimate child. A proposed uniform act on legitimacy, with sections on legitimacy and legitimation, child's right of support and inheritance, enforcement of support obligation against father, and miscellaneous provisions, which include uniformity of interpretation and operation-repeal, is described and the present American laws of illegitimacy are then examined and compared to relevant provisions of the proposed Act. It is concluded that efforts to bring the illegitimate into the second half of this century should be statutory, because only broad, coordinated legislation can assure the uniformity for elimination of the conflict of laws problem. A new draft of uniform legislation should propose a unified view of illegitimacy that centers on the interest of the child and supplants the present piecemeal approach that has resulted from too much concern for the other interests involved, primarily that of the father.

866 Kuchler, Frances W. Law of Engagement and Marriage 1966. New York: Oceana, 1966. xxii, 103 pp.

Provides a summary of legal aspects of marriage in the several states of the U.S.A. Topics include: common-law and statutory marriage, age and consent requirements, void and voidable marriage, rights of engaged couples, antenuptial agreements, proxy and G.I. marriages, annulment, and support obligations.

867 Kummer, Jerome M., ed. Abortion: Legal and Illegal, A Dialogue Between Attorneys and Psychiatrists. Santa Monica, California: The Author, n.d.

Two lawyers and three physicians discuss the proposed liberalization of California's abortion law at a meeting (panel) in 1963. They review the pros and cons from medical-psychiatric, legal, and religious viewpoints. Appendix B is the Amici Curiae Brief submitted by the two panel lawyers to the Supreme Court of the State of California in the case of Shively and Smith vs. Board of Medical Examiners.

868 Kummer, Jerome M. "Criminal Abortion -- A Consideration of Ways to Reduce Incidence," California Med. 95:170-ff., 1961.

Discusses the contradictions between existing abortion laws and current medical attitudes and practice, with reference to the fact that, while the laws have as their basic premise the protection of the mother's health, they do not allow the physician to use his own professional judgment in regard to the interruption of pregnancy. The author contends that the number of criminal abortions can be minimized through the recognition of medical, humanitarian, and eugenic grounds for abortion, the institution of abortion committees in hospitals permitted to perform abortions, and by switching the judgment of humanitarian indications from the medical to the legal profession. Recommended also are abortion consultation centers, extended contraceptive research, and increased sex education for the general public.

869 Kummer, Jerome M., and Leavy, Zad. "Abortionists Are Rarely Convicted," New Med. Materia 4:59-ff., 1962.

It is contended that the number of illegal abortions will not diminish until there is a realistic reform of current abortion statutes. Stressed is the need for sex education programs and abortion counseling centers.

870 Kummer, Jerome M., and Leavy, Zad. "Therapeutic Abortion Law Confusion," J. Amer. Med. Assn. 195:96-ff., 1966.

Discussion of attempted reform of abortion laws in the United States, the puritanical basis of current laws and presentation of some statistics in support of the need for reform. Notes that abortions increase with education level and parity and that the percentage of pregnancies ending in induced abortions is high for younger married or previously married women (28% for ages 16-20), lower for more mature women (12% for ages 31-39), and highest for older women (36% for ages 41-50).

871 Kurtz, Sheldon F. "Old Wine in New Wineskins or Mutual Consent Divorces for New Yorkers," Syracuse Law Rev. 18: 71-88. Fall 1966.

Before New York's divorce law was amended in 1966, New Yorkers could obtain a divorce only after the proven commission of adultery, which was the only technically designated divorce ground. The newly written Section 170 of the New York Domestic Relations Law will now permit divorce on any of six grounds, including abandonment for two or more years, cruel and inhuman treatment by one spouse jeopardizing the physical or mental well-being of the other, spouses having lived apart pursuant to a decree of separation for two years, and spouses having lived separate and apart pursuant to a written agreement of separation for two years. The author discusses some of the questions raised by Section 170 of the new statute, with particular references to problems of separation agreements and the current validity of a bilateral Mexican divorce, which many couples obtained under the old statute. Also reviewed are public policy considerations in separation agreements, problems regarding support and alimony payments when a separation agreement is followed by either a separation or divorce decree and whether refusal to cohabit after demand constitutes desertion.

The author describes the leading New York case involving the validity of bilateral Mexican divorces (Rosenstiel v. Rosenstiel) and includes descriptions of court cases involving many of the above questions. It is concluded that, while mutual consent was not adopted as a grounds of divorce in New York, certainly a mutually agreed upon separation agreement is close in spirit, if not in law.

872 Lader, Lawrence. Abortion. New York: Bobbs-Merrill Co., 1966. viii, 212 pp.

Reviews the religious, legal and medical aspects of the abortion situation in the United States including suggestions for reform. Data from Scandinavia, Eastern Europe and the United States which indicate that the mortality rates and physical complications following hospital abortion are minimal are examined. Report of the psychic sequalae of induced abortion in Scandinavia and the United States illustrates that psychological consequences are mainly the product of a myth. The committee systems are criticized for their lack of uniformity and discrimination against the ward patient. Evolution of American abortion laws is then described with reference to positions of the major religions. The author suggests that the most practical solution is the insistence of medical profession on its rights within the existing laws. He also notes that previous court decisions have established liberal interpretations in several states and that through a series of test cases further liberalization could be effected.

873 Lamm, Richard D., et al. "The Legislative Process in Changing Therapeutic Abortion Laws: The Colorado Experience," Amer. J. Orthopsychiatry 39(4):684-90. July 1969.

There is a growing belief in the United States generally, and in the medical professions specifically, that abortion is essentially a medical matter. However, each one of the 50 states has laws severely limiting the circumstances in which a doctor may perform abortions. Reform of these laws is a political product, purchased in the political marketplace, paid for with political dollars and sometimes political lives. This paper examines the successful progress of a liberalized law through the legislature of Colorado, the first of a growing number of states to pass abortion law reform.

874 Landis, Judson T. "Attitudes and Policies Concerning Marriages Among High School Students," Marr. Fam. Living 18(2):128-36. May 1956.

A report on responses to a questionnaire on student marriages sent to the 469 public senior high schools in California. Analysis is based on 205 schools which gave complete marriage information on the upper three grades and on the 286 schools giving complete information on school policy toward marriage and the teaching of family living courses. 35.8% of all high schools in California were enrolled in these schools. Findings: (1) 90% of the schools had had one or more student marriages during the previous year (1954); (2) 2,044 females and 220 males had married. (Comparisons are made with Ivins' study in New Mexico.) (3) Majority of females married out-of-school males while majority of males married in-school girls. (4) The drop-out rate was high among the girls who had married. (5) 142 schools take no action when students marry; 248 did not require school attendance after marriage; 106 principals have conferences with the student, and spouse, and parents. Some principals encourage withdrawal or transfer; work out problems on individual basis; have counseling; and/or remove certain privileges. (6) In general administrators take a negative attitude toward student marriages. (7) Few principals were planning changes in policy for dealing with high school marriages but changes being planned were of a discriminatory type. (8) 178 principals regarded married students a problem because they believed they (a) discuss sexual experiences with unmarried students; (b) were irregular in attendance and had a high dropout rate; (c) encouraged single students to marry; and (d) were a classroom problem. (9) 103 schools request or pressure the girls to withdraw at pregnancy and 32 more expel students at pregnancy. (10) 76% of the schools offer courses in family living usually at the senior year and in 1953-54, 20,378 students were enrolled in these courses. The incidence of high school marriages shows a common situation existing in almost all schools in the state, and point to the need for careful evaluation of present policies and the introduction of constructive action for meeting student needs.

875 Landis, Judson T. "Attitudes of Individual California Physicians and Policies of State Medical Societies on Vasectomy for Birth Control," J. Marr. Fam. 28(3):277-83. August 1966.

Statistics are lacking on the frequency of vasectomy for birth control, because operations are performed in doctor's offices and reporting of such operations is not required. A questionnaire was sent to 1,501 active physicians in a two-county medical society asking for information on the number of vasectomies performed, whether doctors approve the vasectomy for birth control, whether they believe the operation to be legal, how successful they have found the operation to be in preventing conception, and their success in reversing the operation. A questionnaire was also sent to the 50 state medical associations to determine their policies on vasectomy as birth control.

876 Landis, Judson T., and Poffenberger, Thomas. "The Marital and Sexual Adjustment of 330 Couples Who Chose Vasectomy as a Form of Birth Control," J. Marr. Fam. 27(1):57-58. February 1965.

A questionnaire study was made of 330 couples who had chosen vasectomy as a means of birth control. The couples gave economic considerations as important in their decision to choose sterilization and to have vasectomy rather than salpingectomy. The respondents reported great improvement in their sex life following the operation; and, in retrospect, almost all were glad that they had had the vasectomy.

877 Langer, Elinor. "Birth Control: U.S. Programs Off to Slow Start," Science 156(3776):756-67. May 12,1967.

The author describes and analyzes the financial and operational problems that have plagued government involvement in family planning programs since early 1966, when HEW issued a policy statement on birth control and pledged federal support and action. Discussed are HEW's belief in comprehensive health programs, the funding proposals and opposition of Senator Tydings, OEO activities and its unified community action approach, and the usefulness of birth control as an anti-poverty measure. The author concludes that, considering the ineffectiveness and bureaucratic sluggishness of federal action thus far in the area of family planning programs, OEO's comparative energy and innovative approaches should not be undermined by heavy involvement with the cautious and slow-moving Public Health Service.

878 Larsen, Nils P. "Field Experiment in Proper Birth Spacing. Its Effect on the Health Problems of Mothers and Infants," Human Fertility 9(1):1-5, 1944.

The sugar plantations of Hawaii, with a laboring population of about 80,000, have a medical and health service provided by the owners which has offered the women birth-control information and material for many years. Since this did not prove to be sufficiently dependable, it was supplemented with surgical sterilization, performed immediately after childbirth, where the number of children was as large as seemed desirable. In 1936 there were 140 such sterilizations, in 1943 there were 110.

879 Larsen, Paul. "Trends and Developments in Oregon Family Law: Parental Rights and Child Welfare," Oregon Law Rev. 43:97-134. February 1964.

The purpose of this article is to discuss a selection of recent Oregon decisions and legislation relating to divorce, custody, adoption and the juvenile court. Certain important changes in the roles of the trial judge and the attorney in this area of the law are identified, particularly the increasing reliance by the Oregon Supreme Court on the trial judge to deal with all family-law problems, and the subtle changes taking place in the attorney's contribution to the solution of such problems.

880 Lauth, E.J. "Liberal Abortion Laws: The Antithesis of the Practice of Medicine," J. Florida Med. Assn. 54:918-ff., 1967.

The author argues against the liberalization of abortion laws on the grounds that it is the duty of a physician to preserve life; that life begins at the moment of conception; that it is the legal, and not the medical profession that should govern abortion legislation; that liberal abortion laws do not lessen criminal abortions and that abortions do not remove causes of rape, incest or foetal deformities. It is suggested that the power of the State might increase in the area of the right to live as a consequence of liberal abortion laws.

881 "Law of Criminal Abortion: An Analysis of Proposed Reform," Indiana Law J. 32:193-ff., 1957.

Discussed are the statutes on abortion, the rationale behind them and the problem of their enforcement. After a review of the possibilities and arguments for and against reform, it is concluded that public opinion will determine the extent of changes in these laws.

882 Leasure, J. William. "Some Economic Benefits of Birth Prevention," Milbank Memorial Fund Quart. 45(4):417-25. October 1967.

Society has a right to be concerned about the size of families, since after the birth of a child the taxpayers (local, state, and federal) will spend money on that child for education, health, and welfare. If the child had not been born, these funds would represent a reduction in government expenditures over what would otherwise have been spent. A proposal is made along these lines. If a female in the lower-income group successfully limits her family to two or three children, the typical middle-class family size, then society could afford to provide as an incentive some of the savings to the taxpayers resulting from the prevention of an additional fourth or fifth child. This payment would be derived from the savings for the taxpayers over the 18 years or so following a birth, i.e., the time when the child is dependent and not working. After that time, the child becomes an adult and contributes to society by working and paying taxes. This scheme is not to be interpreted as an effort to eliminate the poor. The proposed payments should be interpreted as an effort to enable families to have more time and money to spend on the existing children who, as a consequence, will have a greater likelihood of leaving the ranks of the poor. It would enable the children of the poor to receive during their school age years some of the benefits enjoyed by the children of the middle-class. These expenditures, therefore, can be regarded as an investment in people in addition to being a savings for the taxpayers.

883 Leavy, Zad. "Criminal Abortion: Facing the Facts," Los Angeles Bar Bull. 34:355-ff., 1959.

The author examines the more restrictive abortion statutes and emphasize their ineffectiveness in limiting the number of criminal abortions and problems of enforcement. The gap between policy and practice indicates that an informed public and the medical and legal professions must work toward clarification and liberalization of these statutes.

884 Leavy, Zad, and Kummer, Jerome M. "Abortion and the Population Crisis; Therapeutic Abortion and the Law; Some New Approaches," Ohio Law J. 27:647-ff., 1966.

The authors review such aspects of the abortion problem as the question of accepted medical practice, the use of medical and humanitarian indications for abortion, abortion as an increasingly popular method of birth control, and abortion law reform in other countries in order to demonstrate the need in this country for liberalization of current abortion statutes. The general public, as well as the news media in their editorials, have shown interest in such liberalization, and several court decisions are cited to indicate the possibility for change.

885 Leavy, Zad, and Kummer, Jerome M. "Criminal Abortion: A Failure of Law; Needless Suffering and Death Result from the Drastic Restrictions Placed on Therapeutic Abortions by the Laws of Most American States," J. Amer. Bar Assn. 50: 52-55. January 1964.

The problems relating to criminal abortion are of the utmost complexity from social, legal, and medical viewpoints, and airing these problems is a prerequisite to any attempt at solution. The law concerning therapeutic abortion needs to be changed to bring it into conformity with responsible medical attitudes and practices. It is the practice in many hospitals to perform abortions for reasons other than to save the life of the mother. An official change in the law would greatly reduce the death rate due to illegal abortions performed by incompetent persons.

886 Leavy, Zad, and Kummer, Jerome M. "Criminal Abortion: Human Hardship and Unyielding Laws," Southern California Law Rev. 35:123-ff. Winter 1962.

This paper suggests that the first approach to solving the criminal abortion problem is through a cautious modification of a confusing and unrealistic statute, the restrictiveness and unequal application of which continue as a restraining porticullis to other potential solutions. The article relates some facts about abortions by first providing a description of the problem and reviewing the laws, court decisions and rationale behind the laws (especially religious influence). Calls for a modification of existing laws, as criminal abortion is undoubtedly stimulated by the pressure of these stringent laws and by their loose enforcement. The authors compare American with foreign laws and practices. New legislation in other countries resulted in a rise in the incidence of legal abortion and a substantial reduction in the numbers of criminal abortions. Finally, the authors discuss and evaluate recent efforts to modify the California law with special emphasis on the Knox Bill, and suggest preventive measures to accompany legislative changes.

887 Lee, N.H. _Acquaintance Networks in the Social Structure of Abortion_. Doctoral Thesis, Harvard University, 1967.

An analysis of interviews with 25 women and questionnaire responses from 89 of 114 women who had illegal abortions. Discussed are the characteristics of the informants; age, education, employment, place of residence, religion and number of previous terminated pregnancies. Most of the women stated that their decision to have an abortion was based on their unreadiness to accept the responsibility of a child. Also examined are the price ranges of abortions, the places where the abortions were performed, methods used and most common reactions felt after the operation. Immediately following the abortion, most of the women said that they improved their contraceptive practices; however 26 women reported second abortions.

888 Lee, R.E. _North Carolina Family Law_. Third edition. Three Vols. Winston-Salem: Wake Forest College Bookstore, 1963.

The author's present effort has been to clarify, where possible, the law relating to family life in North Carolina and to present in as simple language as accuracy will permit these principles as of the present time. Family Law is now so controlled by statutes that it can no longer be classified as a "common law" subject. It is a subject requiring attentiveness to the statutes and decisions of a particular state.

889 Lidz, Ruth W. "Emotional Factors in the Success of Contraception," Fertility and Sterility 20(5):761-71. October 1969.

Women's use of contraception is influenced by positive and negative, conscious and subconscious attitudes and feelings toward sexuality, pregnancy, childbirth, parenthood, and, particularly, infertility. Women positively motivated toward contraception are those who are: (1) satisfied with their completed family; (2) sexually adjusted and in no hurry to have children, or wishing to postpone the next child; (3) fearful of pregnancy; (4) fearful of childbirth; (5) neurotic and fearful of the dependency of a child; and (6) desirous of being men, including certain homosexuals. Negative reactions to birth control may be seen in women who: (1) have made a marginal sexual adjustment; (2) have a special investment in pregnancy as a creative process; (3) started contraception for financial reasons only, or to please the husband; (4) feel that having children is the only true meaning in life and whose emotional satisfaction comes from babies and young children; and (5) are lonely, depressive, and deprived, and who want a child to satisfy their own emptiness. This study is based on a small number of women attending the Family Planning Clinic at the hospital of the Yale University School of Medicine, and taking contraceptive pills or using the IUD.

890 Lief, Harold I. "The Physician and Family Planning," J. Amer. Med. Assn. 197(8):128-32, 1966.

The physician should aid in the implementation of family planning programs. To do so, he must acquaint himself with the various contraceptive techniques and devices and learn their proper use, and he must counsel patients about their use and benefits with regard to the number and timing of births. He may be motivated to participate in such programs once he is informed of the magnitude of the population problem, and the disastrous consequences of unplanned and numerous births with regard to sexual and marital adjustment and family unity.

891 Linford, Orma. "The Mormons and the Law: The Polygamy Cases," Utah Law Rev. 9:308-70, 1964 and 9:543-91, 1965.

The author, in an extensive review, examines the content and application of the federal anti-polygamy statutes and Supreme Court decisions in the Mormon cases of the second half of the nineteenth century. The analysis is made with a view of the total damage done to the Mormon community, and the author feels that this view, which combines an informed, intelligent understanding of the Mormon experience and condition with an understanding of the cumulative effect of the anti-polygamy legislation, has been overlooked by students of this area of constitutional law. Included in Part I are sections on the Mormon "patriarchal marriage;" the 1862 Act; the Edmunds Act; and the Edmunds-Tucker Act. The latter were congressional actions against polygamy during the period 1856-1887. Also discussed in Part I are the criminal prosecutions of polygamy during this period -- the Reynolds case and those cases dealing with unlawful cohabitation and adultery. Part II includes sections on the civil disabilities of Mormons during the late nineteenth century -- disfranchisement, disqualification from office, jury duty, inheritance and naturalization -- occurring as a result of polygamy problems; the Church Escheat cases are also described.

892 Lion, F.D. "Abortion and Theology," in Guttmacher,A.F., ed. The Case for Legalized Abortion Now. Berkeley: Diablo Press, 1967.

It is contended that the quality of life takes precedence over the quantity of life, and the author suggests the legalization of abortion on grounds that are economic, social, eugenic and humanitarian.

893 Liu, William T. "Selected Works on Fertility and Family Planning Studies in the United States 1960-1967," J. Marr. Fam. 30(2):346-66, 1968.

This annotated bibliography is divided into seven sections: (1) demographic aspects of fertility studies; (2) socio-economic aspects of fertility studies; (3) physiological aspects of fertility studies; (4) abortion, adoption and other factors related to family size; (5) family-planning program studies and trends; (6) family size expectations; and (7) population policy.

894 LoGotto, Anthony F. "Artificial Insemination, I. Legal Aspects," The Catholic Lawyer 1(3):172-83. July 1955.

This article highlights some of the legal involvements created by artificial insemination of human beings. It reviews the precedents of court cases involving the questions of legitimacy, adultery, liability of physician, and liability of donor from as early as 1883. The existing statutes of legislature and efforts to initiate legislature is included. A brief history of the artificial insemination of human beings and the 1955 statistics on artificial insemination are given.

895 LoGotto, Anthony F. "Artificial Insemination, II. Ethical and Sociological Aspects," The Catholic Lawyer 1(4):267-80. October 1955.

The subject of artificial insemination poses complex legal problems, and of greater concern, involvements of an ethical and sociological nature. Father LoGotto attacks the proponents of artificial insemination by donor (AID) from a moral, sociological and psychological viewpoint and contends that these considerations should dissuade the prudent man from the practice or the recommending of AID.

896 Lohner, R.W. "Therapeutic Abortion in Salt Lake City, 1954-64," Obstet. Gynec. 17:665-ff., 1966.

The author examines the low frequency of therapeutic abortion in three hospitals in Salt Lake City during a ten-year period. A total of 44 therapeutic abortions were recorded in ten years; 32 were performed for medical reasons; eight for psychiatric reasons; and four for fetal indications. In response to the author's questionnaire which was answered by 44 obstetricians and 14 psychiatrists, it was found that gynecologists favored medical reasons for performing therapeutic abortions and 17 out of 37 of them also stated that a suicide threat was a justifiable psychiatric indication. However, only four out of eleven psychiatrists considered that a suicide threat warranted an abortion. The author explains both the low incidence of performed therapeutic abortions and the conservative opinion of medical practitioners as being a result of a predominantly Mormon community where large families are favored and abortions prohibited.

897 Lombard, John F. Family Law. 4 Vols. Boston: Boston Law Book Co., 1967.

Massachusetts practice concerning marriage and divorce, adoption, paternity, blood tests.

898 London, Gary D., and Anderson, Gail V. "Immediate Postpartum Insertion of an Intrauterine Contraceptive Device," Obstet. Gynecol. 30(6):851-54, 1967.

A series of 899 clinic patients had 5,434 months' experience with an IUD [intrauterine device] after postpartum insertion. Ninety-three per cent were able to retain the IUD after one or two insertions; 73% are still participating in the study and using the devices successfully. Only 5% of the devices were removed because of patients' symptoms or requests. The uncorrected pregnancy rate has been approximately 2/100 woman-years of use. The immediate postpartum insertion of the intrauterine contraceptive device was found to be practical and effective.

899 Lorimer, Frank. "Helping Young America to Responsible Parenthood Through Social and Economic Aids," J. Heredity 32(12):449-54. December 1941.

This 1941 article argues for encouraging moderately-sized families with from four to six children, where such a family size does not jeopardize the economic situation of the married couple. Several suggestions to make a moderate family more economically feasible are given: (1) provide maternity leave with pay; (2) increase the opportunity of employment compatible with motherhood, i.e., give preference to teachers who are mothers; (3) cancel one-fourth of payable income tax for each child; (4) develop public provisions for mothers and children; and (5) apply subsidy to reduction of rents in proportion to the number of children, similar to the Swedish system. Socially oriented changes are also suggested: (1) build world order with security against war, since frustration and anxiety depress fertility, i.e., Austria in the thirties; (2) emphasize community values. The need for changes in psychological attitudes is admitted, but the need for economic and social changes should take precedence.

900 Low, Seth. "Note: The Economics of Adoption," Welfare in Rev. 4(3):12-14. March 1966.

An economic evaluation of the practice of child adoption as a means to reduce the cost of public service and financial support for illegitimate children and those from disintegrated families. As a crude estimate of the cost of caring for and rearing a child for one year the figure of $1,000 is used. For those parents adopting children in 1964, the cost of rearing the 18,600 children placed in that year until their 18th birthday is estimated at $311 million. The economic benefit accruing from public adoption service is balanced against the cost of providing this service; this is crudely estimated at a one-time $1,500 per child placed for adoption. Hence, 18 million may be deducted from the estimated benefit of $78,000 obtained by placing 18,600 children for adoption in 1964, which leaves a net benefit to the public of $50 million for this year. Therefore adoption services actually do have significant economic benefits for society as a whole.

901 Lowe, David, and Lowe, Harriet Van Horne. Abortion and the Law. New York: [Pocket Books], 1966. x, 116 pp.

In the United States, one million women, representing all social and economic levels, terminate pregnancies by abortion each year. If the laws were strictly enforced, many persons would be prosecuted each year. The value of a law which is so widely violated must be questioned. It is the purpose of this book to set forth the issues of legalizing abortion as they are argued pro and con by doctors, lawyers, clergymen and nonprofessional people who are directly involved.

902 Lucas, Roy. "Federal Constitutional Limitations on the Enforcement and Administration of State Abortion Statutes," North Carolina Law Rev. 46:730-78. June 1968.

After a review of existing legislation in the states which prohibit abortion except where the health or life of the mother may be jeopardized by continuation of the pregnancy, arguments concerning the constitutionality of the anti-abortion provisions are put forth. It is asserted that a right to abortion, given the consent of the woman and its performance by a licensed physician, can be claimed on the basis of at least related forms within the Bill of Rights and the 14th Amendment framework: a) a fundamental right of marital privacy, human dignity, and personal autonomy; b) as a penumbral right emanating from values embodied in the express provisions of the Bill of Rights themselves; and c) as a necessary and altogether reasonable application of precedent, namely, Griswold v. Connecticut.

903 Lyon, F.A. "Abortion Laws - Inequitable, Inconsistent and Hence Inexcusable," Minnesota Med. 50:17-ff., 1967.

The need for abortion law reform is stressed, with references to the gap between policy and practice as seen in the lack of law enforcement, changing public attitudes toward abortion as evidenced in opinion polls, and endorsement of the ALI's recommendations on abortion by numerous legal and medical societies. The author considers briefly the approaches of other countries to the abortion problem and reviews the situation in this country. Data on therapeutic abortions in New York indicate that their number has declined, and that white, private patients have better access to such abortions than do non-white ward patients.

904 MacCamy, E.T. "Therapeutic Abortions in Seattle," Western J. Surg. Obstet. Gynec. 70:41-ff., 1962.

Statistical report of therapeutic abortions performed in Seattle during 1955 through 1958. The ratio of abortions to deliveries fell from 1:327 in 1945-1954 to 1:457 in the period reported. Other results show that 55% were followed by sterilization.

905 MacNamara, Donald E.J. "Sex Offenses and Sex Offenders," Annals Amer. Acad. Pol. Soc. Sci. 376:148-55. March 1968.

Sex and sex-related conduct is rigidly circumscribed by law in the United States, and rigorous penalties are provided for deviations from the limited forms of sexual expression (or choice of sexual partners) permitted. These laws reflect a puritanical sociosexual culture, but do not accurately depict either the incidence or modes of sexual conduct. They do, however, create a body of sexual offenders (perhaps exaggerated as to numbers and certainly exaggerated as to degree of social danger) who are differentially subjected to sanctions by public, police, courts, and correction authorities. While sex acts committed by force or threat, and sexual advances to very young children, must be restrained by penal sanctions (at least in the absence of effective therapeutic techniques), many of the sex statutes punishing consensual or autoerotic conduct, or nuisance manifestations of minor sexual pathology, might well be repealed. This would permit the development of a legal code more consistent with the changing sociosexual mores and folkways of our culture.

906 Maginnis, P. "Elective Abortion as a Woman's Right," in: Guttmacher, A.F., ed. The Case for Legalized Abortion Now. Berkeley, Calif.: Diablo Press, 1967.

It is contended that restrictive measures placed on abortion only endanger safe medical practices and interfere with the rights of women.

907 Malabre, Alfred L., Jr. "Curbing Latin Births," Wall Street J. 169:1-ff., April 7,1967.

U. S. adopts soft sell to limit family size from Mexico to Chile. Area population rises faster than elsewhere, bringing economic social problems.

908 Malson, D.E. "An Analysis of Legal Problems Resulting from Practice of Artificial Insemination in Oklahoma," J. Oklahoma State Med. Assn. 49(10):396-98. October 1956.

909 Mandy, A.J. "Reflections of a Gynecologist," in: Rosen, H., (ed.) Abortion in America. Boston: Beacon Press, 1967.

The difference between the number of abortions actually performed each year and policy on abortions, the ambiguity of abortion laws and the problem of the availability of clear scientific evidence all point toward conflict for physicians. The author is uncertain as to whether abortion on the ground of fetal pathology is justified, but research into the problem and a liberalization of the laws are needed.

910 Mannes, M. "A Woman Views Abortion," in Guttmacher, A.F., ed. The Case for Legalized Abortion Now. Berkeley: Diablo Press, 1967.

The author argues for the woman's right to make decisions concerning her own biological processes.

911 Mannheimer, Robert E., "Tax Consequences of Divorce Decrees," Iowa Law Rev. 40:543-71. Summer 1955.

Covered in this article, fully but not all-inclusively, are the law, the regulations and the decisions regarding the tax consequences of alimony and child support payments under divorce decree or other written agreement between husband and wife. The author contends that extreme care and caution must be used in drafting divorce decrees which will have tax consequences, and attempts should be made to anticipate tax problems which may grow out of a particular decree.

912 "Marriage of Minors and the Running of the Statute of Limitations," Alabama Law Rev. 18:121. Fall 1965.

Because of the scarcity of decisions interpreting the Alabama statutes removing the "disabilities of minority" of all married persons and widows or widowers over 18 but under 21, the extent of the emancipation of such persons has not been determined. Whether such persons are subject to the various statutes of limitation after marriage in light of these emancipation statutes remains unresolved. Discussed are the inconclusive statutory language involved; the problem of what is meant by the word "disability" itself; the conflicting conclusions of other jurisdictions as to the effect of an emancipation statute on the running of a statute of limitations; differences in views concerning the purposes which the statutes were designed to serve; and the inconsistency of the legislature to consider married persons over 18 but under 21 sufficiently mature to make binding contracts and deeds and sue or be sued in their own names, but not mature enough to know when to bring a suit. The author concludes with mention of comparable problems that may arise in connection with special limitation clauses applying only to very limited classes of claims.

913 Maryland Ad Hoc Committee to Study the Abortion Law. "Recommendation of the Ad Hoc Committee to Study the Abortion Law," Maryland Med. J. 16:12-ff., 1967.

Maryland physicians and the ad hoc Committee urge abortion law reform in recognition of advances in the fields of psychiatry and genetics, which were unknown when the present bill was passed, and on the grounds of the welfare of patients and of the right of a physician to exercise his medical judgments. The Committee proposes that misinterpretation of the new law can be avoided under the guidelines of the Medical and Chirurgical Faculty of the State.

914 May, W.J. "Therapeutic Abortion in North Carolina," North Carolina Med. J. 23:547-ff., 1962.

The author briefly examines the North Carolina statute which tolerates abortion only when necessary to preserve the life of the mother. Also reviewed are the 76 abortions performed at the North Carolina Baptist Hospital during 1945-1961. All abortions were approved by a committee and in 23 cases the indication was hypertensive vascular disease, tuberculosis in 15, rheumatic heart disease in 12 and psychiatric problems in 8. Also examined are the restrictive, conservative attitudes toward abortion and it is the author's contention that the present laws protect society and the physician from liberal thinkers and the uninformed public and therefore should not be changed.

915 Mayer, Michel F. Divorce and Annulment in the 50 States. New York: Arco, 1967. vi, 89 pp.

Divorce is a problem of civil law, and under our Constitution it is a matter for state legislatures. In the early days of our country, state legislatures granted divorces themselves by their own special acts, but this practice is obsolete, and the function is now judicial. Religious divorce is a subject by itself. It is not easy to pigeonhole the various causes for annulment and divorce, since their boundaries often overlap. Conduct may justify a decree in one state on one ground and in another under a separate heading. For example, consistent refusal of sex relations by a spouse may be cruelty or it may be constructive desertion. What is "cruelty" in one state may be "indignities" in another. A course of conduct might lead to divorce on one ground in one state but on a different ground elsewhere. Inflexible rules are difficult to find.

916 Mayhew, Bruce H., Jr. "Behavioral Observability and Compliance with Religious Proscriptions on Birth Control," Soc. Forces 47(1):60-69. September 1968.

Differences in behavioral observability, as determined by the prevalence of religious endogamy, account for differences in compliance with the religious proscription against the use of artificial means of birth control. Data are presented on fertility differences among Negro female members of Roman Catholic (number equals 42) and Pentocostal-Holiness (number equals 57) churches. Differences in behavioral observability for these females are determined by differences in the chuch membership status of their husbands. High behavioral observability systematically predicts high fertility. These findings suggest that a stronger emphasis on the explanatory power of situational or external constraints would be profitable in the study of religious organizations.

917 McCoy, Kenneth D., Jr. "Constitutionality of State Statutes Prohibiting the Dissemination of Birth Control Information," Louisiana Law Rev. 23:773-78. June 1963.

This article argues against the prohibition of the dissemination of birth control information. The end sought by states in restricting noncommercial distribution of birth control information appears to be elimination of what a legislature has deemed unhealthy and immoral influences; the means, criminal sanctions for distributing such information. The author submits that anti-birth control statutes regulating the use or dissemination of information, coupled with the improbability of legislative action to modernize the law in this area, dictates the conclusion that the constitutionality of such statutes will be determined in the near future.

918 McDonald, Donald. "Tax Aspects of Divorce, Separation, Alimony and Support," University Pittsburg Law Rev. 17: 1-19. Fall 1955.

Discussed are the special rules which affect every separation or divorce and the agreements incident thereto contained in the Internal Revenue Code. The basic principles governing these situations are outlined, and then the author examines specific sections of the code pertaining to payments under a support decree, a written separation agreement and a decree of divorce; the purpose of the payments under which they are deductible; the payee and source of payments; "periodic" payments; insurance; annuities; payments from a trust; rules where children are involved; the husband's deduction; settlement by property transfer -- income and basis; current income tax returns and general economic results; gift and estate tax rules; and, finally, problems of local law. It is concluded that the negotiation of any separation agreement should take into account whether the husband or wife is to pay the taxes on the income. This is particularly important because a tax benefit for one party comes only at the tax expense of the other.

919 McElin, T.W. "Control of Therapeutic Abortion in a General Hospital," Clin. Obstet. Gynec. 2:110-ff., 1959.

Report of a ten-year history of therapeutic abortions performed at the Evanston Hospital, Evanston, Illinois is presented. In 1954 the hospital established an abortion committee system composed of two permanent members and three other members appointed by the committee chairman by reason of their knowledge of the medical problem involved in the case. The results of the first five years when abortions were performed with the approval of two consulting physicians are compared to the second five-year period when the committee system was in effect.

920 McVeety, J. "Law and the Single Woman," Women Law J. 53: 10-14. Winter 1967.

At the time of the 1960 census, there were in this country more than twenty-two million single women 14 years of age and over, of whom about eight million were widows and two million were divorcees. Some of the areas in which single people, especially single women, are at a disadvantage, are listed, with special references to the impact of prejudice and inequality. Mentioned are the single woman's problems in qualifying for a maximum real estate mortgage; the double-thinking regarding single women in connection with home-owner's insurance; the inequity single persons meet in giving away their property, should they desire to do so; the blind spots of the Social Security Act insofar as single persons are concerned; unfairness in inheritance matters; and the federal income tax prejudice against single persons. Some of the disadvantages can be corrected by legislation. At a minimum, legislation giving equal inheritance, gift and income tax treatment would be helpful. Were that accomplished, other discriminations might gradually disappear. But until they do, the single woman represents a large disadvantaged group.

921 Mead, Margaret. "Problems of Population Balance," Arch. Environmental Health 13(6):802-4, 1966.

The work of the medical profession in population control and its aid in solving the problems of population balance is discussed.

922 Means, Cyril C. "The Law of New York Concerning Abortion and the Status of the Foetus, 1664-1968: A Case of Cessation of Constitutionality," New York Law Forum 14(3):411-515. Fall 1968.

Under the common law of England, which was introduced into the Province of New York in 1664 and remained in force (on the subject of abortion) through 1829, abortion prior to quickening, with the woman's consent, was not an indictable offense, either in her or in the abortionist. Abortion after quickening, i.e., after the end of the 4th or the beginning of the 5th month of pregnancy, was a misdemeanor on the part of the abortionist, if the fetus died in utero; if the fetus died after birth, it was murder. New York's first abortion statute, the earliest statute dealing with surgical abortion, was enacted in 1829. Under this act, the offense of abortion was expanded to include abortions prior to quickening, while abortion after quickening was elevated from a misdemeanor to a felony. Subsequently, similar statutes were enacted in other States. The author demonstrates that the objective of the abortion statute of 1829 and of its successors to the present day was not the protection of the life of the fetus, but the preservation of the life and health of the pregnant woman under the surgical conditions 140 years ago. He argues that these laws became unconstitutional at that point in time when the risk to life and health associated with legal abortion became smaller than the corresponding risk of pregnancy and childbirth.

923 "Medicolegal Aspects of Abortion," Current Med. 1:21-26. November 1953.

A definition and list of the accepted medical types of abortion are given, followed by a discussion of proximate causation, or the many legal and nonlegal causes, of abortion. The medical aspects of abortion are described, including frequency, elements of proof, complications, and treatment.

924 Meier, C.L. Ohio Family Law. Cincinnati: W.H. Anderson Co., 1963. 830 pp. + 1968 Pocket Supplement.

The first part is the text of laws pertaining to marriage, husband and wife, divorce and alimony, and children. Part II contains the Statutes and Constitutional Provisions.

925 Meier, Gitta. "The Effect of Unwanted Pregnancies on a Relief Load: An Explanatory Study," Eugenics Quart. 8(3): 142-53. September 1961.

This paper presents a method for tracing the incidence and the effect of unwanted pregnancies from the case records of a group of long-term relief clients. The small size of the sample and the special restraints on contraceptive information and counseling peculiar to -- though certainly not limited to -- the county in which the study was undertaken, preclude generalizations to other families of very low socio-economic status or even to long-term relief clients elsewhere. Nevertheless our findings appear to complement the data from recent survey-type and intensive interviews among the former, much larger group. At least for the welfare clients in one locality they also suggest additional explanations for contraceptive failure in terms of the functioning of various professional and social agencies as related to family planning.

926 Meier, Gitta. "Research and Action Programs in Human Fertility Control: A Review of the Literature," Soc. Work 11(3):40-55. July 1966.

The findings and experience of social science research and action programs that have helped to establish agreement regarding the need for systematic family planning programs are reviewed. Considered most important in this respect are studies determining (a) the prevalence of small and moderate size family preferences in the United States, the high incidence of excess fertility along with inadequate knowledge and utilization of contraception among the lowest socio-economic group; (b) the extent of family planning assistance provided by hospitals, health and welfare departments and the relevant professionals and the deficiencies in the services available; (c) the personal and social costs of excess fertility. Research with action programs include projects which have proved the feasibility of providing birth control services to previous non-users or uncommitted users, and the deliberate integration of contraceptive assistance in traditional hospital and public health services. The prevention of adolescent pregnancy and the liberalization of abortion are seen as persisting dilemmas for the community and concerned professionals. Specific new opportunities for constructive intervention by social workers from new developments in fertility control are also reviewed.

927 Meier, Gitta, et al. "Family Planning Assistance of Low Income Psychiatric Patients in General Hospitals: An Exploratory Study," Michigan Med. 66:1071-75. September 1967.

The responsibilities for counseling and referral for family planning services assumed by psychiatric personnel were ascertained as part of a survey of such assistance rendered to non-private, low-income patients in the 20 teaching hospitals of a midwestern metropolitan area in 1964. Some of the factors determining the nature and extent of the assistance provided are discussed.

928 Meleney, Henry E. "Preventive Medical Services for the Family," Milbank Memorial Fund Quart. 27(3):251-59. July 1949.

Among the types of preventive medical services advocated for the family are premarital advice, which should include planned parenthood, and prenatal care.

929 Meloy, Sybil. "Pre-Implantation Fertility Control and the Abortion Laws," Chicago-Kent Law Rev. 41:183-205.Fall 1964. 1964.

The article is concerned with pre-implantation fertility control and the legality of its use under the current abortion laws. There is a brief discussion of pre-implantation means of fertility control, followed by a lengthy description of the two broad categories of abortion statutes in the United States and the classifications of each with specific citations of various state orientations, actual court cases and general legal considerations. The statutes which expressly make pregnancy an element of the offense present the greater number of problems (i.e., proof of pregnancy terminated prior to implantation), and the difficulties of these problems are compounded by the absence of reported cases concerning the legality of pre-implantation fertility control. Considered finally is the Model Penal Code: its hypothetical effect on pre-implantation fertility control, its ambiguities and its possible interpretations. The author concludes that legislatures must make some vital decisions concerning the applicability of their abortion laws to pre-implantation means of fertility control and that the development of such means should not be retarded simply because of legal uncertainties.

930 Mencken, H.L. "Utopia by Sterilization," Popul. Rev. 4(1):17-22. January 1960.

A reprint of a classic satirical essay (1937), in which H.L. Mencken proposes to alleviate the ills of mankind by a widespread policy of sterilization of male sharecroppers and others on a very low standard of living. To protect their rights under the Constitution, sterilization could be voluntary, and an adequate number of volunteers would be obtained by offering a cash honorarium to all those submitting.

931 Mietus, A.C., and Norbert, J. "Criminal Abortion: A Failure of Law or a Challenge to Society," J. Amer. Bar Assn. 51: 924-ff., 1965.

The authors challenge the arguments of those who favor liberal abortion laws and deplore the attack on fetal life. Suggest basic preventive and curative measures be taken which might obviate abortion such as: improvement of legal status of illegitimate children, tax relief as a child subsidy, and adoption services.

932 Minnesota Medicine. [A Group of Articles on Abortion.] Minnesota Med. 50:11-136. January 1967.

Partial contents: Barno, A., Criminal abortion -- deaths and suicides in pregnancy in Minnesota, 1950-1964, pp. 11-16; Hakanson, E.Y., An obstetrician's view of therapeutic abortion, pp. 23-28; Decker, D.G., Medical indications for therapeutic abortion: an obstetrician's view, pp. 29-32; Teeter, R.R., Psychiatric indications for abortion, pp. 49-51; Bernstein, I.C., Psychiatric indications for therapeutic abortion, pp. 51-55; Watson, T., Why therapeutic abortion?, pp. 55-59; Ehrenberg, C.J., Unwanted pregnancies, pp. 61-63; McKelvey, J.L., The abortion problem, pp. 119-26; Bray, P.N., Therapeutic abortion: incidence and indications in Minnesota, pp. 129-36.

933 Mistler, Robert G. "Divorce, Separation and the Federal Income Tax: The ABC's of Alimony, Child Support and Attorney's Fees," University Colorado Law Rev. 39:544-57. Summer 1967.

The problems and suggestions contained in this article are not unique or original, but represent a composite of case law and authority gathered from many sources, selected to acquaint the reader (primarily the general practitioner or the litigation attorney) with fundamental income tax questions encountered in divorce and separation arrangements. Section I covers the Internal Revenue Code's Section 71, with subsections on alimony, alimony trust arrangements and child support. Section II covers property settlements, with subsections on transfer of property in exchange for marital rights and transfer of property held in divided ownership. Section III covers attorney's fees.

934 Monahan, Thomas P. "State Legislation and Control of Marriage," J. Family Law 2:30-42. Spring 1962.

The article begins with a brief discussion of the function of law from a sociological viewpoint. Questions are asked concerning marriage and its legal dissolution, and there follows a history of the change in marriage manners and the growth and variation in marriage legislation since the colonial period, with special reference to the common law marriage. Viewed, with the problems and state orientations of each are such marriage restrictions as social measures, eugenic and health measures, the pre-marital blood test, waiting periods and age at marriage. Although the role of law in the area of marriage can only be limited, the author makes several suggestions which, if implemented, might increase the utility and social relevance of marriage legislation. The author concludes that there is, in the United States, an untouched field for positive action or law in regard to marriage and asks that marriage legislation involve itself with positive measures as opposed to the largely regulatory or prohibitive measures with which it has been concerned in the past.

935 Moore, Bruce E. "Federal Tax Aspects of Divorce," J. Bar Assn. Kansas 35:175-76, 208-11. Fall 1966.

With the implementation of the new Code of Civil Procedure in January of 1964, the Kansas practitioner's need for working knowledge of the federal tax consequences of divorce and separation increased greatly. The author reviews the essentials of a taxable alimony payment and discusses the more common problems which may confront the practitioner in this area, with references to the statutory prerequisites for payment of alimony; alimony agreements (pre-divorce, post-divorce and under separation); decree of support; periodic payments; property settlement and transferred property; fixed child support payments; and form of payments. The author concludes that with the present income tax rates, the economic flavor added by the federal tax aspects of divorce and separation cannot be overemphasized.

936 Moore, Frank I. "A Model for the Selection of Indigenous Personnel for Family Planning Clinics in Low-Income Neighborhoods," Dissertation Abstr. 29B:2104, 1968. Abstract of Ph.D. Thesis, University of Oklahoma, Norman Oklahoma, 1968. 147 pp.

The concept of "New Careers" as a strategy to overcome poverty is gaining acceptance as more evidence is accumulated on the effectiveness of nonprofessional workers in the human services professions. The development of this overall strategy has been impeded by the deficiencies of traditional personnel selection methods which are often not valid predictors of performance in these new job roles. The problem of selective placement within these "New Careers" is virtually unstudied. This study attempts to identify the relevant variables affecting selection for "New Careers" job roles under three major headings: (1) the applicants, (2) the selection team, and (3) the criterion measure used to assess effectiveness for a specified job role. Major attention is given to the question of who should comprise the selection team. This study compares the predictive accuracy of two groups of judges: (1) professionals most likely to be involved in the establishment of a family planning clinic and (2) representatives of the low-income consumers of service. Their task was to select the most effective applicants for positions as auxiliary health workers employed by a family planning clinic. Data was presented which indicated that the criterion measure (the numbers of patients accepting and subsequently keeping either an outreach or follow-up appointment) was discriminating among the auxiliary workers on the basis of differences within the auxiliary group rather than some artifact of the job setting. For the purposes of this study these criterion scores were used to rank the workers on two types of assignments -- patient recruitment (outreach) and patient follow-up. The goal of both assignments was to obtain patient attendance at the family planning clinic, and the percentage of patients keeping appointments in relation to the total number given became the evaluation score. Ranking scores assigned by the two groups of judges were compared to the rankings of all workers at the time of evaluation to determine the predictive accuracy of the selection scores. This study found that professional judges were more accurate in predicting follow-up performance than the nonprofessional judges. However, the accuracy of the two groups was reversed when only the outreach assignments were considered.

937 Moore, J.G., and Randall, J.H. "Trends in Therapeutic Abortion. A Review of 137 Cases," Amer. J. Obstet. Gynec. 63:28-ff., 1952.

A decrease in the ratio of therapeutic abortions to deliveries was evident in Iowa between 1926 and 1950. In a review of 137 cases of therapeutic abortion results indicate that: 92% were Catholic and 94% were married women between the ages of 20 and 35. In more than half of the cases, the abortion was performed after four months of pregnancy and the most frequent reasons were toxemica, tuberculosis and cardiac disease. The mortality rate was 5.1% or seven patients. However, not all the abortions were performed to save the life of the mother as required by Iowa laws. It is the authors' convictions that abortion practices should be limited to strictly medical purposes.

938 Moore, Marvin M. "Antiquated Abortion Laws," Washington Lee Law Rev. 20:250-59. Fall 1963.

This article argues for less rigid abortion statutes. Forty-two jurisdictions permit an abortion only when necessary to preserve the mother's life. Maryland has the most liberal abortion statute: when fetus is dead or no other procedure will secure the mother's safety. Approximately one out of five pregnancies of American women terminates in an unprosecuted illegal abortion, one-quarter of which are performed by the mother herself. Eight thousand women per year die from criminal abortions. Enactments should provide exceptions in four situations: (1) where physical or mental health, considering social and economic factors, may be seriously impaired, (2) where child may be born with grave physical or mental defect, (3) where pregnancy is result of rape, (4) where pregnancy is result of incestuous relationship. Several arguments against liberalizing the abortion laws are refuted. In addition to the exceptions, four suggestions are given for inclusion in an updated abortion statute: (1) three physicians must certify as to the justifying circumstances, (2) after 16th week of gestation no abortion under Act, (3) justification of abortion is an affirmative defense, and burden of proof on accused, (4) physician not guilty of breach of duty, if he conscientiously objects to abortion and informs patient of such objection.

939 Moore, Marvin M. "Case for Marriage by Proxy," Cleveland Mar. Law Rev. 11:313-22. May 1962.

A proxy marriage is one in which an agent represents one of the parties at the marriage ceremony, with the absent party (usually the groom) having selected the proxy and having executed a power of attorney authorizing the latter to act for him. An effort is made to comply with the local statutory formalities for marriage. There is a brief historical outline of this type of marriage, with reference to the various legal and religious changes or restrictions involved and the fact that marriage by proxy is not a new institution. The current status of the proxy marriage is summarized (nine states honor proxy unions formed within their borders, in four the validity of the proxy marriage is unknown, and in the remaining 37 states proxy marriages are invalid) and the laws of the individual states are considered in detail. A proxy marriage may be sustained under either of two theories: that it constitutes a valid common law marriage or that it meets the statutory requirements for a ceremonial marriage. It is concluded that, though only a minority of American jurisdictions sanction marriage by proxy, considerations of logic and public policy indicate that many more should do so. When a state assumes the authority to prescribe the sole conditions under which its inhabitants may enter into so basic a relation as that of marriage, it incurs the responsibility of making certain that this right is barred only for good reason.

940 Moore, Marvin M. "A Defense of First-Cousin Marriage," Cleveland Mar. Law Rev. 10:136-48. January 1961.

Today about half of the states still follow the absurd policy of forbidding the wedding of two healthy persons merely because they are first cousins and allowing two congenitally deaf persons to marry and pass their affliction on to their offspring. Such laws impede human happiness and should be changed.

941 Moore, Marvin M. "Defenses Available in Annulment Actions," J. Fam. Law 7(2):239-96. Summer 1967.

An examination of annulment law, revealing some ambiguities and contradictions, e.g., in some states divorce is allowed for causes such as bigamy, which logically should be grounds only for annulment. Also, nearly every jurisdiction recognizes that an innocent party who is forced into a marriage has grounds for annulment. Yet where the coercion is the bringing of bastardy proceedings against the plaintiff, such coercion is regarded as lawful and is not grounds for annulment. The distinction between void and voidable marriages is traced and the statutory and judge-made defenses to annulment actions are discussed. The following categories of waiver of the right to annul a marriage voidable are examined: (1) waiver through "unclean hands," i.e., some courts consider the plaintiff's hands to be sullied because he acted reprehensibly in having coitus before marriage. In this category, marriages voidable because of fraud, impotence, nonage, and mental incompetency are considered; (2) waiver-through "unclean hands"-of the right to annul marriage void for prior existing marriage, violation of statute or court decree forbidding remarriage during a specified period, and for consanguinity or affinity; (3) waiver-through ratification-of right to annul marriage.

942 Moore, Marvin M. "Legal Action to Stop Our Population Explosion," Cleveland Mar. Law Rev. 12:314-29. May 1963.

In order to slow down the rate of population growth, the author proposes that the federal government disallow income tax deductions for more than two child-dependents, publicize the need and desirability of family limitation, and repeal the section of the United States Code which prohibits the mailing of contraceptive devices, drugs, and literature; and that the states repeal their laws restricting voluntary sterilization, and the advertising and use of contraceptive devices.

943 Moore, Marvin M. "Refusal to Have Children as a Ground for Divorce or Annulment," Cleveland Mar. Law Rev. 14:588-600. September 1965.

This paper examines the circumstances under which a spouse's refusal to have children constitutes ground for divorce or annulment. Discussed are the positions of both the English Court of Appeals and the New Jersey Superior Court on several divorce court cases. The courts confront the question of whether the refusal to have uncontracepted intercourse constitutes a refusal to consummate the marriage and whether the grounds of fraud and cruelty, in connection with refusal of consummation, are causes for annulment or divorce in both English and American jurisdictions.

944 Moore, Marvin M. "Unrealistic Abortion Laws," Criminal Law Bull. 1:3-13. December 1965.

The United States abortion laws are outlined and shown to not be a deterrent to criminal abortion. The author recommends more liberal statutes. Until the legislatures recognize this need, the incessant performance of criminal abortion will continue unabated, and the mortality and misery associated with them will continue to plague society.

945 Morehouse, William M. "The Speaking of Margaret Sanger in the Birth Control Movement from 1916 to 1937," Dissertation Abstr. 29A:989, 1968-1969. Abstract of Ph.D. Thesis, Purdue University, Lafayette, Indiana, 1968. 229 pp.

This investigation purposes a critical examination and evaluation of the public speaking of Mrs. Margaret Sanger as spokesman of the birth control movement from 1916 to 1937. During this period Mrs. Sanger planned, initiated, and conducted a campaign to legalize the dissemination of birth control information and for public acceptance of family planning which developed into a national and international movement. She addressed hundreds of audiences over the twenty-one years studied. The movement's considerable success predicates that the public address of Mrs. Sanger was an important and influential factor in her campaign. The author fortunately interviewed Mrs. Sanger and consulted extensive collections of her public and private papers in the Library of Congress and the Smith College Library. Additional library sources provided information required to place woman, speaking, and movement in proper socio-historical setting. Critical examination and evaluation was based on criteria adapted from Edwin Black's Rhetorical Criticism. Many of Mrs. Sanger's speeches appeared to fall into the category Black termed exhortative oratory which he suggests: urges acceptance of ideas or actions initially considered radical; is primarily emotional in persuasive force; makes frequent use of prophetic utterances; and is characterized by simplicity. The author found that the birth control movement achieved its goals, at least partly, because of the speaking and organizational activities of Mrs. Sanger. Her speeches were appropriate to her radical cause; her speaking cannot be divorced from her organizational efforts. Her agitational tactics were directly related to the tone of many speeches. This gifted, not great, speaker was able to combine her intense belief in her cause with her ability to agitate and her organizational talent to promote the movement's success.

946 Morris, Grant H. "Mental Illness as a Prohibition to the Contracting of Marriage," Syracuse Law Rev. 15:42-55. Fall 1963.

Typical state marriage statutes simply provide in indiscriminate fashion that one or more of the following groups are prohibited from marrying: idiots, insane, weak-minded, lunatics, feeble-minded, imbeciles, persons incapable of contracting, and persons of unsound mind. The purpose of this note is to examine the principles used by the courts in solving cases in this area, regardless of the diversity in the statutes. Courts scrutinize the facts of the particular case before them, searching for such a disparity of age, social position, economic condition before and after the marriage, strength of affection between the parties, length of time the parties knew each other before the marriage, length of time elapsed after the marriage was performed before the suit was brought, and any other factors which would awaken a suspicion of incapacity on one side and imposition on the other. The courts are greatly influenced by the type of proceeding in which the question of the invalidity of the marriage due to mental incapacity is raised and the parties involved in that proceeding. For example, after the death of one of the parties to the marriage, in a case involving the will of the deceased or other property rights of the surviving spouse, the court will rarely nullify the marriage.

947 Morrison, Joseph L. "Illegitimacy, Sterilization, and Racism: A North Carolina Case History," Social Service Rev. 39(1):1-10. March 1965.

An account of attempts to introduce legislation in North Carolina for compulsory sterilization of unwed mothers. The motivations included a concern over rising welfare costs and racial considerations: State Senator Wilbur M. Jolly, sponsor of the bills, is quoted as saying: "We sit by and see almost 20% of the state's Negro children born out of wedlock," North Carolina has a 1929 law, amended in 1933, permitting eugenic sterilization; it is generally considered to be administered in a humane manner. Two bills for compulsory sterilization were presented to the North Carolina legislature: (1) in 1957 by State Senator Jolly; and (2) in 1959 by Jolly and Assemblywoman Rachel D. Davis. Both bills were influenced by the atmosphere prevailing in the South after the Supreme Court 1954 decision on desegregation. Both were defeated through efforts of agencies like the North Carolina

Conference for Social Service, and individuals like John R. Larkins, a Negro employed as a consultant by the North Carolina Department of Public Welfare, who pioneered action to reduce Negro illegitimacy, including a Northampton County pilot project; and Harry Golden, then editor of the Carolina Israelite, who organized a campaign. In 1963, Dr. Davis succeeded in having a bill passed which permits doctors after consulting at least one colleague to perform sterilization thirty days after a request, with special safeguards (including approval of a juvenile court judge) in the case of unwed minor mothers.

948 Mueller, Marti. "Oral Contraceptives: Government-Supported Programs Are Questioned," Science 163:553-55. 7 February 1969.

Since 1966, when the federal government, specifically HEW, became deeply involved in family planning programs for the poor, and a major distributor of the pill, the Food and Drug Administration has expressed concern in regard to the general medical health standards and the uneven monitoring of pill distribution connected to such programs. Discussed are the many difficulties and criticisms HEW-supported family planning programs face and the FDA guide lines and precautionary measures established in 1966 to combat the medical hazards of indiscriminate pill distribution. The author concludes that pressure for safe medical practices is growing and that the major problem is that of jurisdiction or HEW's inability to enforce safety regulations on family planning programs it administers or finances indirectly.

949 Munson, H.B. "Abortion in Modern Times: Thoughts and Comments," South Dakota J. Med. 19(4):23-ff., 1966.

The author cites the injustices of the present abortion statutes in the United States and urges a liberal reform as in the law suggested by the American Law Institute's Model Penal Code.

950 National Institute of Municipal Clerks. Marriage and Divorce: Principal Provisions of the Marriage and Divorce Laws of Various U.S. States and Territories, May 1956. 17 pp. (processed).

Legislation governing marriage pertains to the obtaining of a license, the waiting period, blood tests, minimum age with and without parental consent, consanguinity, and common-law marriage. Legislation on divorce covers residency requirements, the major causes of basing the civil suit, and alimony provisions. Annulment and judicial separation are also included. Data permit a comparison of the states with regard to each provision.

951 Neel, James V. "Some Genetic Aspects of Therapeutic Abortion," Obstet. Gynecol. 30(4):493-97, 1967.

Examples are given of the wide range of recurrent risks which may be encountered in genetic counselling concerning therapeutic abortion. In view of recent and impending legislation legalizing abortion in cases where there is substantial risk of grave physical or mental defect in the child, it is suggested that the American College of Obstetrics and Gynecology establish a special, wide-based committee to lay down more specific guide lines.

952 Nelson, G.A. and Hunter, J.S. "Therapeutic Abortion. A Ten Year Experience," Obstet. Gynec. 9:284-ff., 1957.

Statistical results of 64 therapeutic abortions performed at the Mayo Clinic during 1945-1954 are discussed. Results show that the incidence of toxemia was 17%, cardiovascular disease accounted for 14%, and neurological disease was present in 14%. Other indications considered are: age; distribution; number of children before operation; method; and results.

953 "New Approach to Old Crimes: the Model Penal Code," Notre Dame Lawyer 39:310-ff., 1964.

Abortion law reform brought about by the Model Penal Code's provisions on abortion is criticized on the ground that the question of whether or not abortion constitutes the cessation of human life remains vital and unresolved.

954 New York Academy of Medicine, Committee on Public Health. "Therapeutic Abortion," Bull. New York Acad. Med. 41:406-ff., 1965.

This statement calls for the amendment of the present law on abortion to include the health of the mother and child as medical indications for abortion. Recognizing abortion only to save the life of the mother is in conflict with the attitudes and principles of the public and medical profession. Such narrow permissibility also leads hospitals to arbitrarily restrict the number of therapeutic abortions which it performs in order to protect its good name.

955 New York (State) Legislature. Report of Joint Legislative Committee on Matrimonial and Family Laws. Albany: Legislative Document, 1960, No. 27. 220 pp.

The committee was created in 1956. It has attempted to draft legislation in every field suggested and to incorporate the theories and ideas approved by a majority of those concerned, who have expressed an opinion. This report contains legislative adoptions, and recommendations by the committee on illegitimacy, conciliation, and separation agreements. Also included are Foreign Studies, and a Report of the Council of Churches on Marriage and Divorce in New York State.

956 Newman, L. "Abortion as Folk Medicine," California Health, October - November 1965, p. 75.

The results of a survey administered to 194 women and twelve obstetricians in Contra Costa County, California in 1963-1964 are discussed. The women were interviewed about their feelings on pregnancy, birth, and abortion methods they had used or heard of. Private patients were reluctant to discuss any methods, while clinical patients discussed the more folk-oriented (magical or pseudo-medical) methods freely. The fact that some of these patients consistently attempted abortion, along with their reasons for their attempts, indicates that the abortion was a means of "testing the pregnancy." The reasoning behind this is that the weaker fetus would be dislodged, while the healthier ones could withstand the onslaught of chemicals and athletic activity. The informants did not indicate the feeling that this activity itself might be damaging to the fetus.

957 Newman, L. "Between the Ideal and Reality: Values in American Society," in: Guttmacher, A.F., (ed.) The Case for Legalized Abortion Now. Berkeley, California: Diablo Press, 1967.

The author presents a cultural analysis of the American attitude toward induced abortion. The entire system of illegal abortions exists only as a result of American idealism unlikely to be realized, legislation unlikely to be enforced, and confusion as to the distinction between crime and sin. Opposed to the moral stance is the American tradition of individual non-involvement which is now being broken down by American youth, demanding more congruity between the ideal and the real. The solution to the abortion problem, then, lies in changing American values.

958 Niswander, K.R. "Changing Attitudes Toward Therapeutic Abortion," J. Amer. Med. Assn. 196:1140-ff., 1966.

This study of the therapeutic abortions of 504 women in two Buffalo, New York hospitals from 1943 to 1964 showed a high percentage of unmarried women, women under 20, nulliparous gravida, Jewish women, and gravida afflicted with rubella in the first trimester. Laws should reflect the changing social practice displacing purely medical and psychiatric indications for legal abortion.

959 Niswander, K.R. "Medical Abortion Practices in the United States," in: Smith, D.T., ed. Abortion and the Law. Cleveland: Western Reserve University Press, 1967.

This article notes the high incidence of maternal deaths due to illegal abortions and Gold's N.Y.C. findings that the number of illegal abortions have increased in the last 20 years. The historical practice of abortion in ancient times is reviewed. Social pressure is causing a decrease in medical indications. Psychiatric indications have increased from 10% to 80% in a 20 year period. Eugenic indications, specifically rubella in the 1964 epidemic year, caused 35% of all therapeutic abortions. Since abortion is a major health problem, the laws should be liberalized to deal with it.

960 Niswander, K.R., *et al*. "Therapeutic Abortion: Indications and Technics," *Obstet. Gynec*. 28:124-29, 1966.

This article reviews 504 cases of therapeutic abortions in two Buffalo, New York hospitals from 1943 to 1964. There were 299 abortions for psychiatric and 51 for fetal indications (rubella). The number of abortions increased from 4 per 1000 deliveries in 1943-49 to 4.2 in 1950-59 to 8.4 in 1960-64. Sterilization was performed in thirty *per cent* of the cases.

961 Norton, J.W.R., *et al*. "Twenty-One Years Experience With a Public Health Contraceptive Service," *Amer. J. Pub. Health* 49(8):993-1000, 1959.

A contraceptive service was introduced into the Public Health program in North Carolina in March 1937. The program was re-evaluated after 21 years' experience. Initially, the contraceptive program was isolated from the maternity program then in existence. However, over a period of years there was a natural tendency for the program to become consolidated into the overall maternity program. A review of the status of Public Health maternity programs in the state in 1954 revealed that 74 of the 100 counties in the state provided some obstetric care for the indigent and medically indigent in the area. It is impossible to assess the value of the contraceptive program in the reduction of maternal, perinatal and infant mortality rates, although it is certainly the feeling of those involved in the program that the introduction of the contraceptive program into the state and its coordination with the maternity service has been of some value in reducing these rates.

962 Notestein, Frank W. "The Population Council and the Demographic Crisis of the Less Developed World," *Demography* 5(2):553-60, 1968.

The concerns of the Population Council at its foundings in 1952 were to be with the problems of population growth in poverty areas both at home and abroad. Staff was directed by the trustees to take initiative in the broad fields which in the aggregate constitute the population problem. The author gives an informal account of the ways in which an organization based on such concerns has developed and functioned with some estimate both of the importance of its role and of the possibility of finding solutions to major problems. Discussed are the difficulties faced in 1952 by a private American group confronting the demographic crisis overseas; the Council's concentrations in its early years; activities in the field of family planning and contraceptive technology in developing countries; and the effects of such activities. The Council commenced its work in a field of great sensitivity by first of all seeking to advance training and research in the demographic and bio-medical fields, and it moved into practical action only on the request of governments or of governmental agencies. In both the medical and the social sciences, it has endeavored to channel its resources in ways that would lead to local awareness, local interest and the emergence of a competent local leadership. The author concludes with a brief analysis of the prospects for the resolution of the world demographic crisis.

963 "Now: A Tax Plan That Pays People," U.S. News 60:63. 14 February 1966.

Newest plan to wipe out poverty in the U.S. is a "negative income tax." It would mean checks from the Treasury for those with incomes under the poverty level.

964 "Now It's Official: U.S. Backs Birth-Control Aid," U.S. News 58:64-66. 22 March 1965.

The United States Government is openly offering to help family planning programs both at home and abroad, in order to combat ever-rising relief costs in the United States and the population growth in overseas countries which consumes much of our foreign aid. Almost immediately after Johnson's State-of-the-Union Message, a number of overseas and domestic birth control programs appeared. Tax-supported birth control programs, already in existence in the South, are expected to grow and to expand to the Northern and Western States. Officially, AID authorities in Washington make it clear that U.S. funds will not be used to supply contraceptives in any form to any nation. Instead, funds will go only to nations which request them for "research, training and communications." Such programs may include training of doctors and nurses to teach birth control techniques; furnishing transportation for birth control teams and supplying and distributing information on contraceptive measures. By proposing this sort of aid when asked for abroad and by allocating federal funds directly to locally requested family-planning programs at home, President Johnson moved the Federal Government into an entirely new field.

965 Noyes, Hilda Herrick, and Noyes, George Wallingford. "The Oneida Community Experiment in Stirpiculture," Eugenics Quart. 14(4):282-90. December 1967.

A report on the Oneida Community's experiment in "stirpiculture"(defined by J.H. Noyes, founder of the Community, as "intelligent, well-ordered procreation"). Noyes first proposed "stirpiculture" in 1849; but only in 1868 did conditions in the Community become favorable for the experiment, which was conducted between 1868 and 1879, inclusive, first by Noyes and central members of the Community, then by a Stirpicultural Committee (1875-76), and finally again by the "central members" alone, who decided, in each case, whether applicants for parenthood should or should not be permitted to procede. About 100 men and women took part, of whom 81 became parents, with 58 children born and four stillbirths. Data about the children and the experiment are presented in seven tables and analyzed.

966 O'Brien, Joseph P. The Right of the State to Make Disease an Impediment to Marriage. Washington: Catholic University of America Press, 1952. x, 150 pp.

The first chapter attempts to establish the relative competency of Church and State over marriage, since for the baptized, marriage is a sacrament and the Church has sole power over the sacrament from divine positive law. The second chapter is a summary of the actual legislation in force in the various states, to determine its effects on marriage. The third chapter is a brief exposition of the nature and effects of the diseases mentioned in the laws, to determine their influence on marriage as they affect the health of the other spouse and the possible offspring. The fourth chapter concerns the validity and the lawfulness of such marriages, and the fifth determines the rights of the state in establishing impediments to these marriages, both for the baptized and the unbaptized.

967 O'Bryne, John C. "Escape from Holy Deadlock: Some Current Problems of Divorce," Taxes 45:63-86. January 1967.

In a paper presented at the 19th Federal Tax Conference of the University of Chicago, the author examines the problem of taxation of payments from one spouse to another after divorce or separation. His interest lies in the areas where there is room for much interpretation of the laws, and he makes reference to several recent and noted case histories. Corrective legislation of the uncertainty of the allocation of tax liability is recommended through the American Bar Association omnibus tax bill.

968 O'Gara, James. "Birth Control and Foreign Aid: A Catholic View," Commentary 29(3):258-60. March 1960.

A reply to Davis and Blake ["Birth Control and Public Policy," Commentary 29(2):115-21. February 1960]. Birth control is an issue on which it is impossible to reach the kind of national consensus necessary for successful public policy. It is, therefore, folly to suggest that birth control be made an official, tax-supported part of U.S. policy overseas. Birth control should be left to the foreign nations involved and to the convictions of their own people, while popular support is rallied in this country for that which is really imperative: expanding productive capacity in the underdeveloped nations. To divert attention from this need by a domestic controversy over birth control (in the belief that such a course will help the underdeveloped nations) is folly.

969 O'Hara, James B., and Sanks, T. Howland. "Eugenic Sterilization," Georgetown Law J. 25(1):20-44. Fall 1956.

A survey of the legal history and status of sterilization in the U.S., giving brief mention to therapeutic and contraceptive sterilization and focusing on eugenic and punitive sterilization. In the state courts, sterilization is not a cruel and unusual punishment; nor, even when applied only to inmates of state institutions, a denial of equal protection of the laws; nor, where notice and hearing are provided, a violation of procedural due process of law, though there is some disagreement about requirements with respect to appeal. The U.S. Supreme Court has decided only two sterilization cases: in Buck vs. Bell (1927) the Court held that substantive due process of law was not violated by an order to sterilize an imbecile whose mother and daughter were also imbeciles; the decision in Skinner vs. Oklahoma (1942), in contrast, struck down an Oklahoma statute providing for sterilization of a person thrice convicted of a felony involving moral turpitude, on the ground that the Court had no basis for inferring that the line distinguishing persons subject to the law from other criminals had any significance in eugenics or heredity.

970 Ohio State Law Journal. "Symposium: Population Control," Ohio State Law J. 27:591-690. Fall 1966.

Contents: Ferster, Elyce Z., Eliminating the unfit--is sterilization the answer?; Cook, Robert C., World population prospects; Leavy, Zad, and Kummer, Jerome M., Abortion and the population crisis: therapeutic abortion and the law: some new approaches; Pilpel, Harriet F., Birth control and a new birth of freedom.

971 Okada, L.M. "Use of Matched Pairs in Evaluation of a Birth Control Program," Public Health Reports 84(5):445-50. May 1969.

The District of Columbia Department of Health conducted a study of participants in the birth control program at the D.C. General Hospital. Patients in the program were low-income urban Negro women who had had live deliveries at the hospital during the period November 1964 through December 1965. The study had three main objectives: a) to measure the reduction in pregnancies as a result of participation in the birth control program, b) to determine whether certain demographic characteristics may be related to differential participation in the program, and c) to measure the 'use-effectiveness' or continuation rate of the program. There were 32 pregnancies among the 161 members in the study group, and 75 pregnancies among the 161 members of the control group, a reduction of 57 per cent. Comparisons of pregnancy rates 'before' and 'after' for both groups tend to confirm this conclusion. Although not directly related to the use of matched-pair data, the continuation rate of the participants in the program is presented briefly: 94 per cent of the women were followed up and of them 48 per cent were still using oral pills at eighteen months.

972 Oklahoma State Library, Legislative Reference and Research Division. Resume of Principal Marriage and Divorce Laws of Oklahoma, Oklahoma City, 1965. 81 pp.

A 1963 report prepared by the Office of the Attorney General; legal citations are to the Oklahoma Statutes 1961 and Supplement 1963. Included are sections on incestuous marriages; marriageable age; marriage with consent; application for marriage license; chief grounds for divorce; residency requirements for divorce; remarriage after divorce; divorce by joint petition; marriages by proxy; and marriages between blacks and whites.

973 O'Neill, W.L. Divorce in the Progressive Era. New Haven: Yale University Press, 1967.

The book centers on four major themes: mass divorce as a chapter in the history of the American family; the influence of ideology on family change; the ways in which groups and individuals respond to this kind of social change; and the insights into the popular thought of a period that may emerge from the study of such behavior. The author feels that the divorce crisis needs to be examined in several different ways if we are to understand the social and historical functions of such a controversy. Mass divorce seems to have been not the leading edge of a moral revolution so much as the first of a series of adjustments by which the patriarchal family and the Protestant sexual ethic have accommodated themselves to the demands of an urban, industrial society. The author is particularly interested in the process by which criticisms of the family that express a minority point of view become part of a new consensus, how new definitions of acceptable family patterns are arrived at, and the role that criticism plays in determining what is to be worked into the system. The early years of the twentieth century were crucial, because thereafter it became increasingly clear that nothing would or could be done to control the rising divorce rate. It is felt that these years mark the outer limits of the time during which a decisive change in the public attitude toward divorce took place. Included are chapters on the political economy of love; the origins of the new morality; divorce and the social scientists; and the politics of divorce.

974 Opler, Morris E. "Jicarilla Apache Fertility Aids and Practices for Preventing Conception," Amer. Anthrop. 50: 359-61, 1948.

Conception and birth control consist of *coitus interruptus*, use of herbs, abortion, and various ceremonies.

975 Osborn, Frederick. "The Contribution of Planned Parenthood to the Future of America," Eugenics Rev. 45(3):155-60. October 1953.

This 1953 address, delivered by the Secretary of the American Eugenics Society to the Planned Parenthood Federation of America at its annual meeting, takes issue with some of the arguments advanced by Sir Charles Darwin in *The Next Million Years*. In contrast to Darwin's belief that population limitation would create a family drive which would increase population, the author asserts, with support from trends in Japan and India, that if women had permission to raise only the number of children (approximately 3-4) for which they could adequately care, the population would voluntarily be reduced to replacement level. The issue of race suicide, which initially appears to be supported by France, is refuted with the claim that economic factors and psychological values toward more children can be developed if necessary. The vital job of planning is described as the balancing of population with resources. The danger of race deterioration is shown to be relatively weak through references to the Ulbank study, which revealed that persons with tuberculosis voluntarily have fewer children, and the increase in the number of physicians who are advising individuals as to the genetic possibilities of having defective children. It is concluded that the manner of extension of birth control will be the factor determining the future quality of the race.

976 Osgniach, Augustine J. *The Christian State*. Milwaukee: Bruce Publishing Co., 1943. xix, 356 pp.

Arguments against sterilization and family limitation are included. Birth control is viewed as a menace to private and public morality, marital stability, and the economic welfare of a nation. A policy promoting sterilization is opposed on ethical and practical grounds.

977 "Out of Tune With the Times: The Massachusetts SDP Statute," Boston University Law Rev. 45:391-96. Summer 1965.

The Massachusetts Sexually Dangerous Person Statute fails to protect the constitutional rights of every individual.

978 Overstreet, E.W. "Abortion in North America," in: Proceedings of the Eighth International Conference of the International Planned Parenthood Federation. Hertford, England: International Planned Parenthood Federation, 1967.

This article points to the inconsistencies and hypocrisies of the abortion laws, among other problems of abortion, in the United States. Public opinion favors liberalizing the abortion laws, although not to the extent of unrestricted abortions. It is expected that the problem of illegal abortion will continue until contraceptive education and use become extensive in the United States.

979 Overstreet, E.W., and Traut, H.F. "Indications for Therapeutic Abortion," Postgrad. Med. 9:16-ff., 1951.

This report reviews the 134 therapeutic abortions performed at the University of California Hospital from 1938 to 1947. The ratio of abortions to deliveries during this period was 1:63. Prominent reasons for abortions were 22 cases of toxemia, 21 cases of heart disease, and 18 cases of pulmonary disease. Only eight abortions were performed on psychiatric indications and five on fetal indication, but there appeared to be a downward trend on the number of abortions of medical indications and an increasing incidence on psychiatric indications. In general, the number of abortions was decreasing. Slightly more than one-third of the women had concurrent sterilization. No deaths resulted from the abortions in this study; maternal morbidity was 16%. The unclear laws of California place the obstetrician in a precarious situation when asked for a therapeutic abortion. The relationship between disease and pregnancy should be studied, so that the law may be amended for the good of the public.

980 Overton, Philip R. "Abortion and Texas Law," Texas State J. Med. 58:765. September 1962.

The Texas Penal Code's statute on abortion is reviewed with a description of its six separate articles and the severe penalties imposed on those involved with abortion in any respect other than saving the life of the mother.

981 Packer, H.L. "Therapeutic Abortion: A Problem in Law and Medicine," in: Guttmacher, A.F., ed. The Case for Legalized Abortion Now. Berkeley, Calif.: Diablo Press, 1967.

This study of the procedure in performing therapeutic abortions by 26 California hospitals found a ratio of 1:400 abortions to deliveries. Committees were set up to protect and to restrict physicians. Permission of the obstetrician in charge plus a physician other than the patient's own was required by 24 out of 25 of the hospitals. Present medical practice is often in opposition to the law, and the law should be amended to legalize the present actions.

982 Partington, Donald H. "Incidence of the Death Penalty for Rape in Virginia," Washington and Lee Law Rev. 22:43-75. Spring 1965.

During the period 1908-63, 2,798 men were sentenced to the Virginia State penitentiary and of these, forty-one were executed. All those executed were Negroes.

983 Paul, Julius. "Population 'Quality' and 'Fitness for Parenthood' in the Light of State Eugenic Sterilization Experiences, 1907-66," Popul. Stud. 21(3):295-99. November 1967.

Although the use of state eugenic sterilization laws has declined sharply since the end of World War II, the punitive views of the earlier extreme hereditarians are returning in the new guise of legislative attempts to pass laws that would sterilize mothers of illegitimate children receiving welfare assistance. The author urges a closer examination of the 'right' of procreation, the use of so-called 'consent' procedures in states having sterilization laws, and especially the probable impact of new scientific breakthroughs in medicine, genetics, biochemistry and other fields on individual liberty in America. He believes that the relation between science and public policy will be even more complex and agonizing in the years ahead.

984 Paul, Julius. "The Return of Punitive Sterilization Proposals," Law Society Rev. 3:77-106. August 1968.

Various proposals for punitive, noneugenic sterilization have recently been advanced in at least ten States, although none has been carried out. The proposals involved the inclusion of sterilization as part of a program of punitive action including the loss of welfare benefits, the imprisonment and/or fining of the mother, and the loss of custody of children. The arguments in favor are couched in economic or moral terms, and sometimes, overtly or covertly, are based on racial grounds. Specific bills and judicial rulings are discussed for California, Delaware, Georgia, Illinois, Iowa, Louisiana, Maryland, Mississippi, North Carolina, and Virginia.

985 Pedersen, Margrete. "Status of Women in Private Law," Annals Amer. Acad. Pol. Soc. Sci. 375:44-51. January 1968.

Marriage law, property rights, family support.

986 Perkin, Gordon, and Radel, David. Current Status of Family Planning Programs in the United States. New York: The Ford Foundation, 1966. 22 pp.

The authors summarize present policies and activities of Federal agencies relevant to family planning, consider possible future trends and developments in Federal health policies, programs and legislation, and discuss the extent of available family planning services within the United States. In regard to the availability of family planning services, the authors describe services provided through state and local health departments, hospital family planning programs, privately financed family planning programs, and services provided through private physicians. Emphasized is the fact that within the Federal Government the greatest progress so far has been in the area of new policies rather than in the implementation of programs. There is some evidence to suggest that services are not likely to become available to the extent implied by existing policy statements, since there is presently no requirement that family planning be a part of comprehensive health programs utilizing Federal funds and HEW has indicated that it will exert no pressure on states to participate in family planning programs.

987 Perry, Robert J. "Recent Cases," Catholic University America Law Rev. 6:173-75. May 1957.

It is well settled that a sister state can be required to give full faith and credit to an _ex parte_ divorce decree obtained in another state so long as the party obtaining the divorce is properly a domiciliary of the state granting the divorce. Whether this means that full faith and credit must be given to the foreign decree in its entirety or only to the extent that it adjudicates the marital residence and marital status of the parties is the subject of much dispute.

988 Pfeffer, Leo. _Creeds in Competition: A Creative Force in American Culture_. New York: Harper, 1958. xii, 176 pp.

An examination of the efforts of the major religious forces to shape American culture through governmental action either in the enactment of laws or in the operation of governmental institutions. The book proposes to examine the differing positions taken by the three major faiths on issues of public importance and the arguments presented. Chapter 7, The family and the child, discusses: Church dogma and family welfare; Birth control; Abortion; Euthanasia, sterilization, artificial insemination; Sex education in the public schools; Divorce; Child welfare; Adoption.

989 Phelps, A.W. _Divorce and Alimony in Virginia and West Virginia_. Second Edition. Charlottesville, Va.: Michie, 1963. 557 pp.

Most important sections are marriage (pp. 14-25), prohibition of remarriage (pp. 29-32) and grounds for divorce (pp. 64-88).

990 Pickens, Donald K. "The Sterilization Movement: The Search for Purity in Mind and State," _Phylon_ 28(1):78-94. Spring 1967.

Historical account of changing attitudes, pressure groups, and legal regulation in the United States from the turn of the century to the present.

991 Pilpel, Harriet F. "The Crazy Quilt of our Birth Control Laws," _J. Sex Res._ 1(2):135-42. July 1965.

In 1873, A. Comstock persuaded the Congress of the U.S. to pass a law which forbade the importation and transportation in interstate commerce and in the mails of 'any article whatever for the prevention of conception.' The Comstock Act was passed and has remained unchanged. Shortly after 1873 about 50% of the states adopted laws that in one way or another restricted the prescription, selling, advertising or display of contraceptives. Connecticut took the leadership and passed a law prohibiting the use of contraceptives. Not before June 1965, at the fourth attempt to get the law knocked out, did the U.S. Supreme Court decide that the Connecticut anti-use statute is unconstitutional. Great progress has been made in other states. Mississippi and six other southern states have made, as early as the 1930's, family planning part of their public health services. Many other states now regard the availability of contraceptive information and supplies as part of the rights of those persons who are forced to turn to public assistance for health services, and this, of course, is doing something to cut down on the class discrimination angle which has characterized the enforcement of the birth control law until now. Federal funds are now available on a matching state basis to states that want to adopt planned parenthood programs.

992 Pilpel, Harriet F. "The Legal Status of Contraception," North Carolina Law Rev., April 1944.

The article reviews the provisions of the new North Carolina Abortion Law. The discussion covers various religious, moral, social and legal controversies, the problems involved in interpreting and administering abortion laws, and physical and psychiatric justifications for such laws. The author compares the current abortion laws of different states and attempts to show that any fears or uneasiness about the "liberality" of the new law are unwarranted. It is concluded that, because the burden of implementing the new laws lies with the physician, scrutiny should be given to attitudes and developments within the medical profession.

993 "Planned Parenthood et al. Challenge Maryland Compulsory Birth Control," J. Nat. Med. Assn. 60:524-26. November 1968.

The issue of compulsory birth control is discussed, with reference to a 1967 case in Maryland involving three young mothers found guilty of child neglect solely because their children were born out of wedlock. This new case is historically paradoxical, since it centers on a court-originated move not to make birth control illegal but to make it compulsory. The facts and development of the case are described: the use of a Maryland law permitting a judge to find the mother of an illegitimate child guilty of child neglect; announcement of a plan by county health and welfare officials that would require unwed mothers to seek birth control advice before applying for welfare; and Planned Parenthood defense arguments contending violation of freedom of choice in family planning and right of privacy according to the 14th Amendment. Also discussed in regard to the Planned Parenthood brief are that compulsory birth control for welfare recipients introduces discriminatory legal penalties against one sector of the population, enforcement of such compulsion would violate the confidential doctor-patient relationship, the unconstitutionality of special selection of dependent women for prosecution, and the importance of alerting the public to the facts in the Maryland case, since this challenge, like the anti-birth control Comstock laws, threatens the right to freedom of choice in family planning for all citizens, and not merely for recipients of public assistance.

994 Planned Parenthood Federation of America. "Maternity Care for Wives of Service Men," Human Fertility 7(5):159. October 1942.

A summary statement of legislation requested by the President to provide funds for maternal and child health in production areas, maternity care for wives of men in the armed forces, and the extension of child welfare services in overcrowded areas.

995 Plateris, Alexander. "The Impact of the Amendment of Marriage Laws in Mississippi," J. Marr. Fam. 28(2):206-12. May 1966.

An analysis of the very pronounced decline of the number of marriages in Mississippi after new premarital requirements were introduced on July 1, 1958. The differential impact of this decline on various subgroups of brides and grooms is investigated as well as its repercussions on marriages performed in states adjoining Mississippi. Data from the National Center for Health Statistics and the Mississippi State Board of Health are used.

996 Ploscowe, Morris. <u>Sex and the Law</u>. New York: Prentice-Hall, 1951.

Two things stand out in this survey of the law as to marriage, annulment, divorce, illegitimacy, and sex crimes, namely the limits of effective ordering of conduct through law and the inadequacy of our apparatus of lawmaking under the conditions of today.

997 Ploscowe, Morris. "Sex Offenses in the New Penal Law," <u>Brooklyn Law Rev</u>. 32:274-86. April 1966.

The article deals with the sex offenses provided for by New York State's revised Penal Law of 1965 and the legislation passed to supplement it. The provisions of Article 130, as well as other relevant provisions, are analyzed, and the author concludes with a list of the new law's favorable aspects and those aspects he feels are weak, badly formulated, or contain little understanding of social reality.

998 Ploscowe, Morris. <u>The Truth About Divorce</u>. New York: Hawthorn, 1955. 315 pp.

Where divorce was once a rarity, it now has become commonplace; where it was once a vaguely disreputable institution, it has now become fashionable; where it was once a luxury which only the rich could afford, it has now been brought within the reach of all. Divorce laws and their implementation now render a disservice to family life. They need to be changed so as to strengthen the family as the basic unit of American life rather than serving as a factor in its disintegration. The grounds for divorce, the residence requirements and the restrictions on remarriage in each of the 50 states are listed in outline form.

999 Ploscowe, Morris, and Freed, D.J., eds. <u>Family Law: Cases and Materials</u>. Boston: Little,Brown, 1963. xii, 709 pp.

This casebook reveals the law's approach and remedies in family situations. The legal problems in family relations are considered from a comparative family law position where relevant. The laws, civil contracts, licences, and restraints governing marriage are explored. Grounds for, defenses to, and effects of annulment are examined with consideration of population related issues such as impotency, refusal to have children, and refusal to consummate marriage. Grounds for, defenses against, and effects of divorce are dealt with extensively, including degree of sexual relations and migratory divorce. Marital remedies short of divorce, separation agreements, and problems of marital reconciliation are highlighted. Such population related issues as custody, illegitimacy, and adoption are examined separately.

1000 Polgar, Steven, and Jaffe, Frederick S. "Evaluation and Recordkeeping for U.S. Family Planning Service," _Public Health Reports_ 83(8):639-51. August 1968.

Reviews the major tools for evaluation currently in use (particularly by Planned Parenthood), presents an outline of recordkeeping requirements, and suggests some innovative approaches. Among suggested procedures are estimates of size and characteristics of population in need of services, and measurements of success in: contacting and enrolling indicated population; providing continuity of service; and reducing discrepancy between intended and actual births.

1001 Pope, Hallowell, and Knudsen, Dean D. "Premarital Sexual Norms, The Family and Social Change," _J. Marr. Fam._ 27(3): 314-23. August 1965.

Available data suggest that changes since the 1930's in premarital sexual standards have been limited. There is also continued resistance against permissive trends among the advantaged. Changes have resulted in a convergence on a norm of 'permissiveness with affection' accompanied by a decline in the double standard. Because unwed parenthood threatens family status and honor among advantaged strata, they lessen their commitment to norms of chastity only to the extent that social arrangements permit the disassociation of premarital intercourse and illegitimate birth. Four possible social arrangements are discussed: (1) contraception, (2) abortion, (3) adoption, and (4) post-pregnancy marriage. Within the next generations it is probable that premarital intercourse will become normatively allowed among those who, in addition to being in love, have a commitment to marry. This normative solution reflects an adaptation to permissiveness by the advantaged without threatening their superior social position. 'Permissiveness with contraception' is another likely normative development when complete confidence in contraceptive techniques is gained.

1002 Popenoe, Paul. "Family Ideals of Service Men," Eugenical News 29(3/4):57-58, 1944.

From 432 questionnaires filled out by service men ranging in age from 18 to 23 years, 46% indicated that they preferred a two-child family; 28% desired three; 14%, four; and 3% a single child. 95% of the service men questioned had gone beyond the eighth grade at school. Birthplaces of the service men included 45 states and nine foreign countries. Of 134 who proposed to go back to college after the war, the preferred family size was 2.84±0.07 children. Of 237 who did not intend to go back to college, the preference was 2.88±0.05 children. Since only a minority of these young men desired a family large enough to maintain the population, it is obvious that there is great need for eugenic education if a sound balance of population is to be maintained. Along with such education the author urges that necessary economic, social, and other changes must support the desire for larger families.

1003 "Population Control Takes a Step Forward," Bus. Week, June 1965, p. 108.

Supreme court's ruling against Connecticut's anti-birth control statutes may open the way for mass testing by U.S. drug companies of devices suited for worldwide use.

1004 "The Population Problem -- as Catholics See It," U.S. News 47:122-23. 7 December 1959. Also printed in Worldview 3: 3-4. January 1960.

Statement issued by the Catholic Bishops of the United States concerning birth control as a means of regulating population.

1005 Potter, Robert G., Jr. "Some Comments on the Evidence Pertaining to Family Limitation in the United States," Popul. Stud. 14:40-55, 1960.

Three types of data are reviewed for the contemporary United States. These are: (1) reports of respondents about their own family limitation; (2) incidences of contraception, induced abortion and sterilization, especially in the terminal third of the reproductive period; and (3) the average pregnancy rate, during contraception and its trend with increasing marriage duration. It is found that these data do not support each other and several hypotheses are proposed toward explaining the inconsistency.

1006 Potter, Robert G., Jr., et al. "Knowledge of the Ovulation Cycle and Coital Frequency as Factors Affecting Conception and Contraception," Milbank Memorial Fund Quart. 40(1):46-58. January 1962.

Data is drawn from the Family Growth in Metropolitan America study, a longitudinal survey in which 1,165 couples were interviewed approximately six months after their second birth and then 905 were reinterviewed three years later. During both interviews, detailed histories were collected about contraception and conception delays. In addition, during the second interview, questions were asked regarding beliefs about the timing of the fertile period in the menstrual cycle and use made of these beliefs either to hasten or delay pregnancy. About 50% of the responses about the timing of the fertile period were classified as correct; the remainder were fairly equally divided between classifications of "incorrect" and "don't know". 35% of the respondents report avoiding intercourse during particular times of the month as a means of avoiding pregnancy and most of these couples are correctly informed about the timing of the unsafe period. Only 18% report ever trying to hasten pregnancy by deliberately increasing coital frequency. Coital frequency is not correlated with contraceptive effectiveness, partly for the reason that greater sexual activity does not seem to occasion more frequent chance-taking. Coital frequency is moderately correlated with fecundability but only weakly associated with individual conception delays. Correctness of information about the ovulatory cycle does not appear to affect contraceptive effectiveness except in the case of the rhythm method. The gains in conception ease derived from deliberately increasing coital frequency are difficult to gauge because there are disproportionately many subfecund couples in this group who make special efforts to hurry conception. However, among couples reporting special efforts to hasten pregnancy, those correctly informed about the fertile period average shorter conception delays than those who are misinformed.

1007 Pratt, Frances R. "Programs for Public Health Nurses in Birth Control Work," Amer. J. Public Health 30(9):1096-98. September 1940.

A brief outline of the program of the North Carolina State Board of Health, with emphasis on the duties devolving on public health nurses.

1008 Preece, J.D. "An Obstetrician's View of Abortion," J. Med. Soc. New Jersey 64:648-ff., 1967.

This article argues that physicians should be trying to protect life, not trying to justify destroying it. The support of abortion on emotional, social and economic indications, being coupled with the argument for recognition of fetal reasons is criticized.

1009 "Privacy After Griswold: Constitutional or Natural Law Right?" Northwestern University Law Rev. 60:813-33. January - February 1966.

Supreme court decisions on the individual's right to privacy. Implications of the decision regarding Connecticut's birth control law on possible future litigation on other aspects of marital privacy.

1010 "A Pronouncement: A Policy Statement of the National Council of the Churches of Christ in the U.S.A. " Adopted by the General Board, 23 February 1966.

Approval of contraception but disapproval of abortion by the General Board. However, Churches are not unanimous in this feeling.

1011 Prugh, Peter H. "Patching Up Families: Varied New Programs Aim to Curb Breakdown in Negro Home Life," Wall Street J. 166: 1-ff., 30 November 1965.

1012 Quay, Eugene. "Justifiable Abortion -- Medical and Legal Foundations," Georgetown Law J. 49(2 and 3):173-256, 395-548. Winter 1960 and Spring 1961.

Consideration of provisions on abortion and related offenses in the Model Penal Code approved by the American Law Institute in 1959. Article appraises arguments for adoption against the history of such legislation, the common-law status of abortion, and biological concepts underlying it in Aristotelian philosophy, Roman law, and Christian moral philosophy. Documentation with cases and other citations.

1013 Raffel, Burton. "Annulments for Refusal to Procreate: Judicial Evolution in a Circle," New York State Bar J. 31:391-95, 1959.

In New York annulments for refusal to procreate date, in effect, from Mirizio v. Mirizio [242 N.Y. 74 (1926)]. The case is not direct authority since the plaintiff wife, the party unwilling to cohabit, was suing for support. Yet in sustaining the husband's defense on the ground of the wife's refusal of marital relations (the husband had refused her a religious ceremony and she was replying in kind), the court expressed itself sufficiently broadly to open the way for a long sequence of cases leaning on its quite explicit rationale.

1014 Rainwater, Lee. And the Poor Get Children. Chicago: Quadrangle Books, 1960. 202 pp.

The social-psychological and situational factors preventing efficient family planning based on intensive study of a small purposive sample of low-status couples.

1015 Rames, John O. "Analysis of Wyoming Marriage Statutes, With Some Suggestions for Reform," Land Water Law Rev. 2:177-98, 1967.

Discusses and analyzes in detail the Wyoming statutes concerning the creation of the marriage relationship. Many of these twenty-one sections were enacted during Territorial days and have been brought forward unchanged from the Compiled Laws of 1876. There is a need for clarification of the meaning of some of the existing statutes; the statutes should be supplemented in certain respects; and some of them are obsolete or obsolescent in the light of modern legal and sociological ideas.

1016 Rand, A.T. "Family Planning and Responsibility of the Physician to the Childless Couple," J. National Med. Assn. 39:196-200. September 1947.

1017 Ravenholt, Reimert T. "The AID Population and Family Planning Program -- Goals, Scope, and Progress," Demography 5(2):561-73, 1968.

In January 1965, the Agency for International Development began its program of assistance for population and family planning. During the following three years, AID emerged as the largest single resource for helping less-developed countries. The author describes the evolution of the AID program, the kinds of assistance available, expenditures, basic strategies, methods of evaluation and effects on fertility patterns. It is concluded that the tedious preliminary work has largely been accomplished and that we are now entering an era in which it is socially, legally, technically and fiscally possible to deal with the world population crisis on a scale commensurate with the magnitude and urgency of the problem. The great challenge remains that most people in the developing world are still deprived of the knowledge and means to control their fertility.

1018 Ravenholt, Reimert T. "AID's Family Planning Strategy," Science 163:124-27. 10 January 1969.

In a letter to Science, the author reviews the philosophy and strategy upon which the AID population and family planning program is based. He defines family planning as the many relevant actions contributory to greater use of available services and improved practice of family planning.

Viewed from this perspective, an effective family planning program would include birth control information and education; raising the marriage age; abrogation of pronatalist laws and incentives and the repeal or liberalization of abortion laws. Recommends research studies to be performed as needed to overcome obstacles and for advancement of the program and the extension of family planning information and means to all elements of the population.

1019 Records, John W. "Public Family Planning Services in the South -- A Progress Report," Southern Med. J. 59:379-83. April 1966.

For at least twenty years, seven southern states have included child spacing services in the Maternal and Child Health programs at the state level. These seven states are Florida, Georgia, Mississippi, North Carolina, South Carolina, Alabama, and Virginia. In recent years these states as compared with the remainder, continue to make the greatest progress in providing facilities.

1020 Redmount, Robert S. "Analysis of Marriage Trends and Divorce Policies," Vanderbilt Law Rev. 10:513-51. April 1957.

Since divorce law is the legal expression of the values attached to marriage and supposedly involves an implicit understanding of the marital relationship, the author assesses the roles and meanings of marriage, the sources and consequences of marital disharmony, and the complications of marriage dissolution for the purpose of better orienting legal policy. Part I deals with marriage trends and functions. Included are sections on marriage and property; marriage and economic activity; marriage and procreation; marriage and individual development; marriage, love and companionship; and the role of marriage in western society today. Part II deals with divorce policies, in an attempt to ascertain their fidelity to the reason and experience of marriage. The early development of modern divorce policies and laws; the development of policies and laws on divorce in colonial America and in the United States; the laws of divorce and current realities of marriage; and the search for an enlightened marriage and divorce policy.

1021 Reed, Sheldon C. "New Voluntary Sterilization Law," Eugenics Quart. 9(3):166-67. September 1962.

The State of Virginia has recently become the first state to pass a bill explicitly legalizing voluntary sterilization for other than therapeutic or genetic reasons. The new Virginia statute, as well as other State statutes and their justifications, are described.

1022 Regan, Richard J. "The Connecticut Birth Control Ban and Public Morals," The Catholic Lawyer 7:5-10. Winter 1961.

Reviews criticisms on the constitutionality of the Connecticut legislation which bans the sale, prescription or use of contraceptives. The United States Supreme Court agreed to review the case on an appeal by Dr. Buston, who questions whether the Connecticut birth control legislation is a reasonable exercise of the state police power over the health, safety, morals and welfare of the citizens.

1023 Reiss, Ira L. "Contraceptive Information and Sexual Morality," J. Sex Res. 2(1):51-57. April 1966.

Although conclusive data are not available, the existing evidence indicated that contraceptive knowledge is not a primary cause of sexual behavior. Historically, increases in sexual activity have come before widespread use of contraception. Also, social classes with the best contraceptive information are not necessarily those with the greatest frequency of coitus. Differences in sexual behavior between sexes and races are more attributable to their basic traditional set of values than to their contraceptive knowledge. Contraceptive information is therefore seen as only a secondary factor which would most likely aid primarily those already motivated toward sexual intercourse. While the presence of contraceptive information is not a major cause of coitus, the absence of it is a major cause of premarital pregnancy. The adult members of our society cannot fully withhold contraceptive information, for much of it is transmitted by the peer culture and by books.

Thus adults have the choice of increasing the quantity and quality of such information but not of eliminating it. Relatedly, adults in our society will not radically alter the premarital coital rates by giving or withholding such information -- all they can do is make coitus safer. Whether they should do so is a personal matter.

1024 Reiter, Paul G. "Trends in Abortion Legislation," St. Louis University Law J. 12:260-76. Winter 1967.

A review of the history and rational of criminal abortion legislation, the relation of the law to medical practice, and proposals for legal reform on abortion. The purpose is to determine what interests are to be primarily protected by the law and whether the legal revisions successfully uphold those interests.

1025 Reiterman, Carl. Birth Control Policies and Practices in Fifty-eight California County Welfare Departments. Oakland: Planned Parenthood, Alameda County, 1966. x, 102 pp.

Report on questionnaire survey and other sources of data on practices in 1964 in each of the 58 counties and evaluation of the practices described.

1026 Reimer, Ruth, and Whelpton, P.K. "Factors Affecting Fertility xxvii. Attitudes Toward Restriction of Personal Freedom in Relation to Fertility Planning and Fertility," Milbank Memorial Fund Quart. 33(1):63-111. January 1955.

Hypothesis 7 of the Indianapolis Study of fertility states: "The stronger the feeling that children interfere with personal freedom, the higher the percentage of couples practicing contraception effectively and the smaller the planned family." The (inflated) sample consists of 1,444 relatively fecund couples, and includes couples with and couples without children. A printed questionnaire included structured questions that were intended to yield measures of (1) strength of feeling that children interfere with personal freedom; (2) desire for more time to engage in specified activities; and (3) possible effectiveness of visiting nurses and nurseries in alleviating parents' problems. In addition, interviewers rated couples on "feeling that children restrict freedom." Attitude items fail to yield a unidimensional scale, so response codes are added to get summary indices, then dichotomized, and analyzed with the use of chi-square. A significant relationship is found between items (1) and (2) on one hand and percentage of families successfully planned and size of planned families on the other; but, the direction of the relationship is the reverse of that hypothesized. This is because, for couples with children, the questions asked have little relevance to motivation for fertility control. "They refer rather to the experiences encountered in caring for children." The data elicited by the questions are inadequate to test the hypothesis.

1027 Riley, John W., and White, Matilda. "The Use of Various Methods of Contraception," Amer. Sociol. Rev. 6:890-903. December 1940.

First major empirical national study of the use of contraception in relation to social class, religion and urbanization.

1028 Ritty, Charles J. "Invalidity of Marriage by Reason of Sexual Anomalies," Catholic Law 10:90-108. Spring 1964.

A discourse which argues in favor of establishing sexual anomalies as possible valid grounds for the nullity of marriage. Difficulties in defining the sexual pervert, securing evidence against offenders, establishing judicial criteria for nullity, etc., are discussed. Answers and solutions are sought to these difficulties from three main sources: Canon Law, The Rota, and modern psychiatry. Quotations of canonists, theologists, psychiatrists and psychologists, and references from the Rotal jurisprudence are compared according to their ability to serve as sources of sufficient and valid rationale in establishing sexual anomalies as grounds for invalidating marriage. An attempt is made to reconcile the attitudes of psychiatrists and psychologists (reflecting the modern approach) with that which it appears to invalidate; the traditional approach reflecting church views. It is concluded that one may appeal to either approach and find valid justification for these grounds rather than use one approach to invalidate another.

1029 Roach, Jack L., et al. "The Effects of Race and Socio-Economic Status on Family Planning," J. Health Soc. Behavior 8(1):40-45, 1967.

This paper examines the relative strength of race and socio-economic status as predictors of family planning behavior. Information about the contraceptive behavior of 1,000 clients of a planned parenthood agency was used to determine if differences between races basically reflect socio-economic differences as is usually assumed. It was found that race rather than socio-economic status accounted for most of the variance. The implications of this finding are discussed. It appears necessary to give as much attention to race as to socio-economic status in research on a combined Negro and white population.

1030 Robitscher, J.B. "Sterilization and Abortion," Med. Sci. 16(10):41-ff., 1965.

Physicians who are in favor of liberalized abortion laws should work for reform of such laws through legislative channels as opposed to ignoring present restrictions and performing non-legal abortions.

1031 Rodgers, Cleveland. New York Plans for the Future. New York: Harper, 1943. 293 pp.

The importance of the maintenance of population is stressed in a chapter entitled "Babies and real estate values."

1032 Rodgers, David A., *et al*. "Comparison of Nine Contraceptive Procedures by Couples Changing to Vasectomy or Ovulation Suppression Medication," *J. Sex. Res.* 1(2):87-96. July 1965.

Attitudes regarding nine procedures of contraception (condom, diaphragm, douche, jelly or cream, oral pills, rhythm, tubal ligation, vasectomy, and withdrawal) were obtained from 50 couples immediately after they had arranged with a urologist to perform a vasectomy operation on the husband for contraceptive purposes, and from 47 couples immediately after they had obtained an initial prescription from a gynecologist for contraceptive pills for the wife. Attitudes were quantified by a semantic differential scale consisting of twelve adjective pairs, with which each person described each procedure. Average and standard deviations of each adjective description of each procedure were computed. Data indicate that undesirable characteristics along any of several dimensions are sufficient to make a particular procedure unacceptable to a particular couple (average rating closer to undesirable than desirable on the desirable-undesirable comparison). Effectiveness and cost are of special importance but are not the only considerations in contraceptive choice. The conclusion is suggested that most conventional contraceptive procedures are unsatisfactory in certain significant respects. The result is an underlying cultural discontent with such procedures and a readiness to try other promising techniques even when they entail possible disadvantages or risks.

1033 Rodgers, David A., *et al*. "Prevailing Cultural Attitudes About Vasectomy: A Possible Explanation of Postoperative Psychological Response," *Psychosom. Med.* 29(4):367-75, 1967.

Informational feedback from social encounters has been hypothesized to influence self-concept and personality functioning. Recent experimental and other research studies demonstrate this effect, and therefore suggest that prevalent cultural attitudes about couples who elect vasectomy for contraception, if predominantly derogatory, could initiate or reinforce adverse personality changes. Two cultural subgroups, thought to represent common cultural attitudes, ascribed fewer favorable characteristics to couples using vasectomy than to couples relying on ovulation suppression. These findings are discussed in relation to previously reported evidence of negative personality changes following vasectomy.

1034 Rodgers, David A., and Ziegler, Frederick J. "Social Role Theory, the Marital Relationship, and Use of Ovulation Suppressors," J. Marr. Fam. 30:584-91. November 1968.

The family is interpreted as a social institution that allows sexual gratification with limited biological reproduction. In this context, choice of contraception is examined as a core decision reflecting basic husband-wife dynamics. A reformation of social role theory is presented and is used to infer dynamics involved in contraceptive choice. Data concerning women who continue on contraceptive pills and those who do not, from a four-year prospective intensive study of 39 couples, are shown to be highly consistent with the theory. Conversely, husband-wife dynamics are shown to be highly predictive of which couples will effectively utilize pills and which will not.

1035 Rodgers, William H., Jr., and Rodgers, Linda A. "Disparity Between Due Process and Full Faith and Credit: the Problem of the Somewhere Wife," Columbia Law Rev. 67:1363. December 1967.

Throughout the vagaries of our judicial history the jurisdiction standards of the due process and full faith and credit clauses have often been treated as identical. The distinct purposes of the two clauses have been obscured, or even inverted, in the analyses of the courts. In recent years, however, pressures for solution of recurring practical problems in the field of domestic relations have impelled a judicial re-evaluation. The issues posed extend beyond the academic, almost silly, question of whether a person can be divorced in one state but not in another. The integrity of the administration of the respective states is involved; ultimately, the choice of alternatives must reflect considered value judgements about the ordering of our federal system under the full faith and credit clause. As an alternative to judicial action, untapped sources of legislative power are available to combat the evils that have flourished despite resistance on social fronts. Consequently, the phenomenon so often described as the "somewhere wife" need not continue to demonstrate the peculiarity of our federal system.

1036 Rosen, H., ed. Abortion in America: Medical Psychiatric, Psychiatric, Legal, Anthropological, and Religious Considerations. Boston: Beacon Press, 1967. xix, 368 pp.

Re-issue of 1954 anthology. Estimates illegal abortions in the United States to number annually 200,000 to 1,000,000. Recommends more liberal legislation which would permit abortions for socio-economic reasons, when performed in hospitals. Revised 1967 laws of Colorado and California are discussed.

1037 Rosen, H. "Psychiatric Implications of Abortion: A Case Study in Social Hyprocisy," in: Smith, D.T., (ed.) Abortion and the Law. Cleveland: Western Reserve University Press, 1967.

Ambivalence of physicians toward abortion and extra-legal interpretations of ambiguous abortion statutes have resulted in an abortion problem with many complexities. The author analyzes the various indications used by physicians to request abortions from hospital boards, and contends that these reasons usually include rationalizations and socio-economic bases. Forced marriages, foster homes, orphanages, adoption and a more liberal interpretation of present abortion laws are suggested as possible solutions to the abortion problem.

1038 Rosenbaum, Michael. "Are Family Responsibility Laws Constitutional?" Family Law Quart. 1:55-76. December 1967.

The majority of the states have relative responsibility laws. While these laws have been defended as protecting the public treasury as well as strengthening the family, the constitutionality of the laws is subject to serious question. A strong argument can be made that the relative responsibility laws violate the equal protection clause of the federal constitution. The laws are also subject to constitutional attack on the grounds of violating due process as well as amounting to double taxation. Such constitutional questions are examined after discussions of the origin of family responsibility laws, the administrative costs of enforcing them and their relationship to changing family structure. The author concludes that as the area of public concern and governmental programs increase in the field of social welfare and the family unit composing the society becomes increasingly urban, laws that date back over three hundred years to a society where government was limited and local, serving a then dominant rural population, are anachronist. The relative responsibility laws should be repealed by state legislatures, removed by Congressional action as they relate to federally funded programs, or declared unconstitutional by the courts.

1039 Rosenkranz, Stanley W. "Divorce and the Federal Income Tax," University Florida Law Rev. 16:1-33. Summer 1963.

Discussion of the effect of the federal income tax upon some of the more common problems associated with alimony and property settlements. With high tax rates, a husband who continually paid lump sum alimony without a deduction suffered an extreme financial burden when the alimony was combined with his taxes. In addition, the high tax rates would wipe out a great deal of the economic benefit received by the wife. If not careful an arrangement that requires the wife to include the amount in gross income and give the husband a deduction, could end up giving him no deductions. If the husband and wife are not divorced or legally separated under a judicial decree they are still considered man and wife for judicial purposes. The fair market value of property received by the wife in a property settlement is neither taxable to her nor deductible by the husband.

1040 Rosenwaike, Ira. "Parental Consent Ages as a Factor in State Variation in Bride's Age at Marriage," J. Marr. Fam. 29(3):452-55. August 1967.

While many studies have been made of geographic variation in the age at first marriage, few have considered the effect state laws specifying the minimum legal age at marriage without parental consent can have on comparative age distributions. It is pointed out that, in a state permitting earlier marriage without parental approval, brides have a lower modal age than in a similar area with an older age requirement. Since United States marriage data are compiled on the basis of place of occurrence and since migration for the purpose of marriage is considerable, it is not readily ascertainable what the differences would be if comparisons were made on a residence basis. Comparative age ratios are presented for three states: Pennsylvania, Virginia, and Maryland. It is shown that in Pennsylvania and Virginia, where the specified age is 21, in a recent year (1964) the largest number of girls who married were 21; in Maryland, where the specified age was 18, the modal age at marriage was 18. Despite these apparent differences it is possible that there exists only minimal variation in age at marriage between Maryland and Virginia residents, and less variation between Maryland and Pennsylvania than seems indicated. The parental consent laws, rather than deterring marriage, contribute to migratory marriage. Since these migratory marriages tend to be concentrated at certain ages, they can materially detract from the statistical representativeness of data shown on an occurrence basis. But migration does not explain all the variation.

1041 Rossi, Alice S. "Public Views on Abortion," in: Guttmacher, A.F., ed. The Case for Legalized Abortion Now. Berkeley, Calif.: Diablo Press, 1967.

Reports of findings of the National Opinion Research Center survey of attitudes toward legalized abortion. The sample consisted of 1,484 respondents. Over half the sample agreed with the American Law Institute that medical, humanitarian, and fetal defect indications should be conditions for granting a legal abortion. Less than a quarter felt that economic hardship, pregnancy when a woman does not wish to marry the man with whom she has had sexual relations, or pregnancy when a women does not wish any more children should be legalized indications for abortion. Suggestion that abortion would represent a means of birth control was rejected by a majority of the sample. More liberal views were held by respondents with more education, with less church attendance, and with a more permissive view of pre-marital sex. Catholics were the least liberal in their views, Protestants and agnostics more liberal, and Jews (although there were very few in the sample) the most liberal. By political orientation, independents with liberal leanings were most liberal in their views on legal abortion; liberal and conservative Republicans, conservative independents, and liberal Democrats were less liberal, and conservative Democrats and politically uncommitted were the most conservative.

1042 Russell, Donald H., and Chayet, Neil L. "Abortion Laws and the Physician," New England J. Med. 1027-28: 1250-51. May and June 1967.

Since abortion, legal or illegal, is considered to be a medical practice, it falls within the province of medicine from a technical standpoint, and the law has placed it there in terms of the restrictions and exceptions governing the practice. In Part I, the authors review current laws applying to abortion, with references to the differences in the wording of the statutes, differences regarding the person authorized to perform the operation, and requirements in some states that there be consultation with another physician before the abortion is performed, and recommend that physicians would do well to consider a frame of reference beyond the strictly professional position regarding the many implications of legislative change. In Part II, the proposals for abortion reform are considered. Such reforms would allow for a greater range of professional judgment accompanied by increased social responsibility of physicians for therapeutic abortions, although the authors discuss possible new sources of legal action against the physician which may be brought with reform. It is concluded that all proposals for abortion reform tend to favor the position of medicine and health, but their acceptability and applicability depend upon social and moral sanctions.

1043 Russell, K.P. "Forensic Obstetrics," _California Med._ 91: 117-ff., 1959.

Analysis of the medical and legal aspects of abortion, sterilization and professional liability is given. The author urges the formation of joint committees of physicians and lawyers to study these problem areas.

1044 Russell, K.P. "Therapeutic Abortions in California in 1950," _West. J. Surg. Obstet. Gynaec._ 60:497-ff., 1952.

A survey of therapeutic abortions performed at 61 accredited hospitals in California during 1950. The overall ratio of abortions to deliveries was 1:251, whereas the incidence of therapeutic abortions ranged from 1 per 52 deliveries in a private hospital to 1 per 8196 deliveries in the Los Angeles County Hospital. Over 70% of the abortions were performed on four major indications: neuro-psychiatric diseases, hypertensive-renal diseases, pulmonary tuberculosis and cardiac diseases. Results show that twelve abortions were performed on fetal indications and that one-third of the patients were sterilized at the time of the abortion.

1045 Russell, K.P. "Therapeutic Abortion in a General Hospital," _Amer. J. Obstet. Gynec._ 62:434-ff., 1951.

An analysis of 88 therapeutic abortions performed at a California Hospital during 1944 to 1949. In 1948 a committee was established to approve applications for abortions and since that time the ratio of abortions to deliveries declined from 1:193 prior to 1949 to 1:481 in 1949. Indications for abortions during the five-year period included pulmonary disease 25% of cases, hypertensive disorder 25%, renal disease 25%, nervous and mental disease 15%, and cardiac disease 12%. "Other disease" included one case of rubella. Other results showed the largest number of abortions were performed on 26-30 age group; 84% were performed before the thirteenth week and 49% of the patients were sterilized.

1046 Russell, Maurice V., and Swell, Lila. "A Demonstration Project in Fertility Control," Dissertation Abstr. 26:7479, 1965-66. Abstract of Ph.D. Thesis, Columbia University, New York, New York, 1964. 156 pp.

The overall purpose of the research was to increase the competence of working class Negro mothers in family life planning through the use of small-group educational methods. The specific purposes were: a) to explore and determine what effective procedures could be developed for the recruitment and retainment of the target population; b) to discover the specific barriers to purposive family planning for working class Negro families; c) to determine whether the small-group approach could effect a change in contraceptive behavior among working class Negro women. The limited amount of significant positive change, as measured by the post-group questionnaire and the rating scales in relation to the total number of women who attended some sessions raises some questions as to the feasibility of the small group method with this population for the purpose of helping to increase competence in family planning.

1047 Ryan, John J. "Disinheritance of the Widow in New England," Boston University Law Rev. 44:534-52. Fall 1964.

At common law a widow had an inchoate dower interest in the land owned by her husband during coverture, which assured her some means of support at her husband's death. This interest could not be defeated by her husband's transfer since any subsequent purchaser took the land subject to the wife's right, unless she released her claim to dower. In an effort to extend financial protection to the widow now that land is no longer likely to be the principal asset of a decedent's estate, many state legislatures have enacted statutes permitting her to take a certain portion of the total estate owned by her husband at his death. She may do this even though her husband leaves a will, since the statutes specifically permit her to "waive the will" and take her statutory share. The widow's statutory forced share is generally limited to a portion of the property, real and personal, owned by the husband at death. This permits the husband to make _inter vivos_ transfers of his property without his wife's consent, even though they result in a depletion of her expectant share. Thus, despite the statutory protection granted widows, husbands may successfully disinherit their wives. This note discusses the means by which husbands have accomplished the above objective in New England states. Three of the more popular devices used by the husband are considered, namely, the absolute transfer, the revocable _inter vivos_ trust, and the gift _causa mortis_. New England courts are not in agreement as to the effect of such transfers upon the widow's claims because of the different tests they employ in assessing their validity. It is concluded that if the proposition can be assumed that the statutory forced share is primarily concerned with providing a surviving spouse with financial security, then we have been inept (or apathetic) in attempting to afford protection by means of inflexible statutory devices, or mechanical judicial tests, for they only challenge the ingenuity in devising means to circumvent them.

1048 Ryan, K.J. "Humane Abortion Laws and Health Needs of Society," in: Smith, D.T., ed. _Abortion and the Law_. Cleveland: Western Reserve University Press, 1967.

Abortion law liberalization based on abortion as a measure for population control and a means to minimize the number of criminal abortions is felt to be improbable, and the author argues that the major responsibility for any reform of such laws rests with the physician who has had the most immediate experience with abortion. More probable bases for liberalization or an acceptable abortion code are listed, including a recognition of the legal rights of the fetus and that the health needs of a society are within the scope of a physician's practice.

1049 Rydman, Edward J. Jr. "Factors Related to Family Planning Among Lower-Class Negroes," _Dissertation Abstr._ 26:4113-14, 1965-1966. Abstract of Ph.D. Thesis, Ohio State University, Columbus, Ohio, 1965. 171 pp.

This study was concerned with finding some factors related to family planning among a sampling of lower socio-economic level Negro patients of the Planned Parenthood clinics of Columbus, Ohio and Dallas, Texas. Studies of the lower-class Negro have been inadequate and meager. However, there is general agreement that families in this group are matricentric and that males tend to take a secondary position with regard to responsibility. These and other factors appear to be related to success or failure in family planning. The study reveals what other studies have shown; namely, that there are very few factors which have a strong influence on family planning but many which may have a small influence. The study concludes that with these respondents dependence upon answers to direct questions is apt to provide data which are misleading. An important observation is that these subjects tend to behave in inconsistent ways and inconsistency and successful conception control are incompatible. Additional areas of the cultural and social milieu need further investigation before any reliable or valid conclusions may be drawn concerning the effective or ineffective use of contraception by this group. A number of suggestions, based upon interactionist theory are proposed and recommended for further study.

1050 Sagi, Phillip C., et al. "Contraceptive Effectiveness as a Function of Desired Family Size," Popul. Stud. 15(3):291-96. March 1962.

The inclusive notion of method acceptability has been used as an explanation of variation in willingness to use contraception, the regularity with which contraception is used, and the effectiveness of contraception in preventing pregnancy. With the additional assumption that variation in method acceptability is related to differential motivations to limit numbers and control spacing, two hypotheses are advanced: (1) as the number of children individual couples desire is approached or achieved in practice, the proportion attempting fertility control increases; and (2) the success with which fertility is controlled improves as fertility approaches the number of children desired. These hypotheses are supported strongly by data. Several implications of these relationships are advanced.

1051 Sander, Frank E.A. "Dependency Exemptions for Children of Divorced or Separated Spouses: the New Amendment to the Internal Revenue Code," Taxes 45:710-17. November 1967.

One of the most pervasive and vexing tax problems upon separation or divorce has been the determination of which spouse is entitled to the $600 dependency exemption for children of the marriage. A recent amendment to the Internal Revenue Code (Sec. 152 (e), effective for tax years beginning on or after January 1, 1967), which awards the exemption to that parent who has had custody of a particular child for the greater portion of the year (with two important exceptions), is briefly analyzed in terms of its effect, the basic requirements for application, and still unresolved questions. The author outlines the kind of planning that should take place between the spouses in order to obtain the best over-all tax benefit.

1052 Sanders, Robert I., and Stoiber, Carlton R. "Colorado's New Abortion Law," University Colorado Law Rev. 40:297-312. Winter 1968.

In 1967 the Colorado General Assembly amended the state's abortion statutes, the first significant change in 76 years. The authors discuss, after a brief review of Colorado's previous legislation on abortion, the new provisions and their relation to the Model Penal Code, abortion provisions, immediate and more general problems, benefits and improvements, and the new law in practice. They conclude that, while the changes do not provide a perfect solution, they do represent an important step toward removing an essentially medical problem from the ambit of the criminal law.

1053 Sands, M.S. "Therapeutic Abortion Act," University of California, Los Angeles Law Rev. 13:285-ff., 1966.

The status of abortion laws in other states, abortion's sociologic aspects, and religious positions on abortion are considered in regard to California's proposed Therapeutic Abortion Act and opposition to it. It is contended that institution of the Act would merely bring together past policy on abortion and actual medical practice.

1054 Sarrel, P.M., and Davis, C.D. "The Young Unwed Primipara," Amer. J. Obstet. Gynec. 95:722-ff., 1966.

A follow-up study by the Yale-New Haven Obstetrical Clinic of 100 unwed teenage mothers is cited to demonstrate the need for contraceptive programs for such patients. Ninety-five of the 100 patients had 340 children and nine abortions during the five years following the birth of the first illegitimate child. Only four of the patients had married, some had married but were separated, and, of the 95, only three had received information on birth control.

1055 Savel, Lewis E., and Perlmutter, Irving K. "Therapeutic Abortion and Sterilization Committee: A Three Years' Experience," Amer. J. Obstet. Gynec. 80:1192-99. December 1960.

The absence of a clearly defined legal code and the inadequacies of medical custom in the perplexity of therapeutic abortion and sterilization necessitated the establishment of a Therapeutic Abortion - Sterilization Committee at Newark Beth Israel Hospital. The organization and function of this Committee for the years 1956 through 1958 are described, and the disposition of the 272 requests for permission to perform therapeutic abortion and/or sterilization is analyzed, with references to the processing of requests, age distribution of requests, the major indications approved, and performance incidence.

1056 Schmiedeler, Edgar. Sterilization in the United States. Washington: Family Life Bureau, National Catholic Welfare Conferences, 1943. 38 pp.

Introduction, legal status, the question of heredity, the moral question, the solution.

1057 Schmiedeler, Edgar. The Threat of American Decline. Washington: Family Life Bureau, National Catholic Welfare Conference, 1941. 31 pp.

The danger of population decline, from the Catholic standpoint.

1058 Schorr, Alvin L. Poor Kids: A Report on Children in Poverty. New York: Basic Books, November 1966. 205 pp.

A study of problems associated with the welfare of the 15.6 million children living in poverty in the United States. Includes discussion of family allowances in relation to other forms of aid.

1059 Schottland, Charles I. "Government Economic Programs and Family Life," J. Marr. Fam. 29(1):71-123. February 1967.

The changing roles of government and family are considered. Economic problems of government have a significant impact on the United States family, because of its role as a basic economic institute and a distributor of goods and services. In advanced societies, such as the United States, the family is dependent upon money with which to purchase necessary goods. To maintain such money income, the United States has established a variety of social insurance, public assistance, and service programs. Among these programs, the background and status of social insurance, public assistance, and a variety of specific economic aid ranging from the National School Lunch Program to government savings programs, the Housing and Home Finance Agency, and rent subsidies, are examined. Suggestions for their improvement are presented. Finally, some of the recent proposals now in the political arena, e.g., a guaranteed minimum income, and family allowances, are discussed. A continuing rise in the income of the United States family is predicted, especially as connected with possible implementation of major economic reform, e.g., guaranteed minimum income, and even greater progress and economic security for the United States family is seen to lie ahead.

1060 Schroeder, Oliver C., Jr. "The Laws on Reproduction: Abortion, Sterilization and Insemination," Postgraduate Med. 33:A-64-67. May 1963.

The author reviews the legal status of abortion, sterilization and insemination in the United States. The problem of interpreting abortion statutes is discussed, as well as the fact that most statutes disregard eugenic and socio-economic indications. Legal implications of sterilization present different problems from the abortion issue, and the author outlines the varying legal responses initiated by the three types (therapeutic, eugenic and contraceptive) of sterilization. The article concludes with a brief discussion of artificial insemination, with reference to the legal complications which arise when there is a third-party donor.

1061 Schuler, Ruth V. "Some Aspects of Eugenic Marriage Legislation in the United States," Soc. Service Rev. 14:61-82, 1940.

The earliest statutes merely prohibited the marriage of those with certain disabilities, and penalties were added later. The applicant's own statement was accepted as proof of his fitness to marriage. Adequate measures of enforcement have been enacted only recently. In the present analysis, the various health measures now covered by statute are considered. The elements of an adequate law, with satisfactory enforcement provisions, are discussed under each heading, and a comparison made of the various state laws upon each point in relation to the outline of an adequate statute.

1062 Schur, Edwin M. "Abortion," Annals Amer. Acad. Polit. Soc. Sci. 376:136-47. March 1968.

As part of the increasingly open discussion of sexual matters in our society, new public attention has been focused on the abortion problem. In the United States, induced abortion (which medically can be a simple procedure) has been subject to legal proscription and administrative control. The current narrow legal exception of "therapeutic abortion" does not accord with accepted standards of good medical practice, and is now being challenged by medical practitioners and organizations. Instead of curbing abortion, the criminal law ban simply diverts the demand for such services to illicit sources. The results are: a thriving illegal business; subjection of abortion-seekers to the dangers of criminal abortion; a process of "criminalization"; and - for females in the lower socioeconomic strata - discriminatory treatment, according to their financial and informational resources.

An important trend toward liberalization of abortion laws is related to broader currents of social change in our society -- involving norms governing private sexual behavior, fertility control, and the social roles of females. The keynote of such change is the extension to females of areas of free choice hitherto not accorded them. How far this trend will be carried with respect to freedom of abortion remains to be seen.

1063 Schur, Edwin M. "Abortion and the Social System," Soc. Prob. 3(2):94-99. October 1955.

United States abortion law today is characteristic of that legal disequilibrium which results from disharmony between real forces and verbal formulas. Typical of legal disequilibrium is the widespread evasion of current abortion statutes; yet the law still partly determines behavior. Further, the law has several latent social functions. Abortion, in turn, can be a vital instrument of social control -- preventing serious family disorganization, economic hardship, and diminution of physical health. Recognition of this possibility by legislators may play an important role in fostering social and economic reform.

1064 Schur, Edwin M. Crimes Without Victims. Englewood Cliffs, New Jersey: Prentice-Hall, 1965.

Protestant and Jewish spokesmen seem to uphold the morality of therapeutic abortion at least as it is presently defined by the law. One basis for the Catholic objection has been the belief that the unbaptized child cannot enter Heaven. Presently the major ground is the general Commandment against killing. One slight concession appears in the rule of "double effect." If the good consequences of an action is the one interested, it is allowed even if it may have evil accessory effects. In situations in which it is possible to save only the fetus or the mother, the Catholic doctrine actually gives preference to the life of the fetus. This preference may have made sense when baptism was of primary importance, but that argument is no longer central. Critics have long pointed to the discrepancy between the Catholic position on this subject and its stand on killing in wartime or in self-defense and on capital punishment. In spite of the Catholic position a large number of Catholic women undergo abortions, but mainly those who are religiously inactive.

The devout Catholic couples are being put in a peculiarly difficult position if they want to control their family size with the combined prohibition of abortion and the use of contraceptives. Public pressure by the church for restrictive abortion laws may simply drive many women from the hospital abortions they desire to the more perilous illegal operations: hardly a "moral" effect.

1065 Schuyler, Daniel M., "You'll Never Divorce the Tax Collector--or Even Separate from Him," Illinois Bar J. 55:854-64. June 1967.

A discussion of the tax aspects of divorce and separation in terms of assets commonly involved in property settlements. Income, gift and estate tax consequences of periodic and lump sum cash payments and of transfers of real estate and transfers in trust, as well as life insurance and annuities, are considered. Related to population only with respect to child support. It is best for the wife to receive less alimony and more child support, while it is harder on the husband. More child support is also beneficial, if she plans to remarry. The loss of alimony if she remarries could be a deterrant factor.

1066 Schwartz, Herman. "The Parent or the Fetus? A Survey of Abortion Law Reform," Humanist 27:123-26. July - August 1967.

The author contends that, occasionally, laws set up to solve problems create more problems than they solve, and that this is especially true of our laws on abortion. Criminal sanctions against abortion may well be the most inappropriate for the substantial segment of the population that does not consider abortion immoral but rather both necessary and moral. In light of the above, the author first sets out some of the legal aspects of abortion in the United States, and then some facts about the number and nature of abortions in the country, with a few foreign references. Several of the issues and arguments in the current controversy on abortion are described, and the author concludes with an evaluation of some of the recent proposals for reform and their prospects.

1067 Schwartz, Louis B. "Morals Offenses and the Model Penal Code," Columbia Law Rev. 63:669-80. April 1963.

Reviewed are some of the American Law Institute's Model Penal Code Sections -- specifically, those dealing with flagrant affronts and penalization of private immorality, obscenity, prostitution and abortion -- that venture into the difficult area of morals legislation. The author also offers several general considerations in appraising morals legislation, with special references to the boundary between permissible social controls and constitutionally protected nonconformity.

1068 Schwartz, Richard A. "Psychiatry and the Abortion Laws: An Overview," Comprehensive Psychiatry 9(2):99-117. March 1968.

There are one to one and a half million criminal abortions per year in the United States. Because of restrictive legislation, only 8,000 abortions per year are performed under medically approved conditions. More work is needed among professional and lay groups to bring about needed legislative changes in 40 states. More research is also needed to evaluate the results of changes in abortion laws and to study the problems related to the life outcomes of unwanted children.

1069 Scott, Roger. "Income Tax Consequences of Divorce and Separation," Western Res. Law Rev. 8:517-29. September 1957.

Income tax liability on alimony and support payments is defined by various inter-related provisions of the Internal Revenue Code of 1954. The Code itself makes a general classification of the controlling rules, and the author sketches the Code's primary sections in an outline similar to that employed by the Code so that the manner in which each statutory rule operates in conjunction with the others can be understood. Reference is made to provisions on child support, periodic versus installment payments, the transfer of property, temporary alimony or support payments, and attorney's fees. The author concludes that divorce decrees and separation agreements have acquired income tax consequences which demand caution on the part of the draftsman. When evaluating the respective merits of one arrangement over another, the lawyer must be aware of repercussions which may occur regarding the claiming and proving of child dependency, gains, losses and income from property transferred directly or in trust, and estate and gift tax liabilities.

1070 Seegar, J. King, Jr. "Family Planning and the Role of the Maryland State Department of Health," Maryland Med. J. 16:63-67. September 1967.

An evaluation of the Maryland program indicates that it probably contributed to the decline in Maryland birth rate -- thirteen per cent from 1957 to 1964 and fourteen per cent between 1964 and 1966.

1071 "Selected Tax Aspects of Divorce and Property Settlements," Indiana Law J. 41:732-ff. Summer 1966.

In the relatively few divorce cases where alimony is involved it is an important issue because of the conflicting interests of the parties. The two principle types of alimony are described and the tax consequences are discussed, with sections on the deductibility of alimony payments, the recognition of gain upon lump sum transfers of appreciated property, the proper date for valuation of marital rights, the wife's basis, nontaxable exchanges, nontaxable division of property, conduit trust, deductibility of loss on transfer of depreciated property to wife and deductibility of legal expenses. Section 71 of the 1954 Internal Revenue Code is outlined, and various pertinent court cases are described and evaluated.

1072 Semonche, J.E. "Common-Law Marriage in North Carolina: A Study in Legal History," Amer. J. Legal Hist. 9:320-49. October 1965.

Surveys the legislation and court records of North Carolina from colonial times suggesting a number of conclusions. In colonial North Carolina, though statutes prescribed formalities for entering into the marriage relationship, they did not repeal the common law. Both before 1776 and after 1776 no impediment exists to viewing the common-law marriage, which existed widely, as valid. From 1897 the judicially determined law has been fixed with regard to the substantive recognition of common-law marriage. Recorded cases accept general reputation and cohabitation as evidence of marriage. The testimony which should induce a court to declare against the marriage of the parties and thereby bastardize their issue after deaths, ought to be so overwhelming as to leave not a doubt about the facts thus declared.

1073 Shaffer, Helen B., "Abortion in Law and Medicine," Editorial Research Reports, October 6, 1965, pp. 723-40.

1074 Shearer, Marshall L., et al. "Unexpected Effects of an 'Open Door' Policy on Birth Rates of Women in State Hospitals," Amer. J. Orthopsychiat. 38:413-17. April 1968.

Although the open door policy of the state hospital has resulted in major benefits to patients, it has been accompanied in the population under study by over a threefold (366%) rise in the birth rate of hospitalized women who delivered in Michigan's six major state mental hospitals, and presumably an even greater increase in the overall birth rate. 63.6% of the deliveries were to schizophrenic mothers, but the findings reported in the article are seen in both the schizophrenic and non-schizophrenic groups. While the authors mention factors other than the open door policy which could underlie this rise in the birth rate (the increasing marriage and reproductive rate of schizophrenics in recent years; possible shifts in admission policies so that more younger females are admitted; possibilities that these children, to an unknown extent, were conceived between hospitalizations, within the hospital milieu, or prior to hospitalization rather than occurring in relation to hospitals' open door policies), they feel that the likelihood of heightened birth rates for hospitalized women must be taken into account when considering general open door or leave policies as well as in making decisions for each individual woman patient. Unwanted and uncared for children constitute the major problem, and the authors conclude that women patients and their families must be actively prepared for their leaves and other forms of extended community contact, with strong consideration given the provision of effective contraceptives if these do not violate the patient's wishes.

1075 Shearer, Russell. "The Mutually Acknowledged Relationship of Parent and Child Under Inheritance Tax Statutes," Taxes 39:197-206. March 1961.

Provision of the California Inheritance Tax Law discussed in this article; also the statutes of other states.

1076 Shepherd, Robert E. "Support of Children Born Out of Wedlock: Virginia at the Crossroads," Washington Lee Law Rev. 18:343-50. Fall 1961.

During its 1958 session, the Virginia General Assembly created the Commission to Study Problems Relating to Children Born Out of Wedlock. The Committee's six recommendations, issued after one full year of study, are outlined, and the major portion of the article deals with the second recommendation, that which proposes the enactment of a paternity law for Virginia. There is a brief history of the legislature relating to illegitimacy, beginning with England's Poor Law Act of 1576 up to provisions passed by Virginia's General Assembly in 1954. Some of the financial and social problems of illegitimacy are listed - in Virginia, from 1955 to 1958 approximately 29,100 illegitimate children were born or almost 8% of all births in the State. The paternity bill proposed by the Commission is described in terms of purpose, blood tests and the economic welfare of the child or paternal responsibility. It is concluded that the parents should certainly bear the financial burden of support not only for its punitive value but also because in a large number of cases the father could provide a more satisfactory degree of support than the state is able to do through its welfare agencies.

1077 Sherwin, L., and Overstreet, E.W. "Therapeutic Abortion, Attitudes and Practices of California Physicians," Calif. Med. 105:337-ff., 1966.

Of the 934 California obstetricians sent a questionnaire on attitudes and practices regarding induced abortion, 748 replied. Ninety-one percent were in favor of therapeutic abortion when there is imminent risk of maternal death; 87% when definite risk of shortened maternal life; 67% when there is suicidal risk; 72% when risk of impairment of maternal physical or mental health; 77% when risk of fetal abnormality; 83% after rape or incest; and 21% where there are purely socio-economic grounds. One or another of these indications was used by 81% of the physicians who had performed therapeutic abortions.

1078 Sherwin, R.V. Sex and the Statutory Law. New York: Oceana, 1949. Vol. 1, 99 pp.; Vol. 2, 73 pp.

Description of the statutory treatment of sex in the several states of the United States. Among the topics are fornication, seduction, incest, rape, marriage, adultery, impotency, birth control, sterilization, artificial insemination and prostitution.

1079 Shipman, Gordon, and Tien, H. Yuan. "Nonmarriage and the Waiting Period," J. Marr. Fam. 27(2):277-80. May 1965.

A study based on analysis of data on the applications for marriage licenses of couples in Milwaukee County (1954-62) who never returned to get the license after the 5-day waiting period. They were compared with a like number of couples who secured their licenses and presumably were married, called newlyweds. The first sample were over-represented among Negroes and lower status persons and gave much less information about their wedding plans. There was no difference between the two comparison groups regarding the percent of males under 20 and females under 18 for either whites or Negroes, but the Negroes in both groups had higher percents than whites in the lowest age brackets. Remarriage among whites was definitely associated with nonmarriage after application, but for Negroes the data are inconsistent. The waiting period is not only a time for re-considering a hasty marriage, but a period of grace for proving eligibility for marriage. In general, those who are deflected from marriage by such restrictions seem to be poor risks for a satisfactory marriage.

1080 Shlakman, Vera. "Unmarried Parenthood: An Approach to Social Policy," Soc. Casework 47(8):494-501. October 1966.

While unmarried parenthood cuts across class lines, its incidence, like that of infant mortality and morbidity, chronic illness, birth defects, and school discontinuance, is highest among the poor and the deprived. Unwed parents need special help through a range of social, protective, legal, counseling, and health services. But, otherwise, the major problems of unwed parents blend with those of other groups in the community who are caught in the mesh of poverty. There is a two-track system of social services for unmarried parents and their children. For a few thousand of the white girls there is shelter, medical care, and a therapeutic, helping approach. For the rest, there is little or no service, or a punitive, demoralizing, disabling system of relief that is only now starting to change. The social welfare structure has failed to meet need, partly because social policy has not yet come to grips with the most deprived and oppressed groups, whose unmarried parenthood is but one manifestation of their condition. With the use of remedial and preventive conjoint treatment, there was evidence of new growth in the couple's relationship. Concomitantly, the husband's relationship to his wife became less ambivalent and he began to see her for the first time as a companion and love object. Their interactions became more considered and mature and less tied to fantasy and misconception.

1081 Siegel, Earl., _et al_. "A Longitudinal Assessment of the Characteristics of New Admissions to a Community Family Planning Program," _Amer. J. Public Health_ 54(1)):1864-75, 1968.

Surveys of family planning programs have generally neglected the study of changes in the characteristics of new admissions over a period of time as a clinic develops and matures. This study utilizes not only such an approach, but also compares ever-enrolled women over a seven-year period with the total population in need, in an attempt to measure enrollment effectiveness of the public family planning program in Charlotte, North Carolina. Retrospective data from clinic records of all first admissions to the clinic during the period 1961-1967 were used.

1082 Siegel, I., and Kanter, A.E. "Therepeutic Abortion. A 5-Year Survey at Mount Sinai Hospital," _Chicago Med. School Quart_. 21:14-ff., 1961.

A review of 51 therapeutic abortions performed at Chicago's Mount Sinai Hospital during the period 1955-1959. There was an abortion:delivery ratio of 5:1000, with total deliveries numbering 9,580. Thirty percent of the abortions were performed for psychiatric indications; 20% on the ground of rubella. Sterilization followed 53% of the abortion cases. Each abortion is summarized in terms of age of patient, reproductive history, marital status, race, indication for abortion, length of pregnancy before interruption, and method of abortion.

1083 Sirilla, George M. "Family Planning and the Rights of the Poor," Catholic Law 13:42-51, 89-90. Winter 1967.

This article is concerned with the proposed S. 1676 bill submitted to the 89th Congress by Senator Gruening of Alaska on April 1, 1965. This bill which was directed at population problems in this country and in the world, was discussed, before Senator Gruening's subcommittee, by Mr. William Ball representing the Pennsylvania Catholic Conference and by Fr. Hanley representing the United States' Bishops. In this paper the "Bishops' statement" is considered along with a re-examination of Mr. Ball's "coercion-privacy theory." In addition, state and federal activity in family planning programs is examined.

1084 Sirilla, George M. "Government Policy and Family Planning," Catholic Law 12:203-15. Summer 1966.

In April of 1965, a bill (S.1676) proposing changes in government policy toward population problems was introduced by Alaska's Senator Gruening. The author examines and analyzes the opposing testimony of two Catholic scholars (Dexter L. Hanley and William B. Ball) on S. 1676 and outlines the issues and arguments raised by the specter of governmental activity in family planning problems. Ball's criticism centered on the contention that there would be serious dangers to civil liberty and, especially for the poor, coercion and violations of human privacy if the government intervened in the area of family planning. Hanley's position was that of possible Catholic support for government sponsored family planning programs if adequate provision were made for methods acceptable to the Catholic conscience. The question of governmental endorsement of public immorality, i.e., endorsement of artificial contraception, is reviewed, and the statements of Vatican Council II on government policy and family planning are described in terms of another approach to the above issues. Discussed briefly are four additional problem areas: abortion, international policy, whether the unmarried woman should be a recipient of family planning advice and services, and finally, the extent of the role a Catholic may take in establishing, supporting, or assisting in family planning programs wherein immoral methods would be practiced (the argument from cooperation).

1085 Sixty-Second General Convention of the National Episcopal Church. "Resolution on Abortion-Law Reform." Summary of General Convention Actions, 1967, Seattle, Washington. October 1967.

It was resolved at the 62nd General Convention to support abortion law reform to the extent that it has been clearly demonstrated that the mother's physical health is seriously endangered, that the child will be badly deformed in mind or in body, and that pregnancy has resulted from forcible rape or incest.

1086 Slovenko, Ralph. "Sex Mores and the Enforcement of the Law on Sex Crimes: A Study of the Status Quo," Kansas Law Rev. 15:265-86. March 1967.

It is not the formal law, but rather its actual enforcement, which reflects the mores of a society. Sex offenses, in fact, constitute a very small percentage of the criminal docket in every jurisdiction. Full enforcement of the law occurs only in crimes where force is used, where the offense is directed against children, or where there is a violation of the public sense of decency. As studies show, sex offenders are frightened, guilty, woefully inadequate, commonly harmless people. The method of enforcement of the law on sex in large measure is not inhumane; rather, it is the disposition of those persons who are prosecuted and convicted that is punitive.

1087 Slovenko, R., ed. Sexual Behavior and the Law. Springfield, Ill.: C.C. Thomas, 1965. xxi, 886 pp.

In addition to the general editor, there are forty-seven contributors to this work. The overall purpose of the study is to show how a central activity such as sex affects the law over the time. The point is made that law is ambiguous and vacillating for the simple reason that our attitudes toward sex are ambiguous and vacillating.

1088 Smigel, Erwin O. "The Decline and Fall of the Double Standard," Annals Amer. Acad. Polit. Soc. Sci. 376:6-17. March 1968.

A review of the literature on premarital, heterosexual behavior of young people in the United States from A.C. Kinsey and L.M. Terman through W.E. Moore (Social Change) reveals that the changes in sexual behavior which took place in the 1920's have changed only slightly in the 1960's, and that this slow change is continuing. Causes cited range from the effects of industrialization, e.g., increased geographic and social mobility, urbanization, etc., to increased education and the decline in importance of the role of the family. The belief that a gradual transformation is taking place (except in overtness) rests on a comparison of the early studies on sexual behavior, the data from attitudinal studies researched from 1940 through 1963, and observations of the current scene. Data are tabulated here from four studies: Ira L. Reiss, The Social Context of Premarital Sexual Permissiveness; L. Rockwood and M. Ford, Youth, Marriage, and Parenthood; J. T. Landis, Building a Successful Marriage; and W. Ehrmann, Premarital Dating Behavior. It is concluded from these data that: (1) abstinence and permissiveness with affection are favored standards for males and females; (2) female approval of permissiveness with affection has increased and approval of abstinence has decreased; (3) permissiveness without affection is on the decline; (4) the orthodox double standard is on the decline; (5) the percentage of males who favor permissiveness with affection has increased markedly while the percentage of females in this area remains about the same; and (6) the percentage of both males and females who accept increased permissiveness with affection as their standard has increased. Also, the parent generation is both more conservative than the younger generation and more conservative than it was when it was the younger generation. Some further causes for the change are considered. It is noted that the sexual revolution, if existent, is in terms of frankness about sex and the freedom to discuss it. It is concluded that the double standard is declining but has not yet fallen.

1089 Smit, John William. "A Matched Group Study of Religious Differentials in Fertility and Family Planning," Dissertation Abstr. 25:6107-8, 1964-1965. Abstract of Ph.D. Thesis, University of Michigan, Ann Arbor, Michigan, 1964. 206 pp.

This is a study of the differences between American Catholics and Protestants with respect to fertility and family planning. It establishes that the differences are real and that they do not exist because of any temporary disadvantage of Catholics with respect to socio-economic position or demographic characteristics. The sizes of the differences vary systematically in relation to certain characteristics, although some difference is found in almost every one of a large number of sub-groups in which comparisons are made.

1090 Smith, David T., ed. Abortion and the Law. Cleveland: Western Reserve University Press, 1967. xiii, 237 pp.

A collection of essays presenting representative ideas from the three learned professions involved with the 'abortion problem': religion, medicine and law. Partial contents: George, B. James, Current Abortion Laws: Proposals and Movements for Reform, pp. 1-36; Niswander, Kenneth R., Medical Abortion Practices in the United States, pp. 37-59; Ryan, Kenneth J., Humane Abortion Laws and the Health Needs of Society, pp. 60-71; Rosen, Harold, Psychiatric Implications of Abortion: A Case Study in Social Hypocrisy, pp. 72-106; Drinan, Robert F., The Inviolability of the Rights to be Born, pp. 107-23; Jakobovits, Immanuel, Jewish Views on Abortion, pp. 124-43.

1091 Smith, Elmer M. "Family Planning in a State Welfare Department Program," Public Welf. 24(4):302-5. October 1966.

Notes on the background of legislation enacted by the General Assembly of Iowa in 1965 placing responsibility on the State Department of Social Welfare for providing and making payment for family planning services for certain recipients of public assistance. Information on administrative procedure.

1092 Smith, Eugene Vernest. "Content Analysis of Middle Class Women's Fiction from 1901 to 1960 as Indicative of Changing Cultural Values Related to Middle Class Birthrates," Dissertation Abstr. 22:354-55, 1961. Abstract of Ph.D. Thesis, Purdue University, Lafayette Indiana, 1961. 147 pp.

Objective was to help explain the fertility fluctuations of the United States population in terms of value change. The population is increasingly adopting birth control; therefore the problem was to relate birth control planning (or decision-making) to values. Studied are the values of the "middle class" because this class includes the most important contributors to the fluctuations. The content of 300 Ladies Home Journal fiction stories, using five stories from each of the sixty years from 1901-1960 are analyzed. Word descriptions are treated as indicators of the existence of values and their rate of occurrence are assumed to indicate the degree of importance and acceptance on the part of readers. The single value categories were logically combined into twenty-three value clusters. The data indicated that there was a strong value conflict regarding children from 1910 to about 1937. After 1937 the conflict disappeared. Values which had earlier made children undesirable to the middle classes had, by the late 1930's, made children desirable. There were virtually no values (or "ends") after 1940 which were incompatible with children. Positive values toward children continued to rise from 1910 to the late 1950's, where they levelled off. This levelling off was not because of any apparent return to older values but rather reflected the fact that children are now only one of several means, all of which were being used to attain fusion of the family and loss of individuality.

1093 Smith, Peter. "The History and Future of the Legal Battle Over Birth Control," Cornell Law Quart. 49:275-303. Winter 1964.

The author reviews the legislative and judicial history of the birth control controversy in the United States, focusing particularly on the activities in the area of birth control of the legislatures and courts of the federal government and the states of New York, Massachusetts, and Connecticut. The history and implications of the Poe case are examined, followed by an analysis of the Supreme Court decision in Poe, and a look into the future of the controversy. Although the subject's scientific and religious aspects are only occasionally mentioned, the author contends that the religious aspects of the birth control issue are largely responsible for the emotionalism imbedded in the legal controversy.

1094 Smith, R.N. "A Time to Speak Out," Oklahoma Med. Assn. J. 61:139-ff., 1968.

Physicians in Oklahoma must declare their views on abortion in order to provide guidelines for the state's legislature, which is presently considering liberalization of the abortion statute.

1095 Smith, Ruth Proskaner. "Record-Keeping and Follow-Up in Sterilization Cases," J. Fam. Welf. 5(2):47-50. December 1958.

This is an account of the procedure of record-keeping developed by the Human Betterment Association of America from the time they receive a request for assistance in securing sterilization to the follow-up.

1096 Smith, Virginia. "The Public Health Nurse's Role in Family Planning," Fam. Coordinator 17(1):15-17. January 1968.

An examination of the role of Virginia's public health nurses in family planning. In 1962 the State Health Commissioner announced that his Department would henceforth consider family planning as an integral part of the family health services it provides. Local health departments were asked to take positive action to implement the new policy. With regard to the public health nurse, the new policy has meant that child spacing has become an integral part of each family visit, public health nurses no longer have to wait to be asked for information on family planning, the education of public health nurses had to be supplemented by in-service training to prepare them for competent discussion of all child spacing methods, and there has been a great increase of services for the low-income patient in the Health Department, where either clinic services are provided or prescriptions for oral contraceptives may be filled. The author describes her experiences in the Department and concludes that family planning is viewed by the public health services as a private, personal matter which must be decided by the parents, but parents should have full access to information and services provided by the Health Department.

1097 Sobrero, A.J., and Lewit, S., eds. Advances in Planned Parenthood (v.4): Proceedings of the Sixth Annual Meeting of the American Association of Planned Parenthood Physicians, San Antonio, Texas. 16-17 April 1968. Excerpta Medica International Congress Series No. 177, 1969. 152 pp.

Public health departments have several decided advantages which simplify the referral of patients to a family planning program. Patients themselves can be encouraged to disseminate information about a family planning program; 25% of new admissions to the Muscogee County Family Planning Clinic are currently being referred by former patients. In Muscogee County, where all contraceptive care for women in the lower socio-economic group is provided by the Health Department, new admissions to the family planning clinic increased from 20-30 per month to approximately 120 per month over a four-month period and have remained at this level for 18 months. At the beginning of this 18-month study period, contraceptive care had been initiated for 16.2 percent of the women in the county who would not otherwise have been able to afford it through private physicians. By the end of the 18-month study period, contraceptive care had been initiated for 42.2 percent or 2,955 of the 7,000 women in this target group.

1098 "Social Welfare Aid to Needy Children: Liability of Cohabiting Male for Support " [People v. Shirley (Calif.) 360 P 2d 33], University California Los Angeles Law Rev. 9:261-72. January 1962.

The California Aid to Needy Children program is designed to provide aid to children who have been deprived of the support or care of one or both parents; however, aid will not be given when both parents are in the home unless mental or physical incapacity has deprived the child of support or care. Discussed are some of the program's undesirable incidental effects, and a regulation promulgated by the State Social Welfare Board providing for consideration of the income of a cohabiting male in determining the amount of the ANC grant. Recently the regulation was incorporated into an amendment of the Welfare and Institutions Code. Major problems caused by this regulation are outlined, such as that it provided for consideration of the man's income without placing any obligation of payment on him, that there is no constitutional objection to the statute, difficulties with enforcement, since the statute does not specify methods for insuring the carrying out of the obligation imposed, that no specification is made as to the time when the liability of a person assuming the role of spouse arises, and termination of obligation. However, in principle the statute appears desirable. Its advantage over the previous regulation is the provision for a legal obligation to support, rather than a mere consideration of the income of the common-law stepfather. The California Supreme Court's decision in the case of People v. Shirley is described: the defendant, a recipient of ANC funds, was convicted of grand theft for unlawfully obtaining welfare funds by failing to report income earned by a man living in her home.

1099 Special Committee on Matrimonial Laws . "Statement of Howard Hilton Spellman, Chairman, Before the New York State Joint Legislative Committee on Matrimonial and Family Law," Assn. Bar City New York Record 21:35-46. January 1966.

Emphasis on the desirability of modernizing the divorce law of New York.

1100 Spivak, Jonathan. "Birth Control Push," Wall Street J. 166:1-ff. October 21,1965.

United States is moving to make family planning help available to everyone. Agencies work quietly and shy from controversy.

1101 Spivak, Jonathan. "The '70 Census to Ask Sociological Questions to Aid Great Society," Wall Street J. 167:1-ff. April 14,1966.

Comments on the count-by-mail query on family planning, religion, and other sensitive topics.

1102 Stapper, Erik J. "Constitutional Law-Substantive Due Process-Statute Prohibiting Use of Contraceptives [Connecticut]", Michigan Law Rev. 53:929-31. April 1960.

The author argues against the Connecticut anti-contraceptive statute on the grounds that the law deprives patients of the doctor's best medical advice and restrains the doctor's right to practice his profession. The Connecticut legislation provides protection against two evils: first, the fear of exposing the uninformed person to injurious devices; second, there is the possibility that the availability of contraceptives encourages illicit relationships. Since there are already criminal provisions against adultery and fornication, the author contends that depending on judicial identification and appraisal of the basic rights involved and the degree of judicial scrutiny of everything of public interest served by the statute, the statute may well be termed an unreasonable restraint on the people's civil rights.

1103 Stephenson, H.A. "Therapeutic Abortion," Obstet. Gynec. 4:578-ff., 1954.

The indications and incidence of abortion at Children's Hospital in San Francisco during 1949-53 were studied and the results indicated that in 89 abortions, ten were performed because of tuberculosis, thirty for neurological and psychiatric conditions, and the remainder for a wide range of diseases. Because of this wide range, the author suggests that indications were insufficient and recommends that both patient and physician be informed of rigid legal requirements and that indications be studied by a committee.

1104 "Sterilization: New Arguments," U.S. News 53:55. September 24, 1962.

A Virginia law now sanctions free surgery for needy mothers to prevent further childbirth if they request it.

1105 Stinson, H.W. "Maternity Clinic Services in a Small Community Hospital," Virginia Med. Monthly 89:458-61. August 1962.

Report on 33 months' operation of the contraceptive clinic at Fauquier Hospital, Warrenton, Virginia.

1106 Stix, Regine K. "The Place of Fertility Control in Public Health," Amer. J. Public Health 36(3):209-18, 1946.

In the groups studied, pregnancy rates when no contraception was used showed either no significant group differentials or direct association between fertility and socio-economic status. Total pregnancy rates, however, showed expected inverse associations because of wider and more effective use of contraception among well-to-do couples in urban areas as compared with those of lower economic status and in rural areas. No evidence was found that use of contraception impaired fecundity. Expert advice on contraceptive techniques increased effectiveness of all contraceptive efforts, regardless of type of contraception used. Advice on control of sterility and excess fertility is probably of considerable importance in reducing maternal mortality and morbidity, but more research on this aspect of problem is needed. The U.S. Public Health Service has indicated willingness to consider and approve inclusion of child-spacing services in State Maternal Health programs.

1107 Stix, Regine K., and Notestein, Frank W. Controlled Fertility. An Evaluation of Clinic Service. Baltimore: Williams and Williams Co., 1940. xiv, 201 pp.

Follow-up of 991 females, largely Jewish residents of the Bronx (N.Y.) who had been clients of the Birth Control Clinical Research Bureau in 1931-32, showed that after 15 months only one-third of the women were using the clinic method. Those who persisted had a high degree of protection, but so did those who used other methods. The authors conclude that clinic policies need to be changed in many ways, and particularly with more insistence on the eugenic need of larger families in superior homes. They believe their figures tend "to refute the hypothesis that birth rates declined primarily because of biological changes in the population."

1108 Stokes, Walter R. "Should Mothers Inform Their Teenage Daughters on Contraceptives?" J. Sex Res. 2(1):59-60. April 1966.

Observations in private practice suggest four criteria for providing contraceptive information wisely: (1) parents should agree on it as part of girl's natural growth, (2) childhood sex education should have preceeded it, (3) information should be full and detailed, (4) the cooperation of a sympathetic doctor is advisable. United States daughters do not often approach their mothers about such matters. The Scandinavian countries are far ahead of us here.

Parents there are opposed to promiscuity and provide the information in the hope that it will lead to happy marriage and family life. Scandinavian youth have responded in a mature, responsible way.

1109 Storke, Frederic P. "Incestuous Marriage -- Relic of the Past," University Colorado Law Rev. 36:473-99. Summer 1964.

Although prohibition of marriages between persons who are too closely related in blood is practically universal, many relationships do not fall within the prohibited class in some jurisdictions but do in others. It is contended that a major problem is that of classification: "true" incest, limited to parent-child and brother-sister cases, must be distinguished from "technical" incest, occurring where the relationship is more distant. Conflicts of laws arise when the validity of marriage, technically incestuous by the law of the forum but not by the law of the state of celebration, is challenged. Such legal conflicts all involve cases of technical incest and court decisions have not only been hopelessly inconsistent, but have reflected transfer thinking, in that moral indignation over true incest, or even the concept of true incest, is carried over to cases where the legislature has seen fit to ban marriages of more distant relatives. In light of these trends and problems, the author outlines the history of incest, discusses the scientific and social advisability of prohibiting certain marriages, and places great stress on the importance of understanding the balance between local policy against technical incest and the broad conflicts policy of giving effect to marriages valid where contracted or valid by the law of the domicile. Thirty-eight court cases containing actual conflicts holdings are classified according to the relationship of the parties and the decisions are summarized, after a discussion of the effect of conflicts statutes. It is concluded that no marriage, valid by the law of any state with which it has important contacts, should be stigmatized as incestuous.

1110 Stump, Alfred. "The Law Regarding Sterilization," Indiana State Med. Assn. J. 50(7):836-38. July 1957.

Sterilization performed upon the request and consent of the person sterilized is not defined as a crime in any statute in Indiana. The operation may be performed without the consent of the person to be sterilized if he or she is a mental defective confined to a State institution.

1111 Stycos, J. Mayone. "Population Growth and the Alliance for Progress," Eugenics Quart. 9(4):231-36. December 1962.

Evaluates alternative policies for dealing with mounting rates of natural increase and advocates official sponsorship by the United States Government of research in fertility control.

1112 Sulloway, A.W. "The Legal and Political Aspects of Population Control in the United States," Law and Contemporary Prob. 25(3):217-37. Summer 1960.

Three methods of population control -- sterilization, abortion, contraception -- remain entangled in a maze of legislative prohibition or regulation. The legal and political aspects of these methods are discussed in regard to the limitations they impose on constructive effort in the area of American population control.

1113 "Support and Maintenance -- New York Uniform Support of Dependents Law Held Constitutional " [Landes v. Landes (NY) 135 N E 2d 562], St. John's Law Rev. 31:311-14. May 1957.

After a discussion of the ineffective and expensive remedies available to a dependent where an obligor left the jurisdiction, prior to the enactment of reciprocal support legislation in New York, the state's Uniform Support of Dependents Law -- a simple two-state procedure enabling a dependent residing in one state to enforce support obligations against an obligor residing in another state without the necessity of acquiring a prior in personam judgment -- is evaluated in terms of its new social benefits for the dependent and its basic constitutionality, upheld in the two described court cases. It is concluded that the factual pattern of such cases illustrate the value of reciprocal support laws, but, in a larger sense, demonstrate the propriety of reciprocal legislation which erases artificial barriers erected by state lines.

1114 Swain, Marianne DeGraff, and Kiser, Clyde V. "Social and Psychological Factors Affecting Fertility. xviii. The Interrelation of Fertility, Fertility Planning, and Ego-Centered Interest in Children," Milbank Memorial Fund Quart. 31(1): 51-84, 1953.

The Indianapolis Study data yield only limited support to the hypothesis that the greater the extent to which interest in children is a matter of personal (ego-centered) satisfaction, the higher the proportion of couples practicing contraception effectively and the smaller the planned families.

1115 "Symposium on the Law of Domestic Relations in Oklahoma," Oklahoma Law Rev. 14:281-ff. August 1961.

Contents: Introduction; Breach of promise to marry; Civil marriage requirements; Common-law marriage in Oklahoma; Presumptions of marriage in Oklahoma; Void and voidable marriages; Mutual rights, duties and liabilities of the parties during marriage; Duty to support the family; Rights of married women: liabilities and dealings with third persons; Rights and duties between members of the family and third persons arising from the family relationship; Transactions between husband and wife; Intra-family immunities; Legitimation of offspring; Bastardly proceedings; Adoption; Oklahoma guardianships; Custody; Rights and liabilities of minors; Alimony without divorce; Grounds for divorce in Oklahoma; Defenses to divorce in Oklahoma; Procedural aspects of divorce; Effects of divorce decree; Alimony and the division of jointly acquired property; Foreign divorces; Professional ethics in divorce.

1116 "Symposium on Sex and the Law in Contemporary Perspective," University Colorado Law Rev. 40:178-ff., Winter 1968.

Contents: Editors preface; Law as an instrument of population control, by H.H. Clark, Jr.; The legal enforcement of morality, by H.M. Hefner; Sexual deviation: response to an adaptational crisis, by R. Slovenko; The legacy of Freud--a dilemma for handling offenders in general and sex offenders in particular, by R.G. Fisher; Criminality of voluntary sexual acts in Colorado, by D.P. Stimmel; Transsexuals--their legal sex, by J.P. Holloway.

1117 Taber, Ben Z., and Hodges, Robert M. "The Role of the United States Food and Drug Administration in the Development and Evaluation of Anti-Fertility Agents," Internat. J. Fertility 9(4):579-83. October - December 1964.

Review of legal basis and procedures followed for evaluation (including three phases of tests: human bio-essay; preliminary trials; large-scale clinical trial).

1118 Tainter, Charles W., II. "Marriage to a Paramour After Divorce: The Conflict of Laws," Minnesota Law Rev. 43: 889-98, 1959.

The author examines in detail the extent of the extraterritorial effect of statutes which prohibit marriage by a divorced person to his paramour if the basis for dissolution of the marriage was adultery. This type of statute is found in Louisiana, Pennsylvania and Tennessee. It is concluded that the interests of uniformity and sound policy require that the statutes have effect only in the states which proscribe such marriages, and that an otherwise valid marriage should not be nullified unless the divorcing state was the intended domicile at the time of the second marriage.

1119 "Taxation--Income Tax--Deduction Allowed Husband for Entire Alimony Payment to Wife Unless a Portion Thereof is Specifically Designated for Child Support " [Commissioner v. Lester, 8 Sup Ct 1343], Vanderbilt Law Rev. 15: 298-301. December 1961.

Prior to 1942, there was no provision in the Income Tax Code for a deduction of any alimony payments by the husband. In 1942, Congress shifted the tax burden of alimony to the husband, but the new provision did not apply to any amount which was "fixed" by the decree as payable for the support of minor children and this provision was incorporated essentially unchanged into the 1954 Code. Combined payments to the wife for alimony and child support, with no part of the total amount designated as either, have been held entirely taxable to the husband. Discussed are the litigous difficulties and conflicting court decisions that have arisen where the decree does not distinctly designate alimony and child support but does provide that the total payments be altered upon the happening of some future event. To resolve such problems, the Supreme Court ruled, in Commissioner v. Lester (1961), that the husband may deduct from his gross income payments made to the wife under a divorce decree, except portions thereof which are specifically designated as payable for the support of a minor child. The considerations of the Court in coming to this decision are outlined. The parties to a divorce or separation agreement may now negotiate the tax consequences of child support payments to their mutual advantage, after deciding who will pay the income tax on the money used for such a purpose.

1120 Taylor, Howard C., Jr. "A Family Planning Program Related to Maternity Service," Amer. J. Obstet. Gynec. 95:726-31. July 1, 1966.

The article deals, in a broad sense, with the advantages of a system in which family planning would be treated as an integral part of the health and medical organization for maternity care, as opposed to a program stressing general, perhaps somewhat random public education along with birth control clinics or other services for all who may be inspired to attend as a result of general propaganda. Discussion is divided into four sections: the statistical advantages of the introduction of contraception in the postpartum period; the educational opportunities afforded during pregnancy and the puerperium; an illustrative organization for a pregnancy-postpartum program; and a view of some maternity services about the world with respect to their suitability for a postpartum family planning program. Of the means by which birth control may become general practice, the author contends that a concentration of effort on a single phase of our social organization, that concerned with maternity care, would offer maximum results with a minimum of effort, and that this improved organization of maternity care, integrated carefully with family planning programs, might serve as a very effective restraint on population increase.

1121 Taylor, T.R. "A Lawyer Reviews Plan for Legalized Abortions," Linacre Quart. 26:137-ff., 1959.

The recommendations in regard to abortion of the American Law Institute's Model Penal Code are not seen as a restatement of this country's criminal law on abortion.

1122 TenBroek, Jacobus. "California Dual Systems of Family Law: It's Origin, Development, and Present Status," Stanford Law Rev. 16:257-317. March 1964.

California's family law, particularly that dealing with the child, derives from four principal sources -- the Elizabethan Poor Law, the Aid to Families With Dependent Children Law, the California codes of 1872, and the common law -- and the major gap in terms of provisions and concepts among all four of these legal complexes lies between the two public aid laws on one hand and the codes and common law on the other. The poor law and the AFDC Law deal with conservation of public funds and are heavily political and measurably penal. The other system (codes of 1872 and common law statutes) deals with the distribution of family funds, focuses on the rights and responsibilities of family members, and is civil, nonpolitical and less penal. In Part One of a two part article, the author describes and analyzes England's poor and common laws, with references to parliamentary development of the poor law, poor law assumption of public responsibility and private charity (statute of charitable trusts), the poor law and the statute of labourers, the family law of the poor, and the family relationship laws of the common law, which were primarily the work of the courts and lacked the legislative and public character of poor law concerns. In addition, since New York proved a principal channel by which family law ideas eventually were transmitted to the legal system of California, the author traces the early poor law and common law reception in that state and concludes Part One with a discussion of the development of the Field Draft Codes (Civil Procedure, Criminal Procedure, Political, Penal and Civil Codes) in New York. As embodied and altered in the Field Draft Codes, New York's dual system of family law was later considered by code commissioners and legislators in California.

1123 Thorson, Douglas Y. "An Analysis of the Sources of Continued Controversy Over the Tax Treatment of Family Income," National Tax J. 18:113-32. June 1965.

Main questions are the desirable proper degree and form of differentiation among persons of different marital and family status.

1124 Throckmorton, Robert B. "Legal Problems of Artificial Insemination," J. Iowa State Med. Society 46(10):529-32. October 1956.

The legal rights, obligations and status which a widespread practice of artificial insemination creates are quite unclear because of little litigation and no relevant legislation. The author poses a number of unsolved legal questions involving AID, artificial insemination in which the donor is not the husband and offers suggestions to both physician and patient concerning the precautionary steps that should be taken before and after this procedure. He concludes that, since the few legal cases so far decided are in conflict, the physician should make sure that his patients are made cognizant of the legal uncertainties in AID.

1125 Tietze, Christopher. "Demographic Aspects of Abortion in the United States." Paper Presented at the International Union for the Scientific Study of Population, General Conference, London, 3-11 September 1969.

Reviews the legal status of abortion from the common-law to the present. Reports on public attitudes toward abortion, the frequency of legal and illegal abortions, and the resulting maternal mortality.

1126 Tietze, Christopher. "Introduction to the Statistics of Abortion," in: Engle, E.T., ed. Pregnancy Wastage. Springfield, Ill.: Thomas, 1953.

The term abortion is defined as it applies to the stages of fetal development and the traditional types: spontaneous, therapeutic and illegal. The author states that a statistical study would involve extension of vital registration to include all fetal deaths, but recognizes that is has not been too successful in the past. The limitations and possibilities of approximating the incidence of abortion and maternal mortality are examined and the author feels that there is much to be done to determine the quantitative aspects of pregnancy wastage.

1127 Tietze, Christopher. "Report on a Series of Illegal Abortions Induced by Physicians," Human Biol. 21:60-ff., 1949.

The author reports on a study of 363 illegal abortions performed in 1948, by two physicians in "a large Eastern city." Aspects of the abortions described include fees charged, time of pregnancy interruption, marital status and age of the women (average age 28.6 years), and the nulliparus nature of the group. Of the 363 women, 170 had not been pregnant before, but, in comparison with a group of women having deliveries in the same city, the abortion group had a higher parity. It is contended then, that the abortions were used primarily to limit family size and not as a method of child-spacing.

1128 Tietze, Christopher. "Therapeutic Abortion in the United States," Amer. J. Obstet. Gynec. 101:784-ff., 1968.

Results on data of therapeutic abortions from hospitals responding to the Professional Activities Survey show that the ratio of abortions to deliveries was 1.9:1000 during 1963-1965. The author admits that this sample is somewhat biased in that the hospitals and geographic locations were controlled and therefore, the probable abortion ratio is conjectured to be 2:1000 for all of the United States. Hospitals affiliated with a medical school reported five therapeutic abortions in 1000 deliveries; hospitals with residencies in obstetrics and gynecology, 18 in 1000; and the remaining hospitals only 1.2 in 1000. The most common indication for abortion was psychiatric disease except in 1964 when the risk of fetal abnormalities dominated during the rubella epidemic.

1129 Tietze, Christopher, et al. "The Clinical Effectiveness of the Rhythm Method of Contraception," Fertility and Sterility 2(5):444-50, 1951.

This report covers all the women who attended the Rhythm Clinic at the Free Hospital for Women in Brookline from its inception in 1936 until the summer of 1949; a total of 551, only 409 of whom received instruction and used the method. Rather more than 50 per cent of these 409 women was lost trace of, so that the actual failure rate had to be calculated. The authors give the probable number of accidental pregnancies as 87 which is a high rate of failure and they conclude that the rhythm method offers adequate protection only to rigidly selected cases and in such cases where the prevention of further pregnancies is imperative this method cannot be regarded as adequate.

1130 Tietze, Christopher, and Martin, C.E. "Foetal Deaths, Spontaneous and Induced, in the Urban White Population of the United States," Popul. Stud. 11:170-ff., 1957.

Foetal deaths reported by 1,329 white women interviewed for the Kinsey study are analyzed. The sample is characterized as a group of urban white women, three-fourths of whom have attended college. Total number of pregnancies reported was 2,448, of which 1,571 resulted in live births, 444 by spontaneous foetal deaths, and 708 by induced abortions. Ninety-three percent of the induced abortions were illegally performed. About 90% of all pre-marital and post-marital pregnancies were terminated by induced abortion; 15% of the pregnancies occurring during marriage were ended by induced abortion. It may be inferred that in the segment of the urban white population of the United States between one-fifth and one-fourth of all pregnancies were terminated by induced abortion.

1131 Tinnelly, J.T. "Abortion and Penal Law," Catholic Lawyer 5:187, 1959.

It is suggested that formulation of the Modern Penal Code's proposed abortion statute excluded consideration of ethical and religious principles. Lawyers are urged to take particular care with abortion sections which involve the morality of both the individual and society.

1132 Todd, A.L. "The Senate Looks at Population: Head Counting on Capitol Hill," Population Bull. 22:1054. December 1966.

Report on the 1965-66 hearings inquiring into all aspects of the world population crisis before the Subcommittee on foreign aid expenditures, committee on government operations, U.S. Senate.

1133 Trainer, J.B. "Abortion -- A Problem for Solution," in: Physiologic Foundations for Marriage Counseling. St. Louis: C.V. Mosby, 1965.

Emphasized is the need for abortion in our society, with references to pertinent medical, legal and moral arguments. Discussed briefly are the approaches of Japan and the Scandinavian countries, and the author contends that any solution to the abortion problem will be blocked by what he terms a cultural lag. The status of the fetus, the population explosion and advances in medical technology are also reviewed.

1134 Trout, M. "Therapeutic Abortion Laws Need Therapy," Temple Law Quart. 37:172-ff., 1964.

The medical, religious and socio-economic aspects of abortion laws from a historical perspective are reviewed with reference to the present ambiguity of these laws. The author emphasizes the need for clarification, uniformity and public education.

1135 Trudgeon, Jon H. "Marriage to Foreign Nationals and Federal Income Taxation," AF JAG Law Rev. 10:37-44. March - April 1968.

Discussed is the effect of marriage by a U.S. citizen to a nonresident alien on his income tax status: the new status can cause wide variations in the individual's tax liability. Also considered are the factors that must be considered with regard to the alien's income and the problems connected to the inability of the spouses to file a joint return if either spouse is a nonresident alien for any part of the tax year. Changes in status where there are children involved and use of Head of Household title are discussed, and the author concludes with a description of the kinds of savings available to people in low income groups. The importance of income tax planning and advice before marriage to a foreign national actually occurs is emphasized.

1136 Tryhall, Sylvester W. "The Premarital Law," J. Amer. Med. Assn. 187:900-3. March 21, 1964.

Legal requirements for premarital physical examination and blood tests; and a survey of their effectiveness in Michigan.

1137 Tulkoff, M.S. "Legal and Social Control of Abortion," Kentucky Law J. 40:401-ff., 1952.

The ineffectiveness of legal prohibition and punitive measures as controls of abortion is suggested. The author proposes an additional extra-legal control which would be put into practice by members of the medical profession through programs of public education.

1138 Turtletaub, Harold A. "Misconduct in the Marital Relation: Adultery as a Bar to Dower," University of Miami Law Rev. 13: 83-91. Fall 1958.

The Statute of Westminster, a common law doctrine enacted in 1285, declared that a wife would forfeit her dower if she voluntarily left her husband and committed adultery. The author discusses this ancient statute and its subsequent treatment by the various jurisdictions of the United States, and gives particular emphasis to the status of the rule in Florida, where the court decided that the state's divorce statute was preferable to the provisions of English law and refused to apply the Statute of Westminster. The article concludes with an analysis of the Florida decision and suggestions for further legislation, since neither the common law nor the statutory law of the state makes any provision concerning forfeiture of a widow's intestate interest on the grounds of adultery and the wife, being barred from dower, still may elect to take her intestate share which may be more than dower.

1139 United States Agency for International Development. Office of the War on Hunger. The Population Challenge: U.S. Aid and Family Planning in the Less-Developed Countries. Washington: Government Printing Office, 1967. 20 pp.

Briefly reviews problems associated with world population growth; states AID policy; describes some AID-supported programs.

1140 United States Agency for International Development. Population Branch. Health Service. Assistance for Family Planning Programs in Developing Countries. Washington, 1967. iii, 80 pp.

This is the first over-all report by the Agency for International Development summarizing its assistance for population programs of developing countries. Key data are given here, country by country, on the population growth of these countries, the status of their population programs, and the help being provided to such programs and activities by AID and other institutions and agencies. Assistance for regional population projects is also included.

1141 United States Agency for International Development. Proposed Foreign Aid Program FY 1968. Summary Presentation to the Congress. Washington: Government Printing Office, 1967. vii, 297 pp.

1142 United States Bureau of Labor Statistics. "Family Allowances for Teachers," Monthly Labor Rev. 63(2):242-46. August 1946.

At the close of the scholastic year 1945, family allowances were being paid in at least 34 public-school systems and differentials for married men in 62 such systems.

1143 United States. "Contraceptives: Control of Sale and Display," Internat. Digest Health Legis. 18:444, 1967.

Act of 2 July 1965 in New York State amends the Penal Code to permit pharmacies to sell or distribute contraceptive devices and preparations provided the purchaser is over sixteen years of age. But the display of such articles is not permitted.

1144 United States. Department of Health, Education, and Welfare. Premarital Health Examination Legislation. Public Health Service Publication No. 383. Washington: Government Printing Office, 1954. vi, 114 pp.

This publication includes a table of the approval and effective dates of the premarital laws cited in a paper by Dr. J.K. Schafer on "Premarital Health Examination Legislation - History and Analysis," which was originally published in Public Health Reports (May 1954), and a compilation of the laws in force in 1954 in the forty States and two Territories of the United States requiring blood tests and physical examinations for venereal disease. These laws are reproduced from the various legal reference sources of the States and territories, and citations to these sources are given for each law.

1145 United States. Department of Health, Education, and Welfare. *Report on Family Planning: Activities of the U.S. Department of Health, Education, and Welfare in Family Planning, Fertility, Sterility, and Population Dynamics*. Washington: Government Printing Office, September 1966. vi, 35 pp.

Introduction presents policy statement of January 24, 1966, and subsequent developments. This is the first departmental report on family planning. Department plans to issue a report annually, based on the activities of the operating agencies. Chapters: Welfare Administration; Public Health Service; Office of Education; Food and Drug Administration.

1146 United States. President. *The Foreign Assistance Program: Annual Report to the Congress, Fiscal Year 1968*. Washington: Government Printing Office, 1969. vi, 85 pp.

In his letter of transmittal the President notes a sharpened focus of the aid program on the priority problems of food and population. Text includes brief outline of expenditures in areas of population research and family planning, noted on pp. 9, 11, 26, 29, 31, 32, 34, 37.

1147 "United States: Report of the President's Committee on Population and Family Planning," *Stud. Fam. Planning*, No. 40, April 1969, pp. 1-4.

Summary of main recommendations of the Committee's report: *Population and Family Planning: The Transition from Concern to Action*.

1148 United States. Senate Committee on Government Operations. Subcommittee on Foreign Aid Expenditures. *Population Crisis: Hearings Part 1, November 2 1967 on S. 1676, a Bill to Reorganize the Department of State and the Department of Health, Education and Welfare*. 90th Congress, 1st session. Washington: Superintendent of Documents, 1967. v, 268 pp.

Provides information on family planning programs in the United States.

1149 United States. Senate Committee on Labor and Public Welfare. Subcommittee on Employment, Manpower, and Poverty. _Family Planning Program: Hearings May 10, 1966 on S. 2993, a Bill to Provide Federal Financial Assistance to Public Agencies and Private Nonprofit Organizations to Enable Them to Carry on Comprehensive Family Planning Programs_. 89th Congress 2d session. Washington: Superintendent of Documents, 1966. iv, 135 pp.

1150 United States. Senate Committee on Military Affairs. _Family Allowances: Hearings before a Subcommittee of the Committee on Military Affairs, United States Senate, Seventy-seventh Congress, Second Session, on S. 2467, a Bill to Provide Family Allowances for the Dependents of Enlisted Men of the Army, Navy, Marine Corps, and Coast Guard of the United States, and for Other Purposes_. Washington: Government Printing Office, 1942. 2 Vol.

In addition to the bill itself and the testimony on it, the following four appendices are included: I. Family allowances to dependents of members of the armed forces in the United States during the World War. II. Recommendations of Family Security Committee. III. Canadian system of dependents' allowances. IV. Foreign provisions for the dependents of mobilized men.

1151 United States. Senate Committee on Post Office and Civil Service. _Maternity Leave for Government Employees. Hearings Before a Subcommittee of the Committee on Post Office and Civil Service, United States Senate, Eightieth Congress, Second Session, on S. 784, a Bill to Provide 60 days Maternity Leave per Year for Female Employees Who Have Worked at Least 10 Months for the Government. February 17 and 18, 1948._ Washington: Government Printing Office, 1948. iii, 82 pp.

An international survey of practices is included.

1152 United States. Veterans Administration. Department on Veterans Benefits. _Digest of Inheritance Laws: States and Territories of the United States_. Washington: 1966. vi, 118 pp.

Details given on distribution of personal property to heirs of intestate decedents after deductions of legally established allowances and priority claims; also discusses matters pertaining to administration. Notes on adopted children, posthumous children, illegitimate children, allowances, and advances.

1153 United States. War Department. First Annual Report of the Office of Dependency Benefits, Fiscal Year Ending June 30, 1943. Newark, New Jersey, 1944. 76 pp.

Allowances for the last ten months of the period covered totalled $797,287,649.70, of which the Government contributed $446,822,777.22 and the soldiers $350,464,872.48.

1154 United States. Women's Bureau. Maternity Benefits Under Union Contract Health Insurance Plans. Women's Bureau Bulletin No. 214. Washington: Government Printing Office, 1947. 19 pp.

Analyzes the experience of women under eight plans and tries to evaluate the benefits they received in relation to the costs they incurred.

1155 United States. Women's Bureau. Maternity Protection of Employed Women. Women's Bureau Bulletin No. 240. Washington: Government Printing Office, 1952. 50 pp.

Legislation in the United States and in other countries.

1156 United States. Women's Bureau. Working Mothers and the Need for Child Care Services. Washington: Government Printing Office, 1967. 24 pp.

1157 Vadakin, James C. Family Allowances: An Analysis of Their Development and Implications. Coral Gables: University of Miami Press, 1958. xiii, 185 pp.

The author analyzes the nature of family allowances and the budgetary reasons for their use. Next, he examines historical patterns and foreign experiences and child welfare, demographic, economic, and political aspects. The volume closes with a discussion of implications of the system for the United States and with a series of specific proposals.

1158 Valien, Preston, and Fitzgerald, Alberta Price. "Attitudes of the Negro Mother Toward Birth Control," Amer. J. Sociol. 55:279-83. November 1949.

Descriptive statistical study of the attitude toward birth control and selected demographic variables in a random sample of Negro mothers interviewed in Nashville, Tennessee.

1159 Vanderpool, J.P., and White, R.M., "Psychiatry and the Abortion Problem," Texas Med. 64:48-ff., 1968.

Topics discussed include the legal status of abortion, its psychiatric aspects, and possible methods of resolving the abortion problem, with references to Hall's study which pointed out the disparity of abortion incidence between ward and private patients and a Swedish study which concluded that suicide and refusal of abortion were not necessarily related. It is contended, however, that there may be psychiatric problems arising after refusal of abortion which should not be overlooked or ignored.

1160 Voyles, James. "Changing Abortion Laws in the United States," J. Fam. Law 7(3):496-511. Fall 1967.

Cites some available data on abortions and deaths from illegal abortions, and reviews current state laws on abortion.

1161 Wadlington, Walter. "Shotgun Marriage by Operation of Law," Georgia Law Rev. 1:183-204. Winter 1967.

The practice of the so-called "shot-gun" marriage seems to contradict the thesis that marriage requires free and voluntary consent by both parties. Under the guise of protecting the state's interests in the courtship process or regulating sexual relations outside of marriage, a not-so-subtle use of criminal sanctions has served to force marriage in a number of instances. A general examination of the law dealing with fornication and seduction, and of marriage as a defense is given in this paper. To a great extent, our present law dealing with seduction reflects both confusion as to the exact problems to be solved, and our conditioned response of looking to sanctions such as imprisonment, money damages, or even marriage as the only available tools for the solution of these problems. The author suggests using what might be more effective alternatives in cases where illegitimacy is concerned - adoptive placement, improvement in existing paternity or legitimacy statutes, better dissemination of information, or even abortion, as alternatives either in a specific situation or as a preventive for future difficulties.

1162 Wall, L.A. "Abortions: Ten Years' Experience at Kansas University Medical Center," Amer. J. Obstet. Gynec. 9: 510-ff., 1960.

Statistical results of 927 abortions performed at the Kansas University Medical Center from 1948-1957 are given. Ratio of abortions to deliveries was 1:15.8. With regard to previous abortions, 62% of the patients had had none; 25% had had one; 8% had had two; and 5% had had three or more. In 70% of the cases no reason for abortion was given. There were 66 cases of criminal abortion reported.

1163 Walther, Ewell P., Jr., and Wittman, Phillip A. "Separation and Divorce in Louisiana: A Tax Analysis," Tulane Law Rev. 37:1-48. December 1962.

The problems generated by the tax treatment of alimony and support payments arise primarily from 1) a failure to comply with the literal terms of the statute and 2) a failure to identify clearly the nature of the payments. These two rather broad problem areas are discussed in the light of applicable Louisiana statutory, codal and jurisprudential rules which to a large extent, determine the tax effects in separation and divorce proceedings. Section I covers the effects of payment to wife and children, with subsections on statutory requirements, nature of alimony payments, alimony trusts and child support payments. Section II covers the effects on reporting of income, with subsections on joint returns, community income and dependents' exemptions. Section III covers transfers in satisfaction of property rights or marital rights, with subsections on division of community property, transfers in satisfaction of marital rights and special problems, such as recognition of loss and insurance. Section IV covers gift and estate tax problems, with subsections on gift taxes. Section V covers deduction of attorney and accounting fees, with subsections on husband's attorney and accounting fees, wife's attorney and accounting fees and special Louisiana problems.

1164 Warren, D.C. "Contraceptive Laws in the United States," Medico-Legal J. 129:1-4. January 1964.

State legislatures have found it their duty in most states to regulate the distribution and use of contraceptives. The author reviews state statutory laws in this area, excluding those dealing with abortion and sterilization, and mentions fine-imprisonment penalties under many of the statutes. At time of writing, nineteen states had no specific laws regarding contraceptive devices. In these states, regulation is presumably left to the various cities and counties. Condradictory laws on contraception exist in some form for all other states -- ranging from absolute prohibition, to use of any mechanical or pharmacologic means of birth control, to permitting vending machine sales in places where alcoholic beverages are sold on premises.

1165 Watson, T. "Why Therapeutic Abortion?" Minnesota Med. 50:55-ff., 1967.

Argues for greater involvement of physicians in abortion law reform, and respect by those opposing reform for the ethics of those who do. The moral and medical aspects of therapeutic abortion are reviewed, with a suggestion that sterilization when indicated can reduce the number of or need for such abortions. Stressed also is the necessity of providing the poor with information on methods of birth control.

1166 Weinberg, Meyer. "Concubinage: and Common Law Marriages," Chicago Bar Record 37:436-ff., September 1956.

The author reviews a case involving common law marriage in the Texas Civil Appeals (Nevarez v. Vailon, 1956). The court turned down the woman's appeal to act as the administrator of property of the deceased man with whom she had lived in Mexico for 13 years. She and the deceased had cohabited as man and wife; her children lived in their home and were supported by the deceased. The court claimed that she was not the common law wife of the deceased in Mexico, and accordingly, would not be so recognized in Texas. However, the State of Chihuahua, where she had resided with the deceased, recognizes concubinage, and permits the concubine to inherit a proportion of her partner's estate (less than a wife would receive) provided the couple had been living together at time of death for at least five years. The author emphasizes that concubinage as used in Mexico does not carry a stigma, and not only is recognized by law in the Republic of Mexico but is the relationship of an estimated half a million Mexican couples.

1167 Weinberg, Roy D. Laws Governing Family Planning Dobbs Ferry: Oceana Publications, 1968. v, 118 pp.

The text is devoted to a survey in non-technical language of current American laws pertinent to the problems of planned parenthood, including contraception, sterilization, artificial insemination, and abortion. Appendix presents texts of recent statutes and pronouncements by concerned bodies.

1168 Weinberger, Andrew D. "Interracial Marriage. Its Statutory Prohibition, Genetic Import, and Incidence," J. Sex Res. 2(3):157-68. November 1966.

The individual state laws are quoted and reviewed. It is estimated that there are now 50,000 Negro-white marriages in the United States. The phenomenon of Negroes passing into white society is briefly discussed and estimated.

1169 Wentz, F.K. "Problem of Abortion," Board of Social Ministry, Lutheran Church in America, 1967.

A statement by the Lutheran Board of Social Ministry on abortion. While abortion on demand is rejected on the ground that incipient human life needs protection, reform of current abortion laws is advocated for the legalization of "a carefully defined and socially protected 'compassionate' abortion." Indications for abortion of a eugenic, humanitarian, medical and limited socio-medical nature would come under such reform.

1170 West Virginia. Department of Health. Guidelines and Standards for Family Planning and Child Spacing Clinics. Charleston: 1966. 5 pp.

An Act of the Legislature of West Virginia. Regular Session, 1966, relates to the establishment and operation of clinics for family planning and child spacing. The Department of Health has prepared guidelines for distribution to all county health departments, licensed hospitals, selected physicians, and others.

1171 West Virginia. Legislature. Joint Committee on Government and Finance. Report on Family Planning and Child Spacing, to the West Virginia Legislature, by the Joint Committee on Government and Finance and the Commission on Interstate Cooperation, Charleston, 1966. iii, 67 pp.

1172 Westoff, Charles F., et al. "Oral Contraception, Coital Frequency, and the Time Required to Conceive," Soc. Biol. 16(1):1-10. March 1969.

Average coital frequency was 18-20 per cent higher for women 25-44 years of age using oral contraception compared with those using other methods of contraception or no methods, according to data from the 1965 National Fertility Study. This finding was consistent with the difference between women of comparable age using the pill and those using other methods reinterviewed over a span of six to ten years after the initial interview in the Princeton Fertility Study. For pill users, the mean monthly coital frequency increased 7.1 to 7.5 instead of declining to 6.3, the rate they theoretically might have had if they had not shifted to oral contraception. No difference, however, was found in the time required to conceive between women who discontinued oral contraception and those discontinuing other methods.

1173 Westoff, Charles F., et al. "Social and Psychological Factors Affecting Sterility. xx. The Use Effectiveness and Acceptability of Methods of Fertility Control," Milbank Memorial Fund Quart. 31(3):291-357, 1953.

This report is based upon information supplied by 1,977 wives, in response to detailed questions about their pregnancies and contraceptive histories which ranged over a married period of 12-15 years. Requirements for inclusion in the intensive interview study were the same as those set up for previous reports in this series. All couples represented were native white, Protestant, at least 8th grade graduates, married during the period between 1927 and 1929, never previously married, residents of a large city during most of their life together, and with the husbands under 40 and the wives younger than 30 at the time of their marriage. Definite evidence is shown that there is an inverse association between economic class and the regularity of the use of contraceptive practices. This is reflected in the inverse relation seen (in the pregnancy rates of couples practicing contraception) between family income and number of pregnancies. The condom is used by about 72% of couples, either alone or supplemented by some other means. Diaphragm and jelly, which was used in only 7% of all contraceptive exposures, tends to be used later in the married period, although 35% of all couples were using comparatively ineffective methods after 13 to 15 years of married life. For relatively fecund couples who reported using contraception the general effectiveness is 92%, from the point of view in reduction of uncontrolled fertility. Highly effective techniques include the diaphragm and jelly, the condom, and the condom and douches. Least effective methods included the safe periods, suppositories and douches.

1174 Westoff, Charles F., et al. "Some Estimates of the Reliability of Survey Data on Family Planning," Popul. Stud. 15(1):52-69. July 1961.

An important analysis of the reliability of reports on fetal deaths and contraceptive practice based on reinterviews after three years with the sample of the Princeton Study.

1175 Westoff, Charles F., et al. "The Structure of Attitudes Toward Abortion," Milbank Memorial Fund Quart. 47(1):11-37. January 1969.

Analysis of responses to questions on abortion in the 1965 Princeton National Fertility Study, in which approximately 5,600 married women under age 55 were interviewed, shows that respondents were overwhelmingly predisposed to favor abortion if the pregnant woman's health is endangered. They were opposed if the grounds are that the woman is unmarried, cannot afford another child, or wants no more children. With all six items considered simultaneously, response patterns were distributed according to Guttmann's scalogram analysis. Attitudes toward abortion were most favorable among older women (i.e., more advanced in child-bearing cycle), white, non-Catholic (especially Jewish), and living in urban and suburban areas of the Northeast and Far West. Family income and occupation (except for Catholics), employment of the wife, and expressed desire to have no more children, were also found to be related. Higher approval was also positively associated with use of the contraceptive pill and approval of sterilization. The most important variable was education: except for Catholics, approval progressed with increase in education. (Higher levels of Catholic education may reinforce Catholic attitudes and belief, producing a pattern dissimilar to that of other religions.)

1176 Westoff, Charles F., et al. The Third Child: A Study in the Prediction of Fertility. Princeton: Princeton University Press, 1963.

In 1961, Family Growth in Metropolitan America set forth the first phase of this research -- an interview with 1,165 couples who had recently borne a second child in one of the large metropolitan areas of the United States. It emphasized fertility performance in the early phases of family formation, and attitudes toward further increases in family size at a stage that most recently married American couples reach. In The Third Child the emphasis is on fertility behavior in terms of contraceptive practice, the occurrence of pregnancy and the duration of interpregnancy intervals in the three and a half years following the second birth. It is based on a second interivew with 905 couples (of the original 1,165) three years after the first. Contraceptive effectiveness is found to increase with marriage duration and as couples approach the goal of desired family size.

1177 Westoff, Charles F., and Kiser, Clyde V. "Social and Psychological Factors Affecting Fertility. xxx. An Empirical Re-Examination and Inter-Correlation of Selected Hypothesis Factors," Milbank Memorial Fund Quart. 3(4):421-35, 1953.

This study continues the series of analytical reports based upon data collected in the Indianapolis Study of Social and Psychological Factors Affecting Fertility. The particular hypothesis factors selected for this analysis are: socio-economic status, marital happiness, feeling of personal adequacy, tendency to plan in general, and feeling of economic security. All of the correlation coefficients between hypothesis factors and the two dependent variables of fertility planning and completely planned fertility are fairly low. The maximum proportion of the variations in the dependent variables that can be accounted for by multiple combinations of variable factors is 15% for fertility planning and 12% for the size of the planned family.

1178 Westoff, Charles F., and Ryder, Norman B. "Duration of Use of Oral Contraception in the United States, 1960-65," Public Health Reports 83(4):277-87. April 1968.

An investigation of the discontinuance of oral contraception in 4,810 women under 45 years of age in mid-1965. Discontinuation for reasons connected with the use of the pill (such as side-effects, anxiety regarding failure of the method and fear of forgetting to take it) was distinguished from dropout for extraneous reasons. One-third of the women in the survey who had been taking an oral contraceptive at any time since 1960 had discontinued by the autumn of 1965; of these 80 per cent had stopped because of side effects or other difficulties connected with the pill. The less well educated women tended to have higher dropout rates, but the differences in rates between whites and non-whites were less than might be expected from the educational differences. After discontinuing the pill most of the women resumed their previous contraceptive methods.

1179 Westoff, Charles F., and Ryder, Norman B. "Experience With Oral Contraception in the United States, 1960-1965," Clin. Obstet. Gynec. 11(3):734-52. September 1968.

It was data from the 1965 study [National Fertility Study] that made possible the first systematic attempt to assess the extent of the acceptance and use of oral contraception by the total population of married couples and which permitted various demographic and social analyses. Moreover, reasons for discontinuing the pill and the probability of discontinuation were reviewed. The relationship between the increasing adoption of the pill and the declining fertility of American women has also been explored. The data analyzed here are confined to the 4,808 interviews of married women who were under the age of 45 in mid-1965. Focus is on interrelations of use and age, parity, education, race, and religion.

1180 Westoff, Charles F., and Ryder, Norman B. "Family Limitation in the United States," Paper Presented at the International Union for the Scientific Study of Population, General Conference, London, 3-11 September 1969.

Trends in the extent and efficacy of contraceptive practice in the United States are derived from surveys conducted in 1955, 1960 and 1965. An upward trend in the use of contraception is evident among couples at different ages and among groups classified by religion, race, and education. The pill has become the single most used method while the condom and diaphragm have declined most in use. Sterilization is increasing. There has also been an increase in the effectiveness of family planning.

1181 Westoff, Charles F., and Ryder, Norman B. "Methods of Fertility Control in the United States: 1955, 1960, and 1965," pp. 157-69 in: William T. Lui, ed. Family and Fertility, Notre Dame: Notre Dame University Press, 1967.

This article examines the changes over a decade in the methods of fertility control employed by married couples in the United States, through three comparable National Fertility Studies in 1955, 1960 and 1965. The use of methods of fertility control has increased most for non-whites, Catholics, and young women. The increase of condom and jelly (alone) in 1960 regressed in 1965 and was replaced by oral contraceptives. Varying patterns of change were found for couples of different religions: (1) The pill dominates for the Protestants, while use of the diaphragm and condom have declined and rhythm disappeared; (2) Jewish couples have adopted the pill, but continue to use the diaphragm and condom more than other methods; (3) Catholics increased use of various methods, with a decrease of rhythm method for the pill; the pill is the second method most commonly used and varies with regularity of attendance. In general, the greatest decline, in favor of the pill, is use of diaphragm, followed by rhythm and condom.

1182 Weyrauch, Walter O. "Kinsey Reports and the Legal Mind," University Florida Law Rev. 11:277-86. Fall 1958.

Discussed is the urgent need for use of a more enlightened approach to the problems and realities of sexual behavior by those involved in the legal professions. It is contended that the lawyer, judging values in terms of evidence, trial techniques and procedures, can benefit from material uncovered by the Kinsey Reports, or similar publications which deal with substance not normally disclosed in litigation and resulting judicial opinions, not even those dealing with the problems of marriage, divorce, or sex crimes. The dichotomy between legislative and judicial reaction to sexual issues and law enforcement is described, as well as the fact that a judge's sexual bias is likely to be of strong motivating force in court decision-making. It is concluded that change of laws and legal attitudes based on the sexual beliefs and mores of a pre-scientific era is imperative and that the existence of double standards in society is of direct concern to legal professions, just as to other professions.

1183 "What Did Griswold Do for Doctors?" J. Family Law 6:371-82. Winter 1966.

After mentioning some of the statutes which may apply to physicians who prescribe or furnish contraceptives, this note examines the effect of Griswold v. Connecticut on the physician's legal position and possible future developments of his constitutional rights. In states which have never made specific mention of contraceptives in their "lewd and obscene" statutes, doctors may be in some danger of prosecution. Justice Douglas suggested that perhaps contraception and medical advice concerning contraception are merely ancillatory to the broader right of the married couple to do as they please in their relationship. The existing laws interfere with the Hypocratic Oath and, in a very real sense, interferes with population control. Divorce or Annulment for Impotency? The basis of impotency being a ground for annulment seems to be the assumption that the normal marriage "contract" includes mutual representations that the parties are capable of intercourse. This note briefly considers what constitutes legal impotency; how it is proved; what circumstances may prevent divorce or annulment on this ground; and the question of who may assert impotency.

1184 Whelpton, Paschal, et al. Fertility and Family Planning in the United States. Princeton: Princeton University Press, 1966. xxxiv, 443 pp.

Projections are presented of births and population in the United States to 1985 based on interviews conducted with 3,322 females in 1960 as a follow-up to 1955 interviews on the same sources, in ten Chapters and a Preface. (1) Background of the Study and the Reliability of Birth Expectations -- indicates that most of the information refers to white couples with the wife 18-39 years old. Fertility predictions on the group-wide level are reliable; (2) Ideal, Desired, and Expected Family Size -- shows that attitudes toward family size are associated with demographic variables; (3) Family Size by Religion and Socio-economic Status -- demonstrates that attitudes toward family size are also associated with religious, social and economic variables; (4) Fecundity Impairments -- calculates that 31% of the couples have less than normal ability to have children. The frequency and distribution of contraceptive operations is discussed; (5) The Control of Fertility -- examines the attitudes of wives toward contraception, percent of couples using it, and socio-economic variations on prevalence of use; (6) Family Planning -- figures distribution of various degrees of family planning in terms of religion, education, and number of children desired; (7) Methods and Effectiveness of Contraception -- provides information on the most popular methods of contraception and distribution according to religion. One important finding of the Princeton Study is confirmed: effectiveness of contraception improves as couples approach the number of children they want; (8) Trends and Differentials in the Timing and Spacing of Births -- points out that, while age at marriage and spacing of births differ in the various religious and economic groups, the trend toward earlier childbearing has occurred across the line; (9) White-Nonwhite Differences in Fertility -- studies causes of the higher fertility of non-whites; (10) Family Size and Population Growth in Future Years -- sets forth the methodology of using birth expectations to forecast fertility.

1185 Whelpton, Paschal K., and Kiser, Clyde V. "Social and Psychological Factors Affecting Fertility," Milbank Memorial Fund Quart. 26:182-ff., 1948.

Report of the Study of Social and Psychological Factors Affecting Fertility, done in Indianapolis, based on information obtained from 1,977 native, white, Protestant, married couples with at least an eighth grade education. Examined are the influence of impaired fertility and family planning on reducing the number of births. Contraception and illegal abortion are the causes of 65-72% reduction in the fecundity of couples of normal fertility, and defects in the reproductive system account for a 13-21% reduction in the pregnancy rate for couples with contraception and abortion practiced as observed in the sample. Rates of illegal and therapeutic abortions by pregnancy order are listed.

1186 "Where We Stand on the Question of Therapeutic Abortion," California Med. 106:318-ff., 1967.

The resolutions for abortion reform of the California Medical Association are examined, and the Association's support of the 1967 abortion law reform bill is described.

1187 White, R.B. "Induced Abortions: A Survey of Their Psychiatric Implications, Complications, and Indications," Texas Report Biol. Med. 24:531-ff., 1966.

A survey of the possible and actual (from available data) psychological consequences of abortion. The author lists three factors which would serve to ease or block possible damage: 1) that the woman be given adequate time to consider her decision; 2) that the operation be performed in an emotionally supportive environment; and 3) that adequate psychotherapy be available following the operation.

1188 White, Ruth M., et al. "Family Planning as a Part of Maternal Health Services in a Metropolitan Health Department," Amer. J. Public Health 56(8):1226-31. August 1966.

Report on the provision of contraceptive services as part of the comprehensive maternity care program in Baltimore City Health Department. Sections: Public health nurses and contraceptive services; Family planning clinic dropouts; Preparation and follow-up; Evaluation of program.

1189 Whiteside, Frederick W., Jr. "Ten Years of Kentucky Domestic Relations Law 1955-1965," Kentucky Law J. 54:206-42. Winter 1965.

This article is a follow-up of an article which appeared ten years ago in volume forty-four of The Kentucky Law Journal. In that article a survey was made of five years of domestic relations law in Kentucky. This present article covers a more extensive period of a decade and is more comprehensive. It attempts to analyze the present state of the law, discern the trends, and evaluate the law in light of current sociological concepts. Kentucky's divorce laws are not extreme compared with most states. In regard to the grounds required for divorce and the residence requirements for out-of-state applicants, Kentucky takes a representative middle stand somewhere between New York where divorce is extremely difficult and certain other states where residents and non-residents alike can procure a divorce on minimal grounds. Because of the significance of the family as an integrated social-political institution, socio-economic considerations are of utmost importance. Certainly closer cooperation between lawyers and social workers is to be anticipated.

1190 Whitney, Vincent H. "Fertility Trends and Children's Allowance Programs," in: Burns, Eveline M., (ed.) Children's Allowances and the Economic Welfare of Children: The Report of a Conference. New York: Citizens' Committee for Children of New York, 1968.

There is no direct, conclusive evidence from demographic studies that a broad system of children's allowances will or will not stimulate the birthrate in the United States. This conclusion applies as well to specific groups within the total population -- to rural nonwhite persons, urban blue-collar workers, midwestern welfare recipients, or any other category. The author attempts, nevertheless, to indicate a number of factors that make it reasonable to assume that such a system of allowances would have no important bearing on overall fertility levels, especially if payments were low or moderate. Given the complexity of the causes for specific family size patterns, the single factor of income should not be overemphasized. It is important, but so are other influencing items. Full account must be taken of the non-economic costs of large families, even when income is not a problem. Two central facts are underscored: First, attitudes rooted in normative behavior govern the desire for specific numbers of children. Second, in a technologically advanced society, the general acceptance and use of family planning in married life allows preferences to be translated into accomplishment in terms of completed family size. To show that a system of children's allowances will increase average family size for any group of recipients requires a demonstration that they are effectively isolated from the national norms.

1191 Whitridge, John Jr., and Coleman, Randall C. "Medical and Legal Aspects of Human Sterilization," Maryland State Med. J. 15:61-69. November 1966.

The expressed objectives of those Maryland legislators who have recently sponsored legislation relating to surgical sterilization of humans are five in number: first, sterilization is a desirable and effective method of population control; second, sterilization would be effective in controlling the number of children born to unmarried women; third, if sterilization were given legal status, physicians generally would be less reluctant to carry out the procedure; fourth, legislation would enable the courts to order compulsory sterilization of individuals with certain types of hereditary forms of mental illness, deficiency, etc.; and fifth, an adequate law on sterilization would tend to discourage one marital partner from the sterilization procedure without the consent and knowledge of the other partner. The first two of these objectives are largely medical in nature. The fourth is a combination of medical and legal considerations, and the remaining two principally involve legal aspects. Each objective is discussed in detail, and it is concluded that proposed legislation for compulsory sterilization of humans in certain circumstances would not accomplish the objectives of its proponents, and is both medically and legally unnecessary. Indeed, it may even be restrictive to a point of being more harmful than beneficial. The expense of such a program would be prohibitive, although its positive effects would be only minimal.

1192 Williams, G. "Euthanasia and Abortion," University Colorado Law Rev. 38:178-ff., 1966.

The author stresses the fact that current statutes on abortion were enacted at a time in our medical history when abortions performed even by a qualified physician were dangerous. Medical advances since then have made abortion a safe and non-complex operation, and the outdated statutes now play an important role in the frequency of illegal abortion. The gap between policy and practice and the changing attitudes of the public point toward extended medical indications for abortion.

1193 Willson, J.R. "After Office Hours: Abortion - A Medical Responsibility?" Obstet. Gynec. 30:294-ff., 1967.

The author gives a historical review of induced abortion and discusses current attitudes concerning abortion and their relation to religious precepts and the opinions of physicians on the subject. Stressed is the fact that abortion is a medical problem needing greater involvement of the medical profession. The various indications for abortion are examined, and the author contends that, in order to lessen the number of illegal abortions, the emphasis should be on greater understanding, better educational programs in regard to contraceptive information, and liberalization of present abortion laws to close the wide gap between policy and practice.

1194 Willson, J.R. "Intrauterine Contraceptive Devices in Family Planning," pp. 34-91 in: Third Physicians' Conference on Progress in Conception Control, April 1967, Washington, D.C. Philadelphia: Lippincott Co., 1967.

Modern intrauterine contraceptive devices offer better protection against pregnancy than any other method except oral preparations. The associated complications can be kept at a minimum by the proper selection of patients and by careful insertion. This form of contraception is significant for mass population control and for unmotivated women who cannot use other methods consistently. It is also quite satisfactory for private patients who are willing to accept the slight risk of pregnancy for the constant degree of protection that it affords.

1195 Wilson,D.C. "The Abortion Problem in the General Hospital," in Rosen,H., ed. Abortion in America. Boston: Beacon Press, 1967.

Report of 139 therapeutic abortions performed at the University of Virginia Hospital during 1941-1952. Results show that the ratio of abortions to deliveries is 1:120. Other indications show that medical grounds for abortions decreased while those performed for neuropsychiatric reasons increased slightly during 1946-1950, and fell to zero in 1951-1952. The author urges the establishment of committee systems in hospitals to assist the solution of the problem areas of abortion.

1196 Wilson, D.C. "Psychiatric Implications in Abortions," Virginia Med. Monthly 79:448-ff., 1952.

A study of 200 women involved in either spontaneous or induced abortions is described. The psychological consequences of abortion are emphasized.

1197 Windle, Charles D. "Factors in the Passage of Sterilization Legislation: The Case of Virginia," Public Opinion Quart. 29(2):306-14. Summer 1965.

Factors underlying voting on a voluntary sterilization bill passed by the Virginia legislature in 1962 were examined in formal reports, personal characteristics of legislators, characteristics of regions represented by legislators, and legislators' questionnaire responses. Findings suggest that the bill was carried by the representatives of the poorer, non-urban areas, with high percentages of non-whites and of agricultural and manufacturing employees. These are not the types of backgrounds which have been found favoring freedom in public morals issues; rather, they are the characteristics which have been found regarding economic conservatism and anti-minority voting in southern Democratic 81st Congress Representatives. While much of the public discussion regarding voluntary sterilization sounded as if the conflict was between freedom and public morality, the highly related issues of race-relations and welfare seem in fact to have been more central to the legislative process.

1198 Wisconsin Medical Journal. "Legal Aspects of Abortions," Wisconsin Med. J. 55(1):59-60. January 1956.

Wisconsin's Criminal Code of July 1, 1956 made important changes affecting the legal aspects of abortion, and these changes are described. The new statute (940.04), by the penalties it prescribes, continues to make a distinction between greater and lesser crimes. Intentional destruction of the life of any unborn child equates with a fine of up to $5,000 and imprisonment for up to three years. If the life destroyed is that of a quick child or that of the mother, the imprisonment may be for up to fifteen years. The new statute imposes no penalty if the act causing death of either child or mother involved a therapeutic purpose and was a) performed by a physician, b) was in fact necessary to save the life of the mother, and c) was performed in a licensed maternity hospital except in an emergency.

1199 Wisconsin Medical Journal. "Legal Aspects of Abortions and Miscarriages," Wisconsin Med. J. 54(1):54-55. January 1955.

The two sections of the Wisconsin statutes which deal with the offenses of causing an abortion under illegal circumstances, or of causing a miscarriage, were amended by the 1947 legislature so as to impose more stringent penalties for violations. Both offenses are now felonies, and the amended statutes are quoted in full because of their importance. Statute 340.095 deems an individual guilty of third degree murder if either the living fetus or the mother dies due to abortion, unless such an operation was necessary to preserve the life of the mother or was advised to be necessary for this purpose by two physicians. Statute 351.22 issues a fine not less than $1,000 nor more than $5,000 or imprisonment for not less than one year nor more than three years, or both, for initiating a miscarriage. Destruction of a fetus is a criminal miscarriage only if pregnancy has not advanced sufficiently so that there is a living child, by which is ordinarily meant a fetus at least three months old. The position of the physician in regard to after-treatment of an illegal abortion is described, with references to the need for a consulting physician, statement by the patient and method of reporting the case.

1200 Wolf, Roger C. "Can New Laws Solve the Legal and Psychiatric Problems of Voluntary Sterilization?" J. Urology 93:402-6. March 1965.

The legal and psychiatric aspects of voluntary sterilization -- sterilization for purely contraceptive purposes -- are clarified and related with an eye toward an enabling statute such as that which Virginia and North Carolina have enacted. Examined are the potential psychiatric problems connected to both male and female sterilization and the current legal status of voluntary sterilization in the United States, with special reference to the new and more liberal statutes and physician liability.

1201 Wolf, Sanford R. "The Physician's Influence on the Nonacceptance of Birth Control," Amer. J. Obstet. Gynec. 104(5):752-57. 1 July 1969.

A discussion of repetitive patterns by which physicians unintentionally contribute to their patients' non-acceptance of birth control. The data were derived from observations of doctor-patient transactions, tape recordings of patient interviews and follow-up records from a Prenatal Clinic in Baltimore, Maryland, serving largely lower socio-economic class Negro patients. Examples are: (1) over-enthusiastic or overly authoritarian urging of a particular method, creating suspicion in the patient's mind; (2) alienation resulting from a conversation encouraging contraceptive usage because of broad social needs with which the patient cannot identify; (3) the physician's waiting for the patient to raise the subject of birth control and assuming that she understands the subject if it is not raised; (4) the prevalent attitude of patients regarding the condom as illicit or dirty and the physician's relegating this method to an unimportant level; (5) misconception among patients, frequently due to physician's suggestion, that sterility routinely results from gonorrheal infection; (6) patients' assumption, due to physician's suggestion, that genital injury, even when minor, may result in sterility.

1202 Woodside, Moya. "Sterilization and Social Welfare. A Survey of Current Developments in North Carolina," Eugenics Rev. 40(4):205-10. January 1949.

Considers the extent of the practice in North Carolina, popular attitudes toward sterilization, the practice of various agencies in recommending it, and attitudes of gynecologists.

1203 Woodside, Moya. Sterilization in North Carolina. A Sociological and Psychological Study. Chapel Hill: University of North Carolina Press, 1950. xv, 219 pp.

Reviews the provisions of the sterilization law in North Carolina and its functioning, and includes a follow-up study of forty-eight married sterilized women. The significance of sterilization for eugenics and social planning is also considered.

1204 Wright, Nicholas H., and Bellhouse, H.W. "Family Planning and Public Health in Georgia: An Enlarged Commitment," J. Med. Assn. Georgia 56:120-24. March 1967.

1205 Wright, Nicholas H., and Swartwout, Joseph R. "A Program in Mass Family Planning for the Urban Indigent in a Charity Hospital," Amer. J. Obstet. Gynec. 97(6):181-88, 1967.

In September 1962, a family planning service was begun in the postpartum clinic of Grady Hospital, a municipal institution with 7,000 births yearly. This program was designed to meet the urgent public health and obstetric needs of an indigent population characterized by high maternal mortality rates, high premature and perinatal mortality rates, high birth rates, typical of a population with roots in the rural South, and a clearly expressed desire for accurate information and effective family planning services. During a three year experience in group teaching and mass motivation, policies and procedures appropriate to a public health setting have evolved. The service was voluntary but systematically publicized on the delivery wards, leading to a significant increase in the postpartum return rate. All methods are offered, but acceptance of intrauterine contraception was encouraged by a philosophy of instruction which emphasizes the advantages of this method of contraception rather than "cafeteria choice." An analysis of costs establishes the postpartum setting as a particularly inexpensive one for family planning services.

1206 Wypyski, E.M. The Law of Inheritance in All Fifty States. Revised Edition. New York: Oceana Publications, 1961. 98 pp.

A comprehensive view of the salient features of the current laws of descent and distribution in the United States. Included are chapters on property subject to inheritance; persons entitled to inherit; rights of surviving spouse; rights of children and their descendants, whether natural, adopted, illegitimate or posthumous; rights of surviving parents and brothers, sisters and their descendants; rights of aliens; and estate taxes. There are also charts on the right of dower, curtesy, statutory substitutions; degrees of consanguinity under the Civil Law; spouse's right of election; and inheritance by and from illegitimate children.

1207 Yahraes, Herbert. Planning Your Family. New York: Public Affairs Committee, 1948. 32 pp.

Popular description of the Planned Parenthood movement.

1208 Yerby, Alonzo S. "Public Policy in Regard to Birth-Control Services," New England J. Med. 275:824-25. October 13 1966.

New York City's network of clinical services in family planning, the most extensive of any community in the country, is described, with references to the fact that from 1964 to 1965, the number of patients who sought planning guidance at the clinics of the Department of Hospitals increased 318 per cent, and, of the estimated 165,000 medically indigent or low-income women who are at any given time potential patients for subsidized contraceptive services, approximately 44 per cent are being served at the present time by the city's 67 public and private family planning clinics. The medically important effects of family planning on the community and on the health-services system in general are discussed, and the author concludes with a review of four public policy aspects of the New York City experience which bear emphasis: the lack of controversy surrounding the program since the 1958 battle; the possibility of financing the program on a mass basis; the program's progress despite New York State's strong anti-birth control law before 1965; and, finally, demonstration by the program that large numbers of impoverished patients in all ethnic groups are prepared to utilize modern family planning services if they are provided with even modest amounts of dignity, compassion and skill.

1209 Young, Don J., et al. "Court-Ordered Contraception," J. Amer. Bar Assn. 55:223-26, 1969.

As a technical legal proposition, the power of the juvenile court in dealing with children adjudged to be delinquent is far greater than the powers accorded generally to courts for the purposes of commitment of the mentally retarded. It seems a safe legal conclusion that a juvenile court could, without exceeding its powers, order sterilization of a child under its jurisdiction. Germane to this is the recent case of Ohio v. McLaughlin, 4 Ohio App. 2d 327, 212 N.E. 2d 635 (1965).

III LATIN AMERICA (General)

General population policies

1210 Kahl, Joseph A., and Stycos, J. Mayone. "Filosofia de la Politica Demografica en Latinoamerica," [Rationale of Population Policy in Latin America], El Trimestre Economica 31(3):423-34, July - September, 1964; Also published in Studies in Comparative International Development 1(2), 1965.

Beliefs and values of elites in Latin America lead to the conclusion that organized programs of conception control are either harmful or useless. The backgrounds of these beliefs vary enormously, despite their common conclusion, for some are based on Catholicism, some on elite assumptions about the lower classes, some on nationalism, some on anti-elite forms of radical economic ideology, and some on generalizations about urbanization in the advanced capitalist countries.

1211 Mortara, Giorgio. "Estudios Demograficos Relativos a una Politica de Poblacion en los Paises Latino-Americanos," [Demographic Studies Relating to Population Policy in Latin American Countries], Estadistica 18(69):664-82. December 1960.

The author describes briefly and in simplified form some of the possible and desirable applications of population studies, as basic elements for the orientation of demographic and economic policies in the Latin American countries. He begins by analyzing the demographic characteristics of Latin America, namely, the geographic distribution, natural and migratory increase, racial composition, and demographic growth of the population, in order to lead up to demographic studies, to which the main part of the paper is devoted. In this second part emphasis is placed upon the need for such studies and their utility, and, in addition, specific suggestions are made concerning fields in which such studies could be made and their objectives as well as on the possible directives of a population policy for Latin American countries and on the function of population projections in the preparation of such a policy. Concludes with the hope that the considerations set forth will, together with the data presented, arouse interest in demographic studies, open new roads and suggest other applications of such investigations.

1212 Organization of American States, Department of Social Affairs. "Latin America: Meeting on Population Policies in Relation to

Development in Latin America - Recommendations," Stud. Fam. Planning, No. 25, December 1967, pp. 1-4.
The several recommendations put forth are based on the general proposition that the governments, the private sector, and the international organizations should promote the study of various aspects of population policy in relation to economic and social development and quickly adopt measures to establish or expand activities and programs in this field.

1213 Organization of American States, Department of Social Affairs, et al. Meeting on Population Policies in Relation to Development in Latin America, September 11-16, 1967: Final Report. UP/SER.H/V. REPO/II/17 (English) Rev. [Caracas], October 6, 1967. i, 58 pp.

Contains: introductory material, including the agenda of the meeting; declaration; recommendations; and appendices listing participants, documents registered by the secretariat, procedural rules, and a statement on the bases of agreement of the preparatory seminar.

1214 Pan American Health Organization, Population Information Center. Population Dynamics: Programs of Organizations Engaged in Pan American Cooperation 1965-1966. Washington, 1967.

The Population Information Center has produced two volumes, which include all available information on the policies and program activities of the organizations which are co-operating in the field of population in the Pan-American region. The first volume gives the information classified under the following headings: foundations, universities, U.S. government agencies, international agencies and others. The companion volume gives basically the same information classified under countries. A summary is given showing the considerable assistance efforts made in recent years in different countries.

1215 Stycos, J. Mayone. "Opinions of Latin-American Intellectuals on Population Problems and Birth Control," Annals Amer. Acad. Polit. Soc. Sci. 360:11-26. July 1965.

The problem of birth control in Latin America may be divided into two aspects: (1) population control, and (2) family planning. Reasons for Latin American intellectuals' aversion to population control include the rural frontier mystique--

the more people the more wealth and power--and the population-as-goad theory-deprivation and suffering beget creative solutions. The most characteristic attitude to population control, however, is indifference. Either the population problem is a myth created by the imperialists or it is an economic or political problem which will eventually solve itself as industrialization and education result in a lower fertility rate. Underlying these ideas are the fear of governmental control of human life and the fear that the imperialist nations wish to weaken or castrate the underdeveloped countries' populations, especially those of a different color. Regarding family planning, those in favor of voluntary birth control cite its health, psychological and economic advantages and those against it allege various harmful social, political, moral and physical side effects. Analysis of voting of Latin American governments on World Health Organization and United Nations Organization legislation for technical assistance on birth control shows their negative attitude toward it in the past. This attitude is changing very gradually toward the positive as a result of the rapid expansion of population and abortion figures, reconsideration of the Catholic Church of its attitude, rural urban migration, growing reliance on economic planning, and increased monetary and technical assistance from United States universities and other organizations.

1216 Stycos, J. Mayone. "Problemas Demograficos de America Latina," [Demographic Problems of Latin America], Revista Latinoamericana de Sociologia 2(1):20-26. March 1966.

A paper presented at the Fourth Western Hemisphere Region International Conference for Family Planning at San Juan, Puerto Rico in April 1964. Some hypotheses on demographic problems of Latin America are examined in the light of its high rate of population growth and its relatively low population density. The view that Latin America needs a larger population to solve its problems is found to be erroneous because quicker and more economic plans of regional integration would be more effective in improving Latin America's position in the world. Also, the key demographic problem is the growth rate, not the size or density of the population. Nor can the demographic problems of Latin and North America be regarded as parallel -- there are important differences in class structure, distribution of wealth, and access to markets. Latin America's birth and fertility rates are likely to rise before they decrease; in any case, they will not decrease without concrete policies to that end.

The demographic situation of Latin America is characterized by peculiar combinations of demographic factors: high fertility and moderate mortality; quick population growth and slow economic progress; urbanization without industrialization; low population density and rural overpopulation. These demographic imbalances make the adoption of definite demographic policies a necessity.

1217 Stycos, J. Mayone. "Problems of Population Policies in Latin America." Paper Presented at the International Union for the Scientific Study of Population, General Conference, 3-11 September 1969, London.

The 1960's have seen a breakthrough in the area of population control in Latin America -- on the one hand realization that family planning does not face deep religious and psychological resistance on the part of the general population, and on the other demonstrations that clinical services can be mounted without public resistance and with a certain degree of success. While the acceptance of birth control for family planning has become general among the elite classes of the society, the acceptance of birth control for population planning is much less in evidence. As a consequence of the absence of population policies, the state supported birth control programs are inevitably small, inconspicuous, unimaginative, and incapable of substantially affecting population trends, despite their benefits to health. While there are political risks involved in attempting to formulate population policies, the importance of the problem is such that nations might consider these risks worth taking. Indeed, at this stage, public controversy can do much more good than harm, especially as the trend toward the internationalization of technical assistance on population problems becomes a reality. In the light of a current fashion for educating the lower classes in the need for responsible parenthood, the author urges attention to the equally important need for education on population questions at the top social levels of society.

1218 Union Panamericana; [and] Organizacion de los Estados Americanos. "Politicas de Poblacion en Relacion al Desarrollo en America Latina " [Population Policies in Relation to Development in Latin America], _Boletin: Supplemento de la Revista Interamericana de Ciencias Sociales_. 4(3): i-vii, March 1967.

Includes notes on topics discussed, basis of agreement (resolutions), and participants at preparatory seminar, Washington, February 6-10, 1967, preceding the meeting at Caracas, September 11-16, 1967.

1219 Union Panamericana; [and] Organizacion de los Estados Americanos. "Reunion sobre Politicas de Poblacion en Relacion al Desarrollo en America Latina " [Conference on Population Policies in Relation to Development in Latin America], Revista Interamericana de Ciencias Sociales 4(2):1-72, 1967.

Report on meeting at Caracas, September 11-16, 1967, including principal statements, recommendations, and list of participants. "Declaracion" (findings), deals with the development of human resources, defines a general population policy, discusses such factors connected with population as education, labor force, health, agricultural development, urban development, and general planning, and stresses the importance of research and education in demography. "Recomendaciones" (recommendations), offers some specific suggestions regarding the above findings as well as on international cooperation. It is recommended that the governments of the member countries of the Organization of American States study population problems in the context of social and economic development policies; that the proposed action programs in the sectors of health, family planning, education, labor, agricultural development, regional and urban development, etc., be implemented; that the demographic dynamics and changes in population structure in each member country be examined; that efforts be made toward international cooperation in economics and financing; and that in consideration of the process of economic integration of Latin America, attention be given to the demographic phenomena.

1220 Uribe Cualla, Guillermo. "Algunos Problemas Graves de Eugenesia. Immigracion y Feminismo Moderno " [Some Serious Eugenic Problems. Immigration and Modern Feminism], Rev. Med. Legal Columbia 9(33/34):3-21, 1943.

A very general discussion is given, with quotations from a number of authorities, on questions of immigration, population, family limitation, venereal disease, and the like in South America.

Policies on fertility and family size

1221 Aladar Metall, Rudolf. "O Amparo da Maternidade pelo Seguro Social nos Paeses da America Latina," [The Protection of Maternity in Social Insurance Schemes in the Countries of Latin America], Revista do Trabalho, February 1942, pp. 61-66.

General statement of the need for maternity aid and of modern tendencies in providing it, with some European background, is followed by an analysis of maternity-aid legislation in Argentina.

1222 Arraros, J.E. "Concubinage in Latin America," J. Fam. Law 3:330. Fall 1963.

The article is concerned with the widespread social phenomenon of concubinage in Latin America, concubinage being defined as two persons of the opposite sex living together and procreating and raising children without undergoing a civil or religious marriage ceremony. The pervasiveness of concubinage in Latin America is demonstrated by the use of statistical and United Nations data concerning the number of illegitimate children born in these countries; it is assumed that the great majority of illegitimate births in Latin America can be attributed to concubinal relationships. There is a brief discussion of the reasons for the almost exclusive limitation of concubinage to the impoverished cultures of Latin America. In general, the official attitude toward concubinage has been either unrealistic or nonexistent. However, the author analyzes some of the more recent legal solutions for the concubinage problem, especially concerning the two basic and legally remediable areas of the rights and protection of children and the economic relationship between the parties involved in concubinage. Mentioned are approaches in Cuba, Bolivia, Panama, Venezuela and Puerto Rico, for which several court cases involving concubinage are cited. The author concludes that in some Latin American countries the ill effects of concubinage have yet to be properly attended and that these countries must accommodate legally the reality of their social institutions.

1223 Dehollain, Alejandro. "La Recundidad en America Latina" [Fertility in Latin America], Rev. Latinoamer. Sociol. 1(1):103-8. March 1965.

A discussion of the socioeconomic implications of fertility in Latin America, stating that a policy of population planning is necessary to arrive at a balanced economic development. While research has been carried out which correlates tendencies and levels of fertility with demographic, economic, ethnic, social and cultural factors, opinions and attitudes relative to the formation of a family and the control of birth have not been taken into account. The Latin America Center for Demography (Celade) in conjunction with the International Population Program of Cornell University, under the auspices of the United Nations Population Commission, has now sponsored a project investigating individual motivations and attitudes regarding family planning. National institutes of Argentina, Brazil, Colombia, Costa Rica, Mexico, Panama and Venezuela participated. A questionnaire of 56 questions was used to record conjugal and reproductive histories. The project concentrated mainly on females between the ages of 20 and 50, but in Argentina and a few other countries a group of men was included. The details of this research as carried out in Argentina by the Sociological Institute of the University of Buenos Aires on the population of the metropolitan area of the Federal Capital and in greater Buenos Aires, are considered. The data were being evaluated by Celade by December 1964. A total of 2,121 case histories were obtained from 2,850 homes visited.

1224 DESAL [Centro para el Desarrollo Economico y Social de America Latina]; [and] CELAP [Centro Latinoamericano de Poblacion y Familia]. Iglesia, Poblacion y Familia: Estudios Doctrinales [Church, Population, and Family: Doctrinal Studies], Santiago 1967, 262 pp.

Partial contents: Garcia-Vincente, Juan [Birth regulation in the Catholic Church], pp. 17-40; Bockle, Franz [Birth Regulation: Discussion of the Problem within the Church], pp. 41-74; Depre, Louis [Toward a Reexamination of the Catholic Position on the Control of Natality], pp. 135-66; David, Jacob, S.J. [The Problem of Birth Regulation], pp. 167-76; Van der Marck, Wilhem, O.P. [Regulation of Fertility], pp. 177-92; Perez, Gustavo [Family Planning and Latin American Problems--Views in the Catholic Church in 1965], pp. 193-214; Janssens, Louis [Birth Regulation and Collaboration of Catholics with Non-Catholics], pp. 215-36.

1225 Garcia, Maria Luisa. "Present Situation of Family Planning in Latin America 1968." Paper Presented at the International Union for the Scientific Study of Population, General Conference, 3-11 September 1969, London.

Several conditions are to be met in order that family planning programs be successful: users' interest; a technology of acceptable and efficient contraceptives, and an adequate system of health organization in order to opportunely deliver these contraceptive procedures among the population who would want it. In a great number of Latin American countries, contraceptive methods, IUD and gestagens are accepted and efficient, as shown by the wide experience in their use. International financial support makes acquisition easier. Nevertheless, for their massive application an adequate health organization is needed and these conditions are not observed in most countries. Even for those countries that at present plan official programs, it seems difficult to achieve the intended goals. Anyway, the family planning movement has reached during the last five years an unexpected development in the region and prospects, with exception of Peru and Argentina, seem to be more favourable every time. The passive attitude adopted by governments of 14 countries of not stimulating family planning actions but allowing the establishment of clinics at health centres, financed and directed by private associations, suggest a larger expansion of these activities in the future. The wide divulgation of family planning which is now carried out leads a growing number of women to ask for assistance. Existing clinics are insufficient to meet demand; this could bring about an increase of induced abortion for some time, a phenomenon that seems to have been observed in Chile. Some groups of physicians think of the possibility of incorporating legal abortion in family planning programs, extending its present indications to medical-social cases or to those of failure of contraceptive methods. These groups' opinion is that this would probably be an alternative in case that illegal induced abortion can not be diminished by the use of the contraceptives offered by programs. Nevertheless, the majority's opinion is against this procedure and its massive use in the short run seems little probable. While new methods of fertility control are being investigated, such as pills or capsules of long term micro-doses of gestagens and others, it seems evident that methods used will continue to be IUD and gestagens in woman's contraception. Vasectomy counts with few followers among physicians and users.

1226 International Labour Office. "New Child Welfare Services in Latin America," Industry and Labour 9(7)1:219-20. April 1953.

Covers Colombia, Ecuador, El Salvador, Peru and Venezuela.

1227 Mendoza, Ofelia. "Cultural Factors Affecting Fertility Control in Latin America," p. 175 in: Vol. 2 of United Nations, Department of Economic and Social Affairs, Proceedings of the World Population Conference, Belgrade, 30 August - 10 September 1965. New York: United Nations, 1967.

The complexity of a Latin American fertility control movement cannot be understood without recognition of the cultural differences among the diverse social groups of the twenty countries and Puerto Rico, and their implications in the establishment of local programs.

1228 Mendoza, Ofelia. "Population Growth and Family Planning in Latin America," J. Sex Res. 1(2):161-73. July 1965.

A brief review is made of the present state of family planning and population growth in each of the Latin American countries. Two approaches are distinguished, governmental programs and private associations. One of the areas of immediate concern noted is the increasingly high rates of provoked abortion as a means of fertility control. Recent studies have shown Latin America's 2.5% (3.5% in the Caribbean area) population growth rate to be the highest in the world, and the socioeconomic implications of this demographic explosion are examined. Cultural factors are the main cause for the lack of information in birth control and double moral standards for the high illegitimate birth rate.

1229 Miro, Carmen A. "Los Cambios Demograficos en America Latina y su Influencia " [Demographic Change in Latin America and Its Influence], Santiago: Centro Latinoamericano de Demografia, UN Series A, 68, 1967. 11 pp.

After reviewing the characteristics of the Latin American demographic situation on the basis of fertility statistics and life expectancy rates, the significance of the population growth for per capita income, food supply, and supply in consumer goods, trade, finances and services is pointed out. The United Nations has estimated the population for Latin America at 244 million for 1966 and at more than 363 million for 1980. Urbanization can be expected to continue at an even more rapid pace than at present. A rational way must be found to solve the population problem. Chile, Costa Rica and Honduras have enlisted the help of the Latin American Center for Demography (CELADE) and its subsidiaries in designing family planning programs for them. The Ministry of Health of Colombia has initiated a program to train physicians in methods of family planning. The efforts of other Latin American countries are noted.

1230 Requena B., Mariano. "The Problem of Induced Abortion in Latin America." Paper Presented at the International Union for the Scientific Study of Population, General Conference, 3-11 September 1969, London.

Implicitly or explicitly, all family planning programs in Latin America aim at fighting induced abortion as one of its principal objectives. The hypothesis has been considered--based more on common sense than on scientific facts--that it is enough to offer and encourage the use of efficient contraceptives so that population makes the logical replacement of abortion by contraception. At least considering the experience shown by Chile it is necessary to review this hypothesis and to modify accordingly the programmatic approach. Even though in other circumstances and with legalized abortion, socialist countries, Japan and Scandinavian countries have shown that a first step to fertility control is the use of induced abortion. Countries, the same as cultural socioeconomic groups, seem to follow a natural history which begins with the motivation for family planning, continues with the use of abortion and ends with the use of contraception. In a small experimental area of Santiago, of only 25,000 inhabitants, it has been shown that it is possible to avoid the stage of induced abortion if the program underway is very extensive. Nevertheless, at the national level or even at a city level, it is not possible to repeat this experience due to the high cost and to the quantity of personnel resources which would be required. Even accepting the availability of resources and personnel, their employment can not be accepted if it is compared to the priority of other health programs.

1231 Smith, Anna K. Maternal and Child-Welfare Services in Latin America, from Laws, Official Reports, and Other Sources. Washington: Children's Bureau, 1940. 28 pp.

1232 Smith, Anna K. "Progress in Child Welfare in the American Republics," Child 6(10):256-64. April 1942.

Child welfare developments in the American countries since 1935 are summarized under the following headings: Coordination of child welfare, nutrition, social insurance, maternity insurance, preventive work in connection with social insurance.

1233 Stycos, J. Mayone. "Los Anticonceptivos y el Catolicismo en America Latina " [Contraception and Catholicism in Latin America], Rev. Latinoamer. Sociol. 3(1):41-58. March 1967.

The influence of Catholicism on family size and contraception is studied. A series of surveys has been conducted in Latin American cities within the past few years, most of them sponsored jointly by the United Nations Latin American Demographic Center and the Cornell International Population Program. Some of the results obtained in these surveys are analyzed, and it is found that the average Catholic female wants between three and four children, would favor receiving birth control information, and has practiced or will practice contraception before completion of childbearing. Further, no consistent differences have been found between Catholic and non-Catholic females in attitudes, contraceptive practices, or fertility. It has also been found that, although there is variation in fertility among the different cities and within cities among different educational strata, there is no variation in the expected direction according to religiosity. However, the attitudes and behavior directly relevant to fertility showed consistent relationships with degree of religiosity, as measured by frequency of taking Communion. Thus if Catholicism is having little impact on fertility, it may be partly because the average female is not very "Catholic" by church standards, and partly because the attitudes and practices of the less religious female are not especially effective in the control of fertility.

1234 Stycos, J. Mayone. Human Fertility in Latin America: Sociological Perspectives. Cornell University Press, 1968. 312 pp.

A collection of 18 papers by the author on a wide variety of topics related to Latin American fertility, emphasizing attitudinal and other survey data to demonstrate the relevance of sociological variables to an understanding of fertility levels. Included, too, are papers on population policy.

1235 Stycos, J. Mayone. "Politics and Population Control in Latin America," World Politics 20:66-82. October 1967.

The author attempts to account for the hostile and suspicious reactions in Latin America to the emergence of an official U.S. policy regarding foreign aid on population problems. Expressed Latin American opinions have contained little reference to religious questions and impugn most often the political or economic motives of North America. Two types of data are used: the first drawn primarily from Brazilian newspapers of August 1966, when it was announced in Brazil that the government was planning to seek U.S. assistance in dealing with population problems; the second drawn from 51 interviews conducted with university professors in Columbia during the same month. Included are sections on the role of nationalism, a powerful force cutting across political identifications in Latin America with manifestations somewhat different on the Right than on the Left in regard to the population issue; the role of Marxism, which includes a deep ideological basis for opposition to controls on population growth; and the Malthusian-Marxist controversy. Also discussed is the profound effect Marxian economics and social philosophy have had on Latin American intellectuals and the plausibility of an extensive birth control program in Latin American society. The author concludes that discreet and limited U.S. assistance can be extremely useful and that much of the ideological controversy will fade if controlling the birth rate is spoken of as a factor for balance, planning and progress as opposed to the current feeling that a birth rate reduction means the preservation of the old hierarchy and the implementation of a reactionary, imperialist policy. Intellectuals are especially concerned about the freedom of choice in family matters, but if family planning is viewed as facilitating rational decision-making in the family, socialist opposition to population control will probably decrease.

1236 Stycos J. Mayone. "Survey of Research and Population Control in Latin America," Public Opinion Quart. 28(3):367-72. Fall 1964.

The attitude, use and knowledge (AUK) fertility survey: (1) serves science by showing that social and psychological facts can be collected and interpreted scientifically; (2) demonstrates the existence of a demand in the various underdeveloped countries for birth control; and (3) is a relatively non-controversial method of initiating activity in population control in socio-political settings where direct efforts are not possible. Two types of surveys which will have major impacts in Latin America are (A) an organized international series of attitude, use and knowledge surveys and (B) an as yet unorganized set of studies of induced abortions. The attitude, use and knowledge surveys are to be carried out simultaneously in the major city of the participating countries (to date seven), about 2,000 females 15-49 being systematically sampled in each city. Personal interviews and a basic questionnaire will be used. These surveys are expected to show a motivation for small families combined with ignorance of methods to achieve restricted family size. Research projects utilizing before and after surveys are now under way to determine: (a) the extent of induced abortion in the general population; (b) the extent and speed at which a contraceptive program can reduce (a) and whether this will effect the birth rate; and (c) if a program utilizing intrauterine device has different consequences from those emphasizing oral tablets or the conventional contraceptives.

1237 Tabah, Leon. "Plan de Recherche de Sept Enquêtes Comparatives sur la Fécondité en Amérique Latine " [Research Based on Seven Inquiries on Fertility in Latin America], Population 19(1):95-126. January - March 1964.

A longitudinal study, based on a questionnaire submitted to 2,000 females in each city, was conducted in October 1963 simultaneously in Bogota, Colombia, Buenos Aires, Argentina, Caracas, Venezuela, Mexico City, Mexico, Panama, Rio de Janeiro, Brazil, and San José, Costa Rica, to establish: (1) levels and tendencies of fertility regarding demographic, socioeconomic and cultural variables; (2) opinions and attitudes to the family; and (3) the problems of birth control. The validity of the data depended to a great extent on the degree of accurate recall by the sources. Working hypotheses were formulated regarding both (A) independent and (B) dependent variables. (A) included: (a) the socio-cultural environment, (b) degree of integration of the couple in the environment, (c) degree of marital adjustment, (d) personal attitudes, and (e) the concept of the ideal family. (B) involved: (i) demographic factors, i.e., age of mother, length of marriage; (ii) the psychological predisposition to birth control; (iii) knowledge of birth control methods; (iv) experience with birth control; and (v) degree of efficiency of birth control methods. It is concluded that psychological factors as well as demographic variables are crucial in the study of fertility.

1238 Williams, Murat W. "Health and Social Progress in Latin America," Department of State Bull. 51(1326):747-51. November 23, 1964.

Statement by Deputy Director for coordination, Bureau of Intelligence and Research. "The fields in which the United States can be useful have been expanded and include the all-important question of population."

(Tropical South America)

GENERAL

Policies on fertility and family size

1239 Price, Richard Swee. "Trial Marriage in the Andes," Ethnol. 4(3):310-22. July 1965.

A basic pattern of Quechua courtship and marriage has persisted from pre-Columbian times to the present in an area including Peru, Ecuador, and Bolivia: relatively free adolescent sex relations, a year long pre-marital trial period marked by patrilocal residence and cohabitation of the couple and permitting socially sanctioned separation at any time, and a subsequent marriage ceremony which is binding for life. Early historical sources indicated that while both the Inca and Spanish conquests imposed new marriage ceremonies on the Quechua, neither altered the sociological functions of the persisting basic pattern. Following an historical survey of pre-Inca, Inca, and post-conquest courtship and marriage, a description of present-day patterns in Vicos, Peru are presented, based on recent field research. Trial marriage is analyzed in the context of local social structure and as a final step in the socialization process.

BOLIVIA

Policies on fertility and family size

1240 International Labour Office. "Introduction of a System of Family and Rent Allowances in Bolivia," Industry and Labour 10(5):208-11. September 1953.

By a presidential decree of 17 April 1953, the Bolivian Government set up a system of family allowances, allowances for nursing mothers and rent allowances for workers in factories, mines, and the petroleum and building industries. Family allowances and rent allowances are paid directly by the employer to the employee. The family allowance is 500 bolivianos per month for each child up to 16 years of age or 18 years of age if attending school. The rent allowance is 1000 bolivianos per month. Every insured woman, or wife or concubine of an insured man, is entitled to a nursing allowance of 1000 bolivianos per month for a maximum of one year from the birth of her child.

1241 Medina Ruiz, Hugo. "Organizacion de los Subsidios Familiares y de Lactancia " [The Organization of Family and Maternal Subsidies], Proteccion Soc. 16(195/196):27-41. May - June 1954.

BRAZIL

General population policies

1242 Barretto, Castro. Populacao, Riqueza e Seguranca [Population, Risk and Security]. Rio de Janeiro: Biblioteca do Exercito-Editora, Colcao General Benicio, 1961. 332 pp.

Discussion of population problems and recommendations of policy for Brazil. Deals especially with regional differences in density and resources, the organization of agricultural production, and policy on internal migration and immigration.

1243 Barretto, Castro. Povoamento e Populacao Politica Populacional Brasileira [People and Population: Brazil's Population Policy]. Rio de Janeiro: Jose Olympio, 1951. 411 pp.

A population policy is viewed as a necessary condition for the economic and political development of Brazil. The population could double or triple, given the vast size of the country, its potential riches, proper utilization of its natural resources, and its industrialization. Population increase might be realized by internal growth and a policy encouraging immigration. This policy is contrary to the laissez-faire policy which has long determined the destiny of Brazil's population. This conscious action of increase can be facilitated by the great progress in population research and statistics in recent years which afford a picture of Brazil's demographic structure. This research is employed by the author to examine fertility, the quality and quantity of population, and population distribution in Brazil.

1244 Escritorio de Pesquisa Economica Aplicada. Plano Decenal de Desenvolvimento Economico e Social. Demografia: Diagnostico Preliminar, Macroeconomia [Ten-Year Plan of Economic and Social Development. Demography: Diagnostic Preliminary, the Economy as a Whole]. Brasilia, 1966. 132 pp.

Work paper prepared for the Coordinating Group of the General Planning Sector.

1245 Fischlowitz, Estanislau. "Correlacao entre a Politica Social e Demographique Politique " [Interrelations of Political, Social and Demographic Policy], Revista do Servico Publico 84(2):117-31. August 1959.

A general review of the age structure and growth potential of Brazil, against the background of world trends, and a discussion of the interrelations of population growth and social policy, particularly as to family allowances.

1246 Fischlowitz, Estanislau. "Subsidios para a Politica Demografica " [Bases for a Population Policy], _Rivista do Service Publico_ 93(2):29-48. April - June 1965.

Discusses the "demographic crisis" of Brazil and the nation's population policy, past, present and future.

1247 Lima Camara, Aristoteles de. "Alguns Preparos sobre a Politica Demografica Brasileira " [Some Remarks on Brazilian Demographic Policy], _Revista de Imigracao e Colonizacao_ 2(2-3):812-21. April - July 1941.

The differential increase of the continents and nations is surveyed in relation to the demographic policy of Brazil.

Policies on fertility and family size

1248 Brazil. "Protection of Mothers, Children and Adolescents," _Internat. Digest Health Legis_. 19:707-8, 1968.

Decree No. 58740 of 28 June 1966 has been promulgated pursuant to the provisions of the National Health Code, dated 21 January 1961. The Ministry of Health is to coordinate all national activities in the field of assistance to, and protection of mothers, children and adolescents. The activities pertain to health care prior to marriage and conception and during and after birth, day nurseries, and homes for mothers.

1249 Costa Pacheco, Renato J. "Alguns Aspectos Legais do Casamento no Brasil " [Some Legal Aspects of Marriage in Brazil], _Sociologia_ 16(4):413-16. October 1954.

Analysis of current provisions of Brazil's Constitution and Civil Code, relating to marriage and family. In practice, some of these (optional) provisions are largely ignored, because they go counter to Brazilian national character.

1250 "Family-Wage Allowances: Advantages and Disadvantages," Conjuntura Economica 9:57-62. March 1962.

1251 "Family-Wage Allowances -- Estimates of Their Importance," Conjuntura Economica 10:35-38. December 1963.

All married employees of firms that contribute to a social security scheme are entitled to family-wage allowances in proportion to the number of children up to 14 years of age.

1252 Fischlowitz, Estanislau. "Abonos Familiares " [Family Allowances], Revista do Servico Publico 2(3):22-25; 3(1):23-29. June and July 1943.

The first installment discusses family allowances in Brazil, in light of Decree 12,299 of April 22, 1943, which provides for aid to large families. The second installment considers programs in other countries with conclusions applicable to Brazil.

1253 Fischlowitz, Estanislau. "Protecao a Familia na Legislacao Social Brasileira," [Protection of the Family in the Brazilian Social Legislation], Revista do Servico Publica ano XVII, 4(2):53-60. November 1954.

1254 Hutchinson, Bertram. "Induced Abortion in Brazilian Married Women," Amer. Latina 7(4):21-33. October - December 1964.

Provocation of abortion, by the mother or a third party, is illegal in Brazil, with heightened penalties if grave physical lesion or death occurs; this applies to the medical profession as well except when abortion is necessary to preserve the mother's life or when conception occurred during stupor. Generalized disrespect for law in Brazil makes control difficult and there is not, therefore, effective sanction. In a sample interview of 1,734 married females aged 20-50, 9.2% admitted to at least one induced abortion. The effect of induced abortion on the birth rate is seen as significant. Tables are presented relating induced abortion and live-birth history to age of mother at marriage, mother's skin color, religion, husband's social status, and husband's social status regarding that of wife's father, number of additional children desired, and past and present contraceptive practice.

1255 International Labour Office. "A New Family Allowances Scheme in Brazil," Internat. Labour Rev. 91(2):157-58. February 1965.

The features of a new general scheme for family allowances for wage earners, instituted in Brazil by Act 4266 of October 1963, are described. The scheme pays allowances for each dependent child up to the age of 14, legitimate, recognized, illegitimate or adopted children equally eligible. All wage earners can receive the payments, except for agricultural wage earners, domestic workers, public servants, members of the armed forces and employees of public institutions already covered by an equivalent family benefit system. If both parents are wage earners, benefits are due separately to each of them for each eligible child. Before the institution of the new scheme, payment of allowances was restricted to families with low incomes having eight or more dependent children under 18 years of age, while the 1963 Act covers all wage earners, regardless of the form or value of their remuneration, employed by undertakings subject to the basic insurance law of 1960 -- granted they are not excluded by the above classifications.

1256 Iutaka, Sugiyama. "A Estratificacao Social e o Uso Diferencial de Metodos Anticoncepcionais no Brasil Urbano," [Social Stratification and the Differential Use of Contraceptive Methods in Urban Brazil], Amer. Latina 8(1):101-19. January - March 1965.

Some of the first results of the Comparative Survey on Fertility carried out in Rio de Janeiro are presented. The uses of contraceptive methods according to social stratification are analyzed, using the status of the husband to classify the females in the six different status categories adapted for Brazil by B. Hutchinson in preceding studies. The following variables regarding the use of contraceptive devices are considered: (1) previous thought about the number of children the woman would like to have as an indication of the influence of socio-economic development on the size of the family; (2) information about contraceptive methods; and (3) the acceptance of the idea of birth control which could lead the couple to the use of one or more contraceptive methods. These three factors are analyzed according to social status and age. Financial and health problems are the most important reasons why people think about number of children, and there is a relationship between the acceptance of birth control and social status: the lower the status category, the more important it is to have more children. Though the younger groups tend to use more contraceptive methods, their use is not recent.

1257 Milanesi, M.L. [Induced Abortion], Doctoral Thesis, University of Sao Paulo, 1968.

Results of interviews with 2,857 non-single women, 15 to 20 years of age residing in Sao Paulo. The women reported a total of 9,709 prior pregnancies, 12% of which had ended by spontaneous abortion and 6% by induced abortion. Those reporting a history of induced abortion had a total of 554 induced abortions or 1.8 per woman. Experienced midwives performed 46% of the operations, doctors 37% and the woman herself 11%. Method used was: curettage 60%; oral medication 20%; mechanical methods 15%. The probability of abortion increased with the age of the mother and for women residing in Sao Paulo for ten years or more. Rates were lower for practicing Catholics and for women married in both civil and religious ceremonies. There was little difference between the women with a history of induced abortion and those without a history when compared by number of children, age at marriage, education, and occupation of the woman. 79% of the women with a history of induced abortion reported having used contraceptives at some time, while only 27% of the women with no abortions had ever used contraceptives. 45% of the women with a history of abortion had been using contraceptives at the time of the pregnancy which ended in abortion.

1258 Moura, A.F. [Family Planning in the Ambulatorio de Praia do Pinto], _Rev. Brasil Med_. 24:83-90 and 409-12. February and June 1967.

The majority of slum dwellers do not have knowledge of contraception. They are however receptive to the intra-uterine device and abortion as a means of birth control. Statistics are given on their use. There is also a review of the mechanisms of action of the devices.

1259 Ribeiro, L. [Abortion in the Case of Rape and the Medical Code of Ethics], Hospital 67:19-ff., 1965.

Argues against the present Penal Code of Brazil in which abortion may be performed in pregnancies resulting from rape. The author's opinion that the law should be modified so that abortion on medical or humanitarian indications would no longer be valid is supported by quotes from various members of the legal and medical fields.

1260 Rodriques, O. [Induced Abortion]. Rio de Janeiro: Editora Refrigeracao, 1965.

This study of induced abortion was based on a questionnaire sent to all hospitals in Brazil. Only 25% (46 hospitals) responded to the survey, indicating that in 1964 there were 132,000 deliveries and 30,000 abortions. There was no distinction made as to whether abortions were induced or spontaneous. Thirty-five hospitals reported complications; out of 17,000 abortion cases, 45% of the women suffered hemorrhaging and 6% of all cases were given blood transfusions. From this study it is concluded that the rate of induced abortion in Brazil is inaccurate and that hospital statistics are extremely incomplete.

1261 Sao Paulo. Abonos Familiares [Family Allowances]. Second ed. Ministerio do Trabalho, Industria e Comercio. Instituto Nacional de Tecnologia. Rio de Janeiro: Imprensa Nacional, 1943. 84 pp.

1262 Segadas Viana, J. Lei de Protecao da Familia: Doutrina, Legislacao e Formulario [Law for the Protection of the Family: Doctrine, Legislation, and Formulation]. Rio de Janeiro: Livraria Jacintho Editora, 1942. 229 pp.

COLOMBIA

General population policies

1263 Gaitan Arjona, Jorge. "Despoblacion, Desocupacion, Produccion, Colonizacion, Escuelas " [Depopulation, Unemployment, Production, Colonization, Schools], Anales de Economia y Estadistica 5(16):54-56, 1942.

A program for agrarian reform in Colombia.

1264 Herrera B., Jorge."Tercer Congreso Nacional de Abodados, Alumni de Pontificia Universidad Javeriana: Ponencia sobre Demografia y Desempleo , Segunda Sesion de Estudios, 11 de Octubre" [Third National Congress of Lawyers, Alumni of the State University of Javeriana: Presentation on Demography and Unemployment, Second Study Session, 11 October], Universitas: Ciencias Juridicas y Socioeconomicas (Bogota), No.30, June 1966, pp. 63-72.

Discussion of effects of rapid population growth on proportions of active and inactive population. Presentation of statement of policy for a developing country like Colombia, including: recognition of economic drawbacks of rapid population growth and of social unrest resulting from disparity between rates of population increase and economic output; promotion of family planning by methods approved by the Roman Catholic Church; concerted study of population problems by universities, and by spiritual, political, and economic leaders.

Policies on fertility and family size

1265 Asociacion Colombiana de Facultades de Medicine, Division de Estudios de Poblacion [Preliminary Data From the Abortion Studies], Popayan, Colombia: 1966.

Results of an abortion survey administered by the Asociacion Colombiana de Facultades de Medicina in five Colombian towns. Women in four of the five towns reported a total of 23,155 pregnancies, 3,334 of which resulted in abortion. 348 of these abortions were admittedly induced. In all towns the rate of induced abortion was from 1% - 2%.

1266 Cardona Gonzalez, Ramiro. El Delito de Aborto y sus Consecuencias [The Crime of Abortion and Its Consequences]. Bogota, 1965. 216 pp.

1267 Colombia. "Maternal and Child Health," Internat. Digest Health Legis. 1:177-80, 1949.

Decree No. 2378 of 18 July 1947 establishes the National Institute for Child Welfare. Among the services of the Institute will be: prenuptial consultations, prenatal consultations, restaurant for pregnant women, supervision of births, postnatal consultations, and odontological services for pregnant women.

1268 Colombia. Servicio Nacional de Aprendizaje. Legislacion Sobre el "SENA" y et Subsidio Familiar [Legislation on the National Apprenticeship Service and Family Allowances]. Third ed. Colombia: Medellin, 1965. 71 pp.

Texts of legislation concerning (1) the National Apprenticeship Service of Colombia as the national body responsible for vocational training activities, and (2) the institution of family allowances.

1269 Gamboa, G.R. [Analysis of 100 Cases of Induced Abortion]. Unpublished paper. Bogota, Colombia, 1967.

Report of the Bogota Family Planning Clinic of 100 women with a history of induced abortion. Results indicated are: average age is between 25-34; average number of abortions per woman is 2.4; average number of children is 5.3. The most common reasons for abortion are too many children (14%), economic reasons (10%) and marital difficulties (14%).

1270 Sanin Echeverri, Jaime. "El Subsidio Familiar y su Aplicacion en Colombia " [The Family Subsidy and Its Use in Colombia], Universidad Pontifica Bolivariana 22(81):462-68. May - August 1958.

ECUADOR

Policies on fertility and family size

1271 Cruz Cueva, José. "Conveniencia o Inconveniencia de Limitar la Natalidad " [Advantages and Disadvantages of Limiting Natality], Anales 93(348):95-110, 1964.

PERU

Policies on fertility and family size

1272 Bambaren, Carlos A., "La Practica del Certificado Medico Prenupcial en el Peru," [The Practice of Prenuptial Medical Certification in Peru], La Cronica Medica 58:34-43. February 1941.

1273 Chaplin, David. "Some Institutional Determinants of Fertility in Peru," Unpublished Manuscript. April 1968.

Laws designed to promote maternity do so only by default since the higher fertility of the disemployed women will occur outside the protection of adequate medical and welfare institutions.

1274 Hall, M-Francoise. "Family Planning in Lima, Peru," Milbank Memorial Fund Quart. 43(4):100-16, 1965.

A study was made of the pregnancy histories and contraceptive practices of a random sample of 500 women in Lima, Peru chosen by an area cluster sampling method which gave an overrepresentation of the higher socioeconomic levels. For the five years preceding the interview, the percent of pregnancies ending in abortion was found to be 19, 20 and 15 at the upper, middle, and lower socioeconomic levels respectively. Total abortion rate was thought to be high and to include many provoked but not admitted abortions. Suspicion was substantiated when abortion rates were tabulated by age of female and order of pregnancy. It was found that provoked abortions are a means of fertility control in Lima, especially at the high and middle socioeconomic levels, and that recourse to provoked abortions occurs mainly in females over 30 who already have three to four children. Contraception was found to be widely practiced, especially by the upper and middle socioeconomic groups. In all social groups, the majority of the females were in favor of family limitation.

1275 Peru. "Contraceptives: Prohibition of Manufacture," Internat. Digest Health Legis. 10:529, 1959.

Executive Resolution No. 93-DGS of 5 August 1958 prohibits the manufacture of mechanical contraceptives which are not intended to prevent disease.

VENEZUELA

Policies on fertility and family size

1276 Angulo-Arvelo, L.A. "Actitudes ante la Fecundidad en General y Particularmente en Venezuela " [Attitudes Toward Fertility in General and in Venezuela Particularly], Asuntos Sociales 2(7):31-79. June 1966.

1277 Lopez, Dario Merchan. "First Results of Birth Control in Concepcion Palacios Maternity, Caracas, Venezuela," Caribbean Med. J. 26(1/4):107-13, 1967.

Intrauterine contraceptives (Margulies V and Lippes Loops II) were inserted 66 times in 65 women, within the ages of 22 to 45 years with an average of 30.9 years. These women previously had delivered from 1 to 13 children with an average of 6 children each. Two women did not return and one was passed to the oral method. After insertion, 90% of the women reported a little bleeding and slight pain. Nearly all the women reported that their first menstruation was quite abundant. No pregnancy has been observed up to date, either intrauterine or extrauterine.

1278 Mejia, Abel. "La Explosion Demografica Venezolana y el Control de la Natalidad " [The Demographic Explosion in Venezuela and the Control of Natality], Asuntos Sociales 2(5):5-15. December 1965.

Includes section on the control of natality: ideological attitudes and the position of the government and religious bodies.

1279 Quijada, Hernan. "Control de la Natalidad " [Birth Control], Asuntos Sociales 3(10):67-71. March 1967.

Article reprinted from the daily, La Esfera (Caracas), February 26, 1962. Author, Director de Asuntos Sociales e Institutos Autonomos, Ministerio de Sanidad y Asistencia Social, advocates birth control as a means of improving the quality of social and economic life. Stresses need to coordinate psychological and religious approaches with socioeconomic and medical.

1280 Paez, Celis Julio. "Algunas Ideas Para Una Politica de Desarrollo de la Poblacion de Venezuela " [Some Ideas for a Developmental Policy for the Population of Venezuela], Ciencias Sociales 4(1):49-68. June 1968.

The population of Venezuela increased from 1,700,000 in 1873 (the first Census) to 7,500,000 in 1961. Since 1920, the mortality rate has drastically dropped while the birth rate has remained high, resulting in an annual increase of 3.55 *per cent*. The rural sector cannot absorb the growing work force, there is high unemployment, and the increasing migration to cities has resulted in family degradation, delinquency, and other problems. To meet the numerous problems, a population and family policy is proposed which would aim to reduce fertility, eliminate concubinage, raise the age of marriage, plan human resources, reform the work situation, and alter migration so as to obtain a regional equilibrium. Such a policy requires a central organization for coordination and planning under the President of the Republic.

(Middle America - Mainland)

COSTA RICA

Policies on fertility and family size

1281 Amador-Guevara,Jose,*et al*."Neustro Problema Demografico" [Our Demographic Problem],Rev.Med.Costa Rica 24:339-60,1966.

The problem of voluntary illegal abortion is a familiar expression of over-population and constitutes one of the most serious public health problems clinically and financially. Its cause lies in emotional, cultural, and economic problems.

1282 Lopez Cordova,Ernesto R. *Consideraciones Legal Relativas a la Inseminacion Artificial en los Seres Humanos* [Legal Considerations Concerning Artificial Insemination in Human Beings]. Guatemala: Universidad de San Carlos de Guatemala, 1965. iv, 87 pp.

HONDURAS

Policies on fertility and family size

1283 Faraj, R.E. [Abortion - Medico-Social Factors]. Paper presented at the Fourth IPPF Conference for the Western Hemisphere Region, San Juan, Puerto Rico, April 19-26, 1964.

A study of the characteristics of 602 abortion cases treated in the Social Security Hospital in Tegucigalpa. There was no distinction made between induced and spontaneous abortion due to the reluctance of women to admit having induced abortions. The ratio of abortions to deliveries was 17.5: 100 -- the same figure reported at San Felipe Hospital, Tegucigalpa and corresponding to the 15:100 rate reported at San Jose hospital in Costa Rica. The women were between the ages of 20-29 years (54.7%) and 30-39 years (36.4%). 44.7% were married, 55.3% were single. Maternal deaths resulting from abortion was 2.9 per 1000, whereas deaths resulting from birth was 0.6 per 1000. The author urges increased legislation to protect the mother and a contraceptive education for both children and adults.

1284 Honduras. "Physicians and Medical Ethics," Internat. Digest Health Legis. 16:313-29, 1965.

Decree No. 94 of 25 June 1964 promulgates a legal code governing physicians in their relations with patients and colleagues. Two sections of Part 4 pertain to fertility. One section forbids artificial insemination outside of marriage; and sterilization or therapeutic abortion without the written consent of the patient and her husband or nearest relative and certification from a medical committee. The other section requires a physician to use all means to dissuade a person from carrying out his plans to marry when he suffers from a contagious disease.

1285 Honduras. "Sanitary Code," Internat. Digest Health Legis. 18:717-ff., 1967.

Decree No. 75 of 14 November 1966 promulgates the Sanitary Code. Among its contents are the establishment of departments within the Secretariat of Public Health and Social Welfare to provide care to mothers during pregnancy, childbirth and puerperium and to establish maternity homes.

MEXICO

General population policies

1286 Banco Nacional de Mexico. "The Human Factor in Mexico's Economic Development," Rev. Econ. Situation of Mexico 35 (406):3-4. September 1959.

A plea of educational as well as financial aid for the agricultural population.

1287 Banco Nacional de Mexico. "The Population Problem in Mexico," Rev. Econ. Situation of Mexico 34(391):3-5. June 1958.

Notes on growth rates, rural-urban migration, and recommendations for policy.

1288 Consejo Obrero Nacional. Principal Problems of Agriculture and Economy on the American Continent. Mexico, D.F., 1942. 62 pp.

Points of view presented for the consideration of the Second Inter-American Agricultural Conference by the National Labor Council of Mexico and the Federation of Latin American Labor. See especially the statements of policy on the rural population, immigration, and settlement.

1289 Instituto del Seguro Social. Mexico y la Seguridad Social. Tomo III. Construcciones y Sistemas de Proteccion Social [Mexico and Social Security. Vol. III. Achievements and Systems of Social Protection]. Mexico, D.F., 1953.

Part II is devoted to a comparative analysis of the principal characteristics of the systems of protection against the conventional bio-economic risks in different countries of the world. Chapters on: disability, old age, death, illness in general, maternity, occupational hazards, unemployment, and family allowances.

1290 International Labour Office. "New Population Act in Mexico " (Act published in Diario official, 27 December 1947). Internat. Labour Rev. 57(5):503-5. May 1948.

This Act repeals the previous Act of 1936, and prolongs the operation of the regulations under the Migration Act of 1932 until fresh regulations are issued, as well as that of the classified schedule for 1947. The Act contains five main chapters, concerning organization and scope, general population policy, immigration, emigration, and sanctions.

1291 Irigoyen, Ulises. "Politica Demografica " [Population Policy], Revista de Economia 4(2):112-18.

1292 Loyo, Gilberto. "Esquema Demografico de Mexico " [A Demographic Plan for Mexico], pp. 673-796, discussion pp. 797-839 in: Segundo Congreso Mexicano de Ciencias Sociales. Memoria Vol. 3, 1946.

The first section contains a general discussion of demographic terms and data, including a comparison of trends in vital rates in Mexico with those of other countries. More detailed consideration is given to population problems in Mexico: trends in growth, including immigration; housing in relation to population increase; the sex, age, and marital structure of the population; social and economic characteristics; factors to be considered in a population policy; the problem of immigration and bases for an immigration policy.

1293 Ortego San Vincente, Alejandro. La Politica Demografica de Mexico a Traves de Sus Leyes [The Demographic Policies of Mexico as Mirrored in its Laws]. Mexico, 1954. 248 pp.

Compilation and synthesis of regulations and laws on demographic matters that have governed in Mexico from the Cadiz Constitution of 1812, to the present year. pp. 89-206.

1294 Pan American Union. "Mexico's New Population Law," Bull. Pan American Union 82(3):172. March 1948.

Summary of the provisions of a new law that went into effect at the beginning of 1948. The opening paragraphs of the decree explain the nation's aim as an increase of population through natural increase -- including health measure to lower infant and child mortality rates -- and migration. Included in the law is a provision for the registration of all citizens and foreigners.

1295 Yllanes Ramos, Fernando. "The Social Rights Enshrined in the Mexican Constitution in 1917," Internat. Labour Rev. 96:590-608. December 1967.

Policies governing population are of several kinds and include maternity benefits, equal pay regardless of sex, social security, provisions for workers' housing, "family patrimony," and health.

Policies on fertility and family size

1296 Borah, Woodrow, and Cook, Sherburne F. "Marriage and Legitimacy in Mexican Culture: Mexico and California," California Law Rev. 54:946-1008. May 1966.

Historical examination of the formation of patterns of marriage and legitimacy in Mexico, with particular attention to characteristics found among Mexican-Americans in Santa Clara County, California.

1297 Echegollen Melo, Alonso. Aborto y Feticido [Abortion and Feticide]. Mexico, D.F.: Universidad Nacional Autonoma de Mexico, 1952. 63 pp. Thesis (licenciatura en durecho).

1298 Garcia Contreras, Francisco de A. Algunas Consideraciones Doctrinales y Juridico-Sociales Sobre el Salario [Some Doctrinal and Legal-Social Considerations on Wages]. Universidad Nacional Autonoma de Mexico, Facultad de Derecho y Ciencias Sociales. Mexico, 1944. 63 pp.

1299 Martinez, Pedro Daneil. "Population Growth and Family Planning," Public Health Report 81:712-14. August 1966; Also in Salud Publica Mexico 7:99-101. January - February 1965.

1300 Mateos Fournier, M. "La Planeacion Familiar y el Control de la Concepcion, en Relacion con le Presion Demografica " [Family Planning and Conception-Control in Relation to Overpopulation], Medico 17(1):93-101, 1967; Also in Ginec. Obstet. Mexico 20:365-82. May - June 1965.

Reviews arguments for restriction of families by conception-control and suggests formation of National Council for impartial study of population problems.

1301 Moore, Wilbert E. "Attitudes of Mexican Factory Toward Fertility Control," pp. 74-101 in: Approaches to Problems of High Fertility in Agrarian Societies. New York: Milbank Memorial Fund, 1952.

Reports the results of a study conducted in 1948 and 1949 in two villages and two factories of the "Zone" of Atlixco, State of Pueblo, Mexico. Interviews with 597 males of rather homogeneous economic status are used to test five principal questions concerning industrialization, secularization, and attitudes to fertility control.

1302 Nutini, Hugo G., "Polygyny in a Tlaxcalan Community," Ethnology 4(2):123-47. April 1965.

An article based on the municipality of Juan Cuamatzi, better known as San Bernardino Contla, in the state of Tlaxcala, Mexico, population 10,058. Of the 2,360 married males, 9% were involved in illegal, but socially recognized polygynous unions. The practice is not associated with low economic status or any specific social, economic or occupational group. Of the 209 polygynous unions only seven involve more than two wives and these are frowned upon. There are 42 unitary bigamous unions (husband and co-wives live in same household); 40 binary bigamous unions (co-wives live within walking distance of each other); and 120 satellite bigamous unions (co-wives live in different settlements and the husband resides permanently with one wife and visits the other two or three times a week). Integration into the community in the first two unions works smoothly, though there may be some tensions in the latter case.

1303 Pastrana Ibarra Vasques, Ofelia. Las Signaciones Familiares Resuelven la Cuestion Social? [Will Family Allowances Solve the Social Question?] Mexico, 1951. 80 pp.

1304 Remirez Cabanas C., Julio. La Sterilizacion y el Derecho Penal, en Mexico: la Ley 121 y su Reglamento del Estado de Veracruz [Sterilization and the Penal Law in Mexico: Law 121 and Its Operation in the State of Veracruz]. Mexico, 1941. 52 pp.

The law on sterilization and the problem in Mexico, with comparative data from other countries.

1305 Trigueros, G. "La Proteccion Infantil como Base de Campana Social Eugenesica " [Protection of the Child as the Basis of a Campaign for Social Eugenics]. Pediatria de las Americas 4:401-14. July 15, 1946.

PANAMA

Policies on fertility and family size

1306 Panama. "Control of Prostitution," Internat. Digest Health Legis. 3:226, 1951-52.

Decree No. 149 of 20 May 1949 prohibits prostitution in towns and populated areas as well as all places designated by the Public Health Technical Council. Penal provisions are provided for illicit prostitution, procuring, sodomy and other sexual perversions as well as disobedience of orders during hospitalization or treatment for venereal disease.

(Temperate South America)

ARGENTINA

General population policies

1307 Araoz Alfaro, Gregario. Politica Demografica, Natalidad y Mortalidad [Population Policy, Fertility and Mortality]. Buenos Aires: "Coni", 1940. 58 pp.

Demographic, economic, moral, and legislative factors are outlines as the basis of a demographic policy to be developed in intimate connection with economic, educational, and social policies. Special emphasis is placed on Argentine problems and needs.

1308 Instituto Alejandro E., Bunge de Investigaciones Economicas y Sociales, "Estudio del Plan de Govierno 1947-1951 " [A Study of the Government's Plan for 1947-1951]. Revista de Economia Argentina 45(341):391-97; 45(342):429-34. November - December 1946.

A discussion of the demographic sections of the five-year plan proposed by the Poder Executive Nacional. The subjects discussed include marriage, fertility, mortality, immigration and colonization.

1309 Llorens, Emilio and Correa Avila, Carlos. Demografia Argentina. Esbozo de una Politica Demografica [The Demography of Argentina. Outline of a Demographic Policy]. Buenos Aires: Universidad Nacional de Buenos Aires, Facultad de Ciencias Economicas, 1948. 140 pp.

Consideration of the national population situation, the economic and social characteristics of the population, and the population problem precedes sections on future population, the basis of policy, and means to increase nuptiality and fertility and to decrease mortality.

1310 Lugones, C.C. "Algunas Aspectos de Muestro Problema Demografico " [The Population Problem in Argentina], Archivos Argentinos Pediatria 15:455-62. May 1941.

1311 Museo Social. "Primer Congresso Argentino de Poblacion, Celebrado en Buenos Aires los Dias 26, 29, 30, y 31 Octubre de 1940 " [First Argentine Population Congress, Buenos Aires, October 26, 29-31, 1940]. Boletin del Museo Social Argentino, November - December 1940, pp. 345-92.

The Congress recommended marriage loans, family allowances, education of the public in problems of sex and hygiene in order to increase the birth rate, and specific health and welfare measures.

1312 Quiros, Carlos B. de. Problemas Demograficos Argentinos: Sociologia, Estadistics, Eugenesia, Derecho, Legislacion [Argentine Demographic Problems: Sociology, Statistics, Eugenics, Law, Legislation], Buenos Aires: Talleres Graficos "Cruz del Sur," 1942. 148 pp.

A comparative statistical study of the decline of mortality and factors responsible for it is followed by a more detailed discussion of fertility, infant mortality, eugenics, and population policy in the Argentine.

Policies on fertility and family size

1313 Argentina. "Family Allowances for Railwaymen in Argentina," Internat. Labour Rev. 51:792-93, 1946.

A decree of 3 July 1944 regulates the payment of family allowances to railwaymen, numbering about 150,000 wage earners and salaried employees. Payments are made to those persons earning less than 300 pesos a month and having in their care legitimate, legitimated, illegitimate, abandoned or orphaned children under 16 years of age or under 18 years of age if attending school. Payments per month are in the amount of five pesos for the wife, three pesos for the first child, four pesos for the second child, five pesos for the third child, six pesos for the fourth child, seven pesos for the fifth child, and eight pesos for each child beyond the fifth one.

1314 Argentina. "Pre-Marital Examination," Internat. Digest Health Legis. 3:141, 1951-52.

Order No. 20,693 of 25 October 1949 provides for the establishment of the Department of Pre-Marital Examination attached to the Social Hygiene Administration.

1315 Argentina. Comision Nacional de la Desnatalidad. La Desnatalidad y et Problema Demografico Argentino [Fertility Decline and the Demographic Problem of Argentina]. Buenos Aires: Direccion Nacional de Salud Publica. Informe, 2. 1945. 86 pp.

1316 Argentina. Ministerio de Salud Publica de la Nacion, Direccion de Codigo y Legislacion Sanitaria. Eugenesia y Derecho [Eugenics and the Law]. Buenos Aires: Imprenta Central del Ministerio de Salud Publica de la Nacion, 1950. 88 pp.

This work consists of a detailed critical examination of four proposed laws which were presented on 25 March 1949 to the Minister of Public Health by the Argentine Society of Eugenics. The origins of the subject studied are first dealt with. Following this the four laws are in turn analysed and commented upon. The laws are entitled: "Proposed law relating to the hygienic prevention of venereal and related diseases," "Proposed law relating to sex education and eugenics" (followed by "Principles and aspects of sex education, designed to serve as the basis of a general plan and to lead to the production of analytical programs for sex education and eugenics"), "Proposed law relating to the pre-marriage certificate, the prohibition of marriage on grounds of ill-health, and factors leading to nullity of marriage and divorce," and "Proposed law relating to the suppression of the offences of infecting with venereal disease, touting [rufianismo], procuring, and traffic in women and homosexuals." The texts of the proposed legislation mentioned above are reproduced in an appendix, preceded by an introductory letter and a description of the purposes of the legislation.

1317 Basile, C. [The Medico-Social Problem of Abortion in an Area of Greater Buenos Airs], Prensa Med. Argent. 50:1497-ff., 1963.

An analysis of 4,543 abortion cases treated at the Gregorio Araoz Clinic in Buenos Aires during a ten-year period. Reported were 2,925 cases of incomplete abortion, 303 cases of complete abortions, 426 cases of abortion with accompanying complications and 889 cases of threatened abortion. The abortion rate was one per every six births and the mortality rate for all abortions was 3.7 per 1000, and for abortions with complications, 39 per 1000. The author argues for more liberal legislation of abortion laws in the hope that the incidence of illegal abortion will diminish.

1318 Calandra, D. [Criminal Abortion], Prensa Med. Argent. 48: 3187-ff., 1961.

Discussion of the conditions leading to criminal abortion -- the medical, eugenic, social, demographic, and psychological reasons. Attention is given to the possible methods of inducing mortality and morbidity resulting from abortion. This decrease could be effected through a reduction of pregnancies through sterilization and contraception, or through a reduction of induced abortions through legal repression, social legislation or elevation of the socio-economic conditions.

1319 Casiello, Francisco. "Proteccion a la Familia Argentina " [Protection of the Argentine Family], Revista de Economia Argentina, February 1943, pp. 46-53.

This survey of the problem includes an analysis of existing schemes, suggestions for a new scheme, and comparable statistics on the operation of family allowance systems in eight other countries.

1320 Correa Avila, Carlos. "Doctrina y Realidad del Problema Social en Argentina " [Basic Principles and Actual Status of Social Problems in Argentina], Revista de Economia Argentina Ano 34, 50(397-99):69-77. July - September 1951.

Views the basic cause of social problems in Argentina as "the crisis of the family" or limitation of births. Urges policy for increased fertility.

1321 Do Pico, A. [Criminal Abortion: Concept and Definition], Prensa Med. Argent. 48:3197-ff., 1961.

According to Article 86 of the Argentine Penal Code, occasions when the interruption of pregnancy is not a criminal abortion are: if the objective is to save the life of the mother; if performed in anticipation of the birth of the fetus; or if an already dead fetus is to be extracted. Abortion is also permitted if the pregnancy results from a violation or transgression on the privacy of an idiot or demented woman.

1322 Gomez-Ferrarotti, Nydia. [Study of Abortion and Its Variables, Including Methods of Family Planning], Rev. Argent. Soc. Obstet. Ginec. 611:277-ff., 1964.

A study of pregnancy histories based on interviews with 600 women between ages 35 and 49 who were patients at Rawson Hospital in wards other than Obstetric, Gynecologic or Psychiatric. The total sample number decreased to 508 when sterile women and women without a history of sexual experience were omitted. A total of 2,161 previous pregnancies including 1,448 deliveries, 113 spontaneous abortions, 582 illegal abortions and 18 therapeutic abortions were reported. The pregnancy and abortion histories of married women, concubines and single women are compared indicating that the highest rate of abortion is found among single women, followed closely by concubines, and lowest among married women. At the time of conception, some form of contraception was being used in about half the cases. But only nineteen *per cent* of the pregnancies are defined as "planned". The most common form of contraception was *coitus interruptus*.

1323 Iriarte, J.A. [The Punishability of Abortion], Prensa Med. Argent. 48:3194-ff., 1961.

Discussion of the penalties imposed upon those violating the Argentine Penal Code. The punishments vary depending on whether the abortion was performed with the woman's consent and whether the woman was harmed by the operation. Several things must be proved in court: the existence of the pregnancy; signs of violent expulsion of the fetus; stage of pregnancy; conditions causing the pregnancy; whether the mother or someone else had induced the abortion; and other circumstances which determine the character and seriousness of the crime.

1324 Lazcano, Carlos A. *La Fecundacion Artificial* [Artificial Insemination]. Cordoba: Republica Argentina, Impr. de la Universidad, 1951. 53 pp.

1325 Memeladorff, Francisco. "La Implantacion de Subsidios Familiares " [The Introduction of Family Subsidies], Revista de Ciencias Economicas 28(225):311-42. April 1940.

A system of family allowances is advocated for Argentina.

1326 Review of the River Plate. "Family Allowances for Workers," Rev. River Plate 122(3296):16-17; 22-24. July 19, 1957.

Texts and discussion of two decrees of the Argentine Government, dated July 11, 1957, establishing family allowances in industrial establishments and commercial firms in Argentina retroactive to January 1, 1957.

1327 Revista de Economia Argentina. "La Implantacion del Salario Familiar " [The Introduction of Family Wages], Revista de Economia Argentina 40(280):321-22. October 1941.

This is a discussion of a petition to the Argentine Chamber of Deputies by the Central Board of the Argentine Catholic Action for ratification of a law granting family allowances to all workers.

1328 Stabile, Blanca. "The Working Woman in the Argentine Economy: Particularly with Regard to Equality of Remuneration, Employment Opportunities, Standards of Skill and Maternity Protection," Internat. Labour Rev. 85:122-28, 1962.

The increasingly important role being played by women in the Argentine economy is described. The author examines briefly the status of women workers in the country, with particular references to equality of remuneration, employment opportunities, standards of skill and maternity protection.

CHILE

General population policies

1329 Del Rio C., and Raimundo, J. Manual de Derecho Penal [Manual of Penal Law]. Santiago, 1947.

Chapters 7 and 8 under the Part on Special Crimes discuss laws relating to abortion, rape, desertion, incest, sodomy, prostitution, adultery, illegal marriage, infanticide, castration and related matters.

1330 Romero, Hernan. "Hacia una Politica de Poblacion " [Toward a Population Policy], Revista Medica de Chile 93:669-77. October 1965.

Argues for a comprehensive policy to reduce natality, improve the health and welfare of the family, and to ensure full utilization of resources and that the rising expectations are adequately met.

1331 Valdivieso, Ramón. "Politica de Poblacion y Salud Publica en Chile " [The Policy of Population and Public Health in Chile], Rev. Med. Chile 95(4):220-26, 1967.

The share of Chile in the problem of human population explosion is presented. Insufficient supply of prime commodities has caused malnutrition and disease resulting in high rate of mortality. The need for birth control and improvement of the economy to improve the health and general well being of common workers was indicated. The Eighth World Conference on the International Federation of Family Planning was held in Chile and suggestions were made to meet the problems arising from human overpopulation.

Policies on fertility and family size

1332 Armijo, Rolando. "Abortion in Latin America," in: Proceedings of the Eighth International Conference of the International Planned Parenthood Federation. Hertford, England: International Planned Parenthood Federation, 1967.

The dimension of the incidence of criminal abortion in Latin America is shown by several studies. Also discussed are the Chilean reports on the factors associated with post-abortal complications and the results of the contraceptive program established in Santiago in 1964. A decrease both in the number of hospital admissions for abortion and in the birth rate was reported in Santiago in 1965.

1333 Armijo, Rolando, and Monreal, Tegualda. "Epidemiologia del Aborto Provocado en Santiago " [Epidemiology of Induced Abortion in Santiago, Chile], Rev. Med. Chile 92(7):548-57, 1964. Also in: J. Sex Res. 1:143-ff., 1965.

Starting from data of the 1960 Census, a random sample of 2500 homes in urban Santiago (population 2,200,000) was developed. From this sample, women aged 20-45 years were interviewed in their homes concerning their induced abortions and contraceptive practices. This report is based on tabulations of the first 580 records, out of a total of 1800 records, which were collected. The 580 records reveal a total of 734 abortions, of which 495 were induced. The other major findings are as follows: (1) 50 per cent of all women exhibit a history of abortion and 27.2 per cent a history of induced abortion; (2) Of the women exhibiting a history of induced abortion, 72.9 per cent had undergone up to three operations. At the other extreme, 5.6 per cent had had from ten to seventeen induced abortions; (3) An apparent concentration of induced abortion among married women was observed. In our sample 76.2 per cent of women were married and they accounted for 85 per cent of the abortions; (4) Abortion according to age appears to be concentrated in women in the 25 to 29 year age group, with a rate of 77 per 1000 person-years at risk. This age group is closely followed by the 20 to 24 and 30 to 34 year age groups. The cumulative rate for all ages observed was 173 per 1000 person-years at risk; (5) Induced abortion was present in all the social categories, the lower income groups being most significantly affected; (6) In more than one half of induced abortions the reasons alleged were economic; (7) Of the 734 abortions recorded, 58 per cent had not received hospital care. Of this proportion, a marked predominance of induced abortions was noted. On the basis of this ratio the real figure of abortions occurring in Santiago could be estimated at nearly 50,000 per annum; (8) 38 per cent of sexually active women use some type of contraceptive method; (9) 76.8 per cent of the women surveyed were in favour of family planning. 72.5 per cent were in favour of legalization of abortion in certain circumstances.

1334 Armijo, Rolando, and Monreal, Tequalda. "The Problem of Induced Abortion in Chile," Milbank Memorial Fund Quart. 43:263-ff., 1965.

Data provided by retrospective interviews with women aged 20 to 45 in Santiago, Concepcion, and Antofagasta in 1961. Total sample size was 3800. 41% of the women admitted having at least one abortion, either spontaneous or induced; 23% admitted having an induced abortion. The abortion rate was highest for women aged 25 to 29, who were married or were "concubines," who had one to three living children, and were members of the lower and mid-lower class. Reasons most commonly given for having induced abortion were economic (48%), followed by health (11%) and a large family (11%). In 80% of the abortion cases, the sexual partner had been consulted and approved of the abortion. Abortion rates were highest in Antofagasta and lowest in Concepcion (which reported the greatest number of children per woman).

1335 Armijo, Rolando, and Requena B., Mariano. "Epidemiological Aspects of Abortion." Paper Presented at the Meetings of the American Public Health Association, San Francisco, October 31, 1966.

The authors examine the progress of epidemiological studies of abortion in Chile and review the data of early hospital studies, of the retrospective interview studies of Armijo and Monreal, and of Requena, and the prospective study of abortion in the labor camps of the ENDESA (National Electricity Organization and Co.) presently underway.

1336 Avendano, Onofre, and Faundes-Latham, Anibal. "A Contraceptive Program in a Latin American Urban Community: Policy, Objectives and Facts," in: Vol. 2, pp. 313-14 of United Nations Department of Economic and Social Affairs, Proceedings of the World Population Conference, Belgrade, 30 August - 10 September, 1965. 4 Vols. New York: United Nations, 1967.

The Comite Chileno de Proteccion de la Familia in close cooperation with the National Health Service seeks to prevent criminal abortion by means of extensive use of contraception. The estimate is one abortion for every two live births and that two out of three abortions are criminally induced.

1337 Cruz-Coke, R. "The Population Explosion in Chile," Lancet, No. 7409, August 28 1965, pp. 434-35.

Notes on trends in birth rates and on legislation concerning family allowances (1953) and prenatal bonuses payable from the fourth month of pregnancy (1961) and then from the first month (1964). Estimate of small total effect of new policy, beginning July 1, 1965, for giving contraceptive information to married women free through the national health service.

1338 Faundez, N., *et al*. [Epidemiology of Abortions in Concepcion], Demografie 8:349-ff., 1966.

An epidemiological study of induced abortion was made in the province of Concepcion with a population of over 600,000 people. Results show that the greatest abortion risk was found among married, middle-class women, age 24 years with a maximum of three children. Reasons most frequently stated for abortion were economic conditions, large family size and health problems. Although the majority of women in Concepcion favored family planning and legalized abortion, contraception was not frequently used except in the upper classes. Sexual relations started at an earlier age in lower socio-economic groups but the sexual contacts were more frequent among couples of higher social status. Authors urge more liberal and realistic abortion statutes as a needed solution to the etiology of induced abortions.

1339 Mallet S., Armando. "Regimen Chileno de Subsidios Familiares para Empleados " [Family Allowances in Chile], Chile, Ministerio de Salubridad, Prevision y Asistencia Social, Prevision Social , November 1941 - February 1942.

An analysis of the existing legislation and operation, with proposals for new legislation.

1340 Puga, J., _et al_. [Effects of Application and Diffusion of Birth Control Systems in the Hospital Area North of Santiago de Chile and in the Women Treated in the Obstetrics Clinic in the University of Chile], _Rev. Chile Obstet. Ginec_. 32: 220-27, 1967.

1341 Requena B., Mariano. [Problem of Induced Abortion in a Working Class Population of Santiago. Use and Attitudes Toward the Use of Contraceptives]. Paper Presented at the Chilean Society of Public Health, July 19, 1965.

Discussion of induced abortion and attitudes toward contraception among 580 women in a working class district of Santiago. The women who resort to induced abortions were mostly between the ages of 20 and 29 whose husbands were unemployed at the time of pregnancy, who had lived most of their lives in Santiago, with a slightly higher standard of living. Marital status and religion had little effect on the incidence of abortion; however, abortion was more frequent for women with 4-6 children, for women who had had previous abortions, and for women who had used some form of contraception prior to pregnancy. 18% of the women had used contraceptives but had used ineffective methods. They frequently knew of more reliable means but their husbands' attitudes influenced their acceptance of these methods.

1342 Requena B., Mariano. "Social and Economic Correlates of Induced Abortion in Santiago, Chile," _Demography_ 2:33-49, 1965.

A random sample of women of fertile age was studied by means of questionnaires and interviews. This report is on a subsample composed of women from the lower socioeconomic strata, in which the frequency of induced abortion is higher than for the total sample. The risk of abortion is found to be unrelated to the woman's civil status, schooling, and frequency of sexual relations. The risk is higher for women who are: employed as unskilled manual workers rather than as housewives, white-collar workers, or professionals; Catholic rather than Protestant; and the contraceptors rather than the non-contraceptors. Among Catholics, the risk is correlated with frequency of church attendance.

1343 Requena B., Mariano. "Studies of Family Planning in the Quinta Normal District of Santiago," Milbank Memorial Fund Quart. 43(4) Part II,: 69-99. October 1965.

Part of a study in Santiago on the epidemiology of induced abortion, attitudes toward and opinion of birth control, prevalence of contraceptive practice, and preferred contraceptive. Results were: (1) the population studied practice birth control based on induced abortion (30%); and 18% practiced contraception, but only 4.5% used effective measures. (2) Women who practice birth control belong to the high segment of the lower socioeconomic and cultural level. The lower-class do not practice even induced abortion. (3) There is a significant difference between the knowledge of contraceptive methods (90%) and their actual use (4.5%). A striking lack of communication was found between males and females. Females preferred contraceptives which did not demand their active participation and which were not directly connected with the sexual act, i.e., intrauterine devices and pills.

1344 Romero, Hernan. "El Control de la Natalidad " [Birth Control], Santiago, Editorial Universitaria, 1964, 82 pp.

1345 Romero, Hernan, and Vildosola, J. [Introduction to the Problem of Abortions], Rev. Chile Higiene Med. Prevent. 14:197-ff., 1952.

A review of a study of abortion based on interviews with 3038 women. Statistical data indicate: 1038 women admitted to hospitals for delivery and 1000 women treated in hospitals for complicated abortion had had 6232 previous livebirths and 2276 previous abortions. 460 of the 1000 women treated for abortions were thought to have had spontaneous abortions and 540 were thought to have had induced abortions. Induced abortions accounted for 66% of the single women's abortions and 47% of married women's abortions.

1346 Rosselot, J., et al. "Informe Sobre Politica del Servicio Nacional de Salud Para Regular la Natalidad en Chile " [Report on the Policy of the National Health Service on Birth Control in Chile], Revista Medica de Chile 94:744-50. November 1966.

1347 Viel V., Benjamin. "Family Planning in Chile," J. Sex Res. 3(4):284-94. November 1967.

The rapid increase of the Chilean population during the last 50 years has been due primarily to the continuous decline of the death rate, together with a continuing high birth rate. There has also been an increase in the number of females reaching childbearing age due to a decrease in infant mortality. Lastly, the considerable shortening of the period of lactation has also contributed to the high birth rate. In the past the sole way of reducing the number of children was illegal induced abortion. The numbers of such abortions have been increasing since 1938, and complications caused by this operation have been a major cause of hospitalization. In order to counteract the epidemic character of illegal induced abortions, the medical profession initiated a family planning program in 1964. Intra-uterine devices and birth control pills have been offered to the public. An analysis of the results obtained in the city of Santiago after 1.5 years of work indicates that there is good reason to be optimistic about the effectiveness of the program. A decline in the birth rate and a marked decline in the number of hospitalized abortion cases has been noted in places in which a successful family planning plan has been put into operation. A post-partum program offering intra-uterine devices immediately after delivery or after curettage due to abortion has been added to the family planning program since 1966. This new policy appears to be very successful.

1348 Viel V., Benjamin. "Results of a Family Planning Program in the Western Area of the City of Santiago," Amer. J. Public Health 59(10):1898-1909. October 1969.

A total of 20,416 women, representing 18.5 per cent of the women of fertile age living in the western district of Santiago, had accepted IUDs as of June 1967 over a 39-month period. The contraceptive services were offered with an educational campaign starting in April 1964, and supplemented in April 1966 by a program of IUD insertion after delivery or after abortion prior to discharge from the hospital. Acceptance among women hospitalized for abortion was three times higher than for women hospitalized for delivery. As a result of the program, hospital admissions for abortion were reduced by an estimated 32 per cent (minimum) to 52 per cent (maximum), or a reduction at the minimum level of 2,746 abortions and a saving of 8,238 hospital bed days.

Birth rates also appear to be declining in the district since the inception of the program in 1964. Retention rates were highest for post-abortion insertions and for insertions not associated with a pregnancy, and lowest for early post-partum insertions. Nevertheless, the author recommends early insertions after delivery should be made because many women fail to return to the hospital after they are discharged.

PARAGUAY

General population policies

1349 President. Plan Quinquena 1943-1948 de Reconstruccion Nacional [The Quinquennial Plan of National Reconstruction, 1943-1948]. Asuncion: Departamento Nacional de Prensa y Propaganda, 1944. 25 pp.

Sections on agrarian policy, pp. 12-14, and public health, pp. 21-23.

Policies on fertility and family size

1350 Paraguay. "Prevention of Venereal Disease," Internat. Digest Health Legis. 3:520-25, 1951-52.

Decree No. 2436 of 10 January 1951 established regulations for the prevention of venereal disease. Part Nine of the Act requires clinical and serological tests for both parties to a marriage and authorizes the Ministry of Public Health to provide them free of charge. Part Eleven of the Act prohibits prostitution as a means of livelihood and repeals all other Acts regulating prostitution.

URUGUAY

Policies on fertility and family size

1351 International Labour Office. "Family Allowances in Uruguay," Internat. Labour Rev. 50(2):251-52, August 1944 and 51(2): 234-35, February 1945.

A decree of the Uruguayan government of May 17, 1944, established the regulations for the operation of equalization funds for the payment of family allowances in accordance with the provisions of Act No. 10,449 of November 12, 1943. These regulations are summarized in detail.

1352 Rios, Bruno G. "El Aborto Criminal. Responsabilidad del Medico " [Criminal Abortion. Responsibility of the Physician], Anales de la Facultad de Medicina de Montevideo 49:156-64, 1964.

Reviews existing legal reasons for induced abortion and concludes that except where the life of the mother is threatened abortion should not be permitted.

1353 Rozada, I. "The Situation of Voluntary Abortion in Uruguay." Paper Presented at the Fourth IPPF Conference for the Western Hemisphere Region, San Juan, Puerto Rico, April 19-26, 1964.

This article examines three methods used in Uruguay to approximate the abortion rate. Known abortion clinics were observed and a daily chart was recorded of the women who visited these centers. Examination of their bank accounts revealed when the abortions had been performed. Anesthesia sales were analyzed and pregnancy histories were obtained from clinics and private physicians. 68% of the women admitted having had abortions. Each method gave the same figure: 150,000 induced abortions per year or three for each live-birth. 58% of the women stated that they had no knowledge of contraceptive techniques. Of those who used them, 78.3 per cent used them incorrectly. A family planning program available to all is recommended.

1354 Turenne, Augusto. El Contralor de la Concepcion. Necesidad y Urgencia e Implantario en la Republica Oriental del Uruguay [Birth Control: Necessity and Urgency of Policy in Uruguay]. Montevideo: Ministerio de Salud Publica, 1942. 146 pp.

In 1936 the Ministry of Public Health named a Commission on Eugenics, particularly to deal with induced abortions which are estimated to be nearly 50% of the number of live births. The Commission's chairman reviews the possibilities of birth control as a means of dealing with this problem and also of reducing the high number of illegitimate births. He concludes that the social and economic advantages of a population policy based on quality not quantity would also be great, considers the objections of Roman Catholics and others, and calls on the medical profession to act.

(Carribean)

GENERAL

General population policies

1355 Roberts, George W. "Some Demographic Considerations of West Indian Federation," _Soc. Econ. Stud._ 6(2):262-85. June 1957.

Outline of the historical background and principal features of present rapid rates of increase and consideration of the interdependence of policies directed toward controlling migration, mortality, and fertility.

1356 Joint Committee to Examine the Question of Overpopulation and to Make Recommendations for Dealing with this Problem. _Report of the Committee_. Barbados, 1954. 7 pp.

1357 United Nations. Technical Assistance Administration. _Report to the Government of Barbados on Research and Action Programmes for Reduction of Population Pressure_ by Margaret S. Hagood. TAA/BAR/1. May 29, 1956. 16 pp.

Policies on fertility and family size

1358 Back, Kurt W. "A Model of Family Planning Experiments: The Lessons of the Puerto Rican and Jamaican Studies," *Marr. Fam. Living* 25(1):14-19. February 1963.

A discussion of the results of two controlled field experiments in family planning in Puerto Rico and Jamaica, noting the implications of these studies for the conduct of future experiments. The following lessons were derived from these studies: only a minimum proportion of anticipated difficulties with conducting the programs actually happened; the existence of a birth control program was more important than the specific shape of the program; the differential needs of different population groups can be distinguished and the type of work necessary for each determined; and a continuing organization is necessary and must either be maintained separately or coordinated with existing set-ups. Three sets of conditions influencing the change in contraceptive behavior are isolated: individual variables, social variables, and transformation or decision variables. It is suggested that an ideal study would have to combine these ingredients in two ways: by the assessment of these conditions within the society and by planning a program which takes all of them into account. A comprehensive program would select societies in different stages of acceptance of family limitation, both according to distribution of individuals and according to social supports, and then determine the effects of different efforts to reduce the birth rate.

1359 Farley, John U., and Leavitt, Harold J. "Population Control and the Private Sector," *J. Social Issues* 23(4):135-43. October 1967.

Despite the existence of private sector markets for contraceptives in most parts of the world, and despite the fact that most contraceptives are sold through such channels, the private sector has been virtually ignored in population study and in formulation of population programs. A model of consumer acceptance is presented and the role that the private sector plays in the model is examined. Some characteristics of private-sector contraceptive markets in the Caribbean are discussed, along with some important open issues of social science research on the interaction of public and private sector distribution channels.

1360 Goode, William J. "Illegitimacy in the Caribbean Social Structure," Amer. Sociol. Rev. 25:21-30. February 1966.

A study of norms and practices related to legitimacy in the Caribbean is presented to illuminate the operation of its social system. Although Malinowski's Principle of Legitimacy has been challenged, the detailed descriptions of family and courtship patterns in the Caribbean indicate that the Principle is generally valid. The "matrifocal" Caribbean family is a product of an unstable family pattern, in which the mother or grandmother is often in power because no father is there. The courtship pattern is anonymous, so that the young girl must be willing to risk pregnancy in order to establish a basis for a more stable union. Also examined is how courtship relations in the Caribbean may lead to a high illegitimacy rate, even when the norm of legitimacy is accepted.

1361 Patchett, K.W. "Some Aspects of Marriage and Divorce in the West Indies," Internat. Comparative Law Quart. 8:632-77. October 1959.

In 1958 the new Federal Legislature of the West Indies was formally inaugurated and marked a further stage in the political federation of the United Kingdom dependencies in the Caribbean. The colonies have, however, moved towards political maturity largely independent of each other and have also developed legal systems and substantive legal rules on separate and distinctive lines. The author compares some aspects of a branch of law which has received differing treatment by the territories -- the law relating to marriage and divorce. The introduction is designed to indicate some of the factors which have led to divergencies; in Part I, the law relating to matrimonial causes is studied; in Part II, legislation regulating marriages between members of the East Indian population in certain of the territories is compared; and in Part III, a brief survey is attempted of an apparent disregard of the matrimonial law in certain West Indian communities.

1362 Segal, Aaron. "Le Planning Familial dans la Caraibe " [Family Planning in the Caribbean], Les Cahiers du C.E.R.A.G. 15:1-25, 1969.

A summary of the stated and unstated policies on family planning among Caribbean states.

1363 Segal, Aaron, with assistance of Kent C. Earnhardt. Politics and Population in the Caribbean. Institute of Caribbean Studies, University of Puerto Rico, 1969. 158 pp.

The stated and unstated population policies of nine governments or territories in the Caribbean are reviewed. In addition to giving factual information about the population, the population policies, and the family planning programs of these nine areas, a typology of the evolutionary development of family planning is described. Stage one is that of individual (private) activity (e.g., in clinics): Haiti and the Dominican Republic were at this stage in 1967. Stage two is that of indirect government support (e.g., duty-free entry of contraceptives): Curacao, Guadeloupe, and Puerto Rico were at this stage. Stage three is that of full government support of family planning for anti-natalist ends: Barbados reached this stage in 1956, Jamaica in 1966, and Trinidad (nearly) in 1967. The factors seen as making this transition possible are described. It is asserted that the population of the area will double in 25 years, and that there is little evidence that anti-natalist policies will avert disaster.

1364 Smith, M.G. "Political Realities Regarding Family Planning in Caribbean and Adjacent Areas," J. Fam. Welf. 5(1):31-39. September 1958.

Defines the implications of British Caribbean political organization for demographic policy, indicates how a planned parenthood program may be successfully organized within the present framework.

1365 Stycos, J. Mayone. "Experiments in Social Change: The Caribbean Fertility Studies," pp. 305-16, Chpt. in: Kiser, C. V., ed. Research in Family Planning. Princeton: Princeton University Press, 1962. xvi, 664 pp.

Two investigations of fertility control among lower classes have been completed in Puerto Rico and in Jamaica. Each investigation involved a three stage design: (1) unstructured interviews ranging from two to six hours, given to 72 rural and urban couples in Puerto Rico and to 99 Jamaican rural and urban wives and a subsample of 53 husbands; (2) larger sample surveys, using questions more answerable to statistical analysis, and employing, in Jamaica, an area probability of 1400 currently mated urban and rural females and in Puerto Rico, a sample of 888 wives and 322 husbands; and (3) matched or experimently varied groups exposed to varying educational treatments and results, compared with non-treated control groups. Jamaican cases were reinterviewed six weeks, one year, and three years after treatment and Puerto Rican groups six weeks, and one year following treatment. For contrast, Haiti was selected, utilizing the techniques of participant observer and projective testing. Conclusions include: (1) Short exposure programs are effective in precipitating contraceptive behavior, but less so at maintaining it; (2) any stimulus making the issue salient and placing it in a public context of approval by respected groups will precipitate use among that minority psychologically ready; and (3) for sustained contraceptive behavior more intensive type programs would seem required.

1366 Tietze, Christopher, and Alleyne, Charles. "A Family Planning Service in the West Indies," Fertility and Sterility 10(3): 259-71. May - June 1959.

In 1955 a family planning service was instituted in Barbados. 555 women who had visited the clinics and had been fitted with a diaphragm were interviewed in order to evaluate the service's effectiveness. The authors describe the results of these interviews. 63% of the women who were still in need of protection were found to be active cases; the majority of inactive cases had become inactive after using the prescribed method of contraception for only a few months. The pregnancy rate was 17 per 100 years of exposure for women using a diaphragm, while the corresponding rate, based on the experience of all women after attending the clinic (including periods with and without use of a diaphragm), was 29 per 100 years of exposure. The authors estimate that the rate of pregnancy among women who had visited the clinics was reduced by about 60%, compared with the rate expected if they had not visited. This reduction would seem to indicate that the family planning service demonstrated a high degree of effectiveness.

BARBADOS

Policies on fertility and family size

1367 Cummins, G.I.M., *et al*. "Population Control in Barbados," *Amer. J. Public Health* 55:1600-8. October 1965.

In 1951 the Barbadian legislature set up a committee to examine the problem of overpopulation and to make recommendations for dealing with it. The Committee recommended a program of planned parenthood. In May 1954 a voluntary Family Planning Association was formed. This study documents the program, its acceptance by the public, and its effect on population trends in Barbados.

1368 Ebanks, Gosport Edward. "Patterns of Contraceptive Use Among Clients of the Barbados Family Planning Association," *Dissertation Abstr.* 29A:4113, 1968-1969. Abstract of Ph.D. Thesis, Cornell University, Ithaca, New York, 1968. 267 pp.

This is a study of the behavior patterns of lower class Barbadian women during the fecund period of their lives with respect to the introduction of new types of contraceptives within a multiple method family planning program. The behavior patterns of these women are examined through their use of the facilities of The Barbados Family Planning Association (BFPA). The study is developed within a diffusion theoretic framework that focuses on the trial and adoption stages of the diffusion process. The BFPA has followed the policy of making available at nominal cost *all* existing contraceptive methods. This had led to very high drop-out rates after admission and a considerable amount of method changing. However, changes take place generally in the direction of increasing the reliability of the method used. The lower the reliability of the method, the greater the rate of drop-out as well as the rate of change from it. The longer the time spent in the program, the greater the number of methods used; but the longer the time a method is used, the less likely that it will be given up for another method. The transition probabilities for changing from user to non-user in a year do not remain constant over the twelve years for which the program has been in operation. This is also true for changing from non-user to user.

1369 United Nations. Technical Assistance Administration. *The Effectiveness of the Family Planning Service in Barbados*. Prepared for the Government of Barbados by Christopher Tietze, appointed by the ... Report No. TAA/BAR/4. 7 August 1958. 18 pp. processed.

This final report includes findings evaluated on a second visit, March 1-23, 1958, and a report on a follow-up study of about 600 women who had attended the clinics, which was carried out during 1957 and early 1958 by the Barbados Family Planning Association.

1370 United Nations, Technical Assistance Administration. The Family Planning Service in Barbados. Prepared for the Government of Barbados by Christopher Tietze, appointed by the ... Report No. TAA/BAR/2. July 3, 1957. 14 pp. processed.

Report of the first two periods of study, this one from November 21 to December 30, 1956, to evaluate the family planning program sponsored by the Government of Barbados.

CUBA

General population policies

1371 International Labour Office, "Social Policy in Cuba," Industry and Labour 7(3):94-95, 1 February 1952.

Social policy in Cuba aims at preserving social advantages granted workers and extending them in so far as the nation's economic resources will permit. It was shown during the war that the country was poorly equipped to meet national and international crises. It was therefore necessary to organize work on a more scientific basis and to facilitate cooperation between employers and employees. It was also necessary to compile reliable statistics concerning wages, the cost of living and family budgets, and the unemployment situation. In order to solve these matters Cuba has requested technical assistance from the International Labour Organization.

Policies on fertility and family size

1372 Le Riverend, E. "El Divorcio: Derechos Cubano y Puertorriqueno " [Divorce: Cuban and Puerto-Rican Laws], Rev. Jur. UPR 35:535, 1966.

1373 Martinez, Jose Agustin, Aborto Ilicito y Derecho Penal al Aborto [Illegal Abortion and Criminal Law on Abortion], Havana: Bilioteca Juridica de Autores Cubanas y Extranjeros, Vol. 65, 1942.

HAITI

Policies on fertility and family size

1374 Haiti. "Prenuptial Certificate," *Internat. Digest Health Legis.* 14:69, 1963.

Law of 12 September 1961 makes it mandatory for future matrimonial partners to appear, within a maximum period of thirty days preceding the date set for their marriage, before the appointed medical authorities to obtain prenuptial certificate.

JAMAICA

General population policies

1375 Ministry of Development and Welfare. *Jamaica: Five Year Independence Plan, 1963-1968.* A long term development programme. Kingston: Government Printer, 1963. 240 pp.

In much of the first five-year period, emphasis will be particularly directed towards the rural agricultural economy, in a determined effort to reduce rural migration to the overcrowded towns. The Government will encourage the spread of information on, and techniques for, the spacing or limitation of families and will explore new migration outlets. Chapter, Population problems, pp. 7-10, reviews changes 1943-1963 and presents projections 1960-1975 by sex and principal age groups, assuming a net average emigration of ten thousand annually.

Policies on fertility and family size

1376 Cumper, George E. "The Fertility of Common Law Unions in Jamaica," Soc. Econ. Stud. 15:189-202. September 1968.

Argues that common law unions have depressed rather than raised fertility levels as compared with formal marriages, in contradiction to other studies.

1377 Schlesinger, Benjamin. "Divorce in Jamaica: A New Phenomenon?" Indian Sociol. Bull. 5(2):81-85. January 1968.

It is noted that available studies on Jamaican family patterns during 1943-56 did not discuss the question of divorce in Jamaica. From 1960-63 a gradual increase in divorces is observable, with the exception of 1962. The divorce laws of Jamaica are briefly summarized. Grounds for divorce are: nullification; adultery; desertion for a minimum period of three years; cruelty; and uncurable insanity of one marriage partner. Two daily newspapers of Jamaica, The Gleaner and the Star, were examined for divorce reports. Forty reported cases in the Star in the months May - June 1967 were analyzed regarding grounds of divorce, average length of marriage prior to the divorce action, and the average number of children. The most frequent cause of divorce was desertion (22 cases). Quotations from the newspaper articles indicating details of the cases are presented. A thorough study of divorce is needed in order to document this apparently new phenomenon which appears to continue to increase.

1378 Stycos, J. Mayone, and Back, Kurt W. "Contraception and Catholicism in Jamaica," Eugenics Quart. 5(4):216-20, 1958.

In Jamaica where Catholics represent less than a tenth of the population, a sample of the married (common law or in regular liaison) female population was investigated with respect to attitudes toward family planning. No special conservatism among these Roman Catholic versus Protestant women with respect to family planning was found. Hence, no influence of Catholic teaching with respect to family planning among the members of the uneducated test population was demonstrable.

1379 Stycos, J. Mayone, and Back, Kurt W. The Control of Human Fertility in Jamaica, Ithaca, N.Y.: Cornell University Press, 1964. xii, 377 pp.

During the 1950's, a series of studies were conducted to investigate the dynamics of fertility in two underdeveloped areas, Puerto Rico and Jamaica. The form of the study applies to an area characterized by differences in cultural traditions, especially regarding family forms. Jamaica represents in microcosm the twin features of the population explosion -- one of the lowest crude death rates in the world, 8.8 per 1,000 and high fertility, 38.1, with a resulting high rate of natural increase, 29.3. While emigration to the United Kingdom has moderated population increase, population growth has still been very high and events in England propogate to slow down the rate of emigration in coming years. Despite this situation, there was little organized effort to propogate family planning. The study focuses on three separate problems: (1) degree of readiness of the population for contraceptive practices, especially attitudes to family size, and knowledge of and attitudes to birth control; (2) factors affecting fertility, especially urban versus rural residence and marital status; and (3) an experimental program to assess the effects of different educational approaches to the problem of fertility control. To these aspects of the family planning problem is added a discussion of the patterns of mating in Jamaica which provides data not hitherto available. A representative sample survey, involving interviews with 1,359 currently mated females between the ages of 14 and 40 with no more than elementary school education was selected because it represented those females currently exposed to the risk of pregnancy and because females of lesser educational attainments were most likely to have large families. Findings suggest that Jamaican females do not want the large families they typically have: only about 15% of the females who have had four or more children want more. Yet, there is a rather high degree of tolerance for large families if that is the way things work out. It is concluded that there is an excellent base preference for small families, but that Jamaican females need help to turn those preferences into reality. Use of birth control methods was found to be quite low, and knowledge of methods was not well-established, even at a rather primitive level. However, attitudes to the idea of birth control, once it was explained, were favorable, and it is felt that opposition to birth control was not deep rooted in the 33% who expressed some negative attitudes.

1380 Stycos, J. Mayone, and Back, Kurt W. Prospects for Fertility Reduction. New York: The Conservation Foundation, 1957. iv, 113 pp.

In addition to reporting interrelation of social factors, fertility and family planning norms, describes an experiment conducted to introduce family planning.

PUERTO RICO

General population policies

1381 Chase, Stuart. "Operation Bootstrap" in Puerto Rico: Report of Progress, 1951. Prepared for the N.P.A. Business Committee on National Policy. Washington: National Planning Association, 1951. vii, 72 pp.

This analysis of a "Point Four" record proceeds from the population dilemma to the planned industrialization, its origins, its accomplishments, its prospects, and its lessons for other societies.

1382 Senior, Clarence. "Population Pressures and the Future of Puerto Rico," J. Heredity 38(5):131-34, 1947.

A population density of over 600 per square mile creates and aggravates serious social maladjustments. If arable land alone is considered, each person now averages less than half an acre. Infant mortality and maternal death rates are very high. Emigration, though high, affords only minor relief. The author favors a well rounded population policy and program, including industrialization and other means of increasing economic production on idle land; general education; raising the age of marriage; strengthening family ties; emigration; and the spreading of knowledge of modern contraceptive methods among the poor.

1383 Senior, Clarence. "Population Problems in Puerto Rico," Caribbean Econ. Rev. 2(1):113-21. May 1950.

The basis for a broad program, including raising levels of living, education, planned parenthood, and emigration.

Policies on fertility and family size

1384 Back, Kurt W., *et al*. "The Dynamics of Family Planning," *Marr. Fam. Living* 18(3):195-99. August 1956.

A report on 888 lower-class families in Puerto Rico, in 321 families husband and wife were interviewed and in the rest, the wife only. Four types of fertility control were found: (1) the 'never-users' around 50% of the number; (2) sterilized females about 17% of the number; (3) regular-users not more than 10% of the number: and (4) casual users, between 20-25%. Data indicate that though 50% try birth control methods, the number of effective family planners is much smaller. The 'planners' believed in the value of small families, were less traditional in general values, more equalitarian in family organization, had more communication between husband and wife especially with reference to family size ideal, and had the ability to come to a joint decision (can organize effectively in general). The casual user is aware of the pressures of a growing family and will try birth control but lacks the ability to pursue it. The never-user's value system lacks perception on the question of family size, and has the kind of family organization which is inimical to family planning. The overall situation in Puerto Rico is favorable for the development of family planning. Almost everyone knows of at least one method as well as people in the community who use it. The restrictive influence of religion is small. Few people think of birth control as objectionable. Two to three children is considered the ideal family size. However, there is little difference in fertility between those who have and those who have not used birth control methods. In some families where planning is valued but family organization is unable to follow through, sterilization of wife has been the solution. About 17% of all females are sterilized. The latter are on the modern end of a 'traditional-modern' value continuum and had the highest percent of working wives in the group. However, there was little communication between husband and wife in this group, and the husband was dominant. They thus accept the method of birth control that does not entail cooperation.

1385 Back, Kurt W., *et al*. "Population Control in Puerto Rico: The Formal and Informal Framework," *Law and Contemporary Problems* 25:558-76. Summer 1960.

Puerto Rico's concern with its population growth, in conjunction with its respect for the individual and belief in scientific planning, has led to a series of investigations of the general beliefs, attitudes and practices surrounding birth control. These investigations have provided extensive information about family planning in Puerto Rico and have made it possible to put the question into an overall perspective. The authors present an outline of a general logical scheme under which social changes of this nature can profitably be considered, and then discuss the introduction of birth control into Puerto Rico, noting the transition from different stages and describing the present situation. While such legal and institutional changes in a country's birth control program are important, the effect of these changes on the actual birth rate depends on the attitudes and information of individuals and within families. Based on an intensive study conducted by the authors in 1954-55, the level of information about contraception, the influence of religion, and individual motivations are discussed. The high incidence of female sterilization is examined, as well as the extent of use of non-surgical methods of birth control, with reference to the relationship of birth control to the structure of Puerto Rican society. The authors conclude with a discussion of the outlook for the future in Puerto Rico, and contend that, while the ambiguous political and legal position on birth control in the country makes the popular response to a felt need vague and ineffective, given freedom of choice of the people concerned, an effective population program can succeed. There can be witnessed a slow but steady congruence of all the influences making family planning an accepted part of Puerto Rican society.

1386 Back, Kurt W., et al., "The Puerto Rican Field Experiment in Population Control," Hum. Relat. 10(4):315-43, 1957.

A report of an experiment in population control designed to study the determinants of fertility planning in a high-fertility area, discussing the problems of method and introducing experimental precision into field work in population problems, to show how cooperation of the several disciplines can help us to lead the way toward understanding and controlling population changes. It is concluded that even in a field study of family planning it is possible to conduct a controlled experiment, isolating theoretically relevant variables. In this study matched groups of respondents were submitted to educational treatments conforming to an experimental design of content and method, and the effect of these programs was measured. The main implication of the experiment for future educational programs is the need for adaptation of the program to the general demographic situation. It is also necessary to determine what stage in the progress toward family planning has been reached: whether the necessary ground work in values, action potential, and information is missing, whether a favorable predisposition waits to be translated into action, or whether a pattern of family planning has been started and is not stabilized.

1387 Calderon, A.R., Jr. "Filacion en Puerto Rico " [Illegitimacy in Puerto Rico], Rev. C. Abo Puerto Rico 20:103, 287. August 1960.

1388 Cofresi, Emilio. "Differential Fertility in Puerto Rico," Puerto Rico J. Public Health Tropical Med. 25(4):460-80, 1950.

The data were obtained by means of questionnaires after personal interviews with 3,520 married women (including women consensually married, such unions having previously been shown to involve 15.1% of all women). The practice of birth control was more prevalent among urban women and varied proportionally with the family income and educational attainment of the wife. Birth control was more common among women of high fertility because these women turned to it as a check. The two most frequently given reasons for not practicing birth control were ignorance and opposition on the part of the husband; and only a small percentage gave religion as the main reason. The favored method of birth control was mechanical contraceptives; next in popularity was sterilization.

1389 De Alvarado, Carmen R., and Tietze, Christopher. "Birth Control in Puerto Rico," Human Fertility 12(1):15-17, 1947.

Surgical sterilization is almost as popular as contraception among Puerto Rican women, but rare among men. Birth rate has remained unchanged during the past 45 years at about 40 per 1,000 inhabitants.

1390 "El Aborto: Consideraciones Medico-Legales en Torno al Problema en Puerto Rico " [Abortion: Medico-Legal Considerations in Terms of the Problem in Puerto Rico], Rev. Jur. UPR 35:669, 1966.

1391 Hill, Reuben J., et al. The Family and Population Control: A Puerto Rican Experiment in Social Change, Chapel Hill, N.C.: University of North Carolina Press, 1959. xxvi, 481 pp.

The research design included selecting the nuclear family of procreation as the unit of observation, the interactional approach as the frame of reference, and concentrating the study on the lower educational class. The 888 families studied included the Jibaro(traditional, isolated mountain dwellers), the rural lowlands laborers, and the urban laborers. II - Family Goals, Facilitation Mechanisms and Fertility Planning - covers explanatory variables (family size preferences, knowledge of birth control, availability of birth control clinics and female sterilization, psychological, religious and modesty factors in relation to acceptability of birth control, and patterns of marital interaction), and criterion variables (incidence of birth control of various types). Findings include: ambiguity of responses on preferred family size but a tendency to prefer two or three child families; great unevenness in mastery of facilitation mechanisms -- intellectual knowledge is widespread but learned late and covers only a narrow range of methods, psychologically the methods are acceptable and religious objections are also found unimportant; lack of communication between the spouses was found to be important in limiting use of birth control; and about 40% of the families had already had some experience with using birth control. In sum, it would appear that the beginnings of mass utilization of birth control are definitely present, but that effective utilization is still a thing of the future.

1392 Hill, Reuben, _et al_. "Intra-Family Communication and Fertility Planning in Puerto Rico," _Rural Sociol_. 20(3&4): 258-71. September - December 1955.

The nuclear family of procreation was selected as the observational unit, placed in the conceptual framework of the family as an interactive system, comprising (a) status relations, (b) roles and role conceptions, and (c) processes of communication. The focus of the study was then based upon the theory that a family's effectiveness as a planning unit will be a function of its communication system. The problem was one of relating communication between spouses with the use of birth control devices. Findings indicated that communication is low, not only on the questions of birth control, but on the number of children desired, future plans, husband's work and child discipline. The higher the communication scores on the general issues of marriage the higher is the percent of families using birth control methods on a long-term basis. Factors found closely associated with a long-term-use history of birth control measures were wife's perception of husband's attitude regarding family size and birth control. Accuracy of perception by the husband of wife's attitudes towards family size is significantly associated with the choice of non-surgical methods of birth control as opposed to sterilization as a means of fertility control. Female modesty, status differences between husband and wife, and taboos on sex discussion act as barriers to communication.

1393 Kantner, John F., and Stycos, J. Mayone. "A Non-Clinical Approach to Contraception," pp. 573-92, Chpt. in: Kiser, C.V., ed. _Research in Family Planning_. Princeton: Princeton University Press, 1962. xvi, 664 pp.

A study investigating some of the motivational factors at work and the channels of communication used in the Emko contraceptive program in Puerto Rico, especially regarding success in small towns and rural areas in the hands of non-professionals. Municipality leaders are voluntary and their functions are varied. Supervisors, leaders, and users were interviewed in five different situations.

1394 Presser, Harriet B. "Puerto Rico: The Role of Sterilization in Controlling Fertility," Studies in Fam. Planning, No. 45, September 1969, pp. 8-12.

We have estimated that about one-third of all Puerto Rican mothers aged 20 to 49 in 1965 were sterilized. This is twice as high as the estimate of its prevalence in the mid-1950's. Sterilized women in the 1965 sample became sterilized early in the reproductive span: the median age at time of sterilization is 26 and, for women in stable first marriages, the median number of years married when sterilized is six. Only half of the sterilized women had only two or three births. The widespread prevalence and early timing of sterilization suggested that the impact of sterilization on fertility was substantial. To gain some indication of its impact on completed fertility, we compared the mean number of births of sterilized and non-sterilized women by age in 1965. It was speculated that, as a result of sterilization, an average of about two births per mother may have been averted for the cohort of women in their 40's, and perhaps more than two births per mother for younger cohorts. These estimates may be on the conservative side, for the data suggest that sterilized women were more fecund and had greater difficulty controlling their fertility prior to sterilization than did their non-sterilized counterparts. The age-pattern of the decline in Puerto Rican fertility since 1950 provided further evidence of the major role of sterilization as a means of fertility control. There was a notable decline both in marital and total fertility between 1950 and 1960 for women aged 25 to 39. By eliminating some alternative explanations, the decline in both cases was chiefly attributed to the increasing prevalence and, since the mid-1950's, to the earlier timing of sterilization. A secondary factor was the increase in marital instability over this period. The extended age range of the decline in total fertility between 1960 and 1965 to women aged 20 to 44 suggested that induced abortion among young women, and perhaps contraceptive practice by women of all ages, may have recently become important secondary factors in addition to marital instability. The prevalence of other means of fertility control was either indeterminate or would encourage a rise in Puerto Rican fertility.

1395 Stycos, J. Mayone. "Cultural Checks on Birth Control Use in Puerto Rico," pp. 55-65 in: The Interrelations of Demographic, Economic, and Social Problems in Selected Underdeveloped Areas. New York: Milbank Memorial Fund, 1954.

Although there have been broad social changes and favorable conditions for fertility decline in Puerto Rico for several years, the country's birth rate has only very recently shown any signs of dropping. The results of investigations and field studies are used in a discussion of the cultural factors which may be slowing up the acceptance and effective utilization of birth control in Puerto Rico and the incidence of birth control practice on the island is reviewed. Sterilization as an alternative solution is evaluated and the article concludes with a brief description of how research in this area in underdeveloped countries can most profitably proceed.

1396 Stycos, J. Mayone. Family and Fertility in Puerto Rico. New York: Columbia University Press, 1955. xv, 332 pp.

When large families are not particularly desired, and yet the fertility rate remains high, one or more of three causes may be supposed to be in operation: general ignorance of the methods of birth control; lack of the necessary materials; or inability to use the methods effectively. But Puerto Ricans know about contraceptives and can easily obtain them. Why, then, do they not apply birth control effectively? The investigation reveals that some of the reasons are unexpectedly subtle. First, union outside marriage is relatively common; in these circumstances, little interest in family limitation is likely to be shown by the father, who is not bound to support his children indefinitely, and at the same time the mother may want more children -- in order to tie down her partner morally as much as possible. It has been shown in other Caribbean investigations, however, that the breakage of such unions and the formation of new ones does not in itself lead to high fertility, owing to the periods of time that elapse between one "affair" and another. Secondly, strict supervision of young girls leads to a feeling of rebellion on their part and a desire to escape from home by means of an early union or marriage. This desire is usually fulfilled, and then another aspect of their cloistered upbringing shows itself -- namely ignorance of the means of family limitation; this is often not remedied until children have been born. From the man's point of view, the desire to demonstrate virility and to have a son are also factors tending to promote high fertility. Finally, prudishness on the part of both sexes often prevents adequate discussion between them of questions of family building, and lack of communication between husband and wife is perhaps the greatest deterrent to effective birth control practice. The book concludes with some useful suggestions for improving birth control clinics and revising public health measures in Puerto Rico, and for the conduct of future inquiries of a similar kind.

1397 Stycos, J. Mayone. "The Pattern of Birth Control in Puerto Rico," Eugenics Quart. 1(3):176-81. September 1954.

Part of a research project on attitudes on fertility and birth control dealing with differential fertility and the practice and effectiveness of birth control. A sample (number equals 3,000) of Puerto Ricans, married and fertile (at least one pregnancy) was selected from those who entered nine of the public health centers between August - October of 1953. Education is highly correlated within the use of birth control and with age. Thus, use of birth control is most striking among older age groups. In general, because birth control is put to use at older ages or is used ineffectively, its effect on fertility is minimal. The better educated are more successful in birth control. Though the great majority of sample people knew of birth control, the time at which they learned about it was too late in marriage to seriously affect a reduction of the average family size. However, an interest in the small family prevails and an accentuated education program could conceivably accelerate the fertility decline.

1398 Stycos, J. Mayone, et al. "Contraception and Catholicism in Puerto Rico," Milbank Memorial Fund Quart. 34(2):150-59. April 1956.

Analysis of the relationship between religion and attitudes toward ideal family size as achieved by birth control techniques revealed that religious differences either did not exist or were in the unexpected direction. Non-Catholics appeared to be no more liberal in their attitudes than Catholics and in some instances evidence patterns usually associated with Catholics. When religious attendance was controlled, these differences were sustained or enlarged. Attendance at church was usually inversely related to liberal sentiment regarding birth control. Nevertheless, even among church goers, attitudes and behavior were generally in the direction of rational achievement of small family goals. Several interpretations are offered to account for these findings: (1) in Latin American countries Catholics do not take religion as seriously as do Catholics in other areas, especially where the latter are in a minority; (2) a large percent of Catholic adults never attend church, hence, are less exposed to the teachings of the church; and (3) the Protestants, a minority group in Puerto Rico with a high percent of converts and with a much higher clergy-parishioner ratio than is true for Catholics, take their religion more seriously and are susceptible to greater control by the church. Several of the growing Protestant sects oppose birth control.

1399 Stycos, J. Mayone, et al. "Interpersonal Influence in Family Planning in Puerto Rico," pp. 212-21 of Vol. 8 of _Transactions of the Third World Congress of Sociology._ London: International Sociological Association, 1957.

Presents data on the possible effects of different sources of information concerning fertility control.

1400 Stycos, J. Mayone, and Hill, Reuben. "The Prospects of Birth Control in Puerto Rico," _Annals Amer. Acad. Polit. Soc. Sci._ 305:137-44. January 1953.

Puerto Ricans desire to limit their families; religious and moral objections are not great barriers. But superstitious fears, modesty complexes, marital mistrust, lack of equality in marriage, are important in preventing realization of small families. Existing medical and educational services do little to combat anti-contraceptive prejudices but tend to serve those persons without these prejudices. The mass media of communication co-ordinated with discussion groups, sex education, premarital counselling, and an expansion of present facilities might help in a program of population control. Greater use of nurses and female physicians, among other changes, should aid in dealing with the Puerto Rican population in birth control matters.

1401 Tietze, Christopher. "Human Fertility in Puerto Rico," *Amer. J. Sociol.* 53(1):34-40, 1947.

The population of Puerto Rico has increased from 953,000 in 1899 to 1,869,000 in 1940, and is increasing now at an annual rate of 2.2%. With over 600 inhabitants per square mile, it is one of the most densely populated areas in the world. The gross reproduction ratio and the crude birth rate have remained unchanged since 1899. This has resulted from a decline of marital fertility of about 25%, balanced by an increased frequency of the married state. The "fertility ratio" was used to study differential reproduction by residence and color, that is, the number of children under five per 1,000 women aged 15 to 49. The fertility ratio was lowest in the large city of San Juan, and reached a maximum in the most rural areas. The ratio was higher for the Black than the White population. Puerto Ricans are aware of population pressure in their island, and for the last twelve years a number of contraceptive services have been in operation. Voluntary sterilization is also widely practiced.

1402 Tietze, Crhistopher, *et al.* "A Family Planning Service in Rural Puerto Rico," *Amer. J. Obstet. Gynec.* 81(1): 174-82. January 1961.

A total of 1,097 couples, living in a rural area in Puerto Rico, participated in a program offering a choice from among five methods of contraception -- condoms, diaphragm-and-jelly, foam tablets, jelly and syringe, and suppositories. Of this total, 646 couples received instruction and supplies in their homes and 451 couples had clinic service only. Home visits were found to be moderately successful in encouraging regular use of contraception and highly successful in encouraging its continuation. The pregnancy rate of the participating couples after their first pregnancy and prior to admission to the contraceptive service was 83 per 100 years of exposure. Pregnancy rates during use of the five methods prescribed ranged from 28.3 to 42.3 per 100 years of exposure, with condoms offering significantly greater protection than the other four methods combined. Acceptance, as measured by low rates of change to other methods, was far higher for the condom and the diaphragm than for the other three methods.

1403 Wing, Wilson M., et al. "Birth Control in a Rural Area of Puerto Rico," Eugenics Quart.5:154-61, 1958.

The efficacy of several types of contraceptive methods was tested in an area of approximately 20 square miles, located 25 miles from San Juan, Puerto Rico. The Health Department provided adequate supplies of diaphragms, condoms, suppositories, and contraceptive creams and jellies (to be used either with a diaphragm or injected by syringe). The nurse was prepared to give instructions in the rhythm method to patients having religious objections to mechanical methods, but no request for such instruction was made. A change in method was allowed whenever requested. Age-specific, unplanned pregnancy rates following registration with the clinic were compared with rates among women not practicing contraception prior to registration. For age groups below 35 years, the unplanned pregnancy rate was between 40% and 50% of the level of fertility record prior to use of contraceptives. Reasons for 85 unplanned pregnancies of patients using contraceptive methods include noncooperation of the husband, occasional failure to use the available method, and failure to use method because of fear of pain. Only 9% of unplanned pregnancies were thought to be dependent on incorrect use of the method. The authors conclude that at present the most acceptable contraceptive technique in a rural area of Puerto Rico is the condom. Home visits by a nurse in rural areas provide the most effective way of disseminating birth control education.

1404 Zalduondo, Celestina. "A Family Planning Program Using Volunteers as Health Educators," Amer. J. Public Health 54(2):301-7, 1964.

Owing to various obstacles and limiting factors, the Family Planning Association of Puerto Rico has developed an approach to community action for family planning using volunteers. The various elements in this form of community organization are analyzed.

TRINIDAD AND TOBAGO

Policies on fertility and family size

1405 Rodman, Hyman. "Illegitimacy in the Caribbean Social Structure: A Reconsideration," *Amer. Sociol. Rev.* 31:673-83, 1966.

Discussion centers on the controversy regarding whether members of the lower classes in Caribbean societies consider non-legal marital unions and the resulting illegitimate children to be normative or deviant. Data on 176 respondents from Trinidad indicate that members of the lower strata "stretch" their values so that both marriage and the non-legal marital union are part of their normative system. Four hypotheses are tested and validated: that social class status is inversely related to the normative acceptance of non-legal marital unions; that social class status is inversely related to the value stretch; that lower-class men show more normative acceptance of non-legal marital unions than lower-class women; and that lower-class men stretch their values more than lower-class women.

IV AFRICA
(General)

General population policies

1406 Caldwell, J.C., and Okonjo,C., eds. The Population of Tropical Africa. Longmans, Green and Co., 1968. 455 pp.

Publication of almost the complete proceedings of the First African Population Conference, held at the University of Ibadan in 1966. The demographic situation in tropical Africa is examined through descriptions of data collection systems; estimates of fertility, mortality, and population growth; and discussion of migratory movements, urbanization, and the relations between agricultural techniques and population density. A section on population growth and economic development is concerned with governmental population policies, family planning programs, and population training in African universities.

1407 Karstedt, Oskar. Probleme Afrikanischer Eingeborenenpolitik [Problems of Policy for the African Natives]. Kolonialwissenschaftliche Forschungen, Ergebnisse und Probleme, hrsg. im Auftrage des Reichsforschungsrates und der Deutschen Forschungsgemeinschaft, Band 3. Berlin: E.S. Mittler & Sohn, 1942. vi, 162 pp.

See: pp. 57-89, The land and its problems; and pp. 139-56, Considerations for population policy.

1408 Karstedt, Oskar, and Werder, Peter von. Die Afrikanische Arbeiterfrage [African Labor Problems]. Afrika. Handbuch der Praktischen Kolonialwissenschaften, Band 18. Berlin: Walter de Gruyter und Co., 1941. 261 pp.

The labor problem of Africa is due to low density, slow growth, and health deficiencies. Hence social policy in Africa must include population and medical policies in addition to strictly economic measures.

1409 Native Welfare Fund (F.B.I.). _A Work of Cooperation in Development: Fifteen Years' Operation by the Native Welfare Fund in the Congo, Rwanda and Burundi, 1948-1963._ Brussels, 1964. 199 pp.

Sections include: Assistance to peasant settlements, pp 73-75; The fight against the falling birth-rate, pp. 93-98; The fight against the great endemic diseases, pp 98-109.

1410 Olusanya, P.O. "Implications of Population Growth in Nigeria: Some Lessons from the Mauritian Experience," _Nigerian J. Econ. Soc. Stud._ (Ibadan) 8(2):311-29. July 1966.

A study of the demographic experience of Mauritius for the purpose of deriving useful lessons for Nigeria. Topics: Public health and the incidence of mortality in Mauritius; The influence of declining mortality on fertility; The population problem in Mauritius; The Nigerian demographic scene; Growth prospects and implications. In conclusion, Nigeria must choose between two alternatives -- either suspend its public health programmes in order to retard the decline of mortality and thus prevent an increase in the rate of its population growth or initiate as a matter of urgency a national programme of population control.

1411 Prest, A.R. "Population as a Factor in African Development," _United Africa Company Limited, Statistical and Economic Review_ 30:1-16. September 1965.

Initially, section I takes a quick look at some of the principal ways in which economic theory takes cognizance of population changes, paying particular attention to those most relevant to developing economies. Section II reviews the facts, such as are available, about the current population picture in a number of African countries. Section III builds on the theoretical foundation of the first section and the empirical basis of the second to set out the most important policy issues facing African countries in this area.

Policies on fertility and family size

1412 Akinla, Oladele. "Social Obstetrics in Africa. A Strong Indication for Family Planning," West Africa Med. J. 28(2): 47-49, 1969.

The promotion of maternal and child health is a most important aspect of both Preventive Medicine and Obstetrics, and Family Planning is without doubt an essential component of any complete Maternal and Child Health Service. This is especially so in Africa because children and child-bearing women constitute 70-75% of the total population. It is therefore in the context of the promotion of maternal and child health that Family Planning is being and should continue to be preached and practiced.

1413 Aubin, Pierre. "A Propos des Prestations Familiales dans les Territoires Francais d'Afrique Noire," [Family Allowances in the French Territories of Dark Africa], Population 9(1):51-60. January - March 1954.

A brief description of the family allowance system for native government employees in French West and Equatorial Africa and a discussion of the criticisms of the allowance system. In answer to the critics the author defends the principle of family allowances, but indicates that it was an error not to modify an allowance system which was originally devised for a different cultural environment. Help in kind rather than in cash is advocated because it is better suited to the structure of native society. This would include providing free services, such as medical and maternal, as well as free commodities such as clothing for children.

1414 Caldwell, John C. "Anti-Natal Practice in Tropical Africa." Paper presented at the International Union for the Scientific Study of Population, General Conference, 3-11 September 1969, London.

In tropical Africa as a whole the great majority of the population still lives in villages, and a third are found in francophone areas where the use of modern contraceptive methods is certainly less frequent than in the surveyed anglophone areas. Traditional anti-natal practices are probably still used much more extensively for preventing pregnancies under conditions not socially sanctioned than for reducing marital fertility. Perhaps traditional methods keep the birth rate a little below what it would otherwise have been, an impact which is probably less than that of venereal disease - and perhaps modern contraceptives (which have a very uneven impact) have reduced it a fraction of a point. In tropical Africa as a whole only a fraction of one per cent of tropical African married couples are likely to be currently using modern contraceptives. But there are large differentials in contraceptive use. Such use increases with urbanization, length of education, the development of a governmental family planning program and with various other phenomena all of which are markedly on the increase. A measure of these contrasts is provided by data showing that in the 1963-66 period in Ghana attempts at pregnancy prevention within marriage rose from three per cent among rural population, to eight per cent among all urban population, to 33 per cent among the urban elite, and to 44 per cent among the latter where the wife had received any secondary schooling. The 1960 Census Post-enumeration Survey has in fact shown substantial rural-urban and educational fertility differentials in the country, and intra-urban socio-economic ones certainly also exist, but the differentials in age at marriage undoubtedly provide most of the explanation.

1415 Dow, Thomas E., Jr. "Family Planning: Theoretical Considerations and African Models," J. Marr. Fam. 31(2):252-56. May 1969.

A typology is presented to express some of the theoretical possibilities connected with the rate of adoption of family planning in the developing regions. When all the developing regions of the world are considered according to this typology, tropical Africa shows the fewest signs of breaking away from traditional fertility patterns. Surveys in Ghana, Nigeria, and Kenya to determine people's knowledge, attitudes, and practice regarding family size indicate there is substantial interest in contraception throughout the continent, although this interest is not now associated with effective use.

1416 Dursent, Michel. "A Propos des Prestations Familiales dans les Territoires Francais d'Afrique Noire " [On Family Allowances in the French Territories of Black Africa], La Semaine Med., No. 37, October 30, 1954, pp. 938-40.

Criticisms of the allowances in Africa and of some of the difficulties of the system. A main criticism is that under the present code, the program does not have socially favorable consequences without an effort to adapt to the family structure of each area. Recommendations for improvement are to enhance the efficiency of the program through more stringent rules to govern African officials and through more even enforcement of French laws.

1417 Jones, J.D. Rheinallt. "The Development of Central and Southern Africa: Suggestions for Research and Action on Some of the Problems Common to These Territories," South African J. Sci. 44:75-91, 1948.

The lack of population data, the generally low population, the factors which tend to keep down the fertility rate, etc., are discussed.

1418 Piron, Pierre. "Le Mariage Monogamique et le Statut Familial des Indigenes," [Monogamous Marriage and the Family Law of the Natives], Lovania 8:110-43, 1945-1946.

(Western Africa)

GENERAL

Policies on fertility and family size

1419 Parrinder, E.G.S. "Christian Marriage in French West Africa," Africa 17(4):260-68. October 1947.

Policies of Prostestant missions in regard to native marriages and attitudes toward polygamy, divorce, and remarriage are discussed, as well as the role of education and other suggested measures for reform.

DAHOMEY

Policies on fertility and family size

1420 "Changes in the Family Benefit and Workmen's Compensation Scheme in the Republic of Dahomey," Internat. Labour Rev. 88:522-23, 1964.

Four decrees were issued on 4 March 1963, dealing with the raising of contributions to the family benefit scheme, a reduction in the rate of certain family benefits, new arrangements for the payment of the maternity leave allowance, and the fixing of new levels for the working capital funds to be set up for the family benefit branch. Birth grants payable to women workers and the wives of workers for their first three children are reduced from 12,000 to 6,000 C.F.A. francs for the first child and from 6,000 to 3,000 C.F.A. francs for each of the next two children.

GHANA

General population policies

1421 Graft-Johnson, K.T. de. "Population Growth Estimates and the Seven-Year Plan," Econ. Bull. of Ghana 9(2):27-29, 1965.

Discusses quantitative estimates of human resources of Ghana on the basis of the 1948 and 1960 censuses projected to 1970 and their relevance to arguments for a restrictive national population policy as a stimulus for economic development. Discussion also of desirable policy on urbanization.

Policies on fertility and family size

1422 Ollennu, N.A. The Law of Testate and Intestate Succession in Ghana. London: Sweet and Maxwell, 1966. xxv, 332 pp.

The personal law of Ghana is an amalgam emanating from two sources: introduced law, principally English law, and indigeneous law, the customary law. The process of development of the two systems form the subject of Part I of the book. Part II deals with the principles of customary law which regulate intestacy. It brings out clearly the legal obligations of a man, which devolve upon his successor, namely, his obligations to maintain and educate his child, and to maintain and house his wife, in each case according to his station in life.

IVORY COAST

Policies on fertility and family size

1423 Ivory Coast. "Public Health and Population," Internat. Digest Health Legis. 13(1):122, 1962; 16:363-65, 1965; 17:555, 1966.

Decrees No. 60 - 27 of 12 January 1960, No. 64 - 43 of 9 January 1964, and No. 65 - 329 of 28 September 1965 lay down the organization of the central administration of the Ministry of Public Health and Population. The sub-directorate of population is one of the several units concerned with mother and child welfare.

NIGER

Policies on fertility and family size

1424 Niger. "National Service for Mother and Child Welfare," Internat. Digest Health Legis. 18:156, 1967.

Decree No. 64/96/MS of 2 May 1964 establishes the National Service for Mother and Child Welfare. The Service, under the authority of the Director of Public Health, is located in the Ministry of Health. It is responsible, *inter alia*, for the organization and co-ordination, at the national level, of mother and child welfare, for liaison between the centers for mother and child welfare, the Directorate of Health and international organizations, such as UNESCO, and for producing the statistical data needed both by national and international agencies.

NIGERIA

Policies on fertility and family size

Coker, G.B.A. Family Property Among the Yorubas. London: Sweet and Maxwell, Let., 1958. 314 pp.

1425 This book constitutes a survey of the rules and principles of native laws and customs pertaining to family property in Nigeria, with special reference to those of the Yorubas. Included are sections on the impact of English law on native laws and customs, the legal conception of family property, the incidents of family property, special kinds of family property, and the devolution of such property. Native jurisprudence does not recognize individual ownership of land, such ownership as is acknowledged being only vested in the family. Once a woman is married, she becomes a part of her husband's family, and there are few cases of divorce. Marriage attaches the woman more to the husband's family than to the husband himself, since after her husband's death the woman, classified as immovable family property, marries her brother-in-law. Primary native law and custom are susceptible to changing conditions, but the author contends that statutory provisions tend to divest cultures of the incidents of such law and custom. Within available limits, a great deal of modernization is possible without abandoning the fundamental and cultural nature of native property law. Decisions of the courts are recorded in regard to the Yorubas, but dicta in various judgments emphasize the universality of the existence and practice of the Yoruba property holding system.

1426 Okoro, Nwakamma. The Customary Laws of Succession in Eastern Nigeria and the Statutory and Judicial Rules Governing Their Application. London: Sweet and Maxwell, 1966. xv, 249 pp.

This book constitutes the first comprehensive study of contemporary customary laws of succession in Eastern Nigeria. The subject is treated from a lawyer's point of view, since not only are the customary laws discussed but also the impact of legislations and judicial decisions on them. The author begins with a brief ethnographic account of the peoples of Eastern Nigeria and then outlines the functions of property and succession laws in the societies and the people's attitude toward succession disputes, with a classification of their customary laws of succession. There follows an examination of the categories of inheritable property (the estate); the different kinds of individual and group property; the rules of administration of estates; and the rules of testate and intestate succession in the patrilineal, bilineal and matrilineal societies. The dualism of laws in Eastern Nigeria, the general (English) and customary laws, has occasioned, through statutory and judicial rules, conflicts in the choice of the applicable law of succession disputes. These conflicts are analyzed, and the methods under the general law by which the application of customary laws of succession may be excluded or varied are considered. The author concludes with an emphasis on the need for succession law reform in Eastern Nigeria.

1427 Wright, R.D. "A Family Planning Programme for Nigeria," West African Med. J. 17(6):227-29. December 1968.

The Family Planning Council of Nigeria was established in 1963 as a voluntary organization by the Lagos Medical Officer of Health. A KAP survey made in Lagos in 1964 showed the population to be strongly in favor of family planning. The author believes that a nation-wide programme will be possible only through the training of large numbers of nurses, midwives, and paramedical auxiliaries together with a speed-up in the delivery of services. Under the leadership and financing of the Family Planning Council of Nigeria and with the technical assistance of the medical schools, service programmes will be established or expanded in the larger cities. When the stage is reached where rural services are available, chief reliance must inevitably be on midwives and nurses. Another major contribution to a nation-wide family planning program would be the provision of fellowships to doctors and nurses for training in family planning techniques and organization.

SENEGAL

Policies on fertility and family size

1428 Senegal. "Organization of Maternal and Child Welfare," Internat. Digest Health Legis. 15:821-22, 1964.

Decree No. 60 - 247 M.S.A.S. of 13 July 1960 establishes a Department of Maternal and Child Welfare. Among its duties is the safeguarding of the health of the mother during pregnancy.

1429 Senegal. "Reorganization of the Public Health Service of Senegal," Internat. Digest Health Legis. 15:821, 1964.

Decree No. 60 - 107 M.S.A.S. of 9 March 1960 reorganizes the Public Health Service. One of its branches, the Directorate of Public Health, has four divisions, one of which is concerned with demography and population.

TOGO

Policies on fertility and family size

1430 "New Family Benefit Scheme for Civil Servants in Togo," Internat. Labour Rev. 86:502-3, 1963.

By Decree No. 61 - 27 of 16 March 1961 the Togo Government instituted a new scheme of family benefit which included a grant for setting up the home, child allowances, "early years" grants, and a "one-wage" allowance. The child allowance is payable for each child (legitimate, recognized or adopted) up to a maximum of six. The allowance is 24,000 local francs a year for each child until the age of 15 years or to the ages of 17 years or 20 years if an apprentice or in school.

UPPER VOLTA

Policies on fertility and family size

1431 "Changes in Family Allowances in Upper Volta," Internat. Labour Rev. 96:637. December 1967.

Decrees No. 67 - 16 and No. 67 - 57 Pres. DTMO of 11 March 1967 decreases some benefits under the family allowance scheme because of the disturbing financial situation in this branch of social security. The decree abolishes the worker's home allowance, that is the birth allowance granted for each of the worker's first three children by his first wife. Maternity allowance, payable throughout the nine months of pregnancy, is reduced from 6,300 francs to 3,150 francs. Six children is now the limit in qualifying for family allowances. Limits in other African countries are similar: six children in Morocco, four children in Tunisia, and six children in Toga in the case of polygamous families. The grant paid during maternity leave is substantially increased.

1432 Upper Volta. "Duties and Organization of the Ministry of Public Health and Population," Internat. Digest Health Legis. 18:692-93, 1967.

Decree No. 277 PRES. SP.P. of 6 August 1966 lays down the organization of the Ministry. One branch, the General Directorate of Public Health, Population and Social Affairs, is concerned with maternal health as well as other matters.

(Eastern Africa)

GENERAL

General population policies

1433 Penrose, Edith T. "A Great African Project," Scientific Monthly 66(4):332-426. April 1948.

A description of the British Government's plans for the mechanized production of ground nuts in Tanganyika, Northern Rhodesia and Kenya. The advantages of the project are pointed out, among these being the possibility of improving living conditions and relieving population pressure.

Policies on fertility and family size

1434 "Family Planning in East Africa," East African Med. J. 44:447. October 1967.

Family planning programs in East Africa have emphasized use of the IUD, and the effectiveness and problems of this contraceptive method are discussed. The feasibility of use of "the pill" as an alternative method for national programs is examined, and the author contends that a pilot study to investigate large scale distribution of the pill for East Africa would seem to be indicated.

1435 Molnos, Angela. Attitudes Towards Family Planning in East Africa. Ifo-Institut fur Wirtschaftsforschung, Afrika-Studien Nr. 26. Munich: Weltforum Verlag, 1968. 414 pp.

Analysis of a survey of 2,648 boys and girls aged 10-22 in 43 schools in Kenya, Tanganyika, and Uganda, with discussion of the population problem and the traditional and current position of women in East Africa, and suggestions for a psychological approach to family planning promotion. Major findings: The majority of the respondents react positively to the idea of having two or three children. The acceptance of the small family is mainly motivated by the fact that the parents would be able to educate all their children. Whereas the 'naturally' small family is easily accepted, there are specific resistances to a deliberate planning of births. These resistances are rooted in the traditional social structure and the concomitant, still operating religious beliefs. Furthermore, there is a widespread notion of contraceptives sterilizing their users. The resistance to family planning is, however, significantly less frequent among female respondents than male respondents. The higher the educational level of the respondents the more of them show positive attitudes towards family planning. There are significant differences between the attitudes of respondents coming from different tribes.

KENYA

General population policies

1436 British Medical Association, Council of the Kenya Branch. "The Case for the Appointment of a Royal Commission on Health and Population in His Majesty's Dependencies in Africa," East African Medical Journal 25(1):29-73. January 1948.

The rapidly increasing population of East Africa necessitates the promotion of measures for improving the health and welfare of the people. The memorandum is divided into a prefatory note and two parts. Part I contains the proposal for a Royal Commission, and a discussion of the modern conception of health. Part II contains a section on planning.

Policies on fertility and family size

1437 Eraj, Y.A. "The Unplanned Pregnancy," East Africa Med. J. 43:298-ff., 1966.

Kenya statistics for 1964 indicate that the number of deaths resulting from abortion was almost half that of deaths from malaria. The author feels that the medical profession must accept that unplanned pregnancies are a public health hazard and should be accepted and treated as any other social disease.

1438 Kenya. Ministry of Economic Planning and Development. Family Planning in Kenya. A Report Submitted to the Government of the Republic of Kenya by an Advisory Mission of the Population Council of the United States of America. [Nairobi, 1966.] iv, 45 pp.

Outlines the rationale and scope of a government-sponsored program with recommendations concerning organization, methods, evaluation, and financing.

MADAGASCAR

General population policies

1439 Bastian, Georges,"Les Consequences Sociales et Economiques de l'Evolution Démographique " [The Social and Economic Consequences of Demographic Trends]. Bulletin de Madagascar 145:515-19. June 1958.

Notes on problems of governmental planning for the rapidly increasing and predominantly youthful population of Madagascar.

MAURITIUS

General population policies

1440 Titmuss, Richard M., and Abel-Smith, Brian, Social Policies and Population Growth in Mauritius. Report to the Governor. Sessional Paper No. 6 of 1960. London: Methuen, 1961. xviii, 308 pp.

Recommendations are designed actively to assist and not retard the processes of economic growth; to spend less rather than more on public assistance; to prevent rather than treat ill-health; to use more efficiently and more fully the scarce and precious social resources and skills of the community, and, ultimately, to bring about, by calling on the self-discipline of all parents, a more purposeful and dignified family life. For Mauritius to set its governance in this direction it is necessary to accept realistically the facts of population. These are the facts which dominate the present economic situation. Attempts in many of the recommendations and through a combination of social incentives and disincentives to propose measures for slowing down the rate of population growth. As a condition of survival family control must come; but it cannot be imposed. It has to be assisted and given the freedom to develop. For this to happen money must first be spent on providing the necessary information and facilities; on staffing and expanding the health and welfare services through which these facilities may be utilised; and on other essential measures described in this Report. The need for population control is one justification for further public expenditure on social welfare.

RWANDA

General population policies

1441 Bagaragaza, Thadee, Le Plan Rwandais Preparera l'Independance Economique [The Rwanda Plan will Prepare for Economic Independence]. Rwanda Carrefour d'Afrique 66-67:16-21. May-June 1967.

The author is Minister of International Cooperation and Planning. In presenting plans for the next five years, he proposes to meet pressure of population on resources by economic investment and education, and by organizing emigration.

UGANDA

General population policies

1442 Worthington, Edgar G. A Development Plan for Uganda. (With a forword by His Excellency the Governor of Uganda). Entebbe, 1947. xii, 112 pp.

There are tragic lessons to be learned from other parts of the world which have already passed through the stage of development which we see today in Uganda. There were a few far-seeing men in these countries half a century ago who appreciated the biological and political problems which were about to develop, but only now are strenuous efforts being made to redress the balance by concentrating the resources of modern science to bear on the fundamental problem of balance between production and population. The sequence of events which has taken place in India and Egypt must be avoided at all costs in East Africa.

Policies on fertility and family size

1443 Uganda Council of Women. Laws About Marriage in Uganda. Prepared by a Sub-Committee. Kampala, 1961. 19 pp.

The Women's Council of Uganda has attempted a codification of laws on marriage in Uganda. Part I defines the several types of marriage which are possible and Part II defines acts, such as bigamy, which are violations of the marriage rules. The other two parts indicate how divorces may be obtained and the financial arrangements which are possible given breakdown of a marriage.

ZAMBIA

Policies on fertility and family size

1444 Colson, Elizabeth. Marriage and the Family Among the Plateau Tonga of Northern Rhodesia. Manchester: Manchester University Press, 1967. xvi, 379 pp.

The Tonga do not ordinarily seek to justify the importance that they give to fertility and accept it as an ultimate value which is not to be questioned. It is a primary value, and one which takes precedence when it comes in conflict with other values which are otherwise stressed. Thus a man's rights in his wife are subordinated to her right to fertility. The emphasis is in line with the matrilineal nature of the society, the subsistence level of the economy based on agriculture, and the assumption that land is free and plentiful.

(Northern Africa)

ALGERIA

General population policies

1445 "Algérie, Natalité et Politique " [Algeria, Fertility and Policy]. L'Afrique et L'Asie 2:57-63, 1958.

Recommends: an increase in French education especially for women who should develop a sense of being equal to men; and a rise in the standard of living through full employment, improvement of the economy and allowances. But allowances would be contingent upon legal marriage, the mother being 18 years or older at the time of marriage, and the continuation of children in school. Divorced women would be eligible. Because of the disproportion of Muslims to Frenchmen, the measures might serve to lessen Muslim fertility.

1446 Algiers, Secrétariat Social. L'Algérie Surpeuplée. Orientations pour une Politique de Population [Overpopulated Algeria. Points to be Considered in Forming Population Policy]. Algiers: Editions du Secrétariat Social d'Alger, 1958. 319 pp.

Outline of a program for birth limitation by natural method supplemented by a program of family assistance and industrial development.

Policies on fertility and family size

1447 Algeria. Direction Genérale du Plan et des Etudes Economiques. La Régulation des Naissances: Opinions et Attitudes des Couples Algériens [Birth Control: Opinions and Attitudes of Algerian Couples]. Association Algérienne pour la Recherche Démographique, Economique et Sociale, 1968. 128 pp.

A report of findings from a national KAP survey conducted in Algeria 1966-67, with discussion of the implication of these findings for general economic development of Algeria. The first section presents survey results. Just over half of the urban husbands and wives interviewed and just under half of the rural husbands and wives state that they do not want any more children. Urban and rural husbands have lower average ideal numbers of children than their wives. Within the context of the difficulties of defining and then measuring attitudes, the report shows that about half of the urban couples and about one-third of the rural husbands and wives approve of family planning for both spacing and limitation, and another one-fifth to one-third approve of family planning for spacing only. Knowledge of contraceptive methods is fairly limited (56 per cent of the urban wives and 84 per cent of the rural wives do not know any contraceptive method), but considerable interest in learning more about contraception is expressed. Other findings and cross-tabulations by income, parity, and so on, are presented, interspersed with several illustrative quotes from respondents. A second section includes three chapters: the relationships between the economy and demographic characteristics in Algeria, Islam and contraception, and practical implications for a family planning program. Annexes include information on the sample design and field procedures and sets of statistical tables.

1448 Algeria. "Interruption of Pregnancy," Internat. Digest Health Legis. 18:519-20, 1967.

Ordinance No. 65 - 156 of 8 June 1966 amends the Penal Code to provide penalties for abortion except where it is carried to save the life of the mother.

1449 Algeria. "Public Health and Population," Internat. Digest Health Legis. 18:519, 1967.

Decree No. 66 - 68 of 4 April 1966 provides for the reorganization of the external services of the Ministry of Public Health. A departmental directorate of public health and population is established at the chief town of every department.

1450 France. Institut National d'Etudes Démographiques. "La Politique de Sécurité Sociale en Algérie," [Social Security in Algeria], Population 7(1):17-26. January - March 1952.

Including family allowances.

MOROCCO

Policies on fertility and family size

1451 "Enquête d'Opinion sur la Planification Familiale au Maroc (1966)," [Survey of Opinion on Family Planning in Morocco (1966)], Bull. Economique et Social du Maroc 29:95-149. January - June 1967.

Surveys 4,049 couples in nine large villages in Morocco who differ in housing quality. The ideal number of children for women is rarely more than four. About 60 per cent of them are in favor of practicing contraception and desire more information which will assist them in this. The men are more reticent; about a third favor family planning and they are less definite about the ideal number of children. In the urban milieu there is great receptivity to family planning. These matters are particularly important because the population of Morocco, which increased from 6,600,000 in 1935 to 12,323,000 in 1967, is one of the world's most rapidly growing.

1452 Morocco. "Interruption of Pregnancy," Internat. Digest Health Legis. 19:217, 1968.

Crown Decree No. 181 - 66 of 1 July 1967 embodies a law to amend the Penal Code and to repeal the Dahiv of 10 July 1939. Abortion shall not be punished when it is necessary to safeguard the health of the mother.

SUDAN

Policies on fertility and family size

1453 Farran, C. *Matrimonial Laws of the Sudan*. London: Butterworths, 1963. 325 pp.

This book attempts to ascertain and to some extent to evaluate the matrimonial law of the Sudan as it existed in 1962. The main sections of the book are (1) polygamy and the law; (2) "unmixed" marriages, Mohammedan or pagan; (3) mixed marriages, internally and internationally; and (4) residuary. An interesting custom is that a man may continue to be married and be provided with male issue after his death. A younger brother may marry a woman in the name of a brother who died too young to be married. Woman-woman marriage is provided for in the traditions of the tribes; a barren woman-husband may marry another woman-wife and the children of the wife are in law the children of the woman-husband. Divorce rules vary widely among the tribes ranging from a unilateral act of the husband to divorce by agreement to the wife being able to initiate divorce proceedings. Some interesting results of the co-existence of laws are noted. Each tribal area has its own laws on legitimacy. In certain legal systems, a child born a bastard, may gain legitimate status through subsequent events of others. Some of the findings of this study are applicable to areas of Africa beyond the Sudan. The reason is, that two vital areas meet in the Sudan: the Arab North, dominant politically and numerically, looks to Cairo (and to some extent to Mecca); and the Negro South feels at one with such countries as Uganda and the Congo. In addition to legal contributions from these sources, the Sudan has also been left with the legal ideas and procedures of the departed British colonialists. Further, Greeks and Levantines came to the Sudan to trade, missionaries to proselytize, each adding their own complexity to the Sudanese scene, and to the Sudan legal system. The Sudan therefore serves as a useful specimen of African legal geography with regard to matrimonial and other rules.

TUNISIA

Policies on fertility and family size

1454 Gallagher, C.F. Family Planning in Tunisia. (North Africa Series) American Universities Field Staff Reports Service: 12(2), December 1966. 13 pp.

The appearance of serious economic planning in Tunisia at the beginning of this decade underlined the need to control the oncoming demographic wave which threatened developmental goals. The Government scheduled a preliminary and experimental National Family Planning Program from 1964-66, and began a full-scale National Family Planning Campaign in the early summer of 1966. The author discusses the very early history of Tunisian family planning, the results of the two year experimental program, and the change in official attitudes toward birth control. This change stemmed from a speech made by the President of Tunisia in August of 1966, in which the entire governmental policy of birth control was questionned and measures to keep the birth rate from declining further through the favoring of marriage and the setting-up of families were stressed. The speech, which threatened the future of birth control efforts in the country, is explained as a combination of misinformation, external and internal political pressures, and a concern with strengthening the moral content of national orientation. The author concludes with a summary of the basic questions raised by the above about the limits of personal power and arbitrary, off-the-cuff decision-making.

1455 "Tunisie: Deux Annees de Plan Familial " [Tunisia: Two Years of Family Planning], Popul. 22(4):757-60, 1967.

In 1965 and 1966 an experimental program in family planning was introduced in twelve centers of Tunisia, as diverse as Tunis, Makhtar, and Sfax. The diffusion of family planning is found to depend on the organization of the center. For example, the district centers at Kef and Beja provide sterilization operations a little more regularly than the remainder of Tunisia. The characteristics of contraceptors are noted by age, number of offspring, and occupation of the husband. The ideal number of children desired is 3.6 for women less than 25 years of age, 4.0 for women 25-34 years of age, and 4.3 for women over 35 years of age. Ideal number is often expressed as an even rather than an odd number. With regard to spacing, the majority of women favor an interval of five or more years.

1456 Tunisia. "Interruption of Pregnancy," Internat. Digest Health Legis. 17:406, 1966.

Law No. 65 - 24 of 1 July 1965 amends the Penal Code to permit abortion during the first three months and when the parents have at least five living children. Abortion is also permitted when the health of the mother is endangered by the continuation of pregnancy. Abortions must be performed in an authorized clinic or hospital by a physician.

1457 Tunisia. "Prostitution," Internat. Digest Health Legis. 2:452, 1950-51.

Decree of 26 May 1949 strengthens measures to suppress procuring.

1458 Vallin, Jacques. "Planning Familial et Perspective de Population en Tunisie 1966-1975 " [Family Planning and Population Projection in Tunisia, 1966-1975], Tunisienne de Sciences Sociales 5:71-88. January 1968.

Presents projections of total population based on the 1966 census total and the age structure of the 1956 census subjected to alternative hypotheses of mortality and fertility rates varying with levels of intensity of effort in the family planning program.

1459 Vallin, Jacques. "Le Programme Tunisien de Planning Familial," [The Tunisian Program of Family Planning], Servir, Revue Tunisienne du Service Public (5):18-31, 1er semestre, 1969.

A review of Tunisian family planning program experiences, beginning with the experimental phase (1964-1966), and the 1964 KAP survey. This survey shows that 72 per cent of the women aged 30 to 39 do not want any more children. The experimental period produced encouraging results, with 19,770 women accepting IUDs. The national program (mid-1966 to January 1968) saw a slight downturn in results despite an extension in services and areas covered. Some of the downturn may be ascribed to a 1966 pro-natalist speech by President Bourguiba. A revived national program began in January 1968 with the creation of an official Department of Family

Planning. This Direction incorporates administration, training, communications, and statistics sections, which continued to grow and develop in 1968 and 1969. The statistics for 1967 and 1968 do not show increased acceptance of IUDs, but do indicate some increase in the use of pills and increases in female sterilizations (2,438 in 1968) and in social abortions (2,211 in 1968).

1460 Vallin, J., et al. "L'Efficacité de la Contraception Intrauterine dans le Gouvernorat du Kef (Tunisie)," [Effectiveness of Intrauterine Contraception in the District of Kef (Tunisia)], Tunisie Medicale 46:121-31. March - April 1968.

A follow-up study in 1966 of 2,079 women, about half of the total number who had received a first insertion. Data on age of women, number of living children, and retention rates during the first 20 months.

1461 Vallin, Jacques, and Lapham, Robert. "Place du Planning Familial dans L'Evolution Récent de la Natalité en Tunisie" [Place of Family Planning in the Recent Trend in Fertility in Tunisia], Revue Tunisienne de Sciences Sociales 6(17-18): 379-413. June - September 1969.

A paper originally presented at the North African Demographic Colloquium held in Tunis in January 1969, showing trends in Tunisian fertility during the 1960's and discussing possible reasons for fluctuations and for the apparent general decline in the crude birth rate and the general fertility rate. The effects of the marriage-age law of 1964 on marriages in 1963 and 1964 and births in subsequent years are reviewed. The possible effects of contraceptive use on fertility are presented in a context of Tunisian family planning program accomplishments through late 1968, with estimations then made of numbers of births possibly averted by family planning (7,155 in 1968 and 11,477 in 1969, the latter figure representing about five per cent of the expected births in that year).

UNITED ARAB REPUBLIC

General population policies

1462 Al-Khashab, Ahmad. [Population and Social Planning]. Cairo, 1958. 238 pp.

1463 Cleland, W. Wendell. "A Population Plan for Egypt," Milbank Memorial Fund Quart. 22(4):409-23, 1944.

Because of Egypt's rapidly increasing population, poverty and low standard of living, the author suggests that steps be taken to increase and conserve the national wealth; to plan for emigration and to reduce the birth rate through education; raising the standard of living;and, if necessary, legislation designed to restrict propagation of the unfit, limit free social services and raise the age of first marriage.

1464 El-Kammash, Magdi M. Economic Development and Planning in Egypt. Praeger Special Studies in International Economics and Development. New York: Frederick A. Praeger, 1968. xxvi, 409 pp.

Part 2. Some aspects of development of the Egyptian economy, includes chapters: Demographic change; Investment in human resources [with section, Family Planning in Egypt]. Appendixes include note, The implication of Islamic law on population control.

1465 Garzouzi, Eva, Old Ills and New Remedies in Egypt; a Comprehensive Review of the Different Measures Adopted in Recent Years to Deal with the Problems Resulting from Over-Population. Cairo: Dar al Maaref, 1958. 159 pp.

1466 Heller, Peter B. "Demographic Aspects of Development in Contemporary Egypt: An Integrated Study," Dissertation Abstr. 25: 676, 1964-65. Abstract of Ph.D. Thesis, New York University, 1963.

While the previous Farouk governments, dominated by wealthy landowners, were as disinterested in the population problem as in the related mass welfare, the Revolutionary regime has reacted on all fronts. Within a highly centralized, socialized, and secularized framework, the government has instituted far-reaching agrarian policies, five-year development plans, and others for social justice and the general upgrading of the masses. Recently, however, the government, judging these measures to be insufficient, publicly endorsed family planning in order to deliver on its promise of an entirely welfare society for Egyptians. But for essentially the same reasons that have kept the birth rate high, great difficulty is expected in popularizing the birth control movement in the tradition-bound villages, even though the approval of the religion has been secured and cheap and simple methods are available. Yet, there is enough hope in complementary economic, social and especially technical measures to warrant the hypothesis, upheld in this paper, that the worst manifestations of the long-dreaded population explosion will not materialize. This is especially so in the light of the new cult of progress and the desire for self-improvement now apparent.

1467 Nassif, E. "L'Egypte Est-elle Surpeuplée?" [Is Egypt Overpopulated?], Population 5(3):513-32. July-Sept. 1950.

Rapid growth of population is related to agricultural progress since 1921 and future possibilities. The author indicates the demographic policy to be followed in order to lead to an optimum population distribution. He estimates that Egypt is still far from a state of absolute overpopulation, that the standard of living of its inhabitants can be improved, and that it is by no means necessary to encourage the prevention of births.

Policies on fertility and family size

1468 Bardis, Panos D. "Contraception in Ancient Egypt," Indian J. History Med. 12(2):1-3. December 1967.

The ancient Egyptians developed many methods of birth control. As among the Greeks and Romans, most of these formulas involved only the female. The chief contraceptive methods were: (1) ovariotomy; (2) prolonged lactation; (3) sprinkling of the female sex organs with a mixture of a mucilaginous solution and a certain other substance; (4) Kahun Papyrus prescription No. 22 - honey plus natron, the former tending to diminish sperm motility; (5) Kahun prescription No. 21 - crocodile's dung plus a fermented mucilaginous solution (mechanically rather successful, but chemically of doubtful value); (6) fumigation of the womb by means of the seed of a certain grain; and (7) medicated lint tampons, which seem to have influenced the Hebrews' mokh, or "spongy substance."

1469 Bardis, Panos D. "Incest in Ancient Egypt," Indian J. History Med. 12(2)14-20. December 1967.

Ancient Egypt's limited kinship terminology weakens the available evidence regarding incest in Pharaonic times (up to 330 BC). It appears, however, that the Pharaohs did tend to marry their sisters (not their daughters), while brother-sister unions among the common people were rare. In Hellenistic times (330-30 BC), many Ptolemies married their sisters, but the evidence concerning the commoners is inconclusive. During the Roman period (30 BC - 392 AD), incestuous marriages involving brothers and sisters were relatively popular among the masses. Four main theories have been formulated about the origin of Egyptian incest: (1) religious reasons, such as the Osiris-Isis union; (2) emphasis on the purity of the dynastic blood and the succession to the throne; (3) brother-sister marriages to facilitate the transition from matriliny to patriliny; and (4) property continuity. Seven more theories have dealt with the origin of incest taboo. There is no definite evidence that Egyptian incest caused biological defects.

1470 Bardis, Panos D. "Marriage and Family Customs in Ancient Egypt: An Interdisciplinary Study," Soc. Sci. 42(2):104-19. April 1967.

This study deals with circumcision, incest, contraception, ethics, and sex morals in ancient Egypt. The theories explaining the origin of incest in Egypt have stressed religion, the purity of the dynastic blood, the transition to patriliny, and property continuity, which probably is the most scientific explanation. This practice does not seem to have resulted in undesirable biological traits. The main contraceptive techniques were ovariotomy, prolonged lactation, and various rather magical methods involving honey, natron, crocodile's dung, certain grains, lint tampons, acacia tips, colocynth, and dates. The ethical system of ancient Egypt emphasized charity, benevolence, prudence, chastity, social justice, clemency, the love of intellectual pursuits, and the morality of thought and desire. The Book of the Dead contains numerous passages on rewards and punishments. In reality, however, many forms of sexual liberalism were comparatively prevalent in ancient Egypt, including in its temples and tombs.

1471 Egypt. "Closing of Licensed Brothels," Internat. Digest Health Legis. 2, 1950-51.

Proclamation No. 76 of 20 February 1949 requires the closing of all brothels within two months and the prohibition of new ones. Penalties are to be imposed on proprietors and women in such places.

1472 El-Nomrossey, Malik M. "L'Effet des Pilules Contraceptives sur les Femmes en Age d'Etre Fécondables et le Nombre de Leurs Enfants - Une Etude de la Fécondité à Al-Amria " [The Effect of Contraceptive Pills on the Number of Children among Women of Reproductive Age], Egyptian Popul. Fam. Planning Rev. 1(2), December 1968.

1473 Shanawany, Haifaa Abd el Salam. "Family Planning: An Equilibrium Response to Demographic Conditions in the United Arab Republic (Egypt)," Dissertation Abstr. 28A: 3783, 1967-68. Abstract of Ph.D. Thesis, Cornell University, 1967.

The United Arab Republic is presently experiencing an accelerating population growth. Family planning was sought as a solution to demographic conditions, since the country is poor in natural resources, recent technology applied in industry and agriculture is labor saving, and no prospective migration outlet is visualized. Adoption of a family planning policy requires legitimization from the power structure. In the U.A.R. contending forces in politics have traditionally been secular and religious. Study of the opinions of government officials, army officers, members of the National Assembly, intellectuals, and religious leaders, along with content analysis of President Nasser's speeches, show the process of decision making which can delay or precipitate the development of a population control policy. Two years after the adoption of a population control policy, a survey was carried out in 1964 in three Egyptian villages varying in size and type of social and medical services provided. The first and smallest village lacks governmental services, the second has a Health Centre, and the third and largest village is served by a Combined Unit Centre, providing integrated services. For this reason it was expected that the latter village would differ from the others. On reproductive behavior while the villages are similar on most reproductive variables, the third village had the fewest number of live births, a function of greater marital instability rather than of birth control or spacing. On the other hand it ranked highest on responsiveness to birth control even when holding constant structural individual characteristics. Differences in responsiveness might have important implications for policy making in the U.A.R. as to whether communities which already have coordinated services should be accorded priority in the family planning program.

1474 Tomiche, Nada. "En Egypte, Le Gouvernement Devant le Problème Démographique " [The Egyptian Government Faces the Population Problem], Orient No. 3, July 1957. pp. 106-19.

Description of voluntary measures (birth-control propaganda and clinics, raising of age at marriage, marriage counseling, restriction of polygamy and divorce) initiated by official bodies since 1955 and of recommended legal changes. Analysis of response by religious authorities, bourgeoisie, general public. Comparison with policies in China and Iraq.

(Middle Africa)

GENERAL

General population policies

1475 Institut Interafricain du Travail. "Prestations Familiales et Prévoyance Sociale. Colloque des Directeurs des Caisses d'Afrique Equatoriale (Brazzaville 23-25 Juillet 1962)," [Family Allowances and State Insurance. Meeting of the Directors of the Funds for Equatorial Africa (Brazzaville, July 23-25, 1962)]. Bull. de l'Institut Interafricain du Travail 10(1):42-52. February 1963.

Discussion of reciprocity among the states as regards rights, health and social measures, and staff training.

ANGOLA

General population policies

1476 Mendes Correia, A.A. Politica da Populacao nas Colonias [Population Policy in the Colonies]. Sociedade de Geografia da Lisboa. Boletim, Serie 63, Nos. 7, 8.

Colonial policy in Angola, particularly with regard to migration, infant mortality and malnutrition.

CAMEROON

Policies on fertility and family size

1477 Cameroon. "Public Health and Population," Internat. Digest Health Legis. 18:548-49, 1967.

Decree No. 65 - DF - 238 of 4 June 1965 concerns the organization of the Office of the Commissioner General for Public Health and Population. Maternal health is a primary concern. The Office of the Commissioner comprises: (a) the Central Services (the Department of Public Health, the Social Welfare and Population Service and the Sub-Department of Administrative and Financial Affairs); and (b) the External Services (central establishments and territorial establishments). The Social Welfare and Population Service, which is responsible for health and social education, social welfare, the control of social welfare activities, demographic matters, and matters concerning the status of the family, consists of five bureaus (Health and Social Education Bureau, Social Centres Bureau, Social Welfare and Family Bureau, Demographic Bureau, and Community Development and Town Planning Bureau).

CONGO

General population policies

1478 Belgium, Ministere des Colonies. Plan Décennal pour le Développement Economique et Social du Congo Belge [Decennial Plan for the Economic and Social Development of the Belgian Congo]. Brussels: Les Editions de Visscher, 1949. 2 vols. 601 pp.

Statistics on population, health and education are given in tables appended to Volume II.

1479 France, Direction de la Documentation, and Institut National de la Statistique et des Etudes Economiques. Le Plan Développement Economique et Social du Congo Belge [The Ten-Year Plan for the Economic and Social Development of the Belgian Congo]. La Documentation Francaise, Notes et Etudes Documentaires, No. 1479; Série Economique et Financière, 85; Série Outre-Mer, 36. May 11, 1951. 51 pp.

Part I, Section I: The population and its needs.

1480 Goris, Jan-Albert. "Belgian Action in the Congo," Annals of the Amer. Acad. Pol. Soc. Sciences 270: 126-32. July 1950.

Discusses demographic factors and the Belgian policy of dealing with polygamy, migration and education of women.

1481 International Labour Office. "The Conditions of Indigenous Workers in the Belgian Congo in 1944," International Labour Review 53(5-6):340-48. May-June, 1946.

Analysis of an official report on the administration of the Belgian Congo in 1944. Contains material on the manpower situation, migration of indigenous workers, growth of the indigenous population, social problems, and unrest among the natives. The final section considers recent legislation in regard to the labor situation, migration, and social problems.

1482 Vermeulen, V. Deficiences et Dangers de Notre Politique Indigène, Comment y Remédier [Deficiencies and Dangers of Our Policy for the Indigenous Population and How to Remedy Them]. Brussels, 1953. 108 pp.

General conclusions for avoiding a disaster in the case of the Black population of the Belgian Congo.

Policies on fertility and family size

1483 Didier, H. "Les Allocations Familiales au Congo Belge " [Family Allowances in the Belgian Congo], Nouvelle Rev. Francaise d'Outre-Mer 73-75. February 1955.

1484 Sohier, A. Traite Elémentaire de Droit Coutumier du Congo Belge [Basic Characteristics of Common Law in the Belgian Congo]. Bruxelles: Maison Ferdinand Larcier, 1949. 221 pp.

About a quarter of the book is devoted to a study of native common law in regard to marriage and divorce.

1485 Van Wing, J. "La Polygamie au Congo Belge " [Polygamy in the Belgian Congo], Africa 17(2):93-102. April 1947.

Extent and cause of polygamy, and attitude of the Government toward it. While the number of wives held by polygamists has been reduced in the majority of tribes, the number of polygamist husbands has increased. The statistics are derived from the record of supplementary taxes paid on wives beyond the first one. Among the causes of polygamy among the Bantu are: the desire to extend one's personality and to enjoy the honour which comes to the powerful man who multiplies his life through his dependents; sexual needs opposed by certain customs and taboos; the economic advantages offered by the investment of capital in women; the use of women as political links between great chiefs and their vassals; and the lack of other purchasable goods. While the colonial government favors the progressive abandonment of polygamy, no laws directly prohibiting or even restricting it have been passed.

(Southern Africa)

SOUTH AFRICA

General population policies

1486 Reynolds, Rex. Searchlight on South Africa's Native Policy. Pretoria: State Information Office, 1947. 64 pp.

Describes measures undertaken by the Government for the economic and social betterment of both rural and urban native population. The activities include land reclamation, agricultural improvement, health protection, housing and education.

1487 Royal Institute of International Affairs, "The South African Government's Native Policy," Signed D.L.S. World Today 3(10): 445-53. Oct. 1947.

Review of various acts implementing the Government's policy of residential separation and parallel development of the Europeans and natives, with a summary of accomplishments in the fields of native land settlement, education, and public health.

1488 Union of South Africa, South African National Conference on the Post-war Planning of Social Welfare Work. Report of the South African National Conference. (Held at the University of the Witwatersrand, Johannesburg, September 25-29, 1944). Pretoria: Government Printer, 1945. 316 pp.

Contains discussions of family allowances, pp. 72-79, and the problem of rural migration, pp. 286-92.

Policies on fertility and family size

1489 Badenhorst, L.T. "Family Limitation and Methods of Contraception in an Urban Population," Popul. Stud. 16(3): 286-301. March 1963.

Questions are answered regarding family limitation and planning the methods of contraception used by various socio-economic groups: (1) the prevalence of contraception and when practice started; (2) the use of contraception, family planning, and unwanted pregnancies; (3) the incidence of specific means of contraception; and (4) the relationship between types of methods used and various socio-economic characteristics. Data were gathered from a sample of white married females in Johannesburg, South Africa (number totalling 1,022). It was found that: (A) 82% had used contraceptives at some time during their married life, the highest use being among fecund couples. (B) A high percentage of couples used contraceptives before their first pregnancy, and a very small percentage of fecund females never used any form of contraceptive at all during their married lives. Family planning and the spacing of children are widespread and generally accepted by the population. There are still unwanted pregnancies and births and the incidence of family planning practices differ among religious, language, occupation, and income groups. The incidence of the different contraceptive methods (the five most popular being rubber sheath, withdrawal, rhythm, diaphragm, and vaginal jelly, in that order) and types of methods: chemical and appliance, non-appliance, and mixed, also differ significantly among the various socio-economic, especially religious groups.

1490 Hahlo, H.R. The South African Law of Husband and Wife 2nd ed. Juta, 1963.

This book covers South African Marriage Law, including a historical sketch from Roman Law onwards, the formation of marriage, the legal consequences of marriage, marriage by antenuptial contract, separation, the dissolution of marriage by death or divorce, annulment of marriage, and jurisdiction and conflict of laws. The marriage laws vacillate from Roman law where in an informal consent-marriage the woman did not become subject to her husband and could own property, to the Germanic period where the girl's consent was not considered and the husband had unlimited power over the wife, to the Germanic-Franco period where consent of the girl was required and she could have property of her own and so on. The act of marriage is a juristic act in South Africa and involves a status of a public character. South African courts have refused to recognize (a) foreign polygamous marriages; (b) polygamous marriages according to Mohammedan or Hindu custom; and (c) 'native customary unions', contracted between South African natives according to native law and custom. One of the primary ends of marriage is seen as procreation of children. Any condition in general restraint of marriage is void as contrary to public opinion. Marriage brokerage contracts and similar bargains are illegal. Impotence is considered a major ground for annulment except in certain cases when the impotent spouse attempts to have the marriage annulled. A husband must accept his wife as he finds her, unless she was pregnant by illicit intercourse with another man before the marriage, thereby providing grounds for nullity.

1491 Higgins, Edward. "The Bearing of Family Allowances on Family Size in an Urban White Population," Tyds. Maatskap. Navors. 12(2):165-76. May 1962.

A report of a 1957-58 study of 1,022 white married women under the age of 50 to examine reproductive facts, norms, and attitudes among the various socio-economic groups in Johannesburg. It is found that the average white Johannesburg wife would like to have (or have had) four children in her family. This figure is definitely higher than the average size of the urban white family in South Africa today. If family allowances were made available, respondents answered that they would have an average of one more child than they would otherwise have. The Afrikaans-speaking respondents would have larger families than the English-speaking women if family allowances were provided. The lower-blue-collar respondents would have more children than any other occupational group if family allowances were provided. Desired family size, if family allowances were available, was negatively correlated with standard of education and income. Family allowances appeared to make little difference regarding family size to those females who only received a primary school education, while it mattered most to those who had a secondary school education and much less among the college educated females.

1492 Higgins, Edward. "Some Fertility Attitudes Among White Women in Johannesburg," Popul. Stud. 16:70-78, 1962.

Analyzes the replies to certain questions on ideal family size, family planning and the limitation of offspring and attitudes towards the use of contraceptives of 1,022 white married women recently interviewed in a Johannesburg fertility survey. Replies to questions on the above topics are correlated with certain sociological variables such as home language, religion, educational status, family income and occupation. The application of these controls to the sample data revealed some interesting differences in outlook with regard to family size, family planning and the use of contraceptives. Home language and religious affiliation were found to be among the most important variables. Generally speaking, in spite of some significant differences in fertility attitudes between certain groups composing the sample population, there appeared to be a good deal of uniformity with regard to ideal family size, family planning and the use of contraceptives.

1493 Impey, R. Lance. "Sterilization of Women," S. African Med. J. 28(41):872-74, 1954.

The author believes that the complicated problems associated with sterilization (as well as with abortion) demand the attention of the State. The medical grounds for sterilization must remain the responsibility of the medical profession, but it is for the State to say if cognizance should be taken of other indications such as social, economic or eugenic.

1494 "Legal Responsibilities and Liabilities: Intra-Uterine Contraceptive Devices and Oral Contraceptives. Legal Opinion," South African Med. J. 42:278-80. 23 March 1968.

Provides statements of legal opinions regarding the responsibilities and liabilities of a medical practitioner in regard to intra-uterine contraceptive devices and oral contraceptives. Opinions pertain to: the necessity of obtaining the patient's written consent; the necessity of obtaining the husband's consent, either verbally or written; the liability of the physician if the patient becomes pregnant or if the loop accidentally perforates the uterus; and the responsibility of the Medical Defense Union, or other medical protection society, in meeting the costs of legal proceedings related to civil or criminal actions concerning intra-uterine devices.

V ASIA

(General)

General population policies

1495 Balfour, Marshall C. "Population Policy and Population Programmes in Asia Countries," pp. 79-86 in: Thailand, National Research Council, National Seminar on Population Problems of Thailand. Bangkok, 1963.

Short review of policies or their absence in Japan, India, Pakistan, Singapore, Korea, Taiwan, Philippines, and Indonesia.

1496 Balfour, Marshall C., "Research Required for Planning and Policy-Making in the Field of Population," pp. 355-63 in: Thailand, National Research Council, National Seminar on Population Problems of Thailand. Bangkok, 1963.

Studies of demographic trends are essential for adequate planning of development and the designing of population policies. There is also needed research on knowledge, attitudes, and practice of contraception, desired family size, and reasons for desired family size. Consideration of ways of increasing knowledge is also essential.

1497 Borrie, W.D. "The 'Population Explosion' and the Far East: Review Article," Pacific Affairs 33(2):181-91. June 1960.

A number of recent scholarly analytical studies which place population issues in Asia in their proper perspective are discussed. Fifty-five percent of today's world population lives in Asia. By 1980 it is expected to increase by 75%. This assumes continued high birthrates with mortality decreasing. Japan appears to have successfully introduced birth control, but this experience should not be generalized. Her case has special features. On the contrary her most important moral remains the virtual certainty of rapid growth rates in Asia for some decades. Birth control is clearly becoming an international issue. Yet it can clearly not alone cure man's tendency to outstrip available resources. A comprehensive balanced and dynamic development is needed in which population policy takes its rightful place.

WORLD POPULATION POLICY

1498 Chandrasekhar, S. "Population Problems of Asia," Popul. Rev. 7(1):73-81. January 1963.

After presenting several demographic characteristics of various Asian countries, the author reviews the population policies prevailing in Japan, India, China, Indonesia and Pakistan.

1499 Eastman, Nicholson J. "Current Trends in Population Control," Fertility & Sterility 5(5):477-84. September - October 1964.

Results of intensive activity during the first half of the 20th century to control mortality are noted, and current efforts to control fertility in Japan, India, and mainland China are described. The crude birth rate in Japan has been drastically lowered through increased induced abortion; the reasons why this experience is not a suitable prototype for the developing nations are listed. Official Indian policy toward population control and the implementation of the family planning program are summarized. The relative ineffectiveness to date of family planning clinics in India is contrasted with the promise of sterilization campaigns and the mass use of newly developing means of contraception. What little information there is on official birth control activities in China is mentioned.

1500 Kirby, E. Stuart, "An Approach to Population Policy in Asia," Popul. Rev. 1(1):7-11, January 1957.

The U.N. World Population Conference in 1954 found that "the world's 'capital' resources" would maintain the expected population increase until 1980, with the same general standard of living. However, the standard of living must be raised, and is linked with family planning. Economical development is visualized largely in terms of industrialization and urbanization. Population pyramids for developed and underdeveloped areas show marked differences in the age groups, with larger percentages under and over the productive ages in the underdeveloped areas. In approaching the problem of population growth, it is necessary to plan birth control education to plan some degree of freedom of emigration for its moral effect, and to create possibilities for international migration within national boundaries. The large, unplanned families, however, are unable to make the geographical and occupational shifts involved.

1501 Moorthy, K. Krishna, "The Asian Numbers Game," Far Eastern Econ. Rev. 43:101-2. January 16,1964.

Conference convened in New Delhi by the U.N. Economic Commission for Asia and the Far East (ECAFE) voted strongly positive population policies for governments in this region.

1502 Myrdal, Gunnar, Asian Drama: An Inquiry into the Poverty of Nations. New York: Pantheon, 1968. 3 vols. xxx, 2284 pp.

The institutional approach is proposed as an alternative to Western conceptual approaches in this study of post-World-War II development problems in Pakistan, India, Ceylon, Burma, Malaya, Thailand, Indonesia, the Philippines, and--in a few instances--in South Vietnam, Cambodia and Laos. Of demographic policy interest are chapters on Population Policy, in which the rationale of population policy in the South Asian countries and in economically advanced countries today is compared; on Problems of Population Policy, which considers investment in man; health, education, literacy and adult education, the school system; and an appendix on family planning policy in India.

1503 Thompson, Warren, Population and Peace in the Pacific. Chicago: University of Chicago Press, 1946. 397 pp.

The future peace of the world is jeopardized by the fact that the world's population is in a state of unstable equilibrium. Europeans and peoples of European descent have increased enormously during the past 3 centuries but are now levelling off and promise soon to become a static population. On the other hand, Asiatics, having bred up to the limit of their food production, are ready for an "explosive increase" in numbers as soon as improved agricultural and technical methods enable them to secure more food. In 1981 the population of India will be between 680 and 800 millions, that of China between 585 and 700 millions, that of Asia as a whole, approximately 2 billion. These tremendous and, by the end of the century, powerful populations will see across the Pacific the relatively empty continents of North and South America and Australia. Suffering from a chronic internal population pressure, the Asiatics will be tempted to attack, conquer and settle the empty lands. We should immediately open the East Indies and the Oceanic Islands now mandated to Australia and New Zealand to Asiatic emigrants. This will not relieve the population pressure, but it will have an appeasing psychological effect.

Policies on fertility and family size

1504 Balfour, M.C. "Family Planning in Asia," Popul. Stud. 15(2):102-9. November 1961.

From Japan to Pakistan, where recent census data are available in most of the Asian countries, the population far exceeds prior expectations. These countries are beginning to respond to the need and desirability of family planning. Private associations have long been pioneers in this field; their accomplishments are noted, as well as their inadequacy to cope with the present need. Official attitudes in some countries reflect at least a new willingness to study the problem in relation to economic development, while in other countries government policies embrace active and subsidized programs of population control. The problems of implementing government policies and translating them into popular action are discussed. The current status of various methods of limiting fertility, including abortion and sterilization, is described. Because of the growth of favorable public sentiment and government action, a decline in the birth rate in some parts of Asia within the next decade is anticipated.

1505 Chandrasekharan, C. "The Economic Commission for Asia and the Far East Program to Assist Fertility Control," Demography 5(2):651-58, 1968.

The ECAFE program to assist fertility control is vigorous and expanding. It supports national efforts at inducing fertility declines and it contributes to a scientific appreciation and objective solution of the many problems that arise in planning and implementing national family planning programs.

1506 Chandrasekharan, C. "Family Limitation in South and South-East Asia," Paper Presented at the International Union for the Scientific Study of Population, General Conference, 3-11 September 1969.

A major development in the region is the effort at popularization of family planning through national programs and undoubtedly fertility levels in many countries have begun to be affected by such programs. Assessments of the impact which the programs have on the birth rates of these countries poses many challenges to the demographer, and in view of their importance to policy development, it is to be hoped that demographers will engage themselves more and more in problems related to such assessment.

1507 Far Eastern Economic Review, "Urgency of Birth Control in Asia," Far Eastern Econ. Rev. 19(17):518, October 27, 1955.

Notes on problems of India, Japan, and the British colonies.

1508 Fink, Lotte, "Population Policies in India, Pakistan and Japan -- Some Medical Aspects," Australian Outlook, September 1954, pp. 146-57.

The article deals with family planning programs as a measure for population control in India, Pakistan and Japan. A brief outline of population growth rate figures is given for each country, and the Hindu and Moslem attitudes toward birth control are viewed. The history of birth control efforts in India is discussed, beginning with the formation of the Family Planning Society in 1940 and ending with a description of the four ways in which the Association is now active. Discussion of birth control in Pakistan begins with the latest statement on the use of contraceptives issued by the Grand Mufti in 1937 through the founding in 1953, of the National Family Planning Association of Pakistan and the Government's position on the issue. The movement in Japan is dated from Margaret Sanger's first visit to the country in 1922 and discussion ends with the efforts of the Japanese Birth Control League, reorganized in 1947, and the unification of the Family Planning Movement in 1953.

1509 Heenan, Brian, "Curbing Birth Rates," Far Eastern Econ. Rev. 50:514-17. December, 1965.

Discusses the various programs to reduce population increase rates in Asia today -- especially in China and Japan.

1510 Kinch, Arne, "The Role of Man in Family Planning Motivation," J. Fam. Welf. 8(3):39-48, March 1962.

Emphasizing the status of the husband in Ceylonese and other Eastern societies, the author points out the importance of male motivation for family control, if the family planning program is to succeed.

1511 Kirby, E. Stuart, "The New Approach to Population Policy in Asia," Far Eastern Econ. Rev. 19(15):449-52. October 13, 1955.

Discussion of the need for controls to solve the problem of population growth and economic development in Asia. Notes on the recent change in the official Chinese position on contraception.

1512 Kirk, Dudley, "Possible Lessons from Historical Experience for Family Planning Programmes in Asia," pp. 63-66 in: Sixth International Conference on Planned Parenthood, New Delhi, 14-21 February 1959. London: International Planned Parenthood Federation, 1959.

The author is of the view that males are in a better position to help in the family planning movement and should be approached. Furthermore, resources should be devoted to dissemination of information on methods of contraception.

1513 Mendoza-Hoyos, Hernan, Report and Comments on the Visit to Family Planning Programs in: Japan, Republic of Korea, Taiwan, Hong Kong, India, Thailand, Federation of Malaysia, Singapore, October 27-December 23, 1966. [Bogota], Asociacion Colombiana de Facultades de Medicina, Division de Estudios de Poblacion, 1967. v, 51 pp.

Description and evaluation of operation of the programs in several countries.

1514 O'Connor, Ronald W., and O'Connor, Terrence V. "Asian Medical Students and Family Planning: A Study of Knowledge and Attitudes in 33 Medical Colleges," J. Med. Educ. 42(10):949-57, 1967.

A survey of attitudes and knowledge of senior Asian medical students on family planning revealed that in most instances: the students are well aware of the problems of population growth and consider it a national problem; they are not uniformly well informed about the demographic mechanisms involved or the particular medical methodologies available; and there are presently few factors which motivate Asian students to develop competence in family planning. If further emphasis is given the subject of family planning in the university syllabus, and consequently in the curriculum and the examinations, then the existing university system can provide a readily available means for improving the graduating physician's competence in family planning.

1515 Rice, Donald T. "Asian Medical Colleges and Fertility Control," J. Amer. Med. Assn. 204(6):426-30, 1968.

Doctors and nurses must assume an increasing responsibility for designing and supervising the rapidly expanding programs for family planning and population control. This survey concentrates on the medical colleges of India which devote an average of 10.6 hours to the teaching of population dynamics, family planning programs, conception control techniques, and related social, cultural, educational, and motivational aspects. Ward rounds and family planning clinics provide observation and some experience during clerkship and internship. The time assigned to family planning has almost doubled in the past two years, and far exceeds the time allotted in United States and United Kingdom medical schools. Only the two leading medical schools in Taiwan and two in Seoul can match this amount of teaching. These changes indicate a responsiveness to national needs and conditions.

1516 Stone, Abraham, "Fertility Problems in the World Today," Eugenical News 38(3):60-63, 1953.

Recent social interest in population size stems from (1) a widespread realization that it is of benefit to the family for parents to be able to space their children; (2) the knowledge on the part of world leaders and social scientists that the stability of nations is benefited by a better balance between human populations and natural resources. Owing to the progress of modern preventive medicine, mortality rates are decreasing and populations are increasing around the world. For example, in Ceylon, in 1920 the birth rate was 40 per thousand and the death rate, 32 per thousand. In 1950 the birth rate was still about 40 per thousand, but the death rate had been reduced to 12 per thousand owing mainly to the control of malaria. Obviously in an island country, with area and food resources limited, the increased population is of concern to the leaders of the country. A similar situation exists in Japan where widespread abortion is practiced legally, as a drastic attempt to partly solve the population increase problem. In 1951 the government of India requested the author to give advice concerning control of population in that greatly overcrowded country. The author developed the so-called "Bead System" whereby illiterate women could be taught to observe the rhythm method of determining their fertile and infertile periods during the month. Since 1951 the plans proposed by the author have been carried out, and the rhythm method is being widely studied in India. In a trip around the world the author found that the incidence of childlessness in parents desiring children in various countries is about the same, between 10 and 15 per cent. The author found a widespread interest in surgical sterilization in both Japan and India. Such sterilizations, entirely voluntary, were being carried out in both these countries. A better balance between world population and world resources is becoming a public health and medical problem of great importance.

(East Asia)

GENERAL

Policies on fertility and family size

1517 Dreijmanis, John, "Birth Control Policies: Comparison of Chinese and Japanese Policies," Popul. Rev. 12(1-2): January - December 1968.

This article is an exploratory effort in comparative political demography. The birth prevention policies of the People's Republic of China and Japan are analyzed according to the reasons for these policies, their implementation, and their success. At the end, various demographic theories and hypotheses are applied to these two states.

1518 Muramatsu, Minoru, "Family Limitation in East Asia," Paper Presented at the International Union for the Scientific Study of Population, General Conference, 3-11 September 1969.

East Asia as a whole is the region in which family limitation programs have been most successfully conducted. Actual results, or at least the promising signs, of the declines in fertility are already seen in this region. Legal and political attitudes toward fertility control are, in general, favorable. In Korea, Taiwan, Singapore and Malaysia, fertility control is now an official policy of the government. In Japan, the postwar fertility decline has been for the most part an effort on the part of general public. The government has helped speed up this process by incorporating family planning into public health and social welfare. In Mainland China family limitation practice is in use, but its political rationalization is to render necessary service to the people when they ask for it, and the separation of family limitation from the Malthusian overpopulation has been strenuously pursued. In other countries such as Indonesia, Thailand and the Philippines, initial efforts of family planning movements are in progress. The most principal method of contraception in the region has been the IUD.

1519 Nozue, G. "Abortion in the Far East," in: Proceedings of the Eighth International Conference of the International Planned Parenthood Federation, Hertford, England: International Planned Parenthood Federation, 1967.

Although abortion is illegal in Korea and Taiwan, the number performed each year is increasing at a steady rate, while in Japan, where the laws on abortion were reformed in the late 1940's, the number of abortions is decreasing. In 1955, there were 1,170,000 abortions in Japan; in 1965 the country registered only 840,000. Socio-economic reasons account for 63% of Japan's abortions, and less than 15% of all abortion cases involve women who practice birth control on a regular basis.

1520 Takeshita, John Y. "Birth Control in Some of the Developing Countries of the Far East," pp. 168-71 of Vol. 2 in: United Nations Department of Economic and Social Affairs, Proceedings of the World Population Conference, Belgrade, 30 August - 10 September, 1965. New York: United Nations, 1967.

Countries which might be characterized as being in the vanguard of modernization have led others in Asia in the adoption of the small family ideal and of birth control.

(East Asia: Mainland Region)

CHINA

General population policies

1521 Aird, John S. "Population Policy in Mainland China," Popul. Stud. 16(1):38-57. July 1962.

Though the population policies of Communist China have doubtless been influenced by official figures on the rate of growth on China's population, the policies themselves are thus far virtually without demographic significance. There is no reason to believe that the birth control campaign of 1955-58 had any appreciable effect on birth rates even in the urban centers where it was promoted, and there is still less reason to suppose that the anti-Malthusian propaganda before 1955 and since 1958 could have contributed to, or raised the already high level of fertility in mainland China. Like the aspects of domestic policy in mainland China, the population policies of the last thirteen years have been primarily a political phenomenon.

1522 Ali, S.M. "China: Planning for All," Far Eastern Econ. Rev. 45(8):265-ff. August 13, 1964.

Notes from a Peking correspondent on recent trends in governmental policy on family planning and other aspects of population growth indicate that a campaign is in progress to encourage young people to adopt the principles of planned parenthood by marrying late and spacing out births. To the Chinese mind this approach offers an ideal compromise between the somewhat excessive lengths to which the Japanese go in their family planning methods and the unbridled population growth in progress elsewhere in Asia.

1523 Chandrasekhar, S. "China's Population Problems," Popul.Rev. 3(2):17-38. July 1959.

A report based on the 1953-54 census of the Chinese government and a discussion of recent birth control measures and population growth regarding Chinese foreign affairs. Improved sanitary and hygienic facilities, more efficient sewerage and garbage disposal, and better equipped hospitals, have combined in lowering the general death rate and component rates of infant and maternal mortality. The new marriage law as a contributing factor to the higher birth rate is noted. China's population may reach 800 million before 1968. Ambivalent attitudes to birth control were uncovered.

1524 Chen, Ta. "The Foundations of a Sound Social Policy for China," Soc. Forces 26(2):139-45. December 1947.

Maintains that a sound social policy in China necessitates both a thorough study of the social situation before policies are made and the creation of adequate enforcement machinery. The section on "Social policy and population" considers the problem of unifying data-collecting agencies, the advisability of using sampling methods in studying population problems, and the government's attitude toward increase of population and birth control.

1525 Chiang Kai-Shek, Chapters on National Fecundity, Social Welfare, Education, and Health and Happiness. Written by Chiang Kai-Shek as supplement to Dr. Sun Yat-Sen's Lectures on the principle of people's livelihood. Translated by Durham S.F. Chen. Taipei: China Cultural Service, n.d. vi, 108 pp.

Comments written in 1953 to elucidate Dr. Sun's lectures, delivered in 1924. Chapters include: Building up a free and secure society [necessity of industrialization]; National fecundity, social welfare and education [discussion of Malthusian theory, China's population problem, factors affecting the birth rate, and proposed solutions to counter the decline in the birth rate, the problem of old age].

1526 Chou Pei-Yuan, "Population, Production, and Birth Control," Bull. Atomic Scientists 14(8):325, 333, October 1958.

This article is concerned with the relationship of the population of China to her agricultural production and industrial growth. The author mentions that recent advances in medicine and education are gradually affecting contraception methods and he contends that within a reasonably short period of time, the increase in population will become slower, and the standard of living much improved.

1527 Chu Pao-yi, [Refutation of Wu Ching-chao's Slanderous Remarks Against the Chinese People on the Population Issue] Translated from Chinese text in: Tsai Ching Yen Chie [Finance and Economics], No. 1, Feb. 15, 1958. Extracts from China Mainland Magazines, No. 128, May 12, 1958, pp. 17-21.

1528 Coughlin, Richard J. "Population Controls in China," in: Edward Szczepanik, ed. , Symposium on Economic and Social Problems of the Far East, Hong Kong University Press, 1963, ix, 508 pp.

A cultural interpretation of China's population growth, as reported in the recent census. As the Communists came to power and revamped many aspects of Chinese society and culture, the birth rate rose, thus contributing to a great population increase. Recent policies of the Communist government are seen to be attempts to refashion controls on the birth rate as well as to achieve certain economic and political goals.

1529 Djang, T.K. "Social Policy in China," Internat. Labour Rev. 52(5):465-78, November 1945.

The principal trends of social policy in China are discussed, with emphasis upon the four statements of policy adopted by the Sixth Kuomingtang National Congress on May 17, 1945. These statements deal with the growth and distribution of the population, the regulation of conditions of labor, agrarian reform, and the organization of social security in China. The statement on population policy envisages the adoption of a number of measures calculated to increase the population, while ensuring at the same time that satisfactory standards of health and development are maintained. A summary of wartime labor and welfare legislation is presented in an appendix.

1530 Eitner, Hans-Juergen, Changing Population Policy in Communist China. JPRS 8130. Washington: U.S. Joint Publication Research Service, April 19, 1961. i, 10 pp.

China has moved from a position of not recognizing the population problem to vague hints that one exists. Information on family planning is being distributed to married couples. The justification for family planning is twofold: that a smaller number and better spacing of children will ensure better health for mothers; and a smaller number of children provides more favorable conditions for the rearing of each one of them.

1531 Kirby, E. Stuart, "Peiping's Growing Dilemma, Population," Problems of Communism 7:36-41, March - April 1958.

Confronting mainland China has been the growing disparity between the country's population, expected by some to reach 2 billion by 1984, and its available natural resources. The article deals with the two phases of Chinese Communist policy on population control since 1949: doctrinaire opposition, based on Marxist population principles, through 1954 and subsequent encouragement of control, reflecting a retreat from Marxist dogma and the acceptance of a more practical realism. There follows a discussion of Marxist ideology and the propagandistic and psychological values attached to its orthodox view of population control. The author then describes the three main motivations behind the major change in population policy: an increasing recognition of the economic problems inherent to an unchecked growth of population, the use of birth control by the country's upper social stratum, and the need to destroy all foundations and values antithetical to communist ideology and objectives. Birth control could weaken the family system and provide maximum social mobility. Viewed briefly are the "New Marriage Law" of 1950, the publication of articles giving information concerning birth control to the public in 1955, increasingly active efforts by the Ministry of Public Health, and a major national campaign of public education in 1956-57, and finally a reform of abortion regulations also in 1957. The author concludes that, in general, the Chinese Communist ideologists have attempted to be less dogmatic and to adjust party policy in a practically-oriented manner concerning the issue of over-population.

1532 Lal, Amrit, "China's Population Policy," China Report 1(5):25-28, 34, August 1965.

The development of the official approach to mainland China's population problem has been influenced by factors other than the necessity of feeding the people, and the author traces these factors and their relation to population policy from 1949, when the Communists took over the country, to the present. Policy development is divided into four phases: the period of 1949-56, when preference for population increase was directly influenced by immediate aims (consolidation, reclamation, solidification of economy and defense); the period of 1956-58, when self-confidence allowed more attention to be paid to cultural and economic problems; the period of 1958 to the early sixties, when there was an abrupt reversal of policy and a large population was once again favored as a factor of strategic importance; and the most recent period, when the prospect of mass starvation appears to have convinced the communist leaders of the primal necessity of birth control programs. In general, China's population policy since 1949 has wavered between two extremes, the glorification of population and what is termed "contraceptology". Although ideological orthodoxy has always been opposed to birth control, the Chinese are prepared to modify their policies when economic realities take precedence over political or nationalistic gains.

1533 MacDougall, Colina, "China: Population Policies," Far Eastern Econ. Rev. 37(6):242-43, August 9, 1962.

Traces the changes in official policy on population and birth control from the period 1954-57, when the Communist regime advocated birth control for the first time and launched a full-scale campaign for the country, to 1962, when Peking once again gave its official support and encouragement to family planning after several years of rejecting control in favor of doctrinaire ideology and its "great leap" policy. Probable motives behind the most recent statement are outlined, as well as its political and economic implications and major emphasis.

1534 Min Tzu, "It Is Good to Have a Large Population," English translation of article in: Ch'i Hua Ching Chi [Planned Economy], Issue No. 6, June 9, 1958. Extracts from China Mainland Magazines, No. 142, September 15, 1958. pp. 25-32.

Reply to Ma Yin-Ch'u's New theory of population, published in July 5, 1957, issue of Jen Min Jih Pao (Peking), which considered a large population undesirable.

1535 Pressat, Roland, "La Population de la Chine et Son Economie " [The Population and Economy of China], Population 13(4): 569-90, October - December 1958.

The results of an extensive tour of China. Among all the countries subject to population pressure, China is the most significant case, since its people comprise to 25% of the total world population and it is undergoing tremendous social, political and economic changes. In the last year, industry has made steady progress and crops have been excellent. Ideas regarding population have changed, though official policy did not vary. Popular practices and governmental policy are not independent of one another. Data on population and employment are made available only in a sporadic and belated way. (I), "Recent Demographic Facts": mortality has steadily declined and the government is encouraging birth control.

1536 Su Chung, "Facts About China's Population," Peking Rev. 1(18):9-10, July 1, 1958.

An interpretation of the current policy and a rebuttal of old and new Malthusian arguments.

1537 Taeuber, Irene B. "China's Population," Popul. Rev.2(2): 35-41, March 1958.

The announcement by the People's Republic of China, in 1954, that it had a population of 500 million can (despite doubts regarding the completeness and accuracy of the 1953-1954 census) be accepted for operational and planning purposes, as the government itself has accepted them. The birth rate, announced as 37 per 1,000 total population is suspect, regarding the known limitations to public health activities in modern China. A birth rate of 47 and a death rate of 27 are considered plausible. To achieve economic advances, a healthy population is needed. If the government invested large sums in health facilities, personnel, chemicals and medicines, death rates would drop from Eastern to Western levels. The increase in population would create the need for additional food. A failure in economic development, especially the agricultural sector, would mean famines, and a rise in the death rate, retarding in turn economic growth. The government realizes the problem involved, and advocates population control on socio-political grounds. Steps were taken in 1954 and 1956 to spread the use of birth control contraceptives.

1538 Taeuber, Irene B. "Population Policies in Communist China," Popul. Index 22(4):261-74, October 1956.

The article summarizes the available evidence as to Chinese Communist thinking on the population question. It appears that a substantial movement toward encouraging family limitation is under way. This is being accomplished without abandonment of the Marxian position that high growth rates are not a threat to the national economy as a whole. The means by which family limitation is to be achieved is apparently intended to be voluntary 'birth control'. This phrase includes abortion and sterilization, as well as contraception, among its meanings, and there is some indication that restrictions on these two practices are being relaxed. Meanwhile the broader framework of population policy includes encouragement of migration to the sparsely settled border areas, and direct assaults on the family system and the ancient role of women. Whether fertility can be lowered significantly remains to be seen. Shortages of health personnel and facilities are already severe, but the reaction of the traditional rural society to pressures for family planning is less predictable than it once seemed. In the absence of economic collapse, it is to be expected that the Chinese population will grow much larger. Hence, it is probable that there will be firmer and more comprehensive campaigns for reducing family size in future years.

1539 U.S. Joint Publications Research Service, "Premier Chou En-Lai Speaks on Population," Communist China Digest, No. 32, February 14, 1961.

Text of television interview with British correspondent Felix Greene, Peiping, NCNA-English, Nov. 4, 1960. Education on planned parenthood was and continues to be carried out in China mainly to protect the health of mothers and provide favorable conditions for bringing up children, not because of so-called 'population pressure'.

1540 Walker, Kenneth, "Ideology and Economic Discussion in China: Ma Yin-Ch'u on Development Strategy and His Critics," Econ. Develop. Cult. Change 11(2, Pt. 1):113-33. January 1963.

Examination of the content of Ma Yin-ch'u's articles between 1955 and 1960, including those on the interrelations of population and economic development and his policy recommendations.

1541 Wang Tso and Tai Yuan-chen, "Criticism and Appraisal of the 'New Theory of Population'," Translated from the Chinese text in: Ching Chi Yen Chiu [Economic Research], No. 2, Feb. 17, 1958. Extracts from China Mainland Magazines, No. 128, May 12, 1958, pp. 5-16.

Proponents of the New Population Theory such as Fei Hsiao-tung and Wu Ching-ch'ao argue that a large population is incompatible with the goals of socialism and therefore urge a program of birth control. The arguments which they put forth are examined and are found to be the typical Malthusian onces. It is further suggested that birth control is justifiable on other grounds and that a large population is a reality in China and the capital for greater industrialization and agricultural modernization.

1542 Wertheim, W.F. "Recent Trends in China's Population Policy," Sci. Soc. 30(2):129-35, Spring 1966.

An examination of Chinese population policies under Communist rule, based on two visits. A number of analyses of China's overpopulation are considered, and special attention is paid to that of the geographer Pierre Gourou (1948), who contrasted the overintensive use of the lowlands with "unused uplands" and suggested a population transfer from the former to the latter as a remedy, combined with rapid industrialization. During the first visit in 1957, Gourou's recommendations were, unknowingly perhaps, being put into practice, as witnessed by vast reforestation schemes and orchard plantings in mountainous Kwantung province. Industrialization was making rapid progress with the help of Soviet experts, and a third important element of Chinese policy was to increase the yields of traditional lowland crops. During a follow-up visit in August-September, 1964, some changes were noted, although the economical rather than the demographic emphasis on solutions to the overpopulation problems has been maintained. In industry, quality is now stressed at the expense of quantity. In agriculture, there has been a slackening of the work of Gourou's "unused uplands"; stress is laid on the rapid expansion of irrigation and drainage of the lowlands, to increase yields per acre and occupy manpower. However, the possibility of a future switch in policies cannot be excluded.

1543 Wu Ching-ch'ao, "A New Treatise on the Problem of China's Population," Translated from Chinese text in _Hsin Chien She_ [New Construction], Issue No. 3, March 3, 1957, pp. 1-16 in: _Extracts from China Mainland Magazines_.

The author outlines his revised position on population policy. First he repudiates previous errors: i.e., that unemployment was caused by overpopulation and that the birth rate was likely to fall below the replacement level after industrialization. Affirms present views: that the primary need is to increase socialist production by raising productivity rather than the size of the labor force. Mechanization depends on capital accumulation, and is retarded when too many workers have to be absorbed. Estimates desirable rate of population increase on the basis of capital available for socialist construction. Draws comparisons with Soviet and Indian experiences. Outlines investment priorities and advocates birth control for mothers with three children or more. Refutes the appellation of "New Malthusianism" by indicating confidence that food production and living standards will outstrip population growth, as he states they have up to now in Socialist China.

Policies on fertility and family size

1544 Aronowitz, P. "Chinese Succession Law: An Historical Survey," _Portia Law J._ 2:265. Spring 1967.

1545 Chen Ta, "Birth Control, Deferred Marriage, and Population Problems of New China," _The New Reconstruction Monthly_, May 1957, pp. 1-16.

The effective means of lowering the birth rate are considered by the author to be birth control and deferred marriage, although this may take some time. Western and Japanese examples are cited. New China should aim toward a planned growth rather than toward decreasing the population or maintaining the present level. Sterilization and abortion are considered inhumane and ineffective. Raising the age at marriage by increasing educational and employment opportunities for women is considered the most hopeful prospect.

1546 China. People's Republic. CPPCC [Chinese People's Political Consultative Conference] National Committee. [1957 Session of CPPCC National Committee--VI. Birth Control and Population Problems.] [A group of speeches translated and abridged from the Chinese texts in] Jen Min Jih Pao (Peking), March 8, 9, 16, 17, 20, 1957. pp. 1-23 in: Current Background No. 445, April 1957. Summarized in: Liu, Grace "Birth Control in China," New World Rev. 25:22-44. August, 1957.

Contents: Li Teh-chuan [Minister of Public Health], Birth control and planned families; Li Chien-sheng, Do not perform artificial abortion unless absolutely necessary; Shao Li-tzu, Planned parenthood; Chung Hui-lan, Population and birth control; Tseng Cheng-wu, One way of easing overcrowding in urban cities. Policy questions discussed include the intensification of birth control propaganda, raising the legal age of marriage, revision of regulations for abortion and sterilization.

1547 China. People's Republic. Laws, Statutes, etc. Marriage Law of the People's Republic of China with Explanatory Materials. Hong Kong: Foreign Languages Press, 1953. 44 pp. Revised 1959.

Text of law and three explanatory articles.

1548 Chiu, Vermier Y. Marriage Laws and Customs of China. Hong Kong: Institute of Advanced Chinese Studies and Research, New Asia College, Chinese University of Hong Kong [1966].

1549 Chou Hsin-min, "On the Encouragement of Late Marriage and the Statutory Marriage Age," Translation in U.S. American Consulate General, Hong Kong, "Campaign Against Early Marriages," Survey of China Mainland Press, No. 2871, 3 December 1962, pp. 11-15.

The marriage law of the new China stipulates that a boy can get married only after reaching the age of 20 years and a girl only after reaching the age of 18 years. This represents a real effort to legally eradicate the feudal, early marriage system. The new statutory age is worked out by the government in accordance with the principle of opposing early marriage and with due regard to the consciousness of the masses. Both health and career considerations may lead many persons to postpone marriage to an even later age.

1550 Chou Ngo-fen, "Birth Control in China," J. Fam. Welf. 4(1): 17-22. November 1957.

In popularizing and promoting birth control, several steps are being taken. Contraception is being urged by the Ministry of Public Health and medical schools and hospitals are aiding in this. The marriage age is raised to 20 years for males and 18 years for females, and young persons are told of the advantages of late marriage. Abortion is now regarded as a contraceptive method. Sterilization is suggested only when both spouses agree on it.

1551 Chou O-fen, "How to Treat the Question of Contraception," Chung Kuo Ch'ing Nien [China Youth], No. 4, 16 February 1955.

An article by a Chinese Communist, advocating the practice of contraception as a eugenic measure and describing techniques.

1552 Chung Cho-huan, [This is Not an Embarrassing Thing or an Unimportant Matter.] Nan-fang Jih-pao December 1, 1963. Translation in: Survey of China Mainland Press, No. 3128, 30 December 1963, p. 12.

When health workers visited every street and lane to disseminate knowledge of contraception and promote planned childbirth, some people remarked behind their back: 'What an embarrassing thing to talk about childbirth'...a matter of major importance related to the national economy and the livelihood of the people.

1553 Cohen, Jerome A. The Criminal Process in the People's Republic of China, 1949-1963. Cambridge: Harvard University Press, 1968.

The legal attitude to marital offenses is discussed on pages 318-26. Bigamy remains punishable under the new code while adultery is not a penal offense but is subject to control by divorce and "criticism-education."

1554 Current Digest of the Soviet Press, "The Chinese Press on the Problem of Child Birth " [Translation of complete Russian text in: Izvestiia, September 14, 1963, p. 2], Current Digest of the Soviet Press 15(37):15-16, October 9,1963.

Marxism teaches that among the chief tasks related to population problems are the growth of labor productivity and constant concern for raising the living standards of the people, assuming a constant growth of population. Materials recently appearing in the Chinese press advocate contraception and sterilization as methods of solving the population problem and these solutions are incompatible with the Marxist approach.

1555 Etienne, Gilbert, "Quelques Donnees Recentes sur la Population de la Chine " [Recent Statistics on the Population of China] , Popul. 17(3):459-64. July - September 1962.

A demonstration of how, after a brief phase of interior propaganda regarding birth control, the Chinese, without prohibiting contraceptive practices, ceased active propaganda. Statistical population data have continued to be missing since 1958. Even though the Chinese have recently abandoned the pursuit of a birth control campaign, several indices show that the authorities are justifiably preoccupied by the problem. This is doubtless one of the reasons behind the resumption of a birth control campaign, in evidence since the Spring of 1962.

1556 Far Eastern Economic Review, "China: Fewer and Better," By our Shanghai Correspondent. Far Eastern Econ. Rev. 50(2): 47-50, October 14,1965.

Report on current aspects of family planning in Mainland China, including forms of information and propaganda.

1557 Far Eastern Economic Review, "China's Birth Control Campaign," Far Eastern Econ. Rev. 22(14):421-22, April 4,1957.

Discussion includes notes on recent changes of policy on minimum age at marriage, abortion, and sterilization.

1558 Freeberne, Michel, "Birth Control in China," Popul. Stud. 18(1):5-16. July 1964.

China launched her second major birth control compaign during 1962. Such a decision reflected the conflict between the traditional Communist position and the 'neo-Malthusian stand taken in 1957 by Ma Yin-chu with his "New Theory of Population." China has not achieved any breakthrough regarding population control, and moreover, China's second major birth control campaign appears to have lapsed as did the earlier campaign.

1559 Gales, R.R. "Marriage and the Family: Chinese Law," J. Family Law 6:36. Spring 1966.

There is a section on marriage - traditional inter-family contract and rare forms of marriage and an outline of the Nationalist Civil Code of 1931, which presented the first serious challenge to the supremacy of the family. The Communist Marriage Law of 1950 - the first major law promulgated by the Chinese Communist Regime - is explored. This law repudiated the traditional interfamily marriage contract as well as the other forms of traditional marriage. Section on adoption - custom, written law and the unwritten Communist view. Birth control, or a practice which can be construed as something very close to it, was practiced in several ways in traditional China: (1) considered disgraceful for an older woman to become pregnant after first grandchild; (2) lower income groups - abortion or infanticide. Higher income groups tended to stabilize the population: tendency to have large families became mark of wealth. This came down through the years as an additional hindrance to successful birth control in the 20th century.

1560 Harvard University, Center for International Affairs; and East Asian Research Center, Communist China, 1955-1959: Policy Documents with Analysis. Cambridge: Harvard University Press, 1962. xi, 611 pp.

Document 15, "Birth control and planned families," By Madam Li Tehch'uan, pp. 295-99. Translation of speech by the Minister of Health to the third session of the National Committee of the second Chinese People's Political Consultative Conference, March 7, 1957. Text accompanied by prefatory note on changes in official policy, 1954-1959, with references to translations.

1561 Hellstrom, Inger, "The Chinese Family in the Communist Revolution," Acta Sociol. 6(4):256-77, 1962.

An exploration of the family conditions in present-day Communist China regarding their significance in the total social structure and their modern transformation. China before and after Communism is discussed regarding: (1) the general structure of imperial society, (2) family structure in imperial society, (3) changes in the family structure during the Republic, (4) the general social structure after Communism, and (5) familial changes after Communism. It is concluded that the family is no longer an agent of political and social control. The kinship circle functions are now shared by the state, the Party, and the new nuclear type of family. The degree to which the Communists have succeeded in transforming the family, however, is not yet known.

1562 Japan Economy News, "Family Planning in China," Japan Economy News, 20 January 1965.

1563 Kirby, E. Stuart, "China's Population Problem," Far Eastern Econ. Rev. 24(17):513-17. April 24 1958.

An account of the changes in official policy on birth control in 1954.

1564 Kuang Ming Jih Pao, [Further Develop Birth-Control Work in Rural Areas]. English translation of article in Kuang Ming Jih Pao, May 20, 1958. Survey of China Mainland Press, No. 1830, August 12, 1958, pp. 6-7.

Statement of reasons for propagating birth control.

1565 Lal, Amrit, "Fertility Management and Concern with Over-Population in Mainland China," Eugenics Quart. 11(3): 170-74. September 1964.

A discussion of Chinese concepts of population growth, in order to elucidate the evolution of concepts of fertility management in response to overpopulation. It is found that, by 1964, official and public opinion definitely favored fertility management as a state policy, though Communist authorities grasped the significance of fertility management for an urbanizing and industrializing society 'rather late.'

1566 Levi, Werner, "The Family in Modern Chinese Law," Far Eastern Quart. 4:263-73, 1944.

Rules governing matrimony in the new Civil Code (1929-31) set the minimum age at eighteen for the male and sixteen for the female, establish equality between the sexes, abolish the custom of arranged marriages before the children are born, and do not recognize concubinage. Divorce is made easy, and the wife may institute proceedings and have custody of the children just as husbands have their rights.

1567 Majima, Kan, "Chugoku de no Sanji Seigen Ronso " [Discussion on Birth Control in China], Bungei Shunjeu 42(2):144-48. February 1965.

1568 Nossall, Frederick, "How Many Chinese?" Far Eastern Econ. Rev. 39(8):353, 355. February 21, 1963.

Comments on the current campaign to slow down births.

1569 Orleans, Leo A. "Birth Control: Reversal or Postponement?" China Quarterly, No. 3, July - September 1960, pp. 59-70.

Since 1954, China has undergone two radical reversals in its population policy. In September 1954 official advocacy of birth control measures began and continued through much of 1958. Late in 1958 the government reversed itself, reaffirming the thesis that population growth is an asset. Despite such pronouncements it is probable that the government will again advocate birth control when it has the means to implement such a policy and when there is a greater public understanding and acceptance of birth control.

1570 Orleans, Leo A. "Evidence from Chinese Medical Journals on Current Population Policy, China Quarterly (40):137-46. October - December 1969.

A review of mainland China's family planning development to date, based on articles from medical journals. Official Chinese policy has been shrouded in secrecy but both activity and dissemination of birth control information are evident. Sterilizations have never been popular in China, and abortion now appears to be a central means of birth control (although the number of sterilizations per year is rising). During the 1960's the most significant development was the emergence of the IUD as a contraceptive device, with a high proportion of hospitals and medical schools now experimenting with it. While the use of contraceptives does not compare with that of IUDs, their prominent displays have been noted by the press. An increasingly important role has been played by mobile medical teams. At this point, several forces seem to be causing a downward trend in China's birth rate: (1) a high percentage of the population under age 30 is literate, making the introduction of effective birth control measures relatively easy; (2) expanded use of paramedical personnel aids in implementing fertility control; (3) all contraceptive methods, and particularly the IUD, are becoming more available in the rural areas; (4) the number of abortions and sterilizations is apparently increasing.

1571 Orleans, Leo A. "A New Birth Control Campaign?" China Quart., No. 12, October - December 1962. pp. 207-10.

The main effort is to raise the minimum age at marriage through propaganda and persuasion. In the 1950's it was raised to twenty years for the male and eighteen years for the female. Now proposals suggest ages as high as 25-29 years for the male and 23-27 years for the female. There is little prospect that this effort will be any more successful than the earlier effort.

1572 Pei-Yuan, Chou, "Population Production and Birth Control," Bull. Atomic Sci. 14(8):325-33. October 1958.

With the increase of population the country has more mouths to feed and more bodies to clothe, but, on the other hand, with the increase of population there will be more labor at our disposal, and labor will create wealth. While the yearly increase of population in China in the past few years has been about 2%, the average annual increase of agricultural production is about 6% and the yearly industrial growth is more than 15%. Within a reasonably short period the rate of increase of our population will become much slower and then our standard of living will be very much further improved due to the introduction of birth control methods through persuasion and education.

1573 Pierre-Simon, "Le Controle des Naissances en Chine " [Birth Control in China], La Maternite Heureuse, No. 7, December 1958, pp. 1-7.

Report of observations on the contraceptive campaign in 1957 and 1958.

1574 Plotnick, Alan R. "Malthus, Marx and Mao: Red China's Population and Ideology," Challenge 12:9-12. June 1964.

The Chinese have several times reversed their position on population planning, and now are trying to lower the national birthrate but are encountering stubborn resistance from the uneducated, tradition-bound masses.

1575 Pollard, Robert S.W. "Marriage and Divorce in China Now," Plain View 11:54-64. November 1956.

Provisions of the 1950 law and how it works.

1576 Sarker, Subhash Chandra, "Population Planning in China," Popul. Rev. 2(2):49-58. July 1958.

The Chinese Communist government officially adopted a policy of birth control for China in 1955. A population growth rate of 0.5% per year was mentioned as desirable and obtainable by limiting families to three children. Greatest emphasis has been put on delayed marriages and the use of contraceptives. Restrictions on abortions have been lifted, but this has not been publicly emphasized.

1577 Shu Ming-yen, [Several Contraceptives Recommended for General Use], Selections from China Mainland Press, No. 2795, July 24, 1962, p. 15.

1578 Sudarikov, N. "Demokratizacija Semejnobracnogo Zakonodatel' stva Kitajskoj Narodnoj Respubliki," [The Democratization of the Legislation on the Family and Marriage in the People's Republic of China], Sovetskoye Gosudarstvo i Pravd 7:33-40, 1954.

1579 Suyin, Han, "Birth Control in China - Recent Aspects," Eugenics Rev. 52(1):19-22. January 1952.

Birth control was given official approval in China in 1956 though not maximum propaganda. A widespread educational movement was undertaken and contraceptives were made freely available. By 1958 a less positive policy was adopted and continues at present. This was conditioned (1) by psychological resistance to family limitation among peasants who felt that such a government policy must herald the threat of starvation; (2) there is a shortage of manpower in China, and China's wealth is still essentially her manpower since capital accumulation, without machinery, depends on hand labor; and (3) the success of the communes in providing facilities for mothers and children, makes it easier for women to work and have considerable freedom from their children. Thus there is no necessity to limit families but it may often be a convenience. Birth control and abortion are available and are made use of in the cities and factories, and to a much less extent in the communes. Government attitude today is suspended; it does not see birth control as a necessary policy.

1580 Suyin, Han, "The Changing Status of Women, Literacy, Education and Family," J. Sex Res. 3(4):275-83. November 1967.

A report on the Chinese method of tackling the problem of birth control and the situation as regards the relationship between the status of females and the acceptance of family planning as a way of life. In China family planning is related to the need for building up the country and to what is called the mass line. The mass line means that family planning must become a spontaneous yet sophisticated demand from the people concerned, the females, and must never be impressed upon them as a measure necessitated by poverty, need or want. Education in family planning becomes part of the education of the teenager and is related to his social attitudes and becomes a way of life. The stress is on the possibility for females to achieve more by having fewer children. In this area the social organization of the commune has proved of great benefit, because now the 87% of females who live in the villages can get the same advice and care in family planning as the city female can. Family planning was reassessed during the period of bad crops in 1959-61 and in 1962 it was renewed with the emphasis on villages and communes, and education chiefly among the younger age group. Planned parenthood is urged in several forms:

(1) late marriage; (2) for those who get married, contraceptive practice for the first two to three years of marriage; and (3) propaganda directed at changing the ideas of those over 30 years of age. The situation of the national minorities is discussed. Among them the net result has been an increase in the birth rate as well as a decrease in the infant mortality rate. However, family planning is not urged, since they are just being lifted out of poverty and generally live in areas of low population.

1581 Suyin, Han, "Family Planning in China," Eugenics Rev. 49(2): 81-85, 1957.

Madame Li Teh-chuan, the Health Minister, says that there is a definite demand on the part of women for family planning. The difficulties of meeting this demand are related to the deficit of public health personnel, the unavailability of sufficient contraceptive materials, and the size of the population, 83 *per cent* of which is rural. An oral contraceptive, abortion and sterilization are recommended as ways of meeting the demand.

1582 Suyin, Han, "Impact of Culture on Fertility, Recent Developments in China," in: *Proceedings of Seventh Conference of the IPPF*, Singapore, 1963 Amsterdam: Excerpta Medica Foundation, International Congress Series No. 72.

The first birth control campaign began in 1956 and all means of communication was used by the government. It spread from the cities to the rural areas in 1957. The next year it enlisted the support of the Women's Federation of China, an organization that cuts across all strata and which has many purposes. There was a psychological resistance to the program by rural dwellers but with the spread of industrial communes to the countryside and the "work point" system, the resistance declined when large families were now found to be a detriment to economic improvement.

1583 Taeuber, Irene B., and Orleans, Leo A. "National Programmes: Achievements and Problems: Mainland China," pp. 31-54 in: Berelson, Bernard, *et al.* *Family Planning and Population Programme*. Chicago: The University of Chicago Press, 1966.

If the government of China bases its decisions on analyses of the dynamics of its population, programs to reduce birth rates will have increasing priority among the drives toward economic advance and political stability. It appears that population fields are becoming areas for firm decisions rather than arguments on ideology and discussions of policy. Intra-uterine devices, induced abortion, and sterilization permit effective programs and these are acceptable to the Chinese. The dynamics of the Communist system itself may have already transformed youth so deeply that acceptance of delayed marriage and the family of only one or two children may present few problems. There may, of course, be rural-urban differences in this regard.

1584 T'ien Feng-t'iao, "China's Planned Births and Population Increase," Translated from the Chinese from: Jen-min Pao-chien [People's Health Protection],No. 5, May 1, 1959, pp. 1-25 in: U.S. Joint Publications Research Service, New York, Translations on Communist China's Economic Services, 1959. JPRS: 1956-N.

1585 Tien, H. Yuan, "Birth Control in Communist China," China Quart., No. 14, April - June 1963, pp. 218-26.

A critique of two articles in the China Quarterly by Leo Orleans: "Birth Control, Reversal or Postponement?" and "A New Birth Control Campaign?" Main criticisms are that Orleans' analyses are incorrect with regard to 1) the reasons why the early birth control program was terminated, 2) the differential success of that program, and 3) the reasons for the birth control campaigns. Orleans, for example, contends that the first campaign to promote birth control was terminated because the Communists were unwilling to pursue a policy that had failed to produce concrete results and that they would not initiate a new campaign until viable results could be assured. In reply, Tien says that: 1) failure also has no place in the spirit of capitalism; 2) the Chinese Communists are known to have persisted in pursuing certain policies in spite of initial and repeated failures, the best example of which is their now being in power; and 3) the discontinuation of a program may well be merely to make way for the introduction of a new program judged or believed to be equally, if not more, conducive to the realization of the same goal.

1586 Tien, H. Yuan, "Birth Control in Mainland China: Ideology and Politics," Milbank Memorial Fund Quart. 41(3):269-90. July 1963.

This study has two aims; (1) to rectify some of the inaccuracies as regards the inception and evolution of the recent epic birth control campaign in Communist China, and (2) to suggest a more plausible explanation for its subsequent deflation. Both the ideological setting and the political milieu in which the whole episode transpired is taken into account. While ideology is a pervasive force in Communist China, population policies are also politics, and are necessarily and intimately tied to individuals who participate in this oldest form of human drama. A policy and its proponents invariably succeed or fail together on the open stage, especially when high stakes are involved. Careful review of original Communist China sources leads to the conclusion that the issue of birth control was, in the recent past, implicated in a situation where ideology, politics, and personalities were poignantly entangled. For this reason, the vigorous campaign of 1957-1958 was gradually brought to a standstill, though the population problem itself was not entirely or permanently dismissed. In the aftermath of events since 1958, a resumption of birth control activities has occurred. In view of the complexity, delicacy, and enormity of the question of birth control in Communist China, the road to success in fertility control will be neither smooth nor short.

1587 Tien, H. Yuan, "Induced Abortion and Population Control in Mainland China," Marriage and Family Living 25(1):35-43. February 1963.

Publications of Communist China were screened for information relevant to the question: what prospers are there for using induced abortion as the principal means of population control in China? It was found that prior to the 1957 campaign to promote birth control in Communist China, the desirability of induced abortion received scattered comment. But, the keynote of the various discussions was its un-desirability. Nevertheless, induced abortion was legalized in 1953, and rules governing it were further relaxed in 1957, provided: (1) the operation was to take place within three months of gestation, (2) there were no other health impediments, and (3) there had been no abortion during the preceding 12 months. Also, abortions would be allowed without reference to family size. The announcement drew a prompt rebuttal from the Chinese Medical Association which had already made known its opposition.

1588 Tien H. Yuan, "Population Control: Recent Developments in Mainland China," Asian Survey 2(3):12-16. July 1962.

Review of four phases of the 1949-1961 birth control campaign in Mainland China and a report on signs of a new policy of fertility control in 1962 which would promote late marriages. The question remains as to whether postponement of marriage constitutes an effective method of population control, even in the light of the intimate relationship between marriage and childbearing.

1589 Tien H. Yuan, "Sterilization, Oral Contraception, and Population Control in China," Popul. Stud. 18(3):215-35. March 1965.

Since spring of 1962, when China resumed public discussions in favor of late marriage, events have made it clear that this constituted a prologue to a new phase of fertility control activities. Sterilization is being encouraged along with most other contraceptive techniques, with the notable exception of oral contraception. One principal concern is the volume of sterilization needed to reduce fertility to desired levels, not the factors affecting male or female acceptance of it as a method of fertility control. Estimates are made on the basis of the Japanese experience. An intensive review of available Chinese publications also disclosed that oral contraception received attention in 1956 and 1957 through publication and popularization of oral contraceptive recipes of presumed value consisting of ingredients of plant, animal, and mineral origin. This is believed to have resulted from the attempts to change a nation and to cherish her heritage simultaneously. The influence of traditional medicine and its personnel therefore must be reckoned within China today. Yet, ways must be found to make possible the introduction of oral contraceptives of proved value. The earlier interest in oral contraceptives of presumed value has important policy implications for population control.

1590 U.S. American Consulate General, Hong Kong, "The Campaign Against Early Marriage," Survey of China Mainland Press, May 24 and June 13, 1962, pp. 15-19.

In the first place cited are given the text of and some published comment on: [What is the most suitable age for marriage?] Chung-kuo Ch'ing-nien Pao (Peking), April 12, 1962. The author, Dean of Department of Public Health, Peking Medical College, advocates the ages of 25 to 29 for men and 23 to 27 for women. In the second place cited is an unsigned note: [Early marriage is harmful, not beneficial]. Nan-fang Jih-pao (Canton), May 15, 1962. Author calls the statutory ages of 20 for a man and 14 for a woman the minimum possible suitable age for one to get married.

1591 U.S. American Consulate General, Hong Kong. "Campaign Against Early Marriages," Survey of China Mainland Press, No. 2871, December 3, 1962, pp. 9-15.

English translations of two articles: Wang Wen-pin [A talk about the question of age for marriage from the physiological angle.] pp. 9-11. Translation of Chinese text in: Kung-jen Jih-pao (Peking) November 15, 1962; Chou Hsin-min [On the encouragement of late marriage and the statutory marriage age.] pp. 11-15. Translation of Chinese text in: Kung-jen Jih pao (Peking) November 7, 1962.

1592 U.S. American Consulate General, Hong Kong, [For Late Marriage] by Yang Hsiu. Translated from Chinese text in: Chung-kuo Ch'ing-nien [China Youth], No. 11, June 1, 1962. Selections from China Mainland Magazines, No. 322, July 16, 1962, pp. 22-26.

The most suitable age for marriage is assessed from several points of view: intellectual growth, contributions to the motherland, and physical growth and the health of the next generation. From each point of view, it would be better for youths to get married late, i.e., between the ages of 23 and 26 years for women, and between 25 and 29 years for men. After marriage, it is important to practice planned birth or wait for one or two more years before having any children. It is believed that youth will be able to handle their love and marriage correctly provided that ideological education is conducted and concrete guidance and help are given.

1593 U.S. American Consulate General, Hong Kong, [Kwangtung Province Convenes Conference to Exchange Experiences in Work on Planned Childbirth. Program for Planned Childbirth Has Made Great Progress, But Intensified Leadership Over Work Is Urged.] Translation of Chinese text in Canton Nan-Fang Jih-pao, April 14, 1965. Survey of China Mainland Press, No. 1446, April 29, 1965, pp. 19-20.

1594 U.S. American Consulate General, Hong Kong, "Social Problems and Policies. Part 5, Women, Marriage and Family Planning, 1962," Extracts from China Mainland Publications, No. 65, 11 September 1963, pp. 4-7.

Quotations from fifteen published statements advocating later marriage, i.e., between ages 20 and 30.

1595 U. S. American Consulate General, Hong Kong, "Translations of a Group of Articles on Fertility Controls," in: Chung-kuo Fu-nu [Women of China], No. 4, April 1, 1963. Selections from China Mainland Magazines, No. 364, May 13, 1963, pp. 32-39.

Contents: Sung Hung-tsao, Will vasectomy affect health? pp. 32-34; Lu Ta-ch'uan, Before and after I had my vasectomy, pp. 35; Lin Ch'iao-chih, Can late marriage cause difficult labor? pp. 36-37; Fu Lien-chang, The positive significance of planned family, pp. 38-39.

1596 U.S. Department of Agriculture, Report of the China-United States Agricultural Mission. International Agricultural Collaborations, Report No. 2, Office of Foreign Agricultural Relations. Washington: Government Printing Office, 1947. 265 pp.

The need for restricting population is noted.

1597 U.S. Department of State, Bureau of Intelligence and Research, _Chinese Communist World Outlook: a Handbook of Chinese Communist Statements, the Public Record of a Militant Ideology_. Department of State Publication, 7379. Far Eastern Series, 112. Washington: viii, 139 pp.

Section, Social problems and policies includes heading, Population and birth control, containing four pronouncements: Li Te-ch'uan, March 8, 1957; Mao Tse-tung, February 27, 1957; Shanghai Wen Hui Pao, August 14, 1958; Li Fu-ch'un, August 16, 1960.

1598 Wang Chin-shih, "On the Problem of Birth Control," Translated from Chinese text in: _Shih Shih Shou Tse_ [Current Events], Issue No. 24, December 25, 1956, pp. 19-31 in: _Extracts from China Mainland Magazines_, No. 72, March 4, 1957.

Questions and answers on the meaning and purpose of the present official policy of birth limitation.

1599 Woodsworth, K.C. "Family Law and Resolution of Domestic Disputes in the People's Republic of China," _McGill Law J._ 13:169, 1967.

HONG KONG

Policies on fertility and family size

1600 Chun, Daphne, "Family Planning and the Population Problems of Hong Kong," pp. 270-73 in: Vol. 2 of United Nations, Department of Economic and Social Affairs. _Proceedings of the World Population Conference_, Belgrade, 30 August - 10 September, 1965. 4 Vols. New York: United Nations, 1967.

Describes program of Hong Kong Family Planning Association and governmental measures on immigration, housing, health, and children's allowances.

(East Asia: Non-Mainland)

JAPAN

General population policies

1601 Amundson, Robert H. "Japan's Population Problem: a Positive Approach," Rev. Soc. Econ. 15(2):104-17. September 1957.

The purpose of this article is to emphasize a different approach to the solution of Japan's population problem, one which includes an analysis of conditions contributing to population pressure, and the formulation of positive programs based on sound Christian principles.

1602 Burch, Guy I. "Japan: Good Neighbor or Poor Relation?" Popul. Bull. 6(2):9-15. December 1950.

The author discusses the reasons for Japan's multiplying 83,000,000 people, in regard to population limitation and possible ingenuity in production and trade. In April, 1949 the government created a Population Problem Council within the Cabinet. Acting on the recommendations of this council, the Japanese government passed the "Eugenic Protection Law" in June, 1949. This law not only establishes birth control clinics and legalizes sterilization for heredity purposes, but also legalizes abortion for economic reasons. The author contends that those who oppose birth control in Japan should evaluate their decision in the light of the population explosion.

1603 Cook, Robert C. "Population Policy and the Japanese Peace Treaty," Popul. Bull. 7(2):9-16. August 1951.

The author expresses concern that, while the draft of the proposed Japanese peace treaty and specific articles of the United Nations Charter include lofty ideals, they contain no practical statements regarding an effective population policy for Japan. After the war, no measures were taken to reduce the country's high birth rate, and starvation for millions of Japanese appears inevitable unless a balance of births and deaths is programmed through natural means (as written of by Malthus) or through deliberate human action. Discussed are the Japan Diet's legalization of abortion and sterilization in 1949, Puerto Rico's population crisis, the applicability, problems and effectiveness of abortion and sterilization as measures for maintaining balance in populations, and Sweden's nation-wide sterilization law. It is concluded that the United Nations should adopt a population policy relevant and realistic for all of its member nations.

1604 Coyle, David C. "Japan's Population: Past Achievements and New Problems," Popul. Bull. 15:119-36. November 1959.

After an outline of Japanese policy and attitudes regarding population through World War II, with consideration of the push for imperialism versus the problem of economic welfare, and a survey of post war discussion involving both American and Japanese thought on the issue, the author covers Japan's special experience with population control over the years and discusses the reasons for the country's declining birth rates since the last war and future population expectations. The history of birth control in Japan is given, with reference to legal action, public opinion and extent of use, followed by a look at general population statistics and the problem of natural population increase. Prospects and possible solutions are discussed, especially in relation to Japan's surplus of workers and economic development, and the author concludes that the country's population problem is apparently being solved by the people themselves, who will hold down their country's birth rate through westernized techniques and progressive attitudes toward family limitation.

1605 Dore, R.P. "Japanese Rural Fertility: Some Social and Economic Factors," Popul. Stud. 7(1):62-88. July 1953.

Although Japan's rural fertility trends are not yet so clearly marked as fertility trends of the urban population, indications are that the rural or agricultural segment is declining only slowly, if at all. The author examines some social and economic factors influencing rural fertility, with the recognition that it is among this population that traditional beliefs and values have their deepest roots and with a consideration of the possible changes to be brought about by increasing urban industrialization. Reviewed are factors other than birth control affecting rural fertility, the value of children in rural society, ideal family size as demonstrated by rural public opinion surveys, attitudes and access to means of deliberate family limitation, attitudes toward and frequency of abortion, official and public attitudes toward contraception, and recent statistics concerning rural birth rates. The author concludes with a discussion of the reasons why the tendency to limit births is strongest with the middle ranks of farmers and weaker with the poor and the more wealthy and an analysis of future prospects and the government's role in developing policy and encouraging control.

1606 Grajdanzev, Andrew J. "Japan's Ideological Front," Far Eastern Survey 12(9):89-92. May 3,1943.

Current developments in Japanese population goals and policies are summarized on the basis of Japanese sources.

1607 Japan. Jinko Mondai Kenkyusho [Institute of Population Problems], Implications of Population Trends for Planning Social Welfare Services. Tokyo: 1964. ii, 59 pp.

In a paper presented to the Asian Population Conference in New Delhi, 1963, the author presents a case study focusing on the post-World War II demographic experiences in Japan. Some topics discussed are: family planning as a social welfare service; maternal and child welfare; welfare for the aged; social security and community development. It has been realized that the fuller utilization of manpower and manpower development fundamentally depends on the promotion of social welfare in order to adjust to rapid social changes in Japan's post war period.

1608 Japan. Jinko Mondai Kenkyusho [Institute of Population Problems], Sansei Oyobi imin Mondai o Cushin to Suru Tamuson Hakase no Hatsugen to Sono Hankyo [Dr. Thompson's Statements on the Problems of Birth Control and Migration and Their Effects], Series No. 38, Tokyo, 1950, 22 pp.

1609 Japan. Jinko Mondai Kenkyusho [Institute of Population Problems], The Problem of Population and National Development. Tokyo: Institute of Population Problems, Ministry of Health and Welfare, 1964.

Part I, "The Problem of Population and National Development" by Minoru Tachi examines favorable factors and obstacles to the dissemination of family planning and concludes with the statement that the dissemination of family planning can be most effectively realized if closely interwoven in social development programs, particularly in public health and social welfare services. Also,policies designed by the Government are not sufficient unless backed up by the activities of voluntary organizations to permeate the program into daily life. Part II, "The Promotion of Family Planning in Japan and Its Possible Implications" by Minoru Muramatsu reviews the effectiveness of family planning programs among the general public in Japan during the past two decades. The author states that the decision of the Government to promote a contraceptive program was made primarily because of the necessity to offer professional advice on fertility control to those who were already highly motivated toward the planning of family size. Some of the possible implications for the promotion of family planning in general from the Japanese experiences are suggested: to promote contraceptive use with community-centered orientations; with the actual participation of local women's organizations; with the help of social workers; with advice to males on the treatment of sterility; and with the pilot-testing of a practical, effective contraceptive method.

1610 Japan. Jinko Mondai Shingikai [Population Problem Council], _Recommendations of the Population Problem Council in the Cabinet, Japanese Government, November 29, 1949_. Tokyo, 1949. 20 pp.

Specific and generally courageous recommendations with reference to economic development and population control. This is the report to the Cabinet. The Cabinet did not act on the report, and as of April 1950, the Population Problem Council itself passed out of existence.

1611 Japanese Birth Control Institute, "Political Parties on Population Policy," _Japanese Planned Parenthood Quart_. 5(4): 57-ff. October-December 1954.

1612 Kada, Tesuji, "The Family System in Japan," _Nihon Hyoron_, January 1941. This article, in Japanese, is summarized in _Contemporary Japan_ 10(2):237-41. February 1941.

The Japanese Cabinet proposals in favor of the family system through limiting the vote to heads of families is evaluated critically and the need expressed for a broader economic policy to increase the number of large families.

1613 Kitoaka, Juitsu, _Jinko Mondai to Jinko Seisaku_ [Population Problems and Population Policies]. Tokyo, 1948. 238 pp.

Chpts.1-3, General theory and background; 4, Post-war overpopulation; 5, The birth control movement; 6, The policy to increase births; 7, The policy of reducing deaths; 8, Eugenics.

1614 Mitsubishi Economic Research Bureau, "Basic Principles for Population Policy," Monthly Circular: 16-17. March 1941.

1615 Okasaki, Ayami, "Le Probleme et la Politique Demographiques au Japon " [The Problem and Demographic Policy in Japan], Population 7(2):207-26. April - June 1952.

General review of population growth and economic resources from 1603 to 1950, with special emphasis on the period just prior and after World War II. Economic and territorial losses because of the war and a booming population growth necessitated consideration of policy alternatives. Emigration which was very helpful in the past is no longer a possibility and thus reliance is to be placed on birth control. The formation of the Eugenics Protection Commission and its related Eugenics Protection Law, and the surveys by the Japanese Institute of Population Studies on the frequency of contraception and abortion are also discussed.

1616 Robin, Jean, "Le Probleme Demographique au Japon " [The Demographic Problems of Japan], Population 6(2):205-22. April - June 1951.

Part I contains a review of Japanese population during antiquity, the Classical Period (8th-10th centuries), the Middle Ages (11th-16th centuries), the Tokugawa Period (1602-1868), the Meiji Regime (1868-1914), World War I to World War II, and after 1940. The distribution of population, recent fertility and mortality rates, and population projections are also discussed. A review of the economic situation which suggests an imbalance between population and resources is followed by a consideration of policies on emigration and birth control, and the attitudes of political parties and Christianity and Buddhism to birth control.

1617 Royal Institute of International Affairs, "Japan's Prosperity Sphere," Bull. Internat. News 18(9):548-52. May 3, 1941.

Including the population problem and emigration plans.

1618 Taeuber, Irene B. "Japan's Increasing People: Facts, Problems and Policies," Pacific Affairs 23:271-93, 1950.

Population policy has always been a derivative of total national policy. In periods of crisis and depression, democratically-oriented policies based on concepts of individual welfare and social advance have been evolved as solutions to the population problem. In periods of prosperity, expansionist policies have been formulated to advance the political and economic power of the Japanese state without commensurate benefit to other peoples or specific consideration of the individual Japanese families.

1619 Taeuber, Irene B. The Population of Japan. Princeton: Princeton University Press, 1959. xv, 461 pp.

A study about population and socio-economic change during the transition from an agrarian to an urban-industrial society in the Oriental context. Chapter VII - Demography in Peace and War - describes The Demography of War, Problems, Projections, and Policies, and Past and Future.

1620 Terao, Takuma, "Mita Gakkai Sasshi " [The Meaning of Population Policy], Mita Journal of Econ. 48(11):1-14, November 1955.

1621 Thompson, Warren S. "The Need for a Population Policy in Japan," Amer. Sociol. Rev. 15:25-33, 1950.

Encouraging the reduction of births is the only policy which in the long run can be classed as a cure for population pressure. This does not mean that increases in production, expansion of foreign trade, and larger emigration should not be encouraged in all feasible ways. It merely means that as long as there is a relatively high birth rate, population growth will keep pace with or exceed the increase in resources and production.

Policies on fertility and family size

1622 Amano, Fumiko Y. "Family Planning Movement in Japan," Reprint from: Contemporary Japan 23(10-12): 1955. 14 pp.

History of the birth control movement and of governmental policy before World War II, under the Occupation, and since 1952.

1623 Amano, Fumiko Y. "The Role of Midwives in Birth Control," Japan Planned Parenthood Quart. 3(4):42-43, 58. October - December 1952.

1624 American Eugenics Society, "The New Eugenic Protection Law in Japan," Eugenical News 33(1-2):21-23. March - June 1948.

Law establishing the Eugenic Protection Commission and authorizing inducing abortion by licensed physician for health or socioeconomic reasons.

1625 "Asia's Boom in Babies - And Why It's Missing Japan: Government-Backed Legalized Campaign for Birth Control," U.S. News 51:66-67. August 1961.

Shows the effect of induced abortion in reducing the birth rate in Japan.

1626 Bartlett, Christopher, "Planning Japan's Families," Far Eastern Econ. Rev. 54(11):555-59. December 15, 1966.

Summarizes annual statistics on natural increase 1947-1965 and on induced abortions 1949-1965. Considers reasons for trends shown and for changes in government policy.

1627 Beard, Mary R. The Force of Women in Japanese History. Washington: Public Affairs Press, 1953. 196 pp.

Including the story of Shidzue Ishimoto Kato's activities for birth control and ending with the story of overpopulation as the underlying and peculiar problem of Japan.

1628 Blacker, C.P. "Japan's Population Problem," Eugenics Rev. 48:31-39, 1956-57.

Astonishing results, which few people would have dared to predict, have been achieved in introducing to experimental village populations in Japan the principle and methods of family planning. The Japanese government has embarked on an energetic programme of introducing these same methods to the country as a whole, and the last and largest of several surveys suggests that the practice of family planning is fairly rapidly spreading. A government-sponsored policy of facilitating abortion seems to have over-reached itself; the results are now widely criticized. It is impossible to say how successful the new policy -- of substituting the practice of family planning for that of abortion -- will prove to be. It may perhaps be successful beyond what now looks like reasonable expectation and it is not impossible that the gloomy forecasts of demographers that the population of Japan will soon exceed one hundred million may, like other seemingly well-founded forecasts of demographers, be falsified. In no country are the relevant motivations, deriving from both personal and national considerations more powerful than in Japan; in none can the relevant education be conducted with greater freedom from cultural taboos; and in none does population seem more capable of acquiring the new outlook and of learning the new practices.

1629 Boffey, Philip N. "Japan: A Crowded Nation Wants to Boost Its Birthrate," Science 167:960-62, 1969.

For the past two decades Japan has struggled to curb its population growth, and to a large extent it has succeeded. Thus, Minister Eisaku Sato's publicly advocating an increase in Japan's birthrate seems to mark a major reversal of Japan's population policy. Sato noted that Japan's birthrate had fallen below the average for other advanced nations, and he stated that the government would strive to bring it back up to the average level. The recommendations are aimed at alleviating some potentially serious economic and social problems that are related, at least in part to Japan's success at curbing its population growth. The author examines the Japanese situation in detail in regard to the political and economic pressures it presents.

1630 Burch, Thomas K. "Induced Abortion in Japan Under Eugenic Protection Law of 1948," Eugen. Quart. 2(3):140-51, 1955.

At present more than a million Japanese women annually induce abortions to limit families. The Japanese have long practiced abortion and infanticide to conserve resources. By the mid-eighteenth century these practices were so widespread that the government prohibited both. Probably these practices nevertheless continued. Unlike Westerners, Japanese do not regard abortion as seriously immoral. Neither Shinto nor Buddhism categorically opposes abortion. Following World War II economic conditions in Japan were especially harsh. The resulting problems led to passage, in 1948, of the Eugenic Protection Law. This law, as amended, (1) legalizes sterilization in cases in which defective offspring might result or maternal health be endangered; (2) provides for "Eugenic Protection Consultation Offices" to provide advice and information on matters of marriage, eugenics, and family limitation; (3) leaves abortion to discretion of the doctor - with consent of the persons in question. The American occupation authorities adopted a hands-off policy with respect to this legislation. Since passage of the Eugenic Protection Law the number of induced abortions has risen steadily. The chief reasons were economic and because the parents did not want children. According to a study of families given intensive guidance in use of contraceptives, the people made no clearcut distinction between use of contraceptives and abortion as a means of family limitation. Contraceptive failures led to abortion. It was found that couples who resort to abortion more often practice contraception.

1631 Burch, Thomas K. "Patterns of Induced Abortion and Their Socio-Moral Implications in Postwar Japan," Soc. Kompas 3(4): 178-88, 1955-56.

Gives a brief, statistical account of the use of abortion in contemporary Japan, summarizing what seem to be the more significant findings of Japanese research, carried on by

Japanese scholars. This account consists of discussing postwar economic difficulties; the eugenic protection law; incidence of sterilization and abortion under the eugenic protection law; abortion and contraception; abortion and the unmarried; abortion and health; and abortion and population growth. It is unfortunate that the work of Japanese scholars has remained relatively unavailable to the non-Japanese social scientist and medical man, constituting as it does the most extensive and intensive study of the non-therapeutic uses of induced abortion yet made. A brief description of some of the distinctive historical and cultural facts required if the current situation is to be understood, and if reasonable solutions are to be formulated.

1632 Dueholm, Erik. "Japans Liberale Abortlov " [Japan's Liberal Abortion Law], Okonomi og Politik 41(2):172-94, 1967.

1633 Furuya, Y. "A Study of Birth Control in a Model Village," Nippon Jinkogakkai Kiyo 1:1-11. August 1952.

1634 Honda, T. "Sanji Seigen Mondai o Shudai to Suru Jakkan no Jinkorironteki Shosatsu " [Some Considerations Concerning the Contraception Problem from the Standpoint of the Population Problem], Jinko Mondai Kenkyu 5(7-8-9). July - August - September 1947.

1635 "How Japan Solves Population Problem," U.S. News 62:64-65. June 12,1967.

Results of legalized abortion and government encouraged birth control programs in reducing the birth rates. Also there is great financial benefit to the medical profession in performing abortions.

1636 Hunt, Chester L. "Japan's Answer to the Population Explosion," Antioch Rev. 22(4):461-74. Winter 1962-63.

The Japanese birth rate has dropped 50% between 1947 and 1961, from 34.3 to 16.8. This is the result of a major family limitation campaign by the Japanese Government utilizing both contraception and abortion. 1.5 million abortions per year indicates that this has been the major source of family limitation. Contraception has been propagandized but has won only partial acceptance. It is suggested that this is a general feature of Asian countries which have not yet developed the planning attitude toward life required for successful contraceptive practice. There is some ambivalence on population restriction in Japan, but trends indicate a continual decline in the birth rate resulting in stabilized population in 1990.

1637 Japan. "Eugenics and Protection of Maternal Health," Internat. Digest Health Legis. 16:690-99, 1965.

Law No. 156 of 13 July 1948 including amendments up to 21 April 1960 which establishes the Eugenic Protection Commission and the Eugenics Protection Consultation Office and which authorizes the giving of advice on marriage from the eugenics viewpoint, instruction in contraception, and induced abortion for health or socio-economic reasons.

1638 Japan. Jinko Mondai Kenkyusho [Institute of Population Problems]. Ninshin Chusetsu, Datai, Shi-ryuzan, no Wariai ni Kansuru [The Proportion of Terminations of Pregnancy, Abortion, Stillbirth, Miscarriage], Series No. 44, 1950, 4 pp.

1639 Japan. Jinko Mondai Kenkyusho [Institute of Population Problems]. Sanji Seigen Mondai no Jinko Sei-Saku-Teki Kosatsu [Considerations on the Question of Birth Control from the Viewpoint of Population Policy], Series No. 43, July 1949, 46 pp.

1640 Japan. Zaidan Hojin Jinko Mondai Kenkyukai. Jinko Taisaku Linkai [Foundation Institute for Research on Population Problems. Committee on Population Policies]. Jinko Taisaku to Shite no Katei Keikaku no Fukyu ni Kansara Ketsugi [Resolution on Family Planning as a Population Measure]. Tokyo, 1954. 12 pp.

1641 Japan. Zaidan Hojin Jinko Mondai Kenkyukai. Jinko Taisaku Linkai [Foundation Institute for Research on Population Problems. Committee on Population Policies]. Jinko Taisaku to Shite no Katei Keikaku no Fukyu ni Kansuru Ketsugi Setsumei Shiro [Explanatory Material on the Resolution on Promoting Family Planning as a Population Measure]. 1954, 51.

1642 Japan Medical Association, "The Proceedings of the 1st Committee Meeting on the Eugenic Protection Law," J. Japan Med. Assn. 51:295-316. February 1,1964.

1643 Japan. Ministry of Health and Welfare, Jido (kazoku) Teate Seido Kiso Chosa Kekka Nokokusho, 1964 [Statistical Results of a Basic Survey of the System of Family Allowances, 1964]. Tokyo, 1965. 159 pp.

1644 Japan. Ministry of Health and Welfare, Seikatsu Hogo Dotai Chosa Hokoku, 1963 [Survey of Family Allowances in Respect of Low-Income Families in Japan, 1963]. Tokyo, 1965. 57 pp.

1645 "Japan's Dangerous Flowers," Economist 185:599-600. 16 November 1957.

The Anti-Prostitution Law introduced in the Diet in 1955 became effective in March 1957 with penalties for non-compliance postponed to April 1958. It affects 35,000 brothel-keepers and 132,000 prostitutes known as Kiken na Dokubana or Dangerous Poisonous Flowers. Both groups are unionized and they and others oppose the law on economic and moral ground, i.e., rape is lessened by prostitution for sexual satisfaction.

1646 Jira, Lubomir, "K Otazce Aplikace Antikoncepcnich Metod v Japonsku " [Application of Contraceptive Methods in Japan], Demografie 5(2):173-75, 1963.

1647 Karpas, Melvin Ronald, "Moral Attitude Concerning Sex in Japan," Sociol. Bull. 14(1):34-40. March 1965.

In Japan, sexual behavior has been traditionally accepted and respected as part of life, and free from the onus placed on it in the West. This is due to two factors: (1) Traditional religion: Shintoism includes a god of prostitution and worship of phallic symbols for fertility of both fields and womb; (2) Upbringing: Sexual play and references to sexual parts are accepted for children. There are no restrictions on extramarital relations for the Japanese male, although his wife has no such rights. Prostitution is a respected occupation, often used to earn a dowry. With the increase of Western influence since World War I, the Japanese attitude toward sex has been changing. In 1957 a law was passed outlawing prostitution, but enforcement has been lax. Prostitution is a widespread source of income and many families are dependent on it for support. Because the exploited prostitute is regarded with sympathy, the law calls for centers for her rehabilitation, but financial problems are prohibitive. It is too early to adduce the effects of the new moral code on Japanese society.

1648 Kawagoe, Keizo, "On Fertility Control for Poor People in Japan and Osaka," pp. 109-10 in: Sixth International Conference on Planned Parenthood, New Delhi, 14-21 February, 1959. London: International Planned Parenthood Federation, 1959.

Clients in Osaka come to the municipal social welfare office once every month to receive aid money. The author, on the basis of his experience with Osaka City, is convinced that the most effective way to give guidance on fertility control is through special establishments in all municipal social offices.

1649 Kimura, Masabumi, "Induced Abortion in Japan in 1953-54: A Demographic Analysis of Reports from Designated Physicians," Milbank Memorial Fund Quart. 37:154-ff., 1959.

6,932 physicians of the 9,597 authorized to perform abortions in Japan responded to a questionnaire sent out between December 1953 and August 1954. The physicians reported that, of the 6,174 women for whom they had performed abortions, 75% were in the 25-39 year age bracket, 63% had never had an abortion and 8.3% had never been pregnant. 23% wanted an abortion for family limitation, 14% for spacing, 12.5% on economic grounds and 12.2% because of illness.

1650 Kimura, Masabumi, "A Review of Induced Abortion Surveys in Japan," New York: International Union for Scientific Study of Population and Population Association of America, 1961. 10 pp. Paper no.43. Mimeographed.

Surveys conducted in Japan on the prevalence and characteristics of induced abortion are reviewed briefly. The results of a large scale survey carried out in one prefecture are discussed

1651 Kitauka, Juitsu, "How Japan Halved Her Birth Rate in Ten Years," pp. 27-29 in: Sixth International Conference on Planned Parenthood, New Delhi, 14-21 February 1959. London: International Planned Parenthood Federation, 1959.

The author reviews the history of population in Japan and outlines the measures taken to encourage birth control in Japan since the War.

1652 Koya, Yoshio, "Does the Effect of a Family Planning Program Continue?" Eugenics Quart. 11(3):141-47, 1964.

Instruction and guidance in family planning were given over a three-year period to the people in three typical villages in Japan. The present study was planned to investigate whether village wives were still practicing contraception and whether previous instruction to parents was exerting any influence upon the reproductive behavior of younger couples who had married after the close of the program. The data indicate that the educational program was very effective and that the practice of contraception can spread rapidly if people are adequately informed and supplied.

1653 Koya, Yoshio, "Economic Impact of Instruction in Family Planning: A Proposal to the Japanese National Railways," Eugenics Quart. 7(4):212-16. December 1960.

The object of the family planning movement is to regulate number of children born as well as to promote prosperity among the participating families. By improving the health and well-being of employee's families, the Japanese National Railway (JNR) aimed to raise the efficiency of their operation. During the years 1956-1958, 4,294 families were instructed three times or more. Tables are provided to show how far the expenses of management, association and employees were reduced owing to the decrease of the number of births, cases of induced abortion, etc. A graph of projected results of family planning among all male employees of the JNR is also provided. The results given represent one year of study, and show a definite alleviation of monetary burden on JNR employees.

1654 Koya, Yoshio, "Family Planning Among Japanese on Public Relief," Eugenics Quart. 4(1):17-23. March 1957.

The Population Problem Council of Japan in 1949 recommended the dissemination of birth control knowledge to all married couples and to all classes of the nation. A special effort was made recently to enforce a program for dissemination of contraceptive practice among the extremely poor. An experiment and survey was started in 1953 with those who were receiving public relief from the government. An intensive educational program in family planning in a specific test area and a nation-wide survey of families receiving public relief was made. Monthly personal interviews and advice was given but the simpler contraceptive methods were recommended. During the third year there was a 32% decrease in pregnancies from the previous two years of study. The calculation of the pregnancy rate according to the Stix-Notestein method revealed that it decreased from 53.9 for the year previous to the start of the project, to 16.5 for the third year of the study. Instructional emphasis was also placed upon the reduction of induced abortions. These have decreased from 45 to 22 in the course of three years. Family planning seems to be practiced least successfully in the outlying, less civilized rural areas where most of the villages without doctors are found as well as among those embedded in poverty in the cities.

1655 Koya, Yoshio, "Family Planning as Practiced by Japanese National Railways Employees," Eugenics Quart. 13(1): March 1966.

A brief account of family planning as carried out by Japanese National Railways (JNR) employees. The JNR is a semi-governmental organization. It took up family planning as part of its welfare work in 1956 and from then until 1964 has given instructions on family planning to 173,700 of its married employees. The responsibility structure or disseminating family planning information within JNR from JNR President to guidance workers, guidance zones, family groups and households, is considered especially important. The number of large-scale industrial enterprises in Japan following the example of JNR is stated to be steadily on the increase. Labor union chapters and females' societies are included in the regional family planning organization. Physicians (mainly female) and midwives are specially selected and trained to give family guidance, with one midwife being in charge of about 500 households. These family planning measures have resulted in savings for the JNR in various family and child allowances granted to its employees.

1656 Koya, Yoshio, "Family Planning Program in the Japanese National Railways (A Sample of Guidance for Large Population Group)," J. Fam. Welf. 9(4):34-44. June 1963.

Data on developments in the year 1962 and statistical evaluation of achievements, based on comparison of the experience of contraceptors and noncontraceptors.

1657 Koya, Yoshio, "Family Planning Program in a Large Population Group: The Case of the Japanese National Railways," Milbank Memorial Fund Quart. 40(3):319-27. July 1962.

A description of the operation of the family planning committee of the Japanese National Railways and its contribution to the family planning set-up of large population groups. At the end of 1961, 80,000 households were receiving guidance from this organization. A study of those families receiving such guidance for three years and among whom the wife was under 50 years of age reveals that 75% of the wives practiced some form of contraception during the first year. Sterility, subfecundity, and a desire to have children appear to be the major reasons for not using some form of contraception. It is noted that by the third year of the program the birth rate was down to 19.4, a 37% decline in two years. Of course, not all of this decline can be attributed to the program inasmuch as one would expect some decrease in the birth rate over time in a closed cohort population, even in the absence of contraception.

1658 Koya, Yoshio, "Five Years Experiment on Family Planning Among Coal Miners in Joban, Japan," Popul. Stud. 13(2): 157-63. November 1959.

Because of Japan's industrial growth the adoption of a family planning program by an industrial group was considered important. An experiment was started in the Iwasaki District of the Joban coal mine in 1953. The direct object of the study was to ascertain to what extent the high birth rate could be lowered without an increase in induced abortion. The crude birth rate of 33.5 in 1952-53, one year before the program began, decreased to 5.4 in 1957-58, a decline of 84%. This huge decline indicates that by and large the desired family size had been reached. The pregnancy rate decreased from 41.0 in 1952-53 to 15.9 in 1957-58. The annual number of abortions increased during the first year of the study, from 63 to 91, but thereafter declined, reaching a level of 28 or 8.4 per 1,000 population in 1957-58. Of the 28 abortions, 14 involved causes unrelated to birth control. 95.5% of the families exposed to the risk of pregnancy were practicing birth control successfully. There has been an attempt by some persons in the Government to amend the Eugenic Protection Law to counteract the increase in induced abortion in Japan. They claim that there is no relationship between the family planning program and induced abortion. These experiments in the three other villages as well as the one under discussion, show clearly that it is possible to reduce the birth rate simultaneously with a decrease in induced abortion.

1659 Koya, Yoshio, "The Harmful Effects of Induced Abortion," World Med. J. 13:170-ff., 1966.

A preliminary report on a project set up in Japan to analyze the consequences of induced abortion.

1660 Koya, Yoshio, "Lessons From Contraceptive Failure," Popul. Stud. 16(1):4-11 July 1962.

Family planning programs have reduced Japanese fertility: in three rural villages, the crude birth rate declined from 26.7 in 1950 to 13.6 in 1957; in a coal mining area, from 27.6 in 1953 to 13.9 in 1958. The national crude birth rate declined from 33.0 in 1949 to 17.2 in 1957 (a rate of decrease without historical precedent), largely due to use of induced abortion. However, in the experimental areas, where instruction in contraception was given, both birth and abortion rates declined. There is still recourse to abortion in all areas by women who become pregnant accidentally, though using contraception. The main reasons for unwanted pregnancy were miscalculation of the safe period or occasional omission to use contraceptives, as reported by a sample of 4400 women (a 95% response), 50% from areas having lectures on family planning by health center officials. In the instructed areas, 87% were contraceptive users, compared to 52% in non-instructed areas. The more widespread practice in instructed areas dilutes the use effectiveness, so that (except in the early years of marriage) failure rates among users are higher in the instructed than non-instructed areas. Users in non-instructed areas are probably more strongly motivated.

1661 Koya, Yoshio, Pioneering in Family Planning: A Collection of Papers on the Family Planning Programmes and Research Conducted in Japan. New York: Population Research Council, 1963. 173 pp.

Brings together the several studies with which Yoshio Koya has been associated.

1662 Koya, Yoshio,and Koyo, Tomohiko, "The Prevention of Unwanted Pregnancies in a Japanese Village by Contraceptive Foam Tablets," Milbank Memorial Fund Quart. 38(2):167-70. April 1960.

Vaginal foam tablets which produce carbon dioxide when moistened by semen or vaginal fluid are inexpensive, easy to use and easy to learn to use. To determine their effectiveness a brand called Sampoon was distributed without charge to families in a Japanese village with a population of 1,500. The wife was instructed to keep the vial stoppered except during removal of a tablet, and to place a tablet as high as possible in the vagina before each sexual intercourse. No subsequent procedure was prescribed. 82 couples used the tablets for a month or more in the years 1955 to 1958 for a total of 1,809 couple months. 18 pregnancies occurred during the use of the tablets, indicating a rate of 11.9 per 100 couples per year. This was a reduction of 77% from the rate of 52.8 per 100 couples per year of exposure during the 5 years before use of the tablets began. It was somewhat lower than the rate of 13.1 found during the use of condoms in the authors' previous studies. Protection from pregnancy increased with the duration of use, the rate of 15.3 per 100 couples per year in 1955 decreasing to 9.5 in 1958. It is concluded that the contraceptive foam tablets used provide an effective and acceptable method of contraception.

1663 Koya, Yoshio, "The Program for Family Planning in Japan," Eugenical News 38(1):1-3, 1953.

Owing to the great increase in abortions following the war, the Japanese government in 1948 authorized studies in family planning to be made. The Ministry of Health and Welfare chose three typical villages representing mountainous, plain, and coast areas. Physicians and public health nurses visited each of 984 families, recording obstetrical histories, giving information and supplies as to contraception methods. After a ten-month period, 92% of the married fertile families were practising contraception. After 12 months there was observed a reduction to approximately half the expected number of children born. The rate of abortions in the three experimental villages was less than half that estimated for Japan as a whole.

1664 Koya, Yoshio, "Seven Years of a Family Planning Program in Three Typical Japanese Villages," Milbank Memorial Fund Quart. 36(4):363-72. October 1958.

A report of a program which began in 1950 to introduce contraceptive methods to three Japanese villages. Results of this progress check indicate that after seven years contraception was used by 75% of the families exposed to pregnancy and by about 95% of those with four or more children. The net production rate dropped from 1.51 to 0.81. It is estimated that, if an extension of the program to all of Japan could have resulted in the same birth rates as those in the three villages, there might have been in the seven years 3,700,000 fewer unwanted births or 4% of the present population.

1665 Koya, Yoshio, "Some Essential Factors for Fertility Control in Japan," pp. 316-17, Vol. 2 in: United Nations Department of Economic and Social Affairs, Proceedings of the World Population Conference, Belgrade, 30 August- 10 September, 1965. New York: United Nations, 1967.

Induced abortion, already widely used as a method of birth control, was encouraged by the establishment of the Eugenics Protection Law in 1947. A Cabinet decision of 1951 sought to replace the method of induced abortion by encouraging the use of contraceptives. But, once people become accustomed to induced abortion, guiding them to the use of other birth control methods is difficult.

1666 Koya, Yoshio, "Sterilization in Japan," Eugenics Quart. 8(3):135-41, September 1961.

The increase in the number of Japanese sterilizations from 1949 to 1959 is discussed. Data were provided by the physicians designated by the Japan Medical Association. The rise in sterilization cases is attributed to the intense desire of the general public to control family size. Comparisons of sterilization frequency are reported for sex, location, age of mother, number of children, and sex of children. Additional comment is made regarding the psychological effects experienced by the males and females and their spouses. Reported sterilizations totaled 6,000 in 1949 to over 44,000 in 1956. Estimates of the total in Japan, including black market operations, are three to four times this figure. The number of children is a most significant factor in the decision to undergo sterilization. Among the sterilized couples, the modal group had three children, comprising 40% of the families. The existence of a male child is important in the decision to resort to sterilization. Female sterilizations account for more than 95% of the total.

1667 Koya, Y., et al. "A Study of Induced Abortion in Japan and Its Significance," Asian Med. J. 8:265-ff., 1965.

The authors describe a study of 1,382 married women who had legal abortions during the period August 1949 through July, 1950. Distribution was evenly matched in regard to rural areas, medium-sized cities and large metropolitan areas. The average number of abortions per woman varied by community type and was 1.2, 1.3 and 1.4 respectively. Women in the 30 to 39 year old age bracket with two or three children had abortions most frequently and contraception was practiced prior to the abortion by only 27%. At the time they were interviewed for the study, almost 50% of the women were pregnant again, 25% of these within six months after the abortion. 47% reported some type of complication. It is contended that most women wanting abortions are motivated by economic worries; only 17% of the sample indicated health reasons.

1668 Koya, Yoshio, "Why Induced Abortions in Japan Remain High," in: Kiser, C.V., ed. Research in Family Planning. Princeton: Princeton University Press, 1962.

It is contended that Japan's high abortion rate reflects two factors: the acceptance of smaller families by all segments of Japanese society and a lack of contraceptive experience and skill throughout the country. The results of an intensive education program in contraception carried out in three villages and three coal mining districts are described, with references to the decline in birth rate and abortion indicated at the end of the program's fifth year of operation and the problems connected to lowering the number of induced abortions. During the first year there was a 46% increase in the number of abortions and the pre-program abortion level was not matched until the fourth year. Contraceptive failures were the most probable cause for this increase during the primary stages of the program.

1669 Kubo, H., et. al. Family Planning in Japan. Tokyo: Asia Family Planning Association, 1961. 43 pp.

Summarizes the rapid growth of population in Japan with the decrease of death control and the measures taken which have cut the birth rate so heavily. Family planning has grown most rapidly in the salaried groups and in the cities, but the gap between cities and farming and fishing villages is rapidly narrowing. Socioeconomic reasons for practice of birth control are found to be most important in Japan. However, many do not distinguish clearly between conception control and artificial termination of pregnancy. The booklet regards induced abortion as not completely harmless both for medical and humanitarian reasons. The guidance of family planning, both by the Government and by voluntary agencies, is described. Family-planning practices in four districts which have been commended by the Minister of Health are detailed.

1670 Mainichi Newspapers, Population Problems Research Council, Eighth Public Opinion Survey on Family Planning. Tokyo: The Mainichi Newspapers, 1965.

The number of legal abortions performed in Japan has varied, with the highest numbers of more than one million per year during the years 1953-61. For the year 1949 the number was estimated at 246,000 while in 1964 the estimate was 878,000. A study of 3,140 women and the incidence of abortion among them is cited; 32.7% had had more than one abortion, 18 to 24% had had one and 80% of those 20-24 years old had never had an abortion. Wives of men out of work constituted over one-half of the abortion cases, while 40% of the cases involved women whose husbands were white collar workers. 50% of the women using some method of birth control had never experienced abortion; 79% of those not practicing contraception had not had an abortion. Education or age did not appear to have any relation to the frequency of abortion except for women in the 35-39 age bracket, 41% of whom had had an abortion. 16% of all women questioned approved of abortion with no reservations, 62% approved of abortion limited by certain conditions and 14% were not in favor of abortion at all. Economic reasons were felt to be appropriate justification by 47%, while 50% deemed abortion necessary for preservation of the mother's health or life.

1671 Mainichi Newspapers, Population Problems Research Council, Fifth Public Opinion Survey on Birth Control in Japan. Tokyo: The Mainichi Newspapers, 1959. 46 pp.

Results of an opinion survey conducted in Japan by the Mainichi Newspapers are given. In addition to a measurement of the prevalence of birth control, the survey aims to study the people's attitudes on the subject. A random sample of 3,000 married couples was enumerated.

1672 Mainichi Newspapers, Population Problems Research Council, Sixth Opinion Survey on Family Planning and Birth Control: A Preliminary Report. Tokyo: The Mainichi Newspapers, 1962. 33 pp.

Continues survey on prevalence of and attitudes to birth control. Of 2,811 respondents to a question on abortion, 41 per cent report a positive experience, 36 per cent a negative experience, and 23 per cent failed to answer either way. Frequency of abortion is highest in metropolitan areas, in higher educational levels, and among women in the 35-49 age group.

1673 Mainichi Newspapers, Population Problems Research Council, A Survey of Public Opinion in Japan on the Readjustment of Overpopulation. Population Problems Series, No. 3, Tokyo, 1951. 31 pp.

In 1950 a survey was conducted by the Population Problems Research Council of the Mainichi Shimbun to learn the mental attitude of the Japanese toward birth control and also to find out the actual state of affairs in regard to the popularization of its practice. A table showing the demographic and social economic composition of the cases surveyed is given, and the survey's content and findings are outlined and summarized. There are five major sections: Basic Attitude Toward Life, Ideals About the Number of Children to be Had, Pro and Con in Regard to Contraception, Practice of Contraception, and What is Demanded of the Population Policy.

1674 Muramatsu, Minoru, "Action Programmes of Family Planning in Japan," pp. 67-75 in: Muramatsu, Minoru, and Harper, Paul A. eds. Population Dynamics: International Action and Training Programmes. Baltimore: Johns Hopkins Press, 1965.

Some of the important aspects of the various action programs in the field of family planning and fertility control which have been conducted after the war in Japan, mainly by the government but partially by voluntary organizations, are summarized in the first half of this paper.

1675 Muramatsu, Minoru, "The Demographic Aspects of Abortion in Japan," Paper Presented at the International Union for the Scientific Study of Population General Conference, 3-11 September 1969, London.

For the past fifteen years there have been conducted a number of campaigns in this country for the reduction of induced abortions, some sponsored by the Government but mostly by private groups. In such campaigns, various slogans have been employed. Immorality of induced abortion, the danger that the widespread use of induced abortion practice would lead to undermining the respect of life, harmful effects of induced abortion, or sometimes the feeling of international disgrace in having so many abortions-- these have been expressed by campaign leaders. However, induced abortions are still fairly prevalent, though since 1955 their numbers have been decreasing, and the campaigns in general have not yet fully accomplished what they have hoped for. Recently, another factor has been added in this picture. Shortness of immediately available young workers is now a serious concern in certain quarters of society, and the recovery of births is called for by many authorities. Induced abortion should be avoided as rigidly as possible from this viewpoint, too, and a group of social leaders have even attempted to drastically amend the Eugenic Protection Law. However, there also is prevailing an opinion opposed to such an amendment. Opponents usually base their arguments on their conviction that once people have been accustomed to the free availability of abortion, it is not easy to do away with it so quickly. If the legal bases for abortion were tightened strictly, many would undoubtedly go to seek "back street abortionists." Moreover, the very fact that still a large number of abortions are being performed clearly indicates the presence of basic needs for them. Shortage of housing facilities can be a typical example of this kind, and the promotion of social development programs must precede such a manipulation of laws and regulations, they maintain. Faced with the division of opinions among Japanese people, for the time being at least, there will be no drastic change in the legal handling of induced abortion. In the whole process of fertility decline and economic growth in Japan after the war, induced abortion has played a significant part. But at the same time, it is obvious that induced abortion should be regarded only as the last resort. In this country, induced abortion still presents a major social and medical problem. The decline in abortions we have been observing for the past decade or so may further continue, but how far and how fast it will go still remains to be seen. It all depends on how people will react to their traditional value of children when they find themselves amidst the so-called affluence of material goods.

1676 Muramatsu, Minoru, "Effect of Induced Abortion on the Reduction of Births in Japan," Milbank Memorial Fund Quart. 38(2):153-70, April 1960.

An estimation of the number of live births that would have occurred in 1955 in Japan in the absence of induced abortion was made. From the total number of married women, the estimated number of those who did not participate in reproductive activities because of successful contraception or sterilization was subtracted. To those who could participate in reproductive activities, the theoretical age-specific birth rates to be expected in the absence of fertility control practices were applied in order to obtain the expected number of legitimate births in 1955. By applying the ratio of illegitimate births to legitimate births observed in Japan in 1920, the expected number of illegitimate births in the absence of induced abortion was computed. Finally, the number of all live births, legitimate and illegitimate, to be expected if there were no induced abortion at all was estimated by adding up the above two factors. As a conclusion, it can be stated that the number of births in 1955 in Japan would have amounted to twice or more the number actually registered if there were no induced abortion at all. In addition, the reporting of induced abortions to health authorities probably included only 50 to 60% of all cases actually performed.

1677 Muramatsu, Minoru, "Family Planning Practice among the Japanese," Eugenics Quart. 7(1):23-30, March 1960.

A summary of what has been accomplished by a series of field studies known as the test studies of family planning. The studies demonstrated what could be done by an intensive education in family planning and offered the results to the government to promote family planning practices throughout the country. Three groups were selected for the studies: a group of three rural villages, coal-mine workers and people on public relief. Education was conducted at three levels: general, group and individual. Among various methods condoms were usually most popular. Husbands showed relatively great cooperation in the practice of contraception. Births of unwanted children were considerably reduced, though some difficulties were met in reducing induced abortions. Female sterilization increased steadily as the program went on. From other field studies of induced abortion and sterilization it appears that induced abortion, sterilization and contraception constitute alternatives for the spacing and regulation of childbirths. The most significant observation among the Japanese is the strong motivation toward a small family and the actual performance along that line. It is believed that basic education in family planning is more important than the execution of a program designed merely to facilitate its easy practice.

1678 Muramatsu, Minoru, et al. Japan's Experience in Family Planning - Past and Present. Tokyo: Family Planning Federation of Japan, Inc., 1967. 124 pp.

An overview of the demographic situation in Japan is followed by chapters on: social and economic correlates of fertility and family planning; contraception, induced abortion and sterilization; and the postwar movement and program for family planning. In the Appendices are a listing of organizations concerned with family planning and the Eugenics Protection law.

1679 Muramatsu, Minoru, "Policy Measures and Social Changes for Fertility Decline in Japan," pp. 96-ff., of Vol. 2, Proceedings of the World Population Conference, 1965. New York: United Nations, 1967.

Following the passage of Eugenic Protection Law in 1948, the number of induced abortions increased sharply and in 1951-52 the government issued official instructions to implement the dissemination of contraception information through the public health network. However, induced abortion incidence reached a peak in 1955 of 1.17 million. Gradually this figure decreased to 955,000 in 1963. Gross reproduction rate also fell from 2.1 in 1949 to 1.2 in 1955.

1680 Muramatsu, Minoru, "Problems in Procuring Contraceptive Materials in a Rural Area in Japan," pp. 111-24 in: C.V. Kiser, ed. Research in Family Planning. Princeton: Princeton University Press, 1962. xvi, 664 pp.

A study based on a field survey in a rural area in Japan regarding the procurement of contraceptive devices. 472 questionnaires, mostly administered to lower-middle-class couples were used for the analysis. Contraceptives were usually bought by the husband at a pharmacist; the wives obtained them from midwives or local organizations in nearly 50% of the cases and the percentage of chemicals was a little higher than when the responsibility was assigned to the husband. Farming couples with lower social-educational backgrounds and cash incomes generally obtained materials through midwives or organizations. Further expansion of the organizational activities to facilitate the ready procurement of materials at a reduced cost is thus highly desirable, especially for those females whose husbands earn little and are less interested than their wives in the practice of contraception. Results show that couples can afford to pay less than 1% of the average income for materials.

1681 Muramatsu, Minoru, Some Facts About Family Planning in Japan. Population Problems Series, No. 12. Tokyo: Mainichi Newspapers, 1955. x, 120 pp.

Quotes and discusses the Eugenic Protection Law and presents statistical tables on fertility trends since its passage. Summarizes data on organizations concerned with policy on fertility. Literature on recent research and dissemination of findings.

1682 Node, Minoru, "Contraception in Japan: Problems of Motivation and Communication," pp. 551-69 in: C.V. Kiser, ed. Research in Family Planning. Princeton: Princeton University Press, 1962, xvi, 664 pp.

Mass and individual communication have served both to motivate people to accept the movement ideologically and to propagate the technical or medical know how of birth control. The psychology of the Japanese personality is considered a strong factor in that Japanese are generally realistic in their attitude toward daily life, not bound by any religious dogma inconsistent with birth control and benefit from a high diffusion of general education. After the war newspapers served to awaken people to the critical state of overpopulation and to arouse public opinion to favor planned parenthood. Magazines and newspapers were the chief sources of practical knowledge on contraception. A large number of industrial establishments have been positively promoting family planning among their employees as a part of the 'New Life Movement', purported to rationalize individual family life and to raise the living standards. Under the program, family planning is considered a step to modernizing and rationalizing the family life of individual employees.

1683 Ogino, H. [Status of Family Planning in Japan], Sanfujin Jissai 17:578-84, 1968.

1684 Okasaki, Ayanori, A Fertility Survey in Japan of 1952. Tokyo: The Institute of Population Problems, Ministry of Welfare, 1953. 87 pp.

Survey indicates that the Eugenics Protection Act, which makes abortion legally permissible, has had the effect of reducing the birth rate.

1685 Okazaki, Ayanori, "Politique Eugenesique au Japon et Resultats Obtenus" [Eugenic Policy in Japan and Results Obtained], Genus 11(1-4):236-50, 1955.

History of the work of the Eugenic Society of Japan since 1917. The Eugenic Protection Law of 1948 and national experience with respect to sterilizations and abortions, 1949 - June 1954.

1686 Olson, Lawrence, "How the Japanese Divorce: Notes on Divorce and the Family Court in Japan," Reports Service, American Universities Field Staff, East Asia Service 9(8): July 1961.

1687 Ota, Tenrei, Datai Kinshi to Yuseihogoho [The Prohibition of Induced Abortion and the Eugenic Protection Law], Tokyo: Keieishakagaku Kyokai, 1967. 358 pp.

Ota, a gynecologist, is the inventor of the intrauterine ring that bears his name. Few know, however, that he is also a co-sponsor (as a Socialist member of the Lower House in the Diet in the late 1940's) of the original Eugenic

Protection Law. Here he outlines the sponsors' reasons for presenting the law, the compromise version passed in 1948, and revisions made in 1949 and 1952. He discusses comparable legislation passed in Japan in 1940, and recommends future revision. The book contains historical materials on the techniques of induced abortion and contraception in premodern Japan, and a review of the development of the author's own intrauterine device.

1688 Pommerenke, W.T. "Abortion in Japan," Obstet. Gynec. Survey 10:145-ff., 1955.

The author examines the status of abortion in Japan since the liberal Eugenic Protection Law was passed in 1948. Although the total number of abortions per year is almost impossible to ascertain due to under-reporting for purposes of privacy or tax evasion, estimates range from 117,000 to 638,000 for 1951. It is felt that the decrease in Japan's birth rate (29.4 in 1940 to 23.3 in 1952) is due primarily to abortion; Koya places this decrease as 80% abortion and 20% contraception. Approximately 8000 Japanese physicians have been licensed to perform abortions and $5.00 is the average cost of the operation. One study cited indicates that women with two or more children have 40% of all abortions, and statistics from the Welfare Ministry reveal that 77% are performed within the first three months of pregnancy. There is no comprehensive record of morbidity and mortality resulting from abortion in Japan. The author concludes with an analysis of public and official attitudes toward abortion in the country and discusses his own personal experience with centers where abortions are regularly performed.

1689 "Population White Paper," Oriental Economist 27:527-75. October, 1959.

Summary of the report of the Population Problem Council of the Ministry of Welfare.

1690 "Press Review of Population Control," Japan Planned Parenthood Quart. 3(1-3):7-8. January - September 1952.

1691 Riallin, Jean-Louis, "La Prevention des Naissances au Japon: Politique, Intentions, Moyens et Resultats " [Birth Control in Japan: Policy, Purposes, Means and Results], Population 15(2):333-52, April - May 1960.

A record of official action since 1948 and evaluation of the results obtained. Data include findings of the four public opinion surveys by the Population Problems Research Council.

1692 Rouissi, Moncef, "Quelques Resultats de la Politique de Population au Japon: Exemple a Suivre ou Cas Particulier?" [Some Results of the Population Policy in Japan: An Example to be Followed or a Special Case?] Rev. Tunisienne de Sciences Sociales 4(9):177-87, March 1967.

Examines the background and history of the Eugenic Protection Law of 1948. Weighs evidence on the applicability of similar methods in underdeveloped countries of rapid population growth.

1693 Samuel, T.J. "Population Control in Japan: Lessons for India," Eugenics Rev. 58(1):15-22, March 1966.

Socio-economic factors influential in Japan in reducing the crude birth rate of 34.4 in 1947 to 17.2 in 1957 are examined. The psychological impact of Japan's defeat in World War II, and the desire to regain the prewar standard of living or even to raise it also provided incentives to Japanese couples to limit their families. Since there was already an established tradition of family limitation (infanticide and abortion), the Japanese were not reluctant to make use of any available technique. The Japanese government, which had always viewed family limitation with disfavor, assumed a permissive attitude in 1948. All these factors are compared with the situation in India, and it is found that the Japanese experience offers at least two suggestions for fertility control in India: (a) The demographic experiences of several Western countries show that once the people develop a strong motivation for limiting the number of their children, families will be limited. The government of India must create or strengthen this motivation by providing economic incentives for those who limit their families. (b) The introduction of intrauterine devices, which have a low failure rate, is the only way to speed up fertility control through contraception, since the diffusion of effective contraceptive practice is very slow. Other drastic measures, such as voluntary sterilization, may also have to be used in India.

1694 Shinozaki, N. "The Actual State of Birth Control Practice in Adjacent City, Town and Villages of Tokyo: Analysis of the Districts' Character," pp. 62-75 in: Archives of the Population Association of Japan, No. I, 1953.

1695 Steiner, Kurt, "The Revision of the Civil Code of Japan: Provisions Affecting the Family," Far Eastern Quart. 9: 169-84, 1949-50.

The acceptance of the Potsdam Declaration and the enactment of a new constitution raised the question of maintaining or abandoning the family system of the Japanese nation. Most of the changes of the civil code necessitated by the new constitution are closely related to the family system. They, in turn, affected more than sixty other laws which had to be changed or repealed. After some debate, the Parliament by Law No. 222 which became effective January 1, 1948 amended the civil code with regard to the family, making marriage and residence a matter of mutual agreement between potential husband and wife, and equalizing the sexes with respect to property and inheritance and the matter of divorce.

1696 Sutter, Jean, "Les Sterilisations et les Avortements Eugeniques au Japon " [Eugenic Sterilizations and Abortions in Japan], Population 4(4):768-70, October - December 1949.

Discusses the law of June 28, 1948.

1697 Suzumura, M., and Kikuchi, S. "Induced Abortion in Japan - Review of Literature," J. Japanese Obstet. Gynec. Soc. 13:179-ff., 1966.

Total number of induced abortions registered by the Welfare Ministry is about 700,000 to 1,000,000. Several authors, however, suggest that the true number of abortions in Japan may be from 60 to 100% higher. The greatest number of abortions is performed among the 25-29 age group; however, the relative age incidence of abortion is higher in the 30-39 age group. Abortions per 100 births increase steadily with age from a low of 35.1 for the 20-24 age group to a high of 282.2 in the 40-44 age group. 95% of all abortions are performed in the 2nd and 3rd months of gestation. The highest incidence of abortion occurs in the 9th week. One study of 821 abortion cases reported that about 10% of the cases were first pregnancies and that second, third and fourth pregnancies accounted for about 20% each of the sample. 38% of these women had had no previous abortion, 30% had had one previous abortion, and 15% had had two previous abortions. According to one study, 47% of abortions are sought to avoid more children, 46% because of "Disease of the patient herself," and 2% because of out-of-wedlock pregnancy.

1698 Tachi, Minoru, "Contraception in Japan: Problems of Motivation and Communication - Discussion," pp. 551-72 in: C.V. Kiser, ed. Research in Family Planning. Princeton: Princeton University Press, 1962. xvi, 664 pp.

A further elaboration of the 'New Life Movement' in Japan. The Foundation Institution of Research in Population Problems launched its own program of family planning among workers in major industrial establishments to supplement government action. The program also attempted to awaken the workers to the significance and benefits of rational daily life. Guidance workers were sent to company housing areas to hold small group meetings with wives or give individual guidance. Housewives were given guidance on the material aspects of modern life and it was then suggested that the limitation of family size through planning would be more helpful in raising their level of living. It is stressed that family planning can be more effectively promoted when it is carried out as a part of the improvement of family life as a whole.

1699 Tachi, Minoru, "Japan's Population Today," Japan Planned Parenthood Quart. 1(1):3-5, January - March 1950.

Trends and projections of fertility and population size in Japan suggest that there will be a disequilibrium between population and the economy. One approach to this problem is to control population growth by the dissemination of birth control information. On April 15, 1949, the Government established the Population Problems Research Council in the Cabinet with 18 members. One of the recommendations, in its report on November 29, 1949, is that free and voluntary planned parenthood be provided for all classes of people.

1700 Taeuber, Irene B.,and Balfour, Marshall C. "The Control of Fertility in Japan," pp. 102-28 in: Approaches to Problems of High Fertility in Agrarian Societies. New York: Milbank Memorial Fund, 1952.

There has always been fertility control amongst the Japanese population; the patterns of such control were well established by 1920 or 1925. Large parts of the additional control introduced between 1925 and 1950 were associated with the postponement of marriage and the increasing deficits of men. There was a decline in marital fertility, however, and both contraception and abortion were utilized to procure that control. This picture provides no definitive answer as to the history of control in the past, nor does it furnish any firm basis for assessing the future of control. One fact emerges strongly, however. The availability of contraceptive products in the markets and the availability of medical consultation for those willing to take advantage of it do not insure the use of contraception even in a population strongly motivated to limit fertility. Abortion was available in 1950 and it was widely used. It is possible that it had been so selected in the past.

1701 Takeshita, John Y. "Population Control in Japan: A Miracle or Secular Trend," Marr. Fam. Living 25(1):44-52, February 1963.

A discussion of the factors which have made population control more feasible now than ever before in Japan, presenting evidence regarding the diffusion of birth control in the postwar years and the changing pattern of differential fertility. Data from a 1956 study of 1,433 married females in Osaka are reported and shown to be consistent with the trends noted. It is concluded on the basis of these trends that the postwar legislations in Japan probably served to facilitate but not instigate the diffusion of fertility control in the population. Industrial-urban transformation of Japanese society was well advanced so that fertility decline anticipated by the theory of demographic transition was already occurring even while the prewar government was advocating and implementing pronatalist policies. What this implies is that family planning will diffuse throughout the rest of the population as industrial-urban influences diffuse and even if the sponsored programs remain ineffective as some critics believe they are.

1702 Tappe, Friedrich, Soziologie der Japanischen Familie [Sociology of the Japanese Family], Munster: Aschendorffsche Verlagsbuchhandlung, 1955.

This book deals with the main views, ethics, and law of the Japanese family system.

1703 United Nations. "Act No. 216 Promulgated on 24 June 1949 to Amend the Eugenics Protection Act," Yearbook on Human Rights for 1949. pp. 132

1704 Whelpton, P.K. "From Eugenic Abortion and Sterilization to Control of Conception in Japan," Eugenical News 34(3-4): 44-45, September - December 1949.

A discussion of the Japanese Eugenic Protection Law of 1948 and the changes made in the Law during 1949.

1705 Whelpton, P.K. "The Outlook for the Control of Human Fertility in Japan," Amer. Sociol. Rev. 15:34-42, 1950.

After a brief review of the birth rate in Japan from 1870 to 1949, there is a discussion of official and popular attitudes toward population size and fertility control, recent legislation on contraception and fertility, the policy of the Supreme Commander of Allied Powers with regard to fertility limitation, and the future trend of fertility.

1706 Wiegmann, H. "Das Japanische Familien-System Fruher und Heute " [The Japanese Family System in Former Times and Today], Soziale Welt 6:311-17, 1955.

Using the Japanese law as the main source of data, differences between the Japanese family system in feudal days and the present are indicated.

KOREA

Policies on fertility and family size

1707 Bang, Sook. "A Comparative Study of the Effectiveness of a Family Planning Program in Rural Korea," Dissertation Abstr. 29B: 1419-20, 1968. Abstract of D.P.H. Thesis, University of Michigan, 1968.

The program effects were measured both in the aggregate and for individuals. In the latter, our concern was with the interrelationships of changes in the important variables of this study. The data were obtained from surveys conducted before and after two years (1962-64) of program effort in an experimental area (Koryang) and a comparison area (Kimpo). The present analysis is confined to a panel of about 400 women under 50 years of age interviewed in both the "before" and "after" surveys in each area. The findings of this study clearly indicate that an organized family planning program to promote the use of conception control is feasible in rural Korea. Most importantly, this study demonstrates that if we utilize fully and adequately the available resources and techniques it would be possible to control excess fertility now prevalent in Korea, whose population for the most part live in rural areas.

1708 Bang, Sook. "The Koyang Study: Results of Two Action Programs," Stud. Fam. Planning ,April 1966, pp. 5-12.

Results of a study to investigate the possibility of introducing family planning and to make a scientific assessment of any change in fertility behavior after a program of intensive family planning education and contraceptive services, in two rural areas near Seoul, Korea, 1962-64.

1709 Bang, Sook, et al. "A Survey of Fertility and Attitude Toward Family Planning in Rural Korea," Yonsei Med. J. 4:77-102, 1963.

Fertility and attitude toward family planning were studied by interviews among a systematic random sample of about 1000 couples in a Korean rural area. The replies to the five important questions in fertility control were analyzed; the level of fertility, the ideal family size, the family planning limitation factors, the prevalence of conception control and the attitude towards the use of contraceptives. The level of reproductive performance has remained high with the total fertility rate of seven children or more, while their ideal family size was three to five children. Such an excess fertility was not well controlled by delaying of the age of marriage and/or by spacing births; the most prominent factors in limiting family size was the high mortality of children especially in infancy. As the infant mortality rate is declining, family limitation is now practiced by induced abortion. The practice of modern contraceptive methods was low in prevalence.

1710 Cha, Youn-keun, Development of the Korean National Family Planning Programme, 1965, 11 pp. (processed)

A descriptive account of the Korean program, with data on achievements and of two nation-wide KAP surveys.

1711 Chang, Dae Hong, "The Historical Development of the Korean Socio-Family System Since 1392 -- A Legalistic Interpretation," Dissertation Abstr. 25:1964-65. Abstract of Ph.D. Thesis, University of Michigan, 1962.

Within a historical context, Korean society has undergone three major stages of transformation since 1392. Each of these periods witnesses profound changes in the structure and function of the family and social system. The first, called "period of clan recognition" by the author, covers the years between 1392-1910. During this period, the family is recognized only through clan; the family is not legally recognized as a unit of the State. The second period, designated the "period of family recognition," comes about under the Japanese occupation in Korea from 1910 to 1945. It is the first time in Korean history that the family is distinguished as a unit of the State, by law and practice. The third stage, "period of individual recognition," is the current social development in Korea. As is evident in the Constitution and other laws, an increasing emphasis is being placed upon individual rights, freedom, and equality regardless of sex, religion, or social status.

1712 Hahm, Pyong Choon, and Je Jon, Byong, "The Criminality of Abortion in Korea," J. Crim. Law Criminol. Police Sci. 56(1):18-26, March 1965.

Legal norms embody cultural values and traditions of a people. When they are transplanted to an alien culture, they cannot be effective because they are not supported by the values of the receiving culture. In its efforts to modernize its legal system, Korea has modeled its legal system after that of a European country. The system has existed in Korea for fifty or more years, and has yet to be indigenized. It is still European. Abortion takes a special place in the European religio-ethical value system, with its Judaeo-Christian heritage, and cannot occupy the same place in value system of Korea. Should the criminal code of Korea make the same provision for this crime as a European nation? Even if it does, will it be effective? Korea's criminal code contains a provision that makes abortion a punishable offense, except where it is necessary to save the life of a pregnant female. This exception is very narrowly defined. Medical and legal professional groups, which are most closely connected with this problem, in two large urban centers of Korea, were surveyed by multiple-choice questionnaires and interviews. Respondents were chosen by a regular-interval sampling method from the membership lists of the two professional associations. The legal profession was subdivided into judges, prosecutors and practicing lawyers. The moral conviction that abortion is a specie of murder was not strong among the respondents. A criminal law provision that lacks a strong support of public opinion cannot be effective. Ineffectively enforced legal provisions tend to undermine the public's respect for law in general. The law and public opinion must be brought closer together.

1713 Hong, Sung-Bong, "Induced Abortion in Rural Korea," Korean J. Obstet. Gynec. 10:275-ff., 1967.

Report of a study of 2,084 women with a total of 9,800 pregnancies, 9,200 of which resulted in live births, 150 in induced abortions and 450 in spontaneous abortions. Five per cent of the abortion cases indicated at least one previous abortion, and the ratio of abortions to births increased with age, with a maximum of one abortion to four births in the 40-44 year old age bracket. The abortion rate also increased in relation to marriage length, number of pregnancies, number of children and economic level, and among women with no religious affiliation and Buddhists. 63% of the abortions took place in cities, 30% in medium sized towns and only 7% locally, since the sample area had very few medical facilities. Reasons given for the abortions were family planning (90%), child spacing (6%) and other (3%).

1714 Hong, Sung-Bong, Induced Abortion in Seoul, Korea.Seoul: Dong-A Publishing Co., 1966.

The author examines a report of 3,204 married women with 12,400 pregnancies, 10,200 of which resulted in live births, 1,500 in induced abortions and 700 in spontaneous abortions. In comparison with statistics for more recent years, the above figures indicate an increase in abortion rates and a decrease in live births. Results showed an increased abortion rate in relation to length of marriage, pregnancy order, parity and educational level. There was also a higher rate with women married to white collar workers, and with women of the Protestant and Buddhists faiths. Of the abortion cases, 47% of the women had had one abortion and 53% two or more, with 93% reporting that the abortion took place in a private clinic, 4% in hospitals and 3% in homes. Ten per cent reported great feelings of guilt about the abortion, 33% a little guilt and 58% no guilt at all. There appeared to be a decrease in guilt with age and living number of children and an increase in guilt with increased disapproval of the operation.

1715 Hong, Sung-Bong, and Yoon, Joong-Hi, "Male Attitudes Toward Family Planning on the Island of Kangwha-Gun, Korea," Milbank Memorial Fund Quart. 40(4):443-52, October 1962.

One attitudinal question concerned the desire for additional children while another investigated the propensity to use contraception. Relationships between selected characteristics: i.e., father's education, number of living children, number of living sons, the desire for children, were significant at the 0.0001 level, while relationship between similar characteristics and contraception attitudes were significant at the .05 level. Desire for more children varied inversely with the present number of children and age of interviewee and directly with education. Eleven males refused comment on attitudes toward contraception, but of the remaining 108, 74 indicated a positive attitude, 54% desired no additional children while 69% expressed a willingness to use contraception. Such variables as number of children, number of living sons, age, and duration of marriage appear more significantly associated with attitudes towards more children than is education. Education appears more significant than these factors in attitudes towards birth control.

1716 Kang, Yung Sun, et al. [Statistical Studies on the Fertility of Korean Population], Zoologica 3:7-15, 1964.

The results of fertility and amount of birth wastes including abortions, stillbirths and childhood mortality of six groups -- large urban, intermediate urban, agricultural, miner's, fishery's, and island's population -- in Korea were analyzed. Of the women interviewed, 5,787 have answered questions regarding their history of pregnancies and other closely related items. In this study, the fundamental notion of fertility is an actual level of performance in population, based on the number of live births that occur. Urban populations have less children born than in other groups, while women of the fishery's population show the highest fertility. Each complete family in the large urban group has an average of 6.2 live births, whereas the rate is 7.9 in the fishery's population. The difference in birth rate can be attributed to the fact that the urban population has frequently practiced contraception and induced abortion for their birth control. Thus in a large urban group, the rate of abortion and stillbirth is highest of all; the rate of induced abortion reaches 53.6%.

1717 Kang, Yung-Sun, and Cho, Wan Kyoo, "Etude de la Fecondite Feminine Coreenne et Volume des Pertes Causees a la Natalite par L'Avortement, la Mortinatalite et la Mortalite Infantile" [Study of the Fertility of Korean Women and the Reduction in Natality Caused by Abortion, Stillbirth and Infant Mortality], J. Popul. Stud. 4:30-51, 1967.

Study reports the results of an enquiry of 6000 women belonging to different socio-economic levels. Their fertility averages 7.9 children as compared with 6.2 children in Seoul. Induced abortion is very frequent in the urban area. Infant mortality, or death before age four, claims 20.0 per cent of the newborn. This negatively affects the interest in family planning in Korea.

1718 Keeny, S.M. "Korea and Taiwan: the Score for 1966," Stud. Fam. Planning, No. 19, May 1967, pp. 1-7.

The author discusses recent developments in the two pioneering birth control programs of Korea and Taiwan. Approximately 900,000 couples have been served by the Korean government's program since its beginnings in 1963, more than

20% of the couples in the childbearing years. It is contended that this is a remarkable record for a national program. Other indications of rapid changes in the practice of family planning, knowledge about family planning, and attitudes toward family size and planning are evident from comparisons of results of national surveys; although there are some problems about the quality of these surveys, the large and consistent changes over short time periods probably reflect profound and large-scale changes in family values. Figures on IUD insertions, vasectomy cases, the use of traditional contraceptive methods and induced abortions are given, and the possibilities for an expanded pill program are outlined. The author concludes that if the Government continues to back the family planning program as it is doing now, there is a chance that Korea will be the first country in the world to reduce its birth rate rapidly before major industrialization. Family planning efforts in Taiwan benefit from the fact that the country's birth rate has been dropping for the last ten years; thus the aim is to maintain and, if possible, accelerate an already existing trend, which should be much easier than to reverse it. However, with no national policy on family planning, Taiwan works in this area under severe handicaps.

1719 Koh, K.S., and Song, K.Y. "Some Aspects of Fertility and Family Planning in Seoul City, Korea," in: International Union for the Scientific Study of Population, Contributed Papers, Sydney Conference, Australia, 1967.

Report on a 1966 fertility survey (sample basis) undertaken in Seoul City by the Institute of Population Problems. Fertility was sharply reduced by abortions during the one year period examined: one abortion to every three live births was recorded. Age groups were divided into five-year periods, and it was found that the rate of abortion increased with each successive group, with 12 abortions per 100 live births at ages 20 to 24, and 98 per 100 live births at ages 35 to 39. Seoul City's abortion rate approximately doubled the country's abortion rate as a whole in 1964.

1720 Korea. Institute of Population Problems, "Recommendations for Insuring the Effectiveness of the Family Planning Program," J. Popul., Stud. No. 1, 1965 ,pp. 19-27.

Several recommendations are put forth. The program must be widely publicized so as to reach all segments of the population. The importance of a small number of children, whose births are well-spaced, to the health of the mother and the harmony of the family should be noted. Contraceptives must be made widely available and within the financial means of all segments of the population. The recommendations are made by the institute which the government created to advise on the population problem.

1721 Korea. Ministry of Health and Social Affairs, The Findings of the National Survey on Family Planning, 1967. Planned Parenthood Federation of Korea, 1968. 206 pp.

This report summarizes the findings of the KAP survey conducted in April 1967 (the fourth since 1964) by the Family Planning Evaluation Unit of the Ministry of Health and Social Affairs in Korea, for the purpose of assessing the impact of the National Family Planning Program inaugurated in 1962. The nine chapters of the report cover the survey design and procedures; and, by various characteristics of the respondents, trends in knowledge of family planning and of methods of contraception, attitudes toward family planning, trends in concepts of ideal family size, and family planning practices. A chapter on trends in fertility includes brief discussions of births prevented by the intra-uterine contraceptive and vasectomy programs, and of economic gains of the National Family Planning Program. An interview schedule is appended.

1722 Kwon, E-Hyock, et al. [A Study of Acceptability and Effectiveness of Oral Pills (Ovulen) With Women Resident in an Urban Area -- Based on a Program Directed Towards Women Having Discontinued Use of Intra-Uterine Contraception Loops in Sungdong Gu, Seoul, Korea], J. Popul. Stud., No. 6, 1968. pp. 3-48.

Report on survey conducted in November 1966 by the School of Public Health, Seoul National University, in preparation for national use of oral pills to supplement the loop.

1723 Kwon, E-Hyock, and Kang, Kil-Won, "Une Comparison des Attitudes des Hommes et des Femmes Relativement a la Planification de la Famille dans les Regions Urbaines de Coree," [A Comparison of Male and Female Attitudes Relative to Family Planning in Urban Regions of Korea], _J. Popul. Stud._ 4:52-76, 1967.

According to this inquiry conducted in Seoul in 1967 of 200 couples (the women aged 20 to 44 years), 83.5 _per cent_ of the men and 88.5 _per cent_ of the women know about contraceptive procedures, the recourse to which depending on the degree of communication between the spouses. Communication is correlated with the degree of their knowledge.

1724 Park, Kyu Sang, _et al._ "Law for Protecting the Maternal and Children Health and Improving the Quality of the Nation," _J. Popul. Stud._, No. 2, 1966, pp. 151-54.

Proposal by representatives of the Institute of Population Problems for legislation, including provisions for contraceptive control, induced abortion, and sexual sterilization.

1725 Park, Rae-Young, "Fertility Control in Korea: Legal and Institutional Aspects," _J. Popul. Stud._, No. 3, 1966, pp. 129-42.

Describes the history of legal regulation of marriage and the family in Korea, the findings of a recent survey of induced abortion, and the present status of family planning. Outlines provisions of a bill introduced in the national assembly, December 12, 1965, for the protection of maternal and child health and for eugenic improvement.

1726 Ross, J.A., and Bang, S. "The AID Computer Programme, Used to Predict Adoption of Family Planning in Koyant," _Popul. Stud._ 20:61-75, July 1966.

A highly useful computer program has been developed for predicting values of a dependent variable. Basically a sequential analysis of variance, it creates a tree of two-way splits of the sample. Each split maximizes the reduction of unexplained variance in the dependent variable. The program is remarkably sensitive to interactions, since it assumes neither linear relationships, normal distributions, nor homoscedasticity. This program is put to work here on a prediction problem of administrative importance: which women in Korean villages will adopt family planning under a mild program and under an intensive program? Optimum predictors are identified and are arranged in a hierarchy of combinations which give progressively higher predictive accuracy. The best two or three predictors isolate large proportions of women with extremely low adoption rates.

1727 Ross, John A., and Koh, Kap Suk, "The Korean 1968 Fertility and Family Planning Survey," Paper Presented at the International Union for the Scientific Study of Population, General Conference, 3-11 September 1969.

This paper describes the methodology of the Korean 1968 survey, and compares the questionnaire items to those recommended by the Committee on Comparative Studies of Fertility and Family Planning, of the IUSSP. From September 1 - October 31, 1968, the survey covered a total of 8,500 households in 63 sample points, containing 5,400 married women under age 50. A complete household roster was taken, along with births and deaths in the household since January 1, 1965. For each currently married woman below age 50, a full pregnancy history was obtained along with KAP data emphasizing contraceptive practice. For women admitting IUD experience, follow-up information was gathered. Thus a single field operation yielded fertility, KAP, and IUD data. The survey was the latest in a series of eight in Korea. Annual KAP surveys were done from 1964 through 1967 in April, and annual IUD follow-up surveys were done from 1965 through 1967 in the Fall. The decision to make the 1968 survey a multi-purpose one grew out of several considerations.

1728 Ryu, P.K. "The New Korean Criminal Code of 1953 (October 3). An Analysis of Ideologies Embedded in It," J. Crim. Law 48:275-95, September - October 1957.

Korea's new code - the first autonomous modern Korean criminal code - came into force on October 3, 1953, superseding the code imposed by Japan which had been in force in Korea for 40 years. This article presents the leading ideas of the new 1953 code, as they emerged under the impact of the several competing tendencies of the Chinese classical idea, of Anglo-American and of German criminal law. Certain notions of the new code are traceable to Chinese cultural patterns or elements (the two main propositions of which are summarized) as well as several specifically Korean moral patterns, which are listed, although the new code has been influenced mainly by American and German legal ideas, which are examined and analyzed rather extensively. It is concluded that the criminal law must be not a conglomeration of unrelated rules but a product of a considerable "world-view" integrating science and ethics.

1729 Song, Kun-Yong, "Effect of the National Family Planning Program on the Reduction of Births in Korea," _J. Popul. Stud._, No. 1, 1965, pp. 28-38.

Report on the period April 1964 to March 1965. Comparison of actual births with births expected on the basis of "Lorimer's hypothetical model and 0.41 (medium) of annual births per fecund woman in Japan."

1730 Song, Kun-Yong, "Les Effets de la Contraception et de la Sterilite sur la Reduction de la Natalite Chez les Femmes de Seoul " [Effects of Contraception and Sterilization on the Reduction of Births Among Women in Seoul], _J. Popul. Stud._ 4:5-18, 1967.

Report on an inquiry conducted in 1966 in Seoul of 1,638 married women aged 15 to 49 years.

1731 Song, Un Sun, "Marriage and the Family in Korea," _Korean Survey_ 7:4-6, April 1958.

Traditional customs and present-day modifications.

1732 Wadia, Avabai B. "Some Impressions of the Family Planning Programme in South Korea," _J. Fam. Welf._ 12(1):1-10, September 1965.

A group of 15 Indian administrators, clinicians and voluntary workers in family planning visited South Korea at the end of May 1965. The aim of the visit was to study the Korean IUCD program -- how it had been initiated, what types of personnel were needed for it, the kinds of publicity and educational approaches employed, and the problems encountered. Factors which they found as contributing to the success of the program are several: 1) family planning was made an essential part of the 10-year Economic Plan and all ministries were instructed to give their full cooperation to this program; 2) the program is being handled like other public health programs; 3) there is a sense of confidence; 4) there is a full synchronization and dovetailing of the various components of the program; 5) the Planned Parenthood Federation of Korea founded in 1961 has played a key role; and 6) there are important educational and research projects being carried out.

1733 Yang, Jae Mo, et al. "Fertility and Family Planning in Rural Korea," Popul. Stud. 18(3):237-50, March 1965.

In December 1961, the governor of Korea adopted a program of family planning as part of its public health services. In 1962 a pilot research project was begun with the object of demonstrating and assessing what can be achieved through intensive family planning education and services. Wondang Myun near Seoul, with a rural population of 9,000 in villages, was chosen for the study. A baseline survey covering attitudes and practices regarding family planning was made of the population under study, as well as of a similar population in the control area of Kimpo Myun. This report outlines the design, program of education and services, and some preliminary results of the study.

1734 Yang, Jae Mo, "The National Family Planning Programme in Korea," pp. 77-86 in: Muramatsu, M. and Harper, Paul A., eds. Population Dynamics: International Action and Training Programmes. Baltimore: Johns Hopkins Press,1965.

Korea has established national policies and programs in support of family planning movements. The national government included family planning in its Five Year Economic Plan and set as goals the reduction of the rate of population growth to 2.5 per cent by 1966 and 2.0 per cent by 1971. In this study, the year by year progress to the 1966 goal is documented.

1735 Yang, Jae Mo, et al. "The National Family Planning Program as a Strategic Platform for the Improvement of Maternal and Child Health in Korea," Yonsei Med. J. 7:76-85, 1966.

The success of Korea's health program is closely related to the general economic development. In the first five years of the program the group successfully reached by the family planning program was largely the receptive, motivated women in the older child bearing age group. A strategic platform for the success of the next five year plan would be to concentrate on the younger less motivated mothers; to educate them to better family spacing and child care. Inclusion of family planning in a comprehensive, total maternal and child care program seems a rational and effective approach.

1736 Yang, Jae Mo, et al. "Study on a Method to Improve Vital Statistics and Family Planning Simultaneously Among Maternity Cases," Yonsei Med. J. 8:64-70, 1967.

To demonstrate and assess the possibility of improving simultaneously vital statistics and family planning in urban and rural Korea, an action-cum-research project was conducted for a period of one year, from May 1966, to April 1967, over the area covering Kimchun city and a part of surrounding Kumnung Gun, Kyongsangpuk-do province, Korea. A sterilized simple delivery kit was distributed to the expectant mothers in the experimental areas, and its effects on the reporting of vital events such as births and deaths and the acceptance of family planning were compared with the same in the control areas without such an action program. A single delivery kit contained one vinyl sheet for covering and one for lying on, one cotton sheet, a pair of scissors, one foot of thread, two pieces of gauze, a piece of soap, a weight scale and one doubled envelope. From the study, the system of distributing simple hygiene delivery kits to all expectant mothers in an area is an effective method of obtaining accurate statistics of births. It is also effective in the reduction of infant mortality, which in turn, promotes acceptance of family planning in rural Korea.

1737 Yoon, Jong-Joo, "La Preference Accordee par les Familles Coreennes a la Naissance d'Un Garcon et Ses Effets sur la Planification de la Famille et l'Accroissement de la Population " [Preference Accorded by Korean Families to Male Births and Its Effect on Family Planning and the Population Growth], J. Popul. Stud. 4:19-29, 1967.

There is traditional preference for male offspring in Korea. Parents are not disposed to limit their reproduction until they are assured of at least two sons. This results in an increase of completed family size to 4.7 living children and in the annual rate of population growth which is 2.4 per cent annually.

TAIWAN

Policies on fertility and family size

1738 Berelson, Bernard, and Freedman, Ronald, "A Study in Fertility Control," Scientific American 210(5):3-11, May 1964.

The program in Taichung, Taiwan suggests that a planned effort can spread fertility control in a short period of time and economically.

1739 Cernada, George P., and Huang, Tessie, "Taiwan: Training in Family Planning," Stud. Fam. Planning 36:1-6, December 1968.

The most effective family planning programs today owe much of their success to the field workers who make door-to-door rounds of the village or urban households. A report of the progress and training procedures of the Pre-Pregnancy Health (PPH) worker is presented. The working procedure through 1966 has been to concentrate on women with three or more children, at least one of whom is male. About 85% of the women who try the loop have less than junior high school education; over 40% have no formal education; and more than 33% are 30 years of age or older. Data also indicates that one out of three women will probably have tried one method of contraception and one out of ten will have had one or more abortions. The selection of the field worker depends on the candidates emotional maturity, marital status, number of children, contraceptive usage, education, familiarity and is highly selective. The Taiwan curriculum and training program is outlined in detail and new directions to encourage workers to attempt different approaches when results of previous methods fail, are suggested.

1740 Chang, M.C., et al. "Study by Matching of the Demographic Impact of an IUD Program: A Preliminary Report," Milbank Memorial Fund Quart. 47(2):137-57, April 1969.

Acceptors and non-acceptors of the IUD in Taiwan are matched on the basis of age, education, open birth interval and the number of live births. The program is found more attractive to high parity women and although it brought their fertility down sharply after acceptance, the fertility of non-acceptors also declined sharply in the same period -- 1966 to 1968. The net demographic effect of the program is to reduce fertility. The number of births averted per 1000 insertions in Taiwan is 159 the first year (beginning nine months after the insertion), 113 the second year, and 99 the third year.

1741 Chen Shao-hsing, "Prospects for Demographic Controls in Taiwan," Asian Survey 1(6):16-19, August 1961.

Notes on the activities of the Family Planning Association of China, and on official and unofficial attitudes toward government policy on population.

1742 Chow, L.P. "Evaluation of the Family Planning Program in Taiwan, Republic of China," J. Formosan Med. Assn. 67(7): 280-308, 28 July 1968.

For every woman-year of use of the loop, 0.13 births are prevented in the following year, according to estimates based on the program for fertility control in Taiwan. A total of 382,000 loop insertions in the period 1964-67 involved 20 per cent of the eligible women. Assuming current rates of insertion and retention as constants, the proportion of married women of childbearing age with loops in place would remain at about a 14 per cent level. Annual rates of acceptors increased from 3.3 per 100 women in 1964 to 7.9 per 100 in 1967. Although rates of acceptance are positively correlated with age, parity, and education, comparing 1967 with 1964, the rates increased more rapidly for younger women, for those of lower parity, and for women with less education. Termination rates for pregnancy, expulsion, and removal increased from 37 per cent after 12 months to 64 per cent after 36 months, with age and parity as the most important variables. Pregnancy rates were higher for the smaller loops than for the larger sizes, but the differences were small, and removal rates were lower. The rate at which fertility declined in Taiwan has almost doubled since the inception of the program, which is systematically evaluated by the Taiwan Population Studies Center.

1743 Chow, L.P. "A Programme to Control Fertility in Taiwan," Popul. Stud. 19(2):155-66, 1965.

A statistical evaluation of the Family Planning Health Program in Taiwan, using intra-uterine contraceptives. Organization, work procedures, training of personnel, pre-program studies, pre-action surveys, evaluation, analysis and follow-up are delineated. The effort resulted in a 5% reduction of the crude birth rate of the province and 6.3% in Taichung City, in 1964. Summary impressions are: (1) the rate of monthly acceptors of the program increased sharply within a year; (2) the success of the program lies in its careful planning; (3) 93% of the target number of acceptors were reached in 1964; (4) by December 1964, 4% of married females in Taiwan had accepted the device, with a higher percent in Taichung City and a lower percent in Taipei City and Yammingshan Administration; (5) the highest percent of acceptance was in Tachun Township of Changhua County; (6) number of living children and educational level were important in acceptance; (7) 4% of the loops were expelled, 13% removed, and 2% re-inserted. At the time of the interview, 84% of the females were continuous users, with an average of four months use; (8) pregnancy rate per 100 female years was 4; (9) the 1965 target of 100,000 loops is expected to be reached; (10) the bottleneck of the program is uneven distribution of physicians for insertions; and (11) it is hoped that Taiwan may be the first area in the world to show that fertility can be brought down by planned contraceptive efforts.

1744 Chow, L.P. "A Study on the Demographic Impact of an IUD Programme," Popul. Stud. 22(3):347-59, November 1968.

This paper discusses and presents data obtained through various studies and surveys on the effect of the intra-uterine device (IUD) contraceptive program in Taiwan. It has been demonstrated that the fertility of IUD acceptors before first acceptance was 58% higher than that of married women in general and that, after acceptance, it declined by about 76%. The corresponding fertility decline among married women in general was only about 5%. Acceptors (number equals 5,000) had had more recent births, as indicated by their shorter 'open interval' of 20.7 months, compared with 37.4 months among the women in a general survey sample done in 1965. If the fertility of IUD acceptors had declined at the same rate as that of married women in general in the absence of IUD, the insertion of about four IUD's would probably prevent one live birth in the following year. Observation over a longer period, however, is needed to determine the demographic effect of IUD. Data on fertility control practice after termination, type of termination of pregnancies after first acceptance, life-table rates by various socio-demographic characteristics of acceptors, and the 'life expectancy' of the first segment of IUD are also presented.

1745 Chow, L.P., *et al*. "Correlates of IUD Termination in a Mass Family Planning Program: The First Taiwan IUD Follow-up Survey," *Milbank Memorial Fund Quart*. 46(2):215-33, April 1968, Part 1.

To determine the extent of and characteristics associated with IUD loss under actual field conditions, a representative sample of acceptors in Taiwan's island-wide program was interviewed in the latter part of 1965. A major advantage of this survey was the availability of the insertion date (January 1964 - March 1965) from the "coupon" prepared at the time of insertion instead of from the memory of the respondent at time of survey. Computed on a life-table basis, total terminations of the original device were 37.9 per cent after 12 months, 47.9 per cent after 18 months. Corresponding rates in the more favorable Taichung Medical Study were 34.4 and 43.6 per cent respectively. A higher removal rate in Taiwan is the major reason for its higher total termination rate; that is, little difference was found in the pregnancy and expulsion rates, but for the same type of device (Lippes Loop 1) the gross removal rate after 12 months was 25.3 per cent for Taiwan, 18.1 for Taichung. Other major findings are that wife's age and parity are powerfully related (inversely) to each type of termination; that women with induced abortion had significantly lower expulsion (and lower total termination) rates than women without this experience; and that higher educated women had only slightly higher removal and termination rates. Survey findings indicate that the percent "unprotected" among terminated cases varies from about 30 for younger, low-parity women to about 15 among older, high-parity women. However, a significant part of this difference may arise from the fact that younger women were more likely to have adopted the IUD for spacing rather than limiting births.

1746 Chow, L.P., and Freedman, Ronald, "Taiwan: Births Averted by the IUD Program," *Stud. Fam. Planning*, No. 20, June 1967, pp. 7-8.

The net conclusion is that the IUD, despite high termination rates, has a substantial effect in reducing fertility for those persons inserted with it. The next step is to calculate its effect in the total population.

1747 Chow, L.P., and Hsu, S.C. "Taiwan's Population Problem," Popul. Rev. 4(2):17-36, July 1960.

Unprecedented population growth in Taiwan has attracted the attention of demographers. The authors, after giving a brief history of population growth, have analysed the trends in vital rates. Comparison with other economically advanced countries shows that Taiwan has a young population with high fertility. Modern way of life and thinking and increased education and level of living have prepared a basis for people to start thinking in terms of family planning. Thus, a Family Planning Association has been established. The program is discussed and suggestions are given for its success. The authors are for controlling fertility for the sake of better living standards.

1748 Freedman, Ronald, "The Research Challenge to Social Scientists in the Developing Family Planning Programs: The Case of Taiwan," J. Soc. Issues 23(4):165-69, October 1967.

The opportunity to study social change, diffusion, small group processes, etc., in the family planning programs now being organized in many developing countries is emphasized, since experimental treatments of large social collectivities are needed where "social action is both ethical and practical." Reference is made to the article by L.P. Lu, C.H. Chen and L.P. Chow as illustrating "in a specific, simple but important experiment the potential for such studies as part of the family planning program in Taiwan." Taiwan is a favorable setting for population control studies because there have been a series of developments regarding education, mass media circulation, economic development, communications, etc., which are favorable to the development of linkages between the individual and larger social and economical units. On the basis of these developments, fertility would normally decline even before family planning programs, as it did. Previous surveys are cited, and a large scale experiment reported by B. Berelson and R. Freedman ("A Study of Fertility Control," Scientific American 1964, 210, 29-37) was conducted under controlled conditions in the city of Taichung by the provincial health department to bring family planning to the population. It led to an expanded island-wide program. It is noted that while the situation in Taiwan is particularly favorable, it is not unique: there are similar conditions in Korea, and similar programs, on a much larger scale, in India and Pakistan.

1749 Freedman, Ronald, _et al_. "Fertility and Family Planning in Taiwan: A Case Study of the Demographic Transition," _Amer. J. Sociol_. 70(1):16-27, July 1964.

Taiwan is at the stage of the demographic transition in which falling mortality exerts pressures on traditional family forms. There is evidence that efforts are being made to reduce fertility by couples in the latter half of the child-bearing period when they have the moderate number of children and sons most of them want. The extent of such family-limitation efforts, the number of children wanted, and the number of children born are shown to be related to a number of modernization indexes.

1750 Freedman, Ronald, _et al_. "Fertility Trends in Taiwan: Tradition and Change," _Popul. Stud_. 16:219-36, March 1963.

Fertility rates have been falling in Taiwan for several years. The declines appear to be general throughout the island, and are occurring mainly in the age groups above 30, as would be expected if there are beginnings of family limitation. There are indications that the fertility rates are negatively correlated with indices of modernization in local areas. Several pilot studies indicate a consensus in the population on the desirability of a moderate number of children, the desirability of the idea of family planning, a positive valuation of such traditional Chinese values as the joint family and support of parents by their children in old age. In one urban area studied, a substantial minority of wives 25-29 years old have used a family planning method already. The "pre-pregnancy health program" of the Provincial Health Department has been quite successful in providing service to interested couples, and among these couples the program is demonstrably effective in reducing birth rates. Data from the various sources are consistent with the speculation that Taiwanese couples want to use modern family planning methods to maintain elements of the traditional Chinese family in a modern setting.

1751 Freedman, Ronald,and Takeshita, John Y. "Studies of Fertility and Family Limitation in Taiwan," _Eugenics Quart_. 12(4):233-50, December 1965.

Fertility has been falling slowly in Taiwan since 1958 without benefit of any large-scale organized family planning program. Declines begin to appear at age 30 to 34 and then increase sharply with age. Sample surveys were conducted in Taichung (2,432 married females of childbearing age) to study fertility and evaluate the success of a family planning program which might change fertility. The overwhelming appeal of the intrauterine contraceptive devices (IUCD) in this area was clearly demonstrated. 74% of all acceptances of the program up to November 1963 were IUCD cases. The success of the program as a whole depended considerably on the availability of the IUCD with all its advantages. A disproportionate number of acceptances are older wives, having three or more living children, and having at least one living son. Contrary to expectation a larger percent of acceptors were from rural districts than was the case for the eligible females. Thus far the demographic characteristics (wife's age and number of living children) appear to be much more important than the social characteristics (wife's education and residence).

1752 Hsu, S.C. "Report on the Development of the Family Planning Program in Taiwan," Eugenics Quart. 10(3):135-38, 1963.

Taboos against birth control in Taiwan are slowly crumbling because of an increasing population pressure and an active group of people proselytizing in favor of birth control. The significance of this finding is discussed.

1753 Jain, Anrudh K. "Relative Fecundability of Users and Non-Users of Contraception," Soc. Biol. 16(1):39-43, March 1969.

Married women who had used contraception and/or induced abortion after their first pregnancy and prior to becoming acceptors in a family planning program in Taichung had a higher absolute fecundability (177 = 5 per 1,000) than the average for all women (163 = 2) and higher than that for non-acceptors who had not used any contraception (152 = 2). This fecundability differential is understated because women who had been pregnant were excluded. When these women are added, the fecundability of non-acceptors with no previous contraceptive use declines to 143. The author draws two practical implications from his findings that acceptors had a higher fecundability than non-acceptors both at time of marriage and at time of interview: (1) The impact of the program is greater than would be expected on the assumption that acceptors have the same fecundability as non-acceptors; the acceptors have a greater potential for producing births than the other women with lower fecundability. (2) Even if older women with higher parity are more likely to accept the IUCD or other contraceptive methods in a family planning program, it is worthwhile to invest resources in such a program because these women have the potential to produce substantially more births than the average women of their age class. This does not imply that these acceptors would have adopted some method of birth control in the absence of an organized family planning program. The study is based on a probability sample of 2,443 married women, aged 20-39 and living with their husbands, interviewed in 1963 at the end of a year-long family planning program in Taichung, Taiwan, and again in July 1965, to determine whether they had become acceptors in the interval.

1754 Lu, Laura, *et al*. "An Experimental Study of Effect of Group Meetings on the Acceptance of Family Planning in Taiwan," *J. Soc. Issues* 23(4):171-77, October 1967.

The Taiwan family planning program offers the opportunity to study social change diffusion and small group processes in a situation combining social action with experimental design. The present study was directed toward measuring the effect of small group meetings on (a) knowledge of attitudes toward contraception, (b) acceptance of the intrauterine loop, and (c) diffusion of information to contiguous areas. Comparisons based on pre- and post-meeting surveys of the effectiveness in areas having meetings in every *lin* (neighborhood groupings) with area meetings in every other *lin* show that the meetings were significantly and almost equally effective in improving knowledge and acceptance, whether in the saturated or semi-saturated areas.

1755 Potter, Robert G., *et al*. "Taiwan's Family Planning Program," *Science* 160:848-53, May 24, 1968.

The birth rates for women participating in the IUD program in Taiwan have fallen sharply since their initial participation; these rates are between 68 and 78 percent below the rates that would have been expected had there been no IUD program. These and other findings refute the argument that the program is trivial because the participants are too old, too few, or too poorly motivated to practice contraception with any persistence or with any significant effect on fertility.

1756 Ross, John A., et al. "Korea and Taiwan: Review of Progress in 1968," Stud. Fam. Planning 41:1-11, April 1969.

Contains a short discussion of the official policy adopted by Taiwan in 1968.

1757 Takeshita, John Y., et al. "A Study of the Effectiveness of the Pre-Pregnancy Health Program in Taiwan," Eugenics Quart. 11(4):222-33, December 1964.

The Taiwan Provincial Maternal and Child Health Institute has in force a family planning program, known officially as the Pre-Pregnancy Health Program, (PPHP) in 100 or more of the 361 Health stations throughout the island. These stations have as their specific task the introduction of family planning ideas and knowledge of contraceptive methods to married couples, and the promotion of their use; they also make supplies available at home, the health stations, and other places of convenience. Until recently follow-up visits have been required. Between its inception in April 1960 and April 1964, a total of 43,766 cases were brought into the PPHP. Both the pregnancy rate and birth rate of PPHP cases showed substantial reduction, the latter being considerably greater than a control group of matched cases. The findings indicate that the PPHP program has been effective in bringing about definite reduction in fertility among those who are directly exposed to it. The recent introduction of the Lippes Loop has attracted many more cases and has become the method to which many old cases are switching. The effectiveness of the PPHP is expected to be enhanced by this new development. Study is now under way to compare birth rates in townships served by PPH workers as compared with those not served. This should show the total impact of the program - both direct and indirect - on fertility reduction among the people.

(South Asia)

GENERAL

Policies on fertility and family size

1758 Ling, T.O. "Buddhist Factors in Population Growth and Control: A Survey Based on Thailand and Ceylon," Popul. Stud. 23(1):53-60, March 1969.

An attempt to account for high observed fertility rates in Thailand, Cambodia, Ceylon, and Burma in spite of Buddhist religious factors that might have been expected to act as a check.

(South Asia: Middle South Asia)

CEYLON

General population policies

1759 Ceylon. Director of Medical and Sanitary Services, Administration Report...1949. Part IV. Education, Science and Art (B). Colombo: Ceylon Government Press, 1950. 17 pp.

A recorded birth rate of 39.9, a death rate of 12.6, and an annual natural increase of over 200 thousand necessitates careful economic and social planning. The absence of concrete proposals from international organizations is noted.

1760 Commonwealth Consultative Committee on South and South-East Asia, The Colombo Plan for Co-operative Economic Development in South and South-East Asia: Report. Command 8080. London: H.M. Stationery Office, 1950. vi, 101 pp.

The inevitable short-term trend towards larger populations only emphasises the need for rapid development. The additional problem which this increase in population involves may, however, be counter-balanced to some extent by the increased vigour and productivity of the people. In the longer run experience suggests that a general improvement in standards of living eventually exercises a steadying influence on the growth of population.

1761 Sarkar, N.K. "Population Trends and Population Policy in Ceylon," Popul. Stud. 9(3):195-216, March 1956.

Ceylon has a wealth of demographic data unusual in Eastern countries, and the author summarizes the trend of population since the beginning of the present century quite briefly. His chief interest is then to discuss economic policy in relation to communities where the death rate has fallen sharply and fertility remains high. He combats the idea that agriculture should be intensified, on the grounds, *inter alia*, that this would perpetuate the present fertility pattern. He is an ardent advocate of putting industrialization first, and criticizes the Colombo Plan for being too little concerned with this.

Policies on fertility and family size

1762 Ceylon. Family Planning Association, *Provisional Scheme for a Nation-Wide Family Planning Programme in Ceylon, 1966-1976*. 9 (processed).

1763 Ceylon. Ministry of Labour, "The Need for Family Planning," *Ceylon Labour Gazette* 7(9):317-21, September 1956.

Summary of statistics on population growth in relation to employment opportunities and economic development.

1764 Kinch, Arne, "A Preliminary Report From the Sweden-Ceylon Family Planning Pilot Project," pp. 85-102 in: Kiser, C.V., ed. *Research in Family Planning*. Princeton: Princeton University Press, 1962.

The Sweden-Ceylon Family Planning Pilot Project was started in Ceylon in June, 1958 with the object of assessing the attitudes of the people, investigating the possibilities of family planning, and giving instruction in various methods. In a village area and a tea estate, a consensus and an attitude survey were conducted. The Family Welfare Centres established in these areas supplied contraceptives free of charge. Preliminary estimates showed an acceptability of 40 to 50 per cent.

1765 Prince Peter of Greece and Denmark, "Anthropological Research in Ceylon, India and on the Borders of Tibet," *Royal Central Asian Sociol. J.* 45:251-63, July - October 1959.

Economic, social and psychological aspects of polyandry: an address.

1766 Ryan, B. "Hinayana Buddhism and Family Planning in Ceylon," pp. 90-102, in: Milbank Memorial Fund, The Interrelations of Demographic, Economic and Social Problems in Selected Underdeveloped Areas. New York: Milbank Memorial Fund, 1954. 200 pp.

Deals briefly with the textual and metaphysical bearing of Buddhism upon family planning, and more extensively with the results of survey type interviews with eighty-six Buddhists monks or priests (Bhikkus). The scholarly Bhikkus are found to be actively favorable to family planning while the poorly educated ones exhibit a lack of knowledge or lack of interest. The latter group might react passively to a family planning program but they would not be concerned with stimulating ideological opposition.

1767 Ryan, Bryce, "Institutional Factors in Sinhalese Fertility," Milbank Memorial Fund Quart. 30(4):359-81, 1952.

The institutional context of marriage among the Sinhalese is similar to that prevalent in many patriarchal and patrilineal societies. Spouses are surrogates of kin, and the new household is one in an interminable chain of kinship units. The power of kin is expressed strongly in process of marrying, in social relationships and direction of loyalities of the marital household, and in the predominance of paternal kin contacts. Encompassing marriage within the domain of kin effectively shuts out individual choice and romanticism. Such marriages lead to high fertility rates as the economic and social advantages of children, especially sons, are considerable. Women fear the fate of singleness or of a childless wife. Men are driven to marriage by its many advantages or almost, for the male, its total lack of any disadvantages. There is a reluctance among mothers to bear too many children which is not shared by the father, to whom there are no disabilities of parenthood. Care of home and family is much more difficult for the woman than in Western society and many women have really a difficult life as homemakers. Sex education and instruction in contraceptive methods would appear to be valuable knowledge for the Sinhalese peasant to acquire but objections are immediate in that only one of the sexes would derive any advantages from the introduction of such instruction.

1768 Selvaratnam, S. "Family Planning Programme in Ceylon," Paper Presented at the International Union for the Scientific Study of Population, General Conference, 3-11 September 1969.

Pioneer work in family planning was organized and implemented by the Family Planning Association of Ceylon which was founded as a voluntary organization in 1953. In 1958 the Government of Ceylon entered into an agreement with the Government of Sweden for an action cum research program. Today family planning work is a part of the Ministry of Health and is nationwide. But, for a variety of reasons, the adoption of birth control techniques has been extremely low.

1769 Wright, Nicholas H. "Recent Fertility Change in Ceylon and Prospects for the National Family Planning Program," Demography 5(2):745-56, 1968.

A discussion of the apparent trend of declining fertility that began in the early 1950's in Ceylon and an appraisal of the National Family Program initiated in 1966. The crude birth rate decline in Ceylon, during 1953-1963 resulted from changes in the age structure and marital status of women 15 to 49. Marital fertility changed very little during these years but the continuing and increasing decline of the crude birth rate after 1963 is attributed to marital fertility rather than to continuing changes in age-marital structure. The fertility decline after 1963 probably represents the effects of family planning, but not of the National Family Planning Program which began in 1966 and was reaching full development only by mid-1968. While the marital status patterns of the next few years are unknown, it is certain that the relative numbers of women 20-39 will increase, mainly at the lower end of that age distribution. This development will tend to inflate the crude birth rate unless compensated for by reduced marital fertility, continued or increasing postponement of marriage, or an increase in the proportion of single women. The author contends that if current plans are implemented quickly and new proposals for the establishment of family planning services are approved, the present goals of the national program can be attained.

INDIA

General population policies

1770 All India Congress Committee, "All India Seminar on Population -- A Review," AICC Econ. Rev. 15(21):29-32, April 7, 1964.

The All India Seminar on Population, the second of the kind organized by the Institute of Economic Growth, was held from 12 to 14 March 1964. Welcoming the participants to the Seminar, Mr. P.N. Dhar, Director, Institute of Economic Growth, emphasized the need to pass on from aggregative study of demographic data in all India terms to demographic experience and behaviour on regional and state levels. He laid emphasis on the imperative need for studying inter-state variations for the formation of an appropriate population policy. Participants from 23 institutions read papers on inter-state and inter-regional differentials and problems. Authors and summaries are noted.

1771 Blacklock, D.B. "The Population Problem of India," British Med. J. No. 4329, pp. 805-7, December 25, 1943.

Population should be regulated in accordance with the number the land will support.

1772 Bose, Ashish, "The Population Puzzle in India," Econ. Develop. Cult. Change 7(3, Part I):230-48, April 1959.

Discussion of the basis for a population policy for India, including as an interrelated whole industrialization, family planning, and modernization of the villages.

1773 Chand, Gyan, Some Aspects of the Population Problem of India. Bannailli Readership Lectures, University of Patna, March 1954. Bihar: Patna University, 1956. iii, 168 pp.

Six lectures by the head of Economic Section, Cabinet Secretariat; Chapter on population policy discusses correlation of family planning with broad economic and social planning, public health, migration, and research.

1774 Chandrasekhar, S. "A Comment on Dr. Enke's Article," Popul. Rev. 4(2):51-54, July 1960.

Thus far, the various mechanical and chemical contraceptive methods have proved to be impractical due to expense,inconvenience, lack of domestic facilities, and absence of female physicians in India. Enke's plan (bonus for non-pregnant women), as a concrete proposal is welcome. However, putting it into action would involve several difficulties: (1) great administrative expense; (2) possibility of women forgetting to report to the clinics; (3) a great amount of strain on the presently limited personnel; and (4) the hiring of a large clerical staff for record-keeping purposes. Despite the above difficulties, it would be worthwhile for the state governments in India to experiment with it. As for the vasectomy (male sterilization)-bonus scheme, a similar plan has been in operation in Madras since 1958, and only 6,193 sterilizations had been performed in a 19 month period; however, it must be remembered that the scheme was confined to Madras, and that more intensive propaganda would be required "at a dignified level" in order to counteract the feeling that the bonus is a kind of 'bribe'. Also, a great deal of superstition regarding the operation will have to be overcome, as well as a thorough investigation and follow-up on possible after-effects of the operation.

1775 Chandrasekhar, S. "India's Planning Commission's Five-Year Plan and the Population Program," Eugenics Rev. 44:122-25, 1952-53.

Describes the financial outlay, the role of planning in a democracy, agricultural and food policy, the population problem and family planning.

1776 Chandrasekhar, S. India's Population. Fact and Policy. Second revised edition. Chidambaram, India: Indian Institute for Population Studies, 1950. pp. 170.

The book is divided into three parts, namely, "Demographic Fact," "Public Health," and "Toward a National Population Policy." The author suggests that the Central Government should appoint "a Population Commission composed of demographers, economists, sociologists, statisticians, medical authorities and social reformers, with wide terms of reference," to recommend a policy. He further suggests the creation of a Portfolio of Population, or Ministry of Welfare, to deal with both the quantity and the quality of the population, and he goes on to describe the varied functions of such a Ministry, which would include, amongst much else, a Bureau of Marriage.

1777 Chandrasekhar, S. "India's Population: Fact, Problem and Policy," Econ. Rev. 18:139-45, January 26, 1967.

The author begins with a brief historical discussion of world population growth and estimates of future rate increases. General population figures for India are cited, and, in explaining the country's rapidly expanding growth, the author points to age and sex composition as the two basic, biological characteristics influencing the population's birth-death rates and its compositional-structural aspects. Several dynamic features of India's population are mentioned, and the country's central economic problems are examined after a few general comments concerning the qualitative improvement of and the quantitative optimum for population in any society. The author contends that India's basic economic problem is really purely demographic, and unless a National Population policy is a policy of control any economic progress will be negated. He proceeds to define a population policy and then places India's needs within the context of that definition. Views on the relation between birth rate and standard of living are described, and while there is no easy solution to India's population problems, the author lists the five steps usually advocated to meet the problem of overpopulation in an underdeveloped country and the numerous implementation difficulties connected with them. He concludes with a discussion of family planning, specifically, the four categories of scientific birth control and the relevance of each for India.

1778 Chopra, R. "Our Population Problem," In 9 parts. Eastern Economist 42(13, 14, 15, 16, 17, 18, 19, 20, 21):721-23; 780-81; 833-36; 903-4; 973-74; 1037-38; 1097-98; 1143-44; 1147; 1195-96. March 27, April 3, 10, 17, and 24, May 1, 8, 15, and 22, 1964.

A series of articles in the course of which a systematic attempt is being made to determine the nature and dimensions of India's population problem and to suggest an adequate programme for dealing with this problem in a realistic manner.

1779 Choudry, N.K. "A Note on the Dilemma of Planning Population in India," Econ. Develop. Cult. Change 4(1):68-81, Nov. 1955.

The year 1921 has been followed by high and accelerating growth rates for the Indian population. Statistical analysis is offered of the past and projected future Indian population, life expectancies, birth rates, and death rates. Analysis is made of effect of population trends on total consumption in terms of (a) agricultural requirements, and (b) national income requirements. Present and future capital requirements in industry and agriculture are analyzed with special attention to unemployment and underemployment in agriculture. Problems created by the expanding population are discussed in terms of total consumption, savings, investments, and outputs. The problem that this population growth portends is basically one of increasing strains on the economy simultaneously with a reduction in the wherewithal to meet them. Various government sponsored birth control efforts are discussed and their general failure noted. Rapid industrialization may lead to decreased birth rates but the relationship is not clear. The possibility must be admitted that the Indian economy lacks resources for the kind of expansion which would raise the standard of living to the point at which a declining birth rate would lead to population stability.

1780 Commerce (Bombay), "Population Control," Commerce 96(2457): 730, April 19, 1958.

Summarizes a report on government policy and expenditure for population control during 1956-57 and 1957-58.

1781 Das, N.K. "Family Planning and Indian Population Problems," Summarized and reviewed by Satya Sevadeshi. Mysore Econ. Rev. 41(10):2-6, 1956.

The increasing pressure of population on the limited resources of the country has made urgent a program of family planning and population control. The urgency is enhanced further by recognition of the fact that the immediate effect of any large improvement in the economic conditions would be an increase in the growth of members. Because of this the consensus of opinion is now in favour of the adoption of a comprehensive policy of population control as a prior condition for the successful operation of an economic development program.

1782 Davis, Kingsley, "Demographic Fact and Policy in India," Milbank Memorial Fund Quart. 22(3):256-78, 1944.

A rural, illiterate, religious and immobile population with a naturally high fertility rate has acquired a stable government, economy and public health system, largely controlled by outsiders, producing a marked reduction in the normal death rate. The population has risen from about 250 million in 1870 to almost 400 million in 1941. It is likely to increase by hundreds of millions during the next century.

1783 Demeny, Paul, "The Economics of Government Payments to Limit Population: A Comment," Econ. Develop. Cult. Change 9(4, Pt. 1):641-44, July 1961.

Comment on the Economic Costs of the Proposals by S. Enke in his article, "The Economics of Government Payments to Limit Population," Econ. Dev. Cult. Change 8(4, Pt. 1): 339-48, July 1960.

1784 Desai, P.B. "Planning and Population Policy in India," Indian Popul. Bull. 3:217-30, August 1966.

While the population policy dealing with the question of population growth needs to be strengthened and vigorously followed,the other aspects of the demographic phenomena, particularly regional distribution, rural-urban relationships and labor force structure, demand urgent attention. It seems imperative that we have a set of inter-related policies to deal with different aspects of the general population problem. The second point emphasized is that the success of both the planning and the population policy has been affected by the traditional social structure. Planning has built up potentialities of basic overheads in irrigation, transport, power, etc., but these potentialities are tending to remain underutilized on account of insufficient public participation and response. This lack of participation is related to the constraints inherent in the continuing traditional society.

1785 Desai, P.B. "Economic Development and Population Control," Paper presented at the National Conference on Population Policy and Programmes, New Delhi, 19-23 December 1969.

The experience of Indian planning suggests that effective population control, designed to restore the balance between vital rates by reducing the level of fertility, has a positive contribution to make to the process of economic development. A reduction in fertility would make the process of modernization more rapid and certain. It would accelerate the growth of income, make employment more probable for those in the labor-force age group, and it would make the attainment of universal education easier. Finally, it would give women some relief from constant pregnancy, parturition, and child care.

1786 Desai, Sapur Faredum, "Toward a National Population Policy," Indian J. Soc. Work 26(2):129-32, July 1965.

Population theory and population policy are examined in the light of India's practical problems of population structure, unemployment, low health and nutrition, economic underdevelopment, etc. The ineffectiveness of birth control propaganda in the last 10 years is noted. Birth control must reach the masses and this can be achieved by education through social workers, officers and workers of the Panchayat Raj (village government), CD organizations, etc. Eugenic teaching in schools and colleges is advocated, since the problem is seen as not only one of limiting birth, but of limiting procreation to those who are healthy. Suggestions are made regarding eugenics policies and programs concerning (1) population trends and economic and social planning; (2) population and eugenical measures; (3) medical, social and public health measures; and (4) developmental and social psychological, educational practice, and improvement of human relations. A coordinated effort is called for in order to successfully bring national policy to the individual.

1787 Eastern Economist, "Demographic Research," Eastern Economist 33(8):269, August 21, 1956.

Report on the first meeting and constitution of the Demographic

Advisory Committee, appointed by the Government of India to coordinate and direct demographic training. Statements by the Chairman, V.K.R.V. Rao, and by the Union Health Minister, D.P. Karmarkar.

1788 Enke, Stephen, "The Economics of Government Payments to Limit Population," _Econ. Develop. Cult. Change_ 8(4, Part I): 339-48, July 1960.

In over-populated nations, infants at age zero may have a negative economic value, so that the society, through its government may be justified in offering bonuses to married fathers who volunteer for a vasectomy. This negative value of infants arises in countries where the marginal product of labor is a small fraction of consumption per capita, as in the case of India. Moreover, this negative valuation depends on discounting future marginal products and average consumption to the present date, and infants are consumers for many years before they become producers. If an infant's economic value at birth is roughly -$125 in India, where per capita consumption is about $75 a year, a young married father can be paid several hundred dollars for a vasectomy. If the cost of such an operation is $5 or less, resources invested in vasectomies may prove several hundred times more effective in raising future per capita incomes than resources of equivalent value invested in factories, etc.

1789 Enke, Stephen, "Government Bonuses for Smaller Families," _Popul. Rev._ 4:47-54, July 1960.

A discussion of the advantages of awarding government bonuses for family limitation (male vasectomy and/or female pregnancy prevention). If men are to volunteer for sterilization, there must be a powerful counter-inducement, the most effective being one with a money value (e.g., old age pension). In underdeveloped countries, infants can consume more than they produce over their lifetimes; however, these same infants, if born, "may be an economic asset to those parents who live within an extended family." The amount of the bonus awarded to males would vary with age of both spouses, and the number and sex of surviving children, all of which determines the number of extra children the man might be expected to have without sterilization. In the case of women, the government would pay a certain amount per year to remain non-pregnant: this would involve registration and medical examination three times a year with a credit toward a 'blocked' savings account with the State - a positive or omitted examination would forfeit the blocked credits which become payable at 45 years of age. Blocking is necessary to assure permanent prevention, and avoid mere deferring of births. A husband's consent and proof that he had not had a vasectomy would also be required. Hypothetical cases of program costs and economic effectiveness are demonstrated.

1790 Enke, Stephen, "A Rejoinder to Comments on the Superior Effectiveness of Vasectomy-Bonus Schemes," Econ. Develop. Cult. Change 9(4, Part 1): 645-47, July 1961.

Reply to P. Demen's comments in Econ. Develop. Cult. Change 9(4, Part 1):641-44. July 1961. States that Demeny is skeptical regarding claim that, per unit of resources invested, vasectomy-bonus schemes might be several times more effective than traditional development projects in raising per capita income. Specifically he suggests that parts of the alleged "transfer" bonus payment may in fact include an investment opportunity cost because taxpayers will save less. Enke agrees to this possibility but points out that this would not be the case if the initial beneficiaries are the "emerged" urban, middle class couples; if the bonus is paid in goods and services rather than cash; and over the long-run.

1791 Enke, Stephen, "Some Misconceptions of Krueger and Sjaastad Regarding the Vasectomy-Bonus Plan to Reduce Births in Overpopulated and Poor Countries," Econ. Develop. Cult. Change 10(4):427-31, July 1962.

In a rejoinder to the comments of Krueger and Sjaastad, the author supports his previous argument for the vasectomy-bonus plan and questions why Krueger and Sjaastad have not advanced any better plans for controlling the population, which in India alone has been boosted by 30 million infants since the first writing of his articles in 1960. The burden of the complaint was that the vasectomy-bonus plan goes too far, in that it overestimates the value of reducing births and so presumably might overly decrease national populations. The author feels that this is a remote danger, but even with this alleged bias towards too few births, the situation could be modified before the overpopulated countries got their births and deaths into balance.

1792 Enke, Stephen, "Some Reactions to Bonuses for Family Limitation," Popul. Rev. 5(2):33-40, July 1961.

Three objections are discussed: (1) industrialization will so increase India's national income that population control is unnecessary; (2) a scheme equating the marginal return on resources devoted to increasing capital stocks or labor force will maximize aggregate national income and not per capita income; and (3) the suggested bonus payments are not merely transfer costs but also include a measure of lost investment cost. By using the Cobb-Douglas type function, the above arguments are repudiated. By contrasting manipulation of economic factors (e.g., increased national output, invested capital, and increased productivity), with population variables, the original hypothesis is reaffirmed. Further conclusions are: (A)"a baby has a negative value unless its marginal productivity exceeds per capita consumption"; (B) the superiority of the bonus-vasectomy scheme as a means of raising per capita incomes may be even greater than originally claimed; (C) "bonus payments from other curtailed operations would include only a fraction of investment opportunity cost"; (D) a bonus paid in productive goods and services is likely to increase net investment; and (E) using resources in the bonus-vasectomy scheme both retards population growth and increases economic output.

1793 Enke, Stephen, The Worth of Population Control to India: Some Money Measures and Incentive Schemes. Rand Corporation [Series] P - 1649. Santa Barbara, March 20, 1959; Revised May 4, 1959. 29 pp., processed. Also in: Rev. Econ. Statistics 42(2):175-81, May 1960.

In this paper a preliminary attempt is made to estimate the value of permanently preventing a birth, to outline one incentive scheme for husbands and another for wives to reduce births, and to assess the impact of these schemes on the economy's resources and the government finances.

1794 Freymann, Moye W. "Population Control in India," Marr. Fam. Living 25(1):53-61, Feb. 1963.

A discussion of the development of the population control movement in India, reviewing some of the main forces which have acted to control mortality and fertility rates at the levels now existing in India and the stages of development of the Indian national family planning program. It is noted that the population of India was controlled during the last century at a level of almost half of what it is today, primarily by recurring famines. With improvements in technology and disease control, a consistent rise in population has occurred since 1920. A number of potent forces support the present high birth rate in India. On the other hand, the fact that some groups in the population are reducing their fertility, and that factors consistent with such a change exist among other groups, lend support to the proposition that an aggressive national family planning program can hasten an overall decline in birth rate.

1795 Ganguli, B.N. "Introduction to a National Population Policy," Paper presented at the National Conference on Population Policy and Programmes, New Delhi, 19-23 December 1969.

India needs a broadbased population policy for a number of compelling reasons. The policy must aim to achieve a future population which in terms of size and skills increases the prospects of development. Development, following the U.N. principle, means a "faster rate of reduction of the number of people living below an acceptable minimum standard of living than the rate of growth in aggregate income." The policy must aim, too, to lessen the serious problem of rapid urbanization and its concomitant high economic and social costs. Regional planning must be a part of the policy. While family planning should be an integral part of the policy, there should also be considerable investment in child health, nutrition and education.

1796 Ghose, Bimal C. Planning for India. London: Oxford University Press, 1944. iv, 76 pp.

This is an examination of the implications and problems of economic planning, with special reference to the Bombay Plan. Preliminary description of the implications of planning and estimates of the food, clothing, housing, health, and educational needs according to minimum standards to precede the outlining of a series of three five-year "Gosplans" designed to achieve these minimum standards. The major techniques of raising standards is to be through the increased production made possible by rapid industrialization.

1797 Goel, S.C. "A Plea for Population Control," Rural India 18(1):17-22, January 1955.

In India there is a growing need to evolve a rational population policy. The death rate in India indicates a gradual decline mainly due to state welfare measures. But the birth rate has not declined during the last 50 years. The main reasons for high fertility in India are: (1) early marriage which increases the span of reproductive age; (2) the universality of marriage regardless of hygienic, eugenic or economic considerations; and (3) the institution of polygamy, although not practiced on a considerable scale. Control of marriage below 21 years would have controlled births effectively. The provisions of the Sharda Act could be modified and enforced to mobilize and train population in this respect. On the more positive side, propaganda for family planning, spread of education, establishment of family planning centers, easy dissemination of knowledge regarding scientific methods of birth control, establishment of a population research center, facilities for recreational and cultural activities, establishment of health centers and holiday resorts, etc. could achieve the desired results. Regional distribution of the population should be undertaken by the Planning Commission on the basis of a well-planned and comprehensive survey of the country with a special regard to the material resources of each region.

1798 Gopalaswami, R.A. "Family Planning and National Planning," Popul. Rev. 1(1):1-6, Jan. 1957.

A Great Britain Royal Commission on Population a few years ago conducted a survey in which it was found that family planning in Great Britain had decreased the birth rate. Reasons given in Great Britain for family planning included 'more children could not be afforded,' 'to space pregnancies,' and 'health reasons.' All of these are valid for family planning in India. The Second National 5-Year Plan is in operation to create a balance between a low birth rate (without avoidable improvident maternity - births of fourth and higher orders) and a low death rate (without avoidable premature mortality), and to create a better standard of living for the next generation. It is thus clear that the practice of family planning is no longer a matter of purely private interest to married couples. The welfare of the nation as a whole will be promoted or retarded by what every married couple does or fails to do about family planning.

1799 Hallen, G.C. "Population Explosion: Need for Evolving a Scientific Population Policy for India," AICC Econ. Rev. 18(20):23-28, May 1, 1967.

Stresses the multiplicity of factors to be considered. The article begins with a brief outline of Malthusian theory and its relevance to present growth rate figures for population and food supplies. Demographic and national studies are cited to substantiate the author's claim that world populaton is increasing at a much faster rate than production of food. India's situation is examined: its rapidly increasing population, its minimally successful family planning program, its inability to meet food demands, and the application of positive checks. There follows a discussion of two prevalent approaches to population, the transition theory and the theory that population problems have been grossly exaggerated. Both have little pragmatic value in terms of formulating a progressive or realistic population policy for India, and acceptance of the applicability of either would mean that there would be no need to deal with the Malthusian 'devils' at work on the country's modern demographic societal structure. The article concludes with a discussion of some of the many factors which must be considered if there is to be a systematic and scientific effort toward the alleviation of India's population and economic problems.

1800 India. Hyderabad Government, "Population Trends and Family Planning," Hyderabad Government Bull. Econ. Affairs 7(5-6): 170-79, May-June 1954.

There are two opposing viewpoints in formulating a population policy. One is to limit population to the country's agricultural potential and the other is to adjust the food supply to the growing population. All the populationist theories emphasize the former point. On the assumption that the policy of stepping up food-supply to meet the needs of the growing population is adopted, then there are various measures which may be resorted to.

1801 India, Legislature. Council of State, Reconstruction Committee, Second Report on Reconstruction Planning. Delhi: Manager of Publications, 1945. 57 pp.

The general objectives of this plan, including the relief of pressure on the land, are stated, the general principles outlined in major fields of endeavor, and development policy summarized with respects to main subjects, including resettlement, industrial development, agriculture, and public health.

1802 India, Madras (Presidency). Post-War Reconstruction (Co-ordination) Department, Post-War Reconstruction and Development Schemes of the Government of Madras. Madras: Printed by the Superintendent, Government Press, 1945. xix, 198 pp.

A five-year plan, based on the recommendations of a Post-War Reconstruction Committee and the reports of its sub-committees on agriculture, livestock, forests, fisheries, irrigation, industries including the development of electric power, communications, public transport, education, public health and medical relief, questions particularly affecting women, and labor.

1803 India. National Planning Committee, Population: Report of the Sub-Committee. Khushal T. Shah, editor. National Planning Committee Series, 6. Bombay: Vora, 1947. xv, 145 pp.

The National Planning Committee, appointed in 1938, began work in 1939, issued an elaborate and comprehensive questionnaire, and then formed twenty-nine sub-committees. The sub-committee reports were submitted in 1940, but Pandit Nehru, the Chairman, was then imprisoned, so work ceased. The war prolonged the interruption. This final report of the Sub-Committee on Population describes the trends of population, planned food policy, social reform and legislature, unemployment and industries, and social welfare and eugenics, indicating policy implications in all cases. Resolution 4 of the final report was as follows: "In the interests of social economy, family happiness and national planning, family planning and a limitation of children are essential, and the State should adopt a policy to encourage these. It is desirable to lay stress on self-control, as well as to spread knowledge of cheap and safe methods of birth control. Birth control clinics should be established, and other necessary measures taken in this behalf and to prevent the use of advertisement of harmful methods."

1804 India. Orissa Government, Post-War Reconstruction and Development Schemes, Government of Orissa. First Draft. Cuttack: Superintendent, Government Press, 1944. xiii, 423 pp.

This provisional draft for the first five-year plan of development for Orissa includes broad outlines and cost estimates for economic developments in the resettlement of servicemen, industries and industrial training, roads, power development, mining, irrigation, agriculture, education, public health and medical services, etc.

1805 India. Planning Commission, The First Five Year Plan: A Draft Outline. July, 1951. vii, 295 pp.

Part I explains the approach to planning, Part II the salient features of the Five Year Plan, Part III problems of policy and administration. In Part I there is consideration of the bearing of population pressure on development, with the conclusion that population policy is essential to planning. Part II, Ch. 15, "Health," states in its section on family planning, pp. 2-6-7, that there is agreement with the recommendations of the Subcommittee on Population Growth and Family Planning of the Panel of Health Programmes. The further statement is added that "methods of family limitation other than contraceptives should also be investigated. In this connection the question of raising the age of marriage of girls deserves consideration."

1806 India. Planning Commission, The First Five Year Plan. Vol. I. New Delhi: Government of India Press, 1952. xvi, 671 pp.; The First Five Year Plan. Vol. II. Development Schemes ...1952. 165 pp.; Five Year Plan. Progress Report for 1951-52 and 1952-53 ...1953. ii, 174 pp.

The first report notes throughout the relation of population increase to economic, health, and welfare developments, outlines an approach to the problem of population, and assigns to the Department of Health responsibility for field studies. The "Progress report" notes the existence of three experimental centers for pilot studies in family planning methods, the establishment of a Family Planning Section in the Ministry of Health, and the constitution of a Population Research and Programmes Committee. The "Explanatory memorandum" on the budget of the Central Government for 1954-55 (as laid before the Parliament): [1954] notes also the provisions for subsidies to State governments and voluntary organizations from the budget allocations for family planning.

1807 India. Planning Commission, Third Five Year Plan. New Delhi, 1961. xiv, 774 pp.

Chapters include: Employment and manpower; Agricultural labour; Health and family planning [summary of past and planned activities]. Appendix C, Notes on population and employment, discusses projections for the fourth and fifth plans. For a summary and discussion of this report see: Moorthy, K. Krishna, "India's Third Five-Year Plan," Far Eastern Econ. Rev. 33(8):356-61. Aug. 24, 1961.

1808 India Planning Commission, Third Five Year Plan: Summary. Delhi: Director, Publications Division, n.d. [iii], 215 pp.

Chapter, Employment and manpower, presents quantitative estimates on labor force size and growth. Chapter, Health, housing and other welfare services, has section, Health and family planning.

1809 India (Republic) Laws, Statutes, etc. Codified Hindu Law. 1964 Edition. Law Book Company, 1964.

Book is divided into four sections: Hindu Marriage Act, Hindu Succession Act, Hindu Adoptions and Maintenance Act, and Hindu Minority and Guardianship Act. Contains all unrepealed and repealed Acts pertaining to Hindu Laws from 1850 to 1964 and various other useful Appendices. Various sections of Law are illustrated by numerous cases before the courts.

1810 Institute of Economic Growth, India's Population: Some Problems in Perspective Planning. Proceedings of a Seminar [Delhi, India. Mar. 7-8, 1959]. S.N. Agarwala, ed. Bombay: Asia Publishing House, xi, 208 pp.

Papers are grouped under the following headings: Future growth of India's population; Employment aspects of population growth; Population policy for India; Problems of demographic research in India.

1811 Johl, S.S., and Ayalvi, H.S. "Some Socio-Economic Aspects of Population Control in India," J. Fam. Welf. 13(2):61-66, Dec. 1966.

Optimum population standards can now be set and maintained by society and the logistic curve of biological growth of population can be trimmed and trained.

1812 Kamat, Melba,and Kamat, R.G. Suggestions for the Effective Control of Population in India. Bombay: Popular Book Depot, 1959. 32 pp.

The reasons which led the Government of India to organize the services of Family Planning in the Ministry of Health are outlined: the principal object of such planning is to stabilize the population at an appropriate level consistent with the economic policy of raising the standard of life rapidly. Defined is what would constitute a desirable level of population for India's conditions, and there follows a discussion of fecundity in India, with references to [including tables and graphs] birth and death rates; effect on fertility of change in diet; differential fertility among various religious communities; a survey conducted by the Contraceptive Testing Unit in the industrial area of Bombay, which investigated patterns and variability of the menstrual cycle in a group of women, correlation between diet and reproductive ability and the period of inability to conceive after delivery; and frequency of sexual intercourse. Chronic semi-starvation, especially the protein starvation prevalent in India, for a century or more, and perhaps also other conditions have brought about a decrease in fecundity. Therefore, with improvement of the country's standard of living, there will be an increase in the already high birth rate and a decrease in the death rate. Since it is contended that only family planning can control a terrific increase in population, different methods of birth control and their effectiveness are examined, and the importance of research is emphasized. The authors conclude with a list of seven points on which a required program of population control for India should be based and contend that the birth rate can be lowered only if an integrated plan of higher production, full employment, better food, free health service and family planning is organized carefully and carried out with the mobilization of popular support.

1813 Krishnamurthy, K.G. "The Need for a Population Policy and Planned Urban Growth," Paper presented at the National Conference on Population Policy and Programmes, New Delhi, 19-23 December 1969.

The government is attempting to reduce the birth rate from 42 to 25 per 1000 through a "cafeteria approach" to family planning. Along with this general reduction in numbers, there is need to reduce the present 75 to 80 percent of the population dependent on agriculture to 50 percent in the next 15 to 20 years. The surplus population would be redistributed to the urban areas. A reduction in the evils of urbanization and the prevention of the influx of migrants to large metropolitan centers requires identification of all the growth centers in the country. Each growth center should be linked to all the villages within a radius of 15 to 20 miles in terms of transportation and the provision of the amenities of urbanization such as hospitals, schools, shops, etc. Planning for such centers should be done for the next 30 to 40 years.

1814 Krueger, Anne O.,and Sjaastad, Larry A. "Some Limitations of Enke's Economics of Population," Econ. Develop. Cult. Change 10(4):423-26, July 1962.

Issue is taken with S. Enke's formulation of optimal population policy, and shows that, according to all generally acceptable welfare criteria, payment of subsidies to families limiting their size should equal the cost of additional children to society that is not borne by the family having the children. While this criterion leaves a major role to be played by subsidies (and the spread of information) in limiting population growth, it differs significantly from Enke's in that Enke would pay individuals not having children the entire costs to be incurred by the family and society if there were more people. On economic grounds, Enke's criterion would result in a double reward, since families with fewer children woul be able to enjoy increased consumption both because they have fewer dependents, and because a subsidy would again pay them the foregone child's consumption. Fundamental issue is taken with Enke's use of per capita income as the maximum, since it ignores the possibility of people preferring more children. It is shown that welfare will be maximized by a lower per capita income if this results from individuals' preferences for larger families.

1815 Mahajan, V.S. "Population, Employment and Family Planning in India," Indian J. Soc. Work 22(3):253-57, Dec. 1961.

While India's population increased by 39 million between 1891 and 1931, it increased by 81 million between 1931 and 1951. The annual rate of growth between 1931 and 1951 comes to 1.3% and between 1951 and 1961 it comes to 2.2%. It is expected to rise to 2.5% during 1961 to 1971, thereby doubling the population within a period of 25 to 30 years. It is argued that family planning as an instrument of population control cannot be effective unless it reaches remote areas, which, thanks to the spread of health facilities, constitute explosive pockets regarding population growth. On the other hand, more conscious members in the urban areas - upper classes and middle classes - are gradually curtailing the number of children per family. This would lead to population imbalance in the sense that there would be more mentally less-developed people in the society than intelligent ones. It is suggested that the government should devote more attention to programs of family planning, rural development and education, and less to the public sector (heavy industry) program.

1816 Mahalanobis, P.C. "Next Steps in Planning," Sankhya 22(1-2): 143-72, Jan. 1960.

A review of the aims, attainments, and failures of the first and second Indian five-year plans, and the "next steps" needed for the third plan, to begin in 1961. Recommendations include the initiation of a truly national health service with emphasis on establishing a large number of small village units, to provide essential medical and health service and also serve as family planning centers.

1817 Mamoria, C.B. "Our Demographic Situation and Its Solution," AICC Economic Rev. 9:67-74, Aug. 15, 1957.

Universal education, delayed marriage, provision of social security measures, rapid urbanization, death control, together with a corresponding control of births and caste equality and improvement of nutritional standards should all be considered as basic programmes for reducing improvident parenthood and developing new wants, ambitions and pattern of living. A population policy that seeks to provide mere subsistence defeats itself. Education and change in social culture and mores of the society, of course, are the sovereign factors from bringing about a new outlook in the family. Demographic policy must not rest on what Professor Robbins has called a "fodder minimum" for the people but on the amenities, decencies and comforts of a civilized life, made increasingly available for a larger and larger section of the population by rational family planning. Family planning should form an essential part in all our programmes.

1818 Mamoria, C.B. Population and Family Planning in India. Allahabad: Kitab Mahal, 1959. 167 pp.

A comprehensive discussion of the nature of India's population problem and the government's population policy. Aspects considered: history of controls; current issues; methods of contraception; improvement of the quality of the population; present government policy on family planning.

1819 Mamoria, C.B. "Population Planning in India," Modern Rev. 93:21-32, Jan. 1953.

Data on birth and death rates, density of population, and economic resources. Suggests a population policy aimed at:

reducing fertility, raising the age at marriage, raising the level of literacy and recreational pursuits, positive and negative eugenics and agricultural and industrial development.

1820 Mauldin, W. Parker, "The Population of India: Policy, Action and Research," Econ. Digest 3(2):14-31, Summer 1960.

Reviews the provisions made by the Government of India for family planning, research facilities and studies. Birth and death rates and trends are also given.

1821 Mazumdar, Jyoti, and Strommer, Aarno, "Vaestonkehityksesta ja Vaestopolitiikasta Intiassa" [Population Development and Population Policy in India], Chpt. in Eripainos Vaestontutkimuksen Vuosikirjasta [Yearbook of Population Research in Finland], Helsinki: Population Research Institute, 7:9-18, 1961/62.

A condensation of a larger paper on population problems in India, based on population growth data presented in tables and diagrams. It is established that India, with a population of 438 million in 1961, has a long way to go before it will achieve complete economic modernization. For the present, this development is retarded by the steady increase in population which is estimated at between 27.1 and 15.9% for the decade 1966-1976. Latest investigations place the exact birth rate at about 40 per 1,000 and the death rate somewhat over 20 per 1,000, producing a population growth rate of nearly 2% a year. As Indians cannot emigrate in large numbers, it is obvious that the country will not be able to afford many more years of high fertility. The government and the country's intellectual leaders are seriously concerned about the situation and considerable measures have already been taken to retard the process of growth by family planning and other programs, with further measures being prepared. Accordingly, India's population policy is directing its energies to (1) obtaining accurate knowledge of the factors operative in rapid population growth, (2) on determining the techniques of birth control most suitable for Indian conditions and methods of implementing fertility planning, and (3) toward introducing consultation on family planning as a new, essential item of service in public and private hospitals, clinics, and health agencies.

1822 Mitra, Asok, "Population Studies in Population Policy," Paper presented at the National Conference on Population Policy and Programmes, New Delhi, 19-23 December 1969.

There are numerous areas in which demographic research is essential but still rudimentary for development planning. These include: the problem of transfer of agricultural to non-agricultural population as it relates to constraints of consumption and domestic saving; problems of internal migration as they relate to industrial development planning, planning of substantial territories, and studies in levels of living and consumption patterns in rural and urban areas; and public consumption as a concomitant of economic development, mainly education, health, transport, housing, etc.

1823 Mukerjee, Radhakamal, "Address," pp. 6-10 in: Family Planning Association of India, _Report of the Proceedings, Second All India Conference on Family Planning_. Bombay: The Association, 1955. 117 pp.

Universal education, improvement of nutritional standards, delayed marriage, land redistribution, co-operative farming, caste equality and adoption of a scheme of social security should all be considered as basic programs for reducing improvident parenthood and developing new wants, ambitions and patterns of living. In addition, programs of social research on attitudes toward birth control are needed. A social philosophy of democratic values and aspirations allowing the mass of the population a greater sharing of the cultural heritage rather than social defeatism should underlie the ideal and program of family planning.

1824 Mukerjee, Radhakamal, _The Food Supply_. Oxford Pamphlets on Indian Affairs, No. 8. London: Oxford University Press, 1942. 31 pp.

Statistics are marshalled from some of the author's studies to indicate that the present hiatus between increase of population and food supply in India will be enlarged unless adequate policy measures are undertaken immediately. Ten specific suggestions are made for a progressive food policy.

1825 Natarajan, Swaminath, _Social Problems_. Oxford Pamphlets on Indian Affairs, No. 7. London: Oxford University Press, 1942. 32 pp.

After briefly reviewing the Hindu attitude towards caste, the joint family, the status of women, birth control, prostitution, and professional mendicancy, the author concludes that social legislation in India can succeed only on a national scale.

1826 "The Need for Population Policy: Draft Population Policy Resolution," Paper presented at the National Conference on Population Policy and Programmes, New Delhi, 19-21 December 1961.

The enunciation of a population policy is not only urgently needed in view of complex ramifications of the population problems, but is especially warranted by the new orientation of the problem of development. Such a policy must consider both the numbers involved and the distribution and characteristics of such numbers. Because changes occur unceasingly, the policy must be related to the short-term situation and the long-term prospects. The policy must be adapted to regional variations.

1827 Nehru, Jawaharlal, "Inaugural Address at the Sixth International Conference on Planned Parenthood," J. Fam. Welf. 5(3):4-10, March 1959.

Endorses family planning but strongly urges that it be considered as one phase of general economic and social planning.

1828 Nevett, A. Population Explosion or Control? A Study with Special Reference to India. Notre Dame, Indiana: Fides Publishers, Inc., 1964. 224 pp.

A book in 10 chapters on the factors which affect population growth, containing an author's Preface, and extensive statistical and demographic data. (1) General Demographic Survey-discusses resources and population and the accuracy of statistics. (2) Theories of Population Growth - defines overpopulation and considers the advantage of numbers for a population, aging populations, and the ethical problem of population control. (3) India's Population Problem - is concerned with problems special to India and other developing countries, e.g., illiteracy, sex imbalance, unemployment, lack of investment, and the relationship between population and resources.

(4) Attempts at Population Control in India - examines the spread of birth control in the West, especially in Great Britain, education towards birth control, birth control and religion, motives for and success of birth control in India, as well as the methods used, including oral contraceptives, sterilization, abortion and rhythm. Migration is also considered a method of population control. (5) Attitudes to Life and Responsibility - studies the frequent Indian failure in parental and social responsibility, the passivity and the violence of the Indian culture, and other obstacles to the development of responsibility. (6) The Indian Woman and Marriage - describes Hindu ideals and customs regarding marriage and family life, and Gandhi's view of marriage. (7) Age at marriage deals with the legal age of consent in India, the attitude of the Muslims and India's women, social pressure and the effectiveness of the law raising the legal age of marriage and its conflict with the Indian culture, including survey data for the time after 1929.

1829 Nevett, A. Too Many of Us ?: The Indian Population Problem. Poona, 1952. 188 pp.

1830 Panikkar, K.M. Population Problems. Chidambaram, India: Annamalai University, Indian Institute for Population Studies, 1950. 8 pp.

Deals with the necessity for a factual basis for India's population policy.

1831 Political and Economic Planning (PEP). "Population Policies in India and Japan," Planning 21 (378): 33-48. April 4, 1955.

Since 1945, two great countries of Asia, India and Japan, have adopted positive policies to secure lower birth rates and population growth.

They are the first large countries to take this significant step, and their progress is accordingly watched with interest by all those who regard rapid population growth as a threat to the economic well-being of Asia. This broadsheet summarizes the two policies, traces their history, and draws from them lessons that may be helpful to the governments of other countries similarly placed.

1832 Raina, B.L. "Medicine and Family Planning: Some Aspects," Paper presented at the National Conference on Population Policy and Programmes, New Delhi, 19-23 December 1969.

In its essence, medical science is a social science. It is concerned with not only an individual but the total environment of the group of individuals so that the community as a whole may lead a healthy, full, creative and fruitful life. Thus, medicine is a major instrument of social policy. Its existing knowledge and technology and research efforts may aid in bringing about family limitation. Family limitation is a means to the "good life." Currently, the states of India vary greatly in the adoption of the IUCD and sterilizations. Raising the age of marriage and the legalization of induced abortions are also recommended as ways of reducing the fertility level. In changing the patterns of fertility, appropriate attention must be given to the genetic implications.

1833 Raina, B.L. "Population Policy in India," Paper presented at the International Union for the Scientific Study of Population General Conference, 3-11 September 1969.

The policy of limiting births in India plays an essential role in the general plan of economic and social development. This policy includes the pursuit of research by individuals and organizations on the dynamics of fertility. It is recognized that various socio-economic changes may be inducive to an atmosphere of limitation and the actual effects of such changes are being evaluated. A change in fertility involves several related matters: raising the age at marriage, liberalization of the abortion law, education of women, and organizations to popularize the idea of birth control.

1834 Raina, B.L. "Potentialities for Fertility Reduction Under a Planned Economy," Indian Popul. Bull. 3:231-36, August 1966.

After a brief discussion of the aims and principles of planned economic development, the potentialities for fertility reduction in India are examined. Since fertility among the population has been clearly identified as a key problem influencing the process of economic and social transition, the author reviews India's national family planning program, with references to methods of reducing fertility and the possibilities for motivational changes. Outlined are the factors favoring high fertility and those favoring low fertility under a planned economy. Such factors are, in many cases, susceptible to influence by planned governmental action, and the article concludes with an examination of the types of action -- education, organization, supplies and social legislation -- which go into an integrated population program.

1835 Raina, Saraswati, "Demographic Crisis and Family Planning. Summarized and Reviewed by Satya Swadeshi," Mysore Economic Rev. 41(304):10-14, March-April 1956.

After considering the growth of population, the need for family planning, the high maternal and infant mortality, the deficit of doctors and other health practitioners, the author discusses the practical difficulties involved in efforts to improve health and nutrition. Finally, she suggests how the demographic crises may be solved by raising the standard of living and implementing family planning programs.

1836 Rao, R.V. Economic Planning in India. Rajkot: Kitarghar, 1945. 116 pp.

Chapter V, "Population and Planning," considers family limitation and the necessity for both a good economy and a population policy.

1837 Rao, R.V. "The Problem of India's Increasing Numbers: A Plea for an Inter-State Approach," AICC Econ. Rev. 13(6): 10-12, 35, August 7, 1961.

Comparison of census data of 1901 and 1961 for fourteen of the fifteen states of the Indian union (excluding Jammu and Kashmir) on population size, percent increase, and density per square mile, and discussion of the policy implications of the difference observed.

1838 Samuel, T.J. "The Development of India's Policy of Population Control," Milbank Mem. Fund Quart. 44(1):49-68, Part I, Jan. 1966.

An examination of the factors hindering the rapid development of India's population control policies. The development of the present government policy falls into 4 periods: (1) the period of indifference (before 1947); (2) the period of neutrality (1947-1952); (3) the period of experimentation (1952-1961); and (4) the beginning of the policy of population control (1961-1962). During period 1, British indifference to the problem was based on the belief that a population increase contributed to prosperity. Though a favorable climate for a policy of population control developed in the 1950's, it was only in December 1952 that the first 5-year plan allotted money for family planning propaganda and experiments. In period 3, the program remained in the experimental stage. By 1961-62, population control was accepted as "an essential element in the strategy of development" to achieve a faster rate of economic growth, and The Health Survey and Planning Committee (Mudaliar Committee) was appointed in 1961 to develop an adequate program. But the formulation of an effective population control policy remains difficult; in addition to the problems of caste, religion, and language, the low rate of literacy and income, and the attitudes of the population contribute to the government's ambivalent attitude toward the implementation of an effective population control policy. The main factors are: (a) an attitude still prevalent among nationalist leaders that the solution to India's economic problems lies in the exploitation of its natural resources, which are plentiful enough to afford a higher living standard to the masses; (b) economic development is equated with a large labor force; (c) a belief that without a higher standard of living and education population control would fail; (d) the assumption that the birth rate would fall if the standard of living were raised; (e) opposition to the use of contraceptives on moral and health grounds, and an insistence on the preferable application of the rhythm method of birth control; and (f) a lack of support by important leaders on the grounds of interference in the family life.

1839 Sanyal, S.N. "Population Problem of India," Indian Med. Assn. J. 20(5):215-20, March 1951.

India should adopt measures for deliberate restriction of numbers. She must try to influence people through education, teach them to make their sex-life something nobler, i.e., which will help the reproduction of desirable progeny for the future nation, for the future of mankind depends on the quality of human life produced. The best thing for the state to do will be to continue efforts to bring efficient birth control within the reach of the lowest and the least useful classes, for that will solve almost all the problems of overpopulation and incidentally of eugenics.

1840 Sen, Sudhir, Land and Its Problems. Vol. I. Visva-Bharati, Economic Research. Calcutta, 1943. 155 pp.

This study of paddy cultivation in the villages surrounding the Srinketan Institute of Rural Reconstruction in Birbhum, Bengal, assesses the increases in production, income, and welfare that could be secured by the proper maintenance of existing irrigation and drainage works, greater use of manures, the selection and hybridization of seeds, and improved techniques of cultivation.

1841 Sharma, K.K. "Planning for Employment," Ind. J. Comm. 7(28): 15-27, Dec. 1954.

There are three major types of unemployment, viz., (i)cyclical, due to deficiency in demand, (ii) chronic,due to shortage of capital equipment, and (iii) frictional, due to lack of correspondence between demand for and supply of labour in particular jobs. The stabilization of the rate of domestic investment and the stimulation of consumers' demand are the remedies for the first type. The second type exists in underdeveloped countries. Land settlement, mixed farming and industrial development are its remedies. For the third type measures to increase the mobility of labour, training and retraining of workers are suggested. All these three types of unemployment are prevalent in India. The working force has been increasing at the rate of about 250,000 per annum. The deflationary policy since the middle of 1950, the steady migration of workers from villages to towns and an increase in the number of educated persons have also intensified the problem. Remedies suggested include regulated government expenditure, increased investment in the private sector, a policy of controlled deficit financing, encouragement of export industries, a proper population policy and a changed educational pattern. A policy of full employment must be laid down in the Five Year Plan.

1842 Shenoy, B.R. Indian Planning and Economic Development. London: Asia Publishing House, 1963. xi, 152 pp.

Discusses the more important economic policy issues currently facing the country. A diagnosis of the maladies is accompanied by an assessment of the achievements under the prevailing policy measures and is followed by an indication of alternative policy action. The area covered is the experience of the past decade of planning in India and some problems confronting the Third Plan. Includes estimates of employment and unemployment and of population growth.

1843 Sharma, A.D. "Population Policy in India's Third Five Year Plan," Indian J. Econ. 40(156):83-86, July 1959.

Suggests a Population Commission for India and several aspects of a population policy which the Government of India should adopt for the Third Five Year Plan.

1844 Simmons, George B. The Indian Investment in Family Planning. Ph.D. Dissertation, University of California, Berkeley, California, June 1969.

Estimates that the benefit per prevented birth between 1964 and 1990 ranges from 3,534 to 5,800 rupees depending on whether the gain of prevention is reflected in income changes.

1845 Singh, Baljit, Population and Food Planning in India. Bombay: Hind Kitabs Ltd., 1947. vii, 156 pp.

An attempt is made to estimate the future population of India, and assess its food requirements on the basis of a balanced diet. Targets of production have been fixed for the different items and scrutinized at each stage as to their practicality. For a time imports will be necessary but that will be only during the transition period, after which the country can be self-sufficient at a standard of food consumption which will provide enough of the various nutritional elements for all with ease.

1846 Singh, V.B. Some Aspects of Indian Population. Lucknow: Balkrishna Book Co., 1955. 22 pp.

Examines conflicting theories on the 'over-population' of India and proposals for increased agricultural production and family planning to solve the problem.

1847 Singh, J.C. "The Population Problem of India," Modern Rev. 94(5):361-64, November 1953.

It should be recognized that birth control measures alone cannot solve the population problem. It is therefore necessary to concentrate on the second kind of remedies, viz., increased productivity, both in industry and agriculture. The word 'productivity' is deliberately used, for greater production at a higher cost, might lead to further inflation, if the consumer can be coerced to buy at higher prices. In other words, we should aim at a larger output, both in industry and agriculture, with greater efficiency than at present. Moreover, if the system of taxation becomes more equitable and there is better distribution of wealth in the country, if there are wider social security measures and greater spread of knowledge among the masses, their standard of living is bound to rise and with such a rise in the standard of living, the birth rate is likely to decline, as has been the experience of many advanced countries in the West.

1848 Sinha, J.N. "What Price Population Growth?" J. Institute Econ. Res. 1(1):6-14, Jan. 1966.

Analysis in this paper is restricted to...examining the implications of population growth within a limited timespace of 15 to 20 years taking India for the case of study. Sections: trends in population growth and vital rates; prospective changes in vital rates and population action; alternative rates of population growth and required plan efforts; population growth, savings and relative consumption levels.

1849 Sinha, R.K. "Explosive Growth of Population in India," AICC Econ. Rev. 9:17-19, Sept. 1, 1957.

It is a very farsighted idea on the part of our Prime Minister to lay the foundation for developing an alternative source of power from atomic resources. But keeping in view the explosive growth of India's population, it is equally important that along with development plans, that a very high priority is given to planning for population control. Unless plans are made simultaneously for a rapid control of population to a replacement or even below replacement level, it will be difficult to raise the standard of living to any appreciable extent within the next few decades, because any probable advances in agriculture and industry may not be able to keep pace with the rapidly increasing population.

1850 Sivaswamy, K.G. "Indian Agriculture -- Problems and Programmers," Pacific Affairs 23(4):356-70, Dec. 1950.

Agricultural reforms and policies essential to increase domestic productivity to where the increasing population may be maintained without food imports.

1851 Sovani, N.V. "Population Planning in India," Indian J. Econ. 27:299-315, 1946-1947.

The article deals with the possibilities and prospects of population planning in India. After defining the word planning and outlining the conflict between facts and values in the determination of ends and means in social planning, the author's discussion centers around three topics: the Indian environment, the ends to be sought and the means to achieve. Representative growth and reproductive rates are viewed, as well as India's resources and economy, and the author presents some general, social and economic policy objectives that have been evolved and accepted recently through public discussion and by the country's major political parties. The goals of population planning for India are listed in both quantitative and qualitative terms. Evaluated are such quantitative means as increased mortality, increased net emigration and fertility control, with references to possible extent of fertility control, probable effects and factors influencing the spread of contraception throughout India, and such qualitative means as improved health and efficiency of the existing population and possible promotion of desirable biological characteristics.

1852 Srivastava, P.L., ed. A Comparative Study of Four Five-Year Plans. Calcutta: Bookland Private Limited 1965. 270 pp.

Partial contents: Ashok Mehta, "Background of Planning."

1853 Subrahmanyan, V. "Practical Approach to the Food Problem in India," Sci. Cult. 13(6):213-18, 1947.

An annual population increase of 5-6 millions coupled with no increase in agricultural production in the last 30 years has changed India from a food exporter to an importer; when the rains fail, famine results. To increase supplies of food the following recommendations are made: rice parboiling before selling; insect-proof storage facilities so that the excess from good years can be stored; scientific reclamation of partially spoiled grains; increased irrigation projects; increased marine fishing; increased production of leafy vegetables, and improved dehydration and storage techniques of all vegetables and tubers; more basic agricultural research and a policy whereby an owner not making efficient use of the land would forfeit it. Since the required co-operative action for such a program probably could not be attained, government control will be necessary, as will also be true of the problem of the hitherto uncontrolled population increase.

1854 Sur, A.K. "Planning and Poverty in India," Econ. Affairs (1):9-18, 99, January 1964.

Includes sections, The myth of overpopulation; Danger of a smaller population.

1855 Tandon, B.C., ed. The Third Five Year Plan and India's Economic Growth. Allahabad: Chaitanya Publishing House, 1962. 322 pp.

Essays by 28 scholars. Partial contents: C. Chandrasekharan, "Population Control"; Vinod Dubey "Employment Policy"; J.S. Mathur, "Labour Policy".

1856 Vakil, Chandulal N., and Brahmananda, P.R. Planning for a Shortage Economy; the Indian Experiment. Bombay: Vora, 1952. 319 pp.

The object of this book is to emphasize the essential soundness of the Five Year Plan, and to examine the various problems and proposals with a view to making constructive suggestions. One chapter, Population Control and Family Planning, discusses population pressure and shortages, agricultural vs. industrial development, and the need for a population policy.

Policies on fertility and family size

1857 Agarwala, S.N. "Abortion Rate Among a Section of Delhi's Population," Med. Digest 30:1-7, 1962.

A review of the pregnancy histories of 5,912 women attending family planning clinics in Delhi indicates an overall abortion rate of 9 per 100 pregnancies. Results show that rates did not differ significantly when compared by clinic, age, duration of marriage, income, or mother-tongue, but that rates were higher for women with previous contraceptive experience, for those highly educated and for those whose husbands were employed as officers in the Government. Abortion rates rose steeply after clinic attendance.

1858 Agarwala, S.N. "The Arithmetic of Sterilization in India," Eugenics Quart. 13:209-13, 1966.

It has been pointed out by Gopalaswamy that sterilization operations performed at the rate of 5 per 1,000 population per annum for 10 years would reduce birth rate by 12 points. Our calculations show that the decline will be by 11 points under the assumptions made by Gopalaswamy, when the population of India remains fixed over time. If this stationary condition is removed and the calculations are made on the basis of the projected population as given by the Expert Committee on Population, it is found that 28 million operations performed in 10 years will bring down birth rate by only 5.5 points. Calculations also show that if the Government wants to bring down birth and death rates to 16 by 1991, roughly 4 million sterilizations will have to be performed annually during 1961-1966. The number of annual operations will increase to 10 million during 1986-1991. In other words, while all the currently married females of the reproductive age above 42.5 or their husbands will have to be sterilized in 1961, all those above age 22 will have to be operated upon in 1991. This indicates that the Government cannot rely on sterilizations alone, as the number of operations which will have to be performed each year appear beyond the limit of feasibility.

1859 Agarwala, S.N. Attitudes Toward Family Planning in India. Bombay: Asia Publishing House, 1962. ix, 55 pp. Also in: Family Planning News 2(12):239-86, and 3(1):17-24, Dec. 1961 and Jan. 1962.

A brief survey of studies made so far in India on prevailing beliefs and practices related to family planning. Some 26 such studies have been made, but they have not been carried out uniformly and cannot be considered to present an authoritative picture. But the studies do give some idea of the Indian position on family planning which the author sums up thus: People in rural areas consider four children the ideal, while urbanites prefer three. An interval of three to four years is considered desirable in both urban and rural sections. Knowledge about family planning and willingness to learn about it are significantly related to education, age, and number of living children, but not to caste or religion. There is no organized religious or social opposition to family planning. Among married females of reproductive age, knowledge of contraception varies between 10-20 per cent in rural areas, and 20-30 per cent in urban districts. About 70 per cent of women, 35 or older, with four or more children were willing to learn about family planning. The author concludes from the research done at the Institute of Economic Growth in New Delhi that village women are generally unwilling to use modern medicines, including modern contraceptives. He feels it likely that they would use more willingly the indigenous drugs or herbs as contraceptives.

1860 Agarwala, S.N. "Evaluating Effectiveness of the Family Planning Programme," J. Fam. Welf. 8(4):8-19, June 1962. Also published in: Research in Family Planning ed. by Clyde V. Kiser. Princeton: Princeton University Press, 1962, pp. 409.

The objectives and the content of the family planning programme of the Government of India are discussed here. Two categories of indices are presented: the attitudinal, for increasing the effectiveness of the educational programme, and resultant indices to measure the effective progress of the clinic programme in changing the behaviour pattern.

1861 Agarwala, S.N. Family Planning in Selected Villages. Bombay: Asia Publishing House 1963. 88 pp. Also in: Popul. Stud. 15(2):110-20, Nov. 1961.

A family planning attitude survey was conducted in four villages near metropolitan Delhi. Information was obtained through questionnaires from 455 currently married females of reproductive age. Of the women interviewed, 50% were aware of family planning, 19% had knowledge of a method and only 3% used birth control methods. The method most commonly practised was prolonged lactation. Of the women interviewed, 253 were willing to learn about family planning and said there was little opposition from their family members. These women felt that a family should have four children, and spacing between them should be roughly four years.

1862 Agarwala, S.N. Fertility Control Through Contraception: A Study of Family Planning Clinics of Metropolitan Delhi. Delhi: Directorate General of Health Services, Ministry of Health, 1960. 85 pp. Also in: J. Fam. Welf. 6(3):1-20, Mar. 1960.

Deals with persons who visited family planning clinics in metropolitan Delhi from 1955 to 1958. The most important finding is that even without clinical services pregnancies can be reduced if there is sufficient motivation. First priority in India, therefore, should be given to motivating people toward family planning rather than opening clinics, the author concludes. In this study pregnancies are effectively reduced through use of clinically prescribed contraceptives. The group was not typical of India's population, so general conclusions can not be drawn. But results give a measure of likely success for educated and urban India. More than half the patients had had pre-clinical contraceptive experience and had in that way reduced the risk of their pregnancies by nearly 44%. Of those who came to the clinic, 45% could not be brought to use contraception, which does not speak highly of the persuasive power of the clinics.

1863 Agarwala, S.N. "A Follow-Up Study of Intrauterine Contraceptive Devices: An Indian Experience," Eugenics Quart. 15: 41-ff., 1968; Also in: International Union for the Scientific Study of Population, Papers, Sydney Conference, Australia, 21-25 August 1967. pp 424-29.

Follow up of 867 women enrolled in a clinic in Delhi over a period of fifteen months. The majority of women who came for IUCD's were literate, had an average of 4.4 living children, and were wives of white-collar workers. Their average age was 29.5 years and monthly family income was 175 rupees. About 62% had previous contraceptive experience and switched over to the IUCD because they were told it is a better contraceptive. The total dropout rate was 22 by the 12th month and 40 by the 24th month. The expulsion and removal rates by the 24th month of use were 10 and 28 respectively.

1864 Agarwala, S.N. "Some Aspects of the Family Planning Programme," J. Fam. Welf. 12(4):1-4, June 1966.

Discusses needs and goals for launching a broad education - motivation program in India, to increase participation to ten per cent of the population by the end of the Fifth Plan.

1865 Agarwala, S.N. Some Problems of India's Population. Bombay: Vora, 1966. iii, 153 pp.

The Government of India plans to intensify family planning efforts to reduce the birth rate by half in the shortest possible time. With every Five Year Plan, the money allocated for family planning has been increased: Rs. 6.5 million in the First Five Year Plan (1951-56), Rs. 49.5 million in the Second, Rs. 250 million in the Third (with a ceiling of Rs. 500 million) and Rs. 950 million in the Fourth Five Year Plan (1966-71). The earlier plans could not be implemented fully, as only 25 per cent of money allocated was spent during the First, and 30 per cent during the Second Plan. With an unprecedented increase in population obstructing the implementation of programmes of economic development, family planning work must be treated as a national emergency programme. The author suggests that its success depends on the effective cooperation of universities, demographic research organizations and workers in the Community development blocks for family planning educational talks to the villagers.

1866 Agarwala, S.N. "Sterilization as a Population Control Device: Its Economics," Econ. Weekly 16(27):1091-94, July 4, 1964.

Critical examination of quantitative estimates of the probable effect of a government subsidized large-scale sterilization program for husbands of females aged 28-32 in the next five years. Analysis of comparative costs in relation to benefits of alternative methods.

1867 Ahluwalia, Gurdeep, "A Preliminary Report on an Attitude Survey in a C.H.S.F.P. Centre, New Delhi," J. Fam. Welf. 7(4):41-44, June 1961.

The findings of a survey of 100 cases at a Family Planning Clinic in Delhi are presented here. Nearly half the women had a favourable attitude towards sex education for their children. Their attitude towards sterilization was marred with misconceptions.

1868 Allen, LeRoy R. "A Family Planning Study as a Part of a Comprehensive Health Service in a Rural Area," Popul. Rev. 1(1):19-21, Jan. 1957.

An intensive family planning study of 320 potential child-bearing couples in Edayanzathu, India was conducted through the Mother's Clinic to determine attitudes toward family planning and provide information and methods for family planning. The initial interview was held to verify census data regarding family; to determine attitudes toward family planning; to inform the sources about the services in the general health program; and to give specific information regarding family planning aid, where desired. During the current second interviews, more detailed information is being obtained regarding the living situation, socio-economic-status, and knowledge regarding the regulation of frequency of conception, as well as discussing the purpose and desirability of planned families. During this second interview a limited supply of a contraceptive is given to the wife of each couple desiring it. Following the second interview, one or more additional villages will be added to the special study. The family planning assistance is free to the sources, the project being financed for two years by U.S. funds.

1869 Anand, D. "Clinico-Epidemiological Study of Abortion," Indian J. Public Health 9:52-ff., 1965.

A study of the abortion cases admitted to a university hospital in New Delhi during 1956-1963. No efforts were made to differentiate between induced and spontaneous abortions and the ratio of abortions to deliveries was 1:3. Sixty per cent of the women indicated that they did not desire the pregnancy and delayed treatment of the threatening abortion in comparison with the other women. Only 38% of the patients rejecting the pregnancy had used contraceptive methods to prevent it.

1870 Anand, D., and Pannu, S.K. "Village Leaders Camp," J. Fam. Welf. 8(2):19-25, Dec. 1961.

This paper is based on experiences at four village leader camps organised in Najafgarh area, Delhi, and deals with pre-planning of the programme and actual work activity. Recommendations made by the village leaders in various camps regarding the administrative procedures, educational approaches, facilities for service, and training of village persons in the field of family planning are outlined.

1871 Anerjee, S. "Female Sterilization in a Population Control Programme," Indian J. Public Health 9:65-68, April 1965.

1872 Balakrishnan, T.R., and Matthai, R.J. "Evaluation of a Family Planning Publicity Program in India," pp. 413-23 in: International Union for the Scientific Study of Population, Contributed Papers, Sydney Conference, Australia, 21-25 August 1967.

This paper reports some of the findings of a study done to measure the overall effectiveness of an intensive contraceptive publicity program carried out in the Hooghly District in West Bengal, with its main emphasis on the introduction of the intra-uterine devices but including other conventional methods as well. Publicity was concentrated in three major urban areas and media used during the campaign's 63 days included slides in movie theatres, speeches, exhibitions, radio broadcasts by prominent persons, and articles and advertisements in local newspapers. Effects were measured through two sample surveys, a baseline survey before the start of publicity and a survey after the campaign to determine the extent of knowledge and practice of family limitation in the suburban communities of Serampur, Chandernagger and Chinsurah. The authors describe the selection and characteristics of the interviewed couples and then give a brief outline of the survey results, with references to exposure to publicity media, attitudes toward family size, attitudes toward family planning, knowledge of family planning, and practice of family planning. They conclude that the most important finding of their study is the extent of the impact an intensive campaign can have in a rather localized community. A well conceived mass communication program using primarily mass media can effectively increase the awareness of family planning in a rather limited time, although the need for follow-up studies to determine how much retention of interest there has been is emphasized. Interest stimulated should also be studied over a period to determine the extent to which general awareness is translated into a desire to gain more knowledge and the depth to which knowledge acquired results in practice.

1873 Banerjee, G.R. "Prostitution Requires Prohibition," Ind. J. Soc. Work 19(1):11-17, June 1958.

Prevalence of sexual promiscuity has been referred to in the Vedas but prostitution as a legalized institution is a post-Vedic development. Aryan princes patronized courtesans and with the passage of time prostitution turned into a trade. Today there are three categories of prostitutes: (1) those who are exploited by others for earning their livelihood, (2) independent professionals who depend entirely on the profession for their living, (3) amateur prostitutes who have other means of livelihood and indulge in promiscuous sexual intercourse for supplementing their income or for personal satisfaction. Those who once indulge in this profession cannot come out of it even if they wish to as society would not accept them as honorable members. No thorough and serious attempt has ever been made to suppress this institution. Licensing of brothels presupposes their toleration and it carries with it the sanction of the state; other evils, like trafficking in women, procuring and selling them to brothels, are encouraged.

1874 Barve, S.G. With Malice Toward None; A Critique of New India's Plans and Aspirations. London: Asia Publishing House, 1962. xv, 372 pp.

Recommends a vigorous large-scale programme by the federal and state governments in support of family planning.

1875 Basu, R.N. "Evaluation of Family Planning Educational Programme," Indian J. Public Health 6(3):133-40, July 1962.

Presents the findings of an inquiry into the impact of an educational programme undertaken in the Singur Health Centre area in India. Economic reason is reported to be the main factor determining awareness of the need for family limitation. Group discussion was found to be effective.

1876 Basu, R.N. "Some Problems in Relation to the Family Planning Programme," J. Fam. Welf. 8(1):13-18, Sept. 1961.

An account of the problems faced and procedures adopted in educating the people in the adoption of family planning methods.

1877 Basavarajappa, K.G., and Belvalgidad, M.I. "Changes in Age at Marriage of Females and Their Effect on the Birth Rate in India," Eugenics Quart. 14:14-26, 1967.

Though socially raising the minimum age at marriage to 19 or 20 years is a desirable thing, it cannot provide a satisfactory solution to the population problem India is facing today. However, any legislation in favor of it may at least create an awareness among the people of the necessity of raising the present extremely low level of age at marriage.

1878 Bennet, M. Catchatoor, "The Second Report on Family Planning Welfare at Kharaberia and Other Villages in West Bengal, India," Med. Gynaecology Sociol. 3(11-12):323-26, Nov.-Dec. 1968.

Report on characteristics and history of 775 IUD acceptors, 1965-1968, at the Family Planning Clinic in a small village 14 miles from Calcutta, serving an area of 132 surrounding villages.

1879 Bhanoji Rao, V.V. "Population Growth and Family Planning: Some Aspects of Policy for Economic Growth," Asian Studies 6(2):65-77, April 1964.

Discussion of problems related to rapid population growth in India and of government policy on education in fertility control.

1880 Bhouraskar, D.M. "On Improvident Maternity," Indian Econ. J. 7(2):175-96, Oct. 1959.

An examination in quantitative terms of the report by R.A. Gopalswami on the Population Census of India, 1951, and examination of the practicability of the policies advocated for controlling fertility in the 1951-1971 period.

1881 Blacker, C.P. "The Rhythm Method: Two Indian Experiments," Eugenics Rev. 47 (2-3) :93-105,163-72. July-October,1955.

A summary of the commentary upon the WHO publication Final Report on Pilot Studies in Family Planning (New Delhi, 1954), this two-part article is concerned with field experiments with the rhythm method organized by WHO at the request of the Indian Government and carried out in the rural area of Ramanagaram in southern India and the urban Lodi colony on the outskirts of New Delhi. Information was sought on three points: the acceptability of the rhythm method, the effectiveness of the method for those who used it, and (in the case of Ramanagaram) its effectiveness in reducing the birth rate of the community. On the basis of attitude studies that preceded the introduction of the method, it appeared that 75 per cent of the women interviewed in each place were interested in obtaining information about family planning. Of the 1,709 women who expressed an interest in learning the rhythm method, only 68 (4 per cent) were following the method regularly at the end of the observation period of somewhat less than two years. The small amount of evidence that was collected indicated that the number of exposure months per pregnancy was about 50 for those following the method, as compared with about 20 estimated for an unprotected rural Indian population. The birth rate of Ramanagaram rose during the experiment. From these results it is concluded that the evidence as to the acceptability of this particular method was "scarcely favourable".

1882 Bogue, Donald J. "Some Tentative Recommendations for a Sociologically Correct Family Planning Communication and Motivation Program in India," In: Research in Family Planning, ed. by Clyde V. Kiser. Princeton: Princeton University Press, 1962. pp. 503-38.

After a study of fertility researches conducted in India, Latin America and the United States, the author makes 27 recommendations for making the family planning programme sociologically correct and more effective in India.

1883 Chacko, V.I. "Family Planning in Plantations in South India," Paper presented at the National Conference on Population Policy and Programme, New Delhi, 19-23 December 1969.

Under the Plantations Labour Act, 1951, a comprehensive welfare measure provides for maternity benefit, medical care and sickness benefit for workers on plantations having 25 acres and 30 or more employees. Family planning programs are included. Medical centers on the plantations have encouraged workers to undergo vasectomy or tubectomy after they have two or three children by offering different forms of incentives. In Kerala, 30 to 100 rupees are paid for sterilization operations, a day's leave is given for IUCD placement, and sick leave may be used for the sterilization operation. In Mysore, 30 rupees are paid and seven days' leave with full wages are given for a sterilization operation. The programs have not resulted in many sterilizations and do not directly reach the majority of workers who are on plantations smaller than those covered by the Act.

1884 Chambard, Jean-Luc, "Marriages Secondaires et Foires aux Femmes en Inde Centrale " [Second and Fair Marriages of Women in Central India], L'Homme 1(2):51-88, May-Aug. 1961.

A report on a study in social anthropology, kinship and rural economics, based on 2.5 years of observation in a village of Northern Maliva (Central India). The two dominant castes in the village are the Brahmans and the Kirars; the latter are shudras who call themselves fallen Rajputs. The marriage, divorce and remarriage system found among the Kirars is described. The system emphasizes the importance of marital freedom of women. Contrary to the cultural and social pattern accepted among the high sanskritized castes in India, which demand a single marriage for the woman and impose unbreakable widowhood, the Kirars not only allow widows to remarry, but give a woman who feels she is not sufficiently taken care of, or not sexually gratified, the right to leave her husband and consummate a second marriage with another man. This secondary marriage is as legal as the first one, and gives equal rights to the children. The Kirar community is therefore characterised by a circulation and exchange of women, especially when they are young.

1885 Chandrasekhar, S. Demographic Disarmament for India: A Plea for Family Planning. Raopura, Baroda: Sadhana Press, [no date] 39 pp.

Presidential address delivered at the First All-India Conference of The Family Planning Association of India, Bombay, 30th November - 2nd December 1951. A review of the population problem of India and underlying social factors is followed by a discussion of birth control as the most important and possible solution.

1886 Chandrasekhar, S. "Family Planning in an Indian Village: Motivations and Methods," Popul. Rev. 3(1):63-71, Jan. 1959.

This study conducted in Nangadu village in Madras shows that a majority of fathers and mothers accept in theory the desirability of limiting family, mainly for economic and health reasons. The motivation among the rural folk is not strong enough. A tentative conclusion is that the easier and more effective way out is either vasectomy or salpingectomy.

1887 Chandrasekhar, S. "Family Planning in Rural India," Antioch Rev. 19(3):399-411, Fall 1959.

Population control is necessary in India to check decline of an already low standard of living, but successful family planning requires a higher standard of living than exists at present. The wish for family planning, the recognition of the need for it, and the relation between family size and standard of living, may not be present in rural areas. In addition, cultural and other barriers may exist against family planning and the use of certain methods. All of these factors are relevant to the promotion of family planning policy and practice. The establishment of a clinic in a typical caste Hindu village has allowed for some examination of these problems. A survey indicated a large majority who wished to limit family size but were most ignorant of basic rules of personal and public hygiene and lacked knowledge of the reproduction system. Consequently the need for a simple method involving least genital manipulation became evident. Of available methods the clinic found the sponge and foam powder to be most acceptable to women in the village. In a two year period, 94% of married women of childbearing age were persuaded to visit the clinic and accept appliances. Thirty-three percent of these failed to use them and conceived, 25% of these believed they were immune because they were breast-feeding, and 31% found contraception awkward and gave it up. A considerable gap still exists between the successful breakdown of barriers to acceptance of the principle of family planning and actual practice.

1888 Chandrasekhar, S. "How India is Tackling Her Population Problem," Demography 5(2):642-50, 1968.

Today's population policy cannot yield full results at once, but it is encouraging to note that a perceptible beginning in the birth rate is already visible in certain areas where there are dedicated doctors and paramedical personnel, ready supplies, good incentives, excellent administrative machinery, and satisfactory public relations.

1889 Chandrasekhar, S. India's Population Policy and Achievements. Lectures delivered at Centre for Population Studies, Harvard University. Cambridge: Harvard University Press, 1966.

1890 Chandrasekhar, S. Population and Planned Parenthood in India. London: George Allen and Unwin, 1955. xii, 108 pp.

Growth of India's population in terms of her fertility, mortality and social institutions; place of family planning.

1891 Chandrasekhar, S. "The Prospect for Planned Parenthood in India," Pacific Affairs 26(4):318-28, Dec. 1953.

Contends that the motivations for planned parenthood are present in the Indian population and cites studies conducted in several areas of India as evidence. The basic problem is to bring birth control information to the millions to whom the motives for planned parenthood are acceptable.

1892 Chandrasekhar, S. Report on a Survey of Attitudes of Married Couples Towards Family Planning in the Pudupakkam Area of the City of Madras, 1958. Madras: Controller of Stationery and Printing, 1959. 35 pp.

A report on a survey of attitudes towards family planning among 1000 married couples having a monthly income of less than Rs. 200/- in the Pudupakkam area of the City of Madras.

1893 Chandrasekhar, S. "Some Aspects of Family Planning Programme in India," Popul. Rev. 11(2):25-30, July - Dec. 1967.

Notes on current problems, including the need for personnel, for periodic review at the state and district level, and for increased participation by governmental and other bodies. Discussion of alternatives in methodology and strategy.

1894 Chandrasekaran, C. "Cultural Factors and the Propagation of Family Planning in the Indian Setting," pp. 67-71 in: International Conference on Planned Parenthood. New Delhi, 14-21 Feb. 1959. London: International Planned Parenthood Federation, 1959. Also in: J. Fam. Welf. 5(3):43-51, March 1959.

This is an account of the reactions and behaviour of couples to some of the methods of family planning according to two studies carried out by the All India Institute of Hygiene and Public Health, Calcutta. One deals with the educational programme in three specific methods of family planning and the other with the effectiveness of metaxylohydroquinone as an oral contraceptive.

1895 Chandrasekaran, C. "Fertility Trends and National Policy," J. Fam. Welf. 10(3):12-20. March 1964. Also in: Maharashtra Med. J. 11(1):31-39, April 1964.

A review of fertility trends in many countries and of the experience gained in the implementation of the family planning program in India, provides several pointers which can be used for reshaping the national program of family planning in India.

1896 Chandrasekaran, C. "Survey of Family Planning Clinics in Greater Bombay," J. Fam. Welf. 9(3):30-39. March 1963,

A report on the procedure and findings of a survey of family planning clinics in Greater Bombay. Analysis is focused on the rate of admission, sources of referral, the method most often advised, the return of patients for check-up, and the socio-economic status of the clients, etc.

1897 Chandrasekaran, C., and Bebarta, P.C. The Relative Role of Information Sources in the Dissemination of Knowledge of Family Planning Methods in Bombay City. Bombay: Demographic Training and Research Centre, [n.d.] 10 pp. (Mimeographed).

Data collected during a sample survey of 666 women in Bombay City have been analyzed in a comparative study of the role of different communication media in the dissemination of knowledge of family planning methods.

1898 Chandrasekaran, C., and Kuder, Katherine, assisted by V.C. Chidambaram. Family Planning Through Clinics: Report of a Survey of Family Planning Clinics in Greater Bombay. Bombay: Allied Publishers Private, 1965. xxviii, 272 pp.

The report is based on a sample survey of family planning clinics in Greater Bombay. No rural areas are included. The survey began in April 1960 and seems to have been completed at the end of November 1961. During the period there were fifty-three clinics in Greater Bombay. The data come from a fraction of the case-cards in the possession of twelve of these fifty-three clinics. The survey fairly quickly ran into difficulties. A total of 575 women were selected for follow-up and interview. Of these, 207 could not be contacted and five, though contacted, were widowed or refused to be interviewed. Hence the report is based on the follow-up of 363 women. Clinics are not especially successful. About 51% of the women failed to adopt the method recommended to them. Furthermore, women attending clinics over the ten years - 1949-1959 - represent only five per cent of the women in Bombay.

1899 Chaudari, D.H. The Hindu Succession Act. 1956 (Act No. 30 of 1956). Third Edition. Calcutta: Eastern Law House, 1963. xvii, 306 pp.

An exhaustive commentary, explanatory and critical notes, case law, prior acts, table of heirs, table of cases, index, etc.

1900 Chaudhary, R.L. Hindu Woman's Right to Property, Past and Present. Mukhopadhyay, 1961.

1901 Chellaswami, T. "Population Planning in India," Sci. Cult. 19(3):115-20, Sept. 1953.

In India with a high density of population, with high birth rates and death rates, with its small amount of capital and primitive agricultural methods, there is overpopulation for a decent standard of living, and every improvement in social conditions tends to be cancelled out by an increase in population. A population policy, which includes family planning is essential.

1902 Chidambaram, V.C. "Population Dynamics and Family Planning," J. Fam. Welf. 14(1):25-32, Sept. 1967.

Discussion of India's population growth cites limitations of government-sponsored family planning programs and considers additional measures (raising the age at marriage and legislation on abortion) for reduction of the national birth-rate.

1903 Claxton, E., and Watson, D. "The Debate on Legal Abortion," Indian Med. J. 59:120-21, May 1965.

1904 Cook, Robert C. "Report on India. The Bombay Conference," Popul. Bull. 9(1):1-6, Feb. 1953.

Summary of the Third International Conference on Planned Parenthood, Bombay, November 24-29, 1952. Emphasis is on India, particularly the conflicting views and ethical position of governmental persons on fertility control.

1905 Dandekar, Kumudini, "Change in Family Planning Activity in the City of Poona (1951-64)," Paper Presented at the International Union for the Scientific Study of Population General Conference, 3-11 September 1969.

1906 Dandekar, Kumudini, "Family Studies Conducted by the Gokhale Institute of Politics and Economics, Poona," pp. 3-16 In: Research in Family Planning. ed. by Clyde V. Kiser. Princeton: Princeton University Press, 1962.

Reviews a series of ten studies on attitudes toward family planning and three others on the communication of family planning knowledge and techniques, conducted by the Gokhale Institute of Politics and Economics, Poona, India, during 1951-55.

1907 Dandekar, Kumudini, "Population Programmers and Their Effect on Growth Rate," Paper Presented at the National Conference on Population Policy and Programmes, New Delhi, 19-23 Dec. 1969.

The goal is to attain a 37.5 per cent in the birth rate (i.e., from 40 to 25 births per 1000 population) during the decade beginning 1966 or 1968. This decline requires 7 sterilizations (or the equivalent IUD insertions) per thousand population along with the promotion of other contraceptive devices. Some states like Maharashtra, Kerala and Madras have a slight chance of attaining the goal if they continue their efforts of 1967-69. But Uttar Pradesh, Bihar, Rajasthan, Assam and Gujerat, on the basis of past performance, do not stand a chance of doing so. For the entire country, an equivalent of two sterilizations per thousand of population has not yet been attained.

1908 Dandekar, Kumudini, "Possible Targets and Their Attainment in the Field of Family Planning in India During 1966-76," Artha Vijnana 8(3):239-49, Sept. 1966.

This paper is an attempt to estimate the size of work-program, if the birthrate in the country is to be brought down by one third during 1966-76. The size of work-program is assessed only in terms of the number of couples that should stop child-bearing in order to attain the target of reduction in birth-rate by 1976. The calculations are based on the assumption of the necessity to stop child-bearing after the third living child... The methodology to assess the possibilities of attaining the targets has been illustrated with the data for the district of Poona and is followed by a very rough estimate for the country, on the basis of the results obtained for the district.

1909 Dandekar, Kumudini, "Promotion of Family Planning in Rural Areas: A Field Experiment," Artha Vijnana 3(1):24-37, March 1961.

Results of an intensive campaign to popularize vasectomy carried out by a voluntary organization are compared with those of a campaign sponsored by the Government of Maharashtra in South Satara District. The acceptance of vasectomy was not restricted to a few castes or occupational groups nor to the literates.

1910 Dandekar, Kumudini, "Sterilization Programme: Its Size and Effects on Birth Rate," Artha Vijnana 1(3):220-32, Sept. 1959.

An attempt to estimate, on the basis of data on 7,592 married men in six rural localities in 1954-1955: (i) the effect of male sterilization on the annual birth rate, (ii) the total number of such sterilizations that will have to be performed if a programme was adopted for the country as a whole, and (iii) the total number of sterilizations that will have to be conducted periodically. Effect of putting an upper and lower limit to the age of the sterilized is also considered.

1911 Dandekar, Kumudini, "Vasectomy Camps in Maharashtra," Popul. Stud. 17(2):147-54, Nov. 1963.

Sterilization as a method of family planning was found popular in the state of Maharashtra. The government of Maharashtra offered free facilities for male sterilization by holding camps all over the State. A description is given of the socioeconomic, demographic composition of the persons who underwent sterilization in 41 camps held in one district of the state. This district had the largest number of vasectomies in Maharashtra in 1960. 1.2 vasectomies per 1,000 population were conducted in the district. Though the effect of these vasectomies on the birth rate was likely to be small, a climate of opinion favorable to family planning was created in the district.

1912 Dandekar, Kumudini, "Vital Rates and the Efforts at Family Planning in the Various States of India," Artha Vijnana 6(4):290-301, Dec. 1964.

Comparison of birth rates by states in 1941-1950 and 1951-1960 in relation to statistics on inter-state migration, 1951-1961, and intensity of family planning campaign in the states during the first and second five-year plans.

1913 Darbari, B.S. "Sterilization: An Effective Measure of Population Control," Paper Presented at the National Conference on Population Policy and Programmes, New Delhi, 19-23 December 1969.

Estimates that since the program began, the number of births prevented by sterilization has increased from 32,000 in 1961 to 1,417,000 in 1968. Of the couples eligible for sterilization, 10.6 per cent (5.5 millions) have undergone the operation.

1914 Datta, Nalinee, "Influence of Marital Life on the Reproductive Cycles in Women," J. Fam. Welf. 5(4):7-14, June 1959.

This paper discusses the influence of married life on reproductive cycles in women on the basis of records during 1953-56 for 110 middle-class Bengalis in Calcutta. It is suggested that unpredictable variation in menstrual cycles occur more commonly among married women and, hence, the rhythm method should not be recommended to women who cannot afford to risk another conception.

1915 Davis, Kingsley, "Fertility Control and the Demographic Transition in India," pp. 68-89 in: The Interrelation of Demographic, Economic, and Social Problems in Selected Underdeveloped Areas. New York: Milbank Memorial Fund, 1954.

Views India as having a chance to be the first country to achieve a major revolution in human life - the planned diffusion of fertility control in a peasant population prior to the urban-industrial transition.

1916 Demerath, Nicolas J. "Organization and Management Needs of a National Family Planning Program: The Case of India," J. Soc. Issues 23(4):179-94, October 1967.

The efforts by the government to reduce the birth rate in India are examined. India is one of the only two nations in the world (the other is China) in which the central government is pursuing reduction policies. The process of modernization in general is briefly considered. The Indian effort in family planning is analyzed according to three phases, with the use of the concepts of: overloading the elite, organization as blueprint, and organization as action. (1) Stage One (1956-61) was based on "blueprint 1" developed after the Central Ministry of Health received its first appropriation for family planning in 1952. Training and research were emphasized. "Action 1" consisted of initial efforts in establishing rural clinics especially, and hospital sterilization programs. (2) Stage Two (1962-64) consisted of "blueprint 2" which established a goal of reducing the national birth rate from more than 40 births per 1,000 population to 25 per 1,000, hopefully by 1973. Three basic pre-conditions of family planning in terms of education were stressed: group acceptance of smaller family size, personal knowledge of family planning methods, and easy availability of supplies and services for the adult population. "Action 2" is analyzed with special reference to the author's findings regarding the use of the Intra-uterine Contraceptive Device (IUCD), especially the "Lippes loop," which began to be emphasized in 1965. An all-India picture of usage was "very spotty." (3) Stage Three (1966--) includes "blueprint 3" which emphasized the need for decentralization of certain powers, such as grant allocation, to local voluntary organizations and other bodies. Financial recommendations were made. It is yet too soon to evaluate "action 3." The persistent gap between plans and the execution of them is noted, and whether and when the applied social science and management input will be made is problematic, though this is seen as the most critical factor now in Indian family planning accomplishment.

1917 Demographic Research Centre, Attitude to Family Planning. Trivandrum, [n.d.] 9V. Part (1) Trivandrum City. 98 pp. (2) Quilon Town. 66 pp. (3) Alleppy Town. 58 pp. (4) Kottayom Town. 61 pp. (5) Palghat Town. 59 pp. (6) Kozhikode Town. 61 pp. (7) Cannanore. 51 pp. (8) Attingal. 51 pp. (9) Ernakulam. 53 pp. (Pts. 2 to 9 mimeographed).

These reports give the results of a survey conducted in specified towns and cities of Kerala State, India. The report gives the percentage of persons who favour family planning and prefer known methods of contraception. Attempt has also been made to study the differentials in fertility in varying income and occupation groups.

1918 Demographic Research Centre, Trivandrum, "A Study of Persons who have Undergone Sterilization Operation in Kerala," *Popul. Rev.* 6(2):137-42, July 1962.

A presentation of the results of empirical research regarding the socioeconomic and demographic traits of the 14,126 people who underwent sterilization operations in Kerala, derived from data taken from 57 hospitals with sterilization facilities. Offered are descriptions of age composition; sex and religion; educational status; income; occupation; number of children born previously; and number of children living. Data is presented in tabular form. More males undergo the operation than females; males usually undergo the operation after the age of 30, and females between the ages of 25 and 34; the operation is more popular among Hindus than Muslims; the income of those who have undergone the operation is very low; and the number of children for males is 4.4, and 4.9 for females.

1919 Demographic Training Research Centre, Chembur. *Implications of Raising the Female Age at Marriage in India.* Bombay, 1968.

It is established that the female age at marriage in India has been increasing during the past two decades. This change has attracted the attention of demographers because of the possible impact of such an increase on the national birth rate. It has also attracted the attention of policy-makers in the context of their efforts to arrest the increasing rate of growth of population in the country through a reduction in the national birth rate. As a result, the Central Family Planning Council in January 1967, recommended that the Government of India change the law to allow marriage of the female at age 20 rather than 16. Data are presented in support of the argument that raising the age at marriage will both delay the onset of child bearing and reduce the actual reproductive period. Thus a drop in fertility is expected.

1920 Derrett, J.D.M. "Hindu Succession Act, 1956: An Experiment in Social Legislation," Amer. J. Comparative Law 8:485-501, Autumn 1959.

Depicts in outline the pre-existing law in order that the changes in it may be evaluated. The topics discussed are: the statute's applicability to persons and to property; the general scheme of testamentary and intestate succession; disqualifications and limitations upon the right of heirship; and miscellaneous matters.

1921 Derrett, J.D.M. "Statutory Amendments of the Personal Law of Hindus since Indian Independence," Amer. J. Comparative Law 7:380-93, Summer 1958.

Hindu law in India was codified during the period between May, 1955, and December 1956, in four statutes, namely the Hindu Marriage Act (Act No. 25 of 1955), the Hindu Succession Act (Act No. 30 of 1956), the Hindu Minority and Guardianship Act (Act No. 32 of 1956), and finally the Hindu Adoptions and Maintenance Act (Act No. 78 of 1956). The process, which it is convenient to call "codification," lacks some of the characteristics of a conventional code, since there remain important parts of the Hindu law which are untouched by the legislation. But that portion of the system which has been affected has been so radically affected as to render the result almost unrecognizable for what it is: namely the culmination of a long process of modification and reform, both by way of judicial legislation and by statute, of the ancient legal system indigenous to India and known as the dharmasastra. A summary of the motives of the legislators, of the changes they have brought about, and of the results of their work is likely to interest those who use or study "family laws" in codified form. For it is certain that India's experiment is not less remarkable than the enactment of the Code Napoleon, while nothing comparable with it for width of scope or boldness of innovation has been seen in the Anglo-American systems.

1922 Desai, M.P. Population Control: A Modern Shibboleth. Ahmedabad: Navajivan Publishing House, 1959. iv, 53 pp.

Gandhian approach; reprints of articles by a former editor of Harijan.

1923 Dev, A.K. "The Future Programme and Organization of Family Planning," Paper presented at the National Conference on Population Policy and Programmes, New Delhi, 19-23 December 1969.

Population will continue to grow rapidly under current programs set up to control it. There must be a more scientific approach to population control under an autonomous Population Control Commission directly responsible to the Parliament through the Prime Minister in place of the present five tiered Governmental Department. It should be organized on the lines of a supreme H.Q. of a nation at war under a supreme Commander with full authority to command control.

1924 Dev, A.K. "Sterilization as a Technique of Fertility Control," Paper presented at the National Conference on Population Policy and Programmes, New Delhi, 19-23 December 1969.

Sterilization as a technique of fertility control has distinct advantages over all other methods. It is particularly suited for India and as a mass program. The future of the sterilization program lies in female sterilization. Plans must be made to meet the growing demand. In both West Bengal and Maharashtra female sterilization shows a rise both in actual numbers and in ratio to male sterilizations.

1925 Dhruv, Madhuri, "Study of 87 Birth Control Cases with Special Reference to Follow-Up," J. Fam. Welf. 8(4): 38-46, June 1962.

This is a report on a study undertaken in four chawls (old one or two-room residential sheds) in Bombay City to find out difficulties in the use of different methods of conception control and to give suggestions for their better use.

1926 Diwan, Paras, "The Hindu Marriage Act, 1955," Comparative Law Quart. 6:263-72, April 1957.

In all her measures for social and economic reforms, India is confronted with two diametrically opposite views: one making for sweeping reforms and the other for maintaining the status quo. The Hindu Marriage Act has not found favour with the holders of either of the views. Even if it is assumed that the Act does not provide for what it should have, one can feel satisfied in what it has provided. The Act in providing for monogamy as a rule of law for all Hindus and in providing for divorce for all Hindus has certainly brought Hindu law into consonance with other systems of law. At least one great blemish on Hindu social institutions, polygamy, has been removed. Its importance is realized when we recall the havoc it has wrought in the Conflict of Laws.

1927 Dubey, Bhagwant Rao, "Legalizing Abortion," Family Planning News, May 1967, pp. 1-2.

Abortion should be the last resort as a method of family planning. It should be adopted as a social policy only when the majority of people in the procreative age groups is converted to some other method of fertility limitation.

1928 Eastern Economist. "The Population Mix," Eastern Econ. Blue Supplement 6(12):813-14, March 30, 1962.

Includes a summary of recent developments in the Indian government-sponsored family-planning program and of Ministerial recommendations.

1929 Economic Weekly. "Population and Family Planning: A Comment," AICC Econ. Rev. 16(6):6, August 25, 1964.

A note on the setting up of the seven-member Committee by the Union Government to chalk out effective measures to activize the programme of family planning in the country.

1930 Economic Weekly. "The Sterilization Debate " [A Group of Articles.] Economic Weekly 16(35):1445-52, and 16(35-37): 1501-3, August 29 and September 12, 1964.

Contents: Rao, V. Raja, Moonshine on vasectomy; Samuel, T.J., The cheapest method; Bose, Ashish, Cost calculations not enough; Sinha, J.N., Not alternatives, but complements; Prahlad, K., Cost-benefit analysis is necessary; Dheer, R.S., Emphasis motivation, not means.

1931 Family Planning Association of India, "The Place of Family Planning in the Third Five Year Plan," Memorandum presented to the Planning Commission by the Family Planning Association of India. J. Fam. Welf. 6(3):30-47, March 1960.

It is strongly urged that an implementing agency of the highest power and authority be set up to undertake the expansion of family planning under the Third Five Year Plan. Suggestions at other times have been made for a Ministry of Health and Population. It is urged that at least a Commission or autonomous statutory Family Planning Board be appointed with a non-official Chairman. Such a high-powered implementing agency can act effectively to continue and enlarge present schemes, and institute new ones especially those with an economic bias.

1932 Family Planning Association of India. Third All-India Conference on Family Planning: Report of Proceedings, 5-9 January 1957, Calcutta. Calcutta: xx, 155 pp.

Text of papers at the plenary sessions on India are grouped under the main themes: Family planning measures under the Second Five Year Plan; Health and medical aspects of family planning; Population growth in India; Sociological research in attitudes and motivations. An additional section presents three papers on family planning in Egypt and Great Britain.

1933 France, Conseiller Commercial de France, [New Delhi.] "Le Probleme Demographique et la Politique de Limitation des Naissances" [The Demographic Problem and Birth-Control Policy], Problemes Economiques, No. 1095, December 26, 1968, pp. 21-27.

A communique from the French Embassy in New Delhi, dated July 30, 1968. Topics: the scale of the Indian demographic problem; the development of fixed goals for Indian birth control policy; from qualitative to quantitative planning; results of past actions and need for an updating of Indian birth control policy; elements of a "scientific" birth control policy in India; the effort required.

1934 France. [French Embassy at New Delhi.] "La Demographie et la Politique de Limitation des Naissances en Inde " [Demography and Birth-Control Policy in India], Bulletin d'Information Economique du Conseiller Commerical de France a New Delhi. May, 1966. Reprinted in: Problemes Economiques, No. 970, August 4, 1966, pp. 8-12.

Report by the Commercial Counselor at the French Embassy in New Delhi on the evolution of Indian thought, planning, budgetary specifications, and actual installation of family planning centers from 1950 to 1966 and on the objectives of the Fourth Plan (1966-1971).

1935 Freymann, Moye W. "India's Family Planning Programme: Some Lessons Learned," pp. 13-26 in: Muramatsu, M., and Harper, Paul A., eds. Population Dynamics: International Action and Training Programmes. Baltimore: Johns Hopkins University Press, 1965.

From experience in a variety of localities in India a number of broad generalizations are made about the process of family planning program development in a country of this type. Such generalizations are offered with regard to problems of establishing political support for a family planning movement, the roles of pilot projects and social research, and the subject of supporting legislation. Propositions are also offered regarding program evaluation procedures, contraceptive supply lines, contraceptive technology, and the role of doctors. The needs for differentiating educational functions and for providing an optimal organizational environment are also noted.

1936 Freymann, Moye W.,and Lionberger, Herbert F. "A Model for Family Planning Action-Research," pp. 443-61 in: Research in Family Planning, ed. by Clyde V. Kiser. Princeton: Princeton University Press, 1962.

The authors have proposed a tentative model for family planning action research, with special reference to India. Types of research activities which might be undertaken in an action research programme and the nature of staff requirements are discussed. Subsequently, the three phases of the project, viz., the preparatory and implementation stages and the third phase involving the consolidation of research findings are discussed.

1937 Ghosh, J.C. "Family Planning in India," J. Fam. Welf. 2(4): 130-34, May 1956.

A member of the Planning Commission, at the Seminar on Family Planning organized by the Delhi Family Planning Association on the 14th of April 1956, reviews the growth in population and economic development, the early history of interest in family planning, the current interest of the people in family planning, and the efforts made by the Government through the First Five Year Plan.

1938 Ghosh, J.C. "Inaugural Address on Family Planning," J. Fam. Welf. 3(1-2):1-6, Jan. - Feb. 1957.

Address of a member of the Planning Commission to the Third All India Conference on Family Planning, Calcutta, January 1957 in which special attention is given to the recommendations made by the Central Family Planning Board at its first meeting in October, 1956.

1939 Ghosh, Mallika, "The Birth of Family Planning," Paper presented at the National Conference on Population Policy and Programmes, New Delhi, 19-23 December 1969.

The Family Planning Movement began as an individual effort at birth control. It has evolved into an international movement involving governments and voluntary organizations.

1940 Godrej, S.P. "Role of the Industrial Sector in Family Planning," Paper presented at the National Conference on Population on Policy and Programmes, New Delhi, 19-23 December 1969.

The industrial sector is needed for effective implementation of the national family planning program. It is the best organized branch of the Indian economy and it has the capacity, resources, organization and facilities to render greater help in the program. Moreover, this sector comprises nearly 35 million people, of whom 13 million are industrial laborers. The participation of the industrial sector is not only a social obligation but also an economic necessity. A slackening of population growth will bring an increase in per capita disposable income which acts to increase purchasing power in the public, lessen inflation, and raise the standard of living. These results will ameliorate the growing sense of frustration and insecurity.

1941 Gokhale, V.V. "Vasectomy Camps in Ahmednagar District," J. Fam. Welf. 7(1):9-11, September 1960.

Developments that led to the organization of vasectomy camps in the Ahmednagar District, India, are outlined here. Some suggestions are made on the best means of organizing such camps.

1942 Gopalaswami, R.A. "Administrative Implementation of Family Planning Policy," Popul. Rev. 3(1):43-62, January 1959.

The development of national and Madras State concern with population growth and family planning, prior to and during the First and Second Five-Year Plans, is discussed. Controversy over various methods of birth control during the First Five-Year Plan period was the creation of the necessary political climate which is the condition precedent to successful execution of a policy of this kind. A few ineffective birth control clinics had also been established. The family planning program was reevaluated and expanded during the Second Five-Year Plan. A Family Planning Manual was prepared and a few 100,000 copies were sold or distributed throughout Madras State. Statistics on use, adoption, and success of contraception began to accumulate. By the end of the third year (1958), a few thousand sterilizations had been performed in Madras. Fathers were less receptive to contraception than mothers. Planning for the Third Five-Year Plan is discussed. Couples are urged not to have more than three children. Attention is directed to a massive educational and propaganda campaign.

1943 Gopalaswami, R.A. Family Planning. Outlook for Government Action in India. Madras: Controller of Stationery and Printing on behalf of the Government of Madras, 1960. iv, 12 pp. Also pp. 67-81 in: Clyde V. Kiser, ed. Research in Family Planning. Princeton: Princeton University Press, 1962. 662 pp.

The visible results of government action in India during the last few years are very small. But the activities were intentionally limited to the scale of pilot experimentation. Lessons have been learned which are to be used as the basis for extending coverage and intensifying the effort during the next few years. Future success will depend almost entirely on the rapidity with which people can be persuaded to resort to sterilization as a method of family limitation. In this respect, the outlook for government action in India is, at the moment, promising.

1944 Gordon, John E., and Wyon, John B. "A Field Study of Motivation to Family Planning," pp. 72-79 in: International Conference on Planned Parenthood, 6, New Delhi, 14-21 Feb. 1959. London: International Planned Parenthood Federation, 1959.

Family planning programmes have two aspects: first, overcoming the initial inertia to employ such practices and secondly, to continue and maintain a satisfactory level of performance. According to the author, in the population study at Khanna, Punjab, family planning motivation was seen to be higher among older women than among the younger ones. Programmes should be so planned that the younger couples become more highly motivated than the older ones who cannot contribute much to the solution of the problem.

1945 Gore, Sushila, "Review of Abortion as a Method of Population Control," Maharashtra Med. J. 11(2):245-53, May 1964.

1946 Gore, Sushila S. "Safeguards to be Adopted in Sterilization," J. Fam. Welf. 5(2):5-12, December 1958.

Discusses the essential conditions that should be determined before sterilization is advocated as a method of family limitation. According to the author, it is not to be advocated in a mass campaign, for it is beneficial only in selected situations. The author outlines the medical and socio-economic conditions under which sterilization can be recommended.

1947 Gulati, B. "Integration of Family Planning with Maternity and Child Health Services," Paper presented at the National Conference on Population Policy and Programmes, New Delhi. 19-23 December 1969.

The integration of family planning services with maternal and child health services will increase the acceptability of the former because parents will have greater assurance that the survival rate of children born will be greatly increased. Otherwise, it is difficult to argue for family limitation under conditions of an infant mortality rate of 98/1000.

1948 Gupta, P.B. "A Method of Estimating the Reduction in Birth Range by Sterilization of Married Couples," Sankhya Series B 27(3-4):225-50, December 1965.

Adopting a generation approach retrospectively, and using the principles of multiple decrement tables, and on the basis of a given condition of eligibility, a given range of age of wife to come under the scope of sterilization and a given rate at which sterilization is sought to be performed, the proportion of unsterilized married couples at various ages of wife in the reproductive period and at various intervals from the initial year of sterilization are obtained, from which the birth rate (All-India rural) at successive intervals can be calculated.

1949 Gupta, Sunil Kumar, "Gandhye's Attitude to Birth Control," Paper presented at the National Conference on Population Policy and Programmes, New Delhi, 19-23 December 1969.

Gandhi saw the necessity for birth control but he looked with disfavor on artificial methods because of their degrading effect on society and the individual. He advocated Brahmacharya -- self-control -- as the surest and moral method.

1950 Hanif, Waqar, "Attitudes Toward Family Planning," Indian Soc. Res. 3(2):66-69, July 1962.

A study of 100 adults in different sections of Amroha township to ascertain their attitudes regarding birth control and family planning. It was found that 43% were aware of the safe-period method of birth control, the most popular method known. However, "the ideal of limiting the size of the family directly conflicts with the prevailing social values of the people," either for reasons of social pride or because of the view that one must not interfere with the 'scheme of nature.' Almost 34% indicated an ideal family size of five members. Nearly 48% showed knowledge of sterilization and 52% considered abortions as desirable for limiting the size of the family. It is suggested that sex education should be provided for young boys, that females be encouraged to pursue careers so as to increase the marriage age, and that cheap contraceptives be provided.

1951 Haynes, M. Alfred, et al. "A Study on the Effectiveness of Sterilizations in Reducing the Birth Rate," Demography 6(1):1-11, February 1969.

By studying the fertility of a control group with comparable age, income, education, religion, and number of living children, the number of prevented future births per 1,000 women in Kerala couples, one partner of which was sterilized, was estimated. The results were used to project the entire saving in births over a 30-year period; of each year there were one, three, or five sterilizations performed per 1,000 total population. With five sterilizations per 1,000, the reduction in the crude birth rate is estimated as seven points after a decade or nine points after three decades.

1952 Heimsath, Charles H. "The Origin and Enactment of the Indian Age of Consent Bill, 1891," J. Asian Studies 21: 491-504, 1962.

Reviews the arguments pro and con and organizational development to support or oppose the proposals of Behramji Malabari in 1884 for legislation to restrict infant and child marriages, to encourage widow remarriage, and to reward through occupational and educational preferences the unmarried state.

1953 Houghton, Vera, "Planned Parenthood in India," Eugenics Rev. 43(1):33-35, April 1951.

Reviews the efforts of regional and national governments, hospitals and private organizations to disseminate birth control information and materials.

1954 Husain, Mazhar, The Suppression of Immoral Traffic in Women and Girls Act, 1956: With Critical Commentary and Case Law. Calcutta: Eastern Book Company, 1958. 103 pp.

A description of the scope of the Parliamentary Act, its Constitutional validity, and its penal provisions. There are appendices concerning the Acts of four states.

1955 India. Association for Moral and Social Hygiene, Memorandum on Sex Education Placed Before the Education Commission, Government of India. New Delhi: Family Life Institute, March 1965. 32 pp.

A submission to introduce sex education in schools, from primary to college level. Puts forward a syllabus for the various levels and recommendations for the selection and training of suitable teachers.

1956 India. Embassy of India, Washington, D.C. The Quiet Revolution: Family Planning in India. Washington, 1967. 13 pp.

Non-technical statement of government policy. Quotation from Mrs. Indira Gandhi states "Family planning therefore is at the base of our whole endeavor of national development."

1957 India. Laws, Statutes, etc. Child Marriage Restraint Act. Allahabad: Law Publishers, 1963.

1958 India. Laws, Statutes, etc. Commentaries on the Dissolution of Muslim Marriage Act, 1939 (Act VIII of 1939). Calcutta: Eastern Book Company, 1961.

1959 India. Laws, Statutes, etc. Hindu Adoptions and Maintenance Act (Act 78 of 1956). Second Ed. with suppe, 1966. Allahabad Law Book Company, 1966.

1960 India. Laws, Statutes, etc. The Indian Law of Marriage and Divorce. Bombay: Popular Book Company, 1964.

1961 India. Laws, Statutes, etc. Law of Succession. Fourth Edition. Calcutta: Eastern Law, 1957.

1962 India. Madras. [Panchayat Administration.] "Family Planning and Rural Administration in Madras State," Population Rev. 5(1):63-66, January 1961.

Text of instructions to the Panchayat Administration on the intensive scheme for the popularization of surgical methods of family planning.

1963 India. Ministry of Health, Directorate General of Health Services, Family Planning in India: A Review of the Progress in Family Planning Programme April, 1956 - November, 1958. New Delhi: Central Health Education Bureau, 1959. ix, 151 pp.

Review of the accomplishments since the establishment of the Central Family Planning Board, Sept. 1, 1956. Chapters: Early efforts; First five-year plan; Second five-year plan. Appendixes present committee reports, reports from states, and reports from organizational units.

1964 India. Ministry of Health, Proceedings of the First Meeting of the Family Planning Research and Programmes Committee (13th to 18th July, 1953.) Delhi: Manager of Publications, 1954. xx, 78 pp.

This committee, which is appointed, makes recommendations to the Government of India regarding research, experimental and other programs relating to family planning to be adopted and the nature and the amounts of assistance, if any, to be given to existing voluntary organizations in the field of family planning. At its first meeting, the committee emphasized that family planning should be broadly conceived and that a family planning centre would thus include sex education, marriage counselling, marriage hygiene, the spacing of children and advice on such matters as may be necessary to promote the welfare of families. For the immediate future, however, the essential service would be largely advice on family limitation through the spacing of children. The committee surveyed the working of the existing family planning services in the country and made recommendations for their reorganization, for education and research, and suggested the allocation of funds.

1965 India. Ministry of Health, Report of the Family Third Five-Year Plan Committee, 1960. Delhi: n.d. vii, 177 pp.

Includes complete text of recommendations and an appendix of supporting documents. Among these are the results of a questionnaire survey of attitudes toward the government's role in contraceptive planning.

1966 India. Parliamentary and Scientific Committee, Population Control and Family Planning. Delhi: Publications Division, Ministry of Information and Broadcasting. May 1964. 63 pp.

Report based on three meetings of a study group in May and June 1962, and adopted Sept. 19, 1963. The Committee feels that the progress made in the family planning programs is not commensurate with the urgency and need; therefore, some rethinking on the approach, administration and organization of the family planning services is necessary. The main suggestions of the Committee are: the question of forming a separate body to deal with family welfare should receive serious consideration; far more resources should be put into non-clinical systems of education and distribution of contraceptives; greater emphasis should be placed on the male methods as they are easier for distribution and do not need elaborate clinics or organization, indigenous production of rubber contraceptives should receive a high priority; for women and men, who have had all the children they desire, facilities for sterilization should be provided, with adequate medical and psychological safeguards. Vision should be made for the investigation and treatment of sterile couples; and promotion of research and studies should receive high priority in regard to (a) the physiology of reproduction; (b) oral contraceptives; (c) psychological and sociological studies on group and individual attitudes to family planning with particular reference to sterilization, abortion, etc.; and (d) educational materials and techniques of mass communication.

1967 India. Planning Commission, Annual Plan, 1966-67. New Delhi: Government of India Press, 1966. 133 pp.

Section, Family planning, pp. 85-87, give notes on aims, program, and current statistics on family-planning organization.

1968 Indian Conference of Social Work. Family Planning and Social Welfare. Report of subcommittee of the Indian Conference of Social Work submitted to the Lucknow session, December, 1955. Bombay, [1954]. 28 pp.

This memorandum consists of two parts: the first considers the different aspects from which the subject of family planning should be approached, and the second deals with the technical and organizational sides of the question. In addition, sixteen recommendations, based on the findings, are presented.

1969 Indian Institute of Public Opinion, "A Programme for Family Planning for the Fourth Plan: A Proposal for 1966-71, in a Long Range Perspective," Indian Institute of Public Opinion, Quart. Econ. Report 11:21-32, March 1965.

1970 Israel, Sarah, and Kamat, Melba, "A Study of the Effectiveness of Contraceptive Methods in Family Planning Clinics in India," J. Fam. Welf. 5(3):52-61, March 1959. Also in: Sixth International Conference on Planned Parenthood, New Delhi, 14-21 Feb. 1959. London: International Planned Parenthood Federation, 1959.

Assesses the risk of conception involved in the use of certain contraceptive methods. The estimates are based on data collected from 17 family planning clinics.

1971 Jain, S.P. "Fertility Trends in Greater Bombay," pp. 325-36 in: International Union for the Scientific Study of Population, Contributed Papers, Sydney Conference, Australia, 21 to 25 August 1967.

Results of a survey of attitudes to induced abortion administered to a number of women in Bombay. Of those women with some knowledge of contraceptive methods, 16.1% approved of abortion and of them, over half accepted it to avoid an unwanted pregnancy, for economic reasons, or as a woman's right. Those women who objected to induced abortions were of the opinion that it was harmful to the mother's health.

1972 Jain, S.P. "The Strategy for Demographic Impact of the Family Planning Programme," J. Fam. Welf. 13(1):37-46, September 1966.

Discussion of alternatives, with emphasis on motivation and methods, in the Indian government's family-planning campaigns.

1973 Kapadia, K.M. Marriage and Family in India. Bombay: Oxford University Press, 1955.

Surveys the socio-religious and ideological foundations and developments of marriage and family in India, and attempts to trace the impact of modern political and economic ideologies on these institutions. Based on study of Sanskrit texts in original and Arabic texts in translation. Materials also gathered from anthropological accounts of Indian tribes, and from theses prepared at Bombay University.

1974 Kaub, Jurjit, "Socio-Economic Consequences of Liberalisation of Abortion," Paper presented at the National Conference on Population Policy and Programmes, New Delhi, 19-23 December 1969.

Discusses estimates of the number of abortions in various countries of the world, the consequences of liberalized abortion laws, and public attitudes to abortion. Among the recommendations is the preparation of a guide to the revised Indian Abortion Act which should be sent to all physicians, and the development of considerable research on attitudes and practices concerning abortion in India.

1975 Khare, R.S. "A Study of Intrafamily Problems of Motivation in Relation to Family Planning in India," East. Anthrop. 18(2):73-79, May - August 1965.

Some common intrafamilial relationships which are of vital importance to the Family Planning Program in India are discussed regarding husband - wife, parents, and brother and cousins. The intrafamilial motivation pattern in couples has large measures of ambivalence along with feelings of insecurity in independent action; is centered around prevalent notions and preconceptions; and tends to vary in strength with the age of the couple. There is a close relationship with mother-in-law and the desired size of family, and a negative correlation of this relationship with motivation towards family planning in general. Males and females of the same age group tend to form peer groups along sex lines for purposes of opinion formation and practice of family planning. Brother's wives residing close to each other provide another grouping relevant to the spread of family planning which is powerful in influencing the decisions of parents. It is concluded that it is not sufficient to tackle a couple alone in the Indian family if strong and sustaining motivation for the program is to be achieved. Socially and morally every couple is deeply and firmly attached to and dependent upon certain close relatives for family decisions. Parents and peers should be taken into account, and intrafamilial peer groups are equally important.

1976 Krishnamurthy, K.G. "Population Control: Ways and Means," Eastern Economist 43(16):735-37. October 16,1964.

Under the present circumstances, increasing age at marriage or proper propagation of contraceptives alone will not solve the population problem. Considerable emphasis should therefor be given to sterilization in any national program.

1977 Krishnamurthy, K.G. Research in Family Planning in India. Delhi: Sterling Publishers, Ltd., 1968. xv, 108 pp.

The four chapters discuss attitudes, fertility, knowledge about contraception, and the dissemination of information. There is also a brief description of methodology at the end of each chapter to acquaint the family planning worker with research steps.

1978 Kurup, R.S. "Sterilization Operation in Kerala State, India," pp. 440-48 in: International Union for the Scientific Study of Population, Contributed Papers, Sydney Conference, Australia, 21 to 25 August 1967.

The number of male and female sterilizations in Kerala State increased 521 and 158, respectively, in 1957 to 36,102 and 6,532 in 1965. The numbers declined to 21,721 and 4,835 for the first ten months of 1966. The impact on the birth rate was almost negligible.

1979 Kurup, R.S., *et al*. "A Case Study of IUCD Acceptors in Two Hospitals in Trivandrum City - India," Paper presented at the International Union for the Scientific Study of Population General Conference, 3-11 September 1969.

An analysis of the age-composition of the females has revealed that 80% females belong to the age group 20-34 years and 84% are below 35 years. 58% of the women have three or fewer children at the time of IUCD insertion. Comparison with other studies shows that Kerala women adopt IUCD earlier than their counterparts in other areas. 91% of the cases of IUCD insertions are found active after one year. This is a very high percentage compared to results obtained from other studies, but this is not in any way an indication of the level in the State as a whole or in any particular place but is due to the extreme interest taken by the staff of the hospital in the programme.

1980 Kurup, R.S., and Mathen, T.K. "Sterilization as a Method of Family Limitation in Kerala State," [India]. *Popul*. *Rev*. 10:61-68, July 1966.

Kerala State, whose population is growing at the rate of 2.24 percent per annum, began to popularize sterilization as a technique of birth control in 1957. In the beginning a benefit allowance of Rs.25 was given. In 1959 a uniform allowance was set at Rs.15 for men and Rs.20 for women. The number of sterilizations per year rose from 679 in 1957 to 22,000 in 1964. That the rate is accelerating is quite evident: up to May 1965, there were over 13,000 sterilizations. But, thus far sterilization has had little effect on the birth rate. Particulars of sterilized persons are given.

1981 Lakshmanan, M.S. "Prospects of Population Control," *Indian J*. *Econ*. 45(179):411-16, April 1965.

1982 Lakshmi, P. "A Note on the Progress of Sterilization in Madras State," *J*. *Fam*. *Welf*. 8(3):12-17, March 1962.

Discusses the organization and administration of the Madras Government's Intensive Scheme for the Popularization of Surgical Methods, the number of sterilizations performed between 1956 and February 1962, and the objectives set up for 1962.

1983 Lakshminarayana, T. "Government Programmes of Family Planning," pp. 55-58 in: Family Planning Association of India, Report of the Proceedings, Second All India Conference on Family Planning, Bombay: The Association [n.d.] 117 pp. Also in: J. Fam. Welf. 1(2):64-66, January 1955.

Discusses the events leading up to the Government of India's participation in the programme of family planning and population and the specific amounts allocated by the Government for family planning programs and research.

1984 Lippitt, Theodora, "Tubal Ligation as Part of Family Planning in India," Amer. J. Obstet. Gynec. 105(3):434-39, 1 October 1969.

In rural South India, a survey was done to determine the attitudes toward salpingectomy as a means of birth control. Selection of 200 women was made from hospital records; 146 of the selected women were interviewed. The women under study were up to 9 years post-tubal ligation. Educational status was noted to be higher in these patients and the husbands than in the general population. Physical complaints in 27 per cent of the women did not change the favorable attitudes of the women. There was favorable discussion of the operation with neighbors and friends by 97 per cent of the women and 98 per cent would urge others to undergo the operation.

1985 Mahadevan, M.S. "The Conflicting Effects of Family Planning Measures and Maternity Benefit Measures," J. Fam. Welf. 10(4): 40-50, June 1964.

Comment and statistics on the experience of women laborers on tea plantations in Kerala, as regards total births and birth rate, infant mortality, stillbirths, abortions, and miscarriages. Recommends legislation to permit withholding of maternity benefits after birth of third child.

1986 Mahajan, B.M. "On Economics of Sterilization as a Measure of Birth Control," Econ. Affairs 11(1, 2-3, and 4):89-96; 105-14; 193-97, January, February - March, April, 1966.

Evaluation of potential effectiveness of sterilization in India as compared with alternative measures (conventional contraceptives, oral contraceptives, intra-uterine contraceptive devices, induced abortion). Appendix contains statistics on Indian experience compiled from several sources.

1987 Majumdar, M. "Some Aspects of Fertility and Family Planning in the Urban Areas of India," Paper Presented at the International Union for the Scientific Study of Population General Conference, 3-11 September 1969.

1988 Majumdar, Niloy, "India's Population Policy Reconsidered," Econ. Affairs 8(708):333-41, July - August 1963.

Gives reasons for advocating a governmental policy of mass sterilization of female or, preferably, male spouse after birth of second child.

1989 Malhotra, Prabha, and Khan, Lilian, "Family Planning Knowledge and Practices Among Women Attending Some New Delhi M.C.W. Centres," Indian J. Public Health 6(3):121-32, July 1962.

The study is based on a sample of women attending the Maternity and Child Welfare Centres opened by the New Delhi municipality. The extent of awareness of the possibility of family planning, action taken in the matter, and sources of information, etc. are considered.

Ministry of Health to direct the family planning programme under the Second Year Plan. This Board has suggested (i) the formation of an Executive Committee to implement the policy formulation by the Family Planning Board; the appointment of a Family Planning Officer in each State, with a Central subsidy for three years, to coordinate Family Planning activities throughout the State and to act as a liaison officer of the Central Family Planning Organization; (ii) and the provision of financial assistance to voluntary organizations after examining requirement of each case.

1990 Mandelbaum, David G. "Population Problems in India and Pakistan," Far Eastern Survey 18(24):283-87, November 30, 1949.

The facts, the requirements, and the prospects for a solution.

1991 "Marx Wasn't Hungary," Economist 20F:140, April 13, 1963.

Mr. Podyachikh of the Soviet Union has, in the U.N. Population Commission, expressed opposition to United Nations assistance for family planning research. The opposition follows from the classical Marxist arguments that there is no such thing as over-population in an absolute sense and that production can be increased several times to support the population if capitalists restraints on the productivity of land were removed. In this paper, it is argued that birth control is essential to a better standard of living and that this view is shared by the Indian socialists.

1992 Mathen, K.K. "Preliminary Lessons Learned from the Rural Population Control Study of Singur," pp. 33-50, Chpt. in. Research in Family Planning, C.V. Kiser, ed. Princeton University Press, 1962. xvi 664 pp.

The Rural Population Control Study of Singur is an experiment in evolving practical and effective methods of popularizing family planning among rural populations of India. A demographic survey was followed by a preliminary contact survey during which field workers obtained preliminary acquaintance with the couple, gave general talks on the necessity of family planning and economic and health factors and received direct information regarding willingness to learn methods of family planning. Teaching material was designed regarding community beliefs and customs. Of the 1,296 couples in which the wives were in the reproductive period, 997 husbands and 1,002 wives were taught family planning individually or in groups. The pregnancy rate for all the groups practicing different methods, including those who had practiced irregularly, is significantly lower than that of the non-practicing group. Of the three groups of regular users of the three methods, rhythm, foam and rhythm, and foam, the last method is the most effective according to the data regarding the first year of observation.

1993 Mathen, K.K.,and Sen, M. "The Singur Population Study as an Action Research Model for Family Planning," J. Fam. Welf. 10(4):4-15, 1964.

Research in family planning in a village in India, based on a model suggested by Freyman and Lionberger, covered survey of the background factors, operational problems which hinder family planning programs, specific educational techniques, development of action programs.

1994 Mathew, C. "The Population Dilemma and Family Planning Programme in India," Indian J. Soc. Work 22(3):233-38, 1961.

The alarming rate of Indian population growth is due mainly to the steady decline of the death rate in recent years. Projections based on current population increases estimate that at the present rate India will double her numbers in 30 years. Status of family planning in India, its progress under the Five-Year Plans, the research program, and the limitations of the present program are discussed. It is suggested that a course on sex education and family planning methods should be introduced in secondary schools, colleges, and public health institutes.

1995 Mehta, G.L. Understanding India. London: Asia Publishing House, 1959. 287 pp.

Part III, India's planned economy, has section, Family planning in India, including notes on the clinics to be set up under the second five-year plan.

1996 Mehta, T.S., et al. National Seminar on Population Education. National Council of Educational Research and Training, October 1969. 83 pp.

Report of a seminar held 2-3 August 1969 in Bombay, sponsored by the Ministry of Education and Youth Services of India in collaboration with the Ministry of Health and Family Planning. Seven papers review developments in other countries as well as in India, and suggest guidelines for introducing population education in schools. The recommendations of the Seminar provide a basis for India's program in population education.

1997 Mitra, Asok, "How Social Legislation Can Defeat Family Planning," Family Planning News 3(10):225-27, October 1962.

The need to carry the message of family planning to every household and to divert a fraction of India's industrial capacity to the production of contraceptives is discussed. The author emphasizes that it is necessary to ensure that social legislation also moves in step in order to discourage indiscriminate population growth and points out how some of the legislations of the past decade might have had a contrary effect.

1998 Mohan, Raj P. "Factors to Motivation Towards Sterilization in Two Indian Villages," Fam. Life Coordinator 16(1-2): 35-38, 1967.

Forty-nine males in two villages in India were interviewed regarding government encouragement for sterilization to check population growth.

1999 Mohanty, S.P. "A Review of Some Selected Studies on Abortion in India," J. Fam. Welf. 14(4):39-48, June 1968.

In India, there have been some attempts by various authors to study the incidence of abortion and the rates of abortion prevailing in various socio-economic groups in the rural as well as in the urban areas. This paper aims at reviewing such studies carried out in different parts of India and at presenting their findings.

2000 Moizuddin, Mohammad, "Creating a Motivation for Family Planning," J. Fam. Welf. 8(3):44-50, March 1962.

Difficulties in creating motivation for family planning in the general population are outlined here. Some educational methods which may help field workers in inducing people to practice family planning are discussed.

2001 Morrison, William A. "Attitudes of Females Toward Family Planning in a Maharashtrian Village," Milbank Memorial Fund Quart. 35(1):67-81, January 1957.

Number of total offspring, number of living children, number of living male children, age, caste, and number of years married are found to be negatively correlated with desire for more children. Education, age at marriage, and number of total offspring are positively correlated with willingness to use contraceptives.

2002 Morrison, William A. "Attitudes of Males Toward Family Planning in a Western Indian Village," Milbank Memorial Fund Quart. 34(3):272-86, July 1956.

Study of family planning attitudes and practices among males in Badlapur Village, Bombay State, India, was conducted in 1954 (the sample was 124 males out of a universe of 573 married males 15-54 years of age). Number of living children, number of living male children, years married, age and education were found to be negatively correlated with desire for more offspring. Education, number of living children, number of living male offspring and caste were positively correlated with willingness to use contraceptives.

2003 Morrison, W.A. "Family Planning Attitude Prediction, The Social Worker and the Villager," Indian J. Soc. Work 20(3): 137-56, December 1959.

A discussion of the attitudes of the villager towards family planning. It is felt that all efforts to persuade the people to accept known methods of contraception against their volition will be wasted unless the propaganda used is sufficiently well designed and presented to reach and to be meaningful to them. For creating a favorable climate for family planning, illiteracy should be effaced and a general standard of education raised.

2004 Morrison, W.A. "Some Thoughts and Proposals Relating to Educational Programme for Population Control in India," Indian J. Soc. Work 21:321-36, March 1961.

Even though it is based on a small number of cases, the evidence is clear and incontrovertible that the attitudes and values held by members of the several major, socio-economic and cultural groups towards family planning and population control vary tremendously. Because of the many possible different combinations of attitudes and socio-cultural characteristics which exist, it is axiomatic that not one single line of educational propaganda can be satisfactory in changing all the different attitudes towards these subjects held by the different groups.

2005 Murthy, D.V.R. "Evaluation of Family Planning Programme in India," pp. 468-75 in: International Union for the Scientific Study of Population, Contributed Papers, Sydney Conference, Australia, 21-25 August 1967.

The first critical appraisal of the family planning program in India was made in April 1963 and it resulted in a decision to shift the emphasis from a clinical to a non-clinical program. Since then regular evaluations of the IUCD, sterilization and contraceptive programs have been done and the personnel and record-keeping procedures for evaluation have been institutionalized.

2006 Mysore Economic Review. "The Case For and Against Family Planning, with Special Reference to India," Mysore Econ. Rev. 41(5):9-12, May 1955.

2007 Nair, S.P. "Dynamics of Population Control," AICC Econ. Rev. 16(13-15):89-91, January 6,1965.

A contribution to the Durgapur Congress Special Number, centering on the need for accurate demographic statistics, studies of the interrelations of population growth and socio-economic change, and policy on family planning.

2008 Namboodiri, N. Krishnan, "On the Problem of Measuring the Impact of F.P. Action Programmes," J. Fam. Welf. 11(1): 29-35, 1964.

A review of various studies. The main problems of measurement of effectiveness relate to whether the psychological acceptability of family limitation methods and services has increased and whether the wives in child bearing years in that population have become small-family minded.

2009 Nanda, Ved Prakash, "Marriage and Divorce in India: Conflicting Laws," Northwestern University Law Rev. 55:624-47, November - December 1960.

A review of rules under old Hindu laws and the Hindu Marriage Act of 1955, the Sharia and the Muslim Marriage Act of 1939, the Indian Christian Marriage Act of 1872 and the Indian Divorce Act of 1869, the Parsi Marriage and Divorce Act of 1936, and the Special Marriage Act of 1954. Argues that the Legislature should refrain from efforts to codify and unify all the different legal codes which reflect deep-rooted variations in value judgements among India's diverse communities.

2010 Narain, Barkat, "Family Planning and Community Development Program," Kurukshetra 10(9):12-16, June 1962. Also in: J. Fam. Welf. 2(3):85-87, 92, March 1956.

Outline of problems and of measures adopted by the Government of India. Gives particular attention to the roles in family planning work which are performed by two large organizations, the Community Development Programme and the Panchayati Raj.

2011 Narain, Barkat, "Family Planning in Rural India," J. Fam. Welf. 7(3):15-18, March 1961.

The author discusses how the Community Development Programme and the Panchayati Raj Institution can be useful in spreading the message of family planning throughout rural India.

2012 Narain, Govind, "India: The Family Planning Program Since 1965," Studies in Family Planning No. 35: November 1968. pp. 1-12.

Contains some information on newly proposed policies at the state and central levels of government.

2013 Nayak, V.T. "Birth-Control and Gandhian Morality," Indian J. Soc. Work 21(4):373-86, March 1961.

An examination of Gandhi's views of human nature, morality, and birth control. Gandhi saw man as neither pure spirit nor brute; and morality involves man's obligations to understand and fulfill his own nature. Sex is a fine and noble thing which is meant only for the act of creation. Thus, the use of contraceptives is against morality. Hence one must either repudiate and deny all morality in man or give up the contraceptive methods. Use of birth control would encourage self-indulgence and involve moral harm and vice. Gandhi argued that self-restraint was within the capacity of every human being. Hence, he advocated the avoidance of sexual gratification outside the desire for progeny. Also aiding to the solution of the population problem was Gandhi's war on child marriages.

2014 "Notes on the Schemes for Sterilization in Madras State," J. Fam. Welf. 5(2):38-44, December 1958.

Provides some statistics on sterilization in Madras State and gives information on payments to private practitioners and persons for sterilization operations, and outlines the reasons why the sterilization program was introduced.

2015 Notestein, Frank W. "Policy of the Indian Government on Family Limitation," Popul. Index 17(4):254-63, October 1951.

Contains a reprint of a report by a Subcommittee on Population Growth and Family Planning appointed by the Panel on Health Programmes of the National Planning Commission.

2016 Opler, Morris Edward, "Cultural Context and Population Control Programs in Village India," pp. 201-21, in: Count, Earl W.G., and Bowles, Gordon T. , eds. Fact and Theory in Social Science, Syracuse: Syracuse University Press, 1964. xvi, 253 pp.

A ten-year study of a north Indian community of approximately 2,000 demonstrated the influence of many of the obstacles related to birth control. There was a strong accent on the importance of the male and female line. Village exogamy and patrilocal residence took the bride to her husband's village and home. Parents and close relatives were eager to see the girls of the family safely married as early as possible. Once in her new home, the married female's prestige and happiness depended to a considerable extent on producing male issue to insure the continuation of the husband's line. Thus male ascendency, early marriage, the prevalence of the joint family, the emphasis on the family as such, and the need of a female for children (especially sons) to gain an honored place in the family tended to keep the birth rate high, and to obscure the national problem. In the rural environment a large family was an advantage at times of intense agricultural work, a protection in village family rivalries and feuds, provided alternative hands for hereditary family work obligations, and made credit available since repayment duties were shared. On the other hand, the large family (especially the joint family) did have a number of ways in which it controlled sexuality in its younger members. Consequently the immediate effect of an attack upon joint family ideals in the interests of population control may well be an increase in the birth rate. The factors likely to lower the birth rate in India in the near future are increased education (especially for females), the greater control of disease, further industrialization, and the implementation of laws now on the statute books regarding inheritance and relations between the sexes.

2017 Pai, D.N. "Sterilization," Paper presented at the National Conference on Population Policy and Programmes, New Delhi, 19-23 December 1969.

The sterilization programme in India has out-stripped other programs of population control because it is the most easily implemented. In this paper the sterilization program in India, Maharashtra, and Bombay is analyzed with a view to assess its past impact and future potentials.

2018 Pandit, Vijayalakshmi, "Family Planning in India," J. Fam. Welf. 2(5):177-81, July 1956.

In this address delivered at the Annual General Meeting of the Family Planning Association of the United Kingdom held in June, 1956, the High Commissioners for India reviews the development in India of the concept of family planning.

2019 Pareek, Udai, and Kothandapani, V. "Modernization and Attitude Toward Family Size and Family Planning: Analysis of Some Data from India," Soc. Biology 16(1):44-48, March 1969.

An attempt to relate family size preferences and attitude toward birth control with a number of variables such as caste, ethnicity, occupation and education. The sample consisted mainly of farmers, inexperienced and experienced factory workers and urban nonindustrial workers from the "tribal belt" of Bihar, a state in the north-eastern part of India. The data used formed a part of the Harvard Project on the socio-cultural Aspects of Development directed by Alex Inkeles. The data were meticulously collected through a long interview with the help of a precoded interview schedule. The two dependent variables in the study are family size preference and attitude toward family planning. 59% of the people in this sample prefer to have no more than 3 children while 82% prefer no more than 4 children. Several independent variables such as lack of fatalism, education, personal overall modernization.

2020 Patel, Taraben, "Some Reflections on the Attitude of Married Couples Towards Family Planning in Ahmedabad," Sociol. Bull. 12(2):1-13, September 1963.

An analysis of 5% of the 25,000 couples between 21-45 years of age in Ahmedabad, a city of 1,149,852 people, regarding caste or creed, level of education, family in relation to living area, occupation, maintenance of family attitude and economic levels, and their attitude towards family planning. Of the sample (number of cases equalled 1,250) 60.85% knew about birth control, but only 8.75% knew about Family Planning Centers and took some help or advice from them. 52.1%

of the couples knew of the centers but did not utilize them. The three main reasons for non-utilization were no desire to restrict family size, religious or psychic feelings against artificial stoppage of procreation, and fear of public criticism. Only a small number of those believing in family planning were practicing it. Of those who did not believe in family planning, 66% already had sons. Most of these persons believed the number of children to be a matter of fate. None of the couples whose income was over 600 Rs showed disfavor to family planning. For an effective family planning program the following should be done: (a) the popular media should be used to disseminate birth-control knowledge and win favorable popular opinion; (b) sterilization of males as well as females should be encouraged and provision for an easier procedure should be developed; (c) the scope of the family planning centers should be enlarged; (d) establishment of centers should follow population and area density, and home visits should be provided for; and (e) research into methods of birth control and evaluation of the family planning centers should take place.

2021 Pathak, S.H. "Implementation of Family Planning in India. A Critique of Strategy and Approach," Popul. Rev. 12(1-2): 60-68, January - December 1968.

Comments on the draft outline of the Fourth Five-Year Plan.

2022 Pathare, Rajani, "The Family Planning Programme: A Sociological Analysis," Sociol. Bull. 15(2):44-63, September 1966.

Attitudes towards marriage, family life and especially towards the status of women are seen as crucial factors which must be taken into consideration in any program of population control. Tyranny of husbands over their wives in general, and especially over the sex lives of their mates, mitigates against use of contraception by women. The limited success of government and private efforts to introduce family planning are attributed in great measure to this social phenomenon. Interviews with Indian women indicate that although for at least 33.3% of them sex holds no joy, they consider it their duty as good wives to submit to their husbands. Thus, the women, whose part it would be to attend clinics or take contraceptive measures, are forced by cultural pressures into validating themselves by the bearing of male children and by submission to unwanted intercourse.

2023 Pawate, I.S. Daya - Virhaya. Daharwar, India: S.B. Harikar at the Tontadarya Press, 1945.

Concerned with inheritance and succession in India.

2024 Pethe, Vasant P. "A Study of Patients of Family Planning Clinics in Sholapur," J. Fam. Welf. 6(1):17-23, September 1959.

The author analyzes the attendance at two family planning clinics in Sholapur, with reference to the distribution of patients according to community, age at which advice is sought, order of birth, referral agency, previous use of contraceptives and the follow-up of the cases.

2025 Pethe, Vasantkumar, and Gandhi, Vasundhara, Population Crisis in India. Poona: Swas-Grantha-Mala Sholapur, 1954. 46 pp.

A plea for the Family Planning Movement.

2026 Phadnis, S.P. "Family Planning: Motivation and Methods," J. Fam. Welf. 7(2):10-19, December 1960.

This paper reports on a research project to find out the factors which give motivation to family planning and to determine the acceptability and effectiveness of contraceptive methods. The responses of 119 patients attending a family planning clinic at Nagpur, India, obtained through interviews and questionnaires and supplemented by case cards are discussed.

2027 Phadnis, S.P. "Population Control and the Third Plan," J. Fam. Welf. 6(3):55-59, March 1960.

The author discusses the investment programme in the Third Five Year Plan in the context of the population problem and points out some defects in the present family planning programme.

2028 Poffenberger, Thomas, and Patel, Haribhai G. "The Effect of Local Beliefs on Attitudes Toward Vasectomy in Two Indian Villages in Gujarat State," Popul. Rev. 8(2):37-44, July 1964.

In the last few years, India has made a concerted effort to popularize vasectomy as one of the methods to gain population control. In Gujarat State and in other areas of India there exists a little understood semi-religious group made up of impotent or castrated males who dress in female's clothing, and are known as Paviyas, Hijaras or Hijakas. They are generally believed to be incapable of sexual intercourse and are widely known to the villagers of the state. The objective of the study was to determine if there was any association in the minds of village men between this group and the vasectomy operation. A series of questions were asked of a random 10% sample of men in two villages in central Gujarat State (number of cases equalling 46). The background findings were: (1) Over half of the sample had at least some understanding of family planning. (2) 87% knew the government was encouraging men to be sterilized to aid population control. (3) 72% thought the vasectomy would offer economic relief. These percentages indicate that there was knowledge of the government's initiation of a family planning program with the objective of reducing population growth, and that vasectomy was one way recommended by the government to limit family size. Other than this, information tended to be limited and inaccurate. Knowledge of vasectomy was as follows: (A) 58% did not know how a vasectomy was performed. (B) 35% thought it to be painful. (C) 33% believed vasectomy and castration were the same. (D) Nearly 70% were not sure that intercourse would be possible after vasectomy. Attitudes of villagers to vasectomy were as follows: (a) 76% of the respondents reported villagers' attitudes as negative. (b) Of these, 40% (30% of the sample) said that a person who underwent vasectomy would be regarded as a Paviya, female or a castrate. The findings support the hypothesis that local beliefs play a part in shaping attitudes to vasectomy. Many villagers give evidence of associating the operation with castration, impotence and femininity, all of which are symbolized by the Paviya group. Those who make this association clearly do not believe intercourse is possible after the operation.

2029 Ponnamma, K. "Post-Partum Sterilization," _J. Fam. Welf._ 6(1):34-37, September 1959.

The author briefly traces the history of the family planning programme in Kerala State and analyses 700 cases of post-partum sterilizations, with reference to their age, parity, indications and techniques used for the operation.

2030 Ponniah, S., _et al_. "A Report After Two Years' Work on Rural Family Planning Project," _J. Fam. Welf._ 5(4):15-21, June 1959.

This is a report on the acceptance of contab foam tablets in a village in South India. The methodology of the study, difficulties encountered in interviewing, and responses of the sample are discussed. The acceptability of foam tablets was approximately 25% and no satisfactory solution was found to the problem of creating a demand for family planning in rural areas.

2031 "Population Control," _Seminar_ 33:1-56, May 1962.

This issue of the journal is devoted to various aspects of the problem of controlling India's increasing population. The following participants have contributed articles on specified topics: The problem, by Ashish Bose; Immediate measures, by N.V. Sovani; Background, by P.B. Tupta; A rational approach, by S.S. Sokhey; Responsible parenthood, by A.Nevett; Motivation, by M.V. Raman; Public acceptance, by C. Chandrasekaran; Achievements, by B.L. Raina.

2032 Poti, S.J. "An Enquiry into the Prevalence of Contraceptive Practices in Calcutta City," pp. 52-60 in: _Sixth International Conference on Planned Parenthood_. London: The International Planned Parenthood Federation, 1959. Also in: _Studies in Family Planning_. Delhi: Directorate of Health Services, Ministry of Health, Government of India, 1961.

One of the few studies available on the simultaneous interrelation of social status, family planning, and fertility in a high fertility country. Shows a significant practice of fertility control in Calcutta.

2033 Poti, S.J.B., Chakraborti, and Malaker, C.R. "Reliability of Data Relating to Contraceptive Practices," pp. 51-66, Chpt. in: Research in Family Planning, C.V. Kiser, ed. Princeton: Princeton University Press, 1962. xvi, 664 pp.

Data based on an inquiry into the prevalence of contraceptive practices among the Calcutta city population conducted by the Indian Statistical Institute. A master sample of 6,884 couples was used. Results revealed that the reports of the husbands were more dependable than those of the wives. Husbands were cooperative and consequently their reporting errors were mostly ascribable to lapse of recall and could be considerably reduced by appropriate amendments effected by re-interview.

2034 Potter, R.G., et al. "Fetal Wastage in Eleven Punjab Villages," Hum. Biol. 37:262-ff., 1965.

The authors collected, through monthly home visits over a period of three to five years, the pregnancy and menstrual records of 12,000 Punjab women. Eleven villages were selected, seven in which techniques of birth control had been introduced to lower birth rates and four controls in which birth control had not been introduced. Reports of early fetal deaths were deficient, although the retrospective reports of live births and stillbirths were fairly complete. The early fetal death reports equaled only 20% of the rate for prospective cases. There were 31 stillbirths out of 1000 births, and 105 abortions, with a rate of early to late fetal death of 72/35. Three major difficulties were encountered: scheduling home interviews, separating induced from spontaneous abortions, and the hesitancy of the woman interviewed to report early symptoms of pregnancy.

2035 Prabhudesai, Usha, "A Problem in Family Planning Check-Up and Follow-Up Visits," J. Fam. Welf. 6(3):48-50, March 1960.

There are a number of forces working adversely in the way regular follow-up of the family planning cases, especially in places where the average community is conservative and still exercises a strong hold over the individual. India is similar to England, where family planning is comparatively old, in the small per cent of women who return to the clinic after the initial visit.

2036 Prasada, K. "Family Planning Work in Lucknow," Indian Med. Gaz. 89(2):77-84, 1954.

Clinics were held in hospitals starting in March 1951. Publicity work was carried out cautiously at first but later all available means of publicity were fully utilized. In 15 months the total attendance at the four centers for which records are available was 1,647. There was no opposition from any quarter and the response was beyond expectations. It is planned to start work in other cities.

2037 Puri, V.V. "Family Planning in the Municipal Health Services," pp. 85-94 in: Family Planning Association of India. Report of the Proceedings, Second All India Conference on Family Planning, Bombay: The Association, 1955. 117 pp.

The nucleus of an organization for family planning under a Municipality is a maternity home and a maternity and child welfare centre. All the activities should be controlled from this centre. The first maternity home under the Bombay Municipality was opened in the year 1915. Up to 1947, all the maternity, child welfare and family planning activities have been controlled and conducted under the auspices of the maternity homes which constitute centres for family health and planning. A need to open free family planning clinics in the city of Bombay was felt by the Municipal Corporation and the Health authorities. Consequently, two family planning clinics were started in April, 1947 which were the first of their kind in India. Now there are 20 such clinics in the city of greater Bombay. The work done in the Bombay clinics may be divided into three parts, namely, education and publicity, practical instructions to women, and follow up of the cases advised at clinics.

2038 Radhakrishnan, Sarvepalli, "Planned Parenthood," Eugenics Rev. 55(1):15-18, 1953.

Revision of address delivered on 24 November 1952 at the Third International Congress on Planned Parenthood in which the speaker discusses the Hindu view of sex and marriage, the role of intellect in solving human problems, the Gandhian view of birth control, and the traditional Indian attitude of the ideal and the permissible in human conduct.

2039 Raina, B.L. Family at Cross Roads. Hukerikar Memorial Lecture, Series 2, 1966. Dharwar: Janata Shikshana Samiti's Institute of Economic Research, 1967. iv, 13 pp.

Consanguineous marriage, extended and nuclear types of family, family planning, and abortion are among topics discussed in March 20, 1967, address by Director of India's Central Family Planning Institute.

2040 Raina, B.L. "Family Planning Programme in India," pp. 111-21, in: Berelson, Bernard, et al., Family Planning and Population Programme. Chicago: The Chicago University Press, 1966.

A brief account of history of family planning in India, of the structure, target and achievements of the government family planning program to date, and of the tasks ahead.

2041 Raina, B.L. "How Can We Moderate Fertility?" Maharashtra Med. J. 11(1):93-96, April 1964.

2042 Raina, B.L. Possible Effects of Public Policy Measures on Fertility in India. New Delhi: Ministry of Health, 1965. 7 pp. (processed).

2043 Rajan, K.S. Sundara, "India's Population Problem," Finance and Development: The Fund and Bank Review 2(3):144-51.

Outlines the Government of India's family-planning program.

2044 Rama Rau, Dhavanthi, "Family Planning in India," J. Sex Res. 3(4):272-74, November 1967.

Description of goals, targets, activities, and methods of the governmental program.

2045 Ramu, G.N. "Gold Miners and Family Planning," Indian J. Soc. Work 27(4):337-42, 1967.

Three hundred male heads of families among the miners of Kolar Gold Mining Undertakings in Mysore State were interviewed on the subject of family planning. Information was sought on their views on limiting the number of children, the arguments for and against limitation, and the desirability of government intervention.

2046 Ranadive, K.T., et al. "A Socioeconomic Survey of a Population-Group in Relation to Family Planning," Popul. Rev. 5(1):27-38, January 1961.

This survey gives an insight into methods of motivating people to accept family planning, particularly in the context of cultural patterns and habits which act as barriers. A reference has been made to the husband's role in family planning. The survey is based on the results of 1000 questionnaires filled over a period of 42 months in Dadar, Bombay.

2047 Ranganadham, V.V. "Declining Mortality Rates and a Case for Family Planning in India," Indian J. Econ. 47(187): 429-54, April 1967.

2048 Rao, B. Krishna, "Family Planning in the Second Five-Year Plan," J. Fam. Welf. 2(6):213-14, September 1956.

Notes on opening of clinics, training of personnel, propaganda, and research. Also provides information on expenditures by Central Government and State Governments for these aspects of family planning.

2049 Rao, K. "The Impact of Legalization of Induced Abortion," J. Indian Med. Assn. 45:97-ff., 1965.

It is shown that in countries where induced abortions are increasing, specifically where it is illegal, the greatest incidence is found among women with the highest educational level, and abortion increases with the spread of information on family planning, without a parallel spread of effective contraceptive methods. Where wide-spread legal abortion is responsible for large decreases in the birth rate, as in Japan, restriction of legal abortion would only result in an increase in illegal abortions. The abortion situation in Eastern Europe is examined and rates of mortality and morbidity are cited. However, the author concludes that induced abortion as a method of population control in India is not feasible within the context of the available resources of qualified personnel, hospitals and equipment.

2050 Rao, V.V. Bhanoji, "Population Growth and Family Planning: Some Aspects of Policy for Economic Growth," Asian Studies 6:65-77, April 1964.

2051 Rattigan, W.H. A Digest of Civil Law for the Punjah. University Book Agency, 1966.

Includes laws affecting domestic relations.

2052 Rau, B.R.K. "Gandhian Economic Thought and Indian Development," AICC Econ. Rev. 16(19):35-39, March 10,1965.

Advocates intensification of the Government's birth-control education campaign with more allocation of funds and putting pressure on minority groups, now opposing it in hope of increasing their proportionate numbers.

2053 Rele, J.R.,and Patankar, Tara, "Differential Fertility of Contraceptors and Non-Contraceptors," Paper presented at the International Union for the Scientific Study of Population General Conference, 3-11 September 1969, London.

Findings lead us to the conclusion that the fertility of the sterilized couples is significantly higher compared to that of the non-contraceptors. This is because in the case of sterilized couples the birth control is adopted only for the purpose of limiting the family size. It can be recalled that only 14.45 per cent of the sterilized group had used other methods before sterilization, after on an average 2.24 live births. As sterilization is almost irrevocable, it was adopted by persons only after getting four or more children. In fact it was found that 82.9 per cent of the wives in sterilized group had four or more live births. At the same time the average age of the wife at the time of sterilization (couple) was 29, which is rather low, and which helps to confirm the conclusion that sterilized couples were more fertile. In case of wives practising methods other than sterilization the standardized average number of children ever born was 14.92 per cent higher than the non-contraceptors. This tends to indicate that there is no substantial difference between the fertility of the contraceptors using methods other than sterilization and that of the non-contraceptors. The former had resorted to family planning after getting on an average 2.18 children. Nearly 67 per cent of them had accepted contraception before getting three or less children. It can thus be said that this group does not appear as selective as the sterilized group in terms of the level of fertility. It appears that Greater Bombay depicts a stage where those couples with "too many children" are going in for sterilization to limit their family size. Emerging simultaneously is another trend where couples with relatively less number of children are resorting to other conventional contraceptives at somewhat younger ages either for limitation or spacing of births.

2054 Repetto, Robert, "India - A Case Study of the Madras Vasectomy Progress," Studies in Family Planning, May 1968, pp. 8-16.

This case study attempts to demonstrate the value of an explicit decision-making framework in programs surrounded with risk and uncertainty, if for no other reason than to stimulate a closer definition of policy weights and to provide a focus and incentive for the application of data to the decision process. It also demonstrates the important role that private initiative and organizations can play in forwarding a program when administrative structure and personnel are a real constraint.

2055 Roy, A.K. "Hindu Marriage Act, 1955 in the Light of the Institutes of Manu," Indian Law Rev. 9:271-ff. October - December 1957.

2056 Roy Burman, B.K., "Problem of Family Planning Among the Scheduled Tribes of West Bengal," Vanyajati 6(4):161-64, October 1958.

Lack of statistical data hinders the formulation of a successful family planning policy for tribals. Increased decline in the population depends on birth and death rates, and migration: the relative contribution of these factors have not been ascertained. Nevertheless census demographic data show that the problem of planning is not identical in all 41 scheduled tribes of West Bengal. Some general features of the socio-economic life of the tribes discussed give an insight into the problem. Precedence should be given to a cautious and indirect approach in the shape of educational campaigns particularly in the case of most tribes who have a very low percentage of literacy, over the direct introduction of family planning measures.

2057 Salunkhe, G.R. "Family Planning as Understood and Practised in the City of Indore," Indian Sociol. 1(1):59-65, March 1959.

A social survey of ninety-nine families of Indore City, India, regarding the consciousness and practice of family planning among the lower-class, middle-class and upper-class income groups. The structured interview method was employed in the study. It was found that the consciousness of family planning grew with a rise in education and income, but there seemed a general lack of social consciousness as only 35% of the total sample practiced planning. Education and dissemination of knowledge through various ways is suggested.

Cheap and effective contraceptives should be provided by the State Ministry of Health. More financial help should come from the states, and the standard of living should be increased.

2058 Samuel, T.J. "Abortion for Population Control," Family Planning News 7(5):5-ff., 1966.

The author discusses legalizing abortion in India as a method of population control. However, he admits that abortion, although morally acceptable and demographically effective is not economically efficient or medically practicable. If abortion were to be legalized it must be done so at the family's own cost.

2059 Samuel, T.J. "Allocation and Utilization of Resources for Population Control in India," Indian J. Econ. 146(182): 245-62, January 1966.

Discusses the allocation of resources for the population control program in the first four Five Year Plans of India and examines the factors responsible for their underutilization so far in different degrees in different states. Attributes the low allocations of funds for family planning and underutilization of even allocated resources mainly to ambivalent attitude of the government towards the policy of population control.

2060 Samuel, T.J. "The Cost of Children in India," AICC Econ. Rev. October 15,1963, pp. 19-22 and March 24,1964, pp. 31-32.

Discusses the cost to the society, to the parents, and to the nation to produce a child, bring him up, educate him and provide him with the amenities of life on a level available to an average citizen.

2061 Samuel, T.J. "Family Planning and How to Make It Effective," Indian J. Soc. Work 21:223-27, December 1960.

Summarized India's population problem and recommends a tax on excess children to emphasize the seriousness of the problem.

2062 Samuel, T.J. "Motivation for Family Limitation," Eastern Econ. 46:812, April 15, 1966.

Pleads for a combination of fiscal incentives and penalties as part of India's program of family planning education.

2063 Sanual, Hem, "Socio-Economic Indications for Permanent Conception Control," J. Fam. Welf. 5(2):27-37, December 1958.

Dealing with the general implications of sterilization, the author proceeds to study the attitudes of people and the social demand for sterilization on the basis of interviews with some 250 women and their husbands. The author also reports on another study aimed at finding the incidence of sterilization in relation to the number of deliveries, characteristics of the sterilized group, and the after-effects of the operation. The author concludes that sterilization has no ill-effects and promotes family welfare.

2064 Sanyal, S.N. "Attitude Towards Contraceptive Methods," Man in India 42(2):126-38, April - June 1962.

A discussion of attitudes towards different methods of birth control in India, revealing that the best attitude is held regarding oral contraceptives. Trial with oral contraceptives was carried out among middle-class and lower-middle-class people for 2.5 years. The total roll was 727 after two years, and 950 at the end of 2.5 years. Originally there was fear of probable harmful effects, such as permanent sterility, complete cessation of menstruation, and other toxic effects. However, the trial showed a reduction of 60% in the pregnancy ratio. A second trial of two years, under the aegis of the All India Institute of Hygiene and Public Health, in Calcutta, also showed a reduction of 60% in the treatment group, compared to that of the control group.

2065 Sarma, R.S.S. "Demographic Effects of a Large-Scale Sterilization Policy," Artha Vijnana 5(1):17-23, March 1963.

Presents quantitative estimates of effects on birth and growth rates of a policy equivalent to that proposed by Shri R.A. Gopalaswami, that one-tenth of all married couples with wives aged between 25 and 34 years should be taken out of reproduction annually. The implementation of such a policy will result in preventing 1.8 _per cent_ of the total births in the first year. The number of births prevented will gradually rise to 30 _per cent_ in the fifteenth year and remain at the same level thereafter. The rate of population growth will tend to decrease during the fifteen years following the implementation of the policy.

2066 Sastri, L.S. _The Child Marriage Restraint Act_. Third Edition. Revised by S.N. Joshi. Allahabad: Law Book Company, 1962. 55 pp.

2067 Savant, P.K. "Inaugural Address Delivered at the First State Family Planning Conference Held at Nagpur on 9 August 1962," _J. Fam. Welf._ 9(1):11-15, September 1962.

Review by the Minister of Public Health, Government of Maharashtra, on the provisions in the first three Five-Year Plans for family planning, and of the progress made in the State of Maharashtra.

2068 Savkar, D.S. "Population and Planning," _AICC Econ. Rev._ 11(8):21-22. August 15, 1959.

Comment by the Economic Adviser, Reserve Bank of India, on the relation of the 'vital revolution' and the Third Five-Year Plan and on governmental support for family planning.

2069 Saxena, G.B. "Latent Practices of Family Planning and Motivation: a Sample Study in Rural Uttar Pradesh," _Fam. Planning News_ 3(3):57-58, March 1962.

The author points out certain economic and sociological factors relevant to the family planning programme. Information collected from 1,336 rural couples in Uttar Pradesh, India, is discussed briefly.

2070 Saxena, J.N. "Widow's Right of Succession in India," Amer. J. Comparative Law 11:574, Autumn 1962.

This survey of the law of testamentary and intestate succession, affecting a widow in India indicates that the lot of a Christian widow, or a Jewish widow, or a widow who was married under the Special Marriage Act (1872 or 1954), or whose marriage was registered under the Special Marriage Act, 1954, is satisfactory (but for the extreme case in which the husband transfers all his property by will to others than the wife). The position of a Parsi widow (under the special provisions of intestate succession in the Indian Succession Act, 1925, as amended by the Act of 1939), and that of a Hindu widow (under the Hindu Succession Act, 1956), has been greatly improved from what it used to be a few years back, but can by no means be said to be perfect. The laws affecting a Mohammedan widow, however, are certainly outdated and need an early reform. In Independent India, the Hindu law has in many respects been brought up to date. But the Government has been obstinately shy about reforming the Mohammedan Law.

2071 Schorr, B. [Family Planning in India], Sante Publique 9:41-ff., 1966.

The abortion problem is briefly dealt with. The law permits interruption of pregnancy of medical indication, but this is rarely done because of lack of support from public opinion and in the government policy. The incidence of illegal abortion is said to be considerable. Complications of abortion are said to occupy too much of scarce medical facilities. Opinion for legalizing abortion on a more liberal basis has been expressed. A committee to investigate this question was appointed by the Central Government in 1964.

2072 Sen, Hari, "Some Experiments on the Propagation of Family Planning in Yeotmal," J. Fam. Welf. 7(1):33-45, September 1960.

Experiences of the author in promoting awareness and adoption of family planning methods in Yeotmal, India, are described. Some suggestions are made on measures to interest men in the vasectomy operation.

2073 Sen, S.C. "Need for Expansion of India's Family Planning Service," Indian Med. Assn. J. 32 (6):253-55. March 16,1959.

2074 Sen, Sushama, "The Hindu Marriage Act, 1955," Modern Rev. 98:120-24, August 1955.

The Hindu Marriage Act of 1955 has tried to encompass the following questions: (1) the abolition of caste as a necessary requirement of a valid marriage, (2) enforcement of monogamy, (3) divorce or dissolution of marriage on certain grounds, and (4) restraint of child-marriage. Actually the achievement of this legislation lies in codification and unifying the prevalent practices rather than in the introduction of any novel feature. For example, about 80% of the Hindu population has had customary divorce that is extended to the remaining 20%. The Act has been criticized, and much depends on how it is used. The Act is only a stand-by.

2075 Sethi, R.B. Muslim Marriage and Its Dissolution. Second Edition. Allahabad: Law Book Company, 1960.

2076 Shillong. Central Family Planning Association, "Research Study of Causes of Resistance to the Adoption of Family Planning Amongst the Labourers of Assam Tea Gardens," Paper presented at the National Conference on Population Policy and Programmes, New Delhi, 19-23. December, 1969.

This study was undertaken at the request of the Indian Tea Association to learn why the rate of IUD insertions dropped from 21.7 per 1000 in 1965 to 16.9 per 1000 in 1966. The majority of respondents wanted four to six children because of the high child mortality and the belief that their children, especially boys, would be employed on the tea estates and would contribute to the family's income. Majority of women were opposed to monetary rewards for IUD insertions because they treasure children more. Many misconceptions concerning the effects of IUD on health and fecundity prevail.

2077 Sills, David L. "Some Problems and Procedures in Studying Acceptance of Family Planning," Family Planning News 2(3): 49-55, March 1961.

The author has used data collected from 626 women in the Bombay Births Study, undertaken by the Demographic Training and Research Centre, Bombay, to analyze some of the problems in question wording. An "accounting scheme" for ascertaining reasons for accepting or not accepting family planning, as used in the study, is explained.

2078 Singh, Baljit, Five Years of Family Planning in the Countryside. Lucknow: J.K. Institute of Sociology and Human Relations, Lucknow University, 1958. 118 pp.

A sample of 1,453 females (76% of the married females) was selected from 26 villages connected by road or rail to Lucknow or Sittapur. The majority of them and their husbands were Hindu and illiterate. The couples had had no previous experience with birth control and the survey examines the acceptability of various methods. The rhythm method, to which the 1,453 women were first introduced by the use of colored beads, proved the least successful; the main difficulty was inability to count, and only 4.2 per cent of the women used it. Slightly more acceptable was the oil plug method (a cotton pad dipped in oil). The sponge method was better, being regularly or occasionally adopted by 8 per cent of women. The most successful of the four methods was the foam tablet, the distribution of which was begun rather late in the experiment (June 1955): about one in six of the women took to it; and if women wanting more children and those indifferent to family planning (together amounting to 50 per cent of the total) are excluded, one woman in three used these tablets. Four is the optimum number of wanted children. The fourth surviving child seems to focus attention sharply on family limitation. But three children are enough to restrict, in the manner desired by planners, the rate of population growth. Hence there exists at present a disparity between what are called "individual and social optima." Differences are disclosed in the attitude towards family planning: these relate to the parity of mothers, to the ages of husband and wife, to occupation, literacy, and religion (relatively more Muslims than Hindus adopted birth control). Another factor is the distance of the couple's home from the centre providing the contraceptive services. Stress is laid on the importance of a good follow-up system.

2079 Singh, R. "Matrimonial Property Law Among Hindus," J. Family Law 6:129, Spring 1966.

The legal history of India shows the unique independence of Hindu women with regard to their property rights: even under the system of land law,recognition of separate property is found. The author discusses "stridhan" (a term which literally means "woman's property" but has almost acquired a technical meaning with the smrti and other writers) - what constitutes it and how far Hindu law has allowed the married woman to exercise her dominion over it. Also discussed are the contractual obligations of the spouse under past and more recent Hindu laws, with references to ante-nuptial agreements or Law of Sulka, contracts during coverture, torts relating to property and spouses (tortious liability), presumption of advancement between spouses, disposition of property by a married woman, laws relating to gifts among Hindus and gifts between spouses, partition and spouses, property of spouses and their testamentary power, and the respective rights of spouses over matrimonial property in cases of divorce. Provisions and regulation regarding property within the Hindu Marriage Act of 1955 are described.

2080 Sinha, J.N. "Differential Fertility and Family Limitations in an Urban Community of Uttar Pradesh," Popul. Stud. 11(2): 157-69, November 1957.

In this study there is a distinctively negative correlation between income or caste level and fertility resulting in part from differential use of contraception.

2081 "Small Family Norm Committee Report," Family Planning News 9(12):15-16, December 1968.

Recommendations from an Indian "Small Family Norm Committee," 3 January 1967, chaired by Shri Gorind Narain, Secretary of the Ministry of Health and Family Planning, India, to promote economic and social benefits for a small family -- ranging from various compensations for sterilization and tax reform to accentuation of family life education and awards for books on population.

2082 Srinivasan, K. "Demographic Pressure in India and Methods of Control," J. Fam. Welf. 7(1):1-11, June 1960.

Discusses various causes for the recent spurt in the growth of India's population and methods of population control. Suggestions are made to help overcome the difficulties that stand in the way of the success of the family planning program.

2083 Sundaram, Kamakshi, "Family Planning in the Fourth Plan: Without Frills or Fat," Eastern Econ. 47:657, 7 October 1966.

The provision for family planning in the Fourth Plan will be five times what has been spent over the past three Plans put together. It is also intended to cover the whole country with about 5,500 rural family planning centers, 41,000 sub-centers and 1,800 urban centers. This article attempts a practical discussion of the technical implementation of the family planning program and what may be expected with the sanctioned budget based on previous performances.

2084 Sundaram, Kamakshi, "Family Planning in the Fourth Plan II: Much Cry, Little Wool," Eastern Econ. 47: 711-12, 14 October 1966.

Criticism of the organization of the IUCD program and the treatment of family planning as a medical program rather than a community program. Recommends greater utilization of social workers particularly for the evaluation of specific programs.

2085 Sundaram, Kamakshi. "On Legalization of Abortion," Eastern Econ. 43(21):961, 20 November 1964.

Recommends that the Governmental Committee on Abortion define whether abortion is to be a family planning technique or the last resort when other contraception has failed. The former definition simplifies administration of a program and the education of the public.

2086 Sundar, Rao, P.S.S. "Awakening Rural India," J. Fam. Welf. 6(1):24-31, September 1959.

Results of an experiment carried out in a village in South India to measure the acceptability and effectiveness of Contab foam tablets are presented here. Factors operating against the acceptance of conception planning and control are discussed.

2087 Swadeshi, Satya, "Review and Summary of Prize-Winning Essay, Family Planning and National Welfare by Vijay Kekre," Indian J. Soc. Work 23(1):63-68, April 1962.

This essay won the Population Essay Contest in 1956. It contains six sections: (1) population growth and economic development; (2) population control; (3) need for family planning in the villages; (4) attitude of people towards family planning; (5) methods of family planning and their feasibility in India; and (6) conclusions. Several case studies are presented to illustrate the need for child spacing and limitation.

2088 Talwar, Prem P. "A Note on Changes in Age At Marriage of Females and Their Effect on the Birth Rate in India," Eugenics Quart. 14:291-95, 1967.

If Indian women are not allowed to marry before the age of 20, the immediate effect is a decrease of about 10 to 11 births per 1,000 population or a relative reduction of about 25 *per cent*. The long-term effect will be much less. The decrease may range between 8 and 12 *per cent*. The best estimate is a reduction of about 16 *per cent* in the national birth rate.

2089 Thacker, P.V. "The Role of Industry in Population Control," National Conference on Population Policy and Programmes, New Delhi, 19-23 December, 1969.

The Family Planning Movement in the Tata group of industries began 15 to 20 years ago and has moved through three stages: the sympathetic, the active, and the dynamic. Initially the effectiveness of family planning depended on the initiative of the local managers but in July 1967, Tata Industries Limited recommended a uniform policy. Policy included payment of Rs. 200 for a sterilization operation, Rs. 25 for a loop insertion, and leave with wages for four days for a vasectomy and ten days for a tubectomy. Targets were set and educational programs were introduced.

2090 Thapar, Savitri, "Family Planning in India," Popul. Stud. 17(1):4-19. July 1963.

A detailed account of progress since 1925, when the first birth control clinic was opened. Since Governmental condemnation gave way to support 10-15 years ago, the pace of advance has greatly speeded up, but even so it has lagged far behind hopes. Under the current "Third Five Year Plan", emphasis is being placed on education, as motivation for family planning is still low among the general population.

2091 Thomas, P. Indian Women Through the Ages. New York: Asia Publishing House, 1964.

In the Mahabharata the following reference suggests the Hindu attitude toward abortion: "...letting a woman's Rtu (fertile period) go waste was a sin tantamount to embryo-murder".

2092 Thomson, Claire, A Christian Approach to Family Planning. Madras: Christian Medical Association of India, 1963. vi, 44 pp.

Essentially a manual of contraceptive methods. Abortion is condemned, except when necessary to save life. Appendix on sterilization advises caution.

2093 United Nations. The Mysore Population Study. New York: United Nations, 1961, 352 pp.

This is a large-scale intensive sample survey of the fertility in Mysore, India, made under the auspices of the United Nations. It is one of the most comprehensive studies in an underdeveloped area including coverage of a large number of social and economic variables in relation to marriage, fertility, mortality, and family planning. It includes extensive methodological discussions.

2094 United Nations. Programme of Technical Assistance, Report on the Family Planning Programme in India, Prepared for the Government of India by a United Nations Advisory Mission. Report No. TAO/IND/48. New York, United Nations, February 20, 1966. iv, 123 pp.

Chapters: Summary and broad conclusions; Background and main features of the family planning programme in India; Ways of strengthening the organization and administration; Family planning techniques; Supplies and services; Training; Education of the public; Incentives; Research and evaluation;

Programme planning: Social policies to promote family planning and small family norms; International assistance and co-operation; Prospects of curbing population growth; A reinforced program in 1965-66. Appendixes include: Prospective trends in total population, birth rates, rate of population growth, number of births and age distribution in India, 1965-1990.

2095 UNESCO Expert Mission. Preparatory Study of a Pilot Project in the Use of Satellite Communication for National Development Purposes in India. February, 1968.

One section, pp. 13-14, suggests a policy of using satellite communications to help solve the population problem.

2096 University of Lucknow, Demographic Research Centre, "Progress of Family Planning in India - A Comparative Study of States With Special Reference to Uttar Pradesh," Demography Develop. Digest 1(2):277-95, July 1967.

Reports All-India and state statistics, for period 1961-1967, on: family planning expenditures; establishment of urban and rural family planning centers; and progress of sterilization and IUD programs.

2097 Vembu, Elfriede, "How Family Planning Came to India," J. Fam. Welf. 1(5):155-60, July 1955.

Discusses the development of the family planning movement in India from shortly after the founding of the Neo-Malthusian League in England (1877) to 1952.

2098 Villard, Henry H. "A Note on the Economics of Birth Control," Rev. Econ. Statistics 40(1, Part 1):78-79, February 1958.

Estimates of the order of direct and indirect costs for introducing to all couples available birth control devices in India.

2099 Visaria, Pravin, "Population Assumptions and Policy," _Econ. Weekly_ 16(32-33):1339, 1341-44, August 8 1964.

This note examines whether, and how far, the population projections of the Third Plan, made in 1961, stand in need of revision in the light of later developments. It is also intended to: (a) review the implementation of family planning program; and (b) analyze the proposed reorientation of the programme with the objective of achieving a more rapid decline in the rate of growth of population.

2100 Wadia, Avabai B. "The Family Planning Association of India," _J. Fam. Welf._ 7(3):41-48, March 1961.

Discusses the organization of the FPAI and its relationships with the Central and State Governments, and its clinical and educational services.

2101 Wadia, Avabai B. "The History of the Family Planning Association of India," Paper presented at the National Conference on Population Policy and Programmes, New Delhi, 19-23 December 1969.

Traces the history and programs of the Family Planning Association of India from its inception in 1949 to 1969. Most notable is the early efforts in 1950 of the Association to get the Government of India to include family planning included in its over-all plan for development.

2102 Wadia, Avabai B. "Some Socio-Economic Aspects of Family Planning," _J. Fam. Welf._ 3(6):219-24, September 1957.

Notes on the problem in general and the program of the Government Programmes and Research Committee.

2103 Wadia, Avabai B. "Some Thoughts on the Educational Programme for Family Planning," _J. Fam. Welf._ 11(3):13-18, March 1965.

Criticism and suggestion of changes in the family-planning educational campaign of the Government of India under the third five-year plan.

2104 Wallace, Victor H. "Contraception in Relation to Abortion," _J. Fam. Welf._ 7(4):1-13, June 1961.

The author discusses how the use of contraceptives and other educational, economic and social measures can help in reducing the number of induced abortions.

2105 World Health Organization, _Final Report on Pilot Studies in Family Planning_. 2 vols. 36 Appendices. New Delhi: WHO Regional Office of S.E. Asia. Mimeographed, 1954. 132 pp.

Describes results of a program to introduce the "rhythm" method in rural India.

2106 World Health Organization, "Population Control. WHO Undertakes Pilot Study at Request of Government of India," _Chron. World Health Organization_ 6(2):33-34, February 1952.

Describes briefly the one-year pilot study in family planning being undertaken in India.

2107 Wyon, John B., and Gordon, John E. "A Long-Term Prospective-Type Field Study of Population Dynamics in the Punjab, India," pp. 17-32, Chpt. in _Research in Family Planning_ C.V. Kiser, ed. Princeton: Princeton University Press, 1962. xvi,664 pp. 664 pp.

The practical aim was to determine facts on which to build a program for birth control. Villages, (total equalled 8,000) formed the test group for the birth control program. Two sets of villages (total equalling 4,000 each), were controls. Contraceptive methods were used at one time or another by 39% of currently married wives aged 15-44 years. When used regularly, probability of conception was 37% of that of a control population. Nevertheless, no change in birth rate was noted during 4 years of observation. The population of test villages increased by only 0.1% per year. It is concluded that the people were solving their own population problem largely by out-migration to other villages and to cities.

IRAN

Policies on fertility and family size

2108 Behnam, Jamshid, "Population Policy and Family Planning in Iran," pp. 456-61 in: International Union for the Scientific Study of Population, Contributed Papers, Sydney Conference, Australia, 21 to 25 August 1967.

Measures in connection with family planning began in 1957 with the establishment of the Family Health Guidance Association and also the Mother and Child Welfare Department of the Ministry of Health. Official administrative arrangements to devise a population policy began in 1967.

2109 Chasteland, J.C., *et al*. *Etude sur la Fecondite et Quelques Caracteristiques Demographiques des Femmes Mariees dans Quatre Zones Rurales d'Iran* [Study of Fertility and Some Demographic Characteristics of Married Women in Four Rural Areas of Iran], Teheran: University of Teheran, 1968. 317 pp.

The seven chapters are written by different authors. Survey is based on 4,743 married women selected from a universe of 115,100 married women aged 15-49 years, in four rural areas. Past and current fertility, infant mortality, the socio-economic characteristics of the villages, and the demographic opinions and knowledge of the villagers are discussed. The inquiry, which is sponsored by the Iranian Government along with the Population Council and the United Nations, seeks to understand the causes of the high rate of reproduction in order to formulate a birth control policy. The effect of the Koranic laws from the seventh century are considered.

2110 Hinchcliffe, Doreen, "The Iranian Family Protection Act," *Internat. Comparative Law Rev*. 17:516-21, 1968.

The Iranian Family Protection Act is one of the most important statutes to be enacted in the Islamic world in recent years. Its outstanding provisions relate to divorce but other points such as the custody of children and polygamy are also included. The hitherto unprecedented step has been taken of depriving a husband of his right of unilateral repudiation. Henceforth the sole ground for divorce is that the marriage has broken down and that there is no possibility of reconciliation between the spouses. Altogether the Act consists of 23 Articles and one Note.

2111 Maroufi-Bozorgi, Nasser, "Some Socio-Demographic Characteristics of Women Seeking Contraceptive Advice in One of the Southern Clinics of Tehran," pp. 476-82 in: International Union for the Scientific Study of Population, Contributed Papers, Sydney Conference, Australia, 21 to 25 August, 1967.

Study is based on records of 779 women attending the family planning clinic of the Farah Hospital in Tehran from March 1964 to February 1965. As compared with the general female population of Tehran, the clinic cases are concentrated in the 30-39 year age group and in the illiterate educational category. Their husbands are most often craftsmen and are least often professionals. Women seeking contraception are of high parity, their pregnancies averaging 6.4 at ages 25-29 years, 7.8 at ages 30-34 years, and 9.3 at ages 35-39 years.

2112 Pakistan's Family Planning Division, Proposals for Iran's Family Planning Scheme for Current Five Year Plan Period. August 1968. 141 pp.

A detailed set of guidelines and recommendations for launching a family planning program in Iran, prepared primarily by Enver Adil, former Secretary to the Government of Pakistan, Family Planning Division, under the aegis of R.C.D. (Regional Cooperation for Development) Technical Cooperation. Chapters cover approach, orientation, methodology, training schedule, and job descriptions. Tables of targets, financial expenditures for the coil, vasectomy, and conventional contraceptive programs, and sample record-keeping forms are included.

2113 Population Council, "Iran: Report on Population Growth and Family Planning," Stud. Fam. Planning 20:3-6, June 1967.

Summary of a report submitted to the Ministry of Health, Government of Iran, by the Population Council in August 1966. Recommends a policy on family planning.

NEPAL

Policies on fertility and family size

2114 David, A.S. "Nepal: National Development, Population, and Family Planning," Studies in Family Planning, No. 42, May 1969, pp. 6-16.

Following a general description and historical sketch of Nepal, the author discusses the population growth from 1911, the year of the first census of population. Accepting the existing data as the best available, it is noted that the population increased by 66% in the years between 1911 and 1961 and it is estimated that population annual growth rate will continue to increase for each five-year period. Both population size and growth rate will be reduced if fertility begins to decline. A family planning clinic was established in Nepal in 1958 by a volunteer association and in 1965 His Majesty's Government began to offer family planning services in Kathmandu Valley. The current expansion of the official governmental program is presented and the author concludes that the program must be strengthened tremendously if it is to achieve the desired objective of fertility reduction through channels of family planning alone. The author recommends program flexibility; the need for increased social support, financial support; and the need for a closer coordination and involvement of the Nepal Family Planning Association in developing the needed social support through increased educational efforts.

2115 Thakur, H.N. "A Demographic Quest for Family Planning in Nepal," J. Fam. Welf. 11(1):20-28 September 1964.

The Government should initiate programs which lead to family planning, university courses on human reproduction, higher education for more persons, and a higher age at marriage for both sexes. While the average family size is not large (an average of 5.3 persons), the economic resources are inadequate for the existing population. The programs should slow growth.

2116 Toner, Joseph S. "The Problem Ahead," Royal Nepal Econ. 7-8:33-37, January - July 1966.

Advocates governmental support for family planning and for agricultural development.

PAKISTAN

General population policies

2117 Krotki, Karol J. "The Feasibility of an Effective Population Policy for Pakistan," Pakistan Develop. Rev. 4(2): 283-313, Summer 1964.

The purpose of the discussion is threefold; to consider whether or not rapid population growth is an impediment to economic development in Pakistan; to assess the impact of alternative changes in population growth on the size and composition of national development plans; to consider means of manipulating population size and growth. Under the last group of problems, questions will be asked about the effectiveness of a government-directed family-planning program.

Policies on fertility and family size

2118 Adil, Enver, "Measurement of Family Planning Progress in Pakistan," Demography 5(2):659-65, 1968.

In the evaluation of the operational statistics compiled monthly under the Pakistan family planning program a formula has been developed to convert IUCD insertions, sterilization operations and sales of conventional contraceptives into a standard measure of achievement.

2119 Adil, Enver, "Pakistan: The Family Planning Program, 1965-1967," Studies in Fam. Planning, No. 26, January 1967, pp. 4-11.

An examination of Pakistan's Family Planning program under the Third Five-Year Plan. The five-year target of the program is to make family planning services available to all fertile couples in Pakistan and to reduce the birth rate from 50 to 40 per 1,000 population by 1970. The major focus of the plan has been on the IUD and conventional contraceptives. Earlier efforts in family planning and the results of the first two years achievements(1965-1967)are reviewed. A detailed account of the basic elements of the current family planning scheme is given.

2120 Adil, Enver, "The Use of Statistical Guides and Measures of Effectiveness in Determining Government Policy for Influencing Fertility - Pakistan," in: Vol. 2, pp. 63-67 of United Nations Department of Economic and Social Affairs, Proceedings of the World Population Conference, Belgrade, 30 August - 10 September 1965. 4 Vols. New York: United Nations, 1967.

The test of effectiveness of a family planning program is prevention of pregnancies. Methods must be found for inexpensive, prompt assessment of such programs rather than waiting for decennial censuses.

2121 Ahmed, Mohiuddin, and Ahmed, Fatema, "Male Attitudes Toward Family Limitation in East Pakistan," Eugenics Quart. 12(4): 209-26, 1965.

Two opposite forces were found operating in the population on the formation of attitude desire for children. First, demographic forces such as expanding family size, age, and years married tended to depress the desire for additional offspring, but they did not necessarily generate a favorable attitude toward birth control. This is so because people become easily adjusted to changed circumstances, partly as a result of their fatalistic attitude. On the other hand, these tradition-bound people were not arbitrarily opposed to birth control universally. An utter ignorance about birth control as such was their basic problem for a favorable attitude toward effective family limitation.

2122 Awan, Asghari K. Provoked Abortions Amongst 1,447 Married Women, Lahore: Maternity and Child Welfare, 1969. 86 pp. Summarized in: "Attempted Illegal Abortions in 156 Cases of Fetal Loss Occurring Among 1,447 Married Women - Saddar Pregnancy Study (1963-1965)," J. Amer. Med. Women's Assn. 24(7):571-86, July 1969.

The total of 40 illegally induced abortions among 1,447 pregnant women, living in the Saddar Area, Lahore, Pakistan, represents a fetal loss ratio of 70.6 per 1,000 live births. Of these 40 abortions, 28 were admitted by the women, and 12 were diagnosed on the basis of criteria recommended by the World Health Organization. The total fetal loss ratio for this group is 188.5 per 1,000 live births. The estimated incidence of fetal mortality from illegally induced abortions at six weeks gestation is 57.3 per 1,000 pregnancies. On the basis of life table procedures, used in all computations in this report, it is estimated that 35 per cent of all fetal losses occurring before the 28th week of gestation are the result of illegally induced abortions. Most women in the community used "quacks and unqualified healers" to obtain their abortions. The study covered 4,431 women, 10-50 years of age (although no pregnant woman was found below age 14), with husband present. It was sponsored by the Department of Maternal and Child Health of the Institute of Hygiene and Preventive Medicine, Lahore, and the Maternity and Child Welfare Association of Pakistan.

2123 Berleson, Bernard, "Pakistan: The Rural Pilot Family Planning Action Programme at Comilla," Stud. Fam. Planning 3:9-11, 1964.

Reviews the pilot-program on family planning initiated by the Pakistan Academy for Rural Development in March, 1961. The first phase of the program continued until November of that same year and was followed by a reorientation period in which plans were reviewed and revised and personnel changed, and the new program began in mid-1962 and is currently an active force. The Academy's basic position on any form of modernization in the villages is that success depends on training the villagers through their own leaders and on making contraceptive supplies easily available in the village. It was shown that without active and continuous supervision, at least in the first years of operation, the program tends to drop off in effectiveness. Also indicated was that as in other cases, the condom comes to be preferred to the foam tablet as a contraceptive method.

2124 Duke University. Commonwealth-Studies Center, Program in Comparative Studies on Southern Asia, Family Planning Scheme for Pakistan: A Critique of Sources, Conditions, and Issues, with Appended Documents. Durham: Duke University Press, 1966. 569 pp.

2125 Green, Lawrence W., and Krotki, Karol J. "Class and Parity Biases in Family Planning Programs: The Case of Karachi," Eugenics Quart. 15(4):235-51, December 1968.

Specifically, the questions to which this analysis is addressed are: (a) How does the socioeconomic distribution of family planning clients in the early phases of an urban program compare with the socioeconomic distribution of births in the population? (b) How does the parity distribution of family planning clients compare with the distribution of births by parity in the population at large? (c) What are the implications of the comparative distribution of family planners and fertility for population control and program planning? The present findings are from an analysis of 3,422 couples attending the Family Planning Association Model Clinic in Karachi, Pakistan, between 1958 and 1964.

2126 Gustafson, Harold C., et al. "Educational Efforts in the Implementation of Rural Family Planning Programs in East Pakistan," Demography 4(1):81-89, 1967.

The pilot family planning studies reported in this paper were conducted in a rural area adjacent to the city of Dacca in East Pakistan. The field activities in the development of various educational approaches to family planning are described. Three separate geographic areas (from 15,000 to 20,000 population) were each approached in a different way, varying in the number and educational qualifications of the workers and in the degree of involvement of village leadership. Preliminary analyses of field records indicate that these variations of approach apparently have little effect on the percentage of the population willing to accept contraceptive supplies. It is the opinion of the writers that more intensive educational efforts are necessary at the village level to develop social support for continuing use of contraception and to gain adoption of contraception by younger married couples primarily for spacing of births.

2127 Khan, Muhammad K.H. "Measurement of Impact of Family Planning Programme on Fertility in Pakistan," pp. 449-55 in: International Union for the Scientific Study of Population, Contributed Papers, Sydney Conference, Australia, 21 to 25 August 1967.

Recommends successive surveys to ascertain the impact of the family planning program on the birth rate.

2128 Mauldin, W. Parker, "Population and Population Policy in Pakistan," Marr. Fam. Living 25(1):62-68, 1963.

Perhaps nowhere else in the world do such large numbers live in such close proximity as in East Pakistan. In spite of the gross inadequacies of birth and death registration and the hazy concepts of time and age, decennial census data provide a record of population growth in the area that is now Pakistan. Since the turn of the century population has more than doubled, with an increase of 23.7% in the 1951-61 decade. During the First Five-Year Plan, 1955-60,, it became evident that per capita income, estimated at $51.46 in 1960, was increasing slowly, if at all. Concern developed over the impact of population increase on economic development. A special Family Planning meeting was called in February 1958, and by 1960 the government had provided the equivalent of over U.S. $6,000,000 for expenditure on a program of birth control which to date has consisted of: training medical and para-medical personnel; adding family planning services to existing medical centers; undertaking limited clinical studies of newer methods of contraception; small-scale experimentation with mobile audio-visual vans; and limited use of mass media. Perhaps only Japan and India are doing more than Pakistan. Lack of trained personnel and a relatively weak organizational structure are the major obstacles to fuller development of the family planning program.

2129 Pakistan. East Pakistan, Information Department, East Pakistan On Road to Prosperity 1964. Dacca: 1965. 107 pp.

Includes statistics, 1960-1964 on family planning clinics, sterilization operations, numbers trained by family-planning teams, names of cooperating organizations, and public information campaign events.

2130 Pakistan. Family Planning Council, Annual Report on the Working of Pakistan's Family Planning Programme, 1965-66, 1966. 86 pp.

The major focus of the program is on the IUD and conventional contraceptives in order to make family planning services available to all couples by 1970. An account of basic organization and achievements of the program is given.

2131 Pakistan. Family Planning Division, Proposals of the Family Planning Division for Family Planning Sector during the Fourth Five Year Plan (1970-75), Islamabad: 1968. ii, 140 pp.

Chapters: Objectives; Background; Financial implications; Report of the Planning Committee for proposed Population Study Centre and related training, research and evaluation institutions of Pakistan's Family Planning Division; Appendices and annexures; Projected district-wise breakdown of annual expenditure and targets. Tables include Population projections under declining mortality assumption, 1965-1975.

2132 Pakistan. Ministry of Health, Labour and Social Welfare, _Family Planning Scheme for Pakistan During the Third Five Year Plan Period, 1965-1970_. Rawalpindi: 1965. 192 pp.

A detailed presentation of the organization of the program which aims to reach all couples and to reduce the birth rate of Pakistan by twenty _per cent_ in five years.

2133 "Pakistan: Report on the Family Planning Program by the UN/WHO Advisory Mission," _Stud. Fam. Planning_, No. 40, April 1969, pp. 4-10.

Excerpts of Chapters 13 and 14 of the Joint UN/WHO Advisory Mission's final draft report titled, _An Evaluation of the Family Planning Programme of the Government of Pakistan_.

2134 Pakistan. Secretariat. Regional Co-operation for Development, _Seminar on Family Planning, Karachi April 6-8, 1966_. Government of Pakistan Press, 1966. 157 pp.

The Seminar was attended by official delegations of Turkey, Iran and Pakistan, besides experts and foreign consultants engaged in Family Planning work in Pakistan. Report of this Seminar is presented in three parts. The first part includes papers on family planning programme in the three countries and the population policy followed by them, the second part contains papers dealing with Pakistan experience in the field of family planning and the third contains re-research reports, dealing primarily with medical and social problems.

2135 Rauf, Abdur, "Psychological Aspects of Family Planning," _J. Fam. Welf._ 4(3):85-91, March 1958.

The author describes the problem of family size and birth rate as predominantly psychological. He mentions some of the ingredients that constitute the psychological nuclei of a formidable resistance to the forces of family planning in Pakistan.

2136 Robinson, Warren C. "Family Planning in Pakistan's Third Five Year Plan," Pakistan Develop. Rev. 6(2):255-81, Summer 1966.

This paper critically reviews the population policy contained in the Third Five Year Plan of Pakistan and its supporting documents in the light of previous family planning efforts in the country and experience of other countries in the field. The main points of criticism are that the scheme is excessively ambitious, the setting is unfavourable, emphasis on non-clinical methods and conventional contraceptives rather than IUD's is discouraging, evaluation has not been adequately spelled out, supply apparatus is not detailed, and insufficient attention has been given to publicity and propaganda.

2137 Robinson, Warren C. "Pakistan's New National Family Planning Experiment," Eugenics Quart. 13(4):316-25, December 1966.

Describes the Pakistan family planning scheme and analyzes critically its socioeconomic assumptions and the logic of its organizational structure. Finally, it draws some conclusions about probable strengths and weaknesses of the scheme.

2138 Shah, Nasim A., and Cobb, John C. A Preliminary Report on the Use of Oral Contraceptive Pills Synchronized with the Phases of the Moon. Lahore: Medical Social Research Project, January 1963. 51 pp. (mimeographed)

Oral contraceptive pills were taken, synchronizing with phases of the moon and found effective.

2139 Stoeckel, J., and Choudhury, Mogbul A. "Factors Related to Knowledge and Practice of Family Planning in East Pakistani Villages," Soc. Biol. 16(1):29-38, March 1969.

Over two-thirds of the 2,078 married couples living in villages in the Comilla-Kotwali thana knew about family planning, but only one in 20 reported practicing it currently and only one in 14 reported ever having used it. One possible reason for the gap between knowledge and reported practice is that there is a "stigma" associated with family planning and respondents will not admit practicing it. Knowledge, but not practice, was directly associated with occupation and education. Significantly higher proportions of members of cooperatives (11.7 per cent) had ever used contraception, compared with non-members (5.8 per cent), but there was no difference in knowledge and current practice. Among Hindus compared with Moslems, and among couples with four or more children compared with couples with smaller families, contraceptive knowledge and practice was significantly higher. This study was based on interviews conducted in 1967 under the auspices of the Pakistan Academy for Rural Development, Comilla, East Pakistan.

2140 Stoeckel, John E., and Choudhury, Mogbul A. "The Impact of Family Planning on Fertility in a Rural Area of East Pakistan," pp. 432-39 in: International Union for the Scientific Study of Population, Contributed Papers, Sydney Conference, Australia, 21 to 25 August 1967.

Evaluation of the impact of adoption of conventional contraceptives on fertility has been conducted by comparing adopter and non-adopter rates of pregnancy and analyzing trends in pregnancy reduction due to adoption from 1962 through 1966 in selected villages of Comilla-Kotwali thana. The general finding is that the effectiveness of the program resembles a bell shaped curve, i.e., in the initial phases pregnancy reduction increased, reached a plateau, and then declined in the remaining phases.

2141 Stoeckel, John, and Choudhury, Mogbul A. "Pakistan: Response Validity in a KAP Survey," Stud. Fam. Planning 1(47):5-9, November 1969.

An investigation into the rate of false response to questions on "knowledge" and "use" of family planning in a rural sample of known female contraceptive users reveals that while less than ten percent claimed they had no knowledge of family planning, over one-third contended they had never practiced it. There are two important implications of this latter finding. First, the so-called "Asian courtesy bias" would not appear to operate for this rural sample in answering the interviewer. Second, the rate of practice of family planning obtained from KAP surveys in East Pakistan must be questioned. Another observation is that the only demographic and social factors related to false response are family type, age, and duration of marriage.

2142 Waheed, S. "The Role of Government in Family Planning Programmes in Pakistan," pp. 291-93 in: IPPF Sixth International Conference on Planned Parenthood, Report of the Proceedings. New Delhi, 14-21 February 1959. 1959.

2143 Wishik, Samuel M. "Community Programs to Modify Family Size: Indications for Organization and Planning," pp. 198-210 in: Sheps, Mindel and Ridley, Jeanne C., Public Health and Population Change: Current Research Issues. Pittsburgh Press, 1965. xvii, 557 pp.

Paper presents the problems that arise in planning such programs and discusses the questions that need answers. Many of the examples relate particularly to Pakistan, since the writer has recently been working in that country. Topics: Availability of services; Education--motivation; Administration.

2144 Wishik, Samuel M. "Designs for Family Planning Programs and Research in Developing Countries," Amer. J. Public Health 57(1):15-21, January 1967.

Notes of typical difficulties (illiteracy, identification of individuals, inaccurate vital statistics, special health conditions, channels of communication) and on adaptations to cultural and environmental circumstances in Pakistan.

2145 Zucker, Elizabeth, "La Limitation des Naissances au Pakistan" [Birth Limitation in Pakistan], Population 24(5):951-62, 1969.

The ambitious program of Pakistan is to have couples limit and space their births more so that the birth rate may be reduced from 50 to 40 per 1000 by 1970. The budget for the program during 1965-1970 totals 284,000,000 rupees ($60,000,000 U.S.A.). Officially the program is considered a success. A modest estimate is that 981,494 births have been averted by the program for the 2,944,482 couples who have recourse to one of the contraceptive techniques.

(South Asia: South-East Asia)

GENERAL

General population policies

2146 Perkins, Gordon W. "Population Policy and Programs in South East Asia: A Discussion of Limiting Factors," Paper prepared for The Press Foundation of Asia "Beyond Nationalism" Seminar, Bangkok, Thailand, October 14-18, 1968.

Population programs cannot be viewed in isolation. While there is some evidence that an ambitious national program can accelerate or perhaps even initiate a decline in fertility before it would otherwise have occurred, the impact of a program will be much greater if it is accompanied by other changes -- improvements in health, education, employment, and agricultural production, for example. A population program is only one component of total development strategy - but a highly relevant, and heretofore, frequently neglected aspect.

2147 Rueff, Gaston, "Postwar Problems of French Indo-China: Social and Political Aspects," Pacific Affairs 18(3): 229-45, September 1945.

The period of tutelage prior to independence should include comprehensive developments in the fields of public health and sanitation; the replacement of contract labor by non-contract labor; and education. Solutions to the labor problem require the creation of a spontaneous current of emigration between Tongking and Cochin-China which would provide the concerns in the South with an adequate supply of non-contract labor; and the settlement near agricultural concerns of the workers already employed.

BURMA

Policies on fertility and family size

2148 Maung, Maung. Law and Custom in Burma and the Burmese Family. The Hague: Nijhoff,1963.

2149 Wichmann, Arthur A. "Burma: Agriculture, Population and Buddhism," Amer. J. Econ. Sociol. 24:71-83, January 1965.

Considers agricultural output, especially rice, in relation to need. Cultural obstacles to population control arising from Buddhist thought on population are also discussed.

CAMBODIA

Policies on fertility and family size

2150 "Cambodia: The Family Allowances Scheme," Internat. Soc. Security Assn. Bull. 12:41-44, January - February 1959.

INDONESIA

General population policies

2151 Sadli, Mohammad, "Indonesia's Hundred Millions," Far Eastern Econ. Rev. 40:21-23, April 4,1963.

Although Indonesia and particularly the island of Java are often taken as exemplifying the classical Malthusian situation, the official Government attitude since the independence toward Indonesia's population problem has never involved an endorsement of birth control. The author analyzes Indonesia's economic dilemma and population control attitudes in terms of the country's socialist orientation and the place of transmigration, or inter-island migration, in development planning and policy. Discussed are Java's ever-increasing population pressure, possible effective alternatives for the Indonesian government, and some of the social costs connected to the realization of a population control policy in the country. The nature and problems of birth control campaigns in developing nations are viewed in relation to what is being and can be done in Indonesia. The precedents set by other socialist countries applying population control policies to aid efforts toward economic development are described briefly, and the author concludes that, while a program of population control seems inevitable for Indonesia, a nation-wide birth control campaign may have to take second place at present to the improvement of such pressing problems as education and general social development.

Policies on fertility and family size

2152 Singarimbun, Masri, "Family Planning in Indonesia," Bull. Indonesian Econ. Stud.,No. 10, June 1968, pp. 48-55.

Summary of three reports prepared in 1967 and 1968 under auspices of the Indonesian Planned Parenthood Federation on background, activities, and prospects of a national program.

MALAYSIA

Policies on fertility and family size

2153 Cho, Lee-Jay, et al. "Recent Fertility Trends in West Malaysia," Demography 5(2):732-44, 1968.

A statistical study of the decline in fertility underway in Malaysia indicates a significant decrease in urban areas and a likely continuation of this trend as the country undergoes further development and modernization. Malaysia's new National Family Planning Board program is increasingly making contraceptive methods available to the public. Other conditions favorable to fertility decline seem to be present. In fact, West Malaysia seems to meet most of Freedman's "conditions for fertility decline " (i.e., social development, high literacy rate, mortality decline, preference for smaller families). The effects of changes in the age structure, changes in the proportion married, and differences in race on fertility are also examined.

2154 Razak bin Hussein, Tun Abdul, "Government Policy on Birth Control in Malaysia," Kajian Ekonomi Malaysia: J. Econ. Assn. Malaysia 3:3-6, June 1966.

2155 Siraj, M. "Recent Changes in the Administration of Muslim Family Law in Malaysia and Singapore," Internat. Comparative Law Quart. 17:221-32, January 1968.

There is a variety of enactments but since 1952 there has been an attempt to follow a model form of legislation. The enactments deal mainly with the administration of Muslim law. No attempt has been made, except in Sarawak, to codify the Muslim law or to affect legislative changes in it. This paper examines the changes in administration in the Muslim law relating to polygamy, divorce, arbitration in family disputes and related matters.

PHILIPPINES

General population policies

2156 Aromin, Basilio B. "Considerations for a Philippine Population Policy," Philippine Statistician 12(4):122-44, December 1963.

The Philippines should consider seriously and no longer hesitate in formulating a national policy to control population growth. Sections: The scope of a national population policy; research measures; political measures; educational measures; economic measures; parental measures; what method of fertility control should be used; conclusion.

2157 Philippine-United States Agricultural Mission. Report of the Philippine-United States Agricultural Mission. U.S. Office of Foreign Agricultural Relations. I.A.C. Series, No. 3. Washington, 1947. iv, 50 pp.

The historical and high present rate of population increase is noted, but the most effective means for preparing for an increased population that are considered include only more efficient use of present agricultural lands, development of new lands, and greater industrialization. Levels and trends in fertility are not mentioned.

Policies on fertility and family size

2158 Juco, Jorge M. "Some Legal Aspects of Chinese Marriages in the Philippines," Philippine Sociol. Rev. 14(1):57-58, January 1966.

When a Chinese national living in the Philippines desires to marry, the law of the Conflicts Rules of Philippine Private International Law must be applied. According to this law marriage as a status is governed not by the law of domicile but by the law of nationality. The six requisites for a valid marriage according to the Civil Code are enumerated. Generally, aliens must be married in accordance with their national law. However, they may choose to do so under Philippine legal requirements, although they may not be recognized as validly married by the law of their nationality. Their national law governs them even while they are residing in the Philippines in so far as their civil status is concerned.

2159 Madigan, Francis, C.J. "Population Pressures in the Philippines and Some Ethical Aspects of Government Planning," Philippine Statistician 11(2):68-96, June 1962.

Discussion of recent population growth in the Philippines and particularly Cagayan de Oro City and Misamis Oriental Province. Presentation of a Catholic view of policy on fertility control.

2160 Philippines (Republic), Laws, Statutes, etc. Persons and Family Relations. P.C.F., 1952. 13 pp. (processed).

SINGAPORE

Policies on fertility and family size

2161 Djamour, Judith, The Muslim Matrimonial Court in Singapore. London: Athlone Press, 1966. 191 pp.

The efforts to reform the rules of the Malay Muslims resulted in the suppression of polygamy, the introduction of occidental concepts in Malay law, and the creation in 1958 of the Court of Matrimonial Justice in Singapore. Since then the rate of divorce has accelerated. In 1962 it reached 20 per cent of the marriages.

2162 Green, L.C. "Medico-Legal Aspects of Sterilisation," Singapore Med. J. 4:98-112, September 1963.

2163 Singapore Family Planning Association: Twelfth Annual Report. Singapore: 1961. 48 pp.

Report of the Singapore Family Planning Association which shows increasing acceptance of its work after a slow start. The government of Singapore assists the Association by an annual grant. The government's Maternal and Child Health Clinics now include family planning education which complements the work of the Association. A major family planning campaign was conducted by the government in 1960. As a result total clinic attendance increased from 37,965 to 43,974. The Singapore birth rate has dropped from 42.7 in 1957 to 35.5 in 1961. Opposition to family limitation has decreased, partly because the rhythm method, acceptable to certain religious groups, is advocated. The rate of natural increase for the first time in the postwar years dropped to below 3% in 1961. A further decline to 1.5% is deemed essential.

2164 Stockwin, Harvey, "Family Planning," Far Eastern Econ. Rev. 50(6):282-83, November 1965.

Summary of White Paper issued by the Government of Singapore.

2165 Wolfers, D. "The Demographic Effects of a Contraceptive Programme," Popul. Stud. 23:111-40, March 1969.

The author outlines the serious problems involved in the use of past marital fertility rates for the prediction of future potential fertility when calculating the demographic effects of a contraceptive program and presents a new method of calculating such effects, with illustrative data from the Singapore post-partum program at the Kandang Kerbau Hospital. The new method is based on the concept of a 'reproductive unit' of time or the interval between successive recurrences of the same stage of a woman's reproductive cycle, i.e., the interval between conception and conception, delivery and delivery, resumption of a post-partum fecundity between one birth and the next. It is assumed that if a woman uses contraception effectively for a period equal to this unit, a birth is prevented. If she uses it for a proportion of this unit, the probability of a birth being prevented is equal to this proportion. The total period of effective contraceptive use can thus be expressed in terms of reproductive units. Factors taken into consideration include differential fertility between races and ages; the different fertility expectations of women accustomed to using contraception and those who have never used it; differential continuation rates between races and ages; and post-partum infecundity. Results were calculated for two alternative purposes: to determine the total births averted by contraceptive use in the program in isolation and to determine the total births averted after taking into account the probability that respondents in the program might have adopted contraception had the program not come into being.

2166 Wolfers, D. "Evaluation Criteria for a National Family Planning Program," Amer. J. Pub. Health 58(8):1447-51, August 1968.

The expected monthly birth rates in Singapore for the next five years are projected on the assumptions (a) that age specific fertility rates for 1965 will persist unchanged and (b) that the decline in fertility for 1961 to 1965 will continue at the same rate. Actual registered births are observed to be almost identical with projection (b), until twelve months after the commencement in January 1966 of a government family planning program, at which point a sharp downward departure took place. A projection based on the average rate of fertility decline over the last five years would lead to a crude birth rate in 1970 of 25.6; the present rate of decline will have to be approximately doubled to achieve the government's objective of a reduction in crude birth rate to 20 per 1000 in five years.

2167 Wolfers, D. "The Singapore Family Planning Programme: Further Evaluation Data," Paper Presented at the International Union for the Scientific Study of Population, General Conference, 3-11 September 1969.

The first three years of operation of a form of evaluation of the Singapore Government Family Planning Programme are presented. During this period, overall fertility has declined by 23.1% from the 1965 level and 25,400 births have been 'saved'. The decline amongst citizens of the two major minority ethnic groups has been ever higher, of the order of 30%. It is suggested that the method employed provides a basis for apportioning the 'credit' for fertility decline between a family planning programme and the elements of continuous change which may affect fertility behaviour in developing societies. On this basis a little less than 50% of the observed decline appears to be the direct result of additional family planning activity initiated by the Government of Singapore after January 1966.

THAILAND

General population policies

2168 Gille, Halvor, and Balfour, Marshall C. "National Seminar on Population Problems of Thailand: Conclusions of the Seminar," Stud. Fam. Planning No. 4, August 1964. pp. 1-5.

At the concluding session of the Seminar, the question of population policy was discussed under the heading "Does Thailand Need a Population Policy?" Population policy means governmental measures with the aim of affecting population trends. Many types of population policy exist, not only designed to affect fertility but equally well to influence the level of mortality and movement of people from one area of the nation to another. In those terms, it may be agreed that Thailand needs and has a population policy. There are health measures which have greatly affected mortality and thereby the rate of population growth. There are, also, land settlement schemes, industrialization programs, and regional planning, for example, for the Northeast of Thailand. There are measures intended to affect--in many cases, to promote, while in other cases to prevent--population movements from one area of the country to another. With regard to measures to affect the level of fertility, it may even be agreed here that Thailand does need a population policy.

2169 Mintrakinetra, Bancha, "Population Policy," pp. 381-87 in: Thailand, National Research Council, National Seminar on Population Problems of Thailand. Bangkok, 1963.

2170 Raengkham, Thawee, "Does Thailand Need a Population Policy?" pp. 325-44 in: Thailand, National Research Council, National Seminar on Population Problems of Thailand. Bangkok, 1963.

2171 Virawan, Amnuey, "Does Thailand Need a Population Policy?" pp. 345-54 in: Thailand, National Research Council, National Seminar on Population Problems of Thailand. Bangkok, 1963.

2172 Asavasena, Winich, et al. "Family Planning in Thailand: Its Development and Achievement," pp. 335-41 in: Thailand, National Research Council, National Seminar on Population Problems of Thailand, Bangkok, 11-14 October 1965.

2173 Glass, David V. "Notes on the Establishment of a Family Planning Programme," pp. 389-400 in: Thailand, National Research Council, National Seminar on Population Problems of Thailand, Bangkok, 11-14 October 1965.

2174 Hamburger, Ludwig, "Fragmentierte Gesellschaft. Die Strukter Der Thail-Familie " [Fragmented Society: The Structure of the Thai-Family], Koelner Z. Soziol. Soz-Psychol. 17(1):49-72, 1965.

A detailed study of the Thai family structure as the opposite extreme of the pluralist society of the West. The Thai family is a loose accumulation of husbands and blood relatives without cohesion, less firmly constructed even than the modern family of western Europe or the U.S.A. Noted are: the lack of cohesive institutions; the vague family identity; the vague family membership (no clear line between in-wedlock and out-of-wedlock offspring). Polygamy is legal and occurs frequently, marriage is easily formed, without formal ties and religious sanction, and is equally easily dissolved. The historic Thai concept of marriage is that of a relationship for an indeterminate, not necessarily or preferably life-long time span. It is stated that there are no strong ties between parents and children or between related families. There is no tribal identification or sense of family tradition. This loose structure of the family is found to produce a regrettable fragmentation of the Thai society, which has not created any forces or institutions to check, discipline or compensate for these effects. The government is the only apparatus which holds the society together. In contrast to this disintegrated social structure, western society is held up as a system which neutralizes the forces of social fragmentation through rational cohesion and replaces family association with organizational association.

2175 Peng, Jui-Yun, et al. "A Pilot Programme for Family Planning in Thailand: Review of One Year of Operation in Potharam, 1964-65," Parts 1 and 2 Med. Gynaec. and Sociol. 2(7):5-8 and 2(8):7-15, 1967.

Part 1 describes the organization and administration of the family planning program at Potharam, a rural district about 60 miles from Bangkok, undertaken in 1964 by the Government of Thailand with support by the Population Council. Part 2 summarizes findings of a baseline study designed to gather demographic data and information about knowledge, attitudes, and practices in the area of fertility control.

2176 Prachuabmoh, Visid, and Fawcett, James T. "Fertility Control in Rural Thailand: Some Results of Demonstration Project in Potharam District," pp. 492-500 in: International Union for the Scientific Study of Population, Contributed Papers, Sydney Conference, Australia, 21 to 25 August 1967.

Potharam District which is about 60 miles west of Bangkok was the site of surveys on family planning in 1964, 1965 and 1967. Over time there is an increasing knowledge, acceptance and practice of birth control but the fertility rate has not significantly changed.

2177 Smythe, Hugh H. and Sasidhorn, Nibondh, "Population Control in Thailand through Family Sterilization," Amer. J. Econ. Sociol. 24(3):301-6, July 1965.

The Thai government's seminar on population problems, especially family planning, held in 1963, found that contrary to popular belief religion was no bar to the institution of preventive measures to reduce the increasing birthrate. The analysis was based on female sterilization data collected from a sample of 1,908 cases of females operated on at a Bangkok hospital, which showed that there had been an almost uninterrupted increase in the operation since 1957, with more females coming to the hospital for delivery so that the operation could be performed after having the last baby. Females ranged in age from 20 to 40 plus. The majority already had five to six living offspring with three having two and twenty-four having nine to ten. They had been married 3-15 years and monthly earnings averaged $25-50. Husband's occupations were largely reported as laborers, government officials and farmers. Few sterilized females were Catholic or Muslim and most professed to be Buddhists. Females of Chinese extraction were more in favor of sterilization than others. The project aimed at development of a family planning program.

VIETNAM

Policies on fertility and family size

2178 Faurillou, R. "Les Allocations Familiales dans le Sud-Viet Nam " [Family Allowances in South Viet Nam], Bull. Economique de l'Indochine 52(9):300-1, September 1949.

By Decree 268-3099 of September 26, 1947, family allowances were instituted for European employees and Indo-Chinese in industrial and commercial enterprises and the professions. Decree 868 MI/P3 of February 18, 1948, confirmed provisions for South Viet Nam.

2179 International Labour Office, "Family Allowances in Viet-Nam," Industry and Labour 10(6):247-49, 15 September 1953.

The family allowance scheme for workers and salaried employees in private undertakings, which was introduced in Viet-Nam on 26 September 1947, has been completely organized by Ordinance No. 2, on 20 January 1953. Allowances are payable in respect of the following persons: legitimate of chief wife not gainfully employed and dependent children up to the age of 16 years, or 21 years if still in school or unemployable. In addition, the allowance is payable up to the age of 21 years in the case of a female child who devotes herself to household work and looks after at least two children under 10 years of age and dependent on the beneficiary, provided that the beneficiary's spouse is absent or disabled. Family allowances are calculated as a percentage of the basic wage in a given occupation. The rates applicable are: 15 percent for a legitimate or chief wife; 6 percent for every dependent child up to and including the fifth; and 3 percent for every dependent child in excess of five. These are minimum figures. More favorable bases may be adopted by decision of the equalization funds or through collective bargaining. In addition, the equalization funds may grant workers supplementary allowances or increases above those fixed.

(South Asia: South-West Asia)

GENERAL

Policies on fertility and family size

2180 Pettengill, R.B. "Population Control to Accelerate Economic Progress in the Middle East," pp. 79-97 in: Economic Research Institute, American University of Beirut, Middle East Economic Papers, 1961. Daral-Kitab, Lebanon, 1961.

2181 Skaist, Aaron J. "Studies in Ancient Mesopotamian Family Law Pertaining to Marriage and Divorce," Dissertation Abstr. 24:1587-88, 1964. Abstract of Ph.D. Thesis, University of Pennsylvania, 1963. 195 pp.

From the beginning of the third millennium through the middle of the first millennium B.C., the legal literature of all the diverse peoples of the ancient Near East had in common the use of the cuneiform script, the Akkadian language and a similar style of legal document. All of these features however, pertain only to the external form of the laws. In this study one aspect of the laws of the peoples of the ancient Near East namely, the marriage laws, is examined in order to determine if there exists any uniformity in the contents of the laws corresponding to the uniformity in their form. The conclusion is that no single form of marriage existed for the entire ancient Near East. Instead it appears two major traditions co-existed, each within a clearly definable geographic area. This geographic split corresponds closely to the geographic division between the areas dominated in the third millennium by the Sumerians and the Semites respectively.

ISRAEL

Policies on fertility and family size

2182 Bachi, Roberto, and Matras, Judah, "Contraception and Induced Abortions among Jewish Maternity Cases in Israel," Milbank Memorial Fund Quart. 40:206-29, April 1962.

Post-partum interviews were conducted with 3,006 Jewish maternity cases from August 1959 to March 1960. Prior to the present pregnancy, forty-one per cent had used contraception and ten per cent had had an induced abortion. Characteristics of contraceptors and abortees are considered along with their degree of religious observance and place of birth.

2183 Cohen, Gerda L. "Family Planning in Israel," Midstream 12:49-54, June - July 1966.

2184 Halevi, H.S. "The Incidence of Abortion Among Jewish Women in Israel," Amer. J. Pub. Health, May 1958.

Abortion rates, drawn from figures on abortions reported in national hospital statistics, are described for Israeli women and compared by country of origin. During the period 1952-53, the national abortion rate was 150:1000, with rates of 286:1000 for women born in Israel, 189:1000 for women born in Europe and America, and 84:1000 for women born in Asia and Africa. The rates for Asian and African women were compared with length of stay in Israel and it was found that these rates were lower than those for recently arrived immigrants. Induced and spontaneous abortions were not separated in the statistics on hospital admissions, although induced abortions account for a number of admissions.

2185 International Labour Office, "Family Allowances in Israel," Industry and Labour 22(8-9):293-95, 1 November 1959.

Summary of provisions of the amendment of August 3, 1959, to the National Insurance Law of November 18, 1953, for the purpose of setting up allowances for families with four or more children under age 14.

2186 Scheftelowicz, Erwin Elchanan, Jewish Law of Family and Inheritance and Its Application in Palestine. Tel-Aviv: The Author, 1948.

2187 Weisel, D. von. "Legal Consequences of Artificial Insemination," Harefuah 56(7):178-81, 1 April 1959.

LEBANON

Policies on fertility and family size

2188 Asmar, G. [Abortion], J. Med. Lebanon 16:51-ff., 1963.

Any form of induced abortion is forbidden according to Lebanon's Penal Code, and the penalties for such abortions are varied. They depend on whether there is consent from the women for the performance of the abortion, whether there are complications after the abortion, and who performed the abortion -- the women herself, a member of the medical profession, or a third party. Since there is no specific mention in the Penal Code of regulations pertaining to therapeutic abortion, its legal status remains unclear although "reasons of honor" is listed as appropriate cause for sentence mitigation. Single women are, however, not covered by this provision.

2189 Khalaf, Samin, Prostitution in a Changing Society: A Sociological Survey of Legal Prostitution in Beirut. Beirut: Khayats Booksellers and Publishers, 1965. xiv, 163 pp.

2190 Yaukey, David, "Differential Fertility in Lebanon," pp. 125-40, Chpt. in: Kiser, C.V. , ed. Research in Family Planning. Princeton: Princeton University Press, 1962. xvi, 664 pp.

In 1959, about 900 Lebanese females were interviewed about their fertility histories, social backgrounds, fertility-determining behaviors, and attitudes on family size and birth control. The purposive sample included extremes on rural/urban residence and socio-economic status, and included all major Christian and Moslem sects in Lebanon.

SYRIA

Policies on fertility and family size

2191 International Labour Office, "Family Allowances for Civil Servants in Syria," Industry and Labour 8(4):205, August 15, 1952.

Legislative decree No. 146 of 28 February 1952 provides family allowances for civil servants. Family members covered include: the wife, if not herself a civil servant; sons under 18 years of age; sons completing their schooling who are less than 21 years old if in secondary school or less than 26 years old if in a college or university; invalid sons of all ages; unmarried daughters who are not working; divorced or widowed daughters who are without means and dependent on their father. Legitimized natural and adopted children are included. The amount paid varies with the salary grade of the employee.

2192 Syria. "Venereal Disease: Pre-Marital Examinations," Internat. Digest Health Legis. 6:352, 1955.

Legislative Decree No. 34 of 3 March 1953 prohibits the services of the Ministry of Health and Public Assistance from approving reports of pre-marital medical examinations until they are satisfied that a blood examination of the parties concerned has shown them to be free from syphilis.

TURKEY

General population policies

2193 Fisek, N.H. "The Population Policy of Turkey," Paper presented at the International Union for the Scientific Study of Population, General Conference, 3-11 September 1969, London.

A historical review of the reasons why Turkey shifted from a policy of encouraging population to one of discouraging population. Attitudes of political parties are noted.

2194 Turkey State Planning Organization, Development Plan, First Five Years (1963-1967). 1965 Annual Program. Ankara, 1964. 405 pp.

Part 2, Problems related to social structure, has subsections: Population policy; Employment and manpower; Labor and labor problems; Workers employed in foreign countries. pp. 19-27.

2195 Turkey State Planning Organization, First Five Year Development Plan, 1963-1967. 1964 Annual Program. Ankara, 1963. xv, 263 pp.

Part 3, Problems related to social structure, has sections: Population policy; Employment and manpower; Labor and labor problems; Social security.

Policies on fertility and family size

2196 Aral, Namik Z. "The Population Problem in Turkey," Turkish Econ. Rev. 4(6):12-15, September 1963.

Observations on proposals for liberalizing Turkish laws that prohibit the dissemination of contraceptive aids and information.

2197 Berelson, Bernard, "Turkey: National Survey on Population," Stud. Fam. Planning No. 5, December 1964 ,pp. 1-5.

This report, the first of its kind in Turkey, contains findings which have important implications for the development of Turkey's population policy and population program.

2198 Cillov, H. "Attitudes on Family Planning in Turkey," pp. 483-91 in: International Union for the Scientific Study of Population, Contributed Papers. Sydney Conference, Australia, 21 to 25 August 1967.

The danger to Turkey is not overpopulation but the rapid rate of increase. The family planning program is going to attempt to slow down the high rate of increase, given the liberal attitude of the public.

2199 Fisek, Nusret H., and Shorter, Frederic C. "Fertility Control in Turkey," Demography 5(2):578-89, 1968.

The results of some recent studies relating to fertility control carried out by different researchers on Turkey are presented. A general fertility decline, accompanied by major fertility differences among regions which correlate well with socioeconomic and literacy indices is noted. The sale and use of contraceptives and family planning programs since 1965 and the general background of educational and economic development in Turkey may be supportive of an acceleration of the fertility decline in the future. Turkey's government initiated IUD program is discussed with reference to the goals for family planning set in the Second Five-Year Plan.

2200 Shorter, Frederic C. "Information on Fertility, Mortality and Population Growth in Turkey," Popul. Index 34(1):3-21, January - March 1968.

Study refers to the demographic situation in Turkey from 1960 to 1965 as shown by the 1960 Census and recent surveys. By these sources it is estimated that the rates for births, general mortality, and infant mortality, respectively, are 43, 16 and 155 per 1000 population and the expectation of life at birth is 60.3, 57, and 52.2 years for metropolitan, urban, and rural residences, respectively. The population increased from 16,158,000 in 1935 to 31,190,000 in 1965. But the rate of increase declined from 2.85 in 1955-60 to 2.46. The expectation is that birth rates will decline as a result of new policies on contraceptives and abortions, as described.

2201 Stirling, P. "Land, Marriage, and the Law in Turkish Villages," Internat. Soc. Sci. Bull. 9(1):20-33, 1957.

The informal system of social control (morality, custom, etiquette, etc.) is more fundamental to society than the formal legal system of the State (law): (1) it is indispensable to societal continuance; (2) it controls the bulk of everyday activities; and (3) it may make formal law unenforceable. Field work of several months in 1949 and 1952 in two villages of central Turkey provides the author with the knowledge that a number of factors makes the application of the existing laws concerning the inheritance and sale of land very difficult even though the laws are in theory roughly consistent with the informal rules. Since the villagers do not usually bring their disputes concerning the transfer of land to the courts, the formal legal system is relatively irrelevant. Registration of marriage is a legal necessity in Turkey. Though more than half of the marriages are unregistered, they are marriages in all but a legal sense. Some couples separate without obtaining a legal divorce and marry again. Polygamy is not allowed. Only three or four cases seemed to be in each village and in none of these cases did a man have more than two wives. In general, the new laws regarding marriage are in conflict with the informal rules and so are ignored. To be effective a legal system dare not introduce new laws totally or extensively inconsistent with the existing informal system. Social reform through legislative means is not attainable by drastic, wholesale changes ordered by fiat.

2202 Stycos, J. Mayone, "The Potential Role of Turkish Village Opinion Leaders in a Program of Family Planning," Pub. Opin. Quart. 29(1):120-30, Spring 1965.

Results of an extensive public opinion survey regarding probable reactions of Turkish couples to a government program of family planning sponsored by the Research and Measurement Bureau of the Turkish Ministry of Education are reported. The usefulness of mass media and local political and spiritual leaders in such a program was also assessed. 2,744 wives and 2,373 husbands were interviewed in a national sample of households containing a married female aged 20-45. Results show a favorable motivational base on which a family planning program could be built with over 66% desiring a government sponsored birth control program. Public opinion on this subject, however, does not yet exist, and opinions are not especially firm. Since the political (muhtar) and religious (imam) leaders of each village will play a central role in the creation and direction of public opinion regarding any family planning program, an extensive study was made of their opinions regarding change, progress, and family planning. Muhtars and Imams, highly esteemed by the villagers, have attitudes very similar to those of the average villager. Muhtars are the more highly regarded, and are somewhat more favorable to birth control, but few Imams are opposed to a government sponsored program. Professional sources (medical) and authoritative mass media channels seem more influential than local leaders. The program must be carefully planned, for the attitudes of the people toward birth control and family planning are fairly unstable and a poorly contrived educational campaign could turn the villagers against family planning as easily as a well planned campaign could turn them toward it.

2203 Timur, H. "Civil Marriage in Turkey: Difficulties, Causes and Remedies," Internat. Soc. Sci. Bull. 9(1):34-36, 1957.

The adoption of the Swiss Civil Code in Turkey was most remarkable in the aspect of its inclusion of a new system of family law. Available statistics prove that at the present time there are many couples living as man and wife who were never married as prescribed by the Civil Code. The reasons for this are: the cumbersome formalities of a civil marriage, old habits associated with postponing military service and evading the road tax, difficulties associated with the required physical examination, the loss of pension rights to widows and daughters upon marriage, the desire for more solemnity in the marriage service, and the poor communication facilities in some sections of the country. The administration of the family law needs reform to accelerate the acceptance of civil marriage by the people.

2204 Turkey. "Family Planning and Interruption of Pregnancy," *Internat. Digest Health Legis.* 17:985-87, 1966.

Law No. 557 of 1 January 1965 establishes the right of each individual to have the number of children he desires and to procreate at the time of his choice. The right may be exercised solely by the use of contraceptive methods. Abortion and sterilization operations are prohibited except where the life of the mother is endangered by the pregnancy or where there is a high probability of defective offspring. Penalties are provided for the manufacture, sale or distribution of contraceptives which have not been approved by the Ministry of Health and Social Welfare.

2205 Turkey. "Sickness and Maternity Insurance Act," *Resmi Gazete* (Official Gazette) No. 7402, 10 January 1950.

Maternity benefits for an insured woman or the uninsured wife of an insured man shall consist of: ante-natal examinations; medical assistance at confinement; cash allowance for nursing assistance; and payment of compensation to the insured woman for the period of absence from employment before and after confinement.

VI OCEANIA

(General)

General population policies

2206 Karmel, P.H. Population and Policy. Economic Society of Australia and New Zealand, 1949. 23 pp.

A summary of past trends, a review of the present demographic situation in various areas, and an outline of policies.

2207 South Pacific Conference. Second Report by the Secretary-General, South Pacific Commission. Noumea: New Caledonia, 1953. iv, 100 pp.

Population in relation to resources, pp. 27-31. Resolutions on the establishment of demographic services as an aid to the formation of local policy.

(Australia and New Zealand)

AUSTRALIA

General population policies

2208 Australia. Committee of Economic Enquiry, Report of the Committee of Economic Enquiry. In 3 Vols. Canberra, 1965.

Terms of reference of the Committee of economic enquiry: Having in mind that the objectives of the [Australian] Government's economic policy are a high rate of economic and population growth with full employment, increasing productivity, rising standards of living, external viability, and stability of costs and prices, to enquire into and report its findings on the trends in population as a whole, in the work force, and in the distribution of the latter among various sections. Vol. 1. Chapters 1-17, 455 pp, contains the views of the Committee on its Terms of Reference. Chapter, Population and work force, pp. 63-91, has section, Conclusions about the desirable future rate of immigration. Vol. 2. Appendices A-N. 1195 pp., mimeographed. Sets out the more detailed studies the Committee has carried out on the Terms of Reference.

2209 Borrie, W.D. "Australian Population Policy and Its Relation to Asia," The Australian Outlook 4(3):162-69, September 1950.

Since it was believed by Australia's war-time Labour Government that the country required a much larger population than likely to accrue from the natural increase of the Australian-born parents, an immigration program was designed to achieve a constant intake of 70,000 new settlers per year, but which actually resulted in the arrival of a vast influx of immigrants -- double the original target figure -- from the United Kingdom and Europe. Discussed are the problems Australia must face if she is to continue to absorb settlers at such a rapid pace, with references to the difficulty of maintaining a population program over long periods of time, selective migration control, and finally, whether Australia, in employing selective control, would be preventing a solution to Asia's over-population. The author concludes with an analysis of Asia's population problems, and an assessment of Australia's role in a proposed international conference, composed of both white and non-white countries of Southeast Asian and Pacific zones, the purpose of which would be to discuss the demographic implications of current and future economic policies.

2210 Borrie, W.D. _Australian Population Policy and Its Relation to Demographic Problems in Asia_. New York: Institute of Pacific Relations, 1950. 34 pp.

2211 Borrie, W.D. _The Peopling of Australia_. Sydney: University of Sydney, 1958. 24 pp.

Reviews the history of governmental policy on population size and immigration, 1904-1958, in relation to observed growth trends and economic and social assimilation.

2212 Borrie, W.D. "Population Studies and Policy in Australia," _Internat. Soc. Sci. Bull._ 7(2):211-19, 1955.

Official policy. Population studies: official material; unofficial material. The current situation and the future. Assessment.

2213 Brown, R.G. "Social Policy in Australia," _Australian Quart._ 38:82-90, June 1966.

The implications of the Vernon Report (Australia, Committee on Economic Enquiry, _Report_, Canberra, 1965) for social policy-making and the responses of the Government and public to it are considered. The Government appears to have seen policy and variables primarily in economic terms, and the Committee to have accepted this view. Thus there is no comprehensive discussion of the social implications of the economic policies considered, although passing references are made to them. The response of the Government and public comment on the Report was against the development of explicit social policies.

2214 Downing,R.E., ed. "The Vernon Report: Review of the Report of the Committee of Economic Enquiry," Econ. Record 42(97):1-180.

Partial contents: Downing, R.E., Summary of the Report, pp. 1-12; Appleyard, R.T., Population and Work Force, pp. 46-58; Gruen, F.H., The Industrial Pattern the Rural Economy, pp. 79-84; Lydall, H.F., The Economy as a Whole: Policies for Growth, pp. 149-68.

2215 Holmes, MacDonald, "Land and Resources in the Pacific," Hawkesbury Agricultural College J. 40:110-12, August 31, 1943.

The thesis is that the densely populated nations of the world should retain their surplus population. Australia would remain sparsely populated, but would export food and raw materials.

Policies on fertility and family size

2216 "Abortion: Some Ethical and Legal Aspects," Med. J. Australia 1:359-ff., 1968.

Discussion centers on the uncertain status, both medical and legal, of induced abortion in Australia. The author emphasizes that any reform of the country's statutes dealing with abortion or clarification of the medical aspects of abortion must take into account the varying moral views on the issue.

2217 Australia. Commonwealth Bureau of Census and Statistics, Labour Report, 1944, No.34. Canberra: Government Printer, 1946. vi, 161 pp.

The section on "Child endowment," pp. 92-94, includes a brief historical resume and summary statistics, 1941-1945.

2218 Australia. Department of Labor and Industry, Australian Child Endowment Act, April 7, 1941. Sydney: Industrial Gazette, April, 1941.

2219 Australia. Laws, Statutes, Etc., Act Relating to Marriages of Australian Citizens, and Marriages of Members of the Defence Force. Outside Australia. (No. 31, Laws 1955).

2220 Australia. "Vital Statistics: Definitions of Birth and of Still-Birth," Internat. Digest Health Legis. 14:236, 239, 1963.

Act No. 6564 of 24 November 1959 and Act No. 34 of 6 November 1959 consolidate and amend the law relating to the registration of births, deaths and marriages. Legal definition of birth is defined as the complete expulsion or extraction from the mother of a product of conception, of at least 28 weeks gestation, and which afterwards breathed or showed any sign of life. Still-birth is similarly defined except that there is no sign of life; or where length of gestation is not easily ascertainable, it refers to an expelled fetus, dead at birth, which weighs at least two pounds twelve ounces.

2221 "Australian Statute Established Uniform Federal Law for Marital Actions," Harvard Law Rev. 74:424-27, December 1960.

Australian Matrimonial Causes Act of 1959 is a federal statute which supersedes the marital-action laws of the several states and establishes a uniform law for the whole of Australia. Section 8 preempts the states' powers to legislate concerning divorce, annulment, and matters of maintenance. Especially noteworthy features are the law's provisions aimed at saving marriages, which enable a trial judge to act as a conciliator and which authorize government subsidization and court use of marriage-guidance organizations.

2222 Bennett, J.M. "Establishment of Divorce Laws in New South Wales," Sydney Law Rev. 4:241-ff. March 1963.

2223 Beyrer, T.B. "Family Allowances in Australia," Internat. Soc. Security Assn. Bull. 14:45-60, January - February 1961.

2224 Craig, W.H., and Scott, N.F.C. "Maintenance of Concubines," Tasmanian University Law Rev. 1:685-ff. November 1962.

2225 Chambers, D.H. "Treatment of Sexual Offenders in Tasmania," Tasmanian University Law Rev. 1:98-ff. July 1958.

2226 Chappell, D.,and Wilson, P.R. "Public Attitudes to the Reform of the Law Relating to Abortion and Homosexuality," Australian Law J. 42:120, 175, August - September 1968.

2227 Cowen, Z. "Legitimacy, Legitimation and Bigamy: A Commentary on Attorney-General for Victoria v. Commonwealth of Australia [1962] 36 ALJR 104," Australian Law J. 36:239, January 1963.

2228 Davey, Constance M. Children and their Lawmakers: A Social-Historical Survey of the Growth and Development from 1836 to 1950 of South Australian Laws Relating to Children. Griffin, [1956]. xiii, 158 pp.

2229 Day, Alice Taylor, "Divorce Down Under [Australia]," Columbia University Forum 7:19-22, Spring 1964.

As compared with the United States, divorce has a lower incidence in general and occurs later in marriage in Australia. One possible cause might be the "climate" of divorce - its availability and acceptability. Liberal divorce laws cannot be said to cause marital discord, yet by making it easier to dissolve the marriage bond they do encourage the choice of divorce in preference to some other means of coping with marital problems. The laws of Australia are more liberal than those of some states and more stringent than those of other states in the United States. But, generally a longer "cooling off" period is required in Australia before the final decree is granted. Non-legal factors are also possible explanations of the low Australian divorce rate.

2230 Day, Lincoln H. "Patterns of Divorce in Australia and the United States," Amer. Sociol. Rev. 29:509-22. August 1964.

Australians resort to divorce less frequently than do Americans, and generally only after a much longer duration of marriage. This may arise from differences between the two countries in a) the availability of divorce in both existential and normative terms and b) the extent of and handling of marital disharmony. As compared with the general population at various durations of marriage, the divorced are more often childless and of lower fertility.

2231 Dowsett, Wolfred T. "Child Endowment and Income Tax Exemptions," Econ. Record 17(33):239-47, December 1941.

The Federal Child Endowment Act, introduced in the Australian Parliament on March 28 and passed soon after, provided an endowment of five shillings per week for all children but one, under sixteen years of age, regardless of the size of the family income. The cost was to be met by disallowing income tax exemption on eligible children, a pay-roll tax on higher-income brackets, and consolidated revenue. The purpose was to supplement the existing wage policy and indirectly to increase the population. This note compares the direct form of child endowment contemplated in the Act with the prevalent one of exemptions from income taxation for dependent children.

2232 Johnston, S.W. "Control of Human Fertility in Australia: Law and Policy," Med. J. Australia 1:72-ff., 1965.

Discusses abortion as means of fertility control in Australia. The author notes that the law prohibiting abortion is widely disregarded by the Australians, and that it should be repealed and replaced by a more liberal law more in accordance with public opinion.

2233 Medical Journal of Australia, "Therapeutic Abortion and the Law in Western Australia," Med. J. Australia 1(Supplement 2): 16-18, February 12,1966.

2234 Morris, J.H.C. "Australian Matrimonial Causes Act, 1959," Internat. Comparative Law Quart. 11:641-50, July 1962.

2235 Morton, F.D. "Reflections on Some Laws Affecting Conjugal and Family Life," Australian Law J. 31:231-ff., August 1957.

2236 Nygh, P.E. "Living 'Separate and Apart' as a Ground for Dissolution of Marriage in Australia," J. Fam. Law 6:219-29, Winter 1966.

The Australian Parliament in 1959 enacted legislation dealing with the breakdown of marriage. Specifically dealt with were separation by the parties, and the subsequent living apart as grounds for a decree of dissolution. A distinction arises between the American and Australian legislation in that in Australia the separation need not be voluntary on both sides. Some measure of physical separation is required under the law, the only question being one of degree. There are occasions where the petitioner's own conduct may thwart his relief: where it would be contrary to public interest to set that person free to remarry; where the petitioner approaches the court without "clean hands"; and where the petitioner had made reconciliation impossible by consistent misconduct during separation. This adaptation of American legislation and the resultant liberalization of the grounds for divorce has not resulted in an appreciable increase in divorce, as was feared by the statute's critics, but it allows the dissolution for a marriage where this evil is necessary.

2237 Ringwood, Pamela Elsie, "Some Aspects of Wife Desertion," Australian J. Soc. Issues 2(4):42-53, August 1966.

The usefulness of a study of wife desertion in relation to the general questions of marital relations and the law is noted. The exigencies of the deserted wife's situation -- the husband absent and often unavailable for negotiation, greater loss of social security than widowhood, less financial returns from insurance and property than in widowhood -- factors such as these sharply outline characteristics which are true to a lesser degree of family law in general. The proliferation of social and legal remedies is mentioned briefly and their varying aims and methods. The importance is stressed of both legal and social remedies being integrated to form a consistent or at the very least, a non-conflicting pattern of social pressure on the spouses and the family. Both the husband and wife in the present situation are subjected to pressures which pull both to and against reconciliation or even peaceful negotiation. Being human they cannot fit these conflicting pressures into well insulated compartments in their minds and personalities.

2238 Selby, D.M. "Development of Divorce Law in Australia," Modern Law Rev. 29(5):473-91, September 1966.

Little attention has been given to recent developments of matrimonial law in Australia. Since 1959 marriage failure evidenced by five years' separation has been a ground for divorce throughout the Commonwealth. That a common law system is perfectly capable of accommodating legislation for divorce without proof of "fault" has been previously demonstrated in New Zealand and, as the present article shows, has now been confirmed by the Australian experience. There are however some problems in administration of the divorce legislation.

2239 Selby, D.M. "The Federal Matrimonial Causes Bill," Australian Quart. 31:11-21, September 1959.

Proposed reform of the divorce laws.

2240 "Therapeutic Abortion," Med. J. Australia 1:273-ff., 1968.

Recent discussion centering on the 1967 British Abortion Act is reviewed. It is hoped that this review will aid Australia in evaluating its own laws on abortion and in reform of such laws should the need arise.

2241 "Therapeutic Abortion and the Law in Western Australia," Med. J. Australia (Supplement 2) I:16, 1966.

Western Australia's Criminal Code forbids any illegal attempt to induce an abortion whether a woman is pregnant or not pregnant. If, however, the abortion is performed on the grounds of preservation of the mother's life,it is not held to be a criminal act. Abortion performed to preserve the mother's health is not considered legal cause (also in Queensland), but in Australia's other states the laws on abortion may be interpreted more liberally since they do not include clauses pertaining to abortion only for preservation of the life of the mother.

NEW ZEALAND

General population policies

2242 International Labour Office, "Policy and Programmes: New Zealand," Migration 1(2):5-7, March - April 1952.

In 1952, New Zealand's Department of Labour and Employment set up a Cabinet Committee on Immigration to examine all aspects of immigration policy and administration. This article describes some of the problems of and decisions concerning immigrants to New Zealand, with mention of revision of selection criteria, child migration, immigration increases and the assimilation of refugees or non-British citizens and placement and accommodation of new immigrants.

2243 Tocker, A.H. "Population Policy in New Zealand and Elsewhere: A Review of Objectives," New Zealand Geographer 1(2):139-48, October 1945.

The author contends that nowhere is the widespread increase in the collection and use of statistics more apparent, or more valuable, than in the field of population. The growing science of demography now aims to provide a very comprehensive description of many aspects of population and of the changes occurring within them. After a brief discussion of the outstanding features of world population, such as the differences that exist in standards of living and the wide spread in density, the author examines the reasons behind wartime interest in population and the problems connected to projecting population trends. The bulk of the article is concerned with defining the objectives of population policy, primarily objectives of population increase. Included are sections on density and safety, 'optimum' population, and greater equality of distribution. The author concludes with a discussion of policy in New Zealand and the two alternatives the government has if an increase in population is to be effected: natural increase and migration increase.

Policies on fertility and family size

2244 Inglis, Brinsley D. *Family Law in New Zealand*. Wellington: Sweet, 1960. 662 pp.

2245 Inglis, Brinsley D. *Family Law in New Zealand: Supplement 1964* Wellington: Sweet, 1964.

2246 Inglis, Brinsley D. "Recent Developments in Family Law," *New Zealand Law J.* 966:38, 1 February 1966.

2247 Inglis, Brinsley D., and Mercer, A.G., eds. *Family Law Centenary Essays*. Wellington: Sweet, 1968. 153 pp.

A series of public lectures arranged by the Law faculty of Victoria University of Wellington to mark the hundredth anniversary of the passing of New Zealand's first statute on divorce.

2248 Moore, R.W. "Psychiatric and Legal Aspects of Therapeutic Abortion and Sterilization," *New Zealand Med. J.* 58:772-ff., 1959.

The author discusses the question of whether or not there exist psychiatric grounds for therapeutic abortion. She contends that those who argue against the validity of such grounds, who declare that pregnant women rarely commit suicide, must realize the variety of factors which must be considered for each therapeutic abortion case. They must recognize the necessity in certain cases and for good reasons of abortion on the basis of preserving the mother's future health. Socio-economic conditions or the close connection between mental instability of the mother and her external environment are important factors. In addition, the woman with heavy family responsibilities may, with the strain of an unwanted pregnancy, face strong psychiatric problems. It is concluded that with the above aspects of therapeutic abortion in mind, the law should include the use of psychiatric grounds as appropriate medical cause for termination of pregnancy.

2249 New Zealand. Department of External Affairs, _Memorandum of Reciprocal Arrangements Relating to Family Allowances in Northern Ireland and Family Benefits in New Zealand Made by the Ministry of Labour and National Insurance for Northern Ireland with the Consent of the Ministry of Finance for Northern Ireland of the One Part and the Ministry of Social Security in New Zealand of the Other Part_. Publication No. 71, Treaty Series 1949, No. 2. Wellington, 1949. 6 pp.

2250 New Zealand. Laws, Statutes, etc. _Act to Provide for the Payment of Family Benefits in Advance for Housing Purposes_. (No. 106, Laws 1958). Wellington, 1958.

2251 New Zealand. Laws, Statutes, etc. _Law of Adoption in New Zealand_. Wellington, 1952.

2252 Northey, J.F. "Artificial Insemination: A Legal View," _New Zealand Med. J._ 57(322):531-34, December 1958.

2253 Stichbury, P.C. "Therapeutic Abortion in Dunedin Hospital," _New Zealand Med. J._ 60:559-ff., 1961.

An analysis of the frequency and indications for therapeutic abortion over a ten year period at one New Zealand hospital. 80 cases were found in the hospital's records and, broken down into two five year intervals, psychiatric indications increased (12 to 23 cases) and medical indications decreased (6 to 2 cases for TB, 5 to 1 cases for kidney disease, 4 to 1 cases for cardiac disease). The total number of abortions decreased slightly in the second five year period (42 to 38). In order to standardize hospital records and insure equal treatment for all women wanting an abortion, the author recommends the institution of a committee review system for the hospital.

(Polynesia and Micronesia)

GENERAL

General population policies

2254 Sayers, C.E. "Second South Pacific Conference," South Pacific Commission Quart. Bull. 3(2):2-4, April 1953.

A summary of the proceedings, including a report on the session dealing with population pressures and possible solutions, such as birth control, migration, etc.

Policies on fertility and family size

2255 Vayda, Andrew P. "Love in Polynesian Atolls," Man 61:204-5, December 1961.

Two kinds of restrictions upon sexual freedom in Polynesian atolls are discussed: (1) incest tabus and (2) a requirement of 'decent' secrecy about sexual adventures and involvements. It seems warranted to conclude that in the case of those coral atolls with populations so small as to limit severely the number of possible sexual partners for any individual, the incest tabus must be regarded as constituting important restrictions on sexual freedom. In Rakahanga, a small atoll with a single village settlement, the practice observed for sexual concealment is motoro, which consists of the young man's stealthily entering the girl's house late at night when her parents or guardians are asleep. If a motoro visit is detected, the young man is often chased or perhaps beaten by the girl's father, and subject to the gossip and ridicule of the villagers.

WESTERN SAMOA

General population policies

2256 New Zealand. Department of Island Territories, Western Samoa Administered Under Trusteeship Agreement dated 13th December, 1946: Report for the Period of Nine Months from 1st April to 31st December 1950. Wellington, 1951. 76 pp.

The section on Population, pp. 3-4, states that recognition of the demographic situation lies behind all the plans of the Samoan government for economic and social advancement.

VII EUROPE

(General)

General population policies

2257 Cofresi, Emilio, [Demographic Policies in England, Sweden, France and Holland], Ministerie van Maatschappelijk Werk: Afdeling Maatschappelijk Opbouwwerk, Serie B. No. 53, The Hague, 1953. 27 pp.

The policies used have been either expansive, restrictive or a combination of both. The restrictive policies used are birth control and migration, while the expansive policies are family aids and industrialization. Due chiefly to her low birth rate and her need for manpower, France is using every available means to foster population growth. Holland is at the other extreme. With the highest density of population in continental Europe, she is trying to deal with her problem through migration and industrialization. Sweden's case is somewhat different, since she has plenty of land and a low density of population. Hence, she encourages both immigration and reproduction. However, for purely social and humanitarian reasons, she has a birth control program sponsored by the government. In England, again we meet an entirely different situation. Contrary to Sweden, England has a high density of population and a consequent scarcity of available land. Hence, migration and birth control are encouraged. Birth control advice, however, is given by the government only for health reasons. However, for social and humanitarian reasons, a program of family aid also exists -- side by side with the restrictive policies just mentioned.

2258 Digby, Margaret, "Agriculture in the Post-war European Settlement," Fabian Quart. 33:27-34, Spring 1942.

Relief of population pressure is held to be one of the most important aspects of post-war policies for European agriculture.

2259 Glass, David V. "Population Policies," J. Heredity 33(3): 107-12, March 1942.

A general resume of nineteenth century policies is followed by a description of the programs of population encouragement of the immediate pre-war period.

2260 Glass, David V. Population Policies and Movements in Europe. London: Frank Cass & Co., 1967. xvi, 490 pp.

A reprint of a 1940 edition. Eight chapters are preceded by an introduction to the 1967 reprint, a preface to the first edition and an introductory note. (1) Population Movements in England and Wales presents statistics on birth, death and fertility in these areas, discusses contraception and abortion in detail, and notes that the Population Statistics Act, which came into force in July, 1938, makes it possible to calculate accurate reproduction rates and analyze in detail changes in fertility. (2) Introduction to State Intervention traces government population policies from the time of Roman Emperor Augustus through the Middle Ages to the present. (3) France and Belgium, I, discusses the granting of family allowances as part of the official population policies in France and Belgium. (4) France and Belgium, II, examines the general population policies and monetary and non-monetary rewards for high fertility in France and Belgium over the course of history, and describes repressive and positive measures taken. (5) The Italian Struggle for Population deals with the fascist efforts to encourage population growth in Italy. (6) German Policy and the Birth Rate is concerned with the population changes in Germany from 1933 to 1940 and the German struggle to raise the birth rate which had been declining since about 1875. (7) Scandinavia and the Population Question discusses the decline in fertility in these countries and the measures taken by the government to combat it. (8) Nature and Consequences of Population Trends provides an overall summary and some theoretical considerations regarding the policy choice between a stationary population and a population which is allowed to fluctuate within certain defined limits. In most European countries, the population had been declining steadily since the nineteenth century. It is concluded that the implementation of measures to raise fertility will depend on political rather than economic questions.

2261 Heck, Bruno, "Werden die Familien Wirklich Immet Hilfsbedurftiger? Familienpolitik lst Soziale Strukturpolitik. Eine Notwendige Antwort an die Kritiker " [Is the Present-Day Family Becoming Increasingly Impoverished? Family Policy as Social Structure Policy. An Urgent Reply to Critics], Zeitschrift fur Sozialreform, No. 12, 1963. pp. 707-15.

This very general article states the necessity of establishing family policy which views the family as a "social-cultural personality" as well as a biological unit. It also states the need to adopt measures and programs (though nothing concrete is given here) which would ease family problems not by making families more dependent on aid, especially that from the state, but by making them more self-sufficient and by granting them the essential freedom to be able to develop materially and psychologically. Adjustments in income distribution must be made, but mainly, new concepts of the family as a social structural unit and of its accompanying needs must be reached in public thinking and official planning.

2262 International Labour Office, "The European Social Charter and International Labour Standards," Internat. Labour Rev. 84(5):354-75, November 1961.

Description of the background and provisions of the charter adopted at Turin, October 18, 1961, by representatives of the member states of the Council of Europe. Provisions include: the right of the family to social and economic protection; the right of migrant workers and their families to protection; and the application of the social charter to foreigners.

2263 Lindgren, Karl, "Perhekustannusten Tasauksen Taloudellisesta Merkityksesta " [The Economic Significance of the Equalization of Costs of Family Maintenance], Chapter in: Eripainos Vaestontutkimuksen Vuosikirjasta [Yearbook of Population Research in Finland]. Helsinki: Population Research Institute, 8:86-102, 1963/64.

An analysis of the significance of the equalization of the cost of family maintenance in some countries, mainly European, especially regarding the family but in part regarding the economy as a whole. A comparison of the benefits received by the family with the income of the family is made, based on the average wage per month paid by manufacturing industries. The findings show that the size of children's allowances varies greatly in different countries according to wages and number of children. There are countries in which the family allowances actually constitute some kind of family grant, the size of which is almost as big as the wage of the head of the family. This is the situation primarily in France and its neighboring countries, as well as in East European countries. As a rule, children's allowances grow in relation to the size of the family. Low wages and comparatively large family allowances are represented in the main by France and its neighboring countries. The equalization system for the cost of family maintenance is being taken into use in an increasing number of countries. Moreover, in more developed countries the current family policy support system has been expanded and improved. Generally, income redistribution in favor of the family maintenance has a tendency to increase the consumption of necessities and to decrease the consumption of luxury items. A consequence of the structural change in the consumption of necessities is in principle a rise in employment within the capital-dominated branches of industry. If family allowances were limited wholly or partially to payments made by employers, an even clearer influence would in this way be exerted on the labor market. Dependent upon the production structure of the country concerned, a change in consumption could also bring about an augmented demand for import goods, and thus extend its influences also to foreign trade and payment balances.

2264 Lorimer, Frank, "European Governmental Action Regarding Population," _Annals Amer. Acad. Polit. Soc. Sci._ 262:56-61, March 1949.

A survey of governmental policies and programs in various European countries with respect to family allowances, pronatalist programs, and emphasis upon qualitative aspects of population, particularly in their relation to migration policies.

2265 McCleary, G.F. "Pre-War European Population Policies," _Milbank Memor. Fund Quart._ 19(2):105-20, April 1941.

The main provisions of the pro-population policies in Belgium, France, Germany, Italy and Sweden are described as they actually operated before the outbreak of the war. The experiences of the European countries that have adopted population policies seems to support Malthus' conclusion that such measures 'when not mixed with religion... are seldom calculated to answer the end which they aim at.'

2266 Nation und Staat. "Die Bevolkerungspolitische Entwicklung: Nordschleswigs Seit dem Ende des Weltkrieges " [The Development of Population Policy: North Schleswig Since the End of the World War...], (Erhebung des Amts fur Bevolkerungspolitische Fragen der NSDAP) <u>Nation und Staat</u> 15(1):9-15, October 1941.

A short history is presented of the population fluctuation among the Danes and the Germans in the Schleswig area between 1920 (when it was granted to Denmark) and 1941. Rather than outlining any population policies, the article attempts to show that the situation for the German part of the Schleswig population has been unfavorable and as yet unsolved by Denmark, and that many Germans in that area have no citizenship and do not know to which state they belong. As a conclusion, a demand is made that the Schleswig Germans and the area itself be legally and politically incorporated into the German Reich.

2267 Organski, A.F.K. "Population and Politics in Europe," <u>Science</u> 133(3467):1803-7, 1961.

The relationship between population and politics in Europe is of long standing. In the laissez-faire century before World War I, demographic trends influenced European power but political developments had little effect on demographic trends. Immense population growth, unplanned and uncontrolled, was crucial in making Europeans first in power in the world. In the 20th century, the relationship between population and politics has changed. Politics tries to influence demographic trends. But few nations have been successful in adopting a coherent population policy.

2268 Ramneantu, Petru, "Masuri de Politica Demografica si Politica Demografica Totalitara " [Measures of Demographic Policy and Totalitarian Demographic Policy], <u>Buletin Eugenic si Biopolitik</u> 11(1-2-3):29-52, January - March 1940.

Measures discussed include those to reduce mortality, prevent excessive urbanization, adapt density to means of subsistence, increase fertility, and increase the superior and eliminate those with hereditary defect. The demographic policies of France, Belgium, Latvia, Germany, and Italy are analyzed.

2269 Sauvy, Alfred, "Problemes de Population en Communaute Europeenne " [Population Problems in the European Community], Riv. Polit. Econom. 50(3):467-80, March 1959. Italian text, pp. 481-92.

Discussion of the relevance of neo-Malthusianism, the prospects for large-scale migration, the economic burden of the inactive population, and implications of community organization for the members' social security systems.

2270 Stamper, A. [Population Policies in Various European Countries], Lijecnicki Vjesnik 62:559-62, November 1940.

2271 Vaestopoliittisen Tutkimuslaitoksen Julkaisuja. Eripainos Vaestoliiton Vuosikirjasta II. Vaestopolitiikkamme Uusia Muotoja Etsimassa [Finnish Population Association Year Book II. Our Population Policy Looking for New Forms of Activity]. Helsinki, 1948.

The following articles are included: Sukselainen, V.J. [The Child Subsidy System in Finland]; Nieminen, Armas [Origin of a General Child Subsidy System in Sweden and Norway]; Lento, Reino [On the French and Belgian Family Wage Systems]; Nieminen, Armas [Some Features of the Development of Family Wages in Switzerland]; Lento, Reino [What is Demography?]; Lento, Reino [Demographic Research Work and Institutions Engaged in It in Finland and Elsewhere]; Nieminen, Armas [What is the Effect on the Development of Families of the Present Tendency to Urban Expansion?; American Sociological Research into Families]; Von Hertzen, Heikki [Main Trends of Our Population Policy, 1946-1948]; Nykanen, Helmi [Finnish Literature on the Population Problem, Family and Marriage, 1941-1947]; Lento, Reino [On the Migration Movement and Its Causes in Certain Communes of the County of Kuopio, Finland, 1921-1944]; and Nieminen, Armas [On Large Families in the County of Kuopio, Finland Their Housing Conditions, etc.. Comparative Statistical Report].

Policies on fertility and family size

2272 Association des Caisses d'Allocations Familiales, Journees Internationales d'Etudes sur les Prestations Familiales; Communications et Discussions. [International Study Conference on Family Allowances; Papers and Discussions]. Bruxelles: 1952. 237 pp.

2273 Breitenecker, L., and Breitenecker, R. "Abortion in Germanic Lands," in Smith, D.T. Abortion and the Law. Cleveland: Western Reserve University Press, 1967.

Describes the legal status of abortion in Austria, West and East Germany. Austrian law currently forbids abortion except when a danger to the life or health of a pregnant woman exists. A more liberal law is under consideration which would permit abortion if it is performed to avert present danger to life or prolonged damage to health which cannot otherwise be averted. Judgment of this condition would be based upon consideration of the woman's living conditions and her physical and emotional state. The German Criminal Code of 1871 forbids all abortion. A proposed reform of this Code would permit abortion on medical and ethical indications. In 1947, the East German Code provided very liberal medical, socio-medical, ethical and eugenic indications for induced abortion. With improved economic and social conditions in 1950, abortion was restricted to limited medical and eugenic indications. Abortions are performed only with the consent of a commission consisting of physicians, health department representatives, and members of the Democratic Women's League. In Switzerland, abortions may be performed only to prevent danger to the life and health of pregnant women. The law requires the written consent of the woman, the opinion of a second consulting physician, and that the doctor reports the abortion within 24 hours of the operation. Interpretation of the medical indication is considered to be very liberal. Punishment is mitigated if the pregnancy is interrupted because of some emergency.

2274 Darby, Peter, "Legal Abortion," New Society 4(98):16-18, 13 August 1964.

Following a discussion of the consequences of Great Britain's anti-abortion law, experiences of such nations as Sweden and Eastern European countries which have legalized abortion are dealt with. These experiences are seen to be positive, and it is suggested that critics of legalized abortion exaggerate both the physical and psychological consequences of the operation.

2275 Gebauer, Siegfried, Familie und Staat: Handbuch zur Familienpolitik in Europa [The Family and the State: Handbook on Family Policy in Europe]. Heidelberg: Impuls Verlag Heinz Moos, 1961. 144 pp.

2276 Gille, Halvor, "Family Limitation in Europe," Paper presented at the International Union for the Scientific Study of Population, General Conference, 3-11 September 1969., London.

Recent developments in European countries are reviewed with regard to contraception and induced abortion. A number of European countries still have restrictive legislation regarding dissemination of information and services on contraception but contraceptive facilities are increasingly being introduced in public health centres and many places. Information is available only periodically concerning actual practices of contraception but there are indications to show that male methods are still the most widely used in the majority of countries. The use of oral contraceptives is spreading rapidly in a number of countries in Western Europe while preference seems, at least in the USSR, to have been given to the IUD. These two modern methods will rapidly change the contraceptive patterns in Europe and also the role of the medical profession and family planning clinics. Legalized abortions take place in large numbers in most Eastern European countries and sometimes they exceed the number of live births, but some restrictions are being reintroduced in several countries as concern is being expressed about the widespread use of abortions as a means of family limitation. In Northern European countries, and also now in the United Kingdom, legalized abortions are provided on limited grounds including mixed medical-social indications.

2277 Glass, D.V. "Family Limitation in Europe: A Survey of Recent Studies," pp. 231-62 in: Kiser, C.V., ed. Research in Family Planning. Princeton: Princeton University Press, 1962. xvi, 664 pp.

The relative scarcity of systematic information in Europe on family planning is partly a reflection of the limitations of the social scientists. Further, birth control organizations have generally shown little interest in research and in many European countries free access to birth control information is relatively recent. Relatively few countries have laws which definitely prohibit the dissemination of birth control information or the sale of contraceptives, and in those that do (Ireland, Spain and France), the laws are not always strictly enforced. An important need is for a far more systematic compilation, perhaps undertaken jointly with the International Planned Parenthood Federation, of the numbers, types and clientele of clinics and other agencies for giving contraceptive advice in different countries. There is also a need for surveys of the attitudes and practice of private physicians, an examination of the extent to which information is conveyed through the press, and an analysis of the volume and nature of manufacturing, sales and import of various contraceptives. More comprehensive and reliable data on abortion should also be obtained.

2278 Glass, D.V. "Fertility Trends in Europe Since the Second World War," Popul. Stud. 22(1):103-46, March 1968.

Developments since World War II -- largely initiated in the 1930's -- have considerably narrowed the range of fertility in Europe. In many Western and North-Western countries, age at marriage has fallen and the probability of marriage has increased, especially for females. In such countries, too, marital fertility has tended to stabilize and in some cases has risen -- partly but not solely a function of changes in age at marriage. In Southern and Eastern Europe, by contrast, the decline in marital fertility has continued and especially in those Eastern European countries in which the grounds for legal abortion have been greatly extended and where legal abortion has come to be used as a major method of birth prevention. Within some countries there is evidence of a reduction in socio-economic differences in marital fertility. Changes in marriage patterns and in birth spacing, as well as in ultimate family size, combine to make the use of period rates very hazardous in measuring or interpreting fertility trends.

2279 Goetz-Girey, R. "Prestations Familiales et Salaires des Familles dans l'Europe des Six " [Family Allowances and Family Wages in the Europe of the Six], Direction Sociale, No. 7-8 ;July - August 1963, pp. 426-34.

Comparison of basic concepts and financial importance of family subsidies by the state in the separate countries.

2280 Harmsen, H., ed. [Contributions to the Population Development in Soviet Russia, Eastern European Peoples' Republics and Middle Germany, With Special Reference to the Abortion Problem] Hamburg: Akademie fur Staatsmedizin in Hamburg, 1961.

The abortion situation in Bulgaria, Hungary, Poland, Czechoslovakia, Yugoslavia and the German Democratic Republic is discussed in all but four of the papers included in this volume. Each country report is followed by excerpts from the important law texts in German translation, and the papers were written by experts in the field. The Soviet Union's 1955 decree abolishing the country's tight restrictions on abortion is quoted, and the first three chapters involve an analysis of population development in the Soviet Union based mainly on the 1955 census. The final chapter deals with the development and structure of Middle Germany's population.

2281 Herberg, Charlotte von der, "Marriage Laws of Europe," European Rev. 14:32-34, Winter 1963-64.

There is no unified conception of marriage in the European Community. Although the old Napoleonic Code exerted an influence in all six nations, the nations have generally developed different legal systems. It is only in the postwar period that laws have been passed in the Federal Republic of Germany, in France and in the Netherlands, which pay attention to the new position of women in the world. Of special interest to women are comparisons of the nations in terms of: how marriage affects the legal status of the married woman in relation to the unmarried woman and the man; and the principle of equal rights in marriage and family law.

2282 Leclercq, Jacques and Boudet, Robert, Die Lage der Familie in Europa [The Situation of the Family in Europe]. Sonderheft der Zeitschrift "Dokumente", Munchen: Kosel-Verlag, 1952.

An evaluative account of what is happening to the family in Europe, followed by statistics from each European country about living standards, fertility, economics, and national policies for families.

2283 Novak, Franc, "Abortion in Europe," Proceedings of the Eighth International Conference of the International Planned Parenthood Federation, Hertford, England: International Planned Parenthood Federation, 1967.

Economic and social conditions have compelled Europeans to practice birth control. Where contraception is unknown or made difficult by restrictive legislation, abortion is practiced. Eastern Europe has succeeded in minimizing maternal deaths and post-operative complications by the development of an electric vibrating dilator and suction. In Czechoslovakia there were no deaths among 140,000 instances of legal abortion in the years 1963-64. A table on the abortion and contraceptive policies of European countries is included.

2284 Novak, Franc, "Les Problemes de l'Avortement en Europe " [The Problem of Abortion in Europe], Stanovnistuo 5(3): 191-98, July - September 1967.

The annual increase in population in Europe is relatively slight, probably because of recourse to contraceptives and induced abortion, a result of industrialization, and the participation of women in the community and a modification in their social status. Over several decades a number of European countries have passed very liberal legislation on abortion and others have prepared it. There is a brief review of actual laws on abortion and contraception in 27 European countries.

2285 Tietze, Christopher, "Abortion in Europe," Amer. J. Public Health 57:1923-32, 1967.

Legalization of abortion in the European countries is divided into three categories: abortion only on strict medical indications (e.g., Germany and France); for extended medical, eugenic, and humanitarian indications (e.g., the Scandinavian countries); for medical, eugenic, and social indication, or on demand (e.g., Eastern Europe). The incidence of legal abortion, its recent trends and influence on the birth rate, and on illegal abortion, is discussed.

2286 United Nations. Committee on the Status of Women. Creches and Day Nurseries: Note by the Secretary General, No. 6, 1961, 119+56 pp.

International children's centre report of the Seminar on creches [for children of working mothers] held in Paris, France, December 5-7, 1960, as well as a report on creches in four European countries.

2287 United Nations. Economic Commission for Europe, Research and Planning Division, "Taxes on Wages or Employment and Family Allowances in European Countries," Economic Bulletin for Europe 4(2):25-55, First Quarter, 1952.

An analysis of direct taxes paid and family allowances received by the working classes, as well as taxes paid by the employer.

2288 United Nations. Office of Social Affairs, European Seminar on Social Policy in Relation to Changing Family Needs, Arnhem, Netherlands, April 16-26, 1961. Geneva: 1962. i, 153 pp.

2289 Vaestopoliittinen Tutkimuslaitos [Population Research Institute], "Katsauksia," [Surveys], pp. 151-90 in: Vaestopoliittinen Tutkimuslaitos, Vaestontutkimuksen Vuosikirja, 1967-68, Helsinki: 1968. 200 pp.

Contents: "Lapsilisalain Muutosesitykset 1948-67" [Proposed Amendments to the Legislation Relating to the Child Allowance in 1948-1967] by Sirkka-Liisa Kolehmainen, pp. 151-62; "Aidinpalkka " [Mother's Wages] by Antero Peralainen and Jarl Lindgren, pp. 163-71; "Perhekustannusten Tasauksen

Vaihtoehtoja " [Alternative Schemes for the Compensation of Cost of Family Maintenance] by Antero Peralainen, pp. 172-82; "Suhtautuminen Perhepoliittisiin Toimenpiteisiin " [Attitudes Towards Family Policy Measurements] by Heli Ekman, pp. 183-88; "Saksan Liittotasavallan Lapsilisajar-Jestelmaan Ehdotetut Muutokset " [Proposed Amendments Relating to the Family Allowance System in West Germany] by Sirkka-Liisa Kolehmainen, pp. 189-90.

2290 Villanova, Giogio, "Family Allowances in Common Market Countries," Migration News 11(4):14-17, July - August 1962.

Family allowance programs are described as they operate in Germany, France, Belgium, the Netherlands, Luxembourg and Italy. The programs depend upon the social category of the beneficiaries and upon the size of the family for which payments are to be made, and differentiated according to whether they are directed to the entire population of a country, to the active population or to the active salaried population. Comparisons are made among the different systems, and it is concluded that generalization is, without doubt, the aim toward which all present systems should tend. This would also correspond to the general program of standardizing social legislation, which is one of the objects of the Common Market. The unification of the systems should extend and unify the range of application to beneficiaries and attain a unique criterion for attribution of family payments.

(Western Europe)

GENERAL

General population policies

2291 Sauvy, Alfred, "Les Problemes de Population Europeenne: I. Un Plan d'Etudes " [Problems of European Population: I. A Plan for Research], Population 8(1):4-20, 1953.

Needed is a careful study of the problem of overpopulation in Western Europe. The nature of the problem must be spelled out and the extent of overpopulation measured. A number of possible solutions are discussed. A decrease in death rates can never be accepted as a way of reducing the extent of overpopulation. A further decrease in fertility is not feasible. Discussed topics relating to the problem of overpopulation are: 1) the possibility and economic consequences of overseas emigration; 2) the feasibility and effects of international redistribution of population within Europe; 3) factors facilitating or impeding changes in the occupational structure of the population; 4) political, fiscal, and financial policies affecting international trade between Europe and other continents; 5) the role of economic relations between Europe and Africa, and especially N. Africa; 6) economic integration of W. Europe; and 7) increase in productivity, development of natural resources, increase in savings, and expansion of technical education.

Policies on fertility and family size

2292 Caisses d'Allocations Familiales, "Evolution des Prestations Familiales Depuis 1958 " [Development of Family Allowances Since 1958], Bulletin des Caisses d'Allocations Familiales C.A.F. 1-2:5-11, January - February 1966.

2293 Glass, David V. "Family Planning Programmes and Actions in Western Europe," Popul. Stud. 19(3):221-38, March 1966.

Neo-Malthusian organizations for spreading birth control propaganda were created in many West European countries in the 1870's and 1880's. But the birth control movement proper, with its provision of clinics and other means of supplying advice on contraception, began much later -- generally after World War I and largely on a welfare basis, divorced from Malthusianism. Legal and other difficulties impeded progress and conditioned the nature of the movement. Since World War II, however, the relevance of birth control has come increasingly to be recognized and the movement has expanded markedly. In some countries -- especially in France, West Germany and Italy -- there are still legal obstacles, though ways have been found of avoiding them. But even in other countries the direct impact of birth control clinics is far smaller than might have been expected, and married couples still obtain their information on contraception from other sources. In recent years the various national movements have shown a greater interest in the evaluation of their activities. As a result the near future may see substantial changes in their structure and in the approach to their potential clientele.

AUSTRIA

General population policies

2294 Doublet, Jacques, "Politique Demographique en Autriche " [Demographic Policy in Austria], Population 2(2):293-302, April - June 1947.

2295 International Labour Office, "Social Policy of the New Government in Austria," Industry and Labour 9(11-12): 359-60, June 15,1953.

A statement of proposed policies concerning employment, savings, housing, and old-age insurance. In addition, the new government would pay special regard to the protection of the family, and particularly to assistance for large families.

Policies on fertility and family size

2296 Austria, Laws, Statutes, Etc. Beihilfen zur Familienforderung. Kinderbeihilfe, Familienbeihilfe, Mutterbeihilfe, Sauglinsbeihilfe, Geburtenbeihilfe. Mit Erlauterungen von Franz Lechner [Subsidies for the Promotion of the Family. Subsidies for Children, Families, Mothers, Infants, and Confinements. With comments by Franz Lechner]. 3rd ed. Schriftenreihe des Osterreichischen Gewerkschaftsbundes, 55. Vienna: Osterreichischer Gewerkschaftsbund, 1966. 140 pp.

Includes the text of Familienlastenausgleichgesetz [Law for the equalization of family burdens].

2297 Austria. "Maternal and Child Health," Internat. Digest Health Legis. 7:201, 1956.

Federal Law No. 99 of 9 April 1954 lays down principles for assistance to mothers, infants, and young persons and prescribes regulations for the well-being of young persons.

2298 Austria. "Midwives: Regulations," Internat. Digest Health Legis. 5:591-92, 1954.

Decree No. 150 of the Federal Ministry of Social Welfare of 4 September 1953 requires midwives to watch out for tuberculosis in the home of any pregnant woman and to insist upon the need of every pregnant woman to undergo a serological examination for syphilis.

2299 Austria. "Trade in Contraceptives," Internat. Digest Health Legis. 5:591, 1954.

Decree No. 120 of the Federal Ministry of Social Welfare of 26 June 1953 prohibits contraceptives which are harmful to health. Prohibited are the manufacture, importation, sale or use of (a) vaginal specula of less than 10 mm. in diameter and (b) intrauterine pessaries of any kind.

2300 Dammer, D. Vom Heterogenen Familieneinkommen zum Familienlohn [From Heterogeneous Family Income to a Family Wage]. Vienna: Spring 1955. 179 pp.

This volume argues that economists ought to have a systematic view of the role of the family in the economic system; if child rearing, for example, is an economic burden, the state should introduce compensatory measures according to an explicit plan. Family allowances, tax relief, reduced rents and fares are all examined here from this general point of view.

2301 Hansluwka, H. "Divorce in Austria," Paper presented at the International Union for the Scientific Study of Population, General Conference, 3-11 September 1969, London.

Laws governing divorce are reviewed. Review covers 1811 to present. Available information on divorce in Austria since 1924 is analyzed and the influence of certain demographic and socio-economic factors discussed. In Austria, at least 10% of marriages terminate in divorce, this estimate being based on the experience of marriage cohorts 1959-67. Divorce rates are highest for both sexes at young age and decrease with rising age. Gainfully occupied wives take recourse to divorce more frequently than housewives. Duration-specific divorce rates are in Vienna almost three times higher than in the rest of the country. The 1961 population census results draw attention to striking occupational and social class differences in divorce patterns.

2302 Lacinova, Valerie, "Rodinne Pridavky v Rakousku " [Family Allowances in Austria], Demografie 7(1):68-70, 1965.

2303 Osterreichische Institut fur Wirtschaftsforschung. "Familienpolitik in Osterreich " [Family Policy in Austria], Monatsberichte des Osterreichischen Institutes fur Wirtschaftsforschung 39 (8), August 1966.

2304 Pleyl, Josef, "Nyheter Inom Osterrikisk Sociallagsstiftning " [New Social Legislation in Austria], Sociala Meddelanden, No. 5, 1958, pp. 257-64.

Includes a brief review of the new regulations that have been introduced to help families with many children, such as increased children's allowances and tax relief for families with children.

2305 Reichel, Kurt, Der Familienlastenausgleich [Family Allowances]. Vienna: H. Fellerer, 1963. [6], 129 pp.

2306 Schindl, K. "Bevolkerungsbewegung und Soziale Sicherheit " [Population Increase and Social Security], Soziale Sicherheit January, 1955, pp. 1-10.

The demographic situation and family policy in Austria.

BELGIUM

General population policies

2307 Baty, V. "De l'Influence de l'Habitat sur Une Politique de Population " [The Influence of Housing on Population Policy], Rev. Conseil Econ. Wallon, No. 65, November - December 1963, pp. 25-31.

Includes a report on a preliminary questionnaire survey on preferences for housing type and situation and on family size, conducted by the Societe Nationale de la Petite Propriete Terrienne in the Walloon and Flemish areas of Belgium in December 1963.

2308 Belgium. Centrum voor Bevolkingsen Gezinsstudien, "Kroniek Wetgeving. (Teksten Verschenen in het Belgisch Staatsblad Tussen 1-1-1963 en 31-3-1964)," [Legislative Chronicle. (Texts Published in the Belgian Official Gazette between Jan. 1,1963 and March 31,1964], Bevolking en Gezin, No.3 1964, pp.82-90.

Citations are arranged chronologically under the topics: protection of the family; children's allowances; nationality; pensions; social probation system for minor offenders; public health; public housing and small land holdings; disease and invalidity insurance.

2309 Belgium. Ministere de la Sante Publique et de la Famille, Plan de Quinze Ans pour le Ministere de la Sante Publique et de la Famille, 1961-1975 [Fifteen-Year Plan for the Ministry of Public Health and the Family, 1961-1975]. Brussels, 1961. 246 pp.

2310 Bie, Pierre de, "Les Allocations Familiales dans la Perspective de la Politique Familiale et de la Demographie " [Family Allowances in Relation to Family Policy and Demography], Rev. Belge Sec. Soc., November 1960, pp. 1454-61.

Discusses the aims of Belgian family allowances and their adaptation to the arrangements of the Common Market.

2311 Conseil Economique Wallon, [A Group of Articles on the Sauvy Plan], Rev. Conseil Econ. Wallon Nos. 54-55 and 56, January - April and May - June 1962.

Contents: Pressat, Roland [The Problem of the Economy and Population of Wallonia] No. 54-55, January-April 1962, pp. 1-23; Sauvy, Alfred [Conditions of Economic Development and Measures to be Taken for a General Renewal] Ibid., pp. 24-51; [Exposition of Policy Recommendations in Support of Industrial Growth and a Revival of Natality]; [What the Press Thinks of It] Ibid., pp. 52-57; [A Plan of Action for the Renewal of Wallonia] No. 56, May-June, 1962, pp. 1-20.

2312 Conseil Economique Wallon, "Un an Apres..." [One Year After the Sauvy Report], Rev. Conseil Econ. Wallon,No. 62, May-June 1963, pp. 2-20.

Substantial extracts from three addresses at Liege, May 20, 1963. Contents: Sauvy, Alfred [Life and Growth of a Population: Maturity, Old Age, and Youth] pp. 2-11; Servais, Leon [For an Immigration Policy] pp. 12-16; Leburton, Edmund [Our Family Policy] pp. 17-20.

2313 Conseil Economique Wallon, "Un Document Fondamental dans la Ligne du Rapport Sauvy: Le Rapport Delperee " [A Basic Document on the Lines of the Sauvy Report: The Delperee Report], Rev. Conseil Econ. Wallon, No. 57, July - August 1962, pp. 7-24.

The Government, in a declaration before the Parliament, 2 May 1961, recommended the allocation of sufficient resources to meet the costs of an expanded family policy which is based on social justice and which creates the conditions necessary for population growth. Implementation of this declaration resulted in the appointment of a committee on social and family policy, under the direction of M. Delperee, Secretary-General of the Ministry of Social Security, which was charged with formulating a set of recommendations. The committee's report recommends allocations for children by rank in family and birth allowances which should be regionally administered; indirect aides (public services, education, etc.) to child and family; social services; and adjustments in allowances according to regional socio-economic differentials. Recommended, also, are policies to attract immigrants; codes for housing, population and the family; and a policy for old-age security.

2314 Conseil Economique Wallon, "Materiaux pour l'Elaboration d'une Politique Demographique " [Materials for the Development of Population Policy], Rev. Conseil Econ. Wallon, No. 15, July - August 1955, pp. 1-20.

Review of French and Belgian policy and experience. Data on family size in Belgium.

2315 Conseil Economique Wallon, "La Presse devant le Probleme Demographique " [The Press and the Population Problem], Rev. Conseil Econ. Wallon, No. 15, July - August 1955, pp. 29-32.

A summary of recent press discussions of the Wallon problems.

2316 Cordy, Andre, "Pour une Politique Familiale et Demographique Globale " [For an Inclusive Family and Population Policy], Industrie 17(9):635-43, September 1963.

Discussion of the Delperee report. The major burden of financing family allowances for working class people was on their employers in 1961, not on the government. Without greater government support for the social security system as a whole, Belgium could face a serious economic setback. Efficiency must be increased first by seeing that allowances cannot be given just to any family with children, regardless of age or rank in the family. Increased natality must be seen as the way to rejuvenate the aging population. First children make up 50% of the beneficiaries of the present system of allowances.

2317 Dereymaker, R. De Democratie voor een Zware Taak, een Doelmatige Bevolkingspolitiek [The Difficult Task of a Democracy -- An Effective Demographic Policy]. Antwerpen, 1946. 52 pp.

2318 Dereymaker, R. "Quelques Grandeurs Fondamentales pour la Politique de Population " [Some Fundamental Factors for a Population Policy], Bull. Statistique 33(5):477-89, May 1947.

A study of financial factors, such as the distribution of income in relation to size of family, that should be taken into account in developing a population policy for Belgium.

Includes material from the Economic and Social Census of 1937 on incomes of workers in commerce and industry.

2319 Dupreel, Eugene, Le Pluralisme Sociologique; Fondements Scientifiques d'Une Revision des Institutions [Sociological Pluralism; Scientific Bases of a Review of Institutions]. Actualites Sociales. Nouv. Ser. 5. Bruxelles, Office de Publicite, 1945. 80 pp.

Implications for family and demographic policy, pp. 36-38.

2320 Fallon, Valere, Famille et Population [Family and Population]. Tournai: Casterman, 1942. 80 pp.

Evolution, causes and remedies for the population problem.

2321 Laloire, Marcel, "Le Rapport Sauvy " [The Sauvy Report], Rev. Nouvelle 18(4):388-95, April 1962.

Discussion of the Sauvy Report. Two family policies -- one for Wallon, and one for Flanders -- were formulated, taking into account the special needs of each area and each people. The principal plan rests on family allocations. By giving a mother large allowances for second, third, etc., children, she may be encouraged to have more children. Sauvy would like a suppression of the allowance for first children, but such a plan would be politically impossible as most families receive that allowance.

2322 Mols, Roger, "Valeur et Faiblesse du Rapport Sauvy " [Strength and Weakness of the Sauvy Report], Vie Econ. Soc. 33(3):153-82, May 1962.

A descriptive and critical analysis and an evaluation as a whole of the report by Alfred Sauvy, Conditions of Economic Development and Measures to be Taken for a General Renewal [of Wallonia].

2323 Revue Belge de la Securite Sociale, "Politique de la Population et de la Famille " [Policy on Population and the Family], Rev. Belge Sec., Soc. July - August 1962, pp. 921-84.

The Revue editors generally applaud the Delperee Commission report. Principal parts of recommended policies on population and the family are described and assessed. These include: benefits to children; prenatal, maternity and postnatal provisions; employment policy; immigration policy; internal integration; and old-age and social security.

Policies on fertility and family size

2324 Belgium. Association des Caisses d'Allocations Familiales. Journee d'Etudes sur le Theme 'Allocations Familiales et Denatalite' [A Study Conference on 'Family Allowances and Declining Fertility']. Bruxelles: Association des Caisses d'Allocations Familiales, 1953. 100 pp.

2325 Belgium. Comite d'Etude des Problemes de la Denatalite en Belgique, "Le Vieillissement de la Population Belge et le Peril de la Denatalite " [The Aging of the Belgian Population and the Danger of Declining Fertility], From: Bull. Mensuel Centre d'Etudes Documentation Soc. Province Liege, No. 3, March 1953, 55 pp.

2326 Belgium. Laws. Legislation Relative aux Allocations Famiiales pour Travailleurs Salaries; Textes Coordonnes [Legislation Relating to Family Allowances for Wage Earners; Coordinated Texts]. Bruxelles: 1952. 99 pp.

2327 Boogaerts, A. De Kinderbijslagwet voor de Loonarbeiders, Verzameling van de Vigerende wetten en Vitvoeringsbesluiten [Family Allowances for Wage-Workers, a Collection of Laws]. Leuven: Vlaamse Drukkerij, 1947. 144 pp.

2328 Bouzat, P. "Le Probleme de l'Avortement " [The Problem of Abortion], Rev. Droit Penal Criminol. 33(8):703-24, 1963.

The repressive measures intended to lower the number of abortions and the preventive measures of an ethical, economic and social nature. In each of these directions, the measures already taken and those under consideration.

2329 Brat, T., et al. [Female Sterilization. Statistical Analysis, 1961-1966], Bull. Soc. Roy. Belg. Gynec. Obstet. 38:97-107, 1968.

2330 Cliquet, Robert L. "L'Etude de la Fertilite Biologique et de la Contraception dans le Cadre de l'Enquete Nationale (Belge) sur la Fertilite et la Fecondite. Le Materiel et les Methods " [Study of the Biology of Fertility and Contraception in the Course of a National (Belgian) Inquiry on Fertility and Fecundity. The Materials and the Methods], Popul. Fam. 14:43-94, June 1968.

Reports and comments on the statistical analysis of this large inquiry. Develops an elaborate classificatory scheme for fecundity and contraception and considers in detail the appropriate methods for a qualitative analysis of the questionnaires. The classification is influenced by the large U.S.A. studies.

2331 Cliquet, Robert L. "Enquete Nationale sur la Fertilite et la Fecondite de la Femme Mariee en Belgique " [National Inquiry on Fertility and Fecundity of Married Women in Belgium], Popul. Fam. 13:15-35, 1967.

Presents the anthropological objectives of an inquiry on fecundity in 1966 based on a probability sample of 3,000 Belgian women who were living with their husbands. The first part considers the influence of diverse sociocultural variables on fertility. In the second part are statistics on contraceptive practice and comments on the voluntary limitation of potential fertility.

2332 Conseil Economique Wallon, "Bases d'un Regime d'Allocations Familiales Socialement Juste et Demographiquement Efficace " [Basis for a System of Family Allowances Socially Just and Demographically Effective], Rev. Conseil Econ. Wallon, Nos. 24-25, January - April 1957, pp. 1-17.

2333 Conseil Economique Wallon, "La Politique Familiale Belge et la Crise Demographique Wallonne" [Belgian Family Policy and the Demographic Crisis of Wallonia], Rev. Conseil Econ. Wallon,No. 17, November - December 1955, pp. 46-52.

Comparison of French and Belgian family.

2334 Conseil Economique Wallon, "La Wallonie Veut Vivre! Un Plan de Salut Public pour Conjurer la Menace d'une Decadence Demographique" [Wallonia Must Stay Alive! A Public Health Plan to Banish the Menace of a Declining Population], Rev. Conseil Econ. Wallon,No. 20, May - June 1956, pp. 1-30

An outline of statistics on declining natality and a plea for a governmental program of family allowances, birth and prenatal allowances, and marriage loans.

2335 Creutz, E. "Evolution Demographique et Politique des Prestations Familiales en Belgique" [Demographic Change and Policy on Family Allowances in Belgium], Rev. Belge Sec. Soc.,June - July 1966, pp. 639-705.

Presents and discusses statistics on the timing of the increase in natality in Belgium in relation to the increase in the level of family allowances.

2336 Derbroech, G., "La Reforme des Allocations Familiales" [Reform of Family Allowances], C.S.C. Bull. Mensuel Confederation Syndicats Chretiens Belgique,November - December 1956, pp. 399-416.

The legal basis of family allowances and the necessity of a reform to promote a new population policy; modes and finances of such a reform.

2337 Derobert, L. "Les Possibilites Medicales dans la Repression de l'Avortement Criminel" [The Medical Possibilities in the Suppression of Criminal Abortion], Rev. Droit Penal Criminol. 33(8):725-37, 1953.

The problem has differing aspects according to whether the physician is called upon in the capacity of medical practitioner or of expert. In the first case the difficulties are above all ethical, in the second technical.

2338 "Effectif Probable des Enfants Beneficiares d'Allocations Familiales au Cours des Annees 1963 a 1965" [Probable Number of Child Beneficiaries of Family Allowances during 1963 to 1965], Rev. Sec. Soc. 5(3):430-46, March 1963.

Various statistics and procedures are used to estimate the extent of child allowances by the Belgian Government to salaried workers. After assessing data on employment and unemployment and the number of students, infirmed, and young ladies aged 14-21 years remaining at home, the author estimates that the number of youngsters legally entitled to allowances to be 1,610,000 in 1963; 1,648,000 in 1964; and 1,687,000 in 1965.

2339 Fallon, Valere, Allocations Familiales des Non Salaries: le Regime Actuel et le Project, Gouvernemental [Family Allowances for Non-Wage Earners: The Present Status and the Government Project]. Louvain: Societe d'Etudes Morales, Sociales et Juridiques, 1953. 107 pp.

2340 Fallon, Valere, Les Deux Regimes d'Allocations Familiales; Reforme ou Revision? [Two Regimes of Family Allowances; Reform or Revision?]. Louvain: Societe d'Etudes Morales, Sociales et Juridiques, 1952. 36 pp.

2341 Familles dans le Monde, "Mesures en Faveur de la Famille en Belgique" [Measures Favoring the Family in Belgium], Familles dans le Monde,September 1959.,pp. 209-22.

Social insurance, housing, taxes, etc.

2342 Goldschmidt-Clermont, Paul, "The Belgian Social Security Scheme," Internat. Labour Rev. 55(1-2):46-61, January - February 1947.

The Director-General of the Belgian National Social Security Office presents the major provisions of the Belgian scheme and gives the results of its first year of operation. Includes a section on family allowances.

2343 Goldschmidt-Clermont, Paul, "The Family Allowances Scheme in Belgium Today," Soc. Sec. Assn. Bull. 12:211-28, May 1959.

2344 Goldschmidt-Clermont, Paul, "La Population Belge Devant l'Inconnue de Sa Perennite Demographique" [The Population of Belgium Confronted with the Uncertainty of Its Demographic Survival], Industrie 18(4):281-84, April 1964.

Presents the case for regional programs to reinforce pronatal policies. Payments of 7,500 francs should be allocated for each child beginning with the second. This is the opposite of the Sauvy Report which diminishes payments for each succeeding child.

2345 Goldschmidt-Clermont, Paul, "Une Programme D'Action Familiale et Demographique" [A Program of Action for the Family and the Population], Rev. Conseil Econ. Wallon, No. 46, September - October 1960, pp. 5-18.

Proposal to extend the scope of the Belgian decree of April, 1957, on family allowances, from wage- and salary-earners to independent workers.

2346 Goldschmidt-Clermont, Paul, "Le Regime Belge d'Allocations Familiales Peut-il Devenir un Moyen Efficace de la Lutte Contre la Denatalite?" [Can the Belgian System of Family Allowances Become an Effective Means of Combatting the Decline of Fertility?] Bull. Mensuel Centre Etudes Documentation Soc. Province Liege, February 1951, pp. 46-54. Discussion pp. 54-64.

2347 Gossieres, Pierre, "L'Institution des Allocations Familiales en Belgique, Service Public" [Family Allowances as a Belgian Public Service], Rev. Travail 44:445-63, August 1943.

2348 Heuskin, L., and Kiermash, Berger J. "L'Adoption En Belgique" [Adoption in Belgium], Rev. Institut Sociol. 1:61-114, 1967.

Two essential considerations guided this research: learning the volume and the objective data of the institution of adoption with reference to future modifications of its legal status. The legal aspects have been analyzed according to laws of 1940 and 1958 as well as the Harmel draft law of October 30, 1962. Originally, adoption was considered as an institution of legitimation which was rarely used. Its conditions were strict, its effects restricted, and the age of candidates for adoption was high. Gradually, a new institution appeared, whose major characteristic is that it should be contracted for the benefit of the adoptee. It still remained, however, a contract with relatively strict conditions on age and publicity. This system is still in force; but a proposed law has produced some important changes in its essential principles, especially regarding the conditions of the age of candidates and of publicity. Moreover, it has been recommended that legitimation by adoption should confer upon the adoptive family the characteristics of the legitimate family with all the accruing consequences in the areas of persons and property. The age of adoption has been lowered and the prohibition of adoption when legitimate children exist has been suppressed. Moreover, if the parents have been married for over five years, they can adopt simultaneously if one of them has reached the age of 30, regardless of the age of the other. Also, if one spouse is over 35, the other can adopt simultaneously with him, if he is 21 or more. The intention of the law has moved towards encouraging adoption by parents as young as possible. After some commentaries on international legislation, the purely sociological aspects of adoption are reviewed.

2349 Hoorebeke, F. van, and Dumon, F. "La Repression de l'Avortement" [The Suppression of Abortion], Rev. Droit Penal Criminol. 33(8):738-83, 1953.

Problems raised: limits of penal action, legal basis for suppression, dispositions made by diverse legislation, professional secrets of physician and midwife, the problem of allowing certain abortions, the suppression of the attempt, preventive measures.

2350 Houtte, Jean van, "Overzicht Over De Statostoelem Omzale Echtscheiding en Scheiding van Tafel en Bed" [Apercu des Statistiques du Divorce et de la Separation de Corps et de Biens/Statistics on Divorce and'Separation from Bed and Board'], Popul. Fam./Bevolk. Gezin 4:63-69, 1964.

A short survey of the Belgian legislation on divorce and "separation from bed and board" and of the statistical data on these subjects, followed by an exposure of the difference between demographic and juridical statistics. An analysis of both kinds of statistical data suggests some hypotheses and conclusions.

2351 Jacquemijns, Guillaume, Pour ou Contre la Limitation des Naissances [For or Against Birth Control]. Bruxelles, 1952. 66 pp.

2352 Jacquemijns, Guillaume, Opinions au Sujet des Allocations Familiales [Thoughts on the Subject of Family Allowances]. Bruxelles: Institut Universitaire d'Information Sociale et Economique, 1952. 59 pp.

2353 Klein-Vercautere, E. [The Situation of Abortion in Belgium] in: Mehlan, K.H., ed. Internationale Abortsituation, Abortbekampfung, Antikonzeption. Leipzig: Georg Thieme, 1961.

Belgian law forbids any form of interruption of pregnancy, contraceptive information and propaganda; however, the birth rate is one of the lowest in Europe (1947-1958 average 16.8) and families with no children (26.4%) and with one child (28.5%) dominated in 1947, indicating an extensive use of birth control. Abortion, therefore, must commonly occur to counteract ineffective contraceptive methods (rhythm method or coitus interruptus). In the period studied only 165 to 245 persons were prosecuted for criminal abortion yearly and only 44 deaths reported from abortion complications.

2354 Koster, Paul, "Theorie sur les Allocations Familiales " [Theory of Family Allowances], Vie Econ. Soc. 30(1):45-48, January 1959.

Discussion of four fundamental assumptions, of which one is the duty of the nation to assure the maintenance of the population.

2355 Laloire, Marcel, "Objectifs d'une Politique Familiale " [Aims of a Family Policy], Rev. Nouvelle 19(7-8):85-95, July - August 1963.

2356 Laloire, Marcel, "Politique Nataliste ou Politique Familiale?" [Natalist Policy or Family Policy?] Rev. Nouvelle 11(12):541-47, December 1955.

2357 Leburton, Edmond, [Our Family Policy], Rev. Conseil Econ. Wallon No. 62, 1963, pp. 17-20.

Describes measures for the family during 1961 to 1963. Allowances for independent workers are increased to correspond with the rates of salaried workers. Provisions are made for family vacation allowances. Efforts are made to ensure the receipt of benefits by children and orphanages.

2358 Leener, George de, Vingt-Cinq Annees de Regime des Allocations Familiales en Belgique [Twenty-five Years of Family Allowances in Belgium]. Brussels: Office de Publicite, S.C., 1947. 188 pp.

A description of the growth of family allowances in Belgium and an account of the principal legislative acts with respect to them. A number of provisions of the present scheme are described and commented on briefly. References are made in the study to demographic and other objectives of family allowances.

2359 Ligue des Familles Nombreuses de Belgique, Interets Familiaux. Rapport General de la Commission Centrale des Interets Familaux [Matters Pertaining to the Family. General Report of the Central Commission of Matters Pertaining to the Family]. Bruxelles: Ligue des Familles Nombreuses de Belgique, 1945. 323 pp.

2360 Ligue des Familles Nombreuses de Belgique, La Securite Sociale et les Allocations Familiales [Social Security and Family Allowances]. Bruxelles: Ligue des Familles Nombreuses de Belgique, 1945. 65 pp.

2361 "Livelihood Guarantee Funds in Belgium," Internat. Labour Rev. 92:141-47, August 1965.

Payments of supplementary benefits to involuntarily unemployed persons in various sectors of the economy and payment of other social benefits such as retirement bonuses, holiday pay, family supplements.

2362 Moureau, P. "Possibilites de Repression de l'Avortement " [Possibilities for the Suppression of Abortion], Rev. Droit Penal Criminol. 33(8):784-94, 1953.

The fight for the legislative program against abortion meets great difficulties: difficulties of a technical nature that impede the disclosure; difficulties of an ethical and legal nature that prevent the physician from helping the law.

2363 Ockers, Julien, "De Juridische aard van de Kinderbijslag: van Liberaliteit naar Sociaal Recht " [The Legal Basis of Children's Allowances: from Gift to Social Right], Popul. Fam., No. 2, April 1964, pp. 121-40.

A study of the varying legal concepts of children's allowances based on an examination of the writings of Belgian and some French commentators. Three stages are discussed: first, before legal obligation for children's allowances; second, from legal obligation to the establishment of social security; third, under the social security system.

2364 Somerhausen, C. "Les Aspects Medico-Sociaux de la Planification Familiale " [Medico-Social Aspects of Family Planning], Rev. Institut Sociol. 4:785-86, 1966.

A report on a conference organized at Anderlecht (Belgium) by La Famille Heureuse [The Happy Family], a Belgian family planning association on October 23, 1966. M. Graffar (Free University of Brussels, Belgium), reviewed the history of voluntary limitation of births and stressed that it was a cultural rather than biological phenomenon. Julemont, a social science graduate, examined the demographic and sociological aspects of contraception and concluded that family planning originated in rationalism but later developed according to its socioeconomic context. Debauche (Brugman Hospital) noted the psychological importance of the physical equilibrium of marriage partners. The roles of the social assistance worker, marriage counselor and social nurse in family planning were examined by Mmes. Borgers, Apostel and Schepens of La Famille Heureuse. The president, Mme. Weill, explained the purposes and activities of the family planning center.

2365 Spitaels, Guy, L'Annee Social 1962 [The Social Year 1962], Brussels: Editions de l'Institut de Sociologie, 1963. 355 pp.

Fourth annual review, including new sections on Belgian family encouragement policy and on general population policy, pp. 24-115.

2366 Susswein, E. "Family Allowances in Belgium," Popul. Stud. 2(3):278-91, December 1948.

The administration and finances of the scheme are described, and an account is given of the ancillary social services provided by the Equalization Funds which administer the allowances.

2367 Trine, Andre, Les Allocations Familiales [The Family Allowances]. Published with the support of the Association des Secretariats Sociaux d'Employeurs and of the Ligue des Familles Nombreuses. Brussels: Vioburo, 1954. 296 pp.

2368 Walle, E. van de, "La Nuptialite en Belgique de 1846 a 1930 et sa Relation avec le Declin de la Fecondite " [Wedding Frequency in Belgium Between 1846 and 1930 and Its Relation to the Lowering of Fecundity], Popul. Fam./Bevolk. Gezin, 6-7:37-56, 1965.

Belgian matrimonial fecundity for the years 1866, 1900 and 1930 was analyzed by the A.J. Coale method. It is noted that as the number of wives within child-bearing age increases, the actual number of children each of them has decreases. Factors pertaining to the evolution of marriage are discussed, i.e., the lowering of age at marriage, and the decrease in the number of spinsters. It is concluded that simultaneous with the fecundity revolution in Belgium, a slow but profound nuptial revolution occurred.

2369 Watson, Cicely, "A Survey of Recent Belgian Population Policy," Popul. Stud. 8(2):152-87, November 1954.

Belgium has for 50 years experienced a rapidly declining birth rate with a consequent aging of her population. The fall in births and losses due to two wars further unbalanced the age structure. An outline of the development of the present demographic situation stresses the different conditions and the growing disequilibrium between Flemings and Walloons, the latter being more industrialized and having a lower birth rate and higher death rate. Belgian population policy, though rudimentary, has closely paralleled that of France. The most important part is the family allowance system, which has developed and been extended as part of the general system of social security rather than as a part of population policy. This accounts for its failure to change the disequilibrium between Flemings and Walloons. Growth of the family allowance system is traced in some detail, its importance to the worker's budget and cost to the state estimated. Data on number of beneficiaries of various kinds, size of allowances under various regimes, sources of funds, relation of allowances to basic earnings, etc., are presented in 23 tables.

FRANCE

General population policies

2370 Bettelheim, C. "Economic and Social Policy in France," Internat. Labour Rev. 54(3-4):139-59, 1946.

As a part of the post World War II social policy, there was a readjustment of workers' incomes through increases in wages and family allowances. The most important measures are the Order of 28 September 1945 and the Act of 6 August 1946. In addition to raising benefits by about 100%, a new benefit -- pre-natal allowances -- payable from the time of conception was established. Measures are based on health and demographic consideration.

2371 Carnot, Paul, "Le Probleme Qualitatif et Quantitatif de la Reproduction, Renatalite, Immigration, Croisements" [The Qualitative and Quantitative Problem Connected with Reproduction, Rise in Fertility, Immigration, and Inter-Breeding], Paris Med., No. 2, January 11, 1947, pp. 9-12.

2372 Ceccaldi, Dominique, "Role de la Recherche dans le Choix et la Conduite d'une Politique Demographique et Familiale" [The Role of Research in the Choice of and Carrying Out of Population and Family Policy], Familles dans le Monde 8(1):3-13, January - March 1955.

France, which for several years has included demographers as government specialists and has developed a scientific organization (L'Institut National d'Etudes Demographiques), offers a unique opportunity to observe the role of research in the development of demographic and family policy.

2373 Chevalier, Louis, Les Paysans; Etude d'Histoire et d'Economie Rurales [The Peasantry; A Study of History and Rural Economy]. Paris: Societe des Editions Denoel, 1947. 231 pp.

Part II, "Policy Choices," considers the peasants as the source of the quantitative and qualitative renewal of the nation.

2374 Cournil, P. "Donnees d'Une Politique de la Population en France" [Benefits of a Population Policy in France], _Cahiers des Groupes Reconstruction_ 11(31):9-24, April 1956.

2375 Debre, Robert, "Plan de Population" [A Population Plan], _Monde Francais_, December 1946, pp. 464-572.

2376 Debre, Robert and Sauvy, Alfred, _Des Francais pour la France: le Probleme de la Population_ [Frenchmen for France: the Population Problem]. 5th ed. Paris: Gallinard, 1946. 264 pp.

2377 Fage, Anita, "La Revolution Francaise et la Population" [The French Revolution and Population], _Population_ 8(2): 311-38, April - June 1953.

French attitudes and policies concerning population during the Revolution.

2378 France. Direction de la Documentation, _Aspects de la Politique Sociale Francaise: Population et Famille, Problemes, Travail, Emploi, Action Sociale et Sante, Logement, Jeunesse, Justice_ [Aspects of French Social Policy -- Population and Family, Problems, Work Employment, Social Action and Health, Housing, Youth, Law]. Paris: Documentation Francaise, 1967. Variously paged.

Special issue of _Cahiers Francaise_ includes demographic data and information on wages, social services, housing, and education.

2379 France. Haut Comite Consultatif de la Population et de la Famille, Presidence du Conseil, _La Population Francaise. Tome 1. France Metropolitaine. Rapport du..._ [The French Population. Vol. 1. Metropolitan France. Report of the Committee...]. Paris: La Documentation Francaise, 1955. ii, 304 pp.

The prewar situation: demographic analysis and economic implications. Opinion and effective policy on natality up to 1952. Demographic developments since 1939. Objectives and a program for population policy, covering family allowances, protection of children, problems of an aging population, housing, alcoholism, migration movements and distribution, popular information, health measures.

2380 France. Institut National d'Etudes Demographiques, Le Probleme Demographique Francais [The French Demographic Problem]. Cahiers Francais d'Information, No. 118, October 1948, 46 pp.

Part I: Major facts; Part II: Lines of Action; Part III: Conclusion. Among the recommended actions are: a rise in fertility; a decrease in mortality; immigration as industry requires it; and a prolongation of the active life.

2381 France. Institut National d'Etudes Demographiques, Les Travaux du Haut Comite Consultatif de la Population et de la Famille en 1945 [Works of the Chief Consultative Committee on Population and the Family in 1945]. Travaux et Documents, Cahier No. 1. Paris: Presses Universitaires de France, 1946. 48 pp.

Publication of documents that served as the basis for amendments and additions to the Family Code, the statute concerning foreigners in France and certain measures on naturalization, and other social measures. These documents were assembled by A. Landry and J. Doublet.

2382 France. Ministere de la Sante Publique et de la Population, "Rapport Annuel sur l'Activite de l'Education Sanitaire Demographique et Sociale du Ministere de la Sante Publique et de la Population au cours de l'Annee 1951" [Annual Report on the Demographic and Social Health Education Activity of the Minister of Public Health and Population during 1951], Prophylaxie Sanitaire et Morale 24(4):114-24, April 1952.

2383 France. Ministere de la Sante Publique, Service de Documentation, Recueil des Textes Officiels Concernant la Protection de la Sante et de la Famille Promulgues en 1945 [Collection of Official Texts Concerning the Protection of Health and the Family Made Public in 1945]. Paris: Imprimerie Nationale, 1946. 1059 pp.

Decree No. 45-0134, December 24, 1945, relative to the responsibilities of the Minister of Population, is reproduced from the Journal Officiel of December 25, 1945. See also the texts concerning the Institut National d'Etudes Demographiques, pp. 689-91, and the Secretariat General a la Famille et a la Population, pp. 692-740.

2384 France. Ministere de la Sante Publique et de la Population, Service du Documentation, Recueil des Textes Officiels Concernant la Protection de la Sante et de la Famille Promulgues en 1949 [Collection of Official Texts Concerning the Protection of Health and the Family Issued in 1949]. Bulletin de la Ministere de la Sante Publique..., 1949. Paris: Imprimerie Nationale, 1950. 896 pp.

2385 France. Ministere de la Sante Publique et de la Population, Service de Documentation, Recueil des Textes Officiels Concernant la Protection de la Sante et de la Famille Promulgues en 1950 [Collection of Official Texts Concerning the Protection of Health and the Family Issued in 1950]. Bulletin..., 1950. Paris: Imprimerie National, 1951. 701 pp. Also issued in subsequent years.

2386 France. Union Nationale des Caisses d'Allocations Familiales, Guide des Prestations Familiales des Travailleurs Etrangers [Guide to Family Allowances for Foreign Workers]. Paris, 1966. In 2 vols. loose-leaf.

Textbook of social security legislation in France. Includes European Economic Community country agreements in the matter and contains sections on dispositions for Algerian, German, Belgian, Spanish, Italian, Portuguese, Senegalese, Swiss and Tunisian workers, as well as for Luxemburgers and Monegasques.

2387 Germany. Deutsche Arbeitsfront, "Die Bevolkerungspolitische Lage Lothringens am Ende der Franzosischen Herrschaft" [Population Policy in Lorraine at the Close of the French Administration], Wirtschaft und Sozialbericht 4: 94-97, December 1941.

2388 Glass, D.V. "Current Notes on Demography," Eugen. Rev. 37(3):116-23, 1945.

French population statistics, with changes in marriage frequencies, suggest postponement of marriage and of first and second births. The decree law (1939) ranges from birth premiums and family allowances through agricultural loans and income tax rebates to prohibition of abortion and provision in all French schools of instruction on population questions. It extends the scope of pro-natalist legislation and brings monetary assistance above all previous levels. Professor A. Sauvy believes France should have 75 million population, progressing by slow annual increments of 300,000 - 350,000. This growth is attainable through reduction of death rates, yearly immigration of 120,000 - 150,000, plus 150,000 annual births. Immigrants should come, in order, from (1) Belgium and Holland, (2) Spain, (3) Italy, (4) Poland. Assimilation should include an intermediate stage, with limited and easily revocable rights. Employment and production should be increased, balanced with increased consumption; old people should work to supplement their pensions; previous subsidies should be increased; knowledge of population trends should be widespread and demonstrate that everyone benefits through maintenance of population; there should be 3- and 4-child families, and universal suffrage; the mother proxying for children under 10, the father for the remainder of their minority. Glass regards this as the most comprehensive and realistic of French plans and as free from dogmatism, yet quite in the general French tradition. He believes that it would raise the quantity though probably not the quality of the population.

2389 "La Premiere Legislature de la IVe Republique et la Legislation Demographique" [The First Legislature of the IV Republic and Demographic Legislation], Population 6(3): 397-410, July - September 1951.

2390 Le Goherel, R. "Politique Demographique et Familiale" [Demographic and Family Policy], Cahiers Politiques, August - September 1945, pp. 79-85.

2391 Manceau, Bernard, Le Seul Probleme: Prevoyance Familiale, Credits a la Construction, Mutualite, Assurances et Profession [The Only Problem: Provision for the Family, Credits for Building, Assistance, and Insurance]. Paris: Librairie Generale de Droit et de Jurisprudence, 1945. 55 pp.

The population problem is one before which all others appear of secondary importance. This pamphlet pleads for family allowances, housing and insurance. The appendix presents selections from the legal documents, including 1942 modifications.

2392 Moreau, Pierre, "Social Measures on Behalf of the Agricultural Population in France," Bull. Internat. Soc. Sec. Assn. 7(8):283-99, 1954.

Through this special system of social measures, the workers and their families are protected against risks in nature likely to reduce or terminate their earning capacity. The manner in which the system covers the workers' maternity needs and family responsibilities is described. Objectives of the social security plan are defined in Article 1, Ordinance 4, October, 1945.

2393 Musee Social, Guide Pratique des Lois Sociales, l'Aide a la Famille, l'Aide aux Travailleurs [Practical Handbook of Social Laws, Aid to the Family, and to Workers]. Preface by Andre Siegfried. Second, revised ed. Paris: Musee Social, 1943. 232 pp.

Contents: Aids to the Family (family allowances; bonus for the first child; allowances for housewives; aids to unwed mothers and pregnant women; employment of heads of households; loans for the settlement of young, rural couples; endowments and medals for large families; and adoption); housing, medical and welfare assistance; social security; assistance to immigrants; and military allowances and assistance to veterans.

2394 Nizard, A. "La Politique de Population de la France" [French Population Policy]. Paper presented at the International Union for the Scientific Study of Population General Conference, 3-11 September 1969, London.

The first part presents French family policy and more particularly, the evolution of family allowances. The second part describes the general characteristics of the population policy and its historical evolution. The decline in fertility (1.98 children per marriage between the two world wars) lead to government intervention. The third part examines the government action on birth control. In general, French population policy has lost its repressive character and is now more respectful of individual liberty.

2395 Peltier, Roger, "L'Institut National d'Etudes Demographiques--Organisation, Travaux et Resultats"[The National Institute of Demographic Studies--Organization, Work, and Results], Population 4(1):9-38, January - March 1949.

2396 Peyre, Henri, Problemes Francais de Demain; Reflexions a propos d'un Livre Recent [French Problems of Tomorrow; Reflections on a Recent Book]. New York: Moretus Press, 1943. 48 pp.

This book consists of "reflections" on Pierre Maillaud's "France" (Oxford Press, 1942). The discussion concerns primarily the demographic problem, pp. 11-18; the industrial problem, pp. 19-25; and the agricultural problem, pp. 26-35.

2397 Pfeil, Elisabeth, "Die Neueste Entwicklung der Franzosischen Bevolkerungspolitik" [Recent Developments of French Population Policy], Arch. Bevolker. 13:37-41, April 1943.

The new generalization of family compensation in France, the Code de la Famille, which was passed in July 1939 and went into effect January 1940, extended government aid to the families of farm producers, employers, the self-employed and artisans as well as for wage earners and salaried employees as in the old plan. The new plan also set up consultation centers for pregnant women and homes for receiving mothers before and after giving birth, and guaranteed the right of every woman to hospital care one month prior to and following childbirth. The new family aid legislation was divided into five categories: allocations for a single salary; family allocations; allocations for women in the home; allocations for assistance; and a salary for marriages that were less than two years old.

2398 Ponsioen, J.A. "Venster op Frankrijk" [Window on France], Sociol. Gids 1(11):192-93, November 1954.

An account of the French National Institute for Demographic Studies. It was founded by the French Government "to study population in its quantitative and qualitative, static and dynamic aspects;" but it is an independent institute which selects its study themes. Its 27 investigators discuss their research at weekly meetings with the Director, Alfred Sauvy. The research program is centered upon the relations between population structure and human behavior. A systematic survey of 15,000 French families produced data on the number of children desired (2.8), optimum number of children (3 to 6), etc.. Another theme is the relation between ethnic groups in France, particularly important because of France's constant need of foreign workers. Alfred Sauvy has shown that the relative weakness of the economically active strata in the French population makes a considerable immigration necessary; Girard and J. Stoetzel have investigated the attitudes and adaptations of Polish and Italian immigrant workers and their French hosts.

2399 Pundt, A.G. "France's Family Code and the Problem of Depopulation," Soc. Sci. 29(3):170-75, 1954.

The striking recent growth of population in France is linked both to the provisions of the family code and to the broadened and perfected system of social security.

2400 Sauvy, Alfred, La Montee des Jeunes [The Upsurge of Youth]. Paris: Calmann-Levy, 1959. 264 pp.

After a historical review indicating that a fall in births has never brought wealth, the author describes the effort to reverse the trend in France between the two world wars and the enactments supporting an expansionist policy. He then proposes a similar effort to provide suitable education, housing, and employment for the oncoming generation.

2401 Sauvy, Alfred, "La Politique Francaise de Population" [French Population Policy], Rev. Econ. Franco-Suisse 31: 380-83, December 1951.

France delayed the study of population for 100 years. It then acted to strengthen the family and to understand the dynamics of population through several measures around World War II. These include the passing of the Family Code, and the creation of the National Institute of Demographic Studies and the publication of _Population_. Family allocations began and maternity homes were built. Allowances for children and for low-scale workers with families were begun. Result was a forty percent increase in births. The main objective of family allowances is to allow parents to raise their children well.

2402 Sauvy, Alfred, "Population Demandee et Population Effective" [Required Population and Actual Population], _Rev. Sci. Econ._ 38(134):67-84, June 1963.

Consideration of general principles, with illustrations from French experience, of interrelations between population growth and economic and social progress. Conclusion discusses needed research for a social biology.

2403 Tissier, Pierre, _The Government of Vichy_. London: Harrap, 1942. 347 pp.

See especially Part II, Section II, The Renovation of the Population, pp. 150-87; and Section IV, The Return to the Land, pp. 210-32.

Policies on fertility and family size

2404 Aries, P.H. _Histoire des Populations Francaises et de Leurs Attitudes devant la Vie depuis le XVIIIe Siecle_ [History of French Populations and Their Attitudes to Life Since the Eighteenth Century]. Paris: Editions Self, 1948. 569 pp.

Includes historical analysis of attitudes toward family limitation, family size and related matters.

2405 Auclair, M. [The Black Book of Abortion]. Paris: Librairie Artheme Fayard, 1962.

In November, 1960 the author asked for opinions on abortion in "Marie-Claire," a French magazine. There was an initial response of 295 letters, followed by 286 letters in October, 1961, in response to another request. Among the 581 respondents there were 440 married women, 81 single women, 21 divorcees, 8 widows and 31 men who reported knowledge of a total of 2,960 abortions, 2,369 of which were illegal. The appendices include data on the readership of "Marie-Claire" and the terms of the French Health and Penal Codes concerning birth control and abortion. Similar legislation of other countries is briefly reviewed.

2406 Audry, C. "Le Parti Communiste et la Maternite Controlee" [The Communist Party and Birth Control], Temps Modernes, June 1956, pp. 1880-89.

2407 Baudovin, L. "Le Marchandage Juridique de l'Adultere de la Femme au Cours de la Liquidation des Interets Pecuniaires des Epoux en Cas de Separation de Corps," [Judicial Haggling Over Adultery of the Wife in the Course of Liquidating the Financial Interests of the Couple in Case of Physical Separation], Rev. Notariat 64:229, 293-ff., January - February 1962.

2408 Beaujeu-Garnier, J. "Faut-il Autoriser l'Avortement?" [Is it Necessary to Sanction Abortion?] Rev. Polit. Parlementaire, June 1956, pp. 231-39.

Abortion is against morality; but a policy of information on contraceptives is possible.

2409 Beaulieu, Georges de, "La Legislation Familiale, mars, 1950 a janvier, 1952" [Legislation on the Family, March 1950 to January 1952], Pour la Vie, January - March 1952.

2410 Becaud, J., _et al._ _Controle ou Regulation des Naissances?_ [Control or Regulation of Births?] Lyon: Social Chronicle of France, 1963. 109 pp.

A common vision of man brought together a Protestant doctor, two Catholic doctors, a journalist specializing in sociology, and a priest, to discuss birth control. Doctor D., an advocate of natural methods praised the individual doctor-couple discussion; he also preferred centers, and above all information disseminated through para-medical journals. To Doctors F. and M.G., it appears less desirable to concern oneself with the "law of 1920", but the suppression of that law cannot be done without considering the stabilization of the French population. They base their action on their confidence in the possibilities of educating man. F. draws a vivid picture found in the Malthusian mentality which is basically bourgeois and characteristic of modern times among the technically economically developed peoples. Also described is the Catholic position toward marriage.

2411 Bellut, Eugene. "La France A-T-Elle Une Politique Familiale?" [Has France a Family Policy?] _Pour la Vie_, No. 80, March 1960, pp. 1-8.

Discusses the history of the government's attitude toward population. The objective after World War II was to increase the population, hence the system of family allowances in proportion to salaries. The three imperatives at the foundation of the new policy became judicial, economic, and moral in 1957. The three plans are discussed.

2412 Besse, F. "A propos d'un Bilan Financier de la Compensation des Charges Familiales en France," [A Financial Balance Sheet on Family Allowances in France], _Pour la Vie_, No. 3, 1953, pp. 267-77.

2413 Besse, F., "En Quoi les Prestations d'Allocations Familiales et de Securite Social Sont ou Devraient Etre une Redistribution du Revenu National" [The Extent to which Family Allowances and Social Security Do or Should Involve a Redistribution of the National Income], _Formation_, November and December 1953, 8 pp. and 5 pp.

2414 Binder, R. Nos Prisonniers de Guerre et Leurs Familles [Our Prisoners of War and Their Families]. Paris: Imprime Chez Dubois et Bauer, 1942. 80 pp.

This pamphlet, published in Paris in 1942, describes family allowances and other facilities available to prisoners' families.

2415 [Birth Control], Rev. Inform Assist Soc. 17:242-ff., 1967.

Proposal of the Haut Comite Consultatif de la Population et de la Famille recommending that the legal indications for therapeutic abortion be extended to all cases where the mother's health is seriously endangered by the pregnancy. The report urges that severe guarantees be provided to avoid misuse of the more extended indication.

2416 Blacker, C.P. "A New Movement in France," Eugen. Rev. 48:213-21, January 1957.

Efforts to rescind provisions of the law of 1920 proscribing birth control, as led by the La Maternite Heureuse, are described. The position of the Institut National d'Etudes Demographiques, a state sponsored center, is also described.

2417 Blacker, J.G.C. "Social Ambitions of the Bourgeosie in 18th Century France and Their Relation to Family Limitation," Popul. Stud. 11(1):46-63, July 1957.

Relates the family limitation practices of the French bourgeosie to their desire for social mobility for the family.

2418 Bourdon, J. "Avortement et Birth Control" [Abortion and Birth Control], Rev. Polit. Parlementaire, October 1956, pp. 155-60.

Possible demographic consequences of the official sanction of birth control.

2419 Boverat, Fernand, Une Doctrine de Natalite [A Doctrine of Natality]. Paris: Librairie de Medicis, 1944. 40 pp.

2420 Brown, L. Neville, "The Reform of French Matrimonial Property Law," Amer. J. Comp. Law 14:308-22, Spring 1965.

By matrimonial regime is meant the sum of the rules governing the property rights between spouses, rules which may operate both during the subsistence of the marriage and at its termination by death, divorce, or in some other way. The Law of 13 July 1965 has carried out a sweeping reform of the French matrimonial regimes. Over 200 articles of the Civil Code have been recast in what amounts to the most extensive single revision to date of the text of 1804. Among other things, it introduces community of acquisitions as the new legal regime, but it abolishes the time-honored dotal regime and discards the cardinal principle of the immutability of regime. Socially, the reform reflects the continuing advance of French women towards complete legal equality.

2421 Buttler, R. "Jusqu'a Quel Point l'Etat Peut-il Aider la Famille?" [To What Extent Can the State Aid the Family?] Familles dans le Monde 7(3):196-203, 1954.

Discusses the desirable relation of public and private assistance.

2422 Calin, R. [The Family Code, an Expression of New Social and Political Conditions], Roumanie Nouvelle 7(130):1-5, February 1954.

2423 Ceccaldi, Dominique, "Donnees Essentielles d'une Reforme des Prestations Familiales" [Essential Data for a Reform of Family Allowances], Droit Soc.,September - October, November 1955, pp. 441-45, 582-93.

The development of the general level of family allowances since 1946. Should, and can, the general level of family allowances be raised?

2424 Ceccaldi, Dominique, "Family Policy in France," Eugen. Quart. 4(3):148-52, September 1957.

Nine per cent of the national income is allotted by the government to the annual budget for family relief measures. The French experiment is guided by three principles: (1) demographic, aiding the economic condition of the family and thereby raising the birth rate; (2) social justice, enabling all those who work to have a family and to assure provision for the main needs of the family; and (3) psycho-sociological aspects, emphasizing that the family is the natural and fundamental element of the society and has a right to be protected by the society and the State. The various aspects of the family allotment are discussed. The result of France's fifteen year experiment with a family policy has been an increase in the birth rate and an improvement in family conditions accomplished by a redistribution of incomes. The results have been encouraging, but many changes and additions need to be made before the institutions of social protection for the family reach their last stage of development.

2425 Ceccaldi, Dominique, Histoire des Prestations Familiales en France [History of Family Allowances in France]. Paris: Union Nationale des Caisses d'Allocations Familiales, 1957. 165 pp.

In this history of family benefits in France, Ceccaldi attempts to give a faithful picture of a highly complex and varied situation comprising a multiple of philosophical, economic and demographic trends and to show how the present system sprang from a coincidence of social and demographic aims. The work is accompanied by a selective bibliography and a list of the most important dates [1932-1956] in the history of family allowances in France.

2426 Ceccaldi, Dominique, "Le Logement de la Famille du Travailleur dans ses Rapports avec la Politique Generale des Ressources Familiales," [Housing of Workers' Families in Relation to the General Policy of Family Assistance], Pour la Vie, No. 3, 1953, pp. 230-52.

2427 Ceccaldi, Dominique, Politique Francaise de la Famille, Principes, Orientations, Realisations [French Family Policy, Principles, Orientation, Accomplishments]. Toulouse: Privat, 1957. 125 pp.

2428 Ceccaldi, Dominique,and Blondeau, Jacques, "Evolution Comparee des Prestations Familliales, des Salaires et des Prix Depuis 1946" [Comparative Development in Family Allowances, Wages, and Prices Since 1946], Population 10(4):705-11, October - December 1955.

2429 Chamoux, Antoinette, and Dauphin, Cecile, "La Contraception avant la Revolution Francaise: l'Exemple de Chatillon-sur-Seine" [Contraception Before the French Revolution: The Example of Chatillon-on-the-Seine], Ann. Econ. Societes, Civilisations 24(3):662-84, May - June 1969.

Presents the first results of a multidisciplinary inquiry in the region of Chatillon-on-the Seine, launched in 1966. The discovery of a record of the families of this village, which was begun by a local scholar in 1772, permitted investigation of the fertility of 130 marriages formed between 1772 and 1784. The record included an intensive study of the parish registers. The analysis of legitimate fertility at all durations of marriage according to age at marriage and a comparison of these data with comparable studies in other areas of France shows Chatillon-on-the-Seine to have a very low rate before the Revolution which suggests a voluntary limitation of births there. Malthusianism which was strong during the end of the 18th century and the 19th century had not yet come into vogue and thus does not explain the limitation.

2430 Colin, Robert, "La Famille Devant le Probleme du Logement" [The Family and the Housing Problems], Population 4(2): 269-82, April - June 1949.

The housing shortage in France and the recently instituted housing allowances are discussed.

2431 Colin, Robert, "Premier Bilan des Allocations de Logement" [A First Appraisal of Rental Allotments], Population 7(2): 237-48, April - June 1952.

Appraisal of the rental allotments established in 1948 as one of the family subsidies.

2432 Chappaz, G. [Proposal to Prohibit the Free Sale in Pharmacies of Potassium Permanganate Tablets], Bull. Acad. Nat. Med. 149:277-ff., 1965.

A questionnaire was sent to 30 obstetricians in different regions of France dealing with the use of potassium permanganate tablets as an abortifacient. Seventeen responded that they saw on the average of two to three women per year for complications resulting from the use of this tablet; nine saw them occasionally; and four had never seen women for this reason. Twenty-one had seen very grave cases resulting from the use of the tablets, three had seen them exceptionally, and six had never seen grave cases. One death was attributed to the use of the tablets. All felt that potassium permanganate in tablet form was of no use to them for therapeutic reasons, and all felt that the tablets should be banned from free sale in pharmacies.

2433 Charrier, M.A. [Criminal Abortion, National Scourge], J. Med. Bordeaux 124:10-ff., 1947.

Hospital statistics indicate increasing numbers of criminal abortions in France. Methods of minimizing the incidence of such abortions are discussed.

2434 Colloque National, Pour une Politique de l'Enfance dans une France Democratique, Organise a l'Initiative de l'Union des Vaillants et Vaillantes et de l'Ecole et la Nation Paris, 18-24 Avril 1966 [National Conference for a Policy on Children in Democratic France, Organized on the Initiative of the Union of Valor and Bravery and the School and Nation, Paris, 18-24 April 1966]. Paris: Editions Sociales, 1966. 238 pp.

2435 Congres National de la Federation des Familles de France, "Compte Rendu du Congres National de la Federation des Familles de France, Familles Nombreuses et Jeunes Foyers, Lille, les 10, 11 et 12 novembre 1950" [Report of the National Conference of the Federation of Families of France, Large Families, and Youth Homes, Lille, 10th to 12th November, 1950], Pour la Vie, December 1950 - January 1951.

2436 Cook, Robert C., ed. "Children in Spite of Ourselves: France Struggles With a Dilemma," Popul. Bull. 12:109-26, November 1956.

History and development of France's population policy; the issues and personalities involved in the current controversy over the legal status of birth control.

2437 Coudray, P., et al. "Contraception et Avortement. Etude Psycho-Sociologique d'Information et d'Attitudes en Milieu Urbain " [Contraception and Abortion. Psycho-Social Study of Information and Attitudes in an Urban Milieu], Rev. Hygiene Med. Soc. 17(3):269-82, April - May 1969.

2438 Le Couple et la Contraception [The Couple and Contraception], Toulouse: Privat, 1967. 142 pp.

2439 Le Couple et la Limitation des Naissances: Reflexions et Informations sur la Contraception [The Couple and Birth Limitation: Ideas and Information on Contraception]. Paris: P. Lethielleux, 1966. 62 pp.

2440 Daric, Jean, "Social, Demographic and Economic Aspects of the French System of Family Allowances," Bull. Internat. Soc. Sec. Assn. 4(7-8):284-94, July - August 1951.

2441 Delaume, Georges R. "France: Recent Developments in the Law of Alimony Settlements Incidental to Divorce," Amer. J. Comp. Law 5:277-81, 1956.

Pursuant to Article 301, paragraph 1, French Civil Code, the spouse in whose favor the divorce is pronounced may be granted alimony up to and not in excess of one third of the other spouse's income. Traditionally, it is said that this alimony is both "compensatory" and "alimentary" in character. Today, instead of emphasizing the "compensatory" character of alimony, as the courts did until 1949 to validate alimony settlements, they now emphasize the "alimentary" character of alimony to invalidate such settlements. Under the pressure of economic circumstances (inflation and depreciation of the national currency) the courts have felt that a means be found to review alimony settlements as well as judicial alimony. Under the "alimentary" concept of alimony, this power of judicial review could be exercised with less difficulty. Hence the change in the analysis of the juridical nature of alimony.

2442 Delerue, J. [Abortion], J. Sci. Med. Lille 81:520-ff., 1963.

A general discussion of abortion. The issue of professional secrecy is reviewed and the author feels that limiting the number of criminal abortions depends on preventative measures which would combat the economic, social and family situations causing women to seek abortions and on realistic contraceptive education.

2443 Derogy, Jacques, Des Enfants Malgre Nous [Children in Spite of Ourselves]. Paris: Les Editions de Minuit, 1956. 254 pp.

A plea for freedom to disseminate contraceptive information and to sell contraceptive products in France.

2444 Derogy, Jacques, and Lescaut, Paul, Population sur Mesure [Population on Order]. Paris: Le Seuil, 1965. 125 pp.

Discussion of family planning and birth rates in France in relation to population growth and social structure.

2445 Deshaies, G. [Abortion and Sterilization in Psychiatry], Press Med. 68:87-ff., 1960.

Abortion may provide the best answer to the problem of psychiatric contraindicated pregnancy. It is a method of avoiding childbirth; it is not permanent, and its use would lead to far fewer sterilizations. French law should permit abortion due to maternal incapability or danger.

2446 Doublet, Jacques, "Le Controle de l'Emploi des Prestations Familiales" [Control of the Use of Family Allowances], Population 2(1):53-60, January - March 1947.

A study of various proposals concerning family allowances in France.

2447 Doublet, Jacques, "Deux Modalites de la Politique d'Aide a la Famille: Prestations en Especes et Prestation en Nature " [Two Methods of Extending Assistance to Families: Payments in Money and Benefits in Kind], Population 3(4): 651-60, October - December 1948.

Discusses both methods and concludes that to pass judgment on the problem one must examine the aims pursued and take into account the peculiarities and customs of each country concerned.

2448 Doublet, Jacques, "Family Allowances in France," Popul. Stud. 2(2):219-39, September 1948.

Deals with the development and nature of family allowances in France, as well as other benefits given by the French State to those with families. As such services are now intimately connected with the general scheme of social security in France, the place which services designated to aid the family have in the system is explained.

2449 Doublet, Jacques, "La Premiere Legislature de la IVe Republique et la Legislation Demographique" [The First Legislature of the IVth Republic and Demographic Legislation], Population 6(3):397-410, July - September 1951.

2450 Doublet, Jacques, "Les Prestations Familiales et la Loi du 22 aout, 1946" [Family Payments and the Law of August 22, 1946], Droit Soc.,December 1946, pp. 413-20.

2451 Doublet, Jacques, et al. Reflexions sur les Prestations Familiales: Dix Annees de Fonctionnement [Thoughts on Family Allowances: Ten Years' Experience]. Paris: Union National des Caisses d'Allocations Familiales, 1958. 135 pp.

Four lectures on the tenth anniversary of the National Union of Family Allowance Funds of France. Mr. Jacques Doublet, Director - General of Social Security, describes the legislative changes which have been made during these ten years. Mr. Pierre Laroque, Chairman of the Board of Directors of the French National Social Security Fund, analyzes the financial evolution of the system from 1946 to 1956. Mr. Emmanuel Rain, Director - General of the Population and Mutual Aid Department, discusses problems arising out of the social work of the family allowance funds. Finally, Mr. Alfred Sauvy, Director of the National Institute for Demographic Studies, endeavours to define the contribution of family allowances to social progress.

2452 Douriez, P. [Contraception and the Law]. Concours Med. 84:3143-49, May 19, 1962.

2453 Dourlen-Rollier, Anne-Marie, L'Avortement Autorise ou Defendu [Legal and Illegal Abortion]. Paris: Buchet-Chastel, 1965. 192 pp.

The author, legal counsel for the French Movement for Family Planning, compares French legislation on abortion, and its enforcement, with that of Sweden and Switzerland.

2454 Dourlen-Rollier, Anne-Marie, ed. L'Avortement en France: Colloque Organise sous l'Egide du Mouvement Francais pour le Planning Familial [Abortion in France: Colloquium Organized Under the Auspices of the French Family Planning Movement]. Paris: Maloine, 1967. 185 pp.

Report on a colloquium on problems and policies associated with abortion, held at the Center of International Conferences of the Ministry of Foreign Affairs. Participants included physicians, psychiatrists, jurists, demographers, social workers, and sociologists.

2455 Dourlen-Rollier, Anne-Marie [The Situation of Abortion in France] in: Mehlan, K.E. , ed. Internationale Abortsituation, Abortbekampfund, Antikonzeption. Leipzig: Georg Thieme, 1961.

Report on the rigid abortion legislation in France which permits abortion only to save the life of the mother, and after a long procedure. Under 100 therapeutic abortions are performed annually, yet the estimated figure of criminal abortions in France varies between 400,000 and 1,200,000 each year. High statistics on the number of maternal deaths resulting from abortion are given, but the deaths are vastly reduced due to the introduction of antibiotic therapy. The need for contraceptive education and less prohibitive abortion laws are stressed.

2456 Dourlen-Rollier, A.M. La Verite sur l'Avortement [The Truth about Abortion]. Paris: Librarie Maloine, 1963.

The history of abortion legislation and therapuetic abortion in France are reviewed. The problem of illegal abortions and the abortion situation in other European countries and in the United States are also discussed. The author recommends preventive measures for induced abortion including social legislation to alleviate the economic burden of child-bearing and increased education in sexual responsibilities and in contraceptive use.

2457 Drouhet, Pierre, L'Evolution Juridique des Allocations Familiales [The Legal Development of Family Allowances] Paris: L'Edition Sociale Francaise, 1943. 334 pp.

Study of the nature, organization, and progress of the family-allowance movement in France.

2458 Dumolin du Fraisse, G. L'Avortement, en Droit Penal, Depuis le Code de la Famile [Abortion, in Penal Law, Since the Family Code]. Paris: Recueil Sirey, 1944. 213 pp.

2459 Durand, Paul, "Allocations Familiales et Allocation de Salaire Unique" [Family Allowances and Allowance of Special Wages], pp. 19-27 in: Le Nouveau Regime du Travail. Paris: Librairie Sociale et Economique, 1943. 63 pp.

A comparison of provisions in the Code de la Famille and in the Law of February 15, 1941.

2460 Familles dans le Monde. "Mesures en Faveur de la Famille en France" [Measures for the Benefit of Families in France]. Familles dans le Monde,Nos. 2-3, June - September 1960 , pp. 107-30.

2461 Fayot-Petitmaire, M. "De la Sterilisation Feminine Preventive" [On Preventive Sterilization in Women], Semaine Hopitaux Paris 31(71):3804-7, December 2, 1955.

2462 Febvay, M. "Niveau et Evolution de la Fecondite par Categorie Socio-Professionnelle en France" [Birth Rate and Change in a Socio-Professional Category in France] Population 14(4):729-39, October - December 1959.

Evidence that relatively high status groups with lowest pre-war fertility had largest rises after war. Advances the theory that family allowance program produced this effect by providing resources for those most interested in future of their children.

2463 "La Federation des Familles de France Face au Probleme de la Regulation des Naissances" [The Federation of Families in France Face the Problem of Birth Regulation],Pour la Vie 105/106:259-61, 1966.

2464 Feinerman, Danielle, "Enquete sur les Connaissances et Pratiques Contraceptives dans un Groupe de Femmes Encientes" [Enquiry Concerning Knowledge and Practice of Contraception in a Group of Pregnant Women], Fertilite 1(3):41-45, June 1969.

2465 Felgines, Marcel, "Realites Demographiques et Politique Familiale" [Demographic Reality and Family Policy], Vitalite Francaise,No. 488-489, December 1967.

2466 Fischer, G. "La Sterilisation Feminine Preventive en France et a l'Etranger" [Preventive Sterilization of Women in France and Abroad], Concours Med. 77(28): 2831-37, July 9, 1955.

2467 Fournier, E. "Legislation de l'Avortement" [Legislation on Abortion], Bull. Med. 69(3):77-79, April 1955.

2468 France. L'Alliance Nationale Contre la Depopulation, Comment Enrayer la Depopulation de la France [How to Check the Depopulation of France]. Paris: Impr. de Coquemard, 1943. 32 pp.

2469 France. Codes de la Securite Sociale, de la Sante Publique, de la Famille et de l'Aide Sociale [Social Security, Public Health, and Family and Social Assistance Codes], Third edition. Paris: Jurisprudence Generale Dalloz, 1962. 1016 pp.

Published in the collection of Petits Codes Dalloz, this compilation of basic legislation concerning the organization of social security is supplemented, in this new edition, by two parts reproducing the Public Health Code and the Family and Social Assistance Code, for the use of physicians, dentists, medical auxiliaries, pharmacists and social welfare workers who have to know them, and carry out their requirements. A chronological list of legislative texts is included.

2470 France. Comite Central des Allocations Familiales, Le Code de la Famille [The Family Code], Fifth edition. Lille: Imp. Martin - Mamy, 1942. 187 pp.

Preceded by a detailed commentary and followed by interpretative text. Law of July 29, 1939, modified and extended by laws of December 16, 1939; April 24, 1940; November 18, 1940; February 15, 1941; March 29, 1941; November 17, 1941 and February 3, 1942.

2471 France. Commissariat General a la Famille, Les Prisonniers et la Famille [Prisoners and the Family]. Paris: Office de Propagande Generale, 1943. 76 pp.

A multicolored, pictographic presentation of the problem of too few births is followed by a discussion of reforms. The latter includes references to the relevant French laws.

2472 France. "Creches," Internat. Digest Health Legis. 3:478-83, 1951-52.

Order of 18 April 1951 amends Article 3 of the Decree of 21 April 1945 regarding Creches with respect to arrangement of the premises, care of children, staff, and methods of administrative supervision.

2473 France. Direction du Service des Prisonniers de Guerre, Guide Pratique des Familles de Prisonniers de Guerre et des Prisonniers Rapatries, Droits et Avantages [A Practical Guide for Families of Prisoners of War and Repatriated Prisoners, Rights and Benefits]. Paris: Charles-Lavauzelle and Cie., 1944. ix, 160 pp.

Including family allowances and medical and other assistance for families.

2474 France. "Family Planning," Internat. Digest Health Legis. 19:620-21, 1968.

The manufacture and the import of contraceptives, previously forbidden in France, were authorized under a law (No. 67-1176) enacted in December 1967. Contraceptives may be sold in pharmacies only. Some contraceptives will be placed on a special list to be bought by prescription only. Non-emancipated minors will also need the written consent of a parent or guardian. The law specifies that IUDs must be inserted by physicians in hospitals, treatment centers, or other places to be designated by public administrative regulations. Centers of family planning and education, private and public, are to be governed by public administrative regulations. Such centers are prohibited from dispensing contraceptives. All anti-natalist propaganda is specifically prohibited, as is commercial advertising of contraceptives.

2475 France. Haut Comite Consultatif de la Population et de la Famille, La Regulation des Naissances [Regulation of Births]. Paris: La Documentation Francaise, 1967. 82 pp.

2476 France. "Health Register of Prostitutes," Internat. Digest Health Legis. 1:225-26, 1948-50.

Decree No. 47-2253 of 5 November 1947 in application of Act No. 46-795 of 24 April 1946 requires every prostitute to be entered into a central register set up for the entire metropolitan area. The register, which is a social and public health measure, is under authority of the Minister for Social Affairs and Ex-Service men. This decree also supplements Act No. 46 of 13 April 1946 for the closing of brothels and the strengthening of control over traffic in women.

2477 France. Institut National d'Etudes Demographiques, "La Compensation des Charges Familiales en France en 1951" [Family Subsidies in France During 1951], Population 8(1):142-47 and 8(4):781-86, January - March 1953 and October - December 1953.

2478 France. Institut National d'Etudes Demographiques, "La Compensation des Charges Familiales en France en 1953" [Family Subsidies in France During 1953], Population 9(4):734-37, October - December 1954.

2479 France. "La Limitation des Naissances en France" [Limitation of Births in France], Population 11(2):209-34, April - June 1956.

The prospect of liberalization of birth control laws established in 1920 has prompted a reappraisal of data pertaining to the question. The following arguments are advanced by those in favor of these modifications: abortions will occur less frequently, women will have more freedom, French laws will be more similar to those of other countries. It is assumed that fertility will not be reduced as a result of these new laws. However, in reality, it is very difficult to evaluate the consequences of such legislative measures.

The availability of birth control methods will probably reduce the number of births as it cannot be realistically assumed that all unwanted pregnancies end in abortions. Furthermore, since no method is completely safe, abortion can still occur. The Indianapolis study documents the decrease in births which contraceptive methods bring about. In addition, these laws would have psychological consequences and would affect individuals' attitudes. In France, families with three or more children account for 23% of all births. If no family had more than three children, the population would not be replacing itself (net reproduction rate of .84). The comparatively favorable birth-rate experienced by France in recent times results from legislation in favor of large families. Modifications in these laws would lead to an unwanted decrease in the birth rate. Liberalization of existing laws must proceed with caution.

2480 France. Institut National d'Etudes Demographiques, "Rapport de l'Institut National d'Etudes Demographiques a Monsieur le Ministre des Affaires Sociales sur la Regulation des Naissances en France" [Report on Birth Control in France Presented to the Minister of Social Affairs by the National Institute for Demographic Research], Population 21(4): 645-90, July - August 1966.

The report is in two parts. Part 1, a study of the effect on French natality of the adoption of a more liberal policy on birth control, has sections on: abortions in France; effects of a contraceptive method of 100% efficiency on legitimate natality in France; probable effects of the introduction of such a method on illegitimate births, prenuptial conceptions, and nuptiality; probable effects on total natality (legitimate and illegitimate); costs of contraceptive methods when used by a population; conclusion of Part 1 (stressing need for nation-wide sample surveys of couples' fertility and of induced abortion in France). Part 2, necessary regulatory legislative measures to be taken for the development of natality in France has sections on: the psychological environment; information campaign; legislative and regulatory measures (related to housing, education, taxation, military service, women's labor-force participation.

2481 France. Institut National de la Sante et de la Recherche Medicale, Rapport Etabli par la Commission Creee a l'Institut pour Examiner les Consequences Eventuelles sur la Sante de l'Absorption de Produits Anticonceptionnels [Report Submitted by the Committee Established at the National Institute of Health and Medical Research to Examine the Ultimate Consequences on Health of the Use of Contraceptive Products]. Paris, 1966. 5 pp.

2482 France. Institut National de la Statistique et des Etudes Economiques, "Les Charges Sociales dans les Pays de l'O. E.C.E." [Social Charges in the O.E.C.E. Countries], _Etudes Conjoncture_ 9(3):269-84, March 1954.

Including maternity protection, family allowances, etc.

2483 France. Institut National de la Statistique et des Etudes Economiques, "Premiers Resultats Concernant les Depenses des Familles de Salaries de la Region Parisienne, au Printemps 1948" [First Results on the Expenditures of Families With Salaries in the Paris Region, in the Spring of 1948] _Bull. Statistique Generale France_ 37, Supplement: 37-55, January - March 1949.

One of the objectives of the study was to provide a factual basis for government policy in regard to rations and the family.

2484 France. Institut National de la Statistique et des Etudes Economiques, "Des Prestations Familiales" [Family Allowances] Bull. _Mensuel Statistique_ Supplement: April - June 1955. pp. 47-54.

Legislation July 29,1939,to 1946, and since 1946. The family allowance funds. Detailed data on laws, administration, statistics.

2485 France. Institut National de la Statistique et des Etudes Economiques, "Les Prestations Familiales Agricoles" [Agricultural Family Allowances] _Bull. Statistique General France_ 47, Supplement: 28-36, January - March 1949.

Origin, development, finance, functioning, 1940-1947.

2486 France. Laws, Statutes, etc. "Code de la Famille et de l'Aide Sociale" [Family Code and Social Assistance], _J. Officiel Republique Francaise_, Paris, 1956. iv, 138 pp.

2487 France. Laws, Statutes, etc. Code des Prestations Familiales [Code of Family Allowances]. Paris: Revue Generale Securite Sociale, 1947. 19 pp.

2488 France. Laws, Statutes, etc. "Loi No. 46-1835 du 22 aout 1946 Fixant le Regime des Prestations Familiales" [Law No. 46-1835 of 22 August 1946 Fixing the Rules on Family Allowances], Population 1(3):581-86, July - September 1946.

2489 France. Laws, Statutes, etc. "Loi Modifiant et Completant le Decret du 29 juillet 1939, Relatif a la Famille et a la Natalite Francaisses" [Law Modifying and Completing the Decree of July 29, 1939 Relative to the French Family and Fertility], J. Officiel Republique Francaise 62(298):5715-16, November 19, 1940.

A decree signed November 18, 1940 modifies the decree of July 29, 1939 and earlier decrees with reference to the fixation of base wages for commerce and industry and for agriculture. The rates for family allowances are fixed at ten per cent of the average monthly salary for the second child, and twenty for the third and each succeeding child, i.e., ten per cent for two children, thirty per cent for three, and a twenty per cent increase for each child above three.

2490 France. Laws, Statutes, etc. "Population Policy," J. Officiel Republique Francaise, 11 July 1943, p. 1853.

An act of 6 July 1943 amending the legislation concerning the French family and the birth rate provides that in future family allowances will be payable also to relatives in the collateral line, that is, to a brother or sister, uncle or aunt, on behalf of sister or brother, nephew or niece for whose maintenance he or she is permanently and wholly responsible.

2491 France. Laws, Statutes, etc. "Prestations Familiales (Metropole): Volume Arrete a la Date du 14 janvier, 1957" [Family Allowances (Metropolitan France): Record up to January 15, 1957], in: France, Ministere de la Guerre, Bulletin Officiel, Edition Methodique, La Securite Sociale, No. 351. Paris: Charles-Lavauzelle, 1957. 203 pp.

2492 France. Laws, Statutes, etc. Prestations Familiales (Professions Non Agricolis). Edition Nuse a Jour au 15 aout 1959 [Family Allowances (Non-Agricultural Occupations). Edition Issued October 15, 1959], J. Officiel Republique Francaise 1009, Paris, 1959. 139 pp.

2493 France. Laws, Statutes, etc., Securite Sociale [Social Security]. Paris, 1949. 123 pp.

Principal legislative and statutory texts concerning family allowances.

2494 France. Ministere de la Sante Publique et de la Population, Service de Documentation, Recueil des Textes Officiels Concernant la Protection de la Sante et de la Famille Promulgues en 1948 [Collection of Official Texts Concerning the Protection of Health and the Family Made Public in 1948]. Paris: Imprimerie Nationale, 1949. 1072 pp.

Cabinet decrees, and laws, directives, etc., of the following: Directorate of General Administration of Personnel and the Budget; Directorate General of Public Hygiene and Hospitals; Directorate of Social Hygiene; Central Pharmaceutical Service; Directorate General of Population; National School of Health; National Institute of Demographic Studies; National Center of Health, Demographic and Social Education; French Association for the Study of Human Problems; Ministry of France Overseas; Ministry of Reconstruction and Urbanization; and Ministry of Employment and Social Security.

2495 France. "Maternal and Child Health: Pre and Postnatal Examinations," Internat. Digest Health Legis. 16:538-41, 1965.

Order of 22 February 1965 of the Minister of Public Health and Population modifies the conditions for conducting prenatal and postnatal examinations. Prenatal examinations are required before the end of the third month of pregnancy, during the sixth month of pregnancy, and during the first fifteen days of the eighth month of pregnancy. Radiological examinations, serological tests, blood grouping and the search for nephritis, cardiac disorder, and other specific diseases are required. The postnatal examination is compulsory during the eight weeks following the delivery.

2496 France. "Maternal and Child Welfare: Medico-Social Assistance," Internat. Digest Health Legis. 8:275-76, 1957.

Decree No. 56-149 of 24 January 1956 codifies legislation relating to families and social assistance under the name of the Family and Social Assistance Code. Included are: social welfare of the family, material aid to the family especially in matters relating to employment and housing, family education, social welfare of children, prevention of abortions, and social assistance to children.

2497 France. "Maternal and Child Welfare: Miscellaneous Provisions," Internat. Digest Health Legis. 16:100, 1965.

Law No. 64-677 of 6 July 1964 amends provisions of the Public Health Code. Included are provisions for the care of pre-school children and for the costs of maternal and child welfare.

2498 France. Ministere du Travail, Direction Generale de la Securite Sociale, Social Security in France, 1965. 112 pp.

2499 France. Ministere du Travail et de la Securite Sociale, Rapport...de Securite Sociale. Statistiques du 1[er] janvier, 1951 au 31 decembre, 1952. [Report...on Social Security Statistics from January 1, 1951 to December 31, 1952]. Paris, 1953. 90 pp.

2500 France. "Prenuptial Certificate and Child Health Protection," Internat. Digest Health Legis. 16:103-4, 1965.

Decree No. 64-931 of 3 September 1964 states that physicians may issue the prenuptial certificate only after satisfactory results of the radiological and serological examinations of persons planning marriage. Decree also specifies provisions for child care where parents have been refused family allowances because of their unwillingness to accept employment.

2501 Freed, Doris J. "Grounds for Divorce in French and American Law," J. Family Law (1):241-59, Fall 1961.

Comparison of the "peremptory" (adultery and criminal conviction) and "optional" (physical and mental cruelty) grounds for divorce in French law and United States law. Violations of the duties and obligations of marriage are also discussed under cruelty. These duties include fidelity, cohabitation, protection, sexual intercourse, and support and assistance. Two other matters are also discussed. One matter pertains to conduct which is contrary to the dignity of married life: habitual drunkenness, habitual gambling, and drug addiction. The other matter pertains to humiliating words, acts, or conduct.

2502 Geisendorf, W. [Must the Prescription of Oral Contraceptives be Regulated?] Bull. Federation Societes Gynec. Obstet. Langue Francaise 16:3-5, January - March 1964.

2503 Geraud, Roger, La Limitation Medicale des Naissances, Histoire, Biologie, Psychologie, Demographie, Legislation, Doctrines [The Medical Limitation of Births: History, Biology, Psychology, Demography, Legislation, Doctrines]. Revised edition.

2504 Girard, Alain, and Bastide, Henri, "Une Enquete sur l'Efficacite de l'Action Sociale des Caisses d'Allocations Familiales" [An Enquiry into the Efficacy of the Social Action of the Family Allowances Funds], Population 13(1): 39-54, January - March 1958.

Report on a sample survey by the Institut National d'Etudes Demographiques in the first quarter of 1957, covering 623,800 recipients of family allowances in the Paris region, Saint Etiene, Toulouse, and Angers. Describes survey methods, and summarizes and evaluates the findings as to amounts and relative proportions of allowance payments in aid of lodging, vacations, household needs, social services, placement, supplementary allowances, and miscellaneous expenses.

2505 Girard, Alain, and Samuel, Raul, "Une Enquete sur l'Opinion Publique a l'Egard de la Limitation des Naissances" [A Survey of Public Opinion on the Limitation of Births], Population 11(3):481-506, July - September 1956.

Report of a sample survey of 2,432 respondents representative of the sex, age, residential, regional, and occupational distributions of France in May and June 1956. Thirteen questions tested knowledge of birth-rate data, understanding of the attitude toward birth limitation, and approval of proposed policy changes. Presentation of results and analysis of influence of demographic, economic, and social characteristics.

2506 Girard, Alain, and Zucker, Elizabeth, "La Conjoncture Demographique: Regulation de Naissances, Famille, et Natalite: Un Equete Aupres du Publique" [Demographic Conjuncture: Birth-Control, Family and Natality. A Public Survey], Population 23(2):225-64, March - April 1968.

Currently French legislation in demographic matters is of a repressive character. There is, however, an effort to develop positive measures for stimulating fertility and favoring the large family. The success of these efforts are related to the general aspirations of people. In this inquiry, an objective is to learn about actual fertility and desired fertility in relation to several variables. The findings are based on the responses of 2,692 persons located in 187 communities.

2507 Girard, Alain, and Zucker, Elizabeth, "Une Enquete Aupres du Public sur la Structure Familiale et la Prevention des Naissances" [A Public Survey on Family Structure and on Birth Control], Population 22(3):401-54, May - June 1967.

The question of population growth and family planning has become one of the crucial problems; there has been much recent discussion of the issue in France. There are now family planning centers open in France since the law of 1920 which prohibited the publicizing of contraceptive practices has now been revised. In a public survey to examine family structure and the use of birth control measures, 2,519 individuals were interviewed (52% of whom were female) using two forms of a questionnaire. Respondents were asked such questions as how many children they desired, and the data was compared with the results of previous surveys. Questions were asked to determine background information on the respondents and the results are broken down by region, age, occupation, etc. Data were also gathered concerning the actual number of children per family and this was presented in conjunction with the data on the ideal number of children desired. Other questions asked concerned the intervals desired between children, the ideal interval between marriage and first child, and the age at which a woman should have her last child. It was found that in 1966, the number of Frenchmen who felt that the population of France was growing too rapidly rose sharply so that it matched the number who felt that it was at a good level. It was found that 49% of the respondents felt that the government should occupy itself with the question of family planning. It was found that 85% of the women between 20 and 49 years of age had heard discussion of birth control measures in 1966, as compared to 45% of the same age group in 1956. Various questions were asked concerning the regulation of births by the government, the use of contraceptives, etc., and these were tabulated by educational level, occupational level, and age. Questions concerning the frequency of actual abortions and morality of abortion were asked, and it was found that 63% of the respondents thought there were many abortions in France; 45% of the group between 20 and 34 years of age approved of abortion, while 34% of those over 65 did. In general, all the data shows the profound evolution which has taken place in the last few years.

2508 Gloor, P.A. Attitudes Feminines devant la Prevention des Naissances [Female Attitudes Towards Birth Control], Paris: Editions Doin (Deren et Cie), 1968. 200 pp.

2509 Guibal, Jean, La Famille dans la Revolution Nationale [The Family in the National Revolution]. Clermont: F. Sorlot, 1940. 31 pp.

2510 Gynecologie Pratique, "Projet d'Experimentation des Methodes de Contraception et de Leurs Consequences dans un Service de l'Assistance Publique" [Plan of Experimentation in Methods of Contraception and Their Consequences in the Public Health Service], Gynec. Pratique 8(3):201-2, 1957.

2511 Hanon, F. "Reflexion sur la Contraception" [Reflections on Contraception], Sem. Hop. 44(15):998-1004, 1968.

An impending new law in France will permit physicians to furnish or prescribe methods of contraception; it will not oblige the physician to do so. For many physicians this law will create new responsibilities implying concern over medical, socio-economic, religious and moral considerations. No method is entirely without possible disadvantages.

2512 Haury, Paul, "L'Oeuvre Legislative d'Adolphe Landry" [The Legislative Work of Adolphe Landry], Pour la Vie, No. 70, Spring 1957, pp. 265-304.

A documented record of Landry's work for family policy in France.

2513 Henry, Louis, "Mise au Point sur la Natalite Francaise" [Focus on French Natality], Population 9(2):197-226, April - June 1954.

Presentation of data leading to the conclusion that the family legislation adopted in 1939 has brought an increase in the proportion of middle-sized families and an earlier age of marriage. It is in the families of one and two children that legislation has favored the birth of an additional child.

2514 Hervet, Emile, and Lemoine, J.P. [On the Difficulty of Indications for Therapeutic Abortion], Presse Med. 74: 175-ff., 1966.

Reviews a case history of a woman in her fifteenth pregnancy with a history of repeated spontaneous abortions and several experiences with thromboembolism. Out of seven living children, four were hospitalized with psycho-motor retardation. Although a cardiologist referred her for therapeutic abortion, this case did not meet the requirements of French law since thromboembolism does not constitute a direct threat to the mother, and since the disease was not always directly associated with pregnancy. The pregnancy aborted spontaneously and tubal ligation was performed.

2515 Hochard, Jacques, "Role des Prestations Familiales Depuis 1945" [The Role of Family Allowances Since 1945], Rev. Action Populaire No. 191, September - October 1965, pp. 949-64.

Reviews the history of family allowances in France since the mid-nineteenth century and especially since 1946. Estimates their current economic role and social effect. Envisages possible extensions.

2516 Hochard, Jacques, et al. Prestations Familiales, Etudes et Perspectives [Family Allowances, Studies and Perspectives] Paris: Union Nationale des Caisses d'Allocations Familiales, 1957. 179 pp.

2517 [Induced Abortions], Prophyl. Sanit. Morale 35:168-ff., 1963.

Presents statistics on illegal abortions drawn from an article in "Le Monde", a popular news magazine, and Dourlen-Rollier's book, La Verite sur l'Avortement.

2518 International Labour Office, "Family Allowances in France," Internat. Labour Rev. 52:196-210, 1947.

In view of the deliberate policy of the State of making family allowances an essential part of its population policy, it is interesting to note the movement of the birth rate since allowances were first introduced. Studies among groups covered by equalization funds have shown a higher birth rate for members than for the population at large. The interpretation of results, however, involves the consideration of such factors as differences in age, sex, marital condition, etc., and therefore this evidence cannot be considered conclusive. Furthermore, as the birth rate has been falling for most of the period in which allowances have been paid, it is clear that the most that can be said is that the existence of such a system may have prevented an even more drastic fall. It seems reasonable to assume, however, that the much more sharply graduated scale of benefits and the payment of special allowances when the mother remains in the home, are likely to be more effective than the earlier State policy of merely extending coverage. They have altered the character of the system and now, more than ever before, its form is such as to provide a very considerable inducement for the raising of three or more children.

2519 International Labour Office, "Maternity and Child Welfare in France," Internat. Labour Rev. 53(5-6):426, May - June 1946.

An Order, No. 45-2720, dated 2 November 1945, consolidates the essential provisions of various maternity and child welfare measures issued in conformity with the Family Code of 1939. It is hoped that new measures under this Order will help to reduce the infant mortality rate which rose during the war. The social and medical protection of mothers and young children are placed in the hands of regional inspectors of health and social workers. A second Order of the same date extends maternity leave up to eight weeks before and eight weeks after child-delivery, and prohibits the employment of a woman within six weeks after confinement.

2520 Jamet, F. "Contribution a Etude des Motivations de l'Acceptation et du Refus des Methods Anticonceptionelles " [A Contribution to the Study of Motivations for the Acceptance and Refusal of Anti-Conception Methods], Recherche Information Sante Publique 23(6):1333-46, November - December 1968.

Brief review of the most recent knowledge concerning contraception and, especially, concerning motivations, efficiency, and changes in knowledge of this problem in France. After examining legal aspects such as the modifications of the 1920 law and the purposes which they are intended to serve, attention is given to the technical aspect of modern contraceptive techniques -- oral contraceptive, IUDs and other methods. There is a greater and greater interest among the French for a satisfactory contraceptive and an absolute right to its use. The adequacy of the contraceptive profoundly influences motivations to accept or refuse its use.

2521 Jarlot, Georges, Le Code de la Famille: Preoccupation Nataliste ou Politique Familiale? [The Family Code: Preoccupation with Natality or Family Policy?] Le Puy, Editions 10. Mappus, 1943. 155 pp.

This small book, published in the Occupation Period, covers population change, 1801-1940; vital statistics; consequences and causes of decline; the "Code de la Famille"; and the "New regime" since 1940.

2522 Jeannin, G. La Prime a la Premiere Naissance [The Premium for First Births]. Paris: Les Publications Sociales Agricoles, 1941. 22 pp.

A description and evaluation of the law of March 15, 1940, providing for a reward at the first birth under certain specified limitations.

2523 Jourdain, Francois, Les Allocations Familiales en Agriculture: Vos Droits, Vos Devoirs, a Jour au 1er avril 1944 [Family Allowances in Agriculture: Your Rights, Your Duties, April 1, 1944]. Paris: Les Publications Sociales Agricoles, 1944. 45 pp.

2524 Lagroua-Weill-Halle, Marie, La Contraception et Les Francais: Etude sur 7,600 Couples, 1956 to 1966. [Contraception and the French: A Study of 7,600 Couples, 1956 to 1966]. Paris: Maloine, 1967. 240 pp.

This study is based on couples who had come to the medical office of the author for consultation on contraception. Most couples are young and belong to the liberal professions, managerial class, and office workers. Responses to a questionnaire show that one-third planned their family size from the beginning of marriage, 40% of the couples desired two children while 20% desired three children, and economic and religious factors influence the numbers of children in an opposite way. Methods of contraception and their psychological effects are also considered.

2525 Lagroua-Weill-Halle, Marie, "Le Controle de Naissances a l'Etranger et la Loi Francaise de 1920" [Birth Control in Other Countries and the French Law of 1920], Sem. Hop. 29:145-52, 22 March 1953.

2526 Lagroua-Weill-Halle, Marie, La Grand Peur d'Aimer. Journal d'Une Femme Medicin [The Great Fear of Sex. Journal of a Woman Doctor]. Paris: Rene Juliard, 1960. 164 pp.

The author is the President of Maternite Heureuse, the French family planning association. In this book she describes her own emotional conflicts which, in 1953, led her into opposition to orthodox French policies affecting family welfare. In addition there are case histories of the intimate dilemmas and problems of about fifty of her patients.

2527 Lagroua-Weill-Halle,Marie, and Chauchard,Paul. Pour ou Contre la Pilule et le Planning Familial [Attitudes to the Pill and Family Planning].Nancy: Berger-Levrault, 1967. 78 pp.

2528 Landauer, D. von, "Matrimonial Causes in French Law," Internat. Comp. Law Quart.13:6-38,January 1964.

Since the Civil Code of 1804, matrimonial law in France had been applicable to only nationals of the country. A change occurred in 1948 when jurisdiction became generally available to aliens established in France. But the French concept of domicile, which was active between 1550 and 1792 and then lapsed into latency, is again revived. Each person has one and only one domicile. The content of domestic law with regard to divorce, judicial separation, nullity, property, adoption, and maintenance is described. This is followed by a statement of the position of international law on these topics. The description is both comparative and historical.

2529 Laurent, Jean-Charles, Le Divorce. Essai de Sociologie Juridique [Divorce: Essay in Legal Sociology], Paris: Guy Victor, 1964. 158 pp.

2530 Lebel, Roland, "Les Allocations Familiales. Etude Internationale" [Family Allowance Systems. An International Study], Informations Soc. 8(2):126-87, February 1954.

Comparison of the French system with British and other western European solutions.

2531 Lebel, Roland, "Evolution de l'Institution des Allocations Familiales en France" [Developments Since the Beginning of Family Allowances in France], Information Soc. 17(12): 81-95, December 1963.

2532 Lebel, Roland, "Family Allowance," Bull. Internat. Soc. Security Assn. 4(7-8):273-83, July - August 1951.

2533 Ledoux, Georges, Amour et Naissances. Une Synthese Pratique et Morale des Meilleures Methodes Actuelles de Regulation des Naissances [Love and Births: A Practical and Moral Synthesis of Better Methods of Actually Regulating Births]. Paris: P. Tequi, 1967. 223 pp.

2534 Levy-Bruhl, H. Aspects Sociologiques du Droit [Sociological Aspects of Law]. Paris: M. Riviere, 1955.

Chapter 9, titled "Reflections on the Family," describes changes in the actual position of the woman and child in the French family. Employed are historical, legislative, and demographic documents and the proceedings of the colloquium on the family organized by the Center of Sociological Studies in 1954.

2535 Lombois, C. "La Condition Juridique de la Femme Mariee" [The Legal Position of the Married Woman] Rev. Notariat 68:457, 525, May, June - July 1966.

2536 Mahon, R. [Therapeutic Abortion in the Rubella-Pregnancy Association, or the Slaughter of Healthy Infants], J. Med. Bordeaux 139:133-ff., 1962.

Research on the possible effects of rubella in pregnancy is described. The author feels that abortion is never justified for rubella pregnancy cases, even when malformations may have occurred, since the probability of such malformations cannot take precedence over the actuality of human life.

2537 Malezieux, R. La Legislation Sociale des Professions Agricoles [Social Legislation in Agriculture] Paris: Librairie Sociale et Economique, 1946. 180 pp.

Family allowances in agriculture are considered.

2538 Malignac, Georges, "Minimum Vital et Niveau d'Existence Suivant le Nombre d'Enfants" [Subsistence Wage and Standard of Living According to the Number of Children], Population 4(2):249-68, April - June 1949.

In order to determine the adequacy of family allowance in France, the objective needs of families are measured in terms of money value as well as in terms of index numbers.

2539 Manceau, Bernard, Pour la Repopulation: des Assurances Familiales [For the Sake of Repopulation: Family Allowances]. Paris: l'Argus, 1942.

2540 Mayer, P.R. [The Risk of Embryopathy], Concours Med. 85:4433-ff., 1963.

The author evaluates the validity of requests for therapeutic abortion on the ground of fetal damage during the early stages of pregnancy. He argues against the use of such indications and feels that not only are they outside the French law on therapeutic abortion but their acceptance would result in a tremendous increase in the country's abortion rate.

2541 McCloy, Shelby T. "Government Aid to Large Families in Normandy, 1764-1786," Soc. Forces 18(3):418-24, March 1940.

The history of the royal edict of Louis XIV in 1666 providing pensions to large families is sketched, together with its later modifications.

2542 [Medicine and Criminal Abortion], Rev. Praticien 12(6) Suppl: 13, 1962.

The article centers on the 1939 Penal Code of France. The Code forbids all abortion (and attempted abortion) whether or not the woman gives her consent and whether or not the woman is pregnant. Only in cases where there is a grave threat to the woman's life is therapeutic abortion allowed; three physicians must agree on the matter, and one of the three physicians must be listed by the civil Tribunal as an expert. Discussed also are the precautions which should be taken before treating a case of threatened abortion or an abortion case with complications.

2543 Michel, Andree, "Les Aspects Sociologiques de la Motion de Famille dans la Legislation Familiale Francaise" [Sociological Aspects of the Conception of the Family in French Family Legislation], Annee Sociol.,1960, pp. 79-107.

The author shows a tolerance for the unmarried mother, the illegitimate offspring, and the illegitimate family among the urban lower classes. He urges the legislature to extend more and more rights to the unmarried mother and the illegitimate offspring.

2544 Michel-Wolfrom, Helene, et al. Problemes Ethique du Controle des Naissances [Ethical Problems of Birth-Control] Paris: Edouard Privat, n.d., 88 pp.

2545 Mignon, J. "La Regulation des Naissances et les Practiciens" [Birth Control and Doctors], Concours Med. 90(3):513-22, 20 January 1968.

2546 Mossuz, Janine, "La Regulation des Naissances: Les Aspects Politiques du Debat" [Birth Control: Political Aspects of the Debate], Rev. Francaise Sci. Polit. 16(5):913-39, October 1966.

A brief account of the attitudes toward birth control and family planning, from 1920 to the present but chiefly since 1955, of some of the chief elements in French public opinion: the medical profession; political parties and groups; the Catholic church; the French Protestant churches; various Nobel prize winners; some of the popular press.

2547 Pernot, Georges, "La Politique Familiale, Condition du Salut" [Family Policy, a Condition of Safety], Rev. Polit. Idees Institutions, June 1942.

2548 Peron, Yves, "Aspects Demographiques et Economiques des Prestations Familiales" [Demographic and Economic Aspects of Family Allowances], Informations Soc. 20(11):54-70, November 1966.

A statistical review of the first twenty years operations of the government family allowance system in France, 1946-1965, in relation to economic and social change during that period.

2549 Pigeaud, H. "Limites d'une Contraception Legitime" [Limits of a Legitimate Contraception], Lyon Med. 215: 319-32, February 6, 1966.

2550 Pigeaud, H., and Lebrat, J. [Medico-Social Study of 300 Women Hospitalized for Abortion or Its Complication], Lyon Med. 210:501-ff., 1963.

A review of 320 cases of complicated abortions at the Obstetrical Clinic of the Edouard-Herriot Hospital. Induced abortions constituted 190 of these cases; 30 women had induced their abortions without the help of any other person, 72 with the help of a friend or relative, 64 with a member of the medical profession and 21 with the help of a non-defined person. Abortions are classified as to cost and professional status of the women. It was discovered that 34 women paid from 10,000 to 20,000 old francs for the abortion, 6 paid 20,000 to 30,000, 15 paid 30,000 to 50,000 and 4 paid more than 50,000. 182 of the women were classified by profession as follows: workers (110), office workers (12), sales ladies (7), nurses (8), students (2), without profession (48).

2551 Poinso-Chapuis, Germaine, "Une Politique Familiale" [A Family Policy], Pour la Vie, June - July 1950, pp. 24-39.

2552 Pons, S. "II Control delle Nascite et la Legge Frances del 1920" [Birth Control and the French Law of 1920], Minerva Med. 44(40):744-49, May 19, 1953.

2553 Pouillot, Pierre J. Prestations Familiales Agricoles [Agricultural Family Allowances].Paris: Librairies Techniques, 1952. 112 pp.

2554 Pour la Vie, "Debats et Reflexions. Une Authentique Politique Familiale Est-elle Compatible avec le Liberalisme Economique" [Debates and Reflections. Is a Genuine Family Policy Compatible with Economic Liberalism], Pour la Vie,No. 75, December 1958, pp. 431-47.

Annotated quotations from the document, Rapport sur la Situation Financiere (1958), presented to the Minister of Finance and Economic Affairs in compliance with his decision of September 30, 1958.

2555 Pour la Vie, "Orientations de la Politique Familiale dans la Nouvelle Legislature" [Attitudes on Family Policy in the New Legislature], Pour la Vie 68:1-87, March 1957.

Contents: Pernot, Georges, The next ten years; Perrin, Francis, Youth in the atomic age; Savelli, Aime, New observations on family size: some recent statistics; Monnin, Roger, Future of family allowances; Lebel, Roland, Problems and perspectives on social action by the Association on Family Allowances; Hourdin, Georges, The Ministry of Population after some years.

2556 Pour la Vie, "Rapport General de la Commission d'Etude des Problemes de la Famille" [General Report of the Commission for the Study of Family Problems], Pour la Vie, No. 88, March 1962, pp. 1-66.

The complete text of the report of the commission of enquiry into French family policy, appointed under the Fifth Republic in 1960. Sections on: results obtained since 1939, prospects for the next twenty years, principles and measures of proposed policy.

2557 Pour la Vie, "La Regulation des Naissances: Travaux Actuels" [Birth Control: Present Proceedings], Pour la Vie, No. 107-108, 1966-67, pp. 297-454.

2558 Pressat, Roland, [On the Number of Abortions in France], Concours Med. 14:87-ff., 1966.

Data obtained in Hungary where liberal legislation has made it possible to ascertain true abortion rates, since the use of contraceptives is not widespread, are cited in order to refute the given estimate of one to 2.5 million criminal abortions in France per year. In 1956-1957 there were 60 abortions to every 100 live births in Hungary; applying this rate to France, a figure of 500,000 abortions per year is obtained. This must be considered a maximum because the accessibility of abortion in Hungary likely discourages conscientious contraceptive use. The author then cites a study of the pregnancy histories of women in Lyon. This study is considered accurate since the sample was composed of urban, working-class women, those most likely to resort to abortion. The reported incidence of abortion was between 30 and 50% of live births.

2559 Prigent, Robert, "Faut-il Abroger la Loi de 1920?" [Should the 1920 Law be Repealed?] Etudes, March 1966 , pp. 306-18.

Reviews circumstances at the adoption of the French law and its original purposes. Considers its relevance to French conditions in 1966, and recommends clarification and modernization rather than repeal.

2560 Prigent, Robert, "En Moins de 30 Ans, la France a Perdu 3 Millions d'Hommes" [In Less than Thirty Years France has Lost Three Million Men], Forces Nouvelles, No. 87, 6-13 October 1946, pp. 1, 3.

The Minister of Population explains the necessity of the family laws recently voted.

2561 "Problems of Decision-Making in Social Security Administration," Internat. Soc. Sec. Assn. Bull. 17:71-91, March - April 1964.

Family allowances funds in France by Francis Netter; Presentation of a model for the simulation of administrative decisions in the French family allowances funds by Henri Souveton.

2562 Puybasset, Michel, et al. La Regulation des Naissances [Birth Control]. Paris: Documentation Francaise, 1967. 82 pp.

The first part on birth control includes two chapters: one on contraception, including text of proposed changes in legislation; the other on abortion, including data on the problem and text of proposed solutions. Part two deals with complementary measures, discussing why these are needed and what they should be in regard to public information and family policy.

2563 Rain, Emanuel, "La Compensation des Charges Familiales en France en 1950, Bilan General" [Family Subsidies in France in 1950, A General Balance Sheet], Population 6(3):411-24, July - September 1951.

2564 Rain, Emanuel, "La Compensation des Charges Familiales en France en 1951" [Family Subsidies in France in 1951], Population 8(1):142-47, January - March 1953.

2565 Revue des Hautes Etudes Politiques Sociales, Economiques et Financieres, "La Famille dans l'Etat: les Documents Francais" [The Family in the State: French Documents], Rev. Hautes Etudes Polit. Soc. Econ. Finan. 4(7): July 1942. 32 pp.

This brochure covers the various activities undertaken by the Vichy Government to foster the family unit. Statistics and summaries of legislation are included.

2566 Saint-Frison, [Problems Posed by Abortion], Rev. Infirm Assist. Soc. 16:205-ff., 1966.

The number of illegal abortions performed in France has resulted in complex medical and social problems. The author recommends the institution of an extensive social legislation program involving aid for the family, sex education and contraceptive education and feels that such a program would ease the situation.

2567 Sauvy, Alfred, "L'Application du 'Code de la Famille' A-t-ell Contribue au Redressement du Taux de la Natalite en France?" [Has the Application of the "Family Code" Contributed to the Recovery of Fertility in France?] Bull. Mensuel Statistique, February 1951, pp.35-45.

2568 Sauvy, Alfred, "L'Enfant et la Famille devant l'Impot" [The Scale of Taxation in Relation to Size of Family], Population 2(1):31-52, January - March 1947.

Part I is a general discussion of a just and reasonable basis for taxation of income and housing, taking size of family into account. Part II analyzes the payment of taxes on 1947 income, and includes tables showing the tax paid by families with two, three or four children, and taxes imposed on the basis of reductions for the third and fourth child. Later sections deal with the effects of a more equitable tax program upon standards of living.

2569 Sauvy, Alfred, "Fransk Familjepolitik" [French Family Policy], Soc. Medelanden, No. 3, 1957, pp. 152-58.

A review of recent trends in the French birth rate and an estimate of the effect of the family allowance policy.

2570 Sauvy, Alfred, "La Prevention des Naissances dans la Famille" [Family Birth Control], Population 15(1):115-20, January - March 1960.

While the factors which led to the reduction in the number of births in French families in the 19th century are understood, the origins of contraceptive techniques still remain obscure. France was the first nation where the use of contraceptives in the family became sufficiently widespread for this use to be noted statistically by the end of the 18th century. This phenomenon has been given little attention. The Demographic Revolution of Auguste Landry mentions it but does not elaborate. The massive work of Himes, Medical History of Contraception says little about France. The work undertaken by M.L. Henry to reconstruct the movement of the French population in the 18th century is merely discursive. A listing of sources containing documentation from the Middle Ages to the first Empire by H. Bergues is included, with particular attention to 18th century authors who noted the existence of contraceptive techniques. A series of opinions containing various interpretations of the problem are presented: Philippe Aries on "Interpretation for a History of Attitudes"; R.P. Michel Riquet on "The Historical and Catholic Theological Point of View"; Jean Sutter on "On the Diffusion of Contraceptive Techniques"; Louis Henry on "The Use of Reports and Statistics"; and Alfred Sauvy on "An Attempt at a Common Viewpoint." Assembled material and comments will help to connect this historical phase to contemporary problems.

2571 Savatier, R. "Artificial Insemination and the Law of France," pp. 15-19 in: Flood, Peter, ed. New Problems in Medical Ethics, Second Series. Cork: The Mercier Press, 1954. iv, 304 pp.

2572 Schulz, T. "Middle-Class Families in France and in England," Oxford University Institute Statistics Bull. 20:353-72, November 1958.

Information on family size among middle classes in France and the United Kingdom was obtained from birth announcements in two newspapers, The Times and Le Figaro. Large families are found to be more frequent in France. One possible explanation is the difference between the two countries in tax reductions and family allowances according to the person's income and number of children.

2573 Semaines Sociales de France, "Le Catholicisme Social Face aux Grands Courants Contemporains" [Social Catholicism Faced with Modern Important Problems], Lyon: Editions de la Chronique Sociale de France. 413 pp.

Lectures delivered at the 34th Session of the Semaines Sociales de France, held in Paris from 28 July to 2 August 1947, are here reproduced. The agenda of the Session included consideration of Social Catholicism's practical program concerning problems of population and the family.

2574 Semaines Sociales de France. "La Montee des Peuples dans la Communnaute Humaine" [The Upsurge of Peoples in the Human Community], Marches Tropicaux et Mediterraneens 15(718): 1841-44, 15 August 1959.

Text of the conclusions of the 46th session of the Semaines Sociales de France, at Angers, July 11-16, 1959. "Neo-Malthusian solutions" including contraception are rejected in favor of continence and the multiplication of the means of subsistence.

2575 Sexualite et Limitation des Naissances [Sexuality and Birth Limitation],Paris: Artheme Fayard, 1963. 233 pp.

Report of a round table on family planning with the participation of Sutter on the demographic view, Moal on the psychological study, and of the marriage counsellors - Lambert, Lieury, de Lestapis and Beirnaert, M. and G. Abiven suggest that birth regulation is a means and not an end itself in the life of a couple. The moral aspects of contraception are observed from the point of view of theology by Bouchaud and from the civil and political point of view by Debray. Contenson examines thoroughly the Catholic's response to legal contraception and Dubarle discusses biblical testimony on love and fertility.

2576 Siebert, Solande, and Sutter, Jean. "Attitudes Devant la Maternite - Une Enquete a Grenoble" [Attitudes Toward Birth Control: A Study in Grenoble], Population 18(4): 655-82, October - December 1963.

A pilot study conducted in Grenoble, France, in 1961-62, by questionnaire and interviewing. 1,200 females were selected by random sampling: 77% were French nationals; 76% resided in urban communities; 66.3% belonged to the lower social class; and 40% were less than 24 years old. Among contraceptives used, coitus interruptus proved most popular (61%). Factors affecting types of contraception included age, socio-economic-status, economic considerations and religion. Though the birth control pill met with considerable opposition, there was a slight increase in favorable response. 79% of the respondents had had no sex education. Interest in sex problems increased with socio-economic-status.

2577 Simon, Pierre, Le Controle des Naissances: Histoire, Philosophie, Morale [Birth Control: History, Philosophy, Morality], Paris: Payot, 1966. 303 pp.

2578 Soubbotitch, I. "Recent Important Reforms in the French Matrimonial Regime," New York Law Forum 12:245-ff. Summer 1966.

The concept, matrimonial regime, refers to the legal obligations existing between husband and wife. Since the time of Napoleon, there have been few changes in these obligations. Now these obligations are being drastically redefined. While the husband continues to be defined as the "head of the household", much of his authority has been removed. Many financial and other matters, including the disposal of property, requires now the assent of the wife.

2579 Sutter, Jean, and Morin, Francis, "Attitudes Devant la Maternite: Une Enquete a Paris en Service Hospitalier" [Attitudes Toward Maternity: An Enquiry in a Hospital Ward at Paris], Population 15(2):223-44, 1960.

The attitude of 1,000 pregnant women with regard to eventual utilization of the contraceptive pill.

2580 Sutter, Jean, [Results of a Study of Abortion in the Paris Region], Population 5:77-ff., 1950.

The author describes a study of 3,000 Parisian post-abortal cases undertaken during a three year period (1946-49). The objectives of the study were to determine how many cases involved married women and whether the group as a whole was representative of any particular socio-economic level. The cases were classified into three categories: voluntary (47%), therapeutic (1%) and probable or dubious spontaneous abortion (52%). 72% of the abortions took place during the first three months of pregnancy,and 67% of the women were in the 20-33 year-old age group.47% were married,38% single and 15% divorced or widowed. 73% already had one to three children, and almost all of the married women were living with their spouses. Psychological reasons for the abortion were given by 30%, a combination of psychological and economic by 56%. It is concluded that the study was useful in providing some knowledge of the motivations behind induced abortion and that the emphasis now should be on abortion as a social problem with consequences requiring alleviation.

2581 Sutter, Jean, "Va-t-on Diffuser les Methodes Contraceptives en France?" [The Problem of Divulgement of Contraceptive Methods in France] Concours Med. 79(10):1195-99 and 79(11): 1311-13, March 9 and 16, 1957.

2582 Sutter, Jean, and Levy, Claude, "Les Dispenses Civiles au Mariage en France Depuis 1800" [Special Civil Marriage Permits in France Since 1800], Population 14(2):285-304, April - June 1959.

Special licenses are required in France for certain marriages: for males under 18 years and females under 15. Brother-in-law may not marry sister-in-law if their relationship resulted from a previous marriage that ended in divorce. Uncle-neice and aunt-nephew marriages are prohibited except by special dispensation. A man is permitted to marry his daughter-in-law or step-daughter, and a woman her son-in-law or step-son only if the person responsible for the relationship has died. Statistics on each type of special license and motivation for its request are given. In most instances, pregnancy or offspring in common is the motive for application.

2583 Talmy, Robert, Histoire du Mouvement Familiales France, 1896-1939 [History of Action for the Family in France, 1896-1939] Union Nationale des Caisses d'Allocations Familiales, Etudes. Aubenas, 1962. 2 vols. 268 pp.

2584 Texier, G. "The Attitudes of the French as Regards Birth Control," Evolut. Psychiat. 32:715-47, July - September 1967.

Sociological analysis of a referendum organized by a Parisian newspaper.

2585 Thery, Rene, "Le Concubinage en France" [Concubinage in France], Rev. Trimestrielle Droit Civil 59(1):33-52, January - March 1960.

A study of the distribution of couples living in concubinage according to the size of the populated area and the socio-professional category. Based on statistical data from the Census of 1954.

2586 Tune, Andre, "Husband and Wife Under French Law: Past, Present, Future," Univ. Penn. Law Rev. 104:1064-79, January 1956.

The status of the married woman was the result of Roman law, the influence of the Roman Catholic Church, and German customs. Northern and Southern France differed in these influences. The Civil Code provisions defining the wife's status were drafted under Napoleon and reinforced the traditional emphasis. Modifications in the Code in 1938, 1942, and 1945 and the Avant-Projet de Code Civil, which appeared in 1954, have placed the wife on a more equal footing with her husband.

2587 Union Internationale des Organismes Familiaux, Secretariat General, Les Prestations Familiales, Las Prestaciones Familiares [Family Allowances], Paris: Moulins, Impr. Crepin-Leblond, 1952.

2588 Universite de Strasbourg, Institut de Sciences Criminelles et Penitentiares, Recherches sur l'Infanticide (1955-1965) [Research on Infanticide (1955-1965)], Paris: Dalloz, 1968. 418 pp.

2589 Valabregue, Catherine, Controle des Naissances et Planning Familial [Birth Control and Family Planning], Paris: Table Ronde, 1960. 254 pp.

The history of the family planning movement in France is a major aspect of this book. Included are the neo-Malthusian convictions and doctrines of Paul Robin whose influence was felt before 1914, the effects of the 1914-1918 war, and the events which led to the law of July 31, 1920. This law imposed penalties on anyone writing or publicly speaking in favor of anticonception measures. There is a chapter on abortion and others dealing with religious, medical and moral issues. In the first chapter the author deplores the fact that there exists no satisfactory translation into French of the expressions, birth control and family planning. Some French people dislike the idea of adopting into their language yet another Anglicism; others find the word, control, distasteful and the word, planning, severe. In the last chapter, the author suggests the new word - orthogenism. Orthogenism has a central meaning in common with family planning: it stresses the benefits, accruing to family life and to the happiness of the mother, of regulation and design as opposed to anarchy and accident in the timing of conceptions. But the neologism carries a further implication - the essential compatibility of interests between family and nation. The word, orthogenism, also implies a corresponding rejection of the attitude of mind which inspired the law of 1920.

2590 Van Camelbeke, M. [Birth Control in the Face of the Law. Abortion, Sterilization and Contraceptive Practices in Modern Legislation], _Rev. Practicien_ 13:2217-31, 21 June 1963.

2591 Villey, Francois, _Le Complement Familial du Salaire, Etude des Allocations Familiales dans leurs Rapports avec le Salaire_ [The Family Subsidy to Wages: a Study of Family Allowances in Relation to Wages], Paris: Editions Sociales Francaises, 1946. 249 pp.

2592 Vincent, Paul, "La Liberte de la Contraception: Opinion d'un Demographe" [Liberty of Contraception: A Demographer's Opinion], _Temps Mod_. 12(134):1547-60, April 1957.

Statement of the author's reasons for advocating repeal of Articles 3 and 4 of the Law of 1920 and for preparing the public for the responsible use of contraception.

2593 Watson, Cicely, "Birth Control and Abortion in France Since 1939," _Popul. Stud_. 5(3):261-86, March 1952.

Punitive legislation enacted after World War I and the more repressive measures following the Occupation which made abortion a crime against society and the state. Modifications in 1947 permitted therapeutic abortion when approved by three physicians for medical reasons.

2594 Watson, Cicely, "Population Policy in France Family Allowances and Other Benefits," Popul. Stud. 7(3):263-86 and 8(1):46-73, March and July 1954.

Origin and growth of the system; the Code de la Famille, 1939; modifications made by the Vichy Government; Critical discussion of postwar developments, economic aspects, and the significance of the program in relation to the recent rise in French fertility.

2595 Willoughby, Gertrude, "Population Problems and Family Policy in France," Eugen. Rev. 45(2):93-100, July 1953.

France today is directing a larger share of her national income to aiding the family than any other country; nearly half of her total expenditure on social services is paid out in direct money allowances to families. Aid to the family is directed at achieving two ends: a measure of social justice by redistributing the national income in favor of the family; and secondly, by the adjustment of certain allowances, to the encouragement of the birth-rate and the discouragement of abortion. Five separate allowances are being paid today, a maternity allowance, family allowances, a special allowance to the family having only one income earner, allowances paid during pregnancy and a housing allowance. The clear effect of this family policy is a reduction in the abortion rate and infant mortality. It also appears that the policy has influenced a rise in the birth rate.

GERMANY (UNDIVIDED)

General population policies

2596 Berlitz, "Ehestandsdarlehen, Siedlungs, Kinderbeihilfen, Ausbildungsbeihilfen, und Forderung der Landbevolkerung in den Eingegliederten Ostgebieten" [Marriage Loans, Settlement and Children's Aids, Educational Subsidies, and Improvement of the Rural Population in the Incorporated Eastern Areas], Deutsche Steuer-Zeitung 30(5):53-57, February 1, 1941.

The measures stipulated in laws passed in the German Reich from 1935-1941 were to encourage migration of Germans or Aryan-blooded people into the eastern areas of the Reich. There were to be government loans to encourage marriage and state loans toward housing and furnishings. Further aid was to come in the form of single cash allotments per child under 16 in families with at least four children, to be used for child development and settlement. Additional contributions were to be made for the child's education from grammar school through college and for additional housing needs. These measures applied to Aryans only. The Polish areas were to be administered in a different way and their allotments were more limited. Restrictions were also placed on any buying and selling with non-Aryans, though these restrictions decreased, the farther east an Aryan lived from the heart of the Reich.

2597 Bickel, Wilhelm, "Aktive Bevolkerungspolitik?" [An Active Population Policy?], Gewerkschaftliche Rundschau Schweiz 33(6):178-91, 1941.

2598 Boehm, H. "Bevolkerungspolitische Umschau" [Survey of Population Policy], Zeitschrift fur Arztliche Fortbildung 39:274-77, June 15, 1942.

This article mainly presents the results of research concerning marriages, child births and families in different geographic areas in the German Reich. This research was conducted as part of the effort to raise the national birth rate. The differences in statistics resulting from population policy measures toward marriage are given, and a comparison is made of the marriage age and the birth rate for people who had a state loan to encourage marriage and for those who did not. The results were that the marriage age was less and the birth rate higher in the group of people receiving the marriage loan, and that the strongest desire to produce children was among older women in the loan group.

2599 Boekholt, K.W. Bevolkingsleer en Bevolkingspolitiek in den Volkschen Staat [Population Doctrine and Policy in the National State], Gravenhage, Uitgeverij "De Schouw," 1942. 106 pp.

2600 Burgdorfer, Friedrich, "Grundfagen Unseres Volkswachstums und der Deutschen Ostsiedlung" [Basic Questions of Our Population Growth and the German Eastern Settlement], Neues Bauerntum 32(4-5):130-32, April-May 1940.

2601 Burgdorfer, Friedrich, Kinder des Vertrauens. Bevolkerungspolitische Erfolge und Aufgaben im Grossdeutschen Reich [The Children of "Faith in the Future." Accomplishments and Tasks of Population Policy in the Greater Germany], Schriftenreihe der NSDAP, Gruppe III. Volkheit und Glaube, Bd. 6. Berlin: Zentralverlag der NSDAP, 1940.

Previous studies are summarized, and the data made more current. The author estimates that the fertility of 1936 and the mortality of 1932-1934 would eventuate in an increase to 72 million and then a decrease to 66 million in the year 2000 for the Old Reich. In 1939, "replacement" was within 1.2%. The 2-1/4 million children born in the seven years, beyond those that would have been born on the basis of the fertility of 1930-1932, are the "children of the faith in the future." However, it will require an increase of 16% over 1939 in order to maintain stability and compensate for World War I gaps.

2602 Burgdorfer, Friedrich, Land Ohne Bauern -- Volk Ohne Jugend [Land Without Peasants -- People Without Youth], Bildung und Nation, Schriftenreihe zur Nationalpolitischen Erziehung, No. 78-79. Leipzig: Hermann Eichblatt, 1940. 25 pp.

The results of the flight from the land and the restrictions of births are held to necessitate a special population policy for rural people.

2603 Danzer, Paul, and Schmalfuss, Hannes, Das Bevolkerungspolitische ABC [Population Policy ABC], Third ed., Munchen-Berlin: J.F. Lehmann, 1940. 63 pp.

This is a forward to an ABC of population policies which was designed to inform the lay public of the German Reich about the threats of their race's extinction and ways of preventing it, and to arouse in everyone, especially youth, a deep-seated, heartfelt sense of duty and responsibility to devote oneself to correction of this problem.

2604 Graf, Jakob, Vererbungslehre, Rassenkunde und Ergesundheitspflege [Theory of Heredity, Race, Science and Eugenics], Ninth ed. Munchen: Lehmann, 1943. 351 pp.

Part 2, Chapter V, "Volksentartung und Volksaufartung," reproduces the survey of German racial and population policy from the 1936 edition.

2605 Guillebaud, C.W. The Social Policy of Nazi Germany: Current Problems, Cambridge: Cambridge University Press, 1941. 134 pp.

The material for this attempt at a comprehensive and impartial description is drawn primarily from official German sources or the International Labour Office. Population policy is regarded as one of the achievements contributing to the support received by the Nazis from the great mass of the German people.

2606 Hartnacke, Wilhelm, "Die Biologischen Fehlerquellen -- Volksstatistik Weist die Wege zur Sicherung der Volkischen Zukunft" [The Biological Sources of Error -- Population Statistics Show the Way to Security of the National Future], <u>Reich</u> 6:6, 1944.

2607 Heubner, P.L. "Die Bevolkerungspolitik Seckendorffs" [Seckendorff's Population Policy], <u>Arch</u>. <u>Bevolk</u>. 13(2): 110-13, June 1943.

2608 Institute of World Affairs, New School for Social Research, <u>Public Health Administration in Germany, 1919-45</u>. New York, 1945. 48 pp.

Appendices: VI. Marriage Loans, Grants to Large Families; VII. Prevention of Hereditary Diseases; VIII. The Marriage Health Act.

2609 Jacoby, Gerhard, <u>Racial State. The German Nationalities Policy in the Protectorate of Bohemia-Moravia</u>, New York: Institute of Jewish Affairs of the American Jewish Congress and World Jewish Congress, 1944. xii, 355 pp.

Based on a study of primary sources, especially the legal and interpretative publications of the Nazis. Part II, "The Method of Segregation," describes in detail the actual implementation of the theory of a racial hierarchy; and Part III, "The Method of Assimilation," describes the activities oriented toward the assimilation of the Germans and the segregation of the Czechs. Part IV, "The Method of Depopulation," covers the expropriation of the Jews; the depopulation and resettlement policies, involving strategic colonization, agricultural resettlement, colonization by evacuees, forced labor, and manpower exports; and the extinction of the Jews through emigration, forced labor, deportation and actual extermination.

2610 Koch, E.W. "Beschleunigter Aufbau Erbtuchtiger Familien durch Staatliche Nachwuchsversicherung. Vorschlag einer Losung des Geburtenproblems" [Acceleration of the Development of Eugenically Sound Families through Public Measures and Proposal for a Solution of the Birth Problem], _Arch. Bevolk_. 13:121-34, August 1943.

This was a proposal meant to encourage a rising birth rate in Hitler's Germany, quality-wise as well as quantity-wise. The state was to guarantee an insurance program for each of the first three children born into a family, for which insurance a premium of 9% of one's yearly income was to be paid to an insurance company of one's choice. A new feature was the payment of a special insurance sum, equal to one-fifth of the yearly income, to the wife when she gave birth to a child. Benefits would also be paid for more than three children without further payment of a premium. The article then further outlines the different cases of this insurance proposal with the use of tables, examples and greater details.

2611 Koehl, Robert L. _RKFDV: German Resettlement and Population Policy, 1939-1945; A History of the Reich Commission for the Strengthening of Germandom_. Harvard Historical Monographs, 31. Cambridge: Harvard University Press, 1957. xi, 263 pp.

2612 Krannhals, Detlef, "Der Reichsgau Danzig-Westpreussen" [Basic Concepts of Population Policy in Danzig-West Prussia], _Bevolkerungspolitische Grundbegriffe Rasse_ 8(1):18-23, 1941.

An article stating the establishment of Western Prussia as a district of the German Reich as ordered by Hitler in 1939. It then goes on to describe, with the use of tables and photographs, the population densities and other population information of the Nordic and Polish elements of the population in various areas within this region.

2613 Lemkin, Rafal, _Axis Rule in Occupied Europe. Laws of Occupation, Analysis of Government, Proposals for Redress_, Washington: Carnegie Endowment for International Peace, Division of International Law, 1944. xxxviii, 674 pp.

The major part of this volume compresses the text of laws and decrees of the Axis powers, and of their puppet regimes, issued for the government of the areas occupied by their military forces in Europe. Preceding these texts are chapters analyzing the purposes and applications of the measures as parts of a general scheme of conquest. Other chapters show the organization of the occupying government set up in each invaded country and the special measures adopted for it. Demographic policies are covered especially in Part I, "German Techniques of Occupation;" Ch. II, "Police;" Ch. VII, "Labor;" and Ch. IX, "Genocide;" and in Part II, "The Occupied Countries."

2614 Magnussen, Karin, "Krieg und Kriegsfolgen vom Standpunkt der Rassenund Bevolkerungspolitik" [War and the Consequences of War from the Standpoint of Race and Population Policy], Arch. Bevolk. 11:145-68, July 1941.

The quantitative and qualitative effects of the last war and the present war on the German people are analyzed from the short and long range points of view. The problems of racial purity created by this war are discussed. Population policies for the post-war world are outlined, with special reference to Eastern Europe and colonial policy.

2615 Muller, Heinrich, "Volkernaturlichen Wachstums. Zur Methodik der Bevolkerungspolitik" [Populations with Natural Increase. Concerning the Method of Population Policy], Deutsche Biol. 11(12):331-41, December 1942.

2616 Pfeil, Elisabeth, "Zur Bevolkerungspolitischen Lage" [The Current Situation from the Standpoint of Population Policy], Arch. Bevolk. 10(1):45-49, February 1940.

The thesis is that Greater Germany must maintain fertility sufficient for replacement, which it reached for the first time in 1939. Techniques for avoiding the deleterious effects of war on population growth are discussed. In contrast to the situation in World War I, marriages increased sharply in the early months of the present war. Marriage rates increased 22% in the third quarter of 1939 over the third quarter of

1938; in large cities, rates in October 1939 were 48%, and in November 1939, 75%, over the corresponding rates for 1939. The author attributes this to both psychological factors and economic security, measured by the absence of unemployment, and the generosity of the provisions for the families of soldiers.

2617 Plathe, Roderich, "Die Bevolkerungspolitische Lage des Deutschen Bauerntums" [The Situation of the German Peasant in Relation to Population Policy], Neues Bauerntum 32(3): 99-105, March 1940.

2618 Soziale Praxis, "Bevolkerungspolitische Probleme in Elsass und in Lothringen" [Population Problems in Alsace-Lorraine], Soziale Praxis 50(3):101-4, February 1941.

The fertility of this region is discussed with reference to the former French and the present German policies. The results of the German policy are expected to be a "renewed will to live" and hence an increased birth rate.

2619 Wagemann, Ernst F. Wirtschaftpolitische Strategie, von den Obersten Grundsatzen Wirtschaftlicher Staatskunst [The Strategy of Economic Policy...], Second revision. Hamburg: Hanseatische Verlagsanstalt, 1943. 376 pp.

See especially: Part 12, "Neue Entwicklungslinien," on intensity of use of population and capital, organizational forms, labor policies, and agriculture.

2620 "Die Wichtigsten bis Mai 1942 Erlassenen Gesetze und Berordnungen im Nationalsozialistischen Deutschland aus dem Gebiete der Bevolkerungspolitik" [The Most Important Laws and Orders of Germany on Population Policy Issued before May 1942], Arch. Bevolk. 12(5):308-15, November 1942.

From a population policy point of view, the main purpose of the laws and decrees passed by the German Reich in the late

1930's and early 1940's was to increase, and take measures to encourage this increase, of the segment of the population of German or Aryan-related blood, and to suppress the other "races" such as Jews, Gypsies, and Slavs, and carriers of hereditary diseases. This encouragement came mainly from the state subsidies to families, especially to families with greater numbers of children, and state aid in housing and furnishings for people of Aryan blood. There were also restrictions such as that forbidding buying and selling from Jews or non-Aryan merchants.

2621 Ziemer, Gregor, Education for Death; the Making of the Nazi, London: Oxford University Press, 1941.

A study of the techniques by which the Nazis indoctrinate the German youth in order that the boys may become zealous soldiers and the girls equally zealous breeders for Hitler.

2622 Zwiedineck-Sudenhorst, Otto von, "Die Wandlungen der Deutschen Bevolkerungspolitik" [Changes in German Population Policy], Jahrbucher Nationalokonomie Statistik 156:498-506, December 1942.

Policies on fertility and family size

2623 Archiv fur Bevolkerungswissenschaft und Bevolkerungspolitik. "Ausbau der Kinderbeihilfen" [Aid for Children], Arch. Bevolk. 11(1):78-79. March 1941.

The law of December 11, 1940, extended grants to each child of third or higher order regardless of the economic and social status or the occupation of parents. The veto power is retained by the local administrative board with the approval of the NSDAP, and by the health officer.

2624 Archiv fur Bevolkerungswissenschaft und Bevolkerungspolitik. "Nachgetragene Gesetze zur Deutschen Familienpolitik" [Supplemental Laws on German Family Policy], Arch. Bevolk. 12(3-4): 251-52. September 1942.

2625 Berlitz, Erick, "Ehestandsdarlehen und Kinderbeihilfen im Krieg" [Marriage Loans and Family Aids in War], Deutsche Steuer-Zeitung 29(39):459-63, September 28, 1940.

2626 Bohs, Fritz, Der Soziallohn, Seine Bevolkerungspolitische und Sozialpolitische Begrundung im Rahmen Volkswirtschaftlicher Zielsetzung [The Family Allowance; the Basis of Its Population and Social Policy in the Framework of an Economic Goal], Halle Dissertation, 1942. 130 pp.

2627 Germany, Amt fur Arbeitseinsatz der Deautschen Arbeitsfront. "Einheitliche Kinderzuschlage im Offentlichen Dienst" [Supplementary Children's Aid in the Public Service], Monatshefte NS-Sozialpolitik 8(3-4):47-48, February 1941.

A detailed analysis of the fixing of allowances for civil servants at 20 RM per child.

2628 Germany, Amt fur Arbeitseinsatz der Deautschen Arbeitsfront. "Kinderbeihilfen" [Children's Aid], Monatshefte NS-Sozialpolitik 8(5-6):71, March 1941.

A list of cases in which households with fewer than three children are eligible.

2629 Germany, Amt fur Arbeitseinatz der Deautschen Arbeitsfront. "Neue Regelung der Kinderbeihilfen" [New Regulations on Children's Aid], Monatshefte NS-Sozialpolitik 8(1/2):24, January 1941.

Regulations effective January 1, 1941 and extended to families with three children.

2630 Germany. Reichsarbeitsamt, "Gesetz zum Schultze der Erwerbstatigen Mutter. Mutterschutzgesetz vom 17. Mai 1942 nebst Begrundung und Ausfuhrungsverordnung mit Erlauterungen von F.H. Schmidt" [The Law for the Protection of Working Mothers, May 17, 1942, with Administrative Regulations and Explanations by F.H. Schmidt], Reichsarbeitsblatt No. 14, 1942.

2631 Germany. Reichsarbeitsministerium des Reichsversicherungsamts und der Reichsversicherungsanstalt fur Angestellte, "Gesetz zur Erhohung der Einnahmen des Sondervermogens des Reichs fur Ehestandsdarlehen und Kinderbeihipfen, Vom 28, February 1941" [Law for the Increase of Special Funds of the Reich for Marriage Loans and Children's Assistance, February 28, 1941], Reichsarbeitsblatt 8(1):126, March 15, 1941.

2632 Germany. Reichsarbeitsministerium des Reichsversicherungsamts und der Reichsversicherungsanstalt fur Angestellte, "Verordnung zur Einfugrung von Ehestandsdarlehen, Kinderbeihilfen, Einrichtungsdarlehen und Einrichtungszuschussen im Protektorat Bohmen und Mahren, vom 10. February 1941" [Regulations for the Introduction of Marriage Laws, Children's Assistance, Equipment Loans and Subsidies in the Protectorate of Bohemia-Moravia], Reichsarbeitsblatt 7(1):113-14, March 1941.

2633 Germany. Statistiches Reichsamt, "Die Bevolkerungspolitische Bedeutung der Ehestandsdarlehen" [The Significance of the Population Policy of State Loans to Encourage Marriages], Wirtschaft und Statistik 22(2):52-57, February 1942.

2634 Germany. Statistiches Reichsamt, "Die Ehestandsdarlehen im 4. Vierteljahre und im Jahre 1940" [Marriage Loans in the Fourth Quarter and in 1940], Wirtschaft und Statistik 21(5): 107-8, March 1941.

2635 Germany. Statistisches Reichsamt, "Die Ehestandsdarlehen im 4. Vierteljahr und im Jahre 1943" [Marriage Loans in the Fourth Quarter and in the Year 1943], Wirtschaft und Statistik 24(3):50-51, March 1944.

2636 Harmsen, Hans, "Erweiterer Schutz fur Erwerbstatige Mutter" [Measures for the Protection of Working Mothers], Arch. Bevolk. 12(3-4):196-201, September 1942.

2637 Harmsen, Hans, "Notes on Abortion and Birth Control in Germany," Popul. Stud. 3(4):402-5, March 1950.

Traces the laws governing abortion and contraception from the Penal Code of 1871 and amendments of 1926 and 1933 to 1948. Statistics on legal and illegal abortions are also provided.

2638 Harmsen, Hans, "Zur Ungeklarten Large der Ledigen Mutter und des Unehelichen Kindes" [The Uncertain Situation of the Unmarried Mother and the Illegitimate Child], Arch. Bevolk. 10(3):145-53, July 1940.

The premise of this discussion is that military victory is valueless unless it is accompanied by population maintenance. There is a summary of the special provisions being made for the illegitimate and legitimate children of men who die in the present war, and also of official attitudes toward unmarried mothers in the age groups characterized by an excess of women due to the fatalities of World War I.

2639 Houghton, Vera, "Birth Control in Germany, Eugenics Rev. 43(4):185-87, 1951.

Legal restrictions to birth control began in Nazi Germany with a Police Regulation of 21 January 1941 prohibiting the manufacture, advertisement, sale or distribution of contraceptives and abortifacients. These were later incorporated into the Penal Code along with the prohibition of abortion. After the capitulation of Germany, when the Penal Code was replaced by the Control Council Law, the 1941 Regulation continued in effect except in Berlin and the Russian Zone. Subsequently the Regulation was revoked in Hamburg and partially revoked in four other provinces. Criminal abortions are frequent and suggest additional revocations of the 1941 Regulation and the diffusion of contraceptive services. There is now little church opposition to birth control but, even in areas where it is legally permissible, the practical possibilities depend on the cooperation of the medical profession and the consent of husbands.

2640 Kattsoff, Louis O. "Germany's Peace and Population Policy," Soc. Forces 22(44):454-57, 1943.

A quantitative increase in the number of Germans was one objective of Germany's population policy. Another was the repopulation of Central Europe by removing some nationals to other countries and bringing Germans in. The attempt to unify Central Europe under a Greater Germany or under the dominance of Greater Germany, if successful, would be a major political gain and a threat to peace even if Germany is again militarily defeated.

2641 Kesselring, M. "Formende Krafte im Weiblichen Arbeitsdienst. Ein Untersuchender Beitrag zur Volkischen Jugendkunde" [Formative Forces in the Women's Labor Service. A Research Contribution to National Youth Study], Z. Padagogische Psychol. 42:49-68, 1941.

The conclusion of this report is that folk-centered labor service teaches girls the true mission and place of the German woman, the blessing of work in close relationship to children, and respect for the peasantry as the lifesource of the Reich.

2642 Klamm, Heinrich, "Nachwuchssicherung im Landvolk" [Assuring Reproduction of the Agricultural Population], Deutsche Agrarpolitik 1:97, December 1942.

The necessity for maintaining or augmenting the agricultural population of Germany is stressed.

2643 Knodel, John, "Law, Marriage and Illegitimacy in Nineteenth-Century Germany," Popul. Stud. 20(3):279-94, March 1967.

In certain German States in the nineteenth century, laws were passed limiting marriage to persons considered to be morally and financially capable of raising a family. These laws were subsequently repealed. The author studies the marriage and birth rates of the period in order to ascertain how effective the laws were. They appear to have restricted marriage rates, and also to have reduced legitimate birth rates; but much of this reduction was compensated for by a rise in illegitimate births.

2644 Meisinger, "Die Bekampfung der Abtreibung als Politische Aufgabe" [The Campaign Against Abortion as a Political Duty], Deutsche Z. Ges. Gerichtl. Med. 32:226-44, 1940.

2645 Nutt, Elizabeth, Die Bevolkerungspolitischen Auswirkungen des Ehestandsdarlehens [The Effects of Marriage Loans in Population Policy], Berlin: Pfau, 1940. 66 pp.

2646 Reimer, Lydia, La Famille dans l'Allemagne Renovee [The Family in the Renovated Germany], Bruxelles: Maison Internationale d'Edition, 1940. 44 pp.

This is a popular eulogy of the German provisions for the aid of the family and children. It is liberally illustrated.

2647 Richter, Bodo, and Volker, Hans, Das Deutsche Eherecht. Ehegesetz... mit Durchfuhrungs - und Ausfuhrungsbestimmungen sowie die Einfuhrungsvorschriften fur die Ostmark [The German Marriage Law...With Administrative Regulations as well as the Order of Introduction for the Ostmark], Second ed. Berlin: Heymann, 1940. 327 pp.

2648 Schottky, Johannes, "Erfahrungen mit einer Ausgleichkasse der Familienlasten" [Experiences With a Fund for the Equalization of Family Costs], Arch. Bevolk. 10(4):219-33, October 1940.

The provisions and operation of a state hospital fund in Thuringia are analyzed.

2649 Soziale Praxis. "Durchstoss zur Reichsfamilienzulage" [Extension of the German Family Allowance System], Soziale Praxis 50(1):19-20, January 1941.

Summary of law, effective January 1941, extending family allowances regardless of income or occupation and covering children aged sixteen to twenty-one.

2650 Soziale Praxis. "Ehestandsdarlehen" [Marriage Loans], Soziale Praxis 50(3):120 and 50(9):376. February and May 1941.

Summary of marriages and births accompanied by loans in the second, third and fourth quarters of 1940.

2651 Soziale Praxis. "Die Kinderhilfe in Ihrer Neuste Form" [Children's Aid in its Newest Form], Soziale Praxis 50(5): 192-94. March 1941.

Summary of law of January 30, 1941 regulating aid for children. Approximately 2,000,000 families will receive about 50,000,000 Reichsmark in 1941.

2652 United States. Bureau of Labor Statistics. "Measures to Increase Birth Rate in Germany," Monthly Labor Rev. 54(1): 75. January 1942.

German expenditures to increase marriages and births, based on a note in the Deutsche Steuer-Zeitung, September 13, 1941.

2653 United States. Bureau of Labor Statistics. "New Family-Allowance System in Germany," Monthly Labor Rev. 53(5): 1289-90. November 1941.

2654 Wachenheim, Hedwig. "Allowances for Dependents of Mobilized Men in Germany," Internat. Labour Rev. 49(3): 323-38. March 1944.

The main principles of the scheme now in operation are outlined and its practical administration described. Sources used were: Reichsgesetzblatt, Reichsministerial-blatt f.d.i.V. Wirtschaft und Statistik, Soziale Praxis, and Die Deutsche Volkswirt.

GERMANY (FEDERAL REPUBLIC)

Policies on fertility and family size

2655 Anselmino, K.J., and Frangenheim, H. "Zur Problematik der Handhabung der Gesetzlichen Schwangerschaftsunterbrechung in der Bundesrepublik" [Problems of Handling Legal Abortion in the Federal Republic], *Medizinische*, No. 11, 15 March 1958, pp. 445-49.

2656 Barnikel, W. [Legality of Induced Abortion], *Deutsch Med. Wschr*. 90:1635-ff., 1965.

Current legislation on abortion in West Germany is described. The law does not permit the use of social, humanitarian and eugenic grounds but does recognize medical indications.

2657 Beckendorff, H. *Ausgleich der Familienlasten? Finanzwirtschaftliche Probleme einer Kinderbeihilfe* [Equalization of Family Costs? The Financial and Economic Problems of a Family Allowance System], Berlin: Duncker and Humblot, 1953. 112 pp.

2658 Becker, W. [On the Problem of the Ethical Indication], *Med. Klin*. 58:1857-ff., 1963.

The author evaluates the validity of humanitarian indications for abortion. It is contended that pregnancy resulting from rape or other criminal intercourse constitutes an emergency situation and that abortion in these cases is justified.

2659 Becker, W. "Die Sterilisation als Rechtliche und Ethische Frage" [Sterilization as a Legal and Ethical Problem], *Med. Klin*. 61:1352-57, 26 August 1966.

2660 Beckmann, Joachim, *et al*. *Kirche und Geburtenregelung* [The Church and Birth Control], Kassel: Gutersloher Verlagshaus Gerd Mohn, 1962. 72 pp.

Contents: Groeger, Guido N. [Contraception from the Point of View of Marriage Counselling], pp. 5-25; Gesenius, Heinrich [Voluntary Sterilization as a Means of Preventing Conception], pp. 26-31; Beckmann, Joachim [The Attitude of the Church toward the Question of Contraception], pp. 32-51.

2661 Bechtold, L. "Rechtsfragen zur Kunstlichen Befruchtung" [Legal Problems of Artificial Insemination], *Med. Klin.* 49(22):886-88, 28 May 1954.

2662 Bernhard, Paul, "Zur Handhabung der Gesetzlich Erlaubten Schwangerschaftsunterbrechung in der Bundesrepublik" [The Administration of Legally Permitted Abortion in the Federal Republic], *Med. Monatsschrift* 7:421-24, July 1959.

After a comparison of the statistics on legal abortion in the various regions of the Federal Republic for the period 1948-58, the author concludes that, were the country's abortion law followed completely, the optimal number of legal abortions would be 0.10 for every 10,000 citizens. It is felt that this ration, if fulfilled, would not endanger maternal health and that, whenever possible, social deficiencies must be combatted with social measures, and not with an increase in abortions. The current law rejects any abortions performed on a ground other than that of pregnancy constituting threat to mother's health.

2663 Bode, Albrecht, *Soziallohn durch Familienausgleichs-Kassen* [Social Benefits Through Family Equalization Funds], Munchen: W. Steinebach, 1950. 64 pp.

2664 Buhler, Hans H. *Familienpolitik als Einkommens und Eigentumspolitik* [Family Policy as a Policy on Income and Property], Berlin: Duncker and Humblot, 1961. 107 pp.

2665 Buhler, Hans W. "Questiones Politicas" [Political Questions], Rev. Espanola Opin. Pub. 8:282-85, April - June 1967.

A public opinion poll in West Germany on adultery as a delict and on the right to divorce is reported. The question was whether a clause in German law designating adultery a criminal offense should be maintained, more strictly enforced, or abolished. 52% felt it should be maintained; 21% felt it should be more strictly enforced; and 19% felt that it should be abolished; and 9% had no opinion. Differences between male and female respondents, and among age groups, religious groups, occupational groups, and on the basis of marital status are noted.

2666 [Causes of the Abortion Epidemic], Med. Mschr. 19:481, 1965.

The author argues against the view that the extensive use of oral contraceptives has resulted in a growing demand for abortion. Reasons are given to support the pill as a limiting factor in regard to the abortion rate.

2667 Doring, G.K. [Current Forensic Problems in Obstetrics and Gynecology: Contraception, Induced Abortion, and Sterilization], Deutsch Z. Ges. Gerichtl. Med. 55:194-ff., 1964.

The author discusses indications for legal abortion in West Germany. The ethical indication (rape, incest) is disputed. The medical indication is the only one accepted by the law, and it is adoptable in a decreasing number of cases. The social indication cannot be used, neither can risk for fetal damage (rubella, Rh-immunization of the mother). A negative correlation between the relative frequency of legal abortion and the part of the population belonging to the Catholic faith is shown for the different States of the Federation, from 0.12 legal abortions/10,000 population in Saarland with 73% Catholics, to 11.17 legal abortions/10,000 population in Hamburg with 6% Catholics. Author concludes with a general recommendation to improve contraception.

2668 Doring, G.K. [Interruption of Pregnancy and Birth Control], Deutsch Med. Wschr. 82:117-ff., 1957.

Reviews the conclusions reached at a 1956 conference on abortion and birth control in West Germany. The number of legal abortions decreased per 10,000 inhabitants over a four year period from 2.0 approvals and 3.1 applications in 1950 to 0.9 approval and 1.4 rejections in 1954. Abortions occurred least frequently in predominantly Catholic provinces. Those women denied abortions delivered their children and received more intensive care during their pregnancies because of the desire for an abortion. It was concluded that only through programs of birth control can the abortion problem be minimized.

2669 Egner, Erich, "Okonomische Probleme der Familienpolitik" [Economic Problems of Family Policy], Schmollers Jahrbuch 75(2):67-92 and 75(3):67-92, 1955.

Critical analysis of Oeter's theories and proposals for the equalization of the costs of childbearing and child-rearing.

2670 Engisch, K. [Artificial Interruption of Pregnancy in Current Penal Law], Muenchener Med. Wochenschrift 102:130-31, 15 January 1960.

There is no uniform and clear legislation on the interruption of pregnancy in the German Federal Republic. In general only the pure medical indication is valid, and ethical, eugenic and social indications are not applicable. Except in emergency situations, when the surgeon himself can make the decision, a special commission usually makes the decision. The recommendations of the commission for a new Penal Code for the Federal Republic include the ethical indication for abortion.

2671 Familles dans le Monde, "Mesures en Faveur de la Famille dans la Republique Federale Allemande" [Measures Favoring the Family in the Federal Republic of Germany], Familles dans le Monde, September 1957, pp. 179-90.

A monograph followed by a short compilation of the texts of the most important German laws since 1883.

2672 Gamm, Hans-Jochen, "Schwanger-Schaftsunter-Brechung als Religioeses und Erzieherisches Problem" [Abortion as a Religious and Pedagogical Problem], Z. Evang. Ethik. 5: 193-203, 1961.

An overview of the sociological, legal, and medical aspects of abortion together with the religio-philosophical presuppositions underlying the current attitudes toward it. The presuppositions divide into two basic positions: (1) a woman has the right to do with her body what she wishes; and (2) at conception a new life has begun, the willful destruction of which is murder. The common conscience of contemporary society has little natural understanding for the second position. Public education in the grammar and secondary schools (not anti-abortion, but pro-elementary respect for all life as per Albert Schweitzer) is one significant way to meet the problem.

2673 Germany, Berlin. Statistisches Landesamt, "Die Biologischen und Sozialen Auswirkungen des Berliner Familiengrundungsdarlehens" [Biological and Social Effects of the Berlin-Family-Founding Loans], Berliner Statistik Monatsschrift 17(10):270-78, October 1962.

2674 Germany, Federal Republic of, Bundesministerium der Justiz, Gutachten und Stellungnahmen zu Fragen der Strafrechtreform mit Arztlichem Einschlag [Expert Testimony and Opinions on Questions of Legal Reform with Medical Applications], Bonn, 1958. 143 pp. processed.

The questions include: sterilization or castration; refertilization; artificial insemination; abortion.

2675 Germany, Federal Republic of, "Control of Prostitution," Internat. Digest Health Legis. 4:709, 1952-53; 8:402, 1957.

Notice of 5 April 1952 called upon the police to control prostitution in communes of less than 20,000 inhabitants. A Decree of 23 November 1956 strengthens this Notice by prohibiting abortion.

2676 Germany, Federal Republic of, Laws, Statutes, etc. Das Mutterschutzgesetz vom 24, Januar 1952 [The Maternal Protection Law of January 24, 1952], Second edition. Essen: Essener Verlag fur Sozialversicherung, 1953.

2677 Germany, Federal Republic of, "Trade in Contraceptives," Internat. Digest Health Legis. 4:716, 1954.

Police Ordinance of 1 September 1952 makes the manufacture and trade in contraceptives subject to authorization by the Minister of the Interior; and prohibits the manufacture, importation, advertising, or sale of uterine specula of less than 12 mm. in diameter and of intra-uterine pessaries. Their use or the administration of radiation or injections, except where the life or health of the mother is threatened, for the purpose of contraception are forbidden and subject to penal sanctions.

2678 Gesenius, Heinrich, "Zur Frage der Notwendigkeit einer Gesetzlichen Regelung der Freiwilligen Sterilisierung aus Sozialer Indikation" [On the Question of the Urgency of Some Legal Regulation of Voluntary Sterilization on Social Indications], Geburtshilfe und Frauenheilkunde 22(5):421-32, May 1962.

Discussion of the present liberal state of voluntary sterilization and of desirable changes.

2679 Giesen, Dieter, Die Kunstliche Insemination als Ethisches und Rechtliches Problem [Artificial Insemination as an Ethical and Legal Problem], Schriften zum Deutschen und Europaischen Zivil - Handels - und Prozessrecht, Band 18. Bielefeld, E. und W. Gieseking, 1962. 272 pp.

2680 Glaus, A. Zum Problem der Psychiatrisch Indizierten Schwangerschaftsunterbrechung Gemass Artikel 120 StGB Sowie Sterilisierender Operationen bei Mann und Frau im Sinne Einer Interruptionsprophylaxe und Geplanter Elternschaft [On the Problem of the Psychiatrically Indicated Abortion Measures (Article 120 of the Federal Republic Statutes) as Well as Sterilization Operations on Men and Women for the Purpose of Interruption-Prophylaxis and Planned Parenthood], Bern and Stuttgart: Verlag Hans Huber, 1962. 112 pp.

2681 Harmsen, Hans, "Familienlasten-Ausgleich" [Family Allowances], Munchener Med. Wochenschrift 99(23):833-35, 7 June 1957.

2682 Harmsen, Hans, [The Situation of Abortion in the German Federal Republic] in: Mehlan, K.H., ed. Internationale Abortsituation, Abortbekampfund, Antikonzeption. Leipzig: Georg Thieme, 1961.

The development of the existing German law on abortion, which lists only strict medical indications as justification for interruption of pregnancy, is reviewed. Statistics gathered in Hamburg, West Berlin, Lubeck and five West German states indicate that, while there has been a general decrease in the abortion rate since the early fifties, interpretation and application of the law varies in the different states. It is felt that the decrease in the number of abortions is due primarily to greater restrictions on the use of medical indications, and also to increasing skill in treating illness without having to interrupt pregnancy. Mental depression was used most often as the medical indication in 1945-46, general weakness in 1947-51, and heart and circulatory diseases in 1959. Although attempts to estimate the incidence of illegal abortion are not easy, figures of from one to three abortions per live births are given. Statistics also show that married women (75%) have the greatest number of induced abortions, as do women in the 20-30 year old age group.

2683 Herold, G. [On the Problem of Criminal Admissability of Artificial Sterilization According to the Current Legal Situation], Med. Klin. 55:194-97, 29 January 1960.

2684 Hofmann, D. [Investigations on the Frequency of the Causes of Abortion with Consideration of Criminal Abortions. An Analysis of 3033 Cases of Abortion at the Giessen University Hospital, 1945-1960], Med. Klin. 56:821-ff., 1961.

The etiology of spontaneous abortions and the frequency of induced abortions are examined. A graded scale using both the symptomatology and history was employed. Results show 2.9% of all cases are considered absolutely free from suspicion, 65.9% as probably induced abortions and 39.3% as definitely criminal abortions (including 5.6% who admitted a provocation). Age distribution, marital status, occupation of husband and patient and history and clinical course are reviewed.

2685 International Labour Office, "Improved Family Allowances in the Federal Republic of Germany," Internat. Labour Rev. 92(2):152-53, April 1965.

Notes on amendment dated April 5, 1965, to the federal act respecting family allowances of April 14, 1964.

2686 International Labour Office, "Maternity Protection in the Federal Republic of Germany," Industry and Labour 7(10): 385-87, 15 May 1952.

An Act for the protection of working mothers was promulgated in West Germany on 24 January 1952, which succeeds the Maternity Protection Act of 17 May 1942. It limits the kind and conditions of work for women during pregnancy and the nursing period. It continues the provision of maternity leave for four weeks and extends the period of leave for postnatal care from six weeks to eight weeks for nursing mothers and to twelve weeks for nursing mothers of prematurely born infants. Maternity payments are detailed. There are also provisions for rest periods for nursing women, and the protection of employment during pregnancy and for four months following confinement.

2687 Janssen, Fritz, Die Behandlung der Inkikationen zur Schwangerschaftsunterbrechung im Deutschen Strafrecht der Ersten Halfte des 20 Jahrhunderts [Indications for the Interruption of Pregnancy as Treated in the German Criminal Code during the First Half of the 20th Century], [Typescript (carbon) of Inaug. Diss., Munich, in U.S. Library of Congress.] Munchen, 1952. v, 138 pp.

2688 Karpf, Hans J. Die Rechtliche Problematik des Artifiziellen Abortes in Ethisch Indizierten Fallen [The Legal Question of Induced Abortion in Ethically Indicated Cases]. Munich, 1965. 136 pp.

2689 Kepp, R. "Medical and Legal Viewpoints on Induced Abortion and Sexual Sterilization," Med. Welt. 35:1702-8, 31 August 1963.

The proposed new abortion law is outlined with regard to using medical reasons for interrupting pregnancy. Excluded is legal permissibility of inducing abortion where there is expected fetal defect. The addition of a rape clause to the act is advocated.

2690 Kepp, R. [On the Problem of Abortion on Fetal Indication] Med. Klin.55:98-ff., 1960.

Fetal indications for therapeutic abortion are regarded as valid in most cases. The author stresses the difficult judgments involved, and notes that the definition of fetal indications includes serious malformations, hereditary diseases and radiological damage to the embryo.

2691 Kern, Egon, "Ist Unsere Familienpolitik Richtig?" [Is Our Family Policy Correct?] Deutsche Gesellschaft Bevolkerungswissenschaft. 34(1):15-30, July 1966.

2692 Kohlhaas, M. [Is Approval of the Fertilizing Male Also Necessary In Cases of Interruption of Pregnancy on Medical Indication?] Deutsch Med. Wschr. 87:1471-ff., 1962.

The author concludes that the fertilizing male's consent is not necessary in abortion cases unless the woman's life or health is seriously threatened. It is the woman's decision only in all other situations.

2693 Kohlhaas, M. "Die Ungeklarte Rechtslage zur Unfruchtbarmachung" [The Unclarified Legal Position of Sterilization], Munchener Med. Wochenschrift 107:1669-773, 27 August 1965.

2694 Krebs, Heinrich, Bundeskindergeldgesetz [The Federal Family Allowance Law]. Herne: Verlag Neue Wirtschafts-Briefe GmbH, 1966. 140 pp.

Systematic exposition of the provisions and administration of the basic law of April 14, 1964 and as amended on April 5, 1965.

2695 Lauterbach, Herbert, "The German Child Allowances Law, Enacted November 13, 1954: Provisions," Internat. Soc. Security Assn. Bull. 8:184-95, May/June 1955; Also in: Revue du Travail 57(3):434-43, March 1956.

Discusses family assistance before the enactment of the family allowance law, the provisions of the law, statistical data, and correlations with other laws.

2696 Leyser, J. "Equality of the Spouses Under the New German Law," Amer. J. Comparative Law 7:276-87, Spring 1958.

The new law of July 1, 1958 aims at giving effect, in the field of the relations between husband and wife, to the new constitutional principle of equality between the sexes. The statute deals with provisions in the field of civil law and it does not deal with equality of the spouses in other fields. Yet, the changes the statute effects are far-reaching. They concern the personal relations as well as the property relations between husband and wife. For example, the wife is now authorized to share in decisions concerning the matrimonial life, and to undertake a gainful occupation provided it does not interfere with her family duties.

2697 Lippmann, Adolf von, "Von Familienlohn zum Familienlastenausgleich" [From Family Allowances to Equalization of Family Costs], Deutsche Versicherungs-Zeitschrift, October 1953, pp. 218-22.

2698 Ludwig, Philipp, "Probleme der Familienpolitik" [Problems of Family Policy], Soz. Welt. 8(2):129-41, 1957.

In spite of the intellectual, financial and social changes of the last century, the family is still considered the most important institution in human life. The last decades were especially unfavorable for family life. During the pre-industrial period the family was an economic center, and in rural life young children, economically viewed, were not only a burden, but an asset too. Industrialization changed this and the most visible result was a shrinking birthrate. In 1955 in West Germany the birthrate surplus was only 4.9 per 1,000 compared with 14.3 in 1910. At the same time, the number of people 65 and over, living mostly on unproductive pensions jumped from 5% to 10% of the population. This development caused a more and more unfavorable biological structure of the population as a whole. Since World War I, 33 countries started to protect the family by administrative rules. In 1953, West Germany established a ministry for family policy. The development and the freedom of the family are only guaranteed if they are not bought by economic distress. The bases of family support are tax relief and rents for children. The average existence minimum per person is considered to be DM 40.00 ($10.00) per month.

2699 Mayer, A. "Soll die Heterologe Kunstliche Insemination Verboten Werden" [Should Heterologous Artificial Insemination be Forbidden?] Med. Klin. 54(25):1149-56, 19 June 1959.

2700 Mayer, A. "Uber Juristische und Psychologische Fragen der Kunstlichen Samenubertragung" [Legal and Psychological Problems of Artificial Insemination], Munchener Med. Wochenschrift 96(15):393-95; and 96(16):444-47, 9 and 16 April 1954.

2701 Muller-Freienfels, W. "Family Law and the Law of Succession in Germany," Internat. Comparative Law Quart. 16:490, April 1967.

Materials pertain to the Federal Republic as well as undivided Germany. Under Family Law are discussions of engagement, marriage, personal and economic marital relations, dissolution of marriage, and divorce. The Law of Succession is briefly treated.

2702 Naujoks, H. [Interruption of Pregnancy and Sterilization] in: Seitz, L. and Amreich, A.I., eds. _Biologie und Pathologie des Weibes_. Berlin: Urban and Schwarzenberg, 1955.

Germany's Federal Penal Code permits the performance of a therapeutic abortion only when the pregnant woman's life is seriously endangered. The author reviews the validity of different medical indications for abortion, with brief reference to the invalidity of eugenic, social and ethical indications in terms of the law and medical ethics. The methods and consequences of induced abortion are also discussed, and the author concludes with a description of legislation and procedural rules concerning abortion and sterilization in the Federal Republic, Democratic Republic, Switzerland, Holland, Sweden, France and Spain.

2703 Noack, H. "Erfahrung der Leipziger Kommission fur Schwangerschaftsunterbrechung" [Experiences of the Leipzig Commission for Abortion], _Deutsche Gesundheitswesen_ 13(19-20): 592-94, 8 and 15 May 1958.

2704 Oeter, Ferdinand, "Der Ausgleich der Familienlastin" [The Equalization of Family Costs], _Schmollers Jahrbuch_. 78(2):71-97, 1958.

A documented discussion of the basis of postwar Germany policy on family allowances.

2705 Oeter, Ferdinand, _Familienpolitik_ [Family Policy]. Stuttgart: Friedrich Vorwerk, 1954. 235 pp.

Argues in favor of the "Ausgleichung der Familienlasten" (the more equitable distribution of expenses of child rearing). Through differential income taxation and through a specially adapted social security system, some of the cost of upbringing of the children would pass on to childless couples and single persons. At the same time, this would strengthen the position of the family by a wide distribution of property, notably of home ownership. Some such legislation has already been passed by the Bundestag. Oeter's position appears to be in keeping with the German reliance on strong social organization. To the emergent large scale organization of the socialist state, Oeter wishes to juxtapose the small scale organization of the family. The rise of the birth-rate, the generational continuity, "die Harte" (the toughness) engendered by the necessity of adjustment to a cohesive family group, are a few of the many benefits cited in support of this policy.

2706 Schmidt, E. [Interruption of Pregnancy and Sterilization According to Current and Future Law], _Arch Gynaek._ 180: 289-ff., 1951.

Only medical indications for legal abortion, and not social, eugenic or ethical, are permitted according to current German law. However, even though the different States of the Federation agree with the law, some variations do exist in regard to interpretation, practice and procedures. The author views changes in basic concepts unnecessary, but does recommend an improvement in the uniformity of details.

2707 Schreiber, W. _Kindergeld im Sozio-okonomischen Prozess-Familienlastenausgleich als Prozess Zeitlicher Kaufkraft-Umschichtung im Individual-Bereich_ [The Socio-Economic Effect of Children's Allowances: The Equalization of Family Burdens as a Secular Process for Transferring Purchasing Power Among Individuals], _Sozialtheorie und Sozialpolitik_ No. 1 W. Kohlhammer Verlag, 1964. 83 pp.

2708 Schubert, G. [Experiences of a Gynecologist with Abortion Recommendations in Northern Germany], _Internist_ 4:124-ff., 1963.

A review of legal abortion in northern Germany. There was a very high abortion rate after World War II, with Hamburg reporting an incidence of 2,000 between 1948 and 1950; however, the number has decreased considerably during the last decade. The experience of seven Hamburg hospitals is described. Births in these hospitals represented 60% of all live births in the city, and 538 abortions were performed over a three year period (1960-62), accounting for 1.3% of hospital deliveries. The hospitals rejected approximately 30% of recommended abortions. The author concludes with a discussion of the validity of the varying medical and medical-social indications for abortion, and stresses that it is the gynecologist who must make the final decision in regard to whether or not there are valid abortion grounds. The need for preventative measures is also emphasized both to avoid private inducement of abortion if a woman is refused legal interruption and to make advice on contraception more readily available so that repeated unwanted pregnancies can be avoided.

2709 Schubert, G., et al. "Arztliche u. Juristische Probleme zur Frage des Legalen Schwangerschaftsabbruchs" [Medical and Legal Problems on the Question of Legal Abortion], Deutsches Med. J. 15:582-89, 5 September 1964.

2710 Schubert, G., et al. [Problems for the Physician and the Lawyer Regarding Legal Abortion], Deutsch Med. J. 15:582-ff., 1964.

The medico-legal aspects of legal abortion in West Germany where interruption of pregnancy is permissable only when the life or health of the woman is seriously threatened are reviewed. Although the number of legal abortions had decreased since the post-war years, they are still fairly frequent in areas like Hamburg where social factors play a decisive role. The physician has the final decision as to whether to abort and therefore should use this power to refuse all abortions which do not strictly adhere to the law.

2711 Schwalm, G. "Nochmals zu Sterilisation und Kastration in Strafrechtlicher Sich" [More on Sterilization and Castration from the Point of View of Penal Law], Med. Klin. 59: 1520, 18 September 1964.

2712 Schwalm, G. "Sterilisation und Kastration in Strafrechtlicher Sicht" [Sterilization and Castration from the Viewpoint of Penal Law], Med. Klin. 58:1976-78, 29 November 1963.

2713 "Social Security Developments in the Federal Republic of Germany Since 1949," Internat. Labour Rev. 66(5-6):485-501, November 1952.

One of several developments is the improvement of maternity benefits through the Maternity Protection Law passed on January 24, 1952. Benefits are raised from 75% to 100% of the average net earnings of women compulsorily insured for sickness. The maternity benefit is ordinarily payable for six weeks before confinement (or four weeks for domestics) and for six weeks after confinement. Nursing mothers, who are entitled to benefits through the insurance of the husband or father, may receive benefits for up to 12 weeks after confinement. Nursing mothers, who are themselves insured, may receive benefits for up to 26 weeks after confinement.

2714 Stein, Bernhard, Der Familienlohn; Probleme einer Familiengerechten Einkommensgestaltung [The Family Allowance; Problems of a Just Family Income Structure]. Sozialpolitische Schriften, Heft 5. Berlin: Duncker und Humblot, 1956. 268 pp.

2715 Tschoepe, Armin, "Fruehehe Del: Analysen Eines Grenzphaenomens der Familiensoziologie" [Early Marriage During Social Change: Analyses of a Border-Line Phenomenon of Family Sociology], Soz. Welt. 17(4):346-64, 1966.

A definition and analysis of teenage marriage is attempted. Legal age-limits for marriage in 19th and 20th century laws are discussed. Statistical material on teenage marriages in Germany is presented for the years, 1950, 1953, 1959, and 1963. The teenage marriage as a sociological fact is found to pose four sociological problems: as to its cause, whether it is a normal phenomenon, what the circumstances are which lead to the high divorce rate for teenage marriage, and what measures to help or prevent teenage marriages are to be taken. Illegitimate pregnancy as a cause for early marriage is studied in the context of public opinion and family pressure against illegitimate birth. It is seen that German moral values have turned back toward traditional middle class ideals, which have been taken over by the rising working class. However, public opinion surveys show that almost 90% of all married males and 70% of all married females in Germany had sexual intercourse before marriage, which indicates permissiveness of sexual mores. It is asserted that society is not so much concerned with forbidding sex, but with preventing biological creation without the assurance of economic provisions and the existence of a proper 'socializing agency', i.e., the family, for the offspring. Teenage marriage is viewed as a social solution for teenage sex; on the condition that early legal ties are anticipated, in case of pregnancy premarital sex is allowed.

2716 Ussler, Otto von, Massnahmen und Forderungen zum Wirtschaftlichen Ausgleich der Familienlasten unter Berucksichtigung der Bevolkerungswissenschaft [Measures and Requirements for an Economic Equalization of Family Costs from the Point of View of Demography] Hamburg: Veroffentlichungen der Deutschen Gesellschaft fur Bevolkerungswissenschaft e.V. 1955. Processed.

2717 Waidl, E. "Die Gegenwartige Rechtslage der Kunstlichen Fehlgeburt" [Current Status of the Legality of Induced Abortion], Munchener Med. Wochenschrift 100(28):1052-55, 11 July 1958.

2718 Welch, E., and Katsch, H.U. [On the Treatment of Febrile Abortion], Z. Geburtsh Gynak. 132:256-ff., 1950.

During 1926 through 1947 there were 1,208 cases of febrile abortion at the University Hospital of Heidelberg. 1,144 of these cases were light and 64 severe or septic; cause was unknown in 70%, resulted from spontaneous abortion in 5%, criminal abortion in 7%, and physical stress in 18%. The majority of the unknown abortions were probably criminal abortions. The distribution by age groups 18-40 was even. A marked increase in the incidence of febrile abortions was noted in the last two years studied, but sulfonamides and penicillin minimized mortality and duration of hospitalization.

2719 Wingen, Max, _Familienpolitik_: _Ziele_, _Wege_, _Wirkungen_ [Policies Concerning the Family: Objectives, Means, Effects]. Paderborn: Bonifacius, 1964. 284 pp.

2720 Winter, G.E., and Meyran, H.R. [On the Interruption of Pregnancy], _Zbl_. _Gynaek_. 83:1141-ff., 1961.

The incidence of legal abortions in Hamburg is discussed. The author demonstrates that a restrictive attitude against the widening of the indications outside of the medical field is necessary. Intensified contraceptive education is urged.

2721 Wuermeling, H.B. [Legal Abortion on Medical Indications and the Catholic Moral], _Deutsch_ _Z_. _Ges_. _Gerichtl_ _Med_. 55:261-ff., 1964.

In areas where the incidence of legal abortion is high, the proportion of Catholics in that area is low. An operation with the direct purpose of killing the fetus will never be accepted by the Catholic doctrine; however, the situation may change when there are increased possibilities to maintain the life of the aborted fetus outside of the mother.

LUXEMBOURG

Policies on fertility and family size

2722 Luxembourg. Service d'Etudes et de Documentation Economiques and Office de la Statistique Generale, "Les Prestations Familiales" [Family Allowances], _Bull. Service Etudes Documentation Econ. Office Statistique Generale_ 1(3):166-68, July - September 1950.

Data for 1947/48 and 1949 on family allowances.

2723 Wattelar, Christine and Wunsch, Guillaume, _Etude Demographique de la Nuptialite en Belgique_ [Demographic Study of Nuptiality in Belgium], Louvain: Catholic University, 1967. 132 pp.

Little research has been devoted to an analysis of marriage and divorce in Belgium. The present book overcomes this deficiency. The first part discusses the methods employed in analyzing changes in Belgian nuptiality over the past century and regional variations in it. The proportion of first marriages regularly increased with the result that the number of celibates at age fifty years decreased, averaging about nine per cent. This rise in nuptiality is accompanied by a continuous decrease in the age at first marriage. It now averages 24.4 years for the male and 22.5 for the female, being a decrease of 2.5 years and 3.2 years, respectively, since the turn of the century. Along with a decrease in the probability in widowhood and an increase in the length of life, there has been a decided increase in the probability of divorce, its maximum probability being reached after seven or eight years of marriage. About nine to ten per cent of the marriages contracted annually consist of the remarriage of divorcees. Legislation, sociocultural and economic factors exercise considerable influence over nuptiality.

2724 Woronoff, Andre, "Le Mouvement Social en 1946" [The Social Movement in 1946], _Bull. Institut Recherches Econ. Soc._ 13(3):275-98, July 1947.

Including old age pensions, family allowances, etc.

NETHERLANDS

General population policies

2725 Godefroy, J. "Das Landnotproblem in den Niederlanden" [The Problem of the Deficit of Land in the Netherlands], Europe Oeconomica 1(1):43-51, 1943.

2726 Groenman, Sjoerd, "Social Aspects of the Demographic Development in the Netherlands," Plan. Develop. Netherlands 1(1):19-28, 1962.

There are more than 350 people to the kilometer in the Netherlands, and the expected increase of population is one million people for every five years. Population increase had led to the acceptance of planning procedures in public life. The first scarcity is land, and this commodity is carefully managed by physical planning. There was a threat of scarcity of means of existence after World War II, and the collapse of economic relations with Indonesia, but this was countered by economic planning and especially by a policy of industrialization. Since in the "Rim-city Holland," recreational space is scarce and means of subsistence are abundant, the national policy has been to encourage the transfer of sources of subsistence to economically backward areas, where there is no lack of space. The threat of overpopulation has also been met by a policy of emigration overseas. Full employment has necessitated the attraction of labor from Italy and Spain, but of other occupational categories than those who leave the country. Motives for reclamation of the Zudierzee-polders have little to do with population pressure but rather with reduction in length of seadikes, the creation of a fresh-water, shortening of highway routes, recreation and the enlargement of farming units. The polders will also create room for the expansion of urban areas. Other fields of planning are: rural reconstruction, the spread of professional industrial training, the foundation of new technical universities, and the expansion of higher education as a whole.

2727 Philippson, Eva, "Bijdrage over de Bevolkingspolitiek van de Duitse Bezetter in Nederland en de Toepassing in Zijn Beleid" [Contribution to the Study of the Population Policy of the German Occupation in the Netherlands and Its Practical Application], Mens en Maatschappij, September 15, 1951. pp. 297-310.

2728 Steigenga, Willem, ed. Bevolkingsgroei en Maatschappelijke Verantwoordelijkheid [Population Growth and Social Responsibility]. A report of the Dr. Wiardi Beckman Foundation. Maatschappelijke Vraagstukken, I. Amsterdam: De Arbeiderspers, 1955. 229 pp.

A joint report by representatives of the major religious denominations on the Netherlands population problem and alternative policies. Discusses changing attitudes on birth control and mass emigration.

Policies on fertility and family size

2729 Berg, B.S. [Abortion and Sterilization], Arch. Gynaek. 179: 319-ff., 1951.

Reviews the abortion situation in the Netherlands where the Dutch Penal Code makes no provision for the interruption of pregnancy. However, induced abortion performed lege artis by a physician has not been prosecuted. It is indefinite which body decides on the validity of indications.

2730 Berg, J. van den, "Responsible Parenthood," Free Univ. Quart. 9:112-20, 1963.

Theological remarks on the question of birth control are presented which seek to approach the complex problem from the side of theological ethics. First attention is given to the doctrine of marriage itself, then to the idea of parenthood as such, next to the notion of responsibility with regard to parenthood and family planning. Finally it is shown how the idea of responsible parenthood fits into the biblical doctrine of marriage.

2731 Boas, C. van Emde, "The Possibilities and Limitations of Instruction in the Use of Contraceptives," in: Proceedings of the Fourth Conference of the Region for Europe, Near East and Africa of the IPPF. New York: Excerpta Medica Foundation, 1965.

An analysis of the causal relationship between conception and abortion with particular reference to research done at a family planning center in Amsterdam which was undertaken to determine the relation between the frequency of induced abortion and the contraceptive method employed among three sets of women in 1932, 1939 and 1945. Results indicated that the incidence of abortion decreased from 8% in 1932 to 1% in 1939, following instruction in modern contraceptive method, that mainly married women had abortions, and that periodic continence and vaginal douches were responsible for 84% of unwanted pregnancies. A 1960 study involving 103 women seeking abortions, revealed that 41 used no contraceptive method; 39 used bad methods (e.g., coitus interruptus); and 20 used good methods (e.g., cervical cap) . (Forty-eight of the sample were married, 50 were single, and 8 were widowed or divorced.)

2732 Bloemhof, F. Het Vraagstuk der Bewuste Geboortebeperking [The Problem of Birth Control], Nijkerk, 1955. Dissertation.

2733 Blom-Cooper, L.J. "Legal Adoption in the Netherlands," Internat. Comparative Law Quart. 6:543-47, July 1957.

Act No. 42 of January 29, 1956 provides for the legal adoption of children in the Netherlands. Thus, Portugal is now the only Western country without such legal provision. The preparatory work of convincing the Dutch people was done by the F.I.O.M. (Federation of the Institutions for the Unmarried Mother and Her Child). There are various restrictions on legal adoption, including the requirement that the adoptive parents must have been married to each other for at least five years before the application.

2734 Centrum voor Staatkundige Vorming, Geboorteregeling als Middel tot Verlichting van de Bevolkingsdruk in Nederland. Is Bevordering van Staatsweger Geoorloofd of Verwerpelijk ? [Birth Control as a Means of Relieving the Population Pressure in the Netherlands. Is Its Promotion by the State Permissible or To Be Rejected?] The Hague, 1957. 32 pp.

2735 Diels, E., and Groenman, S.J. "Gesprekkan met Gchuwde Vrouwen omtrent Geboorteregeling" [Interviews with Married Women About Birth Control], in: Social Wetenschappelike Venkenningen. Assen: Van Garcum and Co., 1957.

An analysis of questionnaires distributed by Dutch doctors to their patients asking whether family planning has been used and the methods used in relation to religion, education, work status, occupation, and reasons for family planning.

2736 Enschede, C.J. [Abortion on the Medical Indication and Criminal Law], Nederl. T. Geneesk. 110:1349-ff., 1966.

One who violates Dutch law *de facto* may be exempt from prosecution if the action was performed for ethical or medical necessity. Thus, physicians performing an abortion for medical purposes will not be punished.

2737 Heeren, H.J., and Moors, H.G. "Gezinsplanning in Utrecht" [Family Planning in Utrecht], Sociolog. Gids 14(4):210-20 . July - August 1967.

2738 Henny, A.W. "Legal Status of the Married Woman in the Netherlands Before and After January 1, 1957," Phi Delta Delta 36:10, June 1958.

2739 Kirchhoff, Heinz, Bevolkerungspolitik und Geburtenregelung [Population Policy and Birth Control], Vortragsreihe der Niedersachsischen Landesregierung zur Forderung in Niedersachsen, Heft 30. Gottingen: Vendenhoech u. Ruprecht, 1965. 20 pp.

2740 Knibbeler, J.M. "Heeft de Kinderbijslag in Nederland Invloed op de Gezinsgrootle?" [Do Family Allowances in the Netherlands Influence Family Size?] Mens en Mij May 15,1953. pp. 153-73.

2741 Leeuwen, B. van, "Echtscheidingen van Katholieken in Nederland" [Divorce Among Catholics in the Netherlands], Soc. Kompas 1(1):19-24, 1953.

The Central Bureau of Statistics collects data concerning the number of divorces in all municipalities. Since 1951 the data are broken down by religion. The figures for 1951 show that the Catholics are concerned in 25.3% of all divorces, while they are concerned in 33.1% of all marriages (1947). Divorce occurs more frequently among mixed marriages(marriages of a Catholic and a non-Catholic), than among marriages where both are Catholic (1.22% and 0.17% of all marriages in each of the categories). The main factor is probably the instability of mixed marriages. There is an indication that mixed marriages between Catholics and secularists lead to divorce sooner than mixed marriages between Catholics and Protestants. For farmers the divorce rate is relatively low, while for unskilled laborers relatively high.

2742 [Legalization of Induced Abortion, Also on Social Indications], Nederl. T. Geneesk. 110:253-ff., 1966.

Reviews abortion legalization in several countries whose main intent was to reduce the number of criminal abortions, and indicates that this decrease has failed to appear. The Dutch law should not be changed, but attempts to improve social conditions and contraceptive use should be enacted.

2743 Nabrink, G. Population Problems, Family Planning and Sexual Reform in the Netherlands, The Hague: Netherlands Society for Sexual Reforms, 1953. 26 pp.

2744 Netherlands. Gezondheidsraad, "Kunstmatige Inseminatie bij de Mens," Rapport uitgebracht door de Voorzitter van de Gezondheidsraad aan de Minister van Sociale Zaken en Volksgezondheid op 9 September, 1960 [Artificial Insemination in Humans. Report presented by the Chairman of Health Council to the Minister of Social Affairs and Public Health on September 9, 1960], Verslagen en Mededelingen betreffende de Volksgezondheid, No. 6, June 1965, pp. 713-801.

Report on methods and findings of a survey of gynecologists in the Netherlands concerning their experience with insemination by husband and by donor. Topics considered: general view of the problem; somatic, psychic, genetic, medical ethics, and legal aspects. Appendixes on survey methods.

2745 Netherlands. Laws, Statutes, etc. Kinderbijslagwet [Family Allowances] Zwolle: N.E.J. Tjeenk Willink, 1947. 320 pp.

2746 Petersen, William, "Family Subsidies in the Netherlands," Marr. Fam. Living 17(3):260-66, August 1955.

Holland's family endowment policy is being administered against a background of a very high natality, a very low (except for war years) mortality and a sharp deterioration of economy from the country's prewar position. The author's principal concern is whether, under such circumstances, family subsidies affect the birth rate. Holland also affords an example of the interaction between Socialist and Catholic family policies, and of the consequent tendency of family subsidies, once they have been instituted, to grow in size and importance.

2747 Pharmaceutisch Weekblad, "Proposals for Changing Legislation on Contraceptives," Pharmaceutisch Weekblad 100:778-82, 18 June 1965.

2748 Treffers, P.E. "Abortion in Amsterdam," Popul. Stud. 20(3):295-305, March 1967.

Mortality from abortion is low in the Netherlands today, and approximately equal to mortality at delivery. Calculations suggest that about 4,000 abortions occur in Amsterdam every year, of which about 2,100 are induced. The abortion rate shows a very gradual decline after the Second World War. An investigation of the social background of women with induced abortion showed no relationship between occupational group and the incidence of abortion, but a strong negative correlation between religion and abortion.

Abortion was more common among women with disturbed relationships in their own or parental families. Induced abortion usually occurred in pregnancies resulting from failure of contraception; these failures were caused not by lack of knowledge of good contraceptives, but by ineffective practice of contraception. The inability to use contraceptive methods in an effective way is related to a lack of communication between the two partners, and to a negative attitude of the women towards sex. An attempt has been made to formulate a theory of the causes of induced abortion among the women interviewed in Amsterdam.

2749 Treffers, P.E. "Family Size, Contraception, and Birth Rate Before and After the Introduction of a New Method of Family Planning," _J. Marr. Fam._ 30(2):338-45, 1968.

Discusses family size, contraception, and birth rate in the Netherlands before and after the introduction of oral contraception, drawing parallels between developments in the Netherlands and several countries in eastern Europe, particularly Hungary, after legalization of induced abortion.

2750 Treffers, P.E. [Induced Abortion as a Social Problem II. Should Induced Abortion be Legalized?] _T. Soc. Geneesk_ 44:655-ff., 1966.

A statistical study of abortion and birth in various countries with liberal abortion laws is presented. The author's viewpoint is that illegal abortion remains and widespread acceptance of contraception is impeded by the availability of legal abortion. He also argues against the introduction of a medical indication in the strict Dutch law, on the grounds that such a revision could be interpreted so liberally as to allow abortion on demand.

2751 University of Leiden, Institute of Criminal Law and Criminology, _Sexual Crime Today: A Symposium_. Hague: Nijhoff, 1960. 86 pp.

2752 Verwey-Jonker, H. "Social Services in the Netherlands," _J. Marr. Fam._ 17:233-37, 1955.

Aids and measures concerning the family are related to the importance of family life and of religious considerations in the pattern of living in the Netherlands. The aids are also a part of a more general social policy. Aids for the family include family allowances, wage controls, tax exemptions for children, social insurance, and educational subsidies. Such aids rather than birth control are viewed as ways of meeting the problems of large family size.

2753 Watson, A. "Development of Marital Justifications for Malitiosa Desertio in Roman-Dutch Law," Law Quart. Rev. 79:87-97. January 1963.

The Protestant theologians permitted a member of their Church to obtain a divorce if he were deserted by his spouse; or if he felt compelled to leave his spouse on account of her odium religionis. The German jurist Arnisaeus said that the deserted spouse should be allowed the divorce provided that he had not given good cause for the desertion. The Dutch jurists, under Brouwer's leadership, did not recognize constructive desertion. The South African courts initially accepted the Dutch position but later reverted to the view of Arnisaeus.

2754 Winter, E.R. de. "Enkele Aspecten van de Abortus Provocatus" [Some Aspects of Induced Abortion], Deventer. Rotterdam: AE. E. Kluwer, 1966.

A study of medico-legal aspects of the current situation in the Netherlands.

SWITZERLAND

General population policies

2755 Feld, W. "Statistische Unterlagen fur Quantitative Bevolkerungs Politik" [Statistical Foundations for Quantitative Population Policy], Gesund. Wohlfahrt 23(1):35-46, 1943.

2756 Henninger, Wilhelm. "Die Schweiz -- Volksbiologisch Gesehen" [Switzerland -- A Population Viewpoint], Z. Geopolitik 19: 509-13. November 1942.

2757 Michot, Albert, "Politique Sociale et Demographique en Suisse" [Social and Demographic Policy in Switzerland], Population 2(3):533-46, July - September 1947.

A summary description of the demographic situation in Switzerland as a basis for understanding Swiss policy on family allowances, aid to youth, immigration and emigration, social assistance, etc..

2758 Nydegger, Alfred, "Das Problem der Auslandischen Arbeitskrafte im Rahmen der Schweizerischen Konjunkturpolitik" [The Problem of Foreign Labor in Relation to Swiss Social Policy], Schweiz. Z. Volkswirtschaft Statistik 99(3):321-32, September 1963.

2759 Schmid, Werner, Grundzuge einer Gesunden Bevolkerungs und Familienpolitik [Outline of a Sound Population and Family Policy]. Leemann, 1941. 20 pp.

2760 Zeck, Hans F. "Die Bevolkerungspolitischen Massnahmen der Schweiz" [Swiss Population Policy], Arch. Bevolk. 10(3):179-81, July 1940.

A summary of the vital statistics of Switzerland, 1899 to the present, is followed by a brief resume of the taxation policy, family allowances and other devices.

Policies on fertility and family size

2761 Bernhard, Roberto, Die Kunstliche Besamungbeim Menschen im Hinblick auf das Schweizerische Recht [Artificial Insemination in Man in Relation to Swiss Law], H. Schellenberg, 1958. xv, 321 pp.

2762 Cloeren, S., and Mall-Haefeli, M. [The Abortion Problem], Z. Praeventivmed 10:85-ff., 1965.

The author gives a brief description of population development and incidence of and legislation on induced abortion in several countries; discussion then centers on the abortion situation in Switzerland, with particular references to the experience of Basel's University Hospital. The country's abortion rate increased from 1 per 20 births in 1900 to 1 per 8 births for 1960-63, while abortion mortality showed a decrease from 20 per thousand abortions for 1921-46 to 1.3 per thousand for 1947-61. Of all hospitalized abortion cases, 20% admitted that their abortions had been induced and 76% were married; 60% were married in the admittedly induced group and 57% were married among all women of reproductive age in the area. 25% of the aborted married women had occupational work as compared to 9% of all married women. Abortion patients had an average of one child, but almost 50% of the occupational workers had no children. Over 50% of the patients were Catholic, whereas 37% of the total population is Catholic.

2763 David, Jakob, Der Lebensraum der Familie. Eine Studie zur Forderg Einer Grechten Sozialpolitic Zugunsten der Familie [The Living Space of the Family. A Study for the Promotion of a Just Social Policy Favoring the Family]. Sozialpolitische Schriftenreihe des Schweizerischen Katholischen Volks-Vereins, No. 1. Luzern: Rex-Verlag, 1943. 48 pp.

2764 Familles dans le Monde. "Mesures en Faveur de la Famille en Suisse" [Measures to Benefit the Family in Switzerland], Familles dans le Monde, No. 1, March 1961, pp. 30-51.

2765 Geiser, M. [Numbers and Thoughts of the Legal Abortions in Switzerland and Abroad], Schweiz. Med. Wschr. 86:1006-ff., 1956.

By the Swiss Federal penal code, abortion is exempted from penalty if it is performed by a physician when the life or health of the woman is in serious danger. Legal abortions are not reported in all the cantons, and the incidence varies in the ones with available statistics. An overall rise in frequency has occurred during the recent years. The highest ratio per 100 births is reported from Geneva (130-150). The estimated figure for all Switzerland is 10-11. Half of the women who were interrupted in Geneva had come from other cantons or from abroad. The majority of the abortions must have been done on medical-social indication, which is considered to be an almost illicitly liberal interpretation of the law. The author also discusses the psychiatric after-effects of induced abortion from the results of his own study, and from a literature review.

2766 Getaz, D., and Merz, W.R. [Family Planning], Gynaecologia 155:27-ff., 1963.

The authors are primarily concerned with the effectiveness of family planning. They report, too, briefly on the abortion situation in Lausanne and Basel. The abortion rates at Basel's University Clinic are compared for the periods 1941-50 and 1951-60; the number of legal abortions increased from 3% to 5% of the gynecological cases treated although a program in contraception was begun in 1951. The authors also point out that, in Lausanne, increasing the number of legal abortions has not effectively combated the number of illegal abortions.

2767 Glaus, A. [On Induced Abortion and Its Prevention/Including Abortion-Prophylaxis for the Wife or Husband/ from the View-point of a Swiss Psychiatrist According to Art. 20 of the Swiss Penal Code], Internist 4:110-ff., 1963.

The author stresses the magnitude of the induced abortion problem; each year in Switzerland (pop. 5-1/2 million) there are an estimated 52,000 criminal abortions and 8,000 legal abortions. Approximately 4,000 criminal abortions are performed annually in Zurich, which reports the same number of live births per year. The country's Federal Penal Code permits abortion only when the mother's life or health is seriously endangered and then with the consent of two physicians. Eugenic or humanitarian indications are not considered sufficient justification. It is felt that rubella, rape or incest should be valid if they seriously affect the health of the woman, as should some mixed social and medical conditions but never purely social indications alone. The legal status of psychiatric indications is discussed and rules for their use are proposed. In a review of various mental disturbances and disorders, it is found that they rarely result in suicide or any serious damage to the woman's health and thus do not constitute valid indications for abortion. The author concludes with a careful evaluation of the roles of contraception and sterilization as preventative or minimizing measures to combat the abortion problem.

2768 Glaus, A. [The Psychiatric Indication for Interruption of Pregnancy], Schweiz. Med. Wschr. 78:97-ff., 1948.

Abortion is permitted, according to Switzerland's penal code, only with strict medical indications, and correct interpretation of the law involves rare use of psychiatric indications. However, if the applicant's situation is especially serious, involving a high sensitivity to psychological stress, there may be justification for abortion. The author feels that, since decisions on psychiatric indications must be based on difficult prognostic evaluations, it is impossible to avoid some mistakes. Characteristic case reports are cited to illustrate this problem.

2769 Harmsen, H. "Schweizer Volksinitiative fur die Familie" [National Initiative in Switzerland on Behalf of the Family], Arch. Bevolk. 13(2):104-9, June 1943.

2770 Hopf-Van der Elst, H. [The Legal Interruption of Pregnancy], Z. Praventivmed 4:131-ff., 1959.

A report on 185 women who used psychiatric grounds in applying for an abortion at the psychiatric clinic of the University of Lausanne during the years 1949-1952. One hundred applications were rejected, and 85 approved. Most of the women with diagnoses of psychogenic evolution and psychosis were approved, while about half of the women with diagnoses of oligophrenia, neurotic evolution and reactive depression were approved. Those with diagnoses of personality disorders and no psychiatric disorders received approval very rarely. 37% were married, 34% unmarried but had a relationship of some permanence with their sexual partners, and 29% were pregnant as the result of a casual relationship.

2771 Kind, H., and Schorno, O. "Grundsatzliches zur Psychiatrischen Gegutachtung der Schwangerschaftsfahigkeit. Katamnese Unerwunschter Schwangerschaften, deren Unterbrechung Gemass Art. 120 StGB Abgelehnt Worden lst" [Principal Remarks on the Psychiatric Appraisal of Capability of Pregnancy. Catamnesis of Undesired Pregnancies Whose Termination Was Rejected on the Basis of Article 120 of the Penal Code], Schweiz. Med. Wschr. 96:1571-75, November 26, 1966.

2772 Noll, P. [Medical Intervention from the Viewpoint of Criminal Law], Deutsch Z. Ges. Gerichtl Med. 57:12-ff., 1966.

The current legal status of abortion in Switzerland and Germany is reviewed. It is concluded that restrictions on abortion are given a more liberal application than was the intention of the law and that changes in the law are not needed since society always evolves a socially necessary hypocrisy.

2773 Perret-Gentil, Gabrielle, Avortement et Contraception [Abortion and Contraception] Neuchatel, Delachaux and Niestle, 1967. 198 pp.

This Swiss gynecologist who seems to introduce a number of oddities in the cabinet advocates liberal legislation in regard to abortion. But it is important to diffuse methods of contraception very quickly so that women who wish to prevent another pregnancy may do so in lieu of having an abortion.

2774 Reimann-Hunziker, R. "Induced Abortion in Switzerland," in: Proceedings of the Third Conference of the Region for Europe, Near East and Africa of the IPPF. New York: Excerpta Medica Foundation, 1962.

The use of legal abortion as a method of birth control is not recommended, although sterilization in Switzerland is common after the desired number of children is achieved. The author reports that there are approximately 600-700 legal abortions and 600 sterilizations -- 400 women, 200 men -- in Basel each year out of a total population of 250,000, but there has been no observable decrease in criminal abortion.

2775 Roth, F. [Critical Considerations of the Present Practice of Interruption of Pregnancy], Schweiz Med. Wschr. 88: 1251-ff., 1958.

The author describes 1,032 cases of legal induced abortion which demonstrate that indications have changed during the last decade. Women who are married with psycho-reactive disturbances constitute the major abortion category, while internal medical indications rarely justify interruptions at present. The author contends that legal abortion is beginning to become a routine birth control measure, and that, as this is opposed to medical principles, members of the medical professions are tending to object to such abortions. It is stressed that the human-ethical aspects of the abortion problem need greater attention.

2776 Roth, F., and Hofer, H. [Critical Analysis of Interruptions of Pregnancy 1946-1961], Ther. Umsch. 20:350-ff., 1963.

A study of legal abortions in the Canton of Bern in Switzerland indicates an increase in the number from 335 in 1946 to 1,620 in 1961. Based on these figures it is estimated that there were 10,000 abortions for the whole country. Figures on marital status, indications for interruption, mortality and morbidity are reviewed. The authors contend that the social aspects underlying psychiatric indications for abortion should be minimized through better sex education and through widespread contraceptive advice.

2777 Sacchi, Emilio, "La Protezione della Maternita e il Problema Demografico nel Cantone Ticino" [The Protection of Maternity and the Demographic Problem in the Canton of Ticino], Pro Juventute 22(1):17-21, 1941.

2778 Switzerland. "Family Planning," Internat. Digest Health Legis. 17:981, 1966.

Law of 9 January 1965 and Regulation of 26 March 1965 provide for the establishment of a Center on Family Matters and Birth Control under the Department of Social Welfare. The center is to give information on family problems and all types of birth control to persons who visit it.

2779 Switzerland. "Interruption of Pregnancy," Internat. Digest Health Legis. 6:737-40, 1955; 19:237, 1968.

Regulation of 12 December 1953 modifies section 33 of the Law for the application of the Swiss Penal Code of 7 December 1940. Enumerates the procedures governing physicians in authorizing abortions in the Canton of Geneva. Order of 4 January 1966 amends the Order of 12 November 1954 on the legal interruption of pregnancy in the Canton of Vaud. The amendments provide for a list of physicians who can give permission for an abortion; restrict the physician granting permission from performing the abortion; and require female aliens, resident for less than three months in Switzerland, to apply to a special commission when requesting an abortion.

2780 Switzerland. Office Federal des Assurances Sociales, Allocations Familiales aux Travailleurs Agricueil des Dispositions en Vigueur, des Baremes et du Commentaire au 1er janvier 1950 [Family Allowances to Agricultural Workers and Workers in the Mountains...].Birne: 1950, 60 pp.

Gives a systematic survey of the statutes and regulations respecting the federal system of family allowances for agricultural workers and workers in the mountainous regions.

2781 Valliere, Paul des, "Natalite et Defense Nationale" [Fertility and National Defense], Rev. Militaire Suisse 85(12):501-9, 1940.

2782 Veillard, Maurice, "Quelques Caracteristiques de la Protection de l'Enfance et de la Famille en Suisse" [Some Characteristics of the Protection of the Child and the Family in Switzerland], Rev. Econ. Franco-Suisse, December 1951, pp. 385-88.

While in Europe the protection of the family has continuously evolved, Switzerland has not advanced in this area except extremely slowly and its federalism has prevented the development of a homogeneous and national family policy. A special article, appended to the federal constitution in 1945, makes it a duty of the confederation to take into consideration family allowances in all aspects. This is because family allowances do not exist except for salaried workers in six industrial cantons but then the rate is very low. Maternity insurance is not yet general. With regard to the question of housing, some cantons and some well-off communes subsidize the construction of housing for large families. This passivity on the part of the confederation affects Switzerland in not encouraging the birth rate because it fears overpopulation, unemployment and a lowered standard of living.

2783 Weber, Hans, "Der Lebenswille im Viermillionenvolk" [The Will to Live in Four Million People], _Schweizerische Rundschau_ 40(9-10):513-23, January 1941.

Concerning a population policy for Switzerland.

(Southern Europe)

GREECE

Policies on fertility and family size

2784 Valaoras, V.G., _et al_. "Control of Family Size in Greece," _Popul. Stud_. 18(3):265-78, March 1965.

The crude birth rate in Greece has fallen substantially, from its pre-war level, and the net reproduction rate is now below unity. An extensive field study undertaken by the University Office of Demographic Research, during 1962 and 1963, revealed that the low fertility rates in Greece stem from a strong desire of married couples, both in urban and rural areas, to keep the size of their families to a manageable level of about 2-3 children. In the absence of any official guidance, married couples practice several contraceptive methods, haphazardly (mostly _coitus interruptus_ in rural areas and _coitus interruptus_ plus the condom in the cities), but apparently without much success. Finally they revert to induced abortions which, though illegal in Greece, seem to be performed at a much higher scale than admitted in the survey. These findings may point to the need for reconsideration of official population policy in Greece.

ITALY

General population policies

2785 Barbadoro, Aldo, Leggi Demografiche Fasciste; Manuale Teorico-Bratico ad uso Delle Amministrazioni Interessate, delle, Sezioni Provinciali, dei Nuclei Comunali delle Famiglie Numerose e degli enti Ausiliari dello Stato [Fascist Demographic Laws; A Theoretical and Practical Manual for the Use of Interested Administrators of Provincial Sections of the Communal Nuclei of Large Families, and of State Supported Organizations]. Bologna: Cantelli, 1940. 291 pp.

An appendix presents the marriage subsidy law of June 29, 1940.

2786 Battara, P. "Die Bevolkerungspolitik Italiens" [Italian Population Policy], Italien-Jahrbuch 2:99-128, 1940.

2787 Fortunati, P. "L'Importanza delle Colonie per la Scienza e la Politica della Popolazione" [The Importance of Colonies for the Science and the Policy of Population], Annali dell'Africa Italiana 3(Bd. 3), 1940. Also in: Studi di Civilta Fascista, Instituto Nazionale di Cultura Fascista, 1940.

2788 Italy. Istituto Centrale di Statistics, L'Azione Promossa dal Governo Nazionale a Favore dell'Incremento Demografico. Atti del Consiglio Superiore di Statistica, Session Ordinarie, 1940, 1941, 1942 [The Policies Developed by the National Government to Favor Demographic Increase. Proceedings of the Upper Council of Statistics, 1940, 1941, 1942]. Annali di Statistics, Serie VII. Roma, 1943. vii, 287 pp.

The first part is devoted to research on the demographic policy of the Fascist Government, 1932-1939, analogous to the earlier study for the period 1928-1931, published in the Annali di Statistica, Serie VI, Vol. 32. The other parts survey the development of Fascist legislation and the application of the provisions and laws in detail. Finally, there is the report of the meeting of the Consiglio Superiore di Statistica.

2789 Italy. Istituto Centrale di Statistica, "Provvedimenti Demografici del Governo Fascista" [Population Policies of the Fascist Government], Notiziario Demografico 13(5):93, December 1940. See also: Ibid. 13(6):111, December 1940.

2790 Livi, Livio, "Sui Risulti della Politica Demografica in Italia" [Some Results of the Demographic Policy of Italy], Economia 25(1):9-15, January 1940.

2791 Nabholz, Hans, "Die Italienische Sudfrage" [The Question of Southern Italy], Schveizerische Z. Volkswirtschaft Statistik 88(5):405-17, October 1952.

Review of the economic conditions and problems of the rapidly increasing population of Southern Italy and governmental attitudes toward the situation.

2792 Nini, Luigi, "Politica Demografica Fascista" [Fascist Population Policy], Razza e Civilta 2(2):261-77, April 1941.

2793 Vacchini, Alfredo, "La Recente Politique Demographique du Gouvernement Italien" [The Recent Demographic Policy of the Italian Government], Magyar Statistikai Tarsasag 20(3-4):185-200, 1942.

Policies on fertility and family size

2794 Berger, Adolf. "Note on Gellius, N.A. I,6," Amer.J. Philology 67: 320-28, 1946.

Chapter 6 of Book I of the critical edition of Aulus Gellius' Attic Nights, by John C. Rolfe, contains the famous speech of a Roman censor, Q. Metellus, addressed to the people of Rome on the topic De Uxoribus Duocendis. Rolfe's translation treats the speech as being "On Marriage." Berger, in this note, argues that it is not a treatise on marriage in general but an exposition of the reasons why it was the duty of bachelors of Rome to take wives. It is their duty, in the interest of the State, to marry in order to check the declining birth rate caused by the increase of celibacy and the sterility of Roman marriages in the second half of the second century B.C.

2795 Berla, Vittoria O. Demografia e Controllo delle Nascite [Demography and Birth Control]. Rome: Editori Riuniti, 1963. 207 pp.

Chapters on: historical signs of movement toward birth control; birth control and psychology; religious and ethical aspects of birth control; demography and birth control; birth control and scientific research. Appendix contains a survey of marriage legislation, divorce and connected subjects related to population.

2796 Borruso, V. [Practice of Abortion and Birth Control in Sicily]. Palermo: Libri Siciliani, 1967.

Two studies on abortion in Sicily are described. The first involved 50 women selected from the clientele of a private practice and a dispensary who were interviewed concerning their experience with abortion, both induced and spontaneous. Of the women under 40 (30) and the women over 40 (20), 21 and 9 respectively reported a total of 55 and 40 abortions. The average number of pregnancies for each woman was 3.8, the average number of abortions 1.9. 3.1 was the average number of induced abortions for women having had abortions. The second sample involved more than 16,000 women from a Bari maternity hospital. The reported abortion rate for these women was 23 per 100 pregnancies. For all of Sicily, with 100,000 to 110,000 births per year, the above rate corresponds to 50,000 to 55,000 induced abortions per year. The author also includes chapters on the Sicilian folk tradition and abortion, the historical and legislative aspects of abortion and birth control in Sicily, and the legal, social and economic structure of abortion.

2797 Calderan, Beltrao, [Toward a Policy of Family Well-Being. Elements of an Economic and Social Norm in Family Policy]. Studia Sociala Edita ab Instituto Scientiarum Socialium Pontificiae Universitatis Gregorianae, 2. Rome: Librairie Editrice de l'Universite Gregorienne; Louvain: Institut de Recherches Economiques et Sociales de Louvain, 1957. 348 pp.

2798 Calogera, E. "Rilievi Critici e Medico-Legali Sugli Articoli 552 e 553 del Codice-Penale" [Critical Remarks on the Medico-Legal Aspects of Articles 552 and 553 of the Penal Code], Difesa Soc., April-June 1954, pp. 53-62.

Criticism of the articles of the penal code relevant to the practice of contraception.

2799 Campopiano, Renato, La Previdenza Sociale; Manuale delle Assicurazioni Sociali Obbligatorie, degli Assegni Familiari e delle Altre Forme di Previdenza ed Assistenza Gestite dall'Instituto Nazionale della Previdenza Sociale [Social Security; A Manual of Compulsory Social Insurance, Family Assistance, and Other Forms of Social Security and Assistance Administered by the National Institute of Social Security]. 6th ed. Rome, 1952. 442 pp.

2800 Capitani, P.L. and Fabroni, F. "La Sterilizzazione Umana nei suoi Aspetti Medicolegali" [Human Sterilization in Its Medicolegal Aspects], Sezione Medico-Fisica 12:1219-20, 1963.

2801 Castellano, V. [Population Growth, Economic Development and the Dangers of National Policies of Birth Control]. Rome: Instituo di Statistica della Facolta di Scienze Statistiche, Demografiche et Attuariali, 1963. 22 pp.

2802 Cattedra di Diritto Ecclesiastico. Studi in Tema di Diritto di Famiglia [Studies on the Subject of Family Law]. Universita degli Studi di Roma, Instituto di Diritto Pubblico della Facolta di Giurisprudenza, Monografie, n.s. 34. Milan: A. Giuffre, 1967. x, 425 pp.

Partial contents: [The Problem of Birth Control] by A. Sini; [Contribution for a Legal Instruction on the Subject of Artificial Insemination] by F. Santosuosso.

2803 "Changes in the Family Allowance Scheme and in Contributions to the Earnings Supplement Fund in Italy," Internat. Labour Rev. 85:403-6, 1962.

Act No. 1038 of 17 October 1961 raises the ceiling for calculating employer contributions to the fund and increases the age eligibility of children from 14 to 18 years, if not gainfully employed, and from 24 to 26 years if attending a university. Average benefit per child and for the spouse is increased about 5%.

2804 Ciprotti, Pio, "The Case of the Bishop of Prato," Catholic Lawyer 4:244-51, Summer 1958.

The Bishop was tried, February 24 - March 1, 1958, for defamation of character for denouncing as concubinaries a couple married in a civil ceremony.

2805 Colombo, Ugo M. "Politica Assistenziale e Controllo della Nascite" [Assistance Policy and Birth Control], Assistenza d'Oggi No. 2, April 1965.

2806 Damilano, S., et al. "L'Aborto della Republica di San Marino (Ventidue Anni di Osservazioni)" [Abortion in the Republic of San Marino (22 Years of Observations)], Riv. Italiana d'Igiene 26:426-37, September - December 1966.

2807 "Family Allowances in Italy," Internat. Soc. Sec. Assn. Bull. 12:22-26, January - February 1959.

2808 "Fattori Culturali Dei Fattori Economici Sulle Oscillazioni Periodiche Dei Matrimoni" [Influence of Cultural and Economic Factors on Periodic Variations in the Marriage Rate], pp. 187-97, Chpt. in: Studium Sociale: Festschrift fuer Karl Valentin Mueller by Specht, K.G., et al., eds. 1959. xvi, 835 pp.

A study was made of the influence in different parts of Italy of customs connected with religious rules and widespread superstitions on variations in the marriage rate. For an investigation of customs more closely connected with religion, Lent, Holy Week and Easter Week were chosen as characteristic times. Concerning the influence of superstition, certain days of the week (Tuesday and Friday) or of the month (the 13th or the 17th) were chosen since they are commonly considered unlucky. Religious feasts were also taken into consideration to ascertain what influence public holidays may have on fluctuations in the marriage rate. In addition, an analysis was made of monthly variations of marriage rates, in conjunction with economic factors. Results indicate that religious customs and superstitious beliefs have a wide influence in all parts of Italy, affecting the distribution of marriages in the weekly and monthly cycles. Their influence is therefore independent of the varying degrees of socio-economic development. The seasonal cycle, however, is also affected by economic factors which cause a differential in agricultural as compared with industrial regions. The choice of the marriage date thus appears to be chiefly linked with cultural factors which persist in spite of economic development and the general evolution of customs.

2809 Fazzari, C. "Sull'uso di Farmaci Antiovulatori. 3. Aspetti Medico-Legali" [On the Use of Antiovulatory Drugs. 3. Medico-Legal Aspects], Rev. Ostet. Ginec. 20:289-94, April 1965.

2810 Giudici, E. [The Sterilization of Humans and Its Most Recent Medico-Moral Aspects], Minerva Ginec. 11:564-67, July 15, 1959.

2811 Hopkins, Keith, "Contraception in the Roman Empire," Comp. Stud. Soc. Hist. 8(1):124-51, October 1965.

It has long been recognized that upper-class Romans, in their desire for small families, practiced abortion on a large scale. What is not well known is the extent to which they were concerned with contraception. Some of the methods advocated by Greek and Roman doctors could have been very effective, and aspects of ancient contraceptive theory were as advanced as any modern theory before the middle of the 19th century. Such contraceptive theory was part of a literary medical tradition, appearing first in Aristotle and the Hippocratic Corpus; its repeated appearance in fragmentary sources, when considered together with the organization of doctors' training, argues for its significance in medical practice, at least among the upper classes. Nonetheless, the general effect of contraception upon fertility in Rome cannot be seen only in those terms. Many ancient contraceptive methods were ineffective and the rudimentary character of some Romans' knowledge of this subject is highlighted by what seems to be interesting confusion of contraception with abortion, both in method and conceptualization. Now can we assume that Romans who wished to limit their families had recourse to the practice of *coitus interruptus*. It is argued that the practice of all forms of contraception declined in the later Empire.

2812 Hopkins, M.K. "The Age of Roman Girls at Marriage," *Popul. Stud*. 18(3):309-27, 1965.

For Roman girls, the legal minimum age at marriage was 12, but the law provided no sanctions and was contravened. The usual age at puberty (at least for the upper classes) was probably 13+. In fact, menarche was not always a precondition of marriage; nevertheless, marriages were usually consummated immediately. Even if pre-pubertal marriages were regarded by some as deviant, they were not exceptional and were condoned. The usual age of girls at marriage can only be guessed at from the fragmentary literary evidence, but 287 tombstones enable us to tabulate the ages of pagan and Christian girls at marriage. The modal age of the former was 12-15 (43%), for the latter 15-18 (42%). These inscriptions are probably most representative of the urban well-to-do. There is no serious bias toward recording low ages. Men married considerably later than girls and their deaths were recorded by their parents more frequently and until a much later age. This favoritism toward boys, the early age at marriage of girls, the age differential between spouses and the high chances of early widowhood have considerable significance for the study of the Roman family.

2813 Italy. Instituto Centrale di Statistics, "La Consegna delle 'Medaglia d'Onore' alle Madri di Famiglie Numerose" [The Award of Medals of Honor to Mothers of Large Families], Notiziario Demographico 13(2):32, April 1940.

2814 Italy. Instituto Centrale di Statistica, "I Prestiti Matrimoniali Concessi nel 1938 e nel 1939" [Marriage Loans Granted in 1938 and 1939], Notiziario Demographico 13(2):31-32, 1940.

2815 Italy. Instituto Centrale di Statistica, "Premi di Nuzialita e di Natalita nel Periodo 1935-1940" [Premiums for Marriage and Births, 1935-1940], Notiziario Demographico 14(2):30-31, April 1941.

2816 Italy. Instituto Nationale della Previdenza Sociale, Atti delle Giornale Internazionale di Studi sulle Prestazioni Familiare..., Roma, 20-25 Aprile 1953 [Proceedings of the International Congress for the Study of Family Assistance..., Rome, April 20-25, 1953]. Rome, 1953. 428 pp.

2817 Italy. Instituto Nazionale della Previdenza Sociale, Fonti e Forme dell'Assistenza Familiare in Italia [Origins and Forms of Family Assistance in Italy]. Rome, 1953. 166 pp.

2818 Italy. Instituto Nazionale della Previdenza Sociale, Servico Statistico-Attuariale, Notizie Statistiche 1948-1951 [Statistical Notes, 1948-1951]. Rome: Instituto Poligrafico dello Stato, 1953. 43 pp.

Includes provisions for marriage, childbirth and family allowances.

2819 Italy. Laws, Statutes, etc., Assegni Familiari, Leggi, Decreti, Contratti Collettivi e Disposizioni Warie [Family Allowance...]. Rome: Instituto Nazionale della Previdenza Sociale, 1943.

Vol. II includes the laws and regulations for the period July 16, 1941 to July 30, 1943.

2820 Italy. Ministero del Lavoro e della Previdenza Sociale, "Il Sisteme degli Assegni Familiari in Italia" [The Italian System of Family Allowances], Rassegna del Lavoro 13(1-2): 67-99, January - February 1967.

A report to the International Family Security Conference, Geneva, May 1967, attended by the appropriate ministers of France, Western Germany, Great Britain, Italy, Luxembourg, the Low Countries and Switzerland.

2821 Loffredo, Ferdinando E. "Family Services in Italy," J. Marr. Fam. 17:231-32, 1955.

The principal means adopted in Italy to try to meet the needs of the family are the following: family allowances, tax exemptions, improvements in social security allowances, assistance to mothers and children, rent controls, and building controls.

2822 Loffredo, Ferdinando E. "Die Wirtschaftliche Forderung der Familie in Italien" [The Economic Promotion of the Family in Italy], Soz. Fortsch. 4(7-8):171-74, April 1955.

Provided that there is no substantial increase in the birth rate, Italy will enter a period of population decline in several decades. Discussion is divided into sections on family allowance, tax exemption, family assistance, social insurance, housing and family social work. The most effective measures have been those which deal with family allowances. These are paid by the employer in industry and public service for wife and children, under certain conditions also for parents, grandparents, nephews and other relatives of the employee. This system has the purpose of protecting the status of the head of the family. As the allowance per child is fixed, the family's relative income decreases as the number of children increases. Tax income is derived to a greater extent than in most other countries from indirect taxes (sales taxes), which affect families inequitably. Two forms of family assistance established by the Fascist regime have been abolished -- marriage and birth allowances. A typical form of family assistance is Assistance for Mother and Child, administered by the Opera Nazionale Meternita e Infanzia (National Service for Mother and Child). Social security measures are similar to those in other advanced countries. The housing problem is still grave. The housing shortage brought about by the war has slowly risen. The deficit is estimated at 3 million rooms. One form of governmental activity is that of the housing plan of the National Institute for Social Insurance, which is financed by compulsory contributions by employer, employee and the government. A limited number of family social workers has been organized by several housing agencies, agencies for reform in agriculture and for rural resettlement. A policy for achieving effective family advancement would require: (1) greater increase in family allowance than in the basic wage, and substantial increase in the allowance for the wife; (2) the greatest possible decrease of the pressure of indirect taxation, and application of the principle of the family coefficient to all direct, progressive taxes. The probable position of the various political parties toward these measures is set forth.

2823 Magnaghi, Gianfranco, "Gli Assegni Matrimoniali per i Laboratori dell'Industria" [Marriage Allowances for Industrial Laborers], Rev. Internazionale Sci. Soc. 11(1):65-67, January 1940.

Summary of recent Italian provisions on allowances.

2824 Marchi, Umberto M. "Premi di Nuzialita nel Periodo 1935-1941" [Premiums for Marriage in 1935-1941], Notizario Demografico 15(2):32-33, June 1942.

2825 Masini, C.A. "Il Sistema degli Assegni Familiari in Italia e l'Opportunita di una Riforma" [The System of Family Allowances in Italy and the Opportunity for Reform], Previdenza Soc. 18(1):1-18, January - February 1962.

Outlines legislative history of the Law No. 1038 of October 17, 1961. Discusses financial bases and social aims.

2826 Migliorino, Giuseppe, "Problemi Medici, Psicologici, Giuridici, Etici Sollevati Dai Nuovi Contracettivi (A Proposito dell'Enciclica 'Humanae Vitae')" [Medical, Psychological, Juridical, and Ethical Problems Related to Contraceptive Use (A Propos of the Encyclical 'Humanae Vitae')], Ann. Facolta Econ. Commercio 22(2):225-39, 1968.

Examines public reaction to a new oral contraceptive as related to diverse variables (age, social milieu, religion, etc.). Brief discussion of possible effects of its utilization in population programs and on the moral and religious problems resulting from the intransigent position of the Catholic Church. Also a quick overview of genetic and legal problems in Italy.

2827 Oeter, Ferdinand, Il Principio della Famiglia e il Nuovo Ordine Sociale [The Principle of the Family and the New Social Order]. Rome: Previdenza Sociale, 1952. 67 pp.

2828 Palmieri, Luigi, "Considerazioni Cliniche e Medico-Legali Sull'Uso degli Anticoncezionali. Rilievo su un Campione Napoletano" [Clinical and Medico-Legal Considerations in the Use of Birth Control...], Difesa Soc. 45(4):206-24, October - December 1967.

2829 Palmieri, Luigi, "La Medicina ed il Controllo delle Nascite" [Medicine and Birth Control], Difesa Soc. 45(3):225-43, July - September 1966.

2830 Paroli, Augusto, "Maternity Protection in Italy," Internat. Labour Rev. 67(2):156-72, February 1953.

Description of legislation protecting the working woman and her child; reform of 1950 and main features of the new system.

2831 Pasi, Luigi, "Gli Assegni Familiari in Italia nel Decennio 1951-60" [Family Allowances in Italy in the Decade 1951-60], Rassegna di Statistiche del Lavoro 14(3-4):115-22, May - August 1962.

Statistical study of annual data on allowances distributed, by industrial group and income of family head.

2832 Pesce, V.S. "La Necessita in Italia del Controllo delle Vascite" [The Need for Birth Control in Italy], _Minerva Ginec_. 3(11):544-46, September 1951.

2833 Ragazzi, B. Rossi, "Le Conseguenze Sociali del Lavoro Femminile in Relazione alla Recenti Legislazione Fascista" [The Social Consequences of the Labor of Women to Recent Fascist Legislation], in: _Atti della IV Riunione della Societa Italiana di Demografia e Statistics...1939_. Rome, 1940. 218 pp.

2834 Santosuosso, Fernando, _La Fecondazione Artificiale nella Donna: Consequenze della Inseminazione Artificiale per il Diritto Civile, Penale e Canonico_ [Human Artificial Insemination: Consequences in Civil, Criminal and Canon Law]. Milan: Giuffre, 1961. xi, 227 pp.

2835 Sbrocca, L. "Il Problema Etico-Religioso e Guiridico della Fecondazione Artificiale Visto da un Ginecologo" [A Gynecologist's View of the Ethical, Religious and Legal Problem in Artificial Insemination], _Minerva Ginec_. 11(4):158-65, February 28, 1959.

2836 Soziale Praxis, "Familienzuschusse in Italien" [Family Grants in Italy], _Soziale Praxis_ 50(4):137-41, February 1941.

Summary of the Italian Law of August 6, 1940, with tables indicating grants according to occupation, size of family and amount during periods from December 1934 to December 1939.

2837 Tagliacarne, Guglielmo, "La Situation Demographique de l'Italie" [The Demographic Situation in Italy], _Population_ 3(3):467-83, July - September 1948.

2838 Tovo, S. [The Personal Injury -- Articles 549 and 550 of the Penal Code], Minerva Medicoleg. 80:213-ff., 1960.

Articles 549 and 550 of Italy's Penal Code are described. 549 pertains to death or injury of the woman and connects with the terms of Articles 545-46, which relate the punishment (imprisonment for 10 to 15 years or 3 to 8 years) for abortionists who cause personal injury during an abortion with or without the woman's consent. Personal injury is defined, in Article 582, as that which gives rise to a disease of the mind or body. The author contends that pathologic phenomena necessarily involved in the abortion itself may not be considered aggravating "injuries." In addition, it is noted that even the most correct and suitably technical abortion measures cause changes which are mostly traumatic and do not represent aggravating circumstances in criminal abortion. Such changes are usually considered lesions accompanying abortion rather than arising from it. However, Article 549 explanations cannot resolve the problems of Article 550, which concerns acts of abortions upon a woman thought to be pregnant, acts punishable under Article 582.

2839 Tuddo, Angelo de, "Valore Demografico della Prividenza Sociale: l'Assicurazione Nuzialita e Natalita" [The Demographic Value of Social Provisions: Marriage and Birth Insurance], Rev. Italiana Sci. Econ. 12(9):1236-39, September 1940.

PORTUGAL

General population policies

2840 Abecasis, Carlos K. Fundamentos de uma Politica de Povoamento [Foundations of a Population Policy]. Lisbon: Junta de Investigacoes do Ultramar, 1965. 21 pp.

Policies on fertility and family size

2841 Correia, Servulo, [Reflections on Family Allowances], Estudos Soc. Corporativos 6(21):94-120, March 1967.

2842 "Family Allowances for Public Officials and Employees in Portugal," _Internat. Labour Rev._ 48:792-93, 1943.

Family allowances are paid for dependent ascendants and children who reside with the employee. Children are considered dependent until 14 years of age, or, if they continue into higher or collegiate education, until 21 years of age. The allowance is added to the basic wage and the amount per dependent depends on the wages paid the various classes of employees. The highest amount is 70 escudos a month per dependent for those earning over 2000 escudos, but only 30 escudos for those earning under 400 escudos.

2843 Lippmann, Adolf von, "Family Allowances in Portugal," _Internat. Soc. Security Assn. Bull._ 8:456-61, December 1955.

2844 "Mesures en Faveur de la Famille au Portugal" [Measures to Benefit the Family in Portugal], _Familles dans le Monde_, No. 2, June 1961, pp. 105-17.

2845 Portugal. Direccao Geral de Previdencia e Habitacoes Economicas, _Les Allocations Familiales au Portugal_ [Family Allowances in Portugal]. Lisbon, 1959. 26 pp.

2846 Portugal. Laws, statutes, etc. _Abono de Familia: Legislacao, Despachos e Modelo de Regulamento das Caixas de Abono de Familia_ [Family Allowances...]. Lisbon: Imprensa Nacional, 1943. 86 pp.

2847 Portugal. Laws, statutes, etc. _Abono de Familia para as Trabalhadores por Conta Doutrem. Contem a Mais Recente Legislacao_ [Family Allowances for Workers...]. Edited by Joao Raposo. Aveiro: Tip. Minerva Central, 1947. 167 pp.

SPAIN

General population policies

2848 Barata, Jose F.N. Para uma Politica de Populacao [For a Population Policy], Biblioteca do Centro de Estudos Politico-Sociais. Lisbon: CEPS, 1964. 236 pp.

Policies on fertility and family size

2849 Almeida, Joao A. de, O Aborto Consensual: Estudo de Direito Penal e de Politica Criminal [Induced Abortion: Study of Penal Law and Criminal Policy]. Lisbon, 1964. 203 pp.

2850 Bermudez, M. "La Limitacion de la Natalidad Como Remedio de la Superpoblacion" [Birth Control as a Remedy for Over-population], Rev. Sanidad Higiene Pub. 26(9-10):541-48, September - October 1952.

2851 Campo, Salustiano del, "Los Medicos Ante el Problema de la Limitacion de la Natalidad" [Doctors Face the Problem of Birth Control], Rev. Espan. Opin. Pub. 1:27-38, May - August 1965.

Spanish studies of the frequency and intensity of the use of contraceptives are mentioned and a detailed account is given of an inquiry undertaken in 1963 among 161 doctors in Barcelona. Results on the attitudes and opinions of these doctors are presented in seven tables. 47% favored sex education by the family, 20% by the school, 17% by doctors and 13% by religious institutes. Doctors' reasons for limiting families were given as follows: 31% thought contraception justified if the mother were sick or her life would be endangered by conception; 26% if fathers suffered from hereditary disease, or if there was a negative RH factor or hemophilia; 15.3% thought economic reasons sufficient; 2.6% favored contraception to prevent a lowering of the standard of living of families; and 0.7% accepted esthetic reasons of the wife. Figures regarding number of persons consulting doctors in matters of contraception and doctors' estimates for the prevalence of various methods in different social classes are presented and analyzed. The influence of religious factors is discussed on the basis of the doctors' responses and the age factor is considered. The following findings are pointed out: Spanish doctors firmly oppose indiscriminate use of contraceptive methods and the general distribution of information on the subject but recognize that these methods are ever more frequently employed and do not consider this the result of the legal prohibition of prostitution. The majority of respondents were influenced by religious factors in their practice and attitudes regarding contraception.

2852 Chaves y Chaves, Casimiro, El Aborto Segun la Historia, la Razon y el Derecho [Abortion in History, Reason and Law]. Madrid, 1958. 116 pp.

2853 Chaves y Chaves, Casimiro, Delito de Infanticidio [The Crime of Infanticide]. Articulo 410 del Codigo Penal. Madrid, 1955. 130 pp.

2854 Comision Espanola de los Congresos de la Familia Espanola, Familia Espanola [The Spanish Family]. Comision Espanola de los Congresos de la Familia Espanola, No, 31. Madrid, May 1962.

Partial contents: Elorriagaga, Gabriel, "European Families"; Desmotres, Georges, "Birth of a Family Policy in Europe"; Ramos, Enrique, "Present Family Legislation."

2855 Cuello Calon, Eugenico, Tres Emas Penales: El Aborto Criminal, el Problema Penal de la Eutanasia, el Aspecto Penal de la Fecundacion Artificial [Three Judicial Topics: Criminal Abortion, the Judicial Problem of Euthanesia, Judicial Aspects of Artificial Insemination]. Publicaciones del Seminario de Derecho Penal y Criminologia de la Universidad de Barcelona. Barcelona: Bosch, 1955. 200 pp.

2856 Dominguez Carmona, Manuel, "Estudia Demografico de la Nupcialidad Espanola" [Demographic Study of Spanish Nuptiality], Rev. Sanidad Higiene Publ. 42(1-2):133-54, January - February 1968.

Analysis of time trends in marriages obtained from annual numbers of recorded marriages 1901-1965 and from census data on population by marital status. Interpolation of a Gaussian curve yields modal ages of females at marriage for each year. Then follow quantitative estimates of the repercussion of change in average age at marriage on marital fertility. In conclusion, change in numbers of illegitimate births is considered as an index of the population's knowledge of and application of birth control methods.

2857 Fernandez-Ruiz, C. "Campana Contra et Aborto Criminal en el Nuevo Estado" [The Campaign Against Criminal Abortion in the New State], Semana Med. Espan. 3:70-81, January 20, 1940.

2858 Garcia de la Granda, Antonio, "Las Politicas de la Poblacion en Relacion a la Politica de Salarios" [Population Policies in Relation to Wage Policy], Rev. Internacional Sociol. 13 (51):323-51, July - September 1955.

Exposition of pro-natalist policies and the family wage.

2859 Gonzalez-Rothwoss, Mariano, "Los Sistemas de Proteccion a la Familia en la Peninsula Iberica" [Systems of Family Aid in the Iberian Peninsula], Rev. Internacional Sociol. 19(75):381-400, July - September 1961.

Outlines social security and marriage and family benefits in Spain and Portugal.

2860 Lippman, Adolf von, "Family Allowances in Spain," Internat. Soc. Security Assn. Bull. 9:351-62, September - October 1956.

2861 Loffredo, Ferdinando, "Gli Assegni Familiari nella Spagna" [Family Allowances in Spain], Riv. Internazionale Sci. Soc. 11(1):36-47, January 1940.

After mentioning early private systems of family allowances, the decrees and administrative practices of the Franco regime are summarized.

2862 Martinez Val, Jose M. La Eutelegenesia y Su Tratamiento Penal [Artificial Insemination and Its Legal Treatment]. Madrid: Instituto de Estudios Manchegos, 1952. 125 pp.

2863 Mascarenas, C.E. "La Proteccion Penal del Matrimonie en el Proyecto de Nuevo Codigo Penal" [Penal Protection of Marriage in the Plan of the New Penal Code], Rev. DP, April - June 1967.

2864 Morales, J.L. "El Aborto ante la Moral y ante la Ley" [Moral and Legal Aspects of Abortion], Clinica y Laboratorio 57(337):248-71, April 1954.

2865 Neyra Govantes, Gerardo, and Marti Bufill, Jose, Manual Practico de Seguros Sociales. Subsidios Familiares; Seguro de Enfermedad [Practical Manual of Social Security. Family Allowances...]. Madrid: Garcia Enciso, 1949. 126 pp.

The authors give a brief and systematized survey of the various regulations now covering social insurances in Spain, particularly the Decree of 29 December 1948, which increased the benefits of old-age insurance and marriage grants.

2866 Parache, E. [Abortion and Sterilization in Spain], Arch. Gynaek. 180:330-ff., 1951.

A report on the legal status of abortion in Spain. The country's Criminal Code forbids any form of abortion, including therapeutic, and there are no indications accepted by doctors as conforming with medical ethics and the Catholic faith. The author feels that physicians have not been performing induced abortions, since no physician has been prosecuted for doing so. Reference is made to the fact that physicians do induce premature labor after viability of the fetus when considered necessary.

2867 Pernaut, M. "Salario Familiar?" [Family Wage?], Razon y Fe 149(675):313-26, 1954.

Examines the economic and demographic position of contemporary Spain and proposes a special allowance to mothers.

2868 Perpina Rodriguez, A., and Tejedor Escribano, M. "Las Familias Muy Numerosas en Espana: Estudio Sobre los Premios a la Natalidad" [Very Large Families in Spain: Study of the Recompenses for Natality], Rev. Iberoamer. Seguridad Soc. 10:929-59, July - August 1961.

2869 Royo, Doroteo Lopez, and Argos Garcia, Carlos, Legislacion de Ayuda Familiar y Plus Familiar [Legislation on Family Assistance and Related Aid]. Madrid: Delegacion Difusora, 1963. 156 pp.

2870 "Sozialversicherung" [Social Insurance], Soziale Praxis 50(8):328, April 1941.

A brief summary of the Spanish Law of February 22, 1941, increasing the grants to families and aid to children.

2871 Spain. Instituto Nacional de Prevision, Legislacion de Subsidios Familiares. Regimen Obligatorio de Subsidios Familiares. Leys, Reglamento y Desposiciones Complimentarias [Legislation on Family Allowances...]. Madrid: Caja Nacional de Subsidios Familiares, 1940. 207 pp.

2872 Spain. "Suppression of Prostitution," Internat. Digest Health Legis. 8:707, 1957.

Decree-Law of 3 March 1956 prohibits prostitution and the opening of brothels and requires the closing of existing brothels within three months.

YUGOSLAVIA

General population policies

2873 Farkas, V. [Our So-Called Overpopulation and Our Problem of Unemployment], Socijalna Polit. 5(7-8): 50-59. July-August 1955.

2874 Klauzer, Jagoda, "Jedan Aspekt Ocenjivanja Potrebe za Populacionom Politikom u Jugoslaviji" [Evaluation of the Necessity of a Population Policy in Yugoslavia], Stanovnistvo 6(1-2):5-35, January - June 1968.

Yugoslavia does not now have a definite and coherent population policy, and the outlook is not to adopt one until there is an analysis of the actual population dynamics, the factors in their change, and their relationship to social, economic and political facts. With this end in mind, the author examines the birth rates by regions and points to the very high rates in certain provinces. The differences, which are double and even triple between the exceedingly high and low rates, are related to differences in economic development and literacy. Furthermore, high fertility areas also have high general and infant mortality. Measures are required to reduce the high fertility of underdeveloped areas. A population policy should not be isolated but integrated in a general program of economic and social development.

Policies on fertility and family size

2875 Andolsek, L. "Abortion in Yugoslavia," Fam. Planning 14: 93-ff., 1966.

The author divides the abortion problem into four major areas or phases: no contraceptive use and a higher illegal abortion rate than legal abortion rate; development of contraceptive use and legal/illegal abortion rates balanced; contraceptive use influencing a higher rate of legal abortions than illegal; and finally, widely accepted use of contraception with a significant decrease in both types of abortion. It is suggested that Yugoslavia has entered the second phase. Figures on the birth and abortion rates for several regions are cited which indicate a decline in the birth rate and a great increase in the number of abortions.

2876 Bucic, M., et al. [The Problem of Abortion in Birth Control in Yugoslavia], Ann. Med. Leg. 47:513-18, September - October 1967.

2877 Desput, D. [Problem of Abortion from the Legal Point of View], Nasa Zakonitost 8(5):272-81, 1954.

2878 Herak-Szabo, J. "Legal and Illegal Abortion in the People's Republic of Croatia," in: Proceedings of the Third Conference of the Region for Europe, Near East and Africa of the IPPF. New York: Excerpta Medica Foundation, 1962.

Preference for abortion as a method of birth control over contraception is evident in the growing number of legal and illegal abortions. The author stresses the need for continued efforts to disseminate information on contraception and feels that the health of women must be protected by reducing the abortion rate.

2879 Hren, M., et al. "Abortion in Yugoslavia within the Framework of the Themes of the Conference," in: Proceedings of the Fourth Conference of the Region for Europe, Near East and Africa of the IPPF. New York: Excerpta Medica Foundation, 1965.

In 1951, abortion in Yugoslavia was permitted only by special regulation for medical indications. In 1960, the legislation was revised to allow interruption on medical, eugenic, juridicial and social indications. A study of 1,000 women with unwanted pregnancies indicates that although maternal mortality rates have declined since legalization, there has been an increase in psychological consequences. Only 24% were well-adjusted; the others showed neurotic symptoms (25%) and were grouped as emotionally or intellectually immature personalities. According to law, decision to terminate the pregnancy is made upon consultation of a gynecologist and a social worker. 10-20% of all applications have been rejected and follow-up interviews of 762 women whose request had been rejected in 1960 and 1961 indicated that 52.5% and 42% bore a child.

2880 Milosevic, B., et al. "Contraception Versus Abortion," in: Proceedings of the Fourth Conference of the Region for Europe, Near East and Africa of the IPPF. New York: Excerpta Medica Foundation, 1965.

Reference is made to the incidence of legal abortion in Belgrade; there were 9,853 abortions in 1956 and 32,500 in 1963, with a complication rate of 30%. The result of this increase was an emphasis on the use of contraceptives for family planning.

2881 Mladenovic, D. "Kontracepcija" [Contraception], Srpski Arkhiv za Tselokupno Lekarstvo 85 (6): 721-25.June 1957.

2882 Novak, F. "Effects of Legal Abortion on the Health of Mothers in Yugoslavia," in: Proceedings of the Seventh Conference of the IPPF, Singapore, 1963. New York: Excerpta Medica Foundation, 1964.

A report on legalized abortion in Yugoslavia and the role such liberalization has played in reducing the number of deaths due to illegal abortion. In 1961 there were five deaths resulting from 104,668 legal abortions and 90 deaths from 59,835 illegal abortions. The country's birth rate has decreased from 27.0 in 1951 to 22.6 in 1961. The industrial region of Slovenia reported an increase in legal abortions (583 in 1955 to 9,291 in 1961) as well as an increased rate of illegal abortions during the same period (4,958 to 5,565). It is concluded that legalized abortion may have reduced the number of illegal abortions and maternal mortality but it also inhibited contraceptive use.

2883 Trampuz, V. "Limitations in Use of Contraceptives," in: Cassano, C., ed. Research on Steroids, Vol.II. Rome: Il Pensiero Scientifico, 1966.

Report on a program combining oral contraceptives and the IUD among 15,000 women in a Ljubljana district. The program appeared to combat the district's increasing abortion rate, but there was no reduction over a five year period. It is felt that the use of post-coital drugs might bring more success.

2884 Yugoslavia. "Criminal Offenses Against Human Health," _Internat. Digest Health Legis._ 4:449, 1952-53.

Except where induced abortion is necessary to preserve the life or health of the mother, abortion is a penal offense according to a law of 2 March 1951.

2885 Yugoslavia. "Decree Concerning Family Allowances," _Sluzbeni List_ No. 48, October 1951, pp. 557-60.

2886 Yugoslavia. "Interruption of Pregnancy," _Internat. Digest Health Legis._ 4:450-53, 1952-53; 12(1):619-22, 1961.

Decree No. 27 of 11 January 1952 permits induced abortion to preserve the life or health of the mother, where pregnancy is due to a criminal act or may result in a deformed offspring, or, in exceptional cases, where the birth of a child might be harmful to the woman's health because of her living, personal or family situations. This last condition was removed from the exceptional category and made a regular cause by Decree No. 33 of 16 February 1960.

2887 Zikovic, B. [The Problem of Abortion in the Former District of Nova Gradiska], _Lijecn. Vjesn._ 85:1243-ff., 1963.

There were 5,963 births and 3,154 abortions in Nova Gradiska during the period 1959-63, with 1,329 legal abortions, 1,622 illegal and 203 spontaneous. Social indications were used for 1,225 of the legal abortions and medical indications for 104. 841 of all abortions resulted in complications: sterility (93); menstrual disturbances (207); extra-uterine pregnancies (43); and pelvic infection (498). 1962 showed an abortion to birth rate of 1.5:1. The author also notes that there is a national morbidity rate of 27% and a mortality rate of 2% for all cases, and stresses the need for stricter limitations on the use of certain criteria for legal abortion and encouragement of contraceptive practice.

(Eastern Europe)

GENERAL

General population policies

2888 Acsadi, G. "Recent Problems on Population Policies in the European Region of Socialist Countries," Paper presented at the International Union for the Scientific Study of Population, General Conference, 3-11 September, 1969, London.

In the socialist countries of Eastern Europe, population policy is defined as including all social and economic measures affecting even indirectly the characteristics and processes of the population. Because of this broad definition, many issues with regard to policy arise and have to be resolved. At present, the issues concern the employment of women, living conditions, abortion, mortality, and age composition of the population. Each country must independently decide on the content of its policies.

2889 Hooz, Istvan, A Nepesedespolitika Nehany Elmeleti Kerdese [Some Theoretical Problems of Population Policy]. Studia Iuridica Auctoritate Universitatis Pecs Publicata, 47. Budapest: Tankonyvkiato, 1966. 27 pp.

Considers problems to be solved by national population policies in the socialist countries. Contrasts the action of general factors in the structure of society that influence growth rates with direct action to influence population growth for political and economic ends. Suggests scheme for systematic analysis.

2890 Syarcova, H. [Situation and Tasks of Marxist Demography], Demografie 1(1):2-10, 1959.

The starting point in fulfilling ever-increasing tasks of Marxist demography is seen in a fundamental checkup of both its theoretical and methodological bases as well as the screening of its basic problems. Instead of seeking a non-existing population law, Marxist demography has stressed the investigation of concrete population laws as opposed to the bourgeois chaos of biological, psychological and economic factors. Bourgeois theories of sociology fail in trying to depict an all-sided description of the world and its laws and therefore in construing general theory and methodology. On the other hand, historical materialism has become a solid basis for the development of demography as a science. The problem of Marxist demography is seen to be a separation between philosophy dealing with the problems of demography in the highest level of universality and empirical demographic studies. Further concrete tasks are: 1) improvement of statistical methods; 2) struggle against bourgeois objectivism; 3) a Marxist evaluation of population development in Czechoslovakia; 4) the creation of a scientific basis for the socialist population policy; 5) a systematic criticism of the reactionary theories of population; and 6) struggle against revision conceptions reaching the sphere of demographic problems.

Policies on fertility and family size

2891 Brackett, James W., and Huyck, Earl, "The Objectives of Government Policies on Fertility Control in Eastern Europe," Popul. Stud. 16(2):134-46, November 1962.

Some East European demographers now admit that over-population may exist under communism, though only in special circumstances and (of course) different in character from over-population under capitalism. They now seek to determine the best population policy without supposing that the higher fertility is the better. Surveys of family planning have been conducted and studies made of the effectiveness of contraceptives. The birth rate has fallen very markedly during the last ten years in Bulgaria, Czechoslovakia, Hungary, Poland, Rumania and Yugoslavia, although not so far as to eliminate population growth altogether. Only in Albania and East Germany is there no sign of such changes.

2892 Brown, L. Neirlle, "Inheritance and the Communist Legal Order," Soviet Studies 14:295-313, January 1963.

Review of the book by Z. Szirmai, ed. The Law of Inheritance in Eastern Europe and the People's Republic of China. Leyden: A.W. Sythoff, 1961, 364 pp. All the systems are alike in two respects: the imposition of drastic limits on the scope of private fortunes; and the incorporation of considerable Roman law, including English common law. One important difference among them is in the range of relatives entitled on intestacy; in this respect the Rumanian system is most liberal, the Hungarian and Yugoslavian systems come next, while the Russian, Chinese, Czech, and Bulgarian systems are least liberal and exclude all persons but parents and the various generations descending from them. Another important difference is the position of the spouse. Spouses benefit from a system of community of acquests in most of these countries, but not Bulgaria; China has a system of complete community, whereas Poland requires the surviving spouse to elect between successoral and marital claims. Hungarian law gives a spouse a life interest in the whole estate if in need, and several systems grant security of tenure of the family home.

2893 Dzienio, Kazimierz, "Kierunki i Srodki Polityki Natalistycznej na Przykadzie Doswiadczen Wybranych Krajow Socjalistycznych" [Directions and Measures of Birth Policy as Exemplified by the Experience of Some Socialist Countries], Studia Demograficzne No. 17, 1968, pp. 65-85.

The article is devoted to the problem of change in the fertility level of women in some socialist countries in 1955-1963. The conclusion is drawn that, except for GDR, there was a substantial decline in the overall level of fertility. The pattern of the female population by fertility age did not favour that decline. Having examined the systems of material and social assistance for the families having children,the author concludes that the economic stimuli used did not result in any remarkable increase in the level of fertility in the period considered.

2894 Harmsen, Hans, "Die Bedeutung der Aufhebung des Verbotes der Abtreibung in Sowjetrussland fur die Osteuropaischen Volksdemokratien" [The Significance of the Lifting of the Prohibition of Abortion in the USSR for the East European Peoples' Democracies], Ostdeutsche Wissenschaft: Jahrbuch des Ostdeutschen Kulturrates 8:40-47, 1961.

Sections on: Bulgaria, Hungary, Poland, Czechoslovakia and Yugoslavia.

2895 Klinger, A. "Demographic Effects of Abortion Legislation in Some European Socialist Countries," pp. 89-91 in: Vol. 2 of the Proceedings of the World Population Conference, Belgrade. New York: United Nations, 1967.

The liberal abortion laws of the European socialist countries (excluding the German Democratic Republic and Albania) were justified ideologically on the grounds that it is the woman's right to plan the size of her family and that the health of women must be protected from the dangers of criminal abortion. Although criminal abortions still occur, their number has been minimized; Czechoslovakia has an annual rate of approximately 3,000-5,000, Hungary 5,000-6,000. Maternal mortality caused by abortion has become very rare in spite of the increase in the number of legal abortions. The abortion rate per number of women of reproductive age reached its highest level for Hungary in 1963: 70 for every 1000 women between the ages of 15 and 49. Bulgaria had the next highest rate (41), followed by Czechoslovakia (29), Yugoslavia (22) and Poland (21). Women aged 25-29 had the greatest frequency of induced abortions, with 133 per 1000 women in Hungary (1962-63) and 49 per 1000 women in Czechoslovakia (1962). Abortion was most common for women with two children, with 95 per 1000 women in Hungary (1963), less common for women with one child or three or more children, each with 80 per 1000 women, and for women with no children with 23 per 1000 women. Slightly less than 15 percent of all abortions in Hungary involved childless women; in Bulgaria, 23 percent. Countries with higher abortion rates have lower birth rates, whereas decreasing abortion rates have been accompanied by increasing birth rates, as in Czechoslovakia.

2896 Mandic, Oleg, "Law Famiglia Extramatrimoniale" [The Extramarital Family], Sociologia 2(1):195-200, January 1968.

A review article of the book by U. Bosanac, Vanbracna Porodica (The Extramarital Family), Zacabria, Yugoslavia: Edizioni Edok, 1967, which makes some general comments on modern changes affecting the family and the institution of matrimony. While for primitive societies matrimony meant primarily a means of sexual satisfaction, the arrival of Christianity produced the formula: sex + matrimony = family, giving rise to the inequality of females and the paternalistic system. Illegitimacy is viewed in the light of the laws of the classic state concerning (a) the ownership of the means of production and the relationship between owners and non-owners; and (b) the personal status and relations which regulate the perpetuation of an exclusive leadership class who owns the means of production. Bosanac's book analyzes in detail extramarital union in this context. Bosanac is of the opinion that, under modern social conditions, the existence of the family is still necessary. Not so necessary, however, is its legal matrimonial status. Society must protect the progeny whether they issue from marital or extramarital relationships. The cohesiveness of the family, which before was maintained by the marital status, must rather be based on the relationship between progenitors and offspring. Establishment of a family is a private matter rather than an institutional act that has the purpose of maintaining the privileges of a leadership class.

2897 Mehlan, K.H. [The Abortion Situation in the European Socialist Countries], _Zbl_. _Gynaek_. 83:853-ff., 1961.

The results of legalizing abortion in Eastern European socialist countries are: a sharp increase in the number of legal abortions; a decrease in the birth rate; a diminished incidence of criminal abortion with an evidently lower number of maternal deaths due to abortion. The mortality rate after legal abortion in specialized hospitals is 6 per 100,000, and complications have also been minimized. In the realization that the legalization of abortion is not the final solution to illegal abortions, the author advocates family welfare measures, development of counseling centers and sex education.

2898 Mehlan, K.H. _Auswirkungen der Legalisierung des Abortes_ [Effects of the Legalization of Abortion]. Wissenschaftliche Zeitschrift, Karl Marx Universitat, Leipzig. Mathematische-Naturwissenschaftliche Reihe, Sonderband 2, 1963.

Presents information about the scale, motives and consequences of legalized abortion in East European countries.

2899 Mehlan, K.H. "Combating Illegal Abortion in the Socialist Countries of Europe," World Med. J. 13(3):84-87, 1966.

The incidence of total and legal abortion between 1955 and 1964 in Eastern European countries is reviewed and the significant decline in the birth rate following the enactment of liberal legal abortion laws is noted. Noted also is the decline in maternal mortality consequent to legalization of abortion and the author suggests the promotion of contraception counseling centers, sex education and the desirability of children.

2900 Mehlan, K.H. "The Effects of Legalization of Abortion on the Health of Mothers in Eastern Europe," in: Proceedings of the Seventh International Conference of the IPPF, Singapore, February 10-16, 1963. New York: Excerpta Medica Foundation, 1964.

After a brief discussion of the abortion rate in several countries (Hungary, Czechoslovakia, Bulgaria and Poland), the effects of legalization of abortion in Eastern Europe on reducing criminal abortions, on the birth rate, mortality, morbidity, and fertility after abortion, and the development of contraceptive measures are considered. In some socialist countries, abortion was legalized on the basis of concern for the life and health of women and for the equal rights of women. The legalization of abortions in these countries is not a measure of population policy and has nothing to do with neo-malthusianistic tendencies. A continuous decrease in the birth rate is striking in all countries, except in the Soviet Union, following legalization of abortion and the relaxation of indications.

2901 Mehlan, K.H. "Legalisierung der Schwangerschaftunterbrechungen: Ja oder Nein" [Legalization of Abortion: Yes or No], Das Deutsche Gesundheitswesen 15:1206-13, June 9, 1960.

2902 Popescu, T.R. "Dreptul Familiei si Morala Socialista" [Family Law and Socialist Morals], Just. N. 20(1):28-36, 1964.

A presentation of the ways in which fundamental principles of socialist morals are reflected in the rules of family law. Discussed are: comradely mutual aid; love and respect for work; intransigence for laziness; probity, sincerity and moral purity; care for the education of the children as required by socialist morals; socialist patriotism; etc.. The essential identity between communist morals and family law is expressed in the way in which the requirements of these two forms of social consciousness are satisfied. Socialist law refuses to protect actions which contradict socialist morals and punishes deeds, attitudes or conduct infringing on socialist rules of cohabitation.

2903 Potts, Malcolm, "Legal Abortion in Eastern Europe," <u>Eugenics Rev</u>. 59(4):232-50, December 1967.

There is widespread conjecture in England, the United States and some Scandinavian countries about the possible consequences of altering the law relating to abortion. Although the Communist block is set apart by its political systems the nations at the eastern fringe of the Iron Curtain belong to the European cultural tradition. Poland, Czechoslovakia, Hungary and Yugoslavia are industrialized; they have large urban populations; the Christian religion remains a powerful influence. In Poland, Czechoslovakia and Hungary ,the great majority is Roman Catholic and churches are still crowded. The author concludes that: 1. A large percentage of women will resort to abortion in order to avoid having more children than they desire. They will do this whatever their religious or ethnic background. Town dwellers appear to use abortion more than their rural neighbors. Limited accommodation, a society where many women are employed, and a standard of living that is neither very rich nor very poor, contribute to the desire for small families. 2. There appears to be no reason for regarding abortion and contraceptive measures as in any way competitive; in fact, they appear to be complementary in their use. In countries like those of Eastern Europe, where contraceptives have been poorly used and criminal abortions common, the legalization of abortion on social grounds has been associated with very large numbers of operations. At the same time family planning programs have been able to progress. In a nation such as Britain, where the practice of contraception is more general than in many countries and the incidence of criminal abortion correspondingly is lower, it can be predicted that an alteration in the law would not be associated with such a high legal abortion rate as occurred in Eastern Europe. 3. There is no evidence that the abortion laws of Eastern Europe have led any significant proportion of the population to be socially irresponsible or that they have in any way undermined the basis of family life. In cutting down the number of unwanted children they may have contributed to the health and welfare of established families.

2904 "Rapid Falls in Fertility in Recent Years: Some Facts," Eugenics Rev. 55:127, 1963.

Japan is not the only country in which there has been a rapid fall in fertility in recent years. The Japanese birth rate fell from 90 per thousand in 1945-49 to 17 per thousand in 1959-61. However, in most parts of Eastern Europe, birth rates have also been falling at a remarkable rate since about 1950. In Bulgaria, there has been a 28% decline in birth rates since 1947; in Hungary, a 39% decline since 1954; in Poland, a 31% decline since 1952; in Rumania, a 30% decline since 1952; and in Yugoslavia, a decline of 24% since 1952. The variation in the dates of onset may be associated with the change from Stalinism to a less repressive regime. These recent rapid falls in fertility in these Eastern European countries show how forceful state pressure can be in influencing demographic events.

2905 Redei, Jeno, "Hozzaszolas Dr. Miltenyi Karoly: Nepesedespolitikank Idoszeru Kerdesei c. Cikkehez" [Some Remarks on Dr. Karoly Miltenyi's paper, 'Timely Problems of Our Demographic Policy'], Statisztikai Szemle 35(4-5):345-50, April - May 1957.

A statement of the theoretical basis for birth control measures in socialist countries.

2906 Tietze, Christopher, and Lehfeldt, Hans, "Legal Abortion in Eastern Europe," J. Amer. Med. Assn. 175:1149-54, April 1961.

Data are presented on legal and other abortions in Hungary, Czechoslovakia, Bulgaria and Poland, obtained at an International Conference on Abortion Problems and Abortion Control, held in Rostock-Warnemunde, East Germany, in 1960, which was attended by the authors. In addition to the statistics on abortion, legislation, choice and technique of operations, mortality associated with legal abortion, complications and sequelae of abortion are discussed. It is concluded that: (1) legalization of abortion on request or on very broadly interpreted social indications has resulted in a markedly overall decrease in the number of abortions; (2) criminal abortions have declined, but have not been completely replaced by legal abortions; and (3) the risk to life from an abortion, performed by an experienced physician in a hospital on a healthy woman in the first trimester, is far smaller than the risk ordinarily associated with pregnancy and childbirth.

BULGARIA

Policies on fertility and family size

2907 Bulgaria. "Interruption of Pregnancy," Internat. Digest Health Legis. 8:605-8, 1957 and 19:589-602, 1968.

Provides for abortion on request of woman if pregnancy is less than three lunar months' duration. Beyond this time, abortion is permissible if examination in a hospital shows that continuation of the pregnancy and delivery might endanger the woman's life or health. Amendment of the law in 1968 prohibited abortion, except in grave circumstances, for women having no living children. Permission of a special medical board is required by women having only one or two children and by unmarried women.

2908 "Family Policy in Bulgaria," Population 18:354-55, 1963.

Policies on material aid to the family, promulgated by the Consul of Ministers on 28 December 1965, and the Central Committee of the Bulgarian Communist Party, are intended to encourage natality. On January 1,1968, family allowances are 20 levas for the first child, 200 for the second, 500 for the third, and 20 levas for the fourth and later children. Allowances are also provided to meet the costs of health care, education, vacations, and maternity leave.

2909 "Increase in Pensions and Family Allowances in Bulgaria," Internat. Labour Rev. 87:384-86, 1963.

Family allowances were first introduced in 1941. Since then the scheme has been elaborated in various ways. In 1944 the nationality requirement was abolished and legitimate and illegitimate were put on the same footing. In 1951 the Government issued a ukase respecting the encouragement of child-bearing and large families. This scheme was financed from taxation on childless couples; the benefit rates were amended in 1955, 1956, 1957, and finally in 1962. Further, there are birth grants, special allowance to unmarried mothers, and ad hoc help to large families which have encountered economic or other difficulties.

2910 Krinchev, Kh., and Lukarski, D. [The Principle of Paying Monthly Allowances for Children], Trud i Tseni 1(5):33-41, 1959.

2911 Markov, M.A. [Changes in Instruction for Legal Abortion], Akush. Ginek. 3:1-4, 1964.

The law legalizing abortion in Bulgaria in 1956 permits abortion for two major reasons, social and medical. The pregnancy should not be past the third month and the period between pregnancies must be at least 6 months. The widening of the law includes reasonable applications for humanitarian and social indications (many children, deserted women, minors, rape). The law has also been expanded to include abortions after the third month with permission of a new deciding body, if grave social or medical conditions exist.

2912 Markov, M.A. "Meditsinskii Zadachi Pri Novata Pravna Bostanovka na Aborta u Nas" [Medical Aspects of New Laws on Abortion in Bulgaria], Suvremenna Meditsina 8(1):107-11, 1957.

2913 Risoff, Stephen, "New Concept of Ownership and Inheritance," Highlights Mid-Europe 4:101-11, April 1956.

2914 Starkaleff, I., et al. [The Situation of Abortion in People's Republic of Bulgaria] in: Mehlan, K.H., ed. Internationale Abortsituation, Abortbekampfung, Antikonzeption. Leipzig: Georg Thieme, 1961.

A report on induced abortion in Bulgaria. Since 1956 a woman can have an abortion on request provided her pregnancy has not gone beyond the third month, contraindications do not exist, and the operation is performed in a hospital department for obstetrics and gynecology. Prior to 1951 abortion was prohibited, and both the woman and the abortionist were liable to punishment. Abortion is also allowed, in addition to the above, for pregnancies over three months in cases of pelvic inflammatory disease, septic foci or other acute and chronic diseases. During the period 1952-55, the number of hospitalized abortions increased from 16,000 to 19,000 with approximately 40-50 deaths per year. There was a decrease in the number of deaths after the new law with 40,000 hospitalized abortions in 1956, 46,000 in 1957 and 55,000 in 1958. There has been a continuous drop in the country's birth rate from 1952 to 1958 (21.2 to 17.9). Over 67% of the aborted women had two children, 6% three or more, 22% one, and 4% were childless. Only 4.4% of the applicants obtained the abortion after consulting an advisory center. Although no deaths were reported resulting from abortion on request, there was a 1.5% complication rate and a 21.5% complication rate for abortions performed outside a hospital. Abortion on request is viewed as an excellent and safe birth control method pending the use of completely effective contraceptives.

2915 Stoimenov, G., and Sepetliv, D. [Abortions and Frequency of Births], Akush. Ginek. 4:398-ff., 1965.

Four Bulgarian regions, urban and rural, each with a high and low birth rate were studied to determine the relationship of abortions and births. A questionnaire was administered to the 3,000 couples in each region. In both urban areas 33% of the women reported previous abortions, and the rural areas reported 11% and 12%; 20% of the married women had had at least one abortion, 39% in urban regions, 10% in rural. It was shown that the number of abortions increased with higher marriage age and that the average number of childbirths after the abortion was markedly higher in women who had had abortion after the second child (2.109), than for those who had it before the first child (1.508).

2916 Totev, Anastas, "Naselenieto na Bulgariia 1880-1980 (Demografsko-Istoricheski Ocherk)" [The Population of Bulgaria, 1880-1890. (A Demographic and Historical Review], _Godisnik na Sofijskija Universitet, Juridiceski Fakultet_ 59(2):1-59, 1968.

Demographic, historical review of population change for the territory within the present borders. Notes on trends in vital rates, age structure, and internal migration in relation to economic change and industrial distribution. Notes also on decree of December 28, 1967 of the Central Committee of the Bulgarian Communist Party and the Council of Ministers concerning measures for promoting the birth rate.

CZECHOSLOVAKIA

General population policies

2917 Czechoslovakia. National Security Office, _Social Policy in Czechoslovakia_. No. 1, Prague, June 1965. 48 pp.

Contents: Srb, Vladimir, "Population Development between 1945-1964," pp. 1-8, and "Twenty Years of Pension Security, 1945-1965," pp. 9-25; Wynnyczuk, Vladimir, "Maternity Leave: Its Economic and Social Aspects," pp. 26-30; Kucera, Milan, "Development of the Mortality Rate," pp. 31-36, and "Divorces of Young Marriages in Prague," pp. 37-42; Prokopec, Jiri, "Activities of the State Commission on Population," pp. 43-47.

2918 Fajfr, Frantisek, "Aktualne Zadania Poliyki Demograficznej" [The Present Tasks of Population Policy], _Studia Demograficzne_ 1(1):53-59, 1963.

Discussion of two objectives of Czechoslovakian policy: an increase in the birth rate by lightening the economic burdens of working women, and the improvement of mutual relations between the individual and society.

2919 George, Pierre, "La Population de la Tchecoslovaquie" [The Population of Czechoslovakia], _Population_ 2(2):281-92, April - June 1947.

2920 Kazimour, Jan, "Uloha Demografie v Planovanem Hospodarstvi" [The Role Demography Plays in Planned Economy], Demografie 6(1):1-9, 1964.

Topics: general observations and designation of immediate research problems; changes in class structure; typology of families and households; sample censuses; demographic studies for housing projects; manpower planning; projections; evaluation of migration processes; and economic activities of the elderly.

2921 Kucera, Milan, "Populacni Politika Ceskoslovenska" [Population Policy in Czechoslovakia], Demografie 10:307-17, 1968.

From 1918 to 1938 there was not really a population policy in Czechoslovakia except for some assistance to families with children, which was interrupted by the war. Immediately after the war, the favorable growth of population suggested the inadvisability of a natalist policy. Beginning in 1953, the increasing rate of reproduction led officials to act, but timidly, to increase the rate of housing construction and to halt the increasing degradation in the life of numerous families. There developed consciousness of the need for a coherent and efficient family policy. Certain favorable measures were introduced, notably maternity leave after 26 weeks and an increase in family allowances. Other changes are envisioned for 1970: acceleration in housing construction and increased maternity leave.

2922 Michal, Jan M. Central Planning in Czechoslovakia: Organization for Growth in a Mature Economy. Stanford: Stanford University Press, 1960. xiii, 274 pp.

Chapter I, Population and Manpower, discusses trends 1947-1958 and as projected from demographic and employment data; also policy questions, notably on abortion.

2923 Prokopec, Jiri, "Deset Let Prace Statni Populacni Komise" [Ten Years of State Population Commission Activities], Demografie 10(1):13-15, 1968.

The Commission was established to serve the government as an advisory body on all population problems and development. In this function it submits proposals on how to control the population. The Czechoslovak population policy is pronatalist, but the support of families with children is expensive, depending upon economic conditions. The Commission's activities have been relatively successful despite the fact that not all proposals meeting population policy requirements could have been realized. The Secretariat of the Commission carries out wide demographic surveys, participates in the preparations of planned parenthood education programs, has helped to open a consulting office for young couples in Prague and has undertaken a study of the divorce rate in Czechoslovakia. One of the Commission's main tasks is to make the public aware of the country's demographic problems.

2924 Srb, Vladimir, "Population Development and Population Policy in Czechoslovakia," Popul. Stud. 16(2):147-59, November 1962.

This article, written by the Chief of the Demographic Section of the Central Office of State Control and Statistics in Czechoslovakia, gives some details of changes in population, and in the outlook upon it, in a period of transition and in perhaps the most economically developed communist country. The net reproduction rate had actually fallen below unity in the Czech regions by 1960, in spite of family allowances, the rate of which increases with each additional child. A high proportion of mothers work, and efforts are being made to harmonize the interests of society and family.

2925 Srb, Vladimir, "Zasady nasi Soucasne Populacni Politiky" [The Principles of Czechoslovak Population Policy], Demografie 2(1):1-8, 1960.

A discussion of the function of the family under Communism, with particular reference to the pro-natalist measures proposed in directives of the Central Committee of the Communist Party of Czechoslovakia and the Government of the Czechoslovak Republic in October, 1959, to be taken in the period 1960-1965.

Policies on fertility and family size

2926 Cernoch, A., "Experiences in Czechoslovakia with the Effects and Consequences of Legalized Artificial Termination of Pregnancy," p. 314 of Vol. 2 of the Proceedings of the World Population Conference, 1965. New York, United Nations, 1967.

Since Czechoslovakia enacted a law which permits the use of medical indications for abortion as well as abortion for cases deserving special consideration, the legal abortion rate increased during a five year period (1958-62) from 69,000 to 94,000. The highest incidence occurred in 1961-62, the result of an amendment in 1960 abolishing fees and residence requirements. In 1962, stricter criteria were introduced for primi-gravidae, termination was limited to the first trimester of pregnancy and fees were again charged. The number of abortions decreased in 1963 to 71,000, but the number of spontaneous abortions and deaths due to criminal abortions and suicide increased moderately. The author discusses early and late complications, and concludes by recommending that the performance of an abortion should only be permitted with the approval of a special committee set up to protect the health of women and the health of the general population. Such a committee must be aware of the possible negative effect of abortion complications on the biological fertility of women.

2927 Cernoch, A. [Legalized Termination of Pregnancy in Czechoslovakia], Gynaec. 160:293-ff., 1965.

In 1958 Czechoslovakia legalized abortion on medical grounds and for special reasons, and its new law has reduced criminal abortion 65-80% and minimized the number of deaths and complications following abortion. The author stresses that with greater medical knowledge, mortality could be limited to 1 for every 40,000 abortions, with trauma limited to 0.06% and gynecological infection to 3-4%. Certain complications can never be eliminated completely, however, such as parametritis, incompetence of the cervix and difficulties in future pregnancies.

2928 Cernoch, A. [Some Problems Encountered with Artificial Interruption of Pregnancy], Cesk. Gynek.25:646-ff., 1960.

Approximately 120,000 abortions were performed in Czechoslovakia during 1958-59 according to the new 1957 abortion law. There were 9 deaths among the legal abortions, but 32 cases of mortality among the illegal abortions. Complications occurred in 15-20% of the legal interruptions, and the complication risk increased steeply in abortions performed after the 12th week of pregnancy. The author feels that only very important medical indications should be accepted for women wanting abortions after the third month. It was determined that use of contraception was very limited, and the need for sex education and information on contraceptive methods is stressed.

2929 Cernoch, A. [Symposium on the Problems of Induced Abortion and Contraception], Cesk. Gynek. 27:629-ff., 1962.

A review of a 1962 symposium held in Czechoslovakia on abortion and contraception. During the period 1957-62, the birth rate decreased (256,000 in 1957; 238,000 in 1958; and 217,000 in 1962) and the abortion rate increased (8,000 in 1957; 69,000 in 1958; and 90,000 in 1962). However, the number of births increased to 236,000 in 1963, while the number of abortions fell to 71,000. Changes in the number of abortions other than legal were less pronounced, with 29,000 in 1957, 27,000 in 1958, 26,000 in 1962, and 29,000 in 1963. Out of 491,000 legal abortions during the years 1958-63, there were only 13 deaths; most of these abortions were performed on medical indications later in pregnancy. Verified criminal abortions caused 75 deaths, with an estimated mortality rate of 1:500-1000. There are approximately 200 prosecutions annually for abortion. Contraceptive use has been minimal, with little acceptance of modern methods.

2930 Czechoslovakia. "Interruption of Pregnancy," Internat. Digest Health Legis. 10:283-92, 1959; 13:491-92, 1962; 15:80, 1964; 19:173-75, 1968.

The law of 1957 provides for abortion upon the request of the woman and authorization by a special board. Authorization is to be granted on health or other reasons (advanced age, numerous children, loss or disability of spouse, economic problems, etc.). Illegal abortions are punishable under the Penal Code. Subsequent amendments make abortions free of cost, require their performance in a hospital, and, except in the case of women under 18 years of age, set a minimum of three living children as a condition of eligibility.

2931 Czechoslovakia. Laws. _Le Nouveau Code de la Famille en Tchecoslovaquie. Discours du Ministre de la Justice A. Cepicka, et Texte de la Loi_. [The New Family Law in Czechoslovakia. A Speech by the Minister of Justice, A. Cepicka, and Text of the Law]. Prague: 1950. 46 pp.

2932 Czechoslovakia. "Maternity Care," _Internat. Digest Health Legis_. 9:65, 1958.

Free medical care is provided for all infants up to the age of twelve months and, if such care is connected to maternity, to all women.

2933 Czechoslovakia. "Protection of Public Health: Organization of Health Services," _Internat. Digest Health Legis_. 18:60-79, 1967.

Part III provides for the care of children in infants' institutions, children's homes and creches. Creches are established in factories and agricultural cooperatives for the benefit of working mothers.

2934 Czechoslovakia. "Sterilization," _Internat. Digest Health Legis_. 19:175-82, 1968.

Contraceptive sterilization is permissible where the woman already has a number of children -- four children, in the case of women less than 35 years of age and three children, in the case of women more than 35 years of age.

2935 Frejka, T. and Koubek, J. "Les Avortements en Tchecoslovaquie" [Abortions in Czechoslovakia], _Popul. Fam_. 16:1-58, December 1968.

From 1958 to 1967 the number of legal abortions in Czechoslovakia increased from 27,110 to 96,421, the largest number in the decade since the enactment of the liberalized abortion law currently in force. The abortion curve shows two peaks with a trough in 1963-64, attributed by authors to efforts to reduce abortions, which resulted in a decrease in legally induced abortion and an increase in abortions classified as spontaneous. The rise in legally induced abortions in recent years is associated with the increasing numbers of women in the reproductive age groups, particularly young women. Rates of both spontaneous and legally induced abortions increased with age in each year of the decade, with very sharp increases with age among the women with induced abortions. Most abortions were performed on married women. However, among women with induced abortions, the proportion married decreased from 86% to 81% while the proportion single increased from 10% to 13% during the decade. The pattern for spontaneous abortions was similar. Among women with induced abortions in the 15-19 year age group, nine out of ten were single; while among women in the 25-44 year age group, close to nine out of ten were married. In 1959, about one-half of the abortions were performed on women with two children or less. In 1967, the proportion was about two-thirds. The reasons for abortion between 1960 and 1967 have shifted from 45.3% to 29.0% on the grounds of three or more children, and from 12.7% to 20.6% for reasons of health. The proportion of first order abortions has declined over the decade from 63.3% to 55.5% while second to fourth order abortions have increased somewhat.

2936 Haderka, J. [Faked Family Disorders and Differences in Applications for Legal Abortion], <u>Cesk</u>. <u>Gynek</u>. 28:349-ff., 1963.

The author describes the ways in which Czechoslovakia's abortion commission can be mislead, for example, through simulated divorce applications. The problem of combating falsified facts in abortion cases is discussed.

2937 Hermann, Adolf, "Czechoslovakia's Abortion Law," <u>New Society</u> 89:8-9, June 11, 1964.

Some persons claim that the drop in the birth rate to 15.7 babies per 1000 inhabitants in 1962, its lowest point ever, was due to the 1957 law permitting abortions for reasons including the difficult position of the unmarried mother, housing and economic hardships, the existence of several children in the family, and disrupted marriage. However, this is not the case, because the birth rate per 1000 had dropped from a peak of 22 during 1950-54 to 18.9 in 1957, when the law was not in effect. The new law has resulted in the check of illicit operations, but is being used as a substitute for contraception. This can be seen by the fact that out of each 100 pregnancies in 1958, 19 were artificially terminated; the corresponding figure for 1959 was 24.5; for 1960, 26.5; for 1961, 27.7; and for 1962, 26.9. A table gives the number of abortions per 100 pregnancies for eight age groups of mothers in Czech regions and Slovakia in 1961.

2938 Jurcikova, V. "The Effects of Legalization of Abortion," in: Proceedings of the Third Conference of the Region for Europe, Near East and Africa of the IPPF. New York: Excerpta Medica Foundation, 1962.

During the period 1960-61 in Czechoslovakia, no maternal deaths resulting from legal abortion were reported. Nevertheless, the author stresses the importance of preventing unwanted pregnancies, and offers as possible solutions effective and more extensive male and female contraception, aid for families with several children, and increased research on healthy conception.

2939 Kolarova, O.,and Gruber, A. [Problems of Artificial Interruption of Pregnancy in the Region of Southern Moravia], Demografie 7:154-ff., 1965.

The author describes some of the characteristics of those who obtained legal abortions in a region of Czechoslovakia during the period 1958-62. 30 years was the average age, although relative increases were apparent in both the 15-20 and the 40-45 age groups. The number of employed women increased from approximately one-half to approximately two-thirds of the total sample, and the most common ground used when applying for abortion was too many children (40%). Other reasons given were health, illegitimacy, and inadequate housing, in that order. Married women constituted 81-84% of the group, while 11-14% were not married.

2940 Koubek, J. [Abortions and Applications, 1960-1965], Demografie 8:280-ff., 1966.

Five tables are given to demonstrate the development of Czechoslovakia's abortion situation from 1960 to 1965. Figures indicate the number of legal and spontaneous abortions; the number of applicants and percent of accepted applications; the ratio of legal and spontaneous abortions per 1000 inhabitants and per 100 births and 100 terminated pregnancies; the number of spontaneous abortions per 100 total abortions and per 100 births; the distribution of age for aborted women; the incidence in various areas; and the rates of application and acceptance in various areas.

2941 Kurka, J. "O Nekterych Problemech Prayni Odpoved-Nosti Pri Umelem Prerusovani Tehotenstyi" [On Some Problems of Legal Responsibility in Induced Abortion], Cesk. Gynek. 29:713-16, November 1964.

2942 Lacinova, Valerie, "Rodinne Pridavky u Nas a ve Svete" [Family Allowances in Czechoslovakia and Abroad], Demografie 8(1):69-72, 1966.

2943 Lukas, J. "Abortion in Czechoslovakia," in: Sex and Human Relations New York: Excerpta Medica Foundation, 1965.

Czechoslovakia's 1958 abortion law legalized abortion on certain medical and social grounds. Over a five year period (1957-61), abortion incidence increased from 37,500 to 120,500, with the number of deaths resulting from all types of abortion decreasing from 41 to 13. These figures seem to indicate at least some reduction in mortality from criminal abortions. Since 1961, the number of abortions has slightly declined, and the author feels that with more extensive programs in family planning instruction the number will be further reduced.

2944 Mellgren, Arne, [The Czech Abortion Law], Svenska Lakartidningen 58:1798-1804, June 16, 1961.

Summary of legal status and official statistics.

2945 Milinska, I. "Offentliche Familienfursorge, Insbesondere bei Kinderreichen Familien" [Public Family Care, Especially for Large Families], Statisticky Obzor 24(1-2):42-58, June 1943.

2946 Pavek, Frantisek, Manzelstv Ocima Soudce [A Jurist's View of Marriage]. Prague: Nakladatelstvi Politicke Literatury, 1966. 276 pp.

Observations on sociological and psychological aspects of marriage and divorce in Czechoslovakia.

2947 Prokopec, Jiri, "Zkusenosti Interrupcnich Komisi a Soucasna Provadeci Praxe Zakona o Umelem Preruseni Tehotenstvi" [Pregnancy Interruption Committee Experience and Present Practice of the Pregnancy Artificial Interruption Act], Demografie 6(3):242-47, 1964.

Summary of results of a survey by the State Population Commission Secretariat in January 1964 to obtain opinions from chairmen of regional and district pregnancy interruption committees concerning the operation of the Artificial Interruption of Pregnancy Act, in force in Czechoslovakia since 1958.

2948 Schiller, N. [On the New Family Law], Cesk. Pediat. 19: 738-40, August 1964.

2949 Srb, Vladimir, "Une Enquete sur la Prevention des Naissances et le Plan Familial en Tchecoslovaquie" [An Inquiry on Birth Control and Family Planning in Czechoslovakia], Population 19:79-94, 1964.

A study of marriage, contraception and abortion in Czechoslovakia, conducted in 1958-59. 3,191 females with an overrepresentation of the young intelligentsia responded to a questionnaire, which is reproduced. Over 50% of the respondents work. 95% had decided on family size before marriage. Only 46.5% were aware of contraceptives before marriage.

Coitus interruptus (68.3%) and the condom (42.4%) were the most popular methods. 24.7% were indifferent to sex or frigid, largely due to fear of pregnancy. Medical and socio-economic grounds were most frequent for abortion, which is more common since the liberalization of the law in 1958. 23.4% of respondents had aborted before 1958. Attitudes toward abortion were mainly determined by socio-economic factors. Over 50% of the respondents were not opposed to sterilization.

2950 Srb, Vladimir, and Kucera, Milan, "Potratovost v Ceskoslovenska v Letech 1958-1962" [The Abortion Rate in Czechoslovakia from 1958 to 1962], Demografie 5:289-307, 1963.

A Czechoslovakia law of 1957 authorized abortion on the demand of the woman. In this paper, the repercussions of the law are discussed. There has been an increase in abortions and a decrease in births. Altogether, for the period under study, it is estimated that 132,000 births were averted. The legislation has contributed to the liberation of the woman. It is possible that the prolongation in maternity leave which is planned will stimulate natality.

2951 Urban, Rudolf, "The Birth and Abortion Rate in Czechoslovakia," Rev. Soviet Med. Sciences 1(3):24-33, 1964.

Between 1950 and 1960, the number of births in Czechoslovakia declined from 288,000 to 236,000, or from 23/1000 inhabitants to 16/1000. Decline is attributed primarily to the legalization of abortion in 1957. Bohemia and Moravia have shown the greatest decline, from 21/1000 inhabitants in 1950 to 13/1000 in 1960. Prague recorded an extremely low birth rate in 1960, 8/1000. This decline in births has been partially offset by a decrease in the death rate, primarily due to a decrease in infant mortality. In 1937, infant mortality ran as high as 117/1000; by 1963 the rate had declined to 22/1000. There is concern over the declining birth rate. In 1961, the State Population Commission stated in its annual report, "The law (legalizing abortion) has proved to have had a far greater effect on the birth rate than was originally expected. Therefore, ways and means to prevent women from submitting applications for an interruption of pregnancy must be found."

In the Fall of 1963 new restrictions were imposed. As a result, abortions, which had risen to 116,000 in 1962, declined by 16,000 in 1963 while births increased by 18,500. At the same time, spontaneous abortions, which had accounted for only 7.7% of the pregnancies in the period after the legalization of abortion, increased slightly, indicating a tendency to resort to criminal abortion in response to the more conservative attitude toward legal abortions.

2952 Vitak, B.,and Zelenkova, M. "Celostatni Instrucktaz Krajskych Odborniku pro Gynekologii a Porodnistyi a Predsedu Krajskych Interrupcnich Komisi 21. 4. 1964" [National Report of Regional Specialists for Gynecology and Obstetrics and Presidents of Regional Abortion Commissions on 4 April 1964], Cesk. Gynek. 43:763-66, December 1964.

Article deals with the situation regarding abortion 1962-63. There were 18,000 more births in 1963 than the previous year, while legal abortions decreased from almost 90,000 to about 70,000. Other hospitalized abortions increased from 26,000 to over 29,000. The relative increase in criminal abortions 1962-63 is estimated to be 40%. The indication for interruption was medical in 19% and social in 81% (most often more than three children or unmarried motherhood). The change is dependent upon a difference in interpretation of the law. The commissions should act more according to the principles of social humanism, procedures should not make the application of law difficult, and secrecy should be maintained.

2953 Vitak, B.,and Zelenkova, M. "Smernice o Provadeni Sterilizace" [Regulations on Sexual Sterilization], Cesk. Gynek. 32:139-42, February 1967.

2954 Vojta, M. "Populacni, Hlediska ve Zdravotni Peci o zeny a Souvasne Problemy Lidske Reprodukce" [Demographic Considerations in the Medical Care of Women and Contemporary Problems of Human Reproduction], Cesk. Gynek. 27(6-7):456-62, 1962.

Observations on the working of the permissive abortion law, 1958-61, and the effect on natality, perinatal and maternal mortality, reproduction rates, and age structure.

2955 Vojta, M. [The Situation of Abortion in Czechoslovakia], in: Mehlan, K.H., ed. Internationale Abortsituation, Abortbekampfung, Antikonzeption. Leipzig: George Thieme, 1961.

Prior to World War II in Czechoslovakia, the induced abortion rate was estimated to be 300,000 or equal to the live birth rate. However, in 1953, 30,000 hospitalized abortions were reported and approximately the same number of criminal abortions performed outside of hospitals, with 1,500 legal abortions. The new 1957 law brought an increased number of legal abortions (more than 61,000 in 1958) out of 89,000 hospitalized abortions and a decrease in the number of criminal abortions (about 10,000). Introduced along with the abortion law were some pro-natalistic socio-economic reforms; it is believed that the health threat of illegal abortion was minimized by these two efforts. 63 women died from abortion in 1955; 53 in 1956; 29 in 1958; and 14 in 1959, with 4 deaths out of 61,000 legal abortions in 1958; and 5 deaths out of 79,000 legal abortions in 1959. 1958 figures on the reasons for abortion were analyzed: 21% gave health factors, 50% said they had too many children (90% of these women had 4 or more children), 12% gave economic or material reasons, 6% financial or housing problems, and o.3% wanted an abortion because of their unmarried status. 33% considered the husband's consent or opinion unnecessary. Only 6-14% changed their minds about the abortion and completed the pregnancies, and preventative measures offered by the deciding commissions have little effect.

2956 Vojta, M. [Some Questions of Unwanted Pregnancy and Legal Abortion as a Solution at the Present Day], Rev. Czech. Med. 5:207-ff., 1959.

Legal abortion is considered to be only a temporary measure for reducing unwanted births in Czechoslovakia. Knowledge of contraceptive methods is preferred since abortion may have undesired complications. The number of criminal abortions has not been reduced; however, more human consideration of unwanted pregnancy questions has reduced the graver forms of injury to health.

2957 Wolinska, H. [Legal Regulation of Abortion in Czechoslovakia], Prawo i Zycie 5(20):6, October 1960.

2958 Wynnyczuk, Vladimir, "Informacni Pruzkum o Prodlouzene Materske Dovolene ve Vybranych Okresech" [Pilot Survey on Prolonged Maternal Leave in Selected Districts], Demografie 6(4):352-55, 1964.

Report on pilot survey conducted by the Secretariat of the State Population Committee of Czechoslovakia, June 8-13, 1964, to test the operation of Law 58/1964 of the collection of Laws and Ordinances, providing optional lengths of maternal leave for employed women.

2959 Wynnyczuk, Vladimir, "Vysledky Sondaze o Prodlouzene Materske Dovolene ve Vybranych Okresech" [Result of Survey of the Extension of Maternal Leave in Selected Districts], Zpravy Statni Populacni Komise No. 4, 1964, pp. 20-28.

GERMANY (DEMOCRATIC REPUBLIC)

Policies on fertility and family size

2960 Brey, J. [Influence of the Sixth Provision for the Execution of the Law on Mother and Child Protection and the Rights of Woman in Abortions in our Clinic in the Last Five Years], Deutsch Gesundh 16:972-ff., 1961.

An increase in gestational age of hospitalized induced abortion cases followed the introduction of certain welfare laws in the country. A connection is seen between the two events, since cash benefits are to be paid in the third to fourth and in the sixth month of pregnancy according to the new laws, and after their implementation, the incidence of abortion seems to rise at these times.

2961 Fiebich, Kurt, "Statistik als Staatsgeheimnis. Sowjetzonale Bevolkerungspolitik" [Statistics as a State Secret. Population Policy of the Soviet Zone], Die Gegenwart 10(26): 828-29, 1955.

In 1950 the population policies of East Germany aimed at trying to increase the national birth rate in order to compensate for the population deficit caused primarily by the very high death rate during and just after World War II.

Three goals were expounded in the laws passed in 1950: promotion of births in general, promotion of births by unwed mothers by eliminating the difficulties they must endure, and bringing mothers in to the national labor force by providing them with child care centers, kindergartens, etc., even at the place of employment. There was also aid for families with at least three children and special grants to families that gave their nation a child per year. Further aid came in the form of tax deductions, living accomodations, privileged positions in work or among the services at stores and offices, and raising of one's social prestige. Another policy adopted in the 50's aimed at preventing East Germans, especially the young, from leaving the country.

2962 Germany, Democratic Republic of. "Abortion," Internat. Digest Health Legis. 4:58, 1952-53.

By a law of September 1950, abortions are legally permitted where life or health of woman is seriously endangered or where one of the parents has serious hereditary disease. Abortions require permission of a commission of physicians and are to be performed in hospitals. The general restriction on abortions is intended to raise the birth rate.

2963 Germany, Democratic Republic of. "Act Concerning the Protection of Mothers and Children and the Rights of Women," pp. 95-96 in: United Nations, Yearbook on Human Rights for 1950; Also in: Internat. Digest Health Legis. 4:58-60, 1952-53.

The Act, which entered into force on 1 October 1950, is sub-divided into five main parts: public assistance for mothers and children; marriage and the family; working women and their protection; participation of women in public life and in the social life of the community; and final provisions. Part I provides that mothers of large families shall receive a grant at the birth of the third child and of each child thereafter and monthly allowances for the fourth child and each child thereafter until each child has reached fourteen years of age. Between the years 1951 and 1955, certain services and institutions are to be created for the improvement of medical care for children and pregnant women, and general and educational care for children of working mothers. Pregnant women are entitled to five weeks' leave of absence before childbirth and six weeks' leave after the birth of the child and to an allowance during that period equalling the previous average monthly income. The Act provides in Part IV for special training courses for women to enable an adequate proportion of them to participate with men in the administration of the Democratic Republic of Germany. The departments of education and public information, superintendents of schools and teachers must aid mothers in performing their educational duties and in widening their knowledge of the public and social activities of women in the Democratic Republic of Germany and abroad.

2964 Grandke, Anita, _et al_. "Die Oeffentliche Meinung in der Deutschen Demokratischen Republik zur Entwicklung der Familie und des Familienrechts und ihr Einfluss auf den Inhalt des Neuen Familiengesetzbuches " [Public Opinion in the German Democratic Republic and Its Influence on the Development of the Family and the Content of the New Family Law], _Koelner Z. Soziol. Soz. Psychol_., 1967, Supplement 11: 310-22.

A study of the influence of East German public opinion on the new Family Law which became valid on April 1, 1966. The law was preceded by a four months' period of public discussion (April - June 1965). The discussion was led by a commission of 24 political figures representing political parties and social organizations. There were 33,973 discussions, in which 752,671 citizens participated. The discussions revealed public support for the family as a basic social institution and a public demand that the state should do even more than now to support it. Some 220 changes were made in the text of the law through adoptions of public suggestions. Examples include provisions on family names (the paragraph of the draft law which allowed both new spouses to keep their family name and give the children the family name of either was omitted because the public rejected it; but the paragraph which permitted the spouses to adopt the family name of either as their joint name was retained). The discussion also showed that a great majority (85% of workers' families, 86% of clerks, 78.6% of cadres, and 76.7% of intellectuals) had a regime of community property. It was felt that a marriage should be dissolved "when it lost its meaning for the spouses, the children, and society (24,649 divorces were granted in 1963). Marriage counseling bureaus were approved by 90% of a special sample of 790.

2965 Hackel, F., and Schmidl, W. "Die Interruptio aus Internistischer Indikation--Erfahrungsbericht uber 1 1/2 Jahrzehnte Tatigkeit der Schwanter-schaftsunterbrechungs-Kommission in Leipzig" [Abortion on the Basis of Internist's Indications: Report on One and a Half Decades of Activity of the Abortion Committee in Leipzig], Z. Gesamte Innere Med. Ihre Grensgebiete 21 (Supplement):90-93. 1 May 1966.

2966 Hagemeyer, Maria, Der Entwurf des Familiengesetzbuches der Deutschen Demokratischen Republik [The Proposed Family Law of the German Democratic Republic]. Bonn: Bundesministerium fur Gesamtdeutsche Fragen, 1955. 24 pp.

2967 Hagemeyer, Maria, Zum Familienrecht in der Sowjetzone. Der "Entwurf des Familiengesetzbuches" und die "Verordnung uber Eheschliessung und Eheauflosung" [Family Law in the Soviet Zone. The Draft of a Family Law and the Decree on Marriage and Divorce]. Bonn: Bundesministerium fur Gesamtdeutsche Fragen, 1958. 75 pp.

2968 Hohlbein, R. [The Subsequent Fate of Mother and Child After Refused Application for Interruption of Pregnancy], Deutsch Gesundh. 15:188-ff., 1960.

The pregnancies of 828 women who were denied legal abortions, 85 of them by a commission of appeal, are examined. 74 patients could not be located for the follow-up. Of those who did not appeal their cases, 79% went to term, 18% had an abortion and the remaining 3% had premature births. The corresponding figures for the appealing women were 81%, 13%, and 6%, respectively. There were no maternal deaths and the abortion ratio is low when compared with figures for the country. A mortality rate of 0.4% was reported for those women whose application for abortion was approved.

2969 Kraatz, H., and Mosler, W. [The Question of Interruption of Pregnancy and Sterilization in Case of Serologic Incompatibility Between Mother and Child], Zbl. Gynaek. 79: 1317-ff., 1957.

The German law does not permit abortion in cases of threatening or manifest erythroblastosis fetalis unless the mother's physical or mental health is seriously threatened. If the woman is fearful in regard to delivering a stillbirth or a seriously ill child, or other appropriate reasons are given, abortion is usually allowed.

2970 Mehlan, K.H. [Abortion Statistics and Birth Frequency in the German Democratic Republic], Deutsch Gesendh. 10: 1648-ff., 1955.

Article based on 287 hospitals and their experience with deliveries and legal and other hospitalized abortions, and on obstetrical histories of 6,485 women of childbearing age. Estimates are made of the relation between births and all types of abortions during the period 1946-54 in the German Democratic Republic. While the number of legal abortions increased from 1948 to 1950, the number of illegal abortions also increased. The next couple of years showed a decrease in the legal abortion rate as well as a slower decrease in the number of illegal abortions. During the above period, however, there was an increase in the live-birth rate. Possible socio-political explanations for these findings are discussed, with reference to the country's welfare legislation and the abortion situation in other European nations and in the United States.

2971 Mehlan, K.H. [Late Sequels of Legal Abortion], Deutsch Gesundh. 11:876-ff., 1956.

A report of 243 women interviewed and examined five years after a legal abortion on a social indication. 11.5% experienced late complications, but this percentage represents all patient complaints registered with the physician during the examination and their connection with the abortion seems dubious in many cases. Four women were involuntarily sterile after the abortion. While 15% had wanted more children after the operation, 48% had a further pregnancy. Contraceptive knowledge was limited and few used an effective method. No mental traumas resulting from the abortions were determined, other than 10% who felt remorse for the interruption, and the abortions appeared to have no effect on further pregnancies and deliveries.

2972 Mehlan, K.H. [The Picture of Legal Abortion in the German Democratic Republic], Deutsch Gesundh. 13:595-ff., 1958.

Three distinguishable periods in the development of legal abortions in the German Democratic Republic are noted: 1945-1947, low incidence; 1948-1950, a definite increase with the addition of a social indication to the law; 1951-1956, a considerable reduction. An analysis of applications for legal abortions in 1956 indicates the difficulty of obtaining permission for abortion and this has resulted in a hesitancy to apply for abortion even in cases where the health of the mother is seriously endangered. The author urges a more liberal interpretation of the law and greater understanding of the social issues involved, rather than a broadening of legal indications.

2973 Mehlan, K.H. "Reducing Abortion Rate and Increasing Fertility by Social Policy in the German Democratic Republic," pp. 223-27 of: Vol. 2, United Nations, Department of Economic and Social Affairs, Proceedings of the World Population Conference, Belgrade, 30 August - 10 September 1965. New York: United Nations, 1967. 4 Vols.

In an effort to reduce the number of illegal abortions in the German Democratic Republic, abortion on social indications was legalized in 1947. The number of legal abortions increased steadily from 1947 to a maximum of 26,400 in 1950. A restrictive law was instituted in 1950 limiting legal abortions to strict medical and legal grounds. Under this policy, legal abortions have been reduced to 700-800 per year. At the same time, births increased steadily from 1946 until the present number of about 300,000 per year was reached in 1950. A trend toward more births among women in the 15-20 year age group, and toward a proportionately greater number of births of third or greater parity is noted. Hospitalized non-legal abortions have decreased from 61,000 in 1954 to about 40,000 in 1960-62. Based on interviews with 287 gynecologists, estimated unhospitalized non-legal abortions equal 50-100% of all non-legal hospitalized abortions, for a total of one abortion per 4-5 births. Recent increases have been noted in the percent of abortions among 20-25 year old women (68% of all abortions), and in the percent of abortions occurring in the first and second pregnancies (53% of all abortions). Decrease in the number of abortions per births after the third birth is taken as evidence of the effectiveness of social policy instituted in 1950 to reduce the financial strain of large families. The ratio of married to unmarried women terminating their first pregnancy in abortion is 1:1; the ratio for women terminating their first pregnancy in birth is 9:1.

2974 Mehlan, K.H. [The Situation of Abortion in the German Democratic Republic], in: Mehlan, K.H., ed. Internationale Abortsituation, Abortbekampfung, Antikonzeption. Leipzig: Georg Thieme, 1961.

The effects of revision in legislation on the incidence of induced abortion in the German Democratic Republic are examined in this conference report from 1960. During the years following the Second World War when strict legislation was still in effect, the rate of legal abortion was decreasing. When in 1948 medical-social indications were introduced to reduce the high incidence of criminal abortion, the abortion ratio increased. Statistical data indicate the growing number of legal abortions was followed by a decrease in the incidence of illegal abortions. In 1950 the maternal and child welfare legislation was enacted and the social indication was excluded from the law. This resulted in a gradual decrease in the legal abortion ratio. The number of criminal abortions is estimated to be 60,000 per year. During 1956-1958, there were 60-70 deaths yearly as a consequence of illegal abortions.

2975 Mehlan, K.H., and Falkenthal, S. [The Legal Abortion in the German Democratic Republic, Statistics from 1953 to 1962], Deutsch Gesundh. 20:1163-ff., 1965.

The number of women applying for legal abortions decreased by two-thirds during a nine year period (1953-62). Abortion incidence dropped to 0.5 for every 10,000 citizens, although different districts indicate varying frequencies. The rate of complications was 5.2%, with three deaths for 2,219 abortions. The author emphasizes the need for a more liberal interpretation of the law.

2976 Pfeideler, Martin, "Les Lois Sociales, le Code de la Famille et la Politique de la Jeunesse en Zone Sovietique " [The Social Law, the Code of the Family and Policy on Youth in the Soviet Zone], Documentation Francais: Articles et Documents 25,January 1955, pp. 1-4.

All social service agencies are centrally coordinated in the Democratic Republic of Germany. The budget for all allowances, etc., is part of the general government budget. Of three million individuals enjoying social allowances, two million have the minimum allowance. The payments are greater in the Federal Republic. The number receiving aid in the Democratic Republic of Germany is on the decline as a result of efforts by the government to reduce the rolls, and to make all who are capable of working, work, including mothers of very young children. Marriage is discussed, especially the government's role in marriage; the divorce laws; women's rights. Also, the role of communism on the lives of youths and in regard to the church.

2977 Wolinska, H. [Legal Regulation of Abortion in the German Democratic Republic], Prawo i Zycie 5(23):6, November 1960.

2978 Wolter, F. [On the Question of Induced Abortion on Eugenic Indication], Zbl. Gynaek. 76:133-ff., 1954.

Since 1950, legal abortion in East Germany is permitted only on the grounds of serious danger to the health or life of the women, or when there is a risk through heredity of a severe disability. The diversity of interpretation of the last indication is shown by several case histories. Author urges the establishment of firm guidelines and demonstrates the desirability of sterilization following abortion on eugenic indications.

2979 Wolter, F., and Roesler, W. [Problems and Experiences with the Certification and Performance of Interruption of Pregnancy], Deutsch Gesundh. 11:592-ff., 1956.

A review of the literature and a study of 300 cases of legal abortion in East Germany. The correct procedure for the application and certification are described and the author discusses, rather conservatively, the morbidity and mortality resulting from abortion.

HUNGARY

General population policies

2980 Danyi, Dezso, "Nepessegi Nezetek es Nepesedespolitika Magyarorszagon a Kapitalizmus Koraban," [Views on Population and Population Policy in Capitalist Hungary], Demografia 5(2): 143-65, 1962.

Account of changes in views on demography in academic textbooks in Hungary from 1848 to World War II in relation to socio-economic conditions and to actual demographic policy.

2981 Miltenyi, Karoly, "Nepesedespolitikai Jogszabalyok 1945-1958" [Laws and Decrees Relative to Population Policy, 1945-1958], Demografia 2(2-3):379-408, 1959.

A survey of the laws and decrees passed after World War II, as far as they are directly connected with population policy (marriage, divórce, birth, deaths and migration). In connection with the more important measures it refers to the effects measurable by statistical means, always emphasizing, however, that due to the complex character of population processes it is not possible to measure exactly the interconnections when studying the effects. In the surveyed period the provisions covering marriages envisaged above all administrative simplifications; moreover, the legalization of some marriages concluded under extraordinary circumstances as well as the regulation of marriages concluded with foreign citizens or concluded abroad. Legal rules covering divorce have also had a strong impact on the movement of population. The decree of 1945 while considerably adding to, and easing the conditions of dissolving marriage, made possible the dissolution of marriages which had been concluded under quite different economic-social conditions and which had been practically disintegrated during the war or under the effect of the changes following it. The legal rules passed in connection with births and children's policy show a uniform character, aiming consequently at the protection of the interests of the mother (especially of the unmarried mother) responsible for the child. (Such were measures of health, labour benefits, grants under the social insurance scheme and from public funds, increased and quicker legal protection in respect of alimony, equality before the law of children born out of marriage, etc.) At the same time a considerable change can be noted especially as far as practical application is concerned, in connection with birth control, the use of contraceptives and induced abortions. The family allowance has been made uniform and extended over all insured workers and employees.

2982 Miltenyi, Karoly, "Nepesedespolitikank Idoszeru Kerdesei" [Timely Problems of our Demographic Policy], Statisztikai Szemle 35(4-5):333-44, April - May 1957.

An account of demographic measures taken in Hungary in the years 1952-1956 and a criticism of Malthusianism.

2983 Szabady, E. "Les Effets Sociaux et Demographiques d'une Nouvelle Mesure de la Politique Demographique en Hongrie" [The Social and Demographic Effects of a New Type of Demographic Policy in Hungary], Popul. Fam. Bevolk. Gezin No. 18, June 1969.

Policies on fertility and family size

2984 Hungary. "Abortions and Patriotism in Hungary," East Europe 13(4):22-23, 1964.

A writer who applauded the legalization of abortions in 1956 now deplores the fact that Hungary's birth rate is the second lowest in Europe. He says that the people have abused the law, and that their cynicism and moral irresponsibility threaten the very life of the nation.

2985 Argay, I., and Nemecskay, T. [On Birth Control Based on our 10 Year Abortion Data], Orv. Hetil. 105:2067-ff., 1964.

Data on abortion collected during the period 1952-62 in Borsod county are presented. 22,000 births and 21,600 abortions were recorded, with 400 established criminal abortions (22 deaths and approximately 200 other complications), 9,200 "spontaneous" complete or incomplete abortions (6 deaths and more than 700 other complications), and 11,846 legal abortions (2 deaths and 588 other complications), 7% of which were performed on medical indications. The author analyzes the varying types of complications and reviews some case reports on maternal deaths. Although the number of legal abortions has increased, the number of "spontaneous" abortions decreased. Mental or psychological consequences of abortion are denied, and it is felt that the present abortion law should not be abolished, although contraception is preferable to abortion for economical and health reasons. The great number of abortions is not believed to have caused the decline of the birth rate; however, the authors argue that fewer children cause marital instability and more abortions.

2986 Acsadi, Gyorgy, [Family Planning Differences in Rural and Urban Areas], Demografia 12, 1969.

2987 Barsy, G.,and Sarkany, J. [Impact of Induced Abortions on the Birth Rate and Infant Mortality], Demografia 6: 427-ff., 1963.

The recent decrease in Hungary's birth rate (12.9 per 1000 in 1962) is attributed primarily to an increasing abortion rate. Abortion on request of the mother is permitted, and it is used extensively as a means of birth control. Discussion centers on the secondary effects of induced abortion on subsequent pregnancies.

2988 "Birth Control Propaganda," [Campaigns in Hungary and China], East Europe 8:32-34. July 1959.

2989 Danyi, Dezso, "Nepesedespolitikank es a Szuleteseke" [Population Policy and Births], Demografia 7(3-4):429-41, 1964.

Discussion on the principles of Hungarian population policy in the periods 1945-1954 and 1954-1964 in relation to the trend in births. Outline of recommendations for a new population policy for the encouragement of births.

2990 Gaultier, Jean P. "Le Nouveau Code de la Famille en Hongrie" [The New Family Law in Hungary], Pour la Vie,1953, pp. 42-49.

Text of the law of June 6, 1952.

2991 Good, Dorothy, "Some Aspects of Fertility Change in Hungary," Popul. Index 30:137-71, 1964.

At the close of World War II the new government, inheriting family allowances as a war measure, proceeded at first unsystematically with a pro-natalist policy. In 1945 a decree provided privileged status for mothers of six or more dependent children. In 1946 family allowances for workers were established as part of the government system of social insurance; benefits were small and coverage incomplete. Between 1947 and 1951 payments were increased and graduated by birth order, and the coverage was extended to some of the omitted groups; bonuses were allotted to the mothers of seven or more living children; the sale of contraceptives available to women was restricted to pharmacies on prescription only. In 1953 laws on maternal and child welfare were codified and further extended. Family allowances to mothers of single children were dropped; payments to those with two or more were raised. The childless, males aged 20 to 50 and females aged 20 to 45, were taxed. Restrictions on induced abortions, which since 1951 had been treated as criminal offenses, were stiffened. In the 1953 code, induced abortions were forbidden except in the first 28 weeks of pregnancy, after obtaining the approval of an administrative committee, on grounds of health or, exceptionally, on grounds of age or extraordinary personal and family circumstances. The prescription requirement for the sale of contraceptives was removed; lack of publicity and scarcity of supplies, however, limited sales. For the next two years the code remained in force with little change except for slight relaxations in the tax on the childless. The annual total of live births, which had fallen from 1950 to 1952, showed small gains in 1953 and 1954, then in 1955 a downward course. In June 1956 the Government's policy was reoriented, as in the other republics of Eastern Europe, in the direction of a more permissive attitude toward fertility control. Presumably the need for greater participation of women in the labor force, the enhanced demand for skilled workers in the new economic activities, the increasing per capita costs of the welfare services, the housing shortage and perhaps the reduced strategic value of mass armies in the nuclear age had played a part in the decision. In line with the new policy, the tax on the childless was abolished, the lowering of prices for freely sold contraceptives was encouraged, and the law on induced abortion was liberalized. Permissible grounds for personal and family reasons were extended. In contrast to the slight influence on births that the pronatalist policy had had, the putting into effect of the new line in the middle of 1956 was soon followed by a shift in the trend of birth statistics. Annual numbers of live births inclined downward, and those of induced abortions upward in a rise that continued until 1962.

2992 Hirschler, I. [The Situation of Abortion in Hungary], in: Mehlan, K.H., ed. <u>Internationale Abortsituation, Abortbekampfung, Antikonzeption</u> Leipzig: Georg Thieme, 1961.

This 1960 conference report centers on the consequences of Hungary's 1956 law, which permits abortion on request provided the pregnancy has not progressed beyond the third month. Abortion only on medical indication was allowed until 1952, but some liberalization occurred during the next few years with an increase from 0.1 - 0.2 abortions per thousand population to 8.4 in 1956. After the very liberal 1956 law went into effect, there was an even greater increase, with the rate of legal abortions (15.2 per 1000) passing the birth rate (15.1). In 1952 mortality from abortion was 22.0 per thousand, in 1958, 2.1 per thousand. 1957-58 showed 87 abortion deaths, 15 in 269,000 legal abortions and 72 in 77,000 other abortions with only 4 of the 72 lethal abortions judged to have been truly spontaneous. 59 died as a result of septic complications, 28 after self-induced abortion. The rate of morbidity was 1.8% after legal abortions and 6% after other types of abortion. The results of a 1959 sample survey are cited. 75% of the married women used some form of birth control; 49% used contraception, 15% abortion and 36% both. 90% were married, and 67% had at least two children, with an average number for the group of 2.2. The author feels that the remaining high incidence of illegal abortion is due to procedural problems which keep women from trying for a legal abortion, especially when there is a premarital or extramarital pregnancy involved. He suggests that the abortion committees be abolished, since their function is completely formal and recommends some pronatalistic socio-economic reforms as well as more extensive contraceptive programs to minimize the abortion rate.

2993 Hungary. "Interruption of Pregnancy," <u>Internat. Digest Health Legis.</u> 9:536-40, 1958.

Laws of 3 June and 24 June 1956 permit abortion on the woman's request if it is justifiable on health or socio-economic grounds. But abortions must be authorized by a special board which is obliged to try to convince the woman of the advisability of keeping her child when it appears expedient to do so and to inform her of the possible prejudicial effects of abortion on her health. Abortions for socio-economic reasons are limited to the first twelve weeks of pregnancy.

2994 Hungary. "Maternal Health," <u>Internat. Digest Health Legis.</u> 2:598-99, 1950-51.

Law of 12 December 1949 describes the duties of midwives and physicians to women and their offspring at birth and in terms of pre-natal and post-natal care.

2995 Hungary. "Sale of Contraceptives," <u>Internat. Digest Health Legis</u>. 1:177, 1949-50.

Law dated 5 October 1949 restricts the sale of vaginal caps, pessaries, and other similar contraceptives to pharmacists and other medical establishments on the prescription of a physician.

2996 International Labour Office. "Maternity and Child Welfare in Hungary," <u>Industry and Labour</u> 9(9):286-88. 1 May 1953.

In 1953 the Hungarian Council of Ministers increased maternity and child welfare benefits. In the area of medical assistance, expectant mothers are now entitled to three prenatal examinations, a free layette, a maternity grant, and aid from a visiting nurse during the entire period of pregnancy. The maternity grant is 700 forints for the first child and it is increased from 500 to 600 forints for each succeeding child. The cost of confinement in a clinic or hospital is covered under social insurance. There are special benefits for the working woman. Maternity leave is allowed her for 12 weeks, or for 16 weeks in special cases. If covered by social insurance, she is entitled to a pregnancy and confinement grant equal to 12 weeks wages, in addition to the maternity grant. The working mother can take leave for as much as an hour and a half each day, with pay, to nurse her baby or visit it at the local creche. She may also obtain a sickness benefit in order to attend an ill child at home. Family allowances are paid according to the number of children. Nothing is allowed for one child except in the case of a woman living alone. The forints per child ranges from 37.5 if there are two children to 112.50 if there are twelve children. For each child beyond twelve the payment is 210 forints. In order to meet the additional costs of these measures, a special tax is imposed on men between 20 and 50 years of age and women between 20 and 45 years of age who have no children. This tax is fixed at four percent of wages and salaries.

2997 Jirka, Ferenc, ed. <u>A Csaladi Potlek Szabalyai</u> [The Family Supplement Rules]. Tarsadalombiztositasi Kezikonyv Szakszervezeti Aktivistaknak. Budapest: Szakszervezetek Orszagos Tanacsa Tarsadalombiztositasi Foosztalya, 1960. 117 pp.

2998 Locsei, Pal, "Rechtlich Geschiedene und Tatsaechlich Geschiedene im II. Budapester Bezirk" [The Legally Divorced and the Actually Divorced in the IInd District of Budapest], Koelner Z. Soziol. und Soz. Psychol. 19(4):672-97, December 1967.

A research project inquiring into the incidence of divorce and separation of nonlegalized marriage (the living together of two sex partners not married to each other) among 4,283 males and females 15 years or above, who constitute 4.8% of all private households in the 2nd Budapest Administrative District. Census statistics were supplemented by interview survey. The following categories of marital status were noted: (a) actually and legally divorced without any marital relationship; (b) divorced, but living with a "sex partner" in an illegitimate marital relationship; (c) separated, but not legally divorced and not maintaining an illegitimate marital relationship; (d) not legally divorced but living in an illegitimate marital relationship. Legally divorced refers to divorce by juridical decree. Respondents were selected from a sample of 90 various size apartment houses and 1-family and 2-family homes in the 2nd District of Budapest. The juridical and demographic dimensions of the research population were analyzed separately from the sociological dimensions and results were compared. Of the 294 respondents who were considered divorced, 57.2% were actually as well as legally divorced and not involved in any marital relationship whatsoever. 80 persons (27.2%) were legitimately married but living apart from their spouses. 21 (7.1%) were illegitimately living with one partner while legally married to another. It is stated that those in this latter group are to be considered juridically as well as actually married to their illegitimate partners. The incongruence between legal and actual marital status was examined and its implications were discussed. Almost 50% of all partners in broken marriages have an incongruent marital status. Permanent incongruence in family status emerges as a social phenomenon. The overwhelming majority of these people are manual workers, while a small minority are nonmanual. They show an indifference to or conscious rejection of the traditional norms of divorce and remarriage. A control study was carried out subsequently in the 4th Budapest District, a typical white-collar area. 58% of these respondents were found to have an incongruent marital status. Of these, 38% have been living for 5 years or more in this situation. A national study is urged in which demographers, jurists, and sociologists should cooperate to gain more insight into the marital facts of Hungarian society.

2999 Miltenyi, K. [Demographic Significance of Induced Abortions], Demografia 7:419-ff., 1964.

The author examines abortion as a method of birth control in Hungary indicating that the pregnancy rate has remained stable since 1957, but an increasing percentage of pregnancies are interrupted by abortion. The economic factors influencing birth control indicate that there is an inverse correlation between income and the tendency to bear two or more children. Finally, the medical consequences of abortion are observed and it is shown that the ratio of premature births is 40-50% higher among women with previous histories of induced abortion.

3000 Miltenyi, K. [Induced Abortions in Hungary During the Years 1957-1959], Demografia 3:424-ff., 1960.

1957 data on induced abortions are compared to 1959 data on induced abortions. The number of induced abortions in Hungary increased from 123,000 in 1957 to 152,000 in 1959; the number of live births in 1959 was 151,000. A rise in the number and frequency of induced abortion was apparent for all age groups, with the greatest increases for 25-29 year olds (95 to 122 abortions per 1000 women). 90% of the women were married in both years studied, and the number of expected abortions for 50 year old women increased from 1.69 (1957) to 2.08 (1959). The average number of abortions for women having abortions rose from 1.83 to 1.97. 11% were nulliparous, 28% had one living child, and 30% had two and three or more. There has been a decrease in the average number of living children from 1.65 to 1.54 for working women and from 2.58 to 2.35 for non-working women. From figures on the sale of contraceptives and the increased number of pregnancies, the author concludes that modern contraceptive methods have not yet been fully utilized in Hungary.

3001 Miltenyi, Karoly, "Nepesedespolitikank Nehany Kerdese" [A Few Problems of Hungary's Demographic Policy], Demografia 1(1):7-26, 1958.

A survey of natural increase in Hungary since 1946 and of policy affecting fertility, especially the law of 1953 banning birth control and the liberalization of the law effected by the decree of 1956. Presents data on the trend in abortions and recommendations for extending contraception.

3002 Miltenyi, Karoly, "Social and Psychological Factors Affecting Fertility in a Legalized Abortion System," p. 318 of Vol. 2 in: Proceedings of the World Population Conference, Belgrade, 30 August-10 September 1965. New York: United Nations, 1967. 4 Vols.

Study analyzes the results of two surveys, identical as to tenor and method, the basis of which was the interrogation in 1960 of 26,100 and in 1964 of 27,900 childbearing females. After a methodological introduction, the study investigates the impact of socio-psychological factors on birth control, by the ratio of childbearing and surgically aborting females.

3003 Miltenyi, K., and Szabady, E. [The Problem of Abortion in Hungary; Demographic and Health Aspects], Demografia 7: 303-ff., 1964.

Reviews the abortion bill issued in June 1956 which permits termination of pregnancy at the request of the woman up to the third month of gestation. The purpose of the decree was to reduce the number of unwanted children and the incidence of complications caused by criminal abortion. Since the legislation of abortion the birth rate has declined by 60,000 to 70,000, and the average family size has decreased. Mortability rates for legal abortions were 0.5 per 10,000 in 1962. However, in 1963, 1.5% of women having induced abortions suffered complications requiring hospitalization. Also reported were higher prematurity rates after induced abortions. Abortion did not affect the rate of spontaneous abortions. Abortion has not served to minimize the number of pregnancies per year and efforts for wide contraceptive use have failed.

3004 Ozsvath, I., and Rado, S. [Experience with Interruption of Pregnancy], Nepegeszsegugy 42:121-ff., 1961.

Comparative analysis shows little difference between working class clientele and the general population in marital characteristics, pregnancy history, and the incidence of abortion. Inadequate housing is an important reason for working class abortions.

3005 Piepponen, Paavo, "Vapaa Abortti Unkarissa" [Free Abortion in Hungary], Sosiologia 4:149-55, 1965.

Hungarian studies on abortion are analyzed, and obstetric

cases in Hungary for the years 1955-64 are tabulated. It is found that per 100 live births, 140 induced abortions were performed in 1964. The civil status, number of children, and age of the aborting females were studied, and it was found that 90% of the females were married with 2 to 4 children. Of the total category of married females with 2-4 children, 70-90% were abortion cases, and only 10-30% gave birth to a child in the hospital cases recorded for 1964. It was found that bearing the child is chosen more frequently by younger females, when the number of children is kept constant. Labour force participation, income, and housing status are related to choosing abortion. The motives for abortion are analyzed: 95% of the respondents gave as answers such reasons as present number of children, intervals between births, and poor economy situation. Due to the legalization of abortion, the mortality caused by induced abortion has decreased. In some Hungarian studies cited, an increase is found in spontaneous abortions, premature births, and infant mortality. The population policy in Hungary is crystallized as follows: (1) the number of births should be encouraged with positive means, e.g., economical aid, psychological support, etc.; and (2) the number of induced abortions should be decreased by means of the substitution of contraceptive methods of family planning.

3006 Sos, Erno, "Gli Assegni Familiari in Ungheria " [Family Allowances in Hungary], Le Assicurazioni Sociali 16(1): 60-64. Jan.-Feb., 1940.

Allowances according to the law of 1938 are discussed.

3007 Srb, V. [Abortion in Hungary], Demografie 5:89-ff., 1963.

The author compares, for Hungary and Czechoslovakia, actual numbers and ratio per 1000 women in reproductive age for live births, stillbirths, legal abortions and spontaneous abortions during the period 1958-61. There was an increase in the number of abortions for both countries, but Hungary's ratio more than doubles that of Czechoslovakia. Maternal mortality is also compared for the two countries; Hungary shows 0.24 (1959) and 0.17 (1960) deaths per 1000 abortions, while Czechoslovakia shows 0.7 (both years). The number of condoms and contraceptive jellies sold increased in Hungary over the four years, while the sale of diaphragms remained stable or decreased slightly.

3008 Szabady, Egon, "Csaladtervezesi Trendek: a Magyar Vizsgalat" [Family Planning Trends: the Hungarian Study], Demografia 11(3-4):333-46, 1968.

The paper is concerned with the problems and character of the fertility, family planning and birth control study of 1965/66 and contains some findings and conclusions in connection with family planning practice in Hungary. The study covered 8,800 persons, i.e., 0.5 per cent of the married women in the reproductive age. The author reviews the development of the number of births in the last 15 years and mentions also the efforts of the Hungarian demographers to reveal the causes and circumstances of the decline in fertility. Then follows a brief comparison of some aspects of the sample surveys performed in Hungary and in other countries.

3009 Szabady, Egon, "Magyarorszag Nepesedesi Helyzete: a Csaladtervezes Gazdasagi, Tarsadalmi es Egeszsegugyi Vonatkozasai," [Hungary's Population Position: Economic, Social and Health Issues of Family Planning], Demografia 5(3):325-32, 1962.

3010 Szabady, Egon, "Some Characteristics of Fertility in Hungary after World War II," Paper Presented at the International Union for the Scientific Study of Population General Conference, 3-11 September 1969. London.

In connection with the development of the fertility we are concerned, first of all, with the efficiency of the population policy measures directly connected with it. The introduction of the maternity allowance is a significant progress, it facilitates especially the situation of the employed mothers. It makes it possible for the mothers to stay at home and to care for their children until they reach the age of 2 and a half years, i.e., during a period which is the most important for the supply of the child and in which the engagement of the mother in the working place and at home imposes the greatest burden on her. Measures have been taken to increase the family allowance and to extend its coverage. As a result it may be hoped that the improvement of fertility, which started in 1966-67, will continue also in the future.

3011 Szendi, B., et al. [23,300 Induced Abortions Reflected by Method of Interruption and Early Complications], Z. Aertzl Fortbild 54:751-ff., 1960.

3.5% of 23,300 legal abortions performed during the period 1956-59 in a "Komitat" of 500,000 people were on medical indications, the remainder on social indications. The rate of pregnancies per 1000 population increased from 30 to 33, but the birth rate decreased from 20 to 15. It could not be determined whether the number of illegal abortions decreased, although maternal mortality caused by such abortions remained the same. There was no observable increase in contraceptive use despite a program of propaganda. 3/4 of the abortions were performed before the 8th week of pregnancy, and only 0.3% after the twelfth week. One death was reported, a second trimester abortion with cervical rupture and peritonitis. 3.8% involved primary complications, such as fever and hemorrhage, 2.1% involved recurretage.

3012 Szendi, B., and Lakatos, L. [Maternal Death in Relation to the Obstetric Cases of 10 Years in Bekes County], Nepegeszsegugy 45:24-ff., 1964.

The author analyzes maternal deaths occurring during the years 1950-60 in Bekes County (pop. about 500,000). The number of pregnancies was reported at 137,000, with 90,000 births, 46,000 abortions (28,000 legal), and 600 ectopics. The total maternal mortality was 5.2/10,000 pregnancies, with a corresponding ratio for the whole country of 6.8 (34.4 in the 1930's). Childbirth was responsible for 41 deaths (4.6/10,000 births) and abortion for 28 (5.8/10,000), only two of which were legal (0.7/10,000). After the 1956 law went into operation, deaths caused by illegal abortion decreased in number, although there is still a substantial number of illegal abortions. Maternal deaths occur generally after self-induced abortion with primitive mechanical means, such as infected roots, bicycle spikes, etc.

3013 Zoltan, I. [On the Importance of Psychic Factors in the Pregnancy], _Z. Aertzl Fortbild_ 56:1159-ff., 1962.

The author reviews figures on 1,465 legal abortions. No maternal deaths were reported, while 93.5% were performed on social indications and 2.2% involved complications. It is suggested that mental illness is more likely with the continuation of an unwanted pregnancy than with an induced abortion. Despite liberal laws, there is still a large number of illegal abortions, especially when the pregnancy is the result of extramarital conception.

POLAND

General population policies

3014 Miklasz, Constant, "La Population Polonaise: Doctrines, Politique et Conflits Religieux" [The Polish Population: Tenets, Policy and Religious Conflicts], _Population_ 15(2): 317-32, April - May 1960.

A critical study, including notes on growth since 1945; the laws of 1956 and 1960 on abortion and conflicts with the Catholic Church; policies concerning excess rural population in the successive economic plans; and controversies over the application of Marxist prescriptions.

3015 Ministry of Foreign Affairs, _German Occupation of Poland_. New York: Greyston, 1941. 240 pp.

Policies of population transfers and forced labor receive brief mention. The appendices present English translations of German administrative promulgations.

3016 Planansky, K. [Need of Effective Internal Population Policy], _Lekarz Wojskowy_ 34:161, February-April 1942.

3017 Polish Research Centre (London), German Failures in Poland: Natural Obstacles to Nazi Population Policy. London: Cornwall Press, 1942. 30 pp.

Policies on fertility and family size

3018 Gorecki, Jan, "Divorce in Poland -- A Socio-Legal Study," Acta Sociol. 10(1-2):68-80, 1967.

Following a pilot study in 1961-1963, 153 divorce trials were observed and 84 conciliatory sessions were attended. 41 divorce judges were interviewed as were 60 divorce lawyers in different parts of Poland. A sample of 323 Cracow law students was questioned and interviews by the Warsaw Public Opinion Research Center with a representative sample of 2,355 Poles, as well as court records, were used. The Polish divorce law intends the granting of divorce when the marriage is completely and permanently broken except when the interests of children would be adversely affected or when it would benefit a guilty party without the consent of the innocent partner (the Polish "recrimination rule," a use of the word "recrimination" with a meaning different from Anglo-Saxon legal language). The first purpose of the legislation is that divorce be granted if the breakdown appears complete. This purpose is achieved in about 99% of the cases in the Cracow Court; but many couples whose married life broke down do not divorce for religious, social and economic reasons. Lack of money, however, does not seem to be a barrier to court action. The second purpose of the divorce law, that divorce be granted only if the breakdown is really complete, is examined from a sample of 58 contested and 70 uncontested cases and found to be fulfilled except for 1 to 6% of the cases. The third purpose, to achieve reconciliation, is achieved in 3.4 to 3.9% of successful reconciliation sessions, a percent higher than indicated by the literature. The fourth purpose, as expressed in the "recrimination rule," which accounts for most of the dismissals of divorce actions, seems to be about equally supported and rejected by public opinion.

3019 Gorecki, Jan, "Recrimination in Eastern Europe: An Empirical Study of Polish Divorce Law," Amer. J. Comp. Law 14:603, 1965-66.

The recrimination rule is that the spouse solely guilty of the marital breakdown cannot claim divorce. This rule, introduced for the first time in the Marriage Law of 1945, was subsequently enacted in the Family Code of 1950 as well as the Family and Guardianship Code of 1964. In this paper, there is an evaluation of how well and through what means the purposes of the law are achieved.

3020 Holyst, B. [Some Criminologic and Criminalistic Aspects of Infanticide], Panstwo i Prawo 14(12):1035-44, December 1959.

3021 Institut National d'Etudes Demographiques, "Textes Etrangers. Pologne, Decret No. 270 du 25 Septembre 1945, Code des Mariages" [Polish Decree No. 270 of 25th September 1945, Marriage Code], Population 2:402-5, April - June 1947.

3022 Kozlowska, Ewa, [Legal Age of Marriage and Social, Legal and Demographic Problems], Stud. Demograficzne 10:81-96, 1966.

Examines problems resulting from the Polish law of 1965 fixing the age at marriage to 21 years for the man and 18 years for the woman. Notes the law's repercussions on the rate of nuptuality, illegitimate births and marital fertility. Also observes its effects on marital stability, with reference to the increased divorce rate of young marriages.

3023 Krotkiewska, Lidia, Warunki Dopuszczalnosci Przerywania Ciazy; Teksty i Komentarz [Conditions Warranting Abortion; Texts and Commentary]. 2nd ed., rev. and enl. Warsaw: Panstwowy Zaklad Wydawn. Lekarskich, 1959. 54 pp.

3024 Lakomy, T. [The Problem of Artificial Abortions -- Based upon the Material from the Clinic of Obstetrics and Gynecology of the Gdansk Medical School], Ginek. Pol. 35:413-ff., 1964.

A report on data obtained from 5,609 abortion patients or patients treated for post-abortal complications at the II Clinic during the period 1956-61 . Abortions performed on social indications increased from 25.7% to 84.6%, while those performed on medical indications increased from 2.04% to 1.3%. The percent relation of medical indication abortions to social indication abortions decreased from 27.9% to 1.3%. After the legalization act was put into operation, the percentage of criminal abortions to all abortions decreased from 1.02% to 0.05%. Post-abortum complications decreased from 31.6% to 7.4%.

3025 Lasok, D. "The Polish Code of Family Law, 1964," Internat. Comp. Law Quart. 14:1022-28, July 1965.

Since the fundamental statute of 1945 which in some respects revolutionized the pre-war system, family law in Poland had been twice recodified. Both the 1950 and 1964 Codes provide for changes in marriage in terms of its formation, the rights and duties of spouses, matrimonial property, and its dissolution. They also provide for changes in kinship in terms of parent and child relationships, parental rights and duties, adoption, and maintenance.

3026 Laudanska, E. "The Effects of Legalization of Abortions," in: Proceedings of the Third Conference of the Region for Europe, Near East and Africa of the IPPF. New York: Excerpta Medica Foundation, 1962.

Abortion legalization in Poland has improved the conditions of women's health and has been a factor in the reduction of the birth rate from 30.5% per 1000 in 1951 to 22.4% per 1000 in 1961. There is, however, a minimum of statistical data on post-abortal complications, and steps to reduce such complications by appropriate pre- and post-operative measures should be undertaken.

3027 Lesinski, J.,and Lacki, M. [Analysis of Abortion in Poland with Specific Reference to Methods for Control], Pol. Tyg. Lek. 16 :99-ff., 1961.

Results of a survey administered to 11 clinics and hospitals during the period July 1956 to June 1957. A total of 3,393 abortions were reported: 2,874 for social indications, 1,510 for medical reasons. An estimate based on these figures indicates that the abortion rate in Poland was 250,000 to

300,000 per year. During 1951 to 1955 there were 1,200 to 1,400 legal abortions performed per year constituting 0.5% of all estimated abortions. A four part program was instituted to minimize the number of illegal abortions: 1) introduction of contraceptives and birth control information; 2) passage of a bill to legalize abortions for social or economic indications; 3) sex education; and 4) maternity benefits. Results of the program show an increase in legal abortions; however, the total number of abortions obtained remained stable.

3028 Lopatecki, T. and Iwaszkiewicz, J. "10 Lat. Realizacji Ustawy o Dopuszczalnosci Przerwania Ciazy" [Ten Years Experience of the Act on Permissibility of Interruption of Pregnancy], _Wiadomosci Lekarskie_ 20:659-62, April 1, 1967.

3029 Poland. "Interruption of Pregnancy," _Internat. Digest Health Legis._ 7:311-12, 1956; 9:319-23, 1958; 13:140-42, 1962; 14:454, 1963; 15:793-94, 1964.

The Ministry of Health, as of July 27, 1954, authorized abortion where the health of the women would be adversely affected by the continued pregnancy. Amendments to the law granted the right to abortion because of difficult living conditions or rape; required that abortions be performed by qualified physicians; and made illegal abortions punishable under the Penal Code. Further, health services approving or performing abortions are required to give instructions bearing on the problems of birth control and to organize sales stands for contraceptives.

3030 Poland. Laws, Statutes, etc., "Family Code: Act of 27 June 1950," _United Nations Yearbook 1950_, pp. 232-33.

The Code consists of four parts: Part 1, Matrimony; Part 2, Relations between Parents and Children; Part 3, Guardianship. Articles 14-28 of Part 1 define the rights and duties of spouses; they emphasize the equality of husband and wife with regard to marital fidelity, decision-making in the family, meeting the needs of the family, and property.

3031 Poland. Laws, Statutes, etc., Kodeks Rodzinny; Komentarz [The Family Code; A Commentary]. Edited under the direction of Maurycego Grudzinskiego and Jerzego Ignalowecza. Warsaw: Wydawn Prawnicze, 1955. 568 pp.

3032 Poland. Laws, Statutes, etc. [The Family Law]. Warsaw: Polish Institute of International Affairs, 1958. 73 pp.

3033 Poland. Laws, Statutes, etc., "Ustawa z dnia 27 kwietnia 1956 r. o. Warunkach Dopuszczalnosci Przerwania Ciazy" [Law of April 27, 1956, Concerning the Circumstances Under Which Abortion is Permissible], Dziennik Ustew Polskiej Rzeczyposolitei Ludowej (Legal Gazette of the Polish People's Republic) No. 12, May 8, 1956, p. 71

An abortion may be performed by a physician: 1) for medical reasons; 2) because of difficult living conditions of the pregnant woman; and 3) if there is well-founded suspicion that the pregnancy was due to a criminal act.

3034 Seogst, Alfons, "Poland: Children Born Out of Wedlock Under the 1950 Code of Domestic Relations," Highlights Mid-Europe 5:383-94, September - October 1957.

3035 Tarnawski, Z. "Zagadnienie Przerwan Ciazy na Terenie M. St. Warszawy w Latach 1963-1965" [Problem of Pregnancy Interruption in Warsaw in 1963-1965], Ginek. Pol. 38:313-16, March 1967.

Statistical data concerning the number of abortions in gynecological wards in Warsaw shows a steady decrease in the number performed between 1963-65. In comparison with 1963, the number decreased by 16.5%. Analogous decrease of operations was noted in the group of women at the peak of their fertility, the index fell from 51.08 to 43.08 per 1000 women. In spite of the increasing use of contraceptives, the high number of abortions continued with the result that obstetrico-gynecologic service authorities intensifed their efforts to spread family planning. To decrease the number of artificial terminations the knowledge of contraception must be made more widespread in factories and offices.

3036 Winkler, E. "Realizacja Ustawy o Przerywaniu Ciazy na Terenie m. Katowic w Latach 1960-1964" [Application of a Law Permitting Abortions in Katowice in 1960-1964], Zdrowie Publiczne 9:383-86, September 1965.

3037 Wolinska, H. [A Compromise Which Did Not Work: The Third Note on the Law and Conditions Permitting Interruption of Pregnancy], Prawo. i Zycie. 4(16):3, August 1959.

Publication on law, state administration, and socio-economic problems issued by the Polish Lawyers Association.

3038 Wolinska, H. Przerwanie Ciazy w Swietle Prawa Karnego [Abortion in the Light of Penal Law]. Warsaw: Panst wove Wydawx. Naukowe, 1962. 133 pp.

ROMANIA

Policies on fertility and family size

3039 Coja, N., et al. [Lawful Interruption of Pregnancy in the Clinic of Obstetrics and Gynecology, Block No.1, Cluj, during 1958-1961], Obstet. Ginec. 10:207-ff., 1963.

22,803 abortions induced on demand in Clu, Romania from 1958 to 1961 are analyzed. The number of births per year remained constant (slightly over 1000), although the number of abortions increased from 2,881 in 1958 to 7,927 in 1961. 1.5% (35 cases) involved complications requiring hospitalization, with the most frequent being hemorrhage, septic inflammation, and trauma due to uterine perforation.

3040 Cristea, A., et al. [The Causes of Punishable Lethal Abortion and Preventive Measures], Obstet. Ginec. 10:277-ff., 1963.

In 1957, Romania legalized abortion for medical and social reasons providing they are performed within the first three months of pregnancy. Since that time, the number and severity of complications have been reduced. A 1961-62 study of 23 illegal abortion cases is described. Most of the women were between 30 and 40 years of age and had passed beyond the third month of pregnancy; 17 were from rural areas. All but two of the cases involved traumatic injuries, renal insufficiency and infections due primarily to unsanitary conditions. The author stresses the need for health education and contraceptives, legalization of some abortions in the second trimester and centers for prevention of abortion, and recommends an emphasis on rural areas.

3041 Melik,S., and Nemes,P. [Experience Acquired in 8,545 Cases of Interrupted Pregnancies], Obstet. Ginec.10:225-ff., 1963.

A review of 8,545 induced abortion cases performed during the period 1957-61 in Sf. Gheorghe, Romania; 0.3% involved immediate complications (29 cases), with 9 uterine perforations and 11 refractory hemorrhages. 3.05% were hospitalized for immediate and late complications (261 patients), and 199 required a repeated curettage. There were no reported deaths in this series.

3042 Mihaescu, D.V. "Noua Reglementare Privind Intreruperra Cursului Sarcinii si Infractiunea de Avort" [New Regulations Concerning Therapeutic Abortion and Criminal Abortion], Rev. Romana Drept. 23(3):49-60, 1967.

Outlines the recent history of Romanian policy from the decree of 1957 granting full liberty to the new decree for regulation of criminal abortion in 1966.

3043 Pressat, Roland, "La Suppression de l'Avortement Legal en Roumanie: Premiers Effets" [Restriction of Legal Abortion in Romania: Initial Effects], Population 22(6):1116-18, 1967.

The new abortion law of 1967, which makes abortion legal only in hardship cases, had the immediate effect of raising drastically the number and rate of births. In 1966, births numbered about 22,000 per month. Shortly after the new law took effect, the number rose to over 60,000 per month in July and August 1967. By August the birth rate reached 38.9%.

3044 Randal, J. "Romanians Upset by Abortion Ban," New York Times, November 13, 1967.

In an attempt to increase the birth rate of Romania, which had fallen from 35.1 per 1,000 in 1932 to 14.3 per 1,000 in 1965, the government reversed the liberal abortion policy and increased taxes and rent for childless and single persons. The results of the anti-abortion legislation were excessive demands on hospital maternity facilities and a sharp increase in the cost of illegal abortions.

3045 Romania. "Interruption of Pregnancy," Internat. Digest Health Legis. 18:822-37, 1967.

Laws of 29 September and 19 October 1966 prohibit abortion except in hardship cases (pregnancy a threat to the life or health of the woman; the woman is over 45 years of age or already has four or more children under her care; or pregnancy the result of rape or incest). But even in these cases, unless there is extreme medical emergency, the pregnancy can be terminated only in the first three months. The conditions for a therapeutic abortion are given in detail. The Penal Code is amended making punishable abortions performed contrary to the new law.

3046 Romania. [Laws Concerning the Protection of Marriage and the Family and the Interests of the Mother and the Child], Rev. Roumaine Sci. Socia. 11:138-ff., 1967.

Terms of Law No. 36, 1966 for the regulation of the interruption of pregnancy by decree No. 770 of the Grand National Assembly, September 29, 1966. Law No. 37, 1966 which provides for modification of the Penal Code by decree No. 771 adopted September 20, 1966 by the Grand National Assembly regarding conditions for the interruption of pregnancy.

3047 Romania. Laws, Statutes, etc., The Family Code in the Rumanian People's Republic. Bucharest: Foreign Lang. Publ. House, 1958.

Decree No. 4 of January 4, 1954, amended by decree No 4 of April 4, 1956.

3048 Vasiliu, T. "Considerath in Legatura cu Unele Masuri Legislative Menite sa Constibuie la Dezvoltarea si Consolidarea Familiei" [On Some Legal Provisions Destined to Contribute to the Development and Consolidation of the Family]. Just. N. 22(10):3-10, 1966.

To effectuate the constitutional principle of protecting marriage and the family and safeguarding mothers' and children's interests, a number of normative acts have recently been issued regarding: the mother's right to maternity leave; child allowance; medical aid; free tuition; state scholarships; protective measures for expectant and nursing mothers; state family allowance; etc. It is necessary to combat the lack of concern for the family which led to an increase in the number of divorces, the neglect of children's education, etc. Because the legal provisions operating with regard to these matters proved inconsistent with the country's economic and social development, Decree No. 779 of October 7, 1966 introduced important changes to Articles 1, 37, 38, 39, and 41 of the Family Code and Articles 612, 613, 615, 618 and 619 of the Code of Civil Procedure. Under these changes divorce will be given in "exception cases" only, and the seriousness of the divorce motives will be decided at the court's discretion. The divorce procedure has been modified to incorporate a constant effort on the part of the courts to achieve reconciliation of the spouses. New regulations have been introduced governing the right to maintenance of the divorced partner. These changes are examined, particular stress being placed on their social meaning and their important contribution to the consolidation of the family.

(Northern Europe)

GENERAL

General population policies

3049 Philip, D. "Scandinavian Social Policy," India Quart. 11: 137-58, April - June 1955.

Insurance, pensions, assistance and grants; family welfare; housing; and health.

Policies on fertility and family size

3050 Gille, Halvor, "Scandinavian Family Allowances," Eugenics Quart. 1(3):182-90, 1954.

The aim and outstanding features of Scandinavian family welfare policies are discussed and particular emphasis paid to family allowances and its effects upon fertility trends. Family allowances were introduced in Scandinavian countries during 1947-50. During the few years they have been in effect, the decline in marital fertility that started during the post-war period has continued. Whether the decline would have been greater without the new politics is not known. There has been a stable level of fertility in the young marriages in Sweden, but it is too soon to state the significance of this tendency. Although allowances may have had no effect on fertility, it may have had other demographic effects (on differential fertility and mortality). Future studies may reveal these other demographic effects as well as psychological effects on fertility and the family resulting from the family allowances program.

3051 Illiovici, Jean, L'Aide aux Familles en Scandinavie [Family Assistance in Scandinavia]. Collections Informations Sociales. Paris: Union Nationale des Caisses d'Allocations Familiales, 1953. 133 pp.

The measures studied include marriage loans, maternity aid and maternity allowances, family allowances, tax reductions for large families, and others.

3052 Linner, Birgitta, "Sexual Morality and Sexual Reality: The Scandinavian Approach," Amer. J. Orthopsychiat. 36(4):686-93, 1966.

The Scandinavian countries do not offer a unified pattern of norms and behavior; however, the degree of openness with which the issues are discussed is typical. An official attitude has been defined regarding sex education in public schools (including birth control), abortions being legal under certain conditions, and children born out of wedlock being regarded as "legitimate."

3053 Tietze, C. "Legal Abortion in Scandinavia," Quart. Rev. Surgery, Obstet. and Gynec. 16:227-30, October - December 1959.

DENMARK

General population policies

3054 Denmark. Ministeriet for Gronland, Betaenkning Afgivet af den af Gronlands Landsrad den 19 September, 1953 [Report Submitted by the Population Commission Appointed by the Parliament of Greenland, September 19, 1953]. Nedsatte Befolkningskommission. Beretninger vedrorende Gronland (Godthab), No. 6, 1957. 74 pp.

The main part of the report deals with: work plans of the commission; historical background; individual migration; legal bases, including regulations on public assistance for migration; loans and/or contributions to private housing construction in relation to consolidation endeavors; relation of migration to migration destination; future plans for consolidation; related investigations, bases for the commission's appraisal and remarks on the individual places; and resume. Appendix contains texts of reports from 15 communes.

3055 Doublet, Jacques, "Politique Sociale et Demographique au Danemark" [Social and Demographic Policy in Denmark], Population 1(3):489-500, July - September 1946.

3056 Gille, H. "Family Welfare Measures in Denmark," Popul. Stud. 6(2):172-210, November 1952.

A survey of recent developments in the population policy of Denmark. The topics covered include the attitude toward abortion; the provision of ante-natal, post-natal and child welfare services; housing policy; family allowance schemes; and a general summary of the attitude toward population policy.

3057 Mangin, Marie-Reine, "La Politique Neo-Malthusienne au Danemark" [Neo-Malthusian Policy in Denmark], Population 17(1):75-96, January - March 1962.

A study of experience relating to abortion, sterilization, and castration and covering legislation, statistics, and medical complications. Review of policy on sex education, contraceptive propaganda, and sale of products.

Policies on fertility and family size

3058 Bratholm, Anders, "Nye Lovregler om Abortus Provacatus" [New Legislation on Induced Abortion], Nordisk Tidsskrift for Kriminalvidenskab, No. 4, 1956, pp. 338-42.

3059 Christensen, Harold T. "Scandinavian and American Sex Norms: Some Comparisons with Sociological Implications," J. Soc. Issues 22(2):60-75, April 1966.

Both attitudinal and behavioral aspects of premarital sexual intimacy are compared cross-culturally, in order to test hypotheses regarding normative theory. The samples were from sexually permissive Denmark, and moderately and restrictive Midwestern States. The data were gathered by means of questionnaires administered to U.S. subjects, and record linkage involving cross-sections of the populations. Not only were the cultures found to vary on the permissiveness-restrictiveness continuum in the expected direction, but restrictiveness was demonstrated to be associated with greater negative consequences. These and other findings are interpreted as giving support to a theory of normative morality -- where decisions concerning "proper" behavior are arrived at by examining measurable cause-effect relationships, rather than relying upon transcendental assumptions or authoritative pronouncements.

3060 Christiansen, A. "Dansk Betoenkning om Svangerskabsafbrydelse."[Danish Report on Abortion], Barnavard och Ungdomsskydd No. 3, 1955, pp. 94-99.

Present legislation. Development since 1939. Recommendations of the commission of inquiry; governmental recommendations; statistics.

3061 Clemmesen, Carl, "Comment on State of Legal Abortion in Denmark," Amer. J. Psychiat. 112(8):662-63, February 1956.

Discussion of the legal basis and current practice of legal abortion in Denmark.

3062 Denmark. "Administering of Ergot and Ergometrine by Midwives," Internat. Digest Health Legis. 2:204, 1950-51.

Notice No. 62 of 28 February 1949 amending the Instructions of 9 March 1934, relating to all midwives authorized to practice, grants authorization to midwives to administer extract of ergot and to inject ergometrine in certain circumstances.

3063 Denmark. "Family Planning: Approval of and Trade in Oral Gestogens," Internat. Digest Health Legis. 18:583-87, 1967.

Applications for trade in hormone preparations intended for internal use for family planning purposes must be submitted to and approved by the National Health Service.

3064 Denmark. "Health Measures during Pregnancy and Provision of Advice on Family Planning," Internat. Digest Health Legis. 18:581-83, 1967.

Law of 8 June 1966 concerning health measures during pregnancy comprises a first examination carried out by the physician as soon as possible after the beginning of pregnancy; examinations carried out by the midwife in the 20th, 30th, 33rd, 37th and 39th weeks of pregnancy and, if necessary, during the 40th week; and by the physician in the 26th and

35th weeks of pregnancy. Also provides for postnatal examination of the woman and the giving of advice on contraception by the physician.

3065 Denmark. "Interruption of Pregnancy," _Internat. Digest Health Legis_. 8:377-81, 1957.

Law No. 177 of 23 June 1956 permits abortion if the pregnancy is a serious threat to the life, or to the physical or mental health of the woman; is due to rape; may result in a defective offspring; and is performed by a duly licensed physician in a hospital. An abortion for other reasons requires application to a maternity center and approval by a committee of two physicians and the matron of the center, as designated by Law No. 119 of 15 March 1939 and now amended.

3066 Denmark. Justitsministeriet, Kommissionen Angaende Aedring af Svangerskapslovgivningen, "Betaenkning Angaende Aendring af Svangerskapslovgivningen m.v. Afgivet af den af...den 9. Januar 1950 nedsatte Kommission" [Report Concerning Changes in Pregnancy Legislation Rendered by the Commission... Appointed on January 9, 1950]. Betaenkning No. 96/1954. Copenhagen: J.H. Schultz, 1954. 185 pp.

3067 Denmark. Laws, _Adgang til Sterilisation og Kastration; Lov. nr. 176 af 11. Maj. 1935_ [Provisions for Sterilization and Castration; Law No. 176 of May 11, 1935], With commentary and reference by E. Schibbye. Copenhagen, 1952. 102 pp.

3068 Denmark. Social Ministry, _Betaenkning om Familiepolitik. Afg. af det af Socialministeren Nedsat Udvalg_ [Report on Family Policy. Report of the Select Committee of the Social Ministry], Betaenkning 359. Copenhagen, 1964. 108 pp.

3069 Denmark. Socialpolitisk Forening, _Familienpolitik, Hvorfor? Hvordan?_ [Family Policy, Wherefore? How?] Socialpolitisk Forenings Smaskrifter, 32. Copenhagen: I Kommission Hos Det Danske Forlag, 1962. 62 pp.

3070 Denmark. "Sterilization and Castration," Internat. Digest Health Legis. 19:746-49, 1968.

Law No. 234 of 3 June 1967, concerns sterilization and castration. Sterilization is permissible when life or health of woman is endangered by pregnancy; where the legally appointed committee unanimously approves; and where the woman is over 18 years of age, cannot bring further pregnancies to term, or is unfit to give reasonable care to children, or lives in undesirable environmental conditions. Castration must be authorized by the Minister of Social Justice and is permissible for persons over 21 years of age whose sexual instincts make them liable to commit crimes, or cause severe mental suffering or social difficulties.

3071 Freudenthal, P. [Contraception, Abortion Mentality, Prevention Mentality], Ugeskr. Laeg. 127:62-ff., 1965.

The author, a physician, is pessimistic in regard to the current possibilities of increasing knowledge and use of contraception in Denmark through an intensified program of information, propaganda and services, or substituting abortion for contraception.

3072 Freundt, L. "Surveys in Induced and Spontaneous Abortions in the Copenhagen Area," Acta. Psychiat. Scand. 40 (Suppl. 180):235-ff., 1964; also in: Proceedings of the Fourth Conference of the Region for Europe, Near East and Africa of the IPPF. New York: Excerpta Medica Foundation, 1965.

A study of abortion in the Copenhagen area using a sample drawn from 304 women admitted to gynecological departments. 74 legal and 90 spontaneous abortions were used as controls with a group of 132 illegal and presumably illegal abortion cases. Women in the 15-19 year old bracket showed the highest incidence of abortion; 70% of these women had illegal abortions. In addition, single women had twice as many illegal abortions as did married women, and the somatic morbidity was lowest in those having illegal abortions. 89% of the women with illegal abortions had had applications for legal abortion rejected.

3073 Hartmann, G. Boliger og Bordeller, Oversigt over Prostitutionens Former og Tilholdssteder i Kobenhavn til Forskellige Tider [Dwellings and Brothels. A Survey of the Forms and Location of Prostitution in Copenhagen at Different Times]. Copenhagen: Rosenkilde & Bagger, 1949. 128 pp.

A brief historical survey of prostitution in Copenhagen, from the middle ages to the present day, largely based on police records and similar material. It describes changing public and official attitudes toward prostitution, the types and conditions of prostitution and its territorial distribution.

3074 Hoffmeyer, Henrik, "The Danish Mothers' Aid Centers," in: Fifth International Conference for Child Psychiatry. August 1962.

A description of the role and activities of Denmark's Mothers' Aid Centers, which provide financial aid for pregnant women and mothers of small children, adoption placement, assistance with legal abortion and sterilization, information on contraception, family counseling, and education programs for the public relating to pregnancy, motherhood and family life.

3075 Hoffmeyer, Henrik, "Medical Aspects of the Danish Legislation on Abortion," in: Smith, D.T., ed. Abortion and the Law. Cleveland: Western Reserve University Press, 1967.

The circumstances leading to legal abortion in Denmark are defined, as well as those conditions constituting a "grave danger to the woman's life or health." The author describes a survey of women who were refused or granted abortions; five years later 80% indicated that they were satisfied with the course of events.

3076 Hoffmeyer, Henrik, "The Mother and the Family," WHO Seminar on Mental Health and the Family, Athens, April 10-18, 1962.

The author describes past attempts to uplift the mother's position in society, with specific reference to Denmark's Mothers' Aid Centers. Danish policy in general is also evaluated.

3077 Hoffmeyer, Henrik, "Psychological Aspects of Legal Abortion and Contraception," J. Sex Res., February 1968, pp. 7-15.

A summary is made of the incidence of abortions in a number of countries around the world in an attempt to place the problem of legalized abortion within the context of other methods of birth control. The original background of the Danish experience and legislation is described in detail. The Danish experiences show that birth control takes place where the motivation for it exists, and when it does, births will be limited by whatever method is at hand and is acceptable to the group in question. The most important class of women applying for legal abortion consists of married mothers who are living under some form of stress because of poor housing conditions, economic difficulties, marital problems, or ill, defective or difficult children. There are also many applicants whose material situation is quite good. It is concluded that applicants for abortion come because of a conflict between their own interests and those of the child. Included is a figure graph showing the competition between parents and their children with regard to standard of living.

3078 Hoffmeyer, Henrik, [The Situation of Abortion in Denmark], in: Mehlan, K.H., ed. Internationale Abortsituation, Abortbekampfung, Antikonzeption. Leipzig: George Thieme, 1961.

The development of Denmark's legislation on abortion and the present law and its application are described in a 1960 conference report. Medical indications, which include consideration of social factors, are responsible for 80% of the legal abortions, eugenic indications 10%, and juridicial and defect indications a few percent each. The remaining abortions are permitted on mixed indications. In 1955, the legal abortion rate reached a peak, with 70 per 1000 live births, and then decreased in 1958 to 52 per 1000. The number of illegal abortions performed each year has been estimated at 15,000-20,000. Although the number of abortions is surprisingly high for a welfare state like Denmark, it is possible that improved socio-economic conditions have caused a reduction of both legal and illegal abortions during the last years. Plans and already instituted programs to minimize the abortion rate even further are discussed, with references to social support, contraceptive services and sex education.

3079 Hoffmeyer, Henrik, _et al_. "Abortion, Sterilization and Contraception," _J. Sex Res_. 3(1):1-24, February 1967.

The Danish abortion legislation is described, and placed in its historical context. The principle is that termination of pregnancy should only be legal if warranted by special circumstances: (1) according to a medical, including socio-medical, indication where all circumstances of the case, with reference to the conditions under which the female lives, shall be taken under consideration; (2) according to the ethical indication -- cases where the impregnation is a criminal act, e.g., due to intercourse with a girl under 15 years of age; (3) according to the eugenic indication; and (4) in special cases where the female is suffering from serious physical or psychic defects. The philosophy underlying this legislation is that it is the responsibility of the community to help females with unwanted pregnancies. From this point of view, such women should be brought in contact with agencies having the facilities to help and support them. In Denmark the Mothers' Aid Centers, state agencies, staffed with social workers and members of the legal and medical professions, are charged with this task. To these Centers, which are in contact with a considerable number of all pregnant females and families with young children, a female, wishing an abortion, shall apply as a general rule, and special socio-medical boards connected to the Centers make the final decision. Statistical information about the number of legal abortions and the practice of the Mothers' Aid Centers is given, and there is an attempt to estimate the number of illegal abortions. The advice on contraception, offered by the Mothers' Aid Centers to all females, is briefly described, and also legislation on sterilization, especially the way in which the Mothers' Aid Centers administer this legislation. A new Sterilization Bill is sketched.

3080 Hoffmeyer, Henrik,and Norgaard, M. [Incidence of Conception and the Course of Pregnancy. Investigations and Calculations on the Incidence of Illegal Abortions since 1940], _Ugesk. Laeg_. 126:355-ff., 1964.

Data from available sources indicate that 6-10% of all pregnancies end in spontaneous abortion. Using figures from their own and similar investigations on women whose applications for abortion have been denied, the authors estimate the incidence of hospitalization for spontaneous or criminal abortion to be between 50 and 70%. A number of sources were employed to calculate the extreme maximal and minimal values for the incidence of criminal abortion, with the maximal values the most probable if time and geographical variations are stressed. On this basis, the criminal abortion to births percentage was estimated at 3 to 5 per 10 for Copenhagen and in rural areas 1 to 3 per 10. The period 1949-61 showed a decrease of 10-14% in the incidence, mostly in the Copenhagen area. There was a sharp increase during the war which was earlier and more marked than the increase in fertility toward the war's end. The popularity of abortion over contraception is felt to account for the discrepancy between conceptions and births during the war and the 1950's.

3081 Ingerslev, M. "Danish Abortion Laws," _Med. Sci. Law_ 7:77, April 1967.

3082 Jacobsen, K. [The Alcohol Problem and Legal Abortion], _Ugeskr. Laeg._ 126:409-ff., 1964.

936 applications for legal abortion were reviewed, and the author found that approximately 10% of the women included alcoholism of the father as a major reason for wanting an abortion. 50% of the women were self-supporting, or supporting their families, 33% listed housing conditions as miserable, and half mentioned serious economic problems. Of those women listing alcoholism of the father, half reported the alcoholism as having lasted more than five years. Both spouses were often found to be deviant personality types.

3083 Jensen, M.L. "Om Svangerskabsafbrydelse og Svangerskabslovgivning" [Pregnancy Interruption and Legislation], _Ugeskr. Laeg._ 117(3):80-83, January 20, 1955.

3084 Kemp, Tage, "Genetic-Hygienic Experiences in Denmark in Recent Years," _Eugenics Rev._ 49(1):11-18, April 1957.

Summary of experience with sterilization and abortion, 1930-1954, and of genetic-hygienic counseling, 1939-1954. Danish legislation authorized sterilization in 1929 and induced abortion in 1939, on eugenic grounds.

3085 Landergreen, M. [Actual Medical Aspects on the Abortion Problem and Pregnancy Legislation], Ugeskr. Laeg. 129: 434-ff., 1967.

A proposal to liberalize extensively Denmark's abortion law is evaluated by a Danish physician. Discussion is based on an analysis of the development and consequences of the present law and procedures. Because of the medical and other damaging effects involved, abortion on demand is strongly opposed, but the author approves of social indications used before the 12th week of pregnancy for certain groups of women, especially those younger than 18 or older than 40 and those still in school.

3086 Landgreen, A.M. "Sterilisation af Kvinder og Sterilisations Lovgivning" [Sterilization of Women and Sterilization Laws], Bibliotek for Laeger 156:145-84, 1964.

3087 LeMaire, L. "Danish Experiences Regarding the Castration of Sexual Offenders," J. Crim. Law 47:294-ff., September - October 1956.

Since legal castration is considered as particularly expedient in the Scandinavian countries, the author describes Denmark's experiences with its therapeutic castration law, the ultimate of which is solely criminal therapy and not deterrence or punishment. It is felt that although the idea of legal castration was first advanced in the U.S., it is now considered without confidence and sympathy in that country. The provisions of the Danish law are outlined and the author then comments generally in regard to the effects of the operation. A closer analysis of the Danish castration practice, with attention given to the characteristics of sexual offenders (age groups, marital status, mental conditions, motives, previous punishment, etc.) is presented for the period June 1929 to June 1939. The resocializing effect of castration appears to be of a secondary character inasmuch as it is attained after the operation by the liberation from the criminal sexual tendencies and fear and uncertainty thereby caused. In other words, castration can remove a hitherto existing hindrance to social adaptation and thereby eliminate a criminogenic factor, the effect of which need not have been limited to sexual matters. The author concludes that while doubt can arise as to how castration can best accommodate itself with the other reaction remedies available against criminals, there can be no doubt regarding the justification of the operation from the experience gained in Denmark.

3088 Louw, A. [The Motives for Applying for Legal Abortion. A Social Psychiatric Investigation of 400 Women Who Applied for Legal Abortion], Ugeskr. Laeg. 126:412-ff., 1964.

The author analyzed 441 reasons given for wanting abortion expressed in 1959 by 400 women applying for legal abortions in Arhus. Chronic stress caused by sickness and socio-economic conditions was listed by 67%. Fear of the future and the sudden alteration in their situation was listed by most of the women under 20 years (14%) and by unmarried women (25%). The author feels that in an affluent society social pressures cause women to seek abortions and that these types of pressure must be minimized through rational and active family policy and an effective family planning program.

3089 [On Pensions for Spouses and Equality of Male and Female Members under the Pension Fund], Ugeskr. Laeg. 130:1930-32, November 7, 1968.

3090 Ostergaard, E., *et al.* [Legal Induced Abortion in Denmark], Ugeskr. Laeg. 129:1337-ff., 1967.

A review of literature in Denmark over the past 25 years relating to legal abortion. Since definitions have differed as to what constitutes an abortion complication, comparisons of the results of varying investigations are difficult; the complication rate has been reported to be as high as 54%. Mortality for the period 1932-1957 was 18 per 1,000 and for the period 1961-1965 0.4 per 1,000. The primary method used during the first 12 weeks of pregnancy was D. & C.; after the 12th week a wide variety of methods was used, none of which is considered to be ideal. As the pregnancy progresses, there is an increase in the rate of complications.

3091 Skalts, V. "Die Gesetzliche Kastration; 10. Jahrige Erfahrungen mit Gesetzlicher Kastration in Danemark" [Ten Year Experience with Sterilization in Denmark], _Veroffentlichungen aus dem Gebiete des Volksgesundheitsdienstes_ 54:501-600, 1940.

3092 Skalts, V. "Svangerskabslov og Modrehjaelpslov" [The Law Concerning Pregnant Women and Maternal Aid in Denmark], _Soc. Tidsskrift_, February 1957, pp. 1-25.

A detailed presentation of legislation concerning the problems of maternal aid before and after childbirth and the question of abortion. Review of the development of the legislation. Cases in which abortion is authorized.

3093 Skalts, V., _et al_. [Mothers' Aid in Denmark]. Copenhagen: Det Dansk Selskab, 1965.

A pamphlet describing the functions and services of Denmark's Mothers' Aid Centers. These Centers provide financial aid and counseling for single and married pregnant women and educational programs in sex and family planning, and administer the country's systems of adoption and abortion. Except for those cases where the mother's life is endangered, when legal abortions can be performed with certification by a senior hospital official, all women wanting abortions must apply to Mothers' Aid Centers. A joint council composed of a social worker, a psychiatrist and a gynecologist attached to each Center makes the decision on each abortion request. Approximately 4,000 abortions are performed legally each year, with 85% approved by the Mothers' Aid joint councils and 15% approved by senior hospital physicians.

3094 Skalts, V., and Norgaard, M. "Abortion Legislation in Denmark," in: Smith, D.I., ed. _Abortion and the Law_. Cleveland: Western Reserve University Press, 1967.

Description of Danish laws on legal and criminal abortion and of the ways in which these laws are interpreted and administered. Denmark's Mothers' Aid Centers, which provide medical, psychiatric and social services for women wanting an abortion, are also discussed. The text of the 1956 Pregnancy Act is included in an appendix.

3095 [Still Too Many Unwanted Pregnancies. A Report from the Mothers' Aid Organization and the Danish Medical Association], Ugeskr. Laeg. 126:1728-ff., 1964.

There has been an increase in the number of extramarital births in Denmark, particularly in young age groups (births to women under 18 number 569 in 1940 and 1,170 in 1962), and an increase in the number of marital births to young teenagers (birth to married women aged 16-17 numbered 238 in 1940 and 786 in 1962). In addition to these increases, the legal and illegal abortion rates have increased, with dangers to maternal health and an unnecessary extra burden on already insufficient hospital resources. The author stresses the need for knowledge and use of contraception in the country, and the importance of an intensified action program dealing with contraceptive problems. Information on existing possibilities for advice on contraception is given, and it is concluded that free contraceptive consultation must be made available for all citizens.

FINLAND

General population policies

3096 Kuusi, Pekka, Social Policies for the Sixties : A Plan for Finland. Translated from the Finnish by Jaakko Railo. Helsinki: Finnish Social Policy Association, 1964. 295 pp.

The author considers the aims of public policy in an economy which is now experiencing a rapid rise in national income and a transition from the dominance of agriculture to expanding industrialization. The place and functions of social policy, how consumption capacity has developed among the non-active population, the need for improvement in the country's social security system, and a detailed inventory of the achievements and shortcomings of Finland's social policy are examined.

3097 Mannio, Niilo A. "Recent Social Developments in Finland," Internat. Labour Rev. 57(1-2):1-14, January - February 1948.

An account of social legislation passed in Finland since the war and its historical background. Includes a summary of rural-urban movements and official population and family policies.

3098 Ministry of Social Affairs, Social Legislation and Work in Finland. Helsinki, 1953. 189 pp.

Chapter 10, "The Population Problem," discusses population policy. It is seen that attempts have been made to influence the growth of population both by measures directly aiming at a rise in the birth rate, and by measures for the benefit in one way or another of children, mothers, and families, which indirectly serve the ends of population policy. Discriminations in tax assessments, housing and colonization policy, the regulation of labor contracts have been used to encourage the growth of families and reduce the advantages attached to the unmarried state and childlessness.

3099 Perdon, Armand,and Tabah, Leon, "La Politique Sociale et Demographique en Finlande" [Social and Demographic Policy in Finland], Population 2(1):105-15, January - March 1947.

Trends in urbanization, nuptiality, mortality and fertility; measures to prevent the decline in population, such as the control of alcoholism, abortion and tuberculosis; family allowances, and a system of differential taxes.

3100 Strommer, Aarno, "Recent Demographic Developments and Population Policies in Finland," Popul. Index 22:3-19, 1956.

Projections of demographic development in Finland stimulated, after 1934, an interest in population policy. Initially, there was a reform in state taxation, the passing of the Maternity Allowance Act, and the appointment of a Population Committee. Subsequently, the Population League, which enjoys semi-official status in the Ministry of Social Affairs, was formed and several other legislative measures were passed: marriage loans, child and family allowances, aids in home management, and birth control techniques. Today, social expenditures comprise 10.3% of the national income of Finland, as compared with 9.5% in Sweden.

Policies on fertility and family size

3101 Aehte, K.A. "Mielisairaus ja Avioliittolaki" [Mental Illness and Marriage Laws], Suomen Laakarilehti 21:1210-12, May 10, 1966.

3102 Allardt, Erik, Miljobetingade Differenser i Skilsmassofrekvensen, Bidrag till Kannedom of Finlands Nature och Folk, Utgifna af Finska Vetenskapssocieteten. Helsingfors, 1953.

An English summary is found in the paper, "The Influence of Different Systems of Social Norms on Divorce Rates in Finland," MFL 17:325-31, November 1955. Studies how different norms and social and cultural conditions influence divorce rates in Finland. Based on secondary sources and opinion polls.

3103 Chambliss, Rollin, "Contributions of the Vital Statistics of Finland to the Study of Factors that Induce Marriage," Amer. Sociol. Rev. 22(1):38-48, February 1957.

The vital statistics of Finland are remarkably accurate and yield important information concerning the factors that induce marriage. With regard to age at first marriage from 1851 to 1953 there is found: (1) a pronounced drop in married age in the 1901-1910 decade; and (2) a continued drop since 1945, reaching an unprecedented young age (men, 24.9; women, 23.2). Explanation for the phenomena are discussed in terms of the heavy emigration of 1901-1910, World War II and population losses, borrowing from future marriage rate, societal opposition to youthful marriages, and social legislation such as loans to establish homes, maternity grants, and state payments for all children.

3104 Finland. "Castration," Internat. Digest Health Legis. 1: 160-63, 1949-50; 2:564-67, 1950-51; 3:160-63, 1951-52.

Decree No. 233 of 5 May 1950, defines the conditions under which the Medical Board is to authorize the operation.

Act No. 84 of 17 February 1950, authorized castration for persons whose sexual impulses are such a danger to others that they require psychiatric hospitalization or who fear that their sexual impulses might lead to crime or mental illness. In the latter instance, the person must request castration, whereas in the former castration does not require personal consent.

3105 Finland. "Interruption of Pregnancy," Internat. Digest Health Legis. 1:158-60, 1949-50; 2:559-64, 1950-51; 3:158-60, 1951-52.

Act No. 82 of 17 February 1950, permits abortion at the request of the woman when continuation of the pregnancy constitutes a serious threat to the physical or mental health of the woman or when pregnancy is due to a criminal act. Interruption of pregnancy is permitted without the woman's consent only in cases of severe mental disorder. Abortions may not be performed after the 4th month except when the woman has not reached the age of 16 before pregnancy or when there are other special circumstances. Decree No. 232 of 5 May 1950, emphasizes the administrative arrangement, particularly the work of the Medical Board and record keeping by the physician.

3106 Finland. "Sterilization," Internat. Digest Health Legis. 1:163-64, 1949-50; 2:562-64, 1950-51.

Act No. 83 of 17 February 1950, and Decree No. 234 of 5 May 1950, provide for sterilization with and without consent of the patient. Consent is not required where there is mental disease or deficiency which would likely appear in the descendants or deprive them of the necessary parental care. Sterilization may be performed at the request of the patient where pregnancy endangers the life or health of the woman, where the mother is likely to transmit mental disease or other grave defect to the descendants, or where the children would be deprived of proper care because of the antisocial life of the parents, their confirmed use of alcohol or narcotics, or their mental incapacity.

3107 Haavio-Mannila, Elina, "Local Homogamy in Finland," Acta Sociol. 8(1-2):155-62, 1964.

Mate selection within the same area was characteristic of old Finnish society, where, in the 19th century, about 80% of marriages were between members of the same rural commune. The percentage of geographically homogamous marriages is declining. This is indicated by data from Finland's Central Statistical Office for the years 1951-1961. In 1961, 64% of marriages were within the same commune. Intermarriages between communes were most frequent in southern and western Finland, in the industrialized, densely populated and economically developed areas, and in the upper social classes. Local homogamy is frequent when spouses belong to different language groups or social classes, i.e., there is status discrepancy. Results are explained in terms of C. Boalt's summation theory: the main principle in mate selection is that the result is equality of the partners.

3108 Hartman, Tor, "Nuptiality and Social Structure," Transact. Westermarck Society 4(2):31-73, 1958-59.

An extensive study of marriage behavior as influenced by social norms, geographic, economic and demographic conditions. (1) The forms of endogamy in Finland are studied through mathematical formulas and on the basis of Finnish statistics. (2) Correlation coefficients on marriage frequency as influenced by contact frequency, sex ratio and economic background are computed for towns, market towns and rural communities. (3) Marriage frequency by age is calculated. (4) An interpretation of the development of marriage frequency from 1880 to 1954 is presented, taking into account the effect of war and changes in the economical standard, as well as changes in the general level of marriage frequency. There is evidence of a very marked village endogamy in the old peasant society of Finland. Through internal migration, a growing percentage of the population came to live in places other than its birth place. As long as the emigrants maintained their village endogamy, the marriage frequency decreased. From 1930 to 1950, the marriage frequency for all single males in towns had increased by 95%, that of rural districts by 50%. The high level of marriage frequency maintained in the beginning of the 1950's is seen as the result of an evolution in process for the last 25 or 30 years. It is suggested that the high marriage frequency is likely to continue for a relatively long period, unless checked by unpredictable changes in the premises of these calculations.

3109 Ingman, O. [On the Influence of Alcohol Abuse of the Husband on the Indications for Abortion], Ann. Chir. Gynaec. Fenn. 55:301-ff., 1966.

1,965 women who applied to the social counseling agency of Helsinki's Association for Population and Family Welfare for a legal abortion were studied to determine the frequency and degree of alcohol abuse of the male partner. The agency granted 965 abortions, after a careful examination of each woman's social background. Psychosomatic exhaustion of the woman caused by her partner's alcoholism was the major indication for abortion. The author stresses the need for preventative measures to limit the number of legal abortions caused by alcoholism of the male.

3110 International Labour Office, "Government Declaration on Social Policy in Finland," Internat. Labour Rev. 44(1): 62-64, July 1941.

A conference held by employees and workers, convened by the Minister of Social Affairs on February 20, 1941, recommended a system of family allowances. (See Finland's Forfattningssamling, 1940, No. 382). The report of the Committee on Population Policy on this subject is also summarized.

3111 Kaprio, Leo,and Rouhunkoski, Mauvi, "On the Marriage Guidance Clinics in Finland," Reprint: Ann. Chir. Gynaec. Fenn. 38, Suppl. 3, 1949. 11 pp.

3112 Katila, O. [On the Finnish Abortion Law and Opinions Regarding the Law of Finnish Mothers], Z. Praeventivmed. 8:206-ff., 1963.

The use of social indications only for abortion is not permitted in Finland, but females below the age of 16 can have their pregnancies interrupted. Interviews with 100 women who had a child at a mature age and with 100 women who had a child before they were 17 revealed that 61 in the first group and 77 in the second considered social indications alone as appropriate justification for abortion, 25 in the first group and 19 in the second viewed abortion as an acceptable method of birth control and 90 in the first group and 97 in the second felt that the age of 16 is adequate or too low as a limit on abortion.

3113 Katila, O.,and Achte, K. [Interruption of Pregnancy and the Psychiatric Indication in Finland], Z. Praeventivmed. 9:167-ff., 1964.

Although the use of social grounds for abortion are not permitted to be used alone according to Finnish law, many psychiatrists write medical certificates in such cases. Finland's abortion rate has increased in recent years to 75 per 1000 births for 1960, and to 230 in Helsinki. A psychiatrist's certificate was used in approximately 60% of the cases. The situation in other countries is described, and the authors criticize the Finnish law and its interpretation in recommending a centralized procedure to make legal application more uniform.

3114 Kauppila, O., et al. [The Effect of the Abortion Act of 1950 on Abortions and Legal Interruptions of Pregnancy in the City of Tampere], Duodecim 78:946-53, 1962.

This is a study of the abortion situation in Tampere over two three-year periods, 1947-1949 and 1957-1959, to identify the effects of the law. In the earlier period, 82% of all pregnancies terminated in birth, 16% in some type of abortion, and 1.5% in legal abortion. In the second period, 83% of all pregnancies terminated in birth, 14% in some type of abortion, and 2.9% in legal abortion. The author notes that although the general abortion rate is higher in Tampere than in other Finnish cities, the legal abortion rate is much lower. Unmarried women composed 16% of the women receiving legal abortions in the first period, and 20% in the second period. The incidence of general abortions increased in the lowest social group (group IV), but fell sharply in group III in which the incidence of legal abortions showed the maximum increase.

3115 Kettunen, I. [The Question of Interruption of Pregnancy], Duodecim 80:581-ff., 1964.

The abortion rate per 1000 births was 75 in 1960 and 68 in 1963, representing increases from 32 in 1951 and 46 in 1956. 60% of the legal abortions performed in 1962 involved psychiatric indications, with the most common diagnosis being "reactio neurotico-depressive." Only a very small number of the cases involved psychosis. The author questions the use of some psychiatric indications as consituting "serious illness."

3116 Lindgren, Karl, "Nakokohtia Lapsilisan Porrastamisesta" [On the Differentiation of Family Allowance], Sosiologia 1:19-24, 1964.

If the [state] family allowance is uniform for each dependent child, it will cover a gradually decreasing proportion of the total expenditure on children. This is due to the fact that the expenditure on children rises not only with the number of children but also with their age. Even if the rate is increased progressively for each additional child, the result is generally the same. As long as additional children are born, the aggregate expenditure on children could remain at about the same size, if the progression rate is high enough. In this respect the interpregnancy interval plays a decisive role. As soon as the family stops having children the expenditure grows faster than the social contribution to the childrens' expenditure, because the consumption of the growing children increases but the sum of family allowances remains constant. If a given proportion of the social contribution to the expenditure on children remains unchanged for as long as the upkeep of the children is in the hands of the parents, then it would be more purposive to increase the family allowance in relation to the age of the child and not to the number of children in the family.

3117 Nieminen, Armas, "Esiaviol-Listen Raskauksien Yleisyydesta Suomessa" [Premarital Pregnancy in Finland], Sosiologia 1: 14-18, 1964. Also in: Acta Sociol. 7(4):225-28, 1963.

The distribution of premarital pregnancy in Finland is studied for the years 1939-1961. Relevant vital statistics have only been available in Finland since 1939. Premarital pregnancy is defined according to the birth of a child to a woman less than 8 months after marriage. The number of premarital pregnancies in a given year is compared with the average number of marriages for that year and the previous year. The lowest frequencies of premarital pregnancy occurred during the war years (only 19% in 1942). The frequency increased after the war up until 1952, after which time it remained stable at the 36% level. In the 1940's premarital pregnancies were more common in the rural regions than in the cities, but no great rural/urban differences are evident during the last years of the period studied. In the country as well as in the city, in about every third marriage the bride is pregnant at the time of the marriage. Premarital pregnancy is most common among wives under 25 years of age; during the last years under study about 40% of these wives were pregnant at the time of marriage, while among those wives between 40-44 years of age the corresponding occurrence was about 10%. Comparisons on the basis of seven rather than eight months after marriage change the picture very little. Illegitimate births are on the decline in Finland, e.g., from 8.4% in 1921-30 to 4.3% in 1951-60. The data are reviewed in the light of attitudes toward premarital cohabitation in Finnish peasant communities before industrialization. Engagement was often regarded as more important than a church wedding; therefore cohabitation would often begin before the wedding. The important social norm was that, whenever possible, the future parents should get married. There is also some evidence that "trial" marriages, i.e., the wedding took place only after fertility was assured (fertility being an important economic factor) or when it became certain that couples were sexually compatible. The patterns of more recent time reflect the attitudes toward and advances in birth control methods.

3118 Nieminen, Armas, Taistelu Sukupuolimorallista [The Battle Over Sexual Morality, Problems of Marriage and Sex in Finland, from Approximately 1860-1920]. Helsinki: Werner Soderstrom Oy., 1951.

Studies the development of the attitudes toward premarital and extra-marital relations in Finland. Based on literature, legislation, ethnography, folklore, and criminal statistics.

3119 Olki, M. [The Situation of Abortion in Finland], in :Mehlan, K.H., ed. Internationale Abortsituation, Abortbekampfung, Antikonzeption. Leipzig: Georg Thieme, 1961.

A 1960 conference report on the abortion situation in Finland. The country liberalized its abortion laws in 1950 because of the frequency and the number of complications of illegal abortion. Three years before this change (1947), 50-70% of the estimated 20,000 abortions performed were thought to be criminal, there were 139 deaths from abortion (1.9%), and the only legal justification was that of saving the mother's life. There are three major indications under the new law: medical, with consideration of difficult living conditions; humanitarian and ethical; and eugenic. Two specially authorized physicians make the decision on each case, unless mainly social indications are being used or there is an appeal, when the National Board of Health decides. In addition to legislation, prevention of unwanted pregnancies has been promoted by state and private programs in contraception, sex education and family counseling; the important role played by the Finnish Family Association in this work is stressed. The rate of legal abortion increased, during the years 1951-58, from 31.3 to 60.0 per 1000 births; the mortality rate is low, with 18 deaths for the period 1950-57 (6.6 per 1000 abortions). During 1950-51, the major indication (about 50%) was somatic illness, with mental illness or weakness constituting 33% of the indications used; there was an opposite distribution for 1953-57. The rate of legal abortion varies greatly among the different regions of the country; the industrialized province of the capital has a much higher rate (more than one abortion per 9 pregnancies) than the rural north (one abortion per 62 pregnancies).

3120 Olki, M.,and Krokfors, E. "Erfahrungen uber Aborte an der Universitatsfrauenklinik zu Helsinki im Hahre 1959" [Results about Abortion in the Helsinki University Women's Clinic for the Year 1959], <u>Gynaecologia</u> 154(1):54-61, 1962.

Report on all cases of abortion treated during the year 1959 at the I and II Gynaecological Clinic of the Central Hospital of the University of Helsinki, totaling 1,891 cases,all confirmed by pathologic-anatomical diagnosis. The highest frequency of abortions is found in the age group of 25-29 years, but even the age group of 20-24 has a high frequency. The most serious cases are also found in the first group. The author concludes that criminal abortions are more common in younger than in older women and that complete abortions increase with age.

3121 Rauramo, L.,and Gronroos, M. [The Extent to which Women Requesting Therapeutic Abortion Actually Had Deliveries after a Negative Decision by the Social Advice Centre], Ann. Chir. Gynaec. Fenn. 50:246-ff., 1961.

Women whose request for abortion was refused by the Turku Social Advice Center during the years 1952-58 were studied in regard to the outcome of their pregnancies. Official records were used, and pregnancy outcome was determined in 856 cases, with no obtainable information in 32 cases. While 81% of women under 35 gave birth to the child, 66% of women over 35 completed the pregnancy. Parity did not appear to influence whether or not the pregnancy was carried to delivery, since the Centre has tried to approve requests from mothers with several children. 15% of the applications made by unmarried women were approved, but unmarried women completed their pregnancies as often as married women. Reactions causing the request for interruption at the beginning of the pregnancy were found to be of short duration, and such factors as family income, means or debts had no definite influence on the pregnancy's later history.

3122 Rauramo, L.,and Gronroos, M. [Social Structure of Case Material Seen at Social Consulting Bureaus], Duodecim 76: 190-ff., 1960.

A report on 1,525 abortion applicants at the Finnish Population Association's counseling bureau. 86% were married, 10% unmarried and 4% widowed or divorced. 74% had no vocational training and 47% had spouses who were unskilled workers. Only 2% had higher education, and 36% reported an unhappy childhood. 17% had experienced a previous spontaneous abortion, 62 women had already had a legal abortion, 58% used contraceptives on a regular or intermittent basis, and over 50% of those who had not used contraceptives felt that it is the husband's responsibility to prevent pregnancy. A great number of the applicants stressed their economic problems, such as the high cost of housing for larger families.

3123 Rauramo, L.,and Gronroos, M. [Subjective and Objective Motivation for Legal Abortion at a Social Advice Centre], Ann. Chir. Gynaec. Fenn. 49:1-ff., 1960.

A study of 1,525 abortion applicants at Finland's Turku Social Advice Centre for the period 1952-58. The Centre approved 568 applications and rejected 957. Higher parity was related to approval and accompanying sterilization. Rejections were more frequent for single, divorced, widowed, Para I and younger women, as well as in cases of more advanced pregnancies. There were 407 purely medical indications and 509 socio-medical indications among the approved cases. The authors also classified the subjective motivations for all of the applications: 889 reasons were linked to the man involved, 1,574 reasons were linked chiefly to the woman herself, and 953 involved both.

3124 Rauramo, L.,and Vataja, U. "Laillisista Raskaudenkeskeyttamisista Ennen Yuonna 1950 Annettua Lakia ja Sen Jalkeen" [Lawful Abortions Performed Before and After the Act Enforced in 1950], Duodecim 71(1-2):248-60, 1955.

3125 Strommer, Aarno, "Kirjallisutta Suomalaisen Vaestontut Kimuksen Alalta Vuosina 1953-1959" [Literature on Finnish Population Research in 1953-1959], pp. 166-87, Chpt. in: Eripsinos Vaestontutkimksen Vuosikirhasta [Yearbook of Population Research in Finland], Helsinki: Population Research Institute, 1960

A 328-item bibliography of research by individual Finnish scholars and institutions classified under headings A to R. Section M is entitled, Policies in Relation to Family Development (Fertility) and Maintenance (Migration).

3126 Sukselainen, V.J. Perhesuhteet Tulo-Jaomaisuusverotuksessa [Family Considerations in Income and Property Taxation]. Vaestopoliittisen Tutkimuslaitoksen Julkaisuja, Sarja A:1 [Population Policy Research Institute, Publications, Series A:1]. Helsinki, 1946. 222 pp.

A study of the principles of tax legislation with particular reference to the experience of Finland. The discussion emphasizes the problem of applying a progressive scale of taxation and the advantages of using the individual rather than the family group as the basis of assessment in a progressive scale of taxation. Finally, the use of taxation as a means of carrying population policy is considered.

3127 Sukselainen, V.J. [The Leveling of the Cost of Parenthood], Population Policy Research Institute, Publications, Series A:4. Helsinki: Werner Soderstrom Osakeyhtio, 1950. 210 pp.

A detailed analysis of family allowances and discussion of various methods and purposes. The final chapter considers the policy from the standpoint of the Finnish national economy.

3128 Turunen, Aarno, "Bevolkerungspolitische Cesichtspunkte in der Geburtslehre-Gorsshung" [Viewpoints of Population Policy in Obstetrical Research], Periodical Finnish Med. Society, 1942, pp. 214-26.

3129 Vaestopoliittisen Tutkimuslaitoksen Julkaisuja [Population Policy Research Institute], Vaestonkehityksen ja Avioliiton Ongelmia [Problems of Population Development and Marriage]. Helsinki: Population League Yearbook, III, 1951. 225 pp.

Contents include: Sukselainen, V.J., "Can the Leveling of Family Expenses be Fitted in Within the Sphere of Social Welfare?"; Niemineva, Kalevi, "The Development of Marriage Guidance Clinics in Finland"; Kaprio, Leo A. and Niemineva, Kalevi, "On the Background of the Abortion Problem"; Valvanne, Leena, "On the Social and Health Background of Birth Control in Finland"; and Nykanen, Helmi, "Finnish Literature on the Population Problem, Family and Marriage, 1948-1949".

3130 Visuri, Elina, "Raskauden Ja Synnytyksen Aiheuttamat Kustannukset" [The Cost of Pregnancy and Childbirth in Finland], pp. 101-20, Chpt. in: Eripainos Vaestontutkimuksen Vuosikirjasta [Yearbook of Population Research in Finland]. Helsinki: Population Research Institute, 1960.

The social legislation of Finland provides for support to expectant mothers in the form of both material and medical help. Maternity welfare centers have been set up, each with an MD and a trained midwife, to be consulted by any mother residing in the country. The aid of the maternity welfare centers, given without cost, has, in recent years, reached as many as 95% of all mothers. Owing to the fact that subsidies are paid to hospitals by the community, it has been possible to set the cost of deliveries affected in them fairly low. A maternity allowance, usually in the form of a parcel containing a basic supply of baby clothing, or alternatively as an equivalent sum of money ($14), is given to every mother who has consulted an MD or a maternity welfare center before the fifth month of her pregnancy. For families with several children there is a body of trained communal housekeepers to help them during the mother's absence. Those of small means are to receive this help free of cost. In the new health insurance plan, submitted recently to the Council of State, a compensation for the cost of childbirth is included as well as one for earnings lost during the necessary maternity leave. This will probably be granted for six weeks before and six weeks after childbirth. The Finnish Population and Family Welfare League studied the question of the cost of childbirth by sending a questionnaire in 1959 to about 16,000 mothers of newborn children, covering nearly all parts of the country. From the results it was evident that the cost of pregnancy and childbirth for those families where the newborn child was the first was higher than that borne by families where it was a subsequent one. The expenses for rural mothers were smaller than those for urban mothers. There were distinct divergences between the mothers in the amounts of money they spent on medicines, places of delivery (hospital or home) and in the extent to which they received domestic help. Likewise, in the amounts of money spent on the child's equipment there appeared variations traceable to differences in standard of living.

IRELAND

General population policies

3131 Commission on Emigration and Other Population Problems, *Report, 1948-1954*. Dublin: Stationery Office, 1955. xii, 418 pp.

Majority report contains chapters on the following topics: population structure and trend; economic background; marriages and conjugal status; births, fertility and family size; deaths; emigration, immigration and internal migration; population and economic and social development; and population policy. It concludes with recommendations and suggestions. Minority reports include those of Most Rev. Dr. C. Lucey and Mr. James Meenan.

3132 Kaim-Caudle, P.R. Social Policy in the Irish Republic. Library of Social Policy and Administration. London: Routledge and Kegan Paul, 1967. 120 pp.

This book examines the health services, social insurance, social assistance, family allowances and housing. Discussion of the social services is introduced by an outline of the environment in which social policy operates -- the political system, social implications of the demographic characteristics and the country's economy.

Policies on fertility and family size

3133 Davitt, Cahir, "Some Aspects of the Constitution and the Law in Relation to Marriage," with Comments by Vincent Grogan and others. Studies 57:6-33, Spring 1968.

Although the Irish High Court has the jurisdiction to issue a decree effecting a judicial separation, and can entertain suits for nullity of marriage, restitution of conjugal rights and "jactitation of marriage," it has no jurisdiction, nor has any court in Ireland ever had, to dissolve a marriage, even one in which the parties are not Catholic, that has been validly contracted so as to leave either spouse free to marry someone else. The author gives a brief historical survey of the several transfers of jurisdiction of matrimonial causes in Ireland; the law which the High Court now administers in this respect is the same law the courts of the Church of Ireland administered up to 1870. Discussed are voidable marriages under the current ecclesiastical law, with references to pertinent court decisions; "clandestine marriages," which is another way in which Irish Catholics can find themselves legally married and canonically single; and judgments in foreign divorce cases. The author concludes with a review of parliamentary powers in regard to marriage before 1937 and the 1937 Constitution. In the report of the Committee on the Constitution, it was recommended that divorce be permitted a vinculo where not inconsistent with the discipline of the religion in accordance with which the parties were married. The recommendation can be implemented only by the decision of the people expressed in a Referendum, and it is felt that the people should be put in a position to compare rationally, the social harm which can result from the availability of divorce a vinculo with that which can result from the existence in the community of many broken marriages.

3134 "A Family Allowances Act in Ireland," Internat. Labour Rev. 50:397-98, 1946.

The Family Allowances Act of 1944 provides allowances of 2s. 6d. weekly for each qualified child in excess of two under 16 years of age normally residing in the same household. There is no means test, but to offset the benefit accruing to the taxpaying class, the income tax allowance in respect of each benefiting child is reduced by 20 pounds (in other words, the net taxable income is increased by 20 pounds). The cost of the scheme in a full year is estimated at 2,250,000 pounds; the present year's cost, however, is estimated at 1,500,000 pounds. The funds required for the operation of the scheme will be voted by Parliament. According to the Minister of Industry and Commerce, who is responsible for the administration of the Act, a non-contributory scheme was adopted because a contributory scheme would be too limited in scope; under the latter, contributions could be made only by employed people working for wages, and a large proportion of the population are not wage earners.

3135 Ireland. Children's Allowances (Amendment) Bill, 1946, as Passed by Both Houses of the Oireachtas. Dublin: Stationery Office, 1946.

3136 Ireland. Laws, Statutes, etc., Act to Provide for the Adoption of Children (No. 25, Acts 1952). Dublin: Stationery Office, 1952.

3137 Lee, G.A. "Irish Matrimonial Laws and the Marital Status," No. Ireland Law Quart. 16:387-ff. September 1965.

3138 "Legal Status of Married Women," Ir. Jur. 21-22:49-ff., 1955-56.

3139 McLaughlin, Patrick J. "Ireland and the World Population Problem," pp. 163-74 in: Capuchin Annual, 1962. Dublin, 1962. 512 pp.

A discussion of the relevance of the Papal Encyclical, Mater et Magistra, to Catholic teaching on the ethics of birth limitation and other approaches to the problem of resources.

3140 Phelan, A. "Proof of Irish Marriages," Law J. 106:422, July 6, 1956.

NORWAY

General population policies

3141 Doublet, Jacques ,and Palmstrom, H. "Problemes Demographiques en Norvege" [Demographic Problems in Norway], Population 1(4):651-62, October - December 1946.

3142 Engelsmann, Robert, "Die Bevolkerungspolitische Lage Norwegens Nach dem Stand des Jahres 1940" [The Position of Norway's Population Policy, 1940], Arch. Bevolk. 14(1-2): 37-55, September 1944.

Policies on fertility and family size

3143 Akman, F. "A Comparative Study of the Norwegian and Turkish Family Laws," Women Law J. 51:14-ff. Winter 1965.

3144 As, Berit,and Tiller, Per Olav, "Marriage -- A Value of the Social Scientist," Acta. Sociol. 8(1-2):7-14, 1964.

A discussion of the motivations young people have when they decide to marry, from a research and theoretical point of view. The differences in the pros and cons regarding marriage are analyzed and the significance of the sex role in this context is pointed out. An atmosphere of rationality is found to surround the decision to marry. It is stated that without conscious awareness of cultural norms, class values and personal idiosyncracies, no purposeful research is possible.

3145 Bruusgaard, C. [The Situation of Abortion in Norway], in: Mehlan, K.H., ed. Internationale Abortsituation, Abortbekampfung, Antikonzeption. Leipzig: Georg Thieme, 1961.

Presents the Norwegian law on abortion first enforced in 1963. The law allows interruption only in the first trimester of pregnancy (unless there is a special reason meriting interruption later) for medical indications when fetal illness or defect is likely. Abortion is also possible when the pregnancy is the result of a criminal act; social conditions are considered in addition to medical indications. The author gives statistics on the abortion situation in Norway from 1956.

3146 "Children's Allowances in Norway," Internat. Labour Rev. 56:345, 1952.

A national scheme of children's allowances was established in Norway by an Act of 26 October 1946, the first payments falling due for the last quarter of 1946. A children's allowance is payable, in respect of the second and following children under 16, to every person residing in Norway who has the care of such children. At least one of the parents of the child must be a Norwegian citizen, but an allowance may also be paid in respect of a child of foreign parentage, by virtue of a treaty of reciprocity. An allowance is payable also for the first or only child in certain cases, namely (a) where the parents are separated; (b) where one or both of the parents are dead; (c) where the parents are not husband and wife, provided that the child is cared for by one of them. As a rule, the recipient of the allowance is the mother. No allowance is payable if for more than three months, the child is wholly maintained by the State, a commune or an insurance fund. The allowance is payable in addition to the children's supplements attached to old-age pensions, sickness benefit and unemployment benefit.

3147 Haffner, J. [The New Abortion Law Enforced], T. Norsk. Laeg. 84:361-ff., 1964.

The Norwegian abortion law was enacted in 1960 and enforced in 1964. This editorial criticizes some lack of clarity in the wording of the law and points out that the law does not allow abortion on social indications alone. As it enacts principles that have been followed by physicians for more than 15 years, it is not believed that the enforcement shall cause any major change in the frequency of legal abortions. Abortion cases should not be given special priority in admission to hospitals, but should be treated as any other patient who asks for medical care.

3148 International Labour Office, "The Question of Family Wages in Norway," Industry and Labour 7(4):138-40, February 1952.

The question of family wages, or wages adjusted to the breadwinner's family responsibilities, have been examined by a governmental committee which recently issued a long report on the matter. This committee was formed because it was thought that the sharp price increase, following devaluation in 1949 and the reduction of subsidies on certain consumer goods in the spring of 1950, was harder on wage earners with families than on single persons. The committee recommends special measures to assist families.

3149 Iversen, T. [The New Abortion Law], Sykepleine 53:6-ff., 1966.

A report on Norway's new abortion law, which was approved in 1960. Legal abortion is allowed for three major indications: when the mother's health is seriously endangered (living conditions must be considered); when fetal illness or defect is likely; and when pregnancy occurs as a result of rape, incest or other criminal intercourse. In most cases, the pregnancy cannot have progressed beyond the 12th week, and two designated physicians (one the chief gynecologist of an approved hospital) make the final decision. The author feels that a psychiatric specialist is often needed and that psychiatric treatment, family counseling or other therapy should be made available for every case of abortion if the intention of the law is observed.

3150 Kolstad, P. "Therapeutic Abortion: A Clinical Study Based upon 968 Cases from a Norwegian Hospital, 1940-53," Acta. Obstet. Gynec. Scand. 36(Supple. 6), 1957.

Study of 968 applications for abortion submitted to the Gynecology Department of Drammen Hospital in Drammen, Norway, from 1940 to 1953. 83% of the applicants were married; 16% were single. The average age was 33 years for married women and 22 years for single women. Married women most often had from 1 to 3 living children. Women from urban areas and from the working class had relatively greater frequency of applications. 7.4% of the applicants admitted had had a previous induced abortion. 714 of the applications were granted; 254 refused. Over the ten years covered by the study, the number of women who applied and were granted abortions rose steadily. At the same time, the indications for interruption of pregnancy have changed in relative importance, with the diminished use of medico-somatic indications and increased use of medical-psychiatric and medical-social indications. Among women with social-medical indications, housing conditions, unsatisfactory economy, unsatisfactory conditions in the home (including reports of alcohol abuse), and numerous family were the main difficulties referred to. Of the 662 patients who had legal abortions, 264 were sterilized. Of the 398 who were not sterilized, 162 were lost to follow-up. Of the remaining 236, 115 reported a later pregnancy, 50 of these pregnancies terminated in delivery, 45 in legal abortion, 6 in illegal abortion and 7 in spontaneous abortion. Of the 254 patients refused abortion, pregnancy outcome is known in 166 cases. 86% of these pregnancies ended in delivery,9% ended in illegal abortion, 4% ended in spontaneous abortion, and in 1%, the women concerned were not pregnant. 135 women whose pregnancies were interrupted described their reactions to the abortion. 83% were glad, without reserve; 10% were satisfied but doubtful; 4% were not happy but knew the abortion was necessary; and 4% were repentant. 113 women whose pregnancies were not interrupted and who carried their pregnancies to term also described their reactions. 84% were glad the pregnancy was not interrupted; 9% were uncertain as to their feelings; and 7% were discontented with the decision of the hospital.

3151 Norway. Departementet for Sociale Saker, _Familienpolitikk og Barnevern i Norge_ [Family Policy and Child Welfare in Norway]. Oslo, 1948. 38 pp.

3152 Norway. "Interruption of Pregnancy," _Internat. Digest Health Legis_. 16:148-54, 1965.

Law No. 2 of 11 November 1960, and Crown Decree of 20 December 1963, regarding abortion. Woman may apply for induction of abortion when continued pregnancy is a serious danger to her life or health, might result in grave illness of serious physical or mental defect in the child, or where pregnancy is the result of a criminal act. Living conditions which might adversely affect the woman's health are to be considered. The operation must be performed in a licensed hospital and when possible by a specialist in surgery or gynecology.

3153 Norway. Justis Departement, Innstilling fra Straffelovradet (det Sakkyndige rad for Strafferettslige Sporsmal) om Adgangen til a Avbryte Svangerskap, Avgilt 1 Juni, 1956 [Report from the Council on Penal Law (the Experts' Council for the Problems of the Penal Law) Concerning the Availability of Interrupting Pregnancy, Rendered June 1, 1956], Trondheim: Trykt i Aktietrykkerieti Trondhjem, 1956. 122 pp.

3154 Norway. Komiteen for Internasjonale Sosialpolitiske Saker, [Family and Child Welfare in Norway, A Survey]. Oslo, 1949. 55 pp.

3155 Palmstrom, H. "Les Allocations Familiales" [Family Allowances], Population 1(4):660-62, October - December 1946.

3156 Strom, A., "Om Adgangen til a Avbryte Svangerskap" [So-Called Availability of Pregnancy Interruption], Tidsskrift for den Norske Laeg. 77(7):293-95, April 1, 1957.

SWEDEN

General population policies

3157 Andreen, P.G. "Befolkningsfragen och Skattepolitiken" [Population Questions and Fiscal Policies]. Svensk Tidskrift No. 8, 1955.

3158 Antoni, N. [Concrete Proposals for the Solution of the Population Problem], Svenska Lakartidn. 38:1333-34, June 13, 1941.

3159 Berglund, A. "Schwedens Befolkerungspolitik" [Sweden's Population Policy], Z. Geopolitik 23:399-405, July 1952.

In 1934, a population commission was established to investigate the reasons for a lowering birth rate and to prepare measures to counteract it. A rising birth rate and economy dulled public interest until the early 1940's, when the lowering birth rate re-awakened public concern and led to the founding of a permanent population board as a government agency. In the late 1930's and early 1940's a series of laws were passed, including children's allowances, public social institutions, such as child care centers and kindergartens, prevention of dismissing pregnant women from work, etc. In 1945, consultation centers were established for women seeking legal abortion, and in 1946, a liberal abortion law was passed. The need to consider the birth and family problems as a complex social-biological phenomenon and not on the basis of the old form of welfare population policies is also stressed here.

3160 Biorck, G. Vart Folk och Var Framted [Our Population and Our Future]. Stockholm: Meden, 1940. 112 pp.

3161 Birth Control Federation of America, "Notes from Sweden," Human Fertility 6(3):93-94, June 1941.

From reports by Gunnar Myrdal and Max Hodann on Swedish population policy during the war.

3162 Dickson, Harald, "Sweden Plans Its Housing Policy," Public Utility Economics 23(4):417-27, November 1947.

A discussion of Sweden's housing program, including the nature of the housing subsidy to families with children.

3163 Gille, Halvor, "Recent Developments in Swedish Population Policy: Part I," Popul. Stud. 2(1):3-70, June 1948.

An account of recent developments in Swedish population policy, with particular reference to the work and consequences of the second Swedish Royal Commission, appointed in 1941. After discussing the main characteristics of present Swedish policy and the considerations by which it has been influenced, the author surveys the various measures introduced, or under discussion, to meet special needs, including marriage loans and loans to individuals with university or similar training, measures designed to reduce the pressures which lead women to seek abortions, and the comprehensive scheme of maternity benefits likely to come into operation soon. In addition, the author analyzes the system of grants in aid of specific items in current family expenses, including, in particular, rent rebates. The details of all the relevant measures are given, and the author traces the various stages of their evolution.

3164 Gille, Halvor, "Recent Developments in Swedish Population Policy, Part II," Popul. Stud. 2(2):129-84, September 1948.

The present section describes various collective schemes for maternity and child welfare, and the nature of the allowances for children. Provisions aiming to overcome manpower difficulties in industry and the home are discussed, including immigration, the rationalization of household work, and home help services. The proposal for a Population Institute is considered, and the cost of the various measures of Swedish population policy is estimated.

3165 Gille, Halvor, Svensk Befolkningspolitik [Sweden's Population Policy]. Arbejds-og Socialministeriernes Okonomisk-Statistiske Undersogelser, No. 13. Kobenhavn: Socialt Tidsskrift, I Kommission hosThaning & Appel, 1949, 96 pp. Also in: Socialt Tidsskrift 25:193-283, May 1949.

In 1935, Sweden set up a population commission to deal with the problem of a lowering birth rate. In 1941, the government established a permanent Population Board, which tried to base its population measures on three factors: demographic, social, and a sense of justice and fairness to all families concerned. The government decided to grant compensation for children in the form of a direct cash contribution per child rather than graduating salaries or taxation on the basis of a family's burdens. In 1945-46, a series of reform laws were enacted, which included: more liberal abortion laws, sex education in the schools, free guidance and easier access to birth control measures, prevention of dismissing women due to marriage or pregnancy, free school meals and vacation transportation for all children, and extensive care and benefits for mothers and children. Other reforms came in later years.

3166 Hohman, Helen F. "Social Democracy in Sweden," Soc. Security Bull. 3(2):3-10, February 1940.

This summary statement includes a consideration of the population policies of Sweden.

3167 Hyrenius, Hannes J. Livsvilja eller Folkdod. Kortfattad Framstallning av Sveriges Befolkningsproblem [Life or Death. Survey of the Swedish Population Problem]. Lund: Sundqvist och Emond, 1941. 160 pp.

3168 Mundebo, Ingemar, Ny Kris i Befolkningsfragen? [New Crisis in the Population Question?]. Stockholm: Raben & Sjogren, 1962. 103 pp.

A survey of Swedish population policy and statistics since 1900.

3169 Myrdal, Alva, Nation and Family: The Swedish Experiment in Democratic Family and Population Policy. New York: Harper, 1941. Paperback, Cambridge: M.I.T. Press, 1968.

The general thesis is that "a population policy can be nothing less than a social policy at large;" the population problem "concerns the very foundation of the social structure and... calls for nothing less than complete social redirection." Part I, Problems and Principles, analyzes the demographic situation of Sweden and its historical development in relation to the awakening of public interest in the quantitative and qualitative aspects of population policy. The goals for a population policy, the means for achieving them, and the importance of aids in kind instead of in cash are then presented on the basis of Swedish experience. Part II, Provisions in Sweden, describes in detail the various aspects of the Swedish plans and developments up to the summer of 1939. The specific chapters are as follows: Official Programs and Legislative Acts; Educational Preparation for Family Life; Planning the Size of Family; Economics of Homemaking; Housing for Families; Feeding a Nation; Health for the Nation; Provisions for Childbearing; The Incomplete Family; Social Security and Social Care of the Handicapped; Opportunities for Education; Recreation and the Family; and One Sex a Social Problem.

3170 Quensel, Carl-Erik, "Levnadskostnadernas Stegring och Skatteberakning ur Befolkningspolitisk Synpunkt" [Increase in the Cost of Living and the Calculation of Taxes from the Point of View of Population Policy], Svensk Tidskrift 29(1):51-54, 1942.

3171 Socialstyrelsen, "Socialstyrelsens Utlatande Angaende Befolkningspolitikens Organisation" [The Social Board's Report on the Organization of a Population Policy], Sociala Meddelenden 57(1):8-15, 1947.

Policies on fertility and family size

3172 Aren, P.,and Amark, C. "The Prognosis in Cases in Which Legal Abortion Has Been Granted But Not Carried Out," Acta. Psych. Neurol. Scand. 36:203-ff., 1961.

The authors describe Sweden's abortion laws and permissible indications and then report on the outcome of 244 cases in the Stockholm and Uppsala areas. Out of this group, 162 completed the pregnancy and 142 kept the child, 33 had illegal or spontaneous abortions, 30 had legal abortions not registered with the Medical Board, 7 were not pregnant and 10 could not be contacted for information. The 162 women who did give birth were interviewed in their homes and asked about their psychological, social and obstetrical-gynecological difficulties . 106 were married, 26 unmarried and 10 divorced. 20% used mental illness as the indication for abortion, 48% used weakness, 13% foreseen weakness and 19% hereditary risk. 71 women voluntarily refrained from having the abortion (17 of whom also refrained because sterilization was a condition for granting their applications), 36 refrained as a result of persuasion by a gynecologist, and 35 had advanced too far in their pregnancies. In addition, 38% felt guilty about the operation, and only 6% regretted giving birth. The number of complications was no greater than in ordinary obstetrical cases.

3173 Berg, G. "Abortfragan" [The Problem of Abortion], Svenska Lakartidn. 50(16):875-76, April 17, 1953.

3174 Berg, G. "Abortfragan i Riksdagen" [Parliamentary Debate on Abortion]. Svenska Lakartidn. 50(7):373-79, February 13, 1953.

3175 Berg, G. "Betankande Avgivet av 1950 ars Abortutredning" [The Question of Abortion; Statement of the Committee Appointed in 1950]. Svenska Lakartidn. 50(44):2279-85, October 30, 1953.

3176 Berglund, A. [Problem of Encouraging Large Families in Sweden], Svenska Lakartidn. 38:581-84, March 7, 1941.

3177 Borell, U. "Abortion for Controlled Medico-Social Indications in Sweden," Med. Gynaec. Sociol. 3:90-ff., 1968.

The author reviews the legal status of abortion in Sweden, and discusses its incidence, the procedure of examination and decision, and the socio-economic and medical measures undertaken in the country to decrease the total number of induced abortions.

3178 Borell, U. "Legal Abortions in Sweden," World Med. J. 13(3):72-ff., 1966.

Swedish legislation on abortion is described, with reference to the ways in which the laws are implemented. Legal abortion is permitted for five indications: medical, medico-social, Socio-medical, eugenic and humanitarian; it can be obtained with two physicians' certificates or with approval of the National Board of Health. Combined with the country's abortion legislation is social legislation intended to minimize the need for and frequency of abortions. The author includes data on the characteristics of women receiving legal abortions.

3179 Ekblad, Martin, Induced Abortion on Psychiatric Grounds: A Follow-up Study of 479 Women. Copenhagen: Munksgaard, 1955. 238 pp.

Some effects of the Swedish Abortion Act have recently been evaluated, affording results of eugenic and social interest. The Act was passed in 1938 and amended in 1946, since which year pregnancy may legally be terminated in Sweden on therapeutic, social-medical, humanitarian and eugenic grounds. Before the Act was passed illegal abortion had reached alarming proportions; it was calculated that in the year 1930 there were twenty abortions for every 100 live births. Since 1938 the number of legally produced abortions has increased, so that by 1951 they amounted to 6,328, i.e., 5.75 for every 100 live births. Only 18% of the married women had had four or more children, so that few worn-out mothers of very large social problem families are included. Follow-up data show that a considerable number of women who have had a legal abortion subsequently become pregnant within the next two years. There were 156 such pregnancies for the 479 subjects studied.

3180 Erkkila, S. "Insemination som ett Social-Medicinskt och Familjirattslight Problem" [Insemination as a Problem in Social Medicine and Family Law], Soc. Med. Tidskrift 33(9): 359-63, November 1956.

3181 Erlander, Tage, "Swedish Social Policy in Wartime," Internat. Labour Rev. 47(3):297-311, March 1943.

The war developments are described against the background of the developments of the 1930's. The social policy of the public authorities has continued to be focused on the family and children, with allowances of all types devised to be more favorable to persons with many dependents than to single persons. A new committee is now working on the population question in order to apply the lessons of the war-time experience to the future.

3182 Evang, K. "Sterilisasjon efter Lov av 1. VI. 1934 om Adgang tip Sterilisasjon M.V." [Sterilization According to the Law of 1 June, 1934, on Permission for Sterilization], Nord. Med. 54(49):1826-29, December 8, 1955.

3183 Fischer, Gerhard, [The Problem of Large Families and Lower Levels of Living; a Proposal for Taxing the Childless], Svenska Lakartidn. 38:293-305, February 7, 1941.

3184 Forssman, H. "Sterilisering och Befolkningspolitik" [Sterilization and Population Policy]. Soc. Med. Tidskrift 35(4): 131-38, April 1958.

3185 Frey, T.S. "Abortdiskussionen" [The Discussion on Abortion]. Svenska Lakartidn. 50(13):697-704, March 27, 1953.

3186 Furuhjelm, Mirjam, "Dagens Abortsituation och Vagen ut" [The Present Abortion Situation and Remedial Measures]. Svenska Lakartidn. 52(9):524-30, March 4, 1955.

3187 Greenberg, D.S. "Birth Control: Swedish Government Has Ambitious Program to Offer Help to Underdeveloped Nations," Science 137(3535):1038-39, September 28, 1962.

Description of the program of the Ceylon project undertaken in 1958 and of the recently formed Swedish Agency for International Assistance.

3188 Gyllensward, Curt, [Extinction or Explosion of the Population: Birth Control in Sweden with Particular Reference to Its Consequences and Significance for Population Development], _Acta_. _Paediat_. _Scand_. 56(2):198-210, 1967.

The experience gained in Sweden shows that with a rising standard of living and with increasing enlightenment, women desire and practice birth control.

3189 Hofsten, Nils von, "Sterilization in Sweden," _J_. _Heredity_ 40(9):243-47, 1949.

A total of 15,486 sterilizations have been performed under Sweden's sterilization law passed in 1935 and expanded in 1941. The law provides for voluntary operation, but sterilization of feebleminded persons may be decided without their consent. It recognizes eugenic, social and therapeutic grounds.

3190 Hojer, K.J. _Samhallet och Barnen: Svensk Lagstiftning till Skydd och Stod for Barn och Familj_ [Society and Children: Swedish Legislation for the Protection and Support of Child and Family]. 4th ed. Stockholm: Norstedt, 1955. 374 pp.

3191 Hultgren, G. "Legala Aborter och Steriliseringar ar 1953" [Legal Abortions and Sterilization, 1953]. _Svenska Lakartidn_. 52(9):531-39, March 4, 1955.

3192 Hultgren, G. [Refused Application for Legal Abortion Statistical Study Regarding 4,274 Women Whose Application Was Refused by the Swedish National Board of Health], _Nord_. _Med_. 62:1182-ff., 1959.

A study of 4,389 women refused a legal abortion by the National Board of Health during the years 1954-1956. Information was not available for 144 of these women, and one unmarried 19 year old committed suicide one month after her application was denied, but of the remaining 4,274, 85.6% completed their pregnancies and 14.4% had an abortion. The abortion rate was 15.7% in Stockholm and 13.6% in other parts of Sweden. After deducting the estimated proportion of spontaneous abortions, the author calculated the criminal abortion rate as 12.5 - 13.5% in Stockholm, 10 - 11% elsewhere in Sweden, and 11 - 12% in the country as a whole.

3193 Hultin, M., and Ottosson, J.O. [In-Patient Observation of Abortion Applicants], _Svenska_ _Lakartidn_. 59:1365-ff., 1962.

166 women referred to a psychiatric hospital ward for observation by the National Board of Health were studied; the Board, in making a decision on legal abortion applications which involve psychiatric indications, refers approximately 2-3% of all the applicants to such wards. The authors analyzed the personal and social characteristics of the group and used a matched group without the observation as a control. 13% of the women referred gave up their applications, 27% were given only a new out-patient examination, and a complete observation was carried out for 60%. The decision on abortion was delayed by the referral about four weeks in most cases, with stays in the ward varying between 2 and 49 days. 59% received final approval of their applications (62% in the control group). 26% of the women who were rejected had an abortion, illegally induced in 80% of the cases. Of the women admitted to the hospital, 8% agreed to continue their pregnancies during the stay, and, of the women who gave up their applications, approximately half delivered and half went on to have spontaneous or illegal abortions. Most of the women referred to the psychiatric ward were unhappy about it initially, with a low motivation for therapy, but over 50% felt grateful afterward and thought the experience worthwhile. It is concluded that such referrals can be very useful in some cases, as an aid in the decision-making process when the need for legal abortion is legally or medically doubtful and as a measure to give women an opportunity to escape from their environmental pressures into the therapeutic and neutral hospital atmosphere.

3194 Inghe, G. [The Social Condition of the Abortion Patients], Acta. Obstet. Gynec. Scand. 22:123-ff., 1942.

787 women were interviewed at a Stockholm hospital after treatment and care for abortion and over 4,000 hospital records were reviewed for social data in an attempt to determine the social conditions of women having abortions. 46% of the women were married, 51% unmarried, and an estimated 80% of the total number of abortions were induced. The abortion rate was higher for married women and highest in the 20-25 year old age group. Abortions occurred most frequently in the 2nd to 4th month of pregnancy. The ratio of abortions to pregnancies was highest with unmarried women, and, of the out-of-wedlock pregnancies, 33% ended in marriage and childbirth, 33% in out-of-wedlock birth and 33% in abortion. The abortion rate was higher for women who had moved to Stockholm as opposed to those who were born in Stockholm, and higher for women in occupational work. If the married women had not resorted to abortion, the number of children in their families would have been raised to an above average level. 80% of the aborted women had used some kind of contraception, primarily the condom (40%) and coitus interruptus (70%), but only 12% of the couples using condoms had done so consistently.

3195 Jonsson, G. [The Social-Psychological Background to the Woman's Desire for Abortion], Acta. Obstet. Gynec. Scand. 22:175-ff., 1942.

787 women, hospitalized in Stockholm for abortion, were interviewed; abortion was considered to have been induced in most cases. Approximately 50% were married, legally or common-law, and 37% of the unmarried women were involved in a permanent relationship. Only 7% had become pregnant during casual relationships. Of the unmarried women, about two-thirds reported that marriage was impossible because of external social conditions, such as lack of money, unemployment or threat of dismissal. The male partner became alienated with knowledge of the pregnancy in over 50% of all the cases and in two-thirds of the unmarried cases. Two-thirds of the women under 25 complained that their parents would not give them support. One-third of all the women were completely unaware of the dangers of induced abortion, and about 50% were unaware of the existing possibilities for socio-economic support. Only 33% had seen a doctor before the abortion and most of these only to have the pregnancy

diagnosed. Reasons given for the abortion by the unmarried women included economic (55%), social disgrace (44%),"convenience" (15%),and difficulties in self-support for an unmarried mother (15%). Reasons given by the married women included economic (75%), limitation of family size (50%), and concern for the child's future (20%).

3196 Kalvesten, Anna-Lisa, "Family Policy in Sweden," Marr. Fam. Living 17(3):250-54, August 1955.

In 1934 Gunnar and Alva Myrdal wrote The Re-population Crisis, which highlighted Sweden's population decline and influenced legislative enactments creating the Population Commission in 1935. Research by the Commission pointed to the unequal costs for different strata and families of different sizes in rearing children, and was instrumental in legislative approval of a family policy which sought to stimulate fertility by providing subsidies and grants to encourage marriages, help meet the cost of housing a family and assist with meeting the health, educational and recreational needs of mothers, families, and children.

3197 Lindberg, B.J. "Den Medicinska Linjen i Abortfragan" [The Medical Stand on Abortion], Svenska Lakartidn. 51(47): 2968-81, November 19, 1954.

3198 Mann, William E. "Sexual Standards and Trends in Sweden," J. Sex Res. 3(3):191-200, August 1967.

A report on sexual trends in Sweden, based on a two week visit to the country for research, interviews and examination of published material, with the purpose of determining whether Sweden can provide, in matters of sex, a potential matrix for Canada. The image of Sweden as a haven for liberal sexual attitudes is confirmed by recent events, such as the publication of Erotic Minorities, by Lars Ullerstam, with its plea for all kinds of deviant sexual behavior, and of two volumes of admitted pornography (Love I and Love II), which were not censored. But other data indicate that Sweden, too, has its confusions and controversies. Abortion is legal, but sectors of the Lutheran Church and other conservative elements still oppose it, and the state itself, while permitting abortions on reasonable wide grounds, does not encourage them. The National Association for Sex Education, started in 1933, has provided contraceptives for females over 15. The law permits sterilization (1000 to 2000 annually) and castration (8 males and no females in 1961). Sex education in the schools has been compulsory since 1938, but Birgitta Linner estimates that only 50-60% of the students actually get a thorough sex education. Pre- or extra-marital sexual activity is confined to youth and the unmarried, according to Anna-Lisa Kalveston, in The Social Structure of Sweden (mimeographed, Swedish Institute, 1962), who states that there is nothing to suggest a greater prevalence of "free love" among married people in Sweden than elsewhere. Several studies (Joachim Israel of Uppsala Univ., on conscripts; S.L. Carlson of Uppsala Univ., on high school students; and Malmnas on unmarried women in Uinisterium Medici, 1963) indicate a gradual extension of sexual permissiveness. A campaign by several physicians against sexual permissiveness as causing a rise in venereal diseases has been "extravagantly attacked" in the major newspapers. The usual sociological explanations of Sweden's sexual mores are: (1) industrialization, urbanization and secularization concommitant to the early achievement of an affluent society; and (2) membership in the Lutheran state church, the traditional guardian of morals, is largely nominal.

3199 Oden, Olof, "Abortfragan" [Abortion Questions], Soc. Med. Tidskrift 33(9):351-58, September 1956.

3200 Persson, Konrad, "Social Welfare in Sweden," Soc. Sec. Bull. 12(4):16-18, 24 April 1949.

Includes sections on child allowances and health insurance. Under the new obligatory system of insurance, which was to be effective in 1950, assistance is provided during pregnancy and childbirth. General child allowances are paid at the rate of 260 kroner a year to practically every child in the country. Special child allowances, up to a maximum of 420 kroner per year, are payable for the upbringing and subsistence of certain groups of children -- for example, the children of widows and invalids.

3201 Rapoport, J.L. "American Abortion Applicants in Sweden," Arch. Gen. Psychiat. 13:24-ff., 1965.

This study of 56 interviewed applicants from the U.S. for abortion in Sweden found that all were from the upper-economic, educated classes and that most were 21-30 year old single women motivated by social disgrace. The interviews plus psychological testing such as the Pregnancy Research Questionnaire and the MMPI revealed more depressive symptoms than high anxiety, although the psychosomatic anxiety symptoms during pregnancy were higher than in a control group. Permission for abortion in Sweden was given to only eight women; abortion was performed elsewhere on twelve women; birth was followed by adoption in the case of three women; and no follow-up data is available for the remaining 33.

3202 Sjovall, A. [Abortion and Sterilization in Sweden], Arch. Gynaek. 180:324-ff., 1951.

A review of legal abortion in Sweden over the period 1935-50, permissible indications being medical, medical-social, eugenic and humanitarian. The rate of legal abortions has increased considerably since 1942, particularly after a 1946 amendment which extended the medical-social indication to include "anticipated weakness." For 1936-42, the percent of abortions to births was 0.5; for 1949, 4.5. The number of illegal abortions has not decreased correspondingly, while the total mortality in 12,827 abortions was 0.59% for 1935-47 and 0.36% in 7,537 abortions for 1945-47. The author's data shows a 16% rate of primary complications. Four personal recommendations are given: that the extended socio-medical indication be abolished; that social indications, if the above extension remains, be judged by the National Board of Health rather than by two physicians; that there be two ways of authorizing abortion (on advice of two physicians or the National Board of Health with a written certificate from one physician, the latter choice requiring two physicians also); and that abortion only be permitted after the 20th week on other than purely medical indications, since the "pregnancy depression" vanishes parallel to the molimina in early pregnancy.

3203 "Sterilization Laws in Sweden," Lancet 243:106-7, July 25, 1942.

The author outlines the development of sterilization laws in Scandinavia, particularly in Sweden, since 1920, when Denmark's government was urged to legalize sterilization of any abnormal person if he, or those responsible for him, applied for it. In 1934, Sweden passed a law regulating the sterilization of mental defectives who were too low-grade to give valid consent to the operation; the Swedish population commission, in reporting on the results of this law, felt that guarantees against sterilization of responsible persons on inadequate grounds were needed far more than measures to protect those incompetent to give consent. A new law was passed in 1941, which defined the conditions for which sterilization could be performed with the consent of the patient, and which provided for the operation to be performed without consent in those incompetent to give it. The author gives a description of the 1941 law, with references to sterilization on eugenic and social grounds; the need for consent of the medical council (unless there are urgent medical grounds); regulations on where the operation can be performed; possibilities for appeal if an application is rejected by the medical council; and those eligible to apply for sterilization (spouse, physician, poor-law authority for those under poor-law care, etc.).

3204 Sutter, Jean, "Bilan de la Politique Neo-Malthusienne en Suede (1937-1957)" [An Appraisal of the Neo-Malthusian Policy of Sweden, 1939-1957], Population 15(4):677-701, August - September 1960; Also in: Concours Med. 84:399-404, January 20, 1962.

A survey of general principles and principal results under the headings: Sex Education; Propaganda for Birth Limitation; Legal Abortions; and Sterilizations and Castrations.

3205 Svenson, Gote, "Familjepolitisk Facit" [Achievements in the Field of Family Policy], Sociala Mederlanden No. 2, February, 1958, pp. 73-81.

Family policy issues decided during the 1957 session of the Riksdag are evaluated and further reforms suggested.

3206 Sweden. Befolkningsutredningen, 1941, Betankande om Atgarder for Beredande av Vila och Rekreation at Modrar och Barn, Avgivet av 1941 ars Befolkningsutredning [Report on Measures to Provide Rest and Recreation for Mothers and Children, by the 1941 Population Commission]. Statens Offentliga Utredninger 1945:55. Stockholm: K.L. Beckmans Boktryckeri, 1945. 173 pp.

Contents: Free travel for children and caretakers; Assistance for vacations for housewives; Assistance for vacation homes.

3207 Sweden. Befolkningsutredning, 1941, Den Familjevardande Socialpolitiken en Redogorelse Utarbetad av 1941 ars Bevolkningsutredning [The Social Policy of Family Care. A Report by the 1941 Population Commission]. Statens Offentliga Utredningar 1946:17. Stockholm: K.L. Beckmans Boktryckeri, 1946. 132 pp.

3208 Sweden. Befolkningsutredning, 1941, Utredning och Forslag Angaende Planmassigt Sparande for Familjebildning och Statens Bosattningslan, Avgivna av 1941 ars Befolkningsutredning [Report and Proposals Concerning Planned Savings for Housing and Government Loans for Household Equipment, by the 1941 Population Commission]. Statens Offentliga Utredningar 1943:18. Stockholm: K.L. Beckmans Boktryckeri, 1943. 68 pp.

3209 Sweden. Befolkningsutredning, 1941, Utredning och Forslag Angaende Statsbidrag till Social Hemhjalpsverks amhet Avgivna av 1941 ars Befolkningsutredning [Report and Proposals Concerning Governmental Assistance for Social Welfare Aid to Families, by the 1941 Population Commission]. Statens Offentliga Utredningar 1943: 15. Stockholm: K.L. Beckmans Boktryckeri, 1943. 87 pp.

3210 Sweden. Befolkningsutredning, 1941, Utredning och Lekskolor m.m. Avgivna av 1941 ars Befolkningsutredning [Report and Proposals Concerning Governmental Assistance for Day Nurseries and Nursery Schools, etc., by the 1941 Population Commission]. Statens Offentliga Utredningar 1943:9. Stockholm: K.L. Beckmans Boktryckeri, 1943. 100 pp.

3211 Sweden. Befolkningsutredning, 1951, _Socialvardens Omfattning och Kostnader efter 1930. En Statistisk Oversikt Utarbetad av 1941 ars Befolkningsutredning_ [Extent and Costs of Social Care Since 1930. A Statistical Survey by the 1941 Population Commission]. _Statens Offentliga Utredningar_ 1944:33. Stockholm: K.L. Beckmans Boktryckeri, 1944. 69 pp.

Contains tables showing the costs of various types of allowances for single years, 1930-1941.

3212 Sweden. "Castration and Sterilization," _Internat. Digest Health Legis_. 17:155, 1966.

Laws of 1941 and 1944 are amended to reduce the prison sentence from one year to six months for persons who perform operations in contravention of the law.

3213 Sweden. Department of the Interior, [The Abortion Issue. Report Submitted by the 1950 Abortion Committee]. Stockholm: _Statens Offentliga Utredningar_ 1953:29. Inrikesdepartementet, 1953. 298 pp.

Reports the problem of induced abortion in Sweden. The risk of illegal abortion is no longer great, and probably decreasing. In legal abortion, only mortality is specifically investigated. There were 46 deaths in 28,447 abortions, 1946-1951 (1.6 per thousand). Combined, abortion and sterilization had a higher mortality (2.5 per thousand) than abortion alone (0.9). In 1949-51, the total mortality had decreased to 1.1 per thousand, and the mortality in abortion alone to 0.6 per thousand. Sweden's mortality in childbirth was, in 1950, also 0.6 per thousand. From an analysis of the indications for abortion as defined in the law and as applied in practice, it is concluded that environmental factors only have been determinant in the decision on abortion. Social and conventional factors alone very rarely seem to have been accepted as indications for abortion. According to the report, induced abortion cannot be accepted as a method for birth control, and, in spite of a demonstrated and almost universal knowledge (especially of _coitus interruptus_ and condom), the contraceptive use is still very unsatisfactory in groups with high risk of unwanted pregnancy. An extended free contraceptive service is recommended.

3214 Sweden. Department of Social Welfare, [Report on the Abortion Question Submitted by the 1941 Population Commission]. Stockholm: Statens Offentliga Utredningar 1944:51. Socialdepartementet, 1944.

A report on the results of a 1941 investigation made by Sweden's Population Commission on the induced abortion situation in the country, especially the motives for illegal abortion and the possibilities for assisting, socially and financially, those women who want an abortion. The Commission recommended that special consultation centers for pregnant women be established and staffed by gynecologists, psychiatrists and specially trained social workers. It also suggested the kinds of socio-economic relief which might help the pregnant woman. Eight appendices give most of the statistical material gathered.

3215 Sweden. "Interruption of Pregnancy," Internat. Digest Health Legis. 8:110, 1957; 17:152, 1966; 18:179, 1967.

Laws of 9 September 1938, and 21 December 1945, were amended in 1955, 1963, 1964 and 1965, to permit abortion also when it is likely that a deformed child would be born or when pregnancy is the result of a crime. In administering the laws on abortion, a committee on social psychiatry is now authorized to supervise matters.

3216 Sweden. Laws, Statutes, etc., Familjestod. Utgivningstid Mars 1966 [Family Assistance. Report of March 1966]. Sociallagarna, 7. Lund: H. Ohlsson, 1966. 224 pp.

3217 Sweden. Okat Stod till Barnafamiljer. Promemoria avg. av Familjeberedningen [Increased Support for Families with Children. Concluding Memorandum on Family Policy]. Statens Offentliga Utredningar 1964:36. Stockholm, 1964. 148 pp.

3218 Sweden. "Sale or Trade in Contraceptives," Internat. Digest Health Legis. 2(4):617, 1951; 4:284, 1952-53; 11:522-23, 1960.

Decree No. 567 of 9 September 1938, is amended by Decree of 4 March, 1949, permitting sale of contraceptives in places other than pharmacies upon authorization from the police. Subsequent amendments in 1951 and 1959 require that contraceptives sold in pharmacies and other authorized places be of the type approved by the Royal Medical Board, prohibit door-to-door hawking of contraceptives, and set a fine or prison sentence for persons acting contrary to the regulations.

3219 Sweden. Socialstyrelsen, "De Allmanna Barnbidragen" [General Children's Allowances], Sociala Med. No. 10, 1947, pp. 881-86.

This article describes a system of children's allowances introduced in Sweden in January 1948, according to which every child under 16 years of age gets an allowance of 260 kronor a year, payable quarterly by a postal check to its mother. There is no previous examination of the need for economic help in order to guarantee the status of allowances as family policy and not poor relief. The buying power of the allowance may be something like $150 in the United States, although the official exchange rate gives only about $70. The allowances are exempt from taxation. They partially replace a previous system with tax-free deductions dependent upon the number of children in the family. For this reason, their additional effect is to some extent reduced, but they will mean a general gain except for a rather small fraction of the population with high incomes.

3220 Sweden. Socialstyrelsen, "Ett Ars Erfarenhet av de All-Manna Barnbidragen" [A Year's Experience of the General Child Allowances], Sociala Med. 59(4):262-66, 1949.

Report on amount spent in 1948 and general results of the program.

3221 Sweden. Socialstyrelsen, "Modrahjalpen Omprovas" [Reform of Maternity Aid], Sociala Med. No. 11, 1951, pp. 784-87.

Recommendations for achieving uniformity in amounts given and for increasing the aid.

3222 Sweden. Socialstyrelsen, "Modrahjalpen 10 Ar" [10th Year of Maternity Aid], Sociala Med. 58(12):923-29, 1948.

Purpose of the Decree on Maternity Aid, which was put into operation in 1937; family allowances granted; and amount spent in 1947.

3223 Sweden. Socialstyrelsen, "Modrahjalpen under Ar 1951" [Maternity Aid in 1951], Sociala Med. No. 7, 1952, pp. 469-77.

3224 Sweden. Socialstyrelsen, "Modrahjalpen under Forsta Halvaret 1947" [Maternity Aid during the First Half of 1947], Sociala Med. 58(1):27-28, 1948.

The number of applications for maternity aid dealt with during the first half of 1947 was about 54% of the number of live births. The number of applications granted was about 47% of the number of live births.

3225 Sweden. Socialstyrelsen, Samhallets Barnarard ar 1946 [The Protection of Children in 1946]. Stockholm: Sveriges Officiella Statistik Socialvard, 1950. xi, 98 pp.

Emphasis on the problems and care of the illegitimate.

3226 Sweden. Socialstyrelsen, Samhallet och Barnfamiljerna. Betankande av 1954 ars Familjeutredning [The Community and Families with Children. Report of the 1954 Family Committee]. Statens Offentliga Utredningar 1955:29. Stockholm: 1955. 294 pp.

3227 Sweden. Socialstyrelsen, "Cad Kostardet Att Ha Barn?" [What Does It Cost to Have Children?] Sociala Med. No. 5, 1951, pp. 327-36.

An analysis of the increase necessary to permit a family to enjoy an unchanged level of living and the proportion of income expended on children.

3228 Sweden. Socialstyrelsen, "Vissa Barnfamiljers Bostadsforhallanden" [The Housing Conditions of Families with Children]. Sociala Med. 58(5):346-55, 1948.

Report of an inquiry in 30-odd municipalities with a combined population of about 85,000 in order to elucidate certain questions in connection with the planned housing allowances to families with at least two small children.

3229 Sweden. Statistiska Centralbyran, "Statistiska Centralbyrans Utlatande over Familjeutredningens Betankande Samhallet och Barnfamiljerna" [Central Bureau of Statistics on the Demographic Statistics Presented in the Report of the 1954 Family Policy Committee], Statistisk Tidskrift 5(4):220-24, April 1956.

3230 Swedish Institute for Cultural Relations with Foreign Countries, Therapeutic Abortion and the Law in Sweden. Stockholm, 1964. 9 pp.

Law on abortion passed January 1, 1939, with subsequent amendments in 1946 and June 1963.

3231 Swedish Population Commission. [Report on the Sex Questions]. Statens Offentliga Utredningar 1936:59. Translated and edited by Virginia C. Hamilton. Baltimore: Williams and Wilkins, 1940. 182 pp.

The present work is a somewhat abridged translation of a report on the sex question produced by the Commission. It includes, besides a general analysis of this problem-complex, certain proposals for reorganizing sex instructions in the schools. The Appendices, which deal with certain aspects of the material, have been omitted because of lack of space. Part I of this translation, "The Decline of Natality in Sweden and Its Causes," describes the decline of fertility and related demographic changes in Sweden and weighs the importance of various causal factors. Part II, "The Ethical Principles Involved in the Question of Contraception," evaluates the trend toward the rationalization of reproduction from the standpoint of social-ethical values and logic. Part III, "The Practical Values of Contraception," discusses the interrelationships of effective fertility and the control of fertility with innate ability, individual medical and hygienic factors, psychological factors, the costs of rearing children, income, unemployment, food consumption and housing. Consideration is given to the desirability of increasing marriages, the complex problems of extramarital relationships, the elimination of abortion, and, finally, the demographic effects on the future of the nation. Part IV concerns an "Evaluation of the Methods of Contraception," while Part V describes "The Campaign Against Venereal Disease." Part VI, "Sex Enlightenment: Its Organization in a Broadened and Improved Education for Parenthood," presents proposals for action by the State, and emphasizes the great importance of broadened and improved training for parenthood.

3232 Uhrus, Kerstin, "Some Aspects of the Swedish Law Governing Termination of Pregnancy," Lancet No. 7372, December 12, 1964, pp. 1292-93.

Presents and comments on statistics on induced abortions and sequelae before and after the addition of a paragraph in 1963, giving five medico-social grounds for abortion, in the Act passed in 1946.

3233 Zetterberg, Hans L. Om Sexualiivet i Sverige: Varderingar, Normer, Beteenden i Sociologisk Tolkning [About Sexual Life in Sweden: Values, Norms and Behavior in Sociological Interpretation]. Utbildningsdepartementet, Statens Offentliga Utredningar 1969: 2.179 pp.

This report on sexual attitudes and behavior is based on interviews with a national sample of 200 men and women in Sweden, 18-59 years of age, in early 1967. Answers to the more sensitive questions were obtained by means of a questionnaire, filled out by the respondent after an oral interview and placed in a sealed box carried by the interviewer. The response rates were high, with only 7.1% refusing the interview and only 1.5% not going on to the questionnaire. The following are some of the major findings. When asked, "How important is it to use contraceptives when one does not want a child?" about 71% of the respondents stated that they "should absolutely be used each time," 23% said that one should use them but that occasional non-use was permissible, 2% said that it was not important, and 4% were opposed to the use of contraceptives. At their most recent coitus, 73% of all respondents had used some method of contraception and 27% admitted that they had used nothing. These percentages are based on couples exposed to the risk of unwanted pregnancy, not including those wanting a child, not able to have one, or women already pregnant. Among methods used, the condom occupied first place (38%), followed by _coitus interruptus_ (17%), oral tablets (14%), and diaphragm (8%). About 8% had relied on other methods and more than one person in ten reported combined use of several methods. Oral tablets were reported three times as often by respondents under 30 years of age than by older persons. Conversely, _coitus interruptus_ was used more often by the older couples. The median age at first coitus reported by persons under 30 years of age was 16.6 years for boys and 17.2 for girls. Most girls had their first coitus with a male older than themselves, but almost one-third of the boys with an older female. About 84% of the respondents reported use of contraception at their first coitus, most often condom (54%) or _coitus interruptus_ (26%). Other methods were rarely used at first coitus.

UNITED KINGDOM

General population policies

3234 Arden-Close, Charles, "A Satisfactory Population for Britain," _Eugenics Rev._ 42:23-24, 1950-51.

Recommends as policy objectives a population of about 37 million, which would be supported by an importation of about one-third of its food needs.

3235 Binney, Cecil, "Eugenic Aspects of the English Criminal Law," _Eugenics Rev._ 60:118-28, June 1968.

An examination of the eugenic aspects of the English criminal law; first presented as a paper at a members' meeting of the Eugenics Society in January 1945. It is noted that English criminal law began to take cognizance of moral and sexual questions fairly late, first during the Reformation and then, more seriously, in the Victorian age. Until then, they were largely the province of the Church and its courts.

Various aspects of the English criminal law are examined with reference to eugenics: 1) immigration laws -- they favor the entry of less valuable aliens; 2) Offenses Against the Person Act of 1861 -- it is, on the whole neutral but it forbids sterilization even when it may be eugenically desirable; 3) contraception -- freedom to use contraceptives enables prospective parents to make eugenic decisions; 4) abortion -- present prohibition has dysgenic effects; 5) bigamy -- a neutral law; 6) homosexuality -- its penalization is dysgenic because conviction brands a man for life; 7) incest -- prohibitions should be strengthened, in spite of conflicting evidence; 8) offenses against young girls -- the age of consent should not be raised; and 9) intercourse with mental defectives -- the law is too difficult to enforce.

3236 Cadbury, L.J. "Population Changes and Economics," Eugenics Rev. 34(1):13-18, April 1942.

An argument for a positive population policy.

3237 Cook, Robert C. "Great Britain at the Crossroads: A Dilemma of Industrialization," Popul. Bull. 10(3):29-39, May 1954.

Since Great Britain is the most highly urbanized nation in the world and capable of producing only about one-half of its food needs, intense pressure for dispersal of population and industry from the country and for a realistic, effective policy on population is ever-increasing. The author outlines,using pertinent tables,graphs and surveys, population growth statistics, changes in fertility rates, extent of birth control practice, the change age of the population and connected economic consequences, birth and death rates, and immigration/migration patterns to the present time and then describes the four major factors -- other than age -- which will influence Britain's future population. The Royal Population Commission's conclusions are listed and the author discusses current population pressure and its economic effect on the country's export market and balance of payments. It is concluded that the economic and population problems of Britain will not be resolved through existing lines of development and that official recommendations must be used as guide lines for the future.

3238 Elton, G.R. "An Early Tudor Law," Econ. History Rev. 6:55-67, August 1953.

This article traces the growth of the legislation on relief in England from 1531-1601, the principles of which were subsequently developed and applied down to 1834. The three most important of these principles were: work must be provided for those who cannot find it; begging is wrong and the helpless must be a charge of the community; and the parish is to be the organization responsible for the task, with the justices of the peace as supervisors. The Act of 1536, often regarded as marking the beginning of the real Tudor poor law, made a distinction between those able to work and those unable to work, and, in addition, offered a thorough and logical classification of the poor. Under this Act, the poor were to be given free medical attention at public expense. Drafts of varying effectiveness were applied to implement the Act, and more legislation was required (and existed) to prevent de-population and other similar problems, since the 1536 Act was intended to cure symptoms only.

3239 Ensor, R.C. "The Problems of Quantity and Quality in the British Population," Eugenics Rev. 42(3):128-35, October 1950.

The Royal Commission on Population proposed that any policy for increasing population should aim to increase it not at one level but at all levels. As a corollary, and in addition to the flat-rate allowances to help parents in the lowest income groups, it proposed to help parents in the higher groups by remission of income tax proportionate to their incomes.

3240 Eugenics Society, "That the Population of the United Kingdom Should be Stabilized at 40 Million -- A Debate," Eugenics Rev. 49(4):173-86, January 1958.

The debate is initiated by C.P. Blacker, who advocates a Forty-Three Year Commonwealth Plan, the object of which would be to enlarge to the maximum the contribution to the world's population made by the Commonwealth as a whole, while at the same time benefiting the United Kingdom. Plan calls for a program designed to raise fertility in, and promote emigration from, the United Kingdom. By the end of the century, the objective would be to stabilize population in the United Kingdom at the 1900 level -- 38 million. The more vigorous the two movements (natural increase and the accompanying emigration), the better for the Commonwealth as a whole. Three arguments are offered in favor of such a Commonwealth plan: eugenic, economic and strategic. Several arguments in opposition are provided by other debaters.

3241 Fabian Society (London), Population and the People: A National Policy. London: The Fabian Society and G. Allen and Unwin Ltd., 1945. 60 pp.

The statement on national policy by the Fabian Society was prepared as a memorandum of evidence for the Royal Commission on Population. Utilizing a sociological approach, the Committee examines the economic and social factors operating as obstacles to parenthood and surveys public services in aid of parenthood, equality of educational opportunity and housing and town planning. In its positive analysis, the Committee concludes that it is desirable and indeed essential in the national interest that the present decline in the birth rate should be arrested and that the net reproduction rate be restored at least to unity, and if possible to 1.15 or 1.2. Final consideration is given to methods of implementing policy and to immigration and emigration.

3242 Glenday, Roy G. "Location of Industry," Royal Society Arts 91(4637):246-53, April 16, 1943. Discussion, pp. 253-55.

The growth of population and the trends in its distribution are sketched from the seventeenth century to the present, with particular reference to the trends within Britain and the policies discussed or adopted to control those trends. Two main problems of the future are outlined: first, what is likely to be the probable size and quality of the population which has to be located? And second, what is the probable direction likely to be taken by the forces of economic evolution so far as provision of occupation for that population is concerned?

3243 Grebenik, E. "Two Reports on Population," Economica 17(65):91-107, February 1950.

Discusses the problem of measuring population change in Great Britain, prospects for future growth, and the problem of population policy, largely on the basis of two reports: "Population Policy in Great Britain," by Political and Economic Planning, and the "Report" of the Royal Commission on Population.

3244 Lafitte, Francois, "Family Allowances and Eugenics," Eugenics Rev. 33:67-72, October 1941.

The suggestion that England should follow a policy of family allowance in order to alter the current differential birth rate is analyzed critically on the basis of the fact that intellectual differences are not class characteristics. More fundamental reforms of the economic system are held essential if increased birth rates and eugenic aims are to be achieved.

3245 Medical Planning Research, "Medical Planning Research: Interim General Report," Lancet 243(6221):599-622, Supplement, November 21, 1942.

This synthesis of proposals offered by members of the group is concerned with the probable postwar pattern of society in which medicine will have to function, and the special measures which should be taken to achieve the highest measure of positive mental and physical health. A longterm planned population policy for Britain is considered essential. Family allowances, free education, planned housing, and wider education are suggested as methods of planning and controlling the population trend. Control of population distribution is also urged. Part One discusses in detail general measures of social security. Part Two explains the administrative and functional organization of the proposed health service which is to be a corporate body.

3246 "Memorandum to the Royal Commission on Population," Eugenics Rev. 37(3):92-104, 1945.

Parenthood is not deterred by a good environment. Inculcate an eugenic conscience; make universally accessible knowledge of regulation of pregnancies; and permit voluntary sterilization of hereditary defectives. We believe this procedure will not induce race suicide, because the philoprogenitive instincts are powerful; it is but environmental restrictions which make it seem weak. Hence, quality parenthood should be brought to equation with prospective parenthood through proper social and economic conditions. This requires a flat family allowance with graded additions and encouragement of early marriage; recognition of the cost of education; and a housing program facilitating residential mobility with increase in family size but no rent increase. Whether social-problem people are the lowest end of a continuous curve or a distinct sub-population is uncertain, but they are highly fertile. Much research is needed in this field. Eugenic propaganda is heeded by the eugenically worthwhile, but disregarded by defectives at whom it is aimed. Pre-marital health examinations should be voluntary, but universally practiced. Vital need for collection of comprehensive and accurate data on population trends should be met by a creation of an Imperial Institute of Demographic Studies.

3247 Notestein, Frank W. "The Report of the Royal Commission on Population: A Review," _Popul. Stud._ 3(3):232-40, December 1949.

The author surveys the Report and assesses the significance of the Commission's findings in the field of demographic analysis and policy.

3248 Political and Economic Planning (PEP), _Population Policy in Great Britain_. London, 1948. 227 pp.

A survey of population trends in Great Britain as a basis for a population policy that will be concerned with quality as well as numbers.

3249 Ross, Rhona, "Population Policy in Great Britain," _South African J. Economics_ 17(3):320-28, September 1949.

Based on the "Report" of the Royal Commission on Population.

3250 United Kingdom. House of Lords, "World Population and World Resources," Parliamentary Debates 187(63):108-20; 123-200, April 28, 1954.

Debate initiated by Viscount Samuel covering the British and international activities underway to advance development throughout the world and in specific areas, and the absence of need for additional specific attention by the House of Lords.

3251 United Kingdom. Royal Commission on Population, Report. London: His Majesty's Stationery Office, 1949.

The Royal Commission on Population was appointed, in March, 1944, to examine the facts relating to the present population trends in Great Britain; to investigate the causes of these trends and to consider their probable consequences; to consider what measures, if any, should be taken in the national interest to influence the future trend of population; and to make recommendations. In this report, the Commission's major concern is the country's decreasing birth rate; the widespread practice of family limitation is viewed as the cause of this decrease. The bulk of the report is directed to proposals for encouraging families large enough to ensure that the population is maintained. Stressed is the need to change attitudes on family size and to reduce the economic and social pressures on large families. The Commission emphasizes the importance of mistakes in social and economic policy, mistakes which, it contends, might mean the difference between population growth and decline.

Policies on fertility and family size

3252 "Abortion Act Will Become Effective Next April," Brit. Med. J. 4:303-ff., 1967.

The provisions of the recent British Abortion Act are reviewed. There is also a discussion of the opposition of the Royal College of Obstetricians and Gynaecologists and the British Medical Association of the section permitting abortion on the ground of risk to the physical or mental health of any existing children in the family.

3253 "Abortion Law," Brit. Med. J. 1:1009-ff., 1965.

Several proposals to reform Britain's Abortion Law are expressed in an editorial. Urges that the reform be phrased in positive, general language rather than the present negative terms. This manner would permit the law to be adapted to advances in medical science.

3254 Abortion Law Reform Association, A Guide to the Abortion Act 1967. London: Abortion Law Reform Association, 1967.

This booklet was compiled to facilitate better comprehension of the provisions of the British Abortion Act of 1967. Its contents include the full text of the Act and excerpts from the Statutory Regulations. The main clauses of the Act are supplemented by legal and medical statements from the Reports of the British Medical Association Committee on therapeutic abortion and also from advice issued by the Medical Protection Society and the Medical Defense Union.

3255 Abortion Law Reform Association, Survey on Abortion. [London], July 1966. 4 pp. plus 16 tables.

Study carried out for the Abortion Law Reform Association by National Opinion Polls Limited.

3256 "Abortions. First Notifications," The Economist, Nov. 2, 1968.

Discusses the status of abortion immediately following the enactment of the Abortion Act of April, 1967. It was found that a more liberal abortion law enabled a new class of women to apply for abortions, but had little effect on those women obtaining criminal abortion.

3257 Abse, Leo, "Infanticide and British Law," Clin. Pediat. 6: 316-17, May 1967.

A Bill introduced in Parliament on June 23, 1965, and now under consideration for passage in the United Kingdom, with the exception of Northern Ireland, would remove the penalty of life imprisonment from the statute on infanticide. The offense of infanticide would then be included among those offenses which are triable summarily with the consent of the accused. Newspapers would be prohibited from giving any account of infanticide which would identify the accused mother. The view is that infanticide results from mental illness.

3258 Addison, P.H. "Legal Aspects of Sterilization and Contraception," Medico-Legal J. 35:164-67, 1967.

Outlines current practices of medical practitioners in Great Britain and their legal basis.

3259 Andrew, J.H. "Family Planning in the Army: Setting up a Family Planning Clinic in the Forces," Proc. Proc. Royal Society Med. 61:247-48, March 1968.

3260 Anton, A.E., and Francescakis, P. "Modern Scots 'Runaway Marriage'", Jurid. Rev. 1958:253, December 1958.

3261 Archbishop of Canterbury's Group on the Divorce Law, Putting Asunder: a Divorce Law for Contemporary Society [Great Britain]: the Report of a Group Appointed by the Archbishop of Canterbury in January 1964. 1966. ix + 172 pp.

3262 Baird, D. "Sterilization and Therapeutic Abortion in Aberdeen," Brit. J. Psychiat. 113:701-ff., 1967.

Abortion is permitted in Scotland if a doctor, after consultation, decides that the disadvantages of continuing the pregnancy are greater than those of ending it. In his decision there should be no separation of the medical and social aspects of the case. A report on Aberdeen women indicated the largest families were among semi-skilled or unskilled workers, and among those who married before 20 or after the start of the first pregnancy. Also, a limited use of effective contraceptive methods was found in these groups.

3263 Banks, Joseph Ambrose, Prosperity and Parenthood. A Study of Family Planning Among the Victorian Middle Classes. New York: Grove Press, 1954.

An attempt to explain why English middle classes began to practise family limitation between 1860 and 1870, based on a review of literature of the nineteenth century covering expectancies of middle-class living, expenditure on principal items of household budget, and the "birth control" controversy. Uses household manuals, diaries, books, and articles in contemporary periodicals.

3264 Banks, Joseph Ambrose,and Banks, Olive, Feminism and Family Planning in Victorian England. New York: Schocken Books, 1964. xi + 142 pp.

The introduction sets the study in the context of world movement for population control. This is a sequel to Prosperity and Parenthood by J.A. Banks (1954); in 9 chapters presenting: (1) Fertility and Feminine Protest, considers various hypothesis regarding fertility decline in 19th century England, and presents a methodological case for considering the feminist movement and the emancipation of females as causal factors; (2) The Rights of Woman Discussion, surveys the literature on women's rights from 1792-1869 and shows that there was no discussion of the right of women to control their own fertility. (3) The Scope of Reform, outlines the problems of females in the middle years of the century regarding the development of an organized movement to introduce reforms between 1850 and 1870. (4) The Consequences of Reform, considers whether the fall in family size in the 1860's and 1870's was an unanticipated consequence of the changes in position of females set under way in the previous period and decides that the evidence does not justify this conclusion. (9) Emancipation and Family Size, returns to the methodological issues raised in (1) and concludes that the kind of emancipation entailed by the notion of family planning was independent of the intentions and activities of feminists. The conclusion asserts that taken together Prosperity and Parenthood and Feminism and Family Planning show that the important issue is the male's attitude to his family regarding what he should struggle to achieve in material terms and that therefore world population programs should direct their energies to this issue.

3265 Barnes, Joan, Family Allowances. London: Conservative Political Centre, News and Views Service. July 1958. 35 pp.

Development and present system of allowances.

3266 Bartholomew, Geoffrey W. "The Legal Control of Birth Control," Singapore Med. J. 1(2):53-58, June 1960.

Discussion of the attitude of the English common law toward consummation of marriage, cruelty, assault, and abortion.

3267 Bevan, H.K. "Limitations on the Right of an Impotent Spouse to Petition for Nullity," Law Quart. Rev. 76:267, April 1960.

The decision of the Court of Appeal in Harthan v. Harthan that an impotent spouse may petition for a decree of nullity on the ground of his or her own impotence has secured for itself a firm niche in the law of nullity. However, the author contends that inadequate consideration has hitherto been given to the possible exceptions to this main rule as laid down by the Court. It is submitted that there are three exceptions to the right to plead one's own impotence, two of them being specific rules of the canon law and the third a general, residuary exception, i.e., it may be unjust in particular circumstances for the impotent spouse to sue. The author analyzes the two exceptions at canon law, since Harthan v. Harthan has firmly established the principle that the pre-Reformation canon law relating to the right to plead one's own impotence has not been modified either by the statute or the common law of England, and examines some other circumstances under which a spouse might not be allowed to rely on his own impotence as a ground for nullity.

3268 Beveridge, William, "Eugenics in England. The Eugenic Aspects of Children's Allowances," Eugenical News 28(3):36-39, 1943.

The Beveridge Report proposes a system of children's allowances providing 9 shillings per week for 2nd and later children. The author believes that these allowances will have a positive eugenic effect upon the quality of the population since they will encourage begetting of children by parents who would otherwise restrict their family for economic reasons. It is a well-known fact that there is an inverse ratio between number of children and economic success of the family. The plan of children's allowances will tend to correct this error in our modern society and thus have a beneficial eugenic influence.

3269 Blacker, C.P. "Voluntary Sterilization for Family Welfare. A Proposal by the Simon Population Trust," Lancet, April 30, 1966. pp. 971-74.

Text of statement advocating such sterilization.

3270 Blacker, C.P. and Pell, John H. "Sterilization of Women," British Med. J. 1(5643):566-67, March 1969.

The Royal College of Obstetricians and Gynaecologists carried out "a survey among practicing gynecologists in order to determine (a) their own views and practice about sterilization of women, and (b) the extent to which this operation was being carried out in National Health Service Hospitals." The survey covered the year 1966 only. Questionnaires were sent to 1,401 of whom 882 replied. "Of those replying to the questionnaire (63 per cent), 96 per cent said they were not debarred by any matter of principle from carrying out the operation of sterilization of women, 83 per cent were prepared to carry out the operation at their own discretion without seeking a second opinion, and 99 per cent made it routine practice to obtain the written consent of both husband and wife except in cases of emergency... Out of the total of 198,218 admissions to the obstetrical and gynecological wards during [1966] 3,997 (2.02 per cent) were sterilized by some form of tubal interruption." There was a difference in practice in different hospitals, however, the range varying from 1 per cent to 4 per cent.

3271 Booker, H.S., "Income Tax and Family Allowances in Britain," Popul. Stud. 3(3):241-47, Dec. 1949.

The author traces the effect of changes in the rate of income tax, and of income-tax rebates for children between 1938 and 1948, and shows that recent movements in these rates have worsened the position of taxpayers with children relative to childless taxpayers.

3272 Boreham, John, "The Pressure of Population," New Society 7(179):9-12, March 1966.

Most major social policy issues depend on the number of people such policy is intended to deal with. Questions raised are: Can the guesswork be taken out of speculations about the future population?; and What is the guesswork, or are the estimates which can be deserving merit? Population forecasts are examined to assess established trends as well as anticipated possibilities. The examination extends to the cities in which a future population can be expected to live.

3273 Brain, Lord, "Medical Issues in Abortion Law Reform," British Med. J. No. 5489, March 19, 1966, pp.727-29.

Discusses twelve questions raised by the legislative proposals introduced in Parliament by Lord Silkin in 1966.

3274 British Information Services, Britain's Charter of Social Security: 1948. New York: British Information Services, 1948. 24 pp.

Contains a section on the Family Allowances Act, pp. 14-15.

3275 British Information Services. Reference Division, Social Services in Britain. Great Britain, 1948 [?]. 31 pp.

Explains the history and provisions of Britain's official social services, including family allowances and marriage guidance.

3276 British Medical Association, "British Medical Association Report on Abortion," Brit. Med. J. No. 5504:6, July 2, 1966.

Comment on proposals contained in two reports on Lord Silkin's Abortion Bill, of which the texts are reproduced or summarized: (1) Therapeutic abortion: report by British Medical Association Special Committee, Ibid., pp. 40-44; (2) Summary of memorandum by the Royal Medico-Psychological Association, Ibid., p. 44.

3277 British Medical Association. "Legality of Sterilization: A New Outlook," Brit. Med. J. No. 5211:1516-18, Nov. 19, 1960.

It is possible to summarize the pith of the English counsel's opinion as follows: An operation for sterilization is not unlawful whether it is performed on therapeutic or eugenic grounds or for other reasons, provided there is full and valid consent to the operation by the patient concerned. This proposition, however, has no direct judicial authority to support it, because it has never been tested in the courts. The Scottish counsel summarize their opinion of the position in Scottish law in these words: "We have formed the opinion that, if a sterilization were performed with the full consent of the patient by a responsible surgeon and if the reason for doing it was substantial and not obviously immoral by present-day standards, it is exceedingly improbable that the Court would hold the act to be criminal".

3278 British Medical Association, "Medical Termination of Pregnancy Bill. View of the British Medical Association and the Royal College of Obstetricians and Gynaecologists," Brit. Med. J. No. 5530:1649-50, Dec. 1966.

Text of bill introduced in Parliament June 15, 1966, and subsequent amendments, and of B.M.A. document of approval.

3279 British Medical Association, "Parliament. Lords Reconsider Lord Silkin's Abortion Bill," Brit. Med. J. No. 5484, Feb. 12, 1966, pp. 430-32.

Report on debate, Feb. 1, 3, and 7, 1966.

3280 Caecus, "Law and Abortion," Med. World 98:309-ff., 1963.

Examines the evolution of the British law on abortion: the offenses against the Person Act of 1861 which prohibits abortion; the infanticide and child destruction laws of 1922 which recognized the possible mental instability of a woman who has just given birth; the Bourne case of 1938 which lends a new liberal interpretation of abortion statutes. Concludes that a more liberal law might replace the Offenses Against the Person legislation on abortion.

3281 Cambridge University, Faculty of Law. Department of Criminal Science, Sexual Offences. London: Macmillan. 1957.

3282 Cartter, Allan M. "Income-Tax Allowances and the Family in Great Britain,: Popul. Stud. 6(3):218-32, March 1953.

Examines the position of the family under existing income tax regulations, discussing the program of tax reliefs and allowances and that of family allowances.

3283 Clark, Colin, and Trueman, A.F. "The High Cost of Government," Economic News 16(4-5):1-4, April-May 1947.

Principally an analysis of Commonwealth expenditures and estimated tax requirements, contains data on maternity allowances paid during 1942-1947.

3284 Clarke, John J. Social Welfare. London: Pitman, 1954. x, 420 pp.

Pp. 108-118, National assistance and family allowances, before and after the Beveridge Plan and the Family Allowances Act of 1945.

3285 "Colloquim on Family Law," J. Soc. Pub. TL 8:166, June 1965.

Social Insurance and the Family by O. Aikin; Discussion by H.K. Bevan; Economic Aspects of Death in the Family by O.M. Stone; Discussion by J.C. Hall; Economic Aspects of the Breakdown of Marriage Other Than on Death by P.M. Bromley; Discussion by L.N. Brown.

3286 "Control of Abortion in Private Practice," Brit. Med. J. 1:706-ff., 1967.

Britain's new Abortion Act is debated in Parliament.

3287 Crane, F.R. "Family Provision on Death in English Law," New York Univ. Law Rev. 35:984-1000, May 1960.

Considers the content and working of the Inheritance (family provision) Act, 1938, and the Amendments made thereto by the Interstates' Estates Act, 1952.

3288 Darby, P. "Legal Abortion?" Medico-Legal J. 34:96-107, 1966.

On the basis of hospital admissions for a variety of abortion cases, estimates incidence of abortion in Britain at 100,000 cases per year. A survey in 1950 of 1,600 - 1,700 admissions showed that 90% were procured, 80% of the patients married and 39% had at least one child. Urges legislation to solve the problem of criminal abortion.

3289 Dickens, Bernard M. Abortion and the Law. London: MacGibbon and Kee, 1966. 219 pp.

Reviews the evolution of abortion laws in England from the Act of 1803, which made abortion a crime on a statutory basis, to the Offences Against the Person Act of 1861. The Bourne case and that of Rex v. Newton and Stungo are cited to illustrate the recent interpretations of the law. Extensive disregard of the law, and enforcement in less than 1% of cases which occur make the law ineffective in preventing illegal abortion. Court records of 1949-63 show that of 806 cases (277 men, 579 women) only 62.5% were sentenced and of that number 67% were imprisoned from six months to two years. Steps toward reform with reference to Bills of 1961 and 1965 by G. Williams and Lord Silkin are discussed and the author suggests that legal abortion is not the solution to illegal abortion; that there is a need for cheap, simple and effective contraception and slow reform stressing extension of medical indications rather than the more controversial issue of legislation.

3290 Diggory, P.L.C. "Some Experiences of Therapeutic Abortion," The Lancet 1(7600):873-75, 26 April 1969.

The Abortion Act of 1967 has meant that therapeutic abortion is now an accepted medical procedure in Britain. A personal series of 1,000 cases is described. Simple curettage was chosen in 77 per cent of cases and hysterotomy in 16 per cent. There were few complications and none was serious. Details of contraceptive practices were available for 249 women: 48 per cent had probably not been using any method at the time of conception. There is some evidence that the more literate, middle-class woman may be in a better position to get an abortion. Abortion clinics within the National Health Service is one way of getting round the problems of variations in abortion policy.

3291 Douglas, J.W.B., and Rowntree, Griselda, "Supplementary Maternal and Child Health Services. Part I. Post-Natal Care. Part II. Nurseries," Popul. Stud. 3(2):205-26, Sept. 1949.

A questionnaire survey of the social and economic aspects of childbearing in Great Britain was carried out in 1946 by a Joint Committee of the Royal College of Obstetricians and Gynaecologists and the Population Investigation Committee. A follow-up study of the same sample of mothers and babies was undertaken in 1948 in which the mothers were asked questions relating to post-natal care and ill-health attributed by them to childbearing. Only 45% had had a post-natal examination; 40% suffered maternal morbidity. The inference is that the present low incidence of examinations is a cause of avoidable maternal ill-health and a serious defect in Britain's maternity services. Questions were also asked in the second survey on attendance at infant welfare centers and use of nurseries. Results indicate that only 3% of all mothers had sent their children to either day or residential nurseries before their second birthday. The author concludes that the low attendance at nurseries can be attributed to the high risk of infectious diseases among children attending nurseries. In these circumstances further research is required into preventative measures designed to reduce the excessive risks of infection among the nursery population

3292 Dowse, R.E., and Peel, J. "The Politics of Birth Control," Polit. Stud. 3(2):179-97, June 1965.

The politics of birth control has been dominated in the United Kingdom by the influence of the middle class, and this paper traces the development of a sectarian and universalistic ideology into a looser commitment to birth control. As a pressure group, birth control dates back to 1877, through the action of the Malthusian League. In spite of their efforts to promote specialized clinics under Ministry of Health auspices, the birth controllers gained little sympathy within the Labor Party, though some support for their ideas was gathered after 1925. In 1930, five organizations amalgamated into the National Birth Control Association, which was able to co-operate more and more with local authorities in setting up voluntary clinics. The efficacy of the birth controllers was due to their influence on the Labor Party, on the Ministry of Health and local authorities, and to the erosion of some medical and religious prejudices.

3293 Dworkin, Ronald, "Lord Devlin and the Enforcement of Morals," Yale Law J. 75:986-1005, May 1966.

A review and assessment of Devlin's views on the right of the State to impose criminal sanctions on homosexuality, prostitution, and the publication of pornography. These views are contained in a book of essays by Devlin. The two chief arguments for criminal sanctions are: (1) society's right to protect its own existence; and (2) the majority's right to follow its own moral convictions in defending its social environment from change it opposes.

3294 Economist (London), "Artificial Insemination: a Timid Report," Economist 196:464, July 30, 1960.

Comment on and estimates of such births in the past twenty years.

3295 Economist (London), "Income Tax Weddings," Economist 187:19, April 5, 1958.

Since the war, couples in U.K. who marry before the end of the financial year obtain a benefit. This benefit is the increase, on marriage, of £ 100 in tax free allowances for the whole year in which the marriage takes place. For anyone earning over about £ 800 a year, a wedding before the end of the financial year brings a bonus of £ 42 10s. The result is a tendency for many couples to marry several months earlier than they ordinarily would.

3296 Eddy, J.P. "Law and Homosexuality," Crim. Law Rev. 1956:22, Jan. 1956.

3297 Eekelaar, J.M. "Crisis in Divorce Law: England and France," Internat. Comp. Law Quart. 15:875-96, July 1966.

With particular reference to the *Gollins v. Gollins* and *Williams v. Williams* divorce cases, the author concludes that what is now the sole issue in cruelty cases, and one of the necessary issues in desertion cases, is of such a nature that it is neither proper nor feasible that a court should refuse decrees, well knowing that reconciliation is impossible. Immediate divorces on apparently trivial grounds would be undesirable; thus, the author recommends a three-year delay under mutual or judicial separation which would not only give a concrete criterion according to which marriages would be dissolved, but might also have the effect of saving marriages now irretrievably broken by hasty initiation of legal proceedings.

3298 Emerson, R.G. "Family Planning in the Army: General Review of Needs and Methods," Proc. Royal Society Med. 61:243-46, March 1968.

3299 England. Parliament, House of Commons, "Family Allowances Bill," Parliamentary Debates, House of Commons 408:2259-2370, March 8, 1945.

General debate in the House of Commons on the second reading of the bill, which provides for the payment by the Minister of National Insurance of an allowance for each family at the rate of 5 shillings for each child except the first or only child.

3300 "Family Disendowment," Economist 224:388-89, July 1967.

Critical of the government's family allowance scheme, as giving inadequate benefits to children below the poverty line.

3301 "The Family Planning Act," Lancet 2:34, July 1968.

Examines the progress of the Family Planning Act of 1967 sponsored by Mr. Edwin Brooks. Of the 204 local health authorities in England and Wales, 49 are providing a family planning service, 38 of which are using the F.P.A. as their agents to provide a full family planning service; 117 are providing a restrictive service under which either the authority provides or uses the F.P.A. to provide service for a) sick only, b) sick and needy, c) only married; 32 are not implementing the act but the F.P.A. is having discussions with eight of them.

3302 Family Planning Association Working Party (The Lafitte Committee), Family Planning in the Sixties. London: Family Planning Association, 1963.

This report provides detailed facts about family planning clinics in Great Britain, their aims, their finance, management and work; and information about the people of the United Kingdom regarding their contraceptive habits and the advice they seek and obtain. It also explains just what reorganization it considers desirable so that the F.P.A. may increase its services in the coming years.

3303 Ferguson, S.M., and Fitzgerald, H. Studies in the Social Services. Civil Series, published in conjunction with Longmans, Green and Co. London: H.M. Stationery Office, 1954.

A successor to Problems of Social Policy, by Professor Titmuss, this volume takes the family as its theme and discusses the efforts required to help it to bear the strains of war. Many of the subjects considered against a wartime background retain their relevance today.

3304 Ferris, P. The Nameless: Abortion in Britain Today. London: Hutchinson and Co., Ltd., 1966.

British law, its interpretations, lack of enforcement, and ineffectiveness and the reform efforts of such a group as the Abortion Law Reform Association are reviewed. It is pointed out that liberalization of present laws would not change the practice of those physicians who find the abortion procedure repugnant or contrary to the purpose of medicine and that the National Health Service policy and that of some physicians of offering contraception advice only for medical indications further hinders attempts to reduce illegal abortion.

3305 Finestein, Israel, "An Aspect of the Jews and English Marriage Laws During the Emancipation: The Prohibited Degrees," Jewish J. Sociol. 7(1):3-21, June 1965.

Until 1835 the right of the Jews to marry validly in English law in accordance with their own rules as to the prohibited degrees does not appear to have been put in issue or openly debated. Lord Lyndhurst's Marriage Act of 1835 declared "All marriages which shall hereafter be celebrated between persons with the prohibited degrees of consanguinity or affinity shall be absolutely null and void..." The object of the Act was principally to render void a marriage between the widower and his deceased wife's sister. Neither the Mosaic code nor rabbinic law excludes marriage with the deceased wife's sister. In 1907, after 70 years of contention, Parliament finally legalized marriage with the deceased husband's brother. Likewise, ecclesiastical law, adopted into English law, prohibited marriage between uncle and niece a union not prohibited in the Mosaic code or by rabbinic law. In 1931 Parliament legalized marriage with a niece or nephew by marriage, but marriage with a niece or nephew of blood remains void.

3306 "The First Year of the Abortion Act," Lancet 1(7600): 867-68, April 1969.

The number of abortions performed in the first year after the passage of the British Abortion Act of 1967, an estimated 35,000, far surpassed expectations. The increased burden put on their National Health Service resources caused many gynecologists to restrict the number of beds available for abortion patients and the patient load problem was exacerbated by a number of gynecologists who, for various reasons, refused to perform abortions. Patients had then to go to doctors with an already heavy patient load or to private hospitals and nursing homes. The standards of many of these private establishments have been called into question. To alleviate the problem of women who cannot obtain abortions in their own N.H.S. districts, pregnancy advisory services have been established in Birmingham and London. The Representative Body of the British Medical Association expressed disapproval of the Abortion Act. Noting that in recent studies, a large number of girls and women reported using no contraceptive, it is suggested that the "real solution" to this problem "lies in better instruction of the young in matters of sexual life and responsibility and fuller guidance in contraceptive practices."

3307 Fisher, R.A. "The Birthrate and Family Allowances," Agenda 2(2):124-33, May 1943.

A discussion of the broad relationships between standards of living, declining fertility, the maintenance of peace, and the deterring effects of modern conditions on child-bearing precedes the suggestion of a plan of family allowances. It is held that an effective nationwide system of allowances would equalize the opportunities for social promotion, and aid in the solution of the eugenic problem through decreasing the trend for social strata to be differentiated on the basis of both innate abilities and low fertility.

3308 Fisher, R.A. "Family Allowances in the Contemporary Economic Situation," Eugen. Rev. 60:109-17, 1968.

This is an address to the Eugenics Society, 12th April 1932. Reviews the demographic and economic situation in Great Britain and sets forth the policy of the Eugenics Society on family allowances. Observing that the allowance system is now only an indirect one making payments for the children of the unemployed and the relief recipients, it recommends that the act and cares of parenthood be regarded as a social service which is provided for directly rather than indirectly as in the past. The nation can continue to exist by proper reproduction.

3309 "Fleet Marriages and Gretna Green," Just. Peace 124:250, April 16, 1960.

3310 Florence, Lella Secor, Progress Report on Birth Control. London: Heinemann, 1956. 260 pp.

A survey of the 2,257 new patients who came to the Birmingham Family Planning Clinic during the year 1948. The book is divided into seven chapters dealing in turn with the early history of the movement, types of patients, methods and clinic procedures, description of the survey and what it attempted to find out, consideration of "failures" and their causes, the value of information as obtained from the case cards and from interviews; finally, and perhaps the most valuable chapter of all, an evaluation of the present situation with regard to birth control.

3311 Fox, T. "Family Planning in Great Britain," Public Health 82:111-15, March 1968.

The author defines family planning as something separate from population control -- one is concerned only with the welfare of a particular family, the other with the welfare of the community. The goal of family planners is to distribute the information and supplies which people need to control their fertility. Several impractical fertility controls are discussed briefly: abortion; postponement of marriage; abstinence; coitus interruptus and condoms. The three most effective, medical methods recommended are the cap, the oral pill and the intra-uterine device. Supports the ministry's request that health authorities should themselves take the initiative and urges that hospitals, general practitioners and clinics provide all the information and services available to the public.

3312 Fraser, Hugh Macnee, "The Law of Succession in Scotland," Scottish Bankers 56:122-31, Nov. 1964.

3313 Gaveson, R.H., and Crane, F.R., eds. Century of Family Law, 1857-1957. London: Sweet, 1957.

3314 Goodhart, C.B. "The Frequency of Illegal Abortion," Eugen. Rev. 53:197-200, January 1964.

Other persons estimate that there may be between 50,000 and 100,000 illegal abortions in Great Britain each year and that the morbidity and maternal mortality from them are high. But the number of deaths attributed to procured abortions in the Ministry of Health's Reports on Confidential Enquiries into Maternal Deaths in England and Wales shows that the risks to life are not much greater than in normal childbirth, in which the maternal mortality rate -- 32.6 per 100,000 births -- is very low. Concludes that either the competence of the abortionist has been underrated or the number of abortions seriously exaggerated.

3315 Great Britain. Commission on Homosexual Offences and Prostitution, The Wolfenden Report. authorized Amer. ed. New York: Stein and Day, Inc., 1963. 243 pp.

3316 Great Britain. Home Office [England and Wales], and the Scottish Home Department, Report of the Departmental Committee on Human Artificial Insemination Presented to Parliament...July 1960. Cmd. 1105 London: H.M. Stationery Office, 1960. vi, 98 pp.

Report by the Chairman of the Committee, the Earl of Feversham, surveys the existing practice and legal consequences in Great Britain, with numerical estimates, and gives the Committee's views and recommendations. Appendixes include a summary of law and practice in eighteen countries.

3317 Great Britain. Law Commission, Reform of the Grounds of Divorce, the Field of Choice: Report on a Reference under Section 3(1) (e) of the Law Commissions Act 1965. Command 3123. London: H.M. Stationery Office, 1966.

3318 Great Britain, Laws, Statutes, etc., Act to Consolidate the Statute Law of England and Wales Relating to Sexual Crimes, to the Abduction, Procuration and Prostitution of Women and to Kindred Offenses. Ch. 69, Acts, 1956. London: H.M. Stationery Office, 1956.

3319 Great Britain, Laws, Statutes, etc., Act to Make as Respects England and Wales, Further Provision against Loitering or Soliciting in Public Places for the Purpose of Prostitution. Ch. 57 Acts 1959. London: H.M. Stationery Office, 1959.

3320 Great Britain, Laws, Statutes, etc., Sexual Offences Act, 1956. London: Butterworth and Company, 1957.

3321 Grebenik, E., and Parry, Dorothy J. "The Maternity Services in England and Wales before the War," Agenda 2(2):133-46, May 1943.

This report on the local maternity and pre-natal services permissable or actually operative in prewar England is a summary of an investigation started under the auspices of the Population Investigation Committee, and completed under those of the Social Research Division of the London School of Economics.

3322 Green, A. Romney, "Social Reconstruction by the Regulation of Incomes," Econ. J. 52:37-44, 1942.

Proposes a minimum income which would supersede and cancel all forms of public relief and pensions. Such an income arrangement would eliminate the growing demand for family allowances as a way of halting the falling birth rate.

3323 Hall, J.C. "Marriage by Proxy--Refusal to Consummate--Choice of Law," [Ponticelli v. Ponticelli 1958 2 W. L R 439], Cambridge Law J. 1958:146-48, November 1958.

Discussed is a case in which an Italian, who had settled in England and acquired an English domicile, was married to a young girl living in Italy by means of a ceremony conducted there by proxy in his absence. The husband petitioned for a decree of nullity after the girl made it clear that she had been forced into the marriage by relatives and intended to return to Italy as soon as possible. There was no doubt that the marriage must be recognized; whether it was voidable, however, on the ground of wilful refusal to consummate depended on which law, Italian or English, was to apply and on this there was little authority. Once the lex loci had been rejected the English law was applied and a decree could therefore be granted. The author feels that this solution, while clearly is to be welcomed, is not entirely free from difficulty. It is still uncertain whether the reference should be to the law of the husband's domicile at the time of marriage or to the law of the intended matrimonial domicile in a case of difference. Nor is it clear whether an English court would be prepared to apply any principle uniformly.

3324 Hall, J.C. Sources of Family Law. Cambridge: Cambridge University Press, 1966. 514 pp.

Family law is described as parts of the general corpus of law which have an especially close bearing on the family as such, either by postulating requirements for recognition of the union between its initial members, or by determining rights and duties between those members and between them and their offspring, or by providing means for the family's artificial termination. The author attempts to portray the broad principles of British family law rather than its finer details, and includes chapters on marriage (engagement contracts, capacity to marry, formalities of marriage, annulment); husband and wife (the right of consortium, maintenance, property rights, tort and contract, judicial separation, magistrates' matrimonial jurisdiction); parent and child (legitimacy, custody, parental obligations, guardianship, wards of court, adoption, the illegitimate child); and divorce (grounds, hearing of the petition, the decree, ancillary relief, proposals for reform). Indices of selected statutes, orders and court cases are also included.

3325 Harrod, R.F. "Memoranda," pp. 77-120 in: Great Britain, Royal Commission on Population, Memoranda Presented to the Royal Commission. Papers of the Royal Commission on Population. Vol. V. London: H.M. Stationery Office, 1950. iv, 120 pp.

A survey of the present situation in regard to declining fertility, the problem, and the governing principles for remedies precedes a proposal for universal endowment of children. The original submission was in August, 1944. There is a supplementary submission, December, 1944.

3326 Hartley, Shirley M. "The Amazing Rise of Illegitimacy in Great Britain," Soc. Forces 44(4):533-45, June 1966.

Demographic analysis of data of illegitimacy in England and Wales for the 25 years ending in 1962 reveals: (1) a tripling of the rate; (2) a postwar decrease of over 10 years with a new rise in the rate in excess of anything previously experienced; (3)greatest increases in the rates are not found in the very youngest groups but, rather, in the 25-34 year old age groups; (4) some parallel with the rise in US illegitimacy rates; and (5) a more moderate rise in premaritally conceived legitimate maternities. An examination is made of various personal, social structural and cultural forces which may be contributing to the rise in illegitimate births. It is suggested that the rise of individualism together with the increased protection of the Welfare State may be reducing the motivation to prevent illegitimacy.

3327 Havard, J.D.J. "Therapeutic Abortion," Crim. Law Rev., Sept. 1958, p. 600.

Statutory recognition of medical indications for therapeutic abortion is urged. Reference is given to the case of Rex v. Newton and Stungo in which the physician was convicted of manslaughter because he did not act in good faith in inducing abortion and had not followed accepted medical practice.

3328 Hemphill, R.E. "The Abortion Bill," Lancet No. 7485, Feb. 11, 1967, pp. 324-26.

Comment on the debates in the House of Commons on the Termination of Pregnancy Bill. Expresses fear that the Bill will increase demand for abortion, strain medical facilities, result in carelessness in contraceptive use, and increase materialism in family values.

3329 Henderson, A. "The Cost of Children," Part I. Popul. Stud. 3(2):130-150, Sept. 1949.

A study of the cost of living of families of different sizes in the attempt to "assess the effect of the addition of one or more children on the distribution of expenditure." The data were secured from two prewar budget inquiries in Great Britain. This section of the report describes the data and methods of procedure, and analyzes the effect of number of children on eleven categories of expenditure.

3330 Henderson, A. "The Cost of Children," Parts II and III. Popul. Stud. 4(3):267-98, Dec. 1950.

Estimates the compensating variation of income which will be necessary to keep the standard of living of a family constant when a child is born to the family. Various methods of estimation are tried, and an attempt is made to calculate the cost of a child in 1948, after allowances have been made for services provided by the government.

3331 Henry, Louis, "A Propos d'une Enquete sur la Contraception en Grande-Bretagne" [An Investigation of Contraception in Great Britain], Population 17(1):65-74, 1962.

A presentation and discussion of the results of a national poll on the practice of contraception in Great Britain, undertaken in 1959-1960 by the Population Investigation Committee (N=3,000 respondents aged 16-59 years). It was found that use of contraceptives depended on: general attitude regarding birth control, socio-professional status, and religion, but especially on age; the younger the respondents and the more recently married, the more recourse to contraception is taken. Results indicated that contraception is: (1) the most frequent among respondents who unreservedly approve of birth control (80.5% versus 35.6% of disapprovers); (2) more frequent in the middle classes (73.9%) than among skilled or semi-skilled workers (69.2% and 61.7%, respectively); (3) more frequent among Protestants (70.1%) than Catholics (47%), as predicted (but with a greater difference in older marriages than in recent ones); (4) more frequent among males than females (72.4% versus 62.9%) - a difference which did not vary with age or length of marriage, thus implying a certain amount of dissimulation among respondents; and (5) effective to a very high degree, with very little social class differences (91.8% of middle-class respondents 88.3% of skilled workers, 87% of unskilled workers).

3332 Hierarchy of England and Wales, "The Population Report. A Statement from the Hierarchy," The Tablet, April 14, 1951. Reproduced in Eugenics Rev. 43(2):94-95, July 1951.

A statement of Catholic opposition to the Report because of its secular orientation and its advocacy of "artificial contraception" which is "intrinsically evil." The major editorial of this issue of the Eugenics Review is a summary and critique of this Catholic critique.

3333 "Homicide and Abortion in England and Ireland," J. Crim. Law 21:362, Oct.-Dec. 1957.

There is uniformity in the theory of abortion laws in England and Ireland but differences arise in the application and interpretation of these laws, e.g., in Ireland the attitudes of the Catholic Church influence the practice of the law.

3334 Houghton, Vera, "Medical Termination of Pregnancy Bill," Eugenics Rev. 53:93-95, July 1961.

Reviews the medical termination of pregnancy bill reintroduced in the Commons in February, 1961, whose main purpose is to bring statute law into line with what case law has been since the Rex v. Bourne judgement of 1939. It also seeks to extend the grounds for legal termination of pregnancy. The more controversial part of the Bill was, as expected, the additional grounds for lawful abortion; in the belief that there would be grave risk of the child being grossly deformed or physically or mentally malformed to the extent that he would require constant hospital treatment or special care; or in the belief that the person became pregnant as a result of rape or is of unsound mind. A discussion of these issues urges the passage of this reform bill.

3335 Hubback, Eva M. "Family Allowances in War-Time," Eugenics Rev. 33(1):13-16, April 1941.

There has been increasing support in Britain for a scheme of Family Allowances due to the fact that war conditions greatly strengthen the national social conscience and the need for such a scheme. The author reviews recent figures as to child-dependency and the cost of living and contends that Family Allowances constitute the only way in which these problems can be satisfactorily dealt with. The costs of a Government scheme are estimated, and it is felt that any scheme introduced must be of a simple nature, with a suggested sum of five shillings per week for each dependent child. Schemes to encourage births in those economic sections of the community that spend more than this amount on their childrens' needs must wait, but once Family Allowances have become familiar,schemes such as the establishment of mutual insurance pools for different economic grades could be superimposed on a flat-rate scheme. An interesting light should be shed on the differential birth rate once the minimum of physical needs have been guaranteed to all children.

3336 Hughes, G. "Crime of Incest," J. Crim. Law 55:322-31, Sept. 1964.

A brief survey of the literature on incest is presented in

an attempt to evaluate the existing criminal law. The author contends that while there are very real harmful effects produced by incest activity both in the immediate impacts on members of the family circle and in the wider social sense of tending to destroy the family as a functioning social unit and that the incest situation is indeed a proper subject for criminal prohibition, the typical state of incest laws in common-law systems are clumsy and imprecise in their impact on the evils produced by such behavior. Existing statutes display unreflecting vestiges of primitive taboo attitudes toward incest and the author proposes a model incest prohibition based on his feeling that the primary need in this area is for protection of the younger female members of the family circle.

3337 Inge, W.R. "The Future of England," Fortnightly 917 N.S.: 288-93, May 1943.

Less industry and population are predicted for the England of the future. The Beveridge Report is attacked, particularly those sections dealing with family allowances.

3338 International Labour Office, "The British Family Allowances Act, 1945," Internat. Labour Rev. 52(5):548-49, Nov. 1945.

A summary of the major provisions of the Act.

3339 Jackson, Margaret H. "A Medical Service for the Treatment of Involuntary Sterility," Eugenics Rev. 36(4):117-25, Jan. 1945.

A discussion of the work of clinics in England, the growth of the service, the nature of the examinations made, and some of the findings and results.

3340 Jackson, Margaret N. "Family Planning in England and India," J. Sex Research 3(4):269-71, Nov. 1967.

A description of family planning work in England for problem families followed by a description of a visit to India and the work being done there in family spacing and limitation. In England local authorities are required by the Ministry of Health to see that adequate facilities are available for all couples who need contraceptive advice for medical or socioeconomic reasons. The Family Planning Association has more than 600 clinics; nearly all prescribe and advise on oral contraceptives and about 25% fit intra-uterine devices. Abortion is briefly discussed. Dismay is expressed at the lack of success with family planning programs in India, where "Abraham Stone failed to make any impact with the rhythm method, the cap and condom reach only a few, sterilization comes too late in reproductive life to do more than ruffle the surface, and abortion is still underground." The intra-uterine device promises to be the way out, and the program was started with enthusiasm, but without adequate or long-range planning, with the result that things are not going too well.

3341 Jeger, Lena M. "The Politics of Family Planning," Polit. Quart. 33(1):48-58, Jan.-March 1962.

The author examines the rapid social acceptability of birth control in Great Britain and questions its political non-recognition. The birth control movement's progress is traced from the Bradlaugh and Besant trial in 1877 through the Family Planning Association's work. The author states that the inconsistencies of domestic political attitudes are reflected in Britain's contributions to the world population program, and urges that the social responsibility of Britain and other Western countries be realized both in domestic and world politics.

3342 Jenkins, Alic, Law for the Rich: A Plea for the Reform of the Abortion Law. London: Gollancz, 1960. 95 pp.

Description of the efforts of the Abortion Law Reform Association to secure reform of the law against abortion in Great Britain. The Association upholds the principle that it is the woman's right to decide whether or not to allow the pregnancy to continue.

3343 Joint Committee of the Royal College of Obstetricians and Gynaecologists and the Population Investigation Committee. "A Survey of Childbearing in Britain," Popul. Stud. 1(1): 99-136, June 1947.

This article is a preliminary report of a questionnaire inquiry into the social and economic factors associated with pregnancy and childbearing in Great Britain. The inquiry was planned to obtain information about expenditure during and after pregnancy, the availability of the maternity services to different social classes and in different parts of the country, the use made of them, the need for extra domestic help for expectant and nursing mothers, and other similar questions; it was felt by the Joint Committee that only in studying these basic problems could effective policies for removing the deterrents to parenthood and increasing the availability of maternity services be formulated. A total of 13,687 mothers cooperated in the survey, and six different occupational groups were covered. The general conclusions were that there is still great inequality in the care received by different social groups and that, in certain respects (particularly postnatal care of the mother and the provision of analgesia), there is room for considerable improvements for all classes. The costs of childbearing are so high that they are likely to deter many mothers, of all classes, from having children. While the lower social groups spend in actual figures less than the more prosperous, in proportion to total income the working-class family is almost certainly paying much more. The inquiry shows that the drain of family expenditure begins sharply at the birth of the first child and that children, in this sense, are one of the major causes of poverty.

3344 Jones, D. Caradog, "Family Allowances," Nature 149(3789): 656-58, June 13, 1942.

This discussion of the official memorandum on the subject (Parliamentary Paper, Command 6354) mentions briefly the implications of family allowance schemes for population policy.

3345 Lafitte, Francois. "Family Planning Clinics," New Society 2(57):14-15, Oct. 31, 1963.

An extract from Family Planning in the Sixties (Family Planning Association Working Party, United Kingdom) suggesting that family planning clinics should improve and involve husbands more closely. It is easier to continue to operate as a service for a female minority. However, giving choice and information regarding both female and male birth control methods would be in line with preference of most Britons and would be in the direction of more comprehensive service of family planning needs. Choice of family planning methods is widening; clientele in family planning clinics is changing in the direction of younger, recently married couples. Needs are outlined as: (1) fuller appreciation of the educative aspects of family planning clinic work, (2) fuller appreciation of the passive and permissive role of the medical experts in family planning, and (3) improvement of family planning clinic services by (a) better timekeeping, (b) appointment systems, and (c) improved psychological atmosphere.

3346 Lafitte, Francois, "The Users of Birth Control Clinics," Popul. Stud. 16(1):12-30, July 1962.

At the request of the British Family Planning Association a Working Party is inquiring into the Association's work and organization. In 1960 the Working Party conducted a national survey of the accomplishments, organization and financing of the network of voluntary birth control clinics which the association established chiefly since 1958. Clinic users (virtually all women in 1960) differed from the majority of birth control users in that they preferred, or at least were advised to try, a minority method - the female cap - which is only slowly gaining in popularity. Clinics recommended this method to virtually all clients, whether newly-wed or mothers of large families and were consulted by about 1 in every 9 women marrying during the year and by between 1 - 1.5% of wives at each later stage of family building. Among clinic users (1) non-manual occupations are more strongly represented, and unskilled and semi-skilled less strongly represented, than in the general population; and (2) many are not beginners, but want to try a different method. 33.3% of new clients are women who have not yet borne a child, usually young and newly-weds, whose growing population among clients is altering the nature of clinic work. Regionally there is evidence of increasing conservatism in clinic work and clientele as one moves from London to Scotland.

3347 Lancet, Family Allowances. Aylesbury, England: Lancet, 1940. 32 pp.

Family allowances schemes already operating in England are summarized.

3348 Lang, L.P., and Richardson, K.D. "The Implications of a Rising Female Sterilization Rate," J. Obstet. Gynaecol. Brit. Commonw. 75(9):972-75, 1968.

The number of female sterilization operations performed in a large provincial obstetric and gynecological unit increased from 54 in 1962 to 144 in 1966. In both years reviewed, the majority of patients had had 4 or more pregnancies. There was no change in the indications for the operation in the 2 years. In both years the complication rate was 17% and only 30% of the patients were discharged by the 7th post-operative day.

3349 Land, Hilary, "Provision for Large Families," New Society 8(217):795-96, Nov. 24, 1966.

A random sample of 150 large families in London forms the basis for an examination of aid to those who must have government support to feed and clothe their children. 86 families from all social classes were interviewed regarding government subsidies and family income. Research shows that apart from housing, the primary problem is administering of services in such a way as to insure that all families needing them are aware of their accessibility. Various methods of filling the "information gap" in this area are suggested, and it is stressed that beyond this the central problem is still the size of family allowances and basic wages.

3350 Latey, W. "Recognition of Foreign Decrees of Divorce," Internat. Comparative Law Quart. 16:982-996, Oct. 1967.

In the case of Indyka v. Indyka, 1967, the House of Lords made legal history. Though adhering to the rigid principle of domicile as the test of jurisdiction for domestic cases of divorce in England, the Lordships unanimously decided that a foreign divorce between a wife living all her life in the country whose court pronounced the divorce, and a husband who was a national of that country but acquired domicile of choice in England, should be recognized here. An important factor for determination should be the substantial connection of the married couple with the country in which the divorce was pronounced.

3351 Leach, Gerald, "Experts in Secret Government Talks on Population Control," The Observer, 5 Oct., 1969.

A secret committee of senior civil servants has been meeting for over a year to advise the Government on Britain's population growth, with a view to seeing how it might be controlled if necessary. The existence of this group is the first firm evidence of high-level Government concern on population matters. The last comparable move was the 1949 Royal Commission on Population, which recommended that population growth should be stabilized by Government policies. Its findings were ignored. The growing consensus among population experts is that governments can exert such pressures only through scores of minor thrusts, and that many of these could be steps to increase social justice.

3352 Lees, Dennis, "Poor Families and Fiscal Reform," Lloyds Bank Rev.,October 1967, pp. 1-15.

Concerns proposals to adjust the present child tax allowances and family allowances. Possibilities of a negative income tax.

3353 "Legal Abortion," Mental Health 20:86-103, Autumn 1961.

Contents: The case for reform, by Kenneth Robinson; Legal aspects of abortion by Glanville Williams; The case against termination on psychiatric grounds by J.V. O'Sullivan and L. Fairfield; Abortion law in other countries.

3354 "Legalized Abortion," Medico-Legal J.34:45-47, 1966.

This editorial argues against the given figure of 100,000 criminal abortions per year as cited in the Report of the Royal College of Obstetricians and Gynaecologists, 1966. The author states that the majority of gynecologists in England see no urgent need for abortion law reform and urges the prevention of liberalizing the laws.

3355 Lewis-Fanning, E. Report on an Inquiry into Family Limitation and Its Influence on Human Fertility During the Past Fifty Years. Papers of the Royal Commission on Population, Vol. I. London: H.M.S.O., 1949. xvi + 202 pp.

This detailed enquiry was carried out by the Royal College of Obstetricians and Gynaecologists at the request of the Royal Commission on Population. The questions to which the Royal Commission particularly needed answers indicate clearly the scope of the enquiry now under review. They are as follows: How extensively is birth control practised?; In what proportions are the different methods of birth control practised?; Are there important differences between different social groups in the extent of the practice of birth control, or in the choice of method?; To what extent is birth control, as practised, effective?; What is the extent of involuntary fertility?; Does the practice of birth control affect the power to reproduce?; How important is abortion as a method of birth prevention?; What is the proportion of "unplanned pregnancies"?; What is the proportion of "unwanted children"?; What are the chief reasons given for using birth control? A questionnaire was designed and launched by a special sub-committee of the R.C.O.G. so that answers to these questions might be elicited from a suitable cross section of the population. Accordingly, between August 1946 and June 1947 inclusive, some 11,078 married women were questioned by members of the staff of voluntary and municipal hospitals and by a certain number of general practitioners and health visitors in chosen representative areas throughout the country.

3356 Leys, D. "Legalising Abortion," Lancet 1:384-ff., 1967.

The author argues that evidence stated to maintain the present abortion law is medically and scientifically unsound. Those prohibiting hospital abortion, he contends, must accept the responsibility for the births of unwanted children and the social inequities of the current system.

3357 Lister, J. "Abortion," New Eng. J. Med. 274:957, 1966.

A survey of public opinion in Britain before the passage of the new abortion bill.

3358 London. Liberal Publication Department. Family Allowances and Social Security -- Lady Rhys-Williams' Scheme. London: Liberal Publication Department, 1944. 24 pp.

Proposals for unifying income-tax allowances with social-security benefits, including family allowances, for the purpose of effecting a more equitable income distribution between persons without dependents and those with family responsibilities.

3359 Mackesy, A.N. "Criminal Law and the Woman Seducer--the Sexual Offences Act 1956," Crim. Law R. 1956:446, 529, and 798, July-August and December 1956.

3360 Manchester, A.H. "Marriage or Prison: the Case of the Reluctant Bridegroom," Modern Law Rev. 29:622-34, Nov. 1966.

English authority concerning the effect of duress on the validity of marriage is quite scarce and so far as some of the early cases are concerned, unreliable. Therefore, the recent judgement in Buckland v. Buckland is of interest on several counts. It is both the first reported English case to offer a tolerably comprehensive guide to the principles which are applicable in such cases and it is the first reported case before an English court in which a male petitioner has sought the annulment of his marriage on the grounds of duress and where the grounds of such duress have been the arrest and possible imprisonment of the petitioner.

3361 Mann, M. "Royal Commission on Marriage and Divorce: Jurisdiction of the English Courts and Recognition of Foreign Decrees," Modern Law Rev. 21(1):1-18, Jan. 1958.

The author examines the recommendations of the Royal Commission on Marriage and Divorce regarding matrimonial jurisdiction and the recognition of the jurisdiction of other countries. Each of these areas is subdivided into portions dealing with divorce and nullity, and the Commission's order of examination is followed, with observations on the more important and controversial recommendations. It is concluded that if one agrees with the Commission that recognition of foreign matrimonial decrees should be based upon reciprocity the problem of the recognition of foreign decrees becomes subservient to that of determining the jurisdiction of the English court. The fundamental difficulty in making that determination lies in attempting to reconcile two conflicting desires: first, the desire to avoid the creation of limping marriages by pronouncing decrees which stand litle chance of recognition abroad. Second, the desire to grant matrimonial relief to those who one conceives should be entitled to it. If the English courts could grant a decree only when both parties were citizens of the United Kingdom and Colonies, who were domiciled and resident in England,it could be guaranteed that an English decree would receive almost universal recognition. This would fulfill the first desire, but only at the expense of the second. The author contends that a simple compromise must be sought, and that it is far from clear whether the Commission's recommendations have served to reconcile the two conflicting desires.

3362 Mathew, J. "The Present State of the Law of Abortion," Med. Sci. Law 4:170-75, July 1964.

The fears of physicians concerning the legality of inducing abortion may be allayed by consistent interpretations of the law. Cites the legal position as represented in the Offenses Against the Person Act of 1861, the Infant Life (Preservation) Act of 1929, and the Case of Rex v. Bourne, 1938.

3363 McGregor, O.R. "The Morton Commission: A Social and Historical Commentary," Brit. J. Sociol. 7:171-93, September 1956.

An assessment of the work and significance of the Morton Commission in the light of the history of divorce in England. The leading Protestant country in Europe was little affected by the Reformation, as far as divorce was concerned; the ecclesiastical courts maintained jurisdiction over marriage and divorce, and the theory of indissolubility of marriage prevalent in medieval times was retained. After the Reformation, those who wished to be divorced had to secure a Private Act of Parliament. The Marriage Act of 1753 provided two important principles: (1) marriage became for the first time a public and certain contract; and (2) the right to determine what constituted a valid marriage was removed from the Church and assumed by the state. By 1836, citizens had a choice of a religious or civil marriage ceremony. The Act of 1857 created a new Court for Divorce and Matrimonial Causes to which was transferred all jurisdiction at that time exercised in matrimonial matters by the Ecclesiastical Courts in England. The Act was criticized on two grounds: (1) it sanctioned two standards of morality by making divorce easier for men than for women; and (2) the cost of divorce was so high as to deny legal remedies to working people. By the beginning of the 20th century, there were two systems of resolving matrimonial difficulties: the affluent used the Divorce Court, and the poor went to the magistrate's courts and obtained separation orders. Subsequent acts placed men and women on equal footing and increased the grounds for divorce, but no steps were taken to make the Divorce Court accessible to the poor. The principal change in the present century has been the innovations of the legal aid system of 1949, which gave access to the Divorce Court to all citizens. The central issue confronting the Morton Commission was whether to keep the matrimonial offense as the basis of divorce law.

3364 "Medical Aspects of Divorce and Nullity of Marriage," <u>Brit</u>. <u>Med</u>. <u>J</u>. 5550:491-93, 1967.

An attempt is here made to indicate the sort of questions on which a medical practitioner is likely to be called upon to give evidence of his expert opinion in suits in which different matrimonial offences are alleged.

3365 Medical Defense Union, "The Abortion Act 1967 - Memorandum from Medical Defense Union," <u>Brit</u>. <u>Med</u>. <u>J</u>. 1:759-ff., 1968.

Discusses several different sections of the New British Abortion Act effective April, 1968. The meaning of key terms, legal implications, the consent of the patient and her husband, and the role of the practitioner are examined. Regarding the question of priority in the use of hospital beds, abortion patients should not be categorized separately, but the gynecologist's task is to deal with each patient according to the needs of her particular case.

3366 Medical Women's Federation, "Abortion Law Reform," <u>Brit. Med</u>. <u>J</u>. 2:1512-ff., 1966.

A subcommittee of the Medical Women's Federation proposes that the new abortion bill in Great Britain include one general clause covering indications for interruption of pregnancy and that the specific grounds should not be listed. They feel that illegal abortion cannot be minimized unless the new law is supplemented by adequate medical and social services including greater sex education and expansion of clinics providing contraceptive advice.

3367 Micklewright, F.H. Amphlett, "A Legal Layman and the Street Offences Bill," <u>Plain View</u> 12:193-99, Winter 1959.

3368 Micklewright, F.H. Amphlett, "Sex Laws in Modern England," <u>Plain View</u> 13:32-41, May 1960.

3369 Mills, Wilfrid, "Intrauterine Contraception in the National Health Service," The Lancet No. 7410, Sept. 4, 1965, pp. 485-86.

This is an account of 341 hospital outpatients fitted with 353 intrauterine devices between June 9, 1964, and July 28, 1965. Notes on organization and method, results, conclusions.

3370 Muller-Freienfels, W. "Equality of Husband and Wife in Family Law," Internat. Comp. Law Quart. 8:249-67, April 1959.

After discussing the principle of equality of husband and wife in current societies, often reformulated in terms of the protection of the family as a social unit, the author examines the equality of spouses in their personal relations, with reference to the doubtful value of statutory regulation in this area and the rules governing the power of decision with the family. The equality of spouses in matrimonial property law is then discussed, with sections on the community of acquisitions or separation of property with equalization of gains between the spouses and the privileged position of the surviving spouse in the law of succession. The author concludes that the question of how to balance in detail the inevitable inequalities of the sexes will remain one of the great problems of the future, even in those countries where the claims of suffragettes shall have become more and more completely satisfied. Efforts in this direction have also to be combined with pedagogic points of view from a psychotactical platform. The ultimate aim should be that of not so much establishing the utmost pure equality of men and women, but rather differentiating, in the spirit of just equality, more exactly and reasonably.

3371 Northern Ireland, Government, Family Allowances Act, Northern Ireland, 1945. Public and General Acts, 1946, Ch. 19. Belfast: H.M. Stationery Office, 1946.

3372 "Notification of Abortions," Brit. Med. J. 1:531-ff., 1968.

Criticizes the provision of Abortion Act of 1967 which would allow police to have access to records in cases of therapeutic abortions. This proposal violates the right of confidential relationship of patient and physician.

3373 Paulsen, Monrad G. "Divorce-Canterbury Style," Valpariso Univ. Law Rev. 1:93-100, Fall 1966.

Legal, sociological and theological implications of the British report titled, Putting Asunder, prepared by a group appointed by the Archbishop of Canterbury and chaired by Dr. Robert Mortimer.

3374 Payne, J.D. "Artificial Insemination Heterologous and the Matrimonial Offense of Adultery in the United Kingdom," North Carolina Law Rev. 40:111-14, Dec. 1961.

A discussion of the British legal experiences with artificial insemination. Several court cases are renewed leading to the conclusion that AID should neither be prohibited nor even regulated by law. In the context of matrimonial law, the committee appointed in 1958 to investigate the practice of human artificial insemination and its legal consequences, accepts the conclusion of the Royal Commission on Marriage and Divorce (1951-1955) that a clear distinction exists between artificial insemination and adultery. The department committee also endorsed the recommendation of the Royal Commission that artificial insemination of the wife without the consent of the husband be made a new and separate ground for judicial separation or divorce.

3375 Peberdy, Mary, "Family Planning as Social Medicine," Lancet 7556:1363-65, 1968.

Family planning means far more than giving advice on contraception. A main purpose is to encourage a sense of responsibility towards reproduction and so strengthen the family. The care of teenagers and young people is a great challenge to those interested in family-planning policy. In any age group all who are about to marry should be able to get counsel. The timing and spacing of births is the essence of family planning; if advice is given on the prevention of pregnancy, there must also be help for those who are having difficulty in starting a baby. Must consider family limitation, whether by contraception or by operations such as vasectomy. These procedures concern lawyers, teachers, politicians, administrators, scientists, and nurses, but most of all the medical profession, who cannot escape this responsibility.

3376 Peel, John, "Contraception and the Medical Profession," Popul. Stud. 18(2):133-45, Nov. 1964.

Family limitation is currently regarded as an important element in preventive medicine and the provision of contraceptive advice an appropriate item in the range of paramedical services which the general practitioner is increasingly being called upon to provide. Medical hostility has, nevertheless, been a major impediment in the development of the English birth control movement. This paper describes the changing attitude of the profession to this subject and attempts to assess the contribution made by physicians to the spread of birth control knowledge and to the advance of contraceptive technique.

3377 Peel, John, "A Fertility Control Experiment Among Problem Families," Med. Officer 116(27):357-58, 1966.

This paper describes and evaluates a domiciliary birth control programme based on traditional method of contraception and operated on a paramedical basis by male social workers.

3378 Peel, John, "A Male-Oriented Fertility Control Experiment," Practitioner 202:677-81, May 1969.

A male-oriented traditional contraceptive method (condom) was found to be as effective as prescribed contraceptives in a group of fertile couples of low socio-economic status and a high rate of mobility. Home visits by a social worker bringing supplies, first at monthly intervals and then at bi-monthly intervals, were discontinued at the end of one year, after which the supplies were mailed. Of the 50 couples originally in the study, conducted in Hull, England, 27 remained in the study at the end of three years. Among the 53 couples currently in the study, 4 pregnancies had occurred, instead of an expected 81 pregnancies.

3379 Peel, John, "The Manufacture and Retailing of Contraceptives in England," Popul. Stud. 17(2):113-26, Nov. 1963.

A survey of the origin and development of the contraceptive trade in Great Britain, together with an assessment of the contribution of commercial interests to the dissemination of birth control knowledge and the development of contraceptive technique. The contemporary status of the £ 20 million/ per year trade in commercial contraceptives is also examined. It is concluded that, in the absence of medical leadership, commercial concerns were almost wholly responsible for satisfying the demand for birth control techniques which developed in Great Britain after 1878.

3380 Peel, J.,and Potts, M. "Demographic Aspects of Abortion in Britain," Paper Presented at the International Union for the Scientific Study of Population General Conference, 3-11 September 1969, London.

Britain is the first country in the world to have introduced a permissive abortion law within a society where contraceptive practice amongst married couples is firmly established and where the two-child family norm is already being displaced. The Abortion Act which was passed on 27 October 1967 avoids the cumbersome delaying procedures characteristic of Scandinavian law. In the first year of its existence, there were 37,736 abortions. These are analyzed by age and other traits. The passage of the Act seems to have brought about new attitudes to contraception.

3381 Peel, John,and Schenk, Faith, "Domiciliary Birth Control: A New Dimension in Negative Eugenics," Eugen. Rev. 57(2): 67-71, June 1965.

Assessment of demographic results in first 50 cases referred in a scheme for providing contraceptive advice by home visitors to problem families in cooperation with local health and welfare services in Newcastle and Southampton, England.

3382 "Policy Orientation in Matrimonial Property Law," [Richards v. Richards (1958) 1 W L R 1116] Modern Law Rev. 22:207, March 1959.

The author contends that with the continuing high degree of marriage-instability and the resulting number of economic claims between husband and wife, it is becoming increasingly evident that some attempt must be made to analyze the underlying policy-orientation of recent decisions. Only through a clearer articulation of the goals toward which the courts are reaching, and a more explicit analysis of how they put their policies into effect, can the traditional formulae achieve any predictive value. The Court of Appeal decision of Richards v. Richards (1958) is described since at least three of the underlying policies of modern law are inherent, in one form or another, in it. The three social policies are examined and the course of each through the related fields of matrimonial law is plotted. It is felt that the courts must focus on the increasing democratization of the family, since both wives and children are playing an increasing role in supporting their families; this democratization is seen in the common modern use of the joint tenancy and feminine contribution to the purchase of marital property.

3383 Pond, D.A., "No Questions Asked?" Lancet 1:611-ff., 1967.

Several problems raised by Britain's new abortion bill are examined. The role of the physician involves a difficult decision of whether to perform an operation like abortion, on which only he is qualified to perform. Questions on the duty of the physician and on the qualifications of the physician in evaluating the psychiatric and social implications of the abortion are considered.

3384 "Population, Births, and Abortions," Lancet 2(7610):52, July 1969.

An abstract of the latest Registrar General's Quarterly Return for England and Wales which includes population projections, and figures for births and for abortions in 1968.

3385 Puxon, C.M. The Family and the Law: The Laws of Marriage, Separation and Divorce. Bristol: MacGibbon and Kee, 1967.

3386 Puxson, H., and Dawkins, S. "Non-Consummation of Marriage," Med. Sci. Law 4:15, Jan. 1964.

3387 Pyke, Margaret, "Family Planning: An Assessment," Eugenics Rev. 55(2):71-79, July 1963.

The text of the 1963 Galton lecture, reviewing the development of the family planning movement in the United Kingdom from its beginnings with T. Malthus, J. Bentham and especially Place, who in 1822 wrote and distributed handbills giving contraceptive information. The Bradlaugh-Besant trial gave an impetus to the decline in the birth-rate which fell from 35 per thousand to 14.9 in 1933 (in 1963 it was 17.1). The work of M. Stopes and the Malthus League led to the foundation of the first birth control clinic in England in 1921. In 1930 the Family Planning Association was founded, under the name of the National Birth Control Clinic, with the permissive authority of the Ministry of Health. The growth of the Association has been rapid, and in the first part of a Working Party-produced Report in 1962, shows a professional and salaried staff, in clinics of 450 physicians and 600 nurses as well as numerous part-time assistants. The Report concludes with the Population Investigation Committee that some 87% of couples married 10 years ago used birth control.

3388 Pyke, Margaret, "Family Planning: the Past and the Future," Eugenics Rev. 44(4):197-201, Jan. 1953.

History, activities, and program of the Family Planning Association of Great Britain.

3389 Rathbone, Eleanor F. Family Allowances. London: Allen and Unwin, 1949. xiii, 293 pp.

A new third edition of the Disinherited family. Includes a new chapter on The family allowances movement, 1924-1947, by Eva M. Hubback.

3390 Rathbone, Eleanor, "Immediate Prospects for Family Allowances," pp. 62-64 in: Highway, Workers Educational Association. London, Feb. 1945.

Reviews the beginnings of the family-allowance movement in Great Britain, takes up the question of allocations in cash or in kind, and appeals for higher grants than those provided in the present British bill for such allowances.

3391 Reading, Marquess of, "Some Legal Aspects of A.I.D.," Oxford Lawyer 2nd Issue, 1958, pp. 5-7, 9.

Discussion of problems created by artificial insemination by donor under present English law.

3392 Robinson, John A.T. Abortion: Beyond Law Reform. London: Abortion Law Reform Association [1966].

Lecture delivered by the Bishop of Woolwich on October 22nd, 1966 to a meeting of the Abortion Law Reform Association.

3393 Robinson, K. "The Case for Reform," Ment. Health 20:88, 1961.

The outcome of the author's Medical Termination of Pregnancy Bill proposed to the House of Commons in 1961 is examined. The author contends that the current abortion legislation of Great Britain has long since ceased to reflect public opinion or to govern common practice and urges reform.

3394 Robinson, Kenneth. "Parliamentary and Public Attitudes," pp. 451-460, Chpt. in: Ismond Rose, ed. The Pathology and Treatment of Sexual Deviation. New York: Oxford U. Press, 1964, xvi + 510 pp.

A discussion of Parliament's approach to problems of sexual deviation, especially homosexuality, regarding its tendency to lag behind, rather than lead public opinion. Parliamentary acts regarding sexual deviation are dealt with. Debates over the Wolfenden Report indicated that there was a recognition that there must be legal reform, not only rectifying the existing situation, but also creating a new attitude of public opinion to homosexuality.

3395 Rodger, T. Ferguson, "Attitudes Toward Abortion," Amer. J. Psychiat. 125(6):804-8, 1968.

The Abortion Act, which recently became law in Great Britain, has clarified previous uncertainty about the legal grounds for abortion. It is pointed out, however, that it has also raised new issues involving the rights of the unborn child, reflecting contemporary views on what may be called the "gift of life."

3396 Rowntree, Griselda, "The Finances of Founding a Family," Scottish J. Polit. Econ. 1(1):201-32, Oct. 1954.

Description of a sample survey of 362 Aberdeen families having a first or second child in the early 1950's. Summary of results and discussion of implications for social policy, particularly maternity benefits.

3397 Rowntree, Griselda, "Supplementary Child Health Services. Part III. Infant Welfare Centres," Popul. Stud. 3(4):375-85, March 1950.

Since the work of the Infant Welfare Centres in education and preventative medicine can only be fully effective if the great majority of all mothers can be persuaded to make regular attendances, the author gives an account of attendance at these centres between 1946 and 1948, based on data from the 1948 Follow-up Survey to the Maternity Survey of 1946. The Maternity Survey was primarily concerned with the social problems associated with maternity among the 13,687 mothers in the national sample who had been confined in the week of March 3-9, 1946 and dealt only briefly with the use of infant welfare centres for the supervision of the health and welfare of the babies in the sample. 4,703 mothers of surviving children were asked, in the 1948 Survey, how many weeks old their children were at the first visit to the centre and how many times they had attended in the periods between March 1946 and February 1947 and between March 1947 and February 1948. The author includes sections on the accuracy of the data; the use of the centres; the date of first attendance; the frequency of attendances; and factors influencing the habitual use of the centres. There were 4,690 children about whom information on the use of centres was available; the proportion who had been taken to the centres at least once before their second birthday was approximately 68.7%. The average date of the first attendance was 7 weeks after the date of delivery, and there was only a small proportion of mothers who attended frequently in the first year and who continued to make regular use of the centres in the second.

3398 Rowntree, Griselda, and Carrier, Norman H. "The Resort to Divorce in England and Wales, 1858-1957," Popul. Stud. 11(3): 188-233, March 1958.

A statistical analysis of the increasing divorce rate in England and Wales is part of a continuing study of marriage and divorce initiated by the Population Investigation Committee of the University of London in 1953. Analysis is based on legal petitions for divorce rather than decrees granted because the latter is subject to procedural bottlenecks and demands such persistence and legal ability as to discourage many petitioners; petitioning seems a better indicator of demand for divorce. Changes in divorce law since 1857 are summarized and alterations in the public acceptance of divorce are discussed. Petitions filed per year per 10,000 married women aged 15-49 have risen from 0.83 in 1861-65 to 1.80 in 1911, 7.50 in 1931, and 37.98 in 1956. The maximum rate was 67.69 in 1947. The authors discuss various factors believed responsible for this 50-fold increase: a 5-fold rise was due to lowered formal barriers and legal aid for the poor, while the remaining 10-fold increase was attributable to the changing climate of opinion. Since published statistics include very few cross tabulations, a detailed picture of changes necessitates going back to original records. This was done for 1871 (285 cases) and 1951 (systematic sample of 1,813 from 38,382 cases), showing the change from predominantly well-to-do and frequently childless couples in 1871 to a divorcing population in 1951 which had nearly the same occupational characteristics as the general population and a somewhat larger proportion of childlessness (26.4% to 21.5%) than those still married. Mid-20th century cohort analysis indicates that the rate of petitioning will probably increase at a decreasing rate and may even stabilize at its present level.

3399 Rowntree, Griselda, and Pierce, Rachel M. "Birth Control in Great Britain," Popul. Stud. 15(1):3-31 and 15(2):121-60, 1961.

First reports on a new national British study on family planning and fertility. Part I is Attitudes and Practice. Part II is Contraceptive Methods Used by Couples Married in the Last Thirty Years. Respondents are participants in the Population Investigation Committee's nationally representative Marriage Survey. In contrast to U.S. patterns, withdrawal (*coitus interruptus*) was almost as popular in Britain as the sheath (or condom), each of these methods being adopted at some time by nearly 50% of the users. The safe period or rhythm method (16%), the cap (11%) and soluble pessaries (10%), were much less important. An analysis of the general experience of individual users shows a small but significant cohort trend away from the method of withdrawal and towards the use of the cap. It was unusual for even the sophisticated group of avowed users (who were more extensively questioned than the reticent) to obtain contraceptive advice from professional sources. Over 70% of the avowed users, married for at least 10 years, adopted only one method during their married lives and the remainder, who often began by using coitus interruptus finally switched to the more reliable appliance methods, notably the cap or chemicals. A social class analysis of the users who started contraception at marriage illustrates how the general trend from withdrawal to cap was spreading through our society: among these early starters, non-manual couples and especially those recently married used the cap much more often than the other manual group, with the skilled manual in an intermediate position. An examination of the conformity of Roman Catholics to their Church's teaching on contraception suggests that their degree of devotion to their faith was a crucial factor in determining their behavior. Though there were distinct trends over time and the pattern of methods used differed significantly with class and religion, these were on the whole minor variations.

3400 Royal College of Obstetricians and Gynaecologists and British Medical Association, "Joint Statement on Abortion," Lancet 1:339-ff., 1967.

Proposes several amendments to the new Abortion Bill: that therapeutic abortion is legal only if performed under the supervision of or by a registered medical practitioner in an accredited hospital or nursing home following consultation and agreement of at least one professional colleague who has also examined the patient, and that the law be clarified so that a physician who terminates a pregnancy under the above conditions and in good faith, and in the interests of the physical or mental health of the mother be regarded as acting lawfully. The total environment of the mother must be taken into account.

3401 Royal Medico-Psychological Association, "Memorandum on Therapeutic Abortion," Brit. J. Psychiat. 112(491):1071-73, 1966.

Report of the Royal Medico-Psychological Association's position on therapeutic abortion. The position includes the general view that, in addition to traditionally accepted medical and psychiatric criteria, all social circumstances should be taken into account when a psychiatrist is deciding whether or not a therapeutic abortion is justified. The Association recommends changes and clarification in existing laws on medically induced abortions and sees as necessary the inclusion of a eugenic ground for abortion. It also recommends, among other more specific measures, that severely subnormal pregnant women or pregnant women suffering from severe mental illness be *prima facie* cases for therapeutic abortion (although conditions of some lesser degree of subnormality, psychopathic disorder or other mental illness should not be regarded as automatically providing grounds for termination) and that emotional overstrain in the pregnant woman be considered, with this provision also applying to such situations as the pregnancy of a young unmarried girl, a pregnancy resulting from rape, or a pregnancy of a woman beset by very disturbing marital or family conflicts. All recommendations are subject to the provision that therapeutic abortion should always be voluntary and at the request of the pregnant woman herself, with agreement of the husband.

3402 Royal Society of Health, *Family Planning: Report of the Royal Society of Health Conference on Family Planning for Britain, 1968*. London: The Royal Society, 1968. 120 pp.

Contains six major papers and discussion dealing with various aspects of family planning as a public health service: W. Edgar, "The Case for Family Planning as a Public Health Service"; D. Morgan, "The Municipal Family Planning Clinic in Action: Domiciliary Services"; G. Sanctuary, "Community Needs for Family Planning Services"; W. Turner, "Blueprint for Establishing the Clinic"; A. Wiseman, "The Municipal Family Planning Clinic in Action: The Clinic."

3403 Royal Society of Medicine, "The Law Relating to Abortion," *Proc. Royal Society Med.* 55:373-76, May 1962.

3404 Rushton, D.I. "Effects of Legalizing Abortions," *Lancet* 7544:692-93, 1963.

States that legalization has reduced criminal abortions.

3405 Samuels, A. "The National Health Service (Family Planning) Act 1967," *Med. Sci. Law* 7:177-80, Oct. 1967.

3406 Scott, J.S. "Implication of Abortion Law Reform," Nursing Times 62:1478-80, Nov. 11, 1966.

An argument against the proposed statute before Parliament in relation to abortion, allowing termination of pregnancy on social indications. The author divides the indications given for abortion into three categories: maternal illness, gross fetal abnormality or high risk of deformity, and social grounds or abortion on demand and he states his personal position on each category. Abortion due to foetal or social reasons is on a par with legalized infanticide and euthanasia and should not be considered in isolation from these other forms of killing. The author urges those who sympathize with his views to write to their member of Parliament to prevent this Act from ever reaching the statute book.

3407 Scottish Advisory Council on Child Care, Prevention of Neglect of Children Commission, Prevention of Neglect of Children: Report. [London]: H.M. Stationery Office, 1963. 26 pp.

3408 Shachor-Landau, C. "Recent Developments in the Law of the Matrimonial Home in England and Israel," Internat. Comp. Law Quart. 6:61, Jan. 1957.

3409 Sheehy, G. "Male Psychical Impotence in Judicial Proceedings," Jurist 20:253, July 1960.

3410 Silkin, Sam, "Divorce by Consent," Socialist Commentary October 1963, pp. 20-22.

Need in Great Britain for legislation which failed passage in 1963; what it would imply.

3411 Simms, Madeleine, "Abortion - A Note on Some Recent Developments in Britain," Brit. J. Criminol. 4(5):491-93, July 1964.

After noting the recommendations in favor of abortion law reform contained in the report of the British Governments Interdepartmental Committee on Abortion published in 1939, the three outstanding events in the public debate regarding abortion law reform that took place in the United Kingdom during 1963 are discussed: (1) The study of 44 female abortionists in prison undertaken by Moya Woodside and published in The Howard J. 11(2) ("Attitudes of Women Abortionists"). This concluded, contrary to popular belief, that financial gain was not the main motive in these females' activities; greater weight was attached to "compassion and feminine solidarity"; (2) The fierce controversy regarding the validity of psychiatric indications for abortion, which raged for many weeks (20/7/63-2/11/63) in the Brit. Med. J. following an article by Myre Sim entitled "Abortion and the Psychiatrist." He suggested abortion was essentially a socioeconomic problem, and that there were no psychiatric grounds for termination.

3412 Socialist Party of Great Britain, Family Allowances: A Socialist Analysis. London: R.E. Taylor and Son, Ltd. 1944. 15 pp.

3413 Stewart, C.M. "Family Allowances Statistics in Great Britain," Popul. Stud. 16(3):210-18, March 1963.

Description of the provisions of the law introduced in 1946 and of the records kept. Illustration of the possibilities and limitations of these for cohort analysis of family formation.

3414 Stock, Mary, "The Malthusian Devil in Chains," Polit. Quart. 21(1):9-19, Jan.-March 1950.

A survey of England's population problem based on the "Report" of the Royal Commission on Population.

3415 Stone, O.M. "Public Policy and the Purpose of Getting Married," [Silver v. Silver (1955) 1 W L R 728] Modern Law Rev. 18:607, Nov. 1955.

The author contends that the British Nationality Act of 1948, which provides citizenship on application to any woman who has married a citizen of the United Kingdom and Colonies be repealed in order to avoid its misuse by spurious marriages performed solely for the purpose of obtaining British nationality. Particular reference is given to the Silver v. Silver case in which the parties did not wish to become husband and wife, but rather desired the incidental advantage which the law attributes to a foreign spouse. The author concludes that permission to reside in Great Britain should of necessity be granted to wives of British citizens, but the matter of nationality should await the conclusion of proper inquiries in the interests of both public security and public morals.

3416 Summerskill, Edith C. Wanted - Babies. Trenchant Examination of a Grave National Problem. London, 1943. 12 pp.

3417 Swingler, Nicholas, "The Streetwalkers Return," New Society 13(329):81-83, Jan. 1969.

An account of prostitution in England since the Street Offenses Act of 1959, which was passed to drive prostitutes off the street. Ten years later, it is clear that it has failed to do so. The prostitutes are back on the streets of London and other English towns for a variety of reasons, chiefly economic. The street offers the best chance to attract clients, especially for the growing number of prostitutes who operate from cars. The police are less active in harrassing than private vigilance agents, because the law provides a number of loopholes. Stiffer punishment for "soliciting" has, however, made relations between prostitutes and police less friendly. Alternatives to the street are offered by pubs, clubs and cafes, as well as the peculiarly English systems of advertising on cards exhibited in stores selling newspapers, candy and cigaretts. A London "card girl" stated that she made 400 pounds ($1,000) a week and took a two weeks' vacation; a Bradford "mobile" prostitute has an average daily income of 12 pounds ($30). A new law sponsored by Lord Chorley intends to make the prostitute's client also liable to punishment; on the other hand, the Swedish psychiatrist Lars Ullerstam suggests that the social function of the prostitute in providing sexual satisfaction should be recognized officially.

3418 Titmuss, Richard M. "Parenthood and Social Change," Lancet 255(6534):797-801, Nov. 20, 1948.

Fertility trends and changing family size are related to trends in social policies in Great Britain as a background to the main argument, which is that public opinion and policy are not based on consideration of the family but on the view that the nation is "a collection of individuals."

3419 Tout, Herbert, "A Statisticcal Note on Family Allowances," Econ. J. 50(197):51-59, March 1940.

The proportion of families and persons living below a defined "poverty line" is presented for Bristol, based on a 1937 social survey of one working-class house in twenty in the Bristol urban area. The high proportion of all children living in families below the poverty level leads to a suggested scheme of family allowances, primarily as a war measure rather than one of population policy. Calculations are made as to the cost of certain allowances schemes.

3420 Tredgold, R.F. "The Abortion Bill," Lancet 1:448, 1967.

The number of unwanted pregnancies and the need for abortions have been steadily increasing. The author feels that the underlying causes of such pregnancies will be only slightly minimized by the new Abortion Bill and stresses the importance of research into adolescent behavior in order to alter current trends and apathy.

3421 United Kingdom. "Abortion," Internat. Digest Health Legis. 19:887, 1968.

Act of 27 October 1967 amends law of abortion relative to physicians to make lawful abortion when two practitioners are of the opinion that pregnancy is a risk to health or life of the mother or of existing children or that there is a risk of the child being born deformed. Induced abortions must be carried out in a hospital.

3422 United Kingdom. _Act to Provide for the Payment of Family Allowances_. Acts of 1945, Ch. 41.

3423 United Kingdom. Chancellor of the Exchequer. _Family Allowances. Memorandum_..., Command 6354, 1942. London, 1942.

The White Paper, presented to Parliament by the Chancellor of the Exchequer on May 8,1942, outlines the case for family allowances, estimates the number which would be included on the basis of different assumptions as to coverage, and estimates the gross and net costs of the various plans.

3424 United Kingdom. "Family Planning," _Internat. Digest Health Legis_. 19:884, 1968.

Act dated 28 June 1967 empowers local authorities in England and Wales to make arrangements, with the approval of the Minister of Health and, to the extent that the latter directs, for the provision of advice on contraception, the medical examination of persons seeking such advice, and the supply of contraceptive substances and appliances.

3425 United Kingdom, Home Department Committee on Grants for the Development of Marriage Guidance, _Report_. Parliament Command Papers, 7566. London: H.M. Stationery Office, 1948.

It is recommended that the experimental work in marriage guidance now being undertaken by private organizations should be helped from public funds, and should receive some form of official supervision.

3426 United Kingdom. House of Commons, "Abortion Administration in NHS Hospitals," _Lancet_ 1:516-ff., 1967.

A 10% sample inquiry was used to estimate discharges after abortions from National Health Service Hospitals over a four year period (1961-64). 69,000 discharges were estimated for 1961, with 2,900 septic abortion cases and 2,300 therapeutic abortions, while the estimate for 1964 was 75,000, with 3,000 septic abortions and 3,300 therapeutic.

3427 United Kingdom. Inter-Departmental Committee on Social Insurance and Allied Services, Social Insurance and Allied Services. Report by Sir William Beveridge. [American ed. Reproduced photographically from the English edition and published by arrangement with His Majesty's Stationery Office.] New York: Macmillan, 1942. 299 pp.

An inter-departmental Committee on Social Insurance and Allied Services was appointed in June, 1941. The report written by Sir William Beveridge, includes recommendations for the improvement of the social insurance system, the introduction or improvement of state provisions for allowance for dependent children, and health and rehabilitation services. The goal is the elimination of want through the provision of subsistence to all; it is to be achieved by a double redistribution of income through social insurance and children's allowances. Specific recommendations include minimum allowances for all children beyond the first, to be paid for from the National Exchequer, as well as a system of marriage and maternity grants. Concern over the population prospects for Britain is implicit throughout the report.

3428 United Kingdom. "Interruption of Pregnancy," Internat. Digest Health Legis. 19:887-89, 1968.

The British Abortion Act of 1967 provides for the termination of pregnancy if two physicians agree that the continuance of the pregnancy would constitute a greater risk than its termination to the life of the pregnant woman, or of injury to her physical or mental health or to that of her children, taking into account the woman's present and future environment. Abortion is also permitted to prevent the birth of a child likely to be seriously handicapped, either physically or mentally. The operation must be performed in National Health Service hospitals or in other officially approved places.

3429 United Kingdom. Ministry of National Insurance, Family Allowances Act. June, 1946. London: H.M. Stationery Office, 1946.

3430 United Kingdom. Ministry of National Insurance, Family Allowances and National Insurance Bill, 1952; Report on the Financial Provisions of the Bill. By the Government Actuary. Command 8518. London: H.M. Stationery Office, 1952. 7 pp.

3431 United Kingdom. Office of the Minister of Reconstruction, Social Insurance. London: H.M. Stationery Office, 1944. 95 pp.

This two-part White Paper contains the British Government's proposals for family, social, and national assistance, thus completing the tasks implicit in the Beveridge Report. The Government's plan for family allowances is presented in Part I of the present White Paper. A uniform allowance of 5s. a week is to be paid for each child in a family, except the first, while the child is under the school-leaving age, or is at school or apprenticed and under 17 years of age. The allowance is granted for stepchildren, adopted children and grandchildren. The cost of family allowances is to be borne entirely from taxation and is expected to amount to 57 million a year at the outset. In addition, free meals and free milk are to be provided by the State for all school children in schools maintained or subsidized by the public authority.

3432 United Kingdom. The Royal Commission on Marriage and Divorce, Report. London: H.M. Stationery Office, 1956. ix, 404 pp.

The Commission favors marriage guidance and conciliation and recommends grants by the State to private organizations engaged in this kind of work. The grounds for divorce and nullity are slightly modified. It did not accept the suggestion of approving nullification when a respondent has been sterilized.

3433 United Kingdom. Royal Commission on Population, Papers, Vol. IV. Reports of the Biological and Medical Committee. London: H.M. Stationery Office, 1950. 52 pp.

The present report is divided into three sections. The first summarizes what is known about the extent, causes and possible lines of treatment of reproductive wastage, under which term the authors include loss of potential citizens by abortion, stillbirth and infant mortality. Two salient points: first, that the trend in the frequency of all these conditions has, throughout this century, but particularly during the last decade, consistently been in a downward direction; secondly, that in spite of this general improvement, the difference in their relative frequency in the Registrar-General's five "Social Classes" remains as great as ever, which suggests that by still further approximating the diet and environment of families in the lower groups to those in the higher, some further reduction of reproductive wastage could be achieved. The next section of the report considers how far the decline in the birth-rate in Great Britain in the last 80 years should be attributed to a decline in reproductive capacity and how far to the spread of deliberate family limitation and, after considering evidence both from this country and America, the conclusion is reached that "while it is not possible to exclude some decline in reproductive capacity, there is no definite evidence that such a decline has occurred." There is, however, clear evidence that the use of contraceptives does not impair fertility. Finally, in the third section, the problem of involuntary childlessness is considered and an attempt made to assess its frequency; a figure in the region of 8 per cent of all married couples being given.

3434 United Kingdom. "Trade in Contraceptives," Internat. Digest Health Legis. 4(2):284, 1953.

Order of Royal Medical Board dated 28 February 1951 authorizing trade.

3435 United States Bureau of Labor Statistics. "Developments in Family Allowances in Great Britain," Monthly Labor Rev. 53 (3):720-22, Sept. 1941.

The program of the National Executive Committee of the British Labor Party is summarized.

3436 Vandyk, N.D., "Family Allowances," Brit. J. Sociol. 7(1): 34-45, March 1956.

A review of the experience of Great Britain, 1946-1954, and discussion of the comparative merits of family allowances and of tax allowances as a means of encouraging fertility.

3437 Waismaa, Usko, "Some Achievements and Objectives of Population Policy in England," in: [Population Policy Research Institute], [Problems of Population Development and Marriage]. Helsinki: Population League Yearbook, III, 1951. 225 pp.

3438 Ward, Audry W.M. "General Practitioners and Family Planning in Sheffield," J. Biosoc. Sci. 1(1):15-22, Jan. 1969.

A questionnaire was mailed to a randomly selected sample consisting of 50% of the general medical practitioners on the Sheffield Executive Council list in April 1967, inquiring regarding the advice they give about family planning; 90% responded; 78% of these suggest contraceptive measures on their own initiative. 93% of the respondents will on occasion advise patients directly; 7% tend to refer patients to the Family Planning Association. Of those who advise directly, only 78% suggest contraceptive measures on their own initiative. Several different methods may be prescribed by these physicians: 92% prefer to prescribe the pill, 40% the condom, 26% the diaphragm, 26% the safe period, 11% the Intra Uterine Device, and 6% a chemical spermicide. 32% of the respondents had training in contraceptive methods. Physicians trained in Ireland were less likely to suggest contraceptive measures on their own initiative or to prescribe the pill, and more likely to prescribe the safe period than physicians trained elsewhere in the British Isles. No questions were asked about the religious affiliation of the physicians. It seems that most physicians follow the recommendation of the 1949 Royal Commission on population that "the giving of advice on contraception to married persons who wanted it should be accepted as a duty of the National Health Service and the initial duty to give advice should rest with the family physician."

3439 Watson, J.S., "Family Planning in the Army: the Role of the General Practitioner in Family Planning," Proc. Royal Society Med. 61:248-50, Mar. 1968.

3440 Webb, P.M., "Breakdown Versus Fault - Recent Changes in United Kingdom and New Zealand Divorce Law," Internat. Comp. Law Quart. 14:194-205, Jan. 1965.

In 1963 the New Zealand divorce law was revised in the Matrimonial Proceedings Act, 1968, which came into force on January 1, 1965. At the same time in England the Matrimonial Causes Act, 1963, made a number of amendments to the law of that country. A comparison of the doctrine of the matrimonial offense, of the breakdown of marriage and the "scope of collusion" dealt with by both makes an interesting study, particularly in considering the extent to which the basic principles on which the dissolution of a marriage is permitted, differ between the two countries.

3441 Williams, D.G.T., "Sex and Morals in the Criminal Law, 1954-1963," Crim. Law Rev. 1964:253, April 1964.

3442 Williams, Glanville, "Legal and Illegal Abortion," Brit. J. Criminol. 4(6):557-69, Oct. 1964.

An abortion may be legally performed in the United Kingdom if it is instrumental in preserving the mother's life or health, without reference to longevity. The law does not take into account sociomedical indications; it fails to deal with cases where the mother may be healthy enough to bear the child but not healthy enough to rear it. The law does not really allow practitioners to do what they think best for their patients in this area. Consequently there are a large number of criminal abortions, between 10,000 and 100,000 annually. The only way to prevent them is to allow an MD to abort a foetus at his discretion.

3443 Williams, Glanville, "The Legalization of Medical Abortion," Eugen. Rev. 56(1):19-25, April 1964.

Discussion of recent attempts to modify the legal prohibition of abortion in Great Britain and of arguments for and against liberalization.

3444 Willmott, Peter, "Kinship and Social Legislation," Brit. J. Sociol. 9:126-42, June 1958.

Only in recent years has the impression that the family unit is confined to parents and dependent children in urban industrial societies been challenged by several field inquiries. These inquiries have suggested that the kindred may be an important source of companionship and support in such societies. The author attempts to determine how far the stereotype of the small family unit is upheld in social legislation, i.e., how far kinship rights and obligations are recognized outside a small isolated unit of parents and young children. The current legal conception generally deals with the 'family' in the more limited sense, with the greater part of 'family law' in Britain concerned with relations between husband and wife, to a lesser extent between parents and children, and little about wider kinship rights and duties. However, for three centuries, under the Poor Law, the range of responsibility was a good deal wider. The 1948 National Assistance Act represented a sharp break with a conception of kinship liability which had persisted in substantially the same form since the beginning of the seventeenth century. The Beveridge Report, which proposed the final abolition of the Poor Law, is described, with references to how the conception of liability has changed in the eyes of the Government and its advisors. The provision for dependent relatives is examined, and the author discusses which kinship obligations the State does acknowledge and in what circumstances it acknowledges them, with references to the national insurance scheme, war pensions, legal aid and income tax. Also described is the place of kinship rights in the law of intestacy. It is concluded that kinship relationships outside the immediate family still figure in law and administration, although there is an absence of any consistent view of the issue, with disagreements relating to what constitutes dependency and who is eligible. What is needed is more factual information about which obligations are actually undertaken in British society so that social administration can be brought into line with customary practice.

3445 Wilson, K., "Fertility in Newcastle-Upon-Tyne," Med. Gynaec. Sociol. 3(8):246-51, Aug. 1968.

Analysis of marriage-conception intervals of 4,327 primiparae who had a spontaneous delivery of a live birth in the period 1960-1964, by age at marriage, social class, and religion. Comparison with findings of other surveys on incidence of contraception.

3446 Winnett, Arthur R., Divorce and Remarriage in Anglicanism. New York: St. Martin's Press 1958. xii + 284 pp.

A survey of the Church of England from the Reformation to the present in respect to divorce and remarriage. Two views are traced deriving from: (1) the pre-Reformation Western tradition marriage once validly contracted is indissoluble; and (2) from the Continental Reformers who regarded marriage dissolvable by unfaithfulness or desertion. The failure of the Reformation Legum to become law led the Church of England to adopt the Canons of 1604 disallowing divorce a vinculo. Many Anglicans held to the dissolution thesis. During the 17th century an almost equal division between indissolubilists/non-indissolubilists prevailed among Anglican divines. In the 18th century the non-indissolubilists prevailed. The Divorce Bill of 1875 brought the problem to discussion, and it is presented in detail. New Testament criticism of the 19th and early 20th centuries brought the Matthaean Exception for questioning. The controversy now centered on whether Jesus in his teaching on marriage was stating a law or setting forth an ideal. The course of the controversy is traced through 1957 with some attention paid to important U.S. Canons of 1946.

3447 Wolfenden, John, "Evolution of British Attitudes Toward Homosexuality," Amer. J. Psychiat. 125(6):792-97, 1968.

Explains the thinking behind the recommendations of the British departmental committee which examined the law and practice relating to homosexual offenses and prostitution. The function of the criminal law is to preserve public order and decency and to protect the weak from exploitation rather than to impose a particular pattern of moral behavior. It follows, then, that there are areas of life which are no concern of the criminal law even though they may be of significant moral concern to individuals and to society.

3448 Woodside, M., Attitudes of Women Abortionists. London: Howard League for Penal Reform, 1963.

The attitudes and characteristics of 44 women who were convicted and sentenced to prison terms for performing illegal abortions are described. Twenty-two were over 60 years of age, all were or had been married and two-thirds were from the working class. The syringe method of inducing abortion was utilized by 80%; the women reported ten deaths. The major motive expressed for performing abortions was to "help" women with unwanted pregnancies and only nominal fees were charged in most cases. Almost all of the women were aware of the illegality of their actions but did not view the abortions as wrong.

3449 Woodside, Moya, "The Contraceptive Practices of an English Working-Class Group. Human Fert. 12(1):11-14, 1947.

In 200 London working-class couples, coitus interruptus was found to be the commonest method of contraception, with condom second. Only 29% were listed as "successful planners." Of 278 children, 91 were specifically planned, 147 unplanned but welcome, 32 unwanted, 8 "no information."

3450 Young, Freda, "The British Experiment in Family Allowances," Soc. Service Rev. 23(1):67-73, March 1949.

Examines the background of the passage of the Family Allowance Act of 1945 and assesses the first results.

VIII UNION OF SOVIET SOCIALIST REPUBLICS

General population policies

3451 Balagushkin, E.G., "The Building of Communism and the Evolution of Family and Marital Relations," Soviet Sociol. 1(3):42-47, Winter 1962-63.

The author examines the changes in the Soviet family as a social unit and the evolution of the family collective. The Party Program indicates specific directions to be followed for the elimination of the residual inequality of women in everyday life. Its three major emphases are: curtailing the woman's work at home by increasing the amount of power available for housework; building enterprises, i.e., restaurants, serving the household; and expanding the system of child care institutions. The Program envisages a rapid rise in consumption at public expense and, during the next 20 years, a gradual transition toward public maintenance of children and all individuals incapable of employment. The separate household will be replaced by large public industry, and the period of the building of communism will witness further reinforcement of the family unit on the basis of improvement of family welfare resulting from betterment and refinement of the functioning of such units.

3452 Bilinsky, Yaroslav, "The Soviet Education Laws of 1958-59 and Soviet Nationality Policy," Soviet Stud. 14:138-57, October 1962.

The adoption of Thesis No. 19 in 1959 shows that policy-making under Krushchev was no longer as rigid as in the last years of Stalin's rule. Furthermore, the reception that was accorded Thesis No. 19 proves that after more than forty years of Soviet rule a great many Soviet citizens still dislike and resist attempts at fusing them into a single nation with a single language -- whether Russian or "zonal."

3453 Brackett, James W., "Demographic Trends and Population Policy in the Soviet Union," pp. 487-589 in: United States, Cong. Joint Economic Com., Dimensions of Soviet Economic Power. Washington: Superintendent of Documents, 1962.

The present Soviet population policy is too often summed up by quoting Khrushchev's 1956 pronouncement that even if 100 million persons were added to the Soviet population, this still would not be enough. An official population policy has many facets. The current population policy in the Soviet Union, insofar as it applies to fertility, can probably best be described as passive. There are contravening forces in the country which make extremely difficult the adoption of a definite program to raise or lower the birth rate. The Soviet Union does have several laws which are sometimes interpreted as being a part of her population policy, but they are either leftover measures from past action programs or laws put into effect to accomplish some purpose unrelated to a population policy. For example, the current family allowance and income tax provisions are left over from the program introduced in 1944 to raise the war-depressed birth rate. The monetary rewards for having children, however, have been reduced over the years, and probably are no longer significant incentives. The purpose of the liberalization of the abortion laws in the mid-1950's apparently was to curb the substantial health hazard created by the large numbers of illegal abortions by permitting abortions to be performed in hospitals by qualified medical personnel. The campaigns for the dissemination of the knowledge and mechanical means of birth control were reportedly initiated as part of a program to curb the abortion rate. In the area of mortality, the Soviet policy is far from passive. The Soviet Government is committed to the policy of lowering mortality and to implement this policy medical facilities are constantly being improved and expanded. The Soviet Government pursues a very strict policy of preventing her citizens from emigrating. Except in very unusual circumstances, residents of the Soviet Union are not given permission to leave the country for the purpose of establishing residence abroad and, in fact, until quite recently, Soviet citizens were rarely permitted to go abroad as tourists.

3454 Brackett, James W., "The Evolution of Marxist Theories of Population: Marxism Recognizes the Population Problem," Demography 5(1):158-73, 1968.

The Soviet Union is cautiously evolving a new policy in the population field. In November, 1965, the Soviet intellectual newspaper, Literaturnaya Gazeta, published the first of a series of papers calling for a new interpretation of the population problems in developing countries. The dialogue was also carried on in magazines intended for foreign consumption. In 1966, in the General Assembly of the United Nations, the Soviet Union supported the resolution that gave the Secretary-General rather broad authority in the population field, stating that it was gratifying that the United Nations had finally come around to the Soviet view that family planning was no substitute for economic and social progress and that it was therefore proper for states to formulate their own population policies. These events indicate that the Soviet Union is in the process of evolving a new policy in the population field. Their actions to date have been cautious, but then it is not in the nature of governments to make radical shifts in policy.

3455 Cook, Robert C., "Soviet Population Policy," Popul. Bull. 8(3):17-27, August 1952.

Traces the changing attitudes of the Soviet Union toward marriage, the family, divorce, abortion and contraception, from the Code of Laws of 1926 through 1952. Suggests that changes were influenced by the drastic decline in the birth rate from 45 per thousand in 1926 to 30 per thousand in 1935.

3456 Cook, Robert C.,(ed.), "Soviet Population Theory from Marx to Kosygin: A Demographic Turning Point," Popul. Bull. 23: 85-115, October 1967.

Focuses on the debate evoked by newly-conceded views appearing in Soviet periodicals that a world population crisis exists, in conflict with Marxist theory that excess population is an imperfection of capitalism.

3457 Engberg, Eugenie.[Social Legislation in the Soviet Union]. Copenhagen: Socialt Tidsskrift, 1946. 96 pp.

The Soviet Union, unlike the West, has a high stable rate of employment, and, in its recent history, needed to increase its production drastically, which created new sources of work and put new demands on the labor force, both quantitatively and qualitatively. To meet these needs, the Soviet government established an extensive state aid program, which included equalization of labor rights for men and women; absorption of invalids, pregnant women and mothers, and pensionists into the labor force without suffering loss of salary or pensions; and maintenance of a sufficient work force in vital areas by making length of a person's employment in the same place as one of the main determinants of the amount of aid, pension and sick pay. There was compensation for housing and children as well as extensive insurance and preventive health programs. All of this aid was geared toward freeing every available person for the labor force, as was so badly needed.

3458 Griffin, J.A., "About Turn: Soviet Law of Inheritance," Amer. J. Comparative Law 10:431-45, Autumn 1961.

An examination of the manner in which inheritance has been treated by the communist governments of Russia since 1917. The author reviews the abolition of inheritance period (1917-1921), when the government maintained that retention of inheritance practices would be inconsistent with the ordained abolition of unearned income; the first official recognition of inheritance rights in 1922, with the "New Economic Policy" and the 1922 Civil Code, which made inheritance possible within a narrowly defined area (maximum permissible amount of the estate remained at 10,000 rubles, severe restriction of the class of persons entitled to take); the period up to the reform of 1945, during which only one change was made relating solely to the group of beneficiaries entitled to take although trends in governmental attitudes toward ownership at this time favored further relaxation; and finally, the Edict of the Federal Presidium of March 14, 1945, which reformed and codified the law relating to succession. Most of the provisions of the Edict are still in force, and represent, with the abolition of the inheritance tax in 1943, reform in many significant respects, particularly in the rules establishing the group of capable heirs. Features of the 1945 Edict are described, with sections on intestate succession; testate succession; "opening of the succession", acceptance, and the administration of estates; escheat to the State; marital property; and farming property. The author concludes that the liberalization of the Soviet rules on inheritance must not be overestimated, since the restrictions upon the acquisition of private property which still exist in Russia result in inheritance having a far different operation from that in Western countries. However, over the last forty years, a period during which Russian society is supposed to have been moving closer and closer to the ideal state of communism, soviet law has changed its attitude toward inheritance from abolition to comprehensive recognition.

3459 Heer, David M., "The Demographic Transition in the Russian Empire and the Soviet Union," J. Soc. History 1(3):193-240, Spring 1968.

A discussion of the demographic transition in the Russian Empire and the USSR from 1861 to 1965 in the light of a general theory relating education to fertility. The theory states that the direct effect of education, i.e., an increase in level of living, augments fertility, but that since several indirect effects of education are inimical to high fertility, usually education relates inversely to fertility. Among the indirect effects of education most inimical to high fertility are mortality decline, increase in educational attainment, development of social security systems, and urbanization. The changes in these direct and indirect effects of education are charted for Russia and the USSR. Also traced are the possible effects on fertility change of various governmental policies such as P.A. Stolypin's agricultural reforms, and Soviet policies toward birth control, subsidies for child-rearing, housing and the employment of women.

3460 Juviler, Peter, "Soviet Families," Survey 60:51-61, July 1966.

Does the Soviet regime seek to destroy the family (as a unit of parents and children) in the USSR, i.e., to end its socialization functions? Some Western writers hypothesize that this is so. They base their predictions of socialized upbringing on an article written by the economist and social researcher, Stanislav Gustafovich Strumilin, who urged that children be raised apart from their parents from infancy in the "living and working communes," where he envisaged Soviet people as living a few decades hence. To test this hypothesis of the "withering away" of the family, use was made of texts of decrees unobtainable in the U.S.A., extensive interviews with Soviet experts and officials, published sources, and impressions of family life in the USSR. Testing points were: ideology, educational policy, housing policy, marriage and divorce laws, sexual morality, and trends in family structure and relations. Results tend to refute the hypothesis. N. Khrushchev and the ideologists rebuffed Strumilin. Khrushchev's 1956-1961 proposals, which ended up advocating a mass system of boarding schools, had fallen through by 1963-64. Experimental housing projects for the future provide family apartments and day schools. Neither the piecemeal revisions in divorce law, nor the concessions such as raising the ban, in 1955, on nontherapeutic abortions, nor the strictures on the widespread lapses from conventional sexual morality among the youth, indicate the abandonment of a conservative approach to family problems. Limited statistical data on family size, marriage, birth rates and divorce, plus the limited findings in Anatol Georgevich Kharchev's "Marriage and the Family in the USSR" (Moscow, 1964) indicate, rather, that the main trend in family functions, structure, and relations today add up to a continuation of the transformation of Soviet families from characteristically extended and authoritarian to characteristically nuclear (though not isolated) and more egalitarian.

3461 "Krasougolnaia Problem Demografii" [Crucial Problem of Population], <u>Voproci Economiki</u> 4:152-54, April 1968.

Soviet demography strongly stresses fundamental research on population growth. Inspired by foreign experiences, notably in France and the United States, it places importance on research on opinions of families concerning the ideal number of children and how these ideals were formed. The Soviets face a dilemma: the effort to establish a common demographic policy for regions which differ extremely in rates of reproduction and in population philosophy. On the other hand, the system of family allowances seems only weakly to stimulate births. A population policy should be an appropriate family policy.

3462 Perevedentsev, V., "Concerning Demographic Ignorance and the Problem of the Birth Rate," <u>Current Digest of the Soviet Press</u> 18(32):8-9, 1966. English translation of Russian text in: <u>Literaturnaia Gazeta</u> (Moscow), August 13, 1966, p. 2.

Observations on the need for a demographic institute to study characteristics of population and processes of redistribution and replacement in the USSR as a basis for determining optimal growth rates and measures to influence the birth rate.

3463 Popov, A., "The Present-Day Malthusians -- Apologists for Colonialism and a 'Positions of Strength' Policy," Internat. Affairs, October 1956, pp. 56-66.

The author takes issue with Malthusian theories, i.e., that human population grows in a geometric progression and doubles every 25 years, while the means of subsistence at best grow only in an arithmetic progression, and, more specifically, with the idea that the cause of tensions leading to war is the pressure of surplus population. Modern Malthusians are attempting to depict the socialist countries, most of which have a rapidly increasing population, as a threat to the capitalist world; in addition, the real reasons for the poverty of the colonial world are falsified. Increases in population for China, Russia and Japan are viewed as vital to their labor forces.

3464 Sauvy, Alfred, "Population et Doctrine de Population en Union Sovietique" [Population and Population Doctrine in the Soviet Union]. Population 7(1):146-48, January - March 1952.

3465 Schlesinger, Rudolf,(ed.), Changing Attitudes in Soviet Russia: Documents and Readings. London: Routledge and K. Paul, 1949.

Vol. I, The Family in the USSR : Part I, Fundamental Attitudes and First Revolutionary Legislation, includes the original family code of 1918, the land code of 1922, the civil code of 1922, and the abortion decree of 1920; Part II, The 1926 Family Code and the Practical Application of Soviet Family Law; and Part III, New Trends After the Stabilization of Soviet Society, cover laws, discussion, explanation and criticisms. The major contents are translations of Russian documents.

Policies on fertility and family size

3466 Abt, John J., "Social Insurance, How It Operates in the USSR," Soviet Russia Today 16:14, 26 June 1947.

Information on the administration and operation of the insurance fund, which finances disability, illness, maternity and old-age benefits and family allowances.

3467 American Review on the Soviet Union, "Supreme Soviet Increases Aid for Mothers and Children, Makes Changes in Divorce Laws and Other Procedures Governing Family Relationships," Amer. Rev. Soviet Union 6(1):69-76, November 1944.

Text of the decree issued July 8, 1944, by the Presidium of the Supreme Soviet.

3468 Arab-Ogly, E., "Russia: Facing the Facts," Atlas 12(3):24-26, 1966. Translated from Literaturnaia Gazeta, Moscow.

A scientific population policy which encourages both an increase in the birth rate in some cases and a substantial reduction in others may serve as an important secondary means for markedly accelerating social progress.

3469 Bjork, Lief, Wages, Prices and Social Legislation in the Soviet Union. London: Dennis Dobson, 1953. Translated from the Swedish by M.A. Michael. 199 pp.

Chapter 10, Social Benefits, gives a brief resume of social insurance benefit during pregnancy and childbirth, of assistance for lone mothers and those with large families, and of institutions caring for children.

3470 Bogorad, Victor, "La Legislation Sovietique de la Famille et son Evolution" [Soviet Family Legislation and Its Evolution]. Cahiers du Musee Social, No. 5-6, 1952, pp. 149-56.

3471 Bouteiller, Georges de. "Les Assurances Sociales en USSR" [Social Security in the USSR], Institut d' Etude de l'Economie Sovietique et del Economies Planifee, Econ. Sovietique Econ. Planifees, No. 9, April 1950, pp. 3-12.

Family allowances, pp. 5-6.

3472 Chambre, H., "L'Evolution de la Legislation Familiale Sovietique de 1917 a 1952" [The Development of Soviet Family Legislation from 1917 to 1952]. Rev. Action Populaire November 1953, pp. 801-16.

3473 Chernetskii, O.E. [Organization of Work for the Reduction of Abortions], Sovet. Zdravookr. 20(6):20-22, 1961.

3474 Coser, Lewis A., "Some Aspects of Soviet Family Policy," Amer. J. Sociol. 56(5):424-38, 1951.

The family is being strengthened in the Soviet Union partly because the decision-makers desire an increase in the birth rate. The new family policy abolishes de facto marriage, provides state support to children of unmarried mothers, and sets up a system of child allowances which ranges from 80 rubles per month for the fourth child to 300 rubles for the eleventh child. The premium paid at the birth of a child increases from 400 rubles for the third child to 1300 rubles for the fourth child and to 5000 rubles for the eleventh child.

3475 Field, Mark G., "The Relegalization of Abortion in Soviet Russia," New Eng. J. Med. 255:421-ff., 1956.

Soviet legislation of abortion falls into four periods. From 1917 to 1920, legislation of the Czarist regime remained in effect and abortion was not legal under any circumstances. On November 18, 1920, a decree legalized abortion, provided it was performed by a doctor in a Soviet hospital. The government felt that by introducing social legislation for the protection of maternity and infancy, the demand for abortions would eventually disappear. In 1927, doctors noted that the number of abortions in towns and villages had increased significantly, but that legalized abortion had not led to a decrease in the growth of the population. Citing statistics from Moscow, 1922-1926, it was noted that the absolute number of abortions had increased 400%, but that the rate of incomplete abortions (presumably secret) had decreased from 46% to 20% of all abortions. They felt that the legalization of abortion had led to a decrease of secret abortions and their complications. In spite of the fact that public opinion favored the liberal abortion laws, a decree of 1936 limited indications for legal abortion to situations where pregnancy threatened the life or health of the mother, or where the fetus might suffer from hereditary defect. Both the abortionist and the woman undergoing the abortion were subject to punishment. This more restrictive decree was accompanied by social legislation intended to aid the pregnant woman and the mother. In 1955, abortion was again legalized when performed in a hospital by a doctor.

3476 Frank, Peter, "Soviet Divorce," New Society 8(215):718-19, November 10, 1966.

A summary of and a commentary on the published results of research by the Soviet scholar A.G. Kharchev. Statistics on divorce relate to an analysis of the reasons for the breakdown of 1,000 marriages in Leningrad, probably in 1962 or 1963. Additional information derives from interviews with a sample of 52 males and 68 females. In general, the divorce rate in the USSR is rising rapidly and this is causing concern. Statistics for Leningrad, however, may not be typical. In 64.1% of cases conflict started within the first 2 years of marriage. The problem of domestic overcrowding is reflected in divorce figures. Only 5.1% of couples in the larger sample had their own flat or house. 71.2% made do with a single room or, more rarely, two rooms in a communal flat. Almost 31.7% did not have their own accommodation and so lived with parents, in a hostel, or rented a room or 'corner' in someone else's flat. Nearly half the couples (49.5%) had one child and in 40.6% of the cases where there were children their upbringing had been left to "Granny" (babushka). Few couples shared leisure activities and inadequate leisure facilities was one of causes cited by Kharchev for the breakdown of marriage. Apart from this and alcoholism ("the most dangerous enemy of the Soviet family and communist morality"), other problems which will have to be tackled include: a quantitative and qualitative improvement of public service institutes, and more and better sex education in the schools. Premarital sexual promiscuity also frequently leads to unsatisfactory marriages. Resort to the collective for help in patching up a flagging marriage, according to those interviewed, had little success.

3477 Grouler, A., "L'Evolution du Droit de la Famille en U.S.S.R." [The Development of Family Law in Russia]. Bull. Trimestriel Societe Legis. Comparee No. 34, July - December 1946.

The principal phases of the development of family laws; the ordinance of the Presidium of the Supreme Council on July 8, 1944.

3478 Heer, David M., "Abortion, Contraception, and Population Policy in the Soviet Union," Demography 2:531-39, 1965. Also in: Soviet Stud. 17(1):76-83, July 1965.

Current Soviet doctrine makes clear that regulation of population growth is a function of the state. Official population policy seems antinatalist because of abortion legislation and research on contraception, but statements of leaders indicate the contrary. The stated ideal of Soviet population policy is at least to preserve the present rather substantial birthrate. Statistics on the number of legal abortions are not available. No decline of the birthrate following legalization of induced abortion has been shown, but may be explained by the altered sex-ratio after World War II. There is reason to believe that the abortions have had a significant depressant effect on fertility. It can be deducted from the data that the number of abortions would be somewhat higher than the number of live births. Limited data are available on the use of contraception in the U.S.S.R. In a study published in 1961, 52% of women requesting abortion did not use any type of contraception. Documentation is presented that the consensus is that the abortion rate is too high and that there is need of furthering contraception, which does not necessarily involve a contradiction in the population policy.

3479 Heer, David M., and Bryden, Judith G., "Family Allowances and Fertility in the Soviet Union," Soviet Stud. 18:153-63, October 1966; or "Family Allowances and Population Policy in the USSR," J. Marr. Fam. 28(4): 514-19, 1966.

Although Western scholars have assumed the Soviet family allowance program to be a strong stimulant to Soviet fertility, the value of a typical family allowance relative to the average wage has declined dramatically since 1944. Currently, family allowances form a much smaller percent of total national income in the USSR than in other nations with family allowance programs. One may conclude that the Soviet government does not wish to encourage a rise in fertility. Included are figures on family allowances and monetary awards to mothers of large families at various dates, 1944-64, with international comparisons.

3480 Hedge, T.S., "Family Relations in the USSR," ISCUS, Summer 1955.

Laws relating to marriage and the family.

3481 Institute for the Study of the History and Culture of the U.S.S.R., "A Soviet Decree on Abortion," Bull. of the Institute... 1(6):32-33, September 1954.

The Presidium of the Supreme Soviet today published a decree legalizing abortions in hospitals and other recognized medical institutions. Such abortions have been forbidden for twenty years, but a decree of August 1954 gave women the right to perform abortions upon themselves. The new decree says that the measures carried out by the Soviet state for the encouragement of motherhood and the welfare of children, together with the constant improvement in the status of women, now makes it possible to drop the legal prohibition. The decree was unexpected because the government is at present trying to bring about a rise in the birth rate. Illegal abortions are frequently reported from many parts of the Soviet Union and persons without special medical qualifications will still be held criminally responsible if they conduct abortions.

3482 "Increased State Aid for Mothers and Children in the USSR," Internat. Labour Rev. 50:396-97, 1944.

A decree promulgated in the U.S.S.R. on July 8, 1944 amended the regulations concerning allowances for mothers and maternity protection, and provided for the extension of the network of institutions for the protection of mothers and children. Under the decree, the allowances to mothers of large families are now payable from the birth of the third child, instead of the seventh child as under the decree of June 27, 1936. The payment consists of a single grant on the birth of the child and a monthly allowance beginning with the second year of the child's life and continuing until it reaches the age of 5.

3483 International Labour Office, "Social Insurance in the Soviet Union," Internat. Labour Rev.55(3-4):261-73, March-April 1947.

Includes a statement of the provisions for family allowances.

3484 Iurburgskii, L., "Adoption Under Soviet Family Law," Soviet Rev. 5:14-18, Summer 1964.

In conjunction with the fact that final work on the draft of the proposed Principles of Legislation of the USSR and the Union Republics on Marriage and the Family is now in process, it would be desirable that all the basic provisions of principle on the institution of adoption be reflected therein. Specifically, it is absolutely essential that the Principles state the purposes for which adoption is permitted, who may adopt, the circumstances under which adoption of children with living parents is permissible, the legal consequences of adoption and the procedure under which cancellation of adoption may occur. The statutory policy that adoption may be carried out solely in the interests of the children plays a major role in decisions by the agencies of guardianship and wardship with respect to adoption.

3485 Johnson, E.L., "Matrimonial Property in Soviet Law," Internat. Comp. Law Quart. 16:1106-34, October 1967.

Comparative lawyers will recognize the Soviet matrimonial regime as one of community of acquests, a system which with numerous individual variations applies in many jurisdictions and is thought by many jurists to correspond more than any other system with the conception of marriage commonly held in modern times. Under a system of community of acquests each spouse benefits from the work of the other, and where the wife is occupied with domestic duties and the care of children she gets the benefit of her husband's professional activities and is at no disadvantage in this respect as she is under a regime of strict separation. Moreover, the fact that each spouse retains full control over property owned before marriage and over property received under wills and intestacies and by means of donations during the marriage reflects the modern aversion to the idea of marriage as a means to the acquisition of property. To this extent Soviet law and practice are in accord with much progressive thinking in western countries.

3486 Kaverin, V., "Marriage Law and Illegitimacy's Stigma; a Dispute; a Case is Heard: Witnesses for the Prosecution," Current Dig. Soviet Press 12:13-15, June 1960.

3487 Konius, E.M. Puti Razvitiia Sovetskoi Okhrany Materinstva, 1917-1940 [History of the Development of Soviet Protection of Mothers and Children, 1917-1940]. Moscow: Central Institute for the Betterment of the Medical Profession, 1954. 402 pp.

Based on the material organized for a scientific conference under the editorship of V.P. Lebedevoi and G.N. Speranskogo. In the series, outlines for the history of pediatrics.

3488 Kopelianskaia, Sof'ia Evseevna, Prava Materi i Rebenka [Rights of Mother and Child]. Moscow, 1953. 131 pp.

Laws on maternal and child welfare.

3489 Krasnopolsky, A., and Sverdlov, G. The Protection of the Rights of Mother and Child in the USSR .Moscow: Foreign Languages Publishing House, 1953. 80 pp.

Chapters deal with principles of policy; labor legislation; mothers' allowances; health services; protection of rights of mother and child in the family; parentless children; and honors conferred on Soviet mothers. The authors are Soviet lawyers; scientific workers of the Law Institute of the Academy of Sciences of the USSR.

3490 Mandel'chtam, A.E., "La Lutte Contre la Sterilite Feminine. Problemes Cliniques et d'Organisation" [The Campaign Against Female Sterility. Clinical and Organizational Problems]. Documents Sovietiques Obstet. Gynec. No. 4, April 1954. 7 pp., processed.

3491 Mazur, Peter, "Birth Control and Regional Differentials in the Soviet Union," Popul. Stud. 22(3):319-33, November 1968.

The study's objective centered on an exploration of the influences upon the fertility of women living in regions with widespread use of birth control as compared to the fertility of women living in regions with no effective forms or program of family planning. From the 1959 census, 149 politico-administrative areas were analyzed in terms of the urban-rural residence dichotomy. It was found that the effects on fertility of education, literacy, economic dependency of the woman and marital status depended on the region-residence category under investigation. Education plays an important role in fertility in terms of the educational differential between the sexes. The study failed to produce evidence that economic dependency of the woman relates to fertility, although there were tentative findings concerning the rural sector of the birth control region. It is concluded, from the analysis of the seven Southern Republics examined, that the most practical method for fertility reduction would emphasize an indirect approach to family planning through a breakdown of the literacy gap between men and women and greater restrictions for marriage.

3492 Mendel'son, G.A., Otvetstvennost' za Proizvodstvo Nezakonnogo Aborta po Sovetskomu Ugolovnomu pravu: v Svete Ukaza Presidiuma Verkhovnogo Soveta USSR ot 23 noiabria 1955 g. "Ob Otmene Zapreshchenila Abortov" [Responsibility for Producing Illegal Abortion in Soviet Criminal Law: According to the Decree of the Presidium of the Supreme Soviet of the USSR, November 23, 1955, "Revocation of the Prohibition of Abortions"]. Moscow: Izd-vo Mosk. Univ., 1957. 60 pp.

On November 23,1955, the Presidium of the USSR Supreme Soviet revoked the prohibition on abortion which was passed in 1936. Operations to terminate pregnancy by artificial means are permitted only in hospitals and other medical establishments in accordance with instructions of the Ministry of Health. Under the decree it remains a criminal offense for persons without special medical training to perform abortions and also for doctors who perform abortions outside hospitals or other medical establishments.

3493 Mironenko, Y., "The Evolution of Soviet Family Law," Inst. Study USSR Bull. 8:33-40, May 1966.

3494 "New Laws About the Family in Russia," Soc. Serv. Rev. 18: 374-75, 1944.

A new law of the Supreme Soviet on marriage, divorce, the family and motherhood aims to surround the family with more external obligations than it has ever known since the coming of the Soviets and to lighten the economic burden of parents. The aim, too, is to make the individual family the basic and all-powerful pillar of society in order to increase the heavily depleted population of the country. Under the new law there is more restraint with regard to obtaining divorce.

3495 Nikonchik, O.K. [Further Measures to Reduce the Number of Abortions], Akush. Ginek. 39:92-ff., 1963.

The problem of limiting the number of abortions since their legalization in 1955 is discussed. The author notes that the new law reduced abortion mortality (250% during the years 1955-61) but did not lower the birth rate. Abortion limitation measures have included the promotion and extended use of contraceptives, public contraceptive education programs and sex education in the schools. A study of 3,085 women using some form of birth control indicated a 95.5% effectiveness.

3496 Nikonchik, O.K. [Problem of the Contraception and of the Organization of Abortion Control in the U.S.S.R.], Akush. Ginek. 35:3-6, November-December 1959.

3497 Nikonchik, O.K. [Protection of Women's Health in the U.S.S.R.], Sovet. Zdravookhr. 24:3-ff., 1965.

A very general review concerning the protection of the woman's health in the USSR. The country provides for 227,100 abortion cases in its hospitals according to the number of beds available for such cases, and 109,400 gynecological cases. Abortions appear to occur most frequently in the 33-45 age group; use of contraceptives is stated to be 94-96% effective. There was a ten time decrease in fatal abortions from 1955 to 1963, and the author contends that utilization of the vacuum aspiration method will minimize the problem of uterus perforation in abortion cases.

3498 "Obstetrics and Gynacecology in the USSR," WHO Chron. 20: 56-ff., 1966.

The status of abortion in the USSR is reviewed. The procedure for obtaining an abortion includes confirmation of pregnancy by a physician in a woman's polyclinic, an attempt by the physician to change the woman's decision regarding the abortion, and, if the woman persists, referral by the physician to a gynecological unit where the abortion is performed. 85% of all abortions are hospital cases, and the remaining 15% not performed in a hospital but occurring at home include those of a spontaneous nature.

3499 Okasaki, Ayanori [The Population Situation in the Soviet Union], pp. 59-62 in: Japan, Welfare Ministry, Annual Reports of the Institute of Population Problems No. 2, Tokyo, 1957. 77 pp.

Primarily an account of Soviet policy and practice concerning abortion since 1920, and the possibility of estimating the effects on the birth rate.

3500 Orlova, Nina, "Marriage and Divorce in the USSR," Monthly Rev. 13:416-23, January 1962.

3501 Petersen, William, "The Evolution of Soviet Family Policy," Prob. Communism, September-October 1956, pp. 29-35.

During the period from the 1917 Revolution to the first Five-Year Plan, the major stress was placed on breaking down intergenerational continuity in order to attract more young people away from their conservative parents to the revolutionary party. From the early 1930's on, however, the regime began once more to encourage continuity between father and son, since by this time, some of the post-revolutionary generation could be counted upon to support the party's rule. The return to a stronger family, moreover, was necessary as a way of replacing the millions who died as victims of the forcible collectivization of agriculture and, later, as casualties of the war of 1941-45. Thus, in broad terms, the Soviet regime shifted from a family policy calculated to help establish its rule within Russia to one designed to furnish the larger population requisite to a strong internal economy and, especially, an effective foreign policy.

3502 Planned Parenthood Federation of America, "Russia's New Laws on Marriage, the Family and Protection of Mother and Child," Human Fert. 9(3):86-89, September 1944.

3503 Prudkova, Nina, "New Soviet Family Law," J. Amer.Bar Assn. 50: 363-65, April 1964.

In 1944 the Presidium of the U.S.S.R. Supreme Soviet issued a decree increasing state aid to pregnant women, mothers of large families and single mothers and strengthening maternity and child protection. This decree introduced a series of new legal norms not provided for by the previous code of laws on marriage and the family. The decree also abolished the juridical concept of "marriage de facto" and it introduced restrictions in granting divorces. These and other matters are now being evaluated as work proceeds on the draft of the new "Principles of Legislation of the USSR and Union Republics on Marriage and the Family."

3504 Sadvokasova, E.A., "Metropriiatiia po Ogranicheniia Rozhdaemosti i ikh Vliianie na Vosproizvodstvo Naseleniia" [Measures on Limiting the Birth Rate and Their Effect on Population Reproduction]. Sovet. Zdravookhr. 25:16-22, 1966.

3505 Sadvokasova, E.A., "Po povodu stat'i D. Heer, 'Abort Protivozachatochnye Sredstva i Politika Naseleniai v Sovetskom Soiuze,' Zhurnal 'Demography', Publication of the Population Association of America, 1965, v. 2" [With Regard to the Article by D. Heer "Abortion, Contraception and Population Policy in the Soviet Union" from the Journal Demography Vol. 2, 1965]. Sovet. Zdravookhr. 52:71-72, 1966.

3506 Sadvokasova, E.A. [Some Social and Hygienic Aspects of a Study of Abortion], Sovet. Zdravookhr. 22:46-ff., 1963.

26,000 questionnaires were sent out during the period 1958-59 for the purposes of determining whether there is a relationship between abortion and fertility rates. Results showed that women in urban areas have lower fertility and higher abortion rates than do women in rural areas. The author classified the abortion grounds into four groups: socio-economic constituted 35% of city abortions and 26% of rural abortions; purely economic constituted 16.5% of city and 18% of rural; lack of suitable family (unwed mothers, etc.) constituted 36.9% of city and 45.2% of rural; and medical (no percentages listed). Women in the 20-39 year age bracket had the greatest number of abortions. Contraceptives as well as abortion are recommended as means of effective birth control.

3507 Shibaeva, A.N. [Some Forms of Propaganda for Contraceptives], Fel'dsher i Akusherka 27(5):50-52, May 1962.

3508 Shinn, William T., "The Law of the Russian Peasant Household," Slavic Rev. 20:601-21, December 1961.

The development of the customary law of the household from the period of its initial recognition in the nineteenth century to its present embodiment in Soviet collective-farm law is the subject of this essay. The discussion concentrates on the internal relationships within the household itself, touching only in passing on its relationships with the commune, the collective farm, and the government.

3509 Sicard, Emile, "Droit Prive: U.S.S.R. Loi du 8 Juillet 1944 Concernant les Meres, les Enfants, le Mariage et le Divorce" [Civil Law: The Soviet Law of July 8, 1944, Concerning Mothers, Children, Marriage and Divorce]. Sociol. Droit Slaves 2(3):334-41, June-August 1946.

3510 Smith, A.K., Health and Welfare Services for Mothers and Children in the Union of the Soviet Socialist Republics. Washington: Children's Bureau, 1945. 40 pp.

3511 "Soviet Family Legislation," Nature 170:274, August 1952.

After having passed its revolutionary period -- which, a posteriori, is explained by the consideration that it was necessary in order to break up some millions of unfree relationships and to establish the principle of equality of the sexes -- Soviet legislation, as enacted in the period 1936-45, has come to conclusions very similar to those current in other advanced industrial countries.

3512 Sverdlov, G.M., Sovetskie Zakony o Brake i Sem'e [Soviet Laws Concerning Marriage and the Family]. Vsesoiuznoe Obshchestvo po Rasprostraneniiu Politicheskikh i Nauchnykh Znanii Ser. 2, No. 30. Moscow: Izd-vo "Znanie," 1955. 38 pp.

3513 Tay, Alice E., "Law of Inheritance in the New Russian Civil Code of 1964," Internat. Comp. Law Quart. 17:472-500, April 1968.

Soviet laws are no longer temporary concessions to a "dying" past or simplified slogans propagandizing the future; they are fast becoming stable arrangements for living in the present. The Fundamentals of the Civil Code promulgated by the All-Union Supreme Soviet in 1961 and the detailed Civil Codes adopted by various Soviet republics since then reflect this change very fully. In them we will find the most detailed provisions for inheritance yet made in the Soviet Union, provisions that extend and consolidate a trend going back to 1936, and which now can be discussed as law and not merely as a symptom of Soviet political and economic attitudes.

3514 United States Embassy, Moscow, "Edict of Supreme Soviet of the USSR on the Increase of State Aid for Mothers and Children," Information Bull. 4(84):1-5, July 25, 1944.

3515 "USSR and the Family," Eugen. Rev. 48:7. April 1956.

At the Communist Party's Twentieth Congress a change of policy regarding the position of the family in the social structure of the U.S.S.R. was announced by N. Khrushchev. Briefly stated the new policy amounts to freeing the parents completely from all family responsibilities as soon as the child is weaned. The child then goes to a full-time nursery, kindergarten and, upon reaching the age of seven, to a boarding school "24 hours a day, 52 weeks in a year" until the age of eighteen. The intention is for this to become universal although the spread must necessarily be slow -- and much opposition will come from many quarters. The policy amounts to a complete reversal of the encouragement of family life, which has held for many years past, and represents a return to the attempt made to abolish the family altogether which followed the Revolution of 1917.

3516 Verbenko, A.A., *et al.*, "K Voprosu Organizatsii bor'by s Abortami" [On the Problem of Organizing Abortion Control], *Voprosy Okhrany Materinstva i Detstva* 10:80-83, August 1965.

The author discusses the means of reducing abortions since the law legalizing abortions was passed in 1955. In an experiment with propaganda and education in the use of contraceptives, 2,000 women were observed, none of whom had previously used contraceptives. The effectiveness of contraceptives averaged 82-86%. Figures for 1962 compared with those for 1960 indicate that abortions declined in five of the seven cities, in four by 7-10%. The authors advise education in the use of new and more effective mechanical and chemical contraceptives.

3517 Wolinska, H. [The Legal Regulation of Abortion in the Union of Soviet Socialist Republics], *Prawo i Zycie* 5(22):6-ff., 1960.

A historical review of the legal status of abortion in the USSR, with references to the 1922 and 1926 penal codes, which involved penalties only for abortions performed by non-medical personnel; the 1936 law, which involved penalties for the patient; for medical personnel performing abortions in a clinic or hospital and for anyone performing an abortion without appropriate medical facilities; and the law of 1954, which amended the 1936 statute to exclude the pregnant woman's responsibility for her actions. The 1936 law, however, provided for abortions where pregnancy endangered the woman's life or health. In 1955, a law was passed which permits abortion only in medical facilities and doctors who perform abortions outside a clinic and under unhealthful conditions are liable to fines and imprisonment.

3518 World Health Organization. "Obstetrics and Gynecology in the USSR," WHO Chron. 20(2): 56-60. February 1966.

Summary of findings of a WHO-sponsored seminar that visited the USSR in 1964. Includes section on contraception and abortion policy and practice.

3519 Zaidman, H. [The Fight Against Abortion in the USSR], Gynec. Prat. 17: 83-ff., 1967.

Abortion in the USSR is discouraged at this time, and the problem of decreasing the number of criminal abortions is being combated. The use of contraception and the importance of health education are emphasized, with references to educational activities concerning contraception in hospitals, clinics, factories and the schools. Through such activities the public is presently becoming more aware that contraceptive use can be effective, simple and cheap. The author describes the various methods of contraception as produced in the country and makes note of the kinds of research and experimentation progressing in this area. A study of 3,085 contraceptive users is cited; the contraceptives proved 96.5% (average) effective.

APPENDIX I

ABBREVIATIONS AND FULL TITLES OF JOURNALS

Acta. Obstet. Gynec. Scand.
ACTA OBSTRETRICIA ET GYNECOLOGIA SCANDINAVICA (Stockholm)
Acta Paediat. Scand.
ACTA PAEDIATRICA SCANDINAVICA (Stockholm)
Acta. Psych. Neurol. Scand.
ACTA PSYCHIATRICA ET NEUROLOGICA SCANDINAVICA (Copenhagen)
Acta Sociol.
ACTA SOCIOLOGICA: SCANDINAVIAN REVIEW OF SOCIOLOGY (Copenhagen)
AF JAG Law Rev.
AIR FORCE JUDGE ADVOCATE GENERAL LAW REVIEW (Washington)
Affaires Danubiennes
AFFAIRES DANUBIENNES: REVUE DE l'EUROPE CENTRAL ET DU SUD-EST (Bucharest)
Africa
AFRICA: JOURNAL OF THE INTERNATIONAL AFRICAN INSTITUTE (London)
L'Afrique et L'Asie
L'AFRIQUE ET L'ASIE (Paris)
Agenda
AGENDA (London)
AICC Econ. Rev.
ALL INDIA CONGRESS COMMITTEE ECONOMIC REVIEW (New Delhi)
Akush. Ginek.
AKUSHERSTUO I GINEKOLOGIIA: SUPPLEMENT TO SUVREMENNA MEDITSINA (Sophia)
Alabama Law Rev.
ALABAMA LAW REVIEW (University, Alabama)
Albany Law Rev.
ALBANY LAW REVIEW (Albany, N.Y.)
Alberta Law Rev.
ALBERTA LAW REVIEW (Edmonton)
Amer. Anthrop.
AMERICAN ANTHROPOLOGIST (Washington)
Amer. Behavioral Scientist
AMERICAN BEHAVIORAL SCIENTIST (Beverly Hills)
Amer. Cath. Sociol. Rev.
AMERICAN CATHOLIC SOCIOLOGICAL REVIEW (Chicago)
Amer. Eccl. Rev.
AMERICAN ECCLESIASTICAL REVIEW (Washington)
Amer. J. Comp. Law
AMERICAN JOURNAL OF COMPARATIVE LAW (Ann Arbor)
Amer. J. Econ. Sociol.
AMERICAN JOURNAL OF ECONOMICS AND SOCIOLOGY (New York)

APPENDIX I

Amer. J. Legal Hist.
AMERICAN JOURNAL OF LEGAL HISTORY (Philadelphia)
Amer. J. Obstet. Gynec.
AMERICAN JOURNAL OF OBSTETRICS AND GYNECOLOGY (St. Louis)
Amer. J. Orthopsychiat.
AMERICAN JOURNAL OF ORTHOPSYCHIATRY (New York)
Amer. J. Philology
AMERICAN JOURNAL OF PHILOLOGY (Baltimore)
Amer. J. Psychiat.
AMERICAN JOURNAL OF PSYCHIATRY (Hanover, N.H.)
Amer. J. Pub. Health
AMERICAN JOURNAL OF PUBLIC HEALTH AND THE NATION'S HEALTH (New York)
Amer. J. Sociol.
AMERICAN JOURNAL OF SOCIOLOGY (Chicago)
Amer. Latina
AMERICA LATINA (Rio de Janeiro)
Amer. Rev. Soviet Union
AMERICAN REVIEW ON THE SOVIET UNION (New York)
Amer. Sociol. Rev.
AMERICAN SOCIOLOGICAL REVIEW (New York)
America
AMERICA, A CATHOLIC REVIEW OF THE WEEK (New York)
Anales
ANALES (Quito, Ecuador)
Anales de Economia y Estadistica
ANALES DE ECONOMIA Y ESTADISTICA (Bogota)
Anales de la Facultad de Medicina de Montevideo
ANALES DE LA FACULTAD DE MEDICINA DE MONTEVIDEO (Montevideo)
Ann. Amer. Acad. Polit. Soc. Sci.
ANNALS OF THE AMERICAN ACADEMY OF POLITICAL AND SOCIAL SCIENCE (Philadelphia)
Ann. Chir. Gynaec. Fenn.
ANNALES CHIRURGIAE ET GYNAECOLOGIAE FENNIAE (Helsinki)
Ann. Econ. Societes, Civilisations
ANNALES ECONOMIES, SOCIETES, CIVILISATIONS (Paris)
Ann. Facolta Econ. Commercio
ANNALI DELLA FACOLTA DI ECONOMIA E COMMERCIO (Bari, Italy)
Ann. Med. Leg.
ANNALES DE MEDECINE LEGALE (Paris)
Annals New York Acad. Sciences
ANNALS OF THE NEW YORK ACADEMY OF SCIENCES (New York)
Annee Sociol.
ANNEE SOCIOLOGIQUE (Paris)
Antioch Rev.
ANTIOCH REVIEW (Yellow Springs, Ohio)
Applied Therapeutics
APPLIED THERAPEUTICS (Washington)

ABBREVIATIONS AND FULL TITLES OF JOURNALS

Arch. Bevolk.
ARCHIV FUR BEVOLKERUNGSWISSENSCHAFT UND BEVOLKERUNGSPOLITIK (Berlin)
Arch. Environmental Health
ARCHIVES OF ENVIRONMENTAL HEALTH (Chicago)
Arch. Gen. Psychiat.
ARCHIVES OF GENERAL PSYCHIATRY (Chicago)
Arch. Gynaek.
ARCHIV FUER GYNAEKOLOGIE (Berlin)
Archives of the Population Association of Japan
ARCHIVES OF THE POPULATION ASSOCIATION OF JAPAN (Tokyo)
Archivos Argentinos Pediatria
ARCHIVOS ARGENTINOS DE PEDIATRIA (Buenos Aires)
Arizona Law Rev.
ARIZONA LAW REVIEW (Tucson)
Arizona's Health
ARIZONA'S HEALTH (Phoenix)
Arkansas Med. Assn. J.
ARKANSAS MEDICAL ASSOCIATION JOURNAL (Fort Smith, Ark.)
Artha Vijnana
ARTHA VIJNANA (Poona)
Asian Med. J.
ASIAN MEDICAL JOURNAL (Tokyo)
Asian Stud.
ASIAN STUDIES (Bombay)
Asian Survey
ASIAN SURVEY (Berkeley)
Assicurazioni Soc.
LE ASSICURAZIONI SOCIALI (Rome)
Assistenza d'Oggi
ASSISTENZA D'OGGI (Rome)
Assn. Bar City New York Record
ASSOCIATION OF THE BAR OF THE CITY OF NEW YORK RECORD (New York)
Asuntos Sociales
ASUNTOS SOCIALES (Caracas)
Atlantic Monthly
ATLANTIC MONTHLY (Boston)
Australian J. Soc. Issues
AUSTRALIAN JOURNAL OF SOCIAL ISSUES (Sydney)
Australian Law J.
AUSTRALIAN LAW JOURNAL (Sydney)
Australian Outlook
AUSTRALIAN OUTLOOK (Sydney)
Australian Quart.
AUSTRALIAN QUARTERLY (Sydney)
Barnavard Ungdomeskydd
BARNAVARD OCH UNGDOMESKYDD (Stockholm)
Berliner Statistik Monatsschrift
BERLINER STATISTIK MONATSSCHRIFT (Berlin)

Bevolkerungspolitische Grundbegriffe Rasse
  BEVOLKERUNGSPOLITISCHE GRUNDBEGRIFFE RASSE
Bevolking en Gezin
  BEVOLKING EN GEZIN, POPULATION ET FAMILLE (Brussels)
Bibliotek for Laeger
  BIBLIOTEK FOR LAEGER (Copenhagen)
Bioscience
  BIOSCIENCE (Washington)
Bol. Inst. Derecho Comp. Mexico
  BOLETIN INSTITUTO DE DERECHO COMPARADO DE MEXICO (Mexico City)
Boletin del Museo Social Argentino
  BOLETIN DEL MUSEO SOCIAL ARGENTINO (Buenos Aires)
Boletim de la Sociedade de Geografia da Lisboa
  BOLETIM DE LA SOCIEDADE DE GEOGRAFIA DA LISBOA (Lisbon)
Boletin: Supplemento de la Revista Interamericana de Ciencias Sociales
  BOLETIN: SUPPLEMENTO DE LA REVISTA INTERAMERICANA DE CIENCIAS SOCIALES (Washington)
Boston University Law Rev.
  BOSTON UNIVERSITY LAW REVIEW (Boston)
Brit. J. Criminol.
  BRITISH JOURNAL OF CRIMINOLOGY (London)
Brit. J. Psychiat.
  BRITISH JOURNAL OF PSYCHIATRY (London)
Brit. J. Sociol.
  BRITISH JOURNAL OF SOCIOLOGY (London)
Brit. Med. J.
  BRITISH MEDICAL JOURNAL (London)
Brooklyn Law Rev.
  BROOKLYN LAW REVIEW (Brooklyn)
Buletin Eugenic si Biopolitik
  BULETIN EUGENIC SI BIOPOLITIK (Cluj)
Bull. Acad. Nat. Med.
  BULLETIN DE L'ACADEMIE NATIONALE DE MEDECINE (Paris)
Bull. Atomic Sci.
  BULLETIN OF THE ATOMIC SCIENTISTS (Chicago)
Bull. Caisses d'Allocations Familiales
  BULLETIN DES CAISSES D'ALLOCATIONS FAMILIALES (Paris)
Bull. Econ. Indochine
  BULLETIN ECONOMIQUE DE L'INDO-CHINE (Paris)
Bull. Economique et Social du Maroc
  BULLETIN ECONOMIQUE ET SOCIAL DU MAROC (Rabat)
Bull. Federation Societes Bynec. Obstet. Langue Francaise
  BULLETIN DE LA FEDERATION DES SOCIETES DE GYNECOLOGIE ET D'OBSTETIQUE DE LANGUE FRANCAISE (Paris)
Bull. Indonesian Econ. Stud.
  BULLETIN OF INDONESIAN ECONOMIC STUDIES (Canberra)
Bull. de l'Institut Interafricain du Travail
  BULLETIN DE L'INSTITUT INTERAFRICAIN DU TRAVAIL (Brazzaville)

Bull. Institut Recherches Econ. Soc.
BULLETIN DE L'INSTITUT DE RECHERCHES ECONOMIQUES ET SOCIALES (Louvain)
Bull. Internat. News
BULLETIN OF INTERNATIONAL NEWS (London)
Bull. Internat. Soc. Sec. Assn.
BULLETIN OF THE INTERNATIONAL SOCIAL SECURITY ASSOCIATION (Geneva)
Bull. Med.
BULLETIN MEDICAL (Paris)
Bull. Mensuel du Centre d'Etudes Documentation Soc. Province Liege
BULLETIN MENSUEL DU CENTRE D'ETUDES DOCUMENTATION SOCIAL PROVINCE LIEGE (Liege)
Bull. Mensuel Statistique
BULLETIN MENSUEL STATISTIQUE (Paris)
Bull. Millard Fillmore Hosp.
BULLETIN OF THE MILLARD FILLMORE HOSPITAL (Buffalo, N.Y.)
Bull. New York Acad. Med.
BULLETIN OF THE NEW YORK ACADEMY OF MEDICINE (New York)
Bull. Pan American Union
BULLETIN OF THE PAN AMERICAN UNION (Washington)
Bull. Res. Coun. Israel
BULLETIN OF THE RESEARCH COUNCIL OF ISRAEL (Jerusalem)
Bull. Service Etudes Documentation Econ. Office Statistique Generale
BULLETIN DU SERVICE D'ETUDES ET DE DOCUMENTATION ECONOMIQUES ET DE L'OFFICE DE LA STATISTIQUE GENERALE (Paris)
Bull. Soc. Roy. Belg. Gynec. Obstet.
BULLETIN DE LA SOCIETE ROYALE BELGE DE GYNECOLOGIE ET D'OBSTETRIQUE (Brussels)
Bull. Statistique
BULLETIN STATISTIQUE GENERALE FRANCE (Paris)
Bull. Trimestriel Societe Legis. Comparee
BULLETIN TRIMESTRIEL DE LA SOCIETE DE LEGISLATION COMPAREE (Paris)
Bulletin d'Information Economique du Conseiller Commercial de France a New Delhi
BULLETIN D'INFORMATION ECONOMIQUE DU CONSEILLER COMMERCIAL DE FRANCE A NEW DELHI (New Delhi)
Bulletin de Madagascar
BULLETIN DE MADAGASCAR (Tananarive)
Bungei Shunjeu
BUNGEI SHUNJEU (Tokyo)
Bus. Week
BUSINESS WEEK (Greenwich, Conn.)
Les Cahiers du C.E.R.A.G.
LES CAHIERS DU C.E.R.A.G.
Cahiers de Droit
CAHIERS DE DROIT (Paris)

Cahiers des Groupes Reconstruction
  CAHIERS DES GROUPES RECONSTRUCTION (Paris)
Cahiers Musee Soc.
  CAHIERS DU MUSEE SOCIAL (Paris)
Cahiers Politiques
  CAHIERS POLITIQUES (Paris)
California Law Rev.
  CALIFORNIA LAW REVIEW (Berkeley)
California Med.
  CALIFORNIA MEDICINE (San Francisco)
California Western Law Rev.
  CALIFORNIA WESTERN LAW REVIEW (San Diego)
California's Health
  CALIFORNIA'S HEALTH (Sacramento)
Cambridge Law J.
  CAMBRIDGE LAW JOURNAL (Cambridge, England)
Canadian J. Econ.
  CANADIAN JOURNAL OF ECONOMICS AND POLITICAL SCIENCE (Toronto)
Canadian J. Public Health
  CANADIAN JOURNAL OF PUBLIC HEALTH (Toronto)
Canadian Med. Assn. J.
  CANADIAN MEDICAL ASSOCIATION JOURNAL (Toronto)
Canton Nan-Fang Jih-pao
  CANTON NAN-FANG JIH-PAO (Hong Kong)
Caribbean Econ. Rev.
  CARIBBEAN ECONOMIC REVIEW (Port-of-Spain)
Caribbean Med. J.
  CARIBBEAN MEDICAL JOURNAL (Port-of-Spain)
Catholic Law.
  CATHOLIC LAWYER (Brooklyn)
Catholic University Law Rev.
  CATHOLIC UNIVERSITY OF AMERICA LAW REVIEW (Washington)
Cesk. Gynek.
  CESKOSLOVENSKA GYNAEKOLOGIE (Prague)
Cesk. Pediat.
  CESKOSLOVENSKA PEDIATRIE (Prague)
Ceylon Labour Gazette
  CEYLON LABOUR GAZETTE (Colombo)
Challenge
  CHALLENGE (London)
Chicago Bar Record
  CHICAGO BAR RECORD (Chicago)
Chicago-Kent Law Rev.
  CHICAGO-KENT LAW REVIEW (Chicago)
Chicago Med. School Quart.
  CHICAGO MEDICAL SCHOOL QUARTERLY (Chicago)
Child
  CHILD (Washington)
China Quart.
  CHINA QUARTERLY (Shanghai)

China Report
  CHINA REPORT (New Delhi)
Christian Century
  CHRISTIAN CENTURY: AN ECUMENICAL WEEKLY (Chicago)
Chron. World Health Organization
  CHRONICLE OF THE WORLD HEALTH ORGANIZATION (Geneva)
Chung Kuo Ch'ing Nien
  CHUNG KUO CH'ING NIEN (Peking)
Ciencias Sociales
  CIENCIAS SOCIALES (Medellin, Columbia)
Cincinnati Law Rev.
  CINCINNATI LAW REVIEW (Cincinnati)
Cleveland Mar. Law Rev.
  CLEVELAND-MARSHALL LAW REVIEW (Cleveland)
Clin. Obstet. Bynec.
  CLINICAL OBSTETRICS AND GYNECOLOGY (New York)
Clin. Pediat.
  CLINICAL PEDIATRICS (London)
Clinica y Laboratorio
  CLINICA Y LABORATORIO, REVISTA MENSUAL ESPANOLA DE CIENCIAS MEDICAS (Saragossa)
Columbia Forum
  COLUMBIA COLLEGE FORUM ON DEMOCRACY PROCEEDINGS (New York)
Columbia Law Rev.
  COLUMBIA LAW REVIEW (New York)
Columbia Univ. Forum
  COLUMBIA UNIVERSITY FORUM (New York)
Commentary
  COMMENTARY (New York)
Commerce
  COMMERCE (Bombay)
Commonweal
  COMMONWEAL (New York)
Communist China Digest
  COMMUNIST CHINA DIGEST (Washington)
Comp. Stud. Soc. Hist.
  COMPARATIVE STUDIES IN SOCIETY AND HISTORY (London)
Comp. Legis. Internat. Law
  COMPARATIVE LEGISLATION AND INTERNATIONAL LAW
Comprehensive Psychiatry
  COMPREHENSIVE PSYCHIATRY (New York)
Concours Med.
  CONCOURS MEDICAL (Paris)
Confluent
  CONFLUENT (Rabat)
Cong. Quart. Weekly Rept.
  CONGRESSIONAL QUARTERLY WEEKLY REPORT (Washington)
Conjuntura Economica
  CONJUNTURU ECONOMICA (Rio de Janeiro)

Conn. Med.
  CONNECTICUT MEDICINE (New Haven)
Connecticut Bar J.
  CONNECTICUT BAR JOURNAL (Bridgeport)
Contemporary Japan
  CONTEMPORARY JAPAN: REVIEW OF JAPANESE AFFAIRS (Tokyo)
Cornell Law Quart.
  CORNELL LAW QUARTERLY (Ithaca, N.Y.)
Crim. Law Quart.
  CRIMINAL LAW QUARTERLY (Ontario)
Crim. Law Rev.
  CRIMINAL LAW REVIEW (London)
Criminal Law Bull.
  CRIMINAL LAW BULLETIN (Boston)
La Cronica Medica
  LA CRONICA MEDICA (Lima)
Current Dig. Soviet Press
  CURRENT DIGEST OF THE SOVIET PRESS (Washington)
Current Med.
  CURRENT MEDICINE (Los Angeles)
Daedalus
  DAEDALUS (Cambridge, Mass.)
Demografia
  DEMOGRAFIA (Budapest)
Demografie
  DEMOGRAFIE (Prague)
Demographe
  LE DEMOGRAPHE (Paris)
Demography
  DEMOGRAPHY (Washington)
Demography Develop. Dig.
  DEMOGRAPHY AND DEVELOPMENT DIGEST (Lucknow)
Dept. State Bull.
  U.S. DEPARTMENT OF STATE BULLETIN (Washington)
Deutsche Agrarpolitik
  DEUTSCHE AGRARPOLITIK (Berlin)
Deutsche Biol.
  BEUTSCHE BIOLOGIE (Berlin)
Deutsche Gesellschaft Bevolkerungswissenschaft
  DEUTSCHE GESELLSCHAFT BEVOLKERUNGSWISSENSCHAFT (Berlin)
Deutsche Gesundh.
  DAS DEUTSCHE GESUNDHEITSWESEN (Berlin)
Deutsche Med. J.
  DEUTSCHES MEDIZINISCHES JOURNAL (Berlin)
Deutsche Med. Wschr.
  DEUTSCHE MEDIZINISCHE WOCHENSCHRIFT (Stuttgart)
Deutsche Steuer-Zeitung
  DEUTSCHE STEUER-ZEITUNG (Heidelberg)
Deutsche Versicherungs-Zeitschrift
  DEUTSCHE VERSICHERUNGSZEITSCHRIFT (Bielefeld, Germany)

ABBREVIATIONS AND FULL TITLES OF JOURNALS

Deutche Z. Ges. Gerichtl. Med.
DEUTSCHE ZEITSCHRIFT FUR DIE GESAMTE GERICHTLICHE MEDIZIN (Berlin)
Developpement & Civilisations
DEVELOPPEMENT ET CIVILISATIONS (Paris)
Difesa Soc.
DIFESA SOCIALE (Rome)
Direction Sociale
DIRECTION SOCIALE (Paris)
Dissertation Abstr.
DISSERTATION ABSTRACTS (Ann Arbor)
Documentation Francaise: Articles et Documents
DOCUMENTATION FRANCAISE: ARTICLES ET DOCUMENTS (Paris)
Documents Sovietiques Obstet. Gynec.
DOCUMENTS SOVIETIQUES D'OBSTETRIQUE ET DE GYNECOLOGIE (Moscow)
Droit Soc.
DROIT SOCIAL (Paris)
Duodecim
DUODECIM (Helsinki)
Dziennik Ustew Polskiej Rzeczypospolitei Ludowej
DZIENNIK USTEW POLSKIEJ RZECZYPOSPOLITEI LUDOWEJ (Warsaw)
East Africa Med. J.
EAST AFRICAN MEDICAL JOURNAL (Nairobi)
East. Anthrop.
EASTERN ANTHROPOLOGIST (Lucknow)
East. Econ.
EASTERN ECONOMIST (Delhi)
East. Econ. Blue Supplement
EASTERN ECONOMIST BLUE SUPPLEMENT (Delhi)
East Europe
EAST EUROPE (New York)
Econ. Affairs
ECONOMIC AFFAIRS (Calcutta)
Econ. Bull. Europe
ECONOMIC BULLETIN FOR EUROPE (Geneva)
Econ. Bull. of Ghana
ECONOMIC BULLETIN OF GHANA (Accra)
Econ. Develop. Cult. Change
ECONOMIC DEVELOPMENT AND CULTURAL CHANGE (Chicago)
Econ. Dig.
ECONOMIC DIGEST (London)
Econ. History Rev.
ECONOMIC HISTORY REVIEW (London)
Econ. J.
ECONOMIC JOURNAL (London)
Econ. News
ECONOMIC NEWS (Brisbane)
Econ. Record
ECONOMIC RECORD (Melbourne)

APPENDIX I

Econ. Rev.
  ECONOMIC REVIEW (Hong Kong)
Econ. Sovietique Econ. Planifiees
  ECONOMIE SOVIETIQUE ET ECONOMIE PLANIFIEES (Paris)
Econ. Weekly
  ECONOMIC WEEKLY (Bombay)
Economia
  ECONOMIA (Rome)
Economist
  ECONOMIST (London)
Editorial Research Reports
  EDITORIAL RESEARCH REPORTS (Washington)
Egyptian Popul. Fam. Planning Rev.
  EGYPTIAN POPULATION AND FAMILY PLANNING REVIEW (Cairo)
Estadistica
  ESTADISTICA (Bogota)
Estudos Soc. Corporativos
  ESTUDOS SOCIAIS CORPORATIVOS (Lisbon)
ETC
  ETC (San Francisco)
Ethnol.
  ETHNOLOGY (Pittsburgh)
Etudes
  ETUDES (Paris)
Etudes Conjoncture
  ETUDES ET CONJONCTURE (Paris)
Eugen. News
  EUGENICAL NEWS (New York)
Eugen. Quart.
  EUGENICS QUARTERLY (New York)
Eugen. Rev.
  EUGENICS REVIEW (Oxford)
Europe Oeconomica
  EUROPE OECONOMICA (Amsterdam)
European Rev.
  EUROPEAN REVIEW (London)
Evolut. Psychiat.
  EVOLUTION PSYCHIATRIQUE (Paris)
Extracts from China Mainland Magazines
  EXTRACTS FROM CHINA MAINLAND MAGAZINES (Hong Kong)
Extracts from China Mainland Publications
  EXTRACTS FROM CHINA MAINLAND PUBLICATIONS (Hong Kong)
Fabian Quart.
  FABIAN QUARTERLY (London)
Fam. Coordinator
  FAMILY COORDINATOR (Minneapolis)
Fam. Law Quart.
  FAMILY LAW QUARTERLY (Chicago)
Fam. Life Coordinator
  FAMILY LIFE COORDINATOR (Minneapolis)

ABBREVIATIONS AND FULL TITLES OF JOURNALS

Fam. Monde
  FAMILLES DANS LE MONDE (Paris)
Fam. Plan.
  FAMILY PLANNING (London)
Fam. Plan. News
  FAMILY PLANNING NEWS (New Delhi)
Fam. Planning Perspectives
  FAMILY PLANNING PERSPECTIVES (New York)
Far East. Survey
  FAR EASTERN SURVEY (New York)
Far Eastern Econ. Rev.
  FAR EASTERN ECONOMIC REVIEW (Hong Kong)
Far Eastern Quart.
  FAR EASTERN QUARTERLY (Ann Arbor)
Fel'dsher i Akusherka
  FEL'DSHER I AKUSHERKA (Moscow)
Fertilite
  FERTILITE (Paris)
Fertility and Sterility
  FERTILITY AND STERILITY (Baltimore)
Finance Develop.: Fund Bank Rev.
  FINANCE AND DEVELOPMENT: THE FUND AND BANK REVIEW (Washington)
Forces Nouvelles
  FORCES NOUVELLES (Paris)
Foreign Affairs
  FOREIGN AFFAIRS (New York)
Foreign Policy Bull.
  FOREIGN POLICY BULLETIN (New York)
Formation
  FORMATION PROFESSIONNELLE (Paris)
Fortnightly
  FORTNIGHTLY (London)
Free Univ. Quart.
  FREE UNIVERSITY QUARTERLY (Amsterdam)
Geburtshilfe und Frauenheilkunde
  GEBURTSHILFE UND FRAVENHEILKUNDE (Stuttgart)
Die Gegenwart
  DIE GEGENWART (Berlin)
Genus
  GENUS (Rome)
Georgetown Law J.
  GEORGETOWN LAW JOURNAL (Washington)
Georgia Law Rev.
  GEORGIA LAW REVIEW (Athens, Ga.)
Gereformeerd Theol. Tijd.
  GEREFORMEERD THEOLOGISCH TIJDSCHRIFT (Heusden)
Gesund. Wohlfahrt
  GESUNDHEIT UND WOHLFAHRT (Zurich)
Gesundheitsfursorge - Gesundheitspolitik
  GESHUNDHEITSFURSORGE - GESUNDHEITSPOLITIK (Berlin)

Gewerkschaftliche Rundschau Schweiz
  GEWERKSCHAFTLICHE RUNDSCHAU FUR DIE SCHWEIZ (Bern)
Ginec. Obstet. Mexico
  GINECOLOGIA Y OBSTETRICA DE MEXICO (Mexico)
Ginek. Pol.
  GINEKOLOGJA POLSKA (Warsaw)
Godisnik na Sofijskija Universitet Juridiceski Fakultet
  GODISNIK NA SOFIJSKIJA UNIVERSITET JURIDICESKI FAKULTET (Sofia)
Gordon Rev.
  GORDON REVIEW (Wenham, Mass.)
Gynaec.
  GYNAECOLOGIA (Basel)
Gynec. Prat.
  GYNECOLOGIE PRATIQUE (Paris)
Harefuah
  HAREFUAH (Tel-Aviv)
Harvard J. Legis.
  HARVARD JOURNAL ON LEGISLATION (Cambridge, Mass.)
Harvard Law Rev.
  HARVARD LAW REVIEW (Cambridge, Mass.)
Hawkesburg Agricultural College J.
  HAWKESBURG AGRICULTURAL COLLEGE JOURNAL (Sydney)
Health, Education, and Welfare Indicators
  HEALTH, EDUCATION, AND WELFARE INDICATORS (Washington)
Higher Education and Research in the Netherlands
  HIGHER EDUCATION AND RESEARCH IN THE NETHERLANDS (The Hague)
Highlights Mid-Europe
  HIGHLIGHTS MID-EUROPE
L'Homme
  L'HOMME (Paris)
Hosp. Progr.
  HOSPITAL PROGRESS (St. Louis)
Hospital
  HOSPITAL (Rio de Janeiro)
Hsin Chien She
  HSIN CHIEN SHE (Peiking)
Hum. Biol.
  HUMAN BIOLOGY (Detroit)
Hum. Relat.
  HUMAN RELATIONS (London)
Human Fert.
  HUMAN FERTILITY (Baltimore)
Humanist
  HUMANIST (Schenectady, N.Y.)
Hyderabad Government Bull. Econ. Affairs
  HYDERABAD GOVERNMENT BULLETIN ON ECONOMIC AFFAIRS (Hyderabad, India)
Illinois Bar J.
  ILLINOIS BAR JOURNAL (Springfield, Illinois)

ABBREVIATIONS AND FULL TITLES OF JOURNALS

Illinois Med. J.
  ILLINOIS MEDICAL JOURNAL (Chicago)
Impact of Science on Society
  IMPACT OF SCIENCE ON SOCIETY (New York)
Ind. J. Comm.
  INDIAN JOURNAL OF COMMERCE (Allahabad)
India Quart.
  INDIA QUARTERLY (New Delhi)
Indian Econ. J.
  INDIAN ECONOMIC SOCIETY JOURNAL (Bombay)
Indian Institute Pub. Opin. Quart. Econ. Rep.
  INDIAN INSTITUTE OF PUBLIC OPINION. QUARTERLY ECONOMIC REPORT (New Delhi)
Indian J. Econ.
  INDIAN JOURNAL OF ECONOMICS (Allahabad)
Indian J. History Med.
  INDIAN JOURNAL OF THE HISTORY OF MEDICINE (Madras)
Indian J. Pub. Health
  INDIAN JOURNAL OF PUBLIC HEALTH (Calcutta)
Ind. J. Soc. Work
  INDIAN JOURNAL OF SOCIAL WORK (Bombay)
Indian Law Rev.
  INDIAN LAW REVIEW (Calcutta)
Indian Med. Assn. J.
  INDIAN MEDICAL ASSOCIATION JOURNAL (Calcutta)
Indian Med. Gaz.
  INDIAN MEDICAL GAZETTE (Calcutta)
Indian Med. J.
  INDIAN MEDICAL JOURNAL (Allahabad)
Indian Popul. Bull.
  INDIAN POPULATION BULLETIN (New Delhi)
Indian Soc. Res.
  INDIAN SOCIOLOGICAL REVIEW (Lucknow)
Indian Sociol.
  INDIAN SOCIOLOGIST (Paris)
Indian Sociol. Bull.
  INDIAN SOCIOLOGICAL BULLETIN (Raleigh)
Indiana Law J.
  INDIANA LAW JOURNAL (Bloomington)
Indiana State Med. Assn. J.
  INDIANA STATE MEDICAL ASSOCIATION JOU NAL (Fort Wayne)
Industrie
  INDUSTRIE (Paris)
Industry Labour
  INDUSTRY AND LABOUR (Geneva)
Informaciones Sociales
  INFORMACIONES SOCIALES (Lima)
Information Bull.
  INFORMATION BULLETIN FOR THE SOUTHERN HEMISPHERE (La Plata, Argentina)

Informations Soc.
  INFORMATIONS SOCIALES (Paris)
Internat. Affairs
  INTERNATIONAL AFFAIRS (London)
Internat. Comp. Law Quart.
  INTERNATIONAL AND COMPARATIVE LAW QUARTERLY (London)
Internat. Comp. Law Rev.
  INTERNATIONAL AND COMPARATIVE LAW QUARTERLY (London)
Internat. Develop. Rev.
  INTERNATIONAL DEVELOPMENT REVIEW (Washington)
Internat. Dig. Health Legis.
  INTERNATIONAL DIGEST OF HEALTH LEGISLATION (Geneva)
Internat. J. Fertility
  INTERNATIONAL JOURNAL OF FERTILITY (Springfield, Mass.)
Internat. J. Soc. Psychiat.
  INTERNATIONAL JOURNAL OF SOCIAL PSYCHIATRY (London)
Internat. Labour Rev.
  INTERNATIONAL LABOUR REVIEW (Geneva)
Internat. Rev. Criminal Policy
  INTERNATIONAL REVIEW OF CRIMINAL POLICY (New York)
Internat. Soc. Sec. Assn. Bull.
  INTERNATIONAL SOCIAL SECURITY ASSOCIATION BULLETIN (Montreal)
Internat. Soc. Sci. Bull.
  INTERNATIONAL SOCIAL SCIENCE BULLETIN (Paris)
Internat. Soc. Sci. J.
  INTERNATIONAL SOCIAL SCIENCE JOURNAL (New York)
Internist
  INTERNIST (Berlin)
Iowa Law Rev.
  IOWA LAW REVIEW (Iowa City)
Ir. Jur.
  IRISH JURIST (Dublin)
Irish Theological Quart.
  IRISH THEOLOGICAL QUARTERLY (Dublin)
ISCUS
  INDO-SOVIET CULTURAL SOCIETY BULLETIN (New Delhi)
Isvestia
  IZVETIIA (Moscow)
Italien Jahrbuch
  ITALIEN JAHRBUCH (Essen)
J. Amer. Bar Assn.
  JOURNAL OF THE AMERICAN BAR ASSOCIATION (Chicago)
J. Amer. Coll. Health Assn.
  JOURNAL OF THE AMERICAL COLLEGE HEALTH ASSOCIATION (Evanston, Illinois)
J. Amer. Med. Assn.
  JOURNAL OF THE AMERICAN MEDICAL ASSOCIATION (Chicago)
J. Amer. Med. Wom. Assn.
  JOURNAL OF THE AMERICAN MEDICAL WOMEN'S ASSOCIATION(Nashville)

ABBREVIATIONS AND FULL TITLES OF JOURNALS

J. Asian Stud.
JOURNAL OF ASIAN STUDIES (Ann Arbor)
J. Bar Assn. Kansas
JOURNAL OF THE BAR ASSOCIATION OF THE STATE OF KANSAS (Topeka)
J. Biosoc. Sci.
JOURNAL OF BIOSOCIAL SCIENCE (Oxford)
J. Chron. Dis.
JOURNAL OF CHRONIC DISEASES (St. Louis)
J. Crim. Law
JOURNAL OF CRIMINAL LAW (London)
J. Crim. Law Criminol. Police Sci.
JOURNAL OF CRIMINAL LAW, CRIMINOLOGY AND POLICE SCIENCE (Chicago)
J. Fam. Law
JOURNAL OF FAMILY LAW (Louisville)
J. Fam. Welf.
JOURNAL OF FAMILY WELFARE (Bombay)
J. Florida Med. Assn.
JOURNAL OF THE FLORIDA MEDICAL ASSOCIATION (Jacksonville)
J. For. Sci.
JOURNAL OF FORENSIC SCIENCES (Chicago)
J. Formosan Med. Assn.
JOURNAL OF THE FORMOSAN MEDICAL ASSOCIATION (Taipei)
J. Health Soc. Behavior
JOURNAL OF HEALTH AND SOCIAL BEHAVIOUR (Washington)
J. Heredity
JOURNAL OF HEREDITY (Washington)
J. Indian Med. Assn.
JOURNAL OF THE INDIAN MEDICAL ASSOCIATION (Calcutta)
J. Institute Econ. Res.
JOURNAL OF THE INSTITUTE OF ECONOMIC RESEARCH (Mysore)
J. Internat. Fed. Gynaecol. Obstet.
JOURNAL OF THE INTERNATIONAL FEDERATION OF GYNAECOLOGY AND OBSTETRICS (Naples)
J. Iowa State Med. Society
JOURNAL OF THE IOWA STATE MEDICAL SOCIETY (Des Moines)
J. Japan Med. Assn.
JOURNAL OF THE JAPAN MEDICAL ASSOCIATION (Tokyo)
J. Japanese Obstet. Gynec. Soc.
JOURNAL OF THE JAPANESE OBSTETRICAL AND GYNECOLOGICAL SOCIETY (Tokyo)
J. Marketing Research
JOURNAL OF MARKETING RESEARCH (Chicago)
J. Marr. Fam.
JOURNAL OF MARRIAGE AND THE FAMILY (Minneapolis)
J. Marr. Fam. Living
JOURNAL OF MARRIAGE AND FAMILY LIVING (Minneapolis)
J. Med. Assn. Georgia
JOURNAL OF THE MEDICAL ASSOCIATION OF GEORGIA (Atlanta)

APPENDIX I

J. Med. Bordeaux
  J. MEDICIN DE LA GIRONDE BORDEAUX (Bordeaux)
J. Med. Educ.
  JOURNAL OF MEDICAL EDUCATION (Chicago)
J. Med. Lebanon
  JOURNAL MEDICAL LIBANAIS (Beirut)
J. Med. Soc. New Jersey
  JOURNAL OF THE MEDICAL SOCIETY OF NEW JERSEY (Trenton)
J. Mississippi Med. Assn.
  JOURNAL OF THE MISSISSIPPI STATE MEDICAL ASSOCIATION (Jackson)
J. Mount Sinai Hosp. N.Y.
  JOURNAL OF THE MOUNT SINAI HOSPITAL OF NEW YORK (New York)
J. Nat. Med. Assn.
  JOURNAL OF THE NATIONAL MEDICAL ASSOCIATION (New York)
J. Obstet. Gyn. Brit. Commonw.
  JOURNAL OF OBSTETRICS AND GYNAECOLOGY OF THE BRITISH COMMONWEALTH (London)
J. Officiel Republique Francaise
  JOURNAL OFFICIEL DE LA REPUBLIQUE FRANCAISE (Paris)
J. Oklahoma State Med. Assn.
  JOURNAL OF THE OKLAHOMA STATE MEDICAL ASSOCIATION (Oklahoma City)
J. Popul. Stud.
  JOURNAL OF POPULATION STUDIES (Seoul)
J. Public Law
  JOURNAL OF PUBLIC LAW (Atlanta, Ga.)
J. Sci. Med. Lille
  JOURNAL DES SCIENCE MEDICALES DE LILLE (Lille)
J. Sci. Study Relig.
  JOURNAL FOR THE SCIENTIFIC STUDY OF RELIGION (Notre Dame, Ind.)
J. Sex Res.
  JOURNAL OF SEX RESEARCH (New York)
J. Soc. Hist.
  JOURNAL OF SOCIAL HISTORY (Berkeley)
J. Soc. Hyg.
  JOURNAL OF SOCIAL HYGIENE (Baltimore)
J. Soc. Issues
  JOURNAL OF SOCIAL ISSUES (Ann Arbor)
J. Soc. Pub. TL
  JOURNAL OF THE SOCIETY OF PUBLIC TEACHERS OF LAW (London)
J. Urology
  JOURNAL OF UROLOGY (Baltimore)
J. Washington Acad. Sci.
  JOURNAL OF THE WASHINGTON ACADEMY OF SCIENCES (Washington)
Jahrbucher Nationalokonomie Statistik
  JAHRBUCHER FUR NATIONALOKONOMIE UND STATISTIK (Jena)
Japan Economy News
  JAPAN ECONOMY NEWS (Tokyo)

Japan Planned Parenthood Quart.
  JAPAN PLANNED PARENTHOOD QUARTERLY (Tokyo)
Jen-min Pao-chien
  JEN-MIN PAO-CHIEN (Peking)
Jewish J. Sociol.
  JEWISH JOURNAL OF SOCIOLOGY (London)
Jinko Mondai Kenkyu
  JINKO MONDAI KENKYU (Tokyo)
Jurid. Rev.
  JURIDICIAL REVIEW (Edinburgh)
Jurist
  JURIST (London)
Just. N.
  JUSTICE NEWS
Just. Peace
  JUSTICE OF THE PEACE (London)
Kajian Ekonomi Malaysia: J. Econ. Assn. Malaysia
  KAJIAN EKONOMI MALAYSIA: JOURNAL OF THE ECONOMIC ASSOCIATION OF MALAYSIA (Kerala Lumpur)
Kansas Law Rev.
  KANSAS LAW REVIEW (Topeka)
Kentucky Law J.
  KENTUCKY LAW JOURNAL (Louisville)
Koelner Z. Soziol. Soz-Psychol.
  KOELNER ZEITSCHRIFT FUR SOZIOLOGIE UND SOZIAL-PSYCHOLOGIE (Opladen)
Korean J. Obstet. Gynec.
  KOREAN JOURNAL OF OBSTETRICS AND GYNECOLOGY (Seoul)
Korean Survey
  KOREAN SURVEY (Seoul)
Kurukshetra
  KURUKSHETRA (New Delhi)
Kyklos
  KYKLOS (Bern)
The Lancet
  THE LANCET (London)
Land Water Law Rev.
  LAND AND WATER LAW REVIEW (Laramie, Wyoming)
Law and Contemporary Prob.
  LAW AND CONTEMPORARY PROBLEMS (Durham, North Carolina)
Law J.
  LAW JOURNAL (London)
Law Quart. Rev.
  LAW QUARTERLY REVIEW (London)
Law Society Rev.
  LAW AND SOCIETY REVIEW (Beverly Hills)
Lekarz Wojskowy
  LEKARZ WOJSKOWY (Warsaw)
Life
  LIFE (New York)

Lijecn. Vjesn.
LIJENICKI VJESNIK (Zagreb)
Linacre Quart.
LINACRE QUARTERLY (Milwaukee)
Literaturnaia Gazeta
LITERATURNAYA GAZETA (Moscow)
Lloyds Bank Rev.
LLOYD'S BANK REVIEW (London)
Los Angeles Bar Assn. Bull.
LOS ANGELES BAR ASSOCIATION BULLETIN (Los Angeles)
Louisiana Law Rev.
LOUISIAN LAW REVIEW (Baton Rouge)
Lovania
LOVANIA (Elisabethville)
Loyola Law Rev.
LOYOLA UNIVERSITY LAW REVIEW (New Orleans)
Luth. Quart.
LUTHERN QUARTERLY (Gettysburg)
Lyon Med.
LYON MEDICAL (Lyons)
Mcgill Law J.
McGILL LAW JOURNAL (Montreal)
Magyar Statistikai Tarsasag
MAGYAR STATISTIKAI TARSASAG (Budapest)
Maharashtra Med. J.
MAHARASHTRA MEDICAL JOURNAL (Poona)
Malaya Law Rev.
MALAYA LAW REVIEW (Singapore)
Malayan Econ. Rev.
MALAYAN ECONOMIC REVIEW (Singapore)
Man
MAN (London)
Man India
MAN IN INDIA (Ranchi)
Manitoba Bar News
MANITOBA BAR NEWS (Winnipeg)
Marches Tropicaux Mediterraneens
MARCHES TROPICAUX ET MEDITERRANEENS (Paris)
Marr. Fam. Living
MARRIAGE AND FAMILY LIVING (Minneapolis)
Maryland Med. J.
MARYLAND STATE MEDICAL JOURNAL (Baltimore)
La Maternite Heureuse
LA MATERNITE HEUREUSE (Paris)
Med. Dig.
MEDICAL DIGEST (Bombay)
Med. Gynaec. Sociol.
MEDICAL GYNAECOLOGY AND SOCIOLOGY (Oxford, England)
Med. J. Australia
MEDICAL JOURNAL OF AUSTRALIA (Sydney)

Med. Klin.
  MEDIZINISCHE KLINIK (Berlin)
Med. Mschr.
  MEDIZINISCHE MONATSSCHRIFT (Stuttgart)
Med. Officer
  MEDICAL OFFICER (London)
Med. Opin. Rev.
  MEDICAL OPINION AND REVIEW (New York)
Med. Sci.
  MEDICAL SCIENCE (Toronto)
Med. Sci. Law
  MEDICINE, SCIENCE AND THE LAW (London)
Med. Welt
  MEDIZINISCHE WELT (Stuttgart)
Med. World
  MEDICAL WORLD (London)
Med. World News
  MEDICAL WORLD NEWS (New York)
Medical Care
  MEDICAL CARE (Philadelphia, Pa.)
Medico
  MEDICO (Mannheim, Germany: FR)
Medico-Legal J.
  MEDICO-LEGAL JOURNAL (Cambridge, England)
Medizinische
  MEDIZINISCHE (Jena)
Mens en Mij
  MENS EN MAATSCHAPPIJ (Amsterdam)
Mensuel Statistique
  BULLETIN MENSUEL DE STATISTIQUE (Paris)
Ment. Health
  MENTAL HEALTH (London)
Michigan Law Rev.
  MICHIGAN LAW REVIEW (Ann Arbor)
Michigan Med.
  MICHIGAN MEDICINE (East Lansing)
Mid East, A Middle East-North African Rev.
  MID EAST, A MIDDLE EAST-NORTH AFRICAN REVIEW (Washington)
Midstream
  MIDSTREAM (New York)
Migration
  MIGRATION (The Hague)
Migration News
  MIGRATION NEWS (Geneva)
Milbank Memor. Fund Quart.
  MILBANK MEMORIAL FUND QUARTERLY (New York)
Minerva Ginec.
  MINERVA GINECOLOGICA (Turin)
Minerva Medica
  MINERVA MEDICA (Turin)

Minnesota Law Rev.
MINNESOTA LAW REVIEW (Minneapolis)
Minnesota Med.
MINNESOTA MEDICINE (St. Paul)
Mita Journal of Econ.
MITA GAKKAI ZASSHI/MITA JOURNAL OF ECONOMICS (Tokyo)
Mod. Hosp. Law
MODERN HOSPITAL LAW (St. Louis)
Mod. Hospital
MODERN HOSPITAL (St. Louis)
Modern Law Rev.
MODERN LAW REVIEW (London)
Modern Rev.
MODERN REVIEW (Allahabad)
Monatsberichte des Oesterreichisches Institut fuer Wirtschaftsforschung
MONATSBERICHTE DES OESTERREICHISCHES INSTITUT FUER WIRTSCHAFTSFORSCHUNG (Vienna)
Monatshefte NS-Sozialpolit.
MONATSHEFTE FUR NS-SOZIALPOLITIK (Stuttgart)
Monde Francais
MONDE FRANCAIS (Paris)
Monthly Circular
MONTHLY CIRCULAR (Geneva)
Monthly Labor Rev.
MONTHLY LABOR REVIEW (Washington)
Monthly Rev.
MONTHLY REVIEW (London)
Muenchen. Med. Wochenschr.
MUENCHENER MEDIZINISCHE WOCHENSCHRIFT (Munich)
Mysore Econ. Rev.
MYSORE ECONOMIC REVIEW (Bangalore)
Nasa Zakonitost
NASA ZAKONITOST (Zagreb)
Nat. Tax J.
NATIONAL TAX JOURNAL (Chicago)
Nation und Staat
NATION UND STAAT (Vienna)
Nature
NATURE (London)
Nederl. T. Geneesk.
NEDERLANDS TIJDSCHRIFT VOOR GENEESKUNDE (Amsterdam)
Nepegeszegugy
NEPEGESZEGUGY (Budapest)
Neues Bauerntum
NEUES BAUERNTUM (Berlin)
New Eng. J. Med.
NEW ENGLAND JOURNAL OF MEDICINE (Boston)
New Med. Materia
NEW MEDICA MATERIA

New Reconstruction Monthly
  NEW RECONSTRUCTION MONTHLY (Peking)
New Society
  NEW SOCIETY (London)
New World Rev.
  NEW WORLD REVIEW (New York)
New York Law Forum
  NEW YORK LAW FORUM (New York)
New York Law Rev.
  NEW YORK UNIVERSITY LAW REVIEW (New York)
New York State Bar J.
  NEW YORK STATE BAR ASSOCIATION JOURNAL (New York)
New Zealand Geographer
  NEW ZEALAND GEOGRAPHER (Christchurch)
New Zealand Med. J.
  NEW ZEALAND MEDICAL JOURNAL (Wellington)
Nigerian J. Econ. Soc. Stud.
  NIGERIAN JOURNAL OF ECONOMICS AND SOCIAL STUDIES (Ibadan)
Nihon Hyoron
  NIHON HYORON (Tokyo)
Nippon Jinkogakkai Kiyo
  NIPPON JINKOGAKKAI KIYO (Tokyo)
No. Ireland Law Quart.
  NORTHERN IRELAND LEGAL QUARTERLY (Belfast)
Nord. Med.
  NORDISK MEDECIN (Stockholm)
Nordisk Tidsskrift Kriminalvidenskab
  NORDISK TIDSSKRIFT FOR KRIMINALVIDENSKAB (Copenhagen)
North Carolina Law Rev.
  NORTH CAROLINA LAW REVIEW (Chapel Hill)
North Carolina Med. J.
  NORTH CAROLINA MEDICAL JOURNAL (Raleigh)
Northwest Med.
  NORTHWEST MEDICINE (Seattle)
Northwestern University Law Rev.
  NORTHWESTERN UNIVERSITY LAW REVIEW (Chicago)
Notizario Demografico
  NOTIZARIO DEMOGRAFICO (Rome)
Notre Dame Lawyer
  NOTRE DAME LAWYER (Notre Dame, Indiana)
Nouvelle Rev. Francaise d'Outre-Mer
  NOUVELLE REVUE FRANCAISE D'OUTRE-MER (Paris)
Nouvelle Revue Theologique
  NOUVELLE REVUE THEOLOGIQUE (Paris)
Nova Scotia Med. Bull.
  NOVA SCOTIA MEDICAL BULLETIN (Halifax)
Nursing Times
  NURSING TIMES (London)
Observateur de l'OCDE
  OBSERVATEUR DE L'OCDE (Paris)

Observer
  OBSERVER (London)
Obstet. Ginec.
  OBSTETRIQUE ET GINECOLOGIE
Obstet. Gynec.
  OBSTETRICS AND GYNECOLOGY (New York)
Obstet. Gynec. Survey
  OBSTETRICAL AND GYNECOLOGICAL SURVEY (Baltimore)
Ohio Law J.
  OHIO LAW JOURNAL (Columbus)
Ohio State Law J.
  OHIO STATE LAW JOURNAL (Columbus)
Oklahoma Law Rev.
  OKLAHOMA LAW REVIEW (Norman, Oklahoma)
Oklahoma Med. Assn. J.
  OKLAHOMA STATE MEDICAL ASSOCIATION JOURNAL (Oklahoma City)
Okonomi og Politik
  OKONOMI OG POLITIK (Copenhagen)
Oregon Law Rev.
  OREGON LAW REVIEW (Eugene)
Orient
  ORINET (Paris)
Oriental Economist
  ORIENTAL ECONOMIST (Tokyo)
Orv. Hetil.
  ORVOSI HETILAP (Budapest)
Ostdeutsche Wissenschaft: Jarbuch des Ostdeutschen Kulturrates
  OSTDEUTSCHE WISSENSCHAFT: JARBUCH DES OSTDEUTSCHEN KULTURRATES (Berlin)
Oxford Lawyer
  OXFORD LAWYER (Oxford)
Oxford University Institute Statistics Bull.
  OXFORD UNIVERSITY INSTITUTE STATISTICS BULLETIN (Oxford)
Pacific Affairs
  PACIFIC AFFAIRS (Honolulu)
Padagogische Psychol.
  PAEDAGOGISCHE PSYCHOLOGIE UND PHYSIOLOGIE (Berlin)
Pakistan Develop. Rev.
  PAKISTAN DEVELOPMENT REVIEW (Karachi)
Pakistan Horizon
  PAKISTAN HORIZON (Karachi)
Panstwo i Prawo
  PANSTWO I PRAWO (Warsaw)
Paris Med.
  PARIS MEDICAL (Paris)
Parliamentary Debates
  PARLIAMENTARY DEBATES, HOUSE OF COMMONS (London)
Past. Psych.
  PASTORAL PSYCHOLOGY (Manhasset, New York)

Pediatria de las Americas
  PEDIATRIA DE LAS AMERICAS (Mexico)
Peking Rev.
  PEKING REVIEW (Peking)
Perspectives in Biology and Medicine
  PERSPECTIVES IN BIOLOGY AND MEDICINE (Chicago)
Pharmaceutisch Weekblad
  PHARMACEUTISCH WEEKBLAD (The Hague)
Phi Delta Phi
  PHI DELTA PHI (Beverly Hills)
Philippine Sociol. Rev.
  PHILIPPINE SOCIOLOGICAL REVIEW (Manila)
Philippine Statistician
  PHILIPPINE STATISTICIAN (Manila)
Phylon
  PHYLON (Atlanta)
Plain View
  PLAIN VIEW (London)
Plan. Develop. Netherlands
  PLANNING AND DEVELOPMENT IN NETHERLANDS (Assen)
Planning
  PLANNING (Chicago)
Pol. Tyg. Lek.
  POLSKI TYODNIK LEKARSKI (Warsaw)
Polit. Quart.
  POLITICAL QUARTERLY (London)
Popul.
  POPULATION (Paris)
Popul. Bull.
  POPULATION BULLETIN (Washington)
Popul. Fam.
  BEVOLKING EN GEZIN, POPULATION ET FAMILLE (Brussels)
Popul. Index
  POPULATION INDEX (Princeton)
Popul. Rev.
  POPULATION REVIEW (Madras)
Popul. Stud.
  POPULATION STUDIES (London)
Portia Law J.
  PORTIA LAW JOURNAL (Concord, New Hampshire)
Postgrad. Med.
  JOURNAL OF POSTGRADUATE MEDICINE (Bombay)
Pour Vie
  POUR LA VIEW (Paris)
Practitioner
  PRACTITIONER (London)
Pratt Planning Pas.
  PRATT PLANNING PAPERS (Brooklyn)
Prawo i Zycie
  PRAWO I ZYCIE (Warsaw)

Praxis
  PRAXIS (Bern)
Prensa Med. Argent.
  PRENSA MEDICA ARGENTINA (Buenos Aires)
Presse Med.
  PRESSE MEDICALE (Paris)
Previdenza Soc.
  PREVIDENZA SOCIALE (Rome)
Pro Juventute
  PRO JUVENTUTE (Zurich)
Prob. Communism
  PROBLEMS OF COMMUNISM (Washington)
Problemes Econ.
  PROBLEMES ECONOMIQUES (Paris)
Proc. Amer. Assn. Pub. Opinion Res.
  PROCEEDINGS OF THE AMERICAN ASSOCIATION FOR PUBLIC OPINION RESEARCH (New York)
Proc. Royal Society Med.
  PROCEEDINGS OF THE ROYAL SOCIETY OF MEDICINE (London)
The Progressive
  THE PROGRESSIVE (Madison, Wisconsin)
Prophyl. Sanit. Morale
  PROPHYLAXIE SANITARE ET MORALE (Paris)
Proteccion Soc.
  PROTECCION SOCIAL (Ciudad Trujillo)
Psychiatry
  PSYCHIATRY (Baltimore)
Psychosom. Med.
  PSYCHOSOMATIC MEDICINE (Washington)
Pub. Health
  PUBLIC HEALTH (London)
Pub. Opin. Quart.
  PUBLIC OPINION QUARTERLY (Princeton)
Public Admin. Survey
  PUBLIC ADMINISTRATION SURVEY (University, Mississippi)
Public Health Reports
  PUBLIC HEALTH REPORTS (Washington)
The Public Interest
  THE PUBLIC INTEREST (New York)
Public Utility Economics
  PUBLIC UTILITY ECONOMICS
Public Welf.
  PUBLIC WELFARE (Chicago)
Puerto Rico J. Public Health Tropical Med.
  PUERTO RICO JOURNAL OF PUBLIC HEALTH AND TROPICAL MEDICINE (New York)
Quart. Rev. Sur. Obstet. Gynec.
  QUARTERLY REVIEW OF SURGERY, OBSTETRICS AND GYNECOLOGY (Washington)
Queens Quart.
  QUEENS QUARTERLY (Kingston, England)

Rass. Ital. Sociol.
  RASSEGNA ITALIANA DI SOCIOLOGICA (Bologna)
Rassegna Lavoro
  RASSEGNA DEL LAVORO (Rome)
Rassegna Statistiche Lavoro
  RASSEGNA DI STATISTICHE DEL LABORO (Rome)
Razon y Fe
  RAZON Y FE, REVISTA MENSUAL (Madrid
Razza e Civilta
  RAZZA E CIVILTA (Rome)
Realist
  REALIST (London)
Recherches Economiques de Louvain
  RECHERCHES ECONOMIQUES DE LOUVAIN (Louvain)
Recherche Information Sante Publique
  RECHERCHE INFORMATION SANTE PUBLIQUE (Paris)
Recueil des Cours
  RECUEIL DES COURS (The Hague)
Reich
  REICH (Munich)
Reichsarbeitsblatt
  REICHSARBEITSBLATT (Berlin)
Relations
  RELATIONS (Montreal)
Reporter
  REPORTER (New York)
Reports Service, American Universities Field Staff, East Asia Service
  REPORTS SERVICE, AMERICAN UNIVERSITIES FIELD STAFF, EAST ASIA SERVICE (Hanover, New Hampshire)
Resmi Gazete
  RESMI GAZETE (Ankara)
Rev. Action Populaire
  REVUE DE L'ACTION POPULAIRE (Rheims)
Rev. Administrative
  REVUE ADMINISTRATIVE (Paris)
Rev. Argent. Soc. Obstet. Ginec.
  REVISTA ARGENTINA DE OBSTETRICA Y GINECOLOGIA (Buenos Aires)
Rev. Belge Sec. Soc.
  REVUE BELGE DE SECURITE SOCIALE (Brussels)
Rev. Brasil Med.
  REVISTA BRASILEIRA DE MEDECINA (Rio de Janeiro)
Rev. C. Abo Puerto Rico
  REVISTA COLEGIO ABO PUERTO RICO (Puerto Rico)
Rev. Chile Higiene Med. Prevent.
  REVISTA CHILENA DE HIGIENE Y MEDICINA PREVENTIVA (Santiago)
Rev. Chile Obstet. Ginec.
  REVISTA CHILENA DE OBSTETRICA Y GINECOLOGIA (Santiago)
Rev. Conseil Econ. Wallon
  REVUE DU CONSEIL ECONOMIQUE WALLON (Liege)

APPENDIX I

Rev. Czech. Med.
  REVIEW OF CZECHOSLOVAK MEDICINE (Prague)
Rev. DP
  REVISTA DE DERECHO PRIVODO (Madrid)
Rev. Droit Penal Criminol.
  REVUE DE DROIT PENAL ET DE CRIMINOLOGIE (Brussels)
Rev. Econ.
  REVUE ECONOMIQUE (Paris)
Rev. Econ. Franco-Suisse
  REVUE ECONOMIQUE FRANCO-SUISSE (Paris)
Rev. Econ. Situation of Mexico
  REVIEW OF THE ECONOMIC SITUATION OF MEXICO (Mexico City)
Rev. Econ. Statistics
  REVIEW OF ECONOMICS AND STATISTICS (Cambridge, Mass.)
Rev. Espan. Opin. Pub.
  REVISTA ESPANOLA DE LA OPINION PUBLICA (Madrid)
Rev. Francaise Sci. Polit.
  REVUE FRANCAISE DE SCIENCE POLITIQUE (Paris)
Rev. Hautes Etudes Polit. Soc. Econ. Finan.
  REVUE DES HAUTES ETUDES POLITIQUE SOCIALES ECONOMIQUE ET FINANCIERES (Paris)
Rev. Hygiene Med. Soc.
  REVUE D'HYGINE ET DE MEDECINE SOCIAL (Paris)
Rev. Iberoamer. Seguridad Soc.
  REVISTA IBEROAMERICANA DE SEGURIDAD SOCIAL (Madrid)
Rev. Infirm. Assist. Soc.
  REVUE DE L'INFIRMIERE ET DE L'ASSISTANTE SOCIALE (Paris)
Rev. Institut Sociol.
  REVUE DE L'INSTITUT DE SOCIOLOGIE (Brussels)
Rev. Int. Sociol.
  REVISTA INTERNACIONAL DE SOCIOLOGIA (Madrid)
Rev. Internazionale Sci. Soc.
  REVISTA INTERNAZIONALE DI SCIENZA SOCIALI (Milan)
Rev. Italiana Sci. Econ.
  REVISTA ITALIANA DI SCIENZE ECONOMIA (Rome)
Rev. Latinoamer. Sociol.
  REVISTA LATINOAMERICANA DE SOCIOLOGIA (Mexico City)
Rev. Med. Chile
  REVISTA MEDICA DA CHILE (Santiago)
Rev. Med. Costa Rica
  REVISTA MEDICA DA COSTA RICA (San Jose)
Rev. Med. Legal Colombia
  REVISTA DE MEDICINA LEGAL DE COLOMBIA (Bogota)
Rev. Militaire Suisse
  REVUE MILITAIRE SUISSE (Lausanne)
Rev. Notariat
  REVUE DU NOTARIAT (Montreal)
Rev. Nouvelle
  REVUE NOUVELLE (Brussels
Rev. Ostet. Ginec.
  REVISTA DI OBSTETRICA Y GINECOLOGIA (Florence)

ABBREVIATIONS AND FULL TITLES OF JOURNALS

Rev. Polit. Idees Institutions
REVUE POLITIQUE DES IDEES ET DES INSTITUTIONS (Paris)
Rev. Polit. Parlementaire
REVUE POLITIQUE ET PARLEMENTAIRE (Paris)
Rev. Practicien
REVUE PRACTICIEN (Paris)
Rev. River Plate
REVIEW OF THE RIVER PLATE (Buenos Aires)
Rev. Romana Drept.
REVISTA ROMANA DE DREPT (Bucharest)
Rev. Roumaine Sci. Socia.
REVUE ROUMAINE DES SCIENCES SOCIALES (Bucharest)
Rev. Sanidad Higiene Pub.
REVISTA DE SANIDAD E HIGIENE PUBLICA (Madrid)
Rev. Sci. Econ.
REVUE DES SCIENCES ECONOMIQUES (Liege)
Revue des Sciences Politiques
REVUE DES SCIENCES POLITIQUES (Paris)
Rev. Sec. Soc.
REVUE DE LA SECURITE SOCIALE (Paris)
Rev. Soc. Econ.
REVIEW OF SOCIAL ECONOMY (Chicago)
Rev. Soviet Med. Sci.
REVIEW OF SOVIET MEDICAL SCIENCES (Munich)
Rev. Travail
REVUE DU TRAVAIL/ ARBEIDSBLAD (Brussels)
Rev. Trimestrielle Droit Civil
REVUE TRIMESTRIELLE DE DROIT CIVIL (Paris)
Rev. Tunisienne de Sciences Sociales
REVUE TUNISIENNE DE SCIENCES SOCIALES (Tunis)
Revista de Ciencias Economicas
REVISTA DE CIENCIAS ECONOMICAS (Buenos Aires)
Revista de Economia
REVISTA DE ECONOMIA (Mexico City)
Revista de Economia Argentina
REVISTA DE ECONOMIA ARGENTINA (Buenos Aires)
Revista de Imigracao e Colonizacao
REVISTA DE IMIGRACAO E COLONIZACAO (Rio de Janeiro)
Revista Interamericana de Ciencias Sociales
REVISTA INTERAMERICANA DE CIENCIAS SOCIALES (Washington)
Revista do Servico Publico
REVISTA DO SERVICO PUBLICO (Rio de Janeiro)
Revista do Trabalho
REVISTA DO TRABALHO (Rio de Janeiro)
Rhode Island Med. J.
RHODE ISLAND MEDICAL JOURNAL (Providence)
Riv. Internazionale Sci. Soc.
RIVISTA INTERNAZIONALE DI SCIENZE SOCIALI (Rome)
Riv. Italiana d'Igene
RIVISTA ITALIANA D'IGENE (Pisa)

Riv. Polit. Econom.
  RIVISTA DI POLITICA ECONOMICA (Rome)
Roumanie Nouvelle
  ROUMANIE NOUVELLE (Bucharest)
Royal Central Asian Sociol. J.
  ROYAL CENTRAL ASIAN SOCIETY JOURNAL (London)
Royal Nepal Econ.
  ROYAL NEPAL ECONOMIST (Kathmandu)
Royal Society Arts
  ROYAL SOCIETY OF ARTS, LONDON JOURNAL (London)
Rural India
  RURAL INDIA (Madras)
Rural Sociol.
  RURAL SOCIOLOGY (Ithaca, New York)
Rwanda Carrefour d'Afrique
  RWANDA CARREFOUR D'AFRIQUE (Kigali, Rwanda)
Salud Publica Mexico
  SALUD PUBLICA DE MEXICO (Mexico City)
Sanfujin Jissai
  SANFUJIN JISSAI (Tokyo)
Sankhya
  SANKHYA: THE INDIAN JOURNAL OF STATISTICS (Calcutta)
Sante Pub.
  SANTE PUBLIQUE (Paris)
Schmollers Jahrbuch
  SCHMOLLERS JAHRBUCH FUR GESETZGEBUND, VERWALTUNG UND
    WOLKSWIRTSCHAFT (Berlin)
Schweiz. Med.
  SCHWEIZERISCHE MEDIZINISCHE WOCHENSCHRIFT (Basel)
Schweiz. Rundschau
  SCHWEIZERISCHE RUNDSCHAU (Zurich)
Schweizerische Z. Volkswirtschaft
  SCHWEIZERISCHE ZEITSCHRIFT FUR VOLKSWIRTSCHAFT UND
    STATISTIK (Basel)
Sci. Cult.
  SCIENCE AND CULTURE (Calcutta)
Sci. Soc.
  SCIENCE AND SOCIETY (New York)
Science
  SCIENCE (Washington)
Scientific Amer.
  SCIENTIFIC AMERICAN (New York)
Scientific Monthly
  SCIENTIFIC MONTHLY (Washington)
Scottish Bankers
  SCOTTISH BANKERS' MAGAZINE (Edinburgh)
Scottish J. Polit. Econ.
  SCOTTISH JOURNAL OF POLITICAL ECONOMY (Edinburgh)
Securite Sociale
  SECURITE SOCIALE (Paris)

ABBREVIATIONS AND FULL TITLES OF JOURNALS

Selections from China Mainland Magazines
SELECTIONS FROM CHINA MAINLAND MAGAZINES (Hong Kong)
Selections from China Mainland Press
SELECTIONS FROM CHINA MAINLAND PRESS (Hong Kong)
Sem. Hop.
SEMAINE DES HOPITAUX DE PARIS (Paris)
La Semaine Med.
LA SEMAINE MEDICALE (Paris)
Semana Med. Espan.
SEMANA MEDICA ESPANOLA (Madrid)
Seminar
SEMINAR (New York)
Servir, Revue Tunisienne du Service Public
SERVIR, REVUE TUNISIENNE DU SERVICE PUBLIC (Tunis)
Sezione Medico-Fisica
SEZIONE MEDICO-FISICA
Singapore Med. J.
SINGAPORE MEDICAL JOURNAL (Singapore)
Sintese Politica Economica Social
SINTESE POLITICA, ECONOMICA, SOCIAL (Rio de Janeiro)
Slavic Rev.
SLAVIC REVIEW (Seattle)
Sluzbeni List
SLUZBENI LIST OPSTINE BECEJ (Becey)
Soc. Action
SOCIAL ACTION (Boston)
Soc. Biol.
SOCIAL BIOLOGY (Chicago)
Soc. Casework
SOCIAL CASEWORK (New York)
Soc. Econ. Stud.
SOCIAL AND ECONOMIC STUDIES (Mona, Jamaica)
Soc. Forces
SOCIAL FORCES (Chapel Hill)
Soc. Kompas
SOCIAL KOMPAS (The Hague)
Soc. Med.
SOCIALA MEDELANDEN (Stockholm)
Soc. Med. Tidskrift
SOCIAL MEDICINSK TIDSKRIFT (Stockholm)
Soc. Order
SOCIAL ORDER (St. Louis)
Soc. Prob.
SOCIAL PROBLEMS (Garden City, New York)
Soc. Sci.
SOCIAL SCIENCE (Winfield, Kansas)
Soc. Sci. Information
SOCIAL SCIENCE INFORMATION (The Hague)

Soc. Sec. Assn. Bull.
  SOCIAL SECURITY ASSOCIATION BULLETIN (New York)
Soc. Sec. Bull.
  SOCIAL SECURITY BULLETIN (Washington)
Soc. Serv.
  SOCIAL SERVICE (Sydney)
Soc. Tidsskrift
  SOCIALT TIDDSSKRIFT (Copenhagen)
Soc. Work
  SOCIAL WORK (New York)
Social Service Rev.
  SOCIAL SERVICE REVIEW (Chicago)
Socialist Commentary
  SOCIALIST COMMENTARY (London)
Socijalna Polit.
  SOCIJALNA POLITIKA (Belgrade)
Sociol. Anal
  SOCIOLOGICAL ANALYSIS (Notre Dame, Indiana)
Sociol. Bull.
  SOCIOLOGICAL BULLETIN (Delhi)
Sociol. Droit Slaves
  SOCIOLOGIE ET DROIT SLAVES (Paris)
Sociol. Gids
  SOCIOLOGISCHE GIDS (Meppel, Netherlands)
Sociol. Soc. Res.
  SOCIOLOGY AND SOCIAL RESEARCH (Los Angeles)
Sociologia
  SOCIOLOGIA (Sao Paulo)
Sosiologia
  SOSIOLOGIA (Helsinki)
S. African Med. J.
  SOUTH AFRICAN MEDICAL JOURNAL (Cape Town)
South African J. Economics
  SOUTH AFRICAN JOURNAL OF ECONOMICS (Johannesburg)
South African J. Sci.
  SOUTH AFRICAN JOURNAL OF SCIENCE (Johannesburg)
South Carolina Law Quart.
  SOUTH CAROLINA LAW QUARTERLY (Columbia)
South Dakota J. Med.
  SOUTH DAKOTA JOURNAL OF MEDICINE AND PHARMACY (Sioux Falls)
South Dakota Law Rev.
  SOUTH DAKOTA LAW REVIEW (Vermillion)
South Pacific Commission Quart. Bull.
  SOUTH PACIFIC COMMISSION QUARTERLY BULLETIN (Haymarket, N.S.W.)
Southern California Law Rev.
  SOUTHERN CALIFORNIA LAW REVIEW (Los Angeles)
Southern Med. J.
  SOUTHERN MEDICAL JOURNAL (Birmingham, Alabama)
Southwestern Law J.
  SOUTHWESTERN LAW JOURNAL (Dallas)

Sovet. Zdravookhr.
  SOVETSKOYE ZDRAVOOKHRANENIE (Moscow)
Sovetskoye Gosudarstvo i Pravo
  SOVETSKOYE GOSUDARSTVO I PRAVO (Moscow)
Soviet Rev.
  SOVIET REVIEW (New York)
Soviet Russia Today
  SOVIET RUSSIA TODAY (New York)
Soviet Sociol.
  SOVIET SOCIOLOGY (White Plains, New York)
Soviet Stud.
  SOVIET STUDIES (Glascow)
Soz. Fortsch.
  SOZIALER FORTSCHRITT (Berlin)
Soz. Welt.
  SOZIALE WELT (Goettingen)
Soziale Praxis
  SOZIALE PRAXIS (Berlin)
Soziale Sicherheit
  SOZIALE SICHERHEIT (Vienna)
Sprawy Miedzynarodowe
  SPRAWY MIEDZYNARODOWE (Warsaw)
Srpski Arkhiv za Tselokupno Lekarstvo
  SRPSKI ARKHIV ZA TSELOKUPNO LEKARSTVO (Belgrade)
St. John's Law Rev.
  ST. JOHN'S LAW REVIEW (New York)
St. Louis University Law J.
  ST. LOUIS UNIVERSITY LAW JOURNAL (St. Louis)
Stanford Law Rev.
  STANFORD LAW REVIEW (Stanford)
Stanovnistvo
  STANOVNISTVO (Belgrade)
State Government
  STATE GOVERNMENT (Denver)
Statistica
  STATISTICA (Bologna)
Statistical Reporter
  STATISTICAL REPORTER (Washington)
Statistisk Tidskrift
  STATISTISK TIDSKRIFT (Stockholm)
Statisticky Obzor
  STATISTICKY OBZOR (Prague)
Statisztikai Szemle
  STATISZTIKAI SZEMLE (Budapest)
Stud. Demograficzne
  STUDIA DEMOGRAFICZNE (Warsaw)
Stud. in Fam. Plan.
  STUDIES IN FAMILY PLANNING (New York)
Studies
  STUDIES (Dublin)

Studies in Comparative International Development
  STUDIES IN COMPARATIVE INTERNATIONAL DEVELOPMENT (Beverly Hills)
Suomen Laakarilehti
  SUOMEN LAAKARILEHTI/FINLANDS LAKARTIDNING (Helsinki)
Survey
  SURVEY (New York)
Survey China Mainland Press
  SURVEY OF CHINA MAINLAND PRESS (Hong Kong)
Suvremenna Meditsina
  SUVREMENNA MEDITSINA (Sophia)
Svensk Tidskrift
  SVENSK TIDSKRIFT (Upsala)
Svenska Lakartidn.
  SVENSKA LAKARTIDNINGEN (Stockholm)
Sydney Law Rev.
  SYDNEY LAW REVIEW (Sydney)
Sykepleine
  SYKEPLEINE (Oslo)
Syracuse Law Rev.
  SYRACUSE LAW REVIEW (Syracuse)
T. Norsk. Laeg.
  TIDSSKRIFT FOR DEN NORSKE LAEGEFORENING (Oslo)
T. Soc. Geneesk.
  TIJDSCHRIFT VOOR SOCIALE GENEESKUNDE (Delft, Netherlands)
Tasmanian Univ. Law Rev.
  TASMANIAN UNIVERSITY LAW REVIEW (Hobart)
Taxes
  TAXES (Chicago)
Temple Law Quart.
  TEMPLE UNIVERSITY LAW QUARTERLY (Philadelphia)
Temps Mod.
  TEMPS MODERNES (Paris)
Texas Law Rev.
  TEXAS LAW REVIEW (Austin)
Texas Report Biol. Med.
  TEXAS REPORTS ON BIOLOGY AND MEDICINE (Galveston)
Texas State J. Med.
  TEXAS STATE JOURNAL OF MEDICINE (Fort Worth)
Theol. Today
  THEOLOGY TODAY (Princeton, New Jersey)
Ther. Umsch.
  THERAPEUTISCHE UMSCHAU UND MEDIZINISCHE BIBLIOGRAPHIE (Bern)
Thought
  THOUGHT (New York)
Time
  TIME (New York)
Transact. Westermarck Society
  TRANSACTIONS OF THE WESTERMARCK SOCIETY (Copenhagen)
El Trimestre Economico
  EL TRIMESTRE ECONOMICO (Mexico City)

Trud i Tseni
TRUD I TSENI (Sofia)
Tulane Law Rev.
TULANE LAW REVIEW (New Orleans)
Tunisie Medicale
TUNISIE MEDICALE (Tunis)
Tunisienne de Sciences Sociales
REVUE TUNISIENNE DE SCIENCES SOCIALES (Tunis)
Turkish Econ. Rev.
TURKISH ECONOMIC REVIEW (Ankara)
Tvds. Maatskap. Navors.
TVDSKRIF VIR MAATSKAPLIKE NAVORSING (Pretoria)
UCLA Law Rev.
UCLA LAW REVIEW (Los Angeles)
Ugeskr. Laeg.
UGESKRIFT FOR LAEGER (Copenhagen)
Umma
UMMA (Dar es Salaam)
United Africa Company Limited, Statistical and Economic Review
UNITED AFRICA COMPANY LIMITED, STATISTICAL AND ECONOMIC REVIEW (London)
Univ. Penn. Law Rev.
UNIVERSITY OF PENNSYLVANIA LAW REVIEW (Philadelphia)
Univ. Pittsburgh Law Rev.
UNIVERSITY OF PITTSBURGH LAW REVIEW (Pittsburgh)
Universidad Pontificia Bolivariana
UNIVERSIDAD PONTIFICIA BOLIVARIANA (Medellin, Colombia)
University Colorado Law Rev.
UNIVERSITY COLORADO LAW REVIEW (Boulder)
University Florida Law Rev.
UNIVERSITY FLORIDA LAW REVIEW (Gainesville)
University Illinois Law Rev.
UNIVERSITY OF ILLINOIS LAW REVIEW (Urbana)
University of Miami Law Rev.
UNIVERSITY OF MIAMI LAW REVIEW (Coral Gables, Florida)
U.S. News
U.S. NEWS AND WORLD REPORT (Washington)
Utah Law Rev.
UTAH LAW REVIEW (Salt Lake City)
Valpariso Univ. Law Rev.
VALPARISO UNIVERSITY LAW REVIEW (Valpariso, Indiana)
Vanderbilt Law Rev.
VANDERBILT LAW REVIEW (Nashville)
Vanyajati
VANYAJATI (New Delhi)
Veroffentlichungen aus dem Gebiete des Volksgesundheitsdienstes
VEROFFENTLICHUNGEN AUS DEM GEBIETE DES VOLKSGESUNDHEIT-SDIENSTES
Verslagen en Mededelingen Betreffende Volksgezondheid
VERSLAGEN EN MEDEDELINGEN BETREFFENDE VOLKSGEZONDHEID (The Hague)

Vie Econ. Soc.
  VIE ECONOMIQUE ET SOCIALE (Antwerp)
Villanova Law Rev.
  VILLANOVA LAW REVIEW (Villanova, Pennsylvania)
Virginia Quart. Rev.
  VIRGINIA QUARTERLY REVIEW (Charlottesville)
Vital Speeches
  VITAL SPEECHES OF THE DAY BY THE LEADING MOULDERS OF
    PUBLIC OPINION (New York)
Vitalite Francaise
  VITALITE FRANCAISE (Paris)
Voproci Econ.
  VOPROCI ECONOMIKI (Moscow)
Voprosy Okhrany Materinstva i Detstva
  VOPROSY OKHRANY MATERINSTVA I DETSTVA (Moscow)
War on Hunger
  WAR ON HUNGER (Washington)
Wash. Lee Law Rev.
  WASHINGTON AND LEE LAW REVIEW (Lexington, Virginia)
Washington University Law Quart.
  WASHINGTON UNIVERSITY LAW QUARTERLY (St. Louis)
Welfare in Rev.
  WELFARE IN REVIEW (Washington)
West Africa Med. J.
  WEST AFRICAN MEDICAL JOURNAL (Ibadan)
West. J. Surg. Obstet. Gynaec.
  WESTERN JOURNAL OF SURGERY, OBSTETRICS AND GYNECOLOGY
    (Portland, Oregon)
Western Law Rev.
  WESTERN RESERVE LAW REVIEW (Cleveland)
WHO Chron.
  WORLD HEALTH ORGANIZATION CHRONICLE (Geneva)
Wiadomosci Lekarskie
  WIADOMOSCI LEKARSKIE (Warsaw)
Wies Wspolczesna
  WIES WSPOLCZESNA (Warsaw)
Wirtschaft und Sozialbericht
  WIRTSCHAFT UND SOZIALBERICHT
Wirtschaft Statistik
  WIRTSCHAFT UND STATISTIC (Stuttgart)
Wisconsin Law Rev.
  WISCONSIN LAW REVIEW (Madison)
Wisconsin Med. J.
  WISCONSIN MEDICAL JOURNAL (Milwaukee)
Women Law J.
  WOMEN LAWYER'S JOURNAL (New York)
World Affairs
  WORLD AFFAIRS (Boston)
World Med.
  WORLD MEDICINE (London)

World Med. J.
  WORLD MEDICAL JOURNAL (New York)
World Politics
  WORLD POLITICS; A QUARTERLY JOURNAL OF INTERNATIONAL
    RELATIONS (New Haven)
World Today
  WORLD TODAY (London)
World View
  WORLD VIEW (New York)
Wyoming Law J.
  WYOMING LAW JOURNAL (Laramie)
Yale Law J.
  YALE LAW JOURNAL (New Haven)
Yonsei Med. J.
  YONSEI MEDICAL JOURNAL (Seoul)
Z. Aertzl. Fortbild.
  ZEITSCHRIFT FUR ARZTLICHE FORTBILDUNG (Jena)
Z. Evang. Ethik.
  ZEITSCHRIFT FUR EVANGELISCHE ETHIK (Guetersloh, Germany: FR)
Z. Geburtsh. Gynak.
  ZEITSCHRIFT FUR GEBURTSHULFE UND GYNAKOLOGIE (Stuttgart)
Z. Geopolitik
  ZEITSCHRIFT FUR GEOPOLITIK (Hessen, Germany: FR)
Z. Gesamte Innere Med. Ihre Grensgebeite
  ZEITSCHRIFT FUR DIE GESAMTE INNERE MEDIZIN UND IHRE
    GRENSGEBIETE (Leipzig)
Z. Praeventivmed.
  ZEITSCHRIFT FUR PRAEVENTIVMEDIZIN/REVUE DE MEDECINE
    PREVENTIVE (Zurich)
Zbl. Gynaek.
  ZBL. GYNAEK.
Zdrowie Publiczne
  ZDROWIE PUBLICZNE (Warsaw)
Zeitschrift Sozialreform
  ZEITSCHRIFT FUR SOZIALREFORM
Zoologica
  ZOOLOGICA (Cassel)
Zpravy Statni Populacni Komise
  ZPRAVY STATNI POPULACNI KOMISE (Prague)

AUTHOR INDEX

(Number next to name refers to item, not page)

AUTHOR INDEX

AUTHOR INDEX

AUTHOR INDEX

AUTHOR INDEX

SUBJECT INDEX

(Number next to subject refers to item, not page)

SUBJECT INDEX

SUBJECT INDEX

SUBJECT INDEX

SUBJECT INDEX

SUBJECT INDEX

SUBJECT INDEX

SUBJECT INDEX

SUBJECT INDEX